INTERVIEWING AND CHANGE STRATEGIES FOR HELPERS

Fundamental Skills and Cognitive Behavioral Interventions

SIXTH EDITION

SHERRY CORMIER
West Virginia University

PAULA S. NURIUS
University of Washington

CYNTHIA J. OSBORN
Kent State University

BROOKS/COLE
CENGAGE Learning

Australia • Brazil • Japan • Korea • Mexico • Singapore • Spain • United Kingdom • United States

BROOKS/COLE
CENGAGE Learning™

Interviewing and Change Strategies for Helpers: Fundamental Skills and Cognitive Behavioral Interventions, **Sixth Edition**

Sherry Cormier, Paula S. Nurius, and Cynthia J. Osborn

Senior Acquisitions Editor:
   Seth Dobrin

Assistant Editor: Christina Ganim

Editorial Assistant: Ashley Cronin

Technology Project Manager: Andrew Keay

Marketing Manager: Karin Sandberg

Marketing Coordinator: Ting Jian Yap

Marketing Communications Manager:
   Shemika Britt

Project Manager, Editorial Production:
   Rita Jaramillo

Creative Director: Rob Hugel

Art Directors: Vernon Boes, Caryl Gorska

Print Buyer: Karen Hunt

Text Permissions Editor: Roberta Broyer

Production Service: Matrix Productions

Copy Editor: Pat Herbst

Cover Designer: Bill Stanton

Cover Image: Masterfile

Compositor: International Typesetting
   and Composition

For product information and technology assistance, contact us at
Cengage Learning Customer & Sales Support, 1-800-354-9706

For permission to use material from this text or product,
submit all requests online at **www.cengage.com/permissions**
Further permissions questions can be emailed to
permissionrequest@cengage.com

Library of Congress Control Number: 2007937693

ISBN-13: 978-0-495-41053-9

ISBN-10: 0-495-41053-5

Brooks/Cole
10 Davis Drive
Belmont, CA 94002-3098
USA

Cengage Learning is a leading provider of customized learning solutions with office locations around the globe, including Singapore, the United Kingdom, Australia, Mexico, Brazil, and Japan. Locate your local office at **international.cengage.com/region**

Cengage Learning products are represented in Canada by Nelson Education, Ltd.

For your course and learning solutions, visit **academic.cengage.com**

Purchase any of our products at your local college store or at our preferred online store **www.ichapters.com**

Printed in the United States of America
3 4 5 6 7 12 11

~

In memory of Bill Keucher and Emma Ruth Osborn,

and in honor of Edith Keucher,

Gwyndolyn Medley Garner, and

Dick Mitchell with grateful

appreciation and affection.

~

About the Authors

Sherry Cormier teaches and supervises in the Department of Counseling, Rehabilitation Counseling, and Counseling Psychology at West Virginia University in Morgantown. She is a licensed psychologist in the state of West Virginia. Her current research and practice interests are in counseling and psychology training and supervision models, issues impacting girls and women, and health and wellness. In her practice and supervision she uses cognitive–behavioral, object-relations, and body-awareness approaches as well as Jungian and transpersonal psychology. She is the mother of two 20-something daughters and the grandmother of a 2-year-old. Her husband is a licensed professional counselor who practices at a pastoral counseling center.

Paula S. Nurius is a professor in the School of Social Work at the University of Washington in Seattle. She brings training and field experience in both psychology and social work to her teaching, practice, and research, with particular concern for vulnerable populations. Her research has focused on schema formation/functioning, perception and responding under conditions of stress and trauma, and interrelationships among violence exposures, mental health, substance use, and personal/social resources on adaptive and maladaptive development. Dr. Nurius's teaching has focused on mental health practice, prevention and health promotion, and research methods. She currently directs an NIMH-funded graduate training program in prevention research and has long-standing interests in fostering linkages between practice and research and among allied disciplines committed to the helping/human services. She enjoys the outdoor life of the Pacific Northwest with her husband, daughter, and schnoodle pup.

Cynthia J. Osborn is an associate professor in the Counseling and Human Development Services graduate program at Kent State University in Kent, Ohio. She is a licensed professional clinical counselor and a certified chemical dependency counselor in Ohio. Her research, clinical practice, and teaching have focused on substance use issues and counselor supervision from the perspectives of motivational interviewing and solution-focused therapy. Additional scholarship has addressed case conceptualization and treatment-planning skills, stamina and resilience in mental health practice, and leadership in the counseling profession. She has served in various leadership capacities in the counseling profession and is currently coeditor of the journal *Counselor Education and Supervision*. She and her husband enjoy traveling, exercising, and the company of their dog, Rudy.

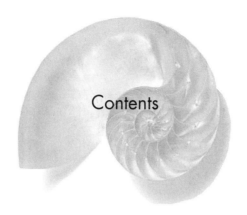

Contents

CHAPTER 10
CLINICAL DECISION MAKING AND TREATMENT PLANNING 271

CHAPTER 11
IMAGERY AND MODELING STRATEGIES 308

CHAPTER 12
REFRAMING, COGNITIVE MODELING, AND PROBLEM-SOLVING STRATEGIES 346

CHAPTER **18**
STRATEGIES FOR WORKING WITH RESISTANCE: SOLUTION-FOCUSED THERAPY AND MOTIVATIONAL INTERVIEWING 562

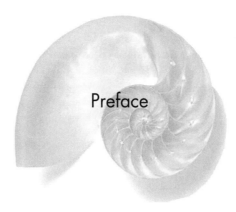

Preface

The sixth edition of *Interviewing and Change Strategies for Helpers* reflects a number of changes! First, and foremost, is a new coauthor: Cynthia J. Osborn. We three authors have found that our collaboration has added new dimensions of complementariness and invigoration to the text. The new edition represents a blending of our expertise in counseling, psychology, social work, and health and human services. Our partnership in these interdisciplinary areas augments the book's responsiveness to the unique perspectives of each discipline while also working at the interface, addressing cross-cutting issues and commitments. This book is intended to be used by *helpers* who are trained in a variety of health and helping-oriented disciplines, including counseling, social work, psychology, and human services and related professions. We recognize that terminology varies across settings. You will see the term *helper* as well as *practitioner, clinician,* and *service provider*.

OUR CONCEPTUAL FOUNDATION

Our conceptual foundation, which we describe in Chapters 1 and 2, reflects four critical areas for helpers from various disciplines: (1) core skills and resources, (2) diversity and ecological models, (3) effectiveness-based practice, and (4) critical thinking and ethical judgment. The core skills that we present cut across all helping disciplines, and in this edition we present them in Chapters 3, "Understanding Nonverbal Behavior," Chapter 4, "Ingredients of an Effective Helping Relationship," Chapter 5, "Listening Responses," and Chapter 6, "Influencing Responses." Diversity and ecological models are presented in Chapters 2, 7, and 8 and also are integrated throughout the book. Chapters 11 through 18 give special attention to the research support for the application of change strategies to diverse groups and the importance of culture and context in applying these and other helping techniques. Effectiveness-based practice is introduced in Chapter 2 and again in Chapters 9 and 10. Recognizing the enormous influence of evidence-based expectations on contemporary practice, we

have incorporated current findings into each of our chapters on cognitive–behavioral change strategies (Chapters 11 through 18).

Layered across all of this is the fourth area of our conceptual model: critical thinking and ethical judgment. We focus on this area specifically in Chapters 1 and 2 and explore these topics again throughout the remainder of the book, for they permeate all of the decisions that helpers face at each phase of the helping process, from establishing the helping relationship, to assessing client problems, setting treatment goals, and selecting, using, and evaluating change intervention strategies. Many users of the text have indicated that combining major stages of the helping process with specific change strategies facilitates integration in students' understanding as well as within and across courses that aim for this bigger picture.

"BUILT-IN" AND SUPPLEMENTAL INSTRUCTIONAL GUIDES

We have retained the specific features of the text that we have learned through feedback make it invaluable as a resource guide—and we have taken this emphasis a step further. We have worked to distinguish this teaching text by providing a rich array of "built-in" exercises, exemplars, and tools to promote and evaluate student comprehension. The book balances attention to conceptual and empirical foundations with an emphasis on real-life factors in practice settings and ample use of examples and how-to guidelines. Chapters are guided by learning outcomes and opportunities to practice with numerous learning activities and guided feedback. Model cases and dialogues are given in each chapter, as well as end-of-chapter evaluations (referred to as "Knowledge and Skill Builders") with feedback, designed to help assess chapter competencies.

In addition, we have developed a range of supplementary materials to enrich the teaching experience. These include an Instructor's Manual, a bank of test questions (which can be used by instructors for course exams or by students in later preparing for accrediting exams). PowerPoint slides for each chapter, and a book-specific website that includes, among other things, online chapter postevaluations for student and instructor access.

NEW TO THE SIXTH EDITION

A considerable amount of new content has been added to this edition—two wholly new chapters as well as expansions and updates and format changes:

1. Responsive to increasing numbers of mandated clients as well as to current efficacy and effectiveness research, we have added a chapter that greatly expands attention to issues of resistance, reactance, reluctance, and ambivalence. Our new Chapter 18 focuses on solution-focused therapy and motivational interviewing as two primary intervention tools, and it examines ways in which helpers may contribute to resistance.

2. Chapter 16, our new chapter on exposure therapies, moves beyond our prior and more limited attention to desensitization, bringing more current thinking about effective ways to handle anxiety and phobias. This chapter was written by Daniel McNeil, PhD, and Brandon Kyle, MS, experts in the application of exposure in both general clinical practice and behavioral medicine settings.

3. We have increased our attention to working with diverse groups. Chapter 2 provides expanded discussion of populations and cultural groups in the United States who have experienced oppression, the concept of multicultural literacy or fluency, guidelines for discussing race/ethnicity in session and for working with culturally diverse clients. The chapter includes a new learning activity to apply these guidelines.

4. Cultural implications of the helping relationship, interviewing skills, assessment, and treatment goals and strategies are presented in Chapters 3 through 10. Research findings and implications for applying change strategies in work with diverse groups are found in Chapters 11 through 18.

5. Chapters 2, 6, and 9 offer expanded consideration of ethical issues. This includes explanation of HIPAA and its implications for record keeping, legal updates on factors such as working with children/adolescents, ethical issues specific to substance abuse counseling, managing multiple dimensions of therapeutic relationships, updates on cybercounseling practices, implications of the American Counseling Association's (2005) revised *Code of Ethics*, discussion of a transcultural ethical decision-making model, and ethical multiculturalism.

6. New material on promoting stamina and resilience to reduce practitioner burnout and compassion fatigue appears in Chapter 2.

7. Consideration of the therapeutic relationship has been expanded (Chapter 4) to include the dynamics of trust and application of control–mastery theory, self–psychology and relational views of the relationship, incorporating cultural variables into the working alliance, and the empirical basis for various relationship conditions toward increasing effectiveness.

8. Expanded discussion of the *DSM-IV TR* in Chapter 7 helps clarify the process of making a diagnosis and addresses advantages and disadvantages of this model.

9. The Person-in-Environment (PIE) classification system, described in Chapters 7 and 8, provides an alternative or complement to the more traditional *DSM-IV TR*. This tool provides greater illumination of contextual factors (a weakness of *DSM-IV TR*) and greater assessment of individual and environmental strengths/resources.

10. Chapters 7 and 8 expand attention to culturally informed assessment interviews and analysis of cases from a variety of perspectives, including a cultural one.

11. Positive psychology is also an emerging third force. Incorporating a strengths-based perspective, this approach promotes balanced attention to assessment of strengths and protective factors alongside client problems or risk factors (Chapters 7 and 8).

12. Facets of neurobiology are addressed, such as the neurobiological basis of empathy, stress responding, and mechanisms responsible for some nonverbal behaviors and responses.

13. In view of increased lethal public violence such as suicide bombings and school shootings, Chapter 8 provides assessment of lethality (danger to self and others) to help recognize warning signs of client lethality.

14. In the change strategy chapters, 11 through 18, updated research boxes on evidence-based change strategies are provided as well as illustrations of findings.

15. Updates on the function of cognitive schemas—including effects of context and "hot" factors such as affect and motivation—in development of client perception-based problems and change strategies are provided in Chapter 13.

16. New developments in counseling/psychotherapy, referred to as third-wave or third-generation interventions, are described, including acceptance and commitment therapy, dialectical behavior therapy, and mindfulness-based cognitive therapy (Chapters 7, 10, 13, 15, 16). These evolving change strategies raise questions about beliefs underlying behavioral and cognitive–behavioral models, and they augment attention to factors such as achieving mindfulness and experiential acceptance.

17. The Instructor's Manual authored by Beth Robinson, PhD, the Test Bank of questions for each chapter, and the book-specific website have been fully updated. In addition, we offer a new resource that can be used for in-class or online teaching formats: a compendium of PowerPoint slides covering major points within each chapter. (These supplements are available to qualified adopters. Please consult your local sales representative for details.)

18. In this edition, each chapter is a self-contained unit, to facilitate teaching in cases where varied combinations of chapters are used. Thus, we list references at the end of each chapter rather than at the back of the book.

19. We have updated many of the references, integrating recent literature, but we have retained references both to valuable older works for which there is no more recent edition and to articles that are classics and provide an important historical perspective.

20. We provide new options for using the book for more specialized needs. Bound versions of Chapter 1–10 are available for courses focusing on interviewing, relationship building, and assessment and treatment planning (ISBN: 0-495-64216-6). Bound versions of Chapter 11–18 are available for courses focusing on empirically supported intervention strategies (ISBN: 0-495-64210-X). Online options allow you to select the chapters you need, add chapters from some other text, and include cases, readings, exercises, and your own original material. (See www.ichapters.com)

PEOPLE WE ACKNOWLEDGE

Over the years, we have been asked, "What is it like to put together a book like this?" Our first response is always, "We require a lot of help." For this edition, we are indebted to a number of people for their wonderful help: to Dr. Beth Robinson for preparation of the Instructor's Manual, Test Bank, and PowerPoint slide resources; to Dr. Daniel McNeil and Brandon Kyle for the new contributed chapter on exposure therapies; to Patricia Russell for manuscript preparation and reference assistance; and to Melanie Scherer, who did mountains of research for updating our research boxes in Chapters 11 through 18.

We are very grateful to the staff at Cengage Learning, particularly to our current and former editors, Marquita Flemming and Lisa Gebo, respectively, for their commitment and enthusiasm. The final form of this book as you, the reader, now see it would not have been possible without the superb efforts of the entire Cengage Learning team including Samantha Shook, Ashley Cronin, Christina Ganim, Bob Kauser, Vernon Boes, Rita Jaramillo, and Karin Sandberg. We are also very appreciative of our talented production coordinator, Merrill Peterson, of Matrix Productions, and our wonderful manuscript editor, Pat Herbst.

We also wish to acknowledge with gratitude the contribution of our manuscript reviewers, who include the following: Kayte Conroy (State University of New York, Buffalo), Gerald Corey (California State University, Fullerton), Rebecca Eberle-Romberger (University of Southern California), Barry Edelstein (West Virginia University), Angela Gillem (Arcadia University), Antonio Gonzales-Prendes (Wayne State University), Bryan Hiebert (University of Calgary), William Kolodinsky (Northern Arizona University), Annette Mahoney (Bowling Green State University), Christopher Mitchell (University of Illinois, Chicago), Eric Ornstein (University of Illinois, Chicago), Eric Patton (Southern State Community College), Richard Craig Williams (Wilmington College), and Geoffrey Yager (University of Cincinnati). For this edition, we also had the benefit of web survey input from a host of instructors. Although they are too numerous to list individually here, we want to acknowledge their unique and valuable contribution. To all of you: Thanks! We could not have done this without your careful and detailed comments and suggestions.

Finally, we also are thankful for the support of our families—particularly our husbands Jay, Jerry, and Dick and our daughters—as well as for the support of colleagues and friends, who also are too numerous to name, but they know who they are!

Sherry Cormier, Paula Nurius & Cynthia Osborn

About the Book Cover

The life of the chambered nautilus, the mollusk that makes its home in the spiral-shaped shell featured on the cover of the book, is fascinating and compelling and captures well the primary message of our book: change and growth. Inside the shell is a series of successively larger compartments, or chambers, each of them a former living space for the mollusk. As the mollusk grows, it forms a new and larger chamber to accommodate its increasing size, and it seals off its previous chamber. It cannot go back to older chambers because they are too small. Because change and growth are constant, it has no choice but to move on. Indeed, the spiral shape of the shell suggests that the chambered nautilus could keep growing forever within its shell, building on its past and gradually forming a more expansive dwelling.

We hope that the skills, strategies, and interventions that we describe in this book will assist professional helpers to guide their clients, using existing resources and strengths, in the construction of new, more accommodating, and healthier living spaces. May the maturing and determined nautilus and its spiral-shaped shell inspire helpers and clients alike in the process of change and growth.

ABOUT THIS BOOK

ENVISION THIS

Imagine yourself as the helper in the following four situations. Try to see, hear, and sense what would be happening to you.

- A 14-year-old boy who is accused of setting fire to his family home walks in defiantly to see you. He has been "mandated" to see you by the judge. He sits down, crosses his arms and legs in front of him, and stares at the ceiling. He is silent after your initial greeting.
- A young woman in her 20s walks in and can't hold back her tears. After a while, she talks about how upset she is feeling. In the last year, three of her close friends died of acquired immune deficiency syndrome (AIDS), and she lost her parents' support because she told them she is a lesbian.
- A Latino and his teenage son come in together, but they are so at odds with each other that they initially refuse to be seen by you in the same room. According to the telephone intake report, they have repeatedly fought about the amount of freedom the son wants and the father is willing to give.
- A middle-aged woman comes in. She has been escorted to your facility by her husband. She is so afraid to go out of her house that she does not drive anymore. In talking with her, you discover that she has confined herself to her home almost exclusively for the last year because of incapacitating anxiety attacks. Her husband recently turned down a lucrative job offer to avoid having to move her into a new environment.

Imagine yourself helping each of these clients. How would you feel? What thoughts would run through your head? How do you see or hear yourself responding? What things about yourself would help you in the interactions? What things would hinder you? What skills would you use to deal with each client? What skills do you lack? What do you observe about the client, and how would your observations affect the help you give? How would you know whether what you were doing was helpful?

Although responding to these kinds of questions may be difficult for you now, it will probably become easier as you go through this book and as you gain experience and feedback. In the following sections we describe the specific emphases and purposes of the text.

A PRACTICE NEXUS FOR THE HELPING PROFESSIONS

During the more than 25-year history of this book, we have learned from our readers and from the changing fields of practice, and our approach has evolved as a result. In Figure 1.1 we illustrate the unique nature of this text in terms of today's *practice nexus*—the interrelation, connections, and interfaces of our field. The figure depicts the relatedness and connection among the four major components of practice knowledge: (1) core skills and resources, (2) critical commitments, (3) effectiveness, and (4) diversity. The components come together to define the central core of what you need for today's practice. So we focus on the "interface"—the area of overlap among the components of practice knowledge—to provide a coherent and unifying foundation. As the figure shows, each component contains specialized content that you will pursue to greater or lesser degrees, depending on the need. And as you specialize, you will certainly find other components of practice that you will need to master. The totality of it all will develop over years of practice training and experience. To begin, however, you need core content, understanding of the interrelatedness, and practical as well as conceptual understanding.

We have found that having a sense of our organizing framework helps readers integrate the parts as they progress chapter by chapter, so let's briefly take a look at the four central components.

Core Skills and Resources
Multiprofessional Relevance
This book has long been adopted for courses in multiple disciplines. Thus, one of our goals is to support the growing multidisciplinary nature of today's practice by focusing on

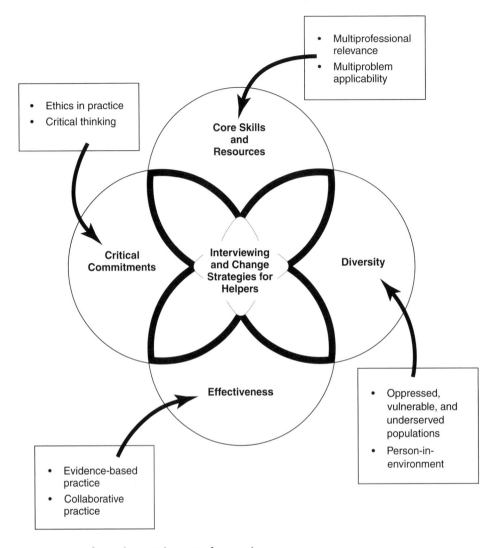

Figure 1.1 A Practice Nexus for Today's Helping Professional

shared knowledge and skills. We provide practice training that is broadly relevant, bridges training backgrounds, and provides a solid foundation on which to build specialized content. The range of settings within which helping services are provided is truly awesome—schools, health service facilities, social service and mental health centers, family service centers, correctional facilities, residential facilities, and independent practices, to name a few. We interchangeably use terms such as *helper, practitioner,* and *clinician,* along with *client* and *service recipient.* These terms are sufficiently widely used to be applicable across a range of settings and service titles. We realize the terminology may be different in your own setting and practice philosophy.

The book is directed (but not restricted) to applying skills within a helper/client dyadic relationship. However, many of the skills and strategies can be used appropriately in other modalities, such as group work, case coordination and advocacy, couple and family counseling, and environmental or organizational interventions. Indeed, we anticipate that you will build on the core knowledge and skills of this book, adding proficiency in other modalities or specializations.

Multiproblem Applicability

Evidence shows that our book stays in the personal libraries of students as they move into their practice careers, in part because the content has broad applicability to populations, practice settings, and modalities (e.g., couples, families, groups). Our selection of models and strategies reflects a predominantly but not exclusively cognitive–behavioral framework. The practice strategies we include recognize that people are active meaning makers, continuously engaged in transactions with the people and places of their lives, and that this meaning making, contextual transaction, and "hot" factors such as goals, values, emotion, and motivation need to be taken into account.

The intervention strategies we have chosen to include share a consistent theory base about ways in which people's thoughts, feelings, and behaviors are interrelated within their daily transactions with their life conditions. It is useful to be aware of the broader array of theoretical orientations. No one approach is going to be sufficient for all needs or all clients, and change strategies are increasingly becoming more integrated to increase their effectiveness and to more fully address the range of problems or vulnerabilities embedded within clients' circumstances. You will see that we integrate dimensions of other approaches into the text (e.g., person-centered, dynamic, solution-focused, relational), and we cite literature on cognitive–behavioral theory and interventions that show how it is evolving (e.g., more inclusive of hot factors, more contextualized, less rationalistic, more meditative) as well as criticisms and limitations. Rather than duplicating this readily available reading, we focus on change strategies reflective of the practice nexus—that is, strategies that are widely used and recognized across disciplines; that have broad applicability across types of problems, service settings, and diverse clientele; that are amenable to teaching clients the reasoning and conduct of strategies to foster long-term self-help; and that have an empirical base that, although not perfect, indicates likely effectiveness and generalizability to helping situations (see Chapters 11–18).

Critical Commitments

Ethics in Practice

Members of the helping professions take their mission, roles, and responsibilities seriously by crafting guidelines in the form of standards for ethics in practice. We have included ethical standards websites for several professions, which will help you better see what is common to and distinct among the perspectives. We speak directly about ethics (Chapter 2). But ethics is not so much a stand-alone factor as one that is interrelated with other critical commitments such as critical thinking as well as with other dimensions of practice, such as diversity, information technology, effectiveness, and practice contexts such as managed care. Thus, information on ethics is interspersed through the book as well as in Chapter 2.

The multifaceted nature of ethics in the practice nexus is illustrated in many of the frameworks developed to help practitioners sort through the various considerations in handling dilemmas. One such framework is Hansen and Goldberg's (1999) seven-category matrix, consisting of moral principles and personal values; clinical and cultural factors; professional codes of ethics; agency or employer policies; federal, state, and local statutes; rules and regulations; and case law. As with other critical commitments, we encourage a proactive, broad view of ethics, and we provide suggested exercises and examples to stimulate thought about grappling with ethical issues and to develop skills in anticipating and solving ethics-related problems.

Critical Thinking

Recent years have underscored the importance of reflective, critical thinking not only in clinical decision making but also as it relates to the full spectrum of practice activities, both within one's own caseload and also as a team member engaged in collective considerations such as case conferencing, program development, and agency policy. Critical thinking involves careful examination of claims, arguments, beliefs, standards, information, interpretations, options, and actions to assess strengths and limitations and yield well-reasoned formulations and answers. Critical thinking is about critiquing (oneself, others, environments) but also about creativity, openness, and tolerance for complexity, ambiguity, and difference. This is part of why we provide examples and exercises, and why we urge skill- and reflection-building activities with your student and professional colleagues. Critical thinking may best be thought of as a skill (or, rather, a set of skills) that can be learned but must be practiced with feedback to become honed and well established.

Our own commitment to critical thinking is one reason we undertake massive literature updates to provide you with sources of evidence, theory, and perspective so that you can evaluate for yourself the strengths and limitations of our and others' claims. Almost all helpers bring profound caring and sincerity to their work, but history and research repeatedly show us that these are not sufficient to avoid bias or errors, ensure provision of helpful services, or guard against inappropriate or harmful practices (Gibbs, 2003; Gibbs & Gambrill, 1999). We also speak to the dimension of critical consciousness—a form of critical thinking directed to more explicit awareness of societal and environmental factors such as power relationships, commonalities, and differences among and within people (Freire, 2005; Reed, Newman, Suarez, & Lewis, 1997). Although critical consciousness requires engagement beyond what any one text or class can achieve, we ask throughout that you be thoughtful about context, difference, and commonality.

Diversity

Oppressed, Vulnerable, and Underserved Populations

As societies become more pluralistic, the helping professions are more aware of the importance of attending to diversity than ever before. We build on the real explosion of information related to diversity and divergent voices, including feminist and multicultural ones, to help increase awareness of inequities and how these affect us and our clients. In addition to being able to identify appropriate counseling strategies for diverse client problems, you should also be able to apply helping skills and strategies carefully and sensitively to a diverse group of clients. Although you yourself may be a gay, Jewish man of middle socioeconomic level or an African American, straight, Protestant woman of upper socioeconomic level, your clients will invariably be somewhat different from you in cultural background—factors such as age, culture, ethnicity, gender, language, disability, race, gender expression, sexual orientation, religion, and socioeconomic level. And even if you and your client share many similarities of background, your client will still have unique characteristics that you must consider.

Although we cannot be prescriptive about the best way to work with all diversity factors, it is important for us to recognize that they exist and that many of the counseling skills and strategies described in this book have been developed by Euro-American men in Western culture and may not be applicable to or sufficient for all clients. For these reasons, in the client descriptions used throughout the text as both model examples and practice ones, we often include cultural referent characteristics of the client such as race, ethnicity, sexual orientation, gender, age, and physical/mental status. Diversity is a focal topic in Chapter 2; but as part of the practice nexus, we interweave diversity throughout the book, such as in examples and literature support regarding interviewing and change strategies with diverse clients.

Person-in-Environment Perspective

Attention to diversity goes beyond differences of peoples. We focus on direct, clinical practice primarily with individuals—assisting them to gain a sense of mastery for dealing with stressful life circumstances and make use of personal and environmental resources to make desired changes in their lives. Although it is beyond the scope of this book to fully cover ecological processes or environmental interventions, we maintain a person-in-environment perspective. We cannot overstate the importance of continually being aware of ways in which problems are embedded within contexts and ways in which environments are contributors to both problems and solutions. Throughout, we emphasize awareness that clients are affected by the contexts in which they live—including familiar elements such as family, neighborhood, work, cultural and identificational groups, regional areas, and countries as well as differences in material, spatial, informational, and sociopolitical resources.

We address issues of environment and transactions between people and their environments (see especially Chapters 7–10). A person-in-environment commitment is also part of what shapes our focus on cognitive–behavioral interventions. Increasingly, cognitive–behavioral interventions reflect an ecological framing—connecting intrapersonal functioning (problematic thoughts, feelings) to individuals' historical and current contexts. This includes attention to factors such as perception and personal meaning, interpersonal transactions that can take on both adaptive and maladaptive forms, and use of learning principles and significant others to initiate and support contextually feasible change.

Effectiveness

Evidence-Based Practice

Today's practice is highly influenced by regulatory requirements and ethical expectations regarding accountability. Use of empirically supported practice and evidence-based decision making has become part of training accreditation requirements as well as work-site expectations, although certainly not without issue. We anticipate that clinical practice in coming years will increasingly be affected (positively and/or negatively) by pressures to demonstrate the evidence base of practice decisions and outcomes, the development and use of practice guidelines, concern for generalizability (e.g., does an intervention appear effective across differing client and situation characteristics?), and efficiency.

We speak to some of the factors to be balanced in this pursuit, particularly in Chapters 9 and 10. We also work to provide pragmatic aids to assist you: We include interviewing and change strategies that have undergone empirical examination, we provide behavioral descriptions of what the strategies entail, we provide updates on literature relevant to current interventions, and we describe concrete tools designed to prepare you to meet today's evidence requirements (see Chapters 11–18). At the same time, we encourage you to recognize the realistic limitations on empirically demonstrable efficacy, the need for new tools (e.g., qualitative, contextually sensitive means of measuring), and emerging or evolving interventions that merit careful consideration.

Collaborative Practice

Significant, sustainable change in people's lives requires much more than a clinician can possibly transact within the limits of formal helping sessions. Collaboration reflects an ethical commitment to self-determination and informed participation, building on strengths toward problem solving, partnering with clients as well as with other resource providers to achieve client goals, an educationally oriented approach that aids clients in their ongoing change efforts, and a pragmatic recognition that effective practice is done not to but with clients. We maintain that, realistically, clients are closest to their own needs and situations. Although this closeness can pose challenges, it nonetheless speaks to the importance of clients bringing their own information, perspectives, and networks to the table, serving as active agents toward realistic change for themselves as people in environments.

These principles have guided many of our choices about what to include here, such as the strengths orientation in assessment (Chapters 7 and 8), emphasis on effective listening (Chapter 5), engagement of clients across the stages of helping (Chapters 3–6), and focus on change strategies that can feasibly be taught, tried out, and judiciously adapted as needed (Chapters 11–18). We also encourage you to consider ways in which activities and other resources within this book or in other sources may be shared with clients. Collaboration applies also to how contemporary professionals work together in practice settings—which are commonly populated by practitioners of varying disciplinary and life experience backgrounds—and to the need to be trained in the practice nexus to "work in the interface." Consider, for instance, the team of people needed to work with high-risk families—perhaps a child counselor, a family therapy social worker, a psychologist or a psychiatrist if testing or medications are indicated, a vocational worker, a case coordinator, and perhaps other specialists (in, for example, translation, disability, violence, chemical dependency, or school liaison).

TODAY'S PRACTICE NEXUS IN THE MANAGED CARE CONTEXT

The impact of the managed care movement on the helping professions is nearly unparalleled. Effects and implications reverberate throughout the practice nexus, raising new ethical dilemmas; diversity-related challenges; influences on core practice activities, including how a problem is articulated and interventions are selected; and, of course, expectations regarding outcomes and effectiveness. This book responds to the realities of today's professional practice by attending to many of these issues and focusing on practice tools and strategies that you will need for defensible, sustainable practice within managed care and related systems of service delivery. Rather than being fixed, this approach involves wide-ranging balances (e.g., the use of short-term, empirically supported treatments balanced with the need to adapt interventions to be appropriate to the needs and environmental characteristics of a diverse clientele) common across the helping professions.

Let's consider a case example and the multiple levels of practice nexus consideration it may require:

> After a licensed psychologist has completed the initially allocated 10 sessions of treatment, the managed care organization (MCO) denies additional sessions for an indigent, adult, Native American client with a history of severe sexual abuse and, at times, manipulative, suicidal gestures. Before the client is informed of this decision, she experiences a suicidal crisis and makes an emergency call to her psychologist, requesting a session later that day. Prior to meeting with the client, the psychologist attempts to obtain authorization from the MCO for at least one additional session. The regular case manager and departmental supervisor are both on vacation. On the basis of a limited understanding of the client, the interim case manager insists that this suicidal crisis is a manipulative gesture and refuses to authorize additional sessions. (Hansen & Goldberg, 1999, p. 495)

Needless to say, many elements are involved here. Critical commitments such as concern about ethical practice and critical consciousness intersect with diversity. For example, to what extent may factors be operating that have historically resulted in lower-socioeconomic-status people of color being viewed in more pathological and decontextualized terms as well as underserved by mental health systems? Are there ways to engage the interim case manager toward a more complete understanding of the client that may result in a different interpretation? Several current and earlier problems are implicated. How might thinking about multiple professional sources expand the spectrum of resources to consider? How was the case originally framed in terms of primary problems to address and selected change strategies? Are there evidence-based alternatives or extensions to the original change strategies that can defensibly be argued toward addressing this multiproblem case? With a collaborative working philosophy in mind, are there ways to engage with the client and, possibly, with her support network to solve the constraints, identify her strengths (including gains the client may have made in her therapeutic work thus far), and generate immediate or longer-term sources of assistance? Clearly, there are no simple solutions, but there are layers of connections. Awareness of these may aid you to think in different ways about clients and options, and to work flexibly on behalf of those who come to you for help.

AN OVERVIEW OF HELPING

A helping professional is someone who helps with the exploration and resolution of issues and problems presented by a client: the person who is seeking help. We identify four primary stages of helping:

1. Establishing an effective therapeutic relationship
2. Assessment and goal setting
3. Strategy selection and implementation
4. Evaluation and termination

The first stage of the helping process, *establishing an effective therapeutic relationship* with the client, is based primarily on client- or person-centered therapy (Rogers, 1951) and more recently on social influence theory (Strong, Welsh, Corcoran, & Hoyt, 1992) and on psychoanalytic theory (Gelso & Hayes, 1998; Safran & Muran, 2000). We present skills for this stage in Chapters 3–6. The potential value of a sound relationship base cannot be overlooked because the relationship is the specific part of the process that conveys the counselor's interest in and acceptance of the client as a unique and worthwhile person and builds sufficient trust for eventual self-disclosure and self-revelation to occur. For some clients, working with a counselor who stays primarily in this stage may be useful and sufficient. For other clients, the relationship part of therapy is necessary but not sufficient to help them with the kinds of choices and changes they seek to make. These clients need additional kinds of action or intervention strategies.

The second stage of helping, *assessment and goal setting,* often begins with or shortly after relationship building. In both stages, the practitioner is interested mainly in helping clients *explore* themselves and their concerns. Assessment is designed to help both the clinician and the client obtain a better picture, idea, or grasp of what is happening with the client and what prompted the client to seek the services of a helper at this time. The information gleaned from assessment is extremely valuable in planning strategies and can also be used to manage resistance. We describe assessment strategies in Chapters 7 and 8. As the problems and issues are identified and defined, the practitioner and client also work through the process of developing outcome goals. Outcome goals are the specific results that the client would like to occur as a result of counseling. Outcome goals also provide useful information for planning action strategies (see Chapter 9).

In the third stage of helping, *strategy selection and implementation,* the counselor's task is to help with client understanding and related action. Insight can be useful, but insight alone is far less useful than insight accompanied by a supporting plan that helps the client translate new or different understandings into observable and specific actions or behaviors. Toward this end, the counselor and client select and sequence a plan of action: intervention strategies that are based on the assessment data and are designed to help the client achieve the designated goals. In developing action plans, it is important to select plans that relate to the identified concerns and goals and that are not in conflict with the client's primary beliefs and values (see Chapters 10–18).

The last major phase of helping, *evaluation and termination,* involves, first, assessing the effectiveness of the helper's interventions and the progress the client has made toward the desired goals (see Chapter 9). This kind of evaluation assists you in knowing when to terminate the process to revamp your action plans. Also, clients, who can easily become discouraged during the change process, often find observable and concrete signs of progress to be quite reinforcing. Our listing of evaluation as the last stage of helping can inadvertently suggest that gauging effectiveness comes late or near the end of counseling. However, if we are not making effective progress in developing a collaborative, therapeutic relationship or in understanding the perspective of a client, we need to be aware of this right away. In reality, we are and need to be explicitly evaluating effectiveness throughout the helping process and also sharing our observations as part of our collaborative relationship with clients. Indeed, there is some flow and interrelationship among all four stages. In other words, elements of these stages are present throughout the helping process, with varying degrees of emphasis. As

Waehler and Lenox (1994) point out, "Counseling participants do not go through a discrete state of relationship building and then 'graduate' to undertaking assessment as stage models imply" (p. 19). Each stage is interconnected to the others. For example, during the assessment and goal-setting stage, the relationship process is still attended to, and termination may be discussed early in the relationship.

Just as there are stages and processes associated with helping, helpers also have stages and themes as they enter the helping profession, seek training, encounter clients, and gain supervised experience. In an award-winning study now summarized in a book, Skovholt and Rønnestad (1995) explored the development of helping professionals over the life span of their careers. They found that practitioners progress through eight stages from the time they select helping as a career to the point where they are experienced practitioners. These eight stages of professional development can be described as follows:

1. Conventional stage
2. Transition to professional training stage
3. Imitation of experts stage
4. Conditional autonomy stage
5. Exploration stage
6. Integration stage
7. Individuation stage
8. Integrity stage

Skovholt (2001) expands on these stages and related factors in the development of practitioners, looking toward fostering "resilient practitioners."

Like the stages of helping, the eight professional development stages are interconnected. At each stage, certain themes most concern helpers. For example, an entry-level practitioner is necessarily more concerned with skill development than with individual identity as a helper. Entry-level helpers are also more likely to model the behaviors they see in expert teachers and supervisors. Farther along the career path, different themes and concerns emerge.

We point this progression out as part of our reasoning for focusing on cognitive–behavioral theories and models of practice. Evidence suggests that at earlier stages of development (as in courses for which this book is designed), detailed knowledge and the opportunity to achieve some initial depth of skills in applying and adapting practice methods match the learning needs and priorities of becoming an effective helper and feeling competent in one's work. Thus, although you will need to become familiar with the wider array of practice models and with their relative strengths and limitations as part of your longer-range professional development, our emphasis at this stage is on core tools and skills.

We selected the cognitive–behavioral framework as the focus for change strategies for this reason and because of its consistency with priorities within the practice nexus. Two major practice theorists, Prochaska and Norcross (2007), have described cognitive–behavioral therapies in general as the fastest-growing and most heavily researched orientations in the contemporary scene—the "blue-chip" selection for the next five years in terms of likelihood of growing. Some reasons for this popularity are the commitment of cognitive–behavioral framework to psychotherapy integration, its dedication to empirical evaluation, and its psychoeducational approach, which makes it more accessible for direct use by clients (e.g., self-help formats, access through the Internet, and availability in computer-assisted mediums). Cognitive methods are commonly blended with other therapies, a process consistent with current experimentation with integrative treatment models that build upon complementary strengths of differing approaches. This blended strategy is popular in societies outside the United States (providing a wider cultural and contextual base for evaluation) and is increasingly being used to treat serious and chronic disorders.

Although these factors have influenced our choice to focus on cognitive–behavioral strategies, every practice method has flaws and limitations, and we do not argue for "card-carrying" adherence to a single perspective. Current estimates place the number of therapies in the hundreds—not a realistic number to review. However, a more limited set of therapies or therapy clusters are commonly grouped as the central ones. Prochaska and Norcross (2007) provide a systematic review of the central tenets of each, including critiques and case examples. They include familiar, long-standing therapeutic approaches such as psychodynamic, existential, behavioral, and systemic as well as more recent developments into multicultural, gender-sensitive, constructivist, and integrative approaches. In a related vein, Norcross, Beutler, and Levant (2005) provide a compilation in which experts in varied therapeutic areas examine nine core questions about evidence-based practices, illuminating some areas of convergence or similarity as well as contention or significant differences.

THE INTERWEAVE OF INTERVIEWING AND CHANGE STRATEGIES

Although interviewing and change strategies are often separated into different courses due to scheduling logistics, they are integrally related to each other, ebbing and flowing across the stages of the helping process. Rather than focusing on interviewing and change strategies in two discrete books, we aim for applied coherence by combining them, as well as combining content on practice knowledge with activities to enhance skill building. The arena of professional helping practice is highly dynamic. An important part of currency is staying abreast of key debates and developments to inform your ongoing selections and training.

Complementary to this breadth of exposure and comparative analysis is a more in-depth description of the knowledge, skills, and tools that operationalize and translate theory into action. These goals permeate our text. In the first six chapters we present what we call "fundamental skills" for understanding nonverbal behavior and establishing an effective helping relationship, and we describe verbal responses useful for practitioners of varying theoretical orientations. We discuss clinician and client nonverbal communication patterns and behaviors in Chapter 3; the facilitative relationship, conditions of empathy, genuineness, and positive regard in Chapter 4; and the microskills associated with listening and conveying basic or reciprocal empathy in Chapter 5. Expanding on the notion of helping as an influence process, we also present microskills associated with influencing, challenging, and conveying advanced or additive empathy in Chapter 6.

We hope that in this book you will find training experiences that further your personal growth, develop your helping skills, and provide ways for you to evaluate your effectiveness. Personal growth is the most elusive and most difficult to define of these three areas. Although it is beyond the scope of this book to focus primarily on self-development, you may engage in self-exploration as you go through certain parts of the text, including refinement of your working model of practice and of your identity as a practicing professional. It is essential that you seek out additional experiences in which you can receive feedback from others about yourself, your strengths, and some behaviors that may interfere with counseling. These experiences might be field-based or classroom activities, feedback, growth groups, and personal counseling. It is well documented that a counselor's warmth, empathy, and positive regard can contribute to client change (see Chapter 4). We feel that your demonstration of these relationship conditions will enhance the way you use the skills and strategies that we present.

Above all, we want to convey that our book is about the *practical application* of selected skills and strategies. Our coverage of theoretical and research concepts is limited because they are covered adequately in other texts; we believe that bringing together knowledge and skill building will be useful to your professional development.

FORMAT OF THE BOOK

Our learning format is designed to help you demonstrate and measure your use of the helping competencies that we present. Each chapter includes the following elements: a brief introduction, Learning Outcomes, content material interspersed with model examples, Learning Activities with feedback, a role-play interview assessment, and a Knowledge and Skill Builder component to assist you in gauging your retention and understanding of the chapter's content. People who have participated in field-testing our text tell us that using these activities helps them get involved and interact with the material.

You can complete the chapters by yourself or in a class. If you feel you need to go over an activity several times, do so! If part of the material is familiar, jump ahead. We have taken care to include references to assist you in further reading at any point. Throughout each chapter, your performance on the Learning Activities and self-evaluations will be a clue to the pace at which you can work through the chapter. To help you use the book's format to your advantage, we will explain each of its components briefly.

Learning Outcomes

As we developed each chapter, we had certain goals in mind. For each major topic, there are certain concepts and skills to be learned. At the beginning of each chapter you will find "Learning Outcomes"—a list of the kinds of things that you can learn from the chapter. The use of outcome goals for learning is similar to the use of goals in the helping process. The Learning Outcomes provide cues for your end results and serve as benchmarks by which you can assess your own progress. As you will see in Chapter 9, an objective or goal contains three parts:

1. Behavior, or what is to be learned or performed
2. Level of performance, or how much or how often the behavior is to be demonstrated
3. Conditions of performance, or the circumstances or situations under which the behavior can be performed

Part 1 of a learning goal refers to what you should learn or demonstrate. Parts 2 and 3 are concerned with evaluation of performance. The evaluative parts of a Learning Outcome, such as the suggested level of performance, may seem a bit hard-nosed. However, setting outcome goals with a fairly high mastery level may result in improved performance. We state the Learning Outcomes at the beginning of each chapter so you know what to be thinking about as you make your way through the chapter. The Learning Outcomes are directly linked to the self-evaluation exercises called "Knowledge and Skill Builders," which are listed at the end of each chapter to help you assess your progress.

Learning Activities

Learning Activities that reflect a chapter's Learning Outcome goals are interspersed throughout each chapter. These activities, which are intended to provide both practice and feedback, consist of model examples, exercises, and feedback. You can use them in several ways. Many of the exercises suggest that you write your responses. Your written responses can help you or your instructor check the accuracy and specificity of your work. You may take a piece of paper and actually write the responses down. Or you may prefer to think through an activity and just consider your responses.

Some exercises instruct you to imagine yourself in a certain situation and doing certain things. We find that this form of mental rehearsal can help you prepare for the kinds of counseling responses you might use in a particular situation. This type of responding does not require any written responses. However, if it would help you to jot down some notes after the activity is over, go ahead. You are the best person to determine how to use these exercises to your advantage.

Many of the Learning Activities, particularly in the first six chapters, are based on cognitive self-instruction. The objective of this type of activity is to help you not only to acquire the skill by providing you with a description of it, but also to internalize the skill. Some research suggests that this approach may be an important addition to the more common elements of microtraining (modeling, rehearsal, feedback) found to be so helpful in skill acquisition (Morran, Kurpius, Brack, & Brack, 1995). The cognitive learning strategy is designed specifically to help you develop your own way to think about the skill or to put it together in a way that makes sense to you. The Learning Activities of Chapters 5 and 6, for example, provide sample client material to respond to, self-questions to guide readers thinking about and responding to that material, and feedback examples to provide an initial basis of comparison for one's own responses relative to responses we might suggest.

Another kind of Learning Activity involves a more direct rehearsal than do the written or covert exercises. These "overt rehearsal" exercises are designed to help you apply your skills in simulated counseling sessions with a role-play interview. The role-play activities generally involve three persons or roles: a helper, a client, and an observer. Each group should trade roles so that each person can experience the role play from these different perspectives. One person's task is to serve as the helper and practice the skills specified in the instructions. The helper role provides an opportunity to try out the skills in simulated helping situations. A second person, the client, will be counseled during the role play.

We give a note of caution: Potentially conflicting aims must be balanced here. One aim is to strengthen training through supervised opportunities, such as role play, that approximate actual helping scenarios and provide input as well as application experience. However, ethical concerns must also be considered. For example, using a real concern or something a student feels strongly about and can readily envision may help augment the realism of portraying a client. On the other hand, self-disclosures in this context cannot be guaranteed to be held in confidence and may introduce discomfort or influence subsequent evaluation of the student/client by the instructor or by student peers. Alternatives have been suggested, such as the use of actors as clients (see Levitov, Fall, and Jennings, 1999, and Osborn, Dean, and Petruzzi, 2004, for examples and discussion). This approach, of course, raises its own dilemmas and trade-offs.

We recommend group discussion of issues such as these prior to undertaking role-play or other training exercises that raise issues such as privacy and vulnerability. Clear ground rules and safeguards need to be established, whatever the method. Evoking the part of a client reminds us of the difficulty and vulnerability that many clients feel with the self-disclosing and sorting out necessary for the helping process. We are not recommending required self-disclosure or inappropriate introduction of one's personal needs into the educational exchange, but judicious decisions about how to make optimal, appropriate use of experiential and other applied training exercises. Needless to say, we assume that you share a view of professionalism that maintains sensitivity and safeguards, whether as part of a role play, case conferencing, group supervision, or other such activity.

The third person in the role-play exercise is the observer. This is a very important role because it develops and sharpens observational skills that are an important part of effective helping. The observer has three tasks to accomplish. First, this person should observe the process and identify what the client does and how the helper responds. When the helper is rehearsing a particular skill or strategy, the observer can also determine the strengths and limitations of the helper's approach. Second, the observer can provide consultation at any point during the role play if it might help the experience. Such consultation may occur if the helper gets stuck or if the observer perceives that the helper is practicing too many unhelpful behaviors. In this capacity, we have often found it helpful for the observer to serve as a sort of alter ego for the helper. The observer can then become involved in the role play to help give the helper more options or better focus. However, it is important not to take over for the helper in such instances. The third and most important task of the observer is to provide feedback to the helper about his or her performance following the role play. The person who role-played the client may also wish to provide feedback.

Giving useful feedback is itself a skill used in some helping strategies. The feedback that occurs following the role play should be considered just as important as the role play itself. Although everyone involved in the role play will receive feedback after serving as the helper, it is still sometimes difficult to "hear" negative feedback. Sometimes, receptiveness to feedback will depend on the way the observer presents it. We encourage you to make use of these opportunities to practice giving feedback to another person in a constructive, useful manner. Try to make your feedback specific and concise. Remember, the purpose of feedback is to help the helper learn more about the role play; it should not be construed as an opportunity to analyze the helper's personality or lifestyle.

The reverse can also be problematic. Feedback that is overly rosy or assumes too much (such as the helper's intent) is not inherently useful. Persons playing observer or client can offer feedback in the form of questions about the reasoning or the basis for a decision or a direction that the helper took in the role play. This kind of walking through practice judgments can be extremely useful to gaining skills in self-reflection and critical thinking. Establishing a respectful, specific, and constructive tone also furthers discussion of issues that naturally emerge through role playing, such as ethical conundrums or uncertainties.

Another Learning Activity involves having people learn the strategies as partners or in small groups by teaching one another. We suggest that you trade off teaching a strategy to your partner or to the group. Person A might teach covert modeling to Person B, and then Person B teaches Person A muscle relaxation. The "student" can also receive feedback on his or her efforts to apply the new skill. For example, Person B would practice covert modeling (taught by Person A), and Person A would demonstrate the strategy learned from Person B. We learn in multiple ways, and techniques such as this capitalize on learning through teaching/modeling/feedback and learning through observing/applying/trying again with feedback.

The Role of Feedback in Learning Activities

We offer some form of feedback for many of the Learning Activities. For example, if a Learning Activity involves identifying positive and negative examples of a helping conversational style, the feedback will indicate which examples are positive and which are negative. We have attempted in most of our feedback to give some rationale for the responses. In many of the feedback sections, we include several possible responses. Our purpose in including feedback is not for you to find out how many "right" and "wrong" answers you have given in a particular activity. The responses listed in the feedback sections should serve as guidelines for you to code and judge your own responses. With this in mind, we would like you to view the feedback sections not only as sources of information and alternatives, but also as aids to developing the habits of mindful, reflective practice reasoning and decision making that are part of critical thinking (e.g., "How did I arrive at that conclusion? What other pieces of information might I have sought or paid greater attention to?"). We hope you do not become discouraged when your responses are different from the ones in the feedback sections. We don't expect you to come up with responses identical to ours; some of your responses may be just as good as or better than the ones that we provide. Indeed, judicious adaptation is predicated on the recognition that the specifics of individuals and circumstances must be taken into account to achieve appropriate and effective helping. Also, space does not permit us to list every possibly useful response in the feedback sections for the Learning Activities.

Locating Learning Activities and Feedback Sections in the Text

Usually, a Learning Activity directly follows the related content section. We have positioned the Learning Activities in this way (rather than grouping them at the end of each chapter) to give you an immediate opportunity to work with and apply specific content before moving ahead to new material. Feedback for a Learning Activity is usually separated from the activity itself by a page turn. This is done to encourage you to work through a Learning Activity without scanning down the page to see our response. We believe that this arrangement will help you work independently and will encourage you to develop and rely on your own knowledge base and skills. The Learning Activities and their corresponding feedback sections are numbered to make them easy to match up. In addition to the model examples in most chapters, in Chapters 7–18 we provide model cases consisting of actual interview dialogues between a practitioner and a client we call Isabella. The cases are intended to demonstrate the particular intervention and change strategies being used in those chapters. A unique feature of these model dialogues is inclusion of the practitioner's clinical reasoning prior to the practitioner's responses so as to illustrate the helper's moment-to-moment planning as the sessions unfold.

Knowledge and Skill Builders and Website Resources

At the end of each chapter can be found a self-evaluation component called "Knowledge and Skill Builder," consisting of questions and activities related to the knowledge and skills to be acquired in the chapter. The Knowledge and Skill Builders are also available on our book-specific website, as are chapter website resources. In addition, the website includes extra practice responses on interviewing skills, and multiple-choice quizzes for each chapter. The quizzes can be useful in preparing you for postdegree certification testing.

The Knowledge and Skill Builder questions and activities reflect the conditions specified in the Learning Outcomes listed at the start of each chapter. When the desired outcome is the ability to identify a response in a written statement or case, take some paper and write down your response. However, if the desired outcome is the demonstration of a response in a role play, the evaluation will suggest how you can assess your level of performance by setting up a role-play assessment. Other self-evaluation activities may suggest that you do something or experience something to heighten your awareness of, or information about, the idea or skill to be learned.

The primary purpose of the Knowledge and Skill Builders is to help you assess your competencies after completing the chapters. One way to do this is to check your responses against those provided in the "Feedback for Knowledge and Skill Builder" sections. If you find a great discrepancy, the Knowledge and Skill Builder activities can shed light on areas still troublesome for you. You may wish to improve in these areas by reviewing parts of the chapter, redoing the Learning Activities, or asking for help from your instructor or a colleague.

Additional Practice

You may find some skills more difficult than others to acquire the first time around. People are often chagrined and disappointed when they do not demonstrate a strategy as well as they would like on their first attempt. We ask these individuals whether they hold similar levels of expectation for their clients! You cannot quickly and simply let go of behaviors that you don't find useful and acquire others that are more useful. It may be unrealistic to assume that you will always demonstrate an adequate level of performance on *all* the evaluations on the first go-round. Much covert and overt rehearsal may be necessary before you feel comfortable with skill demonstration in the evaluations. On some occasions, you may need to work through the Learning Activities and Knowledge and Skill Builder activities more than once.

Some Cautions about Using This Format

Although we believe that the format of this book will promote learning, we want you to consider three cautions about using it. First, as you will see, we have defined the skills and strategies in precise and systematic ways to make it easier for you to acquire and develop the skills. However, we do not intend that our definitions and guidelines be used like cookbook instructions, without thought or imagination. Similarly, one change strategy may not work well for all clients. As your helping experience accumulates, you will find that one client does not use a strategy in the same way, at the same pace, or with similar results as another client. In selecting helping strategies, you will find it helpful to be guided by the documentation concerning the ways in which the strategy has been used. But it is just as important to remember that each client may respond in an idiosyncratic manner to any particular approach or that conditions may require judicious adaptation. In short, you will need to identify the potential appropriateness of any given helping strategy but also fit the intervention to the client and context. After you have finished the book, we hope you will be able to select and use appropriate counseling strategies when confronted with a depressed client, an anxious client, a nonassertive client, and so forth. We also hope you will be aware of cases in which approaches and strategies included in this book may not be very useful.

Our definitions, descriptions, and examples will give you methodology and rationale for the various interviewing, relationship-building, and change strategies. But do not see this as formulaic, particularly when applying your skills during the interview process. If something does not seem to be working effectively or is not suited to the people or situation (including your own personality and work style), we hope you will make adjustments, adapting the procedure creatively and judiciously to provide the most appropriate and effective service. Finally, remember that almost anybody can learn and perform a skill as a routine. Similarly, almost anybody can use a spontaneous "fly by the seat of one's pants" approach or strictly adhere to a personal ideology that is resistant to critique. But not everyone shows the willingness and ability to synthesize qualities of the practice nexus—for example, balancing training in specific practice skills with sensitivity and ingenuity in order to continuously assess and collaborate with clients to establish well-suited forms of helping.

One of the most difficult parts of learning clinical helping skills seems to be trusting the skills to work and not being preoccupied with your own performance. Inordinate preoccupation with yourself, your skills, or a particular procedure reduces your ability to relate to and carefully attend to another person or circumstances of the moment. At first, it is natural to focus on the skill or strategy because it is new and feels a little awkward or cumbersome. But once you have learned and practiced a particular skill or strategy, the skills will be there when you need them. Gradually, as you acquire your repertory of skills and strategies, you should be able to change your focus from the procedure to the person. This is another example of what you will undergo as you are challenged, change, and grow as a helping practitioner, responding to the challenge and growth that clients undergo in their own learning and change efforts. New ways of thinking, feeling, relating, and behaving will inherently feel unnatural at first and will require considerable repetition and reinforcement before they become mastered, automatic, and synthesized as a smooth whole rather than a series of discrete steps. We return to these issues in the chapters on change strategies.

Second, remember that helping is a complex process composed of many interrelated parts. Although in this book we present different helping stages, skills, and strategies in separate chapters, in practice there is a meshing of all these components. As an example, the relationship does not stop or diminish in importance when a practitioner and client begin to assess issues, establish goals, or implement strategies. Nor is evaluation something that occurs only when formal helping sessions are terminated. Evaluation involves continual monitoring throughout the helping interaction. Even obtaining a client's commitment to use strategies consistently and to monitor their effects may be aided or hindered by the quality of the relationship and the degree to which client problems and goals have been clearly defined. In the same vein, keep in mind that most client problems are complex and multifaceted. Successful helping may involve changes in the client's feelings, observable behavior, beliefs,

and cognitions. To model some of the skills and procedures you will learn, we include cases and model dialogues in most chapters. These are intended to illustrate one example of a way in which a particular procedure can be used with a client. However, the cases and dialogues have been simplified for demonstration purposes, and the printed words may not communicate the sense of flow and direction that is normally present in practitioner/client interchanges. Again, with actual clients you will encounter more dimensions in the relationship and in a client's concerns than are reflected in the chapter examples.

Our third concern involves the way you approach the examples and practice opportunities in this book. Obviously, reading an example or doing a role-play interview is not as real as seeing an actual client or engaging in a live counseling interaction. However, some practice is necessary in any new learning program. Even if the exercises seem artificial, they probably will help you learn counseling skills. The structured practice opportunities in the book may require a great deal of discipline from you, but the degree to which you can generalize your skills from practice to an actual helping interview may depend on how much you invest in the practice opportunities.

Options for Using the Book

We have written this book in its particular format because each component seems to play a unique role in the learning process. But we are also committed to the idea that each person must determine the most suitable individual method of learning. With this in mind, we suggest a number of ways to use this book. First, you can go through the book and use the entire format in the way it is described in this chapter. If you do this, we suggest that you familiarize yourself carefully with the format as described here. If you want to use this format but do not understand it, it is not likely to be helpful. Another way is to use only certain parts of the format in any combination you choose. You may want to experiment initially to determine which components seem especially useful. For example, you might use the Knowledge and Skill Builder but not complete the chapter Learning Activities, or you might complete the Knowledge and Skill Builders that are available online. Finally, if you prefer a traditional textbook format, you can ignore the Learning Outcomes, Learning Activities, and Knowledge and Skill Builders. Use the book in whatever way is most suitable for your learning strategies.

Throughout the book, icons appear. These identify chapter elements and are designed to help you quickly locate certain kinds of resources or Learning Activities. Specifically, you will see 📓 for Learning Activities, 🔀 for Feedback on Learing Activities, 🐢 for Knowledge and Skill Builders, and 🔀 for Knowledge and Skill Builder Feedback.

EVIDENCE-BASED PRACTICE

Although the goal of integrating research evidence with clinical expertise and client and professional values is long-standing, the focus on and effects of mandates to use evidence-based or effectiveness-supported change strategies have never been stronger. We recognize that this pursuit is complex and has both positive and negative features. Questions like defining what *evidence* means, what qualifies as evidence or as "better" evidence, who is or is not included as either researcher or researched, how meaningful or contextualized any set of findings is, how rigidly or reasonably findings are translated into practice guides, and what impact evidence-based requirements have on dimensions of helping such as fostering the centrality of the helping relationship and attending to the complexity of the client and her or his circumstances, though important, are often insufficiently addressed.

We have worked to achieve a balance. Our format is consistent with evidence-based commitments and curricula in the selection of teaching content that has evidence support and in opportunities for self-evaluation of the extent to which the content and skills are sufficiently mastered. We have focused on cognitive–behavioral interventions in part because of their effectiveness and favorable track record to date, spanning diverse groups and varied settings and problem types. There are large evidence-based collaborations between practice and research groups that can be useful in staying abreast of developments. Examples include the Cochrane Collaboration (www.cochrane.org/) and the Campbell Collaboration (www.campbellcollaboration.org). Similarly, the American Psychological Association and other professional organizations, are working to summarize and update timely findings and make them available to practitioners. At the same time, we recognize that this is an imperfect and highly complex pursuit, one that requires thoughtful attention to the "practice-based evidence" facets of evidence-based practice. As Prochaska and Norcross (2007, p. 545) note, "—there is probably no issue more central to clinicians than the evolution of EBP [evidence-based practice] in mental health." We believe that the content we have selected and the practice and teaching tools we include will help you build your own foundation as a conscientious and effective practitioner.

GLOBALIZATION

"The fabled global community is now upon us" (Marsella, 1998, p. 1282). More than ever, the pluralism of our own nation in terms of cultural, racial, religious, and linguistic diversity is growing, yet so is our global interconnectedness, intensifying through telecommunication, transportation, economic, environmental, political, and social welfare ties. Many of these developments provide new opportunities and productive changes. In addition, we also must increasingly grapple with problems that accompany this intricate web of forces as well as with the pace and stresses of rapid change, such as culture shock and dislocation, migration, acculturation stress, identity confusion, social fragmentation, impoverishment and civil rights abuses, environmental degradation, critical health threats, terrorism, warfare, and beyond. Helping professionals are part of responding to the emergent concerns and needs caused by such factors and events, requiring tools not only for what is known and recognized today but also for continuing changes that we cannot anticipate.

You will see emphasis throughout this book on the use of system and contextual conceptualizations, cultural forces in people's lives and behaviors, cautions about national or ethnocentric bias, and recognizing the relevance of the world outside our borders. In the harried pace of our everyday lives, the global community can seem somewhat remote—compelling in stories we hear on the news but hard to see and feel in some practice arenas. This situation will change in the years to come, as many of the global forces forge ties both planned and unplanned that will illuminate our interconnections. We encourage a global perspective not only because it is realistic but also because we have as much to learn as to share with our international colleagues and neighbors.

INFORMATION TECHNOLOGY IN THE NEW MILLENNIUM

The surging growth of information technology since the first edition of this book is nothing short of phenomenal. You are likely a daily user of computer and related information technology—whether it be personal use such as word processing, e-mail, fax, and the web, or the more-specialized uses in many service settings today, such as client case recording and management information systems that track and coordinate fiscal, administrative, and service activities. We are also seeing the growth of electronic tools for a variety of educational and therapeutic purposes, such as tutorials, interactive simulations, assessment and decision, case coordination or discharge planning, electronic referral and information sites and sources, multisite conferencing and other distance technology, specialized tools aimed to reduce language and disability barriers, and a growing range of virtual technology and other computer-assisted tools intended for direct use with clients.

We encourage your participation both as a helping professional grounded in the knowledge and critical commitments of your discipline and as a technologically savvy user. This approach will require hands-on skills that will allow you to judiciously evaluate the merits of technological tools and information—to query, for example, if any given computer product or information pulled from the web has demonstrated effectiveness. Has this tool been assessed for its appropriateness with people of differing cultural backgrounds? Can it safely be applied in a manner consistent with ethical safeguards?

CHAPTER SUMMARY

We have significantly updated the literature base of this sixth edition. But the pace of change in practice knowledge has never been greater. Throughout your studies and beyond, you will need to be accessing professional resources to maintain currency and evolve your practice perspective and skill base. We strive in this book to integrate components that, in totality, are part of today's well-prepared helping professional. This aim informs what we lay out here as the "practice nexus." We balance this content knowledge with educational supports—such as case examples, specification of practice techniques and how to apply them, attention to diversity factors and how these shape practice approaches, role-play opportunities, and a range of learning and self-evaluation activities. We believe this balance of theory, research, concrete clinical instruction, and engagement activities is optimal for learning. As you work with this book, you may think of ways we can further improve the book, and we welcome your input!

REFERENCES

Freire, P. (2005). *Education for critical consciousness.* New York: Continuum International Publishing Group.

Gelso, C. J., & Hayes, J. A. (1998). *The psychotherapy relationship.* New York: Wiley.

Gibbs, L. E. (2003). *Evidence-based practice for the helping professions: A practical guide with integrated multimedia.* Pacific Grove, CA: Thomson Learning.

Gibbs, L., & Gambrill, E. (1999). *Critical thinking for social workers: Exercises for the helping professions.* Thousand Oaks, CA: Pine Forge Press.

Hansen, N. D., & Goldberg, S. G. (1999). Navigating the nuances: A matrix of considerations for ethical–legal dilemmas. *Professional Psychology: Research and Practice, 30*(5), 495–503.

Levitov, J. E., Fall, K. A., & Jennings, M. C. (1999). Counselor clinical training with client-actors. *Counselor Education and Supervision, 38,* 249–259.

Marsella, A. J. (1998). Toward a "global-community" psychology. *American Psychologist, 53,* 1282–1291.

Morran, K., Kurpius, D., Brack, C., & Brack, G. (1995). A cognitive-skills model for counselor training and supervision. *Journal of Counseling and Development, 73,* 384–389.

Norcross, J. C., Beutler, L. E., & Levant, R. E. (2005). *Evidence-based practices in mental health: Debate and dialogue on the fundamental questions.* Washington, DC: American Psychological Association.

Osborn, C. J., Dean, E. P., & Petruzzi, M. L. (2004). Use of simulated multidisciplinary treatment teams and client actors to teach case conceptualization and treatment planning skills. *Counselor Education and Supervision, 44,* 121–134.

Prochaska, J. O., & Norcross, J. C. (2007). *Systems of psychotherapy: A transtheoretical analysis* (6th ed.). Pacific Grove, CA: Thomson Learning.

Reed, B. G., Newman, P. A., Suarez, Z. E., & Lewis, E. A. (1997). Interpersonal practice beyond diversity and toward social justice: The importance of critical consciousness. In C. D. Garvin & B. A. Seabury (Eds.), *Interpersonal practice in social work: Promoting competence and social justice* (pp. 44–78). Boston: Allyn & Bacon.

Rogers, C. (1951). *Client-centered therapy.* Boston: Houghton Mifflin.

Safran, J. D., & Muran, J. C. (2000). *Negotiating the therapeutic alliance: A relational treatment guide.* New York: Guilford.

Skovholt, T. M. (2001). *The resilient practitioner: Burnout prevention and self-care strategies for counselors, therapists, and health professionals.* Boston: Allyn & Bacon.

Skovholt, T. M., & Rønnestad, M. H. (1995). *The evolving professional self: Stages and themes in therapist and counselor development.* New York: Wiley.

Strong, S. R., Welsh, J., Corcoran, J., & Hoyt, W. (1992). Social psychology and counseling psychology: The history, products, and promise of an interface. *Journal of Counseling Psychology, 39,* 139–157.

Waehler, C. A., & Lenox, R. A. (1994). A concurrent (versus stage) model for conceptualizing and representing the counseling process. *Journal of Counseling and Development, 73,* 17–22.

2

BUILDING YOUR FOUNDATION AS A HELPER

LEARNING OUTCOMES

After completing this chapter, you will be able to

1. Identify attitudes and behaviors about yourself that might aid in or interfere with establishing a positive helping relationship.
2. Identify, in the context of contemporary service provision, issues related to values, diversity, ethics, and stamina that might affect the development of a helping relationship and appropriate services.

Your decision to pursue a career in a helping profession (e.g., social work, counseling, psychology) suggests that you value and are committed to meaningful work. We speculate that working as a helping professional represents for you more than a job or a way to earn a living. It more than likely reflects your desire for your work to become a way of living, a lifestyle. This means that it is important to you that who you are as a professional is consistent with who you are as a person. Being a genuine or authentic person is therefore a priority in the varied roles you serve, both on the job (e.g., supervisee, colleague, resident) and off the job (e.g., friend, spouse/significant other, parent).

Although this chapter and the entire book present and describe strategies for practitioners, we realize that being a helping professional is not simply about implementing techniques. There is more to this work, this lifestyle, than merely selecting and using "tools" from one's clinical "toolbox." Indeed, in her review of the literature on the role and impact of the therapist in the work of psychotherapy, Reupert (2006) observed that "the 'self' or the 'person' of the counsellor is more important than the orientation chosen, or the interventions employed, in both the process and outcome of therapy" (p. 97). She added that "counsellors bring to therapy more than their professional skills and knowledge" (p. 101).

Skills, however, are clearly essential to the work of helping professionals. Without the intentional use of theoretically informed and research-guided practices learned in formal training (e.g., in graduate school) and at professional workshops, our work would be little more than shooting from the hip, relying more on gut and intuition than on discernible, reliable, and perhaps tested skills.

We contend that a helping professional's skills are a combination or an integration of one's "self" or "person" *and* one's training (academic, continuing education, on-the-job) in a behavioral health discipline. Your skill as a practitioner is the outgrowth or product of your personal characteristics (e.g., the values you espouse, the traditions you maintain, the qualities you embody, the decisions you make in your daily life), *and* your knowledge (e.g., what you have learned and what you are continuing to learn in your graduate studies). What you bring to this time of formal preparation (e.g., learning style, values, life experiences) therefore informs the material you are learning, and, in turn, the theories and strategies you are now learning help shape who you are as a person. This dynamic intersection constitutes what we regard as your professional skills—skills that are ever evolving, influenced by life experiences along the way, and subject to ongoing refinement.

This chapter and the entire book are therefore devoted to the skill of the helping professional, that dynamic intersection of person and professional. Indeed, few professions rival helping practice in the importance of understanding oneself, the dynamics of human interaction, the complexity of implementing values and ethics in practice, and the ways in which diversity among us as people contextualizes both problems and solutions. We see all of helping practice as grounded in a framework of the issues addressed in this chapter. Your personal work in sorting through these issues becomes a fundamental part of your professional identity and approach to practice. This is not easy work, but it creates a strong foundation on which you can build an enduring and well-constructed practice, skill, and lifestyle as a helping professional.

SELF-AWARENESS AND INTERPERSONAL AWARENESS

As you grow in your helping profession and as you gain real-life counseling experience, you will become increasingly aware that you are affected by your practice experience.

Clients and circumstances will trigger responses in you or push sensitive buttons that may cause you to react a certain way, to feel a certain way, or even to worry and lose sleep. This happens because we all carry effects from our personal histories and because we care about the well-being of people we work with and about the justness of systems we work in. None of us came from a perfectly healthy or fair past, and we have all learned ways of dealing with ourselves and other persons; some of these ways are healthy and productive, and some are unhealthy and defensive. We are not perfect or without weaknesses, and to be perfect is neither necessary nor realistic. The important point is that we are aware of our own biases and limitations. We are cognizant of the sensitivities that are opened up in us by working with clients, and we acknowledge that we must take responsibility for appropriately managing these sensitivities. Otherwise, we may inadvertently be prioritizing our own needs and thus diluting or misdirecting the capacity that our relationship and helping skills have for meeting *clients'* priorities.

Day (1995) pointed out the importance of examining our motives for even entering the helping profession. He cited three of the most common motivations: (1) to do for others what someone has done for me, (2) to do for others what I wish had been done for me, and (3) to share with others certain insights I have acquired. These are consistent with Kelly's (1995) finding that benevolence, or concern for the welfare of others, was the highest value orientation reported by members of the American Counseling Association. He concluded that "a strong core value of holistic-humanistic empowerment for personal development and interpersonal concern" (p. 652) reflected a predominant value system among counselors. Norcross and Farber (2005) described this value as an intersection of two motives for becoming a helping professional (1) self-healing and self-growth and (2) healing others or altruism.

Day (1995) cautioned that persons motivated to enter the helping profession "encounter several common problems that potentially convert their motivation to ill impact" (p. 109). Specifically, well-intentioned practitioners can become frustrated and discouraged or experience emotional trauma. These feelings can then affect practitioner behavior with clients and lead to pride rather than humility, insistence rather than invitation, telling rather than listening, assuming an expert role rather than collaborating, and making or coercing rather than assisting. Examining our motives for being a helper and the potential of these motives is an important facet of self-awareness. This type of self-check or self-examination can be enhanced by discussing professional motives and plans with a seasoned practitioner (as a client or as a student conducting an informational interview), an academic adviser, or a clinical supervisor.

Brems (2001) offered one way to think about self-awareness, in terms of various dimensions within it and ways in which it interfaces with knowledge and skills in development of competence. None of these dimensions of self-awareness is really independent or separate from others. For example, values and ethics are part of the personal or individual aspects that a practitioner brings to a helping encounter, but these certainly overlap with professional and cultural dimensions we bring as well. At this point in your professional development, there are four specific areas about yourself that we invite you to explore further: openness to learning, competence, power, and values (see also Learning Activity 2.1). Depending on your specific professional discipline or field of practice, there are likely other arear to add to this early list—for example, the insight needed to assess how well suited one is to work in crisis services or with terminally ill people.

Openness to Learning

The task of learning to be a professional helper is never done. Although you may be eager to have formal coursework completed and a graduate degree conferred, the process of professional learning and development has only begun. In your work with clients as a professional helper, you will more than likely realize that there are many things you don't know, things you believe you should have learned during your formal academic training. This is a common experience of practitioners early in their careers (Skovholt & Rønnestad, 1995). Attending professional workshops and conventions (primarily to obtain continuing education units, perhaps), reading scholarly journal articles and books, and participating in ongoing supervision or in your own personal counseling to raise self-awareness will all serve as primary sources of learning and development beyond graduate school.

A willingness and desire to continually learn is an essential disposition for all effective helpers. Stretching one's clinical repertoire and flexing new helping "muscles" or skills serve to prevent stagnation and boredom, ethical misconduct, burnout, and, most important, client deterioration. Skovholt (2001) very aptly described the choice practitioners have in their professional development: "The practitioner can have years of experience—rich, textured, illuminating, practice-changing professional experience in a helping, teaching, or health occupation. Or a person can have one year of experience repeated over and over" (p. 27). Assuming the role of perpetual student, therefore, contributes to the experience of a "rich, textured, illuminating, and practice-changing" career, one that requires of therapists the "courage to move outside their comfort zone" (Bridges, 2005, p. xiii).

A primary source of learning for practitioners is their clients. From their extensive interviews with approximately 100 therapists, Skovholt and Rønnestad (1995) found that a major theme for counselors reflecting on their professional development was that clients are a continuous source of influence and serve as primary teachers. More recently,

LEARNING ACTIVITY 2.1

Survey of Helper Motives and Goals

This activity is designed to help you explore areas of yourself that in some fashion will affect your helping. Take some time to consider these questions at *different points* in your development as a helper. We offer no feedback for this activity, because the responses are yours and yours alone. You may wish to discuss your responses with a peer, a supervisor, or your own therapist.

1. What is it about the helping profession (e.g., social work, counseling, psychology) that is attractive to you or enticing for you?
2. What do you look forward to learning and doing over the next five years?
3. What is anxiety-provoking to you about the work or lifestyle of a professional helper?
4. What are you cautious or hesitant about as you continue in the profession?
5. If you had to select one event in your life or one personal experience that contributed to your decision to pursue the helping profession you are now in, what would that event or experience be?
6. What have you learned about yourself by having experienced tragedy, trauma, or another type of personal

pain at some point in your life? What more do you still have to learn about yourself as a result of such pain?
7. Which of your personal qualities do you believe will serve you well as a helping professional? Why do you believe this?
8. What aspects of yourself (e.g., being "rough around the edges") do you need to work on in order for you to be a helpful practitioner? How do you see yourself addressing these?
9. How do you handle being in conflict? Being confronted? Being evaluated? What defenses do you use in these situations?
10. How would someone who knows you well describe your style of helping or caring?
11. What client populations or client issues do you enjoy working with or look forward to working with? For what reasons?
12. What client populations or client issues are difficult for you to work with or do you foresee as being difficult for you to work with? For what reasons?
13. What are three primary factors that contribute to being an "effective" helper?
14. How will you know when *you* have been an "effective" helper?

Orlinsky, Botermans, Rønnestad, and the SPR Collaborative Research Network (2001) asked approximately 4,900 therapists from more than 13 countries about specific influences (either positive or negative) on their career development. The majority of therapists surveyed were female and reported being influenced by analytic/psychodynamic theories. In addition, the average age of therapists was 42 years, and they had a median of 10 years of experience as a therapist.

Respondents to Orlinsky et al.'s (2001) survey rank ordered (from 0 to 3, with 0 = *no influence*, and 3 = *very positive/negative influence*) each of 14 influences provided, and they indicated that "experience in therapy with patients" was the most important positive influence on their career development (mean score of 2.51). This suggests that helpers benefit personally and professionally when they regard the helping process as an occasion for learning from their clients. Although attending to the client's needs and welfare is the purpose and priority of helping, it appears that helpers around the world are able to derive great satisfaction from working with clients. From Orlinsky et al's study, the second-most-important positive influence reported was "getting formal supervision or consultation" (mean score

of 2.27), followed by "getting personal therapy, analysis, or counselling" (mean score of 2.24). Several of the other noteworthy positive influences (listed in descending order of positive influence) were "experiences in personal life outside of therapy," "having informal case discussion with colleagues," "taking courses or seminars," "reading books or journals relevant to your practice," "giving formal supervision or consultation to others," "working with co-therapists," and "observing therapists in workshops, films, or tape." These "testimonies" from therapists may assist other helpers in their intentional engagement in and reflection on their work, realizing that experienced helpers who have "gone before" do benefit from their work with clients.

It should be evident that clients top the list when it comes to sources of professional development and continuous learning. What other opportunities would we have to sit and listen to an African American male who lives in the Midwest and identifies as Appalachian explain his method of pig farming? When else would we choose to sit in an emergency room and learn the details of her recent sexual assault from a 15-year-old female? If not for our role as professional helper, how else would we be able to witness a father's gradual acceptance of his son's decision to undergo a sex change operation? Living and working as professional helpers affords us the privilege of learning from others. In many respects, our clients represent the best teachers we could ever hope to have. Assuming the posture of lifelong learner and requesting that our clients tutor us on their lives and experiences not only enhances our clinical skills—but can make us better people through reflection, consultation, supervision, and therapy.

Competence

If you attend professional conferences in the helping field today, pick up a current mental health journal, and listen to conversations among faculty and researchers from the helping professions, you will no doubt hear and see numerous references to competence and specific competencies. The idea of professional competence is not new. For example, most state laws stipulate that a licensed helping professional maintain a self-disclosure statement describing his or her areas of competence. In recent years, however, professional competence has received quite a bit of attention and "press" in academic institutions, accrediting bodies, and the scholarly literature. Despite its liberal usage, the term *competence* is often not clearly defined and therefore remains elusive. Does the word imply proficiency, effectiveness, having expertise, or simply meeting minimal standards of practice? Does earning a graduate degree, obtaining licensure as a professional helper, or completing certification in a specialized practice constitute competence? Is competence, once demonstrated, stable and "here to stay"? Is competence—like cultural identity—self-defined, or is it determined only by another person or group (e.g., supervisor, licensure board, or other regulating body)?

Despite these unanswered questions, we view competence as a practitioner's ability to demonstrate certain skills based on his or her knowledge and experience. These skills are, at the very least, consistent with minimal standards of practice agreed upon or codified by a professional body of which the practitioner is a member (e.g., passing a state licensure exam). Preferably, the skills associated with competence reflect the practitioner's pursuit of professional and personal excellence (see Kottler, 2004), attributes often associated with membership in professional honor societies. Nagy (2005) regarded competence as "an ongoing process . . . that . . . is in a constant state of flux and renewal" (p. 29). Competence for us, therefore, is not absolute or stable, is always "under construction," reflects a commitment to excellence, and is determined by more than one person. In addition, as mentioned earlier, competence is a combination of demonstrated skills and knowledge informed by one's personal and professional experience.

Self-awareness is an important aspect of competence and involves a balanced assessment of our strengths and limitations. Our attitudes about ourselves significantly influence the way we behave. If we don't feel competent or valuable as people, we may communicate this attitude to our clients. Or if we don't feel confident about our ability to counsel, we may inadvertently structure the helping process to meet our own self-image or ideological needs or to confirm our negative self-images. An ongoing challenge, therefore, may be to maintain confidence in our own competence.

As Corey and Corey once noted, it is difficult to be an effective helper if you have a "fragile ego" (personal communication, September 29, 1992). We believe that the opposite is also true: someone whose ego is rigid and impervious to change may not be an effective helper. This is not to say that we don't all experience vacillating self-doubt and overconfidence at times, particularly in early stages of a new career. What we want to emphasize, however, is that one sign of competence is knowing when to seek supervision, consultation, or collegial support, instead of pretending to be "bulletproof." We underscore the importance of a generally sturdy self-esteem; the ability to handle complexity and discomfort with flexibility and open-mindedness; a willingness to seek help as needed; and a commitment to lifelong learning (Brems, 2000; Egan, 2007; Kottler, 2004). Competence, therefore, remains a dynamic construct that resists repeated efforts to be tied down and operationalized once and for all. Perhaps like ethical decision making, competence is understood or appreciated only in consultation with another person (e.g., supervisor) and as a result of receiving feedback or input from clients.

Power

When first introduced as a topic for consideration in therapy and other helping relationships, the word *power* often has a negative connotation—that is, it is understood as something that helpers misuse. It is true that power often is associated with authoritative force, undue influence, control, domination, obstruction, and hierarchical positioning. From at least two theoretical perspectives (i.e., narrative therapy and feminist therapy), however, power in the therapeutic process is understood as agency or a dynamic force, and the role of the helper is to equip clients with healthful or salutary power so that clients become *em*powered. Recognizing both positive *and* negative features (or potential uses) of power is therefore essential for all practitioners.

As helpers, we are indeed in a position of authority in relation to clients, and we are obligated by law in certain instances to exert influence over our clients even when they resist. This is true, for example, when we learn of suicidal or homicidal intentions and suspect child or elder abuse/neglect. In these instances, influencing the actions of our clients is done to protect their welfare and that of persons associated with them, such as family members. Clients often initiate contact with us in a state of vulnerability, and the decisions we make concerning client care can be life changing. Because of this, there is an imbalance of power. We evaluate clients' mental health status, make recommendations for their care, and exert our influence to ensure that our recommendations are implemented. Clients in turn are subject to or susceptible to our influence and perhaps feel at times that they have little recourse or say in the decision making. The power vested in us as professional helpers—by virtue of our graduate training, license to practice, length of experience, and areas of expertise, to name a few—is therefore not something to crave or to flaunt. Rather, the power afforded us should be handled with great care and practiced with respect and deep humility.

Despite what are considered conscientious efforts or at least well-meaning intentions, helpers can misuse their power in their work with clients. This is evident when a practitioner attempts to convince a new client that the assigned diagnosis is "right" and that interventions outlined in the preliminary treatment plan are "correct," sending the message that the client "should" participate in care or risks being "noncompliant." A practitioner may also misuse power when others are not consulted in the event of a crisis or an ethical dilemma. This can happen with novice and experienced helpers alike when they think they should be able to handle complex client issues on their own. The seasoned (and perhaps over confident) helper may say, "Heck, I've been doing this for many years. I know what to do. Besides, it'll take too much time to get others involved at this point." The novice helper may think, "I don't want to appear incompetent, so I'll figure this out on my own. Besides, my supervisor is in a meeting." As one clinical director once noted, however, "Because of the responsibility we assume, supervisors are meant to be interrupted."

The misuse of power, therefore, is often subtle and does not pertain exclusively to flagrant behavior (e.g., having sex with clients). We misuse our power when we assume we know more things about a client's situation or experience than is possible or even respectful. For example, saying with certitude that someone is "shy because she is Japanese American" assumes that this person's ethnic/racial heritage is the direct cause of or fully explains a presumed or known interpersonal characteristic. Such an assumption may exemplify "all-knowing" thinking wherein one's frame of reference is considered central or true, and we regard this kind of unchecked certainty as a subtle misuse of power. This type of thinking is evident in clinical decision-making errors, such as selective attention and confirmatory search strategies (Nezu, Nezu, & Lombardo, 2004). When helpers rely only on certain types of information (i.e., selective attention) and seek information that only confirms their initial impressions of clients, we believe they are misusing their power as professionals in their care of clients.

We also misuse our power when we assume a greater degree of intimacy with our clients than has been established.

This is true, for example, when we use a nickname for a client when he or she has not given us permission to do so. We also misuse our power when we assure clients that their difficulties and challenges are manageable although we do not know this to be the case. Statements such as "Everything will be okay" or "Don't worry about it" or "You will get through" when there is little evidence to support them are but a few examples. Offering a client glib or insincere reassurances might be associated with a "savior complex" or the thinking that one has the ability to "cure," "fix," or "solve" a client's concerns. Such a helper may take unwarranted advantage—consciously or not—of the influence processes in a helping relationship by using counseling to convert the client to a lifestyle or an ideology. A helper in recovery from alcoholism may earnestly believe that if her clients simply followed the same program she did to get sober, they too would get sober and remain sober. Another helper may think that if his client would just take her medication as prescribed, she would automatically be stable and not be "recycling" back into the hospital. In these and other instances, it is helpful to be reminded of the observation Bridges (2005) offered: "Therapists possess great power and authority in the treatment relationship, power that may be used for the patient's good or for irreparable harm" (p. 29).

Instead of exerting power, some practitioners may be afraid of power or wish to deny that they are exercising influence as part of their helping role. These practitioners may unwittingly attempt to escape from as much responsibility and participation in counseling as possible. Such a helper avoids forthrightly addressing roles or expectations and avoids expressing opinions. This might be the case when the helper explains to his or her supervisor, "Well, I didn't want to step on the client's toes, so I didn't say anything, even though I didn't really think it would be in his best interest." Professional relationships between helping practitioners and clients have aspects of unequal power of various types (e.g., authority, resources, and vulnerability). To deny or avoid acknowledgment of the power differential limits one's ability to manage this differential as honestly and productively as possible.

Regardless of how power may be misappropriated in a helping relationship (i.e., overextended or not exerted at all), feminist therapy can serve as a helpful resource for practitioners. A hallmark of feminist therapy is its attention to power and the process of power sharing between client and helper (also known as egalitarian practice; see Rader & Gilbert, 2005). A goal of feminist therapy—regardless of the sex of either client or helper—is to help raise the client's awareness of existing and potential resources and skills so that the client is *em*powered to counter or at least to manage difficulties in his or her life. This might involve teaching assertiveness skills to an adult who has experienced repeated emotional abuse from a parent or significant other, helping a client pursue alternative employment, and supporting a young man's efforts to inform his parents of his intention to marry outside the religion in which he was raised. These and other practices can be empowering when conducted in an egalitarian fashion.

Values

The word *value* denotes something that we prize, regard highly, or prefer. *Value* refers to our feelings or attitudes about something and our preferred actions or behaviors. As an example, take a few minutes to think of and perhaps list five things you love to do. Then look over your list to determine how frequently and consistently you actually engage in each of these five actions. Your values are indicated by your frequent and consistent actions (Simon, 1995). Just as "actions speak louder than words," so do your behaviors—more so than your verbal statements—reflect your values. If you say that you value spending time with friends but you hardly ever do this, then other activities and actions probably have more value for you.

In interactions with clients, it is not possible to be "value free" or completely neutral (Corey, Corey, & Callanan, 2007). Although we may think we are capable of not imposing our beliefs and values on others (equating this capability with unconditional positive regard and being nonjudgmental), what we do and say does influence our clients in either positive or negative ways and in more ways than we realize. This can be a difficult lesson to learn because we are not aware of how much of an impact we can have on others, particularly on clients who are in vulnerable positions. Perhaps you can remember a time when, as a result of watching with your supervisor a videotape of a counseling session that you conducted, you realized you had aligned yourself too quickly with a new client (e.g., "How dare your mother say you couldn't do that!") or you realized you may have discounted the client's concerns by engaging in premature and lengthy self-disclosure. Although your initial reaction to your supervisor may have been, "I didn't mean to do that!" you learned (perhaps with some embarrassment) that what you yourself believe influences how you respond to and interact with clients. This means that we cannot view ourselves or our clients as "blank slates"; in other words, we influence our clients and they influence us.

Some practitioners prefer to meet with new clients without first learning something about their clients' background (e.g., not reviewing medical records and/or legal history prior to the intake or first session) in an effort to prevent the formation of any bias, prejudice, or other preconceived notions. Our values, however, permeate every human interaction. Aponte (1994) stated, "Values frame the entire process of therapy. . . . All transactions between therapists and clients involve negotiations about the respective value systems that each party brings into the therapeutic process"

(p. 170). This means in part that interviewers may unintentionally influence a client to embrace their values in subtle ways by what they pay attention to or by nonverbal cues of approval and disapproval (Corey et al., 2007). If clients feel they need the helper's approval, they may act in ways they think will please the helper instead of making choices according to their own value systems.

To help you clarify and reflect on your preconceptions, values, or reactions in different practice situations, we encourage you to engage in Learning Activity 2.2 before you read the remainder of this section. It is intended as a self-check exercise to gauge or evaluate your attitudes and anticipated behaviors in different situations.

It is true that sometimes helpers push values on client because of loyalty to their own perspective or a belief that their values are preferable to the client's. There are several problems with this approach. First, when we push a value onto a client, the client may feel pushed too—either pushed toward or pushed away. Second, the client's uniqueness and strengths are discounted or dismissed when we regard our values as primary and (perhaps unintentionally) strongly encourage the client to consider or even adopt our perspective. Such practice may be likened to indoctrination and therefore is inconsistent with the purpose of any helping relationship. Third, when we impose our own viewpoint, we do not hear the wisdom of our clients, we fail to learn valuable lessons for our own lives, and we undermine a collaborative relationship.

Obviously, not all of our values have an impact on the helping process. The helper who is a pet lover can probably work without any difficulty with a client who has never sought to interact with animals. The helper who does not smoke may be able to provide quality care to a client who smokes two packs of cigarettes a day. Even the clinician who is a strict vegetarian may say that maintaining a strong working alliance with a client who eats red meat on a regular basis is not impossible. Certain values, however, may make it extremely difficult for us to sustain empathy for certain clients. These might be values we would consider inviolate, values we might say comprise our essence or have shaped our identity—values such as the sanctity of human life, belief in a higher power, and the conviction that people create their own destiny (as in "you reap what you sow"). The practitioner whose family member recently died of lung cancer—a family member who never smoked—may therefore find it terribly difficult to remain nonjudgmental of a client who is a two-pack-a-day smoker and does not intend to quit. Likewise, the helper who is an ardent animal lover and a vegan may not be able to provide unconditional positive regard for a client who has a history of torturing and killing animals. Although benevolence may be a primary value of helpers (Kelly, 1995) and provide the impetus for entering a helping profession, a referral may be necessary if from an

LEARNING ACTIVITY   **2.2**   **Personal Values**

 This activity presents descriptions of six clients. If you work through this activity by yourself, we suggest that you imagine yourself counseling each of these clients. Try to generate a vivid picture of yourself and the client in your mind. If you do this activity with a partner, you can role-play the helper while your partner assumes the role of each client. As you imagine or role-play the helper, try to notice your feelings, attitudes, values, and behavior during the visualization or role-play process. After *each* example, stop to think about or discuss these questions:

1. What attitudes and beliefs did you have about the client?
2. Were your beliefs and attitudes based on actual or on presumed information about the client?
3. How did you behave with the client?
4. What values are portrayed by your behavior?
5. Could you work with this client effectively?

There are no right or wrong answers. Feedback to Learning Activity 2.2 can be found later in the chapter.

Client 1

This client is a young woman who is having financial problems. She is the sole supporter of three young children. She earns her living by prostitution and selling drugs. She states that she is concerned about her financial problems but can't make enough money from welfare or from an unskilled job to support her kids.

Client 2

Your client is charged with rape and sexual assault. The client, a man, tells you that he is not to blame for the incident because the victim, a woman, "asked for it."

Client 3

This client is concerned about general feelings of depression. Overweight and unkempt, the client is in poor physical condition and smokes constantly during the interview.

Client 4

The client is a young White woman who comes to you at the college counseling center. She is in tears because her parents threatened to disown her when they learned that her steady male partner is an African American.

Client 5

Your client, a gay man, is angry with his male lover because he found out from a mutual friend that the lover recently slept with another man.

Client 6

The client, an older man, confides in you that he is taking two kinds of medicine for seizures and "thought control." He states that occasionally he believes people are out to get him. He hasn't been employed for some time and is now thinking of returning to the workforce, and he wants your assistance and a letter of reference.

---

ethical standpoint the practitioner is unable to promote and respect a client's welfare (American Counseling Association, 2005; American Psychological Association, 2002; National Association of Social Workers, 1999).

A recent court case, however, suggests that professional helpers may not be able to "excuse" themselves from providing services to clients when issues that arise in the helping process conflict with the helper's values (e.g., religious convictions). Hermann and Herlihy (2006) discussed the 2001 case of *Bruff v. North Mississippi Health Services Inc.*, in which a counselor was dismissed from her position for refusing to continue counseling a client after the client disclosed that she was a lesbian and had requested help to improve her relationship with her partner. The counselor explained that a homosexual lifestyle conflicted with her Christian beliefs and therefore she could not counsel a lesbian client on relationship issues with her significant other. The employer stated that refusing to provide services to this client had a discriminatory effect and resulted in undue hardship on the counselor's colleagues because additional referrals represented a disproportionate workload for them. Although the counselor appealed her termination and subsequently filed suit against her employer, an appeals court determined that making reasonable accommodations for the employee's religious beliefs did not extend to excusing the counselor from working with homosexual clients on relationship issues.

Lum (2004) asserted that although social work values are oriented toward client rights, the collective values of other cultures should also be addressed—values in the areas of family, spirituality and religion, and cultural identity. We agree with Lum, and we have found that a significant issue for many helpers is the capacity to work with clients whose values and lifestyles are different from those of the helpers.

This is the challenge of what Heilman and Witztum (1997) described as value-sensitive therapy. This therapeutic approach requires helpers to be able to

> look at the world through the eyes of the patients—understand their cognitive perspective—and through their hearts—grasp their affective perspective and their way of life—and, perhaps most crucially, to comprehend their behavior and the cultural or social framework in which they will continue to live. (p. 524)

Usually a helper's value system and level of respect for different values are developed during one's formative years and are influenced by such things as family dynamics, religious affiliation, cultural and ethnic background, socioeconomic status, and geographic location. As adults, we bring to the helping situation varying levels of acceptance of human difference. Generally, it is important to be able to expand our level of awareness to understand clients whose beliefs, values, lifestyles, and behaviors are quite different from our own. Otherwise, we run the risk of regarding clients with different values or lifestyles as somehow less sophisticated, knowledgeable, or "correct" than we are or, worse yet, as inferior to us. We do not mean to minimize the difficulty of these challenges. As earnest and open as we may feel, working with value and perspective differences can take subtle, confusing, and challenging forms and may mean that therapeutic goals need to be revised. For example, helping a Filipino American couple deal with current stress in their marriage may not automatically mean that their 2- and 4-year-old children can no longer sleep with them, as has been their custom. Although separate beds for children and their parents may be a value of the helper, it would not be consistent with value-sensitive therapy (Heilman & Witztum, 1997) to force such a value on these clients.

A first step in working through value differences with clients is to acknowledge honestly what your struggle is with a particular issue rather than deny your blind spots, your ignorance, or your feelings (frustration, anxiety, uncertainty, or anger). Thus, if you are adamantly opposed to abortion, you acknowledge your opposition and also your struggle when working with clients who are pro-choice, which may include referring them to other helping sources. However, value differences may not arise until after you have conducted several sessions and once a helping alliance has been established. For example, a client you have worked with for a while and one you have appreciated for her dedication to personal change informs you of her recent "born-again" experience as a Christian and her decision to pursue "evangelical ministry." For you, a devout Jew, this news may not be easy to hear at first. You may even wonder over the next few weeks if you can continue to provide the client with genuine care and unconditional positive regard. A referral may not be possible. The challenge becomes man-

aging and working through different value systems while remaining committed to helping the client achieve her treatment goals. Although you may not agree with the values of her newfound Christianity, you may still be able to help her apply toward her new endeavor the coping skills she learned in her work with you.

We believe it is particularly important for helpers to support the rights of those clients who—because of their physical or mental abilities, age, gender, race, gender expression, or sexual orientation—have traditionally been the recipients of prejudicial responses and often substandard treatment, ranging from negative stereotyping and emotional abuse to physical violence. Despite the enactment of the 1990 Americans with Disabilities Act, persons with physical disabilities (e.g., multiple sclerosis), psychiatric disabilities (e.g., severe depression), or other mental disabilities (e.g., mental retardation) continue to experience barriers to employment due primarily to the stigmatizing attitudes of employers and coworkers (Scheid, 2005). Such discrimination is reflected, for example, in lower wages among persons with psychiatric disabilities who report stigmatizing experiences (Baldwin & Marcus, 2006). In addition, older persons (i.e., those 60 years and older) worldwide experience negative stereotyping, financial or material exploitation, and other forms of abuse (e.g., physical, emotional or psychological, sexual) and neglect (including abandonment). Although reports of elder abuse and neglect in the United States increased by about 20 percent from 2000 to 2004 (National Center on Elder Abuse, 2006), the vast majority of incidents of elder abuse and neglect in the United States go unreported (National Center on Elder Abuse, 1998), attesting to the lack of awareness or concern about the care of a burgeoning aging population that Brownell and Podnicks (2005) referred to as the "Silver Tsunami" (p. 188). Furthermore, despite advances in the 20th century for equal and fair treatment of women, American women still earn comparatively less in wages than their male counterparts; are less likely to be selected for management positions; are more frequent victims of abuse and assault, as well as sexual harassment in the workplace (see Kelly, Kadue, & Mignin, 2005); and are more likely to receive biased treatment in health care (see Munch, 2006), including mental health.

With respect to issues of race, Miller and Garran (2008) maintain that although no one person is responsible for racism's "long history and deep tentacles" (p. 3) in the United States, all helping professionals are responsible for responding to the racism that persists, because "[n]one of us *is a bystander* in a society structured by racism" (p. 2; emphasis theirs). Racism can be direct and overt or indirect and covert; it can also be intentional or unintentional. It exists at individual, group, institutional, and ideological levels; and, as Ridley (2005) indicated, anyone can be a racist, including members of racial minority groups. An example of this is the

March 2007 firing of a well-respected and highly qualified African American high school principal in Chicago, Illinois (Spielman & Donovan, 2007). Despite her record of improved attendance and academic performance in her eight-year tenure as principal, the local school board, chaired by a Hispanic, voted 6–2 in favor of her ouster. The other 5 votes were also cast by Hispanic school board members who reportedly wanted to pave the way for a Hispanic principal at the high school, whose student body is 65 percent Hispanic. Chicago mayor Daley referred to the principal's firing as a "national disgrace."

Gay men, lesbian women, and bisexual women and men also experience many forms of discrimination, such as lack of health care benefits for same-sex partners and difficulties in adopting children so that both partners are recognized as parents. There are persons who continue to view homosexuality and bisexuality as some pathogenic illness or see gay men and lesbian women as "perverted sinners." In addition to encountering homophobic and biphobic attitudes from heterosexual persons, lesbian women, gay men, and bisexual women and men have to contend with heterosexism and the issue of "heterosexual privilege"—that is, the idea that heterosexuality is the more common and therefore the more acceptable sexual orientation. Generally, straight persons do not feel a need to hide their sexual orientation for fear of reprisal; for many lesbian women and gay men, hiding or being "in the closet" for fear of the consequences is a perpetual concern. In the mental health system, treating the presenting problems of lesbian women and gay men is now customary. Some practitioners, however, still make the condition of homosexuality the focus of therapy, a reminder that misinformation and stereotyping still exist. These attitudes extend to variations in gender expression as well.

Sex offenders comprise an unlikely group of persons to consider when addressing issues of discrimination and other forms of unfair treatment. Indeed, many persons may regard those who have committed sex crimes (e.g., rape) as unworthy of fair treatment, having relinquished that opportunity or right when the crime was committed. Professional helpers themselves may not be able to muster the unconditional positive regard needed to provide helpful care to these individuals. Griffin and West (2006) contend, however, that as a group, sex offenders are treated as "outcasts" of many communities, "stigmatized and exiled" by law enforcement personnel, the media, other offenders, and mental health professionals (¶ 1).

Despite compelling evidence that novice and experienced helpers alike can and do experience vicarious trauma in their work with sex offenders (Moulden & Firestone, 2007), Griffin and West (2006) outlined several steps to follow in order to correct myths and misconceptions about offenders of sex-based crimes. These include becoming familiar with outcome research that supports the efficacy of sex offender treatment (e.g., Lösel & Schmucker, 2005), confronting those "who are spreading misinformation or a sensationalized version of the truth" (Griffin & West, section X, ¶ 3), and advocating for treatment on a case-by-case basis. As Griffin and West stated:

> It is irresponsible and illogical in research and practice to group a sex offender who at eighteen years of age had sexual intercourse with his seventeen-year-old girlfriend alongside a sex offender who violently raped and injured a woman. Doing so limits the ability of our society to differentiate between the threats each sex offender may pose in the future. (section X, ¶ 4)

Although many helpers may prefer not to work with sex offenders, it may be that, depending on their work setting (e.g., inpatient psychiatric facility), helpers may not be able to excuse themselves from such work. It may be that a client presenting with depression and substance use concerns, for example, does not disclose that he committed incest 20 years ago (a crime for which he served prison time) until the fifth or sixth counseling session. If a therapeutic relationship has already been established around the issues of substance use and depression, it may be that transferring the client to a new helper would disrupt progress made thus far and even contribute to a worsening rather than an amelioration of client symptoms.

It should be evident that the values we hold about people, life, and the world around us do impact our work as professional helpers. Our views on such things as same-sex partnerships, the death penalty, racial profiling, abortion and when human life begins, illegal immigration, and various religious principles and practices (e.g., not ordaining women in the Roman Catholic Church) will more than likely filter in to our conversations with clients and influence how we provide them with care. Although certain values—and the intensity with which we and our clients ascribe to or endorse such values—may not be cause for concern, others are. As professionals, we are bound to certain codes of ethics. In addition, as persons committed to genuine and authentic practice, we really cannot fake empathy or only pretend to really care about our clients' well-being. The life of a professional helper does require continuing education, supervision and consultation, and self-reflection and "soul searching." It is not for the timid or the faint of heart. Indeed, being a professional helper means that many of our values are continually challenged and that we need to critique (though not necessarily change) some long-held views to be able to effectively care for a variety of clients. Such views might include how we regard persons from different cultures and our impressions of persons from racial or ethnic groups different from our own.

2.2 FEEDBACK
Personal Values

Did your visualizations or role plays reveal to you that you have certain biases and values about sex roles, age, cultures, race, physical appearance, and rape? Do any of your biases reflect your past experiences with a person or an incident? Most people in the helping professions agree that we communicate some of our values to our clients, often unintentionally. Try to identify any values or biases you hold now that could signal disapproval to a client or could keep you from promoting the welfare of your client. With yourself, a peer, or an instructor, work out a plan to reevaluate your biases or to help you prevent yourself from imposing your values on clients.

SERVING DIVERSE POPULATIONS: MULTICULTURAL AND MULTIETHNIC CONSIDERATIONS

Given the increasingly pluralistic world in which we live, we cannot expect to encounter only clients who share our cultural background or who look and sound like us. Being able to provide quality services to a range of persons representing different backgrounds, professing different beliefs, and engaged in different practices is imperative for all helping professionals, regardless of the geographical location (e.g., midwestern states) or setting (e.g., private practice, rural hospital, suburban school) of service delivery. It must be emphasized that there are many forms of human diversity: gender, gender expression, sexual orientation, race, ethnicity, socioeconomic status, religious or spiritual affiliation, physical and mental ability, age, and so on. These and other demographics or characteristics are often referred to as experiences and expressions of culture.

Generally speaking, *culture* can be defined as a common heritage or a collection of beliefs and values that influence traditions, customs, norms or standard practices, and social environments or institutions. The broad term *multicultural* captures the array of human diversity; *multiethnic* is a narrower term focusing on specifically ethnographic characteristics, such as race and ethnicity. *Ethnicity* connotes a shared history, language, and rituals (perhaps by virtue of sharing the same or similar geographical place of origin), and although *race* is often regarded as a biological category (i.e., identifying persons according to genetic traits such as skin color, shape of eyes and nose), it is not. According to the American Psychological Association (2003), "the definition of race is considered to be socially constructed rather than biologically determined" (p. 380). This means that race has more to do with how social groups "are separated, treated as inferior or superior, and given differential access to power and other valued resources" (U.S. Department of Health and Human Services, 2001, p. 9).

Many textbooks addressing diversity and multicultural considerations begin by presenting and discussing group characteristics. For example, ethnographic information may comprise lists of racial and ethnic groups (e.g., African Americans, Asian Americans) and values/beliefs and practices often associated with each group. Learning about and understanding the commonalities of members of a particular cultural group (or "the ties that bind") are important. However, if this nomothetic—broad-brush—approach to understanding diverse populations is the only one discussed, it can promote generalizations and stereotyping, and as a result, helpers may be inclined to interpret an individual client based solely on his or her racial and/or ethnic group membership. This outcome is evident in statements such as "Cuban Americans are political activists" and "Filipino Americans are hard workers." Although these characterizations may apply to many individuals who identify as Cuban American and Filipino American, respectively, they may not necessarily define the individual client seeking mental health services. Assuming that clients who appear to represent a particular cultural, ethnic, or racial group fulfill or meet all of the stereotypical criteria of persons from that particular group "is actually one of the worst manifestations of prejudice" (Brems, 2000, p. 9). Relying only on generalizations about a particular cultural group to define an individual client is just one side of the story.

Neufeldt et al. (2006) regarded a helper's consideration of individual or within-group differences as a "relatively advanced-level multicultural competence" (p. 474). In their study of case conceptualization practices—specifically, the incorporation of diversity issues—they found that only 3 of 17 therapists-in-training considered within-group differences when they were presented with the case of a female Chinese American client. The majority of these therapists-in-training did not consider ways in which this young woman differed from other members of her identified group, a practice Neufeldt et al. regarded as an assumption of homogeneity. Attending to *both* the nomothetic, homogeneous, or general descriptions of a client's cultural group *and* his or her idiographic, idiosyncratic, or unique characterizations is therefore essential in all cross-cultural interactions. As Neufeldt et al. (2006) stated, however, the latter may represent an advanced helper skill.

Practicing Idiographically

We appreciate Ridley's (2005) idiographic perspective, which Ridley states should guide the entire helping process. This perspective regards each client as unique, "a mixture of characteristics and qualities that make him or her unlike anyone else" (p. 85). According to this posture, helpers are attuned to individual differences in clients and fascinated by the idiosyncrasies and personal stories that each client presents and represents. Rather than defining an individual exclusively by his or her cultural group membership or affiliation (similar to defining a client by his or her mental disorder or diagnosis), an idiographic perspective prioritizes the individual who is a member of one or more cultural groups. For example, an idiographic perspective would ask: "Who is this person who happens to be a 75-year-old second-generation Latina American widow who is a mother of 6, grandmother of 10, and whose primary language is Spanish?" Such an approach is consistent with that recommended by former U.S. surgeon general David Satcher in his report on mental health (U.S. Department of Health and Human Services, 1999) when he stated that "There is no 'one size fits all' treatment" (p. 453). Rather, Dr. Satcher emphasized, "[t]o be effective, the diagnosis and treatment of mental illness must be tailored to individual circumstances, while taking into account age, gender, race, and culture and other characteristics that shape a person's image and identity" (p. 456).

A tailored or an idiographic perspective also seeks to understand how an individual defines or identifies his or her own membership in various cultural groups, rather than the helper being the one to assume the meaning membership has for the individual. Certainly the helper will generate assumptions or hypotheses about individual clients; however, these will always remain tentative unless or until they are confirmed by the client. Indeed, cultural identity is always self-defined. An idiographic perspective, therefore, allows clients to formulate and articulate their cultural identity, prioritizing their own values and practices at particular times in their lives.

Ridley (2005) offered five principles of an idiographic perspective in mental health care. First, practitioners should attempt to understand each client from the client's unique frame of reference. This might be similar to regarding each individual as "a self-contained universe with its own laws" (Shontz, 1965, cited in Cone, 2001, p. 14). Asking a light-skinned African American lesbian who lives in a fairly small town in the Midwest what she means by "passing" might be an example. Respecting and seeking to understand the reasons a young soldier has for requesting to return to the battlefront rather than remain at home after recovering from his wounds might be another example. Although the idiographic perspective appears to pertain only to working with individual clients, it does have application to families. For example, in her work with African American families, Boyd-Franklin (2003) stated, "It is far more useful to avoid thinking of the family members in stereotypical ways but to invite them to share their experiences" (p. 185). This practice sounds very similar to that espoused by an idiographic perspective.

A second principle of an idiographic perspective (Ridley, 2005) is that nomothetic, normative information needs to be considered but may not always fit particular individual clients. For example, homelessness does not imply unemployment, drug addiction, or mental illness. One young African American man who spent nights and weekends in a San Francisco shelter and the subway restroom for several months did not "fit the mold" of a "down-and-out" "druggie" or "criminal." Indeed, Christopher Gardner, whose true rags-to-riches story is featured in the motion picture *The Pursuit of Happyness* (Muccino, 2006), broke all the rules of such stereotypes. Although lacking a college education and being the sole care provider for his young son, Mr. Gardner managed to succeed in a nonpaid internship at a top brokerage firm, pass the licensing exam on the first try, eventually get hired by the firm, proceed to establish his own brokerage firm, and eventually become a millionaire. This one example underscores the importance of an idiographic perspective and is consistent with the adage "Don't judge a book by its cover." An inductive (starting from what is unique) rather than a deductive (starting with generalities) approach to understanding a client might thus be more appropriate.

Ridley's (2005) third principle of an idiographic perspective in the helping process is that people are a dynamic blend of multiple roles and identities. He explained:

> A minority client is not merely a representative of a single racial or ethnic group. He or she is a member of a variety of groups, with group identities overlapping to create a blend that is unique and special to that individual. (p. 88)

This is evident in 6.8 million people, or 2.4 percent of the U.S. population, reporting two or more races in the 2000 census (U.S. Census Bureau, 2001), the first time such an option was made available. An astute helper, therefore, will not assume that a new client's racial identity is either Black or White, for example. Rather, the helper may inquire about the intersection of racial/ethnic identities—or, more broadly, about cultural identities—and will elicit the client's own meaning of such an intersection or blending (e.g., how might the son of an Black African father and a White European American mother describe his cultural identity, particularly when influenced by his being raised in Indonesia?). This inquiry may be especially important for mixed-race women (Hall, 2004), and conversations will likely focus on issues of belonging and acceptance, as well as physical appearance.

According to Ridley (2005), the idiographic perspective is compatible with the biopsychosocial model of mental health. This is his fourth principle, and it reinforces a comprehensive or holistic view of individuals. Rather than understanding someone from only one perspective (e.g., medical model), the biopsychosocial model challenges helpers to formulate their understanding of clients from a variety of perspectives. Similarly, the idiographic perspective is transtheoretical, Ridley's fifth and final principle.

This refers to the use of a variety of theoretical orientations and interventions with clients, not just one tried-and-true approach. A helper who identifies with the same general racial/ethnic group as one of his or her clients (e.g., both identify as Native American) may inadvertently assume that a particular therapeutic intervention (e.g., participating in a healing service) may be appropriate for the client based on the helper's own participation in such an activity. An idiographic perspective that is transtheoretical, however, would entertain several possible theories and strategies for the benefit of the individual client, even if such options did not "fit" the helper's own experience as a member of the same general racial/ethnic group.

Guidelines for Practicing Idiographically

To assist helpers in transferring principles to practice, Ridley (2005) developed 12 guidelines for providing idiographic care. These are listed in Box 2.1 and 5 of them are discussed in some detail.

Developing Cultural Self-Awareness

Providing idiographic care implies that helpers remain cognizant of the significance of cultural issues in their interactions with all clients. Indeed, we recommend that helpers regard *all* conversations with clients as "cross-cultural." This means that issues of sex, age, racial and ethnic identity, socioeconomic status, and sexual orientation, to name a few, are *always* pertinent and inform our work with all clients. If, as former U.S. surgeon general Dr. David Satcher stated, "culture counts" (U.S. Department of Health and Human Services, 2001), then cultural factors should always be at the forefront of our awareness in our work with clients and our life as helpers.

Cultural self-awareness includes becoming aware of our hidden prejudices. These might be apparent when we (1) catch ourselves (or someone else catches us) making an inadvertent racial or ethnic slur, (2) become automatically fearful when someone of another race or ethnicity sits next to us on public transportation, or (3) attribute lack of English comprehension to intellectual deficits rather than to English not being someone's primary language. Sue et al. (2007) described these and other actions as examples of racial microaggressions or "brief, everyday exchanges that send denigrating messages to people of color because they belong to a racial minority group" (p. 273). Simply put, microaggressions are often unconsciously delivered verbal and nonverbal put-downs, such as snubs and dismissive looks and gestures.

Whether they were hidden or not, the depth and extent of prejudicial beliefs among certain celebrities in the United States made headline news in late 2006. These could be said to be prime examples of microaggressions. Television actor/comedian Michael Richards, movie actor Mel Gibson, and television actor Isaiah Washington made public comments disparaging African Americans, Jews, and gays, respectively. All three of these men reportedly entered formal treatment after their incidents to address issues of alcoholism, anger, racism, and homophobia. Although the lasting influence of such treatment interventions on their cultural attitudes and behaviors toward others may never be known, we can hope that the news stories generated by their public comments (some might say tirades) served to remind many of the insidious and potentially harmful effects of hidden prejudices. This outcome was certainly evident in early 2007 when radio and television host Don Imus disparaged members of the Rutgers University women's basketball team while on the air. Despite his apologies, his remarks resulted in the cancellation of his nationally syndicated daily television and radio show.

Developing and enhancing cultural self-awareness can be accomplished in a number of different ways. Lee (2001) outlined at least three self-exploration practices for helpers. First, acknowledge and explore your own racial/ethnic identity by asking yourself, for example, "What rights and privileges have I enjoyed as a result of being a White American?" Second, assess your own stage of identity development. For example, you ask yourself, "As a dark-skinned African American, have I adopted what Boyd-Franklin (2003) described as a 'Blacker than thou' mentality by not trusting light-skinned African Americans?" Third, Lee recommended

BOX 2.1	GUIDELINES FOR PRACTICING IDIOGRAPHIC HELPING
1. Develop cultural self-awareness. 2. Avoid imposing one's values on clients. 3. Accept one's naïveté regarding others. 4. Show cultural empathy. 5. Incorporate cultural considerations into counseling. 6. Avoid stereotyping.	7. Determine the relative importance of clients' primary cultural roles. 8. Avoid blaming the victim. 9. Remain flexible in the selection of interventions. 10. Examine counseling theories for bias. 11. Build on clients' strengths. 12. Avoid protecting clients from emotional pain.

Source: Ridley, 2005.

evaluating influences that have shaped you, and evaluating how your attitudes affect the helping process. If self-exploration leads to self-awareness, then helpers are strongly encouraged to engage in activities that challenge long-held stereotypes and broaden their understanding of and appreciation for the experiences of others. Such activities might include cultural immersion experiences, such as attending an international fair and worship services of a religious group different from one's own (e.g., visiting a mosque, temple, or synagogue). Processing these and other experiences is just as important as engaging in the activities. Ridley (2005) recommended seeking therapeutic services (i.e., assuming the role of client) from a professional of another race, someone whose ancestors have not held positions of sociopolitical power. Such a person could serve as a consultant, helping the professional helper reflect on and make meaning of new experiences that may be initially unsettling or at least confusing.

Accepting Naïveté about Others

Although assuming a genuine posture of curiosity about clients is regarded as an essential skill for helpers, it is particularly important when working with persons who are racially or ethnically different from us. Solution-focused and narrative therapies refer to the "not-knowing" (Anderson & Goolishian, 1992) approach wherein the helper conveys genuine intrigue and a sincere desire to be informed by the client without preconceived opinions and expectations about the client. Some might interpret this as helper ignorance and, indeed, it is! It is impossible for anyone to fully understand, let alone know another's experience. Therefore, maintaining a naive, curious, and genuinely ignorant stance with clients actually represents a primary form of respect for the experiences of clients. To do otherwise would be disrespectful and insulting.

Acknowledging our naïveté about the experiences of culturally diverse clients signals our effort to allow clients to be the experts about their self-defined cultural identity, and our willingness to regard them as our "cultural consultants" (Vicary & Andrews, 2000). In so doing, we assume the role of student or pupil of our clients' experiences, receptive to what our clients can teach us or how they can enlighten us about what it must be like to live their lives. This is not to say that we regard an American Indian client, for example, as the representative of, or spokesperson for, *all* Native Americans or American Indians, regardless of his or her geographic region or tribe. What this means is that we invite individual clients to help us understand their unique experiences as members of particular cultural groups and the meanings they have constructed and ascribed to their cultural identities. Learning from our clients in this way may be possible only when we set aside or modify certain expectations (e.g., direct eye contact, use of grammatically

correct English), pause to consider a new or an alternative perspective, and "flex" our empathic "muscles" with each new client or family. As Ridley (2005) pointed out, "Only when counselors accept the limits of their own expertise are they likely to interpret their clients' problems and needs realistically" (p. 95). It may also be that relinquishing the role of the all-knowing expert makes it possible for the helper to envision more realistic goals for the client, as well as offer services that are not unnecessarily intrusive, intensive, or protracted. For example, according to Vicary and Andrews (2000), the therapist's role in certain cultures (e.g., indigenous Australians) may be to *complement* the healing process rather than assume full responsibility for the process of change or recovery.

Determining the Relative Importance of Clients' Primary Cultural Roles

Given the dynamic blend of multiple roles and identities in the increasingly diverse United States and wider world, it seems important to explore with clients how these roles and identities intersect for them. For example, what meaning has a particular client constructed (or what meaning is still "under construction") about being a middle-age White male veteran who was widowed two years ago, is now raising a 15-year-old daughter (the youngest of his three children), and is not able to secure full-time employment at this time because of a medical disability? From an idiographic perspective, this client might be asked about which of his roles and responsibilities is now most important to him. Such an inquiry may also assist in goal formulation and prioritization. For example, does he want to focus his energies during the helping process on how to be an effective single parent? Does he want to discuss what it is like to be a medically disabled war veteran and how such an identity represents a significant shift from his being a physically fit, mobile, and active man able to provide financially for his family? Allowing the client to determine the importance of his or her various roles and responsibilities conveys utmost respect for the client and represents an invitation for the client to teach the helper about the client's idiographic experience and unique cultural identity.

Avoiding Blaming the Victim

Despite fulfilling multicultural competency training and practicing what Heilman and Witztum (1997) described as value-sensitive therapy, helpers may unwittingly blame their racially and ethnically diverse clients for the stressors and challenges they report having experienced. Such blame may be evident when the helper attributes a client's drug use, for example, to his being a young African American man who did not finish high school, grew up in subsidized housing, and was raised by a single mother. Although perhaps not verbalizing the idea, the helper might think to himself or herself, "Well, that explains it all. He's Black and grew up poor. If he had just stayed in school, he could have stayed away from drugs." Unbeknownst to the helper, such thinking may exemplify in part what Ridley (2005) referred to as unintentional racism, a practice he described as "the most insidious form of racial victimization" (p. 39). Such practice not only is conducted on an individual level but is also practiced at the systemic or organizational level. For example, findings from an early study (Pavkov, Lewis, & Lyons, 1989) indicated that race (specifically being Black) was a significant predictor of a diagnosis of schizophrenia in four midwestern state mental health hospitals. Being a member of a racial/ethnic minority group and having a mental illness, therefore, can signify what Gary (2005) termed the "Double Stigma" (p. 981).

Ridley (2005) contended that therapist inaction (e.g., not addressing the issue of race in session) perpetuates the victimization of racial minorities. This might be evident when a helper professes to be "color-blind," implying that the race or ethnicity of others really doesn't matter or is not important. Not only does this discredit Dr. David Satcher's admonition that "culture counts," but it dismisses the very identity of another human being. Indeed, such comments represent the ultimate form of insult. Ridley (2005) cautioned, however, that "White professionals are not the only ones guilty of therapist inaction" (p. 40). He stated that minority professionals can be said to engage in unintentional racism when they "assume they understand the dynamics of racism when they may not" and "posture as experts on treating minority clients" (p. 40) when they have avoided examining their own racism or have failed to become competent in dealing with minority issues.

Unintentional racism may also be evident when minority helpers who speak the same language as their clients assume they understand the meaning of their clients' spoken word. From their interviews with nine family therapists who were fluent in Spanish and worked primarily with Latino clients, Taylor, Gambourg, Rivera, and Laureano (2006) "cautioned against feeling overly competent when conducting therapy in [Spanish]" (p. 436). Simply sharing the same language, they warned, did not make it possible for the helper to understand a client's unique meaning. They did find, however, that therapists who believed their proficiency in Spanish was limited "felt a high level of acceptance, responsiveness, and appreciation among Spanish-speaking clients who otherwise would not be able to receive services" (p. 437). Fluency in the same language may therefore not be essential to establishing rapport and empathy. Regarding each client as unique, however, is essential and serves to guard against unintentional racism and blaming the client for his or her misfortune or stressors.

Avoiding Protecting Clients from Emotional Pain

At the other end of the spectrum of blaming a racial or ethnic minority client's condition or circumstances on his or her status as a member of a racial or ethnic minority group is the practice of shielding the client from emotional pain. This protection may be a form of paternalism that the helper may initially justify as empathy, although others would regard it as condescension. Indeed, Ridley (2005) termed it a "tactical error" to select "interventions that will cause the least pain rather than those that are most appropriate for helping" clients (p. 104). A mixed-race client may need to talk about feeling ostracized by members of the racial groups that comprise his or her identity (see Miville, Constantine, Baysden, & So-Lloyd, 2005). If a helper squelches exploring the issue in some way (e.g., "I'm sure they didn't mean to treat you that way")—all for the sake of protecting the client from what may be regarded as undue distress or pain—the client may interpret this response as not being taken seriously or as an indication that feeling ostracized is not acceptable, and the client's emotional pain may be prolonged.

As mentioned earlier, helpers need to assume the role of learner or student by allowing their clients to teach them about what it's like to live the life of the client. Such helpers will often hear stories that are unsettling—accounts of discrimination and other forms of unfair treatment, for example—that cannot be tidied up for the client and removed from his or her experience. A significant challenge for helpers is to muster what Kenneth Minkoff eloquently phrased as "the courage to join them [clients] in the reality of their despair" (featured in the Mental Illness Education Project, 2000). Doing so is intended not to "fix" or eradicate clients' pain but to provide clients with the company, companionship, and sense of safety that may assist them in becoming able to work through such difficulties. The work and process of healing or recovery is often accompanied by pain, and helpers actually do their clients a disservice when they make the eradication of pain the primary purpose of helping (Ridley, 2005).

Beyond Competencies to Multicultural Literacy and Fluency

For more than 25 years, educators in the helping professions have emphasized the teaching and acquisition of specific competencies deemed essential to work effectively with diverse groups of clients. Several professional organizations have adopted multicultural competencies, including the American Psychological Association (2003), the National Association of Social Workers (2001), and the American Counseling Association (Sue, Arredondo, & McDavis, 1992).

First introduced by Sue et al. (1982), multicultural competencies have been conceptualized according to three domains: *beliefs and attitudes, knowledge,* and *skills.* In developing their set of multicultural counseling competencies, Sue et al. (1992) paired each domain with the three characteristics of a culturally skilled practitioner described by Sue and Sue

(1990): (1) helper's *awareness* of his or her own assumptions, values, and biases; (2) understanding the *worldview* of the client; and (3) developing appropriate *intervention strategies and techniques*. This pairing resulted in nine competency areas. According to this matrix, the multiculturally competent helper is someone who, for example, is aware of his or her own attitudes toward persons of a different ethnic background, including stereotypes or instances of unintentional racism. Each of the three helper characteristics can therefore be thought of as finding expression within each of the three domains.

Numerous studies have sought to determine the impact of multicultural competence on the helping process and client outcome (see Worthington, Soth-McNett, & Noreno, 2007, for a review of the research literature). For example, it appears that therapist multicultural competence does impact client ratings of therapist empathy and general competence (i.e., therapist attractiveness, expertness, and trustworthiness), suggesting an association between therapist multicultural and general competence (Fuertes et al., 2006). In addition, clients-of-color perceptions of therapist multicultural competence increased clients' overall satisfaction with counseling, beyond their ratings of general counselor competence (Constantine, 2002).

These and other research findings are complicated, however, by the lack of clarity as to how competence is defined and who determines competence, as mentioned earlier in this chapter. For example, therapists have been found to rate their multicultural competence significantly higher than do their clients (Fuertes et al., 2006). In addition, Ladany et al. (1997) found no relationship between either self-reported level of racial identity development or self-reported multicultural counseling competence and multicultural case conceptualization ability in an analogue study of 116 therapists-in-training (35 percent of whom were persons of color). Therapists and those in training may therefore overestimate the extent of their multicultural competence, and neither level of racial identity development nor purported multicultural competence may translate into multicultural counseling skill.

Multicultural competencies have been criticized because of what some have interpreted as their doctrinaire or dictatorial nature (Weinrach & Thomas, 2004), as well as their narrow, rigid, and static definition of culture (see Knapik & Miloti, 2006; Taylor et al., 2006). From a constructivistic or socially constructionistic perspective, Taylor et al. noted, "Cultural competence is not a global, measurable phenomenon but a socially constructed notion created by the therapeutic relationship—" (p. 443). This implies that helpers may never "achieve" or "arrive at" competence but are always working toward it or, preferably, working within the "spirit" of multicultural competence. It may also be that a helper's multicultural competence—like empathy—depends on and

is derived (or learned) from one's work with a particular client or clientele at a particular time in the helper's personal and professional life.

For example, a White helper may be challenged to not succumb to certain stereotypes and resentment in her session on a Monday morning with a new African American male client after learning that her sister was assaulted by an African American male the previous weekend. As the session progresses, however (or over several sessions), this same helper may begin to appreciate the struggles of African American men with respect to racial profiling after learning more about her new client's experience with law enforcement officials. Only in hearing his story may she learn about what it must be like for a young Black man to have to "prove" himself in a "White man's world." The necessary "code switching" and his attention to "acceptable" attire as intentional strategies used to negotiate his way in a system she realizes has been oppressive to some persons may thus temper her earlier stereotypical thinking and allow her to work idiographically with this new client.

From this particular example, we may infer that cultural competence has more to do with what Taylor et al. (2006) regarded as "negotiating and co-constructing meaning with clients, rather than superficially speaking the same language and assuming that clients will understand" (p. 437). In addition, the standards and norms that characterize the multicultural counseling competencies may actually be what Taylor et al. describe as "fluid, dynamic, heavily subjective, and humanistic" (p. 430), making it understandable that developing multicultural competence "involves healthy doses of ambiguity, ambivalence, self-questioning, reflection, and ceaseless challenge" (p. 430).

Rather than focusing on "achieving" multicultural "competence," we prefer Lee's (2007) depiction of multicultural "literacy" or what we might also suggest as multicultural fluency. Lee described multicultural literacy as going "beyond mere competency to embracing a way of life that encourages maximum exposure to and understanding of the many-faceted realities of multiculturalism" (p. 261). We understand Lee to mean that as helpers we are always learning and negotiating our way in a world of human diversity, realizing that we cannot work effectively with all individuals (and with the families or systems they represent or are a part of), but that we can learn and speak the language of cultural empathy.

Consistent with Ridley's (2005) notion of idiographic helping, multicultural literacy or fluency does not suggest that as a helper I can understand and connect with every client I am assigned or with every client with whom I come into contact. Rather, literacy and fluency means that I regard each client–helper relationship as a cross-cultural exchange and that I do my best to elicit the unique qualities and capacities of each client within his or her identified socio/political/cultural context (historical, current, and anticipated). It also means that I learn to be literate and fluent by working with and intentionally learning from persons who are different from me. This practice is consistent with Taylor et al.'s (2006) social constructionistic orientation in multicultural helping, and it implies that conversations with one client may generate a different language or dialect than those conversations I have with other clients. The meaning or constructed realities of those conversations are also different from those with other clients. Furthermore, literacy or fluency conveys that my beliefs and attitudes, knowledge, and skills about cultures and the persons who identify with such cultures are always in flux, always in progress, and never established.

Discussing Race and Ethnicity with Clients

In the spirit of multicultural literacy and fluency, we highlight ways in which race and ethnicity in particular (i.e., as two expressions of culture) can be addressed with clients. Cardemil and Battle (2003) offered six general recommendations for practitioners "interested in more fully integrating multicultural issues into their everyday clinical practice" (p. 279). These are listed in Box 2.2 and are discussed in this section. Although there may be some overlap with Ridley's (2005) guidelines for practicing idiographically, we include them here to further underscore the importance of such client–helper conversations.

Suspending Preconceptions about Race/Ethnicity

Because a person's racial or ethnic identity is often not readily known or obvious, it is important to ask clients directly (and early in the process) to describe their racial and/or ethnic identity. "How would you describe your racial or ethnic background?" or "Tell me how you identify your race or ethnicity" would seem to be appropriate ways to elicit such information and meaning from clients. "What do you know about the racial or ethnic backgrounds and values of your parents?" might be another question to pose. This particular question is in response to a finding of Miville et al.'s (2005) study of the experiences of multiracial individuals, that "par-

ents seemed to be the single most influential people in the development and expression of participants' racial identity" (p. 512). Learning of one or both parents' racial or ethnic identity and how the client describes his or her own identity may also enlighten the helper's understanding of relationships within the client's family of origin.

Recognizing Intragroup Racial/Ethnic Differences

In addition to asking clients about their racial/ethnic identity, it is recommended that helpers ask clients how their racial/ethnic identity has developed and has changed over the years. Such practice provides the opportunity to learn more about the unique ways in which clients understand or identify themselves in relation to other members of their racial/ethnic group. Indeed, Cardemil and Battle (2003) suggested that racial identity development and acculturation (i.e., the gradual physical, biological, cultural, and psychological changes that take place in individuals and groups when contact between two cultural groups takes place) are the two prominent ways in which individuals from the same racial/ethnic group may differ from one another. When working with Latino clients, for example, Taylor et al. (2006) recommended focusing on issues of status, power, pride, and privilege and how these might be related to family income, religion, and educational level within the therapeutic relationship—rather than on skin color.

Considering Client–Helper Racial/Ethnic Differences

Open discussion of racial and ethnic issues (initiated by the helper and including differences between client and helper) appears to be a standard of care when providing services to clients of color, regardless of the race and ethnicity of the helper. Helpers should be prepared, however, for clients who are reluctant to disclose what they consider private information. Some clients may be adamant about not disclosing any private information, doubting that confidentiality will be honored or that the helper will treat them any differently. Ward (2005) proposed a continuum of client disclosure ranging from no disclosing, to superficial disclosing (i.e.,

---

BOX 2.2	RECOMMENDATIONS FOR DISCUSSING RACE AND ETHNICITY IN PSYCHOTHERAPY

1. Suspend preconceptions about clients' race/ethnicity and that of their family members.
2. Recognize that clients may be quite different from other members of their racial/ethnic group.
3. Consider how racial/ethnic differences between therapist and client might affect psychotherapy.

4. Acknowledge that power, privilege, and racism might affect interactions with clients.
5. When in doubt about the importance of race and ethnicity in treatment, err on the side of discussion; be willing to take risks with clients.
6. Keep learning!

Source: Cardemil & Battle, 2003.

presenting information that has no significance to their presenting issues, and information lacking depth and detail), to selective disclosing (e.g., that the client hears voices, but not what the voices tell the client), to open disclosing. Conversations about race/ethnicity and racial and ethnic identity—pertaining to the client, helper, and the client–helper relationship—may follow a similar continuum of disclosure or openness. Multiculturally literate or fluent helpers, therefore, are mindful of such nuances and developmental aspects in the client–helper relationship. They respect the pace of their clients and do not try to push or pressure their clients to "get on board" a definitive plan for change.

Acknowledging the Influence of Power, Privilege, and Racism in Client–Helper Interactions

As helpers, it is important for us to understand how repeated experiences with racism (e.g., racial profiling by police conducting traffic stops) impact our racially and ethnically diverse clients' outlook on life. Such understanding includes the White helper's recognition of the advantages afforded to those who share the dominant culture. These advantages may include never being asked to speak "on behalf" of one's racial/ethnic group; seeing people of one's own race/ethnicity well represented in film, TV, magazines, and other media; and not experiencing what Ogbu (2004) has termed "the burden of 'acting White.'" Although these can be difficult conversations to have with clients, Ridley (2005) stated that "simply demonstrating a willingness to discuss these difficult topics may be the critical component" (p. 282).

Although power, privilege, and racism are often attributed—and rightly so—to the majority or dominant cultural group (e.g., White Americans), Ridley (2005) has proposed that they are also experienced and expressed by members of ethnic and racial minority groups. For example, well-educated African Americans may experience abandonment or betrayal by less-educated African Americans because of the belief that they (the well-educated African Americans) have "joined the enemy" by, for example, learning to "speak proper," moving away from predominantly Black neighborhoods, and working in the "White man's world." Combating racism in the helping process is therefore the responsibility of every mental health professional, regardless of race/ethnicity.

Ridley (2005) acknowledged that "the idea that minorities can be racists may not be popular" (p. 21). He explained, however, that a helper should never

> discount anyone's potential to be a racist simply because of the person's skin color. If we use race as the basis for deciding who is a racist, we are likely to discount the more important issue—that it is actions that make a racist. (p. 21)

Erring on the Side of Discussion and Taking Appropriate Risks

It behooves the helper to broach the topic of race/ethnicity with all clients so as to establish the expectation that "all topics and issues are welcomed here." As Cardemil and Battle (2003) stated, "Broaching the topic directly and matter-of-factly can convey a sense of openness to your client, inviting future discussion on these issues as necessary" (pp. 282–283). In addition, from a postmodern and specifically narrative perspective, Taylor et al. (2006) described the "culturally competent therapist" (or what we might term the multiculturally literate or fluent helper) as one who "can open space for the inclusion of multiple cultural conversations in order to generate dialogues out of restrictive monologues" (p. 433). We agree with these authors and believe that it is better to broach the topic of race and ethnicity than to ignore it altogether.

Keep Learning!

Cardemil and Battle's (2003) final recommendation for discussing race and ethnicity with clients is to continue learning. Although we imagine that no reader would argue with this recommendation and that most helpers would instead wholeheartedly agree with it, we suspect that many may embrace it passively. We acknowledge the ease of maintaining, and perhaps the preference of helpers to maintain, the status quo by conducting therapy according to customary practice (e.g., "I've worked with African American juvenile offenders for years. I already know what works and what doesn't."). But doing so may entail slipping back into familiar stereotypes or unintentionally endorsing new beliefs that turn out to be discriminatory in nature.

For White helpers more so than for helpers of color, race and ethnicity are not necessarily prominent or daily considerations. The recommendation to keep learning, therefore, may be interpreted as beneficial only when the White helper is working with racially and ethnically diverse clients. When new clients are assigned who are Native Americans and Puerto Ricans, for example, the helper's initial reaction may be to rush out and get as many books as possible on Native American and Puerto Rican cultures. Although immersing oneself in such literature is recommended, we caution helpers against relying exclusively or at least primarily on such materials to inform their practice with these new clients. We encourage helpers to learn as much as they can about the experiences of their clients (experiences shaped and informed by their racial/ethnic identities or affiliations) directly from their clients and from the clients' family members. This type of experiential learning is invaluable. As Taylor et al. (2006) suggested, "therapists' development of cultural awareness, sensitivity, and competence will depend heavily on their unique, lived experiences, on their relationships with the clients they serve" (p. 430).

LEARNING ACTIVITY   **2.3**   **Idiographic Helping Applied**

 Read through the following case of Katrina, and then refer back to Ridley's (2005) 12 guidelines for practicing idiographic counseling (Box 2.1) and Cardemil and Battle's (2003) recommendations for discussing race and ethnicity in psychotherapy (Box 2.2). Once you have done so, respond as best you can (by yourself or with a classmate) to the seven questions related to Katrina's case and to your work with her. This might also be an activity for the entire class to engage in.

"Katrina" is a 42-year-old light-skinned African American female who moved from New York City approximately 15 years ago to the small midwestern town where she currently resides. She moved after a failed marriage and a fallout with her mother, and out of a desire to raise her then 3- and 5-year-old sons in a "safer" place. Katrina seeks counseling at this time because of increased stressors at home and at work. She manages a landscaping business and also does home renovation during the off-season.

Katrina discloses that she is lesbian and that her girlfriend, "Elaine," is planning to move out. They had a fight last week, and Katrina states she got enraged when Elaine proposed "cooling things" between the two of them and moving out of the apartment they have shared for two years. "Look, without her I have no one, not one person who really, truly, knows me and accepts me for who I am. Even my sons, I know, think we're freaks . . . they haven't been around for a while . . . and I haven't heard from my mom since last Thanksgiving. This can be too small of a town, you know? Don't get me wrong, there are times when I really like it here and there are some good people around. I get by, you know, I pass, but. . . ."

Questions to Consider

1. What are your initial impressions of Katrina?
2. Given the information presented and using your culturally empathic skills, what do you think life must be like for her?
3. What challenges has she likely encountered and experienced over at least the past 15 years?
4. How would you begin a conversation with Katrina?
5. What questions might you ask or what things might you say that you believe would help you and Katrina establish initial rapport?
6. What additional information would you like for Katrina to share with you that would help you understand or resonate with her self-described cultural identity? How might the imparting of this information represent a risk for you?
7. Select at least 3 of Ridley's (2005) 12 guidelines for practicing idiographic counseling (listed in Box 2.1.), and apply them to your work with Katrina. For example, what things do you think would be helpful for *you* to do to enhance *your own* cultural self-awareness as you continue working with Katrina?

ETHICAL ISSUES

We believe that ethical practice is the foundation, the cornerstone, of all helping professions and is therefore at the very heart of what we do as professionals. Without the awareness of and the adherence to or the incorporation of the principles and guidelines of professional ethics, we are at the very least isolated practitioners, if not persons without a profession. As mentioned earlier in this chapter, professional helping is an intimate business: we are in close contact (both in proximity and at an affective level) with other persons; and we engage other people during critical, life-changing moments, occasions when these individuals (our clients) are vulnerable, impressionable, and susceptible to the harmful mental and physical consequences of their illness (e.g., dangerous to themselves or to others). How we conduct ourselves as professional helpers therefore has a significant impact on the lives of other persons and can sometimes be a matter of life or death (e.g., ordering involuntary psychiatric hospitalization, reporting suspicion of child abuse). This work is definitely not for the faint of heart, and we discuss the hazards of the profession in more detail at the end of this chapter.

We believe that being a professional helper is not simply a matter of earning a graduate degree from a mental health program or in a behavioral science discipline. It is also not restricted to passing a multiple-choice state licensure exam and being able to sign off on clinical documentation with your academic credentials (e.g., MA, MSW, or PhD) and your professional credentials (e.g., LISW, LPC, or LMFT). These examples signify a professional helper in name only, the bare minimum of what one needs in order to earn the legal right to practice as a professional helper.

The word *professional* in the phrase *professional helper* actually signifies or reflects who the helper is as a person, including such things as the helper's communication and interactional style, mannerisms, how he or she wrestles with and manages personal demands and dilemmas, and his or her decision-making and problem-solving methods. This means that we cannot separate or segregate who we are as persons from who we are as professionals. Indeed, practicing as a professional helper—a practice conducted and lived out purposefully and authentically—demands the helper's whole self, not just a part or piece or slice of the helper. Who we are as helpers is therefore not simply determined by who we are "on the clock" or "on the job," including how we conduct ourselves with clients and colleagues. Rather, being a professional helper requires the investment of a person's "whole" self—that is, the integration or intersection of (1) one's personal life and private self and (2) one's professional life and public self. In our opinion, this work is more of a lifestyle than a job, so being a professional helper is an identity we take with us wherever we go. Perhaps there is never a time when we are not professional helpers—it is an identity that defines both our personal and our professional conduct.

Ethics—or, more correctly, ethical practice—is therefore very much influenced by who we are as persons, what we believe and what we sanction. Ethical practice consists of much more than knowing and having memorized ethical codes and guidelines or key vocabulary (the cognitive mechanics, if you will, of ethical practice). Instead, ethical practice represents the helper's behavior as a professional, the visible demonstration of his or her identity as a professional helper and the meaning the helper ascribes to that identity. For such practice to be genuine and credible, the helper must understand the need or the rationale for such behavior. The explanation that a particular behavior is simply either ethical or unethical bespeaks ignorance or a lack of appreciation for the necessity of certain professional behaviors.

For example, a member of your weekly therapy group informs you that he felt snubbed when you did not speak to him at the mall last weekend. Responding with "It wouldn't be ethical for me to initiate contact with you outside our sessions" or "I'm not allowed to meet with my clients outside the agency" or "My supervisor would be very upset with me if she knew I had talked with you out in public" would fail to explain the purpose of your behavior. It also would suggest a lack of ownership of or identification with such practice (i.e., "I'm not allowed" insinuates involuntary behavior). A better explanation for your behavior to the client might be "I respect your privacy enough that I would not want to publicize how I know you." Rather than referring to "rules" or mandatory codes, this response indicates an understanding of ethical practice as primarily that of protecting or enhancing the client's well-being. It also signals your adoption or integration of such behavior so that it is not inconsistent with your own beliefs and values.

Returning to the notion of the connection or intersection of helper values and ethical conduct, Okun and Kantrowitz (2008) stated that

> those helpers whose behavior is consistent with their definition of helping, who are committed to examining their own behaviors and motives, and who seek consultation from others are less likely to function unethically than those who are closed to such reflections. (p. 292)

This suggests that values endorsed or prioritized by helpers—both on and off the job—do impact helper professional behavior. Indeed, Bass and Quimby (2006) argued that "professional judgments are influenced by personal values" (p. 78). We believe, therefore, that when the (personal) values of helpers are consistent with professional standards of conduct, helpers are more likely to interact genuinely and credibly with clients and other professionals. According to the Preamble of the *Code of Ethics* of the National Association of Social Workers (NASW, 1999), such practice would reflect the value of integrity (one of six core values listed). Put in another way, consistency of personal values and professional conduct signals an authentic lifestyle of helping.

Ethics are usually understood as professional standards regarding what is deemed (1) correct, appropriate, proper, or acceptable behavior, and (2) incorrect, inappropriate, improper, or unacceptable professional behavior. Behaviors that comprise professional conduct are typically determined by a group of persons (e.g., ethics committee) charged with the task of outlining the behavioral expectations of members of a particular organization or profession. Ethical codes are thus the product of a collective gathering and consensual validation of professional members of an organization or profession and are intended to guide professional conduct, discharge of duties, and the resolution of moral dilemmas. These codes include the American Counseling Association's (ACA; 2005) *ACA Code of Ethics*, the American Psychological Association's (APA; 2002) *Ethical Principles of Psychologists and Code of Conduct* (hereinafter referred to as APA's *Ethics Code*), and the NASW's (1999) *Code of Ethics*. Marriage and family therapists, rehabilitation counselors, school counselors, health care providers, and other helping professionals have their own sets of ethical standards. For a list of websites where codes of ethics and related standards of professional practice can be read, see the Appendix, which follows Chapter 18.

Ethical Values and Principles

All helping practitioners should be familiar with the ethical codes of their respective professions. As already mentioned, however, simply knowing the codes does not ensure ethical conduct. It is the helper who embraces, intentionally reflects on, and honors the values of helping (e.g., care and concern for the welfare of others, openness to learning) who is often more ethical than the one who has simply memorized and can recite ethical codes. The Preamble of the ACA (2005) *Code of Ethics* captures this sentiment in the statement:

> Professional values are an important way of living out an ethical commitment. Values inform principles. Inherently held values that guide our behaviors or exceed prescribed behaviors are deeply ingrained in the counselor and developed out of personal dedication, rather than the mandatory requirement of an external organization. (p. 3)

As we have emphasized throughout this chapter, our values about diversity, power, relationships, the helping process, religion and spirituality, and competence, to name a few, influence and guide our professional behavior. Simply practicing a certain way because "I have to" (insinuating a lack of agreement or at least an incongruence between values and actual practice) does not engender confidence in the helper's dedication to a lifestyle of helping. Considering the values and principles of ethical practice is therefore appropriate, and doing so in this chapter prior to discussing specific ethical issues is intended to inform and guide (perhaps even structure) the decision-making process of each issue.

Using extant data derived from in-depth interviews with 10 therapists (7 women, 3 men; all European American) who were nominated and deemed by their peers as "the best of the best," Jennings, Sovereign, Bottorff, Mussell, and Vye (2005) identified nine themes or ethical values held by these "master therapists." Because the original study (Jennings & Skovholt, 1999) did not focus specifically on ethics, transcripts of the therapist interviews were compared with ethical values embedded in ethical codes (e.g., APA's *Ethics Code,* 2002) and in ethical principles articulated in the scholarly literature (e.g., Kitchener, 2000). The resulting nine ethical values of well-respected therapists are presented in Box 2.3 and are referenced in the discussions of ethical issues highlighted in the remainder of the "Ethical Issues" section of the chapter.

Client Rights and Welfare

Jennings et al. (2005) grouped the first four ethical values of "master therapists" (i.e., relational connection, autonomy, beneficence, and nonmaleficence) into a category they labeled "building and maintaining interpersonal attachments." It is therefore clear that attending to the relational connection with clients is a primary ethical value. This is demonstrated in the ACA's (2005) listing of "The Counseling Relationship" as the first of eight sections in its *Code of Ethics.* Helpers are obligated to protect the welfare of their clients. In most instances, this means putting the client's needs first. It also means ensuring that you are intellectually and emotionally ready to give the best that you can to each client—or to see that the client has a referral option if seeing you is not in the client's best interests.

The helping relationship needs to be handled in such a way as to protect and promote the client's well-being. Establishing an effective helping relationship entails being open with clients about their rights and options during the course of therapy. Nothing can be more damaging to trust and rapport than to have the client discover midstream that the practitioner is not qualified to help with a particular issue, that the financial costs of therapy or other forms of helping are high, or that services involve certain limitations and that their outcome cannot be guaranteed. Any of these occurrences might help explain what Safran and Muran (2000) described as therapeutic alliance "ruptures." At the outset, the practitioner should provide the client with enough information about therapy to help the client make informed choices (also called "empowered consent").

There appears to be consensus about what should be disclosed to clients, including (1) the kind of service, treatment, or testing being provided (including whether interventions are substantiated in research trials or are more exploratory or innovative in nature); (2) the risks and benefits of the service, treatment, or testing; (3) the logistics involved and the policies of the individual provider or facility regarding the length of appointments, number of sessions, missing appointments, fees, and payment methods; (4) information about the qualifications and practices of the helper (including whether the helper is being directly supervised and the involvement of other professionals who may comprise a multidisciplinary treatment team); (5) risks and benefits of alternatives to the treatment, service, or test or of forgoing it; (6) the meaning, extent, and limits of confidentiality; and (7) emergency procedures (Kitchener, 2000; Pomerantz, 2005). Depending on the diversity factors involved, we would add the importance of identifying available resources and sources of help that may be particularly relevant—for example, indigenous helpers, translators, consultants, and cultural or shared-experience networks or support groups. Pomerantz emphasized that providing clients with these important pieces of information is an ongoing process and that specific topics (e.g., fees, method of payment) should be introduced and discussed with clients sooner than other topics (e.g., total number of sessions anticipated). He characterized this type of sequencing as "increasingly informed consent." Shaw, Chan, Lam, and McDougall (2004), however, found

BOX 2.3	NINE ETHICAL VALUES OF "MASTER THERAPISTS"

1. Relational connection
2. Autonomy
3. Beneficence
4. Nonmaleficence

5. Competence
6. Humility
7. Professional growth
8. Openness to complexity and ambiguity
9. Self-awareness

Source: Jennings et al., 2005.

that among rehabilitation counselors, actual disclosure of essential information (e.g., limits to confidentiality) was not done on a routine basis, placing helpers in the "perilous position of being at high risk for ethical complaints and legal action" (p. 49).

Needless to say, an additional layer of consideration arises when children and adolescents or other vulnerable groups are involved. For example, particular care is needed regarding consent when working with children and adolescents (see Tan, Passerini, & Stewart, 2007), as well as with persons with limited cognitive functioning. Laws are often unclear about whether adolescents should be treated as adults or as children when it comes to consent issues (Koocher, 2003). A recent example of this was the New Hampshire Supreme Court's 2005 ruling *In the Matter of Kathleen Quigley Berg and Eugene E. Berg* that the medical (including therapy) records of minor children could be sealed when one parent demands access to the records for the purpose of litigation (see Wolowitz & Papelian, 2007). As a result of this ruling, it appears that in certain circumstances there could be "mature minors" who would be able to consent to mental health treatment without also having parental consent and that these same children could also claim client–therapist privilege (i.e., deny parental access to therapy information, including therapy records). The implications of this ruling to the practice of professional helping are certainly far-reaching and remain subject to interpretation by other courts.

It is true that children and youth vary greatly in their capacity to provide truly informed consent. Soliciting a young person's *assent* is encouraged (American Academy of Pediatrics Committee on Bioethics, 1995) and the *ACA Code of Ethics* (2005) stipulates this in Standard A.2.d. This means that although some if not many children and adolescents may not be able to provide legal consent, they are able to indicate whether or not they understand what is being proposed. Assent conveys that an individual is willing to accept recommended care after having the opportunity to express his or own wishes, knowing that these wishes will be taken seriously although they will not be given the weight of full consent. Tan et al. (2007) explained that assent allows a young person to participate in decision making without the burden or responsibility for making the choice alone. Kitchener (2000) provided a useful overview of issues regarding informed consent not only with school-age youth and adolescents but with other vulnerable populations as well.

Confidentiality

Closely related to protecting client well-being is the issue of confidentiality. In many respects, confidentiality—or the promise to respect and honor another's privacy—is the foundation or cornerstone of all helping processes (Meer & VandeCreek, 2002). Therapy and other forms of professional helping could not be conducted without the "infra-

structure" or "buttress" of confidentiality, the assurance that both the content and the process of client–helper interactions will be "contained" within established parameters or boundaries of privacy. Helpers who breach client confidences can do serious and often irreparable harm to the helping relationship. Practitioners are generally not free to reveal or disclose information about clients unless they have first received clients' written permission. Exceptions vary from state to state but generally include the following:

- If the client poses a danger to self or others, including but not limited to duty to warn or protect
- If the client waives rights to privilege
- If the helper suspects abuse or neglect of a minor, an older or a disabled person, or a resident of an institution
- If a court orders a helper to make records available
- If the client is deemed to have waived confidentiality by bringing a lawsuit
- If the client is involved in legal action and the client releases records
- If an emergency exists

Other types of exceptions in the course of providing services include clerical staff handling case documents, consultation, and supervision of the professional helper. All these limits should be addressed by helpers, and many require a disclosure statement, which the client is given at the beginning of services.

An issue involving the limits of confidentiality has to do with whether the client who tests positive for the human immunodeficiency virus (HIV) is regarded as a danger to others. Consider the case example presented by Chenneville (2000):

> You have been seeing Michael Smith in therapy for the past 3 months. Michael is 33 years old and has been married for 8 years. He has two children, a boy and girl, ages 3 and 5, respectively. Michael admitted to you in the course of therapy that he had an affair with his neighbor several years ago. His wife never found out about the affair, which lasted approximately 6 months. Michael recently discovered that the woman with whom he had an affair died of AIDS. This prompted Michael to have an HIV test, the results of which were positive. Michael told you he has no intention of telling his wife about his test result. (p. 665)

Take a moment to reflect on the following questions: What are the issues involved in this case? If you had been seeing both Mr. Smith and his wife in couples counseling and he had disclosed this information to you outside of her presence, would you be able to keep this a secret from her? Whether or not you are seeing him in individual or couples counseling, what options are there for intervention? What are the helper's ethical obligations?

The ethical conflicts between duty to protect and duty to maintain confidentiality and work in the client's best interests take many forms. Because states vary as to their laws regarding HIV and confidentiality, and because laws differ in what medical professionals and counseling or psychotherapy professionals are allowed, it is important to be informed about laws in your state. There are complex ethical, legal, and therapeutic issues surrounding this question as well as conflicting positions about how to interpret and apply legal criteria and ethical codes.

Schlossberger and Hecker (1996) concluded that therapists have a legal duty to warn specifically identifiable potential victims of a clear and imminent danger (based on the case of *Tarasoff v. Regents of the University of California*, 1976). Merchant and Patterson (1999) indicated that therapists must act on their duty to warn when (1) a client is engaging in high-risk behaviors, has tested HIV-positive, his or her partners are unaware of test results, and interventions intended to elicit client disclosure of his or her HIV status to at-risk persons have failed; and (2) regardless of the client's HIV status, the client is engaging in high-risk behaviors and has expressed an explicit intent to infect others. Based on this additional information, we encourage you to revisit the case of Michael Smith. What decisions would you make in his case given the information you now know?

Although not often mentioned in mental health practice, federal regulations exist that govern the confidentiality of client and patient records in alcohol and other drug treatment services. Known as 42 CFR (42 Code of Federal Regulations, Part 2), these regulations (Code of Federal Regulations, 2002) were introduced in the early 1970s at a time when treatment for drug dependence was separate from alcohol abuse treatment so that someone contacting a drug treatment center would automatically be identified as having engaged in illegal activity (Fisher & Harrison, 2005). The intent of 42 CFR remains to protect the identity of persons inquiring about and receiving substance use treatment so as to make it easier to access care without concern about stigma.

Professional helpers may think that 42 CFR does not apply to them because they serve only those clients with mental health concerns. However, fairly recent reports suggest that 20 percent of those who sought treatment for a mood disorder also had a substance use disorder (Grant et al., 2004a) and approximately 29 to 48 percent of those with a personality disorder also had either an alcohol or a drug use disorder (Grant et al., 2004b). These prevalence data suggest that "co-occurrence is the rule rather than the exception in psychiatric inpatients and substance abuse settings" (Brems & Johnson, 1997, p. 440). 42 CFR confidentiality regulations are therefore not restricted to chemical dependency treatment facilities; they have implications for mental health practice as well.

A concept similar to confidentiality is that of client privilege. Privilege is the legal right that protects the client from the forced disclosure of personal and sensitive information in legal proceedings. As mentioned earlier in the New Hampshire Supreme Court ruling in the 2005 *Berg* case (see Wolowitz & Papelian, 2007), this legal right may extend to certain "mature minors." In 1996, the U.S. Supreme Court ruled in the case of *Jaffee v. Redmond* that communications between a master's-level social worker and her client were privileged under federal law. Although the Court explained that important public and private interests are served by protecting confidential communications between "psychotherapists" and their clients, some see its practical impact as limited. For one thing, no state legislature licenses "psychotherapists" and the Jaffee court did not define its use of the term. As Shuman and Foote (1999) noted, informing clients that helpers have valuable information, but that courts cannot have that information unless the clients say so, is unlikely to keep the courts at bay. Others, however (e.g., Glosoff, Herlihy, & Spence, 2000), predicted that the Jaffee ruling would serve as a precedent for professional helpers whose state licensure laws do not include privileged communication for their respective professions.

The case of *Jaffee v. Redmond* (1996) reminds helpers to include discussion of likely contexts in which service providers may be expected to disclose information about clients to others. Glosoff et al. (2000) provided seven recommendations for professional helpers who have been asked to divulge confidential client information in a legal or administrative proceeding:

1. Use disclosure/informed-consent statements that explicate the parameters of confidentiality and privileged communication in language that clients can understand.
2. Inform clients of the situation and involve them in the process.
3. Take reasonable steps to protect client confidentiality by securing the assistance of an attorney.
4. Provide minimal disclosure of only essential material. A court order or any other legal requirement to disclose confidential information does not mean that all information must be disclosed. Negotiate with the court the extent of disclosure necessary.
5. With permission, contact the client's attorney to facilitate protection of the client's interests.
6. Document all decisions and actions made, including when each action was taken, what information was disclosed, to whom, and in what form (e.g., verbal testimony, client records, summary reports).
7. Consult with colleagues regarding clinical judgments and with lawyers regarding legal obligations.

Meer and VandeCreek (2002) stated that the concept of confidentiality lends itself well to the Western value of individual rights to privacy and autonomy. When working with diverse clients, therefore, a discussion of the meaning of confidentiality for the client is in order. For example, does the client want to have family members involved in the process of helping? If so, how and to what extent? In addition, the helper must clearly explain to the client the nature of his or her professional obligations so that, for instance, not initiating contact outside of therapy (e.g., inadvertent meeting in the grocery store) does not signal the helper's lack of respect for the client; rather, it actually represents the helper's highest respect for the client because it honors the client's right to disclose in public only if he or she chooses.

Considerations of confidentiality extend not only to clientele served but also to the context of services rendered. Managed mental health care has become the primary or standard milieu for service provision, which heightens the importance of informing clients about the limits of confidentiality. For example, clients may not be aware that insurance companies or HMOs do not necessarily maintain the same level of confidentiality as do professional helpers (Bennett, Bryant, VandenBos, & Greenwood, 1990). In addition, managed care reviewers are not necessarily bound by the same ethical codes or obligations as service providers, and they can breach confidentiality in unsecured forms of communication, such as telephone messages, e-mail messages, and faxes.

Although managed care introduces serious challenges, we urge that you undertake a careful, critical assessment of any workplace. Woody (1999) reminds us that the risk of unintended violations of confidentiality affects us all. Whether you are in a home-based office or in work settings sharing space or equipment, consider the pitfalls associated with shared computers or LANS (local area networks), e-mail accounts, fax machines, mailboxes, and work spaces (whether the family dining table or a conference room) as well as accidental revelation by others (e.g., family members or nontherapist workers).

Documentation, Record Keeping, and the Privacy Act

The ethical issue of record keeping reflects the value of helper competence. According to Mitchell (2007), helpers must keep timely and accurate written records for three primary reasons: fiscal, clinical, and legal accountability. Ethical codes also mandate the need for accurate and timely record keeping. Increasingly, with both government-funded agencies and private health maintenance organizations, written records are becoming a tool for billing as well as for keeping track of client progress. Mitchell (2007) points out that if you don't have records to verify services rendered, both government-funding sources and insurance companies may not pay, or if they do, they may want their money returned until verification of services can be provided.

Record keeping has gained prominence in light of the 1996 enactment of the Health Insurance Portability and Accountability Act (HIPAA) in the United States. Specific information about HIPAA is available at the website www .hhs.gov/ocr/hipaa, and most professional organizations also have HIPAA-related information on their websites. In a nutshell, HIPAA means that helpers must protect the confidentiality of health information they collect, maintain, use, or transmit about clients.

There are two basic components to HIPAA: the Privacy Rule and the Security Rule. The Privacy Rule relates to all protected information in any form—oral, written, and electronic. Under the Privacy Rule, clients are entitled to a written notice about the privacy practices of the helping setting, to review their record, to request a change of information in that record, and to be informed about to whom information has been disclosed. The Privacy Rule is designed to manage *intentional* releases of protected health information (referred to as PHI) by safeguarding and controlling when, under what circumstances, and to whom PHI is released. In contrast, the Security Rule is designed to manage electronic protected health information (referred to as EPHI) from *unintended* or unauthorized disclosure either through security breaches such as computer hackers or through unintended losses such as a natural disaster or a stolen laptop. The Security Rule means that service settings must develop policies and procedures to ensure that appropriate privacy procedures are followed and that potential risks to security are identified. Safeguards are to be implemented particularly in electronic client record and information transmitted by e-mail, cell phones, pagers, and fax machines.

It should go without saying that all forms of documentation must be completed in a timely and accurate manner, conform to confidentiality guidelines, and, with respect to written documentation (e.g., diagnostic intake/assessment reports, case notes, treatment and individualized service plans, discharge summaries), be legible. In addition, all signatures obtained must be original—that is, they cannot be forged. Although these are basic practices and should not require a reminder, it is not uncommon for helpers in the throes of hectic schedules, emergency situations, stress, and exhaustion to overlook adherence to some of these practices from time to time. Indeed, Shaw et al. (2004) found a surprising number of rehabilitation counselors who did not make use of written disclosure statements. Reasons given included (1) the counselors believed that clients preferred oral disclosure, (2) the counselor had not yet developed a form, and (3) the agency did not require such practice.

All forms of clinical documentation need to be written judiciously and carefully. Mitchell (2007) likens record keeping to a "logical, short story" (p. 13) that begins with an assessment, then moves to a plan, notes, case reviews, and termination. Identifying data about the client are recorded initially, as well as appointment times, cancellations, and so on. The intake or the initial history-taking session is recorded next. When writing up an intake or a history, avoid labels, jargon, and inferences. If records were subpoenaed, such statements could appear inflammatory or slanderous. Don't make evaluative statements or clinical judgments without supporting documentation. For example, instead of writing "This client is homicidal," you might write "This client reports engaging in frequent (at least twice daily) fantasies of killing an unidentified or anonymous victim"; or instead of "The client is disoriented," consider "The client could not remember where he was, why he was here, what day it was, and how old he was." The information collected in all of the assessment interviews is reflected in the intake report. Following the intake report, there is also a written treatment plan. Although the specific format of this written plan can vary, it always includes the elements of treatment goals and objectives, interventions designed to achieve such objectives, and diagnostic codes.

It is also important to keep notes of subsequent treatment sessions and of client progress. These can be recorded on a standardized form or in narrative form. Generally, treatment notes are brief and highlight only the major activities of each session and client progress and improvement (or lack of it). These notes are usually started during intakes, and information from the assessment interviews is added. As interviews progress, notations about goals, intervention strategies, and client progress are also included. Again, labels and inferences should always be avoided in written notes and records. Remember that as long as you are being supervised, your supervisor needs to sign off on all progress notes and on treatment plans too. If there are multiple clients, such as a parent and child, or two partners, or a family, keep in mind that separate reports, treatment plans, and progress notes must be written for each person. If one party discusses a related party in the session, do not identify the discussed person by name in the progress note. For example, instead of writing "Betsy talked about the affair that John is having," write "The client discussed the husband's affair." The following list, adapted from the Quin Curtis Center for Psychological Service, Training, and Research of the West Virginia University's Department of Psychology, suggests a model for a progress note that we especially like:

- Session number, start and stop times, diagnostic and procedure codes
- Relevant assessment, current status, dangerousness, current stressors
- Progress toward treatment goals
- Interventions
- Plan
- Assignment
- Signature by clinician and supervisor
- Supervisor note/consultation

Notice that several key components of this kind of progress note are essential for quality control reviews and insurance company reviews. These include the session number, start and stop times, diagnostic and procedures codes, current assessment, and progress or lack of progress toward the achievement of the identified treatment goals. As Mitchell (2007) says, the most helpful progress notes are ones that connect interventions to the treatment plan.

Under HIPAA, progress notes are defined as PHI (protected health information). PHI becomes part of the official client clinical record. PHI includes

- Medication prescription and monitoring
- Counseling session start and stop times
- The modalities and frequencies of treatment given
- Results of clinical tests
- Summaries of diagnosis, functional status, the treatment plan, symptoms, prognosis, and progress to date

HIPAA also allows for practitioners to keep a second set of written notes that are separate from the PHI or clinical record and are referred to as *psychotherapy notes*. By definition, psychotherapy notes *exclude* the elements we listed above. Generally speaking, practitioners who keep psychotherapy notes include more sensitive information. And HIPAA also requires special client authorization for both the disclosure and the use of psychotherapy notes. Client access to psychotherapy notes varies from state to state in the United States. However, because psychotherapy notes may be ordered into a court of law, Mitchell (2007) and others discourage practitioners from keeping a separate set of psychotherapy notes.

It is also important to document in detail anything that has ethical or legal implications, particularly facts about case management. For example, with a client who reports depression and suicidal fantasies, it would be important to note that you conducted a suicide assessment and what its results were, that you consulted with your supervisor, and whether you did anything else to manage the case differently, such as seeing the client more frequently or setting up a contract with the client.

The release of information pertaining to client involvement in therapy is possible only when the client has supplied written permission. Obtaining client consent can at times be a challenge in itself, particularly when the client questions the need for a release of information and may be skeptical of the helper's motives. Completing a detailed release-of-information form, therefore, is essential, and how it is explained to the client may determine whether the client will grant consent and invest himself or herself in the process of helping. To be certain that necessary pieces of information have been addressed, Fisher and Harrison (2005) itemize the 10 "ingredients" of a standard release-of-information form, based on 42 CFR. These are presented in Box 2.4.

| BOX 2.4 | REQUIRED CONTENTS OF A STANDARD RELEASE-OF-INFORMATION FORM |

- Name of program making the disclosure
- Name of individual or organization receiving the disclosure
- Name of client
- Purpose or need for the disclosure
- How much and what kind of information will be disclosed

- A statement that the client may revoke the disclosure at any time
- The date, event, or condition upon which the disclosure expires
- Signature of client and/or authorized person
- Date the consent was signed
- Statement prohibiting redisclosure of information to any other party

Source: Fisher & Harrison, 2005.

When the client terminates, there is also a written record about termination. The termination or discharge report becomes the final piece in the written "short story" about the client. Such closing reports are very important in the event the client returns for additional services and in the event of any future litigation. A typical termination report includes the reason for termination, a summary of progress toward the treatment goals, a final diagnostic impression, and a follow-up plan (Mitchell, 2007, p. 75).

Practitioners also need to be concerned about *retention* of client records. All professional organizations, all states in the United States, and many other countries have regulations about the length of time that practitioners retain client records. HIPAA requires that records be kept for a minimum of six years, many of the states in the United States specify seven years or longer, and professional organizations often have longer lengths of record retention than these. *Discarding client records prior to the specified length of time can result in loss of licensure!* Retention of records applies to electronically stored information as well as paper records.

The records we keep about clients are reviewed by a number of entities, including internal review boards, accrediting bodies, and insurance companies. Regardless of whether you keep electronic or written records, or both, bear in mind Mitchell's (2007) eight assumptions of record keeping (p. 46):

1. The counseling record may be subpoenaed, and the court will need to be able to understand what occurred.
2. The client may present for treatment at a time when you are sick or on vacation and one of your colleagues will need to read your record.
3. The client may read your record.
4. The accuracy of your record is compromised if you wait more than a day to complete it.
5. The record should be the best possible reflection of your professional judgment.
6. Nothing you do with a client is considered a professional service until you enter it in the record.
7. Your record may be selected for an audit to verify a legally reimbursable service.

Multiple Relationships

Dual or multiple relationships arise when the practitioner is in a professional helping relationship with the client and simultaneously or consecutively has one or more other kinds of relationships with that same person, such as an administrative, instructional, supervisory, social, sexual, or business relationship. Multiple role relationships can be subtle and are significant sources of ethical complaints. Such relationships are problematic because they can reduce the counselor's objectivity, confuse the issue, put the client in a position of diminished consent and potential abandonment, foster discomfort, and expose the client and practitioner to negative judgments or responses by others. As much as possible, therefore, professional helpers should avoid becoming involved in dual or multiple relationships with clients.

There are occasions, however, when engaging in multiple relationships with clients is unavoidable. This is particularly true in smaller communities where helpers in therapeutic or other roles are more likely to know clients in other contexts and are less likely to be able to refer clients elsewhere. For example, a male client may be employed as a trainer at the local health club where his therapist is a member. Client and helper may also attend the same church, have children who attend the same elementary school, and may even attend the same 12-step self-help group, such as Alcoholics Anonymous. These and other examples illustrate only a few of the many ways in which our lives intersect with others.

As a fellow human being, someone expected to be familiar with the spectrum of life challenges (e.g., loss, role transitions, illness, tragedy) and thus skilled in empathy, the professional helper should be considered a member of his or her local community and should prioritize involvement in various leisure, philanthropic, and cultural events. To do otherwise suggests a helper unappreciative of and out of touch with common, ordinary, and localized concerns, an isolated or at least detached professional who may not be able to establish meaningful connections with his or her clients. Interactions with clients outside of therapy may therefore not only be inescapable but at times be advisable.

Take, for instance, the client who recently accomplished what for her was the monumental task of earning a four-year college degree as a single parent. Because she regards you as someone who has provided her with helpful professional assistance over the past two years, offering support and encouragement to realize this goal, she invites you to her commencement ceremony and her graduation celebration afterwards with family and friends. Declining her invitation on the grounds that such out-of-session contact would violate professional boundaries may actually strain the ongoing helping relationship you have with her. It is perhaps for this purpose that the ACA (2005) *Code of Ethics* contains a standard that describes potentially beneficial interactions with clients (Standard A.5.d.). Any such "nonprofessional interaction" with a client or former client must be initiated by the client, and the helper must document the rationale, potential benefit, and anticipated consequences of such an interaction.

This "nonprofessional interaction" is what Bridges (2005) characterized as a "boundary crossing"—that is, it is an example of "enactments between the therapist and patient that may or may not be harmful to the therapeutic process" (p. 26). These types of interactions are differentiated from "boundary violations," defined as "egregious and potentially harmful transgression[s] of the therapeutic contract and treatment frame that involve a breach of the fiduciary contract and abuse of the therapist's power" (p. 29). Engaging in a sexual or romantic relationship with a current or former client would be an example of a boundary violation, would not uphold the ethical value of nonmaleficence, and would result in the helper being subject to ethical and legal sanction (e.g., revocation of the helper's state license).

Kitchener (2000) presented three guidelines to determine the potential harmful consequences of participating in a new relationship (either personal or professional) with someone with whom there has been a prior relationship (again, either personal or professional). Based on role theory, she first noted that when differences in expectations and obligations increase, so do the possibilities for misunderstanding, confusion, frustration, and even anger. Second, as the potential for conflicts of interest increases, so does the helper's potential for loss of objectivity about the client's best interests as the helper's own needs become primary. Third, as the helper's power and prestige increase—however unintended this development may be—so does the potential for exploiting and harming the client.

Drawing on the work of several ethicists, Kitchener (2000) identified four reasons to avoid posttherapy relationships. First, a former client may at some point wish to return to therapy with the therapist, which would be prohibited or at least unwise after a posttherapy relationship. Second, the power differential is likely to continue in a posttherapy relationship, leaving the former client vulnerable to exploitation. Clients can develop very strong feelings toward their

therapists that, along with the power differential, may lead to poor objectivity by the former client and can result in exploitation by the therapist. Third, the posttherapy relationship may become strained, and the former client might then reevaluate his or her trust in mental health services and/or helping practitioners. Fourth, therapist objectivity for future professional service, such as testifying in court on the former client's behalf, may be compromised by a posttherapy relationship. Clients may thus withhold information during treatment because they hope or assume that some type of posttherapy relationship will ensue.

In some states, posttherapy relationships are illegal. At least two professional associations allow for posttherapy relationships but only after a required length of time elapses after termination and the therapist is able to document that the purpose of terminating services was not to initiate a post-therapy relationship. The APA's (2002) *Ethics Code* stipulates a two-year "waiting period" after termination, whereas the ACA (2005) *Code of Ethics* prohibits counselors from engaging in a sexual or romantic relationship with a former client whose care was terminated or otherwise discontinued less than five years before the intimate relationship began. We strongly advise, however, that professional helpers not engage in such relationships with a former client at any time, as the NASW (1999) *Code of Ethics* stipulates (see Ethical Standard 1.09).

Under no circumstances should you agree to offer professional services when you can foresee clearly that a prior existing relationship would create harm or injury in any way. Obviously, sexual contact between practitioner and client is never warranted under any circumstance and is explicitly proscribed by all the professional codes of ethics. Smith and Fitzpatrick (1995) addressed the failure to maintain appropriate treatment boundaries by the use of excessive self-disclosure by the practitioner. They noted that this behavior is a common precursor to practitioner-initiated sexual contact: "Typically, there is a gradual erosion of treatment boundaries before sexual activity is initiated. Inappropriate therapist self-disclosure, more than any other kind of boundary violation, most frequently precedes therapist–patient sex" (p. 503).

Referral

Referring a client to another practitioner may be necessary when, for one reason or another, you are not able to provide the service or care that the client requires or when the client wants another helper (Cheston, 1991). If client symptoms persist, another level of care (e.g., hospitalization) may be indicated. Similarly, if a client's needs become increasingly complex and surpass your level of competence, it will be necessary to refer the client to a practitioner whose expertise is likely to address the client's needs. Referrals are mandated when your services could be interrupted because of illness,

This activity, from Kenyon (1999), is designed to help you "walk through" an ethical dilemma relevant to your own practice, consider various dimensions, develop a plan for action, and discuss the plan with your student colleagues and instructor.

The Issue. Describe one ethical dilemma that you find to be particularly troubling in your role as a student or professional in human services. Include as much detail (as many facts) as you can.

Ethical Guidelines. What values, principles, and other guidelines are relevant?

Conflicts. Describe the conflicts. What makes it a dilemma?

Resolving the Conflicts. What assistance have you sought with this decision? Did you get that assistance?

Action Alternatives. What options are there?

Selecting and Evaluating an Action. Has this issue been resolved?

Implications. If it hasn't been resolved, why not? If it has been resolved, what do you think—ethically—of that resolution?

Class Discussion

1. Report the issues and dilemmas you've identified. There will probably be some that are shared among you.
2. On an issue-by-issue basis, explore the ethical guidelines, action alternatives, and selection and evaluation of action.
3. For each issue, is there substantial agreement among you, or do you disagree? Is that disagreement okay, or does it represent an ethical problem?

---

death, relocation, financial limitations, or any other form of unavailability (ACA, 2005).

Careful referral involves more than just giving the client the name of another person or agency. Indeed, Ethical Standard 2.06 of the NASW (1999) *Code of Ethics* states that helpers who refer a client to another professional "should take appropriate steps to facilitate an orderly transfer of responsibility." "Appropriate steps" include explaining to the client the need for the referral, anticipated benefits to the client of such a referral, and providing the client with a choice of service providers who are competent and are qualified to deal with the client's concerns and circumstances. In your recommendations and reasoning, you should respect your client's self-determination, along with the client's interest. However, if clients decline the suggested referrals and you determine that you are no longer able to be of professional assistance to clients, the ACA (2005) *Code of Ethics* states that counselors are to discontinue the relationship (see Standard A.11.b.).

Additional steps to take in the referral process include obtaining written client permission before discussing the case with the new service provider. Meeting jointly or participating in a conference call with the client and the professional to whom you have referred the client is recommended, especially if a client is having difficulty understanding the need for the referral or is reluctant to follow through. Throughout the transfer process, the helper should be prepared to assume the role of client advocate and engage in the practice of brokering. This means that because the client's welfare is the number-one priority, the helper may need to link the client to specific resources in the community (e.g., transportation, child care) to facilitate the client's access to the new

professional's services. To protect against abandonment, the practitioner should follow up with the client to determine if impediments were encountered and if assistance is needed for the client to meet with and establish a connection with the referral source.

Before you read further, we recommend that you pause to review the ethical issues discussed so far. To assist you in taking in and working through the complexities involved in ethical decision making, we invite you to participate in Learning Activity 2.4. You might ask a classmate or other colleague to help you. As you engage in the activity, remember that remaining open to complex and ambiguous issues was an ethical value held by "master therapists" in Jennings et al.'s (2005) qualitative study. This means that ethical decision making does not follow an exact formula and the steps to take are not always readily clear. It is our contention that ethical decision making is never a solo activity and must always involve consultation with a qualified professional.

Emerging Issues in Ethics

Ethical issues are one of the many areas in which our society is changing. Emerging issues include diversification in racial demographics, immigrants from dissimilar parts of the world, the aging of the baby boom generation, new or growing types of counseling issues (e.g., associated with HIV/AIDS, violence, child welfare, technology, the biomedical arena), and factors associated with what appears to be the sedimentation or "settling-in" of managed care.

Cooper and Gottlieb (2000) summarized expected trends in systems of care in coming years that we believe will have implications for ethical practice. These include larger, more multidisciplinary health care practices and fewer independent practices, a growing emphasis on business principles to guide decision-making regarding use of health care resources, and fewer and larger managed care organizations. Two additional predictions are (1) a focus on outcome measurement and attention to evidence regarding which interventions appear to work best with whom, with what type of problem (known as "differential therapies"), and (2) an increased trend toward manualizing (detailing activities, sequences, time periods of specific therapeutic strategies) interventions and specifying those associated with diagnostic categories.

Similarly, from their polling of 62 "experts" in mental health practice about the future of psychotherapy, Norcross, Hedges, and Prochaska (2002) identified four themes they believed accounted for the majority of changes predicted. *Efficiency,* the first theme, underscores the attention to economic issues, such as conducting brief therapies using the least expensive techniques. *Evidence,* the second theme, highlights the growing emphasis on evidence-based practices—that is, those that are informed by the findings of rigorous research. *Evolution,* the third theme, supports the gradual change in theories, building on classical or established theories rather than breaking from them. *Integration,* the fourth theme, speaks to the trend of combining or merging innovative and efficacious methods, such as feminist theory with cognitive–behavioral methods. All four themes have ethical implications, including the use of theoretical approaches (e.g., solution-focused therapy) that may have widespread appeal but lack sound and consistent empirical support (or what some might refer to as "scientific backing"). In addition, what are the ethics involved when practitioners are encouraged to use brief or short-term interventions with clients who have severe and persistent forms of mental illness?

Helpers are increasingly using electronic forms of communication (e.g., e-mail and instant messaging) and record keeping (e.g., digitally recording client information during an intake/assessment). Such means of communication and data storage may expedite certain aspects of the helping process (e.g., e-mailing diagnostic assessments to one's supervisor for his or her review and approval) but may also usher in new ethical considerations (e.g., confidentiality of electronic documents). Some technology applications may not yet have high levels of occurrence (e.g., videoconferencing on mobile phones) but will undoubtedly increase in the future, and others not yet foreseen will emerge (Schoech, 1999).

The ACA (2005) *Code of Ethics* includes an extensive section on technology applications. There are also ethical codes among professional groups that specifically address online counseling (e.g., National Board for Certified Counselors, n.d.), reflecting heightened awareness

and usage of e-therapy, cybercounseling, or web counseling. However, compliance with standards appears to be low. For example, Heinlen, Welfel, Richmond, and Rak (2003) found that of 136 websites offering web counseling through e-mail or chat room, 36 percent claimed no training or credentials in mental health. In addition, Shaw and Shaw (2006) found that only a third of online counselors surveyed required an intake procedure and an electronically signed waiver explaining the limits of confidentiality on the Internet, and fewer than half of online counselors required clients to provide their full names and addresses. Professional helpers are therefore advised to become familiar with ethical guidelines and standards before venturing into electronic forms of interaction with clients. Guidelines include those offered by Kanani and Regehr (2003) for social workers, such as determining whether a helper's state licensure board and liability insurance company recognize such practice and establishing proper boundaries in communication with clients.

Ethical Decision-Making Models

Professional ethical codes provide one set of guidance about ethical expectations, roles, and responsibilities. When grappling with specific ethical dilemmas, however, many practitioners have found that these codes do not always translate into clear decision making or problem solving. This reflects and reinforces what is often experienced as the complexity and ambiguity of ethical practice noted in Jennings et al.'s (2005) study. Thus, there has been considerable effort to devise decision-making tools to assist in systematically sorting out issues, options, and priorities. For example, Kitchener (2000) argued for the need to move from a rulebound approach to ethics to one that focuses on ethical principles, such as autonomy (respect for the right to make one's own decisions if one is competent to do so), nonmaleficence (doing no harm), beneficence (helping others), justice (fairness), and fidelity (honesty, reliability). These and related ethical values or principles (some of which were mentioned earlier in this chapter) have been the basis of several additional models and discussions, focusing largely on a critical–evaluative basis for determining what professional helpers ought to do (see Kitchener, 2000, for a review).

Garcia, Cartwright, Winston, and Borzuchowska (2003) proposed a transcultural integrative model for ethical decision making to be used in the helping professions. Their model is based on the work of Tarvydas (1999), who described a four-stage approach to ethical decision making:

1. Interpret the situation through awareness and fact-finding, such as determining the major stakeholders or persons involved in the dilemma or its outcome.
2. Formulate an ethical decision, such as considering potential positive and negative consequences for each

course of action and consulting supervisors and other knowledgeable professionals.

3. Weigh competing, nonmoral values and affirm the course of action, such as engaging in reflective recognition and analysis of personal blind spots.

4. Plan and execute the selected course of action, such as anticipating personal and contextual barriers and counter measures.

Garcia et al.'s (2003) transcultural integrative model incorporates specific cultural strategies such as reviewing potential discriminatory laws or institutional regulations in processing an ethical dilemma, consulting with cultural experts if necessary, and ensuring that potential courses of action reflect the diverse perspectives of all parties involved. Engaging in these strategies may be a more complex and perhaps time-consuming process. However, we believe that participating in and steering a purposeful, thoughtful, culturally sensitive, and therefore comprehensive approach to an ethical dilemma increases the likelihood of greater clarity about what to do. Furthermore, the decision arrived at may be one that more people (e.g., family members) can support than would have been the case if cultural considerations had not been part of the process.

Drawing on the work of several ethicists, Kenyon (1999) developed a pragmatic model for working through an ethical dilemma. Summarized in Table 2.1, this model walks a practitioner through assessment questions and planning, implementation, and evaluation steps designed to carefully undertake decision making with the best interests of the client in mind. Upon reviewing Kenyon's model, you may decide to return to the case of Michael Smith described earlier in the chapter (see page 34). How might this step-by-step process be used to further clarify the actions to be taken in his case? What additional considerations has this ethical decision-making model raised?

As has been emphasized throughout this chapter, a commitment to ethics is critical to practice but often is complex and difficult. Although ethics involves high levels of abstraction about values, duties, and principles, we hope that Kenyon's (1999) tangible tool will help you hone your ability to undertake reasoning about ethical practice with increasing ease and confidence.

Ethical Multiculturalism

In an effort to integrate two of the four crucial factors addressed thus far in the chapter (i.e., cultural diversity and ethical issues) and to provide yet another model to inform ethical decision making, it seems appropriate to introduce and discuss briefly the concept of ethical multiculturalism. Harper (2006) applied this concept to research in the nursing profession and defined it as "the use of moral reasoning to apply the basic ethical principles of beneficence and respect for persons and communities in a culturally competent manner to research in various societies or cultures" (p. 116).

As can be seen in the visual depiction in Figure 2.1, ethical multiculturalism represents a compromise or a moderate viewpoint between the ethical philosophies of fundamentalism, the view that ethical principles are universal, and relativism, the view that ethical principles are culture-bound and context dependent, and may only be applied to their respective culture. Four helper attributes contribute to the balance of ethical philosophies in ethical multiculturalism, these being cultural competence, beneficence/nonmaleficence, respect for persons and communities, and moral reasoning. These attributes form the fulcrum of Harper's (2006) diagram. The base upon which these attributes are supported represents characteristics and dimensions of multicultural competence: cultural awareness, cultural knowledge, cultural sensitivity, cultural encounters, cultural skill, and knowledge of ethical principles and values.

We appreciate Harper's (2006) discussion and visual depiction of ethical multiculturalism and believe it can be useful to professional helpers in navigating a variety of ethical quandaries and dilemmas. Consider how cultural encounters and cultural sensitivity, for example, can generate and inform respect for persons and communities. In so doing, a balance between or a compromise of a fundamental philosophy and a relativistic philosophy might be achieved. A fundamental philosophy may be likened to a nomothetic (or general) cultural perspective, and a relativistic philosophy may be likened to an idiographic (or unique) cultural perspective.

In many respects, Harper's (2006) model reinforces the wisdom of a both/and approach to the process of helping. To address issues of diversity and ethics, a panoramic view or a contextual stance is essential (e.g., understanding of beliefs and customs shared by a group of persons who have a common heritage; familiarity with ethical values or principles of a profession that have informed specific ethical standards), as is a zoom-in or close-up perspective that considers the unique aspects or the details of a particular client case. Both of these orientations or postures are necessary when we are working with diverse clients who present an array of concerns and who are seen in different types of service delivery venues (e.g., home-based care, correctional facility, place of worship). Furthermore, sociopolitical influences (e.g., racial disparities, responses to natural disasters, economic fluctuations) and global events (e.g., immigration, acts of terrorism) directly affect not only our values and philosophies of helping but also our common or standard practices of care. The challenge for us as helpers, therefore, is to remain (1) open to learning about innovative practices,

TABLE 2.1	An Ethical Decision-Making Model
Step	**Considerations to be addressed**
1. Describe the issue.	Describe the ethical issue or dilemma. Who is involved? What is their involvement? How are they related? Whose dilemma is it? What is involved? What is at risk? What are the relevant situational features? What type of issue is it?
2. Consider ethical guidelines.	Consider all available ethical guidelines and legal standards. Identify your own personal values relevant to the issue. Identify societal or community values relevant to the issue. Identify relevant professional standards. Identify relevant laws and regulations. Apply these guidelines.
3. Examine the conflicts.	Examine any conflicts. Describe the conflicts you are experiencing internally. Describe the conflicts you are experiencing that are external. Decide whether you can minimize any of these conflicts.
4. Resolve the conflicts.	Seek assistance with your decision if needed. Consult with colleagues, faculty, or supervisors. Review relevant professional literature. Seek consultation from professional organizations or available ethics committees.
5. Generate action alternatives.	Generate all possible courses of action.
6. Examine and evaluate the action alternatives.	Consider the client's and all other participants' preferences based on a full understanding of their values and ethical beliefs. Eliminate alternatives that are inconsistent with the client's and significant others' values and beliefs. Eliminate alternatives that are inconsistent with other relevant guidelines. Eliminate alternatives for which there are no resources or support. Eliminate remaining action alternatives that don't pass tests based on the ethical principles of universality, publicity, and justice. Predict the possible consequences of the remaining acceptable action alternatives. Prioritize (rank) the remaining acceptable action alternatives.
7. Select and evaluate the preferred action.	Select the best course of action. Evaluate your decision.
8. Plan the action.	Develop an action plan and implement the action.
9. Evaluate the outcome.	Evaluate the action taken and the outcome.
10. Examine the implications.	What have you learned? Are there implications for future ethical decision making?

Source: What Would You Do? by P. Kenyon ©1999. Reprinted with permission of Brooks/Cole, an imprint of the Wadsworth Group, a division of Thomson Learning.

(2) committed to personal and professional edification, and (3) comfortable with or at least tolerant of ambiguity or "not knowing." At the same time we need to honor and abide by certain foundations, restrictions, and guidelines of professional helping defined by our professional associations and by state and federal laws. The latter might also include standards of care established by helping professionals within a specific locale or community (e.g., protocol for handling psychiatric crises and other emergencies within a rural area).

Remaining attentive and responsive to these multiple considerations is not an easy task. Balancing our many roles and responsibilities is a perpetual challenge. Managing complexities and navigating our way through changes in our professional lives may not be too unlike the challenges faced by our clients in their personal lives. We can therefore gain further appreciation for what our clients experience and empathize with their circumstances. In addition, as persons who have selected a profession committed to human growth and development—that is, to change!—it is rather unlikely that we would be content with perpetual stability, predictability, and routine in the work that we do. Actually, being fascinated with change, fascinated by its complexities and by the array of possibilities for change, is probably what

Balance = Protection, Preservation, Dignity, Value

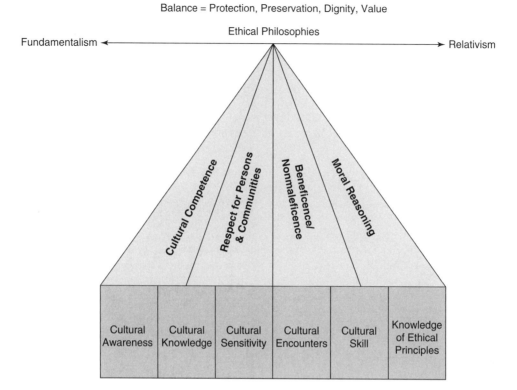

Figure 2.1 Model of Ethical Multiculturalism
Source: Adapted from "Ethical multiculturalism: An evolutionary concept analysis," by M. G. Harper, 2006, *Advances in Nursing Science, 29,* p. 114. Used with permission of author.

attracted us to a helping profession in the first place. Living a life without too much change, therefore, would be mundane and boring for us.

Given the challenges of practicing as an effective helper, how does one maintain energy and retain a sense of enthusiasm for this work? What makes it possible for a professional helper to be multiculturally literate or fluent? How does one pursue consistency between personal values and ethical conduct? How is one able to determine that a review of ethical guidelines and codes and consultation with another professional has been sufficient to warrant making a decision on a particular case? These and other questions related to the challenges of actual practice necessitate a consideration of stamina and resilience for helpers.

PROMOTING STAMINA AND RESILIENCE TO REDUCE BURNOUT AND COMPASSION FATIGUE

Given the many facets of practicing as a professional helper, it is understandable how such a lifestyle can be exhausting at times. It is! Skovholt (2001) said this loud and clear in his listing and descriptions of not one but *twenty* hazards of practicing as a helping professional. Among these are (1)

providing constant empathy, interpersonal sensitivity, and one-way caring; (2) realizing that one's effectiveness is difficult to measure and thus remains elusive; and (3) working with clients who are not "honor students" and whose readiness to change lags behind our own hopes and desires for them. These and other consequences of "emotional labor" (Wharton, 1993) may lead to burnout and compassion fatigue. *Burnout* is a general term that describes emotional depletion, a lack of caring or empathy for clients, and a diminishing sense of personal accomplishment. Jenaro, Flores, and Arias (2007) characterized burnout "as an answer to chronic labor stress that is composed of negative attitudes and feelings toward coworkers and one's job role, as well as feelings of emotional exhaustion" (p. 80). Compassion fatigue can signal the onset of burnout and is regarded as mental and physical exhaustion resulting from taking better care of others than you do of yourself.

We may not have been fully briefed about the hazards of practicing as professional helpers before we submitted our own versions of informed consent and "signed up" for this career. Indeed, it may not be until later in one's formal training (e.g., during practicum and internship) that a novice helper actually experiences some of the stresses and strains that are a part of such a lifestyle. But knowing about all the challenges may not have kept us away anyway, and perhaps some attraction to the challenge of this work spurred us to seek out this particular profession in the first place. It may also be that we are hardier than we realize and that it takes only a few reminders of our competence here and there—including some client "success stories"—to keep us going. Reframing our goals as helping clients manage or otherwise live with concerns rather than fixing, curing, or even solving difficulties may help us remain invested in this important work. There are, however, certain things we can do to help cultivate our resilience and stamina for providing professional care to others.

In a study by Turner et al. (2005), psychology interns reported several self-care strategies they frequently used because they were effective. These included activities undertaken while at their internship site and activities engaged in when not "on the job." Activities interns engaged in at their internship site included consulting with fellow interns, obtaining clinical supervision, diversifying internship activities, and setting realistic internship goals. Activities interns participated in during their personal time included obtaining support from family and friends, engaging in pleasurable activities outside of internship, using humor, getting a sufficient amount of sleep, and engaging in physical exercise. Turner et al. encouraged interns to be intentional about participating in self-care strategies because "self-care is a life-long process and not limited to the internship year" (p. 679). Similarly, Jenaro et al. (2007) emphasized the importance of an appropriate balance between work and private life throughout one's career. Concentrating only on active coping strategies at work, they noted, may actually "exacerbate the psychological tiredness of the worker" (p. 85). Engaging in relaxing activities during one's leisure time is therefore important because these "off-the-clock" activities serve to address the emotional exhaustion that has been found to be the primary culprit of burnout (see Wallace & Brinkerhoff, 1991).

Osborn (2004) identified seven salutary suggestions for stamina for those who serve in the helping professions. These recommendations are intended to assist helpers not only remain vigilant about the hazards of professional helping, such as compassion fatigue, but also maintain their resolve for rewarding work. Based on a review of the scholarly literature and reflections on her clinical practice, Osborn's recommendations comprise a proactive rather than a reactive or preventive approach and are intended to shift attention from a deficiency or pathological perspective (i.e., "burnout prevention") to a strengths or competency-based orientation (i.e., "stamina promotion"). Stamina is likened to resilience and endurance, not in spite of hardship but in the midst of challenges. Each suggestion for stamina corresponds to the seven letters in the word *stamina,* thus creating the acronym STAMINA. These are presented in Box 2.5.

The first ingredient of stamina is *selectivity,* or the practice of intentionally choosing and focusing one's daily activities. Similar to the adage "Pick your fights," selectivity reminds helpers that they cannot be experts in everything and so must concentrate their efforts only on certain causes, a few areas of expertise, and specific practices. Doing otherwise is likely to crumble your credibility and jeopardize your ability to stay on task and provide meaningful care to the clients entrusted to you. In addition, attempting to develop competence in many areas is likely to result in being known as a "jack of all trades and master of none." We recommend, therefore, that you select two or three areas of expertise and pursue intensive training and credentialing in these areas.

Temporal sensitivity refers to the need to always be mindful of the constraints on one's time—as well as those of the clients we serve—and to use the time granted to us wisely. Although such restrictions may be issued by a third entity (e.g., insurance company), we can view them as opportunities to be at our best in what we do, to practice intentional or purposeful therapy, and to focus our efforts on joining or being with our clients in the present moment. Spending too much time trying to reconstruct past events or identifying "reasons" or causes for the client's condition may not be helpful to clients at certain points in their care (e.g., when attempting to establish rapport). Redirecting your own as well as the client's focus on current undertakings and future possibilities may be more worthwhile.

Although many practitioners strive for independent licensure in their respective profession, this designation actually reflects higher levels of responsibility, ethics, and accountability than the levels expected of those who are in training and are receiving mandatory supervision. You may think twice, therefore, about quickening your pace to earn this credential! *Accountability,* however, which is the third ingredient

---

BOX 2.5	SEVEN INGREDIENTS OF HELPER STAMINA
Selectivity	**M**easurement and **M**anagement
Temporal Sensitivity	**I**nquisitiveness
Accountability	**N**egotiation
	Acknowledgment of **A**gency
Source: Osborn, 2004.	

of stamina, is an attribute and skill required of all helpers. According to Osborn (2004), accountability

> refers in part to being able to practice according to a justifiable, ethical, and theoretically guided, and research-informed defense—one that has merit and makes sense not only to the counselor's clients or the counselor him- or herself, but also to the group of professionals of which the counselor is a part. (p. 323)

This means, for instance, that stamina is maintained when professional helpers become multiculturally literate or fluent, actively involve themselves in a professional association, and abide by ethical standards and codes rather than seeking "lone ranger" status that does not require routine professional consultation and peer supervision. Only by consulting the scholarly literature on a particular clinical topic, attending continuing education seminars, and engaging in discussions with colleagues about standards of care will you be able to substantiate treatment decisions you have made or, for example, the proposal you developed for an innovative treatment program at your agency.

The fourth ingredient of stamina is the *measurement* and *management* of one's skills, talents, resources, and strengths. This means, in part, that helpers protect and preserve those things that are valuable to them and that serve to strengthen their undivided attention to and conscientious care of clients. Maintaining healthy boundaries with clients, engaging in personal therapy, and limiting the amount of volunteer or pro bono services extended are a few examples of measuring and managing one's resources. Generating realistic goals with clients and clarifying with your supervisor your exact role and responsibilities are two more. Compared to selectivity, Osborn (2004) stated, "measurement and management pertains to holding on to and accentuating the resources associated with the selections already made" (p. 324). This ingredient, therefore, is intended to assist practitioners in navigating their daily interactions and expectations.

The fifth ingredient of stamina, *inquisitiveness,* draws on and makes use of the trait that many helpers share—that is, curiosity about other people and intrigue about how they function. Think back for a moment to when you first decided you wanted to practice as a professional helper. What was your motivation then? What contributed to your decision? We suspect that your response to these questions includes an interest in human behavior (maybe you are, like many professional helpers, "people watchers"), a fascination with human development and change, and a desire to participate in intimate interactions with people so as to provide them with appropriate professional assistance.

Ridley's (2005) idiographic counseling taps into this trait in helpers by encouraging a fascination with and a desire to learn about persons from diverse backgrounds. An erosion of inquisitiveness is a sure sign of exhaustion, a depletion of a helper's resources, and possibly impairment, the last

identified as an ethical issue by several professional associations (e.g., ACA, 2005; NASW, 1999). It may be evidenced in the use of the same treatment plan for all clients seen (rather than individualizing care maps) and beginning to refer to clients by their diagnosis (e.g., "my bipolar client" or "the borderline group member"). We encourage you to assume the role of student in your interactions with your clients, inviting them to teach you what it is like and what it has been like to have lived their lives. Regarding each client as a one-of-a-kind story with lessons to convey can assist in this process.

Negotiation, the sixth ingredient of stamina, refers to "one's ability to be flexible, to engage in give-and-take, without 'giving in'" (Osborn, 2004, p. 325). This appears to resonate with Newman's (2005) definition of *resilience* as "the human ability to adapt in the face of tragedy, trauma, adversity, hardship, and ongoing significant life stressors" (p. 227). Reevaluating what has become a confining job description, becoming more assertive on a treatment team so as to advocate for a particular client's needs, and expanding rather than throwing away your repertoire of skills may be some examples of negotiation at work in your daily responsibilities. Soliciting feedback from your direct supervisor about your work performance and opportunities for career advancement may also offer insight about alterations you can make in your helping style. In addition, inviting clients to comment on your work with them (e.g., "How has my work with you been helpful?" and "What are some things I could have done to be of better assistance?") can help you negotiate with them the nature and direction of your therapeutic relationship.

The final ingredient of stamina reflects what we believe is an essential skill of all helpers: *acknowledging agency* in others. This is very similar to remaining hopeful about another's capacity for positive change, or what Miller (2000) termed "other-efficacy"—that is, having confidence in another's abilities. Rather than believing that you have the "answers" for clients or that you have somehow been vested with the all-knowing powers to determine what is best for clients, an acknowledgment of the client's agency means in part that you are able to draw on and make use of the client's own resources, which is certainly consistent with multicultural literacy or fluency. We know that helpers must intervene and make decisions on behalf of the client so as to protect the client's welfare. This is certainly the case when clients are presenting with suicidal and/or homicidal ideation. Acknowledging the client's agency, however, reflects the helper's hope and confidence in the client's potential, potential that the client may not be able to grasp or appreciate at a particular moment. Making use of the client and helper's combined resources therefore supports and promotes the client's well-being.

The need for helper stamina is evident in the reflections of a bereaved father that Neimeyer (1998) shared and that are

BOX 2.6	STORY OF THE THREE-SIDED HOUSE

Steve Ryan, a bereaved father, wrote the following metaphoric account of his life in the aftermath of the death of his 2-year-old son, Sean, from complications following a kidney transplant.

I am building a three-sided house.

It is not a good design. With one side open to the weather, it will never offer complete shelter from life's cold winds. Four sides would be much better, but there is no foundation on one side, and so three walls are all I have to work with.

I am building this place from the rubble of the house I used to own. . . . It had four good walls and would, I thought, survive the most violent storm. It did not. A storm beyond my understanding tore my house apart and left the fragments lying on the ground around me. . . . And so I must rebuild. Not,

as so many onlookers would suggest, because I need shelter once again. The storm now travels within me, and there is no shelter from the tempest behind doors or walls.

Who can show me how to build here now? There are no architects, no experts in designing three-sided houses. Why is it then that so many people seem to have advice for me? "Move on," they say, quite convinced that another house can replace the one I lost. . . . I grow weary of consultations based on murky insight, delivered with such confidence.

. . . [And yet] among those who wish to see my house rise again[,] there are real heroes too. People who are not daunted by the wreckage. It is not a pleasant role for them to play because the dust clings to those who come to see and it will not wash off when they go home. . . . Above all they know how difficult this task is, and no suggestion comes from them about how far along I ought to be.

Source: Neimeyer, 1998.

---

presented in Box 2.6. This man's story underscores the importance of walking alongside and waiting with our clients rather than trying to "fix" them or "solve" their concerns. Before reading further, take a moment to read this father's reflections.

Having read this father's reflections, you may need to pause for a moment. Some of what he has to say is not easy to hear. His grief is quite evident.

Once you have paused to reflect on his words (perhaps rereading his reflections), what thoughts come to mind about your intended style of helping? What wisdom might he be conveying to you as you prepare for the work and lifestyle of a professional helper? How would you propose to offer help to this man at this time in his life? What would you tell him if you were working with him? In addition, what ingredients of stamina might you need to intentionally make use of as you work with this father? What aspects of temporal sensitivity or negotiation, for example, might be especially helpful to you?

As we ourselves read and reflect on his words, it seems that this father's loss cannot be "fixed" and that he resents the well-meaning advice others have offered. As much as we'd like to think of ourselves as problem solvers, we realize that some hurts and pains simply cannot be "solved." This father may experience living in the metaphoric "three-sided house" for some time, and no one can build a fourth wall for him—that is, his son will never be restored, will not be brought back to life. This father and all the clients we work with are in charge of constructing their own lives (the ethical value or principle of autonomy that we must honor when working with them); they are the carpenters. As professional helpers, we may be likened to their apprentices or at times

consulting architects, but they themselves know best the constructed and reconstructed lives and houses that will "fit" them.

In addition, clients need helpers who are "not daunted by the wreckage," helpers who are able to deal with and make meaning from the "dust that clings" to them from the stories they (i.e., the helpers) have witnessed and indirectly participated in. Our clients deserve helpers who can demonstrate what Kenneth Minkoff characterized as "the courage to join them [clients] in the reality of their despair" (see Mental Illness Education Project, 2000).

Incorporating the seven ingredients of stamina, therefore, may assist you in tempering the effects of this demanding work, work that is not for the faint of heart. Specifically, we encourage you to establish your own "board of advisers" with whom you can consult on a regular basis. These persons would include trusted friends, family members, a supervisor, respected colleagues, and your own therapist. Surrounding yourself with such a support system is essential. Engaging in specific self-care activities is also essential. These might include physical exercise, meditation, reading self-help books and leisure material (e.g., novels), maintaining a hobby, taking breaks from work (e.g., vacations), and spending time outdoors—all things we encourage our clients to do!

CHAPTER SUMMARY

Part of being an effective helper is knowing yourself so that you can use yourself as a creative, critical thinker who can work with clients toward meeting their goals. This self-awareness includes insight into your values, strengths, and challenges but also extends to a fuller awareness of how you as an individual helper and change agent are part of the process of change for clients. Each of us brings a somewhat unique set of connections among knowledge, skills, commitments, diversity, and collaborative effectiveness. Ideally, awareness of these connections enables you to respond to each client as a unique person, to develop understanding of clients who have values different from yours, and to work in adaptive, collaborative ways with clients whose heritage may differ from your own in one or more significant ways. Finally, your self-awareness and context awareness should foster an appreciation of the balances to be struck in applying an ethical code of behavior in today's practice and pursuing an active role as a lifelong learner to contemporize and strengthen practice.

When lived authentically and intentionally, the lifestyle of a professional helper can be extremely rewarding. This line of work affords us the privilege of being part of the lives of many different individuals and their families. We are in many ways their guests; they extend to us an invitation to witness and share in their struggles and accomplishments. Participating in what may be characterized as sacred conversations with our clients is not something we should ever take for granted or otherwise minimize. It is something to always value and protect. We do this by learning from and with our clients, honoring their experiences and stories, upholding ethical guidelines as professional helpers, and investing in our own nurturance and self-care as a result. Establishing now a firm foundation of balanced other- and self-care is therefore essential. We trust that as you continue to build on this foundation, you will realize the many professional and personal benefits of this line of work.

REFERENCES

American Academy of Pediatrics Committee on Bioethics. (1995). Informed consent, parental permission, and assent in pediatric practice. *Pediatrics, 95,* 314–317.

American Counseling Association. (2005). *ACA code of ethics.* Alexandria, VA: Author.

American Psychological Association. (2002). *Ethical principles of psychologists and code of conduct.* Washington, DC: Author.

American Psychological Association. (2003). Guidelines on multicultural education, training, research, practice, and organizational change for psychologists. *American Psychologist, 58,* 377–402.

Anderson, H., & Goolishian, H. (1992). The client is the expert: A not-knowing approach to therapy. In S. McNamee & K. J. Gergen (Eds.), *Therapy as social construction* (pp. 25–39). Newbury Park, CA: Sage.

Aponte, H. J. (1994). *Bread and spirit: Therapy with the new poor: Diversity of race, culture, and values.* New York: Norton.

Baldwin, M. L., & Marcus, S. C. (2006). Perceived and measured stigma among workers with serious mental illness. *Psychiatric Services, 57,* 388–392.

Bass, B. A., & Quimby, J. L. (2006). Addressing secrets in couples counseling: An alternative approach to informed consent. *The Family Journal, 14,* 77–80.

Bennett, B. E., Bryant, B. K., VandenBos, G. R., & Greenwood, A. (1990). *Professional liability and risk management.* Washington, DC: American Psychological Association.

Boyd-Franklin, N. (2003). *Black families in therapy: Understanding the African American experience* (2nd ed.). New York: Guilford.

Brems, C. (2000). *Dealing with challenges in psychotherapy and counseling.* Belmont, CA: Brooks/Cole.

Brems, C. (2001). *Basic skills in psychotherapy and counseling.* Belmont, CA: Brooks/Cole.

Brems, C., & Johnson, M. E. (1997). Clinical implications of the co-occurrence of substance use and other psychiatric disorders. *Professional Psychology: Research and Practice, 28,* 437–447.

Bridges, N. A. (2005). *Moving beyond the comfort zone in psychotherapy.* Lanham, MD: Jason Aronson/Rowan & Littlefield.

Brownell, P., & Podnicks, E. (2005). Long-overdue recognition for the critical issue of elder abuse and neglect: A global policy and practice perspective. *Brief Treatment and Crisis Intervention, 5,* 187–191.

Cardemil, E. V., & Battle, C. L. (2003). Guess who's coming to therapy? Getting comfortable with conversations about race and ethnicity in psychotherapy. *Professional Psychology: Research and Practice, 34,* 278–286.

Chenneville, T. (2000). HIV, confidentiality, and duty to protect: A decision-making model. *Professional Psychology: Research and Practice, 31,* 661–670.

Cheston, S. E. (1991). *Making effective referrals: The therapeutic process.* New York: Gardner.

Code of Federal Regulations. (2002). *Part 2: Confidentiality of alcohol and drug abuse patient records,* 7-26. Washington, DC: U.S. Government Printing Office. Retrieved March 30, 2007, from http://www.access.gpo.gov/nara/cfr/waisidx_02/42cfr2_02.html

Cone, J. D. (2001). *Evaluating outcomes: Empirical tools for effective practice.* Washington, DC: American Psychological Association.

Constantine, M. G. (2002). Predictors of satisfaction with counseling: Racial and ethnic minority clients' attitudes toward counseling and ratings of their counselors' general and multicultural counseling competence. *Journal of Counseling Psychology, 49,* 255–263.

Cooper, C., & Gottlieb, M. C. (2000). Ethical issues with managed care: Challenges facing counseling psychology. *The Counseling Psychologist, 28,* 179–236.

Corey, G., Corey, M. S., & Callanan, P. (2007). *Issues and ethics in the helping professions* (7th ed.). Belmont, CA: Brooks/Cole–Thomson.

Day, J. (1995). Obligation and motivation: Obstacles and resources for counselor well-being and effectiveness. *Journal of Counseling and Development, 73,* 108–110.

Egan, G. (2007). *The skilled helper: A problem-management and opportunity-development approach to helping.* Belmont, CA: Thomson Brooks/Cole.

Fisher, G. L., & Harrison, T. C. (2005). *Substance abuse: Information for school counselors, social workers, therapists, and counselors* (3rd ed.). Boston: Pearson Education.

Fuertes, J. N., Stracuzzi, T. I., Bennett, J., Scheinholtz, J., Mislowack, A., Hersh, M., & Cheng, D. (2006). Therapist multicultural competency: A study of therapy dyads. *Psychotherapy: Theory, Research, Practice, Training, 43,* 480–490.

Garcia, J. G., Cartwright, B., Winston, S. M., & Borzuchowska, B. (2003). A transcultural integrative model for ethical decision making in counseling. *Journal of Counseling and Development, 81,* 268–277.

Gary, F. A. (2005). Stigma: Barrier to mental health care among ethnic minorities. *Issues in Mental Health Nursing, 26,* 979–999.

Glosoff, H. L., Herlihy, B., & Spence, E. B. (2000). Privileged communication in the counselor–client relationship. *Journal of Counseling and Development, 78,* 454–462.

Grant, B. F., Stinson, F. S., Dawson, D. A., Chou, S. P., Dufour, M. C., Compton, W., Pickering, R. P., & Kaplan, K. (2004b). Prevalence and co-occurrence of substance use disorders and independent mood and anxiety disorders. *Archives of General Psychiatry, 61,* 807–816.

Grant, B. F., Stinson, F. S., Dawson, D. A., Chou, S. P., Ruan, W. J., & Pickering, R. P. (2004a). Co-occurrence of 12-month alcohol and drug use disorders and personality disorders in the United States. *Archives of General Psychiatry, 61,* 361–368.

Griffin, M. P., & West, D. A. (2006). The lowest of the low? Addressing the disparity between community view, public policy, and treatment effectiveness for sex offenders [Electronic version]. *Law and Psychology Review, 30,* 143–169.

Hall, C. C. I. (2004). Mixed-race women: One more mountain to climb. *Women and Therapy, 27*(1–2), 237–246.

Harper, M. G. (2006). Ethical multiculturalism: An evolutionary concept analysis. *Advances in Nursing Science, 29,* 110–124.

Heilman, S. C., & Witztum, E. (1997). Value-sensitive therapy: Learning from ultra-orthodox patients. *American Journal of Psychotherapy, 51,* 522–541.

Heinlen, K. T., Welfel, E. R., Richmond, E. N., & Rak, C. F. (2003). The scope of WebCounseling: A survey of services and compliance with NBCC *Standards for the Ethical Practice of WebCounseling. Journal of Counseling and Development, 81,* 61–69.

Hermann, M. A., & Herlihy, B. R. (2006). Legal and ethical implications of refusing to counsel homosexual clients. *Journal of Counseling and Development, 84,* 414–418.

Jaffee v. Redmond, WL 315841 (U.S. June 13, 1996).

Jenaro, C., Flores, N., & Arias, B. (2007). Burnout and coping in human service practitioners. *Professional Psychology: Research and Practice, 38,* 80–87.

Jennings, L., & Skovholt, T. M. (1999). The cognitive, emotional, and relational characteristics of master therapists. *Journal of Counseling Psychology, 46,* 3–11.

Jennings, L., Sovereign, A., Bottorff, N., Mussell, M. P., & Vye, C. (2005). Nine ethical values of master therapists. *Journal of Mental Health Counseling, 27,* 32–47.

Kanani, K., & Regehr, C. (2003). Clinical, ethical, and legal issues in e-therapy. *Families in Society, 84,* 155–162.

Kelly, E. W., Jr. (1995). Counselor values: A national survey. *Journal of Counseling and Development, 73,* 648–653.

Kelly, J. M., Kadue, D. D., & Mignin, R. J. (2005). Sexual harassment in the workplace: A United States perspective. *International Journal of Discrimination and the Law, 7,* 29–85.

Kenyon, P. (1999). *What would you do? An ethical case workbook for human service professionals.* Pacific Grove, CA: Brooks/Cole.

Kitchener, K. S. (2000). *Foundations of ethical practice, research, and teaching in psychology.* Mahwah, NJ: Lawrence Erlbaum.

Knapik, M. T., & Miloti, A. S. (2006). Conceptualizations of competence and culture: Taking up postmodern interest in social interaction. *International Journal for the Advancement of Counseling, 28,* 375–387.

Koocher, G. P. (2003). Ethical issues in psychotherapy with adolescents. *Journal of Clinical Psychology, 59,* 1247–1256.

Kottler, J. A. (2004). *Introduction to therapeutic counseling: Voices from the field* (5th ed.). Pacific Grove, CA: Brooks/Cole–Thomson.

Ladany, N., Inman, A. G., Constantine, M. G., & Hofheinz, E. W. (1997). Supervisee multicultural case conceptualization ability and self-reported multicultural competence as functions of supervisee racial identity and supervisor focus. *Journal of Counseling Psychology, 44,* 284–293.

Lee, C. C. (2001). Defining and responding to racial and ethnic diversity. In D. C. Locke, J. E. Myers, & E. L. Herr (Eds.), *The handbook of counseling* (pp. 581–588). Thousand Oaks, CA: Sage.

Lee, C. C. (2007). Conclusion: A counselor's call to action. In C. C. Lee (Ed.), *Counseling for social justice* (2nd ed., pp. 259–263). Alexandria, VA: American Counseling Association.

Lösel, F., & Schmucker, M. (2005). The effectiveness of treatment for sexual offenders: A comprehensive meta-analysis. *Journal of Experimental Criminology, 1,* 117–146.

Lum, D. (2004). *Social work practice and people of color: A process approach* (5th ed.). Belmont, CA: Brooks/Cole–Thomson.

Meer, D., & VandeCreek, L. (2002). Cultural considerations in release of information. *Ethics and Behavior, 12,* 143–156.

Mental Illness Education Project. (Producer). (2000). *Dual diagnosis: An integrated model for the treatment of people with co-occurring psychiatric and substance disorders. A lecture by Kenneth Minkoff, M.D.* (Video available from Mental Illness Education Project Videos, 22-D Hollywood Ave., Hohokus, NJ 07423).

Merchant, T. P., & Patterson, M. M. (1999). Duty to warn and interventions with HIV-positive clients. *Professional Psychology: Research and Practice, 30,* 180–186.

Miller, J., & Garran, A. M. (2008). *Racism in the United States: Implications for the helping professions.* Belmont, CA: Brooks/Cole–Thomson.

Miller, W. R. (2000). Rediscovering fire: Small interventions, large effects. *Psychology of Addictive Behaviors, 14,* 6–18.

Mitchell, R. W. (2007). *Documentation in counseling records* (3rd ed.). Alexandria, VA: American Counseling Association.

Miville, M. L., Constantine, M. G., Baysden, M. F., & So-Lloyd, G. (2005). Chameleon changes: An exploration of racial identity themes of multiracial people. *Journal of Counseling Psychology, 52,* 507–516.

Moulden, H. M., & Firestone, P. (2007). Vicarious traumatization: The impact on therapists who work with sexual offenders. *Trauma, Violence, and Abuse, 8,* 67–83.

Muccino, G. (Director). (2006). *The pursuit of happyness* [Motion picture]. United States: Columbia Pictures.

Munch, S. (2006). The women's health movement: Making policy, 1970–1995. *Social Work in Health Care, 43,* 17–32.

Nagy, T. F. (2005). Competence. *Journal of Aggression, Maltreatment and Trauma, 11*(1–2), 27–49.

National Association of Social Workers. (1999). *Code of Ethics.* Washington, DC: Author.

National Association of Social Workers. (2001). *NASW standard of cultural competence for social work practice.* Washington DC: NASW Press.

National Board for Certified Counselors. (n.d.). *The practice of Internet counseling.* Retrieved March 30, 2007, from http://www.nbcc.org/webethics2

National Center on Elder Abuse. (1998, September). *The national elder abuse incidence study: Final report.* Retrieved February 17, 2007, from http://www.aoa.gov/eldfam/Elder_Rights/Elder_Abuse/ABuseReport_Full.pdf

National Center on Elder Abuse. (2006, February). *Fact sheet: Abuse of adults aged 60+. 2004 survey of adult protective services.* Retrieved February 17, 2007, from http://www.elderabusecenter.org/

Neimeyer, R. A. (1998). *Lessons of loss: A guide to coping.* New York: McGraw-Hill.

Neufeldt, S. A., Pinterits, E. J., Moleiro, C. M., Lee, T. L., Yang, P. H., Brodie, R. E., & Orliss, M. J. (2006). How do graduate student therapists incorporate diversity factors in case conceptualization? *Psychotherapy: Theory, Research, Practice, Training, 43,* 464–479.

Newman, R. (2005). APA's resilience initiative. *Professional Psychology: Research and Practice, 36,* 227–229.

Nezu, A. M., Nezu, C. M., & Lombardo, E. (2004). *Cognitive–behavioral case formulation and treatment design: A problem-solving approach.* New York: Springer.

Norcross, J. C., & Farber, B. A. (2005). Choosing psychotherapy as a career: Beyond "I want to help people." *Journal of Clinical Psychology: In Session, 61,* 939–943.

Norcross, J. C., Hedges, M., & Prochaska, J. O. (2002). The face of 2010: A Delphi poll on the future of psychotherapy. *Professional Psychology: Research and Practice, 33,* 316–322.

Ogbu, J. U. (2004). Collective identity and the burden of "acting White" in Black history, community, and education. *The Urban Review, 36,* 1–35.

Okun, B. F., & Kantrowitz, R. E. (2008). *Effective helping: Interviewing and counseling techniques* (7th ed.). Belmont, CA: Brooks/Cole–Thomson.

Orlinsky, D. E., Botermans, J., Rønnestad, M. H., & the SPR Collaborative Research Network. (2001). Towards an empirically grounded model of psychotherapy training: Four thousand therapists rate influences on their development. *Australian Psychologist, 36,* 139–148.

Osborn, C. J. (2004). Seven salutary suggestions for counselor stamina. *Journal of Counseling and Development, 82,* 319–328.

Pavkov, T. W., Lewis, D. A., & Lyons, J. S. (1989). Psychiatric diagnoses and racial bias: An empirical investigation. *Professional Psychology: Research and Practice, 20,* 364–368.

Pomerantz, A. M. (2005). Increasingly informed consent: Discussing distinct aspects of psychotherapy at different points in time. *Ethics and Behavior, 15,* 351–360.

Rader, J., & Gilbert, L. A. (2005). The egalitarian relationship in feminist therapy. *Psychology of Women Quarterly, 29,* 427–435.

Reupert, A. (2006). The counsellor's self in therapy: An inevitable presence. *International Journal for the Advancement of Counselling, 28,* 95–105.

Ridley, C. R. (2005). *Overcoming unintentional racism in counseling and therapy: A practitioner's guide to intentional intervention* (2nd ed.). Thousand Oaks, CA: Sage.

Safran, J. D., & Muran, J. C. (2000). *Negotiating the therapeutic alliance: A relational treatment guide.* New York: Guilford.

Scheid, T. L. (2005). Stigma as a barrier to employment: Mental disability and the Americans with Disabilities Act. *International Journal of Law and Psychiatry, 28,* 670–690.

Schlossberger, E., & Hecker, L. (1996). HIV and family therapist's duty to warn: A legal and ethical analysis. *Journal of Marital and Family Therapy, 22,* 27–40.

Schoech, D. (1999). *Human services technology* (2nd ed.). New York: Haworth.

Shaw, H. E., & Shaw, S. F. (2006). Critical issues in online counseling: Assessing current practices with an ethical intent checklist. *Journal of Counseling & Development, 84,* 41–53.

Shaw, L. R., Chan, F., Lam, C. S., & McDougall, A. G. (2004). Professional disclosure practices of rehabilitation counselors. *Rehabilitation Counseling Bulletin, 48,* 38–50.

Shuman, D. W., & Foote, W. (1999). *Jaffee v. Redmond's* impact: Life after the Supreme Court's recognition of a psychotherapist–patient privilege. *Professional Psychology: Research and Practice, 30,* 479–487.

Simon, S. (1995). *Values clarification* (2nd ed.). New York: Warner.

Skovholt, T. M. (2001). *The resilient practitioner: Burnout prevention and self-care strategies for counselors, therapists, teachers, and health professionals.* Boston: Allyn & Bacon.

Skovholt, T. M., & Rønnestad, M. H. (1995). *The evolving professional self: Stages and themes in therapist and counselor development.* New York: Wiley.

Smith, D., & Fitzpatrick, M. (1995). Patient–therapist boundary issues. *Professional Psychology, 26,* 499–506.

Spielman, F., & Donovan, L. (2007, March 2). Daley: Principal's firing 'a disgrace': Mayor wants Curie High chief back—some pin vote on race, personalities. *Chicago Sun Times.* Retrieved July 13, 2007, from http://web.lexis-nexis.com/universe/document?_m=040c9d01584a19dbaea3aba8a40900e7&_docnum=14&wchp=dGLbVzz-zSkVA&_md5=cb0fbfb4dcc85ade5cacb2ee01272a22

Sue, D. W., Arredondo, P., & McDavis, R. J. (1992). Multicultural counseling competencies and standards: A call to the profession. *Journal of Counseling & Development, 70,* 477–486.

Sue, D. W., Bernier, J. E., Durran, A., Feinberg, L., Pedersen, P., Smith, E. J., & Vasquez-Nuttall, E. (1982). Position paper: Cross-cultural counseling competencies. *The Counseling Psychologist, 10,* 45–52.

Sue, D. W., Capodilupo, C. M., Torino, G. C., Bucceri, J. M., Holder, A. M. B., Nadal, K. L., & Esquilin, M. (2007). Racial microaggressions in everyday life: Implications for clinical practice. *American Psychologist, 62,* 271–286.

Sue, D. W., & Sue, D. (1990). *Counseling the culturally different* (2nd ed.). New York: Wiley.

Tan, J. O. A., Passerini, G. E., & Stewart, A. (2007). Consent and confidentiality in clinical work with young people. *Clinical Child Psychiatry and Psychiatry, 12,* 191–210.

Tarasoff v. Regents of the University of California et al., 551 P.2d 334. (1976).

Tarvydas, V. M. (1999). Ethical decision-making processes. In R. R. Cottone & V. M. Tarvydas (Eds.), *Ethical and professional issues in counseling* (pp. 144–154). Upper Saddle River, NJ: Prentice Hall.

Taylor, B. A., Gambourg, M. B., Rivera, M., & Laureano, D. (2006). Constructing cultural competence: Perspectives of family therapists working with Latino families. *The American Journal of Family Therapy, 34,* 429–445.

Turner, J. A., Edwards, L. M., Eicken, I. M., Yokoyama, K., Castro, J. R., Tran, A. N., & Haggins, K. L. (2005). Intern self-care: An exploratory study into strategy use and effectiveness. *Professional Psychology: Research and Practice, 36,* 674–680.

U.S. Census Bureau. (2001). *The two or more races population: 2000* [in the Census 2000 Briefs series]. Retrieved March 3, 2007, from http://www.census.gov/prod/2001pubs/c2kbr01-6.pdf

U.S. Department of Health and Human Services. (1999). *Mental health: A report of the Surgeon General.* Rockville, MD: Author.

U.S. Department of Health and Human Services. (2001). *Mental health: Culture, race, and ethnicity—A supplement to Mental Health: A report of the Surgeon General—Executive Summary.* Rockville, MD: Author.

Vicary, D., & Andrews, H. (2000). Developing a culturally appropriate psychotherapeutic approach with indigenous Australians. *Australian Psychologist, 35,* 181–185.

Wallace, J. E., & Brinkerhoff, M. B. (1991). The measurement of burnout revisited. *Journal of Social Service Research, 14,* 85–111.

Ward, E. C. (2005). Keeping it real: A grounded theory study of African American clients engaging in counseling at a community mental health agency. *Journal of Counseling Psychology, 52,* 471–481.

Weinrach, S. G., & Thomas, K. R. (2004). The AMCD multicultural counseling competencies: A critically flawed initiative. *Journal of Mental Health Counseling, 26,* 81–93.

Wharton, A. S. (1993). The affective consequences of service work: Managing emotions on the job. *Work and Occupations, 20,* 205–232.

Wolowitz, D., & Papelian, J. (2007, Spring). Minor secrets, major headaches: Psychotherapeutic confidentiality after

Berg. *Bar Journal* [publication of the New Hampshire Bar Association], *48*(1), 24–28. Retrieved July 13, 2007, from http://www.nhbar.org/publications/display-journal-issue.asp?id=359

Woody, R. H. (1999). Domestic violations of confidentiality. *Professional Psychology: Research and Practice, 30,* 607–610.

Worthington, R. L., Soth-McNett, A. M., & Moreno, M. V. (2007). Multicultural counseling competencies research: A 20-year content analysis. *Journal of Counseling Psychology, 54,* 351–361.

2   KNOWLEDGE AND SKILL BUILDER

Part One

According to Learning Outcome 1 listed at the beginning of this chapter, you will be able to identify attitudes and behaviors about yourself that could help or interfere with establishing a positive helping relationship. Here, we present a Self-Rating Checklist that refers to characteristics of effective helpers. Use the checklist to assess yourself *now* with respect to these attitudes and behaviors. If you haven't yet had any or much contact with actual clients, try to use the checklist to assess how you believe you would behave in actual interactions. Identify any issues or areas you may need to work on in your development as a helper. Discuss your assessment in small groups or with an instructor, colleague, or supervisor. There is no written feedback for this part of the Knowledge and Skill Builder.

Self-Rating Checklist

Check the items that are most descriptive of you.

A. Openness to Learning Assessment

_____ 1. I have already learned a lot of life lessons, and I believe clients will benefit from hearing my own story of recovery.

_____ 2. I invite clients to comment on their experiences in therapy and how my work has either helped or hindered the process.

_____ 3. I am a member of a professional association that publishes a scholarly journal for its members.

_____ 4. I think that taking notes in supervision is not necessary.

_____ 5. I am considering participating in therapy as a client to learn more about my own developing style of helping.

_____ 6. I routinely solicit feedback from my supervisor and trusted colleagues.

_____ 7. I have attended a professional workshop or conference in the past six months.

_____ 8. I think I've already learned what it is that I need to work on in order to provide good care to my clients. Reviewing audio- or videotapes of my counseling sessions is therefore no longer necessary.

B. Competence Assessment

_____ 1. Constructive negative feedback about myself doesn't make me feel incompetent or uncertain of myself.

_____ 2. I tend to put myself down frequently.

_____ 3. I feel fairly confident about myself as a helper.

_____ 4. I am often preoccupied with thinking that I'm not going to be a competent helper.

_____ 5. When I am involved in a conflict, I don't go out of my way to ignore or avoid it.

_____ 6. When I get positive feedback about myself, I often don't believe it's true.

_____ 7. I set realistic goals for myself as a helper that are within reach.

_____ 8. I believe that a confronting, hostile client could make me feel uneasy or incompetent.

_____ 9. I often find myself apologizing for myself or my behavior.

_____ 10. I'm fairly confident I can or will be a successful helper.

_____ 11. I find myself worrying a lot about "not making it" as a helper.

_____ 12. I'm likely to be a little scared by clients who would idealize me.

_____ 13. A lot of times I will set standards or goals for myself that are too tough to attain.

_____ 14. I tend to avoid negative feedback when I can.

_____ 15. Doing well or being successful does not make me feel uneasy.

C. Power Assessment

_____ 1. If I'm really honest, I think my helping methods are a little superior to other people's.

_____ 2. A lot of times I try to get people to do what I want. I might get pretty defensive or upset if the client disagreed with what I wanted to do or did not follow my direction in the interview.

_____ 3. I believe there is (or will be) a balance in the interviews between my participation and the client's.

_____ 4. I could feel angry when working with a resistant or stubborn client.

_____ 5. I can see that I might be tempted to get some of my own ideology across to the client.

_____ 6. Allowing the client to make certain decisions and not telling him or her what to do is a sign of weakness on the helper's part.

_____ 7. Sometimes I feel impatient with clients who have a different way of looking at the world than I do.

_____ 8. I know there are times when I would be reluctant to refer my client to someone else, especially if the other counselor's style differed from mine.

_____ 9. Sometimes I feel rejecting or intolerant of clients whose values and lifestyles are very different from mine.

_____ 10. It is hard for me to avoid getting into a power struggle with some clients.

Part Two

According to Learning Outcome 2 for this chapter, you will be able to identify issues related to values, diversity, ethics, and stamina that could affect the development of a therapeutic relationship. Here we present seven written case descriptions and a list of seven types of issues. Read each case description carefully; then on the line preceding each case write the letter of the major kinds of issue reflected in the case description. (More than one type of issue may be reflected in each case.) When you are finished, consult the feedback for this part of the Knowledge and Skill Builder.

Type of Issue

A. Values conflict
B. Values stereotyping
C. Ethics—breach of confidentiality
D. Ethics—client welfare and rights
E. Ethics—referral
F. Diversity
G. Stamina

Case Description

_____ 1. You are counseling a client who is in danger of failing high school. The client states that he feels like a failure because all the other students are so smart. In an effort to make him feel better, you

tell him about one of your former clients who also almost flunked out.

_____ 2. A 58-year-old man who is having difficulty adjusting to life without his wife, who died, comes to you for counseling. He has difficulty in discussing his concern or problem with you, and he is not clear about your role as a counselor and what counseling might do for him. He seems to feel that you can give him a tranquilizer. You tell him that you are not able to prescribe medication, and you suggest that he seek the services of a physician.

_____ 3. A colleague who is soon to be married has asked that you cover her on-call duties at the mental agency where both of you work, conduct two of her intake slots, and meet with four of her outpatient clients while she is on her two-week honeymoon. You inform her that you would like to be of assistance but you already have a full caseload and your supervisor has recently expanded your responsibilities at the agency. You suggest to your colleague that she speak with the supervisor both of you share.

_____ 4. A fourth-grade girl is referred to you by her teacher. The teacher states that the girl is doing poorly in class yet seems motivated to learn. After working with the girl for several weeks, including giving a battery of tests, you conclude that she has a severe learning disability. After obtaining her permission to talk to her teacher, you inform her teacher of this and state that the teacher might as well not spend too much more time working on what you believe is a "useless case."

_____ 5. You are counseling a couple who are considering a trial separation because of constant marital problems. You tell them you don't believe separation or divorce is the answer to their problems.

_____ 6. A Euro-American helper states in a staff meeting that "people are just people" and that he does not see the need for all this emphasis in your treatment facility on understanding how clients from diverse racial/ethnic/cultural backgrounds may be affected differently by the therapy process.

_____ 7. A client comes into a mental health center and requests a helper from his own culture. He also indicates that he would consider seeing a helper who is not from his culture but who shares his worldview and has some notion of his cultural struggles. He is told that it shouldn't matter whom he sees because all the therapists on the staff are value-free.

KNOWLEDGE AND SKILL BUILDER **FEEDBACK**

Part Two

This feedback is to assist you with fulfilling Learning Outcome 2 for this chapter.

1. *C: Ethics—breach of confidentiality.* The helper broke the confidence of a former client by revealing his grade difficulties without his consent.

2. *E: Ethics—referral.* The helper did not refer in an ethical or responsible way, because of failure to give the client names of at least several physicians or psychiatrists who might be competent to see the client.

3. *G: Stamina.* Although you want to be attentive to your colleague, you are mindful of your own responsibilities to clients on your caseload. Assuming additional tasks—even for a two-week period—may jeopardize your ability to provide quality care to your own clients.

4. *B: Values stereotyping.* The helper is obviously stereotyping all kids with learning disabilities as useless and hopeless (the "label" is also not helpful or in the client's best interest).

5. *A: Values conflict.* Your values are showing. Although separation and divorce may not be your solution, be careful about persuading clients to pursue your views and answers to issues.

6. *F: Diversity.* The Euro-American helper is ignorant about the importance and influence of racial/ethnic/cultural factors and is not able to see beyond his White privilege of power.

7. *F and B: Diversity and values stereotyping.* The helper ignores the client's racial identity status and also responds in a stereotypical way to his or her request.

3

UNDERSTANDING NONVERBAL BEHAVIOR

LEARNING OUTCOMES

After completing this chapter, you will be able to

1. From a list of client descriptions and nonverbal client behaviors, describe one possible meaning associated with each nonverbal behavior.
2. In an interview situation, identify as many nonverbal behaviors of the person with whom you are communicating as possible. Describe the possible meanings associated with these behaviors. The nonverbal behaviors you identify may come from any one or all four of these categories: (a) kinesics, or body motion; (b) paralinguistics, or voice qualities; (c) proxemics, or room space and distance; (d) the person's general appearance.
3. Demonstrate effective use of helper nonverbal behaviors in a role-play interview.
4. Identify at least three out of four occasions for responding to client nonverbal behavior in an interview.

Knapp and Hall (2006, p. 23) define nonverbal behavior as "all human communication events that transcend spoken or written words." Of course, many nonverbal behaviors are interpreted by verbal symbols. Separating nonverbal from verbal behavior is somewhat artificial because in real life these two dimensions of communication are inseparable, dependent on each other for meaning and interpretation. The nonverbal behaviors we discuss in this chapter are supported by and support the verbal behaviors and skills we describe in the remainder of the book.

Nonverbal behavior plays an important role in our communication and relationships with others. In communicating, we tend to emphasize the spoken word, yet much of the meaning of a message—65 percent or more—is conveyed by our nonverbal behavior (Birdwhistell, 1970). Nonverbal behavior is an important part of helping because of the large amount of information it communicates. Consider the case of Tim, who scheduled an initial appointment at a college counseling center and was 20 minutes late. When he finally arrived, he could not look at the counselor, he spoke in a very soft tone of voice, and his body posture was slumped. During the intake interview, observing his nonverbal behavior, the counselor was not surprised to learn that Tim had been feeling quite blue and reported feeling quite anxious in new situations.

Clients from some cultural groups may place more emphasis on their own nonverbal behavior and that of their helpers. In part, these clients have learned to rely more on nonverbal communication and less on verbal elaborations to explain something or to get a point across (Sue & Sue, 2003). Also, some clients of color have learned that the verbal messages of White people are often less trustworthy than their nonverbal behavior (Sue & Sue, 2003). As a result, it is very important for practitioners to be aware of the ways in which minority clients may interpret nonverbal behavior (Sue & Sue, 2003). The axiom "Actions speak louder than words" is apparent in the following situation: Jon, a young self-identified gay male client, asked Betty, an older female nongay practitioner, about her views on gay marriage. Betty told Jon that she felt okay about gay marriage. However, before speaking, she hesitated, and when speaking, she avoided eye contact with Jon and stammered and stuttered, making lots of speech errors. Additionally, while speaking, she leaned back in her chair away from Jon and slowly moved her chair back slightly. Jon quickly abandoned further discussion of being gay with Betty during the rest of the session, and then, the following week, he failed to show up for their scheduled session.

THE NEUROBIOLOGY OF NONVERBAL BEHAVIOR

Through the pioneering work of Siegel (2006) we have come to understand more about the role of neurobiology in nonverbal behavior. Siegel (2006) defines *interpersonal neurobiology* as movement toward various levels of neural or brain integration or connectedness and wholeness. A major way in which clients achieve neural integration in the helping process is through the processes of verbal and nonverbal communication with the helper. Verbal and nonverbal communication are processed in the brain in the right and left hemispheres. The *right* hemisphere is the one that processes *nonverbal* communication. The *left* hemisphere processes words and meaning—that is, it sends and receives *verbal* communication. It is the right hemisphere of the brain that both sends and receives nonverbal communicative signals such as gestures, voice tone, and facial expressions and also regulates internal emotional or affective states.

For effective *nonverbal* communication to occur, *both* helpers and clients need to be able to access their respective right brain hemispheres, for the signals sent from one person's right hemisphere (for example, the helper's) directly shape the activity of the other person's right hemisphere (the client's). Similarly, as Siegel and Hartzell (2003) note, words from a practitioner's left hemisphere activitate the left hemisphere of the client. The mutual sharing of nonverbal signals forges deep connections between the helper and the client and fosters collaborative communication. If a practitioner is not adept in using his or her right hemisphere in the work of counseling, that practitioner's ability to make a strong interpersonal connection with the client is much more limited. Consider this example: Jose is a client who is right brain dominant. His body language is very expressive. Jose expresses emotions through his voice, gestures, facial expressions, and posture. Jose's helper, Tim, is left brain dominant. Tim is much more attuned to the words, logic, and literality expressed in Jose's verbal communication than to the emotional tone of Jose's expressions. As a result, Jose feels constantly that Tim is missing something in their sessions, and Tim complains to his supervisor that Jose has difficulty understanding what he says to him. These kinds of experiences are likely to lead to some sort of rupture or breakdown in communication between the helper and client.

In addition to nonverbal processing, the brain's right hemisphere also does processing that is holistic and visuospatial and involves nonverbal autobiographical memory. One way in which the lack of bilateral integration—that is, the lack of integration between the two brain hemispheres—may impact clients is by compromising their recall of their own life stories because the linear explanation of the left brain cannot fully access the nonverbal autobiographical details of the right brain (Siegel, 2006). In instances involving problematic attachments and/or instances of trauma, this lack of integration can limit the client's ability to create a coherent narrative about the trauma. If the nonverbal and emotional aspects are not available to the client, or if they flood the client, the client's ability to integrate the narrative into a coherent and resolvable story is severely limited. The client may have difficulty finding words for feelings or putting feelings into words and also may be too overwhelmed with emotion to process the narrative involved in the traumatic experience. In these situations, the client may be especially dependent on the helper's ability to utilize and convey soothing nonverbal messages.

CLIENT NONVERBAL BEHAVIOR

An important part of a practitioner's repertory is the capacity to discriminate various nonverbal behaviors of clients and their possible meanings. Recognizing and exploring client nonverbal cues is important in counseling for several reasons. First, clients' nonverbal behaviors are clues about clients' emotions. Even more generally, nonverbal behaviors are part of clients' expressions of themselves. As Perls states, "Everything the patient does, obvious or concealed, is an expression of the self" (1973, p. 75). Much of a client's nonverbal behavior may be obvious to you but hidden to the client and may be occurring outside of the client's awareness. Passons (1975, p. 102) points out that most clients are more aware of their words than of their nonverbal behavior. Exploring nonverbal communication may give clients a more complete understanding of their behavior.

Nonverbal client cues may represent more "leakage" than client verbal messages do (Ekman & Friesen, 1969). *Leakage* is the communication of messages that are valid yet are not sent intentionally. Passons (1975) suggests that because of this leakage, client nonverbal behavior may often portray the client more accurately than verbal messages (p. 102). A client may come in and *tell* you one story but in nonverbal language convey a completely different story (Erickson, Rossi, & Rossi, 1976). For instance, Roberto is working with Maria and Peter, a married couple who came in for counseling because of "frequent conflicts." Peter verbally professed his love for Maria in the sessions, but whenever he did so, there was a cold tone to his voice, and generally there was an absence of touching of his wife by him. Peter's nonverbal behavior helped Roberto understand why Maria felt that Peter's verbal professions of love were insincere. Nonverbal "leakages" also constitute subtle microaggressions that are likely to occur in cross-cultural counseling—such as "dismissive looks, gestures, and tones"—and are so "pervasive and automatic" that they are often ignored or their importance is denied, especially by the perpetrator(s) (Sue et al., 2007, p. 273). Such microaggressions may be racist, as when a White practitioner stammers and avoids eye contact when working with a client of color. Gender, disability, age, sexual orientation (as we saw in the case of Jon and Betty described above), and other aspects of culture may give rise to them.

Knapp and Hall (2006) point out that nonverbal behavior and verbal behavior are interrelated to such a degree that to consider each of them as separate facets of communication is difficult, for both are involved in sending messages and receiving and interpreting the meaning of messages. Recognizing the ways in which nonverbal cues support verbal messages can be helpful. Knapp and Hall (2006) identify six ways:

1. *Repetition:* The verbal message is to "come in and sit down"; the hand gesture pointing to the room and chair is a nonverbal repeater.

2. *Contradiction:* The verbal message is "I like you," communicated with a frown and an angry tone of voice. Although in this situation the nonverbal behavior often carries more weight than the verbal message, this may vary according to the age and familiarity with the verbal language of the client.

3. *Substitution:* Often a nonverbal message is used in lieu of a verbal one. For example, if you ask a client "How are you?" and you get a smile, the smile substitutes for "Very well today."

4. *Complementation:* A nonverbal message can complement a verbal message by modifying or elaborating the message. For example, if someone is talking about feeling uncomfortable and begins talking faster and making more speech errors, these nonverbal messages add to the verbal one of discomfort. When the nonverbal and verbal behaviors are complementary rather than contradictory, communication goes more smoothly because the accuracy with which messages are decoded is enhanced. In helping interviews, in which clarity of communication is important, helpers need to be attentive to the ways in which nonverbal messages and verbal messages complement each other.

5. *Accent:* Nonverbal messages can emphasize verbal ones and often heighten the impact of verbal messages. For example, if you are expressing verbal concern, your verbal message may come through stronger when accompanied by nonverbal cues such as a furrowing of your brow, a frown, or tears. The *kind* of emotion a person conveys is best detected from the person's facial expressions. The body better conveys the *intensity* of the emotion (Ekman, 1964; Ekman & Friesen, 1967).

6. *Regulation:* Nonverbal communication helps to regulate the flow of conversation. Have you ever noticed the following: when you nod your head at someone after he or she speaks, the person tends to keep talking; but if you look away and shift your body position, the person may stop talking, at least momentarily. Whether we realize it or not, we rely on certain nonverbal cues as feedback for starting or stopping a conversation and for indicating whether the other person is listening. This has important implications in helping interviews, especially when helpers need to convey respect for clients and to listen carefully to client messages, because we make judgments about people based on these regulatory skills. As interviewers, it is important to remember that regulatory skills vary across clients—children are often less skilled in this area than most adult clients—and differ somewhat among various cultural groups.

Identifying the relation between the client's verbal and nonverbal communication may yield a more accurate picture of the client, the client's feelings, and the concerns that have led the client to seek help. In addition, the helper can detect the extent to which the client's nonverbal behavior and verbal behavior match or are congruent. Frequent discrepancies between the client's expressions may indicate ambivalence. Roberto, the counselor in the case involving Peter and Maria (described above), observed and heard Peter revealing more and more of his ambivalence about loving Maria as counseling proceeded.

Nonverbal behavior has received a great deal of attention in recent years in newspapers, magazine articles, and popular books. These publications may have value in increasing awareness of nonverbal behaviors, but the meanings attached to particular behaviors are oversimplified. It is important to note that the meaning of nonverbal behavior will vary with people and situations (contexts). For example, for one person, watering eyes may be a sign of happiness and glee, but for another, it may mean anger, frustration, or trouble with contact lenses, or all of the above. As Knapp and Hall (2006) assert, nonverbal cues rarely have a *single* meaning (p. 20). A person who has a lisp may be dependent; another person with a lisp may have a speech impediment. Twisting, rocking, or squirming in a seat might mean anxiety for one person and a stomach cramp for someone else. Further, the nonverbal behaviors of one culture may have different or even opposite meanings in another culture. Watson (1970) reports significant differences among cultures in nonverbal behaviors such as distance, touch, and eye contact. In some cultures, for example, avoidance of eye contact is regarded as an indication of respect. As Sue and Sue (2003. p. 127) note, "the same nonverbal behavior on the part of an American Indian client may mean something quite different than if it was made by a White person." We caution you to be careful not to assume that nonverbal behavior has the same meaning or effect for everyone. Also remember that for accuracy of interpretation, the nonverbal behavior(s) must be considered in conjunction with the verbal message as well. (See also Learning Activity 3.1, later in this chapter.)

FIVE DIMENSIONS OF NONVERBAL BEHAVIOR

Five dimensions of nonverbal behavior that have significant effects on communication are *kinesics, paralinguistics, proxemics, environmental factors,* and *time.* Body motion, or kinesic behavior, includes gestures, body movements, posture, touch, facial expressions, and eye behavior (Knapp & Hall, 2006). Associated with the work of Birdwhistell (1970), kinesics also involves physical characteristics that remain relatively unchanged during a conversation, such as body physique, height, weight, and general appearance. In addition to observing body motion, helpers also identify nonverbal vocal cues—paralanguage—the "how" of the message. Voice qualities and vocalizations are paralinguistic cues (Trager, 1958). Silent pauses and speech errors can be considered part of paralanguage as well (Knapp & Hall, 2006). Also of interest to helpers is the area of proxemics (Hall, 1966)—that is, one's use of social and personal space. As it affects the helping relationship, proxemics involves the size of the room, seating arrangements, touch, and the distance between helper and client.

Because people react emotionally to their surroundings, perception of one's environment is another important part of nonverbal behavior. Environments can cause clients to feel arousal or boredom and comfort or stress, depending on the degree to which an individual tunes in to or screens out relevant parts of the surroundings. The fifth aspect of nonverbal behavior that Knapp and Hall (2006) discuss involves perception and use of time. Time—promptness or delay in starting and ending sessions, as well as the amount of time spent in communicating with a client about particular topics or events—can be a significant factor in helping.

All five dimensions of nonverbal behavior are affected by cultural affiliation. We discuss all five in greater detail in the remainder of this section.

Kinesics

Kinesics involves the eyes, face, head, gestures, touch, body expressions, and movements. Therapists who are sensitive to the *eye* area of clients may detect various client *emotions* from the eyes. For example, clients may register surprise or fear by raising their eyebrows. Eyebrows may be lowered and drawn together, and the eyes may appear to have a "cold stare" in the presence of client anger. Sadness may be conveyed by tears in the eyes and the drawing up of the inner corners of the eyebrows.

Also significant to counselor/client interactions is *eye contact* (also called "direct mutual gaze"). Eye contact may indicate expressions of feeling, willingness to engage in interpersonal exchange, or a desire to continue or to stop talking. Lack of eye contact or looking away may signal withdrawal, embarrassment, or discomfort (Exline & Winters, 1965). An averted gaze may serve to hide shame over expressing a particular feeling that is seen as culturally or socially taboo. However, for clients from some cultural groups, lack of eye contact has nothing to do with embarrassment or discomfort and may actually be communicative of respect.

In helping interviews, *more mutual gazing* seems to occur in the following situations (as summarized by Knapp and Hall, 2006):

1. Greater physical distance exists between the helper and client.
2. Comfortable, less personal topics are discussed.
3. Interpersonal involvement exists between the helper and client.
4. You are listening rather than talking.
5. You are female.

6. You are from a culture that emphasizes visual contact in interaction.

Less gazing occurs in these situations:

1. The helper and client are physically close.
2. Difficult, intimate topics are being discussed.
3. Either the helper or the client is not interested in the other's reactions.
4. You are talking rather than listening.
5. You are embarrassed, ashamed, or trying to hide something.
6. You are from a culture that has sanctions on visual contact during some kinds of interpersonal interactions.

Less eye contact may be desirable in situations where arousal levels are too high and need to be lowered—for example, when working with an autistic child or with an agitated teenager in a "shame spiral." Unfortunately, helpers all too often equate avoidance of eye contact with disrespect. The meanings and effects of eye contact, however, vary both within and across cultural groups, involving not only frequency and duration of eye contact but also "rules" about where and with whom to maintain eye contact (Knapp & Hall, 2006). For some clients of color, less frequent eye contact is typical of their culture.

The *face* of the other person may be the most important stimulus in an interaction because it is the primary communicator of emotional information (Ekman, 1982). Facial expressions are used to initiate or terminate conversation, provide feedback on the comments of others, underline or support verbal communication, and convey emotions. Most of the time, the face conveys multiple emotions (Ekman, 1982). For example, one emotion may be conveyed in one part of the face and another in a different area. It is rare for a person's face to express only a single emotion at a time. More often than not, the face depicts a blend of varying emotions.

Different facial areas express different emotions. Happiness, surprise, and disgust may be conveyed through the lower face (mouth and jaw region) and the eye area, whereas sadness is conveyed with the eyes. The lower face and brows express anger; fear is usually indicated by the eyes. Although "reading" someone by facial cues alone is difficult, these cues may support other nonverbal indexes of emotion within the context of an interview.

Facial expressions conveying the basic emotions described above do *not* seem to vary much among cultures. In other words, primary or basic emotions such as surprise, anger, disgust, fear, sadness, and happiness do seem to be represented by the same facial expressions across cultures, although individual cultural norms may influence how much and how often such emotions are expressed (Mesquita & Frijda, 1992).

In a similar way, the movements of the *head* can be a rich source for interpreting a person's emotional or affective state. When a person holds his or her head erect, facing the other person in a relaxed way, this posture indicates receptivity to interpersonal communication. Nodding the head up and down implies confirmation or agreement. Shaking the head from left to right may signal disapproval or disagreement. However, in Sri Lanka, shaking the head from side to side indicates agreement, and among Mayan tribe members, jerking the head to the right means "no" (Sue & Sue, 2003, p. 129). Head shaking accompanied by leg movements may connote anger. Holding the head rigidly may mean anxiety or anger, and hanging the head down toward the chest may reflect disapproval or sadness.

The orientation of the *shoulders* may give clues to a person's attitude about interpersonal exchanges. Shoulders leaning forward may indicate eagerness, attentiveness, or receptivity to interpersonal communication. Slouched, stooped, rounded, or turned-away shoulders may mean that the person is not receptive to interpersonal exchanges. This posture also may reflect sadness or ambivalence. Shrugging shoulders may mean uncertainty, puzzlement, ambivalence, or frustration.

Arms and hands can be very expressive of an individual's emotional state. Arms folded across the chest can signal avoidance of interpersonal exchange or reluctance to disclose. Anxiety or anger may be reflected in trembling and fidgety hands or clenching fists. Arms and hands that rarely gesture and are stiffly positioned may mean tension, anxiety, or anger. Relaxed, unfolded arms and hands gesturing during conversation can signal openness to interpersonal involvement or accentuation of points in conversation. The autonomic response of perspiration on the palms can reflect anxiety or arousal.

If the client's *legs and feet* appear comfortable and relaxed, the person may be signaling openness to interpersonal exchange. Shuffling feet or a tapping foot may mean that the person is experiencing some anxiety or impatience, or wants to make a point. Repeatedly crossing and uncrossing the legs may indicate anxiety, depression, or impatience. A person who appears to be very "controlled" or to have "stiff" legs and feet may be uptight, anxious, or closed to an extensive interpersonal exchange.

Touch is also a part of kinesics. As you might imagine, the use of touch is controversial. As of now, there are not many empirical data to guide our thinking about its use in the helping process. One of the issues is that touch itself can range on a continuum from less to more personal touch (see Figure 3.1). The meanings of an interpersonal touch in the helping context vary greatly, depending on "many environmental, personal, and contextual variables" (Knapp & Hall, 2006, p. 281). The type, location, and duration of touch can affect the meaning conveyed to clients. In Figure 3.1, touch that falls in the middle part of the continuum (friendship, warmth) can be misconstrued by clients, and touch that falls in the upper part of the continuum (love, sexual arousal) should always be avoided with clients because it is unethical. For example, Simon (1999) reported that physical contact such as hugging the client is a significant precursor to sexual relationships between helpers and clients. Touch that falls at the lower end of the continuum (functional, professional, social), such as a handshake between helper and client, is usually acceptable. Bear in mind, though, that some clients, especially those with a history of physical or sexual abuse, may shrink from all forms of touch, including a greeting such as a handshake. Also, cultural caveats come into play here as well. Shaking hands using the right hand may be seen as a "sign of peace" in some Muslim and Asian cultures, but touching anyone with the left hand may be seen as an "obscenity" and an "insult" of the worst kind (Sue & Sue, 2003, p. 129). Also, people from cultures accustomed to more contact may be more comfortable with touch than those from noncontact cultures.

Are there ever exceptions to this general rule? Yes! For example, consider the case of a female helper and a female client, both from a contact culture, or the situation of a person who is institutionalized, anxious, and lonely. And sometimes touch is initiated spontaneously by the client. Marguerite, a school counseling student, talked about working with a young girl whose mother had recently died unexpectedly. During the session with Marguerite, the little girl started to cry and, within a moment's time, climbed up on Marguerite's lap. In this situation, it would have been counter therapeutic and punitive to the young girl if Marguerite had immediately removed the child from her lap. She comforted her and waited until her crying subsided, then gently

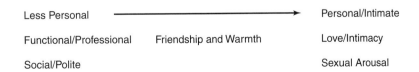

Figure 3.1 Continuum of touch
Source: Adapted from "Touch—A Bonding Gesture," by R. Heslin & T. Alper. In J. M. Wiemann & R. P. Harrison (Eds.), *Nonverbal Interaction.* Copyright © 1983 by Sage Publications.

lifted the child onto the floor next to her, and they did some drawings. Diversity, ethics, values, and critical thinking all come together in making a decision about the use of touch in the helping process. If, for example, you are a male clinician working with an adolescent female who wants to climb on your lap or hug you, different touch boundaries would be necessary than those present in Marguerite's situation.

Most *body movements* do not have precise social meanings. Body movements are learned and culture-specific. The body movements discussed in this section are derived from analyses of (and therefore are most applicable to) White adults from middle and upper socioeconomic classes in the United States.

Body movements are not produced randomly. Instead, they appear to be linked to human speech. From birth, there seems to be an effort to synchronize body movements and speech sounds. In adults, lack of synchrony may be a sign of pathology. Lack of synchrony in body movements and speech between two persons may indicate an absence of listening behavior by both.

One of the most important functions of body movements is *regulation.* Various body movements regulate or maintain an interpersonal interaction. For example, important body movements that accompany the counselor's verbal greeting of a client include eye gaze, smiling, use of hand gestures, and a vertical or sideways motion of the head (Krivonos & Knapp, 1975). Body movements are also useful to terminate an interaction, as at the end of a counseling interview. Nonverbal exit or leave-taking behaviors accompanying a verbal summary statement include decreased eye contact and positioning of your body near the exit encounter. Another way in which body movements regulate an interaction involves *turn taking*—the exchange of speaker and listener roles within a conversation. As Knapp and Hall (2006) observe, "turn-taking behavior is not just an interesting curiosity of human behavior"; it is important because data show that "we seem to base important judgments about others on how the turns are allocated and how smoothly exchanges are accomplished" (p. 424). Effective turn taking is important in a helping interaction because it contributes to the perception that you and the client have a good relationship and that, as the helper, you are a competent communicator. Conversely, ineffective turn taking may mean that a client perceives you as rude (too many interruptions) or as dominating (not enough talk time for the client). The exchange of turns in a helping interview is not only the display of one or more of the signals we just described but also a "jointly negotiated process" between both helper and client (Knapp & Hall, 2006, p. 427). Also, keep in mind that "cultures with different conversational rules and specialized systems of communication like sign language require somewhat different turn-exchange processes" (Knapp & Hall, 2006, p. 425).

In addition to regulation, body movements also serve the function of *adaptors.* Adaptors may include such behaviors as picking, scratching, rubbing, and tapping. In helping, it is important to note the frequency with which a client uses nonverbal adaptors because these behaviors seem to be associated with emotional arousal and psychological discomfort (Ekman, 1982). Body touching may reflect preoccupation with oneself and withdrawal from the interaction at hand. A client who frequently uses adaptors may be uncomfortable with the helper or with the topic of discussion. The helper can use the frequency of client adaptors as an index of the client's overall comfort level during the interview.

Another important aspect of a client's total body is his or her breathing. Changes in breathing rate (slower, faster) or depth (shallower, deeper) provide clues about comfort level, feelings, and significant issues. As clients relax, for example, their breathing usually becomes slower and deeper. Faster, more shallow breathing is more often associated with arousal, distress, discomfort, and anxiety.

Paralinguistics and Silence

Paralinguistics includes such extra linguistic variables as voice level (volume), pitch (intonation), rate of speech, and fluency of speech. Pauses and silence also belong in this category. Paralinguistic cues are cues pertaining to *how* a message is delivered, although occasionally these vocal cues represent *what* is said as well.

Vocal cues are important in helping interactions for several reasons. First, they help to manage the interaction by playing an important role in the exchange of speaker and listener roles—that is, turn taking. Second, vocal characteristics convey data about a client's emotional states. You can identify the presence of basic emotions from a client's vocal cues if you are able to make auditory discriminations. In recognizing emotions from vocal cues, it is also important to be knowledgeable about various vocal characteristics of basic emotions. For example, a client who speaks slowly and softly may be feeling sad or may be reluctant to discuss a sensitive topic. Increased volume and rate of speech are usually signs of anger or happiness, or they may simply reflect cultural norms. Many Arabs, for example, "like to be bathed in sounds" (Sue & Sue, 2003, p. 131). Changes in voice level and pitch should be interpreted along with accompanying changes in topics of conversation and changes in other nonverbal behaviors.

Voice level may vary among cultures. Sue and Sue (2003) point out that some Americans have louder voice levels than people of other cultures. In working with a client, a helper should not automatically conclude that a louder voice means anger or that the client's lower voice volume indicates weakness or shyness (p. 131).

Vocal cues in the form of speech disturbances or aspects of *fluency* in speech also convey important information for therapists, for client anxiety or discomfort is often detected by identifying the type and frequency of client speech errors. Most speech errors become more frequent as anxiety and discomfort increase (Knapp & Hall, 2006).

Pauses and silence are another part of paralinguistics that can give the helper clues about the client. Unfilled pauses, or periods of silence, serve various functions in a helping interview. The purpose of silence often depends on whether the pause is initiated by the helper or by the client. Clients use silence to express emotions, to reflect on an issue, to re-call an idea or feeling, to avoid a topic, or to catch up on the progress of the moment. According to Sue and Sue (2003),

cultures interpret the use of silence differently. The British and Arabs use silence for privacy, while the Russians, French, and Spanish read it as agreement among the parties. . . . In Asian culture, silence is traditionally a sign of respect for elders. Furthermore, silence by many Chinese and Japanese is not a floor-yielding signal inviting others to pick up the conversation. Rather, it may indicate a desire to continue speaking after making a particular point. Often silence is a sign of politeness and respect rather than a lack of desire to continue speaking. (p. 131)

Helper-initiated silences are most effective when used with a particular purpose in mind, such as reducing the helper's level of activity, slowing down the pace of the ses-sion, giving the *client* time to think, or transferring some responsibility to the client through turn yielding or turn de-nying. When therapists pause to meet their own needs—for example, because they do not know what to say next—the effects of silence may or may not be therapeutic. As Cormier and Hackney (2008) observe, when the effect is therapeutic in such instances, the counselor is likely to feel lucky rather than competent. On the other hand, there are instances in counseling sessions when a surprise communication or a moment of intense emotion may result in being at a loss for words. Sometimes in these cases this kind of silence can represent a moment of spontaneous human connection between the practitioner and the client.

An occasion in which silence would *not* be useful would be when a client discloses something very precious and significant, often revealing something that takes great vul-nerability on the client's part. For example, Paul may share with you that he recently was diagnosed as HIV-positive, or Mariko may disclose something about the pain of being the only Japanese American student in her school. In instances like these, silence by the helper often makes the client feel ashamed of the revelation and misunderstood by the helper. Validation of the client's disclosure is essential.

Beginning helpers tend to be quite frightened of any pauses and silent "gaps" in conversation. Even clients can feel awkward during these moments. Yet silence is a useful counseling tool, too useful to overlook or discard because of initial discomfort with it. Generally, instead of jumping in and saying the first thing that comes to mind, the helper needs to keep in mind that it is important to allow silences to occur and to *develop* during a helping session. It is during the development of the silence that clients may reveal their innermost feelings, often conveyed nonverbally rather than verbally. Also, clients may use the period of silence to reflect or to absorb a working moment or moments that have occurred in the session. In these instances, silence offers a way of slowing down the process and bringing attention to the moment. Finally, silence in and of itself can become a significant interpersonal event in the helping relationship. Both the silence and the client's emotions expressed during the silence may be processed and worked through in the helping relationship. For example, consider this scenario: Kim has been working for several months with her client Taja. As Kim learns to talk less and to feel more comfortable with silence and pauses, Taja reveals and discloses more. In their last session, Taja did not immediately respond after Kim asked her what she wanted to discuss. Kim allowed this silent pause to develop. After a few minutes of silence, in which Kim was nonverbally responsive, Taja revealed that she had just discovered she was pregnant and did not know the identity of the baby's father. She did not know how she, as a student, would support a baby. She then followed this disclosure with tears and weeping. This silence became filled with Taja's fear and sadness. After allowing the silence to oc-cur and to develop, Kim was then able to respond and help Taja process her anxiety and sadness surrounding the recent news she had received.

Proxemics

Proxemics concerns the concept of environmental and per-sonal space (Hall, 1966). As it applies to a helping in-teraction, proxemics includes use of space relative to the interviewing room, arrangement of the furniture, seating arrangements, and distance between helper and client. Prox-emics also includes a variable that seems to be important to any human interaction: territoriality. Many people are pos-sessive not only of their belongings but of the space around them. It is important for therapists to communicate nonver-bal sensitivity to a client's need for space. A client who feels that his or her space or territory has been encroached on may behave in ways intended to restore the proper distance. Such behaviors may include looking away or changing the topic to a less personal one.

In helping interviews, a distance of 3 to 4 feet between helper and client seems to be the least anxiety producing and most productive, at least for adult, middle-class Euro-Americans (Lecomte, Bernstein, & Dumont, 1981). For these Americans, closer distances may inhibit verbal produc-tivity, although females in this cultural group are generally more tolerant of less personal space than males, especially when interacting with other females. Disturbed clients also seem to require greater interaction distance. These spatial limits (3 to 4 feet) may be inappropriate for clients of varying ages or cultures. The very young and very old seem to elicit interaction at closer distances. People from "contact" cultures (cultures in which people face one another more directly, interact closer to one another, and use more touch and direct eye contact) may use different distances for interpersonal interactions than people from "noncontact" cultures (Watson, 1970). In short, unlike facial expressions, distance setting has no universals.

Another aspect of proxemics involves seating and furniture arrangement. In some cultures, most helpers prefer a seating arrangement with no intervening desk or objects, although many clients like to have the protective space or "body buffer" of a desk corner and some clients may prefer to sit side by side. Seating and spatial arrangements are an important part of family therapy as well. Successful family therapists pay attention to family proxemics such as the following: How far apart do family members sit from one another? Who sits next to whom? Who stays closest to the therapist? Answers to these questions about family proxemics provide information about family rules, relationships, boundaries, alliances, roles, and so on.

Environment

Helping occurs in an environment—typically an office, although other indoor and outdoor environments can be used. The same surroundings can affect clients in different ways. In a qualitative study of what clients find helpful in psychotherapy, Levin, Butler, and Hill (2006) created a hierarchy of categories that represented what clients found important in therapy. One of the most important categories that emerged from this study was the office environment. Clients indicated that the office environment was a reflection of the care they experienced with the therapist. Clients also noted that they viewed the therapy room as a "projection of the therapist" and that objects in the room such as pictures, furniture, and background music were all useful in helping them feel more relaxed (Levin, Butler, & Hill, 2006, p. 317).

Surroundings are perceived as arousing or nonarousing (Mehrabian, 1976). Environments need to be moderately arousing so that the client feels relaxed enough to explore her or his problems and to self-disclose. If the client feels so comfortable that the desire to work on a problem is inhibited, the helper might consider increasing the arousal cues associated with the surroundings by moving the furniture around, using brighter colors, using more light, or even increasing vocal expressiveness. Therapists who talk louder and faster and use more expressive intonation patterns are greater sources of arousal for those around them (Mehrabian,1976).

Environment is an important issue in working with clients from diverse cultural backgrounds. The idea of coming to an office with a scheduled appointment made in advance is a very Eurocentric notion. For some clients, a walk-in or drop-in visit may be more suitable. Also, for others, having sessions in an out-of-office environment may be desirable. For those clients who do use your office, it is important to think about how suitable your environment is for diverse clients. Racial microaggressions can occur when clients of color are exposed to therapy environments that minimize or devalue the client's race such as the "exclusion of decorations or literature that represents various racial groups" in the counseling room. (Sue et al., 2007, p. 274). The environment also includes the structure and design of buildings and offices that serve clients and the placement of objects within these spaces. Accessibility and barrier-free environmental spaces are especially important when working with clients who may have physical challenges. Consider the parameters of client nonverbal communication in Learning Activity 3.1.

Time

Time has several dimensions that can affect a therapeutic interaction. One of them has to do with the practitioner's and the client's perceptions of time and promptness or delays in initiating or terminating topics and sessions. On the one hand, many clients will feel put off by delays or by rescheduled appointments. On the other hand, if extra time is spent with them, some clients may feel appreciated and valued, but others may perceive the extra time as overly stimulating and may experience the helper as potentially seductive or lacking in boundaries around session management or as unable to manage time limits. Clients may communicate anxiety or resistance by being late or by waiting until the end of a session to bring up a significant topic. Perceptions of time also vary. Some persons have a highly structured view of time, so being "on time" or ready to see the helper (or client) is important to them. Others have a more casual view of time and do not feel offended or put off if the helper is late for the appointment and do not expect the helper to be upset when they arrive later than the designated time.

The concept of time is also greatly shaped by one's cultural affiliation. Traditional U.S. society is often characterized by a preoccupation with time as a linear product and as oriented to the future. In contrast, some American Indians and African Americans value a "present-day" time orientation, and Asian Americans and Hispanics focus on both past and present dimensions of time, reflecting their cultures' traditions of strong respect for ancestors and for the elderly. Such differences in the way individuals view and value time may contribute to discrepancies and misunderstandings in the pace and scheduling of helping sessions.

LEARNING ACTIVITY 3.1 Client Nonverbal Communication

Part One

The purpose of this activity is to have you sample some nonverbal behaviors associated with varying emotions for different regions of the body. You can do this in dyads or in a small group. Act out each of the five emotions listed below, using your face, body, arms, legs, and voice:

1. Sadness, depression
2. Pleasure, satisfaction
3. Anxiety, agitation
4. Anger
5. Confusion, uncertainty

As an example, if the emotion to be portrayed were "surprise," you would show how your eyes, mouth, face, arms, hands, legs and feet, and total body might behave in terms of movement or posture, and you would indicate what your voice level and pitch would be like and how fluent your speech might be. After one person portrays one emotion, other members of the group can share how their nonverbal behaviors associated with the same emotion might differ.

Part Two

This activity will help you develop greater sensitivity to non-verbal behaviors of clients. It can be done in dyads or triads. Select one person to assume the role of the communicator and another to assume the role of the listener. A third person can act as observer. As the communicator, recall recent times when you felt (1) very happy, (2) very sad, and (3) very angry. Your task is to retrieve that experience *nonverbally*. Do *not say* anything to the listener, and do *not* tell the listener in advance which of the three emotions you are going to recall. Simply decide which of the three you will recall; then tell the listener when to begin. The listener's task is to *observe* the communicator, to *note* nonverbal behaviors and changes during the recall, and, from these, to *guess* which of the three emotional experiences the person was retrieving. After about 3 to 4 minutes, stop the interaction to process it. Observers can add behaviors and changes they noted at this time. After the communicator retrieves one of the emotions, switch roles.

HOW TO WORK WITH CLIENT NONVERBAL BEHAVIOR

Various theoretical approaches are used in the helping process. Many of them emphasize the importance of working with clients' nonverbal behavior. For example, behavioral practitioners may recognize and point out particular nonverbal behaviors of a client that constitute effective or ineffective social skills. A client who consistently mumbles and avoids eye contact may find such behaviors detrimental to establishing effective interpersonal relationships. Use of effective nonverbal behaviors also forms a portion of assertion-training programs. Client-centered therapists use clients' nonverbal behaviors as indicators of clients' feelings and emotions. Gestalt therapists help clients recognize their nonverbal behaviors in order to increase awareness of themselves and of conflicts or discrepancies. For example, a client may say, "Yes, I want to get my degree," and at the same time shake his head "no" and lower his voice tone and eyes. Body-oriented therapists actively use body language as a tool for understanding hidden and unresolved "business," conflicts, and armoring. Adlerian counselors use nonverbal reactions of clients as an aid to discovering purposes (often hidden) of behavior and mistaken logic. Family therapists are concerned with a family's nonverbal (analogic) communication as well as with verbal (digital) communication. *Family sculpture* is a tool based on family nonverbal communication (Duhl, Kantor, & Duhl, 1973). Family sculpture is a nonverbal arrangement of people placed in various physical positions in space to represent their relationships to one another. In an extension of this technique, *family choreography* (Papp, 1976), the sculptures or spatial arrangements are purposely moved to realign existing relationships and create new patterns.

Generally, irrespective of a particular theoretical orientation, there are several ways to respond to and work with clients' nonverbal behavior in a helping interview. These include the following:

1. Note or respond to discrepancies, or mixed verbal and nonverbal messages.
2. Respond to or note nonverbal behaviors when the client is silent or not speaking.
3. Use nonverbal behaviors to change the focus of the interview.
4. Work with changes in clients' nonverbal behavior that have occurred in an interview or over a series of sessions.

Nonverbal communication is also a useful way for helpers to note something about the *appropriateness* of a clients' communication style and to observe *how* something is said, not just *what* is said (Sue & Sue, 2003). Such observations may be especially important in working with clients belonging to various ethnic/cultural groups. For example, in traditional Asian culture, *subtlety* in communication versus directness is considered a prized art (Sue & Sue, 2003). These "social rhythms" of communication style vary with the race, culture, ethnicity, and gender of clients. (See Learning Activity 3.2.)

Part One

The purpose of this activity is to practice verbal responses to client nonverbal behaviors. One person portrays a client (1) giving mixed messages, (2) being silent, (3) rambling and delivering a lot of information, and (4) portraying a rather obvious change in nonverbal behavior from the beginning of the interview to the end of the interview. The person playing the helper responds verbally to each of these four portrayals. After going through all these portrayals with an opportunity for the role-play helper to respond to each, switch roles. During these role plays, try to focus primarily on your responses to the other person's nonverbal behavior.

Part Two

With yourself and several colleagues or members of your class to help you, use spatial arrangements to portray your role in your family and to depict your perceptions of your relationship to the other members of your family. Position yourself in a room, and tell the other participants where to position themselves in relation to you and to one another. (If you lack one or two participants, an object can fill a gap.) After the arrangement is complete, look around you. What can you learn about your own family from this aspect of nonverbal behavior? Do you like what you see and feel? If you could change your position in the family, where would you move? What effect would this change have on you and on other family members?

Part Three

In a role-play interaction or helping session in which you function as the helper, watch for some significant nonverbal behavior of the client, such as change in breathing, eye contact, voice tone, and proxemics. (Do not focus on a small nonverbal behavior out of context with the spoken words.) Focus on this behavior by asking the client whether she or he is aware of what is happening to her or his voice, body posture, eyes, or whatever. Do not interpret or assign meaning to the behavior for the client. Notice where your focus takes the client.

Part Four

Contrast the areas of client nonverbal behavior we describe in this chapter—kinesics, paralinguistics, proxemics, environment, and time—for Euro-American and non-Euro-American clients.

Responding to Mixed Messages

The helper can observe the client and see whether the client's words and nonverbal behavior send mixed messages. Contradictory verbal and nonverbal behavior would be apparent with a client who says, "I feel really [pause] excited about the relationship. I've never [pause] experienced anything like this before," while looking down and leaning away. The helper has at least three options for dealing with a verbal/nonverbal discrepancy. The first is to note mentally the discrepancies between what the client says and the nonverbal body and paralinguistic cues with which the client delivers the message. The second option is to describe the discrepancy to the client, as in this example: "You say you are excited about the relationship, but your head was hanging down while you were talking, and you spoke with a lot of hesitation." The third option is to ask the client, "I noticed you looked away and paused as you said that. What does that mean?"

Responding to Nonverbal Behavior during Silence

A practitioner can respond to the nonverbal behavior of the client during periods of silence in the interview. Silence does not mean that nothing is happening! Also remember that silence has different meanings from one culture to another. In some cultures, silence is a sign of respect, not an indication that the client does not wish to talk more (Sue & Sue,

2003). The helper can focus on client nonverbal behavior during silence by noting the silence mentally, by describing the silence to the client, or by asking the client about the meaning of the silence.

Changing the Focus of the Interview

It may be necessary with some clients to change the flow of the interview, because to continue on the same topic may be unproductive. Changing the flow may also be useful when the client is delivering a lot of information or is rambling. In such instances, the helper can distract the client from the verbal content by redirecting the focus to the client's nonverbal behavior.

For "unproductive" content in the client's messages, the helper might say, "Our conversation so far has been dwelling on the death of your brother and your relationship with your parents. Right now, I would like you to focus on what we have been doing while we have been talking. Are you aware of what you have been doing with your hands?"

Such responses can be either productive or detrimental to the progress of therapy. Passons (1975) suggests that these distractions will be useful if they bring the client in touch with "present behavior." If they take the client away from the current flow of feelings, the distractions will be unproductive (p. 105).

Responding to Changes in Client Nonverbal Behavior

For some clients, nonverbal behaviors may be indices of therapeutic change, of conflict, or of underlying emotions and physical reactions outside the client's awareness. Brems (2001) refers to these as "leaks"—that is, to a client's gesture, facial expression, or other body movement that occurs while the client is discussing a particular issue (often in an unemotional or detached way). She provides the following examples of such nonverbal leaks in client communication:

- it is an unusual gesture, expression (facial or voice inflection), or movement that the clinician has not noted in the client before
- it is a quick gesture, expression, or movement that the client tries to hide as soon as it occurred
- it is a gesture, expression, or movement that occurs with some regularity, always in a predictable context
- it is a habitual gesture, expression, or movement that the client does not appear to be aware of and may even deny if asked about. (Brems, 2001, p. 360)

Once the helper observes a nonverbal leak, he or she must make a decision about whether to focus on the leak covertly or overtly, during the current session, or later.

The decision to respond to client nonverbal behavior covertly (with a mental note) or overtly depends not only on your purpose in focusing on nonverbal behavior but also on timing. Passons (1975) believes that helpers need to make overt responses to client nonverbal behavior early in the therapeutic process. Otherwise, when you call attention to something the client is doing nonverbally after the tenth session or so, the client is likely to feel confused and bewildered by what is seen as a change in your approach.

When responding to client nonverbal behavior with immediacy, it is helpful to be descriptive rather than evaluative and to phrase your responses in a tentative way. For example, saying something like "Are you aware that as you're talking, your neck and face are getting red splotches of color?" is likely to be more useful than evaluative and dogmatic comments such as these: "Why is your face getting red?" "You surely do have a red face," or "You're getting so red—you must feel very embarrassed about this." Brems (2001) provides a wonderful example of how one helper responded to leaks in her client's nonverbal behavior:

Clinician: Would you sit back the way you were sitting just a minute ago?

Client: Sit how? (*looks puzzled*)

Clinician: With your legs crossed like that (*models the position*) and your leg swinging. . . .

Client: Why?

Clinician: I'd like to try something with you. . . .

Client: Like that? (*shifts to the "leak" position*)

Clinician: Yeah, that was it. Now swing your lower leg, like that. (*models*)

Client: I really did that?

Clinician: Yes, you really did.

Client: Okay, so now what? (*swinging her leg*)

Clinician: When you were sitting like that you were talking about telling Amy that you would like to end the friendship. I got the feeling that you were communicating something else to her with the way you were holding your body. So I thought maybe you could sit like that again and listen to your body. See if you can identify any sensations you are aware of as you sit that way. . . .

Client: Okay. . . .

Clinician: Go ahead and start swinging your leg, like you did before.

Client: (*complies*)

Clinician: What do you notice in your body?

Client: I don't know. . . . (*tentative and unsure*)

Clinician: Hang in there with me for a moment. I really think this will help us out. Would you, just to give this a fair try, swing your leg a little harder?

Client: Swing harder?

Clinician: Yeah, just put a little more "umph" in that movement.

Client: Okay. . . . (*grins and swings harder*)

Clinician: Okay, now what do you notice in your body?

Client: I'm not sure, but it seems like the right thing to do when I think about Amy right now. (*more forceful voice now*)

Clinician: What feels right about it?

Client: Well, it gives me something to do I guess. (*backs off the affect*) It occupies me with something because this is a tough thing to do, you know, to tell your friend you want out.

Clinician: What thoughts come to mind as you do it, as you swing your leg? (*allowing the detour away from obvious affect for now and going to the cognitive plane, which is more comfortable for the client*)

Client: Oh, I got it; it's like—"Hey Amy, I really wanna kick you out right now!"

Clinician: Were you aware of that thought before?

Client: No. But you know what, it's true. I would like to kick her.*

---

*From *Basic Skills in Psychotherapy and Counseling* (3rd ed.), by Christiane Brems © 2001. Reprinted with permission of Brooks/Cole, an imprint of the Wadsworth Group, a division of Thomson Learning.

HELPER NONVERBAL BEHAVIOR

As a helper, it is important for you to pay attention to your nonverbal behavior. Some kinds of helper nonverbal behavior seem to contribute to a facilitative relationship; other nonverbal behaviors may detract from the relationship. One client described the importance of her therapist's nonverbal behavior in the following way:

> "My therapist was fairly new at the job but it didn't matter. There was something at the core of her being that resonated with what I most needed. I read it in her eyes when she opened the door—she was so open and welcoming and enveloping. I felt at the time that I was basically unlikable, but when she saw me, her eyes would light up." (Simon, 2004, p. 2)

Because much of the research on helpers' nonverbal behavior has been done with ratings of videotapes and photographs, it is difficult to specify precisely what nonverbal behaviors are related to effectiveness. Generally speaking, moderate amounts of eye contact and spatial distance coupled with a body stance that is open, relaxed, and oriented toward the client, accompanying facial expressions that show interest in the client's messages, and an active and energetic voice (and minus distracting nonverbal behaviors such as twiddling thumbs or twirling one's hair) are effective helper behaviors in the nonverbal realm. Also, it is important to remember that the effects of various helper nonverbal behaviors are related to contextual variables in helping, such as type of client, verbal content, timing in session, and client's cultural background.

Two other important aspects of a therapist's nonverbal demeanor that affect a helping relationship are congruence and synchrony.

Congruence

Nonverbal behaviors in conjunction with verbal messages also have some consequences in the relationship, particularly if these messages are mixed, or incongruent. Mixed messages can be confusing to the client. For example, suppose a practitioner says to a client, "I am really interested in how you feel about your parents," while the practitioner's body is turned away from the client with arms folded across the chest. The effect of this inconsistent message on the client could be quite potent. In fact, a *negative nonverbal* message mixed with a *positive verbal* one may have greater effects than the opposite (positive nonverbal and negative verbal). As Gazda and colleagues (2005, p. 80) point out, "When verbal and nonverbal messages are in contradiction, we usually believe the nonverbal message." The client may respond to inconsistent counselor messages by increasing interpersonal distance and may view such messages as indicators of counselor deception. Further, mixed messages may reduce

the extent to which the client feels psychologically close to the helper and perceives the helper as genuine.

Lack of congruence between helper verbal and nonverbal messages can be especially detrimental in cross-cultural helping interactions. Sue and Sue (2003) observe that for many racial/ethnic minority clients there is a "sociopolitical facet" to nonverbal communication (p. 135). Minority clients may intentionally challenge a helper in order to assess the helper's nonverbal message rather than the verbal one. This is done because the nonverbal messages are subject to less conscious control and provide clues to clients about either "conscious deceptions or unconscious bias" on the part of the helper (Sue & Sue, 2003, p. 137). For example, when topics related to a minority client's identity, such as race, are brought up in the session, what the therapist says may oftentimes be negated by his or her nonverbal communication. If this is the case, the minority client will quickly perceive the inconsistency and may conclude that the therapist is incapable of dealing with cultural/racial diversity.

Congruence between helper verbal and nonverbal messages is related to both client and helper ratings of helper effectiveness (Hill, Siegelman, Gronsky, Sturniolo, & Fretz, 1981). The importance of helper congruence, or consistency, among various verbal, kinesic, and paralinguistic behaviors cannot be overemphasized. Congruence between verbal and nonverbal channels seems especially critical when confronting clients or when discussing personal, sensitive, or stressful issues. A useful aspect of congruence involves learning to match the *intensity* of your nonverbal behaviors with those of the client. For example, if you are asking the client to recall a time when she or he felt strong, resourceful, or powerful, it is helpful to convey these feelings by your own nonverbal behaviors. Become more animated, speak louder, and emphasize key words such as *strong* and *powerful*. Many of us overlook one of our most significant tools in achieving congruence—our voice. Changes in pitch, volume, rate of speech, and voice emphasis are particularly useful ways of matching our experience with the experience of clients. Try some of this out in Learning Activity 3.3.

Synchrony

Synchrony is the degree of harmony between a practitioner's and a client's nonverbal behavior. In helping interactions, especially initial ones, it is important to match, or pace, the client's nonverbal behaviors. Mirroring of body posture and other client nonverbal behaviors contributes to rapport and builds empathy. Synchrony does not mean that the helper mimics every move or sound the client makes. It does mean that the practitioner's overall nonverbal demeanor is closely aligned with or very similar to the client's. For example, if

---

LEARNING ACTIVITY **3.3** | **Helper Nonverbal Behavior**

The purpose of this activity is for you to experience the effects of different kinds of nonverbal behavior. You can do this activity in dyads or groups or outside a classroom setting.

1. Observe the response of a person you are talking with when
   a. You look at the person or have relaxed eye contact.
   b. You don't look at the person consistently but instead avert eyes with only occasional glances.
   c. You stare at the person.

   Obtain a reaction from the other person about your behavior.

2. With other people, observe the effects of varying conversational distance. Talk with someone at a distance of (a) 3 feet (about 1 meter), (b) 6 feet (2 meters), and (c) 9 feet (3 meters). Observe the effect these distances have on the person.

3. You can also do the same kind of experimenting with your body posture. For example, contrast the effects of these two body positions in conversation: (a) slouching in seat, leaning back, and turning away from the person, (b) facing the person, learning slightly forward toward the person (from the waist up), and keeping the body relaxed.

---

the client is sitting back in a relaxed position with crossed legs, the helper matches and displays similar body posture and leg movements. Dissynchrony, or lack of pacing, is evident when, for example, a client is leaning back, very relaxed, and the helper is leaning forward, very intently, or when the client has a very sad look on her face and the helper smiles, or when the client speaks in a low, soft voice and the helper responds in a strong, powerful voice. The more nonverbal patterns you can pace, the more powerful the effect will be. However, when learning this skill, it is too overwhelming to try to match many aspects of a client's nonverbal behavior simultaneously. Find an aspect of the client's demeanor, such as voice, body posture, or gestures, that feels natural and comfortable for you to match, and concentrate on synchronizing this one aspect. (See Learning Activity 3.4.)

CHAPTER SUMMARY

This chapter focuses on helper and client nonverbal behavior. The importance of nonverbal communication in helping is illustrated by the trust (or lack of) that both helper and client place in each other's nonverbal messages. Nonverbal behavior may provide a more accurate portrayal of our real selves.

Most nonverbal behaviors are spontaneous and cannot easily be faked. Nonverbal behavior adds significantly to our interpretation of verbal messages. The neurobiology of nonverbal communication suggests that the nonverbal and emotional modes of processing in the brain's right hemisphere support the verbal and linguistic modes of processing in the brain's left hemisphere.

Five significant dimensions of nonverbal behavior are discussed in this chapter: kinesics (face and body expressions), paralinguistics (vocal cues and silence), proxemics (space and distance), environment, and time. Although much popular literature has speculated on the meanings of "body language," in helping interactions helpers must remember that the meaning of nonverbal behavior varies with people, situations, and cultures and, further, cannot be easily interpreted without supporting verbal messages.

This chapter also describes various ways of working with client nonverbal behavior in an interview, including responding to discrepancies between verbal and nonverbal client behavior, responding to silence, using nonverbal behaviors to change the focus of an interview, and responding to client nonverbal "leaks" (changes in nonverbal behavior).

LEARNING ACTIVITY **3.4** | **Observation of Helper and Client Nonverbal Behavior**

The purpose of this activity is to apply the material presented in this chapter in an interview setting. Using the Nonverbal Behavior Checklist on page 70, observe a helper and determine how many behaviors listed on the checklist the helper

demonstrates. In addition, in the role play, see how much you can identify about the client's nonverbal behaviors. Finally, look for evidence of synchrony (pacing) or dissynchrony between the two persons and congruence or incongruence for each person.

These categories of nonverbal behavior also apply to the helper's use of effective nonverbal behavior in the interview. In addition to using nonverbal behaviors that communicate interest and attentiveness, helpers must ensure that their own verbal and nonverbal messages are congruent and that their nonverbal behavior is synchronized with, or matches, the client's nonverbal behavior. Congruence and synchrony contribute in important ways to the building of rapport and empathy within the developing relationship.

REFERENCES

Birdwhistell, R. L. (1970). *Kinesics and context.* Philadelphia: University of Pennsylvania Press.

Brems, C. (2001). *Basic skills in psychotherapy and counseling.* Belmont, CA: Brooks/Cole.

Cormier, S., & Hackney, H. (2008). *Counseling strategies and interventions* (7th ed.). Boston: Allyn & Bacon.

Duhl, F. J., Kantor, D., & Duhl, B. S. (1973). Learning, pace and action in family therapy: A primer of sculpture. In D. A. Bloch (Ed.), *Techniques of family psychotherapy.* New York: Grune & Stratton.

Ekman, P. (1964). Body position, facial expression and verbal behavior during interviews. *Journal of Abnormal and Social Psychology, 68,* 295–301.

Ekman, P. (1982). Methods for measuring facial action. In K. R. Scherer & P. Ekman (Eds.), *Handbook of methods in nonverbal behavior research* (pp. 45–135). New York: Cambridge University Press.

Ekman, P., & Friesen, W. V. (1967). Head and body cues in the judgment of emotion: A reformulation. *Perceptual and Motor Skills, 24,* 711–724.

Ekman, P., & Friesen, W. V. (1969). Nonverbal leakage and clues to deception. *Psychiatry, 32,* 88–106.

Erickson, M. H., Rossi, E., & Rossi, S. (1976). *Hypnotic realities.* New York: Irvington.

Exline, R. V., & Winters, L. C. (1965). Affective relations and mutual glances in dyads. In S. S. Thompkins & C. E. Izard (Eds.), *Affect, cognition, and personality.* New York: Springer.

Gazda, G., Balzer, F., Childers, W., Nealy, A., Phelps, R., & Walters, R. (2005). *Human relations development* (7th ed.). Boston: Allyn & Bacon.

Hall, E. T. (1966). *The hidden dimension.* Garden City, NY: Doubleday.

Hill, C. E., Siegelman, L., Gronsky, B. R., Sturniolo, F., & Fretz, B. R. (1981). Nonverbal communication and counseling outcome. *Journal of Counseling Psychology, 28,* 203–212.

Knapp, M. L., & Hall, J. (2006). *Nonverbal communication in human interaction* (6th ed.). Belmont, CA: Thomson–Wadsworth.

Krivonos, P. D., & Knapp, M. L. (1975). Initiating communication: What do you say when you say hello? *Central States Speech Journal, 26,* 115–125.

Lecomte, C., Bernstein, B. L., & Dumont, F. (1981). Counseling interactions as a function of spatial–environmental conditions. *Journal of Counseling Psychology, 28,* 536–539.

Levin, H., Butler, M., & Hill, T. (2006). What clients find helpful in psychotherapy: Developing principles for facilitating moment-to-moment change. *Journal of Counseling Psychology, 53,* 314–324.

Mehrabian, A. (1976). *Public places and private spaces.* New York: Basic Books.

Mesquita, B., & Frijda, N. (1992). Cultural variations in emotions: A review. *Psychological Bulletin, 112,* 179–204.

Papp, P. (1976). Family choreography. In P. J. Guerin Jr. (Ed.), *Family therapy: Theory and practice* (pp. 465–479). New York: Gardner.

Passons, W. R. (1975). Gestalt approaches in counseling. New York: Holt, Rinehart and Winston.

Perls, F. S. (1973). *The Gestalt approach and eyewitness to therapy.* Palo Alto, CA: Science and Behavior Books.

Siegel, D. J. (2006). An interpersonal neurobiology approach to psychotherapy: Awareness, mirror neurons, and neural plasticity in the development of well-being. *Psychiatric Annals, 36,* 248–256.

Siegel, D. J., & Hartzell, M. (2003). *Parenting from the inside out.* New York: Tarcher/Penguin.

Simon, R. I. (1999). Therapist–patient sex. *Forensic Psychiatry, 22,* 31–47.

Simon, R. (2004, March/April). From the editor. *Psychotherapy Networker,* p. 2.

Sue, D. W., Capodilupo, C. M., Torino, G. C., Bucceri, J. M., Holder, A. M. B., Nadal, K. L., & Esquilin, M. (2007). Racial microaggressions in everyday life: Implications for clinical practice. *American Psychologist, 62,* 271–286.

Sue, D. W., & Sue, D. (2003). *Counseling the culturally diverse* (4th ed.). New York: Wiley.

Trager, G. L. (1958). Paralanguage: A first approximation. *Studies in Linguistics, 13,* 1–12.

Watson, O. M. (1970). *Proxemic behavior: A cross-cultural study.* The Hague: Mouton.

3

Part One

Describe briefly one possible effect or meaning associated with each of the following 10 client nonverbal behaviors (Learning Outcome 1). Speculate on the meaning of the client nonverbal behavior from the client description and context presented. If you wish, write your answers on a piece of paper. Feedback follows the evaluation.

Observed Client   Client Description (Context)
Nonverbal Behavior

1. Lowered eyes—looking down or away

   Client has just described an incestuous relationship with father. She looks away after recounting the episode.

2. Pupil dilation

   Client has just been informed that she will be committed to the state hospital. Her pupils dilate as she sits back and listens.

3. Quivering lower lip or lip biting

   Client has just reported a recent abortion to the helper. As she's finishing, her lip quivers, and she bites it.

4. Nodding head up and down

   Helper has just described reasons for client to stop drinking. Client responds by nodding and saying, "I know that."

5. Shrugging of shoulders

   Helper has just informed client that he is not eligible for services at that agency. Client shrugs shoulders while listening.

6. Fist clenching or holding hands

   Client is describing recent argument with spouse. Her fists are tightly clenched while she relates the incident.

7. Crossing and uncrossing legs

   Helper has just asked client whether he has been taking his medicine as prescribed. Client crosses and uncrosses legs while responding.

8. Stuttering, hesitations, speech errors

   Client hesitates when helper inquires about marital fidelity. Client starts to stutter and makes speech errors when describing extramarital affairs.

9. Moving closer

   As helper self-discloses an episode similar to client's, client moves chair toward helper.

10. Flushing of face and appearance of sweat beads

    Helper has just confronted client about racist remarks. Client's face turns red, and sweat appears on her forehead.

Part Two

Conduct a short interview as a helper, and see how many client nonverbal behaviors of kinesics (body motion), paralinguistics (voice qualities), and proxemics (space) you can identify by debriefing with an observer after the session (Learning Outcome 2). Describe the possible effects or meanings associated with each behavior you identify. Confer with the observer about which nonverbal client behaviors you identified and which you missed.

Part Three

In a role-play interview in which you are the helper, demonstrate effective use of your face and body, your voice, and distance/space/touch (Learning Outcome 3). Be aware of the degree to which your nonverbal behavior matches your words. Also attempt to pace at least one aspect of the client's nonverbal behavior, such as body posture or breathing rate and depth. Use the Nonverbal Behavior Checklist on page 70 to assess your performance from a videotape, or have an observer rate you during your session.

Part Four

Recall the four occasions for responding to client nonverbal behavior:

1. Client's "mixed" (discrepant) verbal and nonverbal message
2. Client's use of silence
3. Changes in client's nonverbal cues—or nonverbal "leaks"
4. Focusing on client's nonverbal behavior to change or redirect the interview

Identify three of the four occasions presented in the following client descriptions, according to Learning Outcome 4:

1. The client says that your feedback doesn't bother him, yet he frowns, looks away, and turns away.
2. The client pauses for a long time after your last question.
3. The client has flooded you with a great deal of information for the last five minutes.
4. The client's face was very animated during the first part of the interview; now the client's face has a very serious look.

3   KNOWLEDGE AND SKILL BUILDER FEEDBACK

Part One

Some of the possible meanings of these client nonverbal behaviors are as follows:

1. This client's lowering of her eyes and looking away probably indicates her *embarrassment* and *discomfort* in discussing this particular problem.
2. Dilation of this client's pupils probably signifies *arousal* and *fear* of being committed to the hospital.
3. The quivering of the client's lower lip and biting of the lip probably denote her *ambivalence* and *sorrow* over her actions.
4. The client's head nodding indicates *agreement* with the helper's rationale for remaining sober.
5. The client's shrugging of the shoulders may indicate *uncertainty* or *reconcilement*.
6. The client's fist clenching probably denotes *anger* with her spouse.
7. The client's crossing and uncrossing of his legs may signify *anxiety* or *discomfort*.
8. The client's hesitation in responding and subsequent stuttering and speech errors may indicate *sensitivity* to this topic as well as *discomfort* in discussing it.
9. The client's moving closer to the helper probably indicates *intrigue* and *identification* with what the helper is revealing.
10. The client's sweating and blushing may be signs of *negative arousal*—that is, *anxiety* and/or *embarrassment* with the counselor's confrontation about the racist remarks.

Part Two

Have the observer debrief you for feedback, or use the Nonverbal Behavior Checklist to recall which nonverbal behaviors you identified.

Part Three

You or your observer can determine which desirable nonverbal behaviors you exhibited as a helper, using the Nonverbal Behavior Checklist.

Part Four

The four possible occasions for responding to client nonverbal cues are these:

1. Responding to a client's mixed message—in this example, the client's frown, break in eye contact, and shift in body position contradict the client's verbal message.
2. Responding to client's silence—in this example the client's pause indicates silence.
3. Responding to client nonverbal behaviors to redirect the interview focus—in this example, to "break up" the flood of client information.
4. Responding to changes in client nonverbal cues or "leaks"—in this example, responding to the change in the client's facial expression.

NONVERBAL BEHAVIOR CHECKLIST

Name of Helper _____

Name of Observer _____

Instructions: During a videotaped or a live interview, use the categories listed below as guides for observing nonverbal behavior. You can use the checklist to observe the helper, the client, or both. Behaviors to be observed are listed in the first column. Check off a behavior when you observe it, and add descriptive comments about it—for example, "Blinking—*excessive*" or "Colors in room—*high arousal*."

Kinesics	**(✓)**	**Comments**
1. *Eyes*		
Eyebrows raised, lowered, or drawn together	___	___
Staring or "glazed" quality	___	___
Blinking—excessive, moderate, or slight	___	___
Moisture, tears	___	___
Pupil dilation	___	___
2. *Face, mouth, head*		
Continuity or changes in facial expression	___	___
Smiling	___	___
Swelling, tightening, or quivering lips	___	___
Changes in skin color	___	___
Flushing, rashes on upper neck, face	___	___
Appearance of sweat beads	___	___
Head nodding	___	___
3. *Body movements, posture, gestures, and touch*		
Body posture—rigid or relaxed	___	___
Continuity or shifts in body posture	___	___
Frequency of body movements—excessive, moderate, or slight	___	___
Gestures—open or closed	___	___
Frequency of nonverbal adaptors (distracting mannerisms)—excessive, moderate, or slight	___	___
Body orientation: direct (facing each other) or sideways	___	___
Breathing—shallow or deep, fast or slow	___	___
Continuity or changes in breathing depth and rate	___	___
Crossed arms or legs	___	___
Greeting touch (handshake)	___	___

3   KNOWLEDGE AND SKILL BUILDER **FEEDBACK**

Paralinguistics

1. Continuity or changes in voice level, pitch, rate of speech   ___ _____
2. Verbal underlining—voice emphasis of particular words/phrases   ___ _____
3. Whispering, inaudibility   ___ _____
4. Directness or lack of directness in speech   ___ _____
5. Speech errors—excessive, moderate, or slight   ___ _____
6. Pauses initiated by helper   ___ _____
7. Pauses initiated by client   ___ _____

Proxemics

1. Continuity or shifts in distance (closer, farther away)   ___ _____
2. Position in room—behind or next to object or person   ___ _____

Environment

1. Arousal (high or low) associated with
   Furniture arrangement   ___ _____
   Colors   ___ _____
   Light   ___ _____
   Overall room   ___ _____
2. Sensitivity to diversity reflected in room décor, pictures, objects   ___ _____

Time

1. Session started promptly or late   ___ _____
2. Promptness or delay in responding to other's communication   ___ _____
3. Continuity or changes in pace of session   ___ _____
4. Session terminated promptly or late   ___ _____

Synchrony and Pacing

1. Synchrony or dissynchrony between nonverbal behaviors and words   ___ _____
2. Pacing or lack of pacing between helper and client nonverbal behavior   ___ _____

Congruence

1. Congruence or discrepancies: nonverbal—between various parts of the body   ___ _____
2. Nonverbal/verbal—between nonverbal behavior and words   ___ _____

Summary

Using your observations of nonverbal behavior and the cultural/contextual variables of the interaction, what conclusions can you make about the helper? The client? The helping relationship? Consider such things as emotions, comfort level, deception, desire for more exchange, and liking.

4

INGREDIENTS OF AN EFFECTIVE HELPING RELATIONSHIP

LEARNING OUTCOMES

After completing this chapter, you will be able to

1. Communicate the three facilitative conditions (empathy, genuineness, and positive regard) to a client in a role-play situation.
2. Match a client description with the corresponding client "test of trust," given six written client descriptions.
3. Identify issues related to transference and counter-transference that might affect the development of the helping relationship, given four written case descriptions.

The quality of the helping relationship remains the foundation on which all other therapeutic activities are built. Norcross (2002a) defines a helping relationship as "the feelings and attitudes that therapist and client have toward one another and the manner in which these are expressed" (p. 7). The last several years have brought renewed acknowledgment of the significance of the most important components of that relationship. The components in the helping relationship that seem to be consistently related to positive therapeutic outcomes include the following and form the focus of this chapter:

1. *Facilitative conditions—empathy, genuineness, and positive regard.* These three therapist qualities, particularly empathy, represent conditions that, if present in the therapist and perceived by the client, contribute a great deal to the development of the relationship.
2. *A working alliance—a relationship in which helper and client collaborate and negotiate their work together toward particular goals and outcomes on an ongoing basis.* The working alliance is characterized by (a) a cognitive component, in which both parties agree to the goals and tasks of counseling, and (b) an affective component, or emotional bond between the helper and client,

characterized by mutual *regard* and *trust.* Regard for the client involves acceptance and caring; trust includes principled behavior, credibility, and reliability.
3. *Transference and countertransference—issues of emotional intensity and objectivity felt by both client and helper.* These issues are usually related to unfinished business with one's family of origin, yet they are triggered by and felt as a real aspect of the therapy relationship. Transference and countertransference *enactments* form the basis of relationship *ruptures. A repair of these ruptures is* a central task of the helper.

THE IMPORTANCE OF THE HELPING RELATIONSHIP

The helping relationship is as important to the overall outcome of the helping process as any particular change or intervention treatment strategy. The power of the helping relationship is acknowledged in nearly all theoretical orientations of psychotherapy; cognitive–behavioral therapy is no exception. For example, when empathy is conveyed to clients, it contributes to the efficacy of cognitive–behavioral therapy interventions (Haaga, Rabois, & Brody, 1999). What makes the helping relationship so powerful for clients? Miller and Baldwin (1987) assert that the power lies in the helper's potential to be healing. *Healing* is a word derived from a term meaning "to make whole." Comas-Diaz (2006) speaks of the universality of healing, noting that "the archetype of the healer is present in many societies" (p. 95). It is through the helping relationship and the interpersonal interactions with the practitioner that clients learn to be whole or integrated. In the relationship clients can experience a healing of the brokenness that often leads them into the helping process in the first place. Yalom (1980) explains the healing process in the therapeutic relationship this way: the helper interacts with the client in a genuine fashion, conveys warmth in a nonpossessive manner, and tries to grasp the meaning of the client's life and experience in order to create a relationship of safety and acceptance.

EMPIRICAL SUPPORT FOR THE HELPING RELATIONSHIP

Harmon, Hawkins, Lambert, Slade, and Whipple (2005) conclude that "empirical support for the importance of the therapeutic relationship in outcome spans more than four decades and hundreds of published research studies" (p. 178). Client ratings of the therapeutic relationship are significantly related to and good predictors of outcomes of therapy, leading these researchers to conclude that when clients respond to treatment negatively, "therapists need to be particularly alert to the client's level of comfort and satisfaction with the therapeutic relationship" (Harmon et al., 2005, p. 179).

In a qualitative study of what clients find helpful in therapy, the therapeutic relationship also emerged as an important component of effectiveness (Levitt, Butler, & Hill, 2006). In this study, clients spoke of their therapeutic relationship "in excess of any other factor" of perceived helpfulness (Levitt et al., 2006, p. 322). This finding was echoed in an outcome study with chronically depressed patients. In this study, the single-best predictor of outcome was the overall degree of emphasis therapists placed on discussing the client–therapist relationship (Vocisano et al., 2004, p. 263). This study also highlighted the importance of the relationship as a key component of change in cognitive–behavioral therapy (Vocisano et al., 2004).

Additional empirical support for the therapeutic relationship comes from the Division 29 Task Force on Empirically Supported Therapy Relationships established by the American Psychological Association. Conclusions from this revealed that for adult treatment, the empathy of the therapist is a particularly important evidence-based factor, with therapist positive regard and congruence closely behind. There is also a wealth of empirical evidence linking the quality of the working alliance to therapeutic outcomes. Managing relationship ruptures and managing countertransference were found to have some empirical support as well. For a complete discussion of these and additional variables, we refer you to Norcross's excellent book, *Psychotherapy Relationships That Work* (2002b).

Currently, research on the therapeutic relationship is leading away from the question "Does the therapeutic relationship work?" and toward the question "How does the therapeutic relationship work for this particular client with this set of issues and this kind of treatment?" (Norcross, 2002a, p. 11). These research-informed conclusions are designed to help practitioners answer the latter question with their clients and to integrate the therapeutic relationship with the specific change interventions or treatment strategies used with clients.

CULTURAL VARIABLES IN THE HELPING RELATIONSHIP

All helping relationships can be considered "cross-cultural" (Comas-Diaz, 2006, p. 82). Comas-Diaz asserts that an effective helping relationship is one that varies from culture to culture. In a ground-breaking article on cultural variations in the therapeutic relationship, she summarizes some of the ways in which the helping relationship is impacted by culture. For example, she notes that some clients from Eastern cultures often expect their helper to conform to a sort of "cultural hierarchy" and regard their helper as an "authority figure" (p. 90). As a result, the nondirective relationship approach of many practitioners can be unsettling to these clients, who prefer a relationship that is more hierarchical (p. 90).

Another way in which some ethnic/racial minority clients may be impacted by the therapeutic relationship has to do with notions of family and extended family. As Comas-Diaz (2006) points out, some clients expect the therapeutic relationship to extend beyond the therapy session and into the structure of the families or their extended support network. Further, clients from indigenous and collectivist cultures may rely on nonverbal communication and pay greater attention to contextual cues in the relationship in order to maintain a harmonious relationship with their helpers. Such clients may feel "put off" by an interpersonal style of relating that is "direct, explicit, and specific" (p. 93).

An important variable that shapes the helping relationship has to do with *microaggressions*—brief, common intentional and unintentional verbal, behavioral, and environmental indignities that convey derogatory slights and insults to the client—often based on some cultural dimension of difference such as race, sexual orientation, disability, and gender (Sue et al., 2007, p. 273). In their thoughtful article, Sue and colleagues note that practitioners often are unaware of their microaggressions—characterized by these authors as *microassaults*, *microinsults*, and *microinvalidations*—in their interactions with clients of color or with clients who differ on other cultural dimensions such as sexual orientation, gender, and disability. As a result, the helping relationship is likely to be impaired in some way(s) when microaggressions occur. Part of the surrounding distress and the resulting power of such microaggressions lies in their invisibility to the practitioner and sometimes to the recipient as well (Sue et al., 2007, p. 275). For example, in the case of racial microaggressions, although the practitioner may find it hard to believe he or she has engaged in an act of racism, discrimination, or prejudice, the recipient of the microaggressive act faces loss of self-esteem, loss of psychic and spiritual energies, and increased levels of anger and mistrust (Sue et al., 2007). Sue and colleagues observe that a "failure to acknowledge the significance of racism within and outside of the therapy session contributes to the breakdown of the alliance between therapist and client. A therapist's willingness to discuss racial matters is of central importance in creating a therapeutic alliance with clients of color" (p. 281).

Comas-Diaz (2006) also emphasizes the importance of recognizing and validating sociopolitical factors in order to solidify the multicultural therapeutic relationship (p. 99). Finally, she notes the ways in which the relationship conditions that we call "facilitative conditions" are also impacted by culture. We explore this topic in greater detail in the following section.

FACILITATIVE CONDITIONS

Facilitative conditions have roots in a counseling theory developed by Rogers (1951), called *client-centered* or *person-centered* therapy. Because this theory is the basis of these fundamental skills, we describe it briefly here.

The first stage of this theory (Rogers, 1942) was known as the *nondirective* period. The helper essentially attended and listened to the client for the purpose of mirroring the client's communication. The second stage of this theory (Rogers, 1951) was known as the *client-centered* period. In this phase, the therapist not only mirrored the client's communication but also reflected underlying or implicit affect or feelings to help clients become more self-actualized or fully functioning people. (This is the basis of current concepts of the skill of empathy, discussed in the next section.) In the most recent stage, known as *person-centered therapy* (Meador & Rogers, 1984; Raskin & Rogers, 1995), therapy is construed as an active partnership between two persons. In this current stage, emphasis is on client growth through *experiencing* of himself or herself and experiencing of the other person in the relationship.

Although client-centered therapy has evolved and changed, certain fundamental tenets have remained the same. One of these is that all people have an inherent tendency to strive toward growth, self-actualization, and self-direction. This tendency is realized when individuals have access to conditions (both within and outside therapy) that nurture growth. In the context of person-centered therapy, client growth is associated with high levels of three core, or facilitative, relationship conditions: *empathy* (accurate understanding), *genuineness* (congruence), and *positive regard* (respect) (Rogers, Gendlin, Kiesler, & Truax, 1967). If these conditions are absent from the therapeutic relationship, clients may fail to grow and may deteriorate (Carkhuff, 1969a, 1969b; Truax & Mitchell, 1971). Presumably, for these conditions to enhance the therapeutic relationship, they must be communicated by the helper *and* perceived by the client (Rogers, 1951, 1957). Clients have reported that these facilitative conditions are among the most helpful experiences for them in the overall helping process (Paulson, Truscott, & Stuart, 1999). It is important to note that, although we (and other authors) discuss each of these three conditions separately, in reality they are not isolated phenomena but in fact interrelated ones (Wickman & Campbell, 2003).

Recent theorists have proposed helping models in which the person-centered approach described above is integrated with empirically supported interventions (Tausch, 1990) and cognitive–behavioral strategies (Tursi & Cochran, 2006). In these models, the helper maintains these core conditions of counseling while implementing various intervention strategies with clients. Tursi and Cochran (2006) point out that cognitive–behavioral tasks occur naturally within the person-centered approach and that knowledge of cognitive–behavioral theory and strategies can actually increase helper empathy. These helping models offer ways to "honor the convergence of literature supporting the efficacy of the core conditions in counseling outcomes as well as a way of counseling that allows counselors a wide range of actions in order to meet a maximal diversity of clients' needs or wants" (Tursi & Cochran, 2006, p. 394). Norcross (2002a) acknowledges what he refers to as "the deep synergy between techniques and the relationship," noting that both intervention strategies and the helping relationship "shape and inform" one another (p. 8). Using helping relationships or intervention strategies alone and in isolation from each other is "incomplete" (Norcross, 2002a, p. 11).

In later writings, Rogers (1977) asserts that empathy, genuineness, and positive regard represent a set of *skills* as well as an attitude on the part of the therapist. In recent years, various persons have developed concrete skills associated with these three core conditions. This delineation of the core conditions into teachable skills has made it possible for people to learn how to communicate empathy, genuineness, and positive regard to clients. In the remainder of the "Facilitative Conditions" section, we describe these three important relationship conditions and associated skills.

Empathy or Accurate Understanding

Empathy may be described as the ability to understand people from their frame of reference rather than your own. Responding to a client empathically may be "an attempt to think *with,* rather than *for* or *about* the client" (Brammer, Abrego, & Shostrom, 1993, p. 98). For example, if a client says, "I've tried to get along with my father, but it doesn't work out. He's too hard on me," an empathic response would be something like "You feel discouraged about your unsuccessful attempts to get along with your father." In contrast, if you say something like "You ought to try harder," you are responding from your frame of reference, not the client's.

Empathy has received a great deal of attention from both researchers and practitioners over the years. We now know that there is even a "brain connection" with empathy! In 1996, a team of neuroscientists discovered brain neurons called "mirror" neurons. Mirror neurons are specifically tailor-made to mirror the emotions and bodily responses of another person. Siegel (2006) observes that these mirror neurons help us create actual body sensations that allow us to resonate with the experiences of the other person. This forms the foundation of the empathic experience in therapy, which is based on the recognition of the self in the other. The resulting potential for empathic attunement with our clients is profound. This empathic mirroring helps clients feel understood, and ultimately it leads to brain changes in clients through the establishment of new neural firing patterns and increased neural integration (Siegel, 2006).

Current concepts also emphasize that empathy is far more than a single concept or skill. Empathy is believed to be a multistage process consisting of multiple elements including affective and cognitive components (Bohart, Elliott, Greenberg, & Watson, 2002). The affective component refers to emotional connectedness between the practitioner and the client, and it involves the helper's ability to identify and contain the feelings and emotions or affective experience of the client. Cognitive empathy is comprised of a more intellectual or reasoned understanding of the client.

Research has abandoned the "uniformity myth" (Kiesler, 1966) with respect to empathy and seeks to determine when empathic understanding is most useful for particular clients and problems and at particular stages in the helping process. As Gladstein (1983, p. 178) observes, "In counseling/psychotherapy, affective and cognitive empathy can be helpful in certain stages, with certain clients, and for certain goals. However, at other times, they can interfere with positive outcomes." Generally, empathy is useful in influencing the quality and effectiveness of the therapeutic relationship. Empathy helps to build rapport and elicit information from clients by showing understanding, demonstrating civility, conveying that both helper and client are working "from the same side," and fostering client goals related to self-exploration (Gladstein, 1983). Bohart et al. (2002) note that the "most consistent evidence is that clients' perceptions that they are understood by their therapist relate to outcome" (p. 101).

Cultural, Person-Centered, and Self-Psychology Views of Empathy

Currently there are multiple explanations for what occurs in the empathic process between helper and client. Here we describe the cultural view of empathy, the person-centered view of empathy, and the self-psychology view of empathy. In our opinion, all three of these views are important for practitioners to be aware of and to incorporate into their therapeutic and relational style.

Ivey, Gluckstern, and Ivey (1993) distinguish between individual and multicultural empathy, saying that the concept of multicultural empathy requires that we understand "different worldviews" from our own (p. 25). The culturally empathic helper responds not only to the client's verbal and nonverbal messages but also to the historical/cultural/ethnic background of the client. Cultural empathy is important because it is considered one of the main foundations of

prosocial behavior and of a justice orientation (Hoffmann, 2000). Ridley and Lingle (1996) note that in cultural empathy, the *affective* component involves the ability of the practitioner to attend to the feeling of a client from another ethnocultural group and the *cognitive* component refers to the practitioner's capacity to understand a racially or ethnically different person's thoughts, feelings, and perspective. A recent study provided empirical validation to this theoretical construct of cultural empathy in the development of the Scale of Ethnocultural Empathy (Yang et al., 2003).

Comas-Diaz (2006) asserts that the practitioner in a multicultural helping relationship, may be able to empathize cognitively or intellectually with the culturally diverse client but may not be able to empathize affectively or emotionally. As an example, consider a practitioner who encounters a client who is an African refugee. The helper may be able to study the client's culture and consult with others who have firsthand knowledge of the client's culture and historical experiences. However, the practitioner may not be able to relate emotionally either to the client's experiences as a refugee or to the practitioner's own emotions that are stirred up in working with this particular client. When affective empathy is missing, cultural misunderstandings abound.

Misunderstandings or breaches of empathy are often a function not just of miscommunications but of differences in understanding styles, nuances, and subtleties of various cultural beliefs, values, and use of language (Sue & Sue, 2003). In an empathic misunderstanding, the helper should acknowledge it and take responsibility for it. Comas-Diaz (2006) concludes that misunderstandings or "missed empathetic opportunities" are prevalent but also subtle in cross-cultural relationships because clients from other cultures frequently communicate indirectly in order to test and assess the practitioner (p. 84).

Rogers's theory of client-centered therapy and his view of the role of empathy in the therapeutic process assume that at the beginning of counseling, a client has a distinct and already fairly complete sense of himself or herself—in Rogers's terms a *self-structure.* This is often true of clients with more "neurotic" or everyday features of presenting problems—that is, they bring problems of living to the helper and at the outset have an intact sense of themselves.

In contrast to the Rogerian view of the function of empathy—which is to help actualize the potential of an already established self-structure—is the view of empathy offered by the self-psychology theory of Kohut (1971b). This view assumes that many clients do not come into therapy with an established sense of self, that they lack a self-structure, and that the function of empathy in particular and of therapy in general is to build on the structure of the client's sense of self by completing a developmental process that was arrested at some time so that the client did not develop a whole sense of self.

LEARNING ACTIVITY   4.1   Validating Empathy

Consider the following case descriptions of clients. What might be the effect on you of hearing each client's issue? What might you try to defend about yourself? How could you work with this to give a validating response to the client instead? Provide an example of such a response. For our feedback on this activity, see page 78.

1. The client expresses a strong sexual interest in you and is mad and upset when she realizes you are not "in love" with her.

2. The client wants to be your favorite client and repeatedly wants to know how special he is to you.
3. The client is a man of Roman Catholic faith who wants to marry a Jewish woman. He is feeling a lot of pressure from his Latino parents, his priest, and his relatives to stop the relationship and find a woman of his own religious faith. He wants you to tell him what to do and is upset when you don't.

Both Rogers (1951, 1957) and Kohut (1971b) have had an enormous impact on our understanding of the role that empathy plays in the development of a positive and authentic sense of self, not only in the normal developmental process but also in the helping relationship. Rogers's emphasis on understanding and acceptance helps clients learn that it is acceptable to be real, to be their true selves. Kohut's emphasis on empathy as a corrective emotional experience allows clients to discover parts of themselves that have been buried or split off and that in counseling can be integrated in a more holistic way. Both Rogers and Kohut stress the importance of a nonjudgmental stance on the part of the helper (Kahn, 1991). It is our position that the views of both of these persons can be used together to create and sustain a facilitative helping relationship. Empathy is conveyed to clients by validating responses, by limit-setting responses, and by the provision of a safe-holding environment (Winnicott, 1958).

Empathy and Validation of Clients' Experience

Both Rogers and Kohut developed their views on empathy from their work with various clients. For Kohut, the turning point was a client who came to each session with bitter accusations toward him. As he stopped trying to explain and interpret her behavior and started to listen, he realized these accusations were her attempts to show him the reality of her very early childhood living with incapacitated caregivers who had been unavailable to her. Kohut surmised that clients show us their needs through their behavior in therapy, giving us clues about what they did not receive from their primary caretakers to develop an adequate sense of self and also about what they need to receive from the helper.

It is important to remember that when a childhood need is not met or is blocked, it simply gets cut off but does not go away; it remains in the person in an often primitive form, which explains why some grown-up clients exhibit behaviors in therapy that can seem very childish. When these needs are chronically frustrated or repressed for the child,

the child grows up with poor self-esteem and an impaired self-structure. Also, the self is split into a *true self*, the capacity to relate to oneself and to others, and a *false self*, an accommodating self that exists mainly to deny one's true needs in order to comply with the needs of the primary caregivers (Winnicott, 1958).

Kohut (1984) believes that empathy—the therapist's acceptance of the client and his or her feelings—is at the core of providing a "corrective emotional experience" for clients. It means avoiding any sort of comment that may sound critical to clients. Because the lack of original empathic acceptance by caregivers has driven parts of the client's self underground, it is important not to repeat this process in helping interactions. Instead, the helper needs to create an opposite set of conditions in which these previously buried aspects of the self can emerge, be accepted, and integrated (Kahn, 1991, pp. 96–97). The way to do this is to let clients know that the way they see themselves and their world "is not being judged but accepted as the most likely way for them to see it, given their individual history" (Kahn, 1991, p. 97).

This is known as a validating response or an *empathic affirmation* (Bohart et al., 2002, p. 101). Validating responses are usually verbal messages from the helper that mirror the client's *experience* (notice the emphasis on *experience* rather than on *words*). This sounds remarkably easy to do but often becomes problematic because of our own woundedness. Too often we fail to validate the client because a button has been pushed in us, and we end up validating or defending ourselves instead. This reaction forms the basis of countertransference, which we discuss later in this chapter. The key to being able to provide validating responses is to be able to contain your own emotional reactions so that they do not get dumped out onto the client. This is especially hard to do when a client pushes your own buttons, and this is why working with yourself and your own "stuff" is so important. (See Learning Activity 4.1.)

Kahn (1991) provides a wonderful illustration of the validating empathic response:

> Recently I had to close my office and see clients in a temporary place. One of my clients refused to meet me there because the parking was too difficult. She was angry and contemptuous that I would even ask her to do such a thing. I committed a whole list of Kohut sins. I told her that the parking was no harder there than anywhere else and that I assumed there was something else underlying her anger. She got angrier and angrier, and finally I did, too. It escalated into a near-disaster. Kohut would have felt his way into her situation and said with warmth and understanding, "I can really see how upsetting it is for you to have the stability of our seeing each other disturbed. I think that figuring out where you'd park really is difficult, and I think there must be a lot of other upsetting things about our having to see each other somewhere else. And I can imagine some of those other things are even harder to talk about than the parking." Had she then kept the fight going, he might have said, "I think it must be really hard to have this move just laid on you without your having any say in the matter. It must seem like just one more instance where you get pushed around, where decisions get made for you, where you have to take it or leave it. It must be very hard."
>
> Had I done that, I might have made it possible for her to explore other feelings—or I might have failed to do so. But whatever the outcome, she would have felt heard and understood. As it was, I became just one more in a long series of people telling her she was doing it wrong. (pp. 103–104)

Teyber (2006) notes that validating responses are especially important when working with clients of color, with gay and lesbian clients, with low-income clients, and with any others who may feel different: "These clients will bring issues of oppression, prejudice, and injustice into the therapeutic process, and their personal experiences have often been invalidated by the dominant culture. These clients in particular will not expect to be heard or understood by the therapist" (pp. 57–58).

Empathy and Limit-Setting Responses

As you can imagine, clients whose primary needs have not been met can present strong needs for immediate gratification to their helpers. As Kahn (1991) explains, "The most primitive side of clients wants to be gratified as *children*; that is, clients want to be hugged, to be told they're wonderful, to be reassured you will protect them and on and on" (p. 99). Part of providing an empathic environment is to reflect the client's wish or desire but not actually provide the gratification. This constitutes a limit-setting response, and, combined with warmth and empathy, it contributes to the client's growth and helps to create an atmosphere of safety. See whether you can spot the difference in the following two examples:

Client: I don't think I do anything very well. No one else seems to think I'm real special either.

Example 1

Helper: Well, you are so special to me.

Example 2

Helper: I can see how that is a very hard thing for you—wanting to feel special and not feeling that way about yourself.

In Example 1, the helper supplies reassurance and gratifies the need, but in doing so, may have closed the door for more explanation of this issue by the client. In Example 2, the helper reflects the client's pain and the client's desire or wishes and leaves the door open for a client response.

Wells and Glickauf-Hughes (1986) note that "for clients with backgrounds of deprivation and/or neglect, limit setting is a needed art of caring, protective containment" (p. 462). Limits may need to be set on behaviors with clients who are prone to acting out—not only because the client is distressed but also because the client's behavior violates your own limits as a helper. If a client repeatedly shouts at you, you may set limits by saying something like "I'm aware of how much you shout at me during our sessions. I know this is your way of showing me something about what has happened to you and how awful you feel about it. Still, in order for me to work effectively with you, I want you to talk to me about your distress without shouting."

We want to emphasize that throughout our discussion of the concept of empathy from the viewpoint of Kohut (1971a, 1984) and self-psychology, we have intentionally used the word *caregivers*. This is consistent with our personal stance, which is that among various ethnic and cultural groups, mothers, fathers, and often grandparents and extended-family members represent the objects healthy children use to develop a cohesive sense of self, and that if self-esteem is impaired or the self needs are blocked, it is the result not of insufficient *mothering* but rather of insufficient and/or inconsistent *caregiving* in general. In Jungian terms, it is the absence of the feminine (or the yang of the yin–yang) in both women and men and in predominantly patriarchal cultures that contributes to the lack of a "cherishing container" for the child (Bion, 1963; Woodman, 1993).

Helms and Cook (1999) add a cautionary note about exploring early childhood events for clients of color. They note that "where early childhood experiences are concerned, it is important for the therapist to remember that experiences that may sound like aberrations to the therapist may be normal for the client in the racial or cultural environment in which he or she was socialized" (p. 136). Moreover, it is important for therapists to be aware of different kinds of families and varying cultural and racial practices in familial roles and child rearing so that the Euro-American family is not used as the standard-bearer for all clients.

FEEDBACK
Validating Empathy

Here are some examples of validating responses. Discuss your emotional reactions and your response with a partner or in a small group.

1. I realize you are disappointed and upset about wanting me to have the same sort of feelings for you that you say you have for me.

2. It is important to you to feel very special to me. I understand this as your way of telling me something about what has been missing for you in your life.

3. I realize you feel caught between two things—your religious and cultural history and your love for this woman. You wish I could tell you what to do, and you're upset with me that I won't.

Empathy and the Holding Environment

The empathic mirroring and limit-setting responses we have described are often referred to as the provision of a therapeutic *holding environment* (Winnicott, 1958). A holding environment means that the therapist conveys in words and/or behavior that he or she knows and understands the deepest feelings and experience of the client and provides a safe and supportive atmosphere in which the client can experience deeply felt emotions. As Cormier and Hackney (2008) note, it means "that the counselor is able to allow and stay with or 'hold' the client's feelings instead of moving away or distancing from the feelings or the client. In doing this, the counselor acts as a *container;* that is, the counselor's comfort in exploring and allowing the emergence of client feelings provides the support to help the client contain or hold various feelings that are often viewed by the client as unsafe" (p. 109). The therapist as a container helps the client to manage what might otherwise be experienced as overwhelming feelings by providing a structure and safe space in having to do so.

Josselson (1992) points out that "of all the ways in which people need each other, holding is the most primary and the least evident," starting with the earliest sensations that infants experience—the sensation of being guarded by strong arms that keep them from falling and also help them to unfold as unique and separate individuals (p. 29). Not only is a child sufficiently nourished in such an environment, but, just as important, the child also feels *real.* As Josselson notes in her seminal work on adult human relationships, this need for holding or groundedness does not disappear as we grow up, although the form of holding for adults may be with institutions, ideas, and words as much as with touch. Individuals who do not experience this sense of holding as children often grow up without a sense of groundedness in their own bodies as well as without a sense of self as separate and unique persons. Often their energy or "life force" is bound up and/or groundless, and they may seek to escape their sense of nothingness by becoming attached to any

number of addictions. Josselson (1992) provides an excellent description of how the process of therapy can support clients' growth through the provision of this sort of holding environment:

> People often come to psychotherapy because they need to be held while they do the work of emotionally growing. They need a structure within which they can experience frightening or warded-off aspects of themselves. They need to know that this structure will not "let them down." They also need to trust that they will not be impinged upon by unwanted advice or by a therapist's conflicts or difficulties. Psychotherapy, because of clinicians' efforts to analyze what takes place, is one of the best understood of holding environments. Therapists "hold" patients as patients confront aspects of their memory and affective life that would be too frightening or overwhelming to face alone. (One of my patients once described her experience of therapy as my sitting with her while she confronts the monsters inside.) Therapists continue to hold patients even as patients rage at them in disappointment, compete with them, envy them, or yearn for them. Adequate holding continues despite the pain of relatedness. (p. 36)

Keep in mind that in various cultures this sort of holding environment is supplied by indigenous healers as well.

Teyber (2006) has noted that the effective holding environment provided by a helper is usually dramatically different from what the young client is experiencing or what an adult client experienced while growing up. For example, if the child was sad, the parent may have responded by withdrawing, by denying the child's feelings, or by responding derisively (Teyber, 2006). In all these parental reactions, the child's feeling was not heard, validated, or "contained"; as a result, the child learned over time to deny or avoid these feelings (thus constituting the "false self" we described earlier). Children are developmentally unable to experience and manage feelings on their own without the presence of another person who can be emotionally present for them and receive and even welcome their feelings. If the parent was unable to help the child hold feelings in this manner, it will be up to the helper to do so. In this way, the helper allows clients to know that he or she can accept their painful feelings and still stay emotionally connected to them (Teyber, 2006). If the helper cannot do so, either because of discomfort with the client's pain or because of feelings that have been "stirred up" in working with the client, this too constitutes a countertransferential reaction.

Teyber's ideas reflect the work of Kohut (1971a, 1971b) on *self-object relationships,* in which the development of the child's sense of *self* depends greatly on the capacity of the child's caretakers, the "*self-objects,*" to fulfill certain psychological functions that the child cannot yet provide for himself or herself. Support and empathy are two of the most important of these psychological functions that the caregiver provides for the developing child. These ongoing supportive and empathic exchanges (or lack thereof) form the basis of the child's psychic infrastructure and impact how the child will be able to relate to himself or herself as well as to others (Cashdan, 1988). Some relationship theorists consider this idea to be Kohut's most important contribution, not only because it explains much about an individual's capacity for relatedness, but also because his notions about the relationship between the child and caregiver have many analogs in the therapeutic relationship between the helper and client. From this perspective, when mis-understandings or empathic breaches occur in counseling, the helper may gently inquire if the current empathic break feels similar in any way to something that occurred in the client's relationship with a caregiver. In fact, in this way, one could look at the healing that occurs in the therapeutic relationship as giving the client "a second developmental chance" (Cashdan, 1988, p. 22).

Genuineness or Congruence

Genuineness—also referred to as *congruence*—is the art of being oneself without being phony or playing a role. Although most practitioners are trained to be professionals, a helper can convey genuineness by being human and by collaborating with the client. Genuineness contributes to an effective therapeutic relationship by reducing the emotional distance between the helper and client and by helping the client to identify with the helper, to perceive the helper as another person similar to the client. The research base suggests that genuineness is more likely to be linked to positive therapeutic outcome when there is a positive association with at least one of the other two facilitative conditions (empathy and/or positive regard) (Klein, Kolden, Michels, & Chisholm-Stockard, 2002). Genuineness has at least four components: supporting nonverbal behaviors, role behavior, consistency, and spontaneity (see also Egan, 2007; Klein et al., 2002).

Supporting Nonverbal Behaviors

Genuineness is communicated by the helper's use of appropriate, or supporting, nonverbal behaviors. Nonverbal behaviors that convey genuineness include eye contact, smiling, and leaning toward the client while sitting. However, these three nonverbal behaviors should be used discreetly and gracefully. For example, direct yet intermittent eye contact is perceived as more indicative of genuineness than is persistent gazing, which clients may interpret as staring. Similarly, continual smiling or leaning forward may be viewed as phony and artificial rather than genuine and sincere. As we mentioned during our discussion of empathy, when establishing rapport, the counselor should display nonverbal behaviors that parallel or match those of the client.

Role Behavior

Counselors who do not overemphasize their role, authority, or status are likely to be perceived as more genuine by clients. Too much emphasis on one's role and position can create excessive and unnecessary emotional distance in the relationship. Clients can feel intimidated or even resentful.

The genuine helper also is someone who is comfortable with himself or herself and with a variety of persons and situations and does not need to "put on" new or different roles to feel or behave comfortably and effectively. As Egan (2007, p. 56) observes, genuine helpers "do not take refuge in the role of counselor. Ideally, relating at deeper levels to others and to the counseling they do are part of their lifestyle, not roles they put on or take off at will."

Consistency

Consistency exists when the helper's words, actions, and feelings match—when they are congruent. For example, when a therapist becomes uncomfortable because of a client's constant verbal assault, she acknowledges this feeling of discomfort, at least to herself, and does not try to cover up or feign comfort when it does not exist. Practitioners who are not aware of their feelings or of discrepancies between their feelings, words, and actions may send mixed, or incongruent, messages to clients—for example, saying, "Sure, go ahead and tell me how you feel about me," while fidgeting or tapping their feet or fingers. Clients are likely to find such messages very confusing and even irritating.

Spontaneity

Spontaneity is the capacity to express oneself naturally without contrived or artificial behaviors. Spontaneity also means being tactful without deliberating about everything you say or do. However, spontaneity does not mean that helpers need to verbalize every passing thought or feeling to clients, particularly negative feelings. Rogers (1957) suggests that helpers express negative feelings to clients only if the feelings are constant and persistent or if they interfere with the helper's ability to convey empathy and positive regard.

Positive Regard

Positive regard, also called *respect,* is the ability to prize or value the client as a person with worth and dignity (Rogers, 1957). Communication of positive regard has a number of important functions in establishing an effective therapeutic relationship, including the communication of willingness to work with the client, interest in the client as a person, and acceptance of the client. Farber and Lane (2002) conclude that existing research data suggest that the "effectiveness of positive regard might lie especially in its ability to facilitate a long-term working relationship" (p. 185). Egan (2007) has identified four components of positive regard: having a sense of commitment to the client, making an effort to understand the client, suspending critical judgment, and showing competence and care. Positive regard also involves expressing warmth to clients (Rogers, 1957; Farber & Lane, 2002).

Commitment

Commitment means you are willing to work with the client and are interested in doing so. It is translated into such actions as being on time for appointments, reserving time for the client's exclusive use, ensuring privacy during sessions, maintaining confidentiality, and applying skills to help the client. Lack of time and lack of concern are two major barriers to communicating a sense of commitment.

Understanding

Clients will feel respected to the degree that they *feel* the helper is trying to understand them and to treat their problems with concern. Helpers can demonstrate their efforts to understand by being empathic, by asking questions designed to elicit information important to the client, and by indicating with comments or actions their interest in understanding the client and the client's cultural heritage and values. Helpers also convey understanding with the use of specific listening responses such as paraphrasing and reflecting client messages.

Nonjudgmental Attitude

A nonjudgmental attitude is the helper's capacity to suspend judgment of the client's actions or motives and to avoid condemning or condoning the client's thoughts, feelings, or actions. It may also be described as the helper's acceptance of the client without conditions or reservations, although it does not mean that the helper supports or agrees with all the client says or does. A helper conveys a nonjudgmental attitude by warmly accepting the client's expressions and experiences without expressing disapproval or criticism. For example, suppose a client states, "I can't help cheating on my wife. I love her, but I've got this need to be with other women." The helper who responds with regard and respect might say something like "You feel pulled between your feelings for your wife and your need for other women." This response neither condones nor criticizes the client's feelings and behaviors. In contrast, a helper who states, "What a mess! You got married because you love your wife. Now you're fooling around with other women," conveys criticism and lack of respect for the client as a unique human being. The experience of having positive regard for clients can also be identified by the presence of certain (covert) thoughts and feelings, such as "I feel good when I'm with this person" or "I don't feel bothered or uncomfortable with what this person is telling me."

Competence and Care

As helpers, we convey positive regard and respect by taking steps to ensure that we are competent and able to work with the clients who come to us for help. This means that we get supervision, consultation, and continuing education to maintain and improve our skills. It also means understanding that we are not know-it-alls and that we keep on learning and growing even after getting our degrees and working in the field. It also means that we act in principled ways with clients. When we are confronted with a client we cannot work with, we use an ethical referral process. Above all else, we do not use clients for our own needs, and we are careful not to behave in any way that would exploit clients. We also are careful to pursue agendas of the client rather than our own (Egan, 2007).

Warmth

According to Goldstein and Higginbotham (1991), without an expression of warmth, particular strategies and helping interventions may be "technically correct but therapeutically impotent" (p. 48). Warmth reduces the impersonal nature or sterility of a given intervention or treatment procedure. In addition, warmth begets warmth. In interactions with hostile or reluctant clients, warmth and caring can speak to the client's anger.

A primary way in which warmth is communicated is with supporting nonverbal behaviors such as voice tone, eye contact, facial animation and expressions, gestures, and touch. Johnson (2006) describes some nonverbal cues that express warmth or coldness. For example, warmth is expressed with a soft tone of voice; a harsh tone of voice reflects coldness. Maintaining some eye contact, smiling, and use of welcoming gestures also reflect warmth. Remember that these behaviors may be interpreted differently by clients from various ethnic, racial, and cultural groups. For example, in some cultures direct eye contact is considered disrespectful, particularly with a person in authority or an elder (Sue & Sue, 2003).

An important aspect of the nonverbal dimension of warmth is touch. In times of emotional stress, many clients welcome a well-intentioned touch. The difficulty with touch is that it may have a meaning to the client different from the meaning you intended to convey. In deciding whether to use touch, it is important to consider the level of trust between you and the client, whether the *client* may perceive the touch as sexual, the client's past history associated with touch (occasionally a client will associate touch with punishment or abuse and will say, "I can't stand to be touched"), and the client's cultural group (whether touch is respectful and valued). Also, because of all the clients who present with trauma history, it is important to observe clear boundaries surrounding touch (Smith & Fitzpatrick, 1995). Check with the client and discuss these boundaries first.

Warmth can also be expressed to clients through selected verbal responses. One way to express warmth is to use enhancing statements (Ivey, D'Andrea, Ivey, & Simek-Morgan, 2002) that portray some positive aspect or attribute about the client, such as "It's great to see how well you're handling this situation," "You're really expressing yourself well," or "You've done a super job on this action plan." Enhancing statements offer positive reinforcement to clients and to be effective must be sincere, deserved, and accurate. Farber and Lane (2002) conclude that it is probably insufficient for helpers to simply feel good about their clients. Instead, helpers need to communicate these positive feelings verbally when they are in the client's presence (though without gushing).

All three of the facilitative conditions, but especially positive regard, are related to the facilitation of the working alliance and the development of trust in the helping relationship. In the next section, we explore how the working alliance is developed, tested, and sustained in the therapeutic process.

THE WORKING ALLIANCE

Horvath and Bedi (2002) point out that the therapeutic alliance has a "lengthy history" in psychotherapy, beginning with the work of Freud, although all therapeutic approaches considered the alliance to be very important. The term *working alliance* was coined by Greenson (1967), who viewed the relationship as a sort of therapeutic collaboration and partnership in which counselor and client pull together in a joint venture, much like rowing a boat.

Three Parts of the Alliance

Bordin (1979) expanded Greenson's work and noted specifically that this alliance comprises three parts:

1. Agreement on therapeutic *goals*
2. Agreement on therapeutic *tasks*
3. An *emotional bond* between client and therapist

Safran and Muran (2006) conceptualize the working alliance as an ongoing process of negotiation between the helper and the client that occurs at both conscious and unconscious levels.

Much research connects the quality of this working alliance to therapeutic outcomes, Overall, these data, summarized by Horvath and Bedi (2002), suggest that such an alliance needs to be founded early in therapy, may wax and wane over time but reemerge during times of crisis, and may be especially influential with the more severe client issues. The working alliance is also affected by the kinds of bonds a client has established as a child with her or his parents. Patterns of attachment are observed in infants, and these patterns are believed to govern adult attachment as well. *Attachment* refers to the client's degree of comfort and trust in a close relationship such as the helping one and also to the extent that the client values relatedness with others. Clients with more difficult attachment styles establish poorer initial alliances with helpers (Horvath & Bedi, 2002).

The working alliance is also impacted by skills of the helper, particularly "negative" behaviors such as exhibiting a "take charge" attitude early in the helping process, displaying a lack of warmth, premature interpretation, and irritability. These data are underscored by interactional data suggesting that what is most important in establishing a positive working alliance is that the helper–client interactions are not "hostile, negative, or competing" (Hovath & Bedi, 2002, p. 59).

The data on the working alliance underscore the importance of revisiting the strength of the alliance throughout the entire helping process, making sure that agreement on the therapeutic tasks and goals remains consistent and that the emotional connection between the helper and client remains strong. A critical element in the efficacy of the therapeutic alliance appears to involve client feedback to helpers about the way clients are experiencing the alliance. Miller, Duncan, Sorrell, and Brown (2005) found that when helpers get client feedback about the quality of the alliance, there is substantial improvement in the outcomes of treatment and in the retention of clients in treatment. These findings were especially true for mandated clients most at risk for treatment failure. Notably, the system developed by Miller, Duncan, Sorrell, and Brown (2005), called the Partners for Change Outcome Management System (PCOMS), involves a brief four-item adult or child Session Rating Scale (see www.talkingcure .com) to assess the therapeutic alliance.

What helper skills promote a strong working alliance? Clients report that feeling understood, supported, and hopeful is connected to the strength of the working alliance, particularly in the early part of the helping process. In addition, the working alliance is also impacted by the client's trust in the helper. As Safran and Muran (2006, p. 289) noted, the alliance highlights the fact that at the most basic level, the client's ability to trust and have faith in the helper plays a pivotal role in the change process.

Practitioners obviously also need to pay attention to the ways in which this working alliance is formed with

LEARNING ACTIVITY **4.2**   Working Alliance

With a partner or in a small group, discuss how the working alliance may be affected by working with clients such as the following.

1. Children
2. Adolescents
3. Elderly

4. Persons with disabilities
5. Men
6. Women
7. Clients of color
8. Gay, lesbian, bisexual, and transgendered clients
9. Clients living in poverty

various clients, particularly clients from various cultural groups (see Learning Activity 4.2). As Berg and Jaya (1993) point out, proper attention to protocol may be very important in forming an initial alliance in diverse helping relationships. They note that "paying proper respect to procedural rules is the first step in achieving a positive therapeutic alliance. *How* the client is shown respect is often more important than *what* the therapist does to help solve problems" (p. 33). The gender of clients may differentially affect the course of the working alliance. Helms and Cook (1999) describe how the working alliance may be affected in cross-racial therapy. They note that "if a bond is formed in cross-racial therapy . . ., the client may have exaggeratedly positive reactions to the therapist because a cross-racial therapy bond may be the first significant nurturing experience that the client has had with a member of the therapist's race" (p. 146).

The emotional bond reflected in the working alliance between the helper and client is greatly impacted by the level of trust between the two participants. In the following section, we discuss ways helpers and develop and nurture trust within the working alliance.

Trust

Trust has been described by clients as a "core trait" in the helping relationship (Levitt, Butler, & Hill, 2006, p. 218). Johnson (2006) points out that trust is a complex construct and consists of multiple elements, including behaving in an ethically and morally justifiable manner, making a good-faith effort to honor one's commitments, and being reliable (p. 94). In a qualitative study, clients deepened their trust in their practitioner after taking a risk to reveal some personal vulnerability and experiencing the therapist's response to the disclosure as caring and respectful (Levitt, Butler, & Hill, 2006). Like many other variables in the helping relationship, trust is an interactional and reciprocal process; the establishment and endurance of trust throughout the relationship can depend on the behaviors and responses of both helpers and clients. However, as with other relationship variables, the responsibility for creating and maintaining trust, especially initially, is in the hands of the helper because

the therapeutic relationship is not a symmetrical one and the helper role has some unique responsibilities associated with it. One of these responsibilities is to behave in ways that are more likely to engender trust.

Establishing Trust

Many clients are likely to find helpers trustworthy, at least at first, because of the status of the helpers' role in society. Clients also are more likely to perceive a helper as trustworthy if she or he has acquired a reputation for honesty and for ethical and professional behavior. Likewise, a negative reputation can erode early trust in a helper. Thus, many clients, particularly those from the dominant cultural group, may put their faith in the helper initially on the basis of role and reputation and, over the course of time, continue to trust the helping professional unless the trust is in some way abused.

Clients who are not from the dominant cultural group may view trustworthiness differently. As LaFromboise and Dixon (1981, p. 135) observe, "A member of the minority group frequently enters the relationship suspending trust until the person proves that he/she is worthy of being trusted." For these and some other clients, helpers may have to earn initial trust and work hard to sustain trust especially as helping progresses. Trust can be difficult to establish yet easily destroyed. Initial trust based on external factors such as the helper's role and reputation must be solidified with appropriate actions and behaviors by the helper that occur during successive interactions.

Johnson (2006) points out that many successive consistent behaviors are necessary to establish trust but just one inconsistent behavior is all it takes to destroy it, and once destroyed or diminished, trust is extremely difficult to rebuild. Trust also can be damaged when the helper acts in any way that abuses the inherent power ascribed to the role as helper. For example, if the helper makes unilateral decisions about the client and the helping process and does not collaborate with the client, this abuse of power will diminish trust. Abuse of power may be particularly damaging when you are working with clients who are from nonmainstream cultural groups and who have been disempowered because of their race, ethnicity, income level, sexual orientation, religion, disability, or gender.

Whether the helper's trustworthiness becomes an issue may also depend on the age of the client, the client's former history with other helpers, and the client's trauma history. Children often trust helpers very readily unless they have had a prior bad experience with a helper in which their trust was violated or unless they have a trauma history. Regardless of age, almost all clients who have trauma histories will have greater issues in trusting a helper than clients who do not.

The behaviors that contribute most importantly to trustworthiness include helper congruence or consistency of verbal and nonverbal behavior, nonverbal acceptance of client disclosures, nonverbal responsiveness and dynamism, dependability and consistency between talk and actions, confidentiality, openness and honesty, accurate and reliable information giving, and nondefensive reflections/interpretations of clients' "tests of trust." Incongruence, judgmental or evaluative reactions, and passivity quickly erode any trust that has developed.

Clients' Tests of Helper Trustworthiness

Trust between helpers and clients does not always develop automatically. Clients need to be assured that the helping process will be structured to meet their needs and that the helper will not take advantage of their vulnerability (Johnson, 2006). Usually clients develop trust after they first scrutinize the helper by engaging in subtle maneuvers to determine the helper's trustworthiness (Levitt, Butler, & Hill, 2006). Fong and Cox (1983) call these maneuvers "tests of trust" and liken them to small trial balloons sent up to "see how they fly" before the client decides whether to send up the big balloon.* Practitioners may be insensitive to such tests of trust and fail to realize that trust is the real concern of the client. Instead of responding to the trust issue or to the process level of the message, helpers may respond just to the content, the surface level of the message.

Another perspective on client tests of trust is offered by *control-mastery theory.* According to this theory, clients are motivated to pursue life-enhancing goals but also are afraid to do so because of "pathogenic beliefs" that tell them that in moving toward their goals, they will endanger themselves or others (Weiss, 2002, p. 2). Weiss (2002) asserts that these pathogenic beliefs are developed in early childhood usually

*This and all other quotations from "Trust as an Underlying Dynamic in the Counseling Process: How Clients Test Trust," by M. L. Fong and B. G. Cox, *The Personnel and Guidance Journal, 62,* pp. 163–166, copyright 1983 by ACA, are reprinted with permission. No further reproduction authorized without written permission of the American Counseling Association.

through traumatic experiences between the child and the caregivers and siblings. For example, if parents neglect a child, the child may develop the pathogenic belief that he or she would and even should be neglected by other people as well, including, of course, the therapist. During the counseling process, clients work to *disprove* these pathogenic beliefs, which are usually unconscious (out of awareness), by testing them in relationship to the helper, hoping that the helper will pass these tests. Typically this testing unfolds in a series of trial actions, usually verbal ones, that, according to the client's beliefs, should impact the helper in a particular way. If the helper does *not* respond in the predictable fashion, the client will perceive the helper as passing the trust test and will feel safer to proceed.

Weiss (2002, p. 2) provides the following example of how this testing may occur in the actual practice process:

> A female (client) who unconsciously believed that she had to comply with male authorities lest she hurt them, felt endangered by her therapy with a male therapist. She feared that she would have to accept poor interpretations or follow bad advice. Her plan for the opening days of therapy was to reassure herself against this danger. She tested her belief that she would hurt the therapist if she disagreed with him. First she tested indirectly, then progressively more directly. The therapist passed her tests; he was not upset, and after about 6 months time the (client) had largely overcome her fear of complying with the therapist, and so became relatively comfortable and cooperative.

We hope that this example makes clear that the helper's task is to decipher what the test of trust is and to respond so that the client's belief is *not confirmed.* If a client believes the helper will be judgmental and rejecting, the helper will consistently show respect and acceptance. If a client believes that the helper will be domineering or autocratic, the helper responds by being unintrusive. Control-mastery theory has been empirically supported from a number of quantitative studies in which both client self-reports and physiological data have been used to determine the effects of this approach on clients (Weiss & Sampson, 1986). From these data, Weiss and Sampson concluded that when helpers pass these tests of client trust, clients feel less anxious and less restricted and show greater insight.

Fong and Cox also observe that some client statements and behaviors are used repeatedly by many clients as tests of trust. They state that "the specific content of clients' questions and statements is unique to individual clients, but the general form that tests of trust take—for example, requesting information or telling a secret—are relatively predictable" (p. 164). Fong and Cox identified six common types of client tests of trust. Table 4.1 summarizes these six tests and presents sample client statements and helpful and nonhelpful helper responses. (See also Learning Activity 4.3.)

TABLE 4.1	Examples of Client Tests of Trust and Helpful and Nonhelpful Practitioner Responses		
Test of trust	**Client statements**	**Nonhelpful responses**	**Helpful responses**
Requesting information ("Can you understand and help me?")	"Have you ever worked with anyone else who seems as mixed up as I am?"	"Yes, all the time." "No, not too often." "Once in a while." "Oh, you're not *that* mixed up."	"Many people I work with often come in feeling confused and overwhelmed. I'm also wondering whether you want to know that I have the experience to help you."
Telling a secret ("Can I be vulnerable with you?")	"I've never been able to tell anyone about this—not even my husband or my priest. But I did have an abortion several years ago. I just was not ready to be a good and loving mother."	"Oh, an abortion—really?" "You haven't even told your husband even though it might be his child too?"	"What you're sharing with me now is our secret, something between me and me."
Asking a favor ("Are you reliable?")	"Could you bring this information (or book) in for me next week?"	Promises to do it but forgets altogether or does not do it when specified	Promises to do it and does it when promised.
Putting oneself down ("Can you accept me?")	"I just couldn't take all the pressure from the constant travel, the competition, the need to always win and be number one. When they offered me the uppers, it seemed like the easiest thing to cope with all this. Now I need more and more of the stuff."	"Don't you know you could hurt yourself if you keep going like this?" "You'll get hurt from this—is it really a smart thing to do?"	"The pressure has gotten so intense it's hard to find a way out from under it."
Inconveniencing the helper ("Do you have consistent limits?")	"Can I use your phone again before we get started?"	"Of course, go ahead—feel free any time." "Absolutely not."	"Marc, the last two times I've seen you, you have started the session by asking to use my phone. When this happens, you and I don't have the full time to use for counseling. Would it be possible for you to make these calls before our session starts, or do we need to change our appointment time?"
Questioning the helper's motives ("Is your caring real?")	"I don't see how you have the energy to see me at the end of the day like this. You must be exhausted after seeing all the other people with problems, too."	"Oh, no, I'm really not." "Yes, I'm pretty tired."	"You're probably feeling unsure about how much energy I have left for you after seeing other people first. One thing about you that helps me keep my energy up is . . ."

1. **Requesting information (or "Can you understand and help me?").** Practitioners need to be alert to whether client questions are searches for factual information or for helper opinions and beliefs. Clients who ask questions like "Do you have children?" or "How long have you been married?" are probably looking for something in addition to the factual response. Most often, they are seeking verification from you that you will be able to understand, to accept, and to help them with their particular set of concerns.

2. **Telling a secret (or "Can I be vulnerable or take risks with you?").** Clients share secrets—very personal aspects of their lives—to test whether they can trust the helper to accept them as they really are, to keep their communications confidential, and to avoid exploiting their vulnerability after they have disclosed very personal concerns. Practitioners need to remember that clients who share secrets are really testing the waters to see how safe it is to self-disclose personal issues.

3. **Asking a favor (or "Are you reliable?").** Clients may ask helpers to perform favors that may or may not be appropriate. According to Fong and Cox (1983, p. 165),

"all requests of clients for a favor should be viewed, especially initially, as potential tests of trust." When clients ask you to lend them a book, or call their boss for them, whether you grant or deny the favor is not as important as how you handle the request and how reliably you follow through with your stated intentions. It is crucial to follow through on reasonable favors you have promised to do. For unreasonable favors, it is important to state tactfully but directly your reason for not granting the favor. Efforts to camouflage the real reason with an excuse or to grant an unreasonable favor grudgingly are just as damaging to trust as is failure to follow through on a favor (Fong & Cox, 1983, p. 165). Asking favors is generally an indication that the client is testing your reliability, dependability, honesty, and directness. A good guideline to follow is "Don't promise more than you can deliver, and be sure to deliver what you have promised as promised."

4. **Putting oneself down (or "Can you accept me?").** Clients put themselves down to test the helper's level of acceptance. This test of trust is designed to help clients determine whether the helper will continue to accept even the parts of them that clients view as bad, negative, or dirty. Often this test of trust is conveyed by

LEARNING ACTIVITY	**4.3**	**Trust**

Part One: Identification of Trust-Related Issues

With a partner or in a small group, develop responses to the following questions:

1. For clients belonging to the mainstream cultural group or from racial/cultural backgrounds similar to your own:

   a. How does trust develop during therapeutic interactions?

   b. How is trust violated during therapeutic interactions?

   c. How does it feel to have your trust in someone else violated?

   d. What are 10 things a helper can do (or 10 behaviors to engage in) to build trust? Of the 10, select 5 that are most important and rank these from 1 (*most critical, top priority to establish trust*) to 5 (*least critical or least priority to establish trust*).

2. Complete the same 4 questions listed above for clients of color or from a racial/cultural background distinctly different from your own.

Part Two: Client Tests of Trust

Listed below are six client descriptions. For each description, identify the content and the process reflected in the test of trust; then write an example of a helping response that could be used appropriately with this type of trust test. You may wish to refer to Table 4.1. The first item is completed as an example. Feedback is provided on page 86.

Example

1. The client asks whether you have seen other people who attempted suicide.

   a. Content: <u>Request for information</u>

   b. Process: <u>Can you understand and help me?</u>

   c. Helper response: <u>"Yes, I have worked with other persons before you who have thought life wasn't worth living. Perhaps this will help you know that I will try to understand what this experience is like for you and will help you try to resolve it in your own best way."</u>

2. The client's phone was disconnected, and the client wants to know whether he can come 10 minutes early to use your phone.

   a. Content: _____

   b. Process: _____

   c. Helper response: _____
   _____

3. The client wonders aloud whether you make enough money as a helper that you would choose this occupation if you had to do it over again.

   a. Content: _____

   b. Process: _____

   c. Helper response: _____
   _____

4. The client states that she must be stupid because she now has to repeat third grade while all the other kids in her class are going on to fourth grade.

   a. Content: _____

   b. Process: _____

   c. Helper response: _____
   _____

5. The client changed the appointment time at the last minute four times in the last several weeks.

   a. Content: _____

   b. Process: _____

   c. Helper response: _____
   _____

6. The client, an Asian American male college student, indicates he is hesitant to speak openly and feels constrained by his concern that his family and friends do not discover he is coming to a counselor. He wonders whom you will tell about his visit to you.

   a. Content: _____

   b. Process: _____

   c. Helper response: _____
   _____

statements or behaviors designed to shock the helper, followed by a careful scrutiny of the helper's verbal and nonverbal reactions. Helpers need to respond neutrally to client self-putdowns rather than condoning or evaluating the client's statements and actions.

5. **Inconveniencing the helper (or "Do you have consistent limits?").** Clients often test trust by creating inconveniences for the helper such as changing appointment times, canceling at the last minute, changing the location of sessions, or asking to make a phone call during the session. Practitioners need to respond directly and openly to the inconvenience, especially if it occurs more than once or twice. When the helper sets limits, clients may begin feeling secure and assured that the helper is dependable and consistent. Setting limits often serves a reciprocal purpose: the clients realize they also can set limits in the

FEEDBACK

Trust

Part Two: Client Tests of Trust

2. a. Content: Asking a favor
   b. Process: Are you reliable and open with me?
   c. Example response: "I know how difficult it can be to manage without a telephone. Unfortunately, I see someone almost up until the minute you arrive for your session, so my office is occupied. There's a pay phone in the outer lobby of the building if you find you need to make a call at a particular time."

3. a. Content: Questioning your motives
   b. Process: Do you really care, or are you just going through the motions?
   c. Example response: "Perhaps, Bill, you're feeling unsure about whether I see people like yourself for the money or because I'm sincerely interested in you. One way in which I really enjoy [value] working with you is. . . ."

4. a. Content: Putting oneself down
   b. Process: Can you accept me even though I'm not too accepting of myself right now?
   c. Example response: "You're feeling pretty upset right now that you're going to be back in the third grade

again. I wonder if you're concerned too about losing friends or making new ones?"

5. a. Content: Inconveniencing you
   b. Process: Do you have consistent limits?
   c. Example response: "Mary, I'm not really sure anymore when to expect you. I noticed you changed your appointment several times in the last few weeks at the last minute. I want to be sure I'm here or available when you do come in, so it would help if you could decide on one time that suits you and then just one backup time in case the first time doesn't work out. If you can give some advance notice of a need to change times, then I won't have to postpone or cancel out on you because of my schedule conflicts."

6. a. Content: Information request
   b. Process: Do you know enough about my cultural background and affiliation for me to be disclosive with you?
   c. Example response: "I understand you are concerned right now about how much you can safely tell me. I respect your wish to keep the visit here just between us."

---

relationship. As an example of this test of trust, consider the client who is repeatedly late to sessions. After three consecutive late starts, the helper mentions "You know, Gary, I've realized that the last three weeks we've got off to quite a late start. This creates problems for me because if we have a full session, it throws the rest of my schedule off. Or if I stop at the designated time, you end up getting shortchanged. Can we start on time, or do we need to reschedule the appointment time?"

6. **Questioning the helper's motives (or "Is your caring real?").** As we mentioned earlier, one aspect of trustworthiness is sincerity. Clients test this aspect of trust by statements and questions designed to answer the question "Do you really care about me, or is it just your job?" Clients may ask about the number of other clients the helper sees or how the helper distinguishes and remembers all his clients or whether the helper thinks about the client during the week (Fong & Cox, 1983). For instance, suppose a client says to her helping professional, "I bet you get tired of listening to people like me all the time." The practitioner may respond with something that affirms her interest in the client, such as "You're feeling unsure about your place here,

wondering whether I really care about you when I see so many other persons. Suzanne, from you I've learned . . ." (the helper then follows through with a personal statement directly related to this client).

Tests of Trust in Cross-Cultural Helping

Tests of trust may occur more frequently and with more emotional intensity in cross-cultural helping, often because clients from nondominant groups experienced or are experiencing oppression, discrimination, and overt and covert racism. As a result, these clients may feel more vulnerable in interpersonal interactions such as helping ones, which involve self-disclosure and an unequal power base. During initial helping interactions, clients with diverse backgrounds are likely to behave in ways that minimize their vulnerability and that maximize their self-protection (Sue & Sue, 2003). In U.S. culture, Euro-American helpers may be viewed automatically as members of the Establishment. As Stevenson and Renard (1993) note, "The dynamics of hostile race relations still exist in our society. It is crucial that therapists question whether these relations are played out in the therapeutic context. . . . [S]ensitivity to oppression issues allows for the building of credibility for psychotherapists which becomes of supreme

LEARNING ACTIVITY   **4.4**   **Transference and Countertransference**

In a small group or with a partner, discuss the likely transference and countertransference reactions you discover in these three cases. Feedback is provided on page 88.

1. The client is upset because you will not give her your home telephone number. She states that although you have a 24-hour on-call answering service, you are not really available to her unless you give her your home number.
2. You are an internship student, and your internship is coming to an end. You have been seeing a client for

weekly sessions during your year-long internship. As termination approaches, the client becomes more and more anxious and angry with you and states that you are letting her down by forming this relationship with her and then leaving.
3. Your client has repeatedly invited you to his house for various social gatherings. Despite all you have said to him about "multiple nonprofessional relationships," he says he still feels that if you really cared about him you would be at his parties.

importance to cross-cultural relationships, especially in the early stages" (pp. 433–434). A therapist's disregard for issues of oppression only fuels a minority client's "legacy of mistrust" (Stevenson & Renard, 1993). We take the position that it may be particularly unwise for clients to trust a helper *initially* until the helper behaviorally *demonstrates* trustworthiness and credibility—specifically until the helper shows that he or she (1) will not re-create an oppressive atmosphere of any kind in the helping interaction; (2) does not engage in discrimination, racist attitudes, and behaviors, and (3) has some understanding and awareness of the client's racial and cultural affiliation.

TRANSFERENCE AND COUNTERTRANSFERENCE: DYSFUNCTIONAL RELATIONAL SCHEMAS

In addition to the facilitative conditions and the working alliance, the helping relationship includes elements that represent what Horvath and Bedi (2002, p. 41) refer to as "still active components of past relationships that both the client and the therapist bring to the current encounter." Historically, dynamically oriented helpers have referred to these components as *transference* and *countertransference*. (See Learning Activity 4.4.) Current interpretations of these two concepts are rooted in what is known as a *relational* model of helping. In a relational model, the emphasis is on the interaction between the two people—for example, the client and the helper—not just on the client. In the helping process, both the helper and the client are seen as participants co-creating enactments that represent configurations of transference and countertransference (Ornstein & Ganzer, 2005, p. 571). Relational models use the term *dysfunctional relational schemas* to describe transferential and countertransferential notions.

Manifestations of Transference

Contemporary definitions of transference suggest that it has two components. One component is the client and the

client's past. As Corey, Corey, and Callanan (2007) suggest, from this perspective, transference is the client's unconscious (or out of awareness) shifting of feelings and fantasies that are reactions to significant others in the client's past onto the helper (p. 48). The second component of transference is the interpersonal dynamic between the helper and client. As Ornstein and Ganzer (2005) observe, from this perspective, transference involves the "here-and-now experience of the client with the therapist who has a role in eliciting and shaping the transference" (p. 567). As an example, a client may have been raised by a caregiver who was emotionally distant and unavailable to respond to the child's feelings. In therapy, the client may be reluctant to deal with feelings. When encouraged to do so by the helper, the client may react by becoming angry or withdrawn.

Transference tends to occur regardless of the gender of the helper (Kahn, 1991) and, according to Kohut (1984), may occur because old unmet needs of the client resurface in the presence of an empathic helper. For example, a recent qualitative study explored 11 dynamically oriented therapists and found that the content of client transference pertained to projections of the feared bad caregiver and the wished-for approving, good caregiver (Gelso, Hill, Mohr, Rochlen, & Zack, 1999). In addition, clients' transferential reactions can include any significant other, not just parents—such as siblings or anyone involved in an earlier and traumatic situation. Transference can be positive, negative, or mixed. A positive transference can strengthen the helping relationship when the practitioner provides missing elements of understanding, impartiality, and reliability (Levitt, Butler, & Hill, 2006, p. 318).

Often the transference (positive or negative) is a form of reenactment of the client's familiar and old pattern or template of relating. The value of it is that through the transference clients may be trying to show how they felt at an earlier time when treated in a particular way. Transference often occurs when the therapist (usually inadvertently) does or says something that triggers unfinished business with the client, often with members of the client's family of origin—parents and siblings or significant others. Helpers can make use of the transference, especially a negative one, by helping clients see that what they expect of us, they also may expect of other people in their lives. If, for example, a client wants to make the helper "look bad," that could be the client's intent with other individuals as well. A recent study (Hoglend et al., 2006) found that clients with troubled family-of-origin issues benefited more from therapy working with transference issues, lending support to the notion that transference is some form of reenactment of impaired object relations.

Management of Transference

Gelso and colleagues (1999) found five consistent ways in which helpers worked with client transference: focusing, interpreting, questioning, teaching, and self-disclosing. Here we describe these ways of managing the transference and offer example responses for each:

1. *Focusing on the immediate relationship*: "I am aware that you seem to be feeling pissed off with me in today's session, and I am wondering what that means."

2. *Interpreting the meaning of the transference:* "Perhaps your feelings of anger toward me are related to the frustration of having your dad be so unavailable for you. And now I am telling you that I will be unavailable during the next month when I have surgery."

3. *Using questions to promote insight:* "Can you recall an earlier time in your life when you felt angry like you do now with me?"

4. *Teaching, advising, and educating about the transference:* "We all have times when we transfer emotional reactions from prior relationships onto other people who are significant to us. Sometimes this occurs in our helping relationship as well. When it does, it is usually useful for us to process this in the session. As I am saying this, are you aware of any particular reactions you are having about me?"

5. *Self-disclosing*: "Sure, there are times for me too when I react to someone in my current life with some unresolved reactions from my past. Sometimes my partner says something that triggers such a response in me. Is this something you have noticed with your partner?"

Relational theorists also acknowledge a constructivist, narrative approach to working with client transference. Rather than responding to the client from an objective and detached position in which the client's reactions are analyzed and/or interpreted, the helper collaboratively works with the client to co-construct a number of different possible realities instead of one "true" interpretation of the client's experience (Ornstein & Ganzer, 2005). Also, as these authors note, what is potentially "transformative" in handling the transference is that the helper "must always view the client's perceptions as plausible given the client's history and lived experience" (p. 567). For example, Renata discloses that she felt disregarded by her mother when growing up and believed that her needs were not important to her mother. Although this statement represents some part of Renata's past experience, it would be wise to wonder aloud with Renata whether she has felt disregarded by the helper as well. Usually, as Teyber (2006) points out, there is "a kernel of truth" in the client's reactions toward the helper, which have in part been evoked by some aspect of the helper's behavior (p. 300).

A final way in which helpers can work with transference issues is by empathically reflecting on the client's desire or wish—for example, the wish to be loved, the wish to be important, and the wish to control. Often the transference acted out by the client not only includes a reenactment of an earlier important relationship but also a replay of how the client wishes it was (Kahn, 1991). With our client Renata in the example above, the helper may say something such as the following: "Renata, I know how hard it was for you to feel overlooked by your mother. I can see that you wish you had been more important to her." Further, using a relational model, the helper may comment on what the client wishes or desires from the helper. With Renata, the helper may say something like "Renata, I can see that in our work together it is important to you to be seen and heard and known accurately by me. Does this resonate with you as well?" Resolution of the transference process seems to occur with increased client insight, more realistic client expectations of the helper, and a more positive client view of himself or herself.

FEEDBACK
4.4   Transference and Countertransference

1. The transference is the client's emotional reaction to not having you available to her at all times. Possible countertransference reactions by you include frustration, anger, and feelings of failure.

2. The transference is the client's feeling of abandonment as termination approaches. Potential countertransference includes sadness, irritation, and pressure.

3. The transference is the client's expectation for you to be socially involved with him. Possible countertransference includes feelings of letting him down, being upset, and impatience.

Helms and Cook (1999) have made an important contribution to the discussion of transference by their suggestion that transference can be racial–cultural as well as parental. They note that helpers should attend to the client's perceptions of the helper's race and culture as part of the potential transferential relationship (p. 138):

> It may be difficult for the client to develop transference related to parents (however "parents" are defined) if racial transference develops as an overriding concern. Under such circumstances, the therapist may come to symbolize whatever past traumatic experiences or socialization—personal or vicarious—that the client or the client's salient identity groups have had with members of the therapist's racial or cultural group(s). Sometimes it is necessary to work through this racial–cultural transference before the more mundane issue of parental transference can even be expected to occur. (p. 138)

Racial–cultural transference may be a particularly salient issue when practitioners are unaware of engaging in behaviors toward clients that express or connote bias and constitute the acts of microaggression discussed earlier in this chapter. Sue et al. (2007) suggest that helpers need to discern and monitor acts of microaggression within the helping relationship in much the same way that we become aware of transference and countertransferential issues (p. 280).

Manifestations of Countertransference

Sheree, a beginning practicum student, finds herself working with Ronnie, a teenage boy who has been mandated to see a counselor. She has seen Ronnie for six sessions. She describes him as "nonresponsive." She states that he sits with his cap down over his eyes so he can't really look at her directly and that he responds with "I don't know" to her inquiries. Sheree feels more and more frustrated. She states that she has tried so hard to establish a good relationship with Ronnie but feels that everything she tries is useless. It seems that Ronnie has succeeded in challenging her need to be helpful to him, and she is finding herself becoming more impatient with him in the sessions. This is an example of countertransference.

Countertransference includes feelings and reactions the therapist has about the client. They may be realistic or characteristic responses, responses to transference, or responses to material and content that trouble the counselor (Kahn, 1991). As Kahn notes, a therapist's countertransference responses can be useful or damaging. He asserts that "at every moment deep characterological, habitual responses lie in wait, looking for an opportunity to express themselves as countertransference" (p. 121). Hurtful countertransference that comes from our own woundedness occurs when (1) we are blinded to an important area of exploration; (2) we focus on an issue more of our own than pertaining to the client; (3) we use the client for vicarious or real gratification; (4) we emit subtle cues that "lead" the client; (5) we make interventions not in the client's best interest, and, most important, (6) we adopt the roles the client wants us to play in his or her old script.

However, as contemporary relational theorists note, not all countertransferential reactions are damaging, problematic, or even undesirable. Countertransference can alert helpers to areas in which they feel stuck or puzzled, and as a result, helpers can begin to sort out what is going on rather than trying to "fix" the uncertainty (Ornstein & Ganzer, 2005). And in some situations it can even be helpful to self-disclose some of your countertransferential reactions in the client's presence as long as this is done without blame for the client and conveyed with respect and regard. In the preceding example, Sheree might find herself wanting to say something to Ronnie like the following: "You know, Ronnie, we have been working together now for about six weeks, and I feel like we are staying in the same place. I don't think we have moved backward, but I also don't think we have moved forward. I think we are just spinning our wheels in the same place, and I wish we could find some way to work together. I wish I could do or say something that would help you feel like coming to see me is worth it." This is a situation that requires much discernment, and for beginning helpers the decision to self-disclose needs to be talked through with a supervisor.

Management of Countertransference

Gelso and Hayes (2002) and Rosenberger and Hayes (2002) reviewed the research on countertransference and concluded that uncontrolled countertransference has an adverse effect on therapy outcome, although they acknowledged that this finding comes from more inferential than from direct empirical data. Regardless, managing countertransference is an important clinical task for practitioners (Gelso, Latts, Gomez, and Fassinger, 2002). In order for us as helpers to manage our countertransference responses therapeutically, we must become aware of what they are and what they mean to us. Gaining awareness is a useful initial step in managing countertransference. When we are unaware of our responses, they may get projected onto or acted out in the therapy session. For example, if Tia is unaware of her covert feelings of aggressiveness surrounding "helpless females," when she encounters a needy, dependent female client, she may behave in a way that conveys disrespect and dislike for the client.

Sometimes a sort of role reversal occurs, and the client is more aware of our own woundedness than we are. In these situations, the client unknowingly becomes the healer and the therapist inappropriately benefits, but the client's growth is stymied. For example, Ricardo may be unaware of his need to talk about himself, fueled by growing up with an inattentive and depressed caregiver. When meeting with his client Anna, she detects Ricardo's tendency to turn the focus onto himself during the session, and she provides support for him to do so!

Often a clue that we are having a countertransference reaction comes from our awareness of strong emotions such as we described in the case involving Sheree. Awareness of countertransference is also dependent on *self-insight*—that is, intentional attention to what is going on inside us (Gelso & Hayes, 2002, p. 277). One of the main reasons why, during and after training, helpers seek and receive individual and group consultation and supervision is that countertransference is inevitable and will occur throughout each helper's professional career. In Box 4.1 we present examples of interpersonal process notes derived from M. Marshak (personal communication, May 11, 1999) that you may find useful for developing awareness of your own reactions to clients. When consultation and supervision do not resolve a helper's reaction, a subsequent step in managing countertransference is to seek personal counseling. It is important for helpers-in-training to make a lifelong commitment to self-awareness. Consultation, supervision, and personal counseling are important components of the self-awareness process.

Being aware of our reactions is the important first step in managing countertransference. A second step is to develop what Gelso et al. (2002, p. 862) call *conceptual understanding*: hunches about what is occurring in the moment in the relationship with the client. This kind of understanding helps to prevent an automatic or reflexive response that may be counterproductive (Teyber, 2006, p. 282). For instance, Tia, in the earlier example, blurts out to a dependent female client, "Hannah, I am sure that you can figure this one out on your own." Alternatively, she may act out her covert aggression by terminating the session early or by being dismissive of the client's concerns. In acting or speaking thoughtlessly, she may inadvertently trigger a reenactment of her client's history—that is, a relational pattern that is similar to an unproductive pattern with a significant person in Hannah's past or current life. In this way, the client's transference may become evoked. For example, the client may feel dismissed by Tia in same way in which the client felt dismissed by her primary caregiver and by her partner and other significant people in her life. (This is an example of the way in which transference and countertransference are often related in the helping relationship.) This scenario points to a third step in the management of countertransference: The helper needs to be willing to examine and to take responsibility for his or her possible contributions to the issues that are emerging between the helper and client. At this point, Tia may say something to her client like the following: "Hannah, I feel like what I just said to you about

---

BOX 4.1   INTERPERSONAL PROCESS NOTES

During sessions, jot down your thoughts, feelings, intuitions, sensations, dreams.

How do feel when you're with this client?

How and where are you blocked with this client?

What is going on between the two of you?

What is going on inside of you when there is a blockage or an issue?

What keeps you from saying what you want to—what you feel?

What keeps you from sitting still and being silent?

How is your therapist activity maintaining the status quo—or moving the client?

What stops the flow in your session?

What disables you?

How is the client using you?

What are the client's expectations that "force" you into a certain mold or way of being with him or her?

What are you doing to the client—are you "forcing" him or her into a certain way of being with you?

What do your *imagination* and your *reveries* tell you about this client?

What symbols come to your mind to describe the process with this client? (Draw something.)

What about this client and session makes you come alive? Makes you "go dead"?

How are you afraid of disappointing the client?

What is lying behind the client's words?

How do you create reflective space in and around the session for both you and the client?

Where does "play" (in the best sense of the word) occur in this session?

Does the language you use reflect your own voice, or does it reflect more of a textbook voice?

What goes on in your body during this session with this client?

What do you do to be seen as an "ideal" person, to avoid carrying "a shadow"?

How are you taking care of yourself in this session with this client?

Source: Abridged from the presentation "The Person of the Analyst," by Mel Marshak, May 11, 1999, Pittsburgh Jung Society. Used with permission of Mel Marshak, PhD.

your concern may have sounded dismissive. I am sorry if this is so. Can you tell me what you experienced when you heard me say that?" Obviously, such a response requires a great deal of *empathy* from the helper. Empathic attunement, both to oneself and to the client, is a fourth step in managing countertransference (Gelso et al., 2002). When the helper's anxiety and/or shame get triggered, however, the helper is likely to respond defensively to the client and to perpetuate the transferential–countertransferential conflict, thus masking any empathy the helper may feel. For this reason, Gelso and colleagues mention *anxiety management* as another important step in managing countertransference.

The final step in managing both transference and countertransference is to develop and use boundaries. Gelso and Hayes (2002) refer to this step as "*self-integration*" and say that in the helping process it "manifests itself as a recognition of ego boundaries or an ability to differentiate self from other" (p. 297). When we are without boundaries in the helping process, we either let too much in from the client's transference reactions, or we send out too much from ourselves to the client, causing the client discomfort and pain. In the first case, we fail to protect ourselves; in the second, we fail to protect the client.

Both scenarios can be managed with the use of internal *protective* and *containing* boundaries (Mellody, 2003). A protective boundary allows you to hold yourself in high esteem even when a client is saying something negative to you. When a client expresses a negative transferential reaction, you can establish a protective boundary for yourself by asking yourself whether the client's reaction is true for you and whether you contributed to the reaction. If you did, it is important to take the client's reaction in and be responsive to it, while recognizing that it does not lessen your self-worth. Establishing a protective boundary is the not the same as walling yourself off. If you withdraw behind a wall of anger, preoccupation, silence, worry, sadness, and so on, nothing the client says or does reaches you (Mellody, 2003). Such a response is tantamount to being dismissive of the client's concern. Walling yourself off is appropriate only when a client is being clearly offensive to you, perhaps shouting an obscenity or a racial slur, and you cannot or choose not to leave (Mellody, 2003).

Protective boundaries are also important to empathic understanding. They allow you to feel the client's feelings without reacting to the feelings as if they belong to you. The containing boundary is what helps us avoid leaking our countertransferential reactions onto the client. Tia, for example, lacked a containing boundary and leaked her feelings of impatience to her client. When we do not have good containing boundaries, it is difficult to provide the sort of holding environment that our clients need, because we have difficulty containing emotional reactions.

Ruptures in the Relationship

At times, tears and ruptures occur in a helping relationship. These ruptures "highlight the tensions that are inherent in negotiating relationships with others" (Safran & Muran, 2000, p. 101). Indicators or markers of ruptures include the client's overt or indirect expressions of negative sentiments, disagreements about the goals or tasks of helping, and avoidance and nonresponsiveness (Safran, Muran, Wallner Samstag, & Stevens, 2002). Also, cross-racial tensions can result in relationship ruptures. As we mentioned earlier, when clients experience racial or other kinds of microaggressions, relationship ruptures are likely to occur.

Research on the effects of relationship ruptures is somewhat limited, but Safran et al. (2002) argue that because much data link the quality of the therapeutic alliance to outcome, the process of repairing relationship ruptures is, by inference, important. Ruptures provide indicators about times when the strength of the working alliance may have waned or instances when agreement on the therapeutic tasks and goals may have drifted.

Safran and Muran (2000) viewed ruptures as windows that let helpers see something about the client's interpersonal relationships (p. 85). Safran and Muran (2006) now describe relationship ruptures as "transference–countertransference enactments" by both the client and the therapist (p. 288). As they explain, clients often reenact an early, difficult, perhaps traumatic life experience and try to pull the helper into assuming a particular role that confirms the client's early experience (p. 85). When helpers allow themselves to get pulled into this role, ruptures result. When a rupture occurs, it can be repaired and begin to heal if the helper can recognize her or his contributions to the rupture and then acknowledge them directly to the client. This acknowledgment provides a new relational experience for the client and is a major way in which the therapeutic relationship becomes healing (Safran & Muran, 2000, p. 88)!

Safran and Muran (2002) distinguish between two types of ruptures in the therapeutic relationship: confrontation ruptures and withdrawal ruptures. In a *confrontation rupture*, the client deals directly with concerns about the relationship by confronting the helper. For example, Francine, the client, has been describing her history with her depressed and unavailable caregiver as well as current events with the same caregiver. Her helper emotionally retreats, shuts down, and does not validate her feelings about these experiences. As a result, Francine asks her practitioner directly why she seems so "nonresponsive."

In a *withdrawal rupture*, clients express their concern about the relationship by "withdrawing, deferring, or even complying" (Safran & Muran, 2006, p. 287). For example, the client, Tepe, has been describing his experiences of being sexually abused by a priest while growing up. Tepe's pain and sadness overwhelm his helper, who jumps in and tries to

TABLE 4.2	Interventions for Repairing Relationship Ruptures

Discuss the here-and-now relationship with your client as it is occurring in the session.
Invite and provide feedback on the therapeutic relationship.
Intentionally explore the client's experiences in therapy.
Attend carefully to the agreement, explicit and implicit, that you and the client make regarding the outcomes of treatment and the strategies designed to achieve these outcomes.
Take responsibility for your contribution to the relationship rupture.
Attend carefully to informed consent; provide a careful rationale for everything you do in the helping process.
Give the client time and space to express negative feelings about the relationship.
Allow the client an opportunity to reveal fears about expressing negative feelings to you.
Provide more positive feedback to the client.
Process issues related to transference.
Be aware of your own countertransference reactions, and seek consultation and supervision to process them.

Source: Harmon et al., 2005, p. 175; Safran et al., 2002, p. 252.

"fix" his feelings. Tepe's failure to show up for the next session signifies an intense withdrawal rupture.

What do those helpers do now about the ruptures? First, they examine their responses to their clients in their last session. This exploration may occur alone or in consultation with a colleague, a supervisor, or a personal therapist. When they realize their contribution to the rupture, they in some way take responsibility for it. When Francine confronts the helper about her nonresponsiveness, the helper addresses the experience directly, saying something like "You know, it's true. When you were talking about all those times your parent was not there for you, I realized that I went away from you and shut down, and in doing so, I also was not there for you. I am sorry about this." Helpers also can repair ruptures by empathizing with the client's experience of or reaction to the rupture (Safran & Muran, 2000, p. 102). For example,

Tepe's helper could say, "I can understand that in our last session I failed to really communicate my acceptance of your pain and sadness about the abuse. Instead I tried to think of a solution. This must have felt like I too was not there for you in some fundamental way because I tuned in to myself then instead of you. I apologize for my lapse."

In order to respond effectively to ruptures, we, as helpers, need to remain open to ourselves and to our own deepest feelings, both past and present, happy and difficult (Safran & Muran, 2000, p. 75). This process of staying open to ourselves requires us to find time or make space in our lives to stay attuned to ourselves and to feel our feelings. Activities such as meditating, deep breathing, movement, and body scans can assist in this process. For a list of additional ways to repair relationship ruptures, see Table 4.2. Learning Activity 4.5 presents guided imagery for working through relationship ruptures.

LEARNING ACTIVITY **4.5**   **Relationship Ruptures**

This activity uses guided imagery to deal with a rupture in a therapeutic relationship.

To complete this activity, go through each step in your imagination, or have a partner read the steps to you and close your eyes and go through each step; then trade roles with the partner.

1. Bring your attention to yourself. What are you currently experiencing?
2. Bring your attention to your breath. Breathe in peace, and breathe out tension.
3. When you feel ready, picture the last client you saw with whom there was some kind of tension or some breakdown in communication. If you are not yet seeing clients, picture some other person.
4. In your mind's eye, recall how you knew a rupture was going on in the relationship. What were the clues or cues?

5. In your mind's eye, focus on how you responded to the rupture.
6. What happened after your response? See and feel this.
7. Focus on anything you could have done or said to repair the rupture. See and feel this.
8. Bring your attention back to yourself and your breath, and notice how you are feeling now.
9. When you are ready, bring your energy back to the environment and the room, and open your eyes if they were closed.

If you are working with a partner, we suggest you process this imagery with that person. Otherwise, you can process it with yourself. What did you learn from this imagery about ruptures? From this activity can you take something into another relationship to help you repair a rupture? If so, what would it be?

CHAPTER SUMMARY

This chapter describes three major components of the helping relationship: the facilitative conditions of empathy, genuineness, and positive regard; the working alliance; and transference and countertransference. None of these components operates independently from the others, and during the course of therapy, they are connected to and influenced by one another. The three components also are, to some degree, affected by client variables such as type and severity of problem, gender, race, and cultural affiliation, because all helping relationships are also cross-cultural ones. These components contribute to both the effective process and the outcome of therapy and are considered important in all theoretical approaches to helping. In the last decade much empirical support for these aspects of the therapeutic relationship has emerged. As King (1998) observed, whatever else may happen in the helping process, the relationship between therapist and client is always present. One of the helper's biggest responsibilities is to attend to this relationship's quality and health. As a result, it is important to constantly revisit the quality of the working alliance during the helping process to ensure that the relationship is strong and that there is agreement about therapeutic goals and tasks.

REFERENCES

Berg, I., & Jaya, A. (1993). Different and same: Family therapy with Asian-American families. *Journal of Marital and Family Therapy, 19,* 31–38.

Bion, W. R. (1963). *Elements of psychoanalysis.* London: Heinemann.

Bohart, A. C., Elliott, R., Greenberg, L. S., & Watson, J. C. (2002). Empathy. In J. C. Norcross (Ed.)., *Psychotherapy relationships that work: Therapist contributions and responsiveness to patients* (pp. 89–108). New York: Oxford University Press.

Bordin, E. (1979). The generalizability of the psychoanalytic concept of the working alliance. *Psychotherapy: Theory, Research, and Practice, 16,* 252–260.

Brammer, L. M., Abrego, P. J., & Shostrom, E. L. (1993). *Therapeutic psychology: Fundamentals of counseling and psychotherapy* (6th ed.). Englewood Cliffs, NJ: Prentice Hall.

Carkhuff, R. R. (1969a). *Helping and human relations.* Vol.1: *Practice and research.* New York: Holt, Rinehart and Winston.

Carkhuff, R. R. (1969b). *Helping and human relations.* Vol. 2: *Practice and research.* New York: Holt, Rinehart and Winston.

Cashdan, S. (1988). *Object relations therapy: Using the relationship.* New York: Norton.

Comas-Diaz, L. (2006). Cultural variation in the therapeutic relationship. In C. D. Goodheart, A. E. Kazdin, & R. J. Sternberg (Eds.), *Evidence-based psychotherapy: Where practice and research meet* (pp. 81–105). Washington, D. C.: American Psychological Association.

Corey, G., Corey, M., & Callanan, P. (2007). *Issues and ethics in the helping professions* (7th ed.). Pacific Grove, CA: Brooks/Cole.

Cormier, S., & Hackney, H. (2008). *Counseling strategies and interventions* (7th ed.). Boston: Allyn & Bacon.

Egan, G. (2007). *The skilled helper* (8th ed.). Belmont, CA: Thomson–Brooks/Cole.

Farber, B. A., & Lane, J. S. (2002). Positive regard. In J. C. Norcross (Ed.)., *Psychotherapy relationships that work: Therapist contributions and responsiveness to patients* (4th ed., pp. 175–194). New York: Oxford University Press.

Fong, M. L., & Cox, B. G. (1983). Trust as an underlying dynamic in the counseling process: How clients test trust. *Personnel and Guidance Journal, 62,* 163–166.

Gelso, C. J., & Hayes, J. A. (2002). The management of countertransference. In J. C. Norcross (Ed.)., *Psychotherapy relationships that work: Therapist contributions and responsiveness to patients* (pp. 267–284). New York: Oxford University Press.

Gelso, C. J., Hill, C. E., Mohr, J., Rochlen, A., & Zack, J. (1999). Describing the face of transference: Psychodynamic therapists' recollections about transference in cases of successful long-term therapy. *Journal of Counseling Psychology, 46,* 257–267.

Gelso, C. J., Latts, M. G., Gomez, M. J., & Fassinger, R. E. (2002). Countertransference management and therapy outcome: An initial evaluation. *Journal of Clinical Psychology, 58,* 861–867.

Gladstein, G. (1983). Understanding empathy: Integrating counseling, development, and social psychology perspectives. *Journal of Counseling Psychology, 30,* 467–482.

Goldstein, A. P., & Higginbotham, H. N. (1991). Relationship-enhancement methods. In F. H. Kanfer & A. P. Goldstein (Eds.), *Helping people change* (4th ed., pp. 20–69). New York: Pergamon.

Greenson, R. (1967). *The technique and practice of psychoanalysis.* New York: International Universities Press.

Haaga, D. A. F., Rabois, D., & Brody, C. (1999). Cognitive behavior therapy. In M. Hersen & A. Bellack (Eds.), *Handbook of comparative interventions for adult disorders* (2nd ed., pp. 48–61). New York: Wiley.

Harmon, C., Hawkins, E. J., Lambert, M. J, Slade, K., & Whipple, J. L. (2005). Improving outcomes for poorly responding clients: The use of clinical support tools and feedback to clients. *JCLP/InSession, 61,* 175–185.

Helms, J., & Cook, D. (1999). *Using race and culture in counseling and psychotherapy.* Boston: Allyn & Bacon.

Hoffmann, M. L. (2000). *Empathy and moral development.* New York: Cambridge University Press.

Hoglend, P., Amlo, S., Marble, A., Bogwald, K.-P., Sorbye, O., Sjaastad, M. G., & Heyerdahl, O. (2006). Analysis of the patient–therapist relationship in dynamic psychotherapy: An experimental study of transference interpretations. *American Journal of Psychiatry, 163,* 1739–1746.

Horvath, A. O., & Bedi, R. P. (2002). The alliance. In J. C. Norcross (Ed.)., *Psychotherapy relationships that work: Therapist contributions and responsiveness to patients* (pp. 37–70). New York: Oxford University Press.

Ivey, A. E., D'Andrea, M., Ivey, M. B., & Simek-Morgan, L. (2002). *Counseling and psychotherapy: A multicultural perspective* (5th ed.). Boston: Allyn & Bacon.

Ivey, A. E., Gluckstern, N. B., & Ivey, M. B. (1993). *Basic attending skills* (3rd ed.). North Amherst, MA: Microtraining Associates.

Johnson, D. W. (2006). *Reaching out: Interpersonal effectiveness and self-actualization* (9th ed.). Boston: Allyn & Bacon.

Josselson, R. (1992). *The space between us: Exploring the dimensions of human relationships.* San Francisco: Jossey-Bass.

Kahn, M. (1991). *Between therapist and client: The new relationship.* New York: Freeman.

Kiesler, D. J. (1966). Some myths of psychotherapy research and the search for a paradigm. *Psychological Bulletin, 65,* 110–136.

King, J. (1998). Contact and boundaries: A psychology of relationship. *Proceedings of the United States Association of Body Process Conference,* pp. 267–272.

Klein, M. H., Kolden, G. G., Michels, J. L., & Chisholm-Stockard, S. (2002). Congruence. In J. C. Norcross (Ed.)., *Psychotherapy relationships that work: Therapist contributions and responsiveness to patients* (4th ed., pp. 195–216). New York: Oxford University Press.

Kohut, H. (1971a). *The analysis of the self.* New York: International Universities Press.

Kohut, H. (1971b). *The restoration of the self.* New York: International Universities Press.

Kohut, H. (1984). *How does analysis cure?* Chicago: University of Chicago Press.

LaFromboise, T., & Dixon, D. N. (1981). American Indian perception of trustworthiness in a counseling interview. *Journal of Counseling Psychology, 28,* 135–139.

Levitt, H., Butler, M., & Hill, T. (2006). What clients find helpful in psychotherapy: Developing principles for facilitating moment-to-moment change. *Journal of Counseling Psychology, 53,* 314–324.

Meador, B., & Rogers, C. (1984). Person-centered therapy. In R. J. Corsini (Ed.), *Current psychotherapies* (pp. 142–195). Itasca, IL: Peacock.

Mellody, P. (2003). *The intimacy factor.* New York: HarperCollins.

Miller, G. D., & Baldwin, D. C. (1987). Implications of the wounded-healer paradigm for the use of the Self in therapy. *Journal of Psychotherapy and the Family, 3,* 139–151.

Miller, S. D., Duncan, B. L., Sorrell, R., & Brown, G. S. (2005). The Partners for Change Outcome Management System. *Journal of Clinical Psychology/InSession, 61,* 199–208.

Norcross, J. C. (2002a). Empirically supported therapy relationships. In J. C. Norcross (Ed.)., *Psychotherapy relationships that work: Therapist contributions and responsiveness to patients* (pp. 3–16). New York: Oxford University Press.

Norcross, J. C. (Ed.). (2002b). *Psychotherapy relationships that work: Therapist contributions and responsiveness to patients.* New York: Oxford University Press.

Ornstein, E. D., & Ganzer, C. (2005). Relational social work: A model for the future. *Families in Society, 86,* 565–572.

Paulson, B., Truscott, D., & Stuart, J. (1999). Clients' perceptions of helpful experiences in counseling. *Journal of Counseling Psychology, 46,* 317–324.

Raskin, N., & Rogers, C. (1995). Person-centered therapy. In J. Corsini & D. Wedding (Eds.), *Current psychotherapies* (5th ed., pp. 128–161). Itasca, IL: Peacock.

Ridley, C. R., & Lingle, D. W. (1996). Cultural empathy in multicultural counseling: A multidimensional process model. In P. B. Pedersen & J. G. Draguns (Eds.), *Counseling across cultures* (4th ed., pp. 21–46). Thousand Oaks, CA: Sage.

Rogers, C. (1942). *Counseling and psychotherapy.* Boston: Houghton Mifflin.

Rogers, C. (1951). *Client-centered therapy.* Boston: Houghton Mifflin.

Rogers, C. (1957). The necessary and sufficient conditions of therapeutic personality change. *Journal of Consulting Psychology, 21,* 95–103.

Rogers, C. (1977). *Carl Rogers on personal power.* New York: Delacorte Press.

Rogers, C., Gendlin, E., Kiesler, D., & Truax, C. (1967). *The therapeutic relationship and its impact: A study of psychotherapy with schizophrenics.* Madison: University of Wisconsin Press.

Rosenberger, E. W., & Hayes, J. A. (2002). Therapist as subject: A review of the empirical countertransference literature. *Journal of Counseling and Development, 80,* 264–270.

Safran, J., & Muran, J. (2000). *Negotiating the therapeutic alliance: A relational treatment guide.* New York: Guilford Press.

Safran, J., & Muran, J. (2006). Has the concept of the therapeutic alliance outlived its usefulness? *Psychotherapy, 43,* 286–291.

Safran, J., Muran, J., Wallner Samstag, L., & Stevens, C. (2002). Repairing alliance ruptures. In J. C. Norcross (Ed.), *Psychotherapy relationships that work: Therapist contributions and responsiveness to patients* (235–254). New York: Oxford University Press.

Siegel, D. J. (2006). An interpersonal neurobiology approach to psychotherapy: Awareness, mirror neurons, and neural plasticity in the development of well-being. *Psychiatric Annals, 36,* 248–256.

Smith, D., & Fitzpatrick, M. (1995). Patient–therapist boundary issues. *Professional Psychology, 26,* 499–506.

Stevenson, H. C., & Renard, G. (1993). Trusting ole wise ones: Therapeutic use of cultural strengths in African-American families. *Professional Psychology, 24,* 433–442.

Sue, D. W., Capodilupo, C. M., Torino, G. C., Bucceri, J. M., Holder, A. M. B., Nadal, K. L., & Esquilin, M. (2007). Racial microaggressions in everyday life: Implications for clinical practice. *American Psychologist, 62,* 271–286.

Sue, D. W., & Sue, D. (2003). *Counseling the culturally diverse* (4th ed.). New York: Wiley

Tausch, R. (1990). The supplementation of client-centered communication therapy with other validated therapeutic methods: A client-centered necessity. In G. Lietaer, J. Rombauts, & R. Van Balen (Eds.), *Client-centered and experiential psychotherapy in the nineties* (pp. 447–455). Leuven, Belgium: Leuven University Press.

Teyber, E. (2006). *Interpersonal process in psychotherapy* (5th ed.). Belmont, CA: Thomson–Brooks/Cole.

Truax, C. B., & Mitchell, K. M. (1971). Research on certain therapist interpersonal skills in relation to process and outcome. In A. Bergin & S. Garfield (Eds.), *Handbook of psychotherapy and behavior change: An empirical analysis* (pp. 299–344). New York: Wiley.

Tursi, M. M., & Cochran, J. L. (2006). Cognitive–behavioral tasks accomplished in a person-centered relational framework. *Journal of Counseling and Development, 84,* 387–396.

Vocisano, C., Klein, D., Arnow, B., Rivera, C., Blalock, J., Rothbaum, B., et al. (2004). Therapist variables that predict symptom change in psychotherapy with chronically depressed outpatients. *Psychotherapy: Theory, Research, Practice, and Training, 41,* 255–265.

Weiss, J. (2002). Control-mastery theory. *Encyclopedia of Psychotherapy, I,* 1–5.

Weiss, J., Sampson, H., & Mount Zion Psychotherapy Research Group. (1986). *The psychoanalytic process: Theory, clinical observations, and empirical research.* New York: Guilford Press.

Wells, M., & Glickauf-Hughes, C. (1986). Techniques to develop object constancy with borderline clients. *Psychotherapy, 23,* 460–468.

Wickman, S. A., & Campbell, C. (2003). An analysis of how Carl Rogers enacted client-centered conversation with Gloria. *Journal of Counseling and Development, 81,* 178–184.

Winnicott, D. W. (1958). *The maturational processes and the facilitating environment.* New York: International Universities Press.

Woodman, M. (1993). The eternal feminine: Mirror and container. *New Dimensions, 20,* 8–13.

Yalom, I. D. (1980). *Existential psychotherapy.* New York: Basic Books.

Yang, Y-W., Davidson, M. M., Yakushko, O. F., Bielstein Savoy, H., Tan, J. A., & Bleier, J. K. (2003). The scale of ethnocultural empathy: Development, validation, and reliability. *Journal of Counseling Psychology, 50,* 221–234.

4   KNOWLEDGE AND SKILL BUILDER

Part One

According to Learning Outcome 1 for this chapter, you will be able to communicate the three facilitative conditions to a client, given a role-play situation. Complete this activity in triads, one person assuming the role of the helper, another the role of client, and the third the observer. The helper's task is to communicate the behavioral aspects of empathy, genuineness, and positive regard to the client. The client shares a concern with the helper. The observer monitors the interaction, using the accompanying Checklist for Facilitative Conditions as a guide, and provides feedback after completion of the session. Each role play can last 10–15 minutes. Switch roles so each person has an opportunity to play each of the three roles. If you do not have access to another person to serve as an observer, find someone with whom you can engage in a role-played helping interaction. Tape-record your interaction, and use the accompanying checklist as a guide to reviewing your tape.

Checklist for Facilitative Conditions

Helper _____

Observer _____

Instructions: Assess the helper's communication of the three facilitative conditions by circling the number and word that best represent the helper's overall behavior during this session.

Empathy

1. Did the helper indicate a desire to comprehend the client?

1	2	3	4
A little	Somewhat	A great deal	Almost always

2. Did the helper refer to the client's feelings?

1	2	3	4
A little	Somewhat	A great deal	Almost always

3. Did the helper discuss what appeared to be important to the client?

1	2	3	4
A little	Somewhat	A great deal	Almost always

4. Did the helper pace (match) the client's nonverbal behavior?

1	2	3	4
A little	Somewhat	A great deal	Almost always

5. Did the helper show understanding of the client's historical/cultural/ethnic background?

1	2	3	4
A little	Somewhat	A great deal	Almost always

6. Did the helper validate the client's experience?

1	2	3	4
A little	Somewhat	A great deal	Almost always

Genuineness

7. Did the helper avoid overemphasizing her or his role, position, and status?

1	2	3	4
A little	Somewhat	A great deal	Almost always

8. Did the helper exhibit congruence, or consistency, among feelings, words, nonverbal behavior, and actions?

1	2	3	4
A little	Somewhat	A great deal	Almost always

9. Was the helper appropriately spontaneous (for example, also tactful)?

1	2	3	4
A little	Somewhat	A great deal	Almost always

10. Did the helper demonstrate supporting nonverbal behaviors appropriate to the client's culture?

1	2	3	4
A little	Somewhat	A great deal	Almost always

Positive Regard

11. Did the helper demonstrate behaviors related to commitment and willingness to see the client (for example, starting on time, responding with appropriate intensity)?

1	2	3	4
A little	Somewhat	A great deal	Almost always

12. Did the helper respond verbally and nonverbally to the client without judging or evaluating the client?

1	2	3	4
A little	Somewhat	A great deal	Almost always

13. Did the helper convey warmth to the client with supporting nonverbal behaviors (soft voice tone, smiling, eye contact, touch) and verbal responses (enhancing statements)?

1	2	3	4
A little	Somewhat	A great deal	Almost always

Observer comments: _____

_____

_____

_____

_____

Part Two

Listed below are six tests of trust and six client descriptions. Match each test of trust with the corresponding client description (Learning Outcome 2). Feedback for Part Two follows on page 97.

4 KNOWLEDGE AND SKILL BUILDER

Test of Trust
  a. Information request
  b. Telling a secret
  c. Asking a favor
  d. Putting oneself down
  e. Inconveniencing the helper
  f. Questioning the helper's motives

Client Description

1. The client asks you whether you get "burned out" or fatigued talking to people with problems all day. The client also asks you how many clients are in your current caseload, whether you really have enough time to see everyone, and whether you would see someone for a reduced fee.
2. The client is very nondisclosive and reticent but finally tells you that she has been sexually abused by her stepfather and has never told anyone about this before.
3. The client asks to borrow a novel she sees on your desk.
4. The client presents with marital issues, and he wants to know whether you are married or single.
5. The client wants you to see him on the weekend because that would make it easier for him to get to the session.
6. The client says she considers herself a whore because she sleeps around a lot.

Part Three

Learning Outcome 3 asks you to identify issues related to transference and countertransference that might affect the development of the helping relationship, given four written case descriptions. Read each case carefully; then identify in writing the transference/countertransference issue that is reflected in the case description. Feedback follows below.

1. You are leading a problem-solving group in a high school. The members are spending a lot of time talking about the flak they get from their parents. After a while, they start to "get the leader" and complain about all the flak they get from you.
2. You are counseling a person of the other sex who is the same age as yourself. After several weeks of seeing the client, you feel extremely disappointed and let down when the client postpones the next session.
3. You find yourself needing to terminate with a client, but you are reluctant to do so. When the client presses you for a termination date, you find yourself overcome with sadness.
4. One of your clients is constantly writing you little notes and sending you cards basically saying what a wonderful person you are.

4 KNOWLEDGE AND SKILL BUILDER **FEEDBACK**

Part Two

  1. f. Questioning your motives to see whether you really care.
2. b. Telling you a secret, something she perhaps feels embarrassed about.
3. c. Asking you a favor—in this case, probably a reasonable one.
4. a. Requesting information overtly—but covertly wondering whether your personal life is together enough to help the client or whether you have enough significant life experiences similar to his own to help him.
5. e. Trying to inconvenience you to see whether you have limits and how you set and follow through on them.
6. d. Putting herself down by revealing some part of herself that she feels is "bad" and also something that will test your reaction to her.

Part Three

1. *Transference:* The group members seem to be transferring their angry feelings toward their parents onto you.
2. *Countertransference:* You are having an unusually intense emotional reaction to this client (disappointment), which suggests that you are developing some affectionate feelings for the client and countertransference is occurring.
3. *Countertransference:* Some emotional attachment on your part is making it hard for you to "let go" of this particular client (although termination usually does involve a little sadness for all parties).
4. *Transference:* The client is allowing herself to idealize you. At this point, the transference is positive, although it could change.

5

LISTENING RESPONSES

LEARNING OUTCOMES

After completing this chapter, you will be able to

1. From a written list of 12 example listening responses, accurately classify at least 9 of them by type: clarification, paraphrase, reflection, or summarization.
2. From a list of three client statements, write an example of each of the four listening responses for each client statement.
3. In a 15-minute helping interview in which you function as an observer, listen for and record five key aspects of client messages that the helper needs to attend to in order to ensure effective listening.
4. In a 15-minute role-play interview or a conversation in which you function as a listener, demonstrate at least two accurate examples of each of the four listening responses.

"Listening is the art by which we use empathy to reach across the space between us. . . . [G]enuine listening means suspending memory, desire, and judgment—and, for a few moments at least, existing for the other person" (Nichols, 1995, pp. 62, 64). Lindahl (2003) observes that true listening involves our "whole being" (p. 29). The all-encompassing nature of listening is depicted in the Chinese symbol for *listening* shown in Figure 5.1. In the upper left-hand side are squares that represent two ears. Squares in the upper right-hand side represent two eyes. Underneath the "eye" squares is a line that represents "undivided attention," and in the lower right-hand side of the symbol is a curved line that represents the heart. As Lindahl (2003) notes, this symbol "indicates that listening is more than hearing words; it encompasses our ears, eyes, undivided attention, and heart" (p. 29).

THREE STEPS OF LISTENING

Listening is a prerequisite for all other helping responses and strategies. Listening should precede whatever else is done. When a helper fails to listen, the client may be discouraged

from self-exploring, the wrong issue may be discussed, or a strategy may be proposed prematurely.

Listening involves three steps: receiving a message, processing a message, and sending a message (see Figure 5.2). Each client message (verbal or nonverbal) is a stimulus to be received and processed by the helper. When a client sends a message, the helper receives it. Reception of a message is a covert process—that is, we cannot see how or what the helper receives. Failure to receive the entire message may occur when the helper stops attending. Reception of a message may be thought of as *contemplative listening* (Lindahl, 2003). A prerequisite for contemplative listening is the ability to be silent! Interestingly enough, the letters that spell LISTEN also spell SILENT (Lindahl, 2003). When we are truly silent, we are not focused on what we are going to say next. Instead, we are creating space for ourselves to receive a message and for clients to send a message. Unfortunately because our world is so noisy, true silence is uncomfortable for many of us and must be cultivated with daily practice. Turning off cell phones and pagers and sitting silently with oneself for a few minutes a day is a great way to develop contemplative listening skills.

Once a message is received, it must be processed in some way. Processing, like reception, is covert: it goes on within the helper's mind and is not visible to the outside world—except, perhaps, from the helper's nonverbal cues. Processing includes thinking about the message and pondering its meaning. Processing is important because a helper's cognitions, self-talk, and mental (covert) preparation and visualization set the stage for overt responding (Morran, Kurpius, Brack, & Brack, 1995). Errors in message processing often occur when helpers' biases or blind spots prevent them from acknowledging parts of a message or from interpreting a message without distortion. Helpers may hear what they want to hear instead of the actual message sent. Processing a message may be thought of as *reflective listening* (Lindahl, 2003). In reflective listening, we are listening to ourselves and focusing our attention inward in order to develop sensitivity to our internal voice. How do we cultivate reflective listening? Like achieving the silence of contemplative

Ear

Eyes

Undivided
Attention

Heart

Figure 5.1 Chinese symbol for *listening*

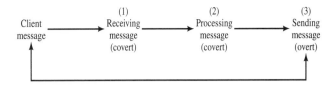

Figure 5.2 Three steps of listening

listening, reflective listening also requires practice. Lindahl (2003) recommends taking a few breaths before responding to a client's message and then, after the breaths, asking oneself, "What wants to be said next?" (instead of "What do *I* want to say?") (p. 32).

The third step of listening involves the verbal and nonverbal messages sent by a helper. Sometimes a helper may receive and process a message accurately but have difficulty sending a message because of lack of skills. Fortunately, you can learn to use listening responses to send messages. When sending messages back to our clients, we are engaging in listening that is *connective*—that is, listening that in some way connects us with our clients (Lindahl, 2003).

This chapter is intended to help you acquire four verbal listening responses that you can use to send messages to a client: clarification, paraphrase, reflection, and summarization. Such responses convey that you are listening to and understanding client messages. Understanding what any client says can be hard. When you are working with clients who are culturally different from you, understanding may be even more challenging because of cultural nuances in communication and expression. As Sue and Sue (2003) note, "While breakdowns in communication often happen between members who share the same culture, the problem becomes exacerbated between people of different racial or ethnic backgrounds" (p. 101).

THE IMPORTANCE OF CLIENTS' STORIES

Ivey, Ivey, and Simek-Morgan (1997) note that listening by the helper helps to bring out the client's story. Listening is healing because it encourages clients to tell their stories. Clients' stories are narratives about their lives and current experiences. From these narratives clients construct their identities and infuse their lives with meaning and purpose (White & Epston, 1990). A good therapist listens to these accounts to help the client recognize how they construct meaning and whether they help or hurt the development of the client's identity. Telling one's own story can also provide emotional relief to a client who has suffered trauma, even a client who is very young or old (Terr, 1990). Stories

provide a way for clients who are suffering from loss—such as a separation or divorce, loss of a job, or death of a significant other—to make sense of the loss (Sedney, Baker, & Gross, 1994). For clients who are dying, stories can bring a sense of closure and also feelings of liberation. Healing is particularly evident if clients describe for the first time "hidden difficulties" or "shame" (Ostaseski, 1994). Each time a story is told, something new is learned, a wound is healed, another part of the story is remembered, or the story teller gains new insight (Lindahl, 2003).

Stories are almost universally present and relevant in various ethnic cultural groups. Helpers need to tune in to many aspects of clients' stories. Ivey and colleagues (1997) recommend listening for the *facts* of the story, for the client's *feelings* about the story, and for the way in which the client *organizes* the story. Sedney and colleagues (1994) recommend listening for how the story is started, for the sequences in the story, and for "hints of anger, regret, and what ifs," as well as for the client's understanding of the story and the role the client plays in it (p. 291). Significant omissions also may provide clues. Ostaseski (1994) comments that helpers must simply trust that some insight will arise for clients just from the telling of the story: "Often the story will deliver what is needed. So pay close attention to whatever you are presented with. Start with that. Take it. Believe it, and see where it leads you" (p. 11).

WHAT DOES LISTENING REQUIRE OF HELPERS?

When someone truly hears us, it is a special gift. We can all recall times when we felt wonderful simply because someone who means something to us stood or sat with us and really listened. Conversely, we also can remember instances in which we felt frustration because someone close to us was inattentive and distracted. Nichols (1995) has referred to listening as a "lost art" because of time pressures that shorten our attention span and impoverish the quality of listening in our lives (p. 2). Lindahl (2003) observes that many of us, including high-powered executives, engage in a great deal of preparation prior to speaking but less than 5 percent of us do a similar amount of preparation prior to listening. This lack of listening can undermine our most prized relationships, contribute to interpersonal conflict, and leave us with a sense of loss. Nichols (1995) observes that this loss is most severe when lack of listening occurs in relationships in which we count on the listener to pay attention, such as in a helping relationship.

In this chapter, we describe four listening responses—clarification, paraphrase, reflections, and summarization—that will help you become a good listener if you learn them. Truly effective listening, however, requires even more from you. It requires you to be fully present to the client and oblivious to distractions—both internal and external. It requires you to create a "holding environment" for clients. The helpers who listen best usually have developed this sort of "mindfulness." They are able to focus very intently on the client. Such mindfulness is especially well developed in Eastern cultures, where people rise at dawn to practice tai chi. Perhaps nowhere is this quality more evident than among helpers who work with dying persons. Ostaseski (1994), director of the San Francisco Zen Hospice Project, discusses mindfulness in the following way:

> We sit at the bedside and we listen. We try to listen with our whole body, not just with our ears. We must perpetually ask ourselves, "Am I fully here? Or am I checking my watch or looking out the window?"
>
> At the heart of it, all we can really offer each other is our full attention. When people are dying, their tolerance for bullshit is minimal. They will quickly sniff out insincerity. Material may arise that we don't particularly like or even strongly dislike. Just as we do in meditation, we need to sit still and listen, not knowing what will come next, to suspend judgment—at least for the moment—so that whatever needs to evolve will be able to do so. (p. 11)

If you feel that mindfulness is a quality you need to develop further in yourself, we encourage you to practice Learning Activity 5.1, adapted from Kabat-Zinn (1993), on a daily basis.

FOUR LISTENING RESPONSES

This chapter is about four listening responses: clarification, paraphrase, reflection, and summarization. *Clarification* begins with a question, often posed after an ambiguous client message. It starts with "Do you mean that" or "Are you saying that" followed by a repetition or rephrasing of all or part of the client's previous message. *Paraphrase* is a rephrasing of the content part of a message—the part that describes a situation, event, person, or idea. *Reflection* is a rephrasing of the client's feelings, or the affect part of the message—the part that reveals the client's feelings about the content. For example, a client may feel discouraged (affect) about not doing well in a class (content). *Summarization* is an extension of the paraphrase and reflection responses; it is a tying together and rephrasing of two or more parts of a message or messages.

To illustrate these four listening responses, here is a client message followed by an example of each response:

Client, a 35-year-old Latina widow, mother of two young children: My whole life fell apart when my husband died. I keep feeling so unsure about my ability to make it on my own and to support my kids. My husband always made all the decisions for me and brought home money every week. Now I haven't slept well for so long, and I'm drinking more heavily—I can't even think straight. My relatives help me as much as they can, but I still feel scared.

Helper clarification: Are you saying that one of the hardest things facing you now is to have enough confidence in yourself?

Helper paraphrase: Since your husband's death you have more responsibilities and decisions on your shoulders, even with the support of relatives.

LEARNING ACTIVITY **5.1** | **Cultivating the Listening Mind**

Part One

Obtain three small objects to eat, such as raisins or M&Ms. Sit in a comfortable position, close your eyes, and focus on your teeth. If wandering thoughts come, let them flow by. Starting with one raisin, slowly lift it to your mouth. Chew it very slowly. Observe your arm lifting the raisin to your mouth. . . . Think about how your hand holds it. . . . Notice how it feels in your mouth. . . . Savor it as you chew it ever so slowly. While doing this, notice your tongue and throat as you very slowly swallow the raisin.

Repeat this process with the next two objects. Afterward, notice what you realize about eating and raisins. What do you usually tune out?

Part Two

Lie still in a comfortable position. Scan your body, starting with your toes and moving very slowly up to the top of your head. Direct your attention to the spot that feels most tense or painful. Put your hand on that spot. Leave it there for a few minutes. Breathe with it. Notice what happens as you go into this part of your body with your breathing and your awareness. You are not trying to change anything. Simply be aware of this place and accept it. Stay with this for a little while, and see what happens to this spot.

Response	Definition	Intended Purpose

TABLE 5.1 Definitions and Intended Purposes of Listening Responses

Response	Definition	Intended Purpose
Clarification	A question beginning with, for example, "Do you mean that" or "Are you saying that" followed by a rephrasing of the client's message	1. To encourage more client elaboration 2. To check out the accuracy of what you heard the client say 3. To clear up vague, confusing messages
Paraphrase (responding to content)	A rephrasing of the content of the client's message	1. To help the client focus on the content of his or her message 2. To highlight content when attention to feelings is premature or self-defeating
Reflection (responding to feelings)	A rephrasing of the affect part of the client's message	1. To encourage the client to express more of his or her feelings 2. To help the client become more aware of the feelings that dominate him or her 3. To help the client acknowledge and manage feelings 4. To help the client discriminate accurately among feelings 5. To help the client feel understood
Summarization	Two or more paraphrases or reflections that condense the client's messages or the session	1. To tie together multiple elements of client messages 2. To identify a common theme or pattern 3. To interrupt excessive rambling 4. To review progress

Helper reflection: You feel worried about having to shoulder all the family responsibilities now.

Helper summarization: Now that your husband has died, you're facing a few things that are very difficult for you right now . . . handling the family responsibilities, making the decisions, trying to take better care of yourself, and dealing with fears that have come up as a result.

Table 5.1 presents definitions and lists the *intended* or hypothesized purposes of the four listening responses. These responses may not produce the same results with all clients. For example, a practitioner may find that reflecting feelings prompts some clients to discuss feelings but that other clients do not even acknowledge the counselor's statement (Uhlemann, Lee, & Martin, 1994). Our point is that we are presenting some "modal" intentions for each listening response; there are exceptions. The listening responses will achieve their intended purposes most of the time. However, other dynamics within an interview may give rise to different client outcomes. Moreover, the effects of these verbal messages may vary because of nonverbal cues that accompany the message. It is helpful to have some rationale in mind for using a response. However, always remember that the effect a response has on the client may not be what you intended to achieve. The guidelines in Table 5.1 should be used tentatively, *subject to modification by particular client reactions.*

In the next three sections we describe the listening responses and present model examples of each response. Opportunities for you to practice each one and receive feedback follow the examples.

THE CLARIFICATION RESPONSE: LISTENING FOR ACCURACY

Because most messages are expressed from the speaker's internal frame of reference, they may seem vague or confusing to the listener. Messages that are particularly likely to be confusing are those that include inclusive terms (*they* and *them*), ambiguous phrases (*you know*), and words with a double meaning (*stoned, trip*). When you aren't sure of the meaning of a message, it is helpful to clarify it. According to Hutchins and Cole-Vaught (1997), a clarification asks the client to elaborate on "a vague, ambiguous, or implied statement." The request for clarification is usually expressed as a question and may begin with phrases such as "Are you saying this" or "Could you try to describe that" or "Can you clarify that."

Purposes of Clarification

Clarification may be used to make the client's previous message explicit and to confirm the accuracy of your perceptions about the message. Clarification is appropriate whenever you aren't sure whether you understand the client's message and you need more elaboration. A second purpose of clarification is to check out what you heard of the client's message. Particularly in the beginning stages of helping, it is important to verify client messages instead of jumping to conclusions. The following example may help you see the value of the clarification response:

Client: Sometimes I just want to get away from it all.

Helper: It sounds like you have to split and be on your own.

Client: No, it's not that. I don't want to be alone. It's just that I wish I could get out from under all this work I have to do.

In that example, the helper drew a quick conclusion about the initial client message that turned out to be inaccurate.

The session might have gone more smoothly if the helper had requested clarification before assuming something about the client, as in this example:

Client: Sometimes I just want to get away from it all.

Helper: Could you describe for me what you mean by "getting away from it all"?

Client: Well, I just have so much work to do—I'm always feeling behind and overloaded. I'd like to get out from under that miserable feeling.

In that case, the clarification helped both persons to establish exactly what was being said and felt. Neither the client nor the helper had to rely on assumptions and inferences that were not explored and confirmed.

A skilled helper uses clarification responses to determine the accuracy of messages as they are received and processed. Otherwise, inaccurate information may not be corrected, and distorted assumptions may remain untested.

Steps in Clarifying

There are four steps in clarifying for accuracy. First, identify the content of the client's verbal and nonverbal messages. Ask yourself, "What has the client told me?" Second, identify any vague or confusing parts of the message that you need to check out for accuracy or elaboration. Third, decide on an appropriate beginning, or sentence stem, for your clarification, such as "Could you describe," "Could you clarify," or "Are you saying." In addition, use your voice to deliver the clarification as a question, not a statement. Fourth, remember to assess the effectiveness of your clarification by listening to and observing the client's response. If your clarification is useful, the client will elaborate on the ambiguous or confusing part of the message. If it is not useful, the client will clam up, ignore your request for clarification, and/or continue to make deletions or omissions. At this point, you can attempt a subsequent clarification or switch to an alternative response.

To decide whether to use clarification, to formulate this response, and to assess its effectiveness, consider the following cognitive learning strategy:

1. What has this client told me?
2. Are there any vague parts or missing pictures in the message that I need to check out? If so, what? If not, I need to decide on another, more suitable response.
3. How can I hear, see, or grasp a way to start this response?
4. How will I know whether my clarification is useful?

Notice how the helper applies this cognitive learning strategy to clarify the client's message in the second example above:

Client: Sometimes I just want to get away from it all.

Helper: [asks and answers covertly]

Self-question 1: What has this client told me?
That she wants to get away from something.

Self-question 2: Are there any vague parts or missing pictures in her message? If so, what? (If not, I'll decide on a more suitable response.)
Yes—I need to check out what she means by "getting away from it all."

Self-question 3: How can I begin a clarification response?
I can see the start of it, hear the start of it, or grasp the start of it. Something like "Well, could you tell me, or could you describe. . . ."

Self-question 4: How will I know that the response will be helpful?
I'll have to see, hear, and grasp whether she elaborates or not. Let's try it. . . .
At this juncture, the helper's covert visualization or self-talk ends, the helper addresses the client, and the client responds:

Helper clarification: Could you describe for me what you mean by "getting away from it all"?

Client response: Well, I just have so much work to do—I'm always feeling behind and overloaded. I'd like to get out from under that miserable feeling.

From the client's response, the helper can determine that the clarification was effective because the client elaborated and added the parts or pictures missing from her previous message. The helper can covertly congratulate himself or herself for not jumping ahead too quickly and for taking the time to check out the client's omission and the resulting ambiguity.

Learning Activity 5.2 gives you an opportunity to try this cognitive learning strategy to develop the skill of clarification.

PARAPHRASE AND REFLECTION: LISTENING FOR UNDERSTANDING

The practitioner needs to listen for information revealed in messages about significant situations and events in the client's life—and for the client's feelings about these events. Ivey and colleagues (1997) talk about this as listening for the main facts of the client's story and for the client's feelings about his or her story. Each client message expresses (directly or indirectly) some information about client situations or concerns and about client feelings. The portion of the message that expresses information or describes a situation or event is called the *content,* or cognitive part, of the message.

LEARNING ACTIVITY **5.2**	**Clarification**

 In this activity, you are presented with three client practice messages.* For each message, develop an example of a clarification response, using the cognitive learning strategy described earlier and outlined in the following example. To internalize this learning strategy, you may wish to talk through these self-questions overtly (aloud) and then covertly (silently to yourself). The end product will be a clarification response that you can say aloud or write down. An example precedes the three practice messages. Feedback is provided on page 104.

Example

Client, a 15-year-old high school student: My grades have really slipped. I don't know why; I just feel so down about everything.

Self-question 1: *What has this client told me?*
That she feels down and rather discouraged.
Self-question 2: *Are there any vague parts or missing pictures to the message that I need to check out? If so, what? (If not, decide on a different response.)*
Yes, several—one is what she feels so down about. Another is what this feeling of being down is like for her.
Self-question 3: *How can I hear, see, or grasp a way to start this response?*
"Are you saying there's something specific?" or "Can you describe this feeling. . . ?"
Self-question 4: *How will I know whether my clarification is useful?*
Say aloud or write an actual clarification response:
"Are you saying there is something specific you feel down about?" or "Could you describe what this feeling of being down is like for you?"

Client Practice Messages

Client 1, a fourth-grader: I don't want to do this dumb homework anyway. I don't care about learning these math problems. Girls don't need to know this anyway.
Self-question 1: *What has this client told me?*
Self-question 2: *Are there any vague parts or missing pictures I need to check out? If so, what?*

Self-question 3: *How can I hear, see, or grasp a way to start my response?*
Actual clarification response: _____

_____

_____

Client 2, a middle-aged man: I'm really discouraged with this physical disability now. I feel like I can't do anything the way I used to. Not only has it affected me in my job, but at home. I just don't feel like I have anything good to offer anyone.

Self-question 1: *What has this client told me?*
Self-question 2: *Are there any vague parts or missing pictures I need to check out? If so, what?*
Self-question 3: *How can I hear, see, or grasp a way to start my response?*
Actual clarification response: _____

_____

_____

Client 3, an older person: The company is going to make me retire even though I don't want to. What will I do with myself then? I find myself just thinking over the good times of the past, not wanting to face the future at all. Sometimes retirement makes me so nervous I can't sleep or eat. My family suggested I see someone about this.

Self-question 1: *What has this client told me?*
Self-question 2: *Are there any vague parts or missing pictures I need to check out? If so, what?*
Self-question 3: *How can I hear, see, or grasp a way to start my response?*
Actual clarification response: _____

_____

_____

The cognitive part of a message includes references to a situation or event, people, objects, or ideas. Another portion of the message may reveal how the client feels about the content; the expression of feelings or an emotional tone is called the *affective* part of the message (Cormier & Hackney, 2008). Generally, the affective part of the verbal message is distinguished by the client's use of an affect or feeling word, such as *happy,* *angry,* or *sad.* However, clients may also express their feelings in less obvious ways, particularly nonverbal behaviors.

The following illustrations may help you distinguish between the content and affective parts of a client's verbal message:

Client, a 6-year-old first-grader: I don't like school. It isn't much fun.

FEEDBACK

5.2   Clarification

 Client 1

Question 1. *What did the client say?*

That she doesn't want to do her math homework—that she thinks it's not important for girls.

Question 2. *Are there any vague parts or missing pictures?*

Yes—whether she really doesn't care about math or whether she's had a bad experience with it and is denying her concern.

Question 3. *How can I see, hear, or grasp a way to start my response?*

Examples of Clarification Responses

"Are you saying that. . . ?"

"Are you saying that you really dislike math or that it's not going as well for you as you would like?"

"Are you saying that math is not too important for you or that it is hard for you?"

Client 2

Question 1. *What did the client say?*

That he feels useless to himself and others.

Question 2. *Are there any vague parts or missing pictures?*

Yes—it's not clear exactly how things are different for him now and also whether it's the disability itself that's bothering him or its effects (inability to get around, reactions of others, and so on).

Question 3. *How can I see, hear, or grasp a way to start my response?*

Examples of Clarification Responses

"Could you clarify. . . ?"

"Could you clarify exactly how things are different for you now from the way they used to be?"

"Are you saying you feel discouraged about having the disability—or about the effects and constraints from it?"

"Are you saying you feel differently about yourself now from the way you used to?"

Client 3

Question 1. *What did the client say?*

He is going to have to retire because of company policy. He doesn't want to retire now and feels upset about this. He's here at his family's suggestion.

Question 2. *Are there any vague parts or missing pictures?*

Yes—he says he feels nervous, although from his description of not eating and sleeping it may be sadness or depression. Also, is he here only because his family sent him or because he feels a need too? Finally, what specifically bothers him about retirement?

Question 3. *How can I hear, see, or grasp a way to start my response?*

Examples of Clarification Responses

"Could you describe. . . ?"

"Would you say you're feeling more nervous or more depressed about your upcoming retirement?"

"Are you saying you're here just because of your family's feelings or because of your feelings too?"

"Could you describe what it is about retiring that worries you?"

The first sentence ("I don't like school") is the affective part of the message. The client's feelings are suggested by the words "don't like." The second sentence ("It isn't much fun") is the content part of the message because it refers to a situation or an event in this child's life—not having fun at school.

Here is another example:

Client, a 20-year-old woman: How can I tell my boyfriend I want to break off our relationship? He will be very upset. I guess I'm afraid to tell him.

In that example, the first two sentences are the content because they describe the situation of wanting to break off a relationship. The third sentence, the affective part, indicates

the client's feelings about this situation—being *afraid* to tell the boyfriend of her intentions.

See whether you can distinguish between the content and affective parts of the next two client messages:

Client 1, a young man: I can't satisfy my partner sexually. It's very frustrating for me.

In that example, the content part is "I can't satisfy my partner sexually." The affective part, or Client 1's feelings about the content, is "It's very *frustrating* for me."

Client 2, an institutionalized man: This place is a trap. It seems like I've been here forever. I'd feel much better if I weren't here.

In that example, Client 2's statements referring to the institution as a trap and being there forever are the content parts of the message. The statement of "feeling better" is the affective part.

The skilled helper tries to listen for both the content and the affective parts of client messages because it is important to deal both with significant situations or relationships and with the client's feelings about the situations. Responding to cognitive or affective messages will direct the focus of the session in different ways. At some points, the helper will respond to content by focusing on events, objects, people, or ideas. At other times, the helper will respond to affect by focusing on the client's feelings and emotions. Generally, the helper can respond to content by using a paraphrase and can respond to affect with a reflection.

Paraphrasing

A paraphrase is a rephrasing of the client's primary words and thoughts. Paraphrasing requires selective attention to the content part of the message and translating the client's key ideas into *your own words*. An effective paraphrase does more than just parrot the words of the client. The rephrase should be carefully worded to lead to further discussion or to increased understanding by the client. It is helpful to stress the most important words and ideas expressed by the client.

Consider this example:

Client: I know it doesn't help my depression to sit around or stay in bed all day.

Helper: You know you need to avoid staying in bed or sitting around all day to help your depression.

The helper merely parroted the client's message. The likely outcome is that the client may respond with a minimal answer such as "I agree" or "That's right" and not elaborate further, or that the client may feel ridiculed by what seems to be an obvious or mimicking response. Here is a more effective paraphrase: "You are aware that you need to get up and move around in order to minimize being depressed."

Purposes of Paraphrasing

The paraphrase serves several purposes in client interactions. First, the paraphrase tells clients that you have understood their communication. If your understanding is complete, clients can expand or clarify their ideas. Second, paraphrasing can encourage client elaboration of a key idea or thought. Clients may talk about an important topic in greater depth. A third reason for using the paraphrase is to help the client focus on a particular situation or event, idea, or behavior. Sometimes, by increasing focus, paraphrasing can help get a client on track. For example, accurate paraphrasing can help stop a client from merely repeating a "story" (Ivey & Ivey,

2007). A fourth purpose is to help clients who need to make decisions. As Ivey and Ivey (2007) observe, paraphrasing is often helpful to clients who have a decision to make, for the repetition of key ideas and phrases clarifies the essence of the problem. Paraphrasing to emphasize content is also useful if attention to affect is premature or counterproductive.

Steps in Paraphrasing

There are five steps in paraphrasing content. First, attend to and recall the message by restating it to yourself covertly. Ask yourself, "What has the client told me?" Second, identify the content part of the message by asking yourself, "What situation, person, object, or idea is discussed in this message?" Third, select an appropriate beginning, or sentence stem, for your paraphrase. Paraphrases can begin with many possible sentence stems. See Table 5.2 for a list of phrases and sentence stems useful for beginning paraphrase and reflection responses.

Fourth, using the sentence stem you selected, translate the key content or constructs into your own words, and express the key content in a paraphrase that you can say aloud. Remember to use your voice so that the paraphrase sounds like a statement, not a question. Fifth, assess the effectiveness of your paraphrase by listening to and observing the client's response. If your paraphrase is accurate, the client will in some way—verbally and/or nonverbally—confirm its accuracy and usefulness.

Consider the following example of the way a helper uses the cognitive learning strategy to formulate a paraphrase:

Client, a 40-year-old Asian American woman [says in a level, monotone voice]: How can I tell my husband I want a divorce? He'll think I'm crazy. I guess I'm just afraid to tell him.

Helper: [asks and answers covertly]

TABLE 5.2	Phrases and Sentence Stems to Introduce Paraphrase and Reflection Responses

It seems like
It appears as though
From my perspective
As I see it
I see what you mean
It looks like
Sounds like
As I hear it
What you're saying is
I hear you saying
Something tells you
You're telling me that
You feel
From my standpoint
I sense that
I have the feeling that

Self-question 1: What has this client told me?
That she wants a divorce and she's afraid to tell her husband because he will think she's crazy.

Self-question 2: What is the content of this message—what person, object, idea, or situation is the client discussing?
She wants a divorce but hasn't told husband because husband will think she's crazy.

Self-question 3: What is an appropriate sentence stem?
I'll go with a stem such as "You think," "I hear you saying," or "It sounds like."

Self-question 4: How can I translate the client's key content into my own words?
Want a divorce = break off, terminate the relationship, split.

Self-question 5: How will I know whether my paraphrase is helpful?
Listen and notice whether the client confirms its accuracy.

At this point the helper's self-talk stops, and the following dialogue ensues:

Helper paraphrase: It sounds like you haven't found a way to tell your husband you want to end the relationship because of his possible reaction. Is that right?

Client: Yeah—I've decided—I've even been to see a lawyer. But I just don't know how to approach him with this. He thinks things are wonderful, and I don't want to dishonor him by divorcing him.

That paraphrase encouraged client elaboration and focus on a main issue.

Learning Activity 5.3 gives you an opportunity to develop your own paraphrase responses.

Reflection and Basic Empathy

The paraphrase is used to restate the *content* part of the message. Although paraphrase and reflection of feelings are not mutually exclusive responses, the reflection of feelings is used to rephrase the *affective* part of the message, the client's emotional tone. A reflection is similar to a paraphrase but different in that a reflection adds to the message an emotional tone or component that is lacking in a paraphrase.

Here are two examples that may illustrate the difference between a paraphrase and a reflection of feelings:

Client: Everything is humdrum. There's nothing new going on, nothing exciting. All my friends are away. I wish I had some money to do something different.

Helper paraphrase: With your friends gone and no money around, there is nothing for you to do right now.

Helper reflection: You feel bored with the way things are for you right now.

Notice the helper's use of the affect word *bored* in the reflection response to tune in to the feelings of the client created by the particular situation.

Purposes of Reflection

The reflection of feelings has five intended purposes. First, reflection is used to encourage clients to express their feelings (both positive and negative) about a particular situation, person, or whatever. Some clients do not readily reveal feelings because they have never learned to do so; other clients hold back feelings until the helper gives permission to focus on them. Expression of feelings is not usually an end in itself; rather, it is a means of helping clients and practitioners understand the scope of the issues or situation. Most if not all the concerns presented by clients involve underlying emotional factors to be resolved. For example, in focusing on feelings, the client may become more aware of lingering feelings about an unfinished situation or of intense feelings that seem to dominate his or her reaction to a situation. Clients may also become aware of mixed, or conflicting, feelings. Clients often express ambivalence about problematic issues. Teyber (2006) identifies two common affective constructions with mixed components: anger-sadness-shame and sadness-anger-guilt. In the first sequence, the primary feeling is often anger, but it is a negative response to hurt or sadness. Often, the experiencing of the anger and sadness provokes shame. In the second sequence, the predominant feeling is sadness, but it is often connected to anger that has been denied because the expression of it produces guilt. These two affective sequences are typically acquired in childhood and are a result of both the rules and the interactions of the family of origin. These affective elements are also strongly influenced by cultural affiliation. As Sue and Sue (2003) note, in Western cultures, which emphasize individualism, the predominant affective reaction following wrongful behavior is *guilt*. However, in some non-Western cultures, such as Asian, Hispanic, and Black, where the psychosocial unit is the family, group, or collective society, the primary affective reaction to wrongful behavior is not guilt but *shame*. Sue and Sue (2003) conclude that "guilt is an individual affect, while shame appears to be a group one" (p. 107).

A second purpose of reflection is to help clients manage feelings. Learning to deal with feelings is especially important when a client experiences an intense emotion such as fear, dependency, or anger. Strong emotions can interfere with a client's ability to make a rational response (cognitive or behavioral) to pressure. Also, when clients are given permission to reveal and release feelings, their energy and well-being are often increased. For example, during and after a crisis or disaster such as an earthquake, terrorist attack, tsunami, or hurricane, people feel overwhelmed by the intensity of their emotions. This feeling can persist for

LEARNING ACTIVITY 5.3 Paraphrase

 In this activity, you are presented with three client practice messages. For each one, develop a paraphrase response, using the cognitive learning strategy outlined in the example below. To internalize this learning strategy, you may wish to talk through these self-questions overtly (aloud) and then covertly (silently). The end product will be a paraphrase response that you can say aloud or write down. Feedback is given on page 108.

Example

Client, a middle-aged graduate student [says in a level, monotone voice]: It's just a rough time for me—trying to work, keeping up with graduate school, and spending time with my family. I keep telling myself it will slow down someday.

Self-question 1: *What has this client told me?*
That it's hard to keep up with everything he has to do.
Self-question 2: *What is the content of this message—what person, object, idea, or situation is the client discussing?*
Trying to keep up with work, school, and family.
Self-question 3: *What is an appropriate sentence stem?*
I'll try a stem like "It sounds like" or "There are".

Actual Paraphrase response: "It sounds like you're having a tough time balancing all your commitments." *or* "There are a lot of demands on your time right now."

Client Practice Statements

Client 1, a 30-year-old woman [says in a level tone without much variation in pitch or tempo]: My husband and I argue all the time about how to manage our kids. He says I always interfere with his discipline. I think he is too harsh with them.

Self-question 1: *What has this client told me?*
Self-question 2: *What is the content of this message—what person, object, idea, or situation is the client discussing?*
Self-question 3: *What is an appropriate sentence stem?*
Actual paraphrase response: _____

_____

Client 2, a 6-year-old boy [says in slow, soft voice with downcast eyes]: I wish I didn't have a little sister. I know my parents love her more than me.

Self-question 1: *What has this client told me?*
Self-question 2: *What is the content of this message—what person, object, idea, or situation is this client discussing?*
Self-question 3: *What is an appropriate sentence stem?*
Actual paraphrase response: _____

_____

Client 3, a college student [says in a level tone with measured words and little change in pitch and inflection]: I've said to my family before, I just can't compete with the other students who aren't blind. There's no way I can keep up with this kind of handicap. I've told them it's natural to be behind and do more poorly.

Self-question 1: *What has this client told me?*
Self-question 2: *What is the content of this message—what person, object, idea, or situation is the client discussing?*
Self-question 3: *What is a useful sentence stem?*
Actual paraphrase response: _____

_____

months or even years after the event. Practitioners who help clients in these sorts of situations do so in part by encouraging them to name, validate, and express their emotions in a safe context (Halpern & Tramontin, 2007).

A third use of reflection is with clients who express negative feelings about therapy or about the helper. When a client becomes angry or upset with the helper or with the help being offered, there is a tendency for the helper to take the client's remarks personally and become defensive. Using reflection in these instances "lessens the possibility of an emotional conflict, which often arises simply because two people are trying to make themselves heard and neither is trying to listen" (Long & Prophit, 1981, p. 89). This use of reflection lets clients know that the helper understands their feelings in such a way that the intensity of the anger is usually diminished. As anger subsides, the client may become more receptive, and the helper can again initiate action-oriented responses or intervention strategies.

Reflection also helps clients discriminate accurately among various feelings. Clients often use feeling words like *anxious* or *nervous* that, on occasion, mask deeper or more intense feelings. Clients may also use an affect word that does not really portray their emotional state accurately. For instance, it is common for a client to say "It's my nerves" or "I'm nervous" to depict other feelings, such as resentment and depression. Other clients may reveal feelings through

FEEDBACK 5.3
Paraphrase

Client 1

Question 1: *What has the client said?*

That she and her husband argue over child rearing.

Question 2: *What is the content of her message?*

As a couple, they have different ideas on who should discipline their kids and how.

Question 3: *What is a useful sentence stem?*

Try "It sounds like" or "Your ideas about discipline are."

Example of Paraphrase Responses

"It sounds like you and your husband disagree a great deal on which one of you should discipline your kids and how it should be done".

"Your ideas about discipline for your kids are really different from your husband's, and this creates disagreements between the two of you."

Client 2

Question 1: *What has this client said?*

He believes his little sister is loved more by his folks than he is, and he wishes she weren't around.

Question 2: *What is the content of this message?*

Client feels "dethroned"—wishes the new "princess" would go away.

Question 3: *What is an appropriate sentence stem?*

I'll try "It seems that" or "I sense that."

Example of Paraphrase Responses

"It seems that you'd like to be 'number one' again in your family."

"I sense you are not sure of your place in your family since your little sister arrived."

Client 3

Question 1: *What has this client said?*

He is behind in school and is not doing as well as his peers because he is blind—a point he has emphasized to his family.

Question 2: *What is the content of this message?*

Client wants to impress on his family that *to him* his blindness is a handicap that interferes with his doing as much or as well as other students.

Question 3: *What is an appropriate sentence stem?*

"It sounds like," "I hear you saying," or "You'd like."

Examples of Paraphrase Responses

"It sounds like it's very important to you that your family realize how tough it is for you to do well in your studies here."

"You'd like your family to realize how difficult it is for you to keep up academically with people who don't have the added problem of being blind."

---

the use of metaphors. For example, a client may say "I feel like the person who rolled down Niagara Falls in a barrel" or "I feel like I just got hit by a Mack truck." Metaphors are important indicators of client emotion. As Ivey, Gluckstern, and Ivey (1993) note, metaphors suggest that much more is going on with the client than just the "surface expression" (p. 71). Accurate reflections of feelings help clients to refine their understanding of various emotional moods.

Finally, reflection of feelings, if used effectively and accurately, helps clients to feel understood. Clients tend to communicate more freely with persons who they feel try to understand them. As Teyber (2006) observes, when understanding is present, "Clients feel that they have been seen and are no longer invisible, alone, strange, or unimportant. At that moment, the client begins to perceive the therapist as

someone who is different from many others in their lives and possibly as someone who can help" (p. 63). The reflection-of-feelings response is the primary verbal tool used to convey basic empathy.

Verbal Means of Conveying Empathy

Consider the following four verbal strategies for conveying empathy:

1. *Show desire to comprehend.* It is necessary not only to convey an accurate understanding from the client's perspective but also to convey your *desire* to comprehend from the client's frame of reference. Recall from our discussion of cultural empathy that this desire includes an understanding not only of the individual

but also of the person's worldview: his or her environmental and sociopolitical context and cultural group. McGill (1992) offers the idea of the *cultural story* as a way to open communication and develop understanding about the client's cultural group:

> The cultural story refers to an ethnic or cultural group's origin, migration, and identity. Within the family, it is used to tell where one's ancestors came from, what kind of people they were and current members are, what issues are important to the family, what good and bad things have happened over time, and what lessons have been learned from their experiences. At the ethnic level, a cultural story tells the group's collective story of how to cope with life and how to respond to pain and trouble. It teaches people how to thrive in a multicultural society and what children should be taught so that they can sustain their ethnic and cultural story. (McGill, 1992, p. 340)

Your desire to comprehend is evidenced by statements indicating your attempts to make sense of the client's world and by clarification and questions about the client's experiences and feelings.

2. *Discuss what is important to the client.* Show by your questions and statements that you are aware of what is most important to the client. Respond in ways that relate to the client's basic problem or complaint. Formulate a brief statement that captures the thoughts and feelings of the client and that is directly related to the client's concerns.

3. Use verbal responses that *refer to client feelings.* One way to define verbal empathy is through the reflection-of-feelings response, which reflects the client's feelings and conveys your awareness of them. This response allows you to focus on the client's feelings by naming or labeling them. It is sometimes called *interchangeable* (Carkhuff, 1969), *basic* (Egan, 2007), or *reciprocal* (Hepworth, Rooney, Dewberry Rooney, Strom-Gottfried, & Larsen, 2006) empathy.

4. Use verbal responses that bridge or *add on to implicit client messages.* Empathy also involves comprehension of the client's innermost thoughts and perspectives even when they are unspoken and implicit. According to Rogers (1977), "The therapist is so much inside the private world of the other that she can clarify not only the messages of which the client is aware but even those just below the level of awareness" (p. 11). The counselor bridges or adds on to client messages by conveying understanding of what the client implies or infers in order to add to the client's frame of reference or to draw out implications of the issue. This is sometimes called *additive* empathy (Carkhuff, 1969, Hepworth et al., 2006) or *advanced* empathy (Egan, 2007). At this level of empathy, the helper uses mild to moderate interpretations of the client's inferred feelings (Hepworth, et al., 2006, p. 522).

Carkhuff and Pierce (1975) developed a Discrimination Inventory that presents a scale for assessing both basic and additive empathy messages. On this scale, helper responses are rated according to one of five levels. Level 3 is considered the *minimally* acceptable response. Level-3 responses on this scale correspond to Carkhuff and Pierce's concept of interchangeable empathy and to Egan's (2007) concept of basic-level empathy. Level 4 corresponds to additive empathy (Carkhuff, 1969) and to advanced empathy (Egan, 2007). Level 5 represents facilitating action.

Carkhuff and Pierce's Discrimination Inventory can be used to discriminate among levels of responses or to rate levels of helper communication. Here are examples of verbal empathic responses at each level:

Client: I've tried to get along with my father, but it doesn't work out. He's too hard on me.

Helper at Level 1: I'm sure it will all work out in time [reassurance and denial]. *Or* You ought to try harder to see his point of view [advice]. *Or* Why can't you two get along? [question].

The Level-1 response is a question, reassurance and denial, or advice.

Helper at Level 2: You're having a hard time getting along with your father.

At Level-2, the response is made to the *content* or cognitive portion of the message; feelings are ignored.

Helper at Level 3: You feel discouraged because your attempts to get along with your father have not been very successful.

The Level-3 response indicates understanding but provides no direction; it is a reflection of feeling and meaning based on the client's explicit message. In other words, a Level-3 response reflects both the feeling and the situation. In this example, "You feel discouraged" is the reflection of the feeling, and "because . . . not very successful" is the reflection of the situation.

Helper at Level 4: You feel discouraged because you can't seem to reach your father. You want him to let up on you.

The Level-4 response indicates understanding and provides some direction. A Level-4 response identifies not only the client's feelings but also the client's deficit that is implied. In a Level-4 response, the client's deficit is personalized—that is, the helper identifies the deficit, as in "you can't reach."

Helper at Level 5: You feel discouraged because you can't seem to reach your father. You want him to let up on you.

One step could be to express your feelings about this to your father.

A Level-5 response contains all elements of a Level-4 response plus at least one action step that the client can take to master the deficit and attain the goal. In this example, the action step is "One step could be to express your feelings about this to your father."

Next, we present information about how to reflect feelings to convey *basic* empathy.

Steps in Reflection of Feelings

Reflecting feelings can be a difficult skill to learn because feelings are often ignored or misunderstood. The reflection of feelings involves six steps, which include identifying the emotional tone of the communication and verbally reflecting the client's feelings in your own words.

1. Listen for feeling words, or affect words, in the client's messages. Positive, negative, and ambivalent feelings are expressed by affect words falling into one of five major categories: anger, fear, conflict, sadness, and happiness. Table 5.3 lists commonly used affect words at three levels of intensity. Becoming acquainted with such words may help you to recognize them in client communications and to expand your own vocabulary for describing emotions. Table 5.4 lists affect words to use with children and teens. With very young children, we recommend using face symbols such as those depicted in Figure 5.3.

TABLE 5.3   Words That Express Feelings

	Feeling category				
Relative intensity of words	**Anger**	**Conflict**	**Fear**	**Happiness**	**Sadness**
Mild feeling	Annoyed Bothered Bugged Irked Irritated Peeved Ticked	Blocked Bound Caught Caught in a bind Pulled	Apprehensive Concerned Tense Tight Uneasy	Amused Anticipating Comfortable Confident Contented Glad Pleased Relieved	Apathetic Bored Confused Disappointed Discontented Mixed up Resigned Unsure
Moderate feeling	Disgusted Hacked Harassed Mad Provoked Put upon Resentful Set up Spiteful Used	Locked Pressured Strained Torn	Afraid Alarmed Anxious Fearful Frightened Shook Threatened Worried	Delighted Eager Happy Hopeful Joyful Surprised Up	Abandoned Burdened Discouraged Distressed Down Drained Empty Hurt Lonely Lost Sad Unhappy Weighted
Intense feeling	Angry Boiled Burned Contemptful Enraged Fuming Furious Hateful Hot Infuriated Pissed Smoldering Steamed	Coerced Ripped Wrenched	Desperate Overwhelmed Panicky Petrified Scared Terrified Terror-stricken Tortured	Bursting Ecstatic Elated Enthusiastic Enthralled Excited Free Fulfilled Moved Proud Terrific Thrilled Turned on	Anguished Crushed Deadened Depressed Despairing Helpless Hopeless Humiliated Miserable Overwhelmed Smothered Tortured

Source: Helping Relationships and Strategies (3rd Ed., p. 72), by D. Hutchins and C. Cole-Vaught. © 1997 by Brooks/Cole, an imprint of the Wadsworth Group, a division of Thomson Learning.

TABLE 5.4	Affect Words and Phrases for Children and Teens			
Anxious	Bored	Childish	Contented or fulfilled	Curious
Depressed	Determined	Disgusted	Doubtful	Embarrassed
Empty	Envious of others	Excited	Furious	Guilty
Hopeful	Humble	Hurt	Irritated	Jealous
Lovable	Mean and destructive	Nervous	Optimistic	Proud
Rebellious	Sad	Safe and secure	Scared or afraid	Silly
Sorry	Strong and capable	Terrified	Thrilled	Warm and cozy
Worried				

Source: Adapted from *Group Activities for Counselors,* by S. Eliot, Spring Valley, CA: Inner Choice Publishing, 1994.

| Strong | Happy | Sad | Angry | Scared | Confused | Weak |

Figure 5.3 Feeling symbols for children
Source: Counseling Children (7th Ed), by C. Thompson and D. Henderson. © 2007. Reprinted with permission of Thomson Learning.

2. Watch the client's nonverbal behavior while he or she is delivering the verbal message. Nonverbal cues such as body posture, facial expression, and voice quality are important indicators of client emotion. In fact, nonverbal behavior is often a more reliable clue because nonverbal behaviors are less easily controlled than words. Observing nonverbal behavior is particularly important when the client's feelings are implied or expressed very subtly.

3. After the feelings reflected by the client's words and nonverbal behavior have been identified, reflect the feelings back to the client, using different words. The choice of words is critical to the effectiveness of this response. Suppose a client feels "annoyed." Interchangeable affect words would be *bothered, irritated,* and *hassled.* Words such as *angry, mad,* and *outraged* probably would convey greater intensity than the client intends to express. With adult clients, it is important for the helper to select affect words that accurately match not only the type but also the intensity of feeling; otherwise, the helper produces an understatement, which can make a client feel ridiculed, or an overstatement, which can make a client feel put off or intimidated. Notice the three levels of feeling in Table 5.3: mild, moderate, and intense. You can also control the intensity of the expressed affect by your choice of a preceding adverb—for example, *somewhat* (weak), *quite* (moderate), or *very* (strong) *upset.* With children, use a word or a symbol that captures their feelings as closely as possible. Study Tables 5.3 and 5.4 carefully so that you can develop an extensive vocabulary of affect words. If you overuse a few common affect words, you will miss the nuances of clients' emotional experiences.

4. Start your reflection statement with an appropriate sentence stem, such as one of the following:

"It *appears* that you are *angry* now."
"It *looks* like you are *angry* now."
"It is *clear* to me that you are *angry* now."
"It *sounds* like you are *angry* now."
"I *hear* you saying you are *angry* now."
"My *ears tell* me that you are *angry* now."
"I can *grasp* your *anger.*"
"You are *feeling angry* now."
"Let's get in *touch* with your *anger.*"

For more sentence stems, refer to Table 5.2.

5. Add the context of the feelings or the situation in which they occur. This addition takes the form of a brief paraphrase. Usually the context can be determined from the content part of the client's message. For example, a client might say, "I just can't take tests. I get so anxious I never do well even though I study a lot." In this message, the affect is anxiety, and the context is test taking. The helper reflects both the affect ("You feel uptight") *and* the context ("whenever you have to take a test").

6. Assess the effectiveness of your reflection after delivering it. Usually, if your reflection accurately identifies the client's feelings, the client will confirm your response by saying something like "Yes, that's right" or "Yes, that's exactly how I feel." If your response is off target, the client

may reply with "Well, it's not quite like that," "I don't feel exactly that way," or "No, I don't feel that way." When the client responds by denying feelings, it may mean your reflection was inaccurate or ill timed. It is very important for helpers to decide when to respond to emotions. Reflection of feelings may be too powerful to be used *frequently* in the very early stage of helping. At that time, overuse of this response may make the client feel uncomfortable, a situation that can result in denial rather than acknowledgment of emotions. But do not ignore the potential impact or usefulness of reflection later on, when focusing on the client's feelings would promote the goals of the session.

In the following example, notice the way in which a helper uses a cognitive learning strategy (adapted from Richardson & Stone, 1981) to formulate a reflection of client feelings:

Client, a White middle-aged man [says in loud, shrill, high-pitched voice, with clenched fists]: You can't imagine what it was like when I found out my wife was cheating on me. I saw red! What should I do—get even, leave her? I'm not sure.

Helper: [asks and answers covertly]

Self-question 1: What overt feeling words has this client used?
None—except for the suggested affect phrase "saw red."

Self-question 2: What feelings are implied in the client's voice and nonverbal behavior?
Anger, outrage, hostility.

Self-question 3: What affect words accurately describe this client's feelings at a similar level of intensity?
"Furious," "angry," "vindictive," "outraged."

Self-question 4: What is an appropriate sentence stem?
Given the client's use of "imagine" and "saw red," I'll try sentence stems like "It seems," "It appears," and "It looks like."

Self-question 5: What is the context, or situation, surrounding his feelings that I'll paraphrase?
The client's discovery that his wife was unfaithful.

Self-question 6: How will I know whether my reflection is accurate and helpful?
Watch and listen for the client's response—whether he confirms or denies the feeling of being angry and vindictive.

Actual Examples of Reflection

"It looks like you're very angry now about your wife's going out on you."

"It appears that you're furious with your wife's actions."

"It seems like you're both angry and vindictive now that you've discovered your wife has been going out with other men."

Suppose that, following the reflection, the client says, "Yes, I'm very angry, for sure. But I don't know about vindictive, though I guess I'd like to make her feel as crappy as I do." The client has confirmed the helper's reflection of the feelings of anger and vindictiveness but also has given a clue that he finds the word *vindictive* too strong *at this time*. The helper picks up on the feelings, noting that the word *vindictive* might be used again later, after the client has sorted through his mixed feelings about his wife's behavior.

Learning Activity 5.4 gives you an opportunity to try to make reflection-of-feelings responses.

SUMMARIZATION: LISTENING FOR PATTERNS AND THEMES

Usually, after a client expresses several messages or talks for a while, the helper is able to spot in the client's messages certain consistencies or patterns, which we refer to as *themes*. The themes of a client's messages are evident in topics that the client continually refers to or brings up in some way. The helper can identify themes by listening to what the client repeats "over and over and with the most intensity" (Carkhuff, Pierce, & Cannon, 1977). The themes indicate what the client is trying to tell us and what the client needs to focus on in the helping sessions. Ivey and colleagues (1997) recommend listening to the *way* the client organizes his or her story (p. 63). The counselor can respond to client themes by using a summarization response. Suppose that you have been working with a young man who, during the last three sessions, has made repeated references to relationships with gay men yet has not really identified this issue intentionally. You could use a summarization to identify the theme from his repeated references by saying something like "I'm aware that during our last few sessions you've spoken consistently about relationships with gay men. Perhaps this is an issue for you that we might want to focus on."

Or suppose that in one session a client has given you several descriptions of different situations in which he feels concerned about how other people perceive him. You might discern that the theme common to all these situations is the client's need for approval from others, or "other-directedness." You could use a summarization such as this to identify this theme: "One thing I see in all three situations you've described is that you seem quite concerned about having the approval of other people. Is this accurate?"

A *summarization* can be defined as two or more paraphrases or reflections that condense the client's messages or the session. Summarization "involves listening to a client over a period of time (from three minutes to a complete session or more), picking out relationships among key issues, and restating them back accurately to the client" (Ivey et al., 1993, p. 92).

LEARNING ACTIVITY	**5.4**	**Reflection of Feelings**

 In this activity, you are presented with three client practice messages. For each message, develop a reflection-of-feelings response, using the cognitive learning strategy (Richardson & Stone, 1981) described earlier and outlined below. To internalize this learning strategy, you may wish to talk through the self-questions overtly (aloud) and then covertly (silently to yourself). The end product will be a reflection-of-feelings response that you can say aloud or write down. An example precedes the practice messages. Feedback is given on page 114.

Example

Client, a 50-year-old steelworker now laid off [says in a loud, critical voice, staring at the ceiling, brow furrowed, eyes squinting]: Now look. What can I do? I've been laid off over a year. I've got no money, no job, and a family to take care of. It's also clear to me that my mind and skills are just wasting away.

Self-question 1: *What overt feeling words did the client use?*
None.
Self-question 2: *What feelings are implied in the client's nonverbal behavior?*
Disgust, anger, upset, frustration, resentment, disillusionment, discouragement.
Self-question 3: *What affect words accurately describe the client's feelings at a similar level of intensity?*
There seem to be two feelings: anger and discouragement. Anger seems to be the stronger emotion of the two.
Self-question 4: *What is an appropriate sentence stem?*
Use stems like "I see you" or "It's clear to me that you" or "From where I'm looking, you." These are similar to the client phrases "now look" and "it's clear."
Self-question 5: *What is the context, or situation, surrounding his feelings that I'll paraphrase?*
Loss of job, no resources, no job prospects in sight.
Reflection-of-feelings response: "I can see you're angry about being out of work and discouraged about the future" or "It looks like you're very upset about having your job and stability taken away from you.

Client Practice Statements

Client 1, an 8-year-old girl [says in a level tone, with measured words, glancing from side to side, lips drawn tightly together, face flushed]: I'm telling you I don't like living at home anymore. I wish I could live with my friend and her parents. I told my mommy that one day I'm going to run away, but she doesn't listen to me.

Self-question 1: *What overt feeling words did the client use?*
Self-question 2: *What feelings are implied in the client's nonverbal behavior?*
Self-question 3: *What are accurate and similar interchangeable affect words?*
Self-question 4: *What is an appropriate sentence stem?*
Self-question 5: *What is the context, or situation, concerning her feelings that I'll paraphrase?*
Actual reflection response: _____

_____

_____

Client 2, a middle-aged man in marital therapy [says in a soft voice with eyes downcast]: As far as I'm concerned, our marriage turned sour last year when my wife went back to work. She's more in touch with her work than with me.

Self-question 1: *What overt feeling words did the client use?*
Self-question 2: *What feelings are implied in the client's nonverbal behavior?*
Self-question 3: *What are accurate and similar interchangeable affect words?*
Self-question 4: *What is an appropriate sentence stem?*
Self-question 5: *What is the context, or situation, surrounding his feelings that I'll paraphrase?*
Actual reflection response: _____

_____

_____

Client 3, an adolescent [says in loud, harsh voice]: Now look, we have too damn many rules around this school. I'm getting the hell out of here. As far as I can see, this place is a dump.

Self-question 1: *What overt feeling words has this client used?*
Self-question 2: *What feelings are implied in the client's nonverbal behavior?*
Self-question 3: *What are accurate and similar interchangeable affect words?*
Self-question 4: *What is an appropriate sentence stem?*
Self-question 5: *What is the context, or situation, surrounding his feelings that I'll paraphrase?*
Actual reflection response: _____

_____

_____

FEEDBACK

5.4

Reflection of Feelings

Client 1

Question 1: *What overt feeling words did the client use?*

"Don't like."

Question 2: *What feelings are implied in the client's nonverbal behavior?*

Upset, irritation, resentment.

Question 3: *What are interchangeable affect words?*

"Bothered," "perturbed," "irritated," "upset."

Question 4: *What sentence stem will I use?*

"Seems like," "It sounds like," or "I hear you saying that."

Question 5: *What is the context, or situation, surrounding her feelings?*

Living at home with her parents.

Actual examples of reflection
"It sounds like you're upset about some things going on at your home now."
"I hear you saying you're bothered about your parents."

Client 2

Question 1: *What overt feeling words did the client use?*

No obvious ones except for the phrases "turned sour" and "more in touch with."

Question 2: *What feelings are implied in the client's nonverbal behavior?*

Sadness, loneliness, hurt.

Question 3: *What are interchangeable affect words?*

"Hurt," "lonely," "left out," "unhappy."

Question 4: *What sentence stem is appropriate?*

"I sense" or "You feel."

Question 5: *What is the context, or situation, surrounding his feelings?*

Wife's return to work.

Actual examples of reflection
"You're feeling left out and lonely since your wife's gone back to work."
"I sense you're feeling hurt and unhappy because your wife seems so interested in her work."

Client 3

Question 1: *What overt feeling words did the client use?*

No obvious ones, but words like "damn," "hell," and "dump" suggest intensity of emotions.

Question 2: *What feelings are implied in the client's nonverbal behavior?*

Anger, frustration.

Question 3: *What are interchangeable affect words?*

"Angry," "offended," "disgusted."

Question 4: *What sentence stem will I use?*

Stems such as "It seems," "It appears," "It looks like," and "I can see."

Question 5: *What is the context, or situation, surrounding the feelings?*

School rules.

Actual examples of reflection
"It looks like you're pretty disgusted now because you see these rules restricting you."
"It seems like you're very angry about having all these rules here at school."

Purposes of Summarization

One purpose of summarization is to tie together multiple elements of client messages. In this case, by extracting meaning from vague and ambiguous messages, summarization can serve as a good feedback tool for the client. A second purpose of summarization is to identify a common theme or pattern that becomes apparent after several messages or sometimes after several sessions. Occasionally, a helper may summarize to interrupt a client's incessant rambling or "storytelling." At such times, summarization is an important focusing tool that brings direction to the interview.

A third use of summarization is to slow the pace of a session that is moving too quickly. In such instances, summaries provide psychological breathing space during the session. A final purpose of a summary is to review progress that has been made during one or more interviews.

A summarization may represent collective rephrasings of either cognitive or affective data, but most summarization responses include references to both cognitive and affective messages, as in the following four examples.

Summarization to Tie Together Multiple Elements of a Client Message

Client, a Native American medical student: All my life I thought I wanted to become a doctor and go back to work on my reservation. Now that I've left home, I'm not sure. I still feel strong ties there that are pulling me back. I hate to let my people down, yet I also feel like there's a lot out here I want to explore first.

Summarization: You're away from the reservation now and are finding so much in this place to explore. At the same time, you're feeling pulled by your lifelong ties to your people and your dream of returning as a doctor.

Summarization to Identify a Theme

Client, a 35-year-old male: One of the reasons we divorced was because she always pushed me. I could never say "no" to her; I always gave in. I guess it's hard for me just to say "no" to requests people make.

Summarization: You're discovering that you tend to give in or not do what you want in many of your significant relationships, not just with your ex-wife.

Summarization to Regulate the Pace of a Session and to Give Focus

Client, a young woman: What a terrible week I had! The water heater broke, the dog got lost, someone stole my wallet, my car ran out of gas, and to top it all off, I gained five pounds. I can't stand myself. It seems like it shows all over me.

Summarization: Let's stop for just a minute before we go on. It seems like you've encountered an unending series of bad events this week.

Summarization to Review Progress

Summarization: Monique, we've got about five minutes left today. It seems like most of the time we've been working on the ways you find to sabotage yourself from doing things you want to do but feel are out of your control. This week I'd like you to work on the following homework before our next session. . . .

That type of summarization is often used as a termination strategy near the end of a session.

Steps in Summarizing

Summarizing requires careful attention to and concentration on the client's verbal and nonverbal messages. Accurate use of this listening response depends on good recall of client behavior, not only within a session but over time—across several sessions or even several months of therapy. Developing a summarization involves the following four steps:

1. Attend to and recall the message or series of messages by restating them to yourself covertly. What has the client been telling you, focusing on, working on? This is a key and difficult step because it requires you to be aware of many, varying verbal and nonverbal messages you have processed *over time*.
2. Identify any apparent patterns, themes, or multiple elements of these messages by asking yourself questions like "What has the client repeated over and over" and "What are the different parts of this puzzle?"
3. Using the sentence stem you've selected, select words to describe the theme or to tie together multiple elements, and say this aloud as your summarization response. Remember to use your voice so that the summarization sounds like a statement, not a question.
4. Assess the effectiveness of your summarization by listening for and observing whether the client confirms or denies the theme or whether the summary adds to or detracts from the focus of the session.

To formulate a summarization, consider the following cognitive learning strategy (Learning Activity 5.5 gives you a chance to try this strategy):

1. What was the client telling me and working on today and over time—that is, what are the *key content* and *key affect?*
2. What has the client repeated over and over today and over time? What *patterns* or *themes* am I seeing?
3. How will I know whether my summarization is useful?

Notice how a helper applies this cognitive learning strategy when developing a summarization in the following example:

Client, a White male fighting alcoholism (he has told you for the last three sessions that his drinking is ruining his family life but he can't stop because it makes him feel better and helps him to handle job stress) [says in low, soft voice, with downcast eyes and stooped shoulders]: I know drinking doesn't really help me in the long run. And it sure doesn't help my family. My wife keeps threatening to leave. I know all this. But it's hard to stay away from the booze. Having a drink makes me feel relieved.

Helper: [asks and answers covertly]

Self-question 1: What has the client been telling me today and over time?
Key content: Results of drinking aren't good for him or his family.

Key affect: Drinking makes him feel better, less anxious.

Self-question 2: What has the client repeated over and over today and over time? What patterns or themes am I seeing? That despite adverse effects and family deterioration, he continues to drink for stress reduction and "medicating" of feelings. Stress reduction through alcohol seems worth more than losing his family.

Suppose that at this time the helper delivered one of the following summarizations to the client:

"Jerry, I sense that you feel it's worth having the hassle of family problems because of the good, calm feelings you get whenever you drink."

"Jerry, you feel that your persistent drinking is creating a lot of difficulties for you in your family, and I sense your reluctance to stop drinking in spite of these adverse effects."

"Jerry, I sense that, despite everything, alcohol feels more satisfying (rewarding) to you than your own family."

If Jerry confirms the theme that alcohol is more important now than his family, the helper can conclude that the summarization was useful. If Jerry denies the theme or issue summarized, the helper can ask Jerry to clarify how the summarization was inaccurate, remembering that the summary may indeed be inaccurate or that Jerry may not be ready to acknowledge the issue at this time.

BARRIERS TO LISTENING

Egan (2007) discusses what he calls the "shadow side" of listening—that is, ways in which the listening process may fail. As he notes, active listening sounds good in theory but in practice is not without "obstacles and distractions" (p. 94). Over the years, we have observed three types of helpers who seem to have very great difficulty listening to clients:

1. *Frenetic helpers:* These helpers are so hyper and so much in motion (internally, externally, or both) that they have great difficulty sitting quietly and taking in clients' stories.
2. *Self-centered helpers:* These helpers are so in love with themselves and so hell-bent on getting their own ideas across that they allow clients little opportunity to tell their own stories.
3. *Self-absorbed helpers:* These helpers often look attentive, but inside they are experiencing so much internal noise that they aren't emotionally available to hear clients.

Egan (2007) points out that evaluations and filters can be obstacles to effective listening. Although it is not possible to suspend judgment completely, most clients have finely tuned antennae that detect evaluative responses—perhaps because they have heard judgment so often in their lives. Clients who have individual or cultural shame are especially likely to shut down when they hear evaluative listening from counselors.

Labels and biases may cause filtered listening (Egan, 2007, pp. 94–95). For example, if you are required to give your client a diagnosis, you may run through possible labels in your head while you are simultaneously trying to listen to the client. Or perhaps someone already labeled the client you are seeing as the "borderline" client or the "dysthymic" client or the "oppositional" kid. An obstacle to listening in each instance is the temptation to look for corroborative behaviors while listening to the client. All of us use filters to structure our worlds, but these filters, if very strong, can inject biased listening into the helping process and foster stereotyping (Egan, 2007, p. 95). Filters often come into play when we are listening to clients who are culturally different from ourselves in some way. Clients who detect "filtered listening" are likely to shut down, feeling it isn't safe to open their hearts and souls to us (Lindahl, 2003). (See Learning Activity 5.6.)

LISTENING WITH DIVERSE GROUPS OF CLIENTS

The listening process in a helping relationship is affected by such factors as the client's age, ethnicity, gender, and languages. Active listening can be a useful way to establish rapport with children and adolescent clients (Thompson & Henderson, 2007). Elderly clients who lack social contacts often long for a good listener.

The listening process itself may conflict with the basic values of some clients of color. As Atkinson, Thompson, and Grant (1993) observe,

Often, in order to encourage self-disclosure, the counseling situation is intentionally designed to be an ambiguous one, one in which the counselor listens empathically and responds only to encourage the client to continue talking. This lack of structure in the counseling process may conflict with need for structure that is a value in many cultures. Racial/ethnic minority clients frequently find the lack of structure confusing, frustrating, and even threatening. (p. 53)

Gender differences also play a role. Some men tend to have a more directive style, asking more questions and doing more interrupting and problem solving, than some women, who may make more reflective statements (Ivey et al., 1997). When working with clients from some cultural groups, the helper may need to adopt a more active style. With some Native American clients, however, the helper will find the capacity to sit silently and be present useful (Ivey et al., 1997, p. 202).

| LEARNING ACTIVITY | **5.5** | **Summarization** |

In this activity, you are presented with three client practice messages. For each message, develop a summarization response using the cognitive learning strategy described earlier and outlined below. To internalize this learning strategy, you may wish to talk through the self-questions overtly (aloud) and then covertly (silently to yourself). The end product will be a summarization response that you can say aloud or write down. An example precedes the practice messages. Feedback is given on page 118.

Example

Client, a 10-year-old girl, at the beginning of the session [says in low, soft voice, with lowered, moist eyes]: I don't understand why my parents can't live together anymore. I'm not blaming anybody, but it just feels very confusing to me.

Same client, near the middle of the same session: I wish they could keep it together. I guess I feel like they can't because they fight about me so much. Maybe I'm the reason they don't want to live together anymore.

Self-question 1: *What has the client been telling me and working on today?*
Key content: She wants her parents to stay together.
Key affect: She feels sad, upset, and responsible.

Self-question 2: *What has the client repeated over and over today and over time? What patterns and themes am I seeing?*
That she's the one who's responsible for her parents' breakup.

Examples of Summarization Response:

"Joan, at the start of our talk today, you were feeling like no one person was responsible for your parents' separation. Now I sense you're saying that you feel responsible."
"Joan, earlier today you indicated you didn't feel like blaming anyone for what's happening to your folks. Now I'm sensing that you're feeling like you're responsible for their breakup."

Client Practice Messages

Client 1, a 30-year-old man who has been blaming himself for his wife's unhappiness [says in low, soft voice with lowered eyes]: I really feel guilty about marrying her in the first place. It wasn't really for love. It was just a convenient thing to do. I feel like I've messed up her life really badly. I also feel obliged to her.

Self-question 1: *What has the client been telling me and working on today?*

Key content: _____

Key affect: _____

Self-question 2: *What has the client repeated over and over today and over time? What patterns or themes am I seeing?*
Summarization response: _____

_____

_____

Client 2, a 35-year-old woman who focuses on how her life has improved since having children [says with alertness and animation]: I never thought I would feel this great. I always thought being a parent would be boring and terribly difficult. It's not, for me. It's fascinating and easy. It makes everything worthwhile.

Self-question 1: *What has this client been telling me and working on today?*

Key content: _____

Key affect: _____

Self-question 2: *What has this client repeated over and over today or over time? What patterns or themes am I seeing?*
Summarization response: _____

_____

_____

Client 3, a 27-year-old woman who has continually focused on her relationships with men and her needs for excitement and stability, at the first session [says with bright eyes and facial animation and in a high-pitched voice]: I've been dating lots and lots of men for the last few years. Most of them have been married. That's great because there are no demands on me.

Same client, at the fourth session [says in a soft voice, with lowered eyes]: It doesn't feel so good anymore. It's not so much fun. Now I guess I miss having some commitment and stability in my life.

Self-question 1: *What has the client been telling me and working on today?*

Key content: _____

Key affect: _____

Self-question 2: *What has the client repeated over and over today or over time. What patterns or themes am I seeing?*
Summarization response: _____

_____

_____

FEEDBACK
Summarization

Client 1

Question 1: *What has the client told me?*

Key content: He married for convenience, not love.

Key affect: Now he feels both guilty and indebted.

Question 2: *What has the client repeated over and over? What patterns or themes do I see?*

Conflicting feelings—feels a strong desire to get out of the marriage yet feels a need to keep relationship going because he feels responsible for his wife's unhappiness.

Examples of Summarization Response

"I sense you're feeling pulled in two different directions. For yourself, you want out of the relationship. For her sake, you feel you should stay in the relationship."

"You're feeling like you've used her for your convenience and because of this you think you owe it to her to keep the relationship going."

"I can grasp how very much you want to pull yourself out of the marriage and also how responsible you feel for your wife's present unhappiness."

Client 2

Question 1: *What has the client told me?*

Key content: Children have made her life better, more worthwhile.

Key affect: Surprise and pleasure.

Question 2: *What has the client repeated over and over? What patterns or themes do I see?*

Being a parent is uplifting and rewarding even though she didn't expect it to be. In addition, her children are very important to her. To some extent, they define her worth and value as a person.

Examples of Summarization Response

"It seems like you're feeling surprise, satisfaction, and relief about finding parenting so much easier and more rewarding than you had expected it would be."

"I hear feelings of surprise and pleasure in your voice as you reveal how great it is to be a parent and how important your children are to you."

"You seem so happy about the way your life is going since you've had children—as if they make you and your life more worthwhile."

Client 3

Question 1: *What has the client told me?*

Key content: She has been dating lots of men who have their own commitments.

Key affect: It used to feel great; now she feels a sense of loss and emptiness.

Question 2: *What has the client repeated over and over? What patterns or themes do I see?*

At first—feelings of pleasure, relief not to have demands in close relationships. Now, feelings are changing, and she feels less satisfied, wants more stability in close relationships.

Examples of Summarization Response

"Lee Ann, originally you said it was great to be going out with a lot of different men who didn't ask much of you. Now you're also feeling it's not so great—it's keeping you from finding some purpose and stability in your life."

"In our first session, you were feeling 'up' about all those relationships with noncommittal men. Now you're feeling like this is interfering with the stability you need and haven't yet found."

"At first it was great to have all this excitement and few demands. Now you're feeling some loss from lack of a more stable, involved relationship."

Another situation in which listening can pose special issues in the helping process arises when clients do not speak standard English, have English as a second language, or do not speak English at all. The counselor may feel that he or she has more trouble listening to such clients, although it is really the clients who suffer the disadvantage. Sue and Sue (2003) note that "the lack of bilingual therapists and the requirement that the culturally different client communicate in English may limit the person's ability to progress in counseling and therapy" (p. 118).

Helms and Cook (1999) also address this issue. They recommend a referral when the language origins of the helper and client differ and when neither party is even partially competent in at least one of the other person's languages

It can be hard to listen to someone who is saying something to you that is difficult for you to hear! In order to be able to listen effectively in these contexts, engage intentionally in conversations with people or classmates who have a point of view different from your own. When responding, do so without defending or justifying your own opinion or position.

One choice you have is to acknowledge the other person's communication. You might say something like "I can see your perspective on this." Or you can let go of the need to respond at all and listen without saying anything in response. As an additional step, try to hold the other person "in the light" and respond with compassion.

One way to work around any listening barrier is to create good protective boundaries for yourself. That way, when someone says something that is hard for you to hear, you can hear it, but the words have no impact on your sense of self-worth. Regardless of whether the message feels true for you or not, it does not undermine your self-esteem.

(p. 194). If a referral is not possible, then an interpreter is needed, although, as Helms and Cook (1999) point out, the use of an interpreter is less than ideal because the helper's lack of language understanding may distort what the client says. If, however, the helper and client have different languages but both are at least somewhat able to understand a "marketplace" language, such as standard English, "then the therapist must learn to recognize some of the speech patterns of the client's at-home culture. This can be done by listening attentively to the client in an effort to discern when the client switches back and forth between the two cultural languages, as well as which emotions seem to accompany the shift" (p. 194).

CHAPTER SUMMARY

We often hear these questions: "What good does all this listening do? How does just rephrasing client messages really help?" In response, let us reiterate the rationale for using listening responses in helping:

1. Listening to clients is a very powerful reinforcer and may strengthen clients' desire to talk about themselves and their concerns. Not listening may prevent clients from sharing relevant information.

2. Listening to a client first may mean a greater chance of responding accurately to the client in later stages of helping, such as problem solving. By jumping to quick solutions without laying a foundation of listening, you may inadvertently ignore the primary issue or propose inadequate and ill-timed action steps (Sommers-Flanagan & Sommers-Flanagan, 2003).

3. Listening encourages the client to assume responsibility for selecting the topic and focus of an interview. Not listening may meet your needs to find information or to solve problems. In doing so, you may portray yourself as an expert rather than a collaborator. Simply asking a series of questions or proposing a series of

action steps in the initial phase of helping can cause the client to perceive you as the expert and can hinder proper development of client self-responsibility in the interview.

4. Good listening and attending skills model socially appropriate behavior for clients (Gazda et al., 2005). Many clients have not yet learned to use the art of listening in their own relationships and social contacts. They are more likely to incorporate these skills to improve their interpersonal relationships when they experience them firsthand through their contact with a significant other, such as a skilled helper.

All these reasons take into account both the gender and the cultural affiliation of the client. Listening may have a differential effect depending on the client's gender and cultural affiliation.

Some helpers can articulate a clear rationale for listening but cannot listen during an interview because of blocks that inhibit effective listening. Some of the most common blocks to listening are these:

1. The tendency to judge and evaluate the client's messages.

2. The tendency to stop attending because of distractions such as noise, the time of day, or the topic.

3. The temptation to ask questions about "missing" pieces of information.

4. The temptation or the pressure that you put on yourself to solve problems, find answers, or somehow "fix" the situation.

5. Your preoccupation with yourself as you try to acquire the skills. Your preoccupation shifts the focus away from the client and actually reduces, rather than increases, your potential for listening. Preparation for effective listening is crucial, but being preoccupied with the technique of listening is not. Preoccupation with listening skills may lessen when you are able to engage in what Lindahl (2003) refers to as contemplative listening, reflective listening, and connective listening.

Effective listening requires an involved yet contained sort of energy that allows you to be fully present to the client. Listening is a process that does not stop after the initial session but continues throughout the entire therapeutic relationship with each client. Listening is a process that not only impacts clients but also impacts ourselves as helpers. We as listeners can be nourished by the listening process and deepen our connectedness to ourselves and to our clients (Lindahl, 2003).

Perhaps the best explanation of the inherent value of listening comes from Remen (1996), in her remarkable book *Kitchen Table Wisdom: Stories That Heal:*

> I suspect that the most basic and powerful way to connect to another person is to listen. Just listen. Perhaps the most important thing we ever give each other is our attention. And especially if it's given from the heart. When people are talking, there's no need to do anything but receive them. Just take them in. Listen to what they're saying. Care about it. (p. 143)

REFERENCES

Atkinson, D. R., Thompson, C. E., & Grant, S. K. (1993). A three-dimensional model for counseling racial/ethnic minorities. *The Counseling Psychologist, 21,* 257–277.

Carkhuff, R. R. (1969). *Helping and human relations.* Vol. 1: *Practice and research.* New York: Holt, Rinehart and Winston.

Carkhuff, R. R. (1993). *The art of helping VII.* Amherst, MA: Human Resource Development Press.

Carkhuff, R. R., & Pierce, R. M. (1975). *Trainer's guide: The art of helping.* Amherst, MA: Human Resource Development Press.

Carkhuff, R. R., Pierce, R. M., & Cannon, J. R. (1977). *The art of helping III.* Amherst, MA: Human Resource Development Press.

Cormier, S., & Hackney, H. (2008). *Counseling strategies and interventions* (7th ed.). Boston: Allyn & Bacon.

Egan, G. (2007). *The skilled helper* (8th ed.). Pacific Grove, CA: Brooks/Cole.

Gazda, G., Balzer, F., Childers, W., Nealy, A., Phelps, R., & Walters, R. (2005). *Human relations development* (7th ed.). Boston: Allyn & Bacon.

Halpern, J., & Tramontin, M. (2007). *Disaster mental health.* Belmont, CA: Thomson–Brooks/Cole.

Helms, J., & Cook, D. (1999). *Using race and culture in counseling and psychotherapy.* Boston: Allyn & Bacon.

Hepworth, D. H., Rooney, R. H., Dewberry Rooney, G., Strom-Gottfried, K., & Larsen, J. (2006). *Direct social work practice* (7th ed.). Belmont, CA: Thomson–Brooks/Cole.

Hutchins, D., & Cole-Vaught, C. (1997). *Helping relationships and strategies* (3rd ed.). Pacific Grove, CA: Brooks/Cole.

Ivey, A. E., Gluckstern, N. B., & Ivey, M. B. (1993). *Basic attending skills* (3rd ed.). North Amherst, MA: Microtraining Associates.

Ivey, A. E., & Ivey, M. B. (2007). *Intentional interviewing and counseling* (6th ed.). Belmont, CA: Thomson–Brooks/Cole.

Ivey, A. E., Ivey, M. B., & Simek-Morgan, L. (1997). *Counseling and psychotherapy: A multicultural perspective* (4th ed.). Boston: Allyn & Bacon.

Kabat-Zinn, J. (1993). Meditation. In B. Moyers (Ed.), *Healing and the mind* (pp. 115–144). New York: Doubleday.

Lindahl, K. (2003). *Practicing the sacred art of listening: The Listening Center Workshop.* Woodstock, VT: Skylight Paths.

Long, L. & Prophit, P. (1981). *Understanding/responding: A communication manual for nurses.* Monterey, CA: Wadsworth Health Sciences.

McGill, D. W. (1992). The cultural story in multicultural family therapy. *Families in Society, 73,* 339–349.

Morran, D. K., Kurpius, D. J., Brack, C., & Brack, G. (1995). A cognitive-skills model for counselor training and supervision. *Journal of Counseling and Development, 73,* 384–389.

Morran, D. K., Kurpius, D. J., Brack, G., & Rozecki, T. G. (1994). Relationship between counselors' clinical hypotheses and client ratings of counselor effectiveness. *Journal of Counseling and Development, 72,* 655–660.

Nichols, M. P. (1995). *The lost art of listening.* New York: Guilford Press.

Ostaseski, F. (1994, December). Stories of lives lived and now ending. *The Sun,* no. 228, 10–13.

Remen, N. (1996). *Kitchen table wisdom: Stories that heal.* New York: Riverhead.

Richardson, B., & Stone, G. L. (1981). Effects of cognitive adjunct procedure within a microtraining situation. *Journal of Counseling Psychology, 28,* 168–175.

Rogers, C. (1977). *Carl Rogers on personal power.* New York: Delacorte Press.

Sedney, M., Baker, J., & Gross, E. (1994). "The story" of a death: Therapeutic considerations with bereaved families. *Journal of Marital and Family Therapy, 20,* 287–296.

Sommers-Flanagan, J., & Sommers-Flanagan, R. (2003). *Clinical interviewing* (3rd ed.). New York: Wiley.

Sue, D. W., & Sue, D. (2003). *Counseling the culturally diverse* (4th ed.). New York: Wiley.

Terr, L. (1990). *Too scared to cry: Psychic trauma in childhood.* New York: Harper & Row.

Teyber, E. (2006). *Interpersonal process in psychotherapy* (5th ed.). Belmont, CA: Thomson–Brooks/Cole.

Thompson, C., & Henderson, D. (2007). *Counseling children* (7th ed.). Belmont, CA: Thomson–Brooks/Cole.

Uhlemann, M., Lee, Y. D., & Martin, J. (1994). Client cognitive responses as a function of quality of counselor verbal responses. *Journal of Counseling and Development, 73,* 198–203.

White, M., & Epston, D. (1990). *Narrative means to therapeutic ends.* New York: Norton.

5   K N O W L E D G E   A N D   S K I L L   B U I L D E R

Part One

Part one allows you to assess your performance on Learning Outcome 1. Classify each of the listening responses in the following list as a clarification, paraphrase, reflection of feelings, or summarization. If you label 9 out of 12 responses correctly, you will have met this objective. Check your answers against those provided in the feedback on page 124.

1. **Client, an older, retired person:** How do they expect me to live on this little bit of Social Security? I've worked hard all my life. Now I have so little to show for it—I've got to choose between heat and food.
   a. Can you tell me who exactly expects you to be able to manage on this amount of money?
   b. All your life you've worked hard, hoping to give yourself a secure future. Now it's very upsetting to have only a little bit of money that can't possibly cover your basic needs.

2. **Client:** I'm having all these horrendous images that keep coming at me. I always thought I had had a happy childhood, but now I'm not so sure.
   a. Can you tell me what you mean by "horrendous images"?
   b. Recently you started to have some very scary memories about your past, and it's made you question how great your childhood really was.

3. **Client:** I feel so nervous when I have to give a speech in front of lots of people.
   a. You feel anxious when you have to talk to a group of people.
   b. You would rather not have to talk in front of large groups.

4. **Client:** I always have a drink when I'm under pressure.
   a. Are you saying that you use alcohol to calm yourself down?
   b. You think alcohol has a calming effect on you.

5. **Client:** I don't know whether I've ever experienced orgasm. My partner thinks I have, though.
   a. Are you saying that you've been trying to have your partner believe you do experience orgasm?
   b. You feel uncertain about whether you've ever really had an orgasm, even though your partner senses that you have.

6. **Client:** I haven't left my house in years. I'm even afraid to go out and get the mail.
   a. You feel panicked and uneasy when you go outside the security of your house.

b. Because of this fear, you've stayed inside your house for a long time.

Part Two

For each of the following three client statements, Learning Outcome 2 asks you to write an example of each of the four listening responses.* In developing these responses, you may find it helpful to use the cognitive learning strategy you practiced earlier for each response. Feedback is provided on page 124.

Client 1, a 28-year-old woman, [says in a high-pitched voice, with crossed legs and lots of nervous twitching in her hands and face]: My life is a shambles. I lost my job. My friends never come around anymore. It's been months now, but I still can't seem to cut down. I can't see clearly. It seems hopeless.

Clarification: _____

Paraphrase: _____

Reflection: _____

Summarization: _____

Client 2, an African American high school sophomore: I can't seem to get along with my mom. She's always harassing me, telling me what to do. Sometimes I get so mad I feel like hitting her, but I don't, because it would only make the situation worse.

Clarification: _____

Paraphrase: _____

Reflection: _____

Summarization: _____

Client 3, a 54-year-old man: Ever since my wife died four months ago, I can't get interested in anything. I don't want to eat or sleep. I'm losing weight. Sometimes I just tell myself I'd be better off if I were dead too.

Clarification: _____

Paraphrase: _____

Reflection: _____

Summarization: _____

Part Three

Part Three gives you an opportunity to develop your ability to observe key aspects of client behavior that must be attended to if you are going to listen effectively:

1. Vague or confusing phrases and messages
2. Expression of key content
3. Use of affect words

---

*The three client messages can be put on audiotape with pauses between statements. Thus, instead of reading each message, you can listen to it and write your response or say it aloud during the pause.

(continued)

(*continued*)

4. Nonverbal behavior illustrative of feeling or mood states
5. Presence of themes or patterns

Learning Outcome 3 asks you to observe these five aspects of a client's behavior during a 15-minute interview conducted by someone else. Record your observations on the accompanying Client Observation Checklist. You can obtain feedback for this activity by having two or more persons observe and rate the same session and comparing your responses.

Client Observation Checklist

Name of Helper _____

Name(s) of Observer(s) _____

Instructions: For each of the five categories of client behavior, write down key client words and descriptions of behavior as it occurs during a short helping interview. (If observers are not available, audiotape or videotape your sessions, and complete the checklist while reviewing the tape.)

1. Vague or confusing   a. _____
   phrases and   b. _____
   messages   c. _____
                             d. _____
                             e. _____

2. Key content   a. _____
   (situation, event,   b. _____
   idea, person)   c. _____
                             d. _____
                             e. _____

3. Affect words used   a. _____
                             b. _____
                             c. _____
                             d. _____
                             e. _____

4. Nonverbal behavior   a. _____
   indicative of   b. _____
   certain feelings   c. _____
                             d. _____
                             e. _____

5. Themes or patterns   a. _____
                             b. _____
                             c. _____

d. _____
e. _____

Observer impressions and comments: _____
_____
_____

Part Four

Part Four gives you a chance to demonstrate the four listening responses. Learning Outcome 4 asks you to conduct a 15-minute role-play interview in which you use at least two examples of each of the four listening responses. Someone can observe your performance, or you can assess yourself from an audiotape of the interview. You or the observer can classify your responses and judge their effectiveness by using the accompanying Listening Checklist. Try to select listening responses to achieve specific purposes. Remember, in order to listen effectively, it is helpful to

1. Refrain from making judgments
2. Resist distractions
3. Avoid asking questions
4. Avoid giving advice
5. Stay focused on the client

Obtain feedback for this activity by noting the categories of responses on the table and their judged effectiveness.

Listening Checklist

Name of Helper _____

Name of Observer _____

Instructions: In the "helper response" column of the table, jot down a few key words from each statement. In the "client responses" column, insert a brief notation of the client's verbal and nonverbal responses. Then use a check (✔) to classify the helper response as a *clarification, paraphrase, reflection of feeling, summarization,* or *other.* Finally, rate the *effectiveness* of each helper response, using the following scale:

1 = *Not effective.* Client ignored helper's message or gave some verbal and nonverbal indication that helper's message was inaccurate and off target.
2 = *Somewhat effective.* Client gave some verbal or nonverbal indication that helper's message was partly right, accurate, on target.
3 = *Very effective.* Client's verbal and nonverbal behavior confirmed that helper's response was very accurate and on target.

5 KNOWLEDGE AND SKILL BUILDER

Remember to watch and listen for the *client's* reaction to the response for your effectiveness rating.

Helper response (key words)	Client response (key words)	Type of helper listening response					Effectiveness of response (determined by client response) Rate from 1 to 3 (3 = *high*)
		Clarification	Paraphrase	Reflection of feelings	Summarization	Other	
1.							
2.							
3.							
4.							
5.							
6.							
7.							
8.							
9.							
10.							
11.							
12.							
13.							
14.							
15.							
16.							
17.							
18.							
19.							
20.							

Observer comments and general observations: _____
_____
_____

5   KNOWLEDGE AND SKILL BUILDER **FEEDBACK**

 Part One

    1. a. Clarification

  b. Summarization

2. a. Clarification

  b. Summarization

3. a. Reflection

  b. Paraphrase

4. a. Clarification

  b. Paraphrase

5. a. Clarification

  b. Reflection

6. a. Reflection

  b. Paraphrase

Part Two

Here are some examples of listening responses. See whether yours are similar.

Client Statement 1

Clarification: "Can you describe what you mean by 'cutting down'?"

Paraphrase: "You seem to realize that your life is not going the way you want it to."

Reflection: "You appear frightened about the chaos in your life, and you seem uncertain of what you can do to straighten it out."

Summarization: "Your whole life seems to be falling apart. Your friends are avoiding you, and now you don't even have a job to go to. Even though you've tried to solve the problem, you can't seem to handle it alone. Coming here to talk is a useful first step in 'clearing up the water' for you."

Client Statement 2

Clarification: "Can you describe what it's like when you don't get along with her?"

Paraphrase: "It appears that your relationship with your mom is deteriorating to the point that you feel you may lose control of yourself."

Reflection: "You feel frustrated and angry with your mom because she's always giving you orders."

Summarization: "It seems like the situation at home with your mom has become intolerable. You can't stand her badgering, and you feel afraid that you might do something you would later regret."

Client Statement 3

Clarification: "Are you saying that since the death of your wife, life has become so miserable that you think of taking your own life?"

Paraphrase: "Your life has lost much of its meaning since your wife's recent death."

Reflection: "It sounds like you're very lonely and depressed since your wife died."

Summarization: "Since your wife died, you've lost interest in living. There's no fun or excitement anymore, and further, you're telling yourself that it's not going to get any better."

CHAPTER

6

INFLUENCING RESPONSES

LEARNING OUTCOMES

After completing this chapter, you will be able to

1. From a written list of 12 influencing responses, identify the 6 influencing responses by type, with at least 9 accurate classifications.
2. With a written list of three client statements, write an example of each of the six influencing responses for each client statement.
3. In a 30-minute helping interview in which you are an observer, listen for and record six key aspects of client behavior that form the basis for influencing responses.
4. Conduct at least one 30-minute helping interview in which you integrate the core skills and knowledge you have acquired so far: ethics, critical commitments, multicultural competencies, nonverbal behavior, relationship variables, listening responses, and influencing responses.

Listening responses are responses to client messages made primarily from the client's point of view or frame of reference. At times in the helping process it is legitimate to move beyond the client's frame of reference and to use responses that include clinician-generated data and perceptions. These *influencing responses* are active rather than passive, and they reflect a helper-directed more than a client-centered style (Ivey & Ivey, 2007). Whereas listening responses from a helper influence the client indirectly, influencing responses from a helper exert a more direct influence on the client. Influencing responses are based as much on the helper's perceptions and hypotheses as on the client's messages and behavior. In this chapter, we present six influencing responses: questions, interpretations (also called additive or advanced empathy), information giving, immediacy, self-disclosure, and confrontation. The general purpose of influencing responses, according to Egan (2007), is to help clients see the need for change and action through a more objective frame of reference.

SOCIAL INFLUENCE IN HELPING

Underlying the six influencing responses is a helping relationship characterized by mutual and complementary influence processes. Indeed, over the last several decades the helping process has been described as a *social influence process*. Based on the work of Strong (1968) and Strong, Welshe, Corcoran, and Hoyt (1992) and drawing from social psychology literature, the social influence model of counseling presumes three factors at work in the helping process:

1. The practitioner establishes a base of influence with clients by the use of legitimate, expert, and referent power to effect attitude change with clients. *Legitimate* power is power that occurs as a result of the helper's role and trustworthiness. *Expert* power results from the helper's competence and expertness. *Referent* power is drawn from dimensions such as interpersonal attractiveness, friendliness, and similarity between helper and client (such as is found in "indigenous" helpers).
2. The practitioner actively uses this influence base to effect attitudinal and behavioral change in clients through the use of behaviors and tools that enhance the helper's expertness, trustworthiness, and interpersonal attractiveness with clients.
3. Clients are responsive to the ideas and recommendations set forth by the practitioners as a function of their sense of dependence on the helper. Dependence is considered to be a motivational factor in this model.

INFLUENCING RESPONSES AND TIMING

The most difficult part of using influencing responses is timing, deciding when to use these responses in the interview. Some helpers tend to jump into influencing responses before they listen and establish rapport with the client. Listening responses generally reflect clients' understanding of themselves. In contrast, influencing responses reflect the helper's understanding of the client. Influencing responses can be used moderately in the interview with most clients as long as the helper is careful to lay the foundation with attending and listening. The listening base can heighten the client's receptivity to an influencing message. If the helper voices his or her opinions and perceptions too quickly, the client may respond with denial, with defensiveness, or even by dropping out of counseling. When this happens, often the helper needs to retreat to a less obtrusive level of influence and do more listening, at least until a strong base of client trust and confidence has been developed.

Influencing responses are considered more directive than listening responses, which are classified as indirective. The directiveness associated with influencing responses has varying effects on clients. Client-related variables that impact the effects and timing of influencing responses include *reactance* and *race and ethnicity*. Reactance has to do with the need to preserve a sense of freedom (J. W. Brehm, 1966; S. S. Brehm, 1976). Clients who are high in reactance are generally oppositional and are motivated to do the opposite of whatever the helper suggests. Reactance is a trait that tends to be consistent across time. Thus clients who are high in reactance are likely to be more "allergic" to influencing responses regardless of the point at which they are introduced in the helping process. With highly reactant clients, usually less directive responses are associated with better therapeutic outcomes (Beutler & Harwood, 2000). A recent study found this to be true for clients with high alcohol use even across different counseling sessions (Karno & Longabaugh, 2005).

Some clients, however, may actually be more comfortable with an active and directive communication style because it is more consistent with their cultural values. Sue and Sue (2003) conclude that "the literature on multicultural counseling/therapy strongly suggests that American Indians, Asian Americans, Black Americans, and Hispanic Americans tend to prefer more active-directive forms of helping than nondirective ones" (p. 144). Some clients of color may feel more comfortable with the use of directive and active skills because these responses provide them with data about the counselor's orientation. Moreover, the use of influencing responses connotes a locus of responsibility that is perhaps more systemic and less person- or individual-centered. This kind of focus is more consistent with the philosophy of many minority clients who have been recipients of societal discrimination and oppression and may view the problem as residing externally or outside of the individual.

WHAT DOES INFLUENCING REQUIRE OF HELPERS?

Accurate and effective listening depends on the ability of helpers to listen to the client and to restrain some of their own energy and expressiveness. In contrast, influencing responses require the helper to be more expressive and more challenging. Egan (2007) describes the use of influencing responses as responding to "sour notes" present in the client's communication and behavior. To use influencing responses effectively, helpers must first provide a supportive and safe environment by listening carefully, and then they must feel comfortable enough with themselves to provide feedback or amplification to the client that the client may not like. Helpers who have esteem issues of their own may find the use of influencing responses difficult, for these responses carry the risk of upsetting a client by what is said or challenged. Ultimately, the use of effective influencing responses requires helpers to feel secure enough about themselves to have their own voice and to tolerate client disapproval and disagreement.

Some helpers prefer to stay in the "safety net" of a more passive attending style. This strategy may be acceptable to some clients, but it may also mean that the helper and client have entered into a covert collusion with each other not to say anything that expresses displeasure or disappointment.

SIX INFLUENCING RESPONSES

We have selected six influencing responses to describe in this chapter. *Questions* are open or closed queries that seek elaboration or information from clients. *Interpretations* are responses that identify themes and patterns, make implied client messages explicit, and often are based on the helper's ideas or hunches about the client. Interpretations are sometimes referred to as *advanced empathic responses* (Egan, 2007) or as *additive empathy* (Hepworth, Rooney, Dewberry Rooney, Strom-Gottfried, & Larsen, 2006). *Information giving* is the communication of data or facts about experiences, events, alternatives, or people. *Immediacy* is a verbal response that describes something while it is occurring within the helping interview. *Self-disclosure* involves sharing of personal information or experiences with the client. *Confrontation,* also called *challenging responses* by Egan (2007), describe patterns of discrepancies and inconsistencies in client behavior and communication.

Notice how these six influencing responses differ in this example:

Client, a 35-year-old Latina widow, mother of two young children: My whole life fell apart when my husband died. I keep feeling so unsure about my ability to make it on my own and to support my kids. My husband always made all the decisions for me. Now, I haven't slept well for so long, and I'm drinking more heavily—I can't even think straight. My relatives help me as much as they can, but I still feel scared.

Helper questions: What sorts of experiences have you had in being on your own—if any? What feels most scary about this?

Helper interpretation: When your husband was alive, you depended on him to take care of you and your children. Now it's up to you, but taking on this role is uncomfortable and also unfamiliar. Perhaps your increased drinking is a way to keep from having to face this. What do you think?

Helper information giving: Perhaps you are still grieving over the loss of your husband. I'm wondering whether there are rituals in your culture as well as certain people who might be helpful to you in your loss.

Helper immediacy: I can sense your vulnerability as you share this with me, and I'm glad you feel comfortable enough with me to let me in on some of it. I think that might help ease some of the burden you are carrying.

Helper self-disclosure: I think I can really understand what you are facing and trying to cope with since your husband died. I also went through a period in my life when I was on my own and responsible for the well-being of me and my two children, and it was a tough time—lots to deal with at once.

Helper confrontation: It seems as if you're dealing with two things in this situation: first, the experience of being on your own for the first time, which feels so new and scary you're unsure you can do it, and second, the reality that, although your relatives help out, the responsibility for you and your children does now rest on your shoulders.

Table 6.1 provides brief definitions and summarizes the intended purposes of those six influencing responses. The intended purposes are presented as tentative guidelines, not as "the truth." In the remainder of this chapter we describe and present model examples of each response and provide opportunities for you to practice each one and receive feedback about your level of skill.

QUESTIONS

Questions are an indispensable part of the interview process. Their effectiveness depends on the type of question that is asked and the frequency of their use. Questions have the potential for establishing desirable or undesirable patterns of interpersonal exchange, depending on the skill of the therapist. Beginning interviewers err by assuming that a helping interview is a series of questions and answers or by asking the wrong kind of question at a particular time. These practices are likely to make the client feel interrogated rather than understood. Even experienced helpers, however, overuse this potentially valuable influencing response. Although asking a question is all too easy to do during silence or when you are at a loss for words, you should not ask questions unless you have in mind a particular purpose for the question. For example, if you are using a question as an open invitation to talk, realize that you are in fact asking the client to initiate a dialogue, and be sure to allow the client to respond.

Open and Closed Questions

Most effective questions are worded in an open-ended fashion: they begin with *what, how, when, where,* or *who.* According to Ivey, Ivey, and Simek-Morgan (2002), the particular word that is used to begin an open-ended question is important. Research has shown that "what" questions tend to elicit facts and information, "how" questions are associated with sequence and process or emotions, and "why" questions produce reasons. Similarly, "when" and "where" questions elicit information about time and place, and "who" questions are associated with information about people. Open-ended questions serve a number of purposes in different situations (Cormier & Hackney, 2008; Ivey & Ivey, 2007):

1. Beginning an interview
2. Encouraging the client to express more information
3. Eliciting examples of particular behaviors, thoughts, or feelings so that the helper can better understand the conditions contributing to the client's concerns
4. Developing client commitment to communicate by inviting the client to talk and guiding the client along a focused interaction

In contrast to open-ended questions, closed (focused) questions can be useful if the practitioner needs a particular fact or seeks a particular bit of information. These questions begin with words such as *are, do, can, is,* and *did,* and they can be answered with "yes," "no," or some other short response. Closed questions are a major tool for obtaining information during the assessment process. Here are three examples of closed questions:

1. Of all the issues we discussed, which bothers you the most?
2. Is there a history of depression in your family?
3. Are you planning to look for a job in the next few months?

Closed questions serve the following purposes:

1. Narrowing the area of discussion by asking the client for a specific response
2. Gathering specific information
3. Identifying parameters of concerns
4. Interrupting an overly talkative client who rambles or "storytells"

Closed questions must be used sparingly within an interview. Too many closed questions may discourage discussion and may subtly give the client permission to avoid sensitive or important topics. Hepworth and colleagues (2006), however, mention an exception to this general guideline. They note that it may be necessary to use more closed questions if the client "has limited conceptual and mental abilities" (p. 139).

TABLE 6.1	Definitions and Intended Purposes of Helper Influencing Responses	
Response	**Definition**	**Intended purpose**
Questions	Open-ended or closed query or inquiry	*Open-ended questions* 1. To begin an interview 2. To encourage client elaboration or to obtain information 3. To elicit specific examples of client's behaviors, feelings, or thoughts 4. To motivate client to communicate *Closed questions* 1. To narrow the topic of discussion 2. To obtain specific information 3. To identify parameters of a problem or issue 4. To interrupt an overly talkative client—for example, to give focus to the session
Interpretation (advanced or additive empathy)	Mirroring of client behaviors, patterns, and feelings, based on implied client messages and the helper's hunches	1. To identify the client's implicit messages 2. To examine client behavior from an alternative view 3. To add to client self-understanding and influence client action
Information giving	Communication of data or facts	1. To identify alternatives 2. To evaluate alternatives 3. To dispel myths 4. To motivate clients to examine issues they may have been avoiding 5. To provide structure at the outset and major transition points in the helping process
Immediacy	Description of feelings or process issues as they are occurring within the helping interview	1. To open up discussion about covert or unexpressed feelings or issues 2. To provide feedback about process or interactions as they occur 3. To help client self-exploration
Self-disclosure	Purposeful revelation of information about oneself through verbal and nonverbal behaviors alliance	1. To build rapport, safety, and trust in the therapeutic process 2. To convey genuineness 3. To model self-disclosure for the client 4. To instill hope and promote feelings of universality 5. To help clients consider other and different alternatives and views
Confrontation	Description of discrepancy/distortions	1. To identify client's mixed (incongruent) messages or distortions 2. To explore other ways of perceiving client's self or situation 3. To influence client to take action

Guidelines for the Use of Questions

Shainberg (1993) observes that "the point of a question is to open a person to [his or her] own process . . . to come in from a different angle than the client" (p. 87). She notes that it is all too easy for helpers to become sloppy or to lack creativity in formulating truly effective questions. The difference between an effective and a poor question, she says, is whether the question enables the client to look at things in a new way or at a deeper level. She notes that "for many clients, being asked a good question is like having some new energy" (p. 88). Shainberg (1993) also mentions two other factors affecting the effectiveness of questions: (1) *frequency* (more does not mean better) and (2) *timing* (stock questions such as "How does this make you feel?" or "What was that like for you?" tend to yield pat answers).

You will use questions more effectively and efficiently if you remember some important guidelines for their use. First, develop questions that center on the client's concerns.

Effective questions arise from what the client has already said, not from the helper's curiosity or need for closure. Second, after a question, use a pause to give the client sufficient time to respond. Remember that the client may not have a ready response. The feeling of having to supply a quick answer may be threatening and may encourage the client to give a response that pleases the helper.

Third, ask only one question at a time. Some interviewers tend to ask multiple questions (two or more) before allowing the client time to respond. We call this tactic "stacking questions." It confuses the client, who may respond only to the least important question in the series. This guideline is especially important when you are working with children and the elderly, for these clients may need more information-processing time.

Fourth, avoid accusatory or antagonistic questions. These are questions that reflect antagonism either because of the helper's voice tone or because of use of the word *why*. You can obtain the same information by asking "what" instead of "why." Accusatory questions can make a client feel defensive.

Finally, avoid relying on questions as a primary response mode during an interview (unless you are doing an intake, taking a history, or conducting an assessment session). Remember that some cultural groups may find questions offensive, intrusive, and lacking in respect. In any culture, consistent overuse of questions can create problems in the therapeutic relationship, such as fostering dependency, promoting the helper as an expert, reducing responsibility and involvement by the client, and creating resentment (Gazda et al., 2005). The feeling of being interrogated may be especially harmful with "reluctant" clients.

Questions are most effective when they provoke new insights and yield new information. To determine whether it is really necessary to use a question at any particular time during a session, ask the question covertly to yourself, and see whether you can answer it for the client. If you can, the question is probably unnecessary, and a different response would be more productive.

Steps in the Use of Questions

There are four steps in formulating effective questions. First, determine the purpose of your question. Is it legitimate and therapeutically useful? Often, before you probe for information, it is therapeutically useful to demonstrate first that you actually heard the client's message. Listening before questioning is particularly important when clients reveal strong emotions. It also helps clients to feel understood rather than interrogated. For this reason, before each of our example questions, (see below), we use a paraphrase or a reflection response. In actual practice, this bridging of listening and influencing responses is very important because it balances the attending and action modes in the interview.

Second, decide what type of question would be most helpful. Open-ended questions foster client exploration. Closed or focused questions should be reserved for times when you want specific information or you need to narrow the area of discussion. Make sure that your question centers on concerns of the client, not issues of interest only to you.

Third, remember to assess the effectiveness of your questioning by determining whether its purpose was achieved. A question is not useful simply because the client answered or responded to it. Fourth, examine how the client responded and the overall explanation, inquiry, and dialogue that ensued as a result of particular questions.

Those four steps are summarized in the following cognitive learning strategy:

1. What is the purpose of my question, and is it therapeutically useful?
2. Can I anticipate the client's answer?
3. Given the purpose, how can I start the wording of my question to be most effective?
4. How will I know whether my question is effective?

Notice how the helper applies this cognitive learning strategy in the following example:

Client: I just don't know where to start. My marriage is falling apart. My mom recently died. And I've been having some difficulties at work.

Helper: [asks and answers covertly]

Self-question: 1. What is the purpose of my question—and is it therapeutically useful?

To get the client to focus more specifically on an issue of great concern to her.

Self-question: 2. Can I anticipate the client's answer?

No.

Self-question: 3. Given the purpose, how can I start the wording of my question to be most effective?

"Which one of these?" "Do you want to discuss _____?"

Self-question: 4. How will I know whether my question is effective?

Examine the client's verbal and nonverbal response and the resulting dialogue, as well as whether the purpose was achieved (whether the client starts to focus on the specific concern).

At this time the helper's covert visualization or self-talk ends, and the following dialogue ensues:

Helper question: Things must feel overwhelming to you right now [reflection]. Of the three concerns you just mentioned, which one is of most concern to you now? [question].

Client response: My marriage. I want to keep it together, but I don't think my husband does [accompanied by direct eye contact; body posture, which had been tense, now starts to relax].

From the client's verbal and nonverbal responses, the helper can conclude that the question was effective because the client focused on a specific concern and did not appear to be threatened by the question. The therapist can now covertly congratulate herself or himself for formulating an effective question with this client.

Learning Activity 6.1 gives you an opportunity to try out this cognitive learning strategy in order to develop effective questions.

INTERPRETATIONS AND ADDITIVE/ADVANCED EMPATHY

Interpretation is a response that calls for understanding and being able to communicate the meaning of a client's messages. In making interpretive statements, the helper uses her or his hunches or ideas to identify patterns and to make implied client messages more explicit. Interpretive responses can be defined in a variety of ways. We define an *interpretation* as a statement that—based on the helper's hunches—identifies behaviors, patterns, goals, wishes, and feelings that are suggested or implied by the client's communication.

Unlike the listening responses (paraphrase, clarification, reflection, and summarization), interpretation deals with the *implicit* part of a message—the part the client does not talk about explicitly or directly. As Brammer, Abrego, and Shostrom (1993) note, when interpreting, a helper will often verbalize issues that the client may have felt only vaguely. Our concept of interpretation is similar to what Egan (2007) calls "advanced accurate empathy," for this response challenges clients to look deeper. Hepworth and associates (2006) refer to interpretive responses as "additive empathy." They note that at this level of empathy, the practitioner uses mild to moderate interpretive responses that accurately identify implicit underlying feelings and/or aspects of the problem, thus enabling the client to get in touch with somewhat deeper feelings and unexplained meanings and purposes of behavior. Further, these interpretive responses may also identify "implicit goals" or actions desired by but perhaps unacknowledged by the client (p. 97). These interpretive responses go beyond the expressed meaning of client messages to partially expressed and implied messages—hence the use of the term "additive" empathy. If these responses are accurate and well timed, clients will gain a new and fresh perspective.

There are many benefits and purposes for which interpretation can be used appropriately in a helping interview. First, effective interpretations can contribute to the development of a positive therapeutic relationship by reinforcing client self-disclosure, enhancing the credibility of the therapist, and communicating therapeutic attitudes to the client (Claiborn, 1982, p. 415). Another purpose of interpretation is to identify patterns between clients' explicit and implicit messages and behaviors. A third purpose is to help clients examine their behavior from a different frame of reference in order to achieve a better understanding of the problem. Finally, almost all interpretations are offered to promote insight. Johnson (2006) observes that interpretation is useful for clients because it leads to insight, and insight is a key to better psychological living and a precursor to effective behavior change.

Here is an example that may help you understand the nature of the interpretation response more clearly:

Client 1, a young woman: Everything is humdrum. There's nothing new going on, nothing exciting. All my friends are away.

Interpretation: You are tired of the same old, same old, the monotony of it all—you feel bored by it, and lonely—perhaps even restless. . . . You wish something new, something different, something exciting would happen in your life. Does this fit with what you are saying?

Sometimes the implicit response may have to do with a cultural aspect of the client's message. Consider the voice of Thad, the only African American student in his communications class: "This is the first class I have ever had to stand up and give a real speech to. And I just feel like I can't do it, it won't be good enough, it won't meet standards, it won't be as good as the other speeches are. . . . It just won't be good enough." The sensitive helper may hear the implied cultural aspect of Thad's message and give an interpretive response similar to the following: "Giving this speech is a first for you, and you feel gripped with doubt and fear about it—in part because this is a new experience for you and also perhaps because you're the only person of color in the room and you're holding yourself to a higher standard."

What Makes Interpretations Work?

During the last few decades, various research studies have explored the interpretive response, although conclusive evidence on this response is limited because of variations in definitions, designs, client differences, timing of the interpretation, and so on (Spiegel & Hill, 1989). Claiborn (1982) proposed three models that account for how interpretations work with clients. The *relationship* model assumes that interpretations work by enhancing the therapeutic relationship. The *content* model assumes that the meaning and wording of the interpretive response effect subsequent change. The *discrepancy* model assumes that the discrepancy between the helper's ideas and the client's ideas motivates the client to change. Spiegel and Hill (1989) conclude that all three models are relevant in

LEARNING ACTIVITY 6.1   Questions

In this activity, you are given three client practice statements. For each client message, develop an example of a question, using the cognitive learning strategy described earlier and outlined below. To internalize this learning strategy, you may wish to talk through the self-questions overtly (aloud) and then covertly. The end product will be a question that you can say aloud or write down. An example precedes the practice messages. Feedback is provided on page 132.

Example

Client 1, a middle-aged White woman: I get so nervous. I'm just a bunch of nerves.

Self-question 1: What is the purpose of my question—and is it therapeutically useful?

The purpose is to ask for examples of times when she is nervous. This is therapeutically useful because it contributes to increased understanding of the problem.

Self-question 2: Can I anticipate the client's answer? No.

Self-question 3: Given the purpose, how can I start the wording of my question to be most effective? "When" or "what."

Actual questions: You say you're feeling pretty upset [reflection]. When do you feel this way? or What are some times when you get this feeling? [question].

Client Practice Messages

The purpose of the question is given to you for each message. Try to develop questions that relate to the stated purposes. Remember to precede your question with a listening response such as a paraphrase or reflection.

Client 1, an older women who is retired from the workforce: To be frank about it, it's been pure hell around my house the last year.

Self-question 1: What is the purpose of my question? To encourage client to elaborate on how and what has been hell for her.

Self-question 2: Can I anticipate the client's answer?

Self-question 3: Given the purpose, how can I start the wording of my question to be most effective?

Actual questions: _____

_____

Client 2, a 40-year-old physically challenged man: Sometimes I feel kind of blue. It goes on for a while. Not every day but sometimes.

Self-question 1: What is the purpose of my question? To find out whether client has noticed anything that makes the "blueness" better.

Self-question 2: Can I anticipate the client's answer?

Self-question 3: Given the purpose, how can I start the wording of my question to be most effective?

Actual questions: _____

_____

Client 3, a 35-year-old African American woman: I feel overwhelmed right now. Too many kids underfoot. Not enough time for me.

Self-question 1: What is the purpose of my question? To find out how many kids are underfoot and in what capacity client is responsible for them.

Self-question 2: Can I anticipate the client's answer?

Self-question 3: Given the purpose, how can I start the wording of my question to be most effective?

Actual questions: _____

_____

---

considering the use and impact of an interpretive response, for each model describes "an aspect that is operative in the process of intervention" (p. 123). In other words, all three models have some clinical relevance to offer.

Ground Rules for Interpreting

According to the *relationship* model, the overall quality of the therapeutic relationship affects the degree to which an interpretation is likely to be useful to the client. As Spiegel and Hill (1989) observe, "The relationship serves as both a *source* of interpretations and is also enhanced by them" (p. 126). Interpretations need to be offered in the context of a safe and empathic contact with the client.

According to the *content* model, the *quality* of your interpretation is as important as the *quantity*. As Spiegel and Hill (1989) note, "More is not always better" (p. 125). Another important aspect of the content of the interpretation is whether your interpretation is based on the client's

---

6.1 FEEDBACK
Questions

Client 1

Sample questions based on defined purpose: It sounds like things have gotten out of hand [paraphrase]. What exactly has been going on that's been so bad for you? *or* How has it been like hell for you? [question].

Client 2

Sample questions based on defined purpose: Now and then you feel kind of down [reflection]. What have you noticed that makes this feeling go away? *or* Have you noticed anything in particular that makes you feel better? [question].

Client 3

Sample questions based on defined purpose: With everyone else to take care of, there's not much time left for you [paraphrase]. Exactly how many kids are underfoot? *or* How many kids are you responsible for? [question].

---

actual message rather than on your own biases and values projected onto the client. You need to be aware of your own blind spots. For example, if you had a bad experience with marriage and are biased against people's getting or staying married, you need to be aware of how this opinion could affect the way you interpret client statements about marriage. If you aren't careful, you could easily advise all marital-counseling clients away from marriage, a bias that might not be in the best interests of many of them.

A third aspect of the content of the interpretation is the way in which the helper phrases the interpretation and offers it to the client. Although preliminary research suggests there is no difference between interpretations offered with absolute and with tentative phrasing (Milne & Dowd, 1983), we believe that in most cases interpretations should be phrased tentatively. Tentative rather than absolute phrasing helps prevent the counselor from engaging in one-upmanship and engendering client resistance or defensiveness to the interpretation. After responding with an interpretation, check out the accuracy of your interpretive response by asking the client whether your message fits. Returning to a clarification is always a useful way to determine whether you have interpreted the message accurately.

Finally, the content of an interpretation must be congruent with the client's cultural affiliations. Because many counseling theories are based on Eurocentric assumptions,

achieving congruence can be a thought-provoking task. It is most important *not* to assume that an interpretation that makes sense to you will make the same sort of sense to a client whose racial, ethnic, and cultural backgrounds vary from your own.

The *discrepancy* model focuses on the *depth* of the interpretation you offer to the client. Depth is the degree of discrepancy between the viewpoint expressed by the helper and the client's beliefs. Presenting clients with a viewpoint discrepant from their own is believed to facilitate change by providing clients with a reconceptualization of the problem (Strong et al., 1992). An important question is to what extent the helper's communicated conceptualization of the issue should differ from the client's beliefs. A study by Claiborn, Ward, and Strong (1981) addressed this concern. The results supported the general assumption that highly discrepant (that is, very deep) interpretations are more likely to be rejected by the client, possibly because they are unacceptable, seem too preposterous, or evoke resistance. In contrast, interpretations that are either congruent with or only slightly discrepant from the client's viewpoint are most likely to prompt change, possibly because these are "more immediately understandable and useful to the clients" (Claiborn et al., 1981, p. 108; Claiborn & Dowd, 1985).

The depth of the interpretation also has some impact on the time at which an interpretation is offered—both within a session and within the overall content of treatment. The client should show some degree of readiness to explore or examine himself or herself before you use interpretation. Generally, an interpretation response is reserved for later, rather than initial, sessions because some data must be gathered as a basis for an interpretive response and because the typical client requires several sessions to become accustomed to the type of material discussed in counseling. The client may be more receptive to your interpretation if she or he is comfortable with the topics being explored and shows some readiness to accept the interpretive response. As Brammer and colleagues (1993, p. 181) note, a helper usually does not interpret until the time when the client can almost formulate the interpretation for herself or himself. Timing within a session is also important. If the helper suspects that the interpretation may produce anxiety or resistance or break the client's "emotional dam," it may be a good idea to postpone it until the beginning of the next session (Brammer et al., 1993).

Client Reactions to Interpretation

Client reactions to interpretation may range from expression of greater self-understanding and release of emotions to less verbal expression and more silence. Generally, the research on interpretation has not *systematically* explored differential client reactions. Research conducted in this area has yielded varying results (Spiegel & Hill, 1989). Based on these studies, Spiegel and Hill (1989) have speculated that an individual client's receptivity to an interpretation has to do with the "client's self-esteem, severity of disturbance, level of cognitive complexity, and psychological mindedness" (p. 1240). To their list, we would also add the client's cultural affiliation as an important moderating variable.

Although the concept of promoting insight, a goal of interpretation, is compatible for some Euro-American clients, insight may not be so valued by other clients. As Sue and Sue (2003) note, "When survival on a day-to-day basis is important, it seems inappropriate for the therapist to use insightful processes" (p. 110). Also, some cultural groups simply do not feel the need to engage in contemplative reflection. Indeed, the very notion of thinking about oneself or one's issues too much is inconsistent for some clients, who may have been taught not to dwell on themselves and their thoughts. Other clients may have learned to gain insight in a solitary manner, as in a "vision quest," rather than with another person such as a helper. In actual practice, you can try to assess the client's receptivity by using a trial interpretation, bearing in mind that the client's initial reaction may change over time.

If interpretation is met initially with defensiveness or hostility, it may be best to drop the issue temporarily and introduce it again later. Repetition is an important concept in the use of interpretations. As Brammer and colleagues observe, "Since a useful and valid interpretation may be resisted, it may be necessary for the counselor to repeat the interpretation at appropriate times, in different forms, and with additional supporting evidence" (1993, p. 183). However, don't push an interpretation on a resistant client without first reexamining the accuracy of your response.

Steps in Interpreting

There are three steps in formulating effective interpretations. First, listen for and identify the *implicit* meaning of the client's communication—what the client conveys subtly and indirectly. Listen for behaviors, patterns, and feelings, as well as for implied goals, actions, and wishes. Second, make sure that your view of the issue, your frame of reference, is relevant to the client's cultural background, keeping in mind some of the precautions we addressed earlier. Finally, examine the effectiveness of your interpretation by assessing the client's reaction to it. Look for nonverbal "recognition" signs such as a smile or contemplative look as well as verbal and behavioral cues that indicate the client is considering the issue from a different frame of reference or that the client may not understand or agree with you.

To formulate an effective interpretation and assess its usefulness, consider the following cognitive learning strategy:

1. What is the implicit part of the client's message?
2. Is my view of this issue culturally relevant for this client?
3. How will I know whether my interpretation is useful?

Notice how a therapist applies this cognitive learning strategy in the following example:

Client, a Euro-American woman: I really don't understand it myself. I can always have good sex whenever we're not at home—even in the car. But at home it's never too good.

Helper: [asks and answers covertly]

Self-question: 1. What is the implicit part of the client's message?

That sex is not good or fulfilling unless it occurs in special, out-of-the-ordinary circumstances or places. Also that the client doesn't understand what exactly is going on with her sexually and perhaps wishes she could have good sex at home as well as in other places.

Self-question: 2. Is my view of this issue culturally relevant for this client?

This client seems relatively comfortable in talking about and disclosing information about her sexual feelings and behaviors. However, be careful not to make any assumptions about the client's sexual orientation. At this point we do not know whether this person is lesbian, bisexual, or straight.

At this point the helper's covert visualization or self-talk ends, and the following dialogue ensues:

Helper interpretation: Ann, I might be wrong about this—it seems that you get psyched up for sex only when it occurs in out-of-the-ordinary places where you feel there's a lot of novelty and excitement. You don't quite understand this yet and perhaps wish you could have great sex at home, too. Does that sound accurate?

Client [lips part, smiles slightly, eyes widen]: Well, I never thought about it quite that way. I guess I do need to feel like there are some thrills around when I do have sex—maybe it's that I find unusual places like the elevator a challenge.

At this point, the practitioner can conclude that the interpretation was effective because of the client's nonverbal "recognition" behavior and because of the client's verbal response suggesting the interpretation was on target. The therapist might continue to help the client explore whether she needs thrills and challenge to function satisfactorily in other areas of her life as well.

Learning Activity 6.2 gives you an opportunity to try out the interpretation response.

LEARNING ACTIVITY 6.2 | Interpretation

Three client practice statements are given in this activity. For each message, develop an example of an interpretation, using the cognitive learning strategy described earlier and outlined below. To internalize this learning strategy, you may want to talk through the self-questions overtly (aloud) and then covertly. The end product will be an interpretation that you can say aloud or write down. An example precedes the practice messages. Feedback follows on page 135.

Example

Client, a young Asian American woman: I don't know what to do. I guess I never thought I'd ever be asked to be a supervisor. I feel so content just being part of the group I work with.

Self-question 1: What is the implicit part of the client's message?
She feels uncertain and perhaps overwhelmed by the thought of this job transition—and perhaps is concerned about losing her place in the group if she moves out of it to become a supervisor.

Self-question 2: Is my view of this issue culturally relevant for this client?
   With her Asian American background, the client may feel more comfortable working in and with a collective group of people.

Actual interpretation response: Despite your obvious success on the job, you seem to be reluctant to move up to a position that requires you to work by yourself. I'm wondering if you are responding in any part to your cultural background, which stresses belonging to a group, and working for the good of the group rather than promoting yourself. Have I heard you accurately or not?

Client Practice Statements

Client 1, a young, Native American woman: I can't stand to be touched anymore by a man. And after I was raped, they wanted me to go see a doctor in this hospital. When I wouldn't, they thought I was crazy. I hope you don't think I'm crazy for that.

Actual interpretation response: _____

_____

_____

Client 2, a 50-year-old Jordanian man: Sure, I seemed upset when I got laid off several years ago. After all, I'd been an industrial engineer for almost 23 years. But I can support my family with my job supervising these custodial workers. So I should be very thankful. Then why do I seem down?

Actual interpretation response: _____

_____

_____

Client 3, a young White man: I have a great time with Susie [his girlfriend], but I've told her I don't want to settle down. She's always so bossy and tries to tell me what to do. She always decides what we're going to do and when and where and so on. I get real upset at her.

Actual interpretation response: _____

_____

_____

INFORMATION GIVING[*]

There are many times in the helping interview when a client may have a legitimate need for information. A client who reports being abused by her partner may need information about her legal rights and alternatives. A client who has recently become physically challenged may need some information about employment and about lifestyle adaptations such as carrying out domestic chores or engaging in sexual relationships. Information giving is an important tool of feminist therapy approaches. Feminist therapists may give information to clients about gender role stereotyping, the impact of cultural conditioning on gender roles, strategies for empowerment, and social/political structures that contribute to disempowerment.

   We define *information giving* as the communication of data or facts about experiences, events, alternatives, or people, and we identify five intended purposes of information giving (see Table 6.1 for a summary). First, information is necessary when

[*]Although this section focuses on the delivery of information within a helping interview, providing clients with informational sources outside the interview is also important. A useful compendium is the *Authoritative Guide to Self Help Resources in Mental Health* (Norcross et al., 2003). This book provides descriptions and ratings of more than 600 books, movies, and websites for many mental health problems and issues.

<table>
<tr><td>

6.2

</td><td>

F E E D B A C K

Interpretation

</td></tr>
</table>

Client 1

Interpretation example: I'm guessing that not only has the rape affected your trust of other men—even doctors—but also that your cultural background is having some effect too. I'm wondering if you would feel safe going to a traditional healer, and one that you know, instead.

Client 2

Interpretation example: It sounds as though when you lost your job as an engineer, you also lost some parts of the role you have learned from your culture about being a man, a husband, and a father. Even though you're glad to have a job, you're sad about these losses and what they mean for you as a man, and as a husband, father, and provider for your family. Does that seem accurate?

Client 3

Interpretation example: You like spending time with Susie, but you feel pressured to settle down with her and are also put off by her bossiness. It sounds like you wish you had more of the control in the relationship. Does that fit with what you are saying?

---

clients do not know their options. Giving information is a way to help them identify possible alternatives. For example, you may be counseling a pregnant client who says she is going to get an abortion because it is her only choice. Although she may eventually decide to pursue this choice, she should be aware of other options before making a final decision.

Second, information giving is helpful when clients are not aware of the possible outcomes of a particular choice or plan of action. Giving information can help them evaluate different choices and actions. For example, if the client is a minor and is not aware that she may need her parents' consent for an abortion, this information may influence her choice.

In the preceding two kinds of situations, information is given to counteract ignorance. Information giving can also be useful to correct invalid or unreliable data or to dispel a myth. In other words, information giving may be necessary when clients are misinformed about something. For example, a pregnant client may decide to have an abortion on the erroneous assumption that an abortion is also a means of subsequent birth control.

A fourth purpose of information giving is to help clients examine issues they have been successfully avoiding. For example, a client who hasn't felt physically well for a year

may be prompted to explore this problem when confronted with information about possible effects of neglected treatment for various illnesses.

A fifth purpose of information giving is to provide clients with structure at major transition points in the helping process such as beginnings and endings. At the outset of counseling, providing information fulfills the ethical responsibility of helpers to inform clients of such things as the purposes, goals, techniques, and benefits and limitations of counseling. Another important component of information giving during the beginning stage of counseling has to do with therapeutic boundaries, confidentiality, limits of confidentiality, and HIPAA (the federal Health Insurance Portability and Accountability Act). Provision of this kind of information at the outset helps to reduce potential ambiguity and anxiety clients may feel as they approach a helper for the first time. A qualitative study found that clients experienced such structure as providing safety and empowerment (Levitt, Butler, & Hill, 2006). As counseling ensues, practitioners provide structure to clients through information giving at different points in the process. For example, helpers need to provide information about any assessment measures or standardized tests to be used as well as about potential treatment goals and treatment plans. Practitioners also are ethically obligated to provide structure and information to clients as termination of the helping process approaches and/or as referrals are needed to other practitioners.

Differences between Giving Information and Giving Advice

It is important to note that giving information differs from giving advice. A person giving advice usually recommends or prescribes a particular solution or course of action for the listener to follow. In contrast, information giving consists of presenting relevant information about an issue or problem. The decision concerning the final course of action—if any—is made by the client.

Consider the differences between the following two helper responses:

Client, a young mother: I find it so difficult to refuse requests made by my child—to say "no" to her—even when I know they are unreasonable requests or could even be dangerous to her.

Helper (advice giving): Why don't you start by saying "no" to her just on one request a day for now—anything that you feel comfortable with refusing—and then see what happens?

Helper (information giving): I think there are two things we could discuss that may be affecting the way you are handling this situation. First, we could talk about what you feel might happen if you say "no". We also need to examine how your requests were handled in your own family when

TABLE 6.2	The "When," "What," and "How" of Information Giving in Helping	
When—recognizing client's need for information	**What—identifying type of information**	**How—delivery of information in an interview**
1. Identify information presently available to client.	1. Identify kind of information useful to client.	1. Avoid jargon.
2. Evaluate client's present information. Is it valid? Data-based? Sufficient?	2. Identify reliable sources of information to validate accuracy of information, including computer sources.	2. Present all the relevant facts; don't protect client from negative information.
3. Wait for client cues of readiness to avoid giving information prematurely.	3. Identify any sequencing of information (option A before option B).	3. Limit amount of information given at one time; don't overload.
	4. Identify cultural relevance of information.	4. Ask for and discuss client's feelings and biases about information.
		5. Know when to stop giving information so action isn't avoided.
		6. Use paper and pencil to highlight key ideas or facts.

you were a child. Very often as parents we repeat with our children the way we were parented—in such an automatic way we don't even realize it's happening.

In the first example, the practitioner recommends action that may or may not be successful. If it works, the client may feel elated and expect the helper to have other magical solutions. If it fails, the client may feel even more discouraged and question whether counseling can really help her resolve this problem. Appropriate and effective information giving indicates what the client *could* ponder or do, not what the client *should* do, and it indicates what the client *might* consider, not *must* consider.

Several dangers associated with advice giving make it a potential trap for helpers. First, the client may reject not only this piece of advice but any other ideas presented by the helper in an effort to establish independence and thwart any conspicuous efforts by the helper to influence or coerce. Second, if the client accepts the advice and the advice leads to an unsatisfactory action, the client is likely to blame the helper and may terminate therapy prematurely. Third, if the client follows the advice and is pleased with the action, the client may become overly dependent on the practitioner and expect, if not demand, more "advice" in subsequent sessions. Finally, there is always the possibility that an occasional client may misinterpret the advice and may cause injury to himself or to herself or to others in trying to comply with it. Sommers-Flanagan and Sommers-Flanagan (2003) point out that in almost all cases, advice giving meets more of the needs of the helper than of the client.

Ground Rules for Giving Information

Information giving is generally considered appropriate when the need for information is directly related to the client's concerns and goals and when the presentation and discussion of information are used to help the client achieve these goals. To use information giving appropriately, a helper should consider: (1) when to give information, (2) what information is needed, and (3) how the information should be delivered. Table 6.2 summarizes the "when," "what," and "how" guidelines for information giving in counseling.

The first guideline, the "when," involves recognizing the client's need for information. If the client does not have all the data or has invalid data, a need exists. To be effective, information giving also must be well timed. The client should indicate receptivity to the information before it is delivered. A client may ignore information if it is introduced too early in the interaction.

The helper also needs to determine what information is useful and relevant to clients. Generally, information is useful if it is something clients are not likely to find on their own and if they have the resources to act on the information. The helper also needs to determine whether the information must be presented sequentially in order to make the most sense to the client. Because clients may remember initial information best, presenting the most significant information *first* may be a good rule of thumb in sequencing information. Finally, in selecting information to give, be careful not to impose information on clients, who are ultimately responsible for deciding what information to use and act on. In other words, information giving should not be used as a forum for the helper to subtly push his or her own values on clients (Egan, 2007).

One of the critical facets of giving information has to do with the cultural appropriateness of the information being given. Lum (2004) observes that much cross-cultural contact involves communicating with people who do not share the same types of information. Also, some research suggests that people in different cultures vary in the types of information they attend to (Basic Behavioral Science Task Force of the National Advisory Mental Health Council, 1996). For example, providing information to a sick client about a traditional physician and medical care setting may be useful if the client is Euro-American. Many non-Euro-American clients, however, may find such information so far removed from their own cultural practices regarding health and illness that the information is simply not useful.

Other cultural mismatches in information giving abound in family therapy. Enmeshment—the concept of a family system lacking clear boundaries between and among individuals—is a prime example. For some Euro-American families, enmeshment is considered a sign of pathology because in enmeshed families, the autonomy of individual members is considered hampered. However, for many Asian families and for some rural Euro-American families, enmeshment is so completely the norm that any other structure of family living is foreign to them; in many of these families, the prevailing culture dictates that the good of the family comes before the individual members' needs and wishes (Berg & Jaya, 1993). If the helper assumes that this behavior is pathological and gives the client information about becoming more "individuated" or "establishing clearer boundaries," the client may feel misunderstood and greatly offended. Sue et al. (2007) characterize this kind of helper behavior as a "racial microaggression"—that is, a brief and common yet derogatory indignity based on the notion that the values and communication styles of the dominant/White culture are the ones that are the standard-bearer and hence are preferred (p. 281). Therefore, these important questions used to be addressed: Given the client's ethnic, racial, and cultural affiliations, what cultural biases are reflected in the information I will give the client? Is this information culturally relevant and appropriate? If you are not careful to assess the assumptions reflected in the information you share with clients, your information may seem irrelevant and your credibility in the client's eyes may be diminished. Because of the effects of globalization, we cannot afford to be culturally obtuse about the kinds of information we make available to clients.

Information Giving through Technology

Information is given to clients not just during sessions but by electronic means. For example, a client who is struggling with having just learned about her malignant brain tumor can benefit from electronic information as well as from what the helper provides during the session. We don't believe that all information should be given to clients electronically, but we do feel that electronic information is going to become increasingly important in the helping process. Many useful websites are now available for clients; also, many community services, referral sources, and information services are now available online (Schoech, 1999). In addition, many types of support groups are available online and may be especially useful for homebound clients (Garvin & Seabury, 1997; Schoech, 1999).

A number of websites deal with information that may be especially pertinent to diverse groups of clients. However, many clients who are outside of mainstream groups, such as some rural, low-income clients, do not have ready access to computer technology because it has not been "shared evenly across all segments of society or in the world" (Garvin & Seabury, 1997, p. 269). In addition to these social justice issues, there are also emerging ethical issues related to providing information by means of computers. As Bloom (2000) points out, "there is no one central repository and distribution point of technological information. . . . [T]he traveler of the information highway is still urged to exercise caution" (p. 188). The quality and accuracy of websites vary tremendously. Some sites may not be suitable for child clients, and many chat rooms contain offensive language.

As Nurius (1999) points out, because there are "no reviewers, editors, or institutional overseers of psychological resources that anyone who cares to can put on-line, each individual must be his or her own judge to a greater extent" in sorting out issues of quality, appropriateness, and accessibility (p. 63). However, the American Psychological Association has created a website to help people evaluate material online: dotcomsense.com.

Schoech (1999) summarizes a number of advantages and disadvantages of computer-based information. Advantages include convenience and flexibility, self-paced time frame, and provision of an educational service to clients. Disadvantages include the lack of regulations and ethical standards, the lack of current research on effectiveness, and procedures that may be overly structured and too mechanical for some clients (p. 129). Some professional organizations in human services have begun to provide standards on the use of information technology in the helping process. We have also found an excellent resource on online mental health resources by Grohol (2004). This reference book is usually updated every year so it contains very current information. For online updates, see the website http://www.insidemh.com.

In the interview itself, the actual delivery of information, the "how" of information giving, is crucial. The information should be discussed in a way that makes it usable to the client and encourages the client to hear and apply the information. Moreover, information should be presented objectively. Don't leave out facts simply because they aren't pleasant. Watch out too for information overload. Most people cannot assimilate a great deal of information at one time. Usually, the more information you give clients, the less they remember. Clients recall information best when you give no more than several pieces at one time.

LEARNING ACTIVITY   6.3   Information Giving

In this activity, three client situations are presented. For each situation, determine what information the client lacks, and develop a suitable information-giving response, using the cognitive learning strategy described earlier and outlined below. To internalize this learning strategy, you may want to talk through these self-questions overtly (aloud) and then covertly. The end product will be an information-giving response that you can say aloud or write down. An example precedes the practice situations. Feedback follows on page 140.

Example

The clients are a married couple in their 30s. Gus is a Euro-American man, and his wife, Asani, is an Asian American woman. They disagree about the way to handle their 4-year-old son. The father believes the boy is a "spoiled brat" and thinks the best way to keep him in line is to give him a spanking. The mother believes that her son is just a "typical boy" and that the best way to handle him is to be respectful. The couple admit that there is little consistency in the way the two of them deal with their son. The typical pattern is for the father to reprimand him and swat him while the mother watches, comforts him, and often intercedes on the child's behalf.

Self-question 1: What information do these clients lack about this issue?
Information about effective parenting and child-rearing skills.

Self-question 2: Given the clients' ethnic, racial, and cultural affiliations, is this information relevant and appropriate?
I have to recognize that the mother and father probably bring different cultural values to this parenting situation. I'm going to have to find information that is appropriate to both value systems, such as the following:

1. All children need some limits at some times.
2. There is a hierarchy in parent/child relationships; children are taught to respect parents, and vice versa.
3. Children function better when their parents work together on their behalf rather than disagreeing all the time, especially in front of the child.

Self-question 3: How can I best sequence this information?
Discuss item 3 first—working together on the child's behalf—and note how each parent's approach reflects his or her own cultural background. Stress that neither approach is right or wrong, but that the approaches are different. Stress points of agreement.

Self-question 4: How can I deliver this information so that the clients are likely to comprehend it?
Present the information in such a way that it appeals to the values of both parents. The mother values understanding, support, and respect; the father values authority, respect, and control.

Self-question 5: What emotional impact is this information likely to have on these clients?
If I frame the information positively, it will appeal to both parents. I have to be careful not to take sides or cause one parent to feel relieved while the other feels anxious, guilty, or put down.

Self-question 6: How will I know whether my information giving has been effective?
I'll watch and listen to their nonverbal and verbal reactions to it to see whether they support the idea. I'll also follow up on their use of the information in a later session.

Example of information-giving response: You know, Asani and Gus, I sense that you are in agreement on the fact that you love your child and want what is best for him. So what I'm going to say next is based on this idea that you are both trying to find a way to do what is best for Timmy. In discussing how you feel about Timmy and his behavior—and this is most important—remember that Timmy will do better if you two can find a way to agree on parenting. I think part of your struggle is that you come from cultures where parenting is viewed in different ways. Perhaps we could talk first about these differences and then find areas where you can agree.

Client Practice Situations

Client 1 is a young Native American man whose driver's license was taken away because of several arrests for driving under the influence of alcohol. He is irate because he doesn't believe drinking a six-pack of beer can interfere with his driving ability. After all, as he says, he has never had an accident. Moreover, he has seen many of his male relatives drive drunk for years without any problem. He believes that losing his license is just another instance of the White man's trying to take away something that justifiably belongs to him.

Information-giving response: _____

_____

_____

Client 2 is an African American male who has been ordered by the court to come in for treatment of heroin addiction. At one point in your treatment group, he talks about his drug use with several of his sexual partners. When you mention something about the risk of AIDS, his response is that it could never happen to him.

Information-giving response: _____

_____

_____

Client 3 is a 35-year-old Euro-American woman with two teenage daughters. She is employed as an executive secretary in a large engineering firm. Her husband is a department store manager. She and her husband have had

a stormy relationship for several years. She wants to get a divorce but is hesitant to do so for fear that she will be labeled a troublemaker and will lose her job. She is also afraid that she will not be able to support her daughters financially on her limited income. However, she indicates that she believes getting a divorce will make her happy and will essentially solve all her own internal conflicts.

Information-giving response: _____

_____

_____

Be aware that information differs in depth and may have an emotional impact on clients. Clients may not react emotionally to relatively simple or factual information such as information about a helping intervention, an occupation, or a résumé. However, clients may react with anger, anxiety, or relief to information that has more depth or far-reaching consequences, such as a biopsy or an HIV test. Ask about and discuss the client's reactions to the information you give. In addition, make an effort to promote client understanding of the information. Avoid jargon in offering explanations. Use paper and pencil as you're giving information to draw a picture or a diagram highlighting the most important points, or give clients paper and pencil so they can write down key ideas. Remember to ask clients to verify their impression of your information either by summarizing it or by repeating it to you. Try to determine too when it's time to stop dealing with information. Continued information giving may reinforce a client's tendency to avoid taking action.

Steps in Information Giving

There are six steps in formulating the *what, when,* and *how* of presenting information to clients. First, assess what information the client lacks about the issue. Second, determine the cultural relevance of any information you plan to share. Third, decide how the information can be sequenced in a way that aids client comprehension and retention. Fourth, consider how you can deliver the information in such a way that the client is likely to comprehend it. Keep in mind that in cross-cultural helping situations, effective delivery requires you to communicate in a language and style that the client can understand.

Fifth, assess the emotional impact the information is likely to have on the client. Sixth, determine whether your infor-

mation giving was effective. Note client reactions to it, and follow up on client use of the information in a subsequent session. Remember too that some clients may "store" information and act on it at a much later date—often even after therapy has terminated. If you have provided information via technology, remember to follow up on it and to ask for the client's reactions, questions, and concerns about it.

To help with your use of information giving, we have put these six steps in the form of questions that you can use as a cognitive learning strategy:

1. What information does this client lack about the issue?
2. Given the client's ethnic, racial, and cultural affiliations, is this information relevant and appropriate?
3. How can I best sequence this information?
4. How can I deliver this information so that the client is likely to comprehend it?
5. What emotional impact is this information likely to have on this client?
6. How will I know whether my information giving has been effective?

Consider the way a helper uses this cognitive learning strategy in the first example of Learning Activity 6.3.

IMMEDIACY

Immediacy is a characteristic of a helper verbal response that describes something *as it occurs* within a session. Immediacy involves self-disclosure but is limited to self-disclosure of *current* feelings or what is occurring at the present in the relationship or the session. When persons avoid being immediate with each other over the course of a developing relationship, distance sets in.

FEEDBACK 6.3
Information Giving

Client 1

Example of information-giving response: I realize this seems to you to be just another example of what white men do to people of your nation that is unjust and unfair. I also realize that you are following what you've seen many of your male relatives do. So I'm sure, based on all this, it does seem hard to believe that drinking a six-pack of beer can interfere with the way you drive. In fact, it can and does affect how you judge things and how quickly you react. Would you be willing to watch a short film clip with me or check out a website to get some additional information?

Client 2

Example of information-giving response: Kevin, when you say this could never happen to you, it makes me wonder what you know about HIV. Do you know any Black men who have tested positive for HIV? And are you aware that the virus can be spread easily through shared needles and also through semen?

Client 3

Example of information-giving response: Leslie, in discussing your situation with you, there are a couple of things I want to mention. First, it might be useful for you to consider seeing a competent lawyer who specializes in divorce mediation. This person could give you detailed information about the legal effects and processes of a divorce. Usually, a person does not lose a job because of a divorce. In many instances, the husband is required to make support payments as long as the children are of minor age, depending on the custody arrangements. I would encourage you to express these same concerns to the lawyer. The other thing I'd like to spend some time discussing is your belief that you will feel very happy after the divorce. That might be very true. It is also important to remember, though, that just the process of ending a relationship—even a bad relationship—can be very unsettling and can bring not only relief but often some feelings of loss and maybe sadness for you and for your children.

In using immediacy in counseling, the therapist reflects on the current aspect of (1) some thought, feeling, or behavior of the *counselor;* (2) some thought, feeling, or behavior of the *client;* or (3) some aspect of the *relationship.* Here are examples of these three categories of immediacy:

1. *Helper immediacy:* The helper reveals his or her own thoughts or feelings in the helping process as they occur "in the moment:"

   "I'm glad to see you today."

   "I'm sorry, I am having difficulty focusing. Let's go over that again."

2. *Client immediacy.* The practitioner provides feedback to the client about some client behavior or feeling as it occurs in the interview:

   "You're fidgeting and seem uncomfortable here right now."

   "You're really smiling now—you must be very pleased about it."

3. *Relationship immediacy.* The helper reveals feelings or thoughts about how he or she experiences the relationship:

   "I'm glad that you're able to share that with me."

   "It makes me feel good that we're getting somewhere today."

Relationship immediacy may include references to specific here-and-now transactions or to the overall pattern or development of the relationship. For example, "I'm aware that right now as I'm talking again, you are looking away and tapping your feet and fingers. I'm wondering if you're feeling impatient with me or if I'm talking too much" (specific transaction). Consider another example in which immediacy is used to focus on the development and pattern of the relationship: "This session feels so good to me. I remember when we first started a few months ago, and it seemed we were both being very careful and having trouble expressing what was on our minds. Today, I'm aware we're not measuring our words so carefully. It feels like there's more comfort between us."

Immediacy is not an end but, rather, a means of helping the practitioner and client work together better. If allowed to become a goal for its own sake, immediacy can be distracting rather than helpful. It is primarily used to address issues in the relationship that, if left unresolved, would interfere with the helping relationship and the therapeutic alliance. Examples of instances in which immediacy might be useful include the following (Egan, 2007):

1. Hesitancy or "carefulness" in speech or behavior ("Juanita, I'm aware that you [or I] seem to be choosing words very carefully right now—as if you [or I] might say something wrong").

2. Hostility, anger, resentment, irritation ("Joe, I'm feeling pretty irritated now because you're indicating you want me to keep this time slot open for you but you may not be able to make it next week. Because you have not kept your appointment for the last two weeks, I'm concerned about what might be happening in our relationship").

3. Feeling of being "stuck"—lack of focus or direction ("Right now I feel like our session is sort of a broken record. We're just like a needle tracking in the same groove without really making any music or going anywhere").

4. Tension and trust ("I'm aware there's some discomfort and tension we're both feeling now—about who we are as people and where this is going and what's going to happen").

Immediacy can also be used to deal with the issues of transference and countertransference.

Immediacy has three purposes. One purpose is to bring out in the open something that you feel about yourself, about the client, or about the relationship that has not been expressed directly. Generally, it is assumed that covert (unexpressed) feelings about the relationship may inhibit effective communication or may prevent further development of the relationship unless the helper recognizes and responds to these feelings. This may be especially important for negative feelings. In this way, immediacy may reduce the distance that overshadows the relationship because of unacknowledged underlying issues.

A second purpose of immediacy is to generate discussion or to provide feedback about some aspects of the relationship or the interactions as they occur. This feedback may include verbal sharing of the helper's feelings or of something the helper sees going on in the interactive process. Immediacy is not used to describe every passing feeling or observation to the client. But when something happens in the process that influences the client's feelings toward counseling, then dealing openly with this issue has high priority. Usually it is up to the helper to initiate discussion of unresolved feelings or issues. Immediacy can be a way to begin such discussion and, if used properly, can strengthen the working alliance.

A third purpose of immediacy is to help clients gain awareness of their relationships to other people and of issues that cause problems for them with other people. Teyber (2006) describes this as the client's *interpersonal style* and identifies three predominant kinds of interpersonal styles: moving toward others, moving away from others, and moving against others. The rationale for this use of immediacy is that clients usually respond to helpers the way they respond to other people in their lives. For example, if Butler is oppositional with the therapist, he is perhaps also oppositional with significant others in his life. If Catherina idealizes the helper, she probably also idealizes other people in her life who are important to her. If Jorge goes out of his way to please the therapist, he most likely works hard to please other people as well. Immediacy can provide a model for clients of how to address and resolve problems in their interpersonal relationships outside of therapy. Individual clients, as well as couples, families, and groups, usually follow the interpersonal model set by the practitioner (Hepworth et al., 2006).

Ground Rules and Client Reactions

Several ground rules can help practitioners use immediacy effectively. First, the helper should describe what she or he sees *as it happens.* If the helper waits until later in the session or until the next interview to describe a feeling or experience, the impact is lost. In addition, feelings about the relationship that are discounted or ignored may build up and eventually be expressed in more intense or distorted ways. The helper who puts off using immediacy to initiate a needed discussion runs the risk of having unresolved feelings or issues damage the relationship.

Second, to reflect the here-and-now of the experience, any immediacy statement should be in the present tense—"I'm feeling uncomfortable now" rather than "I just felt uncomfortable." This models expression of current rather than past feelings for the client.

Further, when referring to your feelings and perceptions, take responsibility for them by using the personal pronoun *I, me,* or *mine,* as in "I'm feeling concerned about you now" instead of "You're making me feel concerned." Expressing your current feelings with "I" language communicates that you are responsible for your feelings and observations, and this may increase the client's receptivity to your immediacy expressions. Also, as in using all other responses, the helper should consider timing. Using a lot of immediacy in an early session may be overwhelming for some clients and can elicit anxiety in either helper or client. Cultural differences also play a role in the decision to use immediacy. Some clients may feel awkward discussing personal feelings or be unwilling to give feedback if solicited by the helper.

As Gazda and associates (2005, p. 205) observe, "It is highly desirable that a strong base relationship exist before using the dimension of immediacy." If a helper uses immediacy and senses that this has threatened or scared the client, then the helper should decide that the client is not yet ready to handle these feelings or issues. And not every feeling or observation a helper has needs to be verbalized to a client. The session does not need to turn into a "heavy" discussion, nor should it resemble a confessional. Generally, immediacy is reserved for initiating exploration of the most significant or most influential feelings or issues. Of course, a helper who never expresses immediacy may be avoiding issues that have a significant effect on the relationship.

Finally, in using immediacy, even if it is well timed, helpers have to be careful that the immediacy response is based on what is actually happening in the relationship rather than being a reflection of their countertransference response to something occurring with the client. For example, Antony is a beginning helper who has just seen one of his very first clients, Marisa. Marisa is very depressed, so he suggests a consultation with the staff psychiatrist. Marisa is receptive to this idea, and Antony schedules this consultation for her after their session the following week. When the time arrives for the consultation, Antony takes Marisa over to the psychiatrist's waiting room, and she is told that due to some scheduling problems she will have to wait at least an hour or longer before the consultation. Marisa becomes upset and lashes out at Antony, saying that she has taken extra time off from work for this consultation and is losing money because of it. Antony reacts on the basis of his first impulse: "Well, if that's the way you feel, you might as well not come back to see me next week." Fortunately, Antony has a safe and trusting relationship with his supervisor and brings this situation up. His supervisor helps Antony to see that what he blurted out was more a reflection of his countertransference and not truly based on what he really felt about Marisa and their relationship. In fact, he likes working with Marisa very much, and she is important to him, but his response was based on his own feeling that he and the helping process were, in his eyes, not more important to her.

One way to prevent a situation like Antony's is to reach for feelings that underlie your immediate experiencing. For example, you may have a superficial level of a feeling such as dislike or boredom but, reaching underneath, discover curiosity or compassion. Or you may feel annoyed at the client for being late but, reaching deeper, feel disappointment that the client isn't more committed to the helping process (Hepworth et al., 2006). Hill (2004) describes this process as recognizing when you are being "hooked" by the client's behavior and then learning how to "pull out" of being hooked (p. 288). She states: "By coming to an understanding of what clients are "pulling" from them, helpers regain objectivity, which permits them to distance themselves from their reactions and begin to help the client" (p. 289).

Steps in Immediacy

The immediacy-influencing response requires a complex set of skills and requires both critical thinking and judicious adaptation. The first step toward immediacy—and an important prerequisite of the actual verbal response—calls for awareness, or the ability to sense what is happening in the interaction. To develop this awareness, you must monitor the flow of the interaction to process what is happening to you, to the client, and to your developing relationship. Awareness also implies that you can read the clues without a great number of decoding errors and without projecting your own biases and blind spots into the interaction.

After developing awareness, the next step is to formulate a verbal response that somehow shares your sense or picture of the process with the client. Sometimes this may include sharing more than one feeling or sharing conflicting feel-

ings. The critical feature of immediacy is its emphasis on the here-and-now—the present.

The third step is to describe the situation or targeted behavior in neutral or descriptive rather than evaluative terms (Hepworth et al., 2006). The fourth step is to identify the specific effect of the problem situation, of the relationship issue, or of the client's behavior on others and on you (Hepworth et al., 2006). You help the client take action by authentically sharing how the client affects you, instead of cajoling, pleading, or directing the client to change, which usually backfires. The last step is to get the client's reactions to your immediacy response. For example, you can ask the client something like "What is your reaction to what I just shared?" If your response is not helpful, the client will most likely shut down, retreat, or even lash out at you. If immediacy is helpful, the client will provide feedback and engage in more exploration.

To formulate an effective immediacy response, consider the following cognitive learning strategy:

1. What is going on right now—in me, with the client, in the process and interaction between us—that needs to be addressed?
2. How can I formulate an immediacy response that addresses this issue in the here-and-now?
3. How can I describe the situation or behavior in a descriptive rather than an evaluative way?
4. How can I identify the specific effect of this situation or behavior?
5. How will I know if my immediacy response is useful to the client?

Notice how the helper uses this cognitive learning strategy for immediacy in the following example.

The client, Isabella, is struggling with a decision about whether to get a job or go back to school. She has been inundating you with e-mails and phone calls between your weekly sessions. This has gone on for several weeks. You are feeling put off by this. You decide during the session to use immediacy to respond because she is also talking about how much difficulty she seems to have in making connections with other people—who just don't seem to be responsive to her.

Helper: [asks and answers covertly]

Self-question 1: What is going on right now that needs to be addressed?

With me—my feelings of moving away from Isabella. With her—her pattern of inundating me with e-mails and phone calls during the week, which I suspect may be happening with other people in her life. Underneath this are probably feelings of anxiety and uncertainty. With the interaction between us—as she increases her requests for my time and energy, I find myself pulling back and giving less.

LEARNING ACTIVITY   **6.4**   **Immediacy**

In this activity, you are given three client practice statements. For each client message, develop an example of an immediacy response. Apply the cognitive learning strategy and the five self-questions listed below to each client statement. Feedback follows on page 144.

Example

The client has come in late for the third time, and you have concerns about this behavior. One concern is that the client's lateness affects your whole schedule, and another is that you feel uncertainty about the client's commitment to the helping process.

Immediacy response: I'm aware that you're having difficulty getting here on time, and I'm feeling uncomfortable about this. I feel uncertain now about when or whether to expect you for your session. I guess I'm also wondering about your commitment to being here. What is your take on this?

Apply the five self-questions to the following three client examples in formulating your immediacy response.

Self-question 1: What is going on right now that needs to be addressed?

Self-question 2: How can I formulate an immediacy response that addresses this issue in the here-and-now?

Self-question 3: How can I describe the situation or behavior in a descriptive versus an evaluative way?

Self-question 4: How can I identify the specific effect of this situation or behavior?

Self-question 5: How will I know if my immediacy response is effective?

Client Examples

Client 1 stops talking whenever you bring up the subject of her academic performance.

Your immediacy response: _____

_____

_____

Client 2 has asked you several questions about your competence and qualifications.

Your immediacy response: _____

_____

_____

Client 3 and you are experiencing a great deal of tension and caution; the two of you seem to be treating each other with kid gloves. You notice physical sensations of tension in your body, and signs of tension are also apparent in the client.

Your immediacy response: _____

_____

_____

Self-question 2: How can I formulate an immediacy response that addresses this issue in the here-and-now?

Use the present tense, and start first with what I'm aware of, such as "I'm aware of some feelings I'm having that might be related to your experiences in connecting with other people."

Self-question 3: How can I describe the situation or behavior in a descriptive rather than an evaluative way?

Take responsibility for my feelings by using an "I" message, describing her behaviors with the e-mails and phone calls without blaming her.

Self-question 4: How can I identify the specific effect of this situation or behavior?

Describe what I see happening in the process—as she requests more of my time and energy with the e-mails and phone calls, I find myself pulling back, giving less, and wondering if this is part of her difficulty in connecting with other people as well.

Self-question 5: How will I know if my immediacy response is useful to her?

I will ask for her feedback at the very end of my immediacy response.

Immediacy response: Isabella, I'm aware of some feelings I'm having that may relate to both your school and work decision and also to your feeling a lack of responsiveness from other people you try to connect with. If you feel willing to hear them, I'd like to share them with you now [pause to get an indicator of her willingness, which often may be nonverbal]. Okay? Well, I'm finding myself pulling back from you and giving you less of my time and energy as you are making more requests of my time through daily e-mails and phone calls asking me what you should do. I'm guessing you're feeling a lot more anxious about this decision than I know. As a result, you are moving toward me with such intensity that I am actually moving back from you when this happens. I wonder if this might also be going on with some of the people in your life you are having trouble connecting to. [pause] What's your reaction to this?

Isabella's response: Well, that's a lot to digest. I guess I never thought of it that way, and I didn't realize it would have that effect. You are right in that I am feeling very uncertain about what step to take next. I've never had much confidence in my ability to make decisions. When I was growing up—I think maybe because I was the "baby" of the family—lots of decisions were made for me. Now, with my parents both dead, it's all up to me, and that feels scary.

Isabella's response suggests she has benefited from the helper's immediacy response in that she is able to begin to explore the idea of having trouble relying on herself for decisions. Although she did not respond to the part about the other people in her life, this may come at a later time in the session or in a subsequent session. Learning Activity 6.4 gives you the opportunity to develop and practice the skills of immediacy using the cognitive learning strategy described earlier.

SELF-DISCLOSURE

Self-disclosure can be direct or indirect. *Direct self-disclosure* is the intentional revelation of information about oneself through the use of self-disclosing statements (Hepworth et al., 2006, p. 107). *Indirect or unintentional self-disclosure* occurs through every word, look, movement, and emotional expression that the helper makes. Our focus in this chapter is on the use of purposeful and direct self-disclosure as a verbal influencing response to achieve certain purposes in the helping process.

Direct self-disclosure is used with clients for several reasons. Conscious use of self-disclosure can build rapport and foster the working alliance by increasing the helper's authenticity, by promoting feelings of universality, and by increasing trust. This purpose of self-disclosure is important with all clients and is perhaps critical with clients from various racial and ethnic groups who may depend on some helper self-disclosure in order to feel safe (Helms & Cook, 1999). The whole idea of self-disclosing intimate aspects of one's life to a stranger such as a therapist may seem inappropriate to clients from some cultural groups who stress friendship as a precondition to self-disclosure (Sue & Sue, 2003). Helms and Cook (1999) provide a useful guideline for the use of self-disclosure in cross-racial helping situations: "If you want clients to tell you *all* about themselves, you must disclose *something* about yourself," but of course do so in a way that does not shift the focus from them to you (p. 191). In this situation, self-disclosure is used to aid client disclosure through modeling by the practitioner.

Another purpose of self-disclosure is to instill hope in clients and to help clients who may feel alone. Also, self-disclosure can be used to help clients consider other and different alternatives and views, and it may be especially suitable to move clients who are stuck in a rut to take some action.

Ground Rules and Client Reactions

Self-disclosure is a complex skill. There are ethical issues surrounding the use of it. Self-disclosure requires critical thinking and judicious adaptation perhaps more than any of the other listening and influencing responses. In part, this degree of forethought is necessary because it is often very tempting for helpers to disclose something about themselves that meets more of their own needs for expression and validation than the client's needs. Such disclosure constitutes a sort of role reversal. There is also the risk of a helper overidentifying with a client and projecting his or her own experiences and feelings onto the client in the self-disclosed material. For example, a client comes in and reports she is in a second marriage and comments, "Aren't second marriages great?" In response the helper self-discloses and says, "Yes, I think so, too. I have no regrets about having divorced my first husband. What about you?" The client looks sad and puzzled by this: "Well, my first husband died in a car wreck." In an example such as this, the thoughtless use of self-disclosure could get the helper into a lot of difficulty. As Simone, McCarthy, and Skay (1998) note, effective self-disclosure ultimately requires "awareness of the ethical and clinical issues related to maintaining professional boundaries and staying focused on the client and the client's needs" (p. 181).

6.4	**F E E D B A C K** **Immediacy**

Here are some expressions of immediacy. See how they compare with yours.

To Client 1: Every time I mention academic performance, like now, you seem to back off from this topic. I'm aware that, during this session, you stop talking when the topic of your grades comes up. Am I hitting a nerve there, or is there something else going on that would help me understand this better?

To Client 2: I'm aware that right now it seems very important to you to find out more about me and my background and qualifications. I'm sensing that you're concerned about how helpful I can be to you and how comfortable you're feeling with me. What's your reaction to this? Maybe you have something you want to share, and, if so, I'd like to hear it.

To Client 3: I'm aware of how physically tight I feel now and how tense you look to me. I'm sensing that we're just not too comfortable with each other yet. We seem to be treating each other in a very fragile and cautious way right now. I'm not sure what this is about. What reactions do you have to this?

Here we provide some ground rules to help you think critically about self-disclosure. The first ground rule pertains to the timing or the decision about *when* to self-disclose to a client. Hepworth and colleagues (2006) suggest that self-disclosure in most instances, is not useful until rapport has been established with the client: "the danger in premature self-disclosure is that such responses can threaten clients and lead to emotional retreat at the very time when it is vital to reduce threat and defensiveness" (p. 108). Remember that self-disclosure is an influencing response, so building a good preliminary base of listening responses with clients is usually a good idea. Another important aspect of the timing of self-disclosure has to do with the helper's awareness of whose needs are being met by the disclosure. A qualitative study found that moderate levels of helper self-disclosure were therapeutically useful and humanizing as long as the disclosure "conveyed concern about the client rather than about the therapist's self interest, bias, or need" (Levitt et al., 2006, p. 320).

The second ground rule has to do with the "breadth" of the disclosure or *how much* disclosure to provide: the amount of information disclosed. Most of the evidence indicates that a moderate amount of disclosure has more positive effects than a high or low level (Edwards & Murdock, 1994). Some self-disclosure may indicate a desire for a close relationship and may increase the client's estimate of the helper's trustworthiness. Some self-disclosure can provide role modeling for clients from cultures with a low level of emotional expressiveness (Lum, 2004). Helpers who disclose very little could add to the role distance between themselves and their clients. At the other extreme, too much disclosure may be counterproductive (Goodyear & Schumate, 1996). The helper who discloses too much may be perceived as lacking in discretion, being untrustworthy, seeming self-preoccupied or needing assistance. A real danger in overdisclosing is the risk of being perceived as needing as much help as the client. This perception could undermine the client's confidence in the helper's ability to be helpful. Also, too much self-disclosure can lead clients who are from cultures unaccustomed to personal sharing to retreat (Lum, 2004).

Excessive self-disclosure may represent a blurring of good treatment boundaries. Greenberg, Rice, and Elliott (1993) refer to the process of too much helper self-disclosure and not enough attention to boundary issues as *promiscuous self-disclosure.* They note that effective use of self-disclosure is based on the helper's accurate awareness of his or her own inner experience (Greenberg et al., 1993). Also, excessive self-disclosure is the most common boundary violation that precedes unethical sexual contact between therapist and client (Smith & Fitzpatrick, 1995).

Another ground rule pertains to the *duration* of self-disclosure—the amount of time used to give information about yourself. Extended periods of helper disclosure will consume time that could be spent in client disclosure. As one person reveals more, the other person will necessarily reveal less. From this perspective, some conciseness in the length of self-disclosive statements seems warranted. Another consideration in duration of self-disclosure is the capacity of the client to use and benefit from the information shared. As Egan (2007) observes, helpers should avoid self-disclosing to the point of adding a burden to an already overwhelmed client. Of course, if the client doesn't seem to respond positively to the self-disclosure, it is best not to use any more of it. And after the self-disclosure, it is wise to make sure that the focus doesn't stay on you but goes back to the client.

A fourth ground rule to consider in using self-disclosure concerns the *depth,* or intimacy, of the information revealed. You should try to make your statements similar in content and mood to the client's messages. Ivey, Gluckstern, and Ivey (1997) suggest that the practitioner's self-disclosure be closely linked to the client's statements. For example:

Client: I feel so down on myself. My partner is so critical of me, and often I think she's right. I really can't do much of anything well.

Helper similar: There have been times when I've also felt down on myself, so I can sense how discouraged you are. Sometimes, too, criticism from someone close to me has made me feel even worse, although I'm learning how to value myself regardless of critical comments from those I care about.

Helper dissimilar: I've felt bummed out too. Sometimes the day just doesn't go well.

Also, there is some evidence that disclosures of a *moderate* amount of intimacy are linked to more positive effects on the helping process (Kim et al., 2003). This same study found that to some degree counselors are able to determine how clients may perceive a particular disclosure and can therefore judge the appropriate amount of disclosure to make (Kim et al., 2003).

The final ground rule involves *with whom* self-disclosure may or may not be feasible. The nature of the client's problems, the client's ego strength, and any diagnoses are all relevant factors to consider. Hepworth and associates (2006) recommend very limited and concrete self-disclosure with clients who are psychotic or have severe and ongoing mental illness. Similarly, Simone and colleagues (1998) found that self-disclosure is not used much with clients diagnosed with personality disorders (Axis II on a *DSM-IV* diagnosis). In particular, clients with a narcissistic personality disorder are unlikely to respond positively to helper self-disclosure. It takes the focus away from them and constitutes a narcissistic wound, a likely reenactment of their old history with significant caregivers. Unfortunately, helpers who themselves have unhealed narcissistic issues may be most likely to use self-disclosure inappropriately and excessively. Self-disclosure is also used less with clients who have been diagnosed with impulse control and conduct disorders.

For some clients, however, the use of self-disclosure is highly indicated. These include clients who are adolescents and some clients of color, who may feel more comfortable and trusting of practitioners who self-disclose. Self-disclosure is also a primary action tool in both individual and group counseling for clients with substance abuse problems. Finally, Simone and colleagues (1998) found that self-disclosure is used most often with clients who have adjustment, anxiety, posttraumatic stress, and mood disorders.

Steps in Self-Disclosure

There are four steps in developing a self-disclosure response. First, assess the purpose of using self-disclosure at this time, and make sure that you're disclosing for the client's benefit and not your own. Simone and colleagues (1998) suggest a series of questions to help you think through the benefits and risks of self-disclosure with a client:

Will my disclosure pull the focus from the client?

Will it blur boundaries?

Will it make the client focus on my needs or feel frightened about my vulnerability?

Will my disclosure cause the client concern about my ability to help?

Will this disclosure improve or diminish our rapport?

Will it help the client look at different viewpoints, or will it confuse the client?

Will the disclosure help the client feel more hopeful and less alone, or could it demoralize the client?

Does this client need me to model disclosure behavior? (p. 182)

Second, assess whether you know enough about the client (and/or the client's diagnosis) to determine if this client can use your self-disclosure to add to insight and to take action. Consider the nature of the client's problems and diagnoses and how this situation may affect the client's ability to use your self-disclosure effectively. Third, assess the timing of the self-disclosure. Note what indicators you have that suggest whether the client is ready to accept your self-disclosure or be put off by it.

Fourth, remember to assess the effectiveness of your self-disclosure. You can follow up on the client's reactions by paraphrasing and reflecting and by open questions. Observe whether the client is receptive to your self-disclosure or seems shut down by it. If the client seems uncomfortable with your self-disclosure or doesn't acknowledge any similarity with his or her own situation, it is best not to make

additional self-disclosures—at least in this session and perhaps not with this client.

To formulate an effective self-disclosure response, consider the following cognitive learning strategy:

1. What is my reason for disclosing now? Is it linked to the client's needs and statements rather than to my own needs and projections?
2. What do I know about this client and the nature of the client's problems and diagnoses? Can this client use the self-disclosure?
3. How do I know if the timing is right for using self-disclosure with this client?
4. How will I know if my self-disclosure is effective?

Notice how the practitioner uses this cognitive learning strategy for self-disclosure in the following example:

Client, a 45-year-old gay man whose partner recently left him: My partner of 20 years has recently left me for another man. I can't help but wonder if he didn't find me attractive anymore. I have been feeling so disgusted with myself. I keep wondering if I should have been doing things differently—if somehow it was my entire fault. It just makes me feel that I must have done something wrong. I keep thinking if only I had done this or done that, he wouldn't have left.

Helper: [asks and answers covertly]

Self-question 1: What is my reason for disclosing now?

My reason for disclosing now is to instill hope in this discouraged client. It is linked to his statements of feeling totally responsible for the breakup of his relationship.

Self-question 2: What do I know about this client and the nature of his problems? Can he effectively use the self-disclosure?

The client is not psychotic or severely mentally ill and does not appear to have an impulse or conduct disorder. I will keep my response short and get the focus back to the client after it.

Self-question 3: How do I know if the timing for self-disclosure is right?

The timing seems okay because the client seems very discouraged and stuck in his discouragement and self-blame.

Self-question 4: How will I know if my self-disclosure is effective?

I will follow up my self-disclosure with a response that returns the focus to the client and checks out his reaction to the self-disclosure.

Helper self-disclosure: Rich, I have been in a similar situation, and it took me a long time to realize that it wasn't my fault, that no matter what or how much I did, my partner

LEARNING ACTIVITY 6.5 Self-Disclosure

 Respond to the following three client situations with a self-disclosing response, using the cognitive learning strategy described earlier and outlined below. Make sure you reveal something about yourself. It might help you to start your statements with "I." Also, try to make your statements concise and similar in content and depth to the client messages and situations. An example is given first, and feedback is provided on page 148.

Example

The client is having a hard time stating specific reasons for seeking counseling, and you have the feeling that a big part of this difficulty may be due to cultural differences between you and the client.

Self-question 1: What is my reason for disclosing now? Is it linked to the client's needs and statements rather than my own needs and projections?

Self-question 2: What do I know about this client and the nature of the client's problems? Can this client use the self-disclosure?

Self-question 3: How do I know if the timing is right for using self-disclosure with this client?

Self-question 4: How will I know if my self-disclosure is effective?

Actual self-disclosure: I know it takes time to get started. I'm reluctant at times to share something that is personal about myself with someone I don't know, and we come from different ethnic groups. I'm wondering if you feel this way too?

Client Practice Messages

Client 1: The client is feeling like a failure because nothing seems to be going well. She states that she "works herself to death" but never feels as though she measures up.

Actual self-disclosure: _____

_____

_____

Client 2: The client is hinting that he has some concerns about sex but does not seem to know how to introduce this concern in the session.

Actual self-disclosure: _____

_____

_____

Client 3: The client has started to become aware of feelings of anger because of racist remarks being made at work and is questioning whether such feelings are legitimate or whether something is wrong with him.

Actual self-disclosure: _____

_____

_____

still would have left. Does my experience have any usefulness for you?

Client response: Well, I'm surprised something like this has happened to you. You seem to have it together. I guess if it could happen to someone like you, maybe it isn't all because of me.

Rich's response seems to confirm the helper's intent of instilling hope and moving him out of his discouragement. In this situation, the use of self-disclosure seemed to be effective. Learning Activity 6.5 gives you the opportunity to develop and practice the skill of self-disclosure.

CONFRONTATION

Confrontation is an influencing response in which the helper describes discrepancies, conflicts, and mixed messages apparent in the client's feelings, thoughts, and actions. Hepworth

and associates (2006) describe the confrontation response in this way: "Similar to interpretation and additive empathy it is a tool to enhance clients' self-awareness and to promote change. Confrontation however involves facing clients with some aspect of their thoughts, feelings, or behaviors that is contributing to or maintaining their difficulties" (p. 528).

Confrontation has several purposes. One purpose is to help clients explore other ways of perceiving themselves or an issue, leading ultimately to different actions or behaviors. Egan (2007) refers to this purpose as challenging the client's "blind spots," things the client fails to see or chooses to ignore (p. 149). This may involve challenging distortions as well as discrepancies. These distortions may be cognitive ones (often the result of inaccurate, incomplete, or erroneous beliefs and information) or affective ones, involving attributions made from inaccurate or erroneous perceptions (Hepworth et al., 2006).

6.5   **FEEDBACK**
Self-Disclosure

Here are some possible examples of counselor self-disclosure for the three client situations. See whether your responses are similar. Your statements will probably reflect more of your own feelings and experiences. Are your statements fairly concise? Are they similar to the client messages in content and intensity?

To Client 1: I sense how difficult it is for you to work so hard and not feel successful. I have also struggled at times with my own high standards and gradually have learned to be more gentle and easier on myself. Is this something you can relate to?

To Client 2: Sometimes I find it hard to start talking about really personal things like sex. I wonder if this is what's happening to you right now.

To Client 3: I can remember times when it has been hard to admit I feel angry. I always used to control it by telling myself I really wasn't angry or that someone really didn't mean to say something offensive to me. Does this feel like what is happening with you?

A second purpose of confrontation is to help the client become more aware of discrepancies or incongruities in thoughts, feelings, and actions. This is important because discrepancies can be indicators of unresolved, contradictory, or suppressed feelings.

Many times during an interview a client may say or do something that is inconsistent. For example, a client says she doesn't want to talk to you because you are a male but then goes ahead and talks to you. In this case, the client's verbal message is inconsistent with her actual behavior. This is an example of an inconsistent, or mixed, message. The purpose of using a confrontation to deal with a mixed message is to describe the discrepancy or contradiction to the client. Often the client is unaware or only vaguely aware of the conflict before the helper points it out. In describing the discrepancy, you will find it helpful to use a confrontation that presents or connects *both* parts of the discrepancy.

Six major types of mixed messages and accompanying descriptions of confrontations are presented as examples (see also Egan, 2007; Ivey & Ivey, 2007).

1. *Verbal and nonverbal behavior*
   a. Client says, "I feel comfortable" (verbal message), but at the same time is fidgeting and twisting her hands (nonverbal message).

Helper confrontation: You say you feel comfortable, and you're also fidgeting and twisting your hands.
   b. Client says, "I feel happy about the relationship being over—it's better this way" (verbal message), but is talking in a slow, low-pitched voice (nonverbal message).

Helper confrontation: You say you're happy it's over, and at the same time your voice suggests you have some other feelings too.

2. *Verbal messages and action steps or behaviors*
   a. Client says, "I'm going to call her" (verbal message), but reports the next week that he did not make the call (action step).

Helper confrontation: You said you would call her, and as of now you haven't done so.
   b. Client says, "Counseling is very important to me" (verbal message), but calls off the next two sessions (behavior).

Helper confrontation: Several weeks ago you said how important counseling is to you; now I'm also aware that you called off our last two meetings.

3. *Two verbal messages* (stated inconsistencies)
   a. Client says, "He's sleeping around with other people. I don't feel bothered [verbal message 1], but I think our relationship should mean more to him than it does" [verbal message 2].

Helper confrontation: First you say you feel okay about his behavior; now you're feeling upset that your relationship is not as important to him as it is to you.
   b. Client says, "I really do love little Georgie [verbal message 1], although he often bugs the hell out of me" [verbal message 2].

Helper confrontation: You seem to be aware that much of the time you love him, and at other times you feel very irritated toward him too.

4. *Two nonverbal messages* (apparent inconsistencies)
   a. Client is smiling (nonverbal message 1) and crying (nonverbal message 2) at the same time.

Helper confrontation: You're smiling and also crying at the same time.
   b. Client is looking directly at helper (nonverbal message 1) and has just moved chair back from helper (nonverbal message 2).

Helper confrontation: You're looking at me while you say this, and at the same time you also moved away.

5. *Two persons* (helper/client, parent/child, teacher/student, spouse/spouse, and so on)
   a. Client's husband lost his job two years ago. Client wants to move; husband wants to stick around near his family.

Helper confrontation: Edie, you'd like to move. Marshall, you're feeling family ties and want to stick around.

b. A woman presents anxiety, depression, and memory loss. You suggest a medical workup to rule out any organic dysfunction, and the client refuses.
    Helper confrontation: Irene, I feel it's very important for us to have a medical workup so we know what to do that will be most helpful for you. You seem to feel very reluctant to have the workup done. How can we work this out?

6. *Verbal message and context or situation*
    a. A child deplores her parents' divorce and states that she wants to help her parents get back together.
        Helper confrontation: Sierra, you say you want to help your parents get back together. At the same time, you had no role in their breakup. How do you put these two things together?
    b. A young couple has had severe conflicts for the past three years, but still they want to have a baby to improve their relationship.
        Helper confrontation: The two of you have separated three times since I've been seeing you in therapy. Now you're saying you want to use a child to improve your relationship. Many couples indicate that having a child and being parents increases stress. How do you put this together?

Ground Rules for Confronting

Confrontation needs to be offered in a way that helps clients examine the consequences of their behavior rather than defend their actions (Johnson, 2006). In other words, confrontation must be used carefully in order not to increase the very behavior or pattern that the helper feels may need to be diminished or modified. The following ground rules may assist you in using this response to help rather than to harm.

First, be aware of your own motives for confronting at any particular time. Although the word itself has a punitive or emotionally charged sound, confrontation in the helping process is not an attack on the client or an opportunity to badger the client (Welfel & Patterson, 2005). Confrontation also is not to be used as a way to ventilate or dump your frustration onto the client. It is a means of offering constructive, growth-directed feedback that is positive in context and intent, not disapproving or critical (Welfel & Patterson, 2005). To emphasize this, Egan (2007) uses the word *challenge* in lieu of *confront*. Ivey and Ivey (2007) describe confrontation as a "supportive" kind of challenge and a "gentle skill that involves listening to the client carefully and respectfully, and then seeking to help the client examine oneself or the situation more fully . . . it is not going against the client, it is going with the client" (p. 263).

To avoid blame, focus on the incongruity as the problem, not on the person, and make sure your supportive stance is reflected in your tone of voice and body language. In describing the distortion or discrepancy, the confrontation should cite a *specific example* of the behavior rather than make a vague inference. A poor confrontation might be "You want people to like you, but your personality turns them off." In this case, the practitioner is making a general inference about the client's personality and also is implying that the client must undergo a major overhaul in order to get along with others. A more helpful confrontation would be "You want people to like you, and at the same time you make frequent remarks about yourself that seem to get in the way and turn people off."

Moreover, before a helper tries to confront a client, rapport and trust should be established. Confrontation probably should not be used unless you, the helper, are willing to maintain or increase your involvement in or commitment to the helping relationship (Johnson, 2006). The primary consideration is to judge what your level of involvement seems to be with each client and adapt accordingly. The stronger the relationship is, the more receptive the client may be to a confrontation.

The *timing* of a confrontation is very important. Because the purpose is to help the person engage in self-examination, try to offer the confrontation at a time when the client is likely to use it. The perceived ability of the client to act on the confrontation should be a major guideline in deciding when to confront. In other words, before you jump in and confront, determine the person's attention level, anxiety level, desire to change, and ability to listen. A confrontation is most likely to be heard when the client feels safe with you; it is less likely to be heard when it occurs early in the relationship. An exception to this general ground rule is in instances of legal violations and danger to self or to others, when confrontation would be mandated earlier in the helping process (Hepworth et al., 2006).

Appropriate use of timing also means that the helper does not confront on a "hit and run" basis (Johnson, 2006). Ample time should be given after the confrontation to allow the client to react to and discuss the effects of this response. For this reason, helpers should avoid confronting near the end of a session.

It is also a good idea not to overload the client with confrontations that make heavy demands in a short time. The rule of "successive approximations" suggests that gradually learning small steps of behaviors is much easier than trying to make big changes overnight. Initially, you may want to confront the person with something that can be managed fairly easily and with some success. Carkhuff (1987) suggests that two successive confrontations may be too intense and should be avoided. With clients who are fragile or clients who are experiencing severe stress or emotional strain, it is wise to avoid using confrontation altogether (Hepworth et al., 2006).

The gender and cultural affiliations of clients also have an impact on the usefulness of the confrontation response. This response may be more suitable for Euro-American male clients, particularly manipulative and acting-out ones (Ivey & Ivey, 2007). Some traditional Asian and Native American clients may view confrontation as disrespectful and insensitive (Sue & Sue, 2003). For *all* clients, it is important to use this response in such a way that the client views you as an *ally,* not an adversary (Welfel & Patterson, 2005).

Finally, acknowledge the limits of confrontation. Confrontation usually brings about client awareness of a discrepancy or conflict. Awareness of discrepancies is an initial step in resolving conflicts. Confrontation, as a single response, may not always bring about resolution of the discrepancy without additional discussion or intervention strategies. Genuine client awareness is often difficult to detect because it may be not an immediate reaction but one that occurs over a period of time.

Client Reactions to Confrontation

Sometimes helpers are afraid to confront because they are uncertain how to handle the client's reactions to the confrontation. Even clients who hear and acknowledge the confrontation may be anxious or upset about the implications.

Hill and Nutt-Williams (2000) note that the empirical evidence surrounding client reactions to confrontation is mixed. A qualitative study also found mixed reviews for the effects of confrontation on clients (Levitt, et al., 2006). In this study, many clients did not have a positive reaction to being challenged by their helper, but there were two notable exceptions: clients who were being manipulative and clients who were avoiding difficult material. These clients felt being challenged was useful for them. One client noted that it was extremely helpful to have a therapist who was "stronger than her eating disorder" (p. 320). For clients who have reasons (often cultural ones) to distrust helpers or for clients such as some adolescents, who may be oppositional, confrontation can produce resistance and lead to poorer client outcomes. Some evidence suggests that in these cases, a process called *motivational interviewing,* which is based on the client-centered listening responses and basic empathy, may yield better client outcomes (Miller & Rollnick, 2002).

Generally, a practitioner can expect four types of client reaction to a confrontation: denial, confusion, false acceptance, or genuine acceptance.

In a denial of the confrontation, the client does not want to acknowledge or agree to the helper's message. A denial may indicate that the client is not ready or tolerant enough to face the discrepant or distorted behavior. Egan (2007, pp. 157–158) lists some specific ways in which the client might deny the confrontation:

1. Discrediting the helper (e.g., "How do you know when you don't even have kids?")
2. Persuading the helper that his or her views are wrong or misinterpreted (e.g., "I didn't mean it that way.")
3. Devaluing the importance of the topic (e.g.,"This isn't worth all this time anyway.")
4. Seeking support elsewhere (e.g., "I told my friends about your comment last week, and none of them had ever noticed that.")
5. Agreeing with the challenger but not acting on the challenge (e.g., "I think you're right. I should speak up and tell how I feel, but I'm not sure I can do that.")

At other times, the client may indicate confusion or uncertainty about the meaning of the confrontation. In some cases, the client may be genuinely confused about what the practitioner is saying. This reaction may indicate that your confrontation was not concise and specific. At other times, the client may use a lack of understanding as a smoke screen—that is, as a way to avoid dealing with the impact of the confrontation.

Sometimes the client may seem to accept the confrontation. Acceptance is usually genuine if the client responds with a sincere desire to examine her or his behavior. Eventually such clients may be able to catch their own discrepancies and confront themselves. But Egan (2007) cautions that false acceptance also can occur, which is another client game. In this case, the client verbally agrees with the helper. However, instead of pursuing the confrontation, the client agrees only to get the helper to leave well enough alone. The risk of having confrontation rejected is greatest among clients who need to be confronted the most but, because they are less likely to engage in self-confrontation and may have lower self-esteem, are more likely to read criticism or blame into this response when none is intended (Hepworth et al., 2006).

There is no set way of dealing with client reactions to confrontation. However, a general guideline is to follow up with basic empathy and go back to the client-oriented listening responses of paraphrase and reflection. A helper can use these responses to lay the foundation before the confrontation and return to this foundation after the confrontation. The sequence might go something like this:

Helper: You seem to feel concerned about your parents' divorce. [reflection]

Client [says in a low, sad voice]: Actually, I feel pretty happy. I'm glad for their sake they got a divorce. [mixed message]

Helper: You say you're happy, and at the same time, from your voice I sense that you feel unhappy. [confrontation]

Client: I don't know what you're talking about, really. [denial]

Helper: I feel that what I just said has upset you. [reflection]

Steps in Confronting

There are four steps in developing effective confrontations.

1. Observe the client carefully to identify the type of discrepancy, or distortions, that the client presents. Listen for a period of time so that you can detect several inconsistencies before jumping in with a confrontation response.
2. Assess the purpose of your confrontation. Make sure that it is based on the client's need to be challenged in some way and not on your need to challenge. Assess whether the relationship is sufficiently safe enough for the client to be able to benefit from the confrontation. Also assess whether the confrontation is appropriate based on the client's race and ethnicity, gender, and age.
3. Summarize the different elements of the discrepancy. In doing so, use a statement that *connects* the parts of the conflict rather than disputes any one part, for the overall aim of confrontation is to resolve conflicts and to achieve integration. A useful summary is "On the one hand, you _____, *and* on the other hand, _____." Notice that the elements are connected with the word *and* rather than with *but* or *yet*. This approach helps you present your confrontation in a descriptive rather than a judgmental way. Make sure that your tone of voice and nonverbal behavior convey concern and caring for the client as well.
4. Remember to assess the effectiveness of your confrontation. A confrontation is effective whenever the client acknowledges the existence of the incongruity or conflict. However, keep in mind that the effectiveness of your confrontation might not be immediate. Watch also for signs that the client may feel defensive or signs indicating indirect reactions to your confrontation. Remember that the client may be adept at masking an overt negative reaction but may subtly withdraw or shut down in the rest of the session if the confrontation has not been well received.

To formulate a confrontation, consider the following cognitive learning strategy:

1. What discrepancy or distortion do I see, hear, or grasp in this client's communication?
2. What is my purpose in confronting the client, and is it useful for this client at this time?
3. How can I summarize the various elements of the discrepancy or distortion?
4. How will I know whether my confrontation is effective?

Notice how a helper uses this cognitive learning strategy for confrontation in the following example:

Client [says in low, soft voice]: It's hard for me to discipline my son. I know I'm too indulgent. I know he needs

limits. But I just don't give him any. I let him do basically whatever he feels like doing.

Helper: [asks and answers covertly]
Self-question 1. What discrepancy or distortion do I see, hear, or grasp in this client's communication?
A discrepancy between two verbal messages and between verbal cues and behavior: client knows son needs limits but doesn't give him any.
Self-question 2. What is my purpose in confronting the client, and is it useful for this client at this time?
My purpose is to challenge the inconsistencies between what this parent actually does with his son and what he wants to do but has not yet been able to do, and to support him in this action. There doesn't appear to be anything about the client that would make him more defensive with the use of this response at this time.
Self-question 3. How can I summarize the various elements of the discrepancy or distortion?
Client believes limits would help son; at the same time, client doesn't follow through.
Self-question 4. How will I know whether my confrontation is effective?
Observe the client's response and see whether he acknowledges the discrepancy.

At this point the helper's self-talk or covert visualization ends, and the following dialogue occurs:

Helper confrontation: William, on the one hand, you feel like having limits would really help your son, and at the same time, he can do whatever he pleases with you. How do you put this together?

Client response: Well, I guess that's right. I do feel strongly that he would benefit from having limits. He gets away with a lot. He's going to become very spoiled, I know. But I just can't seem to "put my foot down" or make him do something.

From the client's response, which confirms the discrepancy, the helper can conclude that the confrontation was initially useful (further discussion of the discrepancy seems necessary to help the client resolve the conflict between feelings and actions).

Learning Activity 6.6 gives you an opportunity to apply this cognitive learning strategy to develop the skill of confrontation.

CHAPTER SUMMARY

Listening responses reflect clients' perceptions of their world. Influencing responses provide alternative ways for clients to view themselves and their world. A change in the client's way of viewing and explaining things may be one indication

LEARNING ACTIVITY   6.6   Confrontation

We give you three client practice statements in this activity. For each message, develop an example of a confrontation, using the cognitive learning strategy described earlier and outlined below. To internalize this learning strategy, you may wish to talk through these self-questions overtly (aloud) and then covertly. The end product will be a confrontation that you can say aloud or write down. An example precedes the practice messages. Feedback follows on page 154.

Example

Client, a Latino college student: I'd like to get through medical school with a flourish. I want to be at the top of my class and achieve a lot. All this partying is getting in my way and preventing me from doing my best work.

Self-question 1: What discrepancy or distortions do I see, hear, or grasp in this client's communication?
A discrepancy between verbal message and behavior. He says he wants to be at the top of his class and at the same time is doing a lot of partying.

Self-question 2: What is my purpose in confronting the client, and is it useful for this client at this time?
My purpose is to help him explore the two different messages in his communication and to do so with sensitivity and respect.

Self-question 3: How can I summarize the various elements of the discrepancy or distortion?
He wants to be at the top of his class and at the same time is doing a lot of partying, which is interfering with his goal.

Actual confrontation response: You're saying that you feel like achieving a lot and being at the top of your class and also that you're doing a lot of partying, which appears to be interfering with this goal. *or* Eduardo, you're saying that

doing well in medical school is very important to you. You have also indicated you are partying instead of studying. How important is being at the top for you?

Client Practice Messages

Client 1, an Asian American graduate student: My wife and child are very important to me. They make me feel it's all worth it. It's just that I know I have to work all the time if I want to make it in my field, and right now I can't be with them as much as I'd like.

Actual confrontation response: _____

_____

_____

Client 2, a 13-year-old African American girl: Sure, it would be nice to have Mom at home when I get there after school. I don't feel lonely. It's just that it would feel so good to have someone close to me there and not to have to spend a couple of hours every day by myself.

Actual confrontation response: _____

_____

_____

Client 3, a Euro-American high school student: My dad thinks it's terribly important for me to get all A's. He thinks I'm not working up to my potential if I get a B. I told him I'd much rather be well rounded and get a few B's and also have time to talk to my friends and play basketball.

Actual confrontation response: _____

_____

_____

of positive movement in counseling. According to Egan (2007), helper statements that move beyond the client's frame of reference are a "bridge" between listening responses and concrete change programs. To be used effectively, influencing responses require a great deal of helper concern and judgment.

Both listening responses and influencing responses reflect two different sorts of helper communication styles. Part of the decision about the timing of these responses involves the helper's awareness of the client's cultural affiliations. As Sue and Sue (2003) note, it is important

for helpers to be able to shift their communication style to meet the unique cultural dimensions of every client. For the most part, although with some exceptions, clients from some culturally diverse groups value influencing responses because they are more directive in nature than listening responses. However, for clients who are highly reactant, the directiveness reflected in influencing responses may thwart therapeutic progress. Part of the practitioner's task is to discern the effects of these responses from clients and adjust his or her counseling style appropriately.

REFERENCES

Basic Behavioral Science Task Force of the National Advisory Mental Health Council. (1996). Thought and communication. *American Psychologist, 51,* 181–189.

Berg, I., & Jaya, A. (1993). Different and same: Family therapy with Asian-American families. *Journal of Marital and Family Therapy, 19,* 31–38.

Beutler, L., & Harwood, T. (2000). *Prescriptive psychotherapy: A practical guide to systematic treatment selection.* New York: Oxford University Press.

Bloom, J. (2000). Technology and web counseling. In H. Hackney (Ed.), *Practice issues for the beginning counselor* (pp. 183–202). Boston: Allyn & Bacon.

Brammer, L. M., Abrego, P. J., & Shostrom, E. I. (1993). *Therapeutic psychology* (6th ed.). Englewood Cliffs, NJ: Prentice Hall.

Brehm, J. W. (1966). *A theory of psychological reactance.* New York: Academic Press.

Brehm, S. S. (1976). *The application of social psychology to clinical practice.* Washington, DC: Hemisphere.

Carkhuff, R. R. (1987). *The art of helping* (6th ed.). Amherst, MA: Human Resource Development Press.

Claiborn, C. D. (1982). Interpretation and change in counseling. *Journal of Counseling Psychology, 29,* 439–453.

Claiborn, C. D., & Dowd, E. T. (1985). Attributional interpretations in counseling: Content versus discrepancy. *Journal of Counseling Psychology, 32,* 188–196.

Claiborn, C. D., Ward, S. R., & Strong, S. R. (1981). Effects of congruence between counselor interpretations and client beliefs. *Journal of Counseling Psychology, 28,* 101–109.

Cormier, S., & Hackney, H. (2008). *Counseling strategies and interventions* (7th ed.). Boston: Allyn & Bacon.

Edwards, C., & Murdock, N. (1994). Characteristics of therapist self-disclosure in the counseling process. *Journal of Counseling and Development, 72,* 384–389.

Egan G. (2007). *The skilled helper* (8th ed.). Pacific Grove, CA: Brooks/Cole.

Garvin, C., & Seabury, B. (1997). *Interpersonal practice in social work: Promoting competence and social justice* (2nd ed.). Boston: Allyn & Bacon.

Gazda, G., Balzer, F., Childers, W., Nealy, A., Phelps, R., & Walters, R. (2005). *Human relations development* (7th ed.). Boston: Allyn & Bacon.

Goodyear, R., & Schumate, J. (1996). Perceived effects of therapist self-disclosure of attraction to clients. *Professional Psychology, 27,* 613–616.

Greenberg, L. S., Rice, L. N., & Elliott, R. (1993). *Facilitating emotional change.* New York: Guilford Press.

Grohol, J. M. (2004). *The insider's guide to mental health resources.* New York: Guilford Press.

Helms, J., & Cook, D. (1999). *Using race and culture in counseling and psychotherapy.* Boston: Allyn & Bacon.

Hepworth, D. H., Rooney, R. H., Dewberry Rooney, G., Strom-Gottfried, K., & Larsen, J. (2006). *Direct social work practice* (7th ed.). Belmont, CA: Thomson–Brooks/Cole.

Hill, C. E. (2004). *Helping skills* (2nd ed.). Washington, D. C: American Psychological Association.

Hill, C. E., & Nutt Williams, S. E. (2000). The process of individual therapy. In S. D. Brown & R.W. Lent (Eds.), *Handbook of counseling psychology* (pp. 670–710). New York: Wiley.

Ivey, A. E., D'Andrea, M., Ivey, M. B., & Simek-Morgan., L. (2002). *Theories of counseling and psychotherapy: A multicultural perspective* (5th ed.). Boston: Allyn & Bacon.

Ivey, A. E., Gluckstern, N. B., & Ivey, M. B. (1997). *Basic influencing skills.* North Amherst, MA: Microtraining Associates.

Ivey, A. E., & Ivey, M. B. (2007). *Intentional interviewing and counseling* (6th ed.). Belmont, CA: Thomson–Brooks/Cole.

Johnson, D. W. (2006). *Reaching out: Interpersonal effectiveness and self actualization* (9th ed.). Boston: Allyn & Bacon.

Karno, M. P., & Longabaugh, R. (2005). Less therapist directiveness is associated with better outcomes among reactant clients. *Journal of Consulting and Clinical Psychology, 73,* 262–267.

Kim, B. S. K., Hill, C. E., Gelso, C. J., Goates, M. K., Asay, P. A., & Harbin, J. M. (2003). Counselor self-disclosure, East Asian American client adherence to Asian cultural values, and counseling process. *Journal of Counseling Psychology, 50,* 324–332.

Levitt, H., Butler, M., & Hill, T. (2006). What clients find helpful in psychotherapy: Developing principles for facilitating moment-to-moment change. *Journal of Counseling Psychology, 53,* 324–324.

Lum, D. (2004). *Social work practice and people of color* (5th ed.). Belmont, CA: Thomson–Brooks/Cole.

Miller, W. R., & Rollnick, S. (2002). *Motivational interviewing* (2nd ed.). New York: Guilford Press.

Milne, C. R., & Dowd, E. T. (1983). Effect of interpretation style on counselor social influence. *Journal of Counseling Psychology, 51,* 603–606.

Norcross, J. C., Santrock, J. W., Campbell, L. E., Smith, T. P, Sommer, R., & Zuckerman, E. L. (2003). *Authoritative guide to self help resources in mental health* (Rev. ed.) New York: Guilford Press.

Nurius, P. S. (1999). Three online books—*Psych Online, Psychological Resources on the WWW,* and *The Insider's Guide to Mental Health Resources. Journal of Technology in Human Services, 16,* 57–64.

Schoech, D. (1999). *Human services technology* (2nd ed.). New York: Haworth.

Shainberg, D. (1993). *Healing in psychotherapy.* Langhorne, PA: Gordon & Breach.

6.6 FEEDBACK

Confrontation

Client 1

Examples of confrontation responses: David, on the one hand, you feel your family is very important, and on the other, you feel your work takes priority over them. How do you put this together? *or* You're saying that your family makes things feel worthwhile for you. At the same time you're indicating you must make it in your field in order to feel worthwhile. How do these two things fit for you?

Client 2

Examples of confrontation responses: Denise, you're saying that you don't feel lonely and also that you wish someone like your mom could be home with you. How do you put this together? *or* It seems as though you're trying to accept your mom's absence and at the same time still feeling like you'd rather have her home with you. I wonder if it does feel kind of lonely sometimes?

Client 3

Examples of confrontation responses: Gary, you're saying that doing a variety of things is more important than getting all A's whereas your father believes that all A's should be your top priority. *or* Gary, you're saying you value variety and balance in your life and your father believes high grades come first. *or* Gary, you want to please your father and make good grades, and at the same time, you want to spend time according to your priorities and values. (*Note:* Do not attempt to confront both discrepancies at once!)

Simone, D. H., McCarthy, P., & Skay, C. (1998). An investigation of client and counselor variables that influence likelihood of counselor self-disclosure. *Journal of Counseling and Development, 76,* 174–182.

Smith, D., & Fitzpatrick, M. (1995). Patient–therapist boundary issues. *Professional Psychology, 26,* 499–506.

Sommers-Flanagan, J., & Sommers-Flanagan, R. (2003). *Clinical interviewing* (3rd ed.). New York: Wiley.

Spiegel, S. B., & Hill, C. E. (1989). Guidelines for research on therapist interpretation: Toward greater methodological rigor and relevance to practice. *Journal of Counseling Psychology, 36,* 121–129.

Strong, S. R. (1968). Counseling: An interpersonal influence process. *Journal of Counseling Psychology, 15,* 215–224.

Strong, S. R., Welsh, J., Corcoran, J., & Hoyt, W. (1992). Social psychology and counseling psychology: The history, products, and promise of an interface. *Journal of Counseling Psychology, 39,* 139–157.

Sue, D. W., Capodilupo, C. M., Torino, G. C., Bucceri, J. M., Holder, A. M. B., Nadal, K. L., & Esquilin, M. (2007). Racial microaggressions in everyday life: Implications for clinical practice. *American Psychologist, 62,* 271–286.

Sue, D. W., & Sue, D. (2003). *Counseling the culturally diverse* (4th ed.). New York: Wiley.

Teyber, E. (2006). *Interpersonal process in therapy* (5th ed.). Belmont, CA: Thomson–Brooks/Cole.

Wehrly, B. (1996). *Pathways to multicultural counseling competence: A Developmental Journey.* Pacific Grove, CA: Brooks/Cole.

Welfel, E., R., & Patterson, L. E. (2005). *The counseling process* (6th ed.). Pacific Grove, CA: Brooks/Cole.

6   KNOWLEDGE AND SKILL BUILDER

Part One

Part one is designed to help you assess your performance on Learning Outcome 1. Identify the type of influencing response—question, interpretation, information giving, immediacy, self-disclosure, confrontation—that is evident in each helper response. Each helper response may be an example of one type of influencing response. If you accurately label 9 out of 12 responses, you will have met this objective. Check your answers against those provided in the feedback on page 160.

1. **Client [talking rapidly, with pressured speech]:** The pressure from my job is starting to get to me. I'm always in a constant rush, trying to hurry and get several things done at the same time. There's never enough time.
   a. Yeah, it sounds like that saying of "The hurrieder I go, the behinder I get." And in your situation, the more you rush, the more pressure you feel, and the more pressure you feel, the more you rush. So you're sort of caught in this ongoing process, and it barely feels tolerable. You'd like to find a way out of it.
   b. It's important you are aware of this. Continued anxiety and stress like this can lead to health problems if they go unchecked.
   c. Now that you are mentioning this, I'm noticing how pressured you seem with me, partly from how fast you're talking and also from how you seem to be hurrying through the session. Does that feel accurate to you?

2. **Client:** I'm tired of sitting home alone, but I feel so uptight when I ask a girl for a date.
   a. You seem to be saying that you feel lonely and also that you're not willing to risk asking a girl to go out with you.
   b. What makes you so anxious when you speak with girls?
   c. I can relate to what you are saying in that I too have had to deal with some fears of my own in meeting new people. One thing that helped me was to join a couple of social and community groups where everyone was new to each other. This helped me practice meeting new people in a low-risk situation—if they didn't like me, I didn't lose much. Although this example isn't specific to dating, I think some of the principles are similar. What do you think?

3. **Client:** I don't know why I tolerate his abuse. I really don't love him.

   a. On the one hand, you say that you don't love him, and on the other hand, you remain in the house and allow him to beat you. How do you put these two things together?
   b. You may be caught up in a vicious cycle about whether your feelings for him, even though they're not love, outweigh your regard for yourself. Does this seem to fit you?
   c. It might be helpful for you to know the process that other women in your shoes go through before they finally get enough courage to leave for good. I'd like to give you the name of someone to talk to at our local domestic violence agency. Also, there are several websites I can give you if you have access to and would like to use the Internet.

4. **Client:** I don't know why we ever got married in the first place. Things were fine for a while, but since we moved, things have just started to fall apart in our marriage.
   a. What qualities attracted you to each other originally?
   b. You're having a difficult time right now, which has led you to question the entire marriage. I wonder whether you would react this way if this present problem wasn't causing such distress.
   c. I too have been in situations like this. When one thing goes wrong, it makes me feel like throwing the whole thing away. Is this something you can relate to in what you are experiencing now with your marriage?

Part Two

For each of the following three client statements, Learning Outcome 2 asks you to write an example of each of the six influencing responses.* In developing these responses, you may find it helpful to use the cognitive learning strategy you practiced earlier for each response. Feedback is provided on page 160.

Client 1, a Euro-American parent [says with loud sighs]: My house looks like a mess. I can't seem to get anything done with these kids always under my feet. I'm afraid that I may lose my temper and hit them one of these days. I just feel so stressed out.

*The three client messages can be put on audiotape with pauses between statements. Then, instead of reading each message, you can listen to it and write your response or say it aloud during the pause.

(continued)

6   KNOWLEDGE AND SKILL BUILDER

(continued)
Question: _____
Interpretation: _____
Information giving: _____
Immediacy: _____
Self-disclosure: _____
Confrontation: _____

Client 2, an African American graduate student: I feel so overwhelmed. I've got books to read, papers to write. My money is running low, and I don't even have a job. Plus, my roommate is thinking of moving out. I just can't seem to get a break—no one goes out of their way to lift a finger to help me.
Question: _____
Interpretation: _____
Information giving: _____
Immediacy: _____
Self-disclosure: _____
Confrontation: _____

Client 3, a young, Native American man: I haven't gotten hooked on this stuff. It doesn't make me feel high, though, just good. All my bad thoughts and all the pain go away when I take it. So why should I give it up? You're not here to make me do it, are you?
Question: _____
Interpretation: _____
Information giving: _____
Immediacy: _____
Self-disclosure: _____
Confrontation: _____

Part Three

Part three gives you an opportunity to develop your skills in observing six key aspects of client behavior that a helper must attend to in order to develop effective and accurate influencing responses. (If observers are not available, audiotape or videotape your sessions, and complete the checklist while reviewing the tape.)

1. Issues and messages that need more elaboration, information, or examples
2. Implicit messages and themes
3. Myths and inaccurate information
4. Feelings and process issues
5. Distorted perceptions and ideas
6. Discrepancies and incongruities

Learning Outcome 3 asks you to observe those six aspects of client behavior during a 30-minute interview. Record your observations on the Client Observation Checklist.

You can obtain feedback for this activity by having two or more persons observe and rate the same session and then compare your responses.

Client Observation Checklist

Name of helper _____
Name(s) of observer(s) _____

Instructions: Write down separate occurrences of each of the six categories of client behavior as they occur during a 30-minute helping interview. (If observers are not available, audiotape or videotape your sessions, and complete the checklist while reviewing the tape.)

1. Issues and messages that need more elaboration, information, or examples

   a. _____
   b. _____
   c. _____
   d. _____

2. Implicit messages and themes

   a. _____
   b. _____
   c. _____
   d. _____

3. Myths and inaccurate information

   a. _____
   b. _____
   c. _____
   d. _____

4. Feelings and process issues

   a. _____
   b. _____
   c. _____
   d. _____

5. Distorted perceptions and ideas

   a. _____
   b. _____
   c. _____
   d. _____

6. Discrepancies and incongruities

   a. _____
   b. _____
   c. _____
   d. _____

6   KNOWLEDGE AND SKILL BUILDER

Part Four

Learning Outcome 4 provides you with an opportunity to integrate the core skills and knowledge you have acquired so far from working with this book. To begin this process, conduct one 30-minute role-play interview. You may want to consider this an initial helping interview in which you are creating rapport and getting to know the "client." Here are the specific tasks for this integrative helping session:

1. Be alert to ethical situations and issues that arise and how you resolve them.
2. Assess the degree to which you are able to conduct this interview in a culturally competent way. Be sensitive not only to cultural competencies, but to any communication and behavior that may be pejorative, biased, or insulting.
3. Assess the key aspects of your nonverbal behavior in the interview.
4. Pay attention to the quality of the helping relationship and specifically to your demonstration of the facilitative conditions of empathy, genuineness, and positive regard.
5. Use as many of the listening and influencing verbal responses as seem appropriate within the time span of this session.

Try to regard this interview as an opportunity to get involved with the person in front of you, not as just another practice. If you feel some discomfort, you may wish to do several more interviews with different kinds of clients. To assess the overall effectiveness of your interview, use the Interview Inventory, which follows. You may wish to make some copies of it.

This inventory has six parts. "Ethical Issues" assesses any ethical issues that arose during the interview and how these were resolved. "Multicultural Competences" assesses 10 aspects of culturally competent interview behaviors. "Nonverbal Behavior" evaluates your use of various nonverbal behaviors. "Relationship Variables" measures aspects of establishing and enhancing a therapeutic relationship. "Verbal Behavior" assesses listening and influencing responses. "Overall Effectiveness" summarizes these preceding parts. To use the inventory for rating, follow the instructions for each part.

Interview Inventory
Interview Number _____ Helper _____
Client _____ Rater _____ Date _____

Ethical Issues

Instructions: List the any ethical issues that came up during the interview, and note how the helper responded to them.

Ethical Issue	Helper Response
1._____	_____
2._____	_____
3._____	_____
4._____	_____

Multicultural Competence*

1. Displayed awareness of his or her own racial and cultural identity development and its impact on the helping process.

Not at all	Minimally	Somewhat	A Great Deal	Almost Always
1	2	3	4	5

2. Was aware of his or her own values, biases, and assumptions about other racial and cultural groups and did not let these biases and assumptions impede the helping process.

Not at all	Minimally	Somewhat	A Great Deal	Almost Always
1	2	3	4	5

3. Exhibited respect for cultural differences among clients.

Not at all	Minimally	Somewhat	A Great Deal	Almost Always
1	2	3	4	5

4. Was aware of the cultural values of each client as well as of the uniqueness of each client within the client's racial and cultural group identification.

Not at all	Minimally	Somewhat	A Great Deal	Almost Always
1	2	3	4	5

5. Was sensitive to nonverbal and paralanguage cross-cultural communication clues.

Not at all	Minimally	Somewhat	A Great Deal	Almost Always
1	2	3	4	5

6. Demonstrated the ability to assess the client's level of acculturation and to use this information in working with the client to implement culturally sensitive helping.

Not at all	Minimally	Somewhat	A Great Deal	Almost Always
1	2	3	4	5

7. Displayed an understanding of how race, ethnicity, and culture influence the treatment, status, and life chances of clients.

Not at all	Minimally	Somewhat	A Great Deal	Almost Always
1	2	3	4	5

(continued)

6   KNOWLEDGE AND SKILL BUILDER

(*continued*)

8. Was able to help the client sort out the degree to which the client's issues or problems are exacerbated by limits and regulations of the larger society.

Not at all	Minimally	Somewhat	A Great Deal	Almost Always
1	2	3	4	5

9. Was able to help the client deal with environmental frustration and oppression.

Not at all	Minimally	Somewhat	A Great Deal	Almost Always
1	2	3	4	5

10. Was able to recognize and work with the client dealing with multiple oppressions.

Not at all	Minimally	Somewhat	A Great Deal	Almost Always
1	2	3	4	5

*Adapted from *Pathways to Multicultural Counseling Competence: A Developmental Journey* (5th ed.), by B. Wehrly, pp. 240–241. Copyright 1996 by Brooks/Cole, an imprint of the Wadsworth Group, a division of Thomson Learning. Adapted with permission.

Nonverbal Behavior

Instructions: Listed below are significant dimensions of nonverbal behavior. Check (✓) any that you observe of the helper, and provide a brief description of the key aspects and appropriateness of the behavior. The first item serves as an example.

Behavior	Check (✓) if observed	Key aspects of behavior
1.	Body posture	Tense, rigid until last
2.	Eye contact	part of session,
3.	Facial expression	then relaxed
4.	Head nodding	
5.	Body posture	
6.	Body movements	
7.	Body orientation	
8.	Gestures	
9.	Nonverbal adaptors	
10.	Voice level and pitch	
11.	Rate of speech	
12.	Verbal underlining (voice emphasis)	
13.	Speech errors	
14.	Pauses, silence	
15.	Distance	
16.	Touch	
17.	Position in room	
18.	Environmental arousal	

19.	Time in starting session
20.	Time in responding to messages
21.	Time in ending session
22.	Autonomic response (e.g., breathing, sweat, skin flush, rash)
23.	Congruence/incongruence between helper verbal and nonverbal behavior
24.	Synchrony/dissynchrony between helper/client nonverbal behaviors
25.	Environmental sensitivity to diverse kinds of clients

Relationship Variables

Instructions: Circle the number that best represents the helper's behavior during the observed interaction.

1. Conveyed accurate understanding of the client and of the client's worldview.

Not at all	Minimally	Somewhat	A Great Deal	Almost Always
1	2	3	4	5

2. Conveyed support and warmth without approving or disapproving of the client.

Not at all	Minimally	Somewhat	A Great Deal	Almost Always
1	2	3	4	5

3. Focused on the person rather than on the procedure or on helper's professional role.

Not at all	Minimally	Somewhat	A Great Deal	Almost Always
1	2	3	4	5

4. Conveyed spontaneity, was not mechanical when responding to client.

Not at all	Minimally	Somewhat	A Great Deal	Almost Always
1	2	3	4	5

5. Responded to feelings and issues as they occurred within the session (that is, in the here-and-now).

Not at all	Minimally	Somewhat	A Great Deal	Almost Always
1	2	3	4	5

6. Displayed comfort and confidence in working with the client.

Not at all	Minimally	Somewhat	A Great Deal	Almost Always
1	2	3	4	5

7. Responded with dynamism and frequency; was not passive.

Not at all	Minimally	Somewhat	A Great Deal	Almost Always
1	2	3	4	5

6   KNOWLEDGE AND SKILL BUILDER

8. Displayed sincerity in intentions and responses.

Not at all	Minimally	Somewhat	A Great Deal	Almost Always
1	2	3	4	5

9. Conveyed friendliness and goodwill in interacting with client.

Not at all	Minimally	Somewhat	A Great Deal	Almost Always
1	2	3	4	5

10. Informed client about expectations and what would or would not happen in session (that is, structuring).

Not at all	Minimally	Somewhat	A Great Deal	Almost Always
1	2	3	4	5

11. Shared similar attitudes, opinions, and experiences with client when appropriate (that is, when such sharing added to, did not detract from, client focus).

Not at all	Minimally	Somewhat	A Great Deal	Almost Always
1	2	3	4	5

Observer comments: _____
_____
_____
_____

Verbal Behavior

Instructions: Check (✓) the type of verbal response represented by each helper statement in the corresponding category on the rating form. At the end of the observation period, tally the total number of checks associated with each verbal response on the chart below.

	Listening responses						Influencing responses				
	Clarification	Paraphrase	Reflecting feeling (basic empathy)	Summarization	Open question	Closed question	Interpretation (advanced empathy)	Information giving	Immediacy	Self-disclosure	Confrontation
1											
2											
3											
4											
5											
6											
7											
8											
9											
10											
11											
12											
13											
14											
15											
16											
17											
18											
19											
20											
Total:											

(continued)

KNOWLEDGE AND SKILL BUILDER

(*continued*)

Overall Effectiveness

Instructions: After all the ratings are completed, look at your ratings in the light of these questions.

1. What ethical dilemmas arose for you, and how did you resolve them?
2. What aspects of multicultural competence do you feel most comfortable with? What parts are still hard for you?
3. Which nonverbal skills were easiest for you to demonstrate? Which ones did you find most difficult to use in the interview?
4. Which relationship variables were easiest for you to demonstrate? Hardest?
5. Examine the total number of verbal responses you used in each category. Did you use responses from each category with the same frequency? Did most of your responses come from one category? Did you seem to avoid using responses from one category? If so, for what reason?
6. Was it easier to integrate the verbal responses or the nonverbal skills?
7. What have you learned about the effectiveness of your interview behavior so far? What do you think you need to improve?

KNOWLEDGE AND SKILL BUILDER **FEEDBACK**

Part One

1. a. Interpretation
   b. Information giving
   c. Immediacy and closed question
2. a. Confrontation
   b. Open question
   c. Self-disclosure and open question
3. a. Confrontation
   b. Interpretation and closed question
   c. Information giving
4. a. Open question
   b. Interpretation
   c. Self-disclosure and closed question

Part Two

Here are some examples of influencing responses. See whether yours are similar.

Client Statement 1

Question: "What exactly would you like to be able to accomplish during the day?" *or* "How could you keep the kids occupied while you do some of your housework?" *or* "When do you feel most like striking the children?" *or* "How could you control your anger?"

Interpretation: "I wonder whether you would be able to accomplish what seems important to you even if the kids weren't always underfoot. Perhaps it's easy to use their presence to account for your lack of accomplishment."

Information giving: "If you believe your problem would be solved by having more time alone, we could discuss some options that seemed to help other women in this situation—things to give you more time alone as well as ways to cope with your anger."

Immediacy: "I can tell from the way you're talking and breathing right now that this stress is very much with you—not just at home but even as we are working together here today."

Self-disclosure: "I know what it is like to feel like your life is spinning out of control, and it's not a pleasant state to be in—for me, it's pretty stressful. How about for you?"

Confrontation: "On the one hand, you seem to be saying the kids are responsible for your difficulties, and on the other, it appears as if you feel you are the one who is out of control."

Client Statement 2

Question: "How could you organize yourself better so that you wouldn't feel so overcome by your studies?" *or* "What kind of work might you do that would fit in with your class schedule?" *or* "How might you cope with these feelings of being so overwhelmed?"

Interpretation: "You seem to feel so discouraged with everything that I imagine it would be easy now to feel justified in giving it all up, quitting grad school altogether."

Information giving: "Perhaps it would be helpful if we talked about some ways to help you with your time and money problems."

6 — KNOWLEDGE AND SKILL BUILDER **FEEDBACK**

Immediacy: "I'm sensing how frustrated you're feeling right now as you talk, and I'm wondering if you're seeing me as someone unwilling to help you."

Self-disclosure: "Wow. I think I know something about what you are saying, how it feels to have the whole world cave in on you at once. It's an awful lot to try to handle."

Confrontation: "You've mentioned several reasons that you feel so overwhelmed now, and at the same time I don't think you mentioned anything you're doing to relieve these feelings."

Client Statement 3

Question: "What do you feel comfortable sharing with me about your pain?"

Interpretation: "Even though you don't feel hooked on this substance, it seems as if using it helps you avoid certain things. Do you think this is so?"

Information giving: "I'm wondering what you would think of the idea of our spending some time talking about other ways to deal with the pain—such as practices and rituals consistent with your own cultural and ethnic background."

Immediacy: "I'm wondering if there is something I'm saying or doing to make you feel like I'm going to be policing your actions as we work together."

Self-disclosure: "I went through a similar way of thinking when I gave up smoking. Cigarettes were always there for me—when nothing else was, they were. In that way, it was hard for me to see what could be so bad about continuing to smoke. Does this fit with what you're feeling in your situation?"

Confrontation: "You're telling me that you're pretty sure you're not hooked on this, and at the same time you recognize it seems to medicate your pain. How do you put these two things together?"

CONCEPTUALIZING AND ASSESSING CLIENT PROBLEMS, CONCERNS, AND CONTEXTS

LEARNING OUTCOMES

After completing this chapter, you will be able to identify each of the following, in writing, using two client case descriptions

1. The client's behaviors
2. Whether the client's behaviors are overt or covert
3. The client's individual and environmental strengths
4. Antecedent contributing conditions
5. Consequences and secondary gains
6. The way each consequence influences the behaviors
7. The sociopolitical context of the issue

Institutionalized patient: Why are people always out to get me?

Student: I can't even talk to my mom. What a hassle!

Physically challenged person: Ever since I had that automobile accident and had to change jobs, I don't seem to be able to get it together.

Older person: I didn't used to worry this much, but with our failing health and the skyrocketing medical costs, I am concerned now.

These client statements are representative of the types of concerns that clients bring to helpers every day. One thing these clients and others have in common is that their initial problem presentation is often vague. A helper can translate vague client concerns into specific problem statements by using certain skills associated with assessment. This chapter presents a conceptual framework that a helper can use to assess clients.

WHAT IS ASSESSMENT?

Assessment, in a nutshell, is about helping a client develop a story. The story involves a number of details and plots, including why the client is coming to see you now, what the client wants from you, and how you can help the client get there. Assessment involves methods, procedures, and tools that are used to collect and process information from which the entire helping program is developed. Interviewing the client and having the client engage in other assessment procedures are only part of the overall assessment process in counseling and therapy. Equally important is the helper's own mental (covert) activity that goes on during the process. The helper typically gathers a great amount of information from clients during this stage of helping. Unless the helper can integrate and synthesize this information, it is of little value and use. The helper's tasks during the assessment process include identifying what information to obtain and how to obtain it, putting the information together in some meaningful way, and using it to generate clinical hunches, or hypotheses, about client issues, hunches that lead to tentative ideas for treatment planning. This mental activity of the helper is called *conceptualization*—which simply means the way the helper thinks about the client's presenting concerns. The assessment methods we describe later in this chapter and our interview assessment model in particular are based on a model of conceptualization we have used over the years in our teaching and in clinical practice.

OUR ASSUMPTIONS ABOUT ASSESSMENT AND COGNITIVE–BEHAVIOR THERAPY

Our model of assessment in helping rests on several assumptions about clients, issues, and behavior that are drawn from the cognitive–behavioral approach. Cognitive–behavior therapy utilizes a variety of techniques and strategies that are based on principles of learning and are designed to produce constructive change in human behaviors. This approach was first developed in the 1950s under the term *behavior therapy* by, among others, Skinner (1986), Wolpe (1992), and Lazarus (2006). Early behavior therapists focused on the importance of changing clients' observable behavior. This is now called the first wave of behavior therapy (Hayes, 2004). Since the 1950s, there have been significant developments in behavior therapy. Among the most important is the emergence of *cognitive–behavior therapy*, which arose in the 1970s as a result of the work of such persons as Bandura (1986), Meichenbaum (2002), and Beck (1991). *Cognitive–behavior therapy*, the second wave of behavior therapy, emphasizes the effects of private events such as cognitions, beliefs, and internal dialogue on resulting feelings and performance. This orientation to change now recognizes that both overt responding (observed behavior) and covert responding (feelings and thoughts) are important targets of change as long as they can be clearly specified. The third wave of behavior therapy includes more recent developments in the field such as *acceptance and commitment therapy* (*ACT*) (Hayes & Strosahl, 2005), *dialectical behavior therapy* (*DBT*) (Linehan, 1993), and *mindfulness-based cognitive therapy* (*MBCT*) (Teasdale et al., 2000). In this section, we explore the links between these three waves of cognitive–behavior therapy and discuss important assumptions about the process of assessing client concerns and issues.

Most Behavior Is Learned

Undesired (maladaptive) behavior is developed, maintained, and subject to alteration or modification in the same manner as normal (adaptive) behavior. Both prosocial and maladaptive behaviors are assumed to be developed and maintained by external environmental events or cues, by external reinforcers, or by internal processes such as cognition, mediation, and problem solving. For the most part, maladaptive behavior is not thought to be a function of physical disease or of underlying intrapsychic conflict. This fundamental assumption means that we do not spend a great deal of time sorting out or focusing on possible unresolved early conflicts or underlying pathological states in the client's story. However, it does not mean that we rule out or overlook possible physiological causes of undesired behavior. For example, clients who complain of "anxiety" and report primarily somatic (body-related) symptoms such as heart palpitations, stomach upset, chest pains, and breathlessness may be chronic hyperventilators, although hyperventilation can be considered only after the client has had a physical examination to rule out cardiopathy. Physical examinations also may reveal the presence of mitral valve heart dysfunction for some individuals who complain of "panic attacks." Other somatic symptoms suggesting anxiety, such as sweating, tachycardia, lightheadedness, and dizziness, could also result from biological disorders such as hypoglycemia, thyroid or other endocrine disorders, or a low-grade infection.

Physiological variables should always be explored in the client's story, particularly when the results of the assessment do not suggest the presence of other specific stimuli associated with the problem behavior. Many psychological disorders have a biological component as well as a learning component. For example, the neurotransmitter serotonin is implicated in both depression and anxiety disorders. Further, the cycling rate of serotonin is affected by genetic markers. Some disorders such as alcoholism and schizophrenia have both genetic and biochemical markers that can increase a person's vulnerability to such a disorder. This is one reason why medical history is assessed during an initial interview. In these situations, evaluation of the client by a physician is warranted.

It is also important to recognize the need for occasional physiological management of psychological issues—for example, in the kinds of disorders mentioned above. Medications may be necessary *in addition to* psychological intervention. Antidepressants are typically recommended for depression in conjunction with cognitive–behavioral and interpersonal therapies. They have been found helpful as a supplement to psychological treatment for some instances of agoraphobia, a disorder typified by a marked fear of being alone or in public places. Furthermore, a biological element seems to be present in many of the psychoses, such as schizophrenia, and these conditions usually require antipsychotic drugs to improve the client's overall level of functioning. Similarly, children with attention-deficit disorder may need stimulant medication.

Problems Are Defined Operationally

Another assumption about cognitive–behavioral assessment is that problems clients bring to counseling are defined operationally. An operational definition functions like a measure, a barometer, or a "behavioral anchor." Operational definitions indicate some very specific behaviors. In contrast, lack of an operational definition usually means that clinicians rely on inferences about vague traits or labels from the client's statement. Mischel (1973, p. 10) has contrasted these two approaches to conceptualization: "The emphasis is on what a person *does* in situations rather than on inferences about what attributes he *has* more globally."

Consider the following example of a way to view a client's concern operationally. In working with the "depressed" client, we would try to define precisely what the client means by "depressed" in order to avoid any misinterpretation of this self-report feeling statement. Instead of viewing the client's issue as "depression," we would try to specify some thoughts, feelings, actions, situations, and persons that are associated with the client's depression. We would also obtain measures of frequency, duration, and intensity of the "depressed mood." We would find out whether the client experiences certain physiological changes during depression, what the client is thinking about while depressed, and what activities and behaviors occur during the depressed periods. In other words, the helper, in conjunction with the client, identifies a series of referents that are indicative of the state of being depressed, anxious, withdrawn, lonely, and so on. The advantage of viewing the problem this way is that vague phenomena are translated into specific and observable experiences. When this occurs, not only we do get a better idea of what is happening with the client, but we also have made the issue potentially measurable, allowing us to assess progress and outcome.

Causes of Client Problems and Therefore Treatments/Interventions Are Multidimensional

Rarely is a client problem caused by only one factor, and rarely does a single, one-dimensional treatment program work in actual practice. For example, with a client, Doug, who reports depression, we may find evidence of biological contributing factors such as Addison's disease (dysfunction of the adrenal gland), of environmental contributing conditions such as being left by his partner after moving to a new town, and of covert contributing factors such as self-deprecatory thoughts and images. Causes and contributing conditions of most client problems are multiple and include overt behavior, environmental events and relationships with others, covert behavior such as beliefs, images, and cognitions, feelings and bodily sensations, and possibly physiological conditions. Intervention is usually more effective when directed toward all these multiple factors. Doug's endocrine level must be restored and maintained. In addition, Doug must be helped to deal with his feelings of rejection and anger about his partner's departure, he needs to develop alternative resources and supports, including self-support, and he needs help in learning how to modify his self-deprecating thoughts and images. He may benefit from the acquisition of problem-solving skills in order to decide the direction he wants his life to take. Also, a focus on his own strengths and coping skills may help give him the confidence he needs to implement this new direction. We also need to consider the effect of Doug's environment. What kind of environmental context (family, community, social, and cultural environment) did he leave? What sort of environmental context does he find or has he not found in his new city? How does this affect his level of depression? Will treatment interventions be solely psychosocial ones, or does he also need medication? The more complete and comprehensive the treatment, the more successful the helping process tends to be, and also the less chance there is of relapse.

Most Problems Occur in a Social Context Known as Ecological or Person-in-Environment

Client problems do not usually occur in a vacuum but are related to observable events (verbal, nonverbal, and motoric responses) and to less visible covert or indirect events (thoughts, images, moods and feelings, body sensations) that precipitate and maintain the problem. These internal and external events are called "antecedents" or "consequences." They are functionally related to the behavior in that they exert control over it, so a change in one of these variables often brings about a change in functionally related variables. Simply put, in assessing a client's story, it is crucial to note how the client's behavior affects the environment and vice versa—how the environment impacts the client's behavior. This functional relationship of behavior and the environment reflects an *ecological* view; it was articulated as early as 1979 and again in 1995 by Bronfenbrenner as well as by Walsh, Craik, and Price (2000) and is consistent with a cognitive–behavioral view of assessment (Bandura, 1986). In an ecological view, the individual client and his or her environment are linked together, so assessment includes not only an individual focus but a contextual focus, including key social settings, events, and resources. Practitioners need to examine the social and cultural contexts of relationships among these key social settings, events, and resources. Whereas the ecological context of issues is important to consider for all clients, the sociopolitical context surrounding the client is especially important for clients who feel marginalized, such as clients of color and clients from minority and oppressed groups.

Some literature also describes the ecological view as a *person-in-environment approach*. The person-in-environment approach is a central feature of the growing edge of practice today (Neufeld et al., 2006). This approach to conceptualizing clients is based on the following two notions:

1. Client concerns do not reside solely within an individual but are embedded within cultural, environmental, and social systems or contexts.
2. There is movement to incorporate a focus on strengths, resources, and coping skills of clients into the assessment and treatment process. This movement is also known as a *strengths perspective* (Saleebey, 2005) which is affiliated with the *positive psychology* movement (Seligman & Csikszentmihalyi, 2000).

Those two assumptions are consistent with current and emerging policy guides on psychology, social work, counseling, and human services curricula as well as multicultural competencies. However, such policy guides do not promote positive psychology or the strengths perspective in a noncritical "across the board" manner. With the exception of self-efficacy, other positive psychology constructs currently lack empirical data (Harris, Thoresen, & Lopez, 2007). Staudt, Howard, and Drake, in a review of the strengths-based empirical literature, concluded that few empirical studies of this approach exist, and of those that do, it is not possible to determine if the outcomes are due to the strengths perspective or to the delivery of additional services (2001). In part, this may be due to the lack of consistent definitions of the meaning and function of *strength* (Oko, 2006). Taylor (2006) notes that the strengths perspective should not be an "end in and of itself" nor should it be used to argue against the neuroscience of mental illness. He advocates for the judicious use of strengths-oriented assessment and treatment in a differential manner (Taylor, 2006). In a similar vein, Harris et al. (2007) assert that identifying and supporting client strengths and resources may provide clients with the motivation they need to reach their goals and that using a strengths perspective in conceptualization of client problems "inherently implies the universe of potential solutions" (p. 5).

In considering the reciprocity of clients and their environments, assessment should include the following two levels:

The individual client, or *Who*

The client's environmental and cultural context, or *Where*

When assessment is conducted on both levels, practitioners obtain a balanced view of the client (Summers, 2006). Next we describe in greater detail the guiding principles of each level of client assessment.

The Individual Client, or *Who*

The individual client brings personal attributes to therapy consisting primarily of covert, internal experiences and overt behaviors. In conceptualizing the client's issues, we assess for four specific modes:

- Feelings or affective modes
- Physiologic sensations or somatic modes
- Thoughts, beliefs, schemas, or cognitive modes
- Actions or behavioral modes

We also assess for protective factors, client strengths, resources, and coping skills within the client's cultural context so that our conceptualization of the client is a balanced one. A focus on client strengths and resources furthers collaboration between helper and client, deemphasizes stigmas associated with client problems and diagnostic labels, and enhances the client's sense of self-efficacy (Hepworth, Rooney, Dewberry Rooney, Strom-Gottfried, & Larsen, 2006). Snyder and Lopez (2007) assert that at the beginning of the 21st century the focus on the positive aspects of mental health clearly lags behind the focus on the negative ones (p. 326).

We also assess for dimensions of the client's problems—that is the rate, magnitude or severity, and duration of the client's behaviors (Haynes, Nelson, Thacher, & Keaweaimoku, 2002). And finally, as Constantine and Sue (2006) note, we cannot separate optimal human functioning from the cultural contexts in which such functioning arises (p. 229). Summers (2006) provides two cases illustrating how the individual characteristics of two different clients, Ralph and Edwardo, affected their prison stay (see Box 7.1).

The Client's Environmental and Cultural Context, or *Where*

Individual clients also bring environmental and cultural variables to helping that affect their presenting issues. For example, a client is a member of some kind of a family system. Depending on the client's culture, the family system has its own structure and values. As well, clients belong to specific social groups, spiritual groups, educational groups, and community groups. Client problems are affected by the larger society and community in which the client lives, such as the government, economy, geography, and religious/spiritual heritage. Clients also are members of one or several cultural groups and are influenced by the structure, socialization, and values of these groups. We refer to environmental and cultural variables that affect client issues as *contextual and relational dimensions* associated with the problem. It is important to assess the impact of these dimensions because "the reason for the client's problems may lie in the *context* rather than with the client" (Summers, 2006, p. 62). The larger social context may also have affected the client's presenting concerns. For example, one client may have experienced loss of employment, disenfranchisement in voting, a poor health care system, and a barely adequate school system. Another client may have experienced a boom in the stock market, preferential political treatment, a first-rate health care system, and a private school (Summers, 2006).

In assessing for contextual and relational dimensions of the client's issues, we look for areas of environmental supports and stressors, risk and protective factors, including places, settings, events, and people who are sources of empowerment and disempowerment (Kemp, Whittaker, & Tracy, 1997). For example, one might ask about the strengths and assets and the weaknesses and the liabilities of the client's environment, and about the extent and availability of family and community resources. If the client is an immigrant or refugee, one might ask how his or her status has been affected by the move. Are there ways to maximize the client's strengths within the environmental context? We cannot overemphasize the importance of assessing the contribution of these environmental variables to identified issues. This sort of assessment helps clients determine, for example, whether an issue may stem from racism and prejudice in *other persons* so that clients or helpers do not inappropriately personalize their concerns.

Imagine that Ralph and Edwardo, described in Box 7.1, are in different environmental settings, and with different contextual and relational variables, even though both are still incarcerated. A key concept of the ecological or person-in-environment approach—is that rather than focusing on just the person *or* the environment, we focus on both and on the interaction between the two (Neufeld et al., 2006, p. 246).

Another aspect of assessing the context includes a *cultural analysis* of client issues. Assessing for cultural data directly

BOX 7.1   THE CASES OF RALPH AND EDWARDO

Ralph had been in prison for some youthful gang activity. While he was there, he took advantage of every opportunity to change. He went to church regularly, developed a personal relationship with a minister who came to the prison often, and obtained his high school diploma. Ralph was a warm, humorous person who attracted many friends. His outgoing personality attracted people to him who ultimately encouraged him and gave him support. During his time in prison, his mother wrote to him often, pleading with him to change his ways. Ralph felt bad about the trouble he had caused his mother, particularly in view of the fact that she had raised him after his father left home, and he saw her letters as a reason to do better. When he left prison, he enrolled in college courses and attached himself to the church, where he was warmly welcomed.

Edwardo was in the same prison for youthful gang activities. He was quiet and retiring and did not attract the attention and support that Ralph had secured for himself. Edwardo attempted to get his high school diploma while in prison, but had trouble asking for help when he needed it and eventually gave the project up in frustration. Preferring not to join groups, he did not go to church or any other group activity that promoted independence and responsibility. Because Edwardo spoke so little and rarely smiled, he was often misunderstood as being hostile. In fact, he felt shy and awkward around other people. Edwardo's mother wrote him regularly, and she too pleaded with him to do better and "turn his life around"; but Edwardo tended to see these letters as nagging and to blame his mother for the fact that his father left when he was very young. He rarely answered her mail. When Edwardo left prison, he moved back with his old friends and resumed his former criminal activities.

This illustration demonstrates how individual characteristics play a role in the outcome for the client. Part of developing a balanced understanding of the client is being able to see what the client brings to the situation and how that interacts with the larger context of his or her life. Ralph brought a personality that attracted others to assist him. He brought a good relationship with his mother and a motivation to do things more constructively. Edwardo brought a more retiring personality, one that was less attractive to others and often misunderstood. Edwardo's interpersonal skills were not as developed as Ralph's. The individual characteristics of Edwardo and Ralph affected the outcome of their prison time.

Now we will look at Edwardo and Ralph differently. For our purposes, let us suppose that Ralph and Edwardo are both warm, humorous people. Both make friends easily and enjoy the company of other people. Each of them is sent to prison for youthful gang activities, but the context is different. Edwardo goes to a prison upstate. It was recently built and the focus is on rehabilitation. There Ed is provided with high school and college classes as well as religious and self-improvement activities. He is able to take advantage of many different programs to further his goals. A supportive counselor works with him to come up with a good set of goals and helps Ed implement these. They meet on a weekly basis. The location of the prison has another advantage. Edwardo is now closer to his father, who lives only a few miles from the prison. His father begins to visit, offering his support and a place for Ed to live when his sentence is completed. Edwardo leaves the prison on a solid footing and continues his work toward a college degree.

Ralph, on the other hand, is sent to an ordinary prison where the counseling staff is overwhelmed. His counselor sees Ralph's potential, but has trouble getting Ralph into high school courses because they are crowded. During the time Ralph is at the prison, the education staff experiences a number of turnovers and layoffs. Ralph never can get into the program and stick to it. He rarely sees his counselor because of the number of inmates with whom the counselor must work. No family member comes to visit Ralph, partly because he has been sent so far from them and partly because they blame him for his incarceration and have lost interest in him. Ralph's mother, sick with severe chronic asthma, rarely writes. There are church services, which Ralph attends regularly, but the prison does not allow inmates to meet the pastors before or after services because of a strict schedule, and the pastors who have formed relationships with inmates come irregularly at other times. When Ralph leaves the prison, he has not completed his high school diploma. He moves near some people he knew in prison, and soon he takes up the criminal activities in which he participated before his incarceration.

Here it is the context that is different. Edwardo finds himself in a supportive context: a counselor who focuses on his goals and sees that these are implemented, plenty of self-improvement opportunities, a warm relationship with his father, a prison committed to education. Ralph, however, finds himself confronted with indifference, lack of supportive programs and activities, an overwhelmed counselor, and a family too distant to give encouragement.

Source: Fundamentals of Case Management Practice (2nd ed.), by N. Summers, pp. 59–60. Copyright © 2006. Reprinted with permission of Thomson–Brooks/Cole.

from clients is an ethical responsibility of helpers. And, further, if it is necessary to ask clients to clarify cultural data for your own understanding, it is important to do so in a way that doesn't burden the client. A model to conduct a through and culturally sensitive assessment has been developed by White Kress, Eriksen, Rayle, and Ford (2005). In this model, the following areas are explored by the clinician with the client:

- Assessment of the client's worldview—that is, how the client sees the world and through what perspectives and lenses.
- Assessment of the client's cultural identity—that is, how the client makes sense of himself or herself culturally and what the client's understanding is (as well as your own understanding) of his or her own level or stage of cultural identity awareness.
- Assessment of the client's level of acculturation—that is, how the client identifies with both former and current cultures and how the client moves through these cultures with resources and/or barriers.
- Assessment of the cultural meaning of the client's issues and presenting symptoms—that is, what the presenting problem means to the client and how the client views it, and what cultural context surrounds the client's concerns.
- Assessment of sources of cultural information available to the client—that is, what information the client reports about areas of his or her life related to both past and current cultural history.
- Assessment of any stigmas associated with the client's concern—that is, what the cultural meaning of the concern is to the client and to his or her cultural community, how the client views seeking help for such concerns, and what the client's experiences are with stigma, prejudice, and discrimination.

In the next section, we expand this model and elaborate on the way in which both individual and environmental aspects of client concerns can be identified in a functional assessment of the antecedents, behaviors, and consequences of a given client's issue.

HOW TO CONDUCT A FUNCTIONAL ASSESSMENT: THE ABC MODEL

Conducting a functional assessment involves obtaining information about the client's story in a very specific way. It means assessing and conceptualizing clinically relevant behaviors within their historical and current context. It involves an analysis of both past and present learning experiences that may be responsible for current presenting issues (Thyer & Myers, 2000). A functional assessment emphasizes the identification of functional relations relevant to a client's problem behaviors and significant and controllable causal variables that impact these problems (Haynes et al., 2002, p. 37). Although there are various methods of assessing client problems—observation, clinical self-report instruments, and so on—in this chapter we emphasize the interview-based functional assessment. The goal of the interview-based functional assessment is to generate causal hunches or hypotheses from information about behaviors, antecedents, and consequences observed by the interviewer; this type of assessment is referred to as the *ABC model* (Tanaka-Matsumi, Seiden, & Lam, 1996, p. 216).

The ABC model of behavior suggests that the *behavior* (B) is influenced by events that precede it, called *antecedents* (A), and by some types of events that follow behavior, called *consequences* (C). An antecedent (A) event is a cue or signal that can tell a person when to behave in a situation. Antecedents are responsible for the behavior being performed in the first place (Spiegler & Guevremont, 2003). A consequence (C) is defined as an event that strengthens or weakens a behavior and determines whether the behavior will occur again (Spiegler & Guevremont, 2003). Notice that these definitions of antecedents and consequences suggest that an individual's behavior is directly related to or influenced by certain stimuli such as the presence of another individual or a particular setting. For example, a behavior that appears to be controlled by antecedent events such as anger may also be maintained or strengthened by consequences such as reactions from other people. Assessment interviews focus on identifying the particular antecedent and consequent events that influence or are functionally related to the client's defined behavior.

As a very simple example of the ABC model, consider a behavior (B) that most of us engage in frequently: talking. Our talking behavior is usually occasioned by certain cues, such as starting a conversation with another person, being asked a question, or being in the presence of a friend. Antecedents that might decrease the likelihood that we will talk may include worry about getting approval for what we say or how we answer the question or being in a hurry to get somewhere. Our talking behavior may be maintained by the verbal and nonverbal attention we receive from another person, which is a very powerful consequence, or reinforcer. Other positive consequences that might maintain our talking behavior may be that we are feeling good or happy and engaging in positive self-statements or evaluations about the usefulness or relevance of what we are saying. We may talk less when the other person's eye contact wanders, although the meaning of eye contact varies across cultures, or when the other person tells us more explicitly that we've talked enough. These are negative consequences (C) or punishments that decrease our talking behavior. Other negative consequences that may decrease our talking behavior could

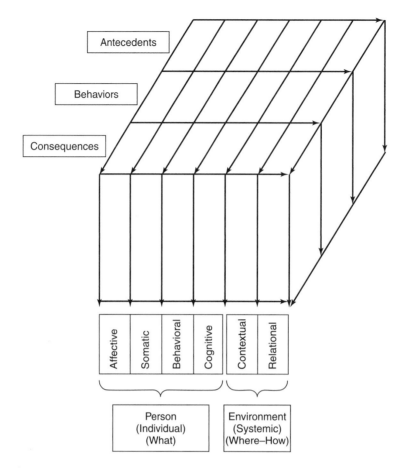

Figure 7.1 The ABC and Person-in-Environment Assessment Model

include bodily sensations of fatigue or vocal hoarseness that occur after we talk for a while, or thoughts and images that what we are saying is of little value to attract the interest of others. As you will see, not only does behavior often vary among clients, but what functions as an antecedent or consequence for one person in one environment is often very different for someone else in a different environment.

Behavior

Behavior can be both overt and covert. *Overt* behavior is behavior that is visible or could be detected by an observer, such as verbal behavior (talking), nonverbal behavior (for example, gesturing or smiling), or motoric behavior (engaging in some action such as walking). *Covert* behavior includes events that are usually internal—inside the client—and are not so readily visible to an observer, who must rely on client self-report and nonverbal behavior to detect them. Examples of covert behavior include thoughts, beliefs, images, feelings, moods, and body sensations.

As we indicated earlier, behavior that clients report rarely occurs in isolated fashion. Most reported undesired behaviors are typically part of a larger chain or set of behaviors.

Moreover, each behavior mentioned usually has more than one component (See Figure 7.1). For example, a client who complains of anxiety or depression is most likely using the label to refer to an experience consisting of an *affective* component (feelings, mood states), a *somatic* component (physiological and body-related sensation), a *behavioral* component (what the client does or doesn't do), and a *cognitive* component (thoughts, beliefs, images, or internal dialogue). Additionally, the experience of anxiety or depression may vary for the client, depending on *contextual* factors (time, place, concurrent events, gender, culture, sociopolitical climate, and environmental events), and on *relational* factors such as the presence or absence of other people. All these components may or may not be related to a particular reported concern.

For example, suppose our client who reports "anxiety" is afraid to venture out in public places except for home and work because of heightened anxiety and/or panic attacks. She is an adult, single woman who still lives at her parental home, and she provides care to her elderly mother, whom she also describes as dependent and helpless. She has lived all of her life in a small, rural community. She reports mistrust of strangers, especially those whom she did not know while growing up. She states she would like to leave and be out on her own and move away, but she is too afraid. Her reported concern of anxiety seems to be part of a chain that starts with a cognitive component in which she thinks worried thoughts and produces images in which she sees herself alone and unable to cope or to get the assistance of others if necessary. These thoughts and images support her underlying cognitive "schema" or structure of limited autonomy.

The cognitive component leads to somatic discomfort and tension and to feelings of apprehension and dread. These three components work together to influence her overt behavior. For the last few years, she has successfully avoided almost all public places. Consequently, she depends on the support of family and friends to help her function adequately in the home and at work and particularly on the few occasions when she attends public activities. This support, though no doubt useful to her, also has helped to maintain her avoidance of public places. These people form her relational network.

At the same time that you see these apparent behaviors of concern, bear in mind there also will be both overt and covert behaviors of this client that represent strengths, resources, and coping skills. The very act of courage it takes to come and see you is an overt behavioral strength and action of initiative. Her recognition of some conflicting feelings and beliefs about her life choices is a covert behavioral strength. Her network of friends and her steady work situation are examples of environmental strengths; being a part of a small, close-knit community can be a cultural strength. It is important to determine the relative importance of each component of the reported behavior in order to select appropriate intervention strategies. It is often valuable to list, in writing, the various components identified for any given behavior. In the following two sections, you will see how antecedents and consequences are functionally related to her behavioral reports.

Antecedents

According to Mischel (1973), behavior is situationally determined. This means that given behaviors tend to occur only in certain situations. For example, most of us brush our teeth in a public or private bathroom rather than during a concert or a spiritual service. Antecedents may elicit emotional and physiological reactions such as anger, fear, joy, headaches, or elevated blood pressure. Antecedents influence behavior by either increasing or decreasing its likelihood of occurrence. For example, a child in a first-grade class may behave differently at school than at home or differently with a substitute than with the regular teacher.

Antecedent events that occur immediately before a specific behavior exert influence on it. Not everything that occurs prior to a behavior, however, is considered an an-

tecedent event—only events that are functionally related to the behavior. Events that are not in temporal proximity to the behavior can similarly increase or decrease the probability that the behavior will occur. Antecedents that occur in immediate temporal proximity to the specified behavior are technically called *stimulus events* (Bijou & Baer, 1976) and include any external or internal event or condition that either cues the behavior or makes it more or less likely to occur under that condition. Antecedents that are temporally distant from the specified behavior are called *setting events* (Kantor, 1970) and include circumstances that the person has recently or previously passed through. Setting events may end well before the behavior, yet, like stimulus events, still aid or inhibit its occurrence. Examples of setting events to consider in assessing client issues are the client's age, developmental stage, and physiological state; characteristics of the client's work, home, or school setting; multicultural factors; and behaviors that emerge to affect subsequent behaviors. Both stimulus and setting antecedent conditions must be identified and defined individually for each client.

Antecedents also usually involve more than one category or type of event. Categories of antecedents may be *affective* (feelings, mood states), *somatic* (physiological and body-related sensations), *behavioral* (verbal, nonverbal, and motoric responses), *cognitive* (schemas, thoughts, beliefs, images, internal dialogue), *contextual* (time, place, multicultural factors, concurrent environmental events), and *relational* (presence or absence of other people). For example, for our client who reported "anxiety," a variety of antecedents may cue or occasion each aspect of the reported behavior—for example, fear of losing control (cognitive/affective); negative self-statements about autonomy and self-efficacy (cognitive); awareness of apprehension-related body sensations, fatigue, and hypoglycemic tendencies (somatic); staying up late and skipping meals (behavioral); being in public places (contextual); and absence of significant others such as friends and siblings, and the demands of her elderly mother (relational).

There also are antecedents that make components of the client's anxiety less likely to occur. These include feeling relaxed (affective), being rested (somatic), eating regularly (behavioral), decreased dependence on her friends (behavioral), decreased fear of separation from mother (affective), positive appraisal of self and others (cognitive), expectation of being able to handle situations (cognitive), absence of need to go to public places or functions (contextual), and being accompanied to a public place by a significant other (relational).

During the assessment phase of the helping process, it is important to identify those antecedent sources that prompt desirable behaviors and those that are related to inappropriate responses. The reason is that during the intervention (treatment) phase, it is important to select strategies that not only aid the occurrence of desirable behavior but also decrease the presence of cues for unwanted behavior.

Consequences

The consequences of a behavior are events that follow a behavior and exert some influence on the behavior, or are functionally related to the behavior. In other words, not everything that follows a behavior is automatically considered a consequence.

Suppose you are counseling a woman who tends occasionally to go on drinking binges. She reports that, after a binge, she feels guilty, regards herself as a bad person, and tends to suffer from insomnia. Although these events are *results* of her binge behavior, they are not consequences unless in some way they directly influence her binges, by maintaining, increasing, or decreasing them. In this case, other events that follow the drinking binges may be the real consequences. For instance, perhaps the client's binges are maintained by the feelings she gets from drinking; perhaps they are temporarily decreased when someone else, such as her partner, notices her behavior and reprimands her for it or refuses to go out with her.

Consequences are categorized as positive or negative. Positive consequences can be referred to technically as *rewards;* negative ones can be labeled *punishers.* Like antecedents, the things that function as consequences will always vary with clients. By definition, positive consequences (rewarding events) will maintain or increase the behavior. Positive consequences often maintain or strengthen behavior by positive reinforcement, which involves the presentation of an overt or covert event following the behavior that increases the likelihood that the behavior will occur again in the future. People tend to repeat behaviors that result in pleasurable effects.

People also tend to engage in behaviors that have some payoffs, or value, even if the behavior is very dysfunctional (such payoffs are called *secondary gains*). For example, a client may abuse alcohol and continue to do so even after she loses her job or her family because she likes the feelings she gets after drinking and because the drinking helps her to avoid responsibility. Another client may continue to verbally abuse his wife despite the strain it causes in their relationship, because the abusive behavior gives him a feeling of power and control. In these two examples, the behavior is often hard to change, because the immediate consequences make the person feel better in some way. As a result, the behavior is reinforced, even if its delayed or long-term effects are unpleasant. In other words, in these examples, the client "values" the behavior that he or she is trying to eliminate. Often the secondary gain, the payoff derived from a manifest problem, is a cover for more severe issues that are not always readily presented by the client. For example, the

husband who verbally abuses his wife may be lacking in self-esteem and may be feeling deeply depressed after the birth of their first child, feeling as if he has somehow "lost" his wife and is no longer the special person in her life. Clients may not always know why they engage in a behavior. Sometimes this knowledge is outside of the client's conscious awareness. Part of doing a good assessment involves making reasons or secondary gains more explicit in the client's story.

Positive consequences can also maintain behavior by negative reinforcement—removal of an unpleasant event following the behavior, thereby increasing the likelihood that the behavior will occur again. People tend to repeat behaviors that get rid of annoying or painful events or effects. They also use negative reinforcement to establish *avoidance* and *escape* behavior. Avoidance behavior is maintained when an *expected* unpleasant event is removed. For example, avoidance of public places is maintained by removal of the expected anxiety associated with public places. Escape behavior is maintained when a negative (unpleasant) event *already occurring* is removed or terminated. For example, punitive behavior toward a child temporarily stops the child's annoying or aversive behaviors. Termination of the unpleasant child behaviors maintains the parental escape behavior.

Negative consequences can weaken or eliminate the behavior. A behavior is typically decreased or weakened (at least temporarily) if it is followed by an unpleasant stimulus or event (punishment), if a positive, or reinforcing, event is removed or terminated (response cost), or if the behavior is no longer followed by reinforcing events (operant extinction). For example, an overweight man may maintain his eating binges because of the feelings of pleasure he receives from eating (a positive reinforcing consequence), or his binges could be maintained because they allow him to escape from a boring work situation (negative reinforcing consequence). In contrast, his wife's reprimands or sarcasm or refusal to go out with him may, at least temporarily, reduce his binges (punishing consequence). Although using negative contingencies to modify behavior has many disadvantages, in real-life settings such as home, work, and school, punishment is widely used to influence the behavior of others. Helpers must be alert to the presence of negative consequences in a client's life and its effects on the client. Helpers also must be careful to avoid the use of any verbal or nonverbal behavior that may seem punitive to a client, because such behavior may contribute to unnecessary problems in the therapeutic relationship and to subsequent client termination of (escape from) therapy.

Consequences also usually involve more than one source or type of event. Like antecedents, categories of consequences may be *affective, somatic, behavioral, cognitive, contextual,* and/or *relational.* For example, for our client who reports "anxiety," the avoidance of public places results in a reduction of anxious feelings (affective), body tension (somatic), and worry about more autonomy (cognitive). Additional consequences that may help to maintain the problem may include avoidance of being in public (behavioral) and increased attention from family and friends (relational). Contextual consequences may include reinforcement of cultural and gender values of being tied to her family of origin, being the family caregiver, and being able to "stay in the nest." It would be inaccurate to simply ask about whatever follows the specified behavior and to automatically classify it as a consequence without determining its particular effect on the behavior. As Cullen (1983, p. 137) notes, "If variables are supposed to be functionally related to behavior when, in fact, they are not, then manipulation of those variables by the client or therapist will, at best, have no effect on the presenting difficulties or, at worst, create even more difficulties."

Occasionally, students seem to confuse consequences as we present the concept in this chapter with the kinds of consequences that are often the results of a behavior—for example, Julie frequently procrastinates on studying and, as a consequence, receives poor grades. Although Julie's poor grades are the result of frequent procrastination, they are not a consequence in the way we are defining *consequence* unless the poor grades in some way increase, decrease, or maintain Julie's procrastination behavior. Otherwise, her poor grades are simply the result of too little studying. One way to distinguish consequences from mere effects of behavior is to remember a principle termed *gradient of reinforcement*. This term refers to the belief that consequences that occur soon after the behavior are likely to have a stronger impact than consequences that occur after a long time has elapsed (Hull, 1980). Poor grades can be so far removed in time from daily studying (or lack of it) that they are unlikely to exert much influence on the student's daily study behavior.

During the assessment phase of helping, it is important to identify those consequences that maintain, increase, or decrease both desirable and undesirable behaviors related to the client's concern. In the intervention (treatment) phase, this information will help you select change strategies that will maintain and increase desirable behaviors and will weaken and decrease undesirable behaviors such as behavioral excesses and deficits. Information about consequences is also useful in planning treatment approaches that rely directly on the use of consequences to help with behavior change, such as self-reward. It is important to reiterate that antecedents, consequences, and components must be assessed and identified for each particular client. Two clients might complain of anxiety or "nerves," and the assessments might reveal very different components of the behavior and different antecedents and consequences. A multicultural focus here is also important: the behaviors, antecedents, and consequences may be affected by the client's cultural affiliations and social–political context. Also remember that there is often some overlap among antecedents, behavior, and consequences. For example, negative

self-statements or irrational beliefs might function in some instances as both antecedents and consequences for a given component of the identified concern.

Consider a college student who reports depression after situations with less-than-desired outcomes, such as asking a girl out and being turned down, getting a test back with a B or C on it, and interviewing for a job and not receiving a subsequent offer of employment. Irrational beliefs may function as an antecedent by cuing, or setting off, the resulting feelings of depression—for example, "Here is a solution that didn't turn out the way I wanted. It's awful; now I feel lousy." Irrational beliefs in the form of self-deprecatory thoughts may function as a consequence by maintaining the feelings of depression for some time even after the situation itself is over—for example, "When things don't turn out the way they should, I'm a failure." At the same time, keep in mind this client has rational and coping beliefs as well as irrational ones, and behavioral, environmental, and cultural strengths as well. These may be less obvious to him than the presenting issues, but part of your task is to help him "uncover" what they are. It is also important to note that most issues presented by clients involve both multiple and complex chains of behavior sequences, so an ABC analysis is conducted on more than one factor. We illustrate this later in the chapter in our model case of Isabella. We also suggest that you work with the material presented in this model by going through the case presented in Learning Activity 7.1. and consult the visual summary given in Figure 7.1.

DIAGNOSTIC CLASSIFICATION OF CLIENT ISSUES

Our emphasis throughout this chapter is on the need to conduct a thorough and precise assessment with each client to be able to define client issues in very concrete ways. In addition, helpers need to be aware that client behaviors can be organized in some form of diagnostic taxonomy (classification). The official classification system is found in the 4th edition of the American Psychiatric Association's *Diagnostic and Statistical Manual of Mental Disorders, (DSM-IV, 1994)* and in the more recent text revision, *DSM-IV TR* (2000). Our interest in this chapter is simply to summarize the basic diagnostic codes and categories found in *DSM-IV* so that the reader will not be caught off guard if a colleague or supervisor begins talking about "Axis I, Axis II," and so on. Obviously, this short explanation is not a substitute for a thorough study of the *DSM-IV* system.

DSM-IV consists largely of descriptions of various mental and psychological disorders broken down into 17 major diagnostic classes, with additional subcategories within these major categories. Specific diagnostic criteria are provided for each category. These criteria are supposed to provide the practitioner with a way to evaluate and classify the client's concerns. The particular evaluation system used by *DSM-IV*

After reading the case of Mrs. Oliverio, complete the following three questions:

1. Based on the case and on your clinical hunches or hypotheses, list what you think are the major issues for Mrs. Oliverio.
2. Examine the issues you named. Do they reflect something about Mrs Oliverio as an individual, something about Mrs. Oliverio's environment, or both?
3. Go through the case again. Then complete as much of the grid in Figure 7.1 as you can from the information you have about the client. Discuss your responses with a classmate or your instructor.

The Case of Mrs. Oliverio

Mrs. Oliverio is a 28-year-old married woman who reports that an excessive fear that her husband will die has led her to seek therapy. She further states that because this is her second marriage, it is important for her to work out her problem so that it doesn't ultimately interfere with her relationship with her husband. However, her husband is a sales representative and occasionally has to attend out-of-town meetings. According to Mrs. Oliverio, whenever he has gone away on a trip during the two years of their marriage, she "goes to pieces" and feels "utterly devastated" because of recurring thoughts that he will die and not return. She states that this is a very intense fear and occurs even when he is gone on short trips, such as a half day or a day. She is not aware of any coping thoughts or behaviors she uses at these times. She indicates that she feels great as soon as her husband gets home. She states that this was also a problem for her in her first marriage, which ended in divorce five years ago. She believes the thoughts occur because her father died unexpectedly when she was 11 years old. Whenever her husband tells her he has to leave, or actually does leave, she reexperiences the pain of being told her father has died. She feels plagued with thoughts that her husband will not return and then feels intense anxiety. She is constantly thinking about never seeing her husband again during these anxiety episodes. According to Mrs. Oliverio, her husband has been very supportive and patient and has spent a considerable amount of time trying to reassure her and to convince her, through reasoning, that

he will return from a trip. She states that this has not helped her to stop worrying excessively that he will die and not return. She also states that in the past few months her husband has canceled several business trips just to avoid putting her through all this pain.

Mrs. Oliverio also reports that this anxiety has resulted in some insomnia during the past two years. She states that as soon as her husband informs her that he must leave town, she has difficulty going to sleep that evening. When he has to be gone on an overnight trip, she doesn't sleep at all. She simply lies in bed and worries about her husband dying and also feels very frustrated that it is getting later and later and that she is still awake. She reports sleeping fairly well as long as her husband is home and a trip is not impending.

Mrs. Oliverio reports that she feels very satisfied with her present marriage except for some occasional times when she finds herself thinking that her husband does not fulfill all her expectations. She is not sure exactly what her expectations are, but she is aware of feeling anger toward him after this happens. When she gets angry, she just "explodes" and feels as though she lashes out at her husband for no apparent reason. She reports that she doesn't like to explode at her husband like this but feels relieved after it happens. She indicates that her husband continues to be very supportive and protective in spite of her occasional outbursts. She suspects the anger may be her way of getting back at him for going away on a trip and leaving her alone. She also expresses feelings of hurt and anger since her father's death in being unable to find a "father substitute." She also reports feeling intense anger toward her ex-husband after the divorce—anger she still sometimes experiences.

Mrs. Oliverio has no children. She is employed in a responsible position as an administrative assistant and makes $35,500 a year. She reports that she enjoys her work, although she constantly worries that her boss might not be pleased with her and that she could lose her job even though her work evaluations have been satisfactory. She reports that another event she has been worried about is the health of her brother, who was injured in a car accident this past year. She further reports that she has an excellent relationship with her brother and strong ties to her church.

is called *multiaxial* because it consists of an assessment on five codes, or *axes:*

Axis I Clinical disorders and other disorders that may be a focus of clinical attention

Axis II Personality disorders and mental retardation

Axis III General medical conditions

Axis IV Psychosocial and environmental problems

Axis V Global assessment of functioning

Axis I comprises the clinical disorders as well as any other disorders that the helper decides are an important focus of clinical attention. Axis I includes disorders typically found in children and adolescents such as learning, communication, developmental, and attention-deficit and disruptive disorders. Also included in Axis I are disorders of adulthood such as cognitive disorders, substance-related disorders, psychotic disorders, mood disorders, anxiety disorders, sexual and gender identity disorders, eating disorders, and sleep disorders. In general, a *clinical disorder* is a pattern of behaviors and psychological symptoms that results in significant distress, impairment, and risk for the individual. For instance, an adult client with Generalized Anxiety Disorder would exhibit excessive worry and anxiety on more days than not for a period of at least six months or more, would find it difficult to manage the worry, and would endorse at least three of six behavioral symptoms including restlessness, fatigue, concentration issues, irritability, muscle tension, and sleep disturbance. These symptoms would cause significant distress or impairment to the client in social, occupational, or other areas of functioning. Each particular clinical disorder is coded on Axis I with a numerical rating. For example, a client with Generalized Anxiety Disorder would receive a code on Axis I of 300.02. If no clinical disorder is present, Axis I is coded V71.09. Remember from our earlier discussion that not all clients will have a pathological or clinical disorder. If the clinician suspects there is a clinical disorder but needs more information about the client before deciding conclusively, then Axis I is coded in the interim as 799.9, which means "diagnosis deferred."

Axis II is used for reporting both mental retardation and personality disorders. The contributors to the *DSM-IV* noted that these two listings were given a separate axis to help ensure that either condition would not be overlooked. *Mental retardation* is a condition characterized by significantly subaverage intellectual functioning with onset prior to age 18 and is accompanied by concurrent deficits or impairments in adaptive functioning. In contrast, *personality disorders* are typically (though not always) diagnosed after the age of 18. Ten possible personality disorders are reported in the *DSM-IV TR* and include such descriptors as *paranoid, schizoid, antisocial, borderline, narcissistic,* and *dependent.* Axis II may also be used to record information about the presence of client defensive mechanisms and maladaptive personality features that are present but not in sufficient strength to warrant a diagnosis of personality disorder. Such personality traits represent longstanding patterns of thinking about and relating to oneself and to one's environment in a variety of contexts. Only when such personality traits create clinically significant distress or impairment do they constitute a personality disorder diagnosis. Personality disorders can be problematic because they represent long-standing patterns of inner experience and behavior that create significant difficulties for the client in areas such as thinking, managing emotions, relationships with others, and

impulse control. Moreover, the pattern reflected in a personality disorder is fairly rigid and invades many contexts across the client's life. If no diagnosis on Axis II is present, the helper uses the code V71.09.

Axis III is used to note current *medical conditions* of the client that are relevant to the understanding and/or management of the client's clinical disorders. Examples of such medical conditions coded on Axis III include infections, endocrine diseases, diseases of the blood, nervous system, circulatory system, respiratory system, digestive system, genitourinary system, skin, musculoskeletal system, and so on. The purpose of Axis III is to promote a thorough assessment and to assess for ways in which general medical conditions can be related to clinical disorders. For example, a client with hypothyroidism may suffer from some sort of depression (coded on Axis I), and the recording of hypothyroidism on Axis III notes the link between the two conditions.

Axis IV is used for reporting *psychosocial and environmental problems* that may influence the diagnosis, treatment, and prognosis of the mental disorder(s) reported in Axis I and Axis II. These include nine general categories relating to negative life events, environmental and familial stresses, and lack of social support (identified by the helper):

Issues with primary support group

Issues related to the social environment

Educational issues

Occupational issues

Housing issues

Economic issues

Issues with access to health care services

Issues related to interaction with the legal system/crime

Other psychosocial and environmental issues

Axis V is used to report the helper's assessment of the client's overall *level of functioning.* This rating is useful in planning treatment and assessing treatment goals. This evaluation is coded on a Global Assessment of Functioning (GAF). The assessment ranges from 0 (*inadequate information*) to 100 (*superior functioning*). Descriptions for all other ratings are as follows:

91–100   Superior functioning in a wide range of activities; life's problems never seem to get out of hand

81–90   Absent or minimal symptoms

71–80   Symptoms, if present, are transient and expectable reactions to stressors

61–70   Some mild symptoms

51–60   Moderate symptoms

41–50	Serious symptoms
31–40	Some impairment in reality testing or communication
21–30	Behavior considerably influenced by delusions or hallucinations or serious impairment in communication or judgment
11–20	Some danger of hurting self or others
1–10	Persistent danger of severely hurting self or others

You will find examples of this multiaxial evaluation system following the analyses of the client cases in this chapter. Of course our brief discussion here is in no way a substitute for familiarizing yourself with the *DSM-IV TR*. In addition, the Canadian Psychological Association has a wide array of fact sheets on various clinical disorders available on their website at http://www.cap.ca/factsheets/main.htm.

In spite of apparent conceptual and practical limitations of diagnosis, the process can aid helpers in assessing target behaviors and in selecting appropriate interventions for treatment. For instance, knowledge about selected features of various types of clinical pathology, such as the usual age of the patient at the onset of some disorder or whether the disorder is more common in men or in women, can aid in assessment. An addition to the *DSM-IV* is its routine inclusion of discussions of age, gender, and cultural implications of the various disorders. For example, it notes under *panic attacks* that in some cultures a panic attack may involve an intense fear of witchcraft or magic, and it reports under *agoraphobia* that in some cultural or ethnic groups the participation of women in public life is restricted.

Selected features of *DSM-IV* are useful for suggesting additional information about behaviors and the controlling variables. For example, the operational criteria found in *DSM-IV* often indicate further target behaviors associated with a particular disorder that should be assessed, and the associated features of a disorder often suggest controlling or contributing variables to be assessed. For instance, if a client describes behaviors related to depression, the helper can use the operational criteria for major depressive episodes to ask about other target behaviors related to depression that the client may not mention. Helpers can also be guided by the associated features of this disorder to question the client about possible controlling variables typically associated with the disorder (for depression, events such as life changes, loss of reinforcers, and family history of depression).

LIMITATIONS OF DIAGNOSIS: CATEGORIES, LABELS, AND GENDER/MULTICULTURAL BIASES

Diagnostic classification presents certain limitations, and these are most apparent when a client is given a diagnostic classification without the benefit of a thorough and complete assessment. The most common criticisms of diagnosis are that it places labels on clients—often meaningless ones—and that the labels themselves are not well defined and do not describe what the clients do or don't do that makes them "histrionic" or "a conduct disorder" and so on. Indeed, some proponents of the strengths perspective we discussed earlier in the chapter question whether formulating diagnoses is in a client's best interest because of potential stigmatization associated with such labels. Also, the current *DSM-IV* system is based on a *categorical* system of classification in which, as you saw from the preceding description of it, clients are diagnosed according to whether they do or do not meet a certain number of criteria for a specific diagnosis. Critics of this system have noted that it does not address the fact that clients receiving the same diagnosis are likely to be quite heterogeneous and also that more than half of our clients are likely to have *comorbid* or coexisting disorders at the same time. Despite the empirical base of the *DSM-IV TR*, the reality is that in actual practice, "pure and uncomplicated symptom pictures are somewhat atypical" (Clark, Watson, & Reynolds, 1995, p. 128). As a result, the categorical system reflected in the *DSM-IV* does not fully reflect the nature of the client's disorders. Future directions in diagnosis of mental disorders are likely to revolve around a *dimensional* approach in which the client's symptoms would be assessed not in categories but along dimensions such as constellation and degree of severity of symptoms (Krueger & Piasecki, 2002; Widiger & Simonsen, 2005).

Also, the process of making diagnoses using the current edition of the diagnostic and statistical manual has come under sharp criticism from members of feminist therapy groups, from persons of color, and from those who are advocates for clients of color (Lopez et al., 2006). For example, feminist therapists assert that the development of clinical disorders in women almost always involves a lack of both real and perceived power in their lives (Brown & Ballou, 1992). These therapists have noted that the concept of "distress," which permeates the traditional diagnostic classification system, reflects a "highly individualized phenomenon" and overlooks distress as "a manifestation of larger social and cultural forces" (Brown, 1992, p. 113).

Brown (1992) argues that a feminist perspective of psychopathology must include the pathology of oppression. The theoretical foundations of psychiatry and psychology underpinning traditional diagnosis "have limited contexts and tend to be ahistorical . . . making invisible the experiences of large segments of the population who have been historically oppressed" (Root, 1992, p. 258). In this model, health is defined not just as an absence of distress "but also as the presence of nonoppressive attitudes and relationships toward other humans, animals, and the planet" (Brown, 1992, p. 112). A feminist model of psychopathology and health also examines the existence and the meaning of particular symptom patterns that may emerge with certain cultural groups. As Root (1992) observes, "For many minority groups, the repeated and/or chronic experience of traumatic events makes it difficult for the individual to believe in anything but unique vulnerability"; this sort of vulnerability "is reinforced in persons who are subject to repeated discrimination or threat, such as anti–gay/lesbian violence, racist-motivated violence, anti-Semitic violence, chronic torture experienced by many Southeast Asian refugees, and repeated interpersonal sexual assault and violence" (p. 244).

In addition to the social–political context described above, a feminist view of psychopathology and health also involves an examination of the social–political context surrounding an individual's expressed behavior. For example, Ross (1990) observes that hearing voices or seeing ghosts is not viewed as a pathological symptom and a sign of psychosis in those cultures that consider such experiences to be indications of *divine favor*. A feminist conception of diagnosis includes cultural relativity and ascertains what is normal for *this* individual, in *this* particular time and place (Brown, 1992, p. 113). Feminist practitioners would ask a client "What has happened to you?" rather than "What is wrong with you?" Similar concerns about bias in diagnosis have been raised by cross-cultural researchers and practitioners.

Kress White and colleagues (2005) note that "research and literature on cross-cultural assessment, diagnosis, and treatment continue to expose the inaccuracy of the DSM system with underrepresented and marginalized groups" (p. 98). Clients from these groups tend to be overdiagnosed, underdiagnosed, or misdiagnosed by clinicians. Misdiagnoses can easily occur when the languages between clinician and client are different and when the services of translators are not available or utilized. Sue and Sue (2003) point out that the history of oppression (described earlier by Brown for women) also affects resulting diagnoses made for clients of color who, because of this history, may be reluctant to self-disclose and, as a result, may be labeled *paranoid*. Sue and Sue (2003), like Brown, argue that diagnosis of clients of color must be understood from a larger social–political perspective. Otherwise, these clients may receive a diagnosis that overlooks the survival and protective value of their behaviors in a racist society. Further, the way in which disorders are experienced by clients varies with things like ethnicity, race, and age. For example, in many parts of Chinese society, the experience of depression is more physical than psychological, and Latino/Latina clients as well as refugees may report symptoms of depressive disorders very differently than Euro-Americans (Kleinman, 2004). Older clients may have more unique presentations of depression as well that impact Axis I diagnoses (Edelstein, Koven, Spira, & Shreve-Neiger, 2003).

Further criticisms of the DSM system have been elaborated by both White Kress and colleagues and by Lopez and colleagues. White Kress and colleagues (2005) view the absence of any culture-bound syndromes related to macrolevel issues such as acculturation adjustments, immigration issues, ethnic–racial identity confusion, or trauma due to racism or violence as a particular limitation of this diagnostic system. Lopez and colleagues (2006) note that in its current form, the DSM system describes a negative syndrome associated with impairment and omits assessment of strengths and processes of change. They recommend widening the diagnostic focus to include criteria for well-being or "flourishing," broadening Axis IV to include psychosocial and environmental resources in addition to the current identification of these stressors, and creation of a new Axis VI to record individual strengths.

In response to these concerns, the contributors to the *DSM-IV* recognize that accurate diagnosis can be challenging "when a clinician from one ethnic or cultural group uses the *DSM-IV* classification to evaluate an individual from a different ethnic or cultural group" (American Psychiatric Association [APA], 1994, p. xiv). They observe that helpers who are not cognizant of the nuances of a client's cultural frame of reference "may incorrectly judge as psychopathology those normal variations in behavior, belief, or experience that are particular to the individual's culture" (p. ix). In the *DSM-IV*, in addition to very brief discussions of age, gender, and cultural features of many of the clinical disorders, there is an appendix that includes a glossary of 12 "culture-bound" syndromes—that is, what the *DSM-IV* (APA, 1994) defines as "localized, folk, diagnostic categories that frame coherent meanings for certain repetitive, patterned, and troubling sets of experiences and observations" (p. 844). Although there is not usually an equivalent found in the *DSM-IV* clinical categories, associated relevant *DSM-IV* categories are also cross-listed with these syndromes. In addition to this glossary, the appendix also includes an outline for a supplemental "cultural formulation" to be used in addition to the multiaxial system. However, as White Kress et al. (2005) note, this glossary is not an exhaustive list and is limited when used for diagnosing clients of color.

INTERFACE OF THE STRENGTHS PERSPECTIVE AND THE DIAGNOSTIC/MEDICAL MODEL: THE PERSON-IN-ENVIRONMENT CLASSIFICATION SYSTEM

Despite the apparent disadvantages of diagnosis, many practitioners find themselves in field placement and work settings in which they are required to make a diagnostic classification of client behaviors. Often, even clients request a diagnosis in order to receive reimbursement from their health insurance carrier for payment made for helping services. This situation is becoming more common with the growth of managed care/HMOs (health maintenance organizations). We believe that when the *DSM-IV* system of classification needs to be used, it should be applied within the context of a complete multifactor and multicultural approach and should not be used as a substitute for an idiographic assessment. (See Learning Activity 7.2.) Some proponents of the strengths perspective that we discussed earlier do not see any compatibility between using a strengths perspective in assessment and using diagnoses that rely on a medical model such as the one reflected in the *DSM-IV*. They argue that formulating diagnoses is not in the client's best interests and promotes stigmatization. We agree with Taylor (2006), who proposes that the strengths perspective and the diagnostic/medical model can be blended in such a way that there is in fact a cooperative relationship among the two perspectives. The strengths perspective is useful because it reminds us that no client should ever be singled out or blamed for having a mental illness. It also reminds us that in spite of issues and struggles, clients are resilient and persons with skills, hopes, and even civil rights. At the same time, as Taylor (2006) observes, findings from neuroscience, genetics, and environmental research point to the role of interacting genes, brain metabolism, and environmental factors in mental health disorders (p. 6).

Because some of the clinical disorders reflected in the *DSM-IV TR* have an associated chemical function and brain structure change associated with them, the information provided by the diagnostic process can be useful in suggesting the need for psychiatric evaluation and/or medical treatment as an ancillary to counseling and therapy. Consider, for example, Mary's client, Joe. Joe is a young man who presents with depression, which he attributes to his recent medical diagnosis of diabetes. His diabetes is not being medically managed nor has he been evaluated or treated medically for depression. Did his depression precede the diabetes, or is it a result of the diabetes? There is some evidence for both possibilities! In either event, Joe is a prime example of a client who could benefit from a referral to a medical practitioner *in addition to* his counseling sessions with Mary.

In general, practitioners need to consider referrals for psychiatric evaluation and/or medical evaluation in the following circumstances:

1. The client presents with a psychiatric emergency—that is, the client's level of functioning is so impaired or the client feels so distressed that he or she cannot perform the daily function of life. Other psychiatric emergencies include instances when a client poses a danger to himself or herself, to someone else, or perhaps even to both self and others.
2. The client presents with symptoms that suggest disease processes in which brain structure and chemical function are apparent. These conditions include mental retardation, attention-deficit disorder, bipolar disorder (known formerly as manic-depressive disorder), mood disorders such as major depression, schizophrenia, dementia,

anxiety disorders, and some conditions related to post-traumatic stress. Practitioners can make such referrals in a humanizing manner, not denying the possibility of impairment or of risk but at the same time recognizing the protective factors, coping skills, and resilience of the individual client.

An alternative to the *DSM-IV* diagnostic system that is preferred by many practitioners who endorse the strengths perspective is the Person-in-Environment (PIE) classification system, developed by Karls and Wandrei (1994). It is an assessment/classification system that helps practitioners understand the interrelationships between the individual clients and the system or environment in which clients reside. Unlike *DSM-IV*, the PIE classification is not considered a diagnostic system. Rather it is a tool that practitioners use to collect relevant assessment information about the client and the client's environment, for the express purpose of facilitating the planning of successful treatment interventions. The PIE assesses these four factors:

Factor I: Social Role Problem Identification

Factor II: Environmental Problem Identification

Factor III: Mental Health Problem Identification

Factor IV: Physical Health Problem Identification

Factors I and II constitute the bulk of the PIE classification. Factor I comprises five levels of assessment: social role, type of interactional difficulty with social role, level of severity, duration of the problem, and the client's ability to cope with the problem. Factor II comprises five levels of assessment: type of environmental problem area, severity of the problem, duration of the problem, client's coping ability, and discrimination experienced by the client. (See Table 7.1 for a complete listing of the dimensions assessed by Factors I and II.) Factor III borrows from the *DSM-IV* by using Axes I and II of the *DSM-IV*, and Factor IV lists physical health problems using the International Classification of Diseases.

Several considerations are worth noting in considering the use of the PIE classification system. One is that this system avoids classifying social roles in a culturally specific context. As a result, Factor I in particular "is limited in clarifying some problems faced by certain culturally diverse groups of people" (Appleby, Colon, & Hamilton, 2001, p. 124). However, Factor II does consider culturally relevant dimensions of environmental problems by assessing discrimination status of each. Second, the judgments involved in the classification and coding are based on the practitioner's perception rather than the client's perceptions. Finally, the delineation of the types of problems is based on the person presenting for treatment—that is, the identified client—and not on other persons who may be contributing to the client's

TABLE 7.1	Summary of Factor I and Factor II of the PIE Classification System

Factor I: Social Role Problem Identification

Type of Problem
Family roles (parent, spouse, child, sibling, other family member, significant other)
Interpersonal roles (lover, friend, neighbor, member, other)
Occupational roles (worker–paid economy, worker–home, worker–volunteer, student, other)
Special life situation roles (consumer, inpatient/client, outpatient/client, probationer/parolee, immigrant–legal, immigrant–undocumented, immigrant–refugee, other)

Type of Interactional Difficulty
Power, ambivalence, responsibility, dependency, loss, isolation, victimization, mixed, other

Level of Severity: 1 to 6 scale
1 = no problem, 2 = low, 3 = moderate, 4 = high, 5 = very high, 6 = catastrophic

Duration Index: 1 to 6 scale
1 = more than five years, 2 = one to five years, 3 = six months to one year, 4 = one to six months, 5 = two weeks to one month, and 6 = less than two weeks

Coping Index: 1 to 6 scale
1 = outstanding, 2 = above average, 3 = adequate, 4 = somewhat inadequate, 5 = inadequate, and 6 = no coping skills

Factor II: Environmental Problem Identification

Type of Environmental Problem Area
Economic/basic needs system, education and training system, judicial and legal system, health, safety, and social services system, voluntary association system, and affectional support system

Discrimination codes for any of these types of environmental problems
Coded by age, ethnicity, color, or language, religion, sex, sexual orientation, lifestyle, noncitizen, veteran
Status (dependency status, disability status, marital status, other)

Severity, Duration, and Coping Skills Indices: 1 to 6 scale
Identical to Factor I

Source: *PIE Manual: Person-in-Environment: The PIE Classification System for Social Functioning Problems,* by J. M. Karls & K. E. Wandrei. Copyright 1994 by National Association of Social Workers. Used with permission.

difficulties. We illustrate the use of the PIE in our model case of Isabella.

MODEL CASE: THE CASE OF ISABELLA

To assist you in conceptualizing client concerns with the models from this chapter, we provide a case illustration followed by two practice cases for you to analyze. The conceptual understanding you should acquire from this chapter will help you actually define client issues and contributing variables with an interview assessment.

The Case

Isabella is a 15-year-old student completing her sophomore year of high school and presently taking a college preparatory curriculum. Her initial statement in the first counseling session is that she is "unhappy" and feels "dissatisfied" with this school experience but feels unable to do anything about it. On further clarification, Isabella reveals that she is unhappy because she doesn't think she is measuring up to her classmates and that she dislikes being with these "top" kids in some of her classes, which are very competitive. She reports particular concern in one math class, which she says

is composed largely of "guys" who are much smarter than she is. She states that she thinks about the fact that "girls are so dumb in math" rather frequently during the class and she feels intimidated. She reports that as soon as she is in this class, she gets anxious and "withdraws." She states that she sometimes gets anxious just thinking about the class, and she says that when this happens she gets "butterflies" in her stomach, her palms get sweaty and cold, and her heart beats faster. When asked what she means by "withdrawing," she says she sits by herself, doesn't talk to her classmates, and doesn't volunteer answers or go to the board. Often, when called on, she says nothing. As a result, she reports, her grades are dropping. She also states that her math teacher has spoken to her several times about her behavior and has tried to help her do better. However, Isabella's nervousness in the class has resulted in her cutting the class whenever she can find any reason to do so, and she has almost used up her number of excused absences from school. She states that her fear of competitive academic situations has been there since junior high, when her parents started to compare her with other students and put "pressure" on her to do well in school so she could go to college. When asked how they pressure her, she says they constantly talk to her about getting good grades, and whenever she doesn't, they lash out at her and withdraw privileges, like her allowance and going out with her friends. She reports a strong network of girlfriends with whom she "hangs out a lot." She reports that during this year, since the classes are tougher and more competitive, school is more of a problem to her and she feels increasingly anxious in certain classes, especially math. Isabella also states that sometimes she thinks she is almost failing on purpose to get back at her parents for their pressure. Isabella reports that all this has made her dissatisfied with school, and she has questioned whether she wants to stay in a college prep curriculum. She has toyed with the idea of going to culinary school instead of going to college. However, she says she is a very indecisive person and does not know what she should do. In addition, she is afraid to decide this because if she changed her curriculum, her parents' response would be very negative. Isabella states that she cannot recall ever having made a decision without her parents' assistance. She feels they often have made decisions for her. She says her parents have never encouraged her to make decisions on her own because they say she might not make the right decision without their help. Isabella is an only child. She indicates that she is constantly afraid of making a bad or wrong choice.

Analysis of the Case

There are three related but distinct concerns for Isabella. First, her "presenting" issue is an academic one (note the corresponding diagnosis on the *DSM-IV* Axis I): she feels anxious about her performance in competitive classes at school, primarily math, and is aware that her grades are dropping in this class. Second, she is generally unsure about her long-term goals and career choice and whether the college prep curriculum she is in is what she wants. (Note the diagnosis of identity problem on Axis I of the *DSM-IV* classification.) She feels indecisive about this particular situation and regards herself as indecisive in many other situations as well. Those two concerns are exacerbated by a third concern: her relationship with her parents. This is coded as a psychosocial and environmental issue on Axis IV of the *DSM-IV* classification. This coding notes the potential influence of this relational situation on the academic and decision-making/identity issues mentioned above.

Next, we use the ABC model presented earlier in the chapter (see Figure 7.1) to analyze these two issues.

Analysis of the School Issue
Relevant Behaviors

Isabella's behaviors at school include

1. Self-defeating labeling of her math class as "competitive" and of herself as "not as smart as the guys."
2. Sitting alone, not volunteering answers in math class, not answering the teacher's questions or going to the board, and cutting class.

Isabella's self-defeating labels are a covert behavior; her sitting alone, not volunteering answers, and cutting class are overt behaviors.

Individual and Environmental Strengths
These include Isabella's help-seeking behavior and the support of her math teacher.

Context of Issue

Antecedent Conditions   Isabella's behaviors at school are cued by certain "competitive" classes, particularly math. Previous antecedent conditions include verbal comparisons about Isabella and her peers made by her parents and verbal pressure for good grades and withholding of privileges for bad grades by her parents. Notice that these antecedent conditions do not occur at the same time. The antecedent of the anxiety in the "competitive" class occurs in proximity to Isabella's problem behaviors and is a "stimulus event." However, the verbal comparisons and parental pressure began several years ago and probably function as a "setting event."

Consequences   Isabella's behaviors at school are maintained by

1. An increased level of attention to her by her math teacher.
2. Feeling relieved of anxiety through avoidance of the situation that elicits anxiety. By not participating in class and by cutting class, Isabella can avoid putting herself in an anxiety-provoking situation.
3. Her poorer grades, possibly because of two payoffs, or secondary gains. First, if her grades get too low, she may not qualify to continue in the college prep curriculum. This would be the "ultimate" way to avoid putting herself in competitive academic situations that elicit anxiety. Second, the lowered grades could also be maintaining her behaviors because she labels the poor grades as a way to "get back at" her parents for their pressure.

Analysis of the Decision-Making Issue
Relevant Behaviors

Isabella's behavior can be described as not making a decision for herself—in this case, about a curriculum change. Depending on the client, issues in making decisions can be either covert or overt. In people who have the skills to make a decision but are blocking themselves because of their "labels" or "internal dialogue" about the decision, the behavior would be designated as covert. A related covert aspect of the decision-making problem may have to do with an underlying cognitive schema of impaired autonomy. A cognitive schema is a belief rooted in a client's developmental history that confirms the client's core belief about oneself. Isabella's

LEARNING ACTIVITY	**7.2**	**Assessment Models**

To help you in conceptualizing a client's issue, we provide two cases. We suggest that you work through the first case completely before going on to the second. After reading each case, respond to the questions following the case by yourself or with a partner. Then compare your responses with the feedback on page 182.

The Case of Ms. Weare and Freddie

Ms. Weare and her 9-year-old son, Freddie, have come to Family Services after Ms. Weare said she had reached her limit with her son and needed to talk to another adult about it. Their initial complaint is that they don't get along with each other. Ms. Weare complains that Freddie doesn't get himself ready in the morning, and this makes her mad. Freddie complains that his mother yells and screams at him frequently. Ms. Weare agrees that she does, especially when it is time for Freddie to leave for school and he isn't ready yet. Freddie agrees that he doesn't get himself ready and points out that he does this just to "get Mom mad." Ms. Weare says this has been going on as long as she can remember. She states that Freddie gets up and usually comes down to breakfast not dressed. After breakfast, Ms. Weare always reminds him to get ready and threatens that she'll yell or hit him if he doesn't. Freddie usually goes back to his room, where, he reports, he just sits around until his mother comes up. Ms. Weare waits until five minutes before the bus comes and then calls Freddie. After he doesn't come down, she goes upstairs and sees that he's not ready. She reports that she gets very mad and yells, "You're dumb. Why do you just sit there? Why can't you dress yourself? You're going to be late for school. Your teacher will blame me, since I'm your mother." She also helps Freddie get ready. So far, he has not been late, but Ms. Weare says she "knows" he will be if she doesn't "nag" him and help him get ready. When asked about the option of removing her help and letting Freddie get ready on his own, she says that he is a smart kid who is doing well in school and that she doesn't want this factor to change. She never finished high school herself, and she doesn't want that to happen to Freddie. She also says that if he didn't have her help, he would probably just stay at home that day and she wouldn't get any of her own work done. On further questioning, Ms. Weare says this behavior does not occur on weekends, only on school days. She states that as a result of this situation, although she's never punished him physically, she feels very nervous and edgy after Freddie leaves for school, often not doing some necessary work because of this feeling. Asked what she means by "nervous" and "edgy," she reports that her body feels tense and jittery all over. She indicates that this reaction does not help her high blood pressure. She reports that Freddie's father is not living at home, so all the child rearing is on her shoulders. Ms. Weare also states that she doesn't spend much time with Freddie at night after school because she does extra work at home at night, for she and Freddie "don't have much money."

DSM-IV Diagnosis for Ms. Weare

Axis I   V61.20, Parent–child relational issue
Axis II   V71.09 (no diagnosis)
Axis III   401.9 (hypertension, essential)
Axis IV   None
Axis V   GAF = 75 (current)

Respond to these questions.

1. What behaviors does Freddie demonstrate in this situation?
2. Is each behavior you have listed overt or covert?
3. What individual and environmental strengths do you see for Freddie?
4. What behaviors does Ms. Weare exhibit in this situation?
5. Is each behavior you have listed overt or covert?
6. What individual and environmental strengths do you see for Ms. Weare?
7. List one or more antecedent conditions that seem to bring about each of Freddie's behaviors.
8. List one or more antecedent conditions that seem to bring about each of Ms. Weare's behaviors.
9. List one or more consequences (including any secondary gains) that influence each of Freddie's behaviors. After each consequence listed, identify how the consequence seems to influence Freddie's behavior.
10. List one or more consequences that seem to influence each of Ms. Weare's behaviors. After each consequence listed, identify how the consequence seems to influence her behavior.
11. Identify aspects of the sociopolitical context that appear to affect Ms. Weare's behavior.

The Case of Mrs. Rodriguez

Mrs. Rodriguez is a 34-year-old Mexican American woman who was a legal immigrant to the United States when she was 10 years of age. She was brought to the emergency room by the police after her bizarre behavior in a local supermarket. According to the police report, Mrs. Rodriguez became very

(continued)

| LEARNING ACTIVITY | 7.2 | **Assessment Models** |

(continued)

aggressive toward another shopper, accusing the man of "following me around and spying on me." When confronted by employees of the store about her charges, she stated, "God speaks to me. I can hear his voice guiding me in my mission." On mental-status examination, the counselor initially notes Mrs. Rodriguez's unkempt appearance. She appears unclean. Her clothing is somewhat disheveled. She seems underweight and looks older than her stated age. Her tense posture seems indicative of her anxious state, and she smiles inappropriately throughout the interview. Her speech is loud and fast, and she constantly glances suspiciously around the room. Her affect is labile, fluctuating from anger to euphoria. On occasion, she looks at the ceiling and spontaneously starts talking. When the helper asks to whom she is speaking, she replies, "Can't you hear him? He's come to save me!" Mrs. Rodriguez is alert and appears to be of average general intelligence. Her attention span is short. She reports no suicidal ideation and denies any past attempts. However, she does express some homicidal feelings for those who "continue to secretly follow me around." When the family members arrive, the helper is able to ascertain that Mrs. Rodriguez has been in psychiatric treatment on and off for the last 10 years. She has been hospitalized several times in the past 10 years during similar episodes of unusual behavior. In addition, she has been treated with several antipsychotic medicines. There is no evidence of any physical disorder or any indication of alcohol or drug abuse. Her husband indicates that she recently stopped

taking her medicine after the death of her sister and up until then had been functioning adequately during the past year without a great deal of impairment although she was not capable of holding regular paid employment outside of the home.

DSM-IV Diagnosis for Mrs. Rodriguez

Axis I   295.30, Schizophrenia, paranoid type
Axis II   V71.09 (no diagnosis)
Axis III   None
Axis IV   Issues with primary social support system (recent death of sister)
Axis V   GAF = 25 (current)

Respond to these questions. See page 182 for feedback.

1. List several of the behaviors that Mrs. Rodriguez demonstrates.

2. Is each behavior you have listed overt or covert?

3. List any individual and environmental strengths you observe.

4. List one or more antecedents that seem to elicit Mrs. Rodriguez's behaviors.

5. List one or more consequences that appear to influence the behaviors, including any secondary gains. Describe how each consequence seems to influence the behavior.

6. Identify aspects of the sociopolitical context that affect her behavior.

---

indecisive behavior seems based on her past learning history of having many decisions either made for her or made with parental assistance. The lack of opportunities she has had to make choices suggests she has not acquired the skills involved in decision making. This issue would be classified as overt.

Individual and Environmental Strengths

Strengths include Isabella's awareness of autonomy issues within herself and with her parents. Another strength is her strong social support network of close girlfriends.

Context of Issue

Antecedent Conditions Isabella's previous decision-making history is the primary antecedent condition. This consists of (1) having decisions made for her and (2) a lack of opportunities to acquire and use the skills of decision making.

Consequences The consequences that seem to be maintaining Isabella's behavior of not deciding include

1. Getting help with her decisions (taking responsibility is apparently aversive)
2. Anticipation of parental negative reactions (punishment) to her decisions through her self-talk
3. Absence of positive consequences or lack of encouragement for any efforts at decision making in the past
4. In the specific decision of a curriculum change, her low grades, which, if they get too bad, may help her avoid making a curriculum decision by automatically disqualifying her from the college prep curriculum

Social–Political Context This part of the assessment addresses the question of how Isabella's presenting issues are a manifestation of the social–political context and structure in which she lives. Isabella's concerns appear to be shaped by a context in which she has been reinforced (and punished) for what she does (or doesn't do). This pattern has led to a devaluing and uncertainty of who she is and what she wants and needs. She appears to feel powerless in her current environment—partly, we suspect, because of the power her parents have exerted over her; partly because of the power exerted by a school system that emphasizes college prep values; and partly because of lessons she has learned from her cultural groups about men, women, and achievement. In her math classroom, the gender context plays a big role. She is literally in the gender minority. She compares herself negatively to the boys in the classroom who hold the power, and she is shut down by her negative comparison. The relevant overt and the covert behaviors that we describe above appear to be tools Isabella is using to cope with this loss and sense of powerlessness as well as ways to attempt to increase the power she has and decrease the power held by other sources of authority.

The *DSM-IV* diagnoses and the Person-in-Environment classification for Isabella follow:

DSM-IV Diagnosis for Isabella

Axis I	V62.3 (academic issue)
	313.82 (identity issue)
Axis II	V71.09 (no diagnosis)
Axis II	None
Axis IV	Issues with primary support system
Axis V	GAF = 65 (current)

Pie Classification for Isabella

Factor I: Social Role Problem Identification

Social role	Type of interactional difficulty	Severity[1]	Duration[2]	Coping[3] index
Family-child	Dependency	3	2	4
Occupational-student	Ambivalence	3	2	4

Factor II: Environmental Problem Identification

Type of problem	Discrimination code	Severity[1]	Duration[2]	Coping[3] index
Education-training	Sex (gender)	3	3	4
Affectional support system	Dependency status	3	2	4

1 = 1–6 scale with 6 being most severe
2 = 1–6 scale with 6 being shortest duration
3 = 1–6 scale with 6 being poorest coping

CHAPTER SUMMARY

Assessment is the basis for development of the entire helping program. Assessment has important informational, educational, and motivational functions in therapy. Although the major part of assessment occurs early in the helping process, to some extent assessment, or identification of client concerns, goes on constantly throughout the process. As the assessment unfolds, the client's story unfolds as well. An important part of assessment is the helper's ability to conceptualize client concerns. Conceptualization models help the practitioner think clearly about the complexity of client issues.

The assessment model described in this chapter is based on several assumptions, including these:

1. Most behavior is learned, although some psychological issues may have biological causes.
2. Causes of issues are multidimensional.
3. Issues need to be viewed operationally, or concretely.
4. Issues occur in a social and cultural context and are affected by internal and external antecedents that are functionally related to or exert influence in various ways.
5. Components of the issue as well as sources of antecedents and consequences can be affective, somatic, behavioral, cognitive, contextual, and relational.
6. In addition to assessment of client issues, a focus on clients' individual and environmental resources and strengths is also important.

Another part of assessment may involve a multiaxial diagnosis of the client. Current diagnosis is based on the *Diagnostic and Statistical Manual of Mental Disorders,* 4th edition, text revision, and involves classifying disorders, medical conditions, and psychosocial and environmental issues, and making a global assessment of current functioning. Diagnosis can be a useful part of assessment. For example, knowledge about selected features of various types of clinical syndromes can add to understanding of a client's concern. However, diagnosis is not an adequate *substitute* for other assessment approaches and is not an effective basis for

FEEDBACK

7.2

Assessment Models

The Case of Ms. Weare and Freddie

1. Freddie's behavior is sitting in his room and not getting ready for school.
2. This is an overt behavior, as it is visible to someone else.
3. Strengths for Freddie include his being smart, doing well in school, and having a mom who believes in him and wants to see him do well academically.
4. Ms. Weare's behaviors are (a) feeling mad and (b) yelling at Freddie.
5. Feeling mad is a covert behavior, as feelings can only be inferred. Yelling is an overt behavior that is visible to someone else.
6. Strengths for Ms. Weare include her decision to seek help and her decision not to try to cope with this situation alone anymore.
7. Receiving a verbal reminder and threat from his mother at breakfast elicits Freddie's behavior.
8. Ms. Weare's behavior seems to be cued by a five-minute period before the bus arrives on school days.
9. Two consequences seem to influence Freddie's behavior of not getting ready for school: (a) he gets help in dressing himself, and this interaction influences his behavior by providing special benefits; (b) he gets some satisfaction from seeing that his mother is upset and is attending to him. These consequences seem to maintain his behavior because of the attention he gets from his mother in these instances. A possible secondary gain is the control he exerts over his mother at these times. According to the case description, he doesn't feel that he gets much attention at other times from his mother.
10. The major consequence that influences Ms. Weare's behavior is that she gets Freddie ready on time and he is not late. This result appears to influence her behavior by helping her avoid being considered a poor mother by herself or by someone else and by helping him succeed in school.
11. This parent–child relational issue is undoubtedly affected by the fact that Ms. Weare is raising her son alone and appears to be living in a fairly isolated social climate with little social support. She also is the sole economic

provider for Freddie, and her behavior and her child rearing are affected by her lack of financial resources. Overall, she appears to feel disempowered in her ability to handle her parental and financial responsibilities.

The Case of Mrs. Rodriguez

1. There are various behaviors for Mrs. Rodriguez: (a) disheveled appearance, (b) inappropriate affect, (c) delusional beliefs, (d) auditory hallucinations, (e) homicidal ideation, (f) noncompliance with treatment (medicine).
2. Disheveled appearance, inappropriate affect, and noncompliance with treatment are overt behaviors—they are observable by others. Delusions, hallucinations, and homicidal ideation are covert behaviors as long as they are not expressed by the client and therefore not visible to someone else. However, when expressed or demonstrated by the client, they become overt behaviors as well.
3. Strengths include a lack of reported suicide ideation and support and care from her extended family.
4. In this case, Mrs. Rodriguez's behaviors appear to be elicited by the cessation of her medication, which is the major antecedent. Apparently, when she stops taking her medicine, an acute psychotic episode results.
5. This periodic discontinuation of her medicine and the subsequent psychotic reaction may be influenced by the attention she receives from the mental health profession, from her family, and even from strangers when she behaves in a psychotic, helpless fashion. Additional possible secondary gains include avoidance of responsibility and of being in control.
6. Identify the sociopolitical context of the issue. In this case it is important to note the potential influence of the cultural–ethnic affiliations of Mrs. Rodriguez. Ideas that may seem delusional in one culture may represent a common belief held by very many persons in another culture. Delusions with a religious thread may be considered a more typical part of religious experience in a particular culture, such as a sign of "divine favor." The skilled helper would take this into consideration in the assessment before settling on a final diagnosis.

---

specifying goals and selecting intervention strategies unless it is part of a comprehensive treatment approach in which issues are identified in a concrete, or operational, manner for each client. An alternative to the *DSM-IV* is the Person-in-Environment (PIE) classification system, which assesses both social role and environmental problems. Research has shown that

both assessment and diagnosis are subject to gender and cultural bias. The skilled practitioner conducts a multi-dimensional assessment process that includes an awareness of the current and historical sociopolitical context in which the client lives and also the client's gender and cultural referent groups.

REFERENCES

American Psychiatric Association. (1994). *Diagnostic and statistical manual of mental disorders* (4th ed.). Washington, DC: Author.

American Psychiatric Association. (2000). *Diagnostic and statistical manual of mental disorders* (4th ed., text revision). Washington DC: Author.

Appleby, G. A., Colon, E., & Hamilton, J. (2001). *Diversity, oppression, and social functioning: Person-in-environment assessment and intervention.* Boston: Allyn & Bacon.

Bandura, A. (1986). *Social foundations of thought and action: A social cognitive theory.* Englewood Cliffs, NJ: Prentice Hall.

Beck, A. T. (1991). *Cognitive therapy and the emotional disorders* (2nd ed.). New York: Penguin.

Bijou, S. W., & Baer, D. M. (1976). *Child development I: A systematic and empirical theory.* Englewood Cliffs, NJ: Prentice Hall.

Bronfenbrenner, U. (1979). *The ecology of human development.* Boston: President and Fellows of Harvard College.

Bronfenbrenner, U. (1995). Developmental ecology through space and time. In P. Moen, G. H. Elder Jr., & K. Luscher (Eds.), *Examining lives in context: Perspectives on the ecology of human development* (pp. 619–648). Washington, DC: American Psychological Association.

Brown, L. S. (1992). Introduction. In L. S. Brown & M. Ballou (Eds.), *Personality and psychopathology: Feminist reappraisals* (pp. 111–115). New York: Guilford Press.

Brown, L. S., & Ballou, M. (1992). *Personality and psychopathology: Feminist reappraisals.* New York: Guilford Press.

Clark, L. A., Watson, D., & Reynolds, S. (1995). Diagnosis and classification of psychopathology: Challenges to the current system and future directions. *Annual Review of Psychology, 46,* 121–153.

Constantine, M. G., & Sue, D. W. (2006). Factors contributing to optimal human functioning in people of color in the United States. *The Counseling Psychologist, 34,* 228–244.

Cullen, C. (1983). Implications of functional analysis. *British Journal of Clinical Psychology, 22,* 137–138.

Edelstein, B., Koven, L., Spira, A., & Shreve-Neiger, A. (2003). Older adults. In M. Hersen & S. M. Turner (Eds). *Diagnostic Interviewing* (3rd. ed., pp. 433–454). New York: Kluwer Academic.

Harris, A. H. S., Thoresen, C. E., & Lopez, S. J. (2007). Integrating positive psychology into counseling: Why and (when appropriate) how. *Journal of Counseling and Development, 85,* 3–13.

Hayes, S. C. (2004). Acceptance and commitment therapy: Relational frame theory and the third wave of behavioral and cognitive therapies. *Behavior Therapy, 35,* 639–665.

Hayes, S. C., & Strosahl, K. D. (2005). *A practical guide to acceptance and commitment therapy.* New York: Springer-Verlag.

Haynes, S. N., Nelson, K. G., Thacher, I., & Keaweaimoku, K. (2002). Outpatient behavioral assessment and treatment target selection. In M. Hersen & L.K. Porzelius (Eds), *Diagnosis, conceptualization, and treatment planning for adults* (pp. 35–70). Mahwah, NJ: Lawrence Erlbaum.

Hepworth, D. H., Rooney, R. H., Dewberry Rooney, G., Strom-Gottfried, K., & Larsen, J. (2006). *Direct social work practice* (7th ed.). Belmont, CA: Thomson–Brooks/Cole.

Hull, C. L. (1980). *A behavior sytem.* New Haven, CT: Yale University Press.

Kantor, J. R. (1970). An analysis of the experimental analysis of behavior (TEAB). *Journal of the Experimental Analysis of Behavior, 13,* 101–108.

Karls J. M., & Wandrei, K. E. (1994). *PIE manual: Person-in-environment: The PIE classification system for social functioning problems.* Washington, DC: National Association of Social Workers.

Kemp, S., Whittaker, J., & Tracy, E. (1997). *Person–environment practice: The social ecology of interpersonal helping.* New York: Aldine de Gruyter.

Kleinman, A. (2004). Culture and depression. *New England Journal of Medicine, 351,* 951–953.

Krueger, R. F. & Piasecki, T. M. (2002). Toward a dimensional and psychometrically informed approach to conceptualizing psychopathology. *Behavior Research and Therapy, 40,* 485–499.

Lazarus, A. (2006). *Brief but comprehensive psychotherapy: The multimodal way.* New York: Springer.

Linehan, M. M. (1993). *Cognitive–behavioral treatment of borderline personality disorder.* New York: Guilford Press.

Lopez, S., Edwards, L., Teramoto Pedrotti, J., Prosser, E., LaRue, S., Spalitto, S., & Ulven, J. (2006). Beyond the *DSM-IV:* Assumptions, alternatives, and alterations. *Journal of Counseling Psychology, 84,* 259–267.

Meichenbaum, D. (2002). *Cognitive–behavior modification: An integrative approach.* New York: Plenum.

Mischel, W. (1973). *Personality and assessment* (2nd ed.). New York: Wiley.

Neufeld, J., Rasmussen, H., Lopez, S., Ryder, J., Magyar-Moe, J., Ford, A., Edwards, L., & Bouwkamp, J. (2006). The engagement model of person–environment interaction. *The Counseling Psychologist, 34,* 245–259.

Oko, J. (2006). Evaluating alternative approaches to social work: A critical review of the strengths perspective. *Families in Society, 87,* 601–611.

Root, M. P. (1992). Reconstructing the impact of trauma on personality. In L. S. Brown & M. Ballou (Eds.),

Personality and psychopathology: Feminist reappraisals (pp. 229–265). New York: Guilford Press.

Ross, C. A. (1990). *Multiple personality disorder: Diagnosis, clinical features and treatment.* New York: Wiley.

Saleebey, D. (2005). *The strengths perspective in social work* (4th ed.). Boston: Allyn & Bacon.

Seligman, M. E. P., & Csikszentmihalyi, M. (2000). Positive psychology: An introduction. *American Psychologist, 55,* 5–14.

Skinner, B. F. (1986). *Beyond freedom and dignity.* New York: Penguin.

Snyder, C. R., & Lopez, S. J. (2007). *Positive psychology.* Thousands Oaks, CA: Sage.

Spiegler, M. D., & Guevremont, D. C. (2003). *Contemporary behavior therapy* (4th ed.). Belmont, CA: Wadsworth.

Staudt, M., Howard, M. O., & Drake, B. (2001). The operationalization, implementation, and effectiveness of the strengths perspective: A review of empirical studies. *Journal of Social Service Research, 27,* 1–21.

Sue, D. W., & Sue, D. (2003). *Counseling the culturally diverse* (4th ed.). New York: Wiley.

Summers, N. (2006). *Fundamentals of case management practice.* (2nd ed.). Belmont, CA: Wadsworth.

Tanaka-Matsumi, J., Seiden, D. Y., & Lam, K. N. (1996). The culturally informed functional assessment (CIFA) interview: A strategy for cross-cultural behavioral practice. *Cognitive and Behavioral Practice, 3,* 215–233.

Taylor, E. H. (2006). The weaknesses of the strengths model: Mental illness as a case in point. *Best Practices in Mental Health, 2,* 1–30.

Teasdale, J., Moore, R., Hayhurst, H., Pope, M., Williams, S., & Segal, Z. (2000). Metacognitive awareness and prevention of relapse in depression: Empirical evidence. *Journal of Consulting and Clinical Psychology, 70,* 275–287.

Thyer, B., & Myers, L. (2000). Approaches to behavior change. In P. Allen-Meares & C. Garvin (Eds.), *Handbook of social work direct practice* (pp. 197–216). Thousand Oaks, CA: Sage.

Walsh, W. B., Craik, K., & Price, R. (Eds.). (2000). *Person–environment psychology: New directions and perspectives* (2nd ed). Mahwah, NJ: Lawrence Erlbaum.

White Kress, V., Eriksen, K., Rayle, A., & Ford, S. (2005). The *DSM-IV TR* and culture: Considerations for counselors. *Journal of Counseling and Development, 83,* 97–104.

Widiger, T. A., & Simonsen, E. (2005). Alternative dimensional models of personality disorders: Finding a common ground. *Journal of Personality Disorders, 19,* 110–130.

Wolpe, J. (1992). *The practice of behavior therapy* (4th ed.). New York: Pergamon.

7 KNOWLEDGE AND SKILL BUILDER

Read the case descriptions of Mr. Huang and of Mr. Robinson; then answer the following questions:

1. What are the client's behaviors?
2. Are the behaviors overt or covert?
3. What are the client's individual and environmental strengths?
4. What are the antecedent conditions of the client's concern?
5. What are the consequences of the behaviors? Secondary gains?
6. In what way do the consequences influence the behaviors?
7. In what ways are the behaviors manifestations of the social–political context?

Answers to these questions are provided in the Feedback section on page 187.

The Case of Mr. Huang

A 69-year-old Asian American man, Mr. Huang, came to counseling because he felt his performance on the job was "slipping." Mr. Huang had a job in a large automobile company. He was responsible for producing new car designs. Mr. Huang revealed that he noticed he had started having trouble about six months before, when the personnel director came in to ask him to fill out retirement papers. Mr. Huang, at the time he sought help, was due to retire in nine months. (The company's policy made it mandatory to retire at age 70). Until this incident with the personnel director and the completion of the papers, Mr. Huang reported, everything seemed to be "okay." He also reported that nothing seemed to be changed in his relationship with his family. However, on some days at work, he reported, he had a great deal of trouble completing any work on his car designs. When asked what he did instead of working on designs, he said, "Worrying." The "worrying" turned out to mean that he was engaging in constant repetitive thoughts about his approaching retirement, such as "I won't be here when this car comes out" and "What will I be without having this job?" Mr. Huang stated that there were times when he spent almost an entire morning or afternoon "dwelling" on these things and that this seemed to occur mostly when he was alone in his office actually working on a car design. As a result, he was not turning in his designs by the specified deadlines. Not meeting his deadlines made him feel more worried. He was especially concerned that he would "bring shame both to his company and to his family who had always been proud of his work record." He was afraid that his present behavior would jeopardize the opinion others had of him, although he didn't report any other possible "costs" to himself. In fact, Mr. Huang said that it was his immediate boss who had suggested, after several talks and lunches, that he use the employee assistance program. Mr. Huang said that his boss had not had any noticeable reactions to his missing deadlines, other than reminding him and being solicitous, as evidenced in the talks and lunches. Mr. Huang reported that he enjoyed this interaction with his boss and often wished he could ask his boss to go out to lunch with him. However, he stated that these meetings had all been at his boss's request. Mr. Huang felt somewhat hesitant about making the request himself. In the last six months, Mr. Huang had never received any sort of reprimand for missing deadlines on his drawings. Still, he was concerned with maintaining his own sense of pride about his work, which he felt might be jeopardized since he'd been having this trouble.

DSM-IV Diagnosis for Mr. Huang

Axis I   309.24, Adjustment disorder with anxiety
Axis II   V71.09 (no diagnosis)
Axis III None
Axis IV   Issues related to the social environment (adjustment to life cycle transition of retirement)
Axis V   GAF = 75 (current)

The Case of Mr. Robinson

This is a complicated case with three presenting issues: (1) work, (2) sexual, and (3) alcohol. We suggest that you complete the analysis of questions 1–6 listed at the beginning of this Knowledge and Skill Builder separately for each of these three concerns. *Question 7 can be completed at the end of the third issue.*

Mr. Robinson, a 30-year-old African American business manager, has been employed by the same large corporation for two years, since his completion of graduate school. During the first session, he reports a chronic feeling of "depression" with his present job. In addition, he mentions a recent loss of interest and pleasure in sexual activity, which he describes as "frustrating." He also relates a dramatic increase in his use of alcohol as a remedy for the current difficulties he is experiencing.

Mr. Robinson has never before been in counseling and admits to feeling "slightly anxious" about this new endeavor. He appears to be having trouble concentrating when asked a question. He traces the beginning of his problems to the completion of his master's degree a little over two years ago. At that time, he states, "Everything was fine." He was working part-time during the day for a local firm and attending

(continued)

(*continued*)

college during the evenings. He had been dating the same woman for a year and a half and reports a great deal of satisfaction in their relationship. Drinking occurred infrequently, usually only during social occasions or a quiet evening alone. On completion of his degree, Mr. Robinson relates, "Things changed. I guess maybe I expected too much too soon." He quit his job in the expectation of finding employment with a larger company. At first there were few offers, and he was beginning to wonder whether he had made a mistake. After several interviews, he was finally offered a job with a business firm that specialized in computer technology, an area in which he was intensely interested. He accepted and was immediately placed in a managerial position. Initially, he was comfortable and felt confident in his new occupation; however, as the weeks and months passed, the competitive nature of the job began to wear him down although he still loves working with computers. He relates that he began to doubt his abilities as a supervisor and began to tell himself that he wasn't as good as the other executives. He began to notice that he was given fewer responsibilities than the other bosses, as well as fewer employees to oversee. He slowly withdrew socially from his colleagues, refusing all social invitations. He states that he began staying awake at night obsessing about what he might be doing wrong. Of course, this lack of sleep decreased his energy level even further and produced a chronic tiredness and lessening of effectiveness and productivity at work. At the same time, his relationship with his girlfriend began to deteriorate slowly. He relates that "She didn't understand what I was going through." Her insistence that his sexual performance was not satisfying her made him even more apprehensive and lowered his self-esteem even further. After a time, his inhibition of sexual desire resulted in inconsistency in maintaining an erection throughout the sexual act. He then saw a doctor,

who said nothing was physically wrong and suggested he talk to someone about the erectile problem. This resulted in an even greater strain on the relationship with his girlfriend, who threatened to "call it quits" if he did not seek treatment for his "problem." He reports that it was at this time that he began to drink more heavily. At first, it was just a few beers at home alone after a day at the office. Gradually, he began to drink during lunch, even though, he states, "I could have stopped if I had wanted to." However, his repeated efforts to reduce his excessive drinking by "going on the wagon" met with little success. He began to need a drink every day in order to function adequately. He was losing days at work, was becoming more argumentative with his friends, and had been involved in several minor traffic accidents. He states he never abused alcohol before, although his grandfather, who helped raise him, was a recovering alcoholic when he was in his later years. Mr. Robinson has gone to a couple of Al Anon meetings. He points out that he has never felt this low before in his life. He reports feeling very pessimistic about his future and doesn't see any way out of his current difficulties. He's fearful that he might make the wrong decisions, and that's why he's come to see a helper at this time in his life.

DSM-IV Diagnosis for Mr. Robinson

Axis I	305.00 Alcohol abuse
	302.72 Male erectile disorder
	311.00 Depressive disorder NOS (not otherwise specified)
Axis II	V71.09 (no diagnosis)
Axis III	None
Axis IV	Issues with primary social support system and occupational problems
Axis V	GAF = 55 (current)

7 KNOWLEDGE AND SKILL BUILDER **FEEDBACK**

The Case of Mr. Huang

1. Mr. Huang's self-reported behaviors include worry about retirement and not doing work on his automobile designs.
2. Worrying about retirement is a covert behavior. Not doing work on designs is an overt behavior.
3. Individual and environmental strengths include Mr. Huang's prior job success and the support of his boss and family.
4. One antecedent condition occurred six months ago, when the personnel director conferred with Mr. Huang about retirement, and papers were filled out. This is an overt antecedent in the form of a setting event. The personnel director's visit seemed to elicit Mr. Huang's worry about retirement and his not doing his designs. A covert antecedent is Mr. Huang's repetitive thoughts about retirement, getting older, and so on. This is a stimulus event.
5. The consequences include Mr. Huang's being excused from meeting his deadlines and receiving extra attention from his boss.
6. Mr. Huang's behaviors appear to be maintained by the consequence of being excused from not meeting his deadlines with only a "reminder." He is receiving some extra attention and concern from his boss, whom he values highly. He may also be missing deadlines and therefore not completing required car designs as a way to avoid or postpone retirement—that is, he may expect that if his designs aren't done, he'll be asked to stay longer until they are completed.
7. The anxiety that Mr. Huang is experiencing surrounding the transition from full-time employment to retirement is a fairly universal reaction to a major life change event. However, in addition to this, Mr. Huang is also affected by his cultural/ethnic affiliation in that he is concerned about maintaining pride and honor, not losing face or shaming the two groups he belongs to—his family and his company. This recognition is an important part of the assessment because it will also be a focus in the intervention phase.

The Case of Mr. Robinson

Analysis of Work Issue

1. Mr. Robinson's behaviors at work include (a) overemphasis on the rivalry that he assumes exists with his fellow administrators and resulting self-doubts about his competence compared with that of his peers and (b) missing days at work because of his feelings of depression as well as his alcohol abuse.
2. His discrediting of his skills is a covert behavior, as is much of his current dejection. Avoiding his job is an overt behavior.
3. Individual and environmental strengths include the fact that Mr. Robinson still likes working with computers—and that he still has his job.
4. The antecedent conditions of Mr. Robinson's difficulties at work are his apparent perceptions surrounding the competitiveness with his coworkers. These perceptions constitute a stimulus event. This apprehension has led him to feel inadequate and fosters his depressive symptomatology. It should be recognized that his occupational concerns arose only after he obtained his present job, one that requires more responsibility than any of his previous positions. Acquisition of this job with its accompanying managerial position is a setting event.
5. The consequences that maintain his difficulties at work are (a) failing to show up for work each day and (b) alcohol abuse.
6. Failing to show up for work each day amounts to a variable-interval schedule of reinforcement, which is quite powerful in maintaining Mr. Robinson's evasion of the workplace. A possible secondary gain of his absenteeism is the resulting decrease in his feelings of incompetence and depression. His abuse of alcohol provides him with a ready-made excuse to miss work whenever necessary or whenever he feels too depressed to go. It should be noted that alcohol as a drug is a central nervous system depressant as well. Alcohol abuse is also a common complication of depressive episodes.

Analysis of Sexual Issue

1. Mr. Robinson's behavior in the sexual area is an apparent loss of interest in or desire for sexual activity, which is a significant change from his previous behavior. His feelings of excitement have been inhibited so that he is unable to attain or maintain an erection throughout the sexual act.
2. The inability to achieve and/or sustain an erection is an overt behavior. We may also assume that whatever Mr. Robinson is telling himself is somehow influencing his observable behavior. His self-talk is a covert behavior.
3. Individual and environmental strengths include the fact that he saw a doctor and that nothing was wrong physically to produce the sexual dysfunction.
4. There are apparently no organic contributing factors. Therefore, it appears likely that the antecedent conditions of Mr. Robinson's current sexual problem are the anxiety and depression associated with the work situation.
5. The consequences maintaining his sexual problem appear to be (a) the lack of reassurance from his girlfriend and (b) his current alcohol abuse.

(continued)

(*continued*)

6. The girlfriend's ultimatum that he begin to regain his normal sexual functioning is creating psychological stress that will continue to prevent and punish adequate sexual response. Although alcohol may serve as a relaxant, it also acts to physiologically depress the usual sexual response.

Analysis of Alcohol Issue

1. Relevant behavior is frequent consumption of alcoholic beverages during the day as well as at night.
2. Although alcohol abuse is certainly an overt behavior, we might also assume that Mr. Robinson is engaging in some self-defeating covert behaviors to sustain his alcohol abuse.
3. Individual and environmental strengths include his reporting of no prior history of substance abuse, his reported familiarity with Al Anon and 12-step programs, and, most important, the fact that he recognizes he has an alcohol issue and is seeking help.
4. It is quite apparent that Mr. Robinson's maladaptive use of alcohol occurred only after his difficulties with his job became overwhelming. It also appears to be linked to the onset of his sexual disorder. There is no history of previous abuse of alcohol or other drugs.
5. Consequences include the payoffs of avoidance of tension, responsibility, and depression related to his job as well as possible increased attention from others.
6. Because he is abusing alcohol, Mr. Robinson has been missing days at work and thus avoids the tension he feels with his job. Alcohol abuse is serving as a negative reinforcer. Moreover, his use of alcohol, which is a depressant, allows him to maintain his self-discrediting behavior, which, owing to the attention he derives from this, may also be maintaining the alcohol abuse. Finally, alcohol may also provide a ready-made reason for his sexual functioning issue with his girlfriend.

7. His issues appear to be affected by the sociopolitical climate in which he works, by his particular life stage of development, and also probably by the history of oppression he has undoubtedly experienced as an African American male. Mr. Robinson made a fairly rapid transition from being a student and working part-time to being a manager in a competitive firm. This progress occurred at a time in which he was also concerned developmentally with issues of identity and intimacy. The difficulties he has encountered have challenged both his concept of himself and his intimate relationship with his girlfriend. Although his firm is competitive, his own sense of vulnerability and his mistrust of himself and of his colleagues have no doubt been affected by his societal experiences of discrimination and oppression. (It is important to recognize that any cultural suspiciousness he feels has been for him an adaptive and healthy mechanism of coping with a host culture different from his own.) His increasing use of alcohol to self-medicate has further exacerbated both his work functioning and his sexual relationship with his girlfriend. His girlfriend appears to be responding to him with threats and intimidation, perhaps in an attempt to control or gain power in the relationship. Indeed, their relationship appears to lack a power base that is shared equally between both partners.

CHAPTER

8

CONDUCTING AN INTERVIEW
ASSESSMENT WITH CLIENTS

LEARNING OUTCOMES

After completing this chapter, you will be able to

1. When given a written description of a selected client, outline in writing at least 2 interview leads for each of the 11 assessment categories that you would explore during an assessment interview with this person.
2. In a 30-minute role-play interview, demonstrate leads and responses associated with 9 out of 11 categories for assessing the client.
3. Given a role-play interview, help the client complete a social network map and an ecomap.

Assessment is a way of identifying and defining a client's concerns in order to make decisions about therapeutic treatment. Various methods are available to help the practitioner identify and define the range and parameters of client issues. These methods include standardized tests, such as interest and personality inventories; psychophysiological assessment, such as monitoring of muscle tension for chronic headaches with an electromyograph (EMG) machine; self-report checklists, such as assertiveness scales and anxiety inventories; observation by others, including observation by the helper or by a significant person in the client's environment; self-observation, in which the client observes and records some aspect of the issue; imagery, in which the client uses fantasy and directed imagery to vicariously experience some aspect of the issue; role playing, in which the client may demonstrate some part of the issue in an in vivo yet simulated enactment; and direct interviewing, in which the client and helper identify concerns through verbal and nonverbal exchanges. All these methods are also used to evaluate client progress during the helping process, in addition to their use in assessment for the purpose of collecting information about clients.

In this chapter we concentrate on direct interviewing, not only because it is the focus of the book but also because it is the one method readily available to all helpers without additional cost in time or money. However, we also mention

ancillary use of some of the other methods named above. In actual practice, it is important not to rely solely on the interview for assessment data but to use several methods of obtaining information about clients. Recent developments in assessment are focused on the use of evidence to support the assessment process. *Evidence-based assessment* involves a decision-making process that targets data from multiple measures (Hunsley & Mash, 2005). Trends in evidence-based assessment point to the need for empirically derived assessment guidelines and for the use of assessment measures that are reliable, valid, and clinically useful (Hunsley & Mash, 2005).

DIRECT ASSESSMENT INTERVIEWING

According to cognitive–behavioral literature, the interview is the most common behavioral assessment instrument. As Sarwer and Sayers point out,

> The behavioral interview is the foundation of the behavioral assessment process. Despite the technological advances in behavioral assessment such as observational coding and analysis, the interview is still the most essential step in examining the reasons for and planning the treatment of patients' difficulties. It is still guided by the need for a clinician to start from the patient's complaints and discover the relations between the person's environment and his or her individual responses to it. (1998, p. 63)

Despite the overwhelming evidence confirming the popularity of the interview as an assessment tool, some persons believe it is the most difficult assessment approach for the helper to enact. Successful assessment interviews require specific guidelines and training in order to obtain accurate and valid information from clients that will make a difference in treatment planning (Edelstein, Koven, Spira, & Shreve-Neiger, 2003).

In this chapter we describe a structure and provide some guidelines to apply in assessment interviews in order to identify and define client issues. This chapter describes interview leads that in applied settings are likely to elicit certain kinds of client information. However, as Sarwer and Sayers (1998) observe, little research on the effects of interview procedures has been conducted. The leads that we suggest are supported more by practical considerations than by empirical data. As a result, you will need to be attentive to the effects of using them with each client. Edelstein and colleagues (2003) note that because the clinical assessment interview relies on client self-report, its accuracy and reliability are very much dependent on the accuracy and veracity of what the client says to the clinician.

INTAKE INTERVIEWS AND HISTORY

Part of assessment involves eliciting information about the client's background, especially as it may relate to *current* concerns. Past, or historical, information is not sought as an end in itself or because the helper is necessarily interested in exploring or focusing on the client's "past" during treatment. Rather, it is used as a part of the overall assessment process that helps the practitioner fit the pieces of the puzzle together concerning the client's presenting issues and current life context. Often a client's current issues are precipitated by events found in the client's history. In no case is this more valid than with clients who have suffered trauma of one kind or another. For example, a 37-year-old woman came to a crisis center because of the sudden onset of extreme anxiety. The interviewer noticed that she was talking in a "little girl" voice and was using gestures that appeared to be very childlike. The clinician commented on this behavior and asked the client how old she felt right now. The client replied, "I'm seven years old," and went on to reveal spontaneously an incident in which she had walked into a room in an aunt's house and found her uncle fondling her cousin. No one had seen her, and she had forgotten this event until the present time. In cases such as this one, history may serve as a retrospective baseline measure for the client and may help to identify cognitive or historical conditions that still exert influence on the current issue and might otherwise be overlooked.

The process of gathering this type of information is called *history taking*. In many agency settings, history taking occurs during an initial interview called an *intake interview*. An intake interview is viewed as informational rather than therapeutic and, to underscore this point, is often conducted by someone other than the practitioner assigned to see the client. In these situations, someone else, such as an intake worker, sees the client for an interview, summarizes the information in writing, and passes the information along to the helper.

In managed care and some state and federally funded mental health programs, intakes often are required before reimbursement for services is given. Sometimes these mandated intake interviews come with a lengthy standardized format that the practitioner must complete with the client in its entirety. In other places, the helpers conduct their own intakes. For helpers who work either in private practice or in a school or agency in which intakes are not required, it is still a good idea to do some history taking with the client

An example of a computer-assisted intake interview is the "computerized assessment system for psychotherapy evaluation and research," called CASPER (Farrell & McCullough-Vaillant, 1996). In this system, 122 intake interview questions covering a wide range (18) of content areas appear on a computer screen. After identifying certain areas of concern, the client rates the severity and duration of each concern, as well as the extent to which he or she wants to focus on a concern in treatment.

A semistructured intake and assessment protocol for child and adolescent clients is the CAFAS—Child and Adolescent Functional Assessment Scale—developed by Hodges (1997). An advantage of this interview protocol is that it assesses for strengths and goals as well as for problems in performance in school, work, home, community, behavior toward others, moods, self-harm, substance use, and thinking. Other examples of interview protocols for child and adolescent clients are found in Morrison and Anders (1999). Edelstein and colleagues (2003) provide examples of interview protocols suitable for older adults. Chief among these more structured interviews is the Structured Clinical Interview for *DSM-IV* disorders, commonly referred to as the SCID-IV (First, Spitzer, Gibbon, & Williams, 1996, 1997). The SCID-IV has good validity and reliability and is used extensively in research on anxiety disorders, personality disorders, and mood disorders. Although it is arguably the most commonly used semistructured interview in clinical settings, the duration of administering it (two hours) prevents even more widespread use.

Various kinds of information can be solicited during history taking, but the most important areas are the following:

1. Identifying information about the client
2. Presenting problems/symptoms including history related to the presenting concerns
3. Past psychiatric and/or counseling history/treatment and previous diagnosis
4. Educational and job history
5. Health and medical history
6. Social/developmental history (including religious, spiritual, and cultural background and affiliations, predominant values, description of past problems, chronological/developmental events, military background, social/leisure activities, present social situation, legal problems, and substance use history)
7. Family, marital, sexual history (including any abuse history, partnered status, and sexual orientation information)

8. Suicidal and/or homicidal ideation
9. Behavioral observations (including assessment of client communication patterns and appearance and demeanor)
10. Goals for counseling and therapy/treatment
11. Diagnostic (DSM) summary

12. Person-in-environment (PIE) classification
13. Results of mental status exam and provisional conceptualization of client

Box 8.1 presents specific questions or content areas to cover for each of those 13 areas.

BOX 8.1	HISTORY-TAKING INTERVIEW CONTENT

1. **Identifying information:** Client's name, address, home and work telephone numbers; name of another person to contact in case of emergency.

Age	Languages
Gender	Disabilities
Ethnicity and indigenous heritage	Occupation
	Citizenship status
Race	

2. **Presenting concerns:** Note the presenting concern (quote the client directly). Do for *each* concern that the client presents:

   When did it start? What other events were occurring at that time?

   How often does it occur?

   What thoughts, feelings, and observable behaviors are associated with it?

   Where and when does it occur most? Least?

   Are there any events or persons that precipitate it? Make it better? Make it worse?

   How much does it interfere with the client's daily functioning?

   What previous solutions/plans have been tried and with what result?

   What made the client decide to seek help at this time (or, if referred, what influenced the referring party to refer the client at this time)?

3. **Past psychiatric/counseling history:** Previous counseling and/or psychological/psychiatric treatment:

   Type of treatment

   Length of treatment

   Treatment place or person

   Presenting concern

   Outcome of treatment and reason for termination

   Previous hospitalization

   Prescription drugs for emotional and or psychological issues

4. **Educational/job history:** Trace academic progress (strengths and weaknesses) from grade school through last level of education completed:

   Relationships with teachers and peers

   Types of jobs held by client and socioeconomic history, current employment, and socioeconomic status

   Length of jobs

Reason for termination or change

Relationships with co-workers

Aspects of work that are most stressful or anxiety producing

Aspects of work that are least stressful or most enjoyable

Overall degree of current job satisfaction

5. **Health/medical history:** Childhood diseases, prior significant illnesses, previous surgeries:

   Current health-related complaints or illnesses (e.g., headache, hypertension)

   Treatment received for current complaints: what type and by whom

   Date of last physical examination and results

   Significant health problems in client's family of origin (parents, grandparents, siblings)

   Client's sleep patterns

   Client's appetite level

   Current medications (including such things as aspirin, vitamins, birth control pills, recreational substance use as well as prescription medications)

   Drug and nondrug allergies

   Disability history

   Client's typical daily diet, including caffeine-containing beverages/food, alcoholic beverages, and use of nicotine or tobacco products

   Exercise patterns

6. **Social/developmental history:** Current life situation (typical day/week, living arrangements, occupation and economic situation, contact with other people):

   Social/leisure time activities, hobbies

   Religious affiliation—childhood and current

   Spiritual beliefs and concerns

   Contacts with people (support systems, family, and friends)

   Community and cultural affiliations

   Military background/history

   Significant events reported for the following developmental periods:

   Preschool (0–6 years)

   Childhood (6–13 years)

   Adolescence (13–21 years)

   Young adulthood (21–30 years)

   Middle adulthood (30–65 years)

   Late adulthood (65 years and over)

   (continued)

| BOX 8.1 | HISTORY-TAKING INTERVIEW CONTENT |

(continued)

7. Family, marital, sexual history: Presence of physical, sexual, and/or emotional abuse from parent, sibling, or someone else:

   How well parents got along with each other

   Identifying information for client's siblings (including those older and younger and the client's birth order or position in family)

   Which sibling was most favored by mother? By father? Least favored by mother? By father?

   Which sibling did client get along with best? Worst?

   History of previous psychiatric illness/hospitalization among members of client's family of origin

   Use of substances in family of origin

   Dating history

   Engagement/marital history—reason for termination of relationship

   Current relationship with intimate partner (how well they get along, problems, stresses, enjoyment, satisfaction, and so on)

   Number and ages of client's children

   Other people living with or visiting family frequently

   Description of previous sexual experience, including first one (note whether heterosexual, homosexual, or bisexual experiences are reported)

   Present sexual activity

   Any present concerns or complaints about sexual attitudes or behaviors

   Current sexual orientation

8. Suicidal and homicidal ideation:

   Presence or absence of suicidal thoughts; if present, explore onset, frequency, antecedent events, duration, and intensity of such thoughts—ranging from *almost never,* to *occasional, weekly,* and/or *daily*

   Presence or absence of suicidal plan; if present, explore details of plan, including method, lethality, availability of method, and timeline of plan

   Prior suicide threats and attempts by the client and also attempts/completions by family members

   Overall suicidal intent—nonexistent, low, moderate, severe

   Presence or absence of homicidal ideation; client attitudes that support or contribute to violence

   Presence or absence of homicidal plan; if present, explore details of plan, including method, means, availability of means, timeline of means, intended victim(s)

   Prior homicidal threats and acts—instances and patterns

   Overall homicidal intent—nonexistent, low, moderate, severe

9. Behavioral observations:

   General appearance and demeanor

   Client communication patterns

10. Goals for counseling and therapy:

    Client's desired results for treatment

    Client's motivation for getting help at this time

11. Diagnostic summary (if applicable) and *DSM-IV* code

    Axis I   Clinical disorders

    Axis II   Personality disorders and mental retardation

    Axis III General medical condition

    Axis IV   Psychosocial and environmental problems (Note: sociopolitical factors can be included here as well.)

    Axis V   Global assessment of functioning (0 to 100 scale)

12. PIE classification (Karls & Wandrei, 1994)

    Factor II: Social Role Problem Identification: – Severity, duration, and coping indices and type of social role problem and type of interactional difficulty

    Factor II: Environmental Problem Identification: – Severity, duration, and coping indices and type of environmental problem area and associated discrimination code

13. Results of mental status exam (if applicable) and provisional conceptualization.

The sequence of obtaining this information in a history or an intake interview is important. Generally, the interviewer begins with the least threatening topics and saves more sensitive topics (such as 6, 7, and 8) until near the end of the session, when a greater degree of rapport has been established and the client feels more at ease about revealing personal information to a total stranger. Not all of this information may be required for all clients. Obviously, this guide will have to be adapted for use with different clients—especially those of varying ages, such as children, adolescents, and the elderly, who may need a simpler way to provide such information and in a shorter amount of time. Learning Activity 8.1 provides an opportunity for you to role-play a history-taking interview.

HANDLING SENSITIVE SUBJECTS IN THE INTERVIEW ASSESSMENT PROCESS

Morrison (1995) has pointed out that some important subjects that come up in intake and assessment interviews can be sensitive for both helpers and clients. This potential sensitivity does not mean that such subjects should be overlooked

---

LEARNING ACTIVITY	**8.1**	**Intake Interviews and History**

 To gain a sense of the process involved in doing an intake or history interview (if you don't already do lots of these on your job!), we suggest you pair up with someone in your class and complete intake/history interviews with each other. Conduct a 30- to 45-minute session, with one person serving as the helper and the other taking the client's role; then switch roles. As the helper, you can use the format in Box 8.1 as a guide. You may wish to jot down some notes.

After the session, it might be helpful to write a summary of the session, using the major categories listed in Box 8.1 as a way to organize your report. Review your report with your instructor. As the client in this particular activity, rather than playing a role, be yourself. Doing so will allow you to respond easily and openly to the helper's questions, and both of you can more readily identify the way in which your particular history has influenced the current issues in your life.

---

or discarded. However, it does mean that the helper should proceed with good judgment and seek consultation about when it is appropriate to assess these areas. On the one hand, it may be seen as voyeuristic if a male counselor asks a young female presenting with an academic/career issue about her sexual practices and activity. On the other hand, if a client comes in and discusses problems in dating persons of the opposite sex and feelings of attraction to same-sex people, not pursuing this subject would be an important omission.

Specific subjects that may fall into the category of sensitive topics include questions about (1) suicidal thoughts and behavior; (2) homicidal ideas and violent behavior; (3) substance use, including alcohol, street drugs, and prescribed medications; (4) sexual issues, including sexual orientation, sexual practices, and sexual problems; and (5) physical, emotional, and sexual abuse, both historic and current. Koven, Shreve-Neiger, and Edelstein (2007) recommend an interviewing strategy for handling sensitive subjects called the "plus minus approach." In this approach, the clinician balances difficult questions with those that are less threatening so that if a client reacts emotionally to a difficult question, the interviewer follows up with a question that is more benign.

A particular category of sensitive subjects has to do with potential lethality or danger to self or others. Interest in this sensitive area has mushroomed with recent events such as suicide bombings and school shootings. Although an in-depth discussion of the assessment of lethality and risk is beyond the scope of this book, we include some brief comments about this topic and recommend additional resources. The MacArthur study of high-risk clients for violence (excluding verbal threats for violence) identified over 100 potential risk factors for violence but found no "magic bullet" predictor of future violence. The findings from this study suggest that a person's propensity for violence is the accumulation and interaction of a number of risk factors including criminological factors (such as prior history of violence and criminality), childhood experiences (such as physical abuse), environmental conditions (such as poverty and unemployment), and clinical risk factors (such as

substance abuse, antisocial personality disorder, persistent violent thoughts and fantasies, and anger control issues). The findings of the MacArthur risk assessment study are summarized in Monahan and colleagues (2001).

In the area of suicide risk assessment, there are several useful structured clinical interview guides to assess potential danger to self. Chief among these are the Adolescent Suicide Assessment Protocol-20 (Fremouw, Strunk, Tyner, & Musick, 2005) and the Suicidal Adult Assessment Protocol (Fremouw, Tyner, Strunk, & Musick, in press). These two protocols present a brief, user-friendly, structured clinical interview designed for practitioners to obtain an initial objective measure of adolescent and adult suicidal risk (Fremouw et al., 2005, p. 207). Both interview protocols include assessment of client demographic factors (such as gender, age, and marital status), historical factors (such as prior attempts, and childhood abuse), clinical items (such as depression and hopelessness, impulsivity, and substance abuse), specific suicidal risk questions (such as thoughts, plans, and intentions), contextual factors (such as firearm access, recent loss, stressors, and social isolation), and protective factors (such as family responsibilities, spiritual and/or religious beliefs, and social support). At the completion of the structured interview, each client is classified according to level of risk; depending on that level of risk, the interviewer will identify various forms of action and intervention such as consultation, increased monitoring, contracting, notification, referrals to other forms of treatment, and elimination of the method of suicide.

MENTAL-STATUS EXAMINATION

After conducting an initial interview, if you are in doubt about the client's psychiatric status or suspicious about the possibility of a cognitive disorder, you may wish to conduct (or refer the client for) a mental-status examination. According to Kaplan and Sadock (1998), the mental-status exam is one that classifies and describes the areas and components of mental functioning involved in making diagnostic impressions and classifications. The major categories covered in a mental-status exam are general description and appearance of the client; mood and affect; perception; thought processes; level of consciousness; orientation to time, place, and people; memory; and impulse control. Additionally, the examiner may note the degree to which the client appeared to report the information accurately and reliably. Of these categories, disturbances in consciousness (which involves ability to perform mental tasks, degree of effort, and degree of fluency/hesitation in task performance) and orientation (whether or not clients know when, where, and who they are and who other people are) are usually indicative of brain impairment or cognitive disorders and require neurological assessment and follow-up as well. Examples of specific mental-status exams for the elderly are given in Hill, Thorn, and Packard (2000): examples of ones for child and adolescent clients can be found in Morrison and Anders's (1999) pragmatic guide.

It is important for practitioners to know enough about the functions and content of a mental-status exam to refer clients who might benefit from this additional assessment procedure. A summary of the content of a brief mental-status exam is given in Box 8.2. For additional information about mental-status examinations and neurophysiological assessment, see Kaplan and Sadock (1998) and Morrison (1995).

History taking (and mental-status exams, if applicable) usually occur near the very beginning of the helping process. After obtaining this sort of preliminary information about the client as well as an idea of the range of presenting complaints, you are ready to do some direct assessment interviewing with the client in order to define the parameters of concerns more specifically.

CULTURAL ISSUES IN INTAKE AND ASSESSMENT INTERVIEWS

It is important to note and account for sources of cultural bias within a traditional intake interview and within assessment interviews in general. Canino and Spurlock (2000) point out that "in some cultures disturbed behavior may be viewed as related to a physical disorder or willfulness"; thus, talking about the behavior is not expected to help

(p. 75). In some cultural groups, there is a sanction against revealing personal information to someone outside the family or extended-family circle. Also, clients' perceptions of what is socially desirable and undesirable behavior as well as their perceptions of psychological distress may reflect values different from the ones held by the practitioner: "Certain cultural factors must be considered in determining the normalcy or pathology of a response. For example, 'hearing the Lord speak' may be a culture-specific impression and therefore nonpathological for some religious groups. An inner-city African American adolescent's statement 'All Whites are out to get us' may actually represent the thinking of the community in which he lives rather than qualify as a sign of paranoia" (Canino & Spurlock, 2000, p. 80).

In interpreting the information received from an intake interview and mental-status exam, remember that some information can have cultural meanings that are unknown to you. For example, some cultures view the child as one year old at the time of birth; other cultures may favor the use of culturally sanctioned healing remedies instead of traditional Western medical or psychological treatment. Also, cultures have different practices regarding discipline of children and adolescents, so what you may view as either indulgent or harsh may not be seen that way by the client and the client's collective community. What constitutes a "family" also varies among cultures; in assessing for family history, it is important to ask about extended-family members who may live outside the household as well as about a parent's significant other. Clients might also report religious and spiritual beliefs that are unfamiliar to the helper, and these can affect the client's help-seeking behavior and perceptions of distress.

Another issue pertaining to cultural dimensions of clients in intake interviews has to do with microaggressions—verbal comments or queries that communicate a derogatory slight or insult to the client (Sue et al., 2007). For example, a culturally insensitive interviewer may actually demonstrate some form of racial or ethnic profiling in an intake interview by assuming something pejorative about the client based solely on the client's race or ethnicity. An example of this would be a practitioner posing more questions about substance use

---

BOX 8.2	SUMMARY OF BRIEF MENTAL-STATUS EXAM
Note the client's physical appearance, including dress, posture, gestures, and facial expressions.	Note whether the client's stream of thought and rate of talking were logical and connected.
Note the client's attitude and response to you, including alertness, motivation, passivity, distance, and warmth.	Note the client's orientation to four issues: people, place, time, and reason for being there (sometimes this is described as "orientation by four").
Note whether there were any client sensory or perceptual behaviors that interfered with the interaction.	Note the client's ability to recall immediate, recent, and past information.
Note the general level of information displayed by the client, including vocabulary, judgment, and abstraction abilities.	

with Native American clients than with other clients and viewing their reports of a nonexistent history with substances as "suspicious" (Sue et al., 2007, p. 282). Another example provided by Sue et al. (2007) of a microaggressive act in an intake interview would be acting on the assumption that Asian Americans and Latino Americans are "foreign born" (p. 282). As Sue and his colleagues (2007) explain, "A female Asian American client arrives for her first therapy session. Her therapist asks her where she is from, and when told 'Philadelphia,' the therapist further probes by asking where she was born. In this case, the therapist has assumed that the Asian American client is not from the United States and has imposed through the use of the second questions the idea that she must be a foreigner" (p. 281).

There are several examples of culturally sensitive interview protocols. One such protocol developed by Hays (2001), uses a framework known as ADDRESSING. This framework calls attention to the following cultural influences:

A   age and generational influences

D   developmental and acquired

D   disabilities

R   religious and spiritual orientation

E   ethnicity

S   socioeconomic status

S   sexual orientation

I   indigenous heritage

N   national origin

G   gender

Another example, developed by Tanaka-Matsumi, Seiden, and Lam (1996), is the Culturally Informed Functional Assessment (CIFA) Interview. Designed to define client issues in a culturally sensitive manner, this interview protocol includes a variety of steps such as assessing the cultural identity and acculturation status of the client, assessing the client's presenting issues with reference to the client's cultural norms, probing explanations of the client's issue and possible solutions to avoid pathologizing seemingly unusual but yet culturally normative responses, and conducting a functional assessment of the client's problem behaviors, and determining whether the client's reactions to controlling variables are similar to or different from customary reactions of one's cultural referent group(s).

ELEVEN CATEGORIES FOR ASSESSING CLIENTS

To help you acquire the skills associated with assessment interviews, we describe 11 categories of information you need to seek from each client. These 11 categories are illustrated and defined in the following list and subsections. They are

also summarized in the Interview Checklist at the end of the chapter (page 222).

1. Explanation of *purpose* of assessment—presenting rationale for assessment interview to the client
2. Identification of *range* of concerns—using leads to help the client identify all the relevant primary and secondary issues to get the "big picture"
3. *Prioritization* and *selection* of issues—using leads to help the client prioritize issues and select the initial area of focus
4. Identification of *present behaviors*—using leads to help the client identify the six components of current behavior(s): affective, somatic, behavioral, cognitive, contextual, and relational
5. Identification of *antecedents*—using leads to help the client identify categories of antecedents and their effect on the current issue
6. Identification of *consequences*—using leads to help the client identify categories of consequences and their influence on the current issue
7. Identification of *secondary gains*—using leads to help the client identify underlying controlling variables that serve as payoffs to maintain the issue
8. Identification of *previous solutions*—using leads to help the client identify previous solutions or attempts to solve the issue and their subsequent effect on the issue
9. Identification of *client individual and environmental strengths and coping skills*—using leads to help the client identify past and present coping or adaptive behavior and how such skills might be used in working with the present issue
10. Identification of the *client's perceptions* of the concern—using leads to help the client describe her or his understanding of the concern
11. Identification of *intensity*—using leads and/or client self-monitoring to identify the impact of the concern on the client's life, including (a) degree of severity and (b) frequency and/or duration of current behaviors

The first three categories—explanation of the purpose of assessment, identification of the range of concerns, and prioritization and selection of issues—are a logical starting place. First, it is helpful to give the client a rationale, a reason for conducting an assessment interview, before gathering information. Next, some time must be spent in helping the client explore all the relevant issues and prioritize issues to work on in order of importance, annoyance, and so on.

The other eight categories follow prioritization and selection. After the helper and client have identified and selected the issues to work on, these eight categories of interviewing leads are used to define and analyze parameters of the issue. The helper will find that the order of the assessment leads varies among clients. A natural sequence will evolve in each interview, and the helper will want to use the leads associated with these content categories in a pattern that fits the flow of the interview and follows the lead of the client. It is important in assessment interviews not to impose your structure at the expense of the client. The amount of time and number of sessions required to obtain this information will vary with the concerns and with clients. It is possible to complete the assessment in one session, but with some clients, an additional interview may be necessary. Although the practitioner may devote several interviews to assessment, the information gathering and hypothesis testing that go on do not automatically stop after these few sessions. Some degree of assessment continues throughout the entire helping process just as the importance of the helping relationship continues throughout this time as well.

Explaining the Purpose of Assessment

In explaining the purpose of assessment, the helper gives the client a rationale for doing an assessment interview. The intent of this first category of assessment is to give the client a "set," or an expectation, of what will occur during the interview and why assessment is important to both client and helper. Explaining the purpose of the interview assessment is especially important in cross-cultural helping because culturally based attitudes weigh heavily in a person's expectations about assessment.

Here is one way the helper can communicate the purpose of the assessment interview: "Today I'd like to focus on some concerns that are bothering you most. In order to find out exactly what you're concerned about, I'll be asking you for some specific kinds of information. This information will help both of us identify what you'd like to work on. How does this sound [or appear] to you?" After presenting the rationale, the helper looks for some confirmation or indication that the client understands the importance of assessing issues.

Identifying the Range of Concerns

In this category, the practitioner uses open-ended leads to help clients identify all the major issues and concerns in their life now. Often clients will initially describe only one concern, and on further inquiry and discussion, the helper discovers a host of other ones, some of which may be more severe or stressful or have greater significance than the one the client originally described. If the helper does not try to get the "big picture," the client may reveal additional concerns either much later in the helping process or not at all. Here are examples of range-of-concerns leads:

"What are your concerns in your life now?"

"Please describe some of the things that seem to be bothering you."

"What are some present stresses in your life?"

"What situations are not going well for you?"

"Tell me about anything else that concerns you now."

After using range-of-concerns leads, the practitioner should look for the client's indication of some general areas of concern or things that are troublesome for the client. An occasional client may not respond affirmatively to these leads. Some clients may be uncertain about what information to share, or clients may be from a cultural group in which it is considered inappropriate to reveal personal information to a stranger. In such cases, the helper may need to use an approach different from verbal questioning. For example, Lazarus (1989) has recommended the use of an "Inner Circle" strategy to help a client disclose concerns. The client is given a picture like this:

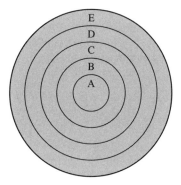

The helper points out that topics in circle A are very personal, whereas topics in circle E are more or less public information. The helper can provide examples of types of topics likely to be in the A circle, such as sexual concerns, feelings of hostility, intimacy problems, and dishonesty. These examples may encourage the client to disclose personal concerns more readily. The helper also emphasizes that progress takes place in the A and B circles and may say things like "I feel we are staying in circle C" or "Do you think you've let me into circle A or B yet?" Sometimes the helper may be able to obtain more specific descriptions from a client by having the client role-play a typical situation.

Exploring the range of concerns is also a way to establish who the appropriate client is. A client may attribute the concern to an event or to another person. For instance, a student may say, "That teacher always picks on me. I can never do anything right in her class." Because most clients seem to have trouble initially "owning" their role in the issue or tend to describe it in a way that minimizes their own contribution, the helper will need to determine who is most invested in having it resolved and who is the real person requesting assistance. Often it is helpful to ask clients who feels it is most important for the concern to be resolved—the client or someone else. It is important for practitioners not to assume that the person who arrives at their office is always the client. The client is the person who wants a change and who seeks assistance for it. In the example above, if the student had desired a change and had requested assistance, the student would be the client; if it were the teacher who wanted a change and requested assistance, the teacher would be the client. Sometimes, however, the helper gets "stuck" in a situation in which a family or a client wants a change and the person whose behavior is to be changed is "sent" as the client. Determining who the appropriate client is can be very important in working with these mandated clients, who are required to see a helper but have little investment in being helped! One strategy that can be useful with clients in these situations is to establish a win–win contract where they agree to talk about what you want to discuss for half the session in exchange for talking (or not talking) about what they want to for the other half of the session.

The question of who is the appropriate client is also tricky when the issue involves two or more persons, such as a relationship, marital, or family issue. In rehabilitation counseling, for example, the client may be not only the individual with a disability but also the client's employer. Many family therapists view family issues as devices for maintaining the status quo of the family and recommend that either the couple or the entire family be involved, rather than one individual.

Prioritizing and Selecting Issues

Rarely do clients or the results of assessment suggest only one area or issue that needs modification or resolution. Typically, a presenting concern turns out to be one of several unresolved issues in the client's life. For example, the assessment of a client who reports depression may also reveal that the client is troubled by her relationship with her teenage daughter. History may reveal that this adult woman was also physically abused as a child. After a client describes all of her or his concerns, the practitioner and client will need to select the issues that best represent the client's purpose for seeking help. The primary question to be answered by these leads is "What is the specific situation the client chooses to start working on?"

Prioritizing issues is an important part of assessment and goal setting. If clients try to tackle too many issues simultaneously, they are likely to soon feel overwhelmed and anxious and may not experience enough success to stay in therapy. Selection of the issue is the client's responsibility, although the helper may help with formulating the client's choice.

The following guidelines form a framework to help clients select and prioritize issues to work on:

1. Start with the presenting issue, the one that best represents the reason the client sought help. Fensterheim (1983, p. 63) observes that relief of the presenting concern often improves the client's level of functioning and may then make other, related issues more accessible to treatment. Leads to use to help determine the initial or presenting issue include "Which issue best represents the reason you are here?" and "Out of all these concerns you've mentioned, identify the one that best reflects your need for assistance."

2. Start with the issue that is primary or most important to the client to resolve. Often this is the one that causes the client the most pain or discomfort or annoyance or is most interfering to the client. Modifying the more important issues seems to lead to lasting change in that area, which may then generalize to other areas. Here are some responses to use to determine the client's most important priority: "How much happiness or relief would you experience if this issue were resolved?" "Of these concerns, which is the most stressful or painful for you?" "Rank order these concerns, starting with the one that is most important for you to resolve to the one least important." "How much sorrow or loss would you experience if you were unable to resolve this issue?"

3. Start with the concern or behavior that has the best chance of being resolved successfully and with the least effort. Some issues/behaviors are more resistant to change than others and require more time and energy to modify. Initially, it is important for the client to be reinforced for seeking help. One significant way to do this is to help the client resolve something that makes a difference without much cost to the client. Responses to determine what issues might be resolved most successfully include "Do you believe there would be any unhappiness or discomfort if you were successful at resolving this concern?" "How likely do you think we are to succeed in resolving this issue or that one?" "Tell me which of these situations you believe you could learn to manage most easily with the greatest success."

4. Start with the issue that needs resolution before other issues can be resolved or mastered. Sometimes the presence of one issue sets off a chain of other ones; when this issue is resolved or eliminated, the other ones either improve or at least move into a position to be explored and modified. Often this concern is one that, in the range of elicited ones, is central or prominent.

5. Giving mandated clients the responsibility for prioritization of concerns is particularly important. This choice allows them to set the agenda and may foster greater cooperation than clinician-directed prioritization of concerns.

Understanding the Present Behaviors

After selecting the initial area of focus, it is important to determine the components of the present behavior. For example, if the identified behavior is "not getting along very well with people at work," with an expected outcome of "improving my relationships with people at work," we would want to identify the client's *feelings* (affect), *body sensations* (somatic phenomena), *actions* (overt behavior), and *thoughts and beliefs* (cognitions) that occur during the situations at work. We would also explore whether these feelings, sensations, actions, and thoughts occurred with *all* people at work or only with *some* people (relationships) and whether they occurred only at work or in *other* settings, at what *times,* and under what *conditions* or with what *concurrent events* (context). Without this sort of exploration, it is impossible to define the behavior operationally (concretely). Furthermore, it is difficult to know whether the client's work concerns result from the client's actions or observable behaviors, from covert responses such as feelings of anger or jealousy, from cognitions and beliefs such as "When I make a mistake at work, it's terrible," from the client's transactions with significant others that suggest an "I'm not okay—they're okay" position, from particular events that occur in certain times or situations during work, as during a team meeting or when working under a supervisor, or from toxic people or environmental conditions in the workplace.

Without this kind of information about when and how the present behavior is manifested, it would be very difficult and even presumptuous to select intervention strategies or approaches. The end result of this kind of specificity is that the behavior is defined or stated in terms such that two or more persons can agree on when it exists. We next describe specific things to explore for each of these six components, and we suggest some leads and responses to further this exploration with clients.

Affect and Mood States

Affective components of behavior include self-reported feelings or mood states, such as "depression," "anxiety," and "happiness." Feelings are generally the result of complex interactions among behavioral, physiological, and cognitive systems rather than unitary experiential processes. Clients often seek help because of this component—that is, they feel bad, uptight, sad, angry, confused, and so on, and they want to get rid of such unpleasant feelings.

One category of things to ask the client about to get a handle on feelings or mood states is feelings about the present behavior. After eliciting feelings, note the content (pleasant/unpleasant) and level of intensity. Remember that positive feelings are as important to identify as negative ones, for they build resources, enhance creative problem solving, increase coping skills, and enhance health (Snyder & Lopez, 2007). Although there are many ways to assess for content and level of intensity of affect, one simple way is to use a checklist such as the Positive and Negative Affect Schedule (Watson, Clark, & Tellegen, 1988) or a rating scale such as the Subjective Units of Distress (SUDS) Scale

(Wolpe, 1990), with 1–10 or a 0–100 range to assess intensity. Example interview leads to assess positive and negative affect are the following:

"How do you feel about this?"

"What kinds of feelings do you have when you do this or when this happens?"

"Describe the kinds of feelings you are aware of when this happens."

"Describe the positive feelings you have associated with this. Also the negative ones."

"On a 10-point scale, with 1 being low and 10 being high, how intense is this feeling?"

"If the number 0 represented no distress, and the number 100 represented severe distress, how would you rate the feeling on this 0 to 100 scale in terms of intensity?"

A second category is concealed or distorted feelings—that is, feelings that the client seems to be hiding from, such as anger, or a feeling like anger that has been distorted into hurt. Below are example responses for this:

"You seem to get headaches every time your husband criticizes you. Describe what feelings these headaches may be masking."

"When you talk about your son, you raise your voice and get a very serious look on your face. What feelings do you have—deep down—about him?"

"You've said you feel hurt and you cry whenever you think about your family. Tune in to any other feelings you have besides hurt."

"You've indicated you feel a little guilty whenever your friends ask you to do something and you don't agree to do it. Try on resentment instead of guilt. Try to get in touch with those feelings now."

The practitioner can always be on the lookout for concealed anger, which is the one emotion that tends to get shoved under the rug more easily than most. In exploring concealed feeling, the clinician needs to pay attention to any discrepancies between the client's verbal and nonverbal expressions of affect. Distorted feelings that are common include reporting the feeling of hurt or anxiety for anger, guilt for resentment, and sometimes anxiety for depression, or vice versa. Remember that clients from some cultures may be reluctant to share feelings, especially vulnerable ones, with someone they don't yet know or trust.

Somatic Sensations

Closely tied to feelings are body sensations. Some clients are very aware of "internal experiencing"; others are not. Some persons are so tuned in to every body sensation that they become somaticizers, while others seem to be switched off "below the head" (Lazarus, 1989). Neither extreme is desirable. Some persons may describe complaints in terms of body sensations rather than as feelings or thoughts—that is, as headaches, dizzy spells, back pain, and so on. Behavior can also be affected by other physiological processes, such as nutrition and diet, exercise and lifestyle, substance use, hormone levels, and physical illness. The helper will want to elicit information about physiological complaints, about lifestyle and nutrition, exercise, substance use, and so on, and about other body sensations relating to the behavior. Some of this information is gathered routinely during the health history portion of the intake interview, but bear in mind that the information obtained from a health history may vary depending on the client's cultural affiliation. Helpers can ask clients who have trouble reporting somatic sensations to focus on their nonverbal behavior or to engage in a period of slow, deep breathing and then to conduct a "body scan." Useful leads to elicit this component of the present behavior include these:

"What goes on inside you when you do this or when this happens?"

"What are you aware of when this occurs?"

"Notice any sensations you experience in your body when this happens."

"When this happens, describe anything that feels bad or uncomfortable inside you—aches, pains, dizziness, and so on."

Overt Behaviors or Motoric Responses

Clients often describe a behavior in very nonbehavioral terms. In other words, they describe a situation or a process without describing their actions or specific behaviors within that event or process. For example, clients may say "I'm not getting along with my partner" or "I feel lousy" or "I have a hard time relating to authority figures" without specifying what they do to get along or not get along or to relate or not relate.

When inquiring about the behavioral domain, the helper will want to elicit descriptions of both the presence and the absence of concrete overt behaviors connected to the issue—that is, what the client does and doesn't do. The helper also needs to be alert to the presence of behavioral *excesses* and *deficits.* Excesses are things that the person does too much or too often or that are too extreme, such as binge eating, excessive crying, or assaultive behavior. Deficits are responses that occur too infrequently or are not in the client's repertory or do not occur in the expected context or conditions, such as failure to initiate requests on one's behalf, inability to talk to one's partner about sexual concerns and desires, or

lack of physical exercise and body conditioning programs. Again, it is important to keep a cultural context in mind here: what might be considered a behavioral excess or deficit in one culture may be different in another. The helper may also wish to inquire about "behavioral opposites" (Lazarus, 1989) by asking about times when the person does *not* behave that way. This is important because you are balancing the assessment interview by focusing on what the client does well, not just on the problematic behaviors. Prosocial behaviors are as important to assess as nonsocial ones. Here are examples of leads to elicit information about overt behaviors and actions:

"Describe what happens in this situation."

"What do you mean when you say you're 'having trouble at work'?"

"What are you doing when this occurs?"

"What do you do when this happens?"

"What effect does this situation have on your behavior?"

"Describe what you did the last few times this occurred."

"If I was photographing this scene, what actions and dialogue would the camera pick up?"

Occasionally the practitioner may want to supplement the information gleaned about behavior from the client's oral self-report with more objective assessment approaches, such as role plays and behavioral observations. These additional assessment devices will help practitioners improve their knowledge of how the client does and doesn't act in the situation and in the environmental setting.

Cognitions, Beliefs, and Internal Dialogue

In the last few years, helpers of almost all orientations have emphasized the relative importance of cognitions or symbolic processes in contributing to, exacerbating, or improving situations that clients report. Unrealistic expectations of oneself and of others are often related to presenting issues, as are disturbing images, self-labeling and self-statements, and cognitive distortions. When the cognitive component is a very strong element of the concern, part of the resulting treatment is usually directed toward this component and involves altering unrealistic ideas and beliefs, cognitive distortions and misconceptions, and dichotomous thinking.

Assessment of the cognitive component is accordingly directed toward exploring the presence of both irrational *and* rational beliefs and images related to the identified issue. Irrational beliefs will later need to be altered. Rational beliefs are also useful during intervention. Remember though that cognitions and belief systems may be quite culturally specific.

Irrational beliefs take many forms, and the most damaging ones seem to be related to automatic thoughts or self-statements and maladaptive assumption such as "shoulds" about oneself, others, relationships, work, and so on, "awfulizing" or "catastrophizing" about things that don't turn out as we expect, "perfectionistc standards" about ourselves that often are projected onto others, and "externalization," the tendency to think that outside events are responsible for our feelings and problems. The practitioner will also want to be alert for the presence of cognitive distortions and misperceptions, such as overgeneralization, exaggeration, and drawing conclusions without supporting data. Underlying these automatic thoughts and assumptions are cognitive schemas. A *schema* is a deep-seated belief about oneself, others, and the world that takes shape in the client's early developmental history and confirms the client's core belief about himself or herself, others, and the world. For example, depressed or anxious clients often focus selectively on cognitive schemas "that mark their vulnerability" (Leahy & Holland, 2000, p. 296).

Although clients may have difficulty verbalizing specific cognitions and beliefs, their nonverbal cues may be important indicators that core beliefs and schemas are being activated in the assessment process. Linscott and DiGiuseppe (1998) note that

> when the therapist has touched on a core-disturbed belief system, the client will frequently exhibit emotional and behavioral reactions. The client who was previously actively engaged in the conversation with the therapist may abruptly begin to avoid the therapist's questions, make little eye contact, evidence disturbed facial expressions, and work to change the subject. Or the client may become enlivened, as if a light bulb has been illuminated by the therapist's inquiries . . . . In addition, the client's sudden anger and confrontational arguments with the therapist may also signal that a core belief has been elicited. (p. 117)

Leads to use to assess the cognitive component include the following:

"What beliefs [or images] do you hold that contribute to this concern? Make it worse? Make it better?"

"When something doesn't turn out the way you want or expect, how do you usually feel?"

"What data do you have to support these beliefs or assumptions?"

"What are you thinking about or dwelling on when this [issue] happens?"

"Please describe what kinds of thoughts or images go through your mind when this occurs."

"Notice what you say to yourself when this happens."

"What do you say to yourself when it doesn't happen [or when you feel better, and so on]?"

"Let's set up a scene. You imagine that you're starting to feel a little upset with yourself. Now run through the scene and relate the images or pictures that come through your mind. Tell me how the scene changes [or relate the thoughts or dialogue—what you say to yourself as the scene ensues]."

"What are your mental commentaries on this situation?"

"What's going through your mind when _____ occurs? Can you recall what you were thinking then?"

Context: Time, Place, Concurrent Events, and Environment

Behaviors occur in a social context, not in a vacuum. Indeed, what often makes a behavior a "problem" is the context surrounding it or the way it is linked to various situations, places, and events. For example, it is not a problem to undress in your home, but the same behavior on a public street in many countries would be called "exhibitionism." In some other cultures, this same behavior might be more commonplace and would not be considered abnormal or maladaptive. Looking at the context surrounding the issue has implications not only for assessment but also for intervention, because a client's cultural background, lifestyle, and values can affect how the client views the issue and also the treatment approach to resolve it.

Assessing the context surrounding the issue is also important because most issues are *situation specific*—that is, they are linked to certain events and situations, and they occur at certain times and places. For example, clients who say "I'm uptight" or "I'm not assertive" usually do not mean they are *always* uptight or nonassertive but, rather, in particular situations or at particular times. It is important that the helper not reinforce the notion or belief in the client that the feeling, cognition, or behavior is pervasive. Otherwise, clients are even more likely to adopt the identity of the "problem" and begin to regard themselves as possessing a particular trait such as "nervousness," "social anxiety," or "nonassertiveness." They are also more likely to incorporate this trait into their lifestyles and daily functioning.

In assessing contextual factors associated with the issue, you are interested in discovering

1. *Situations* or *places* in which the issue usually occurs and situations in which it does not occur (*where* the issue occurs and where it does not).
2. *Times* during which the issue usually occurs and times during which it does not occur (*when* the issue occurs and when it does not).
3. *Concurrent events*—events that typically occur at or near the same time as the issue. This information is important because sometimes it suggests a pattern or a significant chain of events related to the issue that clients might not be aware of or may not report on their own.

4. Any *cultural, ethnic, and racial affiliations,* any particular *values* associated with these affiliations, and how these values affect the client's perception of the issue and of change.

5. *Sociopolitical factors*—that is, the overall zeitgeist of the society in which the client lives, the predominant social and political structures of this society, the major values of these structures, who holds power in these structures, and how all this affects the client.

Here are example responses to elicit information about contextual components of the issue—time, place, and concurrent events:

"Describe some recent situations in which this issue occurred. What are the similarities in these situations? In what situations does this usually occur? Where does this usually occur?"

"Describe some situations when this issue does not occur."

"Can you identify certain times of the day [week, month, and year] when this is more likely to happen? Less likely?"

"Does the same thing happen at other times or in other places?"

"What else is going on when this problem occurs?"

"Describe a typical day for me when you feel 'uptight.'"

"Are you aware of any other events that normally occur at the same time as this issue?"

Assessing the context surrounding the client's problems includes exploring not only the client's "immediate psychosocial environment" but also wider environmental contexts such as cultural affiliation and community (Kemp, Whittaker, & Tracy, 1997, p. 89). Part of your intervention approach often involves helping clients to feel more empowered to act on their own behalf in their environment. Typically, the kinds of environmental systems you assess for during the interview include ones such as neighborhood and community, institutions and organizations, sociocultural-political systems, and person–family support networks. The last one—social networks—we discuss in the next section, on relational aspects of the issue. Within each system, it is important to assess the extent to which the system adds to the client's concerns—as well as the availability of resources within the system to help the client resolve the concerns. Remember that environments can be for better *and* for worse.

A frequently used tool for assessing context and environment is the *ecomap* (see Figure 8.1). The ecomap was originally developed by Hartman as a paper and pencil assessment tool to map the ecological system of an individual client or a family (Hartman, 1979). Preliminary data on the ecomap as an evidence-based assessment tool is provided by

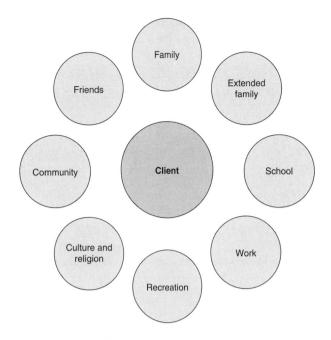

Figure 8.1 Sample Ecomap

Calix (2004). An ecomap is a useful supplement to the interview and a method "for visually documenting the client's relationship with the outside world, including the flow of energy and the nature of relationships experienced" (Kemp et al., 1997, p. 102).

To complete an ecomap, the client writes his or her name, or "me" in a circle in the center of a piece of paper. Then the client identifies and encircles the people, groups, and organizations that are part of his or her current environment—work, day care, family, friends, community groups, religion, school, cultural groups, and so on. These circles can be drawn in any size, and the size may indicate the influence or lack of influence of that environmental system in the client's life. Next, the client draws a series of lines to connect his or her personal circle to the other circles. The type of line that the client draws indicates the client's view of the quality of the relationship with each system. Typically a client is instructed to use solid lines to link his or her own circle to the circles that represent something positive or a strong connection, and to use broken lines to link to circles that represent something negative or a stressful connection. Finally, the client draws wavy lines to the circles that represent something that he or she needs but is not available. We illustrate this process in the model dialogue with our client Isabella later in this chapter (see page 218).

After completing the ecomap, the practitioner can use interview leads like the following ones to complete the picture about the environmental events surrounding the client's concerns:

"Describe the relationship between yourself and all these systems and structures in your current environment."

"How do you experience your current environment? How has this experience been affected by your gender, race, ethnicity, income status, and so on?"

"What is the relationship between you and these larger systems in your ecomap? What has this relationship been like so far in your life? How has this affected your current concerns?"

"Do you feel that you need more relationships with any of these larger systems in your ecomap? If so, what has made it difficult for these relationships to develop?"

"How would you describe the sociopolitical and socioeconomic environment you are in? How has it affected your concerns?"

"How much has your concern been affected by oppression, prejudice, and discrimination in your environment?"

"How has your environment fostered empowerment? Or disempowerment? How has this affected the concerns you are bringing to me?" *

To familiarize yourself with assessing an individual in relationship to her or his environment, complete Learning Activity 8.2.

Relationships, Significant Others, and Social Support

Just as issues are often linked to particular times, places, events, and environmental conditions, they are also often connected to the presence or absence of other people. People around the client can bring about or exacerbate a concern. Someone temporarily or permanently absent from the client's life can have the same effect. Assessing the client's relationships with others is a significant part of many theoretical orientations to counseling, including dynamic theories, Adlerian theory, family systems theory, and behavioral theory.

Interpersonal issues may occur because of a lack of significant others in the client's life, because of the way the client relates to others, or because of the way significant others respond to the client. Consider the role of "other people" in the development of Mario's "school phobia":

Mario, a 9-year-old new arrival from Central America, had moved with his family to a homogeneous neighborhood in which they were the first Spanish-speaking family. Consequently, Mario was one of the few Latino children in his classroom. He soon developed symptoms of school phobia and was referred to an outpatient mental health clinic.

*Adapted from Kemp, Whittaker, & Tracy, 1997, pp. 103–106.

A clinician sensitive to cultural issues chose to work very closely with the school, a decision that facilitated access for Mario to a bicultural, bilingual program. The clinician also realized that Mario was a target of racial slurs and physical attacks by other children on his way to and from school. The school responded to the clinician's request to address these issues at the next parent–teacher conference. With the ongoing support of a dedicated principal, Mario's symptoms abated, and he was able to adjust to his new environment. (Canino & Spurlock, 2000, p. 74).

Other persons involved in the issue often tend to discount their role in it. It is helpful if the practitioner can get a handle on what other persons are involved in the issue, how they perceive the issue, and what they might have to gain or lose from a change in the issue or the client. As Gambrill (1990) observes, such persons may anticipate negative effects of improvement in an issue and covertly try to sabotage the client's best efforts. For example, a husband may preach "equal pay and opportunity" yet secretly sabotage his wife's efforts to move up the career ladder for fear that she will make more money than he does or that she will find her new job opportunities more interesting and rewarding than her relationship with him. Other people can also influence a client's behavior by serving as role models. People whom clients view as significant to them can often have a great motivational effect on clients in this respect.

An important aspect of the relational context of the client's concern has to do with availability and access to resources in the client's social and interpersonal environment, including support from immediate and extended family, friends, neighbors, and people affiliated with the client in work, school, and community organizations. Remember that purposeful, positive relationships are just as important to identify as problematic ones (Snyder & Lopez, 2007).

One specific tool that can supplement the interview leads to understanding about a client's social support system is the *social network map* (Tracey & Whittaker, 1990). It has been used empirically with a variety of client problem situations (Kemp et al., 1997). The social network map is designed to identify both the type and the amount of support the client receives from seven social systems (see Figure 8.2):

1. Household
2. Other Family
3. Work/school
4. Clubs/associations/faith and church groups and organizations
5. Friends
6. Neighbors
7. Formal services and programs, especially community-based

| LEARNING ACTIVITY | **8.2** | **Ecomaps** |

1. Using the ecomap format in Figure 8.1, draw a circle representing yourself in the middle of a piece of paper, and around that circle list the systems that are part of your current environment—for example, work, school, family, friends, religion and cultural groups, community groups, recreation, and extended family.
2. Around each systems draw circles of varying sizes to indicate the degree of influence of that environmental system in your life.
3. Draw a solid line from your circle to any circles that represent systems with which your connection is positive or strong.
4. Draw a broken line from your circle to any circles that represent systems with which your relationship is stressful or negative.
5. Draw a wavy line from your circle to any circles that represent systems that are needed by you but are not available to you.
6. Look over your ecomap. What conclusions can you draw? You may wish to share your conclusions with a classmate.

This list can be modified for any given client, with categories of social support added or deleted.

Using the map displayed in Figure 8.2, "clients are encouraged to write in the people in their social network that fit in each sector. This can be accomplished by drawing in small circles with names to represent women and small squares with names to represent men, or the gender symbols for male and female may be used" (Garvin & Seabury, 1997, p. 197). If necessary, the map can be enlarged for more room. Clients can also use symbols such as arrows to indicate closeness or distance between themselves and their identified circles, as well as the type and direction of help received. Also, as noted by Kemp and associates (1997), clients sometimes list network people or religious or spiritual leaders on the map (p. 117).

Information gleaned from the social network map can be used in helping clients set treatment goals and in planning useful intervention strategies For example, are people in the network draining the client, or is the client a drain on the network? Are there responsive and dependable people in the network whom the client can involve in an intervention plan? Does the client feel "surrounded by a network that is perceived as negative, nonsupportive, or stress-producing?" Or does the client or the network lack skills to access people in the network effectively (Kemp et al., 1997, pp. 117–118)?

Example leads for assessing the relational component of the issue include the following:

"Tell me about the effects this issue has on your relationships with significant others in your life."

"What effects do these significant others have on this concern?"

"Who else is involved in this issue besides you?

How are these persons involved? What would their reaction be if you resolved this issue?"

"From whom do you think you learned to act or think in this way?"

"Describe the persons *present* in your life now who have the greatest positive impact on you. Negative impact?"

"Describe the persons *absent* from your life who have the greatest positive impact on you. Negative impact?"

"What types of social support do you have available in your life right now—too much support or too little?"

"Who do you think you need in your life right now that isn't available to you?"

"Who are the main people in this social support system?"

"Which of these people are there for you? Which of these people are critical of you?"

"What people and social support systems in your life empower you? Disempower you?"

Figure 8.2 Social Network Map
Source: Interpersonal Practice in Social Work (2nd ed.), by C. Garvin & B. Seabury, p. 197. Copyright © 1997 by Allyn & Bacon. Reprinted by permission.

"What things get in your way of using these social support systems and the effective people in them?"

"What people in your life are nourishing to you? Toxic or depleting to you?"

"What people in your life do you look up to? What qualities do they have that help you in your current situation?"

Identifying Antecedents

Antecedents are certain events that happen before and contribute to an issue. Much of the assessment process consists in exploring contributing variables that precede and cue the issue (antecedents) and things that happen after the issue (consequences) that, in some way, influence or maintain it.

Remember that, like behaviors, antecedents (and consequences) are varied and may be affective, somatic, behavioral, cognitive, contextual, or relational. Further, antecedents (and consequences) are likely to differ for each client. Antecedents are both external and internal events that occasion or cue the behaviors and make them more or less likely to occur. Some antecedents occur immediately before (stimulus events); other antecedents (setting events) may have taken place a long time ago.

In helping clients explore antecedents, you are particularly interested in discovering (1) what *current* conditions (covert and overt) exist *before* the issue that make it *more likely* to occur, (2) what *current* conditions (covert and overt) exist that occur *before* the issue that make it *less likely* to occur, and (3) what *previous* conditions, or setting events, exist that *still* influence the issue.

Example leads for identifying antecedents follow and are grouped by category:

Affective

"What are you usually feeling before this happens?"

"When do you recall the first time you felt this way?"

"Describe the feelings that occur before the issue and make it stronger or more constant."

"Identify the feelings that occur before the issue that make it weaker or less intense."

"Tell me about any holdover feelings or unfinished feelings from past events in your life that still affect this issue."

Somatic

"Notice what goes on inside you just before this happens."

"Are you aware of any particular sensations in your body before this happens?"

"Describe any body sensations that occur right before this issue that make it weaker or less intense. Stronger or more intense?"

"Is there anything going on with you physically—an illness or physical condition—or anything about the way you eat, smoke, exercise, and so on, that affects or leads to this issue?"

Behavioral

"If I were photographing this, describe the actions and dialogue the camera would see before this happens."

"Identify any particular behavior patterns that occur right before this happens."

"What do you typically do before this happens?"

"Can you think of anything you do that makes this more likely to occur? Less likely to occur?"

Cognitive

"What kinds of pictures or images do you have before this happens?"

"What are your thoughts before this happens?"

"What are you telling yourself before this happens?"

"Identify any particular beliefs that seem to set the issue off."

"Describe what you think about [see or tell yourself] before the issue occurs that makes it stronger or more likely to occur. Weaker or less likely to occur?"

Contextual

"Has this ever occurred at any other time in your life? If so, describe that."

"How long ago did this happen?"

"Where and when did this occur the first time?"

"Describe how you see those events related to your concern."

"Tell me about anything that happened that seemed to lead up to this."

"When did the issue start—what else was going on in your life at that time?"

"What were the circumstances under which the issue first occurred?"

"What was happening in your life when you first noticed this?"

"Are there any ways in which your cultural affiliation and values contribute to this issue? Make it more likely to occur? Less likely?"

"Are you aware of any events that occurred before this issue that in some way still influence it or set it off?"

"Do you see any particular aspects or structures in your community that have contributed to this issue?"

Relational

"Can you identify any particular people who seem to bring on this issue?"

"Who are you usually with right before or when this occurs?"

"Can you think of any person or any particular reaction from a person that makes this more likely to occur? Less likely?"

"Are there any people or relationships from the past that still influence or set off or lead to this issue in some way?"

"Describe the way people in your social network who hold power have contributed to this issue."

Identifying Consequences

Consequences are external or internal events that influence the current problem by maintaining it, strengthening or increasing it, or weakening or decreasing it. Consequences occur after the problem and are distinguished from results or effects by the fact that they have direct influence by either maintaining or decreasing the problem behaviors in some way.

In helping clients explore consequences, you are interested in discovering both internal and external events that maintain and strengthen the undesired behavior and also events that weaken or decrease it. Example leads for identifying consequences follow and are grouped by category:

Affective

"How do you feel after _____?"

"How does this feeling affect the issue (for example, keep it going, stop it)?"

"Describe any particular feelings or emotions that you have after it that strengthen or weaken it."

Somatic

"What are you aware of inside you just after this happens? How does this affect you?"

"Note any body sensations that seem to occur after the issue that strengthen or weaken it."

"Is there anything you can think of about yourself physically—illnesses, diet, exercise, and so on—that seems to occur after this? How does this affect it?"

Behavioral

"What do you do after this happens, and how does this make the issue worse? Better?"

"How do you usually react after this is over? In what ways does your reaction keep the issue going? Weaken it or stop it?"

"Identify any particular behavior patterns that occur after this. How do these patterns keep the issue going? Stop it?"

Cognitive

"What do you usually think about afterward? How does this affect the issue?"

"What do you picture after this happens?"

"What do you tell yourself after this occurs?"

"Identify any particular thoughts [or beliefs or self-talk] during or after the issue that make it better. Worse?"

"Tell me about any certain thoughts or images you have afterward that either strengthen or weaken the issue."

Contextual

"What happened after this?"

"When does the issue usually stop or go away? Get worse? Get better?"

"Where are you when the issue stops? Gets worse? Gets better?"

"Identify any particular times, places, or events that seem to keep the issue going. Make it worse or better?"

"Tell me about any ways in which your cultural affiliations and values seem to keep this issue going. Stop it or weaken it?"

"Do you think the particular social and political structures of your society or community maintain this issue? How?"

Relational

"Can you identify any particular people who can make the issue worse? Better? Stop it? Keep it going?"

"Can you identify any particular reactions from other people that occur after the issue? In what ways do these reactions affect the issue?"

"Describe how you think this issue is perpetuated by the persons in your social network who hold power."

Identifying Secondary Gains: A Special Case of Consequences

Occasionally clients have a vested interest in maintaining the status quo of the concern because of the payoffs that the issue produces. For example, a client who is overweight may find it difficult to lose weight, not because of unalterable eating and exercise habits but because the extra weight has allowed him to avoid or escape such things as new social situations or sexual relationships and has produced a safe and secure lifestyle that he is reluctant to give up. A child who is constantly disrupting her school classroom may be similarly reluctant to give up such disruptive behavior even though it results in loss of privileges, because it has given her the status of "class clown," resulting in a great deal of peer attention and support.

It is always extremely important to explore with clients the payoffs, or secondary gains, they may be getting from having the issue, because often during the intervention phase such clients seem "resistant." In these cases, the resistance is a sign the payoffs are being threatened. The most common payoffs include money, attention from significant others, immediate gratification of needs, and avoidance of responsibility, security, and control.

Questions you can use to help clients identify possible secondary gains include these:

"The good thing about _____ is . . ."

"What happened afterward that was pleasant?"

"What was unpleasant about what happened?"

"Has your concern ever produced any special advantages or considerations for you?"

"As a consequence of your concern, have you got out of or avoided things or events?"

"Please describe the reactions of others when you do this."

"How does this issue help you?"

"What do you get out of this situation that you don't get out of other situations?"

"Do you notice anything that happens afterward that you try to prolong or to produce?"

"Do you notice anything that occurs afterward that you try to stop or avoid?"

Exploring Previous Solutions

Another important part of the assessment interview is to explore what things the client has already attempted to resolve the concern and with what effect. This information is important for two reasons. First, it helps you to avoid recommendations for resolution that amount to "more of the same." Second, in many instances, solutions attempted by the client either create new concerns or make the existing concern worse.

Garvin and Seabury (1997) note that some clients have the skills and resources to resolve problems but other clients such as "oppressed clients may not have the same resources to cope" (p. 195). If clients cannot find resources or successful solutions, they "may frantically and repeatedly apply unsuccessful strategies" (p. 195). This kind of "amplifying loop results in a vicious cycle of attempts and failures, which ultimately propels the individual into active crisis" (p. 195).

Leads to help the client identify previous solutions include the following:

"How have you dealt with this or other concerns before? What was the effect? What made it work or not work?"

"Tell me about how you have tried to resolve this concern."

"What kinds of things have you done to improve this situation?"

"Describe what you have done that has made the concern better. Worse? Kept it the same?"

"What have others done to help you with this?"

"What has kept the issue from getting worse?"

Identifying the Client's Coping Skills, Individual and Environmental Strengths, and Resources

When clients come to helpers, they usually are in touch with their pain and often only with their pain. Consequently, they are shortsighted and find it hard to believe that they have any internal or external resources that can help them deal with the pain more effectively. In the assessment interview, it is useful to focus not solely on the issues and pains but also on the person's positive assets and resources (which the pain may mask). This sort of focus is the primary one used by feminist helpers; an emphasis is placed on the client's strengths rather than the client's weaknesses. Recent cognitive–behavioral therapists have also placed increasing emphasis on the client's *self-efficacy*—the sense of personal agency and the degree of confidence the client has that she or he can do something. This is also consistent with the strengths perspective and positive psychology. Also, positive cognitive processes such as self-efficacy, learned optimism, and hope reflect ways of thinking that can impact therapeutic outcomes (Snyder & Lopez, 2007). Helpers also should remember that, like many variables, coping skills are culture and gender specific; some men and women may not report using the same coping strategies, just as "effective coping" defined in one cultural system may be different in another one. Coping styles that you consider maladaptive may be adaptive for the client as a way to survive his or her environment (Canino & Spurlock, 2000, p. 66).

Focusing on the client's positive assets achieves several purposes. First, it helps convey to clients that in spite of the psychological pain, they do have internal resources available that they can muster to produce a different outcome. Second, it emphasizes wholeness—the client is *more* than just his or her "problem." Third, it gives you information on potential problems that may crop up during an intervention. Finally, information about the client's past "success stories" may be applicable to current concerns. Such information is extremely useful in planning intervention strategies that are geared to using the kind of problem-solving and coping skills already available in the client's repertoire. Narratives with particular sources of adversity can be revised with the practitioner's help. For example, clients who have experienced trauma can help to heal themselves by telling or drawing the story of the trauma and its key events. It is also important for these clients to put an ending on the story. Clients with trauma histories usually feel helpless in the face of the trauma. As these clients coconstruct their stories, they can also narrate strengths and resources they used to help cope with the trauma. Images of strength are especially important in healing stories of adult survivors.

Information to be assessed in this area includes the following:

1. Behavioral assets and problem-solving skills. When does the client display adaptive behavior instead of problematic behavior? Often this information can be obtained by inquiring about "opposites"—for example, "When don't you act that way?"
2. Cognitive coping skills—such as rational appraisal of a situation, ability to discriminate between rational and irrational thinking, selective attention and feedback from distractions, and the presence of coping or calming self-talk.
3. Self-control and self-management skills—including the client's overall ability to withstand frustration, to assume responsibility for self, to be self-directed, to control undesired behavior by either self-reinforcing or self-punishing consequences, and to perceive the self as being in control rather than being a victim of external circumstances.
4. Environmental strengths and resources. In addition to the three "individual" client strengths described above, it is increasingly important to assess the strengths and resources available within the client's environment. These include not only the support network we mentioned earlier but also such things as availability of adequate employment, housing, transportation, and health care. Environmental strengths also include cultural strengths of belonging to a collective community, such as community cohesiveness, community racial identity, and community resources, groups, and organizations (Kemp et al., 1997). Cultural affiliations can give clients certain "protective" factors that serve as sources of strength when clients experience adversity. Such factors as racial and ethnic pride, spirituality and religion, and interconnectedness of mind, body, and spirit are other examples of culturally protective factors for clients from marginalized groups (Constantine & Sue, 2006).

The following leads are useful in identifying these kinds of individual and environmental strengths and resources:

"What skills or things do you have going for you that might help you with this concern?"

"Describe your strengths or assets that you can use to help resolve this concern."

"When don't you act this way?"

"What kinds of thoughts or self-talk help you handle this better?"

"Notice when don't you think in self-defeating ways."

"What do you say to yourself to cope with a difficult situation?"

"Identify the steps you take in a situation you handle well. What do you think about and what do you do? How could these steps be applied to the present issue?"

"In what situations is it fairly easy for you to manage or control this reaction or behavior?"

"Rate the degree of confidence you have in your capabilities when you are immersed in this situation." (self-efficacy query)

"When you think about this situation, is your expectancy that it will go well or go poorly?" (optimism query)

"Tell me about what kind of resources in any aspect of your community or environment you are currently using."

"What aspects of your community and overall environment do you find helpful?"

"What kinds of things in your community and environment would you describe as strengths or assets?"

"Describe what strengths and resources in your community and environment are available that you need to use more often."

Exploring the Client's Perception of the Concern

Most clients have their own perceptions of and explanations for their concerns. It is important to elicit this information during an assessment session for several reasons. First, it adds to your understanding of the concern. The helper can note which aspects of the concern are stressed and which are ignored during the client's assessment of the issue. Second, this process gives you valuable information about *patient position*, the client's strongly held beliefs and values—in this case, about the nature of the issue. Clients usually allude to such "positions" in the course of presenting their perceptions of concerns. Ignoring the client's position may cause the practitioner to develop a counseling strategy that the client resists because it is incompatible with this "position." You can get a client to describe his or her view of the concern very concisely simply by asking the client to give the concern a one-line title as if it were a movie, play, or book. Another way to elicit the client's perception of the concern is to describe the concern in only one word and then to use the selected word in a sentence. For example, a client may say "guilt" and then "I have a lot of guilt about having an affair." The same client might title the concern "Caught between Two Lovers." This technique works extremely well with children, who typically are quick to think of titles and words without a lot of deliberation. It is also important to recognize the impact of culture, ethnicity, and race on clients' perceptions and reports of concerns. For example, clients from some cultural groups may report the cause of concerns in terms of external factors, supernatural forces, or both. Helpers must not minimize or ridicule such explanations; also, they should incorporate such explanations into the assessment and treatment process.

In the change phase of helping, successful interventions often depend on recognizing and validating the client's "perception of the problem." This emphasis on the client's perspective has made a dramatic impact on the care of elderly clients, but the principle extends to all clients. When clients speak out about their perspectives, there is more collaboration and shared investment in the change process.

Leads to help clients identify and describe their views of concerns include these:

"What is your understanding of this issue?"

"Tell me how you explain this concern to yourself."

"What does the issue mean to you?"

"What is your interpretation [analysis] of this concern?"

"What else is important to you about the concern that we haven't mentioned?"

"Give the issue a title."

"Describe the issue with just one word."

Ascertaining the Intensity of the Concern

It is useful to determine the intensity of the concern. You want to check out how much the concern is affecting the client and the client's daily functioning. If, for example, a client says, "I feel anxious," does the client mean a little anxious or very anxious? Is this person anxious all the time or only some of the time? And does this anxiety affect any of the person's daily activities, such as eating, sleeping, or working? There are two kinds of intensity to assess: the degree or severity and the frequency (how often) and/or duration (how long) of it.

Degree of Intensity

Often it is useful to obtain a client's subjective rating of the degree of discomfort, stress, or intensity of the concern. The helper can use this information to determine how much the concern affects the client and whether the client seems to be incapacitated or immobilized by it. To assess the degree of intensity, the helper can use leads similar to these:

"You say you feel anxious. On a scale from 1 to 10, with 1 being very calm and 10 being extremely anxious, where would you be now?"

"How strong is your feeling when this happens?"

"How has this interfered with your daily activities?"

"How would your life be affected if this issue were not resolved in a year?"

"On a scale from 0 to 100, with 0 being no distress and 100 being extreme distress, where would you place your distress now?"

In assessing degree of intensity, you are looking for a client response that indicates how strong, interfering, or pervasive the concern seems to be.

Frequency and/or Duration

In asking about frequency and duration, your purpose is to have the client identify how often (frequency) and/or how long (duration) the current behaviors occur. Data about how often or how long they occur *before* a change strategy is applied are called *baseline data*. Baseline data provide information about the *present* extent of the problem. They can be used later to compare the extent of the problem before and after a treatment strategy has been used. Leads to assess the frequency and duration of the current behavior include the following:

"How often does this happen?"

"How many times does this occur?"

"How long does this feeling usually stay with you?"

"How much does this go on, say, in an average day?"

Some clients can discuss the severity, frequency, or duration of the behavior during the interview rather easily. However, many clients may be unaware of the number of times the behavior occurs, how much time it occupies, or how intense it is. Most clients can give the helper more accurate information about frequency and duration by engaging in self-monitoring of the behaviors with a written log. Use of logs to supplement the interview data is discussed later in the model dialogue.

Box 8.3 provides a review of the 11 categories of client assessment. This table may help you conceptualize and summarize the types of information you will seek during assessment interviews.

LIMITATIONS OF INTERVIEW LEADS IN ASSESSMENT

The leads we present in this chapter are simply tools that the helper can use to elicit certain kinds of client information. They are designed to be used as a road map to provide some direction for assessment interviews. However, the leads alone are an insufficient basis for assessment because they represent only about half the process at most—the helper responses. The other part of the process is reflected by the responses

BOX 8.3	REVIEW OF 11 ASSESSMENT CATEGORIES		

1. Purpose of assessment
2. Range of concerns
3. Prioritization of issues
4, 5, 6, 7. Identification of:

8. Previous solutions
9. Coping skills and individual and environmental strengths
10. Client perceptions of issue
11. Severity, frequency, duration, of issue

(4.) **Antecedents**	(5.) **Behaviors**	(6.) **Consequences and** (7.) **secondary gains (payoffs)**
Affective	Affective	Affective
Somatic	Somatic	Somatic
Behavioral	Behavioral	Behavioral
Cognitive	Cognitive	Cognitive
Contextual	Contextual	Contextual
Relational	Relational	Relational

these leads generate from the client. A complete interview assessment includes not only asking the right questions but also synthesizing and integrating the client responses.

Think of it this way: In an assessment interview, you are simply *supplementing* your basic skills with some specific leads designed to obtain certain kinds of information. While many of your leads will consist of open-ended questions, even *assessment* interviews should not disintegrate into a question-and-answer or interrogation session. You can obtain information and give the information some meaning through other verbal responses, such as summarization, clarification, confrontation, and reflection. Demonstrating sensitivity is especially important because sometimes during assessment, a client may reveal or even reexperience very traumatic events and memories. The quality of the helping relationship remains very important during assessment interviews. Handling the assessment interview in an understanding and empathic way becomes critical. It is also extremely important to clarify and reflect the information the client gives you before jumping ahead to another question. The model dialogue that follows illustrates this process. (See also Learning Activity 8.3.)

MODEL DIALOGUE FOR INTERVIEW ASSESSMENT: THE CASE OF ISABELLA

To see how these assessment leads are used in an interview, read the following dialogue in the case of Isabella. An explanation of the helper's response and the helper's rationale for using it appears before the responses. Note the *variety* of responses used by the helper.

Helper response 1 is a *rationale* to explain to the client, Isabella, the *purpose* of the assessment interview.

1. **Helper:** Isabella, last week you dropped by to schedule today's appointment, and you mentioned you were feeling unhappy and dissatisfied with school. It might be helpful today to take some time just to explore exactly what is going on with you and school and anything else that concerns you. I'm sure there are ways we can work with this dissatisfaction, but first I think it would be helpful to both of us to get a better idea of what all the issues are for you now. Does this fit with where you want to start today?

Client: Yeah. I guess school is the main problem. It's really bugging me.

Helper response 2 is a lead to help Isabella identify the *range* of her concerns.

2. **Helper:** Okay, you just said school is the *main* concern. From the way you said that and the way you look right now, I have the feeling school isn't the *only* thing you're concerned about in your life.

Client: Well, you're right about that. I'm also kind of not getting along too well with my parents. But that's kind of related to this school thing too.

In the next response, the helper simply *listens* to Isabella and synthesizes what she's saying by using a *paraphrase* response.

3. **Helper:** So from your point of view, the school thing and the issue with your parents are connected.

Client: Yeah, because I'm having trouble in some of my classes. There's too much competition. I feel the other kids are better than I am. I've thought about changing from this college prep program to the work-study program, but I don't know what to do. I don't like to make decisions anyway. At the same time, my parents put a lot of pressure on me to perform well, to make top grades. They have a lot of influence with me. I used to want to do well, but now I'm kind of tired of it all.

In the next response, the helper continues to listen to Isabella and *reflect her feelings*.

LEARNING ACTIVITY   8.3   Interview Assessment

Part One

This activity is designed to assist you in identifying assessment leads in an interview. You are given a helper/client dialogue that consists of an interview with a mother, Ms. Weare, about her relationship with her son Freddie (Chapter 7). For each helper response, your task is to identify and write down the type of assessment lead used by the helper. You may find it helpful to use the Interview Checklist at the end of this chapter as a guide for this activity. There may be more than one example of any given type of lead. Also, identify the listening and influencing responses used by the helper. Feedback follows on page 212.

Dialogue between Ms. Weare and the Helper

1. **Helper:** Hello, Ms. Weare. Could you tell me about some things going on now that are concerning you?
   Client: Not too much. Family Services sent me here.

2. **Helper:** So you're here just because they sent you—or is there something bothering you?
   Client: Well, they don't think my kid and I get along too well. My kid is Freddie.

3. **Helper:** What do you think about the way you and Freddie get along?
   Client: Well, I yell at him a lot. I don't like to do that, but sometimes he gets me so mad. I don't like to, but he needs to learn.

4. **Helper:** So there are times when you get real mad at Freddie and then you yell at him. You don't like to do this, but you see it as a way to help him learn right and wrong.
   Client: That's it. I don't like to, but there are times when he needs to know something. Like yesterday, I bought him new pants, and he came home from school with a big hole in them. Now, I just don't have money to keep buying him new pants.

5. **Helper:** You just mentioned the incident with Freddie's pants. What are some other times that you get mad at Freddie?
   Client: Every morning. Freddie's in fourth grade now. But he still doesn't dress himself in the morning. I want to be a good mother and get him to school on time, and he tries to be late. He waits around not getting dressed.

6. **Helper:** Any other times you can remember getting mad?
   Client: Well, not too long ago he was playing outside and broke a window. I got mad then. But that doesn't happen every day like his not getting dressed does.

7. **Helper:** So one thing that really bothers you is what goes on in the mornings. Tell me exactly what does happen each morning at your house?

Client: Well, I call Freddie to get up and tell him to dress before he comes down for breakfast. He comes down all right—in his pajamas. I warn him after breakfast to get ready. Usually about five minutes before the bus comes, I'll go up. He'll just be sitting in his room! He's still not dressed. I'll yell at him and then dress him so he's not late.

8. **Helper:** And your main feeling at this point is that you're mad. Anything else you feel?
   Client: No, just very mad.

9. **Helper:** And what exactly do you do when you go upstairs and he's not dressed?
   Client: I yell at him. Then I help dress him.

10. **Helper:** What kinds of things do you usually say to him?
    Client: I tell him he's dumb and he's going to be late for school, and that I have to make sure he won't be.

11. **Helper:** You mentioned this happens in the morning. Does this situation go on every morning or only some mornings?
    Client: Just about every morning except weekends.

12. **Helper:** When did these incidents seem to begin?
    Client: Ever since Freddie started going to school.

13. **Helper:** So it appears that this has been going on for about five years, then?
    Client: Yes, I guess so.

14. **Helper:** Okay, now let's go back over this situation. You told me you remind Freddie every morning to get dressed. He never dresses by breakfast. You remind him again. Then, about five minutes before the bus comes, you go upstairs to check on him. When do you notice that you start to feel mad?
    Client: I think about it as soon as I realize it's almost time for the bus to come and Freddie isn't down yet. Then I feel mad.

15. **Helper:** And what exactly do you think about right then?
    Client: Well, that he's probably not dressed and that if I don't go up and help him, he'll be late. Then I'll look like a bad mother if I can't get my son to school on time.

16. **Helper:** So in a sense you actually go help him out so he won't be late. How many times has Freddie ever been late?
    Client: Never.

17. **Helper:** You believe that helping Freddie may prevent him from being late. However, your help also excuses Freddie from having to help himself. What do you think would happen if you stopped going upstairs to check on Freddie in the morning?
    Client: Well, I don't know, but I'm his only parent. Freddie's father isn't around. It's up to me, all by

LEARNING ACTIVITY	8.3	Interview Assessment

myself, to keep Freddie in line. If I didn't go up and if Freddie was late all the time, his teachers might blame me. I wouldn't be a good mother.

18. **Helper:** Of course, we don't *really* know what would happen if you didn't go up and yell at him or help him dress. It might be so different for Freddie after the first day or two he would dress himself. It could be that he thinks it's easier to wait and get your help than to dress himself. He might think that by sitting up there and waiting for you to help, he's getting a special advantage or attention from you.

Client: You mean like he's getting a favor from me?

19. **Helper:** Sure. And when we find a way to get a favor from someone, we usually do as much as we can to keep getting the favor. Ms. Weare, I'd like to ask you about something else. Do you think maybe that you see helping Freddie out as a way to avoid having Freddie be late and then not having someone blame you for this?

Client: Sure. I'd rather help him than get myself in hot water.

20. **Helper:** Okay, so you're concerned about what you think might happen to you if he's late. You see getting him ready on time as a way to prevent you from getting the heat for him.

Client: Yes.

21. **Helper:** How do you usually feel after these incidents in the morning are over?

Client: Well, it upsets me.

22. **Helper:** Okay, you feel upset. Do these feelings seem to make you want to continue or to stop helping Freddie?

Client: Probably to stop. I get worn out. Also, sometimes I don't get my work done then.

23. **Helper:** So helping Freddie so he won't be late and you won't be blamed sort of makes you want to keep on helping him. Yet when you feel upset and worn out afterward, you're tempted to stop helping. Have I heard you accurately?

Client: I guess that could be true.

24. **Helper:** Gee, I imagine that all the responsibility for a 9-year-old boy would start to feel like a pretty heavy burden after a while.

Client: Yeah. I guess a lot of the time it does.

25. **Helper:** Those may be feelings we'll want to talk about more. I'm also wondering whether there are any other things in your life causing you any concern now?

Client: No, this is about it.

26. **Helper:** Ms. Weare, we've been talking a lot about some problem situations you've had with Freddie. Describe some times when the two of you get along okay.

Client: Well, on weekends we do. Freddie dresses himself whenever he gets up. I sleep later.

27. **Helper:** What happens on weekends when the two of you get along better?

Client: Sometimes I'll take him to a movie or a game. And we eat all our meals together. Usually, weekends are pleasant. He can be a good boy, and I don't scream all the time at him.

28. **Helper:** So you realize it is possible for the two of you to get along. How do you feel about my talking with Freddie and then with both of you together?

Client: That's okay.

Part Two

To incorporate the interview leads into your verbal repertoire, we suggest that you try a role-play interview of the case of Ms. Weare (Chapter 7) or the case of Mr. Huang (Chapter 7) with a triad. One person can take the role of the client (Ms. Weare or Mr. Huang); another can be the helper. Your task is to assess the client's concerns using the interview leads described in this chapter. The third person can be the observer, providing feedback to the helper during or following the role play, using the Interview Checklist at the end of the chapter as a guide.

---

4. **Helper:** It seems like you're feeling pretty overwhelmed and discouraged right now.

Client: Yeah, I am [lowers head, eyes, and voice tone].

Helper senses Isabella has strong feelings about these issues and doesn't want to cut them off initially. Helper *instructs* Isabella to continue focusing on the feelings.

5. **Helper:** [Pause]: Let's stay with these feelings for a few minutes and see where they take us.

Client [Pause—eyes fill with tears]: I guess I just feel like all this stuff is coming down on me at once. I'd like to work something out, but I don't know how—or where, even—to start.

Helper continues to *attend,* to *listen,* and to *reflect* the client's current experience.

6. **Helper:** It seems like you feel you're carrying a big load on your shoulders—

Client: Yeah.

FEEDBACK

8.3

Interview Assessment

Part One

Identifications of the responses in the dialogue between Ms. Weare and the helper are as follows:

1. Open-ended question
2. Clarification response
3. Open-ended question
4. Summarization response
5. Paraphrase response and behavior lead: exploration of context
6. Behavior lead: exploration of context
7. Paraphrase response and behavior lead: exploration of overt behavior
8. Reflection-of-feelings response and behavior lead: exploration of affect
9. Behavior lead: exploration of overt behavior
10. Behavior lead: exploration of overt behavior
11. Paraphrase and behavior lead: exploration of context
12. Antecedent lead: context
13. Clarification response
14. Summarization response and antecedent lead: affect
15. Behavior lead: exploration of cognitions
16. Paraphrase and open question responses
17. Consequences: overt behavior
18. Consequences: secondary gains for Freddie
19. Consequences: secondary gains for Ms. Weare
20. Summarization response and exploration of secondary gains for Ms. Weare
21. Consequences: affect
22. Consequences: affect
23. Summarization (of consequences)
24. Reflection-of-feelings response
25. Range-of-concerns lead
26. Coping skills
27. Coping skills
28. Paraphrase and open-ended question

In response 7, the helper *summarizes* Isabella's concerns, then uses a lead to determine whether Isabella has *prioritized* her concerns.

7. **Helper:** I think before we're finished I'd like to come back to these feelings, which seem pretty strong for you now. Before we do, it might help you to think about not having to tackle everything all at once. You know you mentioned three different things that are bothering you—your competitive classes, having trouble making decisions, and not getting along with your parents. Which of these bothers you most?

Client: I'm not really sure. I'm concerned right now about having trouble in my classes. But sometimes I think if I were in another type of curriculum, I wouldn't be so tense about these classes. But I'm sort of worried about deciding to do this.

Helper response 8 is a *clarification*. The helper wants to see whether the client's interest in work-study is real or is a way to avoid the present issue.

8. **Helper:** Do you see getting in the work-study program as a way to get out of your present problem classes, or is it a program that really interests you?

Client: It's a program that interests me. I think sometimes I'd like to get a job after high school instead of going to

college, or maybe just go to culinary school. *But* I've been thinking about this for a year, and I can't decide what to do. I'm not very good at making decisions on my own.

Helper response 9 is a *summarization* and *instruction*. The helper goes back to the three areas of concern. Note that the helper does not draw explicit attention to the client's last self-deprecating statement.

9. **Helper:** Well, your concerns about your present class problems and about making this and other decisions are somewhat related. Your parents tie into this too. Maybe you could explore all concerns and then decide later about what you want to work on first.

Client: That's fine with me.

Helper response 10 is a lead to *identify some present behaviors* related to Isabella's concern about competitive classes. Asking the client for examples can elicit specificity about what does or does not occur during the situation of concern.

10. **Helper:** Okay, give me an example of some trouble you've been having in your most competitive class.

Client: Well, I guess I shut down in these classes. Also, I've been cutting my math classes. It's the worst. My grades are dropping, especially in math class.

Helper response 11 is a *behavior* lead regarding the *context* of the concern to see whether the client's concern occurs at other *times* or other *places.*

11. **Helper:** Where else do you have trouble—in any other classes, or at other times or places outside school?

Client: No, not outside school. And, to some degree, I always feel anxious in any class because of the pressures my parents put on me to get good grades. But my math class is really the worst.

Helper response 12 is a lead to help the client identify *overt behaviors* in math class (*behavioral* component of concern).

12. **Helper:** Describe what happens in your math class that makes it troublesome for you [could also use imagery assessment at this point].

Client: Well, to start with, it's a harder class for me. I have to work harder to do okay. In this class I get nervous whenever I go in it. So I withdraw.

Client's statement "I withdraw" is vague. So helper response 13 is another *overt behavior* lead to help the client specify what she means by "withdrawing." Note that since the helper did not get a complete answer to this after response 8, the same type of lead is used again.

13. **Helper:** What do you do when you withdraw? [This is also an ideal place for a role-play assessment.]

Client: Well, I sit by myself; I don't talk or volunteer answers. Sometimes I don't go to the board or answer when the teacher calls on me.

Now that the client has identified certain overt behaviors associated with the concern, the helper will use a *covert behavior* lead to find out whether there are any predominant *thoughts* the client has during the math class (*cognitive* component of issue).

14. **Helper:** What are you generally thinking about in this class?

Client: What do you mean—am I thinking about math?

The client's response indicated some confusion. The helper will have to use a more specific *covert behavior* lead to assess cognition, along with some *self-disclosure,* to help the client respond more specifically.

15. **Helper:** Well, sometimes when I'm in a situation like a class, there are times when my mind is in the class

and other times I'm thinking about myself or about something else I'm going to do. So I'm wondering what you've noticed you're thinking about during the class.

Client: Well, some of the time I'm thinking about the math problems. Other times I'm thinking about the fact that I'd rather not be in the class and that I'm not as good as the other kids, especially all the guys in it.

The client has started to be more specific, and the helper thinks perhaps there are still other thoughts going on. To explore this possibility, the helper uses another *covert behavior* lead in response 16 to assess *cognition.*

16. **Helper:** What else do you recall that you tell yourself when you're thinking you're not as good as other people?

Client: Well, I think that I don't get grades that are as good as some other students'. My parents have been pointing this out to me since junior high. And in the math class I'm one of four girls. The guys in there are really smart. I just keep thinking how can a girl ever be as smart as a guy in math class? No way. It just doesn't happen.

The client identifies more specific thoughts and also suggests two possible antecedents—parental comparison of her grades and cultural stereotyping (girls shouldn't be as good in math as boys). The helper's records show that the client's test scores and previous grades indicate that she is definitely not "dumb" in math. The helper will *summarize* this and then, in the next few responses, will focus on these and on other possible *antecedents,* such as the nervousness the client mentioned earlier.

17. **Helper:** So what you're telling me is that you believe most of what you've heard from others about yourself and about the fact that girls automatically are not supposed to do too well in math.

Client: Yeah, I guess so, now that you put it like that. I've never given it much thought.

18. **Helper:** Yes. It doesn't sound like you've ever thought about whether *you, Isabella,* really feel this way or whether these feelings are just adopted from things you've heard others tell you.

Client: No, I never have.

19. **Helper:** That's something we'll also probably want to come back to later.

Client: Okay.

20. **Helper:** You know, Isabella, earlier you mentioned that you get nervous about this class. When do you notice that you feel this way—before the class, during the class, or at other times?

Client: Well, right before the class is the worst. About 10 minutes before my English class ends—it's right before math—I start thinking about the math class. Then I get nervous and feel like I wish I didn't have to go. Recently, I've tried to find ways to cut math class.

The helper still needs more information about how and when the nervousness affects the client, so response 21 is another *antecedent* lead.

21. **Helper:** Tell me more about when you feel most nervous and when you don't feel nervous about this class.

Client: Well, I feel worst when I'm actually walking to the class and the class is starting. Once the class starts, I feel better. I don't feel nervous about it when I cut it or at other times. However, once in a while, if someone talks about it or I think about it, I feel a little nervous.

The client has indicated that the nervousness seems to be more of an antecedent than a problem behavior. She has also suggested that cutting class is a consequence that maintains the issue, because she uses this to avoid the math class that brings on the nervousness. The helper realizes at this point that the word *nervous* has not been defined and goes back in the next response to a *covert behavior* lead to find out what Isabella means by *nervous* (affective component).

22. **Helper:** Tell me what you mean by the word *nervous*—what goes on with you when you're nervous?

Client: Well, I get sort of a sick feeling in my stomach, and my hands get all sweaty. My heart starts to pound.

In the next response, the helper continues to *listen* and *paraphrase* to clarify whether the nervousness is experienced somatically.

23. **Helper:** So your nervousness really consists of things you feel going on inside you.

Client: Yeah.

Next the helper will use an *intensity* lead to determine the *severity* of nervousness.

24. **Helper:** How strong is this feeling—a little or very?

Client: Before class, very strong—at other times, just a little.

The client has established that the nervousness seems mainly to be exhibited in somatic forms and is more intense before class. The helper will pursue the relationship between the client's nervousness and overt and covert behaviors described earlier to verify that the nervousness is an *antecedent*. Another *antecedent* lead is used next.

25. **Helper:** Which seems to come first—feeling nervous, not speaking up in class, or thinking about other people being smarter than you?

Client: Well, the nervousness. Because that starts before I get in the class.

The helper will *summarize* this pattern and confirm it with the client in the next response.

26. **Helper:** Let's see. So you feel nervous—like in your stomach and hands—before class and when math class starts. Then during class, on days you go, you start thinking about not being as smart in math as the guys and you don't volunteer answers or don't respond sometimes when called on. But after the class is over, you don't notice the nervousness so much. Have I heard you accurately?

Client: That's pretty much what happens.

The helper has a clue from the client's previous comments that there are other antecedents in addition to nervousness that have to do with the client's concern—such as the role of her parents. The helper will pursue this in the next response, using an *antecedent* lead.

27. **Helper:** Isabella, you mentioned earlier that you have been thinking about not being as smart as some of your friends ever since junior high. When do you recall you really started to dwell on this?

Client: Well, probably in seventh grade.

The helper didn't get sufficient information about what happened to the client in the seventh grade, so another *antecedent* lead will be used to identify this possible *setting event*.

28. **Helper:** What do you recall happened in seventh grade?

Client: Well, my parents said when you start junior high, your grades become really important in order to go to college. So for the last three or four years they have been telling me some of my grades aren't as good as other students'. Also, if I get a B, they will take something away, like going out with my friends.

The helper has no evidence of actual parental reaction but will work with the client's report at this time, because this is how the client perceives parental input. If possible, a parent conference could be arranged later with the client's permission. The parents *seem* to be using negative rather than positive consequences with Isabella to influence her behavior. The helper wants to pursue the relationship between the parents' input and the client's present behavior to determine whether parental reaction is eliciting part of Isabella's present concerns. The helper will use a lead to identify this as a possible *antecedent*.

29. **Helper:** How do you think this reaction of your parents relates to your present problems in your math class?

Client: Well, since I started high school, they have talked more about needing to get better grades for college. And I have to work harder in math class to do this. I guess I feel a lot of pressure to perform—which makes me withdraw and just want to hang it up. Now, of course, my grades are getting worse, not better.

The helper, in the next lead, will *paraphrase* Isabella's previous comment.

30. **Helper:** So the expectations you feel from your parents seem to draw out pressure in you.

Client: Yes, that happens.

In response 31, the helper will explore another possible *antecedent* that Isabella mentioned before—thinking that girls aren't as good as boys in math.

31. **Helper:** Isabella, I'd like to ask you about something else you mentioned earlier that I said we would come back to. You said one thing that you think about in your math class is that you're only one of four girls and that, as a girl, you're not as smart in math as a boy. Do you know what makes you think this way?

Client: I'm not sure. Everyone knows or says that girls have more trouble in math than boys. Even my teacher. He's gone out of his way to try to help me because he knows it's tough for me.

The client has identified a possible consequence of her behavior as teacher attention. The helper will return to this later. First, the helper is going to respond to the client's response that "everyone" has told her this thought. Helpers have a responsibility to point out things that clients have learned from stereotypes or irrational beliefs rather than actual data, as is evident in this case from Isabella's academic record. The helper will use *confrontation* in the next response.

32. **Helper:** You know, studies have shown that when young women drop out of math, science, and engineering programs, they do so not because they're doing poorly but because they don't believe they can do well.* It is evident to me from your records that you have a lot of potential for math.

Client: Really?

Helper response 33 is an *interpretation* to help the client see the relation between overt and covert behaviors.

33. **Helper:** I don't see why not. But lots of times the way someone acts or performs in a situation is affected by how the person thinks about the situation. I think some of the reason you're having more trouble in your math class is that your performance is hindered a little by your nervousness and by the way you put yourself down.

In the next response, the helper *checks out* and *clarifies* the client's reaction to the previous interpretation.

34. **Helper:** I'm wondering now from the way you're looking at me whether this makes any sense or whether what I just said muddies the waters more for you?

Client: No, I guess I was just thinking about things. You mentioned the word *expectations*. But I guess it's not just that my parents expect too much of me. I guess in a way I expect too little of myself. I've never really thought of that before.

35. **Helper:** That's a great observation. In a way the two sets of expectations are probably connected. These are some of the kinds of issues we may want to work on if this track we're on seems to fit for you.

Client: Yeah. Okay, it's a problem.

The helper is going to go back now to pursue possible consequences that are influencing the client's behavior. The next response is a lead to identify *consequences*.

36. **Helper:** Isabella, I'd like to go back to some things you mentioned earlier. For one thing, you said your teacher has gone out of his way to help you. Would you say that your behavior in his class has got you any extra attention or special consideration from him?

Client: Certainly extra attention. He talks to me more frequently. And he doesn't get upset when I don't go to the board.

*From studies conducted at Wellesley College's Center for Research on Women.

Helper response 37 will continue to explore the teacher's behavior as a possible *consequence*.

37. **Helper:** Do you mean he may excuse you from board work?

Client: For sure, and I think he too almost expects me *not* to come up with the answer. Just like I don't expect myself to.

The teacher's behavior may be maintaining the client's overt behaviors in class by giving extra attention to her and by excusing her from some kinds of work. A teacher conference may be necessary at some later point. The helper, in the next two responses, will continue to use other leads to identify possible *consequences*.

38. **Helper:** What do you see you're doing right now that helps you get out of putting yourself through the stress of going to math class?

Client: Do you mean something like cutting class?

39. **Helper:** I think that's perhaps one thing you do to get out of the class. What else?

Client: Nothing I can think of.

The client has identified cutting class as one way to avoid the math class. The helper, in the next response, will suggest another *consequence* that the client mentioned earlier, though not as a way to get out of the stress associated with the class. The helper will suggest that this consequence functions as a *secondary gain,* or *payoff,* in a tentative *interpretation* that is checked out with the client in the next three responses:

40. **Helper:** Well, Isabella, you told me earlier that your grades were dropping in math class. Is it possible that if these grades—and others—drop too much, you'll automatically be dropped from these college prep classes?

Client: That's right.

41. **Helper:** I'm wondering whether one possible reason for letting your grades slide is that it is almost an automatic way for you to get out of these competitive classes.

Client: How so?

42. **Helper:** Well, if you became ineligible for these classes because of your grades, you'd automatically be out of this class and others that you consider competitive and feel nervous about. What do you think about that?

Client: I guess that's true. And then my dilemma is whether I want to stay in this or switch to the work-study program.

In the next response, the helper uses *summarization* and ties together the effects of "dropping grades" to math class and to the earlier-expressed concern of a curriculum-change decision.

43. **Helper:** Right. And letting your grades get too bad will automatically mean that decision is made for you, so you can take yourself off the hook for making that choice. In other words, it's sort of a way that part of you has rather creatively come up with to get yourself out of the hassle of having to decide something you don't really want to be responsible for deciding about.

Client: Wow! Gosh, I guess that might be happening.

44. **Helper:** That's something you can think about. We didn't really spend that much time today exploring the issue of having to make decisions for yourself, so that will probably be something to discuss the next time we get together. I know you have a class coming up in about 10 minutes, so there are just a couple more things we might look at.

Client: Okay—what next?

In the next few responses (45–52), the helper continues to demonstrate *listening responses* and to help Isabella explore *solutions* she's tried already to resolve the issue. They look together at the *effects* of the use of the solutions Isabella identifies.

45. **Helper:** Okay, starting with the nervousness and pressure you feel in math class—is there anything you've attempted to do to get a handle on this concern?

Client: Not really—other than talking to you about it and, of course, cutting class.

46. **Helper:** So cutting class is the only solution you've tried.

Client: Yeah.

47. **Helper:** How do you think this solution has helped?

Client: Well, like I said before—it helps mainly because on the days I don't go, I don't feel uptight.

48. **Helper:** So you see it as a way to get rid of these feelings you don't like.

Client: Yeah, I guess that's it.

49. **Helper:** Can you think of any ways in which this solution has not helped?

Client: Gee, I don't know. Maybe I'm not sure what you're asking.

50. **Helper:** Okay, good point! Sometimes when I try to do something to resolve a concern, it can make the issue better or worse. So I guess what I'm really asking is whether you've noticed that your "solution" of cutting class has in any way made the problem worse or in any way has even contributed to the whole issue?

Client: [Pause] I suppose maybe in a way. [Pause] In that, by cutting class, I miss out on the work, and then I don't have all the input I need for tests and homework, and that doesn't help my poor grades.

51. **Helper:** Okay. That's an interesting idea. You're saying that when you look deeper, your solution also has had some negative effects on one of the issues you're trying to deal with and eliminate.

Client: Yeah. But I guess I'm not sure what else I could do.

52. **Helper:** At this point, you probably are feeling a little bit stuck, like you don't know which other direction or road to take.

Client: Yeah.

At this point, the helper shifts the focus a little to exploration of Isabella's *assets, strengths, and resources.*

53. **Helper:** Well, one thing I sense is that your feelings of being so overwhelmed are sort of covering up the resources and assets you have within you to handle the issue and work it out. For example, can you identify any particular skills or things you have going for you that might help you deal with this issue?

Client: [Pause] Well, are you asking me to tell you what I like about myself?

Clients often talk about their pain or limitations freely but feel reluctant to reveal their strengths, so in the next response, the helper gives Isabella a specific *directive* and *permission* to talk about her *assets.*

54. **Helper:** Sure. Give yourself permission. That's certainly fine in here.

Client: Well, I am pretty responsible. I'm usually fairly loyal and dependable. It's hard to make decisions for myself, but when I say I'm going to do something, I usually do it.

55. **Helper:** Okay, great. So what you're telling me is you're good on follow-through once you decide something is important to you.

Client: Yeah. Mm-hmm. Also, although I'm usually uptight in my math class, I don't have the same feeling in my history class. I'm really doing well in there.

In response 56, the helper will pick up on these "pluses" and use another *coping skills* lead to have the client identify particular ways in which she handles positive situations, especially her history class. If she can demonstrate the steps to succeed in one class, this is useful information that can be applied in a different area. This topic is continued in response 57.

56. **Helper:** So there are some things about school that are going okay for you. You say you're doing well in your history class. What can you think of that you do or don't do to help you perform well in this class?

Client: Well, I go to class, of course, regularly. And I guess I feel like I do well in the reading and writing assignments in there. I don't have the hang-up in there about being one of the few girls.

57. **Helper:** So maybe you can see some of the differences between your history and math classes—and how you handle these. This information is useful because if you can start to identify the things you do and think about in history that make it go so well for you, then you potentially can apply the same process or steps to a more difficult situation, like math class.

Client: That sounds hopeful!

Isabella and the helper have been talking about *individual strengths.* Next (in responses 58–62), the helper will explore any *environmental and cultural strengths and resources* that can help Isabella in this situation.

58. **Helper:** So far we've been talking about your own individual assets. Can you think of any assets or resources—including people—in your immediate environment that could be useful to you in dealing with these concerns?

Client: Well, I mentioned my math teacher. He does go out of his way to help me. He even has given all of us his e-mail address to use if we get stuck on a homework problem, and he has a tutoring session after school every Thursday too. But I haven't used his help too much outside of class.

59. **Helper:** So you rely on him more during class?

Client: Yup.

60. **Helper:** Are there any other people or resources available to you that you may or may not be using?

Client: Hmm.

61. **Helper:** Earlier you mentioned your friends. Do you ever do homework with them or have study groups with them?

Client: No—we mainly just go out on weekends to do things. But I think that might be a good idea, and I think my parents would be in favor of that one too.

62. **Helper:** Anything else you can think of?

Client: Well, I'm kind of stuck; I don't see anything else that could help me right now.

To help Isabella explore contributing conditions of her environment, the helper uses an *ecomap* in responses 63–69.

63. **Helper:** One thing we could start today and finish next time is kind of a chart or drawing. It is actually called an ecomap, and what it does is help us to get a picture about your world and the ways that other people and systems in it can either contribute to your concerns or can be used to help resolve them. Would you like to give this a try with my assistance?

Client: Sure. What do I do—is it like a map of a state or something?

64. **Helper:** Sort of. Here is a piece of paper with a big circle in the center. In that circle simply write your name or "Me." That circle represents you in the center of your world. Then around that center circle which represents you, I would like you to draw other circles—each representing some aspect of your current environment. For example, one circle might be family, one might be extended family, one might be church or religion, another may be friends, while still another would be school, and another could be recreation. Can you think of any other important systems in your current life?

Client: Well let me think. I do some community service—not a lot—but some volunteering at the local boys and girls club.

65. **Helper:** Okay, so maybe another circle would be a community group or community groups such as that boys and girls club you just mentioned. Can you think of any other places or people in your environment that are important to you other than what we have already mentioned? If so, draw a circle there.

Client: Is that it?

66. **Helper:** Not quite. After this, list the names of people, groups, and organizations with-in each circle. Next I'd like you to draw a solid line from yourself to anything (or anyone) you've circled that is positive or represents a strong connection for you.

Client: Okay [draws several solid lines].

67. **Helper:** Almost there. Next, I'd like you to draw a broken line from yourself to anything that feels negative or represents a stressful connection for you.

Client: Okay [continues drawing—this time, broken lines].

68. **Helper:** Last thing—now draw a wavy line from yourself to anything that you need that is not available to you.

Client: Okay, here goes [draws several wavy lines]. That was kind of fun.

69. **Helper:** It *is* fun, and it is also surprising how much information you can get from this.

In the next few responses, the helper tries to elicit *Isabella's perception and assessment of the main issue.*

70. **Helper:** Right. It is. Just a couple more things. Changing the focus a little now, think about the issues that you came in with today—and describe the main issue in one word.

Client: Ooh—that's a hard question!

71. **Helper:** I guess it could be. Take your time. You don't have to rush.

Client: [Pause] Well, how about "can't"?

72. **Helper:** Okay, now, to help me get an idea of what that word means to you, use it in a sentence.

Client: Any sentence?

73. **Helper:** Yeah. Make one up. Maybe the first thing that comes in your head.

Client: Well, "I can't do a lot of things I think I want to or should be able to do."

Next, the helper uses a *confrontation* to depict the incongruity revealed in the sentence Isabella made up about her concern. This theme is continued in response 75.

74. **Helper:** Okay, that's interesting too, because on the one hand, you're saying there are some things you *want* to do

that aren't happening, and on the other hand, you're also saying there are some things that aren't happening that you think you *should* be doing. Now, these are two pretty different things mixed together in the same sentence.

Client: Yeah. [Clarifies.] I think the wanting stuff to happen is from me and the should things are from my parents and my teachers.

75. **Helper:** Okay, so you're identifying part of the whole issue as wanting to please yourself and others at the same time.

Client: Mm-hmm.

In response 76, the helper identifies this issue as an extension of the *secondary gain* mentioned earlier—avoiding deliberate decisions.

For Isabella
Week of Nov. 6–13

Behavior observing	Date	Time	Place	(Frequency/ duration) Number or amount	(Antecedents) What precedes behavior	(Consequences) What follows behavior
1. Thinking of self as not as smart as other students	Mon., Nov. 6	10:00 A.M.	Math class	IIII	Going into class, know have to take test in class.	Leaving class, being with friends.
	Tues., Nov. 7	10:15 A.M.	Math class	IIII IIII	Got test back with a B.	Teacher consoled me.
	Tues., Nov. 7	5:30 P.M.	Home	IIII II	Parents asked about test. Told me to stay home this weekend.	Went to bed.
	Thurs., Nov. 9	9:30 A.M.	English class	II	Thought about having to go to math class.	Got to math class. Had substitute teacher.
	Sun., Nov. 12	9:30 P.M.	Home	III	Thought about school tomorrow.	Went to bed.
2. a. Not volunteering answers	Tues., Nov. 7	10:05 A.M. 10:20	Math class	II	Felt dumb.	Nothing.
b. Not answering teacher questions	Thurs., Nov. 9	10:10 A.M. 10:20 10:40	Math class	III	Felt dumb.	Nothing.
c. Not going to class	Thurs., Nov. 9	10:30 A.M.	Math class	I	Teacher called on me.	Nothing.
	Fri., Nov. 10	10:10 A.M. 10:35 A.M.	Math class	II	Teacher called on me.	Nothing.
	Thurs., Nov. 9	10:45 A.M.	Math class	I	Didn't have a substitute teacher.	Nothing.
	Fri., Nov. 10	10:15 A.M.	Math class	I	Teacher asked girls to go up to board.	Teacher talked to me after class.
3. Cutting class	Wed., Nov. 8	9:55 A.M.	School	1 hour	Didn't want to hassle with class or think about test.	Cut class. Played sick. Went to nurse's office for an hour.

Figure 8.3 Example of a Behavior Log

76. **Helper:** I can see how after a while that would start to feel like so much trouble that it would be easier to try to let situations or decisions get made for you rather than making a conscious or deliberate choice.

In the next two responses, the helper explores the *context* related to these issues and sets up some *self-monitoring* homework to obtain additional information. Note that this is a task likely to appeal to the client's dependability, which she revealed during exploration of *coping skills.*

77. **Helper:** That's something else we'll be coming back to, I'm sure. One last thing before you have to go. Earlier we talked about some specific times and places connected to some of these issues—like where and when you get in the rut of putting yourself down and thinking you're not as smart as other people. What I'd like to do is give you sort of a diary to write in this week to collect some more information about these kinds of problems. Sometimes writing these kinds of things down can help you start making changes and sorting out the issues. You've said that you're pretty dependable. Would doing this appeal to your dependability?

Client: Sure. That's something that wouldn't be too hard for me to do.

78. **Helper:** Okay, let me tell you specifically what to keep track of, and then I'll see you next week—bring this back with you. [Goes over instructions for self-monitoring homework.] (See Isabella's behavior log in Figure 8.3.)

At this time, the helper also has the option of giving Isabella a history questionnaire to complete and/or a brief self-report inventory to complete, such as an anxiety inventory or checklist.

CHAPTER SUMMARY

This chapter focuses on the use of direct interviewing to assess client concerns. In many settings, initial assessment interviews often begin with an intake interview to gather information about the client's presenting issues and primary symptoms as well as information about such areas as previous counseling, social/developmental history, educational/vocational history, health history, and family, relationship, and sexual history. Helpers also assess suicidal and homicidal risk during intake and initial interviews. Intake interviews often yield information that the practitioner can use to develop hypotheses about the nature of the client's issues. History interviews also serve as a retrospective baseline of how the client was functioning before and what events contributed to the present concerns and coping styles. For occasional

clients, intakes or history interviews may be followed by a mental-status exam, which aids the helper in assessing the client's psychiatric status.

In direct assessment interviews, practitioners are interested in defining six components of behavior: affective, somatic, behavioral, cognitive, contextual, and relational. They also seek to identify antecedent events that occur before the issue and cue it, and consequent events that follow the issue and in some way influence it or maintain it. Consequences may include "payoffs," or secondary gains, that give value to the dysfunctional behavior and thus keep the issue going. Antecedents and consequences may also be affective, somatic, behavioral, cognitive, contextual, and relational. Contextual and relational ABCs form the basis of an environmental assessment to determine the ways in which clients' social network (or lack thereof) and environmental barriers and resources affect the issue. Other important components of direct assessment interviewing include identifying previous solutions the client has tried for resolving the issue, exploring individual and environmental strengths, exploring the client's perceptions of the issue, and identifying the frequency, duration, or severity of the concern.

In addition to direct assessment interviewing, other assessment tools include ecomaps, social network maps, role playing, imagery, self-report measures, and self-monitoring. All these techniques can be useful for obtaining more specific information about the identified concerns.

Cultural variables also play a role in assessment interviews. Factors such as age, ethnicity, and race impact both diagnoses and assessment processes. Interviewers need to be culturally sensitive to clients and avoid bias and cultural misunderstandings. Culturally sensitive assessment interview protocols are reviewed in this chapter.

REFERENCES

Calix, A. R. (2004). Is the ecomap a valid and reliable social work tool to measure social support? Unpublished master's thesis, Louisiana State University, Baton Rouge.

Canino, I., & Spurlock, J. (2000). *Culturally diverse children and adolescents: Assessment, diagnosis, and treatment* (2nd ed.). New York: Guilford Press.

Constantine, M., & Sue, D. W. (2006). Factors contributing to optimal human functioning in people of color in the United States. *The Counseling Psychologist, 34,* 228–244.

Edelstein, B., Koven, L., Spira, A., & Shreve-Neiger, A. (2003). Older adults. In M. Hersen & S. M. Turner (Eds.), *Diagnostic interviewing* (3rd ed., pp. 433–454). New York: Kluwer Academic.

Farrell, A. D., & McCullough-Vaillant, L. (1996). Computerized assessment system for psychotherapy evaluation and research (CASPER): Development and current status. In M. J. Miller, K. W. Hammond, & M. M. Hile (Eds.), *Mental health computing* (pp. 34–53). New York: Springer.

Fensterheim, H. (1983). Basic paradigms, behavioral formulation and basic procedures. In H. Fensterheim & H. Glazer (Eds.), *Behavioral psychotherapy: Basic principles and case studies in an integrative clinical model* (pp. 40–87). New York: Brunner/Mazel.

First, M. B., Spitzer, R. L., Gibbon, M., & Williams, J. B. W. (1996). *Structured clinical interview for Axis I Disorders: Patient Edition (SCID-I/P, Version 2.0)*. New York: New York State Psychiatric Institute.

First, M. B., Spitzer, R. L., Gibbon, M., & Williams, J. B. W. (1997). *Structured clinical interview for Axis I Disorders (SCID-I): Clinician Version*. Washington, DC: American Psychiatric Press.

Fremouw, W., Strunk, J. M., Tyner, E. A., & Musick, R. (2005). Adolescent suicide assessment protocol-20. In L. Vandecreek and J. B. Allen (Eds.), *Innovations in clinical practice* (pp. 207–224). Sarasota, FL: Professional Resource Press.

Fremouw, W., Tyner, E. A., Strunk, J. M., & Musick, R. (in press). Suicidal adult assessment protocol—SAAP.

Gambrill, E. D. (1990). *Critical thinking in clinical practice*. San Francisco: Jossey-Bass.

Garvin, C., & Seabury, B. (1997). *Interpersonal practice in social work: Promoting competence and social justice* (2nd ed.). Boston: Allyn & Bacon.

Hartman, A. (1979). The extended family as a resource for change: Ecological approach to family-centered practice. In C. B. Germain (Ed.), *Social work practice: People and environments* (pp. 239–266). New York: Columbia University Press.

Hays, P. (2001). *Addressing cultural complexities in practice: A framework for clinicians and counselors*. Washington, DC: American Psychological Association.

Hepworth, D. H., Rooney, R. H., Dewberry Rooney, G., Strom-Gottfried, K., & Larsen, J. (2006). *Direct social work practice* (7th ed.). Belmont, CA: Thomson–Brooks/Cole.

Hill, R., Thorn, B., & Packard, T. (2000). Counseling older adults: Theoretic and empirical issues in prevention and intervention. In S. Brown & R. Lent (Eds.), *Handbook of counseling psychology* (pp. 499–531). Thousand Oaks, CA: Sage.

Hodges, K. (1997). *Child and adolescent functional assessment scale*. Ann Arbor, MI: Functional Assessment System.

Hunsley, J., & Mash, E. (2005). Introduction to the special section on developing guidelines for the evidence-based assessment (EBA) of adult disorders. *Psychological Assessment, 17,* 251–255.

Kaplan, H. I., & Sadock, B. J. (1998). *Synopsis of psychiatry: Behavioral sciences, clinical psychiatry* (8th ed.). Baltimore: Williams, Lippincott & Wilkins.

Karls, J. M., & Wandrei, K. E. (1994). *PIE Manual: Person-in-environment: The PIE classification system for social functioning problems*. Washington, DC: National Association of Social Workers.

Kemp, S., Whittaker, J., & Tracy, E. (1997). *Person–environment practice: The social ecology of interpersonal helping*. New York: Aldine de Gruyter.

Koven, L., Shreve-Neiger, A., & Edelstein, B. (2007). Interview of older adults. In M. Hersen & J. C. Thomas (Eds.), *Handbook of clinical interviewing with adults* (pp. 392–406). Los Angeles: Sage.

Lazarus, A. A. (1989). *The practice of multimodal therapy*. Baltimore: Johns Hopkins University Press.

Leahy, R., & Holland, S. (2000). *Treatment plans and interventions for depression and anxiety disorders*. New York: Guilford Press.

Linscott, J., & DiGiuseppe, R. (1998). Cognitive assessment. In A. Bellack & M. Hersen (Eds.), *Behavioral assessment* (pp. 104–125). Boston: Allyn & Bacon.

Monahan, J., Steadman, H., Silver, E., Appelbaum, P., Robbins, P., Mulvey, E., et al. (2001). *Rethinking risk assessment of mental disorders and violence*. New York: Oxford University Press.

Morrison, J. (1995). *DSM-IV made easy*. New York: Guilford Press.

Morrison, J., & Anders, T. (1999). *Interviewing children and adolescents*. New York: Guilford Press.

Sarwer, D. B., & Sayers, S. L. (1998). Behavioral interviewing. In A. S. Bellack & M. Hersen (Eds.), *Behavioral assessment: A practical handbook* (4th ed., pp. 63–79). Boston: Allyn & Bacon.

Snyder, C. R., & Lopez, S. J. (2007). *Positive psychology*. Thousand Oaks, CA: Sage.

Sommers-Flanagan, J., & Sommers-Flanagan, R. (2003). *Clinical interviewing* (3rd ed.). New York: Wiley.

Sue, D. W. Capodilupo, C. M., Torino, G. C., Bucceri, J. M., Holder, A. M. B., Nadal, K. L., & Esquilin, M. (2007). Racial microaggressions in everyday life: Implications for clinical practice. *American Psychologist, 62,* 271–286.

Tanaka-Matsumi, J., Seiden, D. Y., & Lam, K. N. (1996). The culturally informed functional assessment (CIFA) interview: A strategy for cross-cultural behavioral practice. *Cognitive and Behavioral Practice, 3,* 215–233.

Tracey, E. M., & Whittaker, J. K. (1990). The social network map: Assessing social support in clinical social work practice. *Families in Society, 71,* 461–470.

Watson, D., Clark, L., & Tellegen, A. (1988). Development and validation of brief measures of positive and negative affect: The PANAS scales. *Journal of Personality and Social Psychology, 54,* 1063–1070.

Wolpe, J. (1990). *The practice of behavior therapy* (4th ed.). New York: Pergamon.

8   KNOWLEDGE AND SKILL BUILDER

Part One

A client is referred to you with a presenting concern of "free-floating," or generalized (pervasive), anxiety. Outline the specific interview leads you would ask during an assessment interview with this client that pertain directly to her presenting component. Your objective (Learning Outcome 1) is to identify at least 2 interview leads for each of the 11 assessment categories described in this chapter and summarized in Box 8.3. Feedback follows on page 228.

Part Two

Using the description of the client in Part One, conduct a 30-minute role-play assessment interview in which your objective is to demonstrate leads and responses associated with at least 9 out of the 11 categories described for assessment (Learning Outcome 2). You can do this activity in a triad in which one person assumes the role of helper, another the "anxious" client, and the third person the role of observer; trade roles two times. If groups are not available, audiotape or videotape your interview.

Use the Interview Checklist below as a guide to assess your performance and to obtain feedback.

After completing your interview, develop some hypotheses, or hunches, about the client. In particular, try to develop "guesses" about

1. Antecedents that cue or set off the anxiety, making its occurrence more likely

2. Consequences that maintain the anxiety, keep it going, or make it worse

3. Consequences that diminish or weaken the anxiety

4. Secondary gains, or payoffs, attached to the anxiety

5. Ways in which the client's "previous solutions" may contribute to the anxiety or make it worse

6. Particular individual and environmental strengths, resources, and coping skills of the client and how these might be best used during treatment/intervention

7. How the client's gender, culture, and environment affect the problem

You may wish to continue this part of the activity in a triad or do it by yourself, jotting down ideas as you proceed. At some point, it may be helpful to share your ideas with your group or your instructor.

Part Three

Conduct a role-play interview with the client from Part One in which you help her complete an ecomap using Figure 8.1 as a guide and a social network map using Figure 8.2 as a guide (Learning Outcome 3). If possible, continue with this activity in your triad and obtain feedback from the observer.

Interview Checklist for Assessing Clients

Scoring		Category of information	Examples of helper leads or responses	Client response
Yes	No			
____	____	1. Explain purpose of assessment interview	"I am going to be asking you more questions than usual so that we can get an idea of what is going on. Getting an accurate picture about your concern will help us to decide what we can do about it. Your input is important."	____ (check if client confirmed understanding of purpose)
____	____	2. Identify range of concerns (if you don't have this information from history)	"What would you like to talk about today?" "What specifically led you to come to see someone now?" "Describe any other issues you haven't mentioned."	____ (check if client described additional concerns)
____	____	3. Prioritize and select primary or most immediate issue to work on	"What issue best represents the reason you are here?" "Of all these concerns, which one is most stressful (or painful) for you?" "Rank order these concerns, starting with the one that is most important for you to resolve to the one least important."	____ (check if client selected issue to focus on)

8	KNOWLEDGE AND SKILL BUILDER

"Tell me which of these issues you believe you could learn to deal with most easily and with the most success."

"Which one of the things we discussed do you see as having the best chance of being solved?"

"Out of all the things we've discussed, describe the one that, when resolved, would have the greatest impact on the rest of the issues."

_____ _____ 4.0. Present behavior

_____ (check if client identified the following components)

4.1. *Affective* aspects: feelings, emotions, mood states

"What are you feeling when this happens?"
"How does this make you feel when this occurs?"
"What other feelings do you have when this occurs?"
"What feelings is this issue hiding or covering up?"
"What positive feelings do you have surrounding this issue?"
"Negative ones?"

_____ (check if client identified positive and negative feelings)

_____ _____ 4.2. *Somatic* aspects: body sensations, physiological responses, organic dysfunction and illness, medications

"What goes on inside you then?"
"What do you notice in your body when this happens?"
"When this happens, are you aware of anything that goes on in your body that feels bad or uncomfortable—aches, pains, and so on?"

_____ (check if client identified body sensations)

_____ _____ 4.3. *Behavioral* aspects: overt behaviors/actions

"In photographing this scene, what actions and dialogue would the camera pick up?"
"What are you doing when this occurs?"
"What do you mean by 'not communicating'?"
"Describe what you did the last few times this occurred."

_____ (check if client identified overt behaviors)

_____ _____ 4.4. *Cognitive* aspects: automatic, helpful, unhelpful, rational, irrational thoughts and beliefs; internal dialogue; perceptions and misperceptions

"What do you say to yourself when this happens?"
"What are you usually thinking about during this problem?"
"What was going through your mind then?"
"What kinds of thoughts can make you feel _____?"
"What beliefs [or images] do you hold that affect this issue?"
Sentence completions: I should _____, people should _____, it would be awful if _____, _____ makes me feel bad.

_____ (check if client identified thoughts, beliefs)

_____ _____ 4.5. *Contextual* aspects: time, place, or setting events

"Describe some recent situations in which the issue occurred. Where were you? When was it?"
"Does this go on all the time or only sometimes?"
"Does the same thing happen at other times or places?"
"At what time does this *not* occur? Places? Situations?"
"What effect does your cultural/ethnic background have on this issue?"
"What effects do the sociopolitical structures of the society in which you live have on this issue?"
"Describe the relationship between yourself, your concerns, and your current environment. We could draw this relationship if you want to see it [using an ecomap]."

_____ (check if client identified time, places, other events)

(continued)

(continued)

_____ _____   **4.6.** *Relational* aspects: other people

"To what extent is your concern affected by oppression and discrimination that you experience in your environment?"

"To what extent does your environment give or deny you access to power, privilege, and resources?"

"What opportunities do you have in your environment for sharing spiritual and cultural values and activities?"

"What effects does this concern have on significant others in your life?"

_____ (check if client identified people)

"What effects do significant others have on this concern?"

"Who else is involved in the concern? How?"

"What persons *present* in your life now have the greatest positive impact on this concern? Negative impact?"

"What about persons *absent* from your life?"

"Let's try filling out this drawing [social network map] to see what types of social support are available in your life right now."

"Who in your life empowers you? Disempowers you? Nourishes you? Feels toxic to you?"

_____ _____   **5.0.** Antecedents—past or current conditions that cue, or set off, the behavior

_____ (check if client identified following antecedent categories)

_____ _____   **5.1.** *Affective* antecedents

"What are you usually feeling before this?"

"When do you recall the first time you felt this way?"

"What are the feelings that occur before the issue and make it more likely to happen? Less likely?"

"Describe any holdover or unfinished feelings from past events in your life that still affect this issue. How?"

_____ (feelings, mood states)

_____ _____   **5.2.** *Somatic* antecedents

"What goes on inside you just before this happens?"

"Are you aware of any particular sensations or discomfort just before the issue occurs or gets worse?"

"Are there any body sensations that seem to occur before the issue or when it starts that make it more likely to occur? Less likely?"

"Is there anything going on with you physically—like illness or a physical condition or in the way you eat or drink—that leads up to this issue?"

_____ (body sensations, physiological responses)

_____ _____   **5.3.** *Behavioral* antecedents

"If I were photographing this, what actions and dialogue would I pick up before this happens?"

"Identify any particular behavior patterns that occur right before this happens."

"What do you typically do before this happens?"

_____ (overt behavior)

_____ _____   **5.4.** *Cognitive* antecedents

"What are your thoughts before this happens?"

"What are you telling yourself before this happens?"

"Can you identify any particular beliefs that seem to set the issue off?"

"What do you think about [or tell yourself] before the issue occurs that makes it more likely to happen? Less likely?"

_____ (thoughts, beliefs, internal dialogue, cognitive schemas)

_____ _____   **5.5.** *Contextual* antecedents

"How long ago did this happen?"

"Has this ever occurred at any other time in your life? If so, describe that."

"Where and when did this occur the first time?"

"What things happened that seemed to lead up to this?"

_____ (time, places, other events)

8 KNOWLEDGE AND SKILL BUILDER

___ ___	5.6. *Relational* antecedents	"What was happening in your life when you first noticed the issue?" "Are there any ways in which your cultural values and affiliations set off this issue? Make it more likely to occur? Less likely?" "How were things different before you had this concern?" "What do you mean, this started 'recently'?" "Are there any people or relationships from past events in your life that still affect this concern? How?" "Identify any particular people that seem to bring on this concern." "Are you usually with certain people right before or when this issue starts?" "Are there any people or relationships from the past that trigger this issue in some way? Who? How?" "How do the people who hold power in your life trigger this issue?"	____ (other people)
___ ___	6.0. Identify consequences of conditions that maintain and strengthen issue or weaken or diminish it		____ (check if client identified following sources of consequences)
___ ___	6.1. *Affective* consequences	"How do you feel after this happens?" "When did you stop feeling this way?" "Are you aware of any particular feelings or reactions you have after the issue that strengthen it? Weaken it?"	____ (feelings, mood states)
___ ___	6.2. *Somatic* consequences	"What are you aware of inside you—sensations in your body—just after this happens?" "How does this affect the issue?" "Are there any sensations inside you that seem to occur after the issue that strengthen or weaken it?" "Is there any physical condition, illness, and so on about yourself that seems to occur after the issue? If so, how does it affect the issue?"	____ (body or internal sensations)
___ ___	6.3. *Behavioral* consequences	"What do you do after this happens, and how does this make the issue better? Worse?" "How do you usually react after this is over?" "In what ways does your reaction keep the issue going? Weaken it or stop it?" "Identify any particular behavior patterns that occur after this." "How do these patterns keep the problem going? Stop it?"	____ (overt responses)
___ ___	6.4. *Cognitive* consequences	"What do you usually think about afterward?" "How does this affect the issue?" "What do you picture after this happens?" "What do you tell yourself after this occurs?" "Identify any particular thoughts [beliefs, self-talk] that make the issue better. Worse?" "Are there certain thoughts or images you have afterward that either strengthen or weaken the issue?"	____ (thoughts, beliefs, internal dialogue)
___ ___	6.5. *Contextual* consequences	"When does this issue usually stop or go away? Get worse? Get better?" "Where are you when the issue stops? Get worse? Get better?"	____ (time, places, other events)

(continued)

8   KNOWLEDGE AND SKILL BUILDER

(continued)

_____ _____		"Identify any particular times, places, or events that seem to keep the issue going. Make it worse or better?"	
		"Are there any ways in which your cultural affiliation and values seem to keep this issue going? Stop it or weaken it?"	
_____ _____	6.6. _Relational_ consequences	"Can you identify any particular reactions from other people that occur following the issue?"	_____ (other people)
		"In what ways do their reactions affect the issue?"	
		"Identify any particular people who can make the issue worse. Better? Stop it? Keep it going?"	
		"How do the people who have power in your life situation perpetuate this concern?"	
_____ _____	7. Identify possible secondary gains	"Has your concern ever produced any special advantages or considerations for you?"	_____ (check if client identified gains from issue)
		"As a consequence of your concern, have you got out of or avoided things or events?"	
		"What do you get out of this situation that you don't get out of other situations?"	
		"Do you notice anything that happens afterward that you try to prolong or to produce?"	
		"Do you notice anything that occurs after the problem that you try to stop or avoid?"	
		"Are there certain feelings or thoughts that go on after the issue that you try to prolong?"	
		"Are there certain feelings or thoughts that go on after the issue that you try to stop or avoid?"	
		"The good thing about _____ [issue] is . . ."	
_____ _____	8. Identify solutions already tried to solve the issue	"How have you dealt with this or other issues before? What was the effect? What made it work or not work?"	_____ (check if client identified prior solutions)
		"How have you tried to resolve this concern?"	
		"What kinds of things have you done to improve this situation?"	
		"What have you done that has made the issue better? Worse? Kept it the same?"	
		"What have others done to help you with this?"	
_____ _____	9. Identify client coping skills, strengths, resources	"What skills or things do you have going for you that might help you with this concern?"	_____ (check if client identified assets, coping skills)
		"Describe a situation when this concern is not interfering."	
		"What strengths or assets can you use to help resolve this?"	
		"When don't you act this way?"	
		"What kinds of thoughts or self-talk help you handle this better?"	
		"When don't you think in self-defeating ways?"	
		"What do you say to yourself to cope with a difficult situation?"	
		"Identify the steps you take in a situation you handle well—what do you think about and what do you do? How could these steps be applied to the present issue?"	
		"What resources are available to you from your community and your environment?"	

8   K N O W L E D G E   A N D   S K I L L   B U I L D E R

		"What kinds of things in your community and environment do you consider to be strengths and assets?"
		"What sorts of positive, purposeful relationships do you have now that help you with this issue?"
		"What do you find meaning in from particular aspects of your culture?"
____ ____	10. Identify client's description/assessment of the issue (note which aspects of issue are stressed and which are ignored)	"What is your understanding of this issue?" "How do you explain this concern to yourself?" "Tell me about what the issue means to you." "What is your interpretation [analysis] of the concern?" "Sum up the issue in just one word." "Give the concern a title."
____ ____	11. Estimate frequency, duration, or severity of behavior/symptoms (assign self-monitoring homework, if useful)	"How often [how much] does this occur during a day? A week?" "How long does this feeling stay with you?" "How many times do you _____ a day? A week?" "To what extent has this interfered with your life? How?" "You say sometimes you feel very anxious. On a scale from 1 to 10, with 1 being very calm and 10 being very anxious, where would you put your feelings?" "What would happen if the issue were not resolved in a year?"

_____ (check if client explained issue)

_____ (check if client estimated amount and/or severity)

Yes   No   **Other skills**

____ ____   12. The helper listened attentively and recalled accurately the information given by the client.

____ ____   13. The helper used basic listening responses to clarify and synthesize the information shared by the client.

____ ____   14. The helper followed the client's lead in determining the sequence or order of the information obtained.

Observer comments: _____

_____

_____

_____

_____

Part One

See whether the interview leads that you generated are similar to the following ones:

"Is this the only issue you're concerned about now in your life, or are there other issues you haven't mentioned yet?" (Range of concerns)

"When you say you feel anxious, what exactly do you mean?" (Behavior—affective component)

"When you feel anxious, what do you experience inside your body?" (Behavior—somatic component)

"When you feel anxious, what exactly are you usually doing?" (Behavior—behavioral component)

"When you feel anxious, what are you typically thinking about [or saying to yourself]?" (Behavior—cognitive component)

"Try to pinpoint exactly what times the anxiety occurs or when it is worse." (Behavior—contextual component)

"Describe where you are or in what situations you find yourself when you get anxious." (Behavior—contextual component)

"Describe what other things are usually going on when you have these feelings." (Behavior—contextual component)

"How would you describe the relationship between yourself and these concerns and your current environment?" (Behavior—contextual component)

"How do your cultural community and affiliation affect this issue?" (Behavior—contextual component)

"Can you tell me what persons are usually around when you feel this way?" (Behavior—relational component)

"How would you describe your support in your life right now?" (Behavior—relational component)

"Who in your life now empowers you? Disempowers you?" (Behavior—relational component)

"Are there any feelings that lead up to this?" (Antecedent—affective)

"What about body sensations that might occur right before these feelings?" (Antecedent—somatic)

"Have you noticed any particular behavioral reactions or patterns that seem to occur right before these feelings?" (Antecedent—behavioral)

"Are there any kinds of thoughts—things you're dwelling on—that seem to lead up to these feelings?" (Antecedent—cognitive)

"When was the first time you noticed these feelings? Where were you?" (Antecedent—contextual)

"Can you recall any other events or times that seem to be related to these feelings?" (Antecedent—contextual)

"Does the presence of any particular people in any way set these feelings off?" (Antecedent—relational)

"Are you aware of any particular other feelings that make the anxiety better or worse?" (Consequence—affective)

"Are you aware of any body sensations or physiological responses that make these feelings better or worse?" (Consequence—somatic)

"Is there anything you can do specifically to make these feelings stronger or weaker?" (Consequence—behavioral)

"Can you identify anything you can think about or focus on that seems to make these feelings better or worse?" (Consequence—cognitive)

"At what times do these feelings diminish or go away? Get worse? In what places? In what situations?" (Consequence—contextual)

"Do certain people you know seem to react in ways that keep these feelings going or make them less intense? If so, how?" (Consequence—relational)

"As a result of this anxiety, have you ever gotten out of or avoided things you dislike?" (Consequence—secondary gain)

"Has this problem with your nerves ever resulted in any special advantages or considerations for you?" (Consequence—secondary gain)

"What have you tried to do to resolve this issue? How have your attempted solutions worked out?" (Previous solutions)

"Describe some times and situations when you don't have these feelings or you feel calm and relaxed. What goes on that is different in these instances?" (Coping skills)

"How have you typically coped with other difficult situations or feelings in your life before?" (Coping skills)

"What resources are available to you from your culture and community that you can use to help with this problem?" (Individual and environmental strengths—coping)

"What kinds of things in your community and environment do you feel are strengths and assets?" (Individual and environmental strengths—coping)

"If you could give this problem a title—as if it were a movie or a book—what would that title be?" (Client perceptions of issue)

"How do you explain these feelings to yourself?" (Client perceptions of issue)

"How many times do these feelings crop up during a given day?" (Frequency of issue)

"How long do these feelings stay with you?" (Duration of issue)

"On a scale from 1 to 10, with 1 being not intense and 10 being very intense, how strong would you say these feelings usually are?" (Severity of issue)

9

IDENTIFYING, DEFINING, AND EVALUATING OUTCOME GOALS

LEARNING OUTCOMES

After completing this chapter, you will be able to

1. Identify a situation about you or your life that you would like to change. Identify, define, and evaluate one desired outcome for this issue, using the Goal-Setting Worksheet in the Knowledge and Skill Builder as a guide.
2. Given a written client case description, describe the steps you would use with this client to explore and define desired outcome goals, with at least 10 of the 13 categories for identifying, defining, and evaluating goals represented in your description.
3. Demonstrate at least 10 of the 13 categories associated with identifying, defining, and evaluating outcome goals, given a role-play interview.
4. With yourself or another person or client, conduct an outcome evaluation of a real or a hypothetical counseling goal, specifying *when, what,* and *how* you would measure the outcome.

Pause for a few minutes to answer the following questions by yourself or with someone else:

1. What is one thing you would like to change about yourself?
2. Suppose you succeeded in accomplishing this change. How would things be different for you?
3. Would this outcome represent a change in yourself or for someone else?
4. What would be some of the risks—to you or others—of this change?
5. What would be your payoffs for making this change?
6. What would you be doing, thinking, or feeling as a result of this change?
7. In what situations would you want to be able to do this?
8. How much or how often would you like to be able to do this?

9. Looking at where you are now and where you'd like to be, are there some steps along the way to get from here to there? If so, rank them in an ordered list ranging from "easiest to do now" to "hardest to do."
10. Identify any obstacles (people, feelings, ideas, situations) that might interfere with the attainment of your goal.
11. Identify any resources (skills, people, knowledge) that you would need to use or acquire to attain your goal.
12. How could you evaluate progress toward this outcome?

These questions reflect the process of identifying, defining, and evaluating goals for counseling. Goals represent desired results or outcomes and function as milestones of client progress. In this chapter we describe and model concrete guidelines you can use to help clients identify, define, and evaluate outcome goals for counseling.

OUTCOME GOALS AND THEIR PURPOSES IN THE HELPING PROCESS

Treatment goals represent results or outcomes described by clients and are a direct outgrowth of the problems identified during the assessment process. Goals have six important purposes:

First, goals provide some directions for helping. Clearly defined goals reflect the areas of client concern that need most immediate attention. Establishing goals can also clarify the client's initial expectations. Goals may help both practitioner and client anticipate more precisely what can and cannot be accomplished through the helping process.

Although each theoretical orientation has its own direction, specifying goals individually for each client helps to ensure that helping is structured specifically to meet the needs of *that* person. Clients are much more likely to support and commit themselves to changes that they create than they are to implement changes imposed by someone else. Without goals, the helping process may be directionless or may be based more on the theoretical biases and personal preferences of the helper. Some clients may go through counseling without realizing that the sessions are devoid of direction or are more consistent with the helper's preferences than with their own needs and aims. In other aspects of our lives, however, most of us would be quite aware of analogous situations. If we boarded a cruise ship destined for a place of our choice and the ship sailed around in circles or the pilots announced a change of destination that they desired, we would be upset and indignant.

Second, goals permit helpers to determine whether they have the skills, competencies, and interests for working with a particular client toward a particular outcome. Given the client's choice of goals and the helper's own values and level of expertise, the helper decides whether to continue working with the client or to refer the client to someone else who may be in a better position to give services.

The third purpose of goals pertains to their role in human cognition and problem solving. Goals help with successful performance and problem resolution because they are usually rehearsed in our working memory and because they direct our attention to the resources and components in our environment that are most likely to help with the solution of a problem. This purpose of goals is quite evident in the performance of successful athletes, who set goals for themselves and then use the goals not only as motivating devices but also as standards against which they rehearse their performance over and over, often cognitively or with imagery. For example, running backs in football constantly "see themselves" getting the ball and running downfield, over and past the goal line. Champion snow skiers are often seen closing their eyes and bobbing their heads in the direction of the course before the race. In the case of helping goals, it is important for clients to be able to visualize and rehearse the target behaviors or end results reflected in their goals.

The fourth purpose of goals is to give the helper some basis for selecting and using particular change strategies and interventions. The changes that the client desires will, to some degree, determine the kinds of action plans and treatment strategies that can be used with some likelihood of success. Without an explicit identification of what the client wants, it is almost impossible to explain and defend one's choice to move in a certain direction or to use one or more change strategies. Without goals, the helper may use a particular approach without any rational basis. Whether the approach will be helpful is left to chance rather than choice.

The fifth and most important purpose of goals has to do with their role in an outcome evaluation. Goals can indicate the difference between what and how much the client is able to do now and what and how much the client would like to do in the future. Keeping the ultimate goal in mind, the helper and client can monitor progress toward the goal and measure the effectiveness of a change intervention. These data provide continuous feedback to both helper and client. The feedback can be used to assess the feasibility of the goal and the effectiveness of the intervention. This feedback illustrates the interrelatedness of the processes of selecting, defining, and evaluating outcome goals.

Finally, goal-planning systems are useful because, like assessment procedures, they are often reactive; clients make progress in change as a result of the goal-planning process itself. Goals induce an expectation for improvement, and purposeful goal setting contributes to a client's sense of hopefulness and well-being. Hope is a major component of a strengths-based helping perspective (Snyder & Lopez, 2007).

CULTURAL ISSUES IN OUTCOME GOALS

Sue and Sue (2003) point out that different cultural groups may require different counseling processes and goals. These authors assert that effectiveness in the helping process is enhanced when helpers define goals "that are consistent with the life experiences and cultural values of the client" (Sue & Sue, 2003, p. 20). They note that the disagreement over potential counseling outcomes increases when the practitioner and client are from different cultures (Sue & Sue, 2003).

Brown (1994) has offered a similar caveat with respect to gender-aware therapy for clients. She suggests that the particular way the helper conceptualizes the case will affect the client's choice of goals. A feminist and a systemic interpretation—which places emphasis on the contribution of external sociopolitical factors—allows clients to have different choices about helping outcomes: "Rather than compliantly taking on tasks assigned by the dominant culture—for example, 'Stop being depressed, become more productive'—a person furnished with this sort of knowledge may develop alternative goals for therapy such as 'Learn to get angry more often and see my connections to other people more clearly'" (Brown, 1994, p. 170). Werner-Wilson, Zimmerman, and Price (1999) discuss another way in which gender may affect selection of treatment goals. They note that in heterosexual-couples therapy, male and female clients may identify different problems and different desired outcomes. Influenced by gender socialization, helpers may not pursue the goals of women clients if they do not recognize the tendency of many women to accommodate (p. 254).

In using cultural awareness to develop goals, the important point for helpers is to be aware of their own values and biases and to avoid deliberately or inadvertently steering the client toward goals that may reflect their own cultural norms rather than the client's expressed wishes. A clear-cut example of this is in respecting a client's preferred sexual orientation when it is different from your own. It is also important to be attentive "to any possible conflicts between the client's own goals and the goals of others" in the client's immediate context, such as school, work, and family (Shiang, 2000, p. 176). For example, a son may define what it means to be a good son in a different way than his parents or his collective cultural group or his religious group.

CHANGE ISSUES IN OUTCOME GOALS

At the simplest level, an outcome goal represents what the client wants to happen as a result of the treatment process. Stated another way, outcome goals are an extension of the types of problems that the client experiences. The desired goals may reflect changes within the individual client, within the client's environment, or within both. The desired changes may be in overt behaviors or situations, in covert behaviors, or in combinations of the two. These outcome goals may be directed at decreasing something, increasing something, developing something, or restructuring something.

Prochaska, DiClemente, and Norcross (1992) have developed a *transtheoretical model of client change*. Their model suggests that a client experiences five stages of change in moving toward a particular outcome:

1. *Precontemplation:* The client is unaware of a need for change or does not intend to change.
2. *Contemplation:* The client is aware of a need for change and thinks seriously about it but has not decided to make it.
3. *Preparation:* The client has decided to take some action in the near future and also has taken some action in the recent past that was not successful.
4. *Action:* The client has begun to engage in successful action steps toward the desired outcome but has not yet attained the outcome.

5. *Maintenance:* The client reaches his or her goals and now works both to prevent backslides and to consolidate changes made in the action phase.

A concrete example of this stage model of change is a person who exhibits verbally abusive behavior toward her or his colleagues. In the *precontemplation* phase, the client either doesn't recognize a need to change her or his abusive behavior or doesn't care about the negative effects of the behavior. This person is content with things the way they are. As the client becomes aware of some of the effects of abusive behavior and starts to think about changing, he or she moves into the *contemplation* phase.

Next, the client attempts some change or problem-solution program but is unsuccessful—yet still plans to take additional action in the near future. This is the *preparation* stage. As the client finds successful ways of modifying his or her abusive behavior and commits to them, the *action* phase is initiated. Finally, the client engages in behaviors to maintain the changes and to prevent recurrence of the abuse; this is the *maintenance* phase.

In recent years, clinical research has provided much empirical support for this model (Prochaska, 2000). The five stages have been found to relate to client self-managed change, treatment intervention, treatment outcome effectiveness, and persistence in therapy. In areas such as weight loss and substance abuse, smoking, hypertension management, and HIV/AIDS, clients who are in or who use these stages have more positive treatment outcomes than those who do not (Prochaska, 2000).

For several reasons, this model has important implications for both goal setting and treatment selection (see Table 9.1). First, as practitioners, we need to have an understanding of

TABLE 9.1	Stages of Change and Corresponding Interventions	
Stage of change	**Interventions**	**Role of helper**
Precontemplation	Be optimistic. Provide rationale for interventions and change. Convey respect and use active listening skills. Increase the pros of change.	Nurturing parent
Contemplation	Educate client about change process. Decrease the disadvantages or costs of change. Support client's ambivalence about change.	Socratic teacher
Preparation	Define, work toward, and evaluate selected outcomes. Present all alternatives. Encourage brief experiments with change.	Experienced coach
Action	Develop cognitions and skills to prevent relapse/ setbacks prior to termination. Review action plan.	Consultant
Maintenance	Provide emotional support	Consultant

what it means to change if we are to effect change in clients. Also, a client's readiness to change is a critical factor in developing outcome goals and selecting intervention strategies. Clients in stage 1, *precontemplation,* come to counseling at someone else's request or under some sort of pressure. Clients in this stage can be difficult to engage, but acknowledging the client's resistance, building a relationship, and increasing the client's awareness of the consequences of his or her behavior may be useful strategies for clients in precontemplation. Clients in stage 2, *contemplation,* may acknowledge the existence of a concern but may not see themselves as part of the solution, at least initially. It is important to recognize the vacillation of these clients, and to remember that ambivalence about change is common. All of us experience what Jungians refer to as "tension of the opposites"—the need to hold on to what is familiar while testing out what is new. Validating the client's ambivalence yet at the same time helping the client increase her or his awareness about the potential benefits of change are helpful tasks for clients in contemplation.

Clients in the stages of *preparation* and *action* acknowledge that there is a problem, see themselves as part of the solution, and are committed to working toward specific outcomes (see Table 9.1). In general, as Smith, Subich, and Kalodner (1995) observe, "Persons further along in the stages seem more likely to progress and benefit from therapy" (p. 35). Clients in the preparation stage intend to take some action soon. They may have already tried something, and they may have a plan (Prochaska, 1999). The helper's task is to help these clients define their goals in specific ways so that progress toward outcomes can be determined. Outcome evaluation is important not only to let clients see their actual progress but also to substantiate the effectiveness of the helping process. Increasingly, mental health providers working in agencies or receiving reimbursement from managed care companies are required to conduct outcome evaluations of the helping process.

Clients in stage 5, *maintenance,* often face difficulties in maintaining changes acquired in the prior stages. It is often easier to prepare and act than to maintain. As clients reach this stage and before they terminate counseling, it is important to work on beliefs and actions to equip them to maintain changes as well as to prevent setbacks and relapses. Maintenance goals and skills are especially important in such areas as substance abuse, mood disorders such as depression, and chronic mental health problems such as schizophrenia. Prochaska (2000, p. 121) regards the role of helper with clients in the action and maintenance stages as that of a "consultant."

An approach that seems particularly useful in working with clients at this last stage of the change model is Marlatt and Gordon's (1985) *relapse prevention model.* This model, which has been used frequently for relapse prevention in addictive behaviors (DeJong, 1994; MacKay & Marlatt, 1990), focuses on helping clients to (1) identify high-risk situations for relapse, (2) acquire behavioral and cognitive coping skills, and (3) attend to issues of balance in lifestyle. A meta-analysis on the relapse prevention model supported the overall effectiveness of relapse prevention in both reducing substance use—especially alcohol—and in improving psychological adjustment. These outcomes were consistent for both inpatient and outpatient settings and for individual, group, and couples treatment modalities (Irvin, Bowers, Dunn, & Wang, 1999).

Table 9.1 summarizes the Prochaska et al. (1992) model and processes described in this section (see also Learning Activity 9.1). It is important for therapists to recognize the stage of change that each client is in, for the kinds of intervention that are required depend on the client's particular stage. Practitioners who are familiar with this model of change can actively use it in the helping process by first identifying the stage a client is in and then applying the appropriate interventions to move the client to the next stage. Prochaska (1999) recommends that helpers set realistic goals for working with clients at each stage. Their main goal should be to try to help a client move to the *next* stage. Helpers, he notes, are increasingly under pressure to produce immediate results; but if this pressure gets transferred to clients, many will get discouraged, become "resistant," and drop out of the helping process altogether (p. 227).

IDENTIFYING OUTCOME GOALS

As practitioners, we need to initiate conversations with clients about the changes they want to make as a result of participating in the helping process with us. In this section we discuss five categories of interview leads for identifying goals. These leads are important parts of the discussion between helper and client about what the client hopes to achieve as a result of counseling. The five categories of leads are associated with identifying client goals. They are leads to

1. Provide a rationale for goal setting
2. Elicit outcome statements
3. State goals in positive terms
4. Determine who owns the goal
5. Weigh advantages and disadvantages of goal attainment

The identification of goals and the associated interview leads are especially useful for clients at the precontemplation and contemplation stages of the Prochaska and associates (1992) change model.

Leads to Provide a Rationale for Goal Setting

The first step in identifying goals is to give the client a *rationale* for setting goals. This statement should describe goals, the purpose for having them, and the client's participation

| LEARNING ACTIVITY | **9.1** | **Stages of Change** |

Match the five client descriptions with the corresponding stage of change. Feedback follows on page 234.

Client Descriptions

1. The client wants to do something soon and may have already tried one plan of action.
2. The client doesn't want to change because of what he would have to give up.
3. The client feels ambivalent about changing in the near future.
4. The client has developed a plan of action.
5. The client has been successful in avoiding drugs over a long period of time.

Stages of Change

a. Precontemplation
b. Contemplation
c. Preparation
d. Action
e. Maintenance

---

in the goal-setting process. The helper's intent is to convey the importance of goals as well as the importance of the client's participation in developing them.

Here is an example of what the helper might say about the purpose of goals: "We've been talking about these two areas that bother you. It might be helpful now to discuss how you would like things to be different. We can develop some goals to work toward during our sessions. These goals will tell us what you want as a result of counseling. So today, let's talk about some things *you* would like to work on." After providing this information, the helper will look for a client response that indicates understanding. If the client seems confused, the helper will need to explain further the purposes of goals and their benefits to the client, or the helper will need to clarify and explore the sources of the client's confusion. This clarification is especially important for clients in the early stages of the Prochaska and associates (1992) model.

Leads to Elicit Outcome Statements

Interview leads are used to help clients identify outcomes that they hope to achieve through counseling. These sorts of leads are useful in helping clients contemplate changes in their life and behavior.

Here are examples of leads that can help clients define goals and express them in outcome statements:

"Suppose some distant relative you haven't seen for a while sees you after counseling. What would be different then from the way things are now?"

"Assuming we are successful, what would you be doing or how would these situations change?"

"What do you expect to accomplish as a result of counseling?"

"Describe how you think counseling can benefit you."

The helper's purpose in using these sorts of leads is to have the client identify some desired outcomes. The helper is looking for some verbal indication of the results the client expects. If the client cannot think of any desired changes or cannot specify a purpose for engaging in therapy, the helper should spend some time in exploring this area with the client. The helper can assist the client in identifying goals in several ways: by assigning homework ("Make a list of what you can do now and what you want to do one year from now"), by using imagery ("Imagine being someone you admire. Who would you be? What would you be doing? How would you be different?"), by additional questioning ("If you could wave a magic wand and have three wishes, what would they be?"), and by self-report questionnaires or inventories.

Leads to State Goals in Positive Terms

An effective outcome goal is stated in positive terms—as what the client wants to do. A positive direction is important because of the role that goal setting plays in human cognition and performance. When a goal is stated positively, clients are more likely to encode and rehearse the things they want to be able to do rather than the things they want to avoid or stop doing. For example, it is fairly easy to generate an image of yourself sitting down and watching TV; however, picturing yourself *not* watching TV is difficult. Instead of forming an image of not watching TV, you are likely to form images (or sounds) related to performing other activities instead, such as reading a book, talking to someone, or being in the TV room and doing something else.

The practitioner will have to help clients "turn around" their initial goal statements, which usually are expressed as something the person doesn't want to do, can't do, or wants to stop doing. Stating goals positively represents a self-affirming position and can be a helpful intervention for clients at the precontemplation and contemplation stages

9.1	**F E E D B A C K** **Stages of Change**
	1. c 2. a 3. b 4. d 5. e

of the change model. If the client responds to the helper's initial leads with a negative answer, the helper can help turn this around by saying something like "That is what you *don't* want to do. Describe what you *do* want to do [think, feel]" or "What will you do instead, and can you see [hear, feel] yourself doing it every time?" or "What do you want things in your life to look like five years from now?"

Leads to Determine Who Owns the Goal

Many clients at the precontemplation stage express goals calling for someone else to change rather than themselves. For example, a teenager says, "I want my mom to stop yelling at me"; a teacher says, "I want this kid to shut up so I can get some teaching done"; a husband says, "I want my wife to quit nagging." The tendency to project the desired change onto someone else is particularly evident when problems involve relationships with two or more persons.

Without discounting the client's feelings, the practitioner needs to help get this tendency turned around. The client is the identified person seeking help and services and is the only person who can make a change. When two or more clients are involved simultaneously in counseling, such as a couple or a family, all identified clients need to contribute to the desired change, not just one party or one "identified patient."

Who owns the change is usually directly related to the degree of *control* or *responsibility* that the client has in the situation and surrounding the change. Suppose you are working with an 8-year-old girl whose parents are getting a divorce. The child says she wants you to help her persuade her parents to stay married. This goal would be very difficult for the child to attain, because she has no responsibility for her parents' relationship.

The practitioner will need to use leads to help clients determine whether they or someone else owns the change and whether anyone else needs to be involved in the goal selection process. If the client steers toward a goal that requires a change by someone else, the practitioner will need to point this out and help the client identify his or her role in the change process.

To help the client explore who owns the change, the helper can use leads similar to these:

"How much control do you have over making this happen?"

"What changes will this goal require of you?"

"What changes will this goal require someone else to make?"

"Can this goal be achieved without the help of anyone else?"

"To whom is this goal most important?"

"Who, specifically, is responsible for making this happen?"

The intent of these leads is to have the client identify a goal that represents change for the client, not for others (unless others are directly affected). If the client persists in selecting a goal that represents change for others rather than for the client, the helper and client will have to decide whether to pursue this goal, to negotiate a reconsidered goal, or to refer the client to another helper.

Leads to Weigh Advantages and Disadvantages of Goal Attainment

It is important to explore the cost/benefit effect of all identified goals—that is, the cost of what is being given up versus the benefit what is being gained from goal attainment. We think of this step as the exploration of *advantages,* or positive effects, and *disadvantages,* or negative effects, of goal attainment. Exploration of advantages and disadvantages helps clients assess the feasibility of the goal and anticipate the consequences; then they can decide whether the change is worth the cost to themselves or to significant others.

Oz (1995) points out that most clients have considered what is attractive about given alternatives and in fact may be "stuck" either because they want to preserve the benefits without incurring any costs or because the choice exposes a values conflict, often between self-denial and costs to a relationship or to self-image (Oz, 1995, p. 81). In identifying goals, the client needs to be aware of possible risks and costs and whether he or she is prepared to take such risks if, in fact, they do occur.

Oz (1995) notes that although the cost factor most often affects a client's eventual choice, it is the factor that the client most often ignores, and inadequate information about costs may lead to postdecisional regret (p. 79). Frequently, the cost factor also fuels client resistance to change, (see Table 9.1).

Generally, the goals that clients select should lead to benefits, not losses. In general, the benefits of change need to outweigh the costs by at least two times in order for the client to move to the preparation and action stages. The advantages and disadvantages associated with goal attainment may be short-term and long-term. The practitioner helps the client identify advantages and disadvantages and then offers options to expand the client's range of possibilities. Sometimes

Desired Changes	Immediate Advantages	Long-Term Advantages	Immediate Disadvantages	Long-Term Disadvantages
1.				
2.				
3.				

Figure 9.1 Form for Recording Advantages and Disadvantages of Identified Goals

it is helpful to create a written list of goals, advantages, and disadvantages that can be expanded or modified at any time (see Figure 9.1).

Leads for Advantages

Most clients can readily predict some positive outcomes from their desired changes. Nevertheless, it is still a good idea for the helper to explore with all clients the positive consequences of the change, for at least four reasons: (1) to determine whether the advantages that the client perceives are indicative of actual likely benefits, (2) to point out other possible advantages for the client or for other persons that have been overlooked, (3) to strengthen the client's incentive to change, and (4) to determine to what degree the identified goal is feasible given the client's overall functioning.

Here are examples of leads that can be used to explore the advantages of client change:

"In what ways is it worthwhile for you to pursue a change?"

"Tell me what you see as the benefits of this change."

"Who would benefit from this change, and how?"

"Describe some positive consequences that may result from this change."

"How would attaining this goal help you?"

"Identify ways in which your life would improve by achieving this goal."

"What good things might result from pursuing this goal or making this change in your life now?"

In using these leads, the helper is looking for some indication that the client is pursuing a goal because of the positive consequences the goal may produce. If the client overlooks some advantages, the helper can describe them to bolster the client's incentive to change.

The inability of a client to identify any benefits of change for himself or herself may be viewed as a signal for caution. It may indicate that the client is attempting to change at someone else's request or that the identified goal is not feasible given the total picture. Suppose a client wants to find a new job while she is also fighting off a life-threatening illness. The desire to secure the new job at this time may be at odds with her desire to regain her health.

Further exploration may indicate that other goals would be more feasible.

Leads for Disadvantages

The helper can use leads to encourage the client to consider risks or side effects that might accompany the desired change or might be the result of giving up the current behavior. Here are some examples of leads that the helper might use to explore the risks or disadvantages of change:

"How could this change make life difficult for you?"

"Will pursuing this change affect your life in any adverse ways?"

"What might be some possible risks of doing this?"

"Identify some possible disadvantages of going in this direction. How willing are you to pay this price?"

"Who might disapprove of this action? How will that disapproval affect you?"

"Describe how this change may limit or constrain you."

"Identify any new problems in living that pursuing this goal could create for you."

The helper is looking for some indication that the client has considered the possible costs associated with the goal. If the client discounts the risks or cannot identify any, the helper can use immediacy or summarization to point out some disadvantages.

Remember to be careful not to coerce or try to persuade the client to pursue another alternative simply because you believe it would be better. Also remember to avoid labels such as "negative" when exploring disadvantages of change.

THE DECISION POINT: CAN YOU HELP THIS CLIENT WITH THIS GOAL?

Most people agree that one of the biggest ethical and, to some extent, legal questions the practitioner faces during the helping process is whether she or he can help a client. The helper and client will need to choose whether to continue with counseling and pursue the selected goals, to continue with counseling but reevaluate the client's initial goals, or to agree that client should seek the services of

LEARNING ACTIVITY 9.2 | Decision Point

 For practice in thinking through the kinds of decisions you may face in the goal-setting process, try this activity. The exercise consists of three hypothetical situations. In each case, assume that you are the helper. Read through the case. Then sit back, close your eyes, and try to imagine being in the room with this client and being faced with this dilemma. How would you feel? what would you say? What would you decide to do? Why? Apply these critical thinking questions to support your decision: What problem are you trying to solve? What perspective are you taking? What assumptions are you making, and what information are you using to arrive at your decision?

There are no right or wrong answers to these questions. You may wish to discuss your responses with classmate, a coworker, or your instructor.

Case 1

You are working with a family with two teenage daughters. The parents and the younger daughter seem closely aligned; the elder daughter is on the periphery of the family. The parents and the younger daughter report that the older daughter's recent behavior is upsetting and embarrassing to them because she recently "came out of the closet" to disclose that she is a lesbian. She has begun to hang out with a few other lesbian young women in the local high school. The parents and younger daughter indicate that they think she is just going through a "phase." They state that they want you to help them get this girl "back in line" with the rest of the family and get her to adopt their values and socially acceptable behavior. Based on the critical thinking questions described above, what do you decide to do, and what are the implications of your decision?

Case 2

You are counseling a fourth-grader. You are the only counselor in this school. One day you notice that this boy seems to be bruised all over. You ask him about this. After much hesitation, the child blurts out that he is often singled out on his way home by two big sixth-grade bullies who pick a fight, beat him up for a while, and then leave him alone until another time. Your client asks you to forget this information. He begs you not to say or do anything for fear of reprisal from these two bullies. He states that he doesn't want to deal with this in counseling and has come to see you about something else. Based on the critical thinking questions described above, what do you decide to do, and what are the implications of your decision?

Case 3

You are working with an elderly man whose relatives are dead. After his wife died six months ago, he moved from their family home to a retirement home. Although the client is relatively young (70) and is in good health and alert, the staff has requested your help because he seems to have become increasingly morbid and discouraged. In talking with you, he indicates that he has sort of given up on everything, including himself, because he doesn't feel he has anything to live for. Consequently, he has stopped going to activities, he isolates himself in his room, and he has even stopped engaging in personal hygiene and grooming, leaving such matters up to the staff. He indicates that he doesn't care to talk with you if these are the kinds of things you want to talk about. Based on the critical thinking questions described above, what do you decide to do, and what are the implications of your decision?

---

another practitioner. These particular decisions are always made on an individual basis and are based on two factors: the helper's *willingness* and *competence* to help the client pursue the selected goals. Willingness involves your interest in working with the client toward identified goals and issues given the overall functioning of the client. Competence involves your skills and knowledge and whether you are familiar with alternative intervention strategies and multiple ways to handle particular concerns (see also Learning Activity 9.2). Referral of a client to some other qualified practitioner may be appropriate in any of the following situations: if you are unable to be objective about the client's concern, if you are unfamiliar with or unable to use a treatment requested by the client, if you would be exceeding your level of competence in working with the client, or if two persons are involved and, because of your emotions or biases, you favor one person over the other.

Assessment of client issues and identification of client goals sometimes reveals that the client needs services or resources that not only are beyond your own competence but are unavailable in the setting in which you work. In these situations, referral involves linking clients to other resource systems, a process referred to as *brokering* (Kirst-Ashman & Hull, 2006). All of the professional codes of ethics discuss reasons for client referral. But providing referral choices is not only an ethical issue; the availability of referral choices may help otherwise reluctant clients to accept therapy.

Helpers have certain responsibilities to clients during the referral process. It is important to explore a client's readiness for a referral and to recognize that the client may already feel attached to you and be reluctant to pursue or accept a referral. Once the client accepts the referral, it is important to be optimistic about the benefits of the referral but not to make unrealistic claims about the referral source (Hepworth, Rooney, Dewberry Rooney, Strom-Gottfried, & Larsen, 2006). It is important to discuss any client anxieties about the new referral source and to provide the client with sufficient information about the referral source. This process will be eased if you ascertained the availability of the new referral sources you are recommending to the client. However, remember under the U.S. privacy act known as HIPAA (Health Insurance Portability and Accountability Act), you cannot disclose information about a client or the client's identity without prior written authorization from the client to do so. After the client accepts the referral, it is wise to follow up with the client to determine if the client actually followed through with the referral.

MODEL DIALOGUE: THE CASE OF ISABELLA

To help you see how leads for identifying goals are used with a client, the case of Isabella is continued here as a dialogue in an interviewing session directed toward goal selection. Helper responses are prefaced by an explanation.

In response 1, the helper starts out with a *review* of the last session.

1. **Helper:** Isabella, last week we talked about some of the things that are going on with you right now that you're concerned about. What do you remember that we talked about?

Client: Well, we talked a lot about my problems in school— like my trouble in my math class. Also about the fact that I can't decide whether or not to switch over to a vocational curriculum—and if I did, my parents would be upset.

2. **Helper:** Yes, that's a good summary. We did talk about a lot of things—such as the pressure and anxiety you feel in competitive situations like your math class and your difficulty in making decisions. I believe we also mentioned that you tend to go out of your way to please others, like your parents, or to avoid making a decision they might not like.

Client: Mm-hmm. I tend to not want to create a hassle. I also just have never made many decisions by myself.

In response 3, the helper moves from problem definition to goal selection. Response 3 consists of an *explanation* about goals and their *purpose*.

3. **Helper:** Yes, I remember you said that last week. I've been thinking that since we've kind of got a handle on the main issues you're concerned about, today it might be helpful to talk about things you might want to happen— or how you'd like things to be different. This way, we know exactly what we can be talking about and working on that will be most helpful to you. How does that sound?

Client: That's okay with me. I mean, do you really think there are some things I can do about these problems?

The client has indicated some uncertainty about possible change. The helper will pursue this in response 4 and indicate more about the *purpose* of goals and possible effects of counseling for Isabella.

4. **Helper:** You seem a little uncertain about how much things can be different. To the extent that you have some control over a situation, it is possible to make some changes. Depending on what kind of changes you want to make, there are some ways we can work together on this. It will take some work on your part too. How do you feel about this?

Client: Okay. I'd like to get out of the rut I'm in.

In response 5, the helper explores the ways in which the client would like to change. The helper uses a lead to *identify client goals.*

5. **Helper:** So you're saying that you don't want to continue to feel stuck. Exactly how would you like things to be different—say, in three months from now—from the way things are now?

Client: I'd like to feel less pressured in school, especially in my math class.

The client has identified one possible goal, although it is stated in negative terms. In response 6, the helper helps the client identify the goal in *positive terms.*

6. **Helper:** Okay, that's something you *don't* want to do. Can you think of another way to say it that would describe what you *do* want to do?

Client: I guess I'd like to feel confident about my ability to handle tough situations like math class.

In the next response, the helper *paraphrases* Isabella's goal and checks it out to see whether she restated it accurately.

7. **Helper:** So you're saying you'd like to feel more positively about yourself in different situations—is that it?

Client: Yeah, I don't know if that is possible, but that's what I would like to have happen.

In responses 8–14, the helper continues to help Isabella *explore and identify desired outcomes.*

8. **Helper:** In a little while we'll take some time to explore just how feasible that might be. Before we do that, let's make sure we don't overlook anything else you'd like to work on. In what other areas is it important to you to make a change or to turn things around for yourself?

Client: I'd like to start making some decisions for myself for a change, but I don't know exactly how to start.

9. **Helper:** Okay, that's part of what we'll do together. We'll look at how you can get started on some of these things. So far, then, you've mentioned two things you'd like to work toward—increasing your confidence in your ability to handle tough situations like math and starting to make some decisions by yourself without relying on help from someone else. Is that about it, or can you think of any other things you'd like to work on?

Client: I guess it's related to making my own decisions, but I'd like to decide whether to stay in this curriculum or switch to the vocational one.

10. **Helper:** So you're concerned also about making a special type of decision about school that affects you now.

Client: That's right. But I'm sort of afraid to, because I know if I decided to switch, my parents would have a terrible reaction when they found out about it.

11. **Helper:** It seems that you're mentioning another situation that we might need to try to get a different handle on. As you mentioned last week, in certain situations, like math class or with your parents, you tend to back off and let other people take over for you.

Client: That's true, and I guess this curriculum thing is an example of it. It's like a lot of things where I do know what I want to do or say but I just don't follow through. Like not telling my parents about my opinion about this college prep curriculum. Or not telling them how their harping at me about grades makes me feel. Or even in math class, just sitting there and sort of letting the teacher do a lot of the work for me when I really do probably know the answer or could go to the board.

12. **Helper:** So what you're saying is that in certain situations with your parents or in math class, you may have an idea or an opinion or a feeling, yet you usually don't express it.

Client: Mm-hmm. Usually I don't because sometimes I'm afraid it might be wrong or I'm afraid my parents would get upset.

13. **Helper:** So the anticipation that you might make a mistake or that your parents might not like it keeps you from expressing yourself in these situations?

Client: I believe so.

14. **Helper:** Then is this another thing that you would like to work on?

Client: Yes, because I realize I can't go on withdrawing forever.

Because Isabella has again stated the outcome in negative terms, in the next four responses (15–18), the helper helps Isabella *restate the goal in positive terms.*

15. **Helper:** Okay, now again you're sort of suggesting a way that you don't want to handle the situation. You don't want to withdraw. Can you describe something you *do* want to do in these situations in a way that you could see, hear, or grasp yourself doing it each time the situation occurs?

Client: I'm not exactly sure what you mean.

16. **Helper:** Well, for instance, suppose I need to lose weight to improve my health. I could say, "I don't want to eat so much, and I don't want to be fat." But that just describes not doing what I've been doing. So it would be more helpful to describe something I'm going to do instead, like "Instead of eating between meals, I'm going to go out for a walk, or talk on the phone, or create a picture of myself in my head as a healthier person."

Client: Oh, yeah, I do see what you mean. So I guess instead of withdrawing, I—well, what is the opposite of that? I guess I think it would be more helpful if I volunteered the answers or gave my ideas or opinions—things like that.

17. **Helper:** Okay, so you're saying that you want to express yourself instead of holding back. Things like expressing opinions, feelings, and things like that.

Client: Yeah.

18. **Helper:** Okay, now we've mentioned three things you want to work on. Anything else?

Client: No, I can't think of anything.

In the next response, the helper asks Isabella to *select one of the goals* to work on initially. Tackling all three outcomes simultaneously could be overwhelming to a client.

19. **Helper:** Okay, as time goes on and we start working on some of these things, you may think of something else—or something we've talked about today may change. What might be helpful now is to decide which of these three things you'd like to work on first.

Client: Gee, that's a hard decision.

In the previous response, Isabella demonstrated in vivo one of her problems: difficulty in making decisions. In the next response, the helper *provides* guidelines to help Isabella make a choice but is careful not to make the decision for her.

20. **Helper:** Well, it's one decision I don't want to make for you. I'd encourage you to start with the area you think is most important to you now—and also maybe one that you feel you could work with successfully.

Client: [Long pause] Can this change too?

21. **Helper:** Sure—we'll start with one thing, and if later on it doesn't feel right, we'll move on.

Client: Okay, Well, I guess it would be the last thing we talked about—starting to express myself in situations where I usually don't.

In the next response, the helper discusses the degree to which Isabella believes the *change represents something she will do* rather than something someone else will do.

22. **Helper:** Okay, sticking with this one area, it seems like these are things that you could make happen without the help of anyone else or without requiring anyone else to change too. Think about that for a minute, and see whether that's the way it feels to you.

Client: [Pause] I guess so. You're saying that I don't need to depend on someone else; it's something I can start doing.

In the next response, the helper shifts to exploring *possible advantages* of goal achievement. Notice that the helper asks the client first to express her opinion about advantages; the helper is giving her in vivo practice in one of the skills related to her goal.

23. **Helper:** One thing I'm wondering about—and this will probably sound silly because in a way it's obvious—but exactly how will making this change help you or benefit you?

Client: Mm. [Pause] I'm thinking. Well, what do you think?

In the previous response, the client shifted responsibility to the helper and "withdrew," as she does in other anxiety-producing situations such as math class and interactions with her parents. In the next response, the helper *summarizes* this behavior pattern.

24. **Helper:** You know, it's interesting; I just asked you for your opinion about something, and instead of sharing it, you asked me to sort of handle it instead. Are you aware of this?

Client: Now that you mention it, I am. But I guess that's what I do so often that it's sort of automatic.

In the next three responses (25–27), the helper does some in vivo assessment of Isabella's problems, which results in information that can be used later for *planning of subgoals and action steps.*

25. **Helper:** Can you run through exactly what you were thinking and feeling just then?

Client: Just that I had a couple of ideas, but then I didn't think they were important enough to mention.

26. **Helper:** I'm wondering if you also may have felt a little concerned about what I would think of your ideas.

Client: [Face flushes.] Well, yeah. I guess it's silly, but yeah.

27. **Helper:** So is this sort of the same thing that happens to you in math class or around your parents?

Client: Yeah—only in those two situations I feel much more uptight than I do here.

In the next four responses, the helper continues to explore *potential advantages* for Isabella of attaining this goal.

28. **Helper:** Okay, that's really helpful because that information gives us some clues on what we'll need to do first in order to help you reach this result. Before we explore that, let's go back and see whether you can think of any ways in which making this change will help you.

Client: I think sometimes I'm like a doormat. I just sit there and let people impose on me. Sometimes I get taken advantage of.

29. **Helper:** So you're saying that at times you feel used as a result?

Client: Yeah. That's a good way to put it. Like with my girlfriends I told you about. Usually we do what they want to on weekends, not necessarily what I want to do, because even with them I withdraw in this way and don't express myself.

30. **Helper:** So you are noticing some patterns here. Okay, other advantages or benefits to you?

Client: I'd become less dependent and more self-reliant. More sure of myself.

31. **Helper:** Okay, that's a good thought. Any other ways that this change would be worthwhile for you, Isabella?

Client: Mm—I can't think of any. That's honest. But if I do, I'll mention them.

In the next responses (32–35), the helper initiates exploration of *possible disadvantages* of this goal.

32. **Helper:** Okay, great! And the ones you've mentioned I think are really important ones. Now, I'd like you to flip the coin, so to speak, and see whether you can think of any disadvantages that could result from moving in this direction.

Client: I can't think of any in math. Well, no, in a way I can. I guess it's sort of the thing to do there. If I start expressing myself more, people might wonder what is going on.

33. **Helper:** So you're concerned about the reaction from some of the other students?

Client: Yeah, in a way. But there are a couple of girls in there who are pretty popular and also made the honor roll. So I don't think it's like I'd be a geek or anything. And actually with my girlfriends, I don't think they would mind if I spoke up; it just hasn't been my pattern with them. So they might be surprised, but I think that would be okay with them.

34. **Helper:** It sounds, then, like you believe that is one disadvantage you could live with. Any other ways in which doing this could affect your life in a less good way—or could create another problem for you?

Client: I think a real issue there is how my parents would react if I started to do some of these things. I don't know. Maybe they would welcome it. But I sort of think they

would consider it a revolt or something on my part and would want to squelch it right away.

35. **Helper:** Are you saying you believe your parents have a stake in keeping you somewhat dependent on them?

Client: Yeah, I do.

This is a difficult issue. Without observing her family, it would be impossible to say whether this is Isabella's perception (and a distorted one) or whether the parents do play a role in this problem. Indeed, from a diagnostic standpoint, family members are often significantly involved when one family member has a dependent personality. The helper thus *reflects both possibilities* in the next response.

36. **Helper:** That may or may not be true. It could be that you see the situation that way and an outsider like me might not see it the same way. On the other hand, it is possible your parents might subtly wish to keep you from growing up too quickly. This might be a potentially serious enough disadvantage for us to consider whether it would be useful for all four of us to sit down and talk together.

Client: Do you think that would help?

In the next two responses, the helper and Isabella continue to discuss potential *disadvantages* related to this goal. Notice that in the next response, instead of answering the client's previous question directly, the helper shifts the responsibility to Isabella and solicits her opinion, again giving her in vivo opportunities to demonstrate one skill related to the goal.

37. **Helper:** What do you think?

Client: I'm not sure. They are sometimes hard to talk to.

38. **Helper:** How would you feel about having a joint session—assuming they were agreeable?

Client: Right now it seems okay. How could it help exactly?

In the following response, the helper changes from an *individual focus* to a *systemic focus,* because the parents may have an investment in keeping Isabella dependent on them or may have given Isabella an injunction: "Don't grow up." The systemic focus avoids blaming any one person.

39. **Helper:** I think you mentioned it earlier. Sometimes when one person in a family changes the way she or

he reacts to the rest of the family, it has a boomerang effect, causing ripples throughout the rest of the family. If that's going to happen in your case, it might be helpful to sit down and talk about it and anticipate the effects, rather than letting you get in the middle of a situation that starts to feel too hard to handle. It could be helpful to your parents too, to explore their role in this whole issue.

Client: I see. Well, where do we go from here?

40. **Helper:** Our time is about up today. Let's get together in a week and map out a plan of action.

(*Note:* The same process of goal identification would also be carried out in subsequent sessions for the other two outcome goals that Isabella identified earlier in this session.)

DEFINING OUTCOME GOALS

Most clients select more than one goal. Ultimately, it may be most realistic for a client to work toward several outcomes. For example, in our model case, Isabella selects three outcome goals: acquiring and demonstrating at least four initiating skills, increasing positive self-talk about her ability to function adequately in competitive situations, and acquiring and using five decision-making skills (see Table 9.5, Isabella's goal chart, on page 260). Selection of one goal may also imply the existence of other goals. For example, if a client states, "I want to get involved in a relationship with a man that is emotionally and sexually satisfying," the client may also need to work on meeting men and on approach behaviors, developing communications skills designed to foster intimacy and learning about what responses might be sexually satisfying.

At first, it is useful to have the client specify one or more desired goals for each separate concern. However, to tackle several outcome goals at one time would be unrealistic. The helper should ask the client to choose one of the outcome goals to pursue first. After identifying an initial outcome goal to work toward, the helper and client can define outcome goals and identify subgoals and action steps. In this section we introduce some interviewing leads that a practitioner can use to help the client

1. Define specific goal-related behaviors
2. Define goal-related conditions and contexts
3. Define a suitable level of change

Then, later in the chapter, we describe leads to help the client

4. Identify subgoals and action steps
5. Sequence subgoals and action steps

6. Identify obstacles to goal achievement
7. Identify resources to facilitate goal achievement

The leads are particularly useful for clients moving from the preparation phase to the action phase of the change model developed by Prochaska and associates (1992). Although we list those seven steps sequentially for learning purposes, and discuss them in separate sections of Chapter 9, in actual practice they occur simultaneously. In other words, clients need to consider the question "What do I want to do?" at the same time they consider the question "How can I tell that I've done it?" In effect, the practitioner helps the client to develop the outcome goals and implement action plans and evaluation plans for assessing those goals at the same time.

Leads to Define Behaviors Related to Goals

Defining goals involves specifying in operational or behavioral terms what the client (whether an individual, group member, or organization) is to *do* as a result of counseling. This part of an outcome goal defines the particular behavior the client is to perform and answers the question "*What will the client do, think, or feel differently?*" Examples of behavior outcome goals include exercising more frequently, asking for help from a teacher, verbal sharing of positive feelings about oneself, and thinking about oneself in positive ways. As you can see, both overt and covert behaviors, including thoughts and feelings, can be included in this part of the outcome goal as long as the behavior is defined by what it means for each client. Defining goals behaviorally makes the goal-setting process specific, and specifically defined goals are more likely than vaguely stated intentions. to create incentives and guide performance. When goals are behaviorally or operationally defined, it is easier to evaluate the effects of your intervention strategy.

Here are some leads a helper can use to identify the behavior part of a goal:

> "When you say you want to, what do you see yourself doing?"
>
> "What could I see you doing, thinking, or feeling as a result of this change?"
>
> "You say you want to be more self-confident. Describe what things would you be thinking and doing as a self-confident person."
>
> "Describe a good (and a poor) example of this goal."
>
> "When you are no longer _____, what will you be doing instead?"
>
> "What will it look like when you are doing this?"

It is important for the helper to continue to pursue these leads until the client can define the overt and covert behaviors associated with the goal. This is not an easy task, for most clients talk about changes in vague or abstract terms. If the client has trouble specifying behaviors, the practitioner can help with further instructions, information giving, or self-disclosing a personal goal. The practitioner can also help with behavioral definitions of the goal by encouraging the client to use action verbs to describe what will be happening when the goal is attained. As we mentioned earlier, it is important to get clients to specify what they *want* to do, not what they don't want or what they want to stop. The goal is usually defined sufficiently when the helper can accurately repeat and paraphrase the client's definition.

Leads to Define the Conditions of an Outcome Goal

The second part of an outcome goal specifies the conditions—that is, the *context* or *circumstances*—where the behavior will occur. This is an important element of an outcome goal for both the client and the helper. The conditions suggest a particular *person* with whom the client may perform the desired behaviors or a particular *setting*, and they answer the question "*Where, when,* and *with whom* is the behavior to occur?" Specifying the conditions of a behavior sets boundaries and helps ensure that the behavior will occur only in desired settings or with desired people and will not generalize to undesired settings. This idea can be illustrated vividly. For example, a woman may wish to increase the number of positive verbal and nonverbal responses she makes toward her partner. In this case, time spent with her partner would be the condition or circumstances in which the behavior occurs. However, if this behavior generalized to include all persons, it might have negative effects on the very relationship that she is trying to improve.

Leads to determine the conditions of the outcome goal include these:

"Where would you like to do this?"

"In what situations do you want to be able to do this?"

"When do you want to do this?"

"Who would you be with when you do this?"

The helper is looking for a response that indicates where or with whom the client will make the change or perform the desired behavior. If the client gives a noncommittal response, the helper may suggest client self-monitoring to obtain these data. The helper can also use self-disclosure and personal examples to demonstrate that a desired behavior may not be appropriate in all situations or with all people.

Leads to Define a Level of Change

The third element of an outcome goal specifies the level or *amount* of the behavioral change. In other words, this part answers the question "*How much* is the client to do or to complete in order to reach the desired goal?" The level of an outcome goal serves as a barometer that measures the extent to which the client will be able to perform the desired behavior. For example, a man may state that he wishes to decrease cigarette smoking. The following week, he may report that he did a pretty good job of cutting down on cigarettes. However, unless he can specify how much he actually decreased smoking, both he and the helper will have difficulty in determining how much the client really completed toward the goal. In this case, the client's level of performance is ambiguous. In contrast, if he had reported that he reduced cigarette smoking by two cigarettes per day in one week, his level of performance could be determined easily. If his goal were to decrease cigarette smoking by eight cigarettes per day, this information would help to determine progress toward the goal. This is a good example of the interrelationship between goal definition and goal evaluation, which we discussed earlier. Setting the level of amount of behavior change reflected in the outcome goal is the part of the goal that enables both the client and the practitioner to determine when the action has been accomplished or the behavior has been changed.

Like the behavior and condition parts of an outcome goal, the level of change should always be established individually for each client, whether the client is an individual, couple, group, or organization. The amount of satisfaction derived from goal attainment often depends on the level of performance established. A suitable level of change will depend on such factors as the present level of the undesired behavior, the present level of the desired behavior, the resources available for change, the client's readiness to change, and the degree to which other conditions or people are maintaining the present level of undesired behavior.

As an example, suppose that a client wants to increase the number of assertive opinions she expresses orally with her husband. If she now withholds all her opinions, her level of change might be stated at a lower level than that defined for another client who already expresses some opinions. And if the client's husband is accustomed to her refraining from giving opinions, this might affect the degree of change made, at least initially. The helper's and client's primary concern is to establish a level that is manageable—that the client can attain with some success.

One way to set the level of a goal that is manageable is to use a scale that identifies a series of *increasingly desired* outcomes for each given area. This concept, introduced by Kiresuk and Sherman (1968), is called "goal-attainment scaling," and it is used more and more in agencies that must demonstrate certain levels of client goal achievement in order to receive or maintain funding and third-party reimbursement. In goal-attainment scaling, the helper and

TABLE 9.2	Goal-Attainment Scale
Date: 10/24/07	**Frequency of checking blood sugar levels**
(−2) Most unfavorable outcome thought likely	Zero per day
(−1) Less than expected success with treatment	One per day
(0) Expected level of treatment success	Two per day
(+1) More than expected success with treatment	Three per day
(+2) Best expected success with treatment	Four per day

client devise five outcomes for a given issue and arrange these outcomes by level or extent of change on a scale in the following order (each outcome is assigned a numerical value): most unfavorable outcome (−2), less than likely expected outcome (−1), most likely or expected outcome (0), more than likely expected outcome (+1), most favorable outcome (+2). Table 9.2 shows an example of a goal-attainment scale (GAS) for a client with diabetes who wants to measure the frequency of daily checking of blood sugar level. A review of the GAS model and similar models is presented by Ogles, Lambert, and Masters (1996). The GAS model can also be used to assess change at the systemic and organizational levels as well as with individual clients. (See Learning Activity 9.3.) Note that the primary purpose of goal-attainment scaling is to assess the amount of client change. We introduce GAS at this point as a way of making outcome goals more explicit; we return to this model later in the chapter when discussing various outcome measures.

Leads for Identifying the Level of Change

In using leads to establish the level of change in the outcome goal, the helper is looking for some indication of the present and future levels of the desired behavior. The level of an outcome goal can be expressed by the number of times, or *frequency,* the client wants to be able to do something. Occasionally, the frequency of an appropriate level may be only one, as when a client's outcome goal is to make one decision about a job change. In this instance, the *occurrence or lack thereof* is the level of change. In other instances, the level of an outcome goal is expressed by the amount of time, or *duration,* the client wants to be able to do something. And in other instances, particularly when the goal behavior reflects a change in emotions, the level is expressed as a rating or scaling, referred to as *intensity.*

Here are some sample leads to establish the level of change:

"How much would you like to be able to do this, compared with how much you're doing it now?" (duration)

"How often do you want to do this?" (frequency)

"From the information you obtained during self-monitoring, you seem to be studying only about an hour a week now. What is a reasonable amount for you to increase this without getting bogged down?" (duration)

"If your feelings are very distressing, say about a 10 on a 1-to-10 scale, where would you like them to be after our work together using this 1-to-10 rating?" (intensity)

The practitioner can help the client establish an appropriate level of change by referring to the self-monitoring data collected during assessment. If the client has not engaged in self-monitoring, it is almost imperative to have the client observe and record present amounts of the undesired behavior and the goal behavior. This information will give some idea of the present level of behavior—that is, the base rate or baseline level. This information is important because the *desired* level should be contrasted with the *present* level of the overt or covert behaviors. A client's data gathering is very useful for defining issues and goals and for monitoring progress toward the goals. This is another example of the way in which goal definition and goal evaluation occur simultaneously in actual practice.

Level as an Indicator of Direction and Type of Change

The level reflected in an outcome goal specifies both the direction and the type of change desired. Consider again the example of the client who wants to be more assertive. If the client's present level of a specified assertive response is zero, then the goal would be to acquire the assertive skill. When the base rate of a behavior is zero, or when the client does not seem to have certain skills in her or his repertory, the goal is stated as acquiring a behavior. If, however, the client wants to improve or increase something that she or he can already do (but at a low level), the goal is stated as increasing a behavior. Increasing or acquiring overt and/or covert behaviors is a goal when the client's concern is a *response deficit,* meaning that the desired response occurs with insufficient intensity or frequency or in inappropriate form. Sometimes, a client has an overt behavioral response in his or her repertoire, but it is masked or inhibited by the presence of certain feelings—in which case the goal would be directed toward the feelings rather than the overt behavior. In this instance, the concern stems from *response inhibition,* and the resulting goal is a disinhibition of the response, usually by the working through of the emotional reactions standing in the way.

In contrast, if the client is doing too much of something and wants to lower the present level, the goal is stated as decreasing a behavior. Decreasing overt and/or covert behaviors is a goal when the client's concern is a *response excess,* meaning that a response occurs so often, so long, with such excessive intensity, or in socially inappropriate contexts that it is often annoying to the client and to others. In situations of response excesses, it is usually the frequency or amount of the response, rather than its form, that is problematic. It is almost always easier to work on developing or increasing a behavior (response increment or acquisition) than on decreasing a response (response decrement). This is another reason to encourage clients to state their goals in *positive* terms, working toward doing something or doing it more, rather than stopping something or doing it less.

Sometimes, the level of change may reflect a *restructuring.* For instance, a client trying to improve grades may desire to replace studying in a crowded room with the TV on with studying in a quiet room free of distractions. This client's goal is stated in terms of restructuring something about her or his environment—in this case, the location of studying. Although this is an example of restructuring an overt behavior, restructuring can be cognitive as well. For example, a client may want to eliminate negative, self-defeating thoughts about taking tests and replace these with positive, self-enhancing thoughts about the capacity to perform adequately in test-taking situations. Restructuring also often takes place during family therapy when boundaries and alliances between and among family members are shifted so that, for instance, a member on the periphery is pulled into the family, triangles are broken up, or overinvolved alliances between two persons are rearranged. Restructuring overt or covert behaviors is a goal when the concern is *inadequate, inappropriate, or defective stimulus control,* meaning that the necessary supporting environmental conditions either are missing or are arranged in such a way as to make it impossible or difficult for the desired behavior to occur.

In some instances, the level of a goal reflects maintenance of a particular overt or covert response at the current rate or frequency or under existing conditions. As you recall from our earlier discussion of client change in this chapter, not all goals will reflect a discrepancy between the client's present and future behavior. Some goals may be directed toward maintaining a desired or satisfying situation or response (stage 5 of the Prochaska change model). Such goals may be stated as, for example, "to maintain my present amount (three hours daily) of studying," "to maintain the present balance in my life between work on weekdays and play on weekends," "to maintain the positive communication I have with my partner in our daily talks," or "to maintain my present level (two a day) of engaging in relaxation sessions." A maintenance goal suggests that the client's present level of behavior is satisfying and sufficient, at least at this time. A maintenance goal may help to put things in perspective by acknowledging the areas of the client's life that are going well. Maintenance goals are also useful and necessary when one of the change goals has been achieved. For example, if a client wanted to improve grades and has done so successfully, then the helper and client need to be concerned about how the client can maintain the improvement. As we mentioned earlier, maintenance goals and programs are often harder to achieve and take greater effort and planning than initial change attempts.

To summarize, the level stated by the outcome goal will usually reflect one of the categories of responses and goals summarized in Table 9.3. Because most clients have more than one outcome goal, a client's objectives may reflect more than one of these directions of change. Knowledge of the direction and level of change defined in the client's goals is important in selecting intervention strategies and assessing the effects of those strategies on the target goals. For example, self-monitoring is used differently depending on whether it is applied to increase or to decrease a response. One change strategy might be used appropriately to help a client acquire responses; another strategy may be needed to help a client restructure some responses.

TABLE 9.3	Categories of Client Goals
A. Response deficit	Response increment
	Response acquisition
B. Response inhibition	Disinhibition of response
	Working through of emotional reactions
C. Response excess	Response decrement
D. Inadequate or inappropriate stimulus control	Response restructuring
E. Maintenance	Response maintenance at current frequency or amount or in current context

It is very important for the helper and client to spend sufficient time on specifying the level of the goal, even if this process seems elusive and difficult. Although our focus in this chapter is on defining goals with individual clients, similar processes occur for defining goals with dyads, groups, and organizations.

IDENTIFYING AND SEQUENCING SUBGOALS AND ACTION STEPS

All of us can probably recall times when we were expected to learn something so fast that the learning experience was overwhelming and produced feelings of frustration, irritation, and discouragement. The change represented by outcome goals can be achieved best if the process is gradual. Any change program should be organized into a sequence that guides the client through small steps toward the ultimate desired behaviors. In defining goals, this gradual learning sequence is achieved by breaking down the outcome goal into a series of smaller goals called *subgoals* or *action steps.* Subgoals help clients move toward the solution of problems in a planned way. The subgoals are usually arranged in a hierarchy, and the client tackles the subgoals at the bottom of the ranked list before attempting the ones near the top. Although an overall outcome goal can provide a "general directive" for change, the specific subgoals may determine a person's immediate activities and degree of effort in making changes.

After the client identifies and selects subgoals, they are ordered as a series of tasks according to their *complexity* and *degree of difficulty and immediacy.* Because some clients are put off by the word *hierarchy,* we use the term *goal pyramid* and pull out an $8\frac{1}{2}$-by-11-inch sheet of paper with a drawing of a pyramid (actually, a triangle!) on it (see Figure 9.2). The first criterion for ranking is the complexity and degree of difficulty of the task. A series of subgoal tasks may represent either increasing requirements of the same (overt or covert) behavior or demonstrations of different behaviors, with simpler and easier responses sequenced before more complex and difficult ones. The second criterion for ranking is immediacy. For this criterion, the client ranks subgoals

according to prerequisite tasks—that is, the tasks that must be done before others can be achieved.

The sequencing of subgoals in order of complexity is based on learning principles called *shaping* and *successive approximations.* Shaping helps someone learn a small amount at a time, with reinforcement or encouragement for each task completed successfully. Gradually, the person learns the entire amount or achieves the overall result through these day-to-day learning experiences that successively approximate the overall outcome. Subgoals are important because "change itself is most typically a small, step by step, back and forth effort at trying new things out, changing, trying new things out and so on—" (Tallman & Bohart, 1999, p. 112).

After all the steps have been identified and sequenced, the client starts to carry out the actions represented by the subgoals, beginning with the initial step and moving on. Usually, it is wise not to attempt a new subgoal until the client successfully completes the task at hand. Progress made on initial and subsequent steps provides useful information about whether the gaps between steps are too large or just right and whether the sequencing of steps is appropriate. As the subgoals are met, they become part of the client's current repertory that can be used in additional change efforts toward the outcome goals.

An example may clarify the process of identifying and sequencing subgoals for a client. Suppose that you are working with a young adult who was diagnosed with juvenile-onset diabetes and advised to monitor and regulate her blood sugar levels. Together, you and the client will determine the tasks the client will need to complete to monitor and regulate her blood sugar levels. These tasks can be stated as subgoals that the client can strive to carry out each day, starting with the initial subgoal, the one that feels most comfortable and easy to achieve, and working the way up the pyramid as each step is successfully completed and maintained in the client's repertory.

Although the achievement of a goal may require multiple action steps, the tasks chosen by two or more clients who have the same or similar goals may be quite different. The helper should be sensitive to individual differences and not impose on the client his or her preferred method for dealing with the issue. Similarly, each client will have a different idea of how subgoals are best sequenced.

The goal pyramid shown in Figure 9.2 illustrates how one particular client who wanted to lose weight sequenced her subgoals. This client's rationale was that if she increased exercise and relaxation *first,* it would be easier for her to alter her eating habits. For her, more difficult and also less immediate goals included restructuring her thoughts about herself as a healthier person and developing social skills necessary to initiate new relationships. The latter subgoal she viewed as the most difficult one because her weight served partly to protect her from social distress situations. After the first

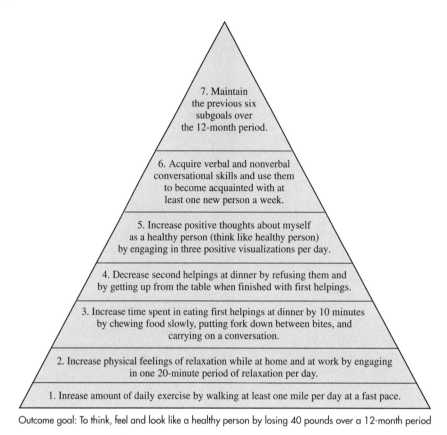

Figure 9.2 Goal Pyramid

six subgoals are achieved, the final subgoal is to keep these actions going for at least a 12-month period. At the top of the pyramid, it is important for the helper to discuss with the client some ways in which she can maintain the subgoals over an extended period of time.

Notice in this example that the outcome goal is stated in positive terms—not "I don't want to be overweight and unhealthy" but "I do want to feel, think, and look like a healthy person." The subgoals represent actions that the client will take to support this desired outcome. Also notice that all the subgoals are stated in the same way as the outcome goal—with the definition of the behaviors to be changed, the level of change, and the conditions or circumstances of change so that the client knows what to do, where, when, with whom, and how much or how often. (See Learning Activity 9.4.)

Leads to Identify Subgoals and Action Steps

To help the client identify appropriate subgoals or action steps, the helper uses leads similar to the following:

"How will you go about doing [or thinking, feeling] this?"

"What exactly do you need to do to make this happen?"

"Let's brainstorm some actions you'll need to take to make your goal work for you."

"What have you done in the past to work toward this goal? How did it help?"

"Let's think of the steps you need to take to get from where you are now to where you want to be."

The helper is always trying to encourage and support client participation and responsibility in goal setting, remembering that clients are more likely to carry out changes that they themselves originate. Occasionally, however, after hearing leads like the ones listed above, some clients are unable to specify any desirable or necessary action steps or subgoals. The helper may then have to use prompts, either asking the client to think of other people who have similar concerns and to identify their strategies for action or providing a statement illustrating an example or model of an action step or subgoal.

Leads to Sequence Subgoals and Action Steps

General leads to use to sequence and rank subgoals include the following:

"Identify your first step."

"What would you be able to do most easily?"

"What would be most difficult?"

"What is most important for you to do now? Least important?"

This activity is an extension of Learning Activity 9.3. Continue the role play, working with the same client on the same goal selected and defined in that activity. Your task as the helper in this activity is to work with the client to generate and sequence subgoals. Use the goal pyramid in Figure 9.2 as a guide. The client assumes the same role as in Activity 9.3, and the observer provides feedback on this process of identifying and sequencing subgoals.

"How could we order these steps to maximize your success in reaching your goal?"

"Let's think of steps you need to take to get from where you are now to where you want to be, and let's arrange them in an order from what seems easiest to you to what seems hardest to you."

"Can you think of some things you need to do before some other things as you make progress toward your goal?"

IDENTIFYING AND ADDRESSING OBSTACLES TO GOAL ACHIEVEMENT

To ensure that the client can complete each subgoal step successfully, it is helpful to identify any *obstacles* that could interfere. Obstacles may include overt and/or covert behavior. *Potential* obstacles to check out with the client include the presence or absence of certain feelings or mood states, thoughts, beliefs and perceptions, other people, and situations or events. Another obstacle could be lack of knowledge or skill. Mitchell, Levin, and Krumboltz (1999) note that deeply held beliefs that see problems as overwhelming or fears about the reactions of others often pose obstacles that block client action steps. Identification of lack of knowledge or skill is important if the client needs information or training before the subgoal action can be attempted. After such obstacles are identified, the client and practitioner can develop a plan that addresses the obstacles so they do not linger as stumbling blocks to change.

Leads to Identify and Address Obstacles

Clients often are not very aware of any factors that might interfere with completing a subgoal, and they may need prompts from the helper, such as the following, to identify obstacles:

"Describe some obstacles you may encounter in trying to take this action."

"What people [feelings, ideas, and situations] might get in the way of getting this done?"

"What or who might prevent you from working on this activity?"

"In what ways might you have difficulty completing this task successfully?"

"Identify information or skills you need in order to complete this action effectively."

Occasionally, the helper may need to point out apparent obstacles that the client overlooks. If significant obstacles are identified, a *plan* to deal with or counteract the effects of these factors needs to be developed. Often this plan resembles an "antisabotage plan" in which helper and client try to predict ways in which the client might not do the desired activity and then work around the possible barriers. Suppose that you explore obstacles with the client who needs to monitor and regulate her blood sugar because she was recently diagnosed with diabetes and wants to improve her health. Perhaps while exploring subgoals, she identifies two factors that might keep her from attending to her blood sugar level: (1) She believes that doing so is not that necessary or relevant to her overall well-being. (2) She is so over-scheduled with school and work that she doesn't have time to monitor her blood sugar. In developing an antisabotage plan, you would need to target both her belief system and her scheduling system in order to get around these obstacles.

IDENTIFYING RESOURCES TO FACILITATE GOAL ACHIEVEMENT

The next step is to identify *resources*—factors that will help the client complete subgoal tasks effectively. Like obstacles, resources include overt and covert behaviors as well as environmental sources. *Potential* resources to explore include feelings, thoughts and belief systems, people, situations, information, and skills. In this step, the practitioner tries to help clients identify already present or developed resources that, if used, can make completion of the subgoal tasks more likely and more successful.

A specific resource involved in attaining desired outcomes is referred to by Bandura (1989) and others as *self-efficacy*. Self-efficacy involves two types of personal expectations that affect goal achievement: (1) an *outcome* expectation and (2) an *efficacy* expectation. The outcome expectation has to do with whether and how much a client believes that engaging in particular behaviors will in fact produce the desired results. In our example about the client with diabetes, the outcome expectation would be the extent to which she believes that the actions represented by the subgoals will help her become a healthier person. The efficacy expectation involves the client's level of confidence regarding how well she can complete the behaviors necessary to reach the desired results.

People in the client's environment, especially those who observe and lend support to the client's goals, are potent resources. Resources may also be found in the client's cultural community—people, situations, events, and so on. For example, a young Latina identifies with Esmeralda, a character in a book that reflects aspects of her cultural community, *The House on Mango Street* (Cisneros, 1984). Like Esmeralda in the book, the client finds a resource in her connection with four skinny trees that grow despite the surrounding concrete. Much like herself, they "do not belong here but are here" (p. 74). She understands that their strength is secret, much like her own, supported by "ferocious roots beneath the ground" (p. 74). This cultural resource helps the client feel empowered enough to take action (Iglesias & Cormier, 2002). Skills of the client or of others in the client's environment—skills such as resilience, persistence, flexibility, and optimism—can also be used as resources.

Leads to Identify Resources

Here are some possible leads:

> "Identify resources you have available to help you as you go through this activity [or action]."
>
> "What specific feelings [or thoughts] are you aware of that might make it easier for you to _____?"
>
> "Tell me about the support system you have from others that you can use to make it easier to _____."
>
> "What skills [or information] do you possess that will help you do _____ more successfully?"
>
> "How much confidence do you have that you can do what it will take for you to _____?"
>
> "To what extent do you believe that these actions will help you do _____?"
>
> "Describe what resources are available to you in your environment and cultures that can help you take this action."

For example, the client with diabetes might identify a friend as a resource she could use for daily monitoring. She might also identify a diabetes support group and her own persistence as additional resources, as well as her weekly prayer or meditative group.

EVALUATION OF OUTCOME GOALS

Good ethical practice calls for helpers to evaluate client achievement (or lack thereof) of outcome goals. Professional codes of ethics specify that practitioners have a responsibility to provide the best and most effective treatments to their clients. Evaluating practice is not only about accounting but also about improving services to clients. A growing body of research suggests that tracking client progress can improve client outcomes (Lambert, Harmon, Slade, Whipple, & Hawkins, 2005).

Doing outcome evaluations also guides treatment planning. Data from outcome evaluations helps determine if there is a need to change the treatment or the intervention. In spite of these reasons, many practitioners resist evaluating outcomes because of the time and complexity involved or because of their philosophy of helping. Not surprisingly to us, in a recent survey of practicing clinicians, those who self-identified as "cognitive–behavioral" were more likely to use outcome measures in their practice (Hatfield & Ogles, 2004). Evidence-based practice is a cornerstone of cognitive–behavioral practitioners. Gibbs (2003) concludes that "the lives of clients are too precious" for helpers simply to assume that an intervention, even with the best of literature support, has had the desired effect (p. 238). In effect, it does little good to establish outcome goals with clients that are not simultaneously evaluated. In the following section, we describe what we believe are pragmatic and cost-effective ways to evaluate outcome goals.

RESPONSE DIMENSIONS OF OUTCOMES: WHAT TO EVALUATE

Goal behaviors are evaluated by measuring the amount or level of the defined behaviors. Three dimensions commonly used to measure the direction and level of change in goal behaviors are frequency, duration, and intensity. You may recall that these three dimensions are reflected by the *level* of the client's outcome goal. Whether one or a combination of these response dimensions is measured depends on the nature of the goal, the method of assessment, and the feasibility of obtaining particular data. It is important to select targets to measure that are the focus of intervention or change strategies so that the targets are valid indicators of the effectiveness of the intervention (Bloom, Fischer, & Orme, 2006). The response dimensions should be individualized, particularly because they vary in the time and effort that they cost the client.

Frequency

Frequency reflects the number (how many, how often) of overt or covert behaviors and is determined by obtaining measures of each occurrence of the goal behavior. Frequency counts are typically used when the goal behavior is discrete and of short duration. Panic episodes and headaches are examples of behaviors that can be monitored with frequency counts. Frequency data can also be obtained from comments written in a diary. For example, the number of positive (or negative) self-statements before and after each snack or bingeing episode, reported in a daily diary, can be tabulated. Occasionally, frequency is simply the presence or absence of a particular behavior, and in this case the level of the goal is referred to as *occurrence.* Occurrence refers to the presence or absence of target behaviors. Checklists can be used to rate the occurrence of behaviors. For example, an older client who has trouble with self-care could use a checklist to rate occurrence of self-care behaviors such as brushing teeth, flossing teeth, taking medicine, washing oneself, and combing hair.

Sometimes, frequency counts should be converted to *percentage data.* For example, knowing the number of times a behavior occurred may not be meaningful unless data are also available on the number of *possible* occurrences of the behavior. For example, data about the number of times an overweight client consumes snacks might be more informative if converted to a percentage. In this example, the client would self-monitor both the number of opportunities to eat snacks and the number of times he or she actually did snack. After these data were collected, they would be converted to a percentage. The advantage of percentage scores is that they indicate whether the change is a function of an actual increase or decrease in the number of times the response occurs or is merely a function of an increase or decrease in the number of opportunities to perform the behavior. Thus, a percentage score may give more accurate and more complete information than a simple frequency count. However, when it is hard to detect the available opportunities or when it is difficult for the client to collect data, percentage scores may not be useful.

Duration

Duration reflects the length of time a particular response or collection of responses occurs. The measurement of duration is appropriate whenever the goal behavior is not discrete and lasts for varying periods. Time spent thinking about one's strengths, the amount of time spent on a task or with another person, the period of time consumed by depressive thoughts, and the amount of time that anxious feelings lasted, for example, can be measured with duration counts. Duration may also involve time *between* an urge and an undesired response, such as the time one holds off before lighting up a cigarette or before eating an unhealthy snack. It also can involve *elapsed* time between a covert behavior such as a thought or intention and an actual response, such as the amount of time before a shy person speaks up in a discussion (sometimes elapsed time is referred to as *latency*).

Measures of both frequency and duration can be obtained in one of two ways: continuous recording or time sampling. If the client obtains data *each time* he or she engages in the goal behavior, the client is collecting data continuously. Continuous recording, however, is sometimes impossible, particularly when the goal behavior occurs very often or when its onset and termination are hard to detect. In such cases, a time-sampling procedure may be more practical.

In time sampling, a day is divided into equal time intervals—90 minutes, 2 hours, or 3 hours, for example. The client keeps track of the frequency or duration of the goal behavior only during randomly selected intervals. When time sampling is used, data should be collected during at least three time intervals every day and during *different* time intervals every day so that representative and unbiased data are recorded. One variation of time sampling is to divide time into intervals and indicate the presence or absence of the target behavior in each interval in an "all or none" manner. If the behavior occurs during the interval, a *yes* is recorded; if it does not occur, a *no* is noted. Time sampling is less precise than continuous recordings of frequency or duration of a behavior, yet it does provide an estimate of the behavior and may be a useful substitute in monitoring high-frequency or nondiscrete target responses.

Intensity

Clients can report the intensity of a behavior or a feeling with some kind of numerical rating. Solution-focused therapists obtain client ratings of intensity by using *scaling questions*—for example, "on a 10-point scale, with 1 being low and 10 being high, rank the degree of anxiety you are experiencing." Another example of an intensity rating is called the SUDS scale, or the Subjective Units of Disturbance scale. On this scale, zero represents *no distress* and 100 represent *severe distress.* These kinds of scales can be used in a helping session or assigned to clients for self-monitoring between sessions. In addition, practitioners can develop more formalized rating scales for clients to use to rate intensity. For example, intensity of anxious feelings can be measured with ratings from 1 (*not anxious*) to 5 (*panic*) on a self-anchored scale.

Cronbach (1990) suggests three ways to decrease sources of error frequently associated with rating scales. First, the helper should be certain that what is to be rated is well defined and specified in the client's language. For example, if a client is to rate depressed thoughts, helper and client need to specify, with examples, what constitutes depressed thoughts (such as "Nothing is going right for me," "I can't do anything right"). These definitions should be tailored to each client, on the basis of an analysis of the client's target behavior and contributing conditions. Second, rating scales should include a description for each point on the scale. For example, episodes of anxious feelings in a particular setting can be rated on a 5-point scale on which 1 represents *little or no anxiety,* 2 equals to *some anxiety,* 3 means *moderately anxious,* 4 represents *strong anxious feelings,* and 5 indicates *very intense anxiety.* Third, rating scales should be unidirectional, starting with 0 or 1. Negative points (points below 0) should not be included. In using these self-anchored scales, it is also important to tell clients that the intervals on the scale are equal—that the difference between 1 and 2, for example, is the same as the difference between 3 and 4 or between 5 and 6 (Corcoran & Fischer, 2000).

One advantage of these sorts of individualized or self-anchored scales is that they can be used at multiple times during a day and the results can be averaged to get a daily single score that can be plotted on a chart or graph for a visual sign of progress (Bloom et al., 2006).

CHOOSING OUTCOME MEASURES: HOW TO EVALUATE OUTCOMES

A major factor facing the typical practitioner in evaluating outcomes is how to choose the most useful measures of outcome. Hatfield and Ogles (2004) conclude from clinician reports that there is a great deal of variability in outcome measures actually used by practitioners and that there is no current "universally accepted measure of outcome" (p. 459). Choosing an outcome measure is not an easy decision. It involves consideration of measures that are (1) psychometrically sound (accurate, reliable, and valid), (2) pragmatic and easy to use, (3) relevant to the client's stated goals, (4) relevant to the client's level of functioning, (5) related to the client's resources and constraints, and (6) relevant to the client's gender and culture. In addition to those factors, Leibert (2006) summarizes a range of issues involved in the selection of outcome measures in an attempt to improve measurement validity. Among his recommendations are the following:

1. Norms for both client and nonclient populations
2. Clear administrative and scoring procedures for before, during, and after treatment
3. Clear operational definition of what is being measured to allow for replication by others
4. Brief enough measures that allow for repeated measurements during the counseling process

In the rest of this section, we discuss ways in which practitioners can use goal-related outcome measures and computer-assisted outcome processes to facilitate the evaluation process. There are three general categories of goal-related outcome measures: (1) individualized outcome assessment such as the goal-attainment scaling system we discussed earlier and client self-monitoring; (2) specific measures of outcome, which typically involve the use of a rapid-assessment instrument (RAI) to assess a given problem area; (3) global measures of outcome, which utilizes instruments that tap into broad problem areas across populations. Practitioners can use any or all of them. It is important to remember that the accuracy of the evaluation process is enhanced when multiple measures of the same goal behavior are used.

Individualized Outcome Assessment

This approach to outcome assessment involves using a measure in which the outcomes are specifically defined for each client. The best-known individualized outcome assessment measure is the goal-attainment scale (Kiresuk & Sherman, 1968) (or some variation thereof), described earlier. The GAS system is especially useful for evaluating individual client change or "target complaints that focus on behaviors that are not necessarily specific to symptoms of diagnosable disorders" (Callaghan, 2001, p. 292). Used extensively with a number of different client populations, the GAS simply requires you to take an outcome goal for any given client and construct a weighted scale of descriptions ranging from the most favorable result (+2) to the least favorable result (−2), with zero representing the expected level of improvement (see Table 9.2 for a review of this process). Using these numerical scores, you can quantify levels of change in outcome goals by transforming the scores to standardized T scores (see also Kiresuk & Sherman, 1968). As Marten and Heimberg (1995) observe, the advantage of the GAS system lies in "its ability to allow practitioners a means of evaluating treatment outcome in an idiographic manner by examining client changes within specific problem areas in a concrete and systematized way" (p. 49). Goal-attainment scaling is also relatively free of bias about client "impairment."

The goal-attainment scale is constructed while the helper and client are developing outcome goals and prior to the beginning of any treatment protocol or change intervention. A particular advantage of this method is that the GAS can be constructed within, rather than outside, the helping situation and with the client's participation and assistance. Therefore, goal-attainment scaling requires almost no extra time from the helper, reinforces the client's role in the change process, and provides a quantifiable method of assessing outcome. Note that although the GAS example we present in Table 9.2 uses *frequency* as the measure of change, you can also construct scales using *duration* and *intensity* as indicators of change. For example, a GAS could be constructed for the *duration or amount* of time a client spends studying or exercising during a given day or week or month. Similarly, a GAS could be constructed to measure the *intensity or severity* of a client's panic attacks on a 100-point SUDS scale. Goal-attainment scaling is useful because each point on the rating scale is described in a quantifiable way, eliminating ambiguity. Another advantage of this system is its applicability to assessing change in couples, families, and organizations, as well as in individual clients (Ogles et al. 2002). However, Ogles et al. (2002) also point out that one disadvantage of a GAS is that it can be harder to score than a standardized assessment tool and may be more difficult to interpret.

Another way in which outcomes specific to individual clients are measured is *self-monitoring* by the clients. Self-monitoring is a process of observing and recording aspects of one's own covert or overt behavior. In evaluating goal behaviors, a client uses self-monitoring to collect data about the number, amount, and severity (frequency, duration, intensity) of the goal behaviors. Self-monitoring is an excellent way to obtain a daily within-person measure of the behavior over days or weeks. It provides an indication of the "temporal patterning" of the behavior as well as of the level of change (Petry, Tennen, & Affleck, 2000, p. 100). Self-monitoring is also an especially good way to collect data about the target behaviors and the environmental and social influences or contributing conditions. The monitoring involves not only noticing occurrences of the goal behavior but also recording them with paper and pencil, mechanical counters, timers, or electronic devices.

Self-monitoring has many advantages, although sometimes the accuracy or reliability of it is doubtful. The accuracy of self-monitoring can be improved when clients are instructed to self-monitor in vivo when the behavior occurs, rather than self-recording at the end of the day, when they are dependent on recall. Using devices such as pagers, hand-held computers, voice mail, and e-mail to cue the client to self-record also may enhance the accuracy of self-monitored data (Cone, 2001).

Self-monitoring can be a reactive process, meaning that the act of counting behaviors can cause behavior to change. An easy way to determine if reactivity is occurring is to watch the data the client self-monitors prior to any treatment intervention—that is, the baseline data. If systematic changes are occurring in the goal behaviors prior to an intervention, there is a pretty good chance that reactivity is occurring. You can reduce reactivity from client self-monitoring in several ways, including asking the client to self-record on a more intermittent basis, having the client use a less obtrusive

counting device, collecting more baseline data and waiting for it to become stable before starting an intervention, and, perhaps most important, comparing the results of client self-monitored data with results of other measures (Bloom, Fischer, & Orme, 2006). In Figure 9.3 we present a sample client self-monitoring evaluation log.

Specific Measures of Outcome

In addition to the individualized outcome assessment measures such as the GAS and client self-monitoring, the helper should consider giving clients paper-and-pencil rapid-assessment instruments (RAIs) that they can complete to provide self-report data about symptom reduction and level of improvement. These instruments focus on specific areas of concern such as anxiety or depression. For a comprehensive compendium of such measures see Corcoran and Fischer's work (2000). These authors provide descriptions of several hundred RAIs for 47 problem areas including profiles of the instruments and information regarding norms, scoring, reliability, validity, and availability. Another source of RAIs is the website http://ericae.net/testcol.htm. Callaghan (2001) describes ways to use RAIs to aggregate and track data across different clients, across therapists, and across varying treatment interventions.

It is important to choose a rapid-assessment instrument that has good psychometric properties; is easy to read, use, and score; and relates directly to the client's identified problems and symptoms at intake and to the stated outcome goals of counseling. For example, the Beck Depression Inventory II (BDI-II) (Beck, Steer, & Brown, 1996) is frequently used with clients who are depressed at intake and want to become less depressed, but it would not be a suitable choice for someone who presents with a different problem such as anxiety, anger control, or marital dissatisfaction. Also, because many of the psychometric properties of RAIs have been normed on Caucasian clients—often middle-class

Day/Time (Frequency)	Event	Intensity Rating (1 to 10 Scale)	Duration
Sat. 2 p.m.	Movie theater	9	10 min.
Sun. 11 a.m.	Church	6	7 min.
Mon. 8 a.m.	Driving	9	5 min.
Tues. 7 p.m.	Restaurant	5	8 min.
Wed. 5 p.m.	Shopping mall	8	8 min.
Thurs. 6 p.m.	Driving	7	7 min.
Fri. 8 a.m.	Driving	6	8 min.
Sat.	Home		None

Figure 9.3 Sample Client Self-Monitoring Evaluation Log of Panic Attacks

college students—caution must be applied when some of these instruments are used with clients of color. If you cannot find a culturally relevant RAI, perhaps you should use goal-attainment scaling instead. Helpers should use RAIs that are as relevant as possible to the client's culture and gender. For example, if you are measuring the stress level of an African American woman, it is better to use the African-American Women's Stress Scale (Watts-Jones, 1990) than some other stress measure.

Cone (2001) points out that most rapid-assessment instruments can be used to assess outcomes at the beginning, mid-point, termination, and follow-up of treatment but cannot be used as repeated daily or weekly measures because they are not sensitive enough to track changes made over short time intervals (p. 49). An exception is the COMPASS tracking system (Howard, Brill, Lueger, & O'Mahoney, 1995). The COMPASS is an outcome assessment system with good psychometric properties that is designed to measure outcomes and the quality of the helping relationship over short, repeated intervals.

Generally speaking, most specific measure of outcome, or rapid-assessment instruments, are easy to use because they are short and do not consume much client time to complete. Another advantage of these measures is that often a great deal of normative data are available for comparison purposes.

Global Measures of Outcome

In addition to RAIs such as the Beck Depression Inventory II (Beck et al., 1996) and the Beck Anxiety Inventory (Beck, 1993), there are RAIs that tap into general levels of client functioning and a range of symptoms. These measures are called *global* outcome measures because they are "designed to be used *across* client diagnoses" (Leibert, 2006, p. 111). RAIs that cover a wide range of symptoms and are thus applicable as global outcome measures include the Derogatis (1983) Symptom Checklist (SCL-90-R), the Derogatis (1993) Brief Symptom Inventory (BSI), and the Behavior and Symptom Identification Scale (Basis-32) (Eisen, Grob, & Klein, 1986). The SCL-90-R and the BSI both have nine subscales and a primary global severity index as well as extensive normative data across a variety of client populations and age groups. The Basis-32 has five subscales and a primary total score although it is used more often in inpatient than in outpatient settings. An outcome measure suitable for evaluating the goals of child and adolescent clients is the Child and Adolescent Functional Assessment Scale (CAFAS) (Hodges, 1997).

Another example of a global measure of outcome is found in the American Psychiatric Association's *Diagnostic and Statistical Manual of Mental Disorders (DSM-IV TR)* (2000), where a Global Assessment of Functioning (GAF) scale is used to report on Axis V. This scale can help to measure the effect of treatment and to track the progress of clients in global terms with the use of a single measure. It rates on a 0-to-100 scale the client's psychological, social, and occupational functioning but not physical or environmental limitations. The GAF scale can be used for ratings at both intake and termination although scant psychometric data are available on the GAF, and it is a very transparent measure (Davis & Meier, 2001).

A limitation of the global measures of outcome is that they do not directly measure the behaviors specified in the client's outcome goals. However, an advantage of these broader and multifaceted RAIs has to do with clinical significance. Within the last 15 years, there has been a major movement in the evaluation of mental health services toward criteria that reflect *clinically* significant outcomes.

Clinical significance refers to the effect of a treatment intervention on a single client, and it denotes improvement in client symptoms and functioning at a level comparable to that of the client's healthy peers. According to Cone (2001), the "simplest way to define clinically significant improvement is to consider a person to have improved when the score on a formal measure, such as the BDI, moves from the clinical to the nonclinical or 'normal' range" (p. 43). So for a client with an initial BDI score of 33 who drops to below a 9, this drop is indicative of clinically significant improvement. There are also statistical ways to define *clinical significance*. Statistically reliable change is change that is greater than would be expected to occur because of behavioral variability and measurement error (Lundervold & Belwood, 2000, p. 96). Clinically significant criteria are applied to each psychotherapy case and not only address the question of the *degree* to which the client makes the specified changes but also the *relevance* of those changes to the client's overall functioning and lifestyle. These criteria are considered to have a high degree of social validity. Increasingly, third-party payers are asking for outcome documentation from practitioners that includes both symptom reduction and data about the client's level of functioning in settings such as work, school, and home.

One brief outcome measure that appears to be reliable, valid, and suitable for repeated measurements, has available software, and provides a statistically derived index of clinical significance is the Outcome Questionnaire (OQ 45) (Lambert et al., 1996). This scale—the subject of much research—measures symptom distress, interpersonal relations, and social role functioning of clients, and it provides a total score. A brief four-item self-report instrument taking less than a minute to complete is the Outcome Rating Scale (ORS) (Miller et al., 2005). The ORS was developed specifically as a valid and reliable short alternative to the OQ 45 and is available in both written and oral forms and in several languages from www.talkingcure.com. Versions of the ORS are also available for children at this website.

Some clients may improve on a general outcome measure but don't reach their goals, whereas other clients, especially in outpatient or EAP (employee assisted programs) settings, may score in the normal range of a general outcome measure. Thus it is important to balance data obtained from the more general outcome measures with specific data tailored to individual clients and their goals.

Computer-Assisted Practice Evaluation Tools

A new development in rapid-assessment inventories is computer-assisted practice evaluation (Nurius & Hudson, 1993). One such package is the Computer Assisted Assessment Package (CAAP) developed by Hudson (1996a). This package, along with an accompanying one called the CASS (Computer Assisted Social Services system) (Hudson, 1996b), stores and administers RAIs directly to clients, scores, interprets scores, prepares graphs of data, and automatically updates a client's file each time a scale is completed. In this system, information is stored so that only the helper or a designated person can access the program and a client's information. These two systems also require minimal knowledge of computers. They are explained and presented as a software program in Bloom and associates (2006); see also the website http://www.ablongman.com/html/bloom/cass .html. Additionally, a web-based system that provides feedback to clinicians on outcome ratings has been developed by the Institute for the Study of Therapeutic Change and is available at www.treatmentoutcomesonline.com. Even more database options are described by Cone (2001), Callaghan (2001), and Nugent, Sieppert, and Hudson (2001).

WHEN TO EVALUATE OUTCOMES

There are several times during which a helper and client can measure progress toward the goal behaviors. Generally, the client's performance should be evaluated before counseling, during counseling or during application of a change strategy, immediately after counseling, and some time after counseling at a follow-up. Repeated measurements of client change may provide more precise data than only two measurement times, such as before and after a change strategy. Moreover, third-party payers are increasingly requiring that practitioners track outcomes for clients over a longer period of time, including and up to a one-year follow-up contact. In some states, Medicaid currently requires five outcome measures to be collected every 90 days.

This form of practice evaluation is based on a single-subject, single-case, or single-system design. Its essential components include "a client, and a repeated administration of the measure over periods of time during which the intervention is absent or present" (Cone, 2001, p. 206). Comparisons and data collected are plotted on graphs for visual observation.

Although there are more sophisticated single-subject designs than what we present here (see Bloom et al., 2006; Cone, 2001; Hayes, Barlow, & Nelson-Gray, 1999; Nugent et al., 2001), the simplest way to do a planned comparison is to compare two key elements of the evaluation—nonintervention and intervention, also called the A–B design (Bloom et al., 2006). This design is useful for busy practitioners with clients in most settings and with any theoretical perspective. Bloom and colleagues assert that although it is not a perfect method, it is a "quantum leap from the subjective or intuitive approaches to evaluating practice commonly used" (p. 495). When it is used with reliable and valid measures, helpers can monitor client progress over time, capture changes in identified goal-related behaviors, and assess the correlation between the timing of the intervention and the onset of any measured change (Bloom et al., 2006).

Measurement before Treatment Strategies: Baseline

A pretreatment measurement evaluates the goal behaviors before treatment. The pretreatment period is a reference point against which therapeutic change in the client's goal behavior can be compared during and after treatment. The length of the pretreatment period can be three days, a week, two weeks, or longer. One criterion for the length of this period is that it should be long enough to contain sufficient data points to serve as a *representative sample* of the client's behavior. For example, with a depressed client, the helper may ask the client to complete self-ratings on mood intensity at several different times during the next week or two. The helper may also ask the client to self-monitor instances or periods of depression that occur during this time. This situation is graphed in Figure 9.4. Notice that several data points are gathered to provide information about the stability of the client's behavior.

Usually, a minimum of three observations is necessary to "provide a reasonably accurate estimate of the pattern of the behavior" (Lundervold & Belwood, 2000, p. 94).

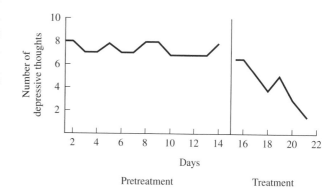

Figure 9.4 Graph of Depressive Thoughts: Pretreatment

If the helper does not collect any pretreatment data at all, determining the magnitude or amount of change that has occurred will be difficult because there are no precounseling data for comparison. The pretreatment period serves as a baseline of reference points, showing where the client is before any treatment or intervention. In Figure 9.4, for example, you can see the number of depressed thoughts that occur for this client in the first two weeks of counseling but before any treatment plan or change intervention is used. In the third week, when the helper introduces and the client works with an intervention such as cognitive restructuring, the client continues to record the number of depressed thoughts. These records, as well as any taken after counseling, can be compared to the baseline data.

Baseline measurement may not be possible with all clients, however. The client's concern may be too urgent or intense to allow you to take the time for gathering baseline data. Baseline measurement is often omitted in crisis situations. In a less urgent type of example, if a client reports "exam panic" and is faced with an immediate and very important test, the helper and client will need to start working to reduce the test anxiety at once. In such cases, the treatment or change strategy must be applied immediately. In these instances, a retrospective baseline may be better than nothing—"retrospective" meaning that the helper and the client establish a picture of what life was like during a relevant window prior to the intake (Abell & Hudson, 2000, p. 542).

Measurement during Treatment Strategies

During the helping process, the helper and client monitor the effects of a designated treatment on the goal behaviors after collecting pretreatment data and selecting an intervention or treatment strategy. The monitoring during the treatment phase is conducted by the continued collection of data on the same behaviors and using the same measures as during the pretreatment period. For example, if the client self-monitored the frequency and duration of self-critical thoughts during the pretreatment period, this self-monitoring would continue during the application of a helping strategy. Or if self-report inventories of the client's social skills were used during the pretreatment period, these same methods would be used to collect data during treatment.

Data collection during treatment is a feedback loop that gives both the helper and the client important information about the usefulness of the selected treatment strategy and the client's demonstration of the goal behavior. Both practitioners and clients alike benefit when feedback about progress is given to them in "real time" (Miller, Duncan, Sorrell, & Brown, 2005). Figure 9.5 shows the data of a client who self-monitored the number of depressed thoughts experienced during the application of two intervention or change strategies: cognitive restructuring and stimulus control. During this phase of data collection, it is important to specify the intervention as clearly as possible (Bloom et al., 2006). Collecting repeated measurements of the goal behavior(s) during treatment provides the most sensitive information about client improvement, or lack thereof.

From a practical standpoint, Lambert and Hawkins (2004) recommend that during treatment, practitioners are wise to administer any measure before counseling sessions rather than after sessions are over. Clients are more likely to complete measures prior to a session, and there is less of a risk that a client's responses given before counseling begins will have been biased or based on the immediate interactions with the practitioner. These authors also assert that client compliance with data collection is enhanced when practitioners take a minute or two during a session to review results and provide feedback to clients about any changes (Lambert & Hawkins, 2004).

If, as the helper, you can't do anything else in the way of data collection, you can be an accountable professional by at least measuring client goal-related outcomes during these two periods—before and during treatment—as we have just described. This enables you to collect data that can benefit clients while treatment is still occurring. The main advantage of collecting outcome data *during* treatment is that the data can provide information about client progress while the client is still in therapy. If a shift in treatment is necessary for client improvement, there is still time to make the shift. However, there is not enough information from those two data periods to tell much about causality. For example, it is hard to know if the change that occurred in the client's goal behaviors was a function of the specific intervention you used or if another event accounted for the observed results.

Although you cannot attribute client change directly to your intervention, this concern has more to do with the conducting of research than of practice evaluation (Bloom et al., 2006). As Nugent and associates (2001) conclude, "given the conflicting demands of science and practice, this may be, except in the most unusual cases, the strongest evidence that can be provided in the practice context" (p. 88). If possible, it is even better to extend data collection to include measurements immediately after a treatment strategy and also when counseling has terminated, as well as at some time after counseling is over—called a follow-up. These added periods of evaluation of the client's goal behaviors help to determine if the observed changes maintain over time (Bloom et al., 2006). They also give us more information about whether the client's changes were achieved at least in part because of the treatment intervention used (although the most conclusive evidence of causality is found with the multiple baseline designs described in the books noted earlier: Bloom et al., 2006; Cone, 2001; Hayes et al., 1999: Nugent et al., 2001).

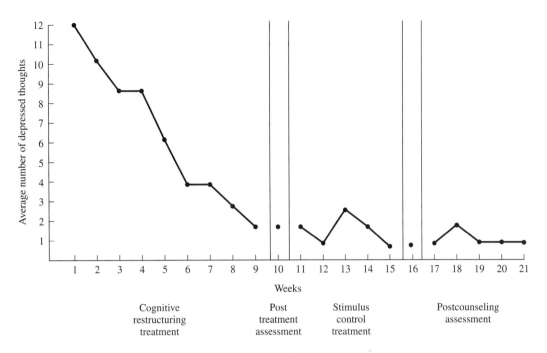

Figure 9.5 Graph of Depressive Thoughts: During Treatment and Posttreatment

Posttreatment: Measurement after Intervention and after Counseling

At the conclusion of a treatment strategy and/or at the conclusion of counseling, the helper and client should conduct a posttreatment measurement to indicate how much the client has achieved the desired results (see also Figure 9.5). Specifically, the data collected during a posttreatment evaluation are used to compare the client's demonstration and level of the goal behavior after treatment with the data collected during the pretreatment period and during treatment.

The posttreatment assessment may occur at the conclusion of a change strategy or at the point when counseling is terminated—or both. For instance, if a helper is using cognitive restructuring to help a client reduce depressed thoughts, the helper and client could collect data on the client's level of depressed thoughts after having finished working with the cognitive restructuring strategy. This assessment may or may not coincide with counseling termination. If the helper plans to use a second treatment strategy, then data would be collected at the conclusion of the cognitive restructuring strategy and prior to the use of another strategy. This example is depicted in Figure 9.5. Notice that the client continued to self-monitor the number of depressed thoughts both between the cognitive restructuring and stimulus control treatments and also after stimulus control, when counseling was terminated.

Ideally, the same types of measures used to collect data before and during counseling should be employed in the posttreatment evaluation. For instance, if the client self-monitored depressed thoughts before and during treatment, then, as Figure 9.5 illustrates, self-monitoring data also would be collected during posttreatment assessment. If the helper had also employed questionnaires such as the Beck Depression Inventory II during the pretreatment period and the treatment or intervention period, these measures would be used during posttreatment data collection as well.

The overall purpose of a posttreatment evaluation is to assess the extent to which the effects of intervention have been maintained at the conclusion of a treatment strategy. Additional information about the maintenance of treatment effects can be gleaned from conducting a follow-up assessment.

Follow-up Assessment

After the helping relationship has terminated, some type of follow-up assessment should be conducted. A helper can conduct both a short-term and a long-term follow-up. A short-term follow-up can occur three to six months after therapy. A long-term follow-up would occur one month to a year (or more) after counseling has been terminated. Generally, the helper should allow sufficient time to elapse before conducting a follow-up to determine the extent to which the client is maintaining desired changes without the helper's assistance.

There are several reasons for conducting follow-up assessments. First, a follow-up can indicate the helper's continued interest in the client's welfare. Second, a follow-up provides information that can be used to compare the client's performance of the goal behavior before and after counseling. Third, a follow-up allows the helper to determine how well the client is able to perform the goal behaviors in his or her own environment without relying on the helper's support and assistance. That last reason reflects one of the most important evaluative questions: Has counseling helped the client to maintain desired behaviors and to prevent the occurrence of undesired ones in some self-directed fashion? As we have indicated, more and more third-party payers are expecting practitioners to provide some follow-up data on client outcomes.

Both short-term and long-term follow-ups can take several forms. The kind of follow-up that a practitioner conducts often depends on the client's availability to participate in a follow-up and the time demands of each situation. Here are some ways in which a follow-up can be conducted:

1. Invite the client in for a follow-up interview. The purpose of the interview is to evaluate how the client is coping with respect to his or her "former" concern or issue. The interview may also involve client demonstrations of the goal behavior in simulated role plays.
2. Mail an inventory or questionnaire to the client, seeking information about her or his current status in relation to the original problem or concern.
3. Send a letter to the client asking about the current status of the problem. Be sure to include a stamped, self-addressed envelope.
4. Telephone the client for an oral report. The letter and telephone report could also incorporate the goal-attainment scale rating if that was used earlier.

These examples represent one-shot follow-up procedures that take the form of a single interview, letter, or telephone call. A more extensive (and sometimes more difficult to obtain) kind of follow-up involves the client's engaging in self-monitoring or self-rating of the goal behavior for a designated time period, such as two or three weeks. Figure 9.6

shows the level of depressed thoughts of a client at a six-month follow-up.

As you can see from the figures, data collected in an outcome evaluation are usually plotted on graphs for visual inspection, giving approximate information and rapid feedback about client goal-related changes. Assessment of changes from graphs is difficult, however, if the patterns are unclear or too variable to offer much meaning. (See Bloom et al., 2006, and Cone, 2001, for additional information about the meanings of graphed data.)

It is also important for helpers to think about introducing and including clients in practice evaluations, stressing that clients can help in monitoring progress. Practice evaluation is used to select and modify workable plans of action. However, challenges to this process occur with clients who are psychotic, cognitively impaired, or literate in languages other than English, as few rapid-assessment inventories have been translated (Callaghan, 2001, p. 296). In these instances, or with clients who may have severe clinical disorders, evaluation strategies often need to be tailored to the individual client. When possible, inform clients that you need to gather facts and that some portion of fact gathering or data collection will continue throughout your contacts together—even during intervention—in order to have "a continuing record of the pulse of the situation" (Bloom et al., 2006, p. 390). In the following model example and dialogue with our client Isabella, we illustrate the interconnected processes of defining and evaluating outcome goals.

MODEL EXAMPLE: THE CASE OF ISABELLA

Isabella's first outcome goal was defined as to acquire and demonstrate a minimum of four initiating skills, including four of the following: (1) asking questions or making reasonable requests, (2) expressing differences of opinion, (3) expressing positive feelings, (4) expressing negative feelings, and (5) volunteering answers or opinions in at least four situations a week with her parents and in math class. This overall goal can be assessed on a goal-attainment scale (Kiresuk & Sherman, 1968). See Table 9.4 on page 259 for Isabella's specific GAS. Additionally, a global outcome measure such as the GAF score from the *DSM-IV TR* or the OQ 45 (Lambert, Okiishi, Finch, & Johnson, 1998) can be used before and during treatment as well to give more general indicators of clinical improvement.

Four subgoals are associated with Isabella's first goal:

1. To decrease anxiety associated with anticipation of failure in math class and rejection by parents from self-ratings of intensity of 70 to 50 on a 100-point scale during the next two weeks of treatment.
2. To increase positive self-talk and thoughts that "girls are capable" in math class and other competitive situations

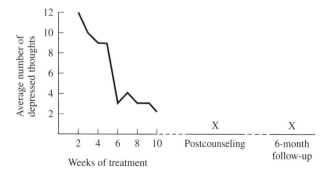

Figure 9.6 Graph of Follow-up Data

from zero or two times a week to four or five times a week over the next two weeks during treatment.

3. To increase attendance in math class from two or three times a week to four or five times a week during treatment.

4. To increase verbal participation and initiation in math class and with her parents from none or once a week to three or four times a week over the next two weeks during treatment. Verbal participation is defined as asking and answering questions with teacher or parents, volunteering answers or offering opinions, or going to the chalkboard. (For a summary of these subgoals, see Table 9.5, Isabella's goal chart, on page 260.)

The helper and Isabella need to establish the method of evaluating progress on each of the four subgoals and to determine the response dimension for each subgoal. For subgoal 1, Isabella could self-monitor intensity of anxiety associated with anticipated failure in math class and rejection from parents, on a scale ranging from 0 to 100. For subgoal 2, we recommend that Isabella self-monitor her self-talk during math class and in other competitive situations. She could be instructed to write (in vivo) her self-talk on note cards during baseline and treatment. Subgoal 3 is to increase her attendance in math class. Isabella could keep a record of the days she attended class, and these data could be verified from the teacher's attendance records, with Isabella's permission. Subgoal 4, verbal participation and initiation in math class and with her parents, also could be self-monitored (in vivo). Isabella could record each time she performed these verbal responses. Again, the same data would be collected before, during, and after an intervention. We illustrate this evaluation process in the following continuation of our model dialogue.

MODEL DIALOGUE: THE CASE OF ISABELLA

The helper starts by *summarizing* the previous session and by checking out whether Isabella's goals have changed in any way. Goal setting is a flexible process, subject to revisions along the way.

1. **Helper:** Okay, Isabella, last week when we talked, just to recap, you mentioned three areas you'd like to work on. Is this still accurate, or have you added anything or modified your thinking in any way about these since we last met?

Client: No, that's still where I want to go right now. And I still want to start with this whole issue of expressing myself and not worrying so much about what other people think. I've been doing a lot of thinking about that this week, and I think I'm really starting to see how much I let other people use me as a doormat and also control my reactions in a lot of ways.

2. **Helper:** Yes, you mentioned some of those things last week. They seem to be giving you some incentive to work on this.

Client: Yeah. I guess I'm finally waking up and starting to feel a little upset about it.

In the next response, the helper explains the *purpose* of the session and solicits Isabella's opinion, again giving her another opportunity to express her opinions.

3. **Helper:** Last week I mentioned it might be helpful to map out a plan of action. How does that sound to you? If it isn't where you want to start, let me know.

Client: No, I do. I've been kind of gearing up for this all week.

In the next two responses, the helper helps Isabella define the *behaviors* associated with the goal—what she will be doing, thinking, and feeling.

4. **Helper:** Okay, last week when we talked about this area of change, you described it as wanting to express yourself more without worrying so much about the reactions of other people. Could you tell me what you mean by expressing yourself—to make sure we're on the same wavelength?

Client: Well, like in math class, I need to volunteer the answers when I know them, and volunteer to go to the board. Also, I hesitate to ask questions. I need to be able to ask a question without worrying if it sounds foolish.

5. **Helper:** You've mentioned three specific ways in math class you want to express yourself [makes a note]. I'm going to jot them down on this paper in case we want to refer to them later. Anything else you can think of about math class?

Client: No, not really. The other situation I have trouble with is with my parents.

"Trouble" is not very specific. Again, a *behavioral definition* of the goal is sought in the next two responses.

6. **Helper:** Okay, "trouble." Again, can you describe exactly how you'd like to express yourself when interacting with them?

Client: Kind of the same stuff. Sometimes I would like to ask them a question. Or ask for help or something. But I don't. I almost never express my ideas or opinions to them, especially if I don't agree with their ideas. I just keep things to myself.

7. **Helper:** So you'd like to be able to make a request, ask a question, talk about your ideas with them, and express disagreement.

Client: Yeah. Wow—sounds hard.

In the following response, the helper prepares Isabella for the idea of working in *small steps* and also explores *conditions (situations, people)* associated with the goal.

8. **Helper:** It will take some time, and we won't try to do everything at once. Just take one step at a time. Now, you've mentioned two different situations where these things are important to you—math class and with your parents. I noticed last week there was one time when you were reluctant to express your opinion to me. Is this something you want to do in any other situations or with any other people?

Client: Well, sure—it does crop up occasionally at different times or with different people, even friends. But it's worse in math and at home. I think if I could do it there, I could do it anywhere.

In the next response, the helper starts to explore the *level* or *desired extent of change.* The helper is attempting to establish a *current base rate* in order to know how much the client is doing now.

9. **Helper:** I'm making a note of this too. Now could you estimate how often you express yourself in the ways you've described above *right now,* either in math class or with your parents, during the course of an average week?

Client: You mean how many times do I do these things during the week?

10. **Helper:** Yes.

Client: Probably almost never—at least not in math class or at home. Maybe once or twice at the most.

The helper continues to help Isabella identify a *practical* and *realistic level of change.*

11. **Helper:** If you express yourself in one of these ways once or twice a week now, how often would you like to be doing this? Think of something that is also practical or realistic.

Client: Mm. Well, I don't really know. Offhand, I'd guess about four or five times a week—that's about once a day, and that would take a lot of energy for me to be able to do that in these situations.

At this point, the *behavior, conditions, and level of change* for this terminal goal are defined. The helper asks Isabella whether this definition is the way she wants it.

12. **Helper:** I'll make a note of this. Check what I have written down—does it seem accurate? [Isabella reads what is listed as the first outcome goal on her goal chart, Table 9.5, on page 260.]

Client: Yeah. Gosh, that sort of makes it official, doesn't it?

This is the second time Isabella has expressed a little hesitation. So in the next response the helper checks out *her feelings* about the process.

13. **Helper:** Yes. I'm wondering what kinds of feelings you are having about what we're doing now.

Client: Kind of good and a little scared too. Like do I really have what it takes to do this?

In the next response, the helper responds to Isabella's concern. Isabella has already selected this goal, yet if she has difficulty later on moving toward it, they will need to explore *what her present behavior is trying to protect.*

14. **Helper:** One thing I am sure of is that you do have the resources inside you to move in this direction as long as this is a direction that is important to you. If we move along and you feel stuck, we'll come back to this and see how you keep getting stuck at this point.

Client: Okay.

Next the helper introduces and *develops a goal-attainment* scale for this particular goal (responses 15–20).

15. **Helper:** Let's spend a little time talking about this particular goal we've just nailed down. I'd like to set up some sort of a system with you in which we rank what you expect or would like to happen, but also the best possible and the least possible success we could have with this goal. This gives us both a concrete target to work toward. How does that sound?

Client: Okay. What exactly do we do?

16. **Helper:** Well, let's start with a range of numbers from −2 to +2. It will look like this [draws the following numbers on a sheet of paper]:

−2

−1

0

+1

+2

Zero represents an acceptable and expected level, one you could live with. What do you think it would be in this case?

Client: I guess maybe doing this at least twice a week—at least once in math and once at home. That would be better than nothing.

17. **Helper:** We'll put that down opposite zero. If that's acceptable, would you say that the four per week you mentioned earlier is more than expected?

Client: Yes.

18. **Helper:** Okay, let's put that down for +1 and how about eight per week for +2. That's sort of in your wildest dreams. How is that?

Client: Let's go for it.

19. **Helper:** Now, if two per week is acceptable for you, what would be less than acceptable—one or zero?

Client: One is better than nothing—zero is just where I am now.

20. **Helper:** So let's put one per week with −1 and none per week with −2. Now we have a way to keep track of your overall progress on this goal. Do you have any questions about this? [See Table 9.4 for the goal-attainment scale for Isabella's first outcome goal.]

Client: No, it seems pretty clear.

In the next response, the helper introduces the idea of *subgoals*, which represent small action steps toward the outcome goal, and asks Isabella to identify the *initial step*, which is subgoal 1 on Table 9.5.

21. **Helper:** Another thing that I think might help with your apprehension is to map out a plan of action. What we've just done is to identify exactly where you want to get to—maybe over the course of the next few months. Instead of trying to get there all at once, let's look at different steps you could take to get there, with the idea of taking just one step at a time, just like climbing a staircase. For instance, what do you think would be your first step—the first thing you would need to do to get started in a direction that moves directly to this result?

Client: Well, the first thing that comes to my mind is needing to be less uptight. I worry about what other people's reactions will be when I do say something.

In the next two responses, the helper helps Isabella define the *behavior and conditions associated with this initial subgoal,* just as she did previously for the outcome goal.

22. **Helper:** So you want to be less uptight and worry less about what other people might think. When you say "other people," do you have any particular persons in mind?

Client: My parents, of course, and to some degree almost anyone that I don't know too well or anyone like my math teacher, who is in a position to evaluate me.

23. **Helper:** So you're talking mainly about lessening these feelings when you're around your parents, your math teacher, or other people who you think are evaluating you.

Client: Yes, I think that's it.

In response 24, the helper is trying to establish the *current level of intensity* associated with Isabella's feelings of being

TABLE 9.4	Goal-Attainment Scale for Isabella's First Outcome Goal	
Date: 2/5/07	**Frequency of verbal initiating skills**
(−2) Most unfavorable outcome	Zero per week
(−1) Less than expected success	One per week — either with parents or in math class
(0) Expected level	Two per week — at least one with parents and at least one in math class
(+1) More than expected success	Four per week — at least two with parents and two in math class
(+2) Best expected success	Eight or more per week — at least four with parents and four in math class

TABLE 9.5 Isabella's Goal Chart	
Outcome Goals	**Related Subgoals**
Goal 1 (B) to acquire and demonstrate a minimum of four different initiating skills (asking a question or making a reasonable request, expressing differences of opinion, expressing positive feelings, expressing negative feelings, volunteering answers or opinions, going to the board in class) (C) in her math class and with her parents (L) in at least 4 situations a week	1. (B) to decrease anxiety associated with anticipation of failure (C) in math class or rejection by parents (L) from a self-rated intensity of 70 to 50 on a 100-point scale during the next 2 weeks 2. (B) to restructure thoughts or self-talk by replacing thoughts that "girls are dumb" with "girls are capable" (C) in math class and in other threatening or competitive situations (L) from 0–2 per day to 4–5 per day 3. (B) to increase attendance (C) at math class (L) from 2–3 times per week to 4–5 times per week 4. (B) to increase verbal participation skills (asking and answering questions, volunteering answers or offering opinions) (C) in math class and with her parents (L) from 0–1 times per day to 3–4 times per day
Goal 2 (B) to increase positive perceptions about herself and her ability to function effectively (C) in competitive situations such as math class (L) by 50% over the next 3 months	1. (B) to eliminate conversations (C) with others in which she discusses her lack of ability (L) from 2–3 per week to 0 per week 2. (B) to increase self-visualizations in which she sees herself as competent and adequate to function independently (C) in competitive situations or with persons in authority (L) from 0 per day to 1–2 per day 3. (B) to identify negative thoughts and increase positive thoughts (C) about herself (L) by 25% in the next 2 weeks
Goal 3 (B) to acquire and use five different decision-making skills (identifying an issue, generating alternatives, evaluating alternatives, selecting the best alternative, and implementing action) (C) at least one of which represents a situation in which significant others have given her their opinion or advice on how to handle it (L) in at least two different situations during a month	1. (B) to decrease thoughts and worry about making a bad choice or poor decision (C) in any decision-making situation (L) by 25% in the next 2 weeks 2. (B) to choose a course of action and implement it (C) in any decision-making situation (L) at least once during the next 2 weeks

Key: B = behavior; C = condition; L = level.

uptight. The helper does this by using an *imagery assessment* in the interview. *Self-reported ratings of intensity* are used in conjunction with the imagery.

24. **Helper:** Now I'm going to ask you to close your eyes and imagine a couple of situations that I'll describe to you. Try to really get involved in the situation—put yourself there. If you feel any nervousness, signal by raising this finger. [The helper shows Isabella the index finger of her right hand and describes three

situations—one related to parents, one related to math class, and one related to a job interview with a prospective employer. In all three situations, Isabella raises her finger. After each situation, the helper stops and asks Isabella to rate the intensity of her anxiety on a SUDS 0-to-100-point scale, zero being *complete calm and relaxation* and 100 being *total panic*.]

After the imagery assessment for base rate, the helper asks Isabella to *specify a desired level of change for this subgoal.*

25. **Helper:** Now, just taking a look at what happened here in terms of the intensity of your feelings, you rated the situation with your parents about 75, the one in math class 70, and the one with the employer 65. Where would you like to see this drop down to during the next couple of weeks?

Client: Oh, I guess about a 10.

It is understandable that someone with fairly intense anxiety wants to get rid of it, and it is possible to achieve that goal within the next few months. However, such goals are more effective when they are *immediate rather than distant.* In the next two responses, the helper asks Isabella to *specify a realistic level of change* for the immediate future.

26. **Helper:** That may be a number to shoot for in the next few months, but I'm thinking that in the next three or four weeks the jump from, say, 70 to 10 is pretty big. Does that gap feel realistic or feasible?

Client: Mm. I guess I was getting ahead of myself.

27. **Helper:** It's important to think about where you want to be in the long run. I'm suggesting three or four weeks mainly so you can start to see some progress and lessening of intensity of these feelings in a fairly short time. What number seems reasonable to you to shoot for in the short run?

Client: Well, maybe a 45 or 50.

At this point, the helper and Isabella continue to *identify other subgoals or intermediate steps* between the initial subgoal and the terminal outcome.

28. **Helper:** That seems real workable. Now, we've sort of mapped out the first step. Let's think of other steps between this first one and this result we've written down here. [Helper and client continue to generate possible action steps. Eventually they select and define the remaining three subgoals shown on Table 9.5, Isabella's goal chart.]

Assuming the remaining subgoals are selected and defined, the next step is to *rank order* or *sequence* the four subgoals and *list them in order on a goal pyramid* like the one shown in Figure 9.2.

29. **Helper:** We've got the first step, and now we've mapped out three more. Consider where you will be after this first step is completed. Which one of the three remaining steps comes next? Let's discuss it, and then we'll fill it in, along with this first step, on a goal pyramid, which you can keep so you know exactly what part of the pyramid you're on and when. [Helper and Isabella continue to rank order subgoals, and Isabella lists them in sequenced order on a goal pyramid.]

In response 30, the helper points out that *subgoals may change in type or sequence.* The helper then shifts the focus to exploration of potential *obstacles for the initial subgoal.*

30. **Helper:** Now we've got our overall plan mapped out. But this can change too. You might find later on that you want to add a step or reorder the steps. Let's go back to your first step—decreasing these feelings of nervousness and worrying less about the reactions of other people. Because this is what you want to start working on this week, describe anything or anybody who might get in your way or would make it difficult for you to work on this.

Client: It is mostly something inside me. In this instance, I guess I am my own worst enemy.

31. **Helper:** So you're saying there don't seem to be any people or situations outside yourself that may be obstacles. If anyone sets up an obstacle course, it will be you.

Client: Yeah. Mostly because I feel I have so little control of those feelings.

The client has identified herself and her perceived lack of control over her feelings as *obstacles.* Later on, the helper will need to help Isabella select and work with one or two *intervention strategies.*

32. **Helper:** So one thing we need to do is to look at ways you can develop skills and know-how to manage these feelings so they don't get the best of you.

Client: I think that would help.

In the next response, the helper explores *existing resources and support systems* that Isabella might use to help her work effectively with the subgoal.

33. **Helper:** That's where I'd like to start in just a minute. Before we do, can you identify any people who could help you with these feelings—or anything else you could think of that might help instead of hinder you?

Client: Well, coming to see you. It helps to know I can count on that. And I have a real good friend who is sort of the opposite of me, and she's real encouraging.

Social allies are an important factor in effecting change, and the helper uses this term in response 34 to underscore this point.

34. **Helper:** Okay, so you've got at least two allies.

Client: Yeah.

In response 35, the helper helps Isabella develop a way to continue the *self-ratings of the intensity* of her nervous feelings. This gives both of them a *benchmark to use in assessing progress and reviewing* the adequacy of the first subgoal selected.

35. **Helper:** The other thing I'd like to mention is a way for you to keep track of any progress you're making. You know how you rated these situations I described today? You could continue to do this by keeping track of situations in which you feel uptight and worry about the reactions of others. Jot down a brief note about what happened and then a number on this 0-to-100 scale that best represents how intense your feelings are at that time. As you do this and bring it back, it will help both of us see exactly what's happening for you on this first step. This will also help us develop a plan of action and modify it if we need to. Does that sound like something you would find agreeable?

Client: Yeah—do I need to do it during the situation or after?

Clients are more likely to do *self-ratings or self-monitoring if it falls into their daily routine,* so this is explored in the next response.

36. **Helper:** What would be most practical for you?

Client: Probably after, because it's hard to write in the middle of it.

The helper encourages Isabella to make her notes soon after the situation is over. *The longer the gap, the less accurate* the data might be.

37. **Helper:** That's fine. Try to write it down as soon as it ends or shortly thereafter, because the longer you wait, the harder it will be to remember. Also, to get an idea of your current level of anxiety, I'd like you to take a

few minutes at the end of our session today to fill out a paper- and-pencil form that asks you some questions about what you may be feeling. There are no right or wrong answers on this, so it's not like a test! I'll be asking you to do this again several times during our work together. Would you feel comfortable doing this?

Before the session ends, they have to work on the *obstacle* Isabella identified earlier—that she is her own worst enemy because her feelings are in control of her.

38. **Helper:** Now, let's go back to that obstacle you mentioned earlier—that your feelings are in control of you. . . .

Upon exploring this issue, the helper will select treatment interventions to use with Isabella.

CHAPTER SUMMARY

The primary purpose of identifying goals is to convey to the client the responsibility and role she or he has in contributing to the results of the helping process. Without active client participation, counseling may be doomed to failure. The selection of goals should reflect *client* choices. Effective goals are consistent with the *client's* cultural identity and belief systems. The helper's role is mainly to use leads that help with goal selection by the client. Together, helper and client explore whether the goal is owned by the client, whether it is realistic, and what advantages and disadvantages are associated with it. If helper and client agree to pursue the identified goals, these goals must be defined clearly and specifically. Throughout this process the client moves along a change continuum ranging from contemplation to preparation and finally to action.

Well-defined goals make it easier to note and assess progress and also aid in guiding the client toward the desired goal(s). A goal is defined when you are able to specify the overt and covert behaviors associated with the goal, the conditions or context in which the goal is to be carried out or achieved, and the level of change. After the outcome goal is defined, helper and client work jointly to identify and sequence subgoals that represent intermediate action steps and lead directly to the goal. Obstacles that might hinder goal attainment and resources that may aid in goal attainment are also explored.

As outcome goals are defined, ways to evaluate progress toward these goals are also incorporated into the helping process. Practice evaluation is an important component of the helping process. Without it, practitioners have no knowledge of how their interventions are working to help clients achieve their outcome goals. Data related to client outcome goals are collected before, during, and after treatment. Individualized, specific, and global measures of goal-related outcomes are used in practice evaluations as outcome indicators. A comprehensive practice evaluation uses multiple measures so that it is multidimensional in scope. When used effectively, outcome measures represent another therapeutic tool available to practitioners.

REFERENCES

Abell, N., & Hudson, W. (2000). Pragmatic applications of single-case and group designs in social work practice evaluation and research. In P. Allen-Meares & C. Garvin (Eds.), *Handbook of social work direct practice* (pp. 535–550). Thousand Oaks, CA: Sage.

American Psychiatric Association. (2000). *Diagnostic and statistical manual of mental disorders* (4th ed., text revision). Washington, DC: Author.

Bandura, A. (1989). Human agency in social cognitive theory. *American Psychologist, 44,* 1175–1185.

Beck, A. T. (1993). *The Beck Anxiety Inventory*. San Antonio: Psychological Corporation, Harcourt Brace.

Beck, A. T., Steer, R. A., & Brown, G. K. (1996). *The Beck Depression Inventory II*. San Antonio: Psychological Corporation, Harcourt Brace.

Bloom, M., Fischer, J., & Orme, J. (2006). *Evaluating practice: Guidelines for the accountable professional* (5th ed.). Boston: Allyn & Bacon.

Brown, L. S. (1994). *Subversive dialogues: Theory in feminist therapy*. New York: Basic.

Callaghan, G. (2001). Demonstrating clinical effectiveness for individual practitioners and clinics. *Professional Psychology, 32,* 289–297.

Cisneros, S. (1984). *The house on Mango Street*. New York: Random House.

Cone, J. D. (2001). *Evaluating outcomes: Empirical tools for effective practice*. Washington, DC: American Psychological Association.

Corcoran, K., & Fischer, J. (2000). *Measures for clinical practice* (3rd ed.). New York: Free Press.

Cronbach, L. J. (1990). *Essentials of psychological testing* (5th ed.). New York: Harper & Row.

Davis, S., & Meier, S. (2001). *The elements of managed care*. Belmont, CA: Wadsworth.

DeJong, W. (1994). Relapse prevention. *International Journal of the Addictions, 29,* 681–705.

Derogatis, L. R. (1983). *SCL-90 R administration, scoring and procedures manual–II*. Towson, MD: Clinical Psychometric Research.

Derogatis, L. R. (1993). *BSI: Administration, scoring, and procedures manual.* (3rd ed.). Minneapolis: National Computer Systems.

Eisen, S. V., Grob, M. C., & Klein, A. A. (1986). BASIS: The development of a self-report measure for psychiatric inpatient evaluation. *The Psychiatric Hospital, 17,* 166–171.

Gibbs, L. E. (2003). *Evidence-based practice for the helping professions: A practical guide with integrated multimedia*. Pacific Grove, CA: Thomson–Brooks/Cole.

Hatfield, D. R., & Ogles, B. M. (2004). The use of outcome measures by psychologists in clinical practice. *Professional Psychology, 35,* 485–491.

Hayes, S. C., Barlow, D. H., & Nelson-Gray, R. D. (1999). *The scientist practitioner: Research and accountability in the age of managed care* (2nd ed.). Boston: Allyn & Bacon.

Hepworth, D. H., Rooney, R. H., Dewberry Rooney, G., Strom-Gottfried, K., & Larsen, J. (2006). *Direct social work practice* (7th ed.). Belmont, CA: Thomson–Brooks/Cole.

Hodges, K. (1997). *Child and adolescent functional assessment scale*. Ann Arbor, MI: Functional Assessment System.

Howard, K., Brill, P., Lueger, R., & O'Mahoney, M. (1995). *Integra outpatient tracking system*. Philadelphia: Compass Information Services.

Hudson, W. W. (1996a). *Computer assisted assessment package*. Tallahassee, FL: WALMYR.

Hudson, W. W. (1996b). *Computer assisted social services*. Tallahassee, FL: WALMYR.

Iglesias, E., & Cormier, S. (2002). The transformation of girls to women: Finding voice and developing strategies for liberation. *Journal of Multicultural Counseling and Development, 4,* 259–271.

Irvin, J., Bowers, C., Dunn, M., & Wang, M. (1999). Efficacy of relapse prevention: A meta-analytic review. *Journal of Consulting and Clinical Psychology, 67,* 563–570.

Kiresuk, T. J., & Sherman, R. E. (1968). Goal attainment scaling: A general method for evaluating comprehensive mental health programs. *Community Mental Health Journal, 4,* 443–453.

Kirst-Ashman, K., & Hull, G. (2006). *Understanding generalist practice* (4th ed.). Pacific Grove, CA: Brooks/Cole–Wadsworth Group.

Lambert, M., Hansen, N., Umphress, V., Lunnen, K., Okiishi, J., Burlingame, et al. (1996). *Administration and scoring manual for the outcome questionnaire (OQ45.2)*. Wilmington, DE: American Professional Credentialing Services.

Lambert, M., Harmon, C., Slade, K., Whipple, J. L., & Hawkins, E. J. (2005). Providing feedback to psychotherapists on their patients' progress. *Journal of Clinical Psychology/In Session, 61,* 165–174.

Lambert, M., & Hawkins, E. (2004). Measuring outcome in professional practice: Considerations in selecting and using brief outcome instruments. *Professional Psychology, 35,* 492–499.

Lambert, M., Okiishi, J., Finch, A., & Johnson, L. (1998). Outcome assessment: From conceptualization to implementation. *Professional Psychology, 29,* 63–70.

Leibert, T. W. (2006). Making change visible: The possibilities in assessing mental health counseling outcomes. *Journal of Counseling and Development, 84,* 108–118.

Lundervold, D., & Belwood, M. (2000). The best kept secret in counseling: Single-case (N = 1) experimental designs. *Journal of Counseling and Development, 79,* 92–102.

MacKay, P., & Marlatt, G. (1990). Maintaining sobriety. *International Journal of the Addictions, 25,* 1257–1276.

Marlatt, G., & Gordon, J. R. (1985). *Relapse prevention.* New York: Guilford Press.

Marten, P., & Heimberg, R. (1995). Toward an integration of independent practice and clinical research. *Professional Psychology, 26,* 48–53.

Miller, S. D., Duncan, B. L., Sorrell, R., & Brown, G. S. (2005). The partners for change outcome management system. *Journal of Clinical Psychology/In Session, 61,* 199–208.

Mitchell, K., Levin, A., & Krumboltz, J. (1999). Planned happenstance: Constructing unexpected career opportunities. *Journal of Counseling and Development, 77,* 115–124.

Nugent, W., Sieppert, J., & Hudson, W. (2001). *Practice evaluation for the 21st century.* Pacific Grove, CA: Brooks/ Cole and Wadsworth.

Nurius, P. S., & Hudson, W. W. (1993). *Human services: Practice evaluation and computers.* Pacific Grove, CA: Brooks/Cole.

Ogles, B., Lambert, M., & Fields, S. (2002). *Essentials of outcome assessment.* New York: Wiley.

Ogles, B., Lambert, M., & Masters, K. (1996). *Assessing outcome in clinical practice.* Boston: Allyn & Bacon.

Oz, S. (1995). A modified balance-sheet procedure for decision making in therapy: Cost–cost comparison. *Professional Psychology, 25,* 78–81.

Petry, N., Tennen, H., & Affleck, J. (2000). Stalking the elusive client variable in psychotherapy research. In

C. Snyder & R. Ingram (Eds.), *Handbook of psychological change* (pp. 89–107). New York: Wiley.

Prochaska, J. (1999). How do people change, and how can we change to help many more people? In M. Hubble, B. Duncan, & S. Miller (Eds.), *The heart and soul of change* (pp. 227–258). Washington, DC: American Psychological Association.

Prochaska, J. (2000). Change at differing stages. In C. Snyder & R. Ingram (Eds.), *Handbook of psychological change* (pp. 109–127). New York: Wiley.

Prochaska, J., DiClemente, C., & Norcross, J. (1992). In search of how people change: Applications to addictive behaviors. *American Psychologist, 47,* 1102–1114.

Shiang, J. (2000). Research and practice: Does culture make a difference? In S. Soldz & L. McCullough (Eds.), *Reconciling empirical knowledge and clinical experience* (pp. 167–196). Washington, DC: American Psychological Association.

Smith, K. J., Subich, L., & Kalodner, C. (1995). The transtheoretical model's stages and processes of change and their relation to premature termination. *Journal of Counseling Psychology, 42,* 34–39.

Snyder, C. R., & Lopez, S. J. (2007). *Positive psychology:* Thousand Oaks, CA: Sage.

Sue, D. W., & Sue, D. (2003). *Counseling the culturally diverse* (4th ed.). New York: Wiley.

Tallman, K., & Bohart, A. C. (1999). The client as a common factor: Clients as self healers. In M. A. Hubble, B. L. Duncan, & S. D. Miller, *The heart and soul of change* (pp. 91–132). Washington, DC: American Psychological Association.

Watts-Jones, D. (1990). Toward a stress scale for African-American women. *Psychology of Women Quarterly, 14,* 271–275.

Werner-Wilson, R., Zimmerman, T., & Price, S. (1999). Are goals and topics influenced by gender and modality in the initial marriage and family therapy session? *Journal of Marital and Family Therapy, 25,* 253–262.

9   K N O W L E D G E   A N D   S K I L L   B U I L D E R

Part One

Learning Outcome 1 asks you to identify a problem for which you identify, define, and evaluate an outcome goal. Use the Goal-Setting Worksheet for this process. You can obtain feedback by sharing your worksheet with a colleague, supervisor, or instructor.

Goal-Setting Worksheet

1. Identify a concern.

2. State the desired outcome of the concern.

3. Assess the desired outcome.
   a. Does it specify what you want to do? (If not, reword it so that you state what you want to do instead of what you don't want to do.)
   b. Is this something you can see (hear, grasp) yourself doing every time?

4. In what ways is achievement of this goal important to you? To others?

5. What will achieving this goal require of you? Of others?

6. To what extent is this goal something you want to do? Something you feel you should do or are expected to do?

7. Is this goal based on
   — Rational, logical ideas?
   — Realistic expectations and ideas?
   — Irrational ideas and beliefs?
   — Logical thinking?
   — Perfectionistic standards (for self or others)?

8. How will achieving this goal help *you*? Help significant others in your life?

9. What problems could achieving this goal create for you? For others?

10. If the goal requires someone else to change, is not realistic or feasible, is not worthwhile, or poses more disadvantages than advantages, rework the goal. Then move on to item 11.

11. As a result of achieving the goal, exactly what will you be
    a. Doing: _____
    b. Thinking: _____
    c. Feeling: _____

12. Specify your goal definition in item 11 by indicating
    a. *Where* this will occur: _____
    b. *When* this will occur: _____

c. *With whom* this will occur: _____
d. *How much or how often* this will occur: _____

13. Develop a plan that specifies *how* you will attain your goal by identifying the action steps to be taken.
    a. _____
    b. _____
    c. _____
    d. _____
    e. _____
    f. _____
    g. _____
    h. _____
    i. _____
    j. _____
    k. _____
    l. _____
    m. _____
    n. _____

14. Check your list of action steps:
    a. Are the gaps between steps small? If not, add a step or two.
    b. Does each step represent only one major activity? Separate every step that does not into two or more steps.
    c. Does each step specify what, where, when, with whom, and how much or how often? If not, go back and define your action steps more concretely.

15. Use the goal pyramid on the page 266 to sequence your list of action steps. Start with the easiest, most immediate step at the bottom of the pyramid, and proceed to the most difficult, least immediate step at the top.

16. Starting with your first action step, brainstorm what could make each action step difficult to carry out or could interfere with doing it successfully. Consider feelings, thoughts, places, people, and lack of knowledge or skills. List the *obstacles* in the space provided on page 266.

17. Starting with your first action step, identify for each action step existing resources such as feelings, thoughts, situations, people and support systems, information, skills, beliefs, and self-confidence that would make it more likely for you to carry out the action or complete it more successfully. List the *resources* in the space provided on page 266.

18. Identify a way to monitor your progress for completion of each action step.

(continued)

KNOWLEDGE AND SKILL BUILDER

(*continued*)

19. Develop a plan to help yourself maintain the action steps
    after you attain them.

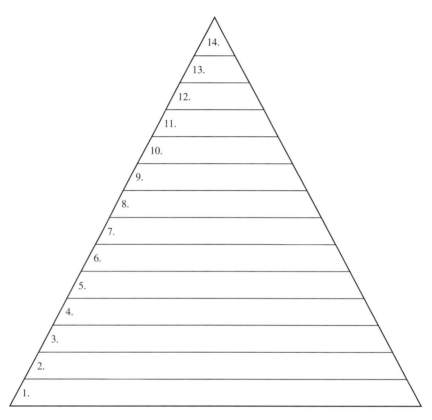

Goal Pyramid

Obstacles		Resources
1.		
2.		
3.		
4.		
5.		
6.		
7.		
8.		
9.		
10.		
11.		
12.		
13.		
14.		

9	K N O W L E D G E A N D S K I L L B U I L D E R

Part Two

In this part of the Knowledge and Skill Builder, we describe the case of Manuel. Assuming that Manuel is your client, describe the steps you would take to help him identify, define, and evaluate desired actions, given his stated problem (Learning Outcome 2). Try to include at least 10 of the 13 steps or categories we described in this chapter for identifying, defining, and evaluating outcome goals. You may want to consult the Interview Checklist for Identifying, Defining, and Evaluating Goals in Part Three for a review of these 13 steps. You can do this activity orally with a partner, in small groups, or by yourself. If you do it by yourself, you may want to jot down your ideas in writing for someone else to assess. Feedback follows on page 270.

The Case of Manuel

Manuel Tréjos is a 52-year-old Latino who is the manager of an advertising firm. He has been with the firm for 17 years and has another 12 years to go before drawing a rather lucrative retirement package. Over the last 3 years, however, Manuel has become increasingly dissatisfied with his job specifically and with work in general. He says he feels as if he wants nothing more than to quit, but he and his wife also want to build up a nest egg for their son's two young children, because their grandchildren are very important to them. Manuel realizes that if he leaves the firm now, he will lose many of his retirement benefits. Manuel defines his problem as feeling burned out with the nine-to-five job routine. He wishes to have more free time, but as the head of his family he also feels a sense of great responsibility to provide financial security.

Part Three

According to Learning Outcome 3, you will be able to demonstrate, in an interview setting, at least 10 of the 13 categories for identifying, defining, and evaluating client outcome goals. We suggest that you complete this part of the Knowledge and Skill Builder in triads. One person assumes the role of the helper and demonstrates helping the client with the goal-setting process in a 30-minute interview. The second person takes the role of the client. You may wish to portray the role and problem described for Manuel Tréjos in Part Two (if you choose to present something unfamiliar to the helper, be sure to inform the helper of your identified problem or concern before you begin). The third person assumes the role of the observer. The observer may act as the helper's alter ego and cue the helper during the role play, if necessary. The observer also provides feedback to the helper after the interview, using as a guide the Interview Checklist for Identifying, Defining, and Evaluating Goals, which follows. If you do not have access to an observer, tape-record your interview so you can assess it yourself.

Interview Checklist for Identifying, Defining, and Evaluating Goals

Instructions: Determine which of the following leads or questions the helper demonstrated. Check each helper question or lead demonstrated. Also check whether the client answered the content of the helper's question. Example leads and questions are provided next to each item of the checklist. These are only suggestions; be alert to other responses used by the helper.

Scoring	Category of information	Examples of helper leads or responses	Client response
___Yes ___No	1. Explain the purpose and importance of having goals or positive outcomes to the client.	"Let's talk about some areas you would like to work on during counseling. This will help us to do things that are related to what you want to accomplish."	___indicates understanding
___Yes ___No	2. Determine *positive* changes desired by client ("I would like" versus "I can't").	"What would you like to be doing [thinking, feeling] differently?" "Suppose some distant relative you haven't seen for a while comes here in several months. What would be different then from the way things are now?" "Assuming we are successful, what do you want to be doing, or how would this change for you?" "In what ways do you want to benefit from counseling?"	___identifies goal in positive terms
___Yes ___No	3. Determine whether the goal selected represents changes owned by the client rather than someone else ("I want to talk to my mom without yelling at her" rather than "I want my mom to stop yelling at me").	"How much control do you have to make this happen?" "Describe what changes this will require of you." "What changes will this require someone else to make?" "Can this be achieved without the help of anyone else?" "To whom is this change most important?"	___identifies who owns the goal

(continued)

9   KNOWLEDGE AND SKILL BUILDER

(continued)

____Yes____No	4. Identify advantages (positive consequences) to client and others of goal achievement.	"In what ways is it worthwhile to you and others to achieve this?" "Describe how achieving this goal will help you." "What problems will continue for you if you don't pursue this goal?" "What are the advantages of achieving this change—for you? For others?" "Identify who will benefit from this change—and how."	____identifies advantages
____Yes____No	5. Identify disadvantages (negative consequences) of goal achievement to client and others.	"Describe any new problems in living that achieving this goal might pose for you." "Identify any disadvantages to going in this direction." "How will achieving this change affect your life in adverse ways?" "How might this change limit or constrain you?"	____identifies disadvantages
____Yes____No	6. Identify what the client will be doing, thinking, or feeling in a concrete, observable way as a result of goal achievement ("I want to be able to talk to my mom without yelling at her," rather than "I want to get along with my mom").	"What do you want to be able to do [think, feel] differently?" "What would I see you doing [thinking, feeling] after this change?" "Describe a good and a poor example of this goal."	____specifies overt and covert behaviors
____Yes____No	7. Specify under what conditions and what situations goals will be achieved: when, where, and with whom ("I want to be able to talk to my mom at home during the next month without yelling at her").	"When do you want to accomplish this goal?" "Where do you want to do this?" "With whom?" "In what situations?"	____specifies people and places
____Yes____No	8. Specify how often or how much the client will do something to achieve goal ("I want to be able to talk to my mom at home during the next month without yelling at her at least once a day").	"How much [or how often] are you doing this [or feeling this way] now?" "What is a realistic increase or decrease?" "How much [or how often] do you want to be doing this to be successful at your goal?" "What amount of change is realistic, considering where you are right now?"	____specifies amount
____Yes____No	9. Identify and list small action steps the client will need to take to reach the goal (that is, break the big goal down into little subgoals). *List of Action Steps* 1. 2. 3. 4. 5.	"How will you go about doing [thinking, feeling] this?" "Identify exactly what you need to do to make this happen." "Let's brainstorm some actions you'll need to take to make your goal work for you." "What have you done in the past to work toward this goal?" "How did it help?" "Let's think of the steps you need to take to get from where you are now to where you want to be."	____lists possible action steps
____Yes____No	10. Sequence the action steps on the goal pyramid (a hierarchy) in terms of a. degree of difficulty (least to most difficult) b. immediacy (most to least immediate)	"Describe your first step. Your last step." "What is most important for you to do soon? Least important?" "How could we order these steps to maximize your success in reaching your goal?" "Let's think of the steps you need to take to get from where you are now to where you want to be and arrange them in an order from what seems easiest to you to the ones that seem hardest."	____assists in rank ordering

9 KNOWLEDGE AND SKILL BUILDER

____Yes____No	11. Identify any people, feelings, or situations that could prevent the client from taking action to reach the goal.	"Tell me about any obstacles you may encounter in trying to take this action." "What people [feelings, ideas, situations] might get in the way of getting this done?" "In what ways could you have difficulty completing this task successfully?"	____identifies possible obstacles
____Yes____No	12. Identify any resources (skill, knowledge, support) that client needs to take action to meet the goal.	"What resources do you have available to help you as you complete this activity?" "What particular thoughts or feelings are you aware of that might make it easier for you to ____?" "What kind of support system do you have from others that you can use to make it easier to ____?" "Describe what skills [or information] you possess that will help you do this more successfully."	____identifies existing resources and supports
____Yes____No	13. Develop a plan to evaluate progress toward the goal.	"Would it be practical for you to rate these feelings [count the times you do this] during the next two weeks? This information will help us determine the progress you are making." "Let's discuss a way you can keep track of how easy or hard it is for you to take these steps this week."	____agrees to monitor in some fashion

Most difficult, least immediate

5

4

3

2

1

Least difficult, most immediate

Part Four

Learning Outcome 4 asks you to conduct an outcome evaluation with yourself, another person, or a client, specifying *what* will be measured, *when* it will be measured, and *how*. Use the following guidelines:

1. Define and give examples of a desired goal behavior.

2. Specify what type of data you or the other person will collect (for example, verbal reports, frequency, duration, intensity, occurrence of the behavior).

3. a. Identify the methods to be used to collect these data (such as self-monitoring, goal-attainment scaling, rapid-assessment inventories, and self-ratings).

   b. For *each* method to be used, describe very specifically the instructions you or the client would need to use this method.

4. Collect data on the goal behaviors at least several times before implementing any treatment (change) strategy (pretreatment).

5. Following pretreatment data collection, implement some treatment strategy for a designated time period. Continue to collect data during the implementation of this treatment strategy.

6. Collect data after treatment. Graph all of your data, or visually inspect them. What do your data suggest about changes in the goal behavior and the effectiveness of your treatment? Share your results with a partner, a colleague, or your instructor.

KNOWLEDGE AND SKILL BUILDER   **FEEDBACK**

Part Two

1. Explain to Manuel the *purpose and importance* of developing goals.

2. Help Manuel state the goal or desired change in *positive terms*.

3. Help Manuel determine whether the goal he is moving toward represents *changes owned by him* and whether such factors are under his control. Probably, giving up his job or taking a leave of absence would be changes under his control.

4. Help Manuel identify *advantages* or *benefits* to be realized by achieving his goal. He seems to be thinking about increased leisure time as a major benefit. Are there others?

5. Help Manuel identify *disadvantages* or *possible costs* of making the desired change. He has mentioned loss of retirement benefits as one cost and subsequent loss of a nest egg for his grandchildren as another. Do the perceived benefits outweigh the costs? What effect would leaving his job have on his wife and family? Would this outcome be consistent with his cultural identity and his beliefs?

6. Help Manuel *define his goal behaviorally* by specifying exactly what he will be doing, thinking, and feeling as a result of goal achievement.

7. Help Manuel specify *where, when,* and *with whom* this will occur.

8. Identify *how much* or *how often* the goal will occur. An option that might be useful for Manuel is to develop and scale five possible outcomes, ranging from *most unfavorable* to *most expected* to *best possible* outcome (goal-attainment scaling).

9. Help Manuel explore and *identify action steps or subgoals* that represent small approximations toward the overall goal. Help him choose action steps that are practical, are based on his resources, and support his values and culture.

10. Help Manuel sequence the action steps according to *immediacy and difficulty* so he knows what step he will take first and what step will be his last one.

11. Explore any *obstacles* that could impede progress toward the goal, such as the presence or absence of certain feelings, ideas, thoughts, situations, responses, people, knowledge, and skills.

12. Explore existing *resources* that could help Manuel complete the action steps more successfully. Like examination of obstacles, exploration of resources also includes assessing the presence or absence of certain feelings, ideas, thoughts, situations, responses, people, knowledge, skills, beliefs, and confidence in pursuing desired outcomes.

13. Help Manuel develop a *plan to review completion of the action steps* and *evaluate progress toward the goal*.

CLINICAL DECISION MAKING AND TREATMENT PLANNING

LEARNING OUTCOMES

After completing this chapter, you will be able to

1. For the client case description of David Chan (Sue & Sue, 1990) and the description of proposed treatment interventions, identify the following:
   a. Ways in which the selected treatment interventions used by the helper failed to address either contextual awareness or consciousness development
   b. How the helper interpreted the client's distress (and perhaps resistance)
   c. Which of Lum's (2004) five interventions (see Box 10.4) the helper could have emphasized
   d. The recommended type, duration, and mode of treatment you would follow as David's helper
2. For the client case of Isabella, using a sample treatment-planning form (see Figure 10.1), develop a written treatment plan that identifies the presenting concern, strengths and resources, goals, measures, and treatment interventions.

Treatment planning is an essential therapeutic activity that includes case conceptualization/formulation, a determination of client goals, and the selection of the most appropriate interventions to help clients meet their goals. It is initiated after a comprehensive client assessment has been conducted (including assessing for client strengths and resources), a preliminary multiaxial diagnosis determined, and available services reviewed and identified. A treatment plan specifies the change interventions (type of treatment) that will help clients reach their stated goals, the specific format or way in which the intervention will be delivered to clients (mode of treatment), activities clients will engage in to realize their goals (client implementation), prognosis, and the frequency and duration of services.

Treatment planning is not a discrete activity that occurs at one point in time. It is a continuous process: the initial plan is revised when new information about the client is received, when the service delivery setting changes or the types of available services are altered or disrupted (e.g., due to funding restrictions), or when the client–helper relationship is at an impasse or experiences what Safran and Muran (2000) characterized as a "rupture." The actual written treatment plan, therefore, can be considered a living document—describing the client's current status as well as the services being rendered—always subject to modification.

Treatment planning is now required by many managed care systems for third-party reimbursement. Its practice, however, should not be regarded as simply fulfilling a funding source's mandate. There are several benefits to treatment planning whether or not an external entity has enforced its practice. First, because the plan is developed jointly by the client and helper, the client's emotional investment in the helping process may increase. Second, treatment planning stimulates the helper's critical thinking and helps to increase the likelihood that the best combination of interventions for a given client with particular outcome goals will be used. Third, developing a treatment plan is like constructing a road map, and the plan itself is intended to keep the process on track—that is, it promotes a structure that ensures that client needs are considered and met as much as possible. Fourth, treatment planning allows different professionals (e.g., members of a multidisciplinary treatment team) to coordinate care for a shared client, and the actual plan serves as the repository, concourse, or forum for their combined services.

COMMON FACTORS AND SPECIFIC INGREDIENTS OF TREATMENT

A central question of treatment planning is "What treatments or change intervention strategies are likely to be useful for this client?" This practical question is an extension of a general, more abstract (some might say existential), and all-encompassing question: "What produces or contributes to change in clients and in treatment outcomes?" Lambert's (1992) early research suggested that client characteristics (or extratherapeutic factors, including social support and cultural composition) account for most (approximately 40%) of client improvement as a result of participating in the helping process. They are followed by the therapeutic relationship (approximately 30%), hope and expectancy factors (15%), and theories and techniques (15%). This means that client characteristics play a pivotal role in the outcomes of any change intervention strategy, regardless of its theoretical base. The quality of the helping relationship is also tremendously important in producing effective outcomes. These four broad contributions have been referred to as common factors in facilitating change.

More recently, Lambert and Ogles (2004) proposed another set of common factors: support, learning, and action factors (see Table 10.1). Unlike the factors that Lambert identified in 1992, each factor in this newer research (2004) is attributable to the therapist, to therapy procedures, and to the client. In addition, Lambert and Ogles presented the three factors sequentially, to indicate their developmental nature. They suggested that certain factors are emphasized at certain points in the helping process and that each factor builds on its predecessor. As Lambert and Ogles explained, "the supportive functions precede changes in beliefs and attitudes, which precede the therapist's attempts to encourage patient action" (pp. 172–173). We would add that the developmental nature of these three common factors appears to be similar to and correspond with the three phases of treatment proposed by Howard, Lueger, Maling, and Martinovich (1993) and by Howard, Moras, Brill, Martinovich, and Lutz (1996): remoralization, remediation, and rehabilitation. Lambert and Ogles's *support factors* are intended to assist the client in experiencing greater well-being, or

remoralization, in the early phase of treatment, including a validation or normalization of his or her experiences (e.g., mitigation of isolation: "I'm not the only who's experienced these symptoms before"). Lambert and Ogles's *learning factors* address the amelioration of symptoms, or *remediation,* the middle phase of treatment when the client is learning to cope with or actively manage stressors. And the intended outcome of Lambert and Ogles's *action factors* is *rehabilitation,* the third phase of treatment proposed by Howard and colleagues. It is at this time that clients are transferring what they've learned in therapy to several areas of their lives in order to improve their overall functioning.

Although common factors should be a focus in clinical decision making, Reid, Kenaley, and Colvin (2004) cautioned against exclusive attention to common factors. In their review of 39 studies (conducted from 1990 to 2001) involving a variety of interventions (e.g., group, individual, case management) delivered specifically by social workers, they found that "common factors may not have been as influential" (p. 77). Differential (rather than equivalent) effects were found in the majority ($n = 30$) of studies, suggesting that specific interventions (e.g., feminist-oriented short-term counseling) delivered in a specified format (e.g., group) and targeting a select clientele (e.g., battered women) contribute to positive client outcomes (e.g., improved self-efficacy, parental reunification). Although their findings did not "deny the importance of common factors in social work" (p. 78), Reid et al. encouraged practitioners to intentionally focus on differential treatments when working with a heterogeneous clientele presenting with idiosyncratic needs and concerns.

TABLE 10.1 Common and Sequential Factors across Therapeutic Treatments		
Support Factors	**Learning Factors**	**Action Factors**
Catharsis	Advice	Behavioral regulation
Identification with therapist	Affective experiencing	Cognitive mastery
Mitigation of isolation	Assimilating problematic experiences	Encouragement of facing fears
Positive relationship	Cognitive learning	Taking risks
Reassurance	Corrective emotional experience	Mastery efforts
Release of tension	Feedback	Modeling
Structure	Insight	Practice
Therapeutic alliance	Rationale	Reality testing
Therapist/client active participation	Exploration of internal frame of reference	Success experience
Therapist expertness	Changing expectations of	Working through
Therapist warmth, respect, empathy, acceptance, genuineness	personal effectiveness	
Trust		

Source: "The Efficacy and Effectiveness of Psychotherapy," by M. J. Lambert & B. M. Ogles, in M. J. Lambert (Ed.), *Bergin and Garfield's Handbook of Psychotherapy and Behavior Change* (5th ed.), p. 173, Table 5.8. Copyright 2004 by Wiley & Sons. Reprinted by permission of the publisher.

FACTORS AFFECTING TREATMENT SELECTION

We believe that clinical decision making and treatment planning involve a consideration of common factors *and* differential interventions. This means that *skilled* helpers are helpers who can attend to both general and specific factors—one type does not take precedence over the other. Although considering both types of factors concurrently is often a challenging and ambiguous process, we believe it is natural, expected, and understandable given the complexities of human nature/behavior. Indeed, there are no treatment-planning "recipes" that, if followed exactly by the clinician, are guaranteed to result in effective care and treatment "success." We would like to think that the allure of working as a professional helper is that there are a variety of persons with whom we can work (i.e., no two clients are alike), the helping process is not intended to be routine or boring, and that there are no easy answers to the multiplicity of concerns that clients present.

Treatment planning can therefore be likened to an adventure, one that the client and helper embark on together and one that requires the joint design and construction of a map rather than reliance on an existing or predetermined set of directions. There are certainly major thoroughfares that need to be traversed (e.g., standards of care, treatment guidelines) and signposts that need to be considered (e.g., assessment of symptoms that meet diagnostic criteria). However, because each client is unique, the methods of transportation and the routes taken to reach the intended destination (the treatment goal) will vary from client to client. Shifting the analogy, we may say that treatment planning requires the helper to be able to see the forest *and* the trees.

In order to embark on the journey of comprehensive treatment planning customized to each client, we need to consider several factors. These include client characteristics, helper characteristics, and practice and documentation guidelines. Although these and other factors (e.g., the therapeutic relationship) might be considered "inextricably intertwined" (Hill, 2005, p. 438), we believe it is helpful to discuss them separately so as to appreciate their interconnections.

Client Characteristics

Client contributions to the helping process have been found to be instrumental to therapeutic change (Lambert, 1992). Indeed, Beutler and Clarkin (1990) proposed that "The characteristics that the patient brings to the treatment experience are the single most powerful sources of influence in the benefit to be achieved by treatment" (p. 31). Similarly, Bergin and Garfield (1994) noted that "It is the client more than the therapist who implements the change process. . . . As therapists have depended more

upon the client's resources, more change seems to occur" (pp. 825–826).

The range of actual and potential client variables to consider in treatment planning is limitless. Characteristics include psychopathology (e.g., symptom severity), sociodemographic descriptors (e.g., sex, age), and personality traits (e.g., sociability), all of which may be invariant (e.g., race and ethnic membership), relatively stable (e.g., socioeconomic status), or quite variable (e.g., motivation for change). Based on an accumulation of research conducted over a number of years, Beutler and his colleagues (Beutler, Clarkin, & Bongar, 2000; Beutler & Harwood, 2000) identified six client characteristics or variables that affect the selection and implementation of treatment strategies: (1) functional impairment, (2) subjective distress, (3) social support, (4) problem complexity/chronicity, (5) reactance/resistance tendencies, and (6) coping styles. Clarkin and Levy (2004) grouped these into three general categories: (1) client impairment (functional impairment, complexity/chronicity); (2) client response(s) to impairment, or what we refer to as symptom management (subjective distress, coping styles, reactance/resistance), and (3) clients' interpersonal context (social support).

Impairment

In general, impairment factors refer primarily to the type, level of severity, and chronicity of symptoms that clients present. These can be attributed to biological or genetic influences (e.g., family history of bipolar disorder), traumatic events (e.g., sexual abuse), learned behavior (e.g., specific phobias), socio-cultural-economic-political influences (e.g., poverty, immigration, oppression), and a combination of two or more. From a cognitive–behavioral perspective, Nezu, Nezu, and Lombardo (2004) differentiated between behavioral deficits (e.g., poor social skills) and behavioral excesses (e.g., compulsive behavior, aggressive actions). They also noted differences between cognitive deficiencies and cognitive distortions. The former refer to the absence of certain thinking processes, such as the failure to realize the consequences of one's actions; the latter refer to errors in cognitive processing, such as irrational beliefs.

The assessment of client impairment is important because, according to Beutler and Harwood (2000), it in turn determines the frequency and intensity of treatment provided. Indeed, the benefits of treatment directly correspond to treatment intensity among functionally impaired clients (p. 74). The Global Assessment of Functioning (GAF) scale (i.e., Axis V) of the *Diagnostic and Statistical Manual of Mental Disorders* (4th ed., text revision; *DSM-IV TR*; American Psychiatric Association, 2000a) is often used to determine a client's level of care and treatment setting, such as whether outpatient or inpatient care is indicated.

To help determine type and level of client impairment, family members and other collaterals should be consulted, as well as professionals who were involved in earlier treatment the client may have received. Medical records of previous mental health treatment should also be obtained. Depending on the complexity of the case, additional professionals should be included in the treatment-planning process and the provision of comprehensive care. For certain presenting disorders, recommendations have been made for the delivery of services by members of a multidisciplinary treatment team. These include eating disorders (American Psychiatric Association, 2000b; Grave, 2005), victims of intimate partner violence (Miller, Veltkamp, Lane, Bilyeu, & Elzie, 2002), and co-occurring disorders (i.e., substance use disorder and mental illness; Mueser, Noordsy, Drake, & Fox, 2003). Particularly when a client is struggling with a severe and persistent mental illness (e.g., schizophrenia), Assertive Community Treatment (ACT) conducted by a team of professionals has established itself as an evidence-based practice (Bond, Drake, Mueser, & Latimer, 2001).

Symptom Management

The ways in which clients experience and express their complaints (e.g., symptoms) and their response to treatment interventions are also important considerations in treatment planning. Three ways in which clients experience and manage their symptoms in and outside of treatment are subjective distress, coping, and reactance/resistance.

Subjective distress typically refers to an individual's internal state rather than his or her observable demonstration of that distress, and it is thus measured according to client report. In addition, Beutler et al. (2000) noted that subjective distress is separate from specific diagnoses and represents transient states of well-being. This means that a client's level of internal distress can be modified and preferably alleviated, depending on the client's investment in the change process. Based on research findings, Beutler et al. (2000) offered three general guidelines for addressing or making use of the client's style of managing his or her own symptoms (p. 63):

1. Moderate distress may be important to sustain commitment and participation in treatment.
2. High initial distress may be an indicator for the use of supportive and self-directed therapy but bears no relationship to the effectiveness of active and therapist-guided interventions.
3. High distress may be an indicator for interpersonally focused interventions, perhaps including group or family formats.

Beutler and Harwood (2000) identified two coping styles that clients use to "reduce uncomfortable experiences": externalized and internalized (p. 80). They stated that "People cope by activating behaviors that range from and combine those that allow direct escape or avoidance of the feared environment (externalizing) and those that allow one to passively and indirectly control internal experiences such as anxiety (internalizing)" (p. 80). It is important for helpers to recognize and differentiate between these two coping styles in order to select treatments that provide clients safe exposure to the experiences that are being avoided (Beutler & Harwood, 2000; Ingram, Hayes, & Scott, 2000). In addition, an assessment of coping style may expand the helper's understanding of the client's cultural background and identity. Research has suggested, for example, that children in collectivist cultures may favor more internalized coping practices (e.g., respect for elders, academic diligence), whereas children in more individualist cultures may exhibit more externalized coping mechanisms (e.g., impulsive behaviors; see Caldwell-Harris & Ayçiçegi, 2006).

Problems associated with externalized coping styles can result from excessive and disruptive behaviors. These persons might be characterized as impatient, hypervigilant, and impulsive, and as thrill-seekers or risk-takers (behaviors that might resemble criteria for conduct disorder). For example, a child who is always "mouthing off" and getting into fights and an adult who is continually berating his or her children are persons with these kinds of behaviors.

Problems associated with internalized coping styles are characterized by the absence of certain activities or an insufficient display of certain behaviors. These persons might be characterized as compliant, dutiful, and overly sensitive to the appraisals of others, and they may have a greater capacity for insight than those with externalized coping styles. They often "tend to inhibit impulses and feelings, have a relatively low need to seek stimulation in their environments, and often are dominated by self-reflective, fearful ruminations and contemplations" (Beutler & Harwood, 2000, p. 81).

Clients may exhibit both coping patterns at different times or with different conflicts, although "most people tend to favor one or the other coping style in treatment-relevant events" (Beutler & Harwood, 2000, p. 82). Generally, treatments based on exposure and skill-building are selected for clients with externalized coping styles, and insight and emotional awareness interventions are selected for clients with internalized coping styles (Beutler & Harwood, 2000, pp. 86–87).

A third means by which clients manage their symptoms—and a client characteristic that affects treatment selection and planning—is reactance or resistance. Beutler and Harwood observed that resistance occurs when a client's "sense of freedom, image of self, safety, psychological integrity or power is threatened" (p. 115). In an interpersonal relationship such as the helping one, resistance suggests the client "is trying to prevent or restore these threatened losses" (p. 115). In this model, resistance may be an enduring aspect of the client's personality or character (a trait) or a situational reaction to feeling threatened (a state; Beutler & Harwood, 2000). When resistance is an enduring client trait, it is often noticeable to the helper at the outset and throughout all phases of the helping process. It can also be identified in the way the client describes and relates to other events and people in her or his life. If the resistance is temporary, it usually occurs in the helping process as a *change* in the client's typical behavior—for example, a client who has normally been punctual starts showing up late for your sessions. In these instances, it is likely that the emerging resistance represents something about the client–helper interaction and may be "an understandable response" to the helper's behaviors or attitudes (Safran & Muran, 2000, p. 50).

Assessing resistance is important because clients with high or recurring levels of resistance benefit from a low level of helper directiveness provided in a safe context (Beutler & Harwood, 2000). An emphasis on support factors (see Table 10.1) with the goal of remoralization is therefore recommended. Clients who are not resistance prone or who have situational and short-term resistance are likely to benefit from more directive interventions such as information giving, interpretations, and structured homework assignments—all of which exemplify the learning and action factors presented in Table 10.1.

One way to tap into the client's overall level of resistance is to assess the client's "reactance level" (J. W. Brehm, 1966; S. S. Brehm, 1976). Psychological reactance is the need to preserve one's freedom. Clients who are high in reactance might be described by some as "oppositional" and often find ways to try to defeat or diffuse the helper, usually by saying or doing the opposite of whatever the helper says. Clients who are low on reactance potential are typically cooperative and comply with the helper's ideas. Helpers can assess this dimension early in the process by noticing whether the client consistently takes positions opposite or complementary to the helper's views and/or by assigning a straightforward task and noticing whether the client carries out or forgets the task.

Interpersonal Context

A primary client characteristic that influences the type and direction of proposed services is social support. As a characteristic that reflects a person's interpersonal context, social support may not always be under the client's direct control. Take for instance the teenager whose parents recently divorced and who as a result has been forced to change high schools midyear because she is now living with her mother in another city. She may lack a ready-made social network, and in response to a number of stressors, she may begin to act out in school, such as by talking back to teachers and initiating fights with peers. Although this young woman may seem to lack control over the availability and quality of

support networks, she might benefit from participating in a counseling group with other teenagers, a group assembled by the school counselor or by another helping professional in the community. The opportunities she is given to "experiment" with new and more socially acceptable behaviors in this group—and the positive feedback she receives from her fellow group members—may assist her in learning ways to interact appropriately and with beneficial effects at school. Her task might be to transfer what she has learned in group to her relationships at school, thus allowing her to realize that she does have some ownership over establishing and maintaining social support.

Access to and interaction with positive social support has been found to improve prognosis, predict treatment outcome, serve as a buffer against relapse, and maintain treatment gains (Beutler et al., 2000). Helpers must therefore assist clients in identifying positive support networks, help them acquire enhanced social skills to effectively interact with such persons, and rehearse behaviors to implement outside of treatment. As in the preceding example, the client's active participation in a counseling group may help her to establish a support outlet, or the helper providing individual care may use the therapeutic relationship to simulate interpersonal interactions outside of treatment (e.g., "So what have you learned about being able to trust me that you can put to use to identify a trustworthy friend?"). Furthermore, the helper can initiate contact with the client's family members and friends to assess the quality of existing social support and can offer psychoeducation, such as conflict resolution, to family members so as to involve them in the client's care. This might entail teaching family members to simply notice positive differences in their loved one's behavior and communicate their observations orally or in writing to the client. Family counseling may also be extended.

Although three categories of client characteristics have been discussed separately (i.e., impairment, symptom management, and interpersonal context), it is necessary for the helper to recognize their interconnections and the meaning of their patterns. Beutler et al. (2000) emphasized the importance of these connections when they stated that "general prognosis is a function of level of the patient's impairment, initial distress, and social support" (p. 112). As a helper, your clinical decision-making skills will enhance as you are able to recognize and interpret the unique configuration of characteristics that each of your clients represents.

Helper Characteristics

Client characteristics are clearly instrumental in the change process. However, helper characteristics also contribute to the process of change. Indeed, Wampold (2001) noted that "the essence of therapy is embodied in the therapist" and that "the person of the therapist is a critical factor in the success of therapy" (p. 202). Like client characteristics, instrumental helper characteristics extend beyond mere so-ciodemographic characteristics such as age, sex, professional degree, and years of practice. Recent research suggests that these therapist factors account for only 5 percent (Wampold & Brown, 2005) to 8 percent (Kim, Wampold, & Bolt, 2006) of client improvement. Additional helper character-istics therefore warrant further attention.

The American Psychological Association's (APA) Presi-dential Task Force on Evidence-Based Practice (2006) iden-tified eight components of clinical expertise. They are pre-sented in Box 10.1. Although they are intended to describe characteristics and skills of psychologists, we believe they ap-ply to all professional helpers and directly impact treatment planning and clinical decision making. Common across all eight components are the helper's ability to (1) be flexible and receptive to feedback (specifically feedback received from clients and supervisors), (2) continually expand and enhance clinical skills, (3) articulate comprehensible clinical recommendations, and (4) be deliberate about identifying and incorporating idiosyncratic and cultural client characteristics throughout the helping process. We next discuss the first three of those four helper characteristics. Attentiveness to cultural considerations is addressed in a later section of this chapter.

Flexibility and Receptivity to Feedback

An essential helper skill is flexibility in the selection of treat-ment interventions so as to accommodate client needs and preferences. This does not mean, as Egan (2007) clarified, "mere randomness or chaos" (p. 43). Rather, helpers are flex-ible within a set of parameters or guidelines (e.g., a specific treatment manual) so as to uphold professional standards that are informed by research and practice. Such flexibil-ity is commensurate with the practice of technical eclecticism wherein the practitioner carefully chooses several theoretical approaches to use in combination for the benefit of a particular client. The APA Presidential Task Force on Evidence-Based Practice (2006) further explicated the practice of clinician flexibility by stating that it is "manifested in tact, tim-ing, pacing, and framing of interventions; maintaining an effective balance between consistency of interventions and responsiveness to patient feedback; and attention to acknowledged and unacknowledged meanings, beliefs, and emotions" (p. 276). In other words, flexibility is the helper's ability to adapt or adjust to client concerns and wishes, as well as to changes in the mechanisms of service delivery (e.g., philosophy of treatment setting, funding sources), "without sacrificing the empirical need for reliability and structure" (Beutler & Harwood, 2000, p. 23). This type of practice is what we have termed "informed improvisation," or creative expression shaped and guided by established and evolving principles of research, theory, and practice.

It is widely held that supervision directly impacts helper skills (see Bernard & Goodyear, 2004). Indeed, the receipt

---

BOX 10.1	COMPONENTS OF CLINICAL EXPERTISE

- Assessment, diagnostic judgment, systematic case formulation, and treatment planning
- Clinical decision making, treatment implementation, and monitoring of client progress
- Interpersonal expertise
- Continual self-reflection and acquisition of skills
- Appropriate evaluation and use of research evidence in both basic and applied psychological science
- Understanding the influence of individual and cul-tural differences on treatment
- Seeking available resources (e.g., consultation, ad-junctive or alternative services) as needed
- Having a cogent rationale for clinical strategies

Source: APA Presidential Task Force on Evidence-Based Practice, 2006.

---

of supervision is required for most practitioners-in-training as they pursue licensure. Ethics committees and licensure boards also routinely prescribe supervision for licensed prac-titioners who have violated ethical guidelines. Supervision, therefore, may be thought of as a corrective intervention. With respect to clinical decision making and treatment planning, emerging research (viz., Lambert et al., 2003) suggests that the clients of helpers who receive specific, concrete, and timely feedback regarding their clients' sta-tus in treatment (e.g., functioning adequately or poorly) and are also provided with clear recommendations (e.g., consider termination, alter treatment plan, present client at case conference) demonstrate positive outcomes compared to clients whose helpers did not receive such feedback. This research is referred to as patient- or client-focused research because the information on client functioning is supplied directly by clients (completing once a week the 45-item Outcome Questionnaire; see http://www.oqmeasures.com). It also appears that therapists who receive specific feedback about the progress made (or lack thereof) by their clients, and who heed the recommendations provided, make judicious use of the duration of therapy. This would include scheduling more therapy sessions when the client is not progressing and scheduling fewer when the client is on track or is progressing. In Lambert et al.'s (2003) research, clients identified early as nonresponders were found to increase their attendance when their therapists followed through with specific feedback pro-vided. Altogether, this research suggests that clients benefit when their helpers make use of supervisory interventions aimed at modifying care plans for individual clients.

Commitment to Expanding and Enhancing Clinical Skills

Skovholt and Jennings (2004) described master therapists as "voracious learners" who have an "appetite for knowledge [that] appears to be an intense source of development" (p. 33). In addition, master therapists value cognitive complexity and the ambiguity of the human condition and are likely to consider multiple criteria in clinical decision making while realizing that clear, absolute, and definitive "answers" may never be determined. This description is similar to that of "intentional learning" reported by Miller (2007) in his study of "passionately committed psychotherapists" practicing in one state's public mental health system. From these depictions, it appears that an important helper characteristic is being committed to skill enhancement and ongoing professional development.

Case conceptualization and treatment planning are specific skills that we believe benefit from constant refinement. Eells, Lombart, Kendjelic, Turner, and Lucas (2005) asked novice therapists (clinical psychology graduate students), experienced therapists (practicing for 10 or more years), and expert therapists (those who had published books or articles on the topic of case formulation) to "think aloud" for about 8 minutes about their conceptualizations of an individual client described to them in writing. Therapists were also asked to talk out loud about how they would treat the client.

Eells et al. (2005) found that the treatment plans of expert therapists were more elaborate and rated as better fitting to their case formulations compared with those of the novice and the experienced therapists. Furthermore, expert therapists were thought to make use of clinical principles, formulation guidelines, or "solution algorithms" as they made decisions of care rather than interpreting client presenting concerns according to their surface features alone. Eells et al. speculated that expert therapists appear to have strong self-monitoring skills, allowing them to detect potential deficits in their practice and make necessary changes or to "calibrate" their skills as a result.

Surprisingly, the case formulations of the novice therapists in Eells et al.'s (2005) study were rated *higher* in overall quality (e.g., comprehensiveness, complexity, precision of language, coherence) than those of the experienced therapists. This should be encouraging information to graduate students! Because of their current investment in formal studies, novice therapists were thought to be able to better calibrate their skills than experienced therapists. The skills of case conceptualization and treatment planning are therefore never "set" or finalized. We believe that helpers are more than likely to provide quality services to clients when they remain dedicated to expanding and enhancing their clinical skills. Your learning, therefore, is never finalized—even after graduation!

Comprehensible Clinical Decision Making

The goal of many students preparing for a career in the helping professions is to obtain a license to practice as a professional helper (e.g., social worker, psychologist, counselor). Newly licensed professionals may pursue independent licensure so as to practice (e.g., diagnose and treat mental disorders) without being supervised. Although obtaining a professional license is a remarkable achievement, practicing as a licensed professional carries with it immense responsibilities. This is similar to the initiation of any new role, such as wife, husband, legally recognized domestic partner, or parent. The wedding day or the day of birth/adoption is cause for celebration. The responsibilities that accompany such roles (may be likened to the "terrible twos" described by parents) often kick in after the "honeymoon."

As a licensed professional, you will be making decisions that affect the lives of many people. As an independently licensed practitioner, your decision alone rather than that of a supervisor may determine whether a client is diagnosed with a personality disorder, involuntarily hospitalized, discharged from residential treatment, or deemed fit to assume legal custody of a child. Your ability to justify your clinical opinions and explain the decisions you have made is therefore critical. There may be no room for relying solely on intuition or on what some might interpret as "wishy-washy" thinking. Instead, you will need to be able to articulate a logical and cogent rationale for your treatment recommendations, and the expectation today is that these recommendations are based on and informed by theory and research. The magnitude of this responsibility is probably apparent when you visualize yourself in the courtroom as an expert witness, providing testimony to a client's mental status.

Not only must your clinical opinions and treatment recommendations be comprehensible to other professionals: they must also make sense to your clients. Discussing the need for and the meaning of a diagnosis to a client, for example, may be time-consuming and perhaps frustrating, but it will likely engender certain benefits. One of these benefits may be that the client becomes more of an active participant in the helping process because he or she now has a better understanding of his or her symptoms and why certain activities need to take place in treatment.

Although we wholeheartedly endorse—indeed, insist on—a collaborative client–helper working relationship, we are clearly aware of the professional helper's responsibility for making treatment decisions. We believe that, as much as possible, helpers should follow the "no surprises" rule when engaging clients in conversations about clinical assessment and treatment planning. This means that the client should not be surprised by the helper's recommendations because the client was kept informed of the helper's thinking and reasoning. It may be that the helper engaged in a "thinking aloud" practice with his or her clients similar to that described in the Eells et al. (2005) study. It is certainly true that the client may not agree with the helper's recommendations or directives—and this is his or her right. However, what the helper should strive for is to avoid hearing the client say, for example, "I really don't know why attending six weekly sessions of group therapy is necessary" or "You never told me you'd need to speak with my partner! Why does she need to be involved in this?" An investment in the formulation and articulation of a clear and cogent rationale for your clinical decisions and treatment recommendations is a sign of an accountable practitioner.

Practice Principles: Research-Informed Treatment

For the past 15 to 20 years, leaders in various mental health professions (namely psychology and psychiatry) have sought to identify a set of principles—based on years of cumulative research findings—that would help practitioners in their treatment selection and implementation. References to these principles have included "empirically validated treatments" (Task Force on Promotion and Dissemination of Psychological Disorders, 1993), "empirically supported treatments" (Chambless & Holon, 1998), "standards of care" (see Granello & Wittmer, 1998), "practice guidelines" (American Psychiatric Association, 2000b), "clinical care pathways" (see De Bleser et al., 2006), and "evidence-based practice" (APA, 2006; Goodheart, Kazdin, & Sternberg, 2006). A registry of evidence-based programs and practices has also been established by the Substance Abuse and Mental Health Services Administration (2006; http://www.nrepp.samhsa.gov/), an agency of the U.S. Department of Health and Human Services (hereafter cited as SAMHSA, 2006). Although intended as a help to practitioners, these efforts have sparked quite a bit of controversy for a number of reasons. We mention four.

First, there are differences of opinion as to the amount of attention given to certain factors (e.g., specific treatment interventions) at the expense of others (e.g., therapeutic relationship). Lambert and Ogles (2004) noted that "technique differences are inseparably bound with therapist and patient differences" (p. 169), and they recommended that future research focus on the "empirically validated psychotherapist" rather than on empirically supported treatment. In a similar vein, Clarkin and Levy (2004) characterized the empirically validated treatment "movement" as an "oversimplification" of clinical practice because "The focus is on treatments, with little attention to patients, therapists, or individual differences" (p. 214), a contention held by Whaley and Davis (2007) because cultural variables are often overlooked. Beutler and Castonguay (2006) mentioned that none of the common and specific principles of change identified from the expanse of research conducted "have been systematically manipulated within experimental studies or sufficiently investigated as potential mediators of change" (p. 8). In other words, widely held factors of change (e.g., client and helper characteristics) have actually *not* been found to be causally related to client improvement in definitive, experimental studies. Beutler and Castonguay recommend, therefore, the use of the term "empirically derived

principles" or "empirically grounded principles" intended to convey theories of practice that are guided or informed by research rather than fully supported or explained by research.

Another reason for controversy in evidence-based practice—related to the first—is that guidelines derived from research findings are often based on homogeneous client samples (or the average effects on heterogeneous client participants). This supports Clarkin and Levy's (2004) contention that "The individualized and more general characteristics of the clients who come for psychotherapy are central to the clinical enterprise of psychotherapy practice and the research investigation of psychotherapy" (p. 216). Take for example research studies that may have included only persons who met criteria for only one *DSM-IV TR* Axis I disorder and excluded persons with more than one Axis I disorder or an Axis I disorder and an Axis II disorder. The treatment guidelines developed from those research findings, therefore, may not be applicable to persons with co-occurring disorders, which may be more the rule or standard than the exception. As Lutz et al. (2006) recommended, ongoing research should "strive to identify and explore, if possible, the differences on an individual patient level" (p. 139).

A third controversial area in evidence-based practice pertains to *how* the "evidence" on which practice is based has been determined (and concurrently, *who* gets to decide what is regarded as "evidence"). For example, should only the findings from randomized clinical/control trials (RCTs) constitute the evidence for treatment practice? Or should findings from studies conducted in applied settings (e.g., a community mental health agency) following normal, routine clinical procedures also be included? The first type of research comprises studies conducted in ideal experimental conditions (e.g., controlled and manualized treatments, random assignment, selected clients and helpers), usually comparing one type of treatment to another or to a control group (e.g., clients on a wait list), or both. These are referred to as *efficacy* studies. The second type of research comprises *effectiveness* studies and does not adhere to the strict (or some might say "sterile") "laboratory" research standards of RCTs. Effectiveness studies (1) exemplify what has been referred to as "pragmatic, utilitarian research" (Sanchez & Turner, 2003, p. 126), (2) may emphasize more idiographic aspects than traditional nomothetic research and, (3) according to Whaley and Davis (2007), have assumed "greater significance" (p. 570) because of their potential to specifically consider cultural factors. A concern about efficacy studies is that their findings may not easily transfer to actual, everyday practice. In a similar vein, a concern about effectiveness studies is that their findings may not be generalizable to other practitioners, treatment facilities, or clients. Hence, the evidence derived from the research question "What works for whom under what conditions?" may have limited utility from either an efficacy or an effectiveness perspective.

A fourth reason for the controversy over evidence-based principles and practices has to do with how they are marketed. Third-party payers and other funding sources—as well as accrediting bodies—have been known to latch on to certain evidence-based treatments because they are viewed as cost-effective and hence "successful." Short-term cognitive–behavioral therapy, for example, may be heralded by certain insurance companies as the "best" treatment for all their providers to practice because, in the long run, it is not as protracted or long-term (and hence expensive) as, say, certain types of expressive–supportive therapies. Clinicians, therefore, may not be receptive to evidence-based practices because they have been mandated by an external entity with little—if any—allowance for the individual style of the helper. Although some helpers may appreciate having a guidebook or a manual to follow when practicing a certain treatment, others may feel controlled, coerced, and "manualized."

We suspect that the controversies surrounding evidence-based practices will continue for some time. Although frustrating for helpers and researchers alike (perhaps for different reasons), we believe there has been merit in this controversy over the past 15 to 20 years. For one thing, the debate may have opened up lines of communication between practitioners and researchers. Second, such conversations have perhaps helped to keep the focus on what is "in the best interest of the client," including prioritizing client experiences of treatment by soliciting their feedback (e.g., patient-focused research; Lambert et al., 2001, 2003; Lutz et al., 2006). And third, discussions about evidence-based practices appear to have ushered in a more integrative or both/and perspective about client care, similar to the common factors *and* differential treatment combination we proposed at the beginning of this chapter. Indeed, the American Psychological Association (APA) recently defined evidence-based practice as "the integration of the best available research with clinical expertise in the context of patient characteristics, culture, and preferences" (APA Presidential Task Force on Evidence-Based Practice, 2006, p. 273).

One example of an integrative approach to evidence-based practice is that of cultural adaptation. This approach was proposed by Whaley and Davis (2007) in an attempt to make research-based interventions more culturally appropriate. They define cultural adaptation as:

> any modification to an evidence-based treatment that involves changes in the approach to service delivery, in the nature of the therapeutic relationship, or in components of the treatment itself to accommodate the cultural beliefs, attitudes, and behaviors of the target population. (pp. 570–571)

Examples of cultural modifications include delivering an evidence-based practice in a client's native language, adding the provision of child care and transportation services to the regimen specified in the treatment manual, and enlisting the assistance of former clients of color trained in data collection methods to conduct field interviews among current clients of color regarding the benefits of treatment.

Castonguay and Beutler's (2006b) promulgation of practice principles also reflects an integrative priority. Their focus on the conditions, aspects, or qualities of treatment that appear to account for positive changes has resulted in guidelines (or flexible heuristics) that encompass not only prescribed interventions often found in treatment manuals, but also client and helper factors, and factors related to the therapeutic relationship or alliance. The current focus, therefore, appears to be on effective treatment that is the product of a confluence of principles—principles that "are more general than a description of techniques and . . . more specific than theoretical formulations" (Beutler & Castonguay, 2006, p. 9). From their focus on four diagnostic dimensions (i.e., dysphoric, anxiety, personality, and substance disorders), Castonguay and Beutler's (2006a) integrative efforts generated 61 principles of therapeutic change, 43 percent of which encompass at least two dimensions. Several principles related to client and therapist characteristics are inferred (e.g., "The benefits of therapy may be enhanced if the therapist is able to tolerate his/her own negative feelings regarding the patient and the treatment process," p. 358) in addition to those that have been observed (e.g., "Clients who have been diagnosed with a personality disorder are less likely to benefit from treatment than those who have not," p. 355). Please consult Castonguay and Beutler's (2006b) book for a comprehensive review of their practice principles.

Two Examples of Evidence-Based Practice

We believe that two treatment approaches—both of which are now considered evidence-based practices—exemplify the benefit of a comprehensive and integrative perspective resulting from ongoing discussions between scientists and practitioners. They have become familiar practices in certain sectors, and the concepts that undergird and guide their respective approaches are not new. However, only in recent years have Assertive Community Treatment (ACT) and Dialectical Behavior Therapy (DBT) gained wide prominence. We discuss each of them briefly and encourage you to complete Learning Activity 10.1 once you have familiarized yourself with ACT and DBT.

Assertive Community Treatment According to Bond et al. (2001), Assertive Community Treatment (ACT) was first developed in the 1970s as an intensive and holistic approach to the treatment of persons with severe and persistent mental illnesses (e.g., schizophrenia, bipolar disorder). Key features of ACT (see Box 10.2) are that integrated services (e.g., medication management, vocational rehabilitation) are provided not by one person but by a group of professionals (e.g., substance abuse counselor, case manager, nurse) who

LEARNING ACTIVITY 10.1 | Compelling Evidence Exercise

This activity is intended to assess your own motivations for adopting and implementing an evidence-based practice. It can also be used as a classroom activity to generate discussion.

Consider for a moment that you are on the clinical staff of a community-based mental health facility serving primarily a low-income population, many of whom have severe and persistent mental illnesses (e.g., schizophrenia, personality disorders). In response to the accrediting body's new policy that all accredited treatment facilities adopt and deliver evidence-based practices as standard service, you have been informed that you will soon become a member of a new Assertive Community Treatment (ACT) team and will need to attend training in Dialectical Behavior Therapy (DBT). Given what you know about ACT and DBT, what "evidence" will convince you that these two treatment approaches will be worth the investment of your time and energy? What information will compel you to adopt and begin implementing these two practices?

Check all of the following that apply, and add your own reasons too.

1. —— Learning about research findings from published clinical trials that justify both ACT and DBT's designation as evidence-based practices.
2. —— Knowing that I will be receiving close supervision and training "tune-ups" in the first few months of using these two approaches.
3. —— Receiving training from seasoned practitioners who themselves have used both ACT and DBT.
4. —— Learning that my salary will remain the same and that I will have to pay for half of the DBT training costs.
5. —— Knowing that I will be part of a team of other clinical staff who will meet at least once a week not only to review client cases but to also offer one another support.

6. —— Learning that after six months of implementing ACT and DBT, our facility saved the county mental health board several thousands of dollars due to our clients needing fewer psychiatric hospital bed stays.
7. —— Hearing the stories of (and even being able to interact with) clients of other treatment facilities who have participated in ACT and DBT and are now managing their symptoms fairly well.
8. —— Receiving training from prominent researchers who have studied ACT and DBT for a number of years.
9. —— Learning that I will be provided with a mobile phone (at no expense to me) so that I can be on call 24 hours once per week.
10. —— Knowing that my current caseload will be reduced and that all members of the ACT team (approximately 6 to 8) will assume responsibility for the same clients (approximately 50 to 60).
11. —— Knowing that DBT is a highly structured approach that holds clients accountable for their behaviors while validating their experiences and circumstance in a nonjudgmental and empathic manner.
12. —— Learning that after six months of implementing ACT and DBT, approximately one-third of the clients our team serves have taken their medications as prescribed and have not been actively suicidal.
13. —— After six months of implementing ACT and DBT, hearing one of my previously hostile and unstable clients describe a recent incident in which he was able to keep his cool after practicing one of his mindfulness exercises.
14. —— ——————————————————
15. —— ——————————————————

work as a team. All team members, therefore, share responsibility for caring for the same clients. It is highly unlikely that persons with severe and persistent mental illnesses initiate and maintain active involvement in formal services. Therefore, the majority (approximately 80 percent) of ACT services are delivered "in the field" or in vivo (i.e., in the community rather than in a clinical setting) so as to engage and remain connected with persons challenged by a multiplicity of concerns and therefore prone to frequent relapses and overall instability. In this manner, ACT is regarded as a proactive, assertive, and persistent treatment approach.

Specific ACT services target what some might consider basic client needs, such as obtaining housing, food, and medical care, as well as managing finances. Although resembling case management, ACT is different from and far more comprehensive than intensive case management in that a range of services is delivered directly to the client (rather than linking the client to other service providers) by members of a team (rather than one case manager). In addition, ACT services are tailored to the individual client, include individual counseling and crisis intervention, and are unlimited. The most encouraging and compelling aspects of ACT are that it has been found to contribute

<table>
<tr><td>

BOX 10.2

KEY PRINCIPLES AND PRACTICES OF ASSERTIVE COMMUNITY TREATMENT (ACT)

- Multidisciplinary staffing
- Integration of services
- Team approach
- Low patient–staff ratios
- Locus of contact in the community
- Medication management
- Focus on everyday problems in living
- Rapid access
- Assertive outreach
- Individualized services
- Time-unlimited services

Source: Bond et al., 2001.
</td></tr>
</table>

to reduced psychiatric hospital stays, increased housing stability, and engaging and retaining clients in mental health services (Bond et al., 2001). For helpers (specifically case managers), the benefits of ACT participation include a decrease in burnout and an increase in job satisfaction (Boyer & Bond, 1999). The Assertive Community Treatment Association (http://www .actassociation.org) was founded in the late 1990s and sponsors an annual conference.

Dialectical Behavior Therapy   Dialectical Behavior Therapy (DBT) was developed by Marsha Linehan (1993) as a highly structured, multimodal treatment program for suicidal clients meeting the criteria of borderline personality disorder (BPD). It is informed by cognitive–behavioral theory, biosocial theory (i.e., biological irregularities combined with certain dysfunctional environments), and Eastern philosophy. Although DBT is now regarded as an evidence-based practice for the treatment of BPD, recent adaptations of DBT have expanded its application to persons with eating disorders (Wisniewski & Kelly, 2003) and to adolescents displaying impulsive and self-destructive behaviors (Grove Street Adolescent Residence of the Bridge of Central Massachusetts Inc., 2004), whether or not BPD or suicidal intent is present.

DBT is a theory- or principle-driven approach, not a protocol-driven treatment (Harned, Banawan, & Lynch, 2006). This means that although DBT is highly structured and calls for the implementation of specific helper skills and client behaviors, it is not a rigid or prescriptive approach, and it fits well with the helper skill of flexibility discussed earlier in the chapter. Indeed, helpers are instructed to provide individualized care and therefore tailor specific practices to the needs of each client.

A guiding premise of DBT is that a convergence or synthesis of what appear to be opposing forces is possible. This process of balancing and regulating conflicting feelings and behaviors is what is meant by *dialectical* in the name DBT.

Take for example an adult woman with a history of sexual and physical abuse who has attempted suicide on several occasions (symptoms or characteristics often associated with BPD). Although she may interpret the violations she experienced as "proof" that she is "not fit to live," she also has a strong desire to experience an intimate connection with another human being, to be loved (a need that might be interpreted by some as an "attachment disorder" or traits of "dependency"). It is not that one experience is "wrong" and the other "right." Rather, both have validity, and in her work with a professional helper, this woman would strive to acknowledge and accept both experiences, live with the tension or paradox (i.e., "not fit to live" vs. someone deserving of love), and arrive at a synthesis of the two polarities (e.g., "I have been violated *and* I am a survivor worthy of love").

As a comprehensive approach, DBT offers an array of behavioral strategies, including problem solving, skills training, contingency management (e.g., behavioral contracting), exposure-based procedures, and cognitive modification. These are complemented by what Linehan (1993) refers to as acceptance-based procedures, such as validation, mindfulness, and distress tolerance. Validation and problem-solving strategies form the core of DBT, and all other strategies are built around them. Validation conveys to the client that the choices he or she has made and the behaviors he or she has engaged in make sense and are understandable, given the client's life situation (i.e., history, current circumstances). Problem solving is undertaken only after validation has been conveyed (it may need to be repeatedly conveyed), and it includes clarifying the primary concern at hand and then generating alternative solutions. One such strategy, chain analysis, involves the development of "an exhaustive, step-by-step description of the chain of events leading up to and following the behavior . . . [so as to examine] a particular instance of a specific dysfunctional behavior in excruciating detail" (Linehan, 1993, p. 258). This exercise not only informs the helper about the client's cognitive schema (e.g., the specific details that are remembered); it also teaches the client important self-observational and self-assessment skills, as well as the connections among many different variables, and it teaches that the client has the ability to exert control over those linkages and create new patterns of behavior.

We believe that both ACT and DBT warrant further consideration by practitioners and scientists/researchers alike. Not only do they have compelling "hard data evidence" to justify their continued practice; they also have practical appeal (i.e., they "make sense," can be implemented in everyday practice settings), and this is not always the case with evidence-based practices.

Adoption and Implementation of Evidence-Based Practice

Torrey et al. (2001) indicated that before clinicians adopt certain evidence-based practices, they must be convinced that the practices are worth learning. This convincing would likely entail outlining the potential benefits of such practices for both clients and helpers when conducted in everyday settings, and not emphasizing "hard data" alone. For example, clinicians "are influenced by compelling vignettes, impressions of the practice seen in action, and a practice ideology, or theory, that resonates with their values and experiences as providers" (p. 47). To facilitate learning, clinicians must have unencumbered access to and involvement in various training mechanisms (e.g., participatory workshops, reading materials) that include opportunities for observation of the skills associated with the practice. And, once the practice has been adopted, clinicians must receive reinforcement over time for their efforts, such as regular supervision and feedback on their activities. Torrey et al. (2001) also noted that "Practices that persist have funding and organizational structures to support the practice. These programs typically have an influential clinical or operational leader who ensures the continuity of the structures and training that maintain the practice" (p. 48).

Researchers and health care administrators cannot expect helpers to automatically and enthusiastically embrace evidence-based practices simply because "the research says so." Rather, adopting and then implementing these practices is a process that requires time, involvement of and collaboration with clinical staff, provision of staff support (e.g., training, ongoing supervision, financial compensation), and evidence beyond research findings. Just as clients engage in a process of personal change—moving through various stages of readiness to change over time—so do practitioners participate in a professional change process when introduced to new practices. Miller, Sorensen, Selzer, and Brigham (2006) likened this process to learning any new skill, which often entails three aids: ground school or basic training (e.g., graduate school, reading, attending workshops), practice with feedback, and coaching or supervision to reinforce correct practice and cultivate enhancement. We believe that researchers, clinical directors, and supervisors need to engage practitioners (as well as the systems or organizations they represent) in a similar stages-of-change process when attempting to disseminate innovative approaches.

To facilitate your further understanding of evidence-based practices and challenges to their implementation, we encourage you to complete Learning Activity 10.1. This activity identifies several aspects of ACT and DBT that may be possible motivations for helpers to adopt their practice.

DECISION RULES IN PLANNING FOR TYPE, DURATION, AND MODE OF TREATMENT

A *decision rule* is a series of mental questions or heuristics that the helper constantly asks himself or herself during interviews in order to match interventions to clients and their identified concerns. Recent formulations of this sort

of helper–client matching have been offered by Nezu et al. (2004) and by Beutler and colleagues (Beutler & Clarkin, 1990; Beutler et al., 2000; Beutler & Harwood, 2000). The American Society of Addiction Medicine (ASAM; Mee-Lee, Shulman, Fishman, Gastfriend, & Griffith, 2001) has published guidelines specific to substance use disorders. Each of these three client-treatment formulations or models is described in this section.

Nezu et al. (2004) describe a problem-solving model of clinical decision making based on cognitive–behavioral principles. Their two-part model consists of case formulation and treatment planning and is influenced by a multiple causality framework (i.e., client concerns have numerous and complex origins or explanations) and a systems perspective. The multiple causality framework suggests that disorders and their symptoms are characterized by either proximal features (i.e., immediate antecedent, such as the presence of a phobic object) or distal features (i.e., developmental history, such as the occurrence of a traumatic event several months or years ago). In planning care, attention is given to client-related variables and environment-related variables within the dimensions of time (i.e., client's current and past functioning) and functionality (i.e., how client and environmental characteristics are interrelated). And, consistent with cognitive–behavioral practice, Nezu and colleagues (Nezu & Nezu, 1995; Nezu et al., 2004) recommend that the helper evaluate the likelihood of potential solution alternatives (i.e., whether proposed goals and interventions will be achieved) by considering the following questions:

1. What is the likelihood that this particular intervention will achieve the specified goal(s)?
2. What is the likelihood that I as the therapist will be able to implement this intervention in its optimal form?
3. What is the likelihood that the client will be able to participate in, understand, and be able to carry out the strategy in its optimal form?
4. What is the likelihood that collaterals (e.g., caregivers, family members) or other health care providers will be able to implement a particular strategy in an optimal way?
5. How much time and effort are required to carry out this intervention?
6. What are the effects of resolving this problem on other client problem areas?

Strengths of the Nezu et al. (2004) model include its foundation in and alignment with cognitive–behavioral therapy (a therapeutic modality endorsed by third-party entities that often require treatment plans) and its comprehensiveness. Concerns about this model are that it may be too complex (i.e., too many variables) for a typical clinician to render it user-friendly and it does not specifically address cultural variables.

The model presented by Beutler and his colleagues (Beutler & Clarkin, 1990; Beutler et al., 2000; Beutler & Harwood, 2000) is an integrated one that considers client predisposing qualities (i.e., problem, personality, and environment), context of treatment (i.e., setting, intensity, mode, and format), and therapist activity and relationship (i.e., therapeutic actions, alliance/relationship factors, and therapist–client matching). In formulating a treatment plan, the clinician selects features of client presentation or functioning (e.g., symptom severity and chronicity, readiness for change) to pair with certain treatment dimensions (e.g., therapist skill, level of directiveness) so as to identify the best client–treatment "match." Strengths of the model are that it has been revised over a period of time according to established and emerging psychotherapy process and outcome research, and that it has been applied specifically to clients with depressive disorders (Beutler et al., 2000).

Since 1991, the American Society of Addiction Medicine (ASAM) has published a clinical guide intended to enhance the use of multidimensional assessments in making decisions about matching patients/clients to appropriate levels of care. Although initially focused on clients with only substance-related concerns, the revised 2nd edition of the *ASAM Patient Placement Criteria for the Treatment of Substance-Related Disorders* (*ASAM PPC-2R*; Mee-Lee et al., 2001) incorporates criteria that address a large subset of individuals with co-occurring disorders or a dual diagnosis (i.e., substance use disorder and mental illness), including what are referred to as dual diagnosis capable programs (substance use remains primary concern) or dual diagnosis enhanced programs (designed for those with more unstable or disabling co-occurring mental disorders). The *ASAM PPC-2R* assesses all clients (both adults and adolescents) on six dimensions: (1) acute intoxication and/or withdrawal potential; (2) biomedical conditions/complications; (3) emotional, behavioral, or cognitive conditions/complications; (4) readiness to change; (5) relapse, continued use, or continued problem potential; and (6) recovery/living environment. Clients are then assigned to one of five basic levels of care that are on a continuum of increasing intensity: (1) early intervention, (2) outpatient treatment, (3) intensive outpatient treatment, (4) residential/inpatient treatment, (5) medically managed intensive inpatient treatment. Although presented as discrete levels, the five levels of care represent benchmarks that can be used to determine client progress. The process of matching clients to type of service is based on the principle of "clinical appropriateness" rather than "medical necessity." The former emphasizes quality and efficiency, in contrast to the latter, which is often associated with restrictions on utilization.

Using the information presented thus far on helper-client treatment matching, review the case of Jane Wiggins presented in Learning Activity 10.2. In order to complete the activity, you may need to refer back to the three models just described.

Type of Treatment

From our review of the three client–treatment matching models, it should be evident that selecting appropriate types of treatment begins with the client or, more precisely, with determining "where the client is." This means assessing the client's current functioning, such as the nature of his or her symptoms (i.e., intensity or level of distress, chronicity, complexity), receptivity to treatment and readiness to change, and resources available (e.g., social support, financial status). Although some helpers may view assessing the client's ability to pay for services as counter to their practice as helpers, the financial information obtained is indeed critical to clinical decision making. Recent findings from a national household survey (SAMHSA, 2006) suggest that the number-one reason individuals have given for not seeking treatment in the past year when mental health needs were present was cost/insurance issues (46.8%). This is followed by not thinking treatment was necessary (or, "I can handle the problem on my own"; 36.7%) and by stigma associated with treatment (23.4%). (We wonder if Jane Wiggins, described in Learning Activity 10.2, may have given any of these reasons, if asked about her reluctance to see a professional helper after being rapped.) Similar reasons have been given by those with substance use issues who knew they needed treatment but did not obtain treatment: not ready to stop using (37.9%), cost/insurance barriers (35.1%), and stigma (e.g., negative opinions from neighbors and community, negative effect on job; 23.9%). Interventions should therefore be selected that take these and other treatment concerns and barriers into consideration. This might mean, for example, recommending less costly services at the initiation of care, such as outpatient versus inpatient treatment. Indeed, the ASAM Patient Placement Criteria state: "For both clinical and financial reasons, the preferred level of care is the least intensive level that meets treatment objectives, while providing safety and security for the patient" (Mee-Lee et al., 2001, pp. 16–17).

When assessing the nature of the client's presenting concerns, recall that Nezu et al. (2004) recommend distinguishing between their *proximal* features (i.e., immediate antecedent, such as the presence of a phobic object) and their *distal* features (i.e., developmental history, such as the occurrence of a traumatic event several months or years ago). This differentiation appears to correspond with Beutler and Clarkin's (1990) assessment of client issues as those involving either symptom distress or symbolic conflicts, which can be determined by asking, "Are these problems simple habits maintained by the environment or are they symbolized expressions of unresolved conflictual experiences?" (p. 226). For example, a teenage girl is referred to you by her mother, who explains that during the last few months her daughter has become more "distant and withdrawn" and has been spending a lot of time on the computer. Although the mother claims to monitor e-mail

| LEARNING ACTIVITY | **10.2** | **Factors Affecting Treatment Selection** |

Using the case of Jane Wiggins, described below, respond to the following questions. You may wish to do this activity with a partner or in a small group.

1. What client characteristics do you see in Jane Wiggins that would affect your choice of treatment intervention strategies and also the overall therapeutic outcomes?
2. How would your training, your theoretical orientation to helping, and your practice setting affect your choice of change intervention strategies?
3. How aware are you of any evidence-based treatments that would be useful here?
4. What questions would you ask about these treatments?
5. If you are not aware of any evidence-based treatments, how could you find some?

The Case of Jane Wiggins

Jane Wiggins is a 34-year-old Euro-American woman living in an isolated rural area. She has been referred to the nearest mental health center because she sought treatment at the local health care clinic following a rape.

She is very suspicious of the helper, who is a Caucasian man, and she talks reluctantly and without much eye contact. Gradually, she reveals that she is married, unemployed, has no children, and lives with her husband, who receives Social Security disability payments because of his very poor health. She has lived in this area all her life. She indicates that she has been followed for the last year by a White man who also grew up in the area. She knows him by name and sight only. In addition to following her, he has sent her numerous letters and has made phone calls containing lewd and suggestive remarks. She indicates that she and her husband went to the sheriff's office several times to complain, but the complaints were never followed up. It appears that this man may be related to a deputy in the sheriff's office.

Several weeks ago her husband went over the hill to a neighbor's house to visit and, unknown to her, left the door unlocked. The man who has been following her apparently was around, noticed the husband's departure, and came into her house and raped her. She says she told no one other than the neighbor and her husband because she feels so ashamed. She indicates she is a very religious person and has been reluctant to go to church or to confide in her minister for fear of what the church people may say. She also has been reluctant to tell her parents and sister, who live nearby, for the same reason. She sees no point in reporting the rape to the authorities because they dismissed her earlier reports.

She feels a lot of guilt about the rape because she thinks she should have been able to prevent it. She has been doing a lot of praying about this. As a few sessions go by, she gradually becomes more open with the helper and indicates she is willing to come back for a few more sessions to deal with her guilt and sadness; she would like to be able to feel happy again and not be so consumed by guilt. She finally discloses she would feel more comfortable talking these things out with another woman, as this is really a "female problem."

and Internet usage, she is concerned about her daughter's cyberspace communications. The presenting concern in this case might be characterized as symptom distress with proximal features. Another teenage girl, however, is brought to you by her mother, who is concerned about her daughter's "distance and withdrawal" not only from her but also from her younger brother. However, the mother notes that this behavior is nothing new; it has been a pattern since she was adopted at age 2 along with her infant brother. In the latter case, the presenting concern might be characterized as more of a symbolic conflict with distal features.

For issues that are primarily symptom based, have proximal features, and involve changes in altering behaviors and cognitions, recommended treatment strategies involve behavioral and cognitive interventions such as DBT's chain analysis, modeling, exposure and graded practice (e.g., systematic desensitization), cognitive restructuring, and self-monitoring, depending on the degree to which symptoms are overt or covert. Overt, external symptoms are more responsive to behavioral strategies; covert symptoms are more responsive to cognitive therapies (Beutler & Clarkin, 1990). Note that symptom distress or a behavioral type of treatment works best with clients who have predominantly externalized coping styles (Beutler & Harwood, 2000). For problems that are primarily conflict based, have distal features, and involve changes in altering feelings, recommended treatment strategies include interventions for enhancing emotional and sensory outcomes (Greenberg & Goldman, 1988), such as reflection of feelings, Gestalt two-chair work or psychodrama, and imagery. Recommended treatment strategies for resolving inner conflict include interpretation, confrontation with care, early recollections, genograms, and two-chair work. Note that these insight-focused treatments work best with clients who have predominantly internalized coping styles (Beutler & Harwood, 2000).

As further guidance for selecting these and other types of interventions, we recommend that you consult the common and sequential listing of treatments presented in Table 10.1. Remember that from a developmental perspective, supportive factors would typically occur in the early phase of treatment and would address such things as concerns related to stigma and the client feeling demoralized. The goal for this phase would be what Howard et al. (1993, 1996) termed "remoralization" and would include strategies such as role induction (i.e, client and helper discussing and agreeing on their mutual and distinct roles, responsibilities, and expectations), further exploration of the client's presenting concerns, and radically accepting or validating the client's experience (a core strategy in DBT). The next phase of treatment would focus on symptomatic relief (or remediation) by implementing learning (or cognitive modification) factors, such as skills training (e.g., emotional regulation through the practice of mindfulness in DBT) or psychoeducation (e.g., the ABC model of Rational-Emotive Behavioral Therapy, REBT), offering advice, and having the client engage in a structured self- and family assessment. Building on what was learned in the second phase of treatment, the third phase would then be devoted to action factors—that is, rehearsing and implementing new behaviors so as to achieve Howard et al.'s goal of rehabilitation.

As discussed earlier in the chapter, treatment planning is a continuous process, an adventure that client and helper undertake as a team. Because the treatment plan is tailored to the individual client, the routes taken to arrive at the client's destination cannot be predetermined. Rather, client and helper jointly construct a map, and the directions are subject to change with each new path traversed. Not all interventions can be identified at the beginning of care; what was thought to have been a beneficial activity during the last treatment plan review (or "rest stop") may now be discarded in favor of another approach in light of client progress, changes in the client's circumstances (e.g., securing employment), and the helper's knowledge and skill enhancement (e.g., completing training in DBT). What is key in selecting appropriate treatment strategies is to remain abreast of the client's case—and by this we mean the full picture (or 3-D photograph) of the client, including history, current status and context (e.g., environmental supports), response to treatment, and revised self-descriptions and aspirations. It is also important to adopt the practice of constant consultation when determining types of treatment. We believe that these clinical decisions are never done solo; rather, they are made in consultation with our clients, with their family members and other collaterals (e.g., referral source, community advocates), and with our colleagues (fellow practitioners, recognized theorists, and published scientists/researchers alike). Yet, as licensed practitioners, our signature on the treatment plan signifies the responsibility we have assumed for the client's professional care. However, that same signature should represent the culmination of conversations with clients, collaterals, and colleagues. Treatment decisions, therefore, are the product of consultative and continuous conversations with key constituents.

Duration of Treatment

How many sessions are necessary for clients to improve in psychotherapy? This question was first introduced by Howard, Kopta, Krause, and Orlinsky (1986) and is referred to as the *dose-effect model*. Their meta-analysis of research studies conducted over a 30-year period and representing 2,431 patients indicated that the majority of patients improved in the first 8 sessions and that by 26 sessions, approximately 75 percent of patients had shown some improvement. Numerous studies since then (e.g., Kadera, Lambert, & Andrews, 1996; Kopta, Howard, Lowry, & Beutler, 1994; Lutz, Lowry, Kopta, Einstein, & Howard, 2001) have upheld these findings for a variety of clients presenting with a range of concerns and receiving services in different treatment settings.

In their review of client length of stay in six different outpatient treatment settings, Hansen, Lambert, and Forman (2002) found that the average number of sessions utilized was 4.3 and the median number of sessions was 3. (It should be noted that these figures do not reflect the 33 percent of clients who remained in treatment for only one session.) The highest average (9.5 sessions) was in a university-supported training clinic, and the lowest average was in a local health maintenance organization (3.3 sessions) and in an employee assistance program (3.6 sessions). Hansen et al. described these utilization numbers as "extremely low" and representing treatment "insufficient by most standards of care" (p. 338). Many health maintenance organizations, however, do limit mental health coverage to 20 sessions or fewer per year and assume that this number of visits represents a "safe harbor" for even those people needing more than the average amount of therapy. Obviously, some clients will need more sessions (e.g., those with severe and persistent mental illnesses), and, lacking their own resources or access to insurance coverage, they will be deprived of needed treatment (as is evident in the SAMHSA, 2006, survey data mentioned earlier). Indigent clients and some clients of color are at greater risk of not having access to mental health services than are clients in more favorable circumstances. It is difficult to make sweeping generalizations about an effective duration for *all* clients; indeed, this is why treatment plans are developed for each individual client. Time should be regarded as a commodity and used judiciously but not at the expense of client need and care.

It is recommended that clients with high levels of impairment be offered more frequent sessions spaced closer together than clients with low levels of impairment. Clients who present with transient situational concerns are good candidates for crisis intervention, but we cannot assume that all clients are automatically good candidates for brief or time-limited therapy. Brief therapy seems to be appropriate for clients who may drop out of therapy early, such as clients who are at the precontemplation stage of the transtheoretical model of change and who have unidimensional symptoms or conflictual issues. Brief therapy may serve as a stepping-stone to more intensive services and may also fit the preferences and belief systems of some clients of color. Overall, we believe that duration of treatment should be a clinical rather than an economic decision. There are ethical issues in providing too little care due to cost containment and too much care under fee-for-service models of reimbursement.

Mode of Treatment

Mode of treatment refers to the mechanism or format of service delivery and typically includes individual treatment, couples and/or family treatment, group treatment, and medication. All these modes have certain advantages.

Individual therapy promotes greater privacy, self-disclosure, sharing, individualized attention, and identification with the helper than the other modes (Beutler & Clarkin, 1990, p. 123). Couples therapy allows for the direct observation of interaction between the partners; deals with both parties, including both "sides" of conflict; and allows for the development of mutual support, communication, and conflict-resolution sources (Beutler & Clarkin, 1990, p. 123). These same advantages are extended to family therapy. A group mode allows for extensive modeling, support, and feedback from others (particularly helpful for those with social phobia and others who could benefit from social skills training). Couples, group, and family interventions are good settings for providing education and skills training. Individual, couple/family, and group modes of treatment do not typically involve adverse side effects, although it goes without saying that not all clients improve with treatment.

Medication management involves the use of psychotropic drugs to help alleviate and/or manage the symptoms of psychological disorders for which there is a clear biochemical imbalance. Generally, these disorders include psychotic conditions, major depression, and bipolar disorders (Thase, 2000). If medication management seems warranted, the client will also need to be evaluated and followed by a physician. Clients rarely learn new ways of problem solving and coping with *just* medication, so some mode of psychotherapy in addition to medication is often warranted. Clients may need to process with nonmedical practitioners the meaning they ascribe to taking medication and how to talk to others (e.g., family members) about their medication. Medications also pose greater risks and adverse side effects to clients than do the other modes of treatment, and prescribing physicians may not take the time to fully discuss these effects with clients. Nonmedical practitioners, therefore, can serve an important educational and supportive function.

The mode of treatment is often indicated by the nature of the client's issue. Although a helper trained primarily in couples- and family- or system-based approaches may view all presenting issues and corresponding interventions as family oriented, an individual format may be conducive for a client in the early phase of treatment (e.g., someone in a precontemplative stage of change). By the same token, another helper trained solely in individual interventions may miss or overlook important group and systemic parts of the issue as well as other nonindividual or collectivist-oriented interventions. The importance of having a multidimensional treatment perspective and remaining flexible cannot be overemphasized!

Given the information presented on decision rules in planning for type, duration, and mode of treatment, we invite you to participate in Learning Activity 10.3. Two cases are presented (Antonio and Mr. Sharn) for you to apply several of the decision rules. Feedback is provided to help you evaluate the rules you selected.

RACIAL, ETHNIC, GENDER, AND OTHER CULTURAL ISSUES IN TREATMENT PLANNING AND SELECTION

It should go without saying that cultural considerations are an indisputable priority in clinical decision making and treatment planning. Culture—broadly defined—is integral to all aspects of the helping process. Race, ethnicity, gender, and other cultural issues (e.g., sexual orientation, religious affiliation, health status, gender expression, socioeconomic status, spirituality) are woven into the very fabric of all helping practices. Helpers must therefore remain vigilant about the cultural background and identity of their clients, how their clients express their cultural identity (whether or not such expression is "obvious," as in client self-report, for example), and the meaning they and their clients attribute to the expression or manifestation of clients' cultural identity. This is true for all clients and helpers because all client–helper interactions are cross-cultural. Although clients and helpers may at times look alike (e.g., members of a similar racial/ethnic group) and may share similar backgrounds, identities, and values, there is no such thing as cultural sameness between clients and helpers. Borrowing from our earlier forest analogy, helpers need to recognize and incorporate into the step-by-step treatment-planning process the idiosyncratic trees that make up the forest.

Many of the strategies described in this chapter are drawn from theoretical positions developed by a (White) founding father or fathers. As a result, the most widely used therapeutic strategies often reflect the dominant values of mainstream culture, defined by "whiteness, middle-class position, youth, able-bodiedness, heterosexuality and maleness" (Brown, 1994, p. 63). Clients who do not have these characteristics are more likely to feel marginalized and may experience what Gary (2005) described as the "double stigma" of being a member of a cultural minority and having a mental illness. This type of stigma may be experienced as public stigma (e.g., institutional racism), self-stigma (e.g., diminished self-efficacy), or family and courtesy stigma (i.e., stigma generalized to a client's family members).

LEARNING ACTIVITY 10.3 Decision Rules in Treatment Planning

 Use the following two case descriptions to identify some decision rules about treatment selection and planning. Respond orally or in writing to the five questions, which represent decision rules about treatment selection. You may want to do this activity with a partner or in a small group. Feedback follows on page 288.

1. What is this client's level of functional impairment? Present data to support your decision. Given the data, what would you recommend about treatment duration for this client?

2. What is this client's predominant coping style—externalized or internalized? Present data to support your decision. Given the data, what type of treatment would you select for this client—behavioral focus or insight-reflective focus?

3. What mode of treatment might work best for this client? Present data to support your choice.

4. How would you assess the client's level of resistance— low or high? Present data to support your choice. Given the data, would you use directive or nondirective intervention strategies?

5. Consider how your training, practice setting, and theoretical orientation(s) to helping might affect your decision about treatment selection.

The Case of Antonio

Antonio is a 15-year-old boy who lives with his dad. His mother kicked him out because he stopped going to school and got in trouble with the law for stealing. His parents are divorced. His dad owns a bar, and Antonio is now staying with his dad but says he doesn't see him much. He says he quit going to school because he didn't have any friends there, his teachers didn't seem to understand him, and he got into trouble all the time for fighting. He spends his time now playing video games, although arrangements have been made for him to be home-schooled for the rest of the year. He denies any substance use. He doesn't understand why he has to see you.

The Case of Mr. Sharn

Mr. Sharn is a 72-year-old man who has come to see you because he has had trouble sleeping and has noticed problems with his memory, problems that he says are unusual. Also, his appetite is poor. He has been retired for seven years and has really enjoyed himself until lately. He and his wife recently returned from visiting their son and grandchildren, who live in a town a few hours away. His other son lives in the same town as Mr. Sharn. Mr. Sharn says he has lots of friends, especially golfing buddies. He reports being close to both sons. He says they had a good visit, but ever since he has been back he has noticed some things about his sleep, memory, and appetite. He does report feeling kind of "blue" but not overwhelmed by it, and he denies any suicidal thoughts. He is hoping you can help him. Although he has never consulted a professional helper before, he doesn't want to burden his wife or his sons with too many problems.

Discrimination and marginalization are particularly evident in the racial disparities that persist in mental health care. These include lower rates of medication management and outpatient utilization after inpatient discharge for racial and ethnic minorities compared to Whites (Virnig et al., 2004), differences in diagnoses according to client race (irrespective of helper race; Neighbors, Trierweiler, Ford, & Muroff, 2003), and greater levels of psychological distress among African Americans both before and after participating in treatment for co-occurring disorders compared to Whites (Grella & Stein, 2006). Furthermore, although a vast majority (85%) of therapists reported having discussions about cultural differences with their clients, these discussions were reported to occur in less than half (43%) of cross-racial/ethnic therapy cases (Maxie, Arnold, & Stephenson, 2006). Helpers of various races and ethnicities may therefore be mindful of racial and ethnic issues in their work, but they may choose not to address such issues directly with their clients (e.g., "She's lived here in the United States for so long and speaks fluent English—I didn't think the fact that she happened to be born in Haiti was really a major issue"), or they may not be able to provide specific culturally appropriate services (e.g., having a staff member who can speak a new client's preferred language).

Typically, traditional treatment planning and selection have not addressed issues of race, gender, and social class— particularly poverty and international perspectives (Brown, 1994). This might be due, in part, to the contention that racially and ethnically diverse participants have not been included in randomized clinical/control trials, the findings of which have supplied the "evidence" for evidence-based practice (Comas-Diaz, 2006; Whaley & Davis, 2007). Indeed, some traditional psychotherapeutic techniques found to be successful with Euro-American clients may be culturally contraindicated for clients who do not fit the dominant and mainstream socio-political-economic culture. These might include certain expressive strategies associated with Gestalt therapy, group work (particularly in the early phase

FEEDBACK

10.3   Decision Rules in Treatment Planning

The Case of Antonio

1. Antonio's functional impairment seems high, due to his family problems, his lack of social support, and his social isolation and withdrawal. As a result, treatment intensity would be increased, with more frequent sessions spaced closer together.
2. Antonio's coping style seems to be externalized. He has been in trouble with the law for stealing and has been in trouble at school for fighting. As a result, your treatment focus would be behavioral.
3. Because of Antonio's family issues, social isolation, and lack of social support, family and group modes of treatment may be better than individual. Individual sessions may be needed at first, however, to establish your credibility and trustworthiness.
4. Antonio's level of resistance appears to be high, and he might be described as being in the precontemplative stage of change (he doesn't know why he has to see you). Nondirective interventions would be more useful.

The Case of Mr. Sharn

1. Mr. Sharn's degree of impairment seems relatively low. He has a supportive and functional family and lots of friends, and he seems to have a good overall support system. So treatment intensity and duration would probably remain at once weekly. Of course, his level of depression would need to be carefully monitored to ensure he is not a danger to himself.
2. Mr. Sharn seems to have a more internalized coping style, for he views himself as the cause of the problems, and he internalizes feelings of distress and sadness.
3. It would be useful to use individual sessions with Mr. Sharn; also, a possible evaluation with a physician may be necessary because of his sleep, appetite, and memory problems.
4. Mr. Sharn's level of resistance is low. He appears to be eager to accept your help, so you can use more directive interventions.

---

of the helping process), disputing what the helper might interpret as irrational thoughts, and identifying a "higher power" in one's recovery from substance dependence. Helpers accustomed to offering these and other strategies to their clients as part of their "standard practice" will need to expand their repertoire so as to accommodate the diverse expressions of culture among their clients. These practices might include prayer and meditation, chanting, consultation with community elders/indigenous healers, drum work, aromatherapy, and home- or community-based visitation. Although some helpers might bristle at the idea of engaging in such practices, Ivey and Brooks-Harris (2005) contend that "Psychotherapy faces a time of major change . . . [that includes] discarding the outmoded concept of self and replacing it with self-in-context, being-in-relation, and person-in-community" (p. 335). A more expansive understanding and practice of helping, therefore, is not only needed but is already at work. We believe it is time for such changes.

Intentional Integration of Cultural Interventions

Nezu (2005) described three barriers that prevent mental health professions from fully incorporating issues of diversity in all aspects of practice: (1) excessive focus on internal psychological processes, (2) the "medicalization" of human behavior, and (3) the ubiquity of unconscious biases against "out-group" members. Perhaps in an effort to address these

and other impediments to adopting a cultural milieu of professional helping, Ivey and Brooks-Harris (2005) presented what we interpret as a preliminary portrait of mainstream multicultural helping. Their description derives from predictions Ivey and Ivey (2000) made about how cultural issues will change the very practice of psychotherapy in the next few decades, predictions Whaley and Davis (2007) would more than likely support. We delineate five features of Ivey and Brooks-Harris's portrait, and we discuss their relevance to clinical decision making and treatment planning: (1) contextual awareness; (2) consciousness development; (3) diffusing distress and reframing resistance; (4) coconstructed, contextual-specific, and collaborative interventions; and (5) therapeutic proactivity. These five features of mainstream multicultural helping are not presented in any order of importance. Specific intervention strategies are discussed in each one.

Contextual Awareness

A multicultural focus in clinical decision making and treatment planning must include a consideration of contextual issues. Such a perspective pertains to the client's past and current environment, especially his or her social system, including (but not limited to) oppressive conditions within the system. Interventions might therefore include conducting a comprehensive assessment of the client's living and working environment (both past and present) with particular attention given to social relationships. In addition to completing a genogram (and not necessarily restricted to biological relations or kin), for example, helpers might ask individual clients and each family member to draw a plan of their house or their current dwelling. Rochkovski (2006) has described this activity, stating that "When we ask a family to 'draw the plan of their house,' previously invisible aspects of the family come to light" (p. 10), such as the types of space(s) involved, how each family member uses the space(s) in the depicted dwelling (as well as the space on the paper on which it is drawn), traffic patterns, furniture, and structure of the house (e.g., shanty, fortress, with/without windows).

Rochkovski (2006) described one family who literally live on garbage (their hut stands on compacted tons of garbage), make their living off the garbage (and so they cannot move), and have metal sheets for their walls and roof. Their interior dwelling, however, consists of two television sets, stereo equipment, separate rooms for each member, and quality bedding. They try to live, therefore, as if they were living at a good address, which may open doors during the helping process, for example, to a consideration of the advantages and disadvantages of a client's collectivist orientation (e.g., value of and commitment to *familia*) when "housed" in an individualist environment (e.g., competitive entrepreneurialism).

Depicting a client's living environment and social system on paper as part of the helping process provides a glimpse into the client's interior and exterior cultural contexts, in some ways consistent with our trees (idiosyncratic or idiographic) *and* forest (nomothetic) analogy. A similar exercise could be undertaken for the client's neighborhood (e.g., "Draw a plan of the block where you live"), work environment (e.g., where offices are located and how office space is used), or school setting (e.g., "Draw for me your classroom" or "Draw a plan of your school cafeteria"). This same exercise could be adapted for clients who do not currently have a home (i.e., depicting the spaces they now occupy and how others may encroach on those spaces).

Contextual awareness also pertains to understanding the helper's context or, more precisely, the social system of the helping process. Interventions might include informing clients about the helper's qualifications (e.g., providing them with a copy of one's professional disclosure statement) as well as disclosing to clients the helper's own cultural identity, background, or context (e.g., "I happen to be legally blind, but I can see the general outlines of faces. I'll probably be squinting quite a bit so I can see more of your facial expressions, and you'll probably see my eyes fluttering from time-to-time as they adjust to the light"). Contextual awareness of the helping process is also furthered by discussing with clients what they will do (i.e., client implementation) and what the helper will do (i.e., helper interventions), the goal being to offer clients what Brown (1994) referred to as empowered consent. We prefer *empowered* consent to *informed* consent because, as Brown pointed out, the word *informed* raises such

questions as "Who is being informed? How? By and about what or whom? Under what conditions of freedom of choice or 'friendly' coercion is consent being given?" (p. 180).

We believe that the helper is acting in good faith to protect clients' rights and welfare by discussing with clients the following kinds of information about treatment strategies:

1. A description of *all* relevant and potentially useful treatment approaches for this particular client with this particular problem
2. A rationale for each procedure
3. A description of the helper's role in each procedure
4. A description of the client's role in each procedure
5. Discomforts or risks that may occur as a result of the procedure
6. Benefits expected to result from the procedure
7. The estimated time and cost of each procedure

Empowered consent is designed to provide complete and meaningful disclosure in a way that supports the client's freedom of choice and may be considered the product of role induction. This practice, therefore, implies collaboration, which we believe is consistent with a mainstream multicultural milieu.

Consciousness Development

Consciousness development is the process of becoming increasingly aware of one's cultural identity and how it is expressed in varying contexts over time. Because "cultural identity is fluid and dynamic and may be differentially invoked, depending on the context and situation" (Lo & Fung, 2003, p. 163), consciousness development is an ongoing activity and is relevant for both client and helper. The client may benefit from exploring internalized conflict/discrepancies that may arise, for example, when familiar surroundings change (e.g., relocation of residence), established relationships require reconfiguration (e.g., family member comes out as gay), or physical appearance and functioning or accustomed mobility are disrupted (e.g., loss of limbs in a freak accident). Validating the client's reactions to these and other changes may be the first step needed to relieve or at least ease what may be feelings of anger or guilt.

An Asian client who was the sole survivor of an automobile accident, for example, may experience "survivor's guilt" and believe that his ensuing depression that has resulted in his unemployment is simply his "bad luck" and "fate." In this instance, the culturally skilled helper may familiarize herself with certain folk beliefs in the client's specific Asian background that may have a salutary connotation and empowering effect. Lo and Fung (2003) made reference to one such Chinese adage: "survivors of great catastrophe will surely have good luck later on." The helper may thus offer this folk belief to the client and suggest that his survival is an example of his ability to withstand the "clutch of fate" and that gratitude for his life might be expressed to a particular deity by helping others (maybe even as a way to earn that deity's favor for future "good luck").

The helper's own consciousness development can occur by conducting what Lo and Fung (2003) described as a Cultural Analysis—that is, a hypothesis-generating strategy for understanding how a client's culture influences self, relationships, and treatment. The goal of such an intervention is to "achieve a more complete and culturally informed psychological understanding of the patient" (p. 166), and components of the analysis can include a sociopolitical history of the client's country of origin, current forces in the host country (e.g., discrimination), and particular dynamics and resources available in the client's local ethnic community. As a means of furthering an appreciation for each client's cultural context and consciousness, Comas-Diaz (2006) described the practice of cultural resonance, which she defined as "the ability to understand clients through clinical skill, cultural competence, and intuition" (p. 94). Integral to this helper skill is the focus on nonverbal communication: "Cultural resonance helps the clinician decipher the client's inner processes and provides information beyond messages that the client communicates verbally" (p. 94).

By engaging the client in a Cultural Analysis and demonstrating cultural resonance, the helper can be said to be assuming one or more culturally appropriate roles. Atkinson, Thompson, and Grant (1993) proposed six roles for helpers to assume in a multicultural helping context (again, which we believe constitutes all client–helper encounters). These are listed in Box 10.3 and represent alternatives to the more conventional role in which many practitioners are trained. In addition, these alternative roles involve helpers more actively in the client's life experiences.

Diffusing Distress and Reframing Resistance

In their vision of a mainstream multicultural milieu, Ivey and Brooks-Harris (2005) stated that "'Disorder' will cease to frame our consciousness about the deeply troubled. Rather, psychotherapy will engage serious client 'dis-stress' and not define it as 'dis-ease'" (p. 335). In addition, client issues and challenges will be understood "as a logical response to developmental history and external social conditions" (p. 335). This depiction implies a prioritization of client strengths, resources, and protective factors, in addition to a consideration of client challenges. Therefore, we would encourage helpers devising treatment plans with clients to intentionally incorporate client assets and resources that, if you recall from Lambert's (1992) research, appear to significantly impact client outcome (i.e., client or extratherapeutic factors account for 40 percent of client improvement during the helping process). The client's spirituality may play an important role in this regard; folk beliefs, mythology, and supernatural forces

may all be significant factors. By embracing a "dis-stress" rather than a "dis-ease" perspective, and helping clients mobilize (indeed, positively exploit) the strengths and resources present in their cultural identity and community, helpers are in essence ushering in a new culture, one that resembles Ivey and Brooks-Harris's (2005) vision of what we have termed a mainstream multicultural milieu in professional helping.

Part of this milieu will be a reframing of resistance as traditionally understood and how it was described earlier in the chapter. Ridley (2005) defined resistance as "countertherapeutic behavior . . . directed toward one goal: the indiscriminate avoidance of the painful requirements of change" (p. 134). He emphasized that resistance, like racism, is a "human motor activity . . . [that] can be observed, repeated, and measured" (p. 134). It "is not an attitude or a psychological state of the client, although resistant attitudes and psychological states are powerful motivators of client behavior" (p. 134). A reframing of resistance views "acts of resistance" as indicators of positive functioning (Brown, 2000, p. 367). Promoting salutary resistance in clients requires helpers who, according to Brown (2000), are "capable of seeing beyond the options presented by the dominant culture" and who are able to identify and support paths of resistance and subversion that may not be authorized by mainstream values (p. 367). For example, at an individual level, this may mean helping the client resist an inequitable contract or workload agreement in her job that has been created without divergent voices and imposed by people who hold the power. Treatment strategies would be selected and implemented toward this act of resistance. At a systems level, both helper and client may need to resist systemwide practices that substitute compliance for difference and agreement for disagreement. From a multicultural perspective, clients' acts of resistance help them feel empowered due to "naming, validating, resisting and subverting external events and influences that are problematic and often oppressive" (Brown, 2000, p. 366).

Coconstructed, Contextual-Specific, and Collaborative Interventions

Depending on the nature of their concerns (e.g., symptom intensity) and their cultural values, clients may present for mental health treatment with the expectation that a "cure" is

---

BOX 10.3	HELPER ROLES

1. Advisor
2. Advocate
3. Facilitator of Indigenous Support Systems
4. Facilitator of Indigenous Healing Systems
5. Consultant
6. Change Agent

Source: Atkinson, Thompson, & Grant, 1993.

possible (indeed, necessary), that the helper is the source of that "remedy," and that the "answer" to "fixing" the clients' concerns can (indeed, must) happen immediately. Such an orientation may be amenable to brief or time-limited cognitive–behavioral interventions, and some helpers may be eager to "jump right on in" and accommodate what might be interpreted as the client's "demands." Although many clients of certain racial/ethnic backgrounds may wait a considerable amount of time before seeking professional help for mental health concerns and thus appear for the first session in a state of crisis (Paniagua, 2005), we would advise helpers not to assume a knee-jerk reaction of "doctor knows best" and proceed in what some might regard as a paternalistic manner of care. Extending treatment without an understanding of or a full appreciation for the client's cultural identity and context is, as we have discussed, inappropriate, inconsistent with professional guidelines (e.g., American Psychological Association, 2003), and potentially unethical (see the National Association of Social Workers' *Code of Ethics*, 1999, Standard 1.05: Cultural Competence and Social Diversity; also see the American Counseling Association's *Code of Ethics*, 2005, B.1.a.: Multicultural/Diversity Considerations).

Clients do need to have their presenting concerns taken seriously (e.g., physical symptoms, even if the helper suspects somatization or malingering). Indeed, when determining appropriate treatment goals, Lo and Fung (2003) emphasized that "the primary principle . . . should be the patient's subjective well-being, conducive to healthy functioning in the patient's environment" (p. 164). However, this does not mean that the helper should presume to know (particularly at the beginning of care) what is "best" for the client. Lo and Fung (2003) recommended a both/and principle of practice in this regard (consistent with the integrative— "trees *and* forest"—perspective emphasized throughout this chapter) in that helpers are able to "recognize and operate within the contrasting frameworks of therapeutic omniscience and naiveté" (p. 161). This means practicing according to one's training and scope of competence (e.g., crisis intervention) while remaining open to the "instruction" of cultural configurations and their meanings for each new, unique client.

Regardless of the client's cultural identity or context, the American Counseling Association's (2005) *Code of Ethics* (A.1.c.) stipulates that "counselors and their clients work jointly in devising integrated counseling plans" and also "regularly review counseling plans to assess their continued viability and effectiveness, respecting the freedom of choice of clients." The selection of treatment goals and strategies, therefore, should be undertaken as a collaborative venture between client and helper. This is accomplished by learning more about the client's cultural identity and context (e.g., language preference, social network and family dynamics, acculturation status, time orientation), engaging in role induction and empowered consent, and possibly consulting with others involved in the client's life (e.g., family members, referral source, family physician). Indeed, the collaborative construction of a treatment plan may extend beyond the client–helper dyad to include the contributions of lay and professional consultants, all of whom would be involved only with the client's expressed permission, of course. When working with Asian American clients, Paniagua (2005) recommended collecting information gradually rather than all at once and planning on several sessions to obtain an adequate amount of necessary and relevant data.

Cognitive–behavioral approaches, in particular, have potential strengths for use with culturally diverse clients (Hays, 2001). These approaches include the emphasis on the uniqueness of the individual and the adaptation of the helping process to meet this uniqueness, a focus on client empowerment, ongoing helper–client collaboration, use of a direct and pragmatic treatment focus, and an emphasis on conscious (versus unconscious) processes and specific (versus abstract) behaviors and treatment protocols (Hays, 2001; Kantrowitz & Ballou, 1992). Lum (2004) described five specific treatment strategies relevant to multicultural practice; they are described in Box 10.4. We believe each of these interventions operates within the framework of client–helper collaboration that includes the coconstruction of a culturally appropriate treatment plan.

Therapeutic Proactivity

To realize the mainstream multicultural milieu that we emphasize here, mental health professionals will need to assume more of a proactive stance than in years past. We believe this is essential to address the prevalent and systemic issues of stigma and discrimination, and thus is consistent with social justice imperatives (see Lee, 2007). This proactive stance will entail engaging in more outreach services (resembling those of Assertive Community Treatment discussed earlier in the chapter), "courting" (*not* coercing) clients once contact has been established to enhance help-seeking behaviors (e.g., "easing into" a system of care by gradually connecting clients with specialized service providers), providing more services in the community (e.g., home-based and mobile/ambulatory care) than exclusively in a professional clinic, and adopting a multicultural philosophy of care that is systemwide or institutional (e.g., the entire staff is trained in and committed to culturally appropriate services). Practices such as these exemplify the helper's role as advocate for societal conditions that unfairly impact clients, a role that will continue to take center stage as mental health care transitions into a multicultural milieu. Ivey and Brooks-Harris (2005) described their vision of this milieu:

> Psychotherapists will recognize the importance of directly attacking systemic issues that affect client development. We will move toward a proactive stance rather than our present reactive stance. We need not expect our clients to work alone.

| BOX 10.4 | FIVE INTERVENTIONS RELEVANT IN MULTICULTURAL PRACTICE |

Liberation (vs. oppression) is the client's experience of release or freedom from oppressive barriers and control when change occurs. For some, it accompanies personal growth and decision-making: The client has decided to no longer submit to oppression. In other cases, liberation occurs under the influence of environmental change; for example, the introduction of a job-training program or the election of an ethnic mayor who makes policy, legislative, and program changes on behalf of people of color.

Empowerment (vs. powerlessness) is a process in which persons who belong to a stigmatized social category can be assisted to develop and increase skills in the exercise of interpersonal influence. Claiming the human right to resources and well-being in society, individuals experience power by mobilizing their resources and changing their situational predicament. The first step to empowerment is to obtain information about resources and rights. Second, by choosing an appropriate path of action, the client participates in a situation in which his or her exercise of power confers palpable benefits. Practical avenues of empowerment include voting, influencing policy, or initiating legislation on the local level.

Parity (vs. exploitation) refers to equality. For people of color, parity entails achieving equal power, value, and rank with others in society and being treated accordingly. Its focal theme is fairness and the entitlement to certain rights. Parity is expressed in terms of resources that guarantee an adequate standard of living, such as entitlement programs (Social Security, Medicare), income maintenance, and medical care.

Maintenance of culture (vs. acculturation) asserts the importance of the ideas, customs, skills, arts, and language of a people. By tracing the history of an ethnic group, helper and client can identify moments of crisis and challenge through which it survived and triumphed. Applying such lessons of history to the present inspires the client to overcome obstacles by drawing on the strength of his or her cultural heritage. Maintenance of culture secures the client's identity as an ethnic individual.

Unique personhood (vs. stereotyping) is an intervention strategy by which stereotypes are transcended. Functional casework maintains that each person is unique in the helping relationship and that there is something extraordinary in each individual. When people of color act to gain freedom from negative social or societal generalizations, they assert their unique personhood and collective ethnic worth.

Source: Social Work Practice and People of Color: A Process–Stage Approach (5th ed.), by D. Lum, pp. 254–262. Copyright 2004. Reprinted with permission of Brooks/Cole–Thomson Learning.

Psychotherapists have an ethical imperative to work toward positive societal change. (pp. 335–336)

Therapeutic proactivity (fueled by the principle of social justice) is needed in light of recent prevalence data suggesting that approximately 30 percent of the U.S. population meet criteria for a *DSM-IV* mental disorder (specifically anxiety, mood, and substance use disorder) in a given 12-month period (Kessler et al., 2005). Only a minority of those with a serious mental disorder, however, received treatment (24 to 40.5 percent), prompting Kessler et al. to argue for practices that will increase access to and demand for treatment by providing care/services in targeted locations intended to reach traditionally underserved groups. In an ethnic-specific mental health program, however, Akutsu, Tsuru, and Chu (2004) reported a 30 percent client attrition rate from prescreening to scheduled intake. Based on their inspection of retained clients, they recommended that the prescreening interviewer be able to speak the client's native language and that this same practitioner continue as the client's intake therapist.

Recruitment and retention of culturally diverse clients can also be accomplished by offering a "gift" at the conclusion of the first session (and perhaps after each of the first few sessions). Although Smolar (2003) described the use of intangible "gifts" (e.g., helper self-disclosure, time, presence), Paniagua (2005) emphasized the extension of tangible gifts to clients—or, what we might refer to as more specific or concrete gifts. Examples of specific and concrete gifts include the helper's explanation about presenting concerns, reassurances, educational literature, and a copy of the helper's professional disclosure statement (to convey the helper's qualifications, which some clients might interpret as reasons to trust in the helper's credibility). These and other gifts may reinforce to the client the helper's genuine concern and investment in the process of care and may also encourage the client to "reciprocate" by investing in the process of change. The American Counseling Association's (2005) *Code of Ethics* acknowledges that "in some cultures, small gifts are a token of respect and showing gratitude" (Section A.10.e.), and some clients may be inclined to offer helpers a tangible gift. Helpers may encourage these clients to instead offer a gift to the process of helping (e.g., implementing a new behavior that has been practiced in therapy with a family member), to another client's efforts to heal (e.g., offering an encouraging word in a group session), or to the treatment facility (e.g., a painting done by the client is placed in the lobby). Reframing the purpose of such gifts and redirecting clients to offer a gift to another recipient (e.g., to themselves, to another client) may be described for clients as an investment in their or another person's "good fortune."

Therapeutic proactivity may also be evidenced in the helper maintaining contact with clients in between sessions (e.g., encouraging clients to telephone the helper at specific times, such as prior to any parasuicidal behavior, as is recommended in Dialectical Behavior Therapy) as well as after the helping process has concluded for the time being. Lo and Fung (2003) referred to this latter practice as keeping the "door ajar"; it may include scheduling "check-in" sessions (possibly held at a community setting, such as the public library) and periodic telephone and e-mail contact. Such practice resembles Cummings's (1995) description of mental health care as the provision of intermittent services across the life span. This means that care is always available and extended, that clients "re-enroll" in the helping process when needs arise (e.g., reactivation of symptoms, major life transitions), and that closure or termination is never permanent. Additional examples of therapeutic proactivity (which Paniagua, 2005, presented as guidelines for preventing client attrition) are listed in Box 10.5. To help you intentionally integrate cultural interventions in your professional practice, we encourage you to participate in Learning Activity 10.4. Before doing so, review the five features of a mainstream multicultural milieu described in this section, as well as the decision rules in treatment planning presented in the preceding section.

THE PROCESS OF TREATMENT PLANNING AND SHARED DECISION MAKING

The choice of appropriate helping strategies is a joint decision in which both client and helper are actively involved. We realize this is an activity that is easier said than done, and the challenge might explain the abundance of what we have heard as lip service paid to client–helper collaboration by many treatment providers. Helpers may speak of establishing rapport with clients but inadvertently "jump in" and begin assigning homework before a client is ready or even willing to consider change. In addition, treatment plans may not always reflect therapeutic collaboration. This is evident when there is a listing of all that the client will do but there is no corresponding list of what the practitioner will do to help the client

implement all that has been planned. A lack of client–helper collaboration is also suspected when, upon inspection of one helper's treatment plans for all clients on his or her roster, one standard plan applied to all clients is discovered. This one-size-fits-all approach to treatment planning overlooks clients' idiosyncratic concerns and resources and yields a predetermined, unilateral, "hand-me-down" plan of care. We believe it is a misuse of the inherent influence of the helping process for the practitioner to select a strategy or to implement a treatment plan independent of the client's input.

Although deliberately engaging clients in treatment decision making and negotiating services can be a time- and energy-consuming process, we are convinced that it is time and energy well spent. Falvey (2001) found that the more time mental health practitioners spent on case conceptualization and treatment-planning activities (approximately 78 to 90 minutes, compared to 60 minutes), the better able they were to make sense of client data and to present information clearly. In another study, Iguchi, Belding, Morral, Lamb, and Husband (1997) found that opioid-dependent clients who participated in an individualized treatment-planning program attended significantly more counseling sessions and demonstrated significant improvement in abstinence rates over time compared to clients enrolled in two other comparison programs. They described the individualized program as a "shaping strategy" because therapists met weekly with clients to establish the following week's behavioral tasks and "were generally free to tailor tasks to suit the needs of individual participants" (p. 423). Therapists were also instructed to reinforce desirable behaviors (i.e., participation in activities inconsistent with drug use), establish easier tasks if clients failed to achieve certain tasks from the previous week, and gradually increase the difficulty of subsequent tasks with the aim of achieving long-term treatment plan goals. From these two studies, it is clear to us that, though

---

BOX 10.5   GENERAL GUIDELINES FOR THE PREVENTION OF ATTRITION

1. Make sure that the client finds what he or she is looking for from a therapist (e.g., acceptance of the client's belief system).
2. Be aware that the client expects a quick solution to his or her problems.
3. Explore the client's expectations regarding therapy.
4. Involve the client's extended family members (including persons related to the client both biologically and non-biologically) in the assessment and treatment process. Remember that with Asian clients, issues of shame and humiliation may preclude the inclusion of nonbiologically related extended family members (e.g., friends).
5. When the length and frequency of treatment sessions are reduced, explain the reasons to the client so that he or she does not perceive the changes as indicating lack of

interest in working with members of the client's cultural group.
6. If paraprofessionals are used, avoid using them too frequently; the client may feel that he or she is being treated as a "second-class client" if he or she is not often seen by a professional.
7. Use a modality of therapy that is directive, active, and structured, and provide a tentative solution to the client's core problem (particularly during the first session).
8. Ensure that all mental health professionals (e.g., psychologists, psychiatrists, social workers) and support staff (e.g., secretaries, receptionists) who come in contact with multicultural clients have had cross-cultural training.

Source: Assessing and Treating Culturally Diverse Clients: A Practical Guide (3rd ed.), by F. A. Paniagua, p. 111, Table 7.1. Copyright 2005 by Sage. Reprinted by permission of the publisher.

LEARNING ACTIVITY   **10.4**   **Gender and Multicultural Factors in Treatment Planning and Selection**

Assume the role of helper, and review the case of Jane Wiggins, a low-income woman living in a rural area (see page 284). Read the case carefully, and identify any multicultural factors that may affect the way in which you work with this woman. Use the five features of a mainstream multicultural milieu described in this section of the chapter (see pages 289 to 293). After this, with a partner or in a small group, identify a treatment plan implementing various interventions that address the multicultural factors you identified. Consider the type, duration, and mode of treatment based on the client's identified concerns and stated goals. Also in your treatment plan, consider what oppressive events Ms. Wiggins needs to be able to name, validate, and resist. Feedback is provided on page 296.

time-intensive, treatment planning that is customized to an individual client and conducted jointly with clients results in greater case formulation clarity for the helper (and we suspect for the client too) and in a realization for the client of his or her treatment goals.

In addition to the benefits demonstrated in research studies, the emphasis on client–helper collaborative treatment planning is related to two separate but very similar movements in the health care industry over the past 10 to 15 years. One has been driven by clients themselves, the other by professionals. Consumer advocacy efforts, such as the National Alliance for the Mentally Ill (http://www.nami.org), have been dedicated to protecting and preserving the rights of clients as full participants in their own care. These efforts have included education for clients, families, and the general public; lobbying for increased and targeted funding of mental health services; and serving in leadership positions (e.g., consumer member of a county mental health board).

Health care professionals have also prioritized the contributions of clients in their own health care decisions. Known in general as shared decision making (Adams & Drake, 2006), this interactive process assumes that both client and helper have important information to contribute to the helping process: helpers have information about and skills in diagnostic assessment, treatment strategies, and interpersonal communication; clients have information about their symptoms, cultural identity and context, and what has been helpful in the past (e.g., coping mechanisms), as well as what they believe will be helpful at this time. Although certain aspects of shared decision making are not without controversy (e.g., "Are persons with severe mental illnesses able to participate rationally and effectively in discussions about their own mental health care?"), the general principle on which it is based—client-centered care—cannot be disputed.

A primary activity in shared decision making is negotiation. To accomplish this, clients are encouraged to be full participants in the process of change and are regarded as "coagents in a problem-solving context" (Young & Flower, 2001, p. 70). According to Adams and Drake (2006), the goal of negotiation is educated decision making "even if the negotiation is to accept negotiations in the first place" (p. 98). They explain this by stating:

The pros and cons of a decision can often be framed to avoid the barrier of illness, stigma or other prejudices that might be preventing the client from engaging with his [or her] practitioner. For each objection to any option in a shared decision-making encounter, thought must be given to strategies that might make the objection less of a threat, or eliminate it altogether. (p. 98)

Applied to individualized treatment planning, shared decision making means that treatment goals and objectives are not imposed on clients; rather, they are negotiated. If a client balks at the helper's initial recommendation, the helper might provide a clearer and more detailed explanation about why he or she thinks this particular strategy would be helpful at this time. If a client remains adamantly opposed to seeing a psychiatrist to determine the appropriateness of psychotropic medication, for example (even after the helper has carefully explained his or her reasons for recommending this), the helper might propose an alternative strategy, such as having the client view a video that features persons who claim to have benefited from taking psychotropic medications, or having the client conduct a search on the Internet to determine the reported benefits and side effects of a particular medication. Certainly the helper needs to uphold professional ethics by not agreeing to substandard care that would knowingly place the client in certain danger. In the previous example, this might mean that the helper offer three options to the client—consult with a psychiatrist, watch the video, or conduct an Internet search—and indicate that the client will need to fulfill one of these in order to continue in this mode and at this level of treatment (e.g., individual outpatient therapy). This is an example of contingency management—that is, contingencies are applied to certain behaviors.

Dialectical Behavior Therapy (DBT) provides a helpful model for client–helper negotiation. In arriving at what Linehan (1993) refers to as "therapeutic agreements," helpers are advised to "avoid unnecessary power struggles" (p. 497). She explains:

If an issue does not seem important, it should not be pursued. Learning how to retreat is very important in DBT, as is choosing battles wisely. The therapist should be prepared, though, to fight and win some battles in order to help the patient. (p. 497)

Throughout the DBT negotiation process, helpers describe and clarify the strategies that are at the client's disposal, the helper's rationale for recommending certain strategies, and the anticipated benefits of such strategies as well as possible risks or shortcomings (empowered consent continually at work!). Helpers also emphasize that it is the client who retains the ability to choose among treatment options (or even to take a vacation from therapy) and that the helper cares about the client, is concerned about his or her well-being, and hopes that any therapeutic impasse can be resolved. The structured and straightforward manner in which DBT is conducted—along with its use of the therapeutic relationship as the medium for change (i.e., constant focus on in-the-moment client–helper interactions)—facilitates collaborative clinical decision making and the completion of a treatment plan. It also serves as a vehicle for clients to learn problem-solving skills along the way—that is, while they are actually in treatment plan negotiations with their helper! This in itself should reinforce to helpers that a written treatment plan is not something to complete and "get out of the way" so as to begin "the real work" of therapy. Rather, as we emphasize throughout this chapter, treatment planning (not just the completion of a written document) is a continuous process, an ongoing activity, that is woven into and apparent in all client–helper interactions.

Many different formats are used to document the negotiated treatment plan, but we believe all must include the following elements, which we have adapted from Maruish (2002, p. 133):

- Referral source and reason for referral
- Presenting complaint and additional/related concerns

- Client strengths and resources
- Client liabilities and potential barriers to treatment
- Multiaxial diagnosis
- Helper and client negotiated goals (vision of client improvement; destination)
- Treatment objectives (means or methods for achieving negotiated goals and arriving at envisioned destination):

— Helper interventions (i.e., specific techniques or strategies that the helper will introduce, conduct, and facilitate)
— Client implementations (i.e., specific activities the client will engage in and fulfill, many of which will correspond to the helper interventions listed)

- Referral for evaluation
- Length, duration, and pace/frequency of treatment
- Criteria for treatment termination or transfer
- Treatment plan review date
- Prognosis (i.e., helper's prediction of client status/improvement by the review date)
- Responsible staff (individual helper, multidisciplinary treatment team members)

Figure 10.1 is a sample outpatient treatment-planning form. It represents many forms currently used by practitioners in various human services settings. You can see that this form incorporates many of the elements listed above. It also serves a variety of functions and ties together the principles and practices emphasized in this chapter.

As we have emphasized, clinical decision making and treatment planning constitute an ongoing, interactive process of

---

TREATMENT PLAN

Client Name: _____   Client File No.: _____

Therapist: _____   Supervisor: _____

Treatment Start Date: _____   Treatment End Date (Est.): _____

Presenting Concerns	Strengths/Resources	Goals and Measures	Therapist Interventions and Client Implementations	Duration
1.				
2.				
3.				
4.				

_____   _____   _____   _____

Client   Parent (if client under 18)   Therapist   Supervisor

Figure 10.1 Sample Treatment-Planning Form
Source: Adapted from Quin Curtis Center for Psychological Service, Training, and Research, Eberly College of Arts and Sciences, West Virginia University. Used with permission of William Fremouw, Ph.D., Director.

FEEDBACK

10.4 Gender and Multicultural Factors in Treatment Planning and Selection

 Consider these guidelines about your plan for Ms. Wiggins:

1. To what extent does your treatment plan reflect a culturally attentive (or perhaps a *culturally resonant*) agreement? How might it even be an example of a mainstream multicultural milieu taking formation? In other words, how has the treatment plan been influenced by Ms. Wiggins's *contextual awareness* and *consciousness development,* or *therapeutic proactivity*? For example, have you considered that Ms. Wiggins is a low-income Euro-American woman who has lived in the same rural community all her life surrounded by family and friends from church? She holds herself responsible for the rape and also feels powerless to get help from local authorities, who in fact have been unresponsive to her requests for assistance.

2. How has your plan addressed the impact of the client's *social system,* including oppressive conditions within that system? Have you noted that Ms. Wiggins is a poor White woman living with a husband on disability due to poor health in a rural area near a small town, that their complaints to local authorities have not been taken seriously, and that the man who raped her is related to a deputy in the sheriff's office? In essence, she feels disempowered and silenced by the system. Also, Ms. Wiggins views the rape at this time as a "female" problem and does not yet really see it as an act of social violence and misuse of power.

3. In what ways has your plan addressed any relevant *indigenous practices, supports,* and *resources*? Ms. Wiggins reports herself to be a very spiritual person who relies on the power of prayer to help her through tough times. How has your plan considered the role of important *subsystems* in the client's life? For this client, the most important subsystems are her family and her church. However, with the exception of her husband, who supports her, she feels cut off from both of these subsystems because of the nature of the issue, her own views about it, and her fears of her friends' and family's reactions.

4. Does your plan reflect the client's view of *health, recovery,* and *ways of solving problems*? For example, spirituality seems to play an important role in the way Ms. Wiggins solves problems. Gender also appears to be an issue. She seems to feel that a female helper would be better equipped to help her with this issue

(consider a referral to a woman helper and/or to a women's support group).

5. Have you considered the *level of acculturation* and any *language preferences* she has (also the use of culturally relevant themes, scripts, proverbs, and metaphors)? Implied in this framework is considering the role of the general history of Ms. Wiggins; the geographic location in which she lives and how long she has lived there; the type of setting; her socioeconomic status, age, gender, and role; and the specific effects of all of this on her language use and comprehension. Ms. Wiggins is a relatively young White woman on a limited and fixed income who has lived all her life in the same area—an isolated rural area near a small town. These demographics make for some interesting contradictions: She feels safe living in this region—safe enough to keep doors unlocked—yet she has been raped. The area is small enough to know who lives in it and who is a stranger, yet she has no support from the local sheriff's office because the assailant in this case (rather than the victim) is a relative of a deputy.

Influenced by the societal and cultural norms of the area, Ms. Wiggins feels ashamed about what has happened to her. All these things are likely to affect your plan. For example, she may not trust you because you are a male and an outsider. Also, she may view you as part of a social system that, in her eyes, is similar to the sheriff's office.

The themes of cultural mistrust and gender-linked shame can be addressed in the types of treatment you use with Ms. Wiggins.

6. How does the proposed *length* of your plan meet the needs and the perspective of Ms. Wiggins? To what extent does her willingness to return for additional sessions depend on the gender of the helper? How will her income and her husband's disability status affect her ability to come in for more sessions? Does your agency offer free services or a sliding scale for low-income clients? If not, how can you be her advocate so she can receive the number of sessions she needs?

7. Did you list some or any of the following *oppressive forces* that Ms. Wiggins needs to name, validate, and resist: local authorities and people in her church and family who would shame her or make her feel guilty about being raped or who would not believe her?

care. However, a tangible document is necessary to record the nature and outcome of these client–helper interactions. Think of this document as a combination syllabus and grade/report card: it reminds client and helper about their joint decisions (e.g., "Okay, what are our respective assignments over the next 15 weeks of the semester?"), guides them on their adventure (i.e., serves as a map), and evaluates (i.e., grades) their progress along the way. Without such a document, both client and helper would likely get confused about the point of their meetings—not to say anything about getting lost!

In order to remain attentive to client needs and preferences, we recommend charting a direct route rather than a scenic route to the client's destination (i.e., treatment goals). Coconstructing and maintaining a written map (treatment plan) are more likely to ensure this expeditious route than is a protracted or long, drawn-out scenic route. The written plan is likely to keep the client and helper "on track." And, as we've noted in this chapter, clients presenting with acute symptoms and clients of various racial/ethnic groups prefer a direct, concrete, clear, and expeditious plan of care. The direct route is also consistent with cognitive–behavioral principles and practices and makes judicious use of time and other resources. For these and other reasons, third-party payers (e.g., insurance companies) require a written and up-dated treatment plan. Can you imagine agreeing to pay for a trip for someone else without that person providing you with an itinerary? This could be likened to writing a blank check! It makes sense, therefore, that insurance companies want to see proof of how their money is being spent. This "proof" is the written treatment plan.

As you inspect the sample treatment plan form in Figure 10.1, notice that it serves to summarize information obtained from the assessment process in which the client's presenting concerns, as well as his or her strengths and resources, have been identified. The form also makes use of the methods of measuring and evaluating client status and progress toward arriving at the destination (or treatment goal). Notice that collaborative decision making emphasized in this chapter is evident in the separation of treatment strategies into "therapist interventions" and "client implementations." The treatment plan form serves many functions and has a wider audience beyond the client and helper. These "audience members" (who have the right and the responsibility to inspect and approve the document) include the client's parent/guardian (if the client is under 18 years of age), the helper's supervisor, and a third party who has been asked to pay the bill (e.g., insurance company representative, county mental health board director). Given these many different eyes reviewing the treatment plan form (now and possibly for years to come), we cannot emphasize enough the importance of accurate, timely, legible, and coherent documentation.

We believe that the process of treatment planning is most effective when the helper actively uses a form such as the one depicted in Figure 10.1 during the assessment, goal-setting, evaluation, and treatment selection sessions. In the spirit of shared decision making, the client needs to be regarded as an active participant in and contributor to the completion of this form. It is also recommended that the form allow for client comments and that, without question, the client's signature and date of signing be documented. Although helpers would first need to consult agency and third-party payer policies, as well as state law, consideration may be given to supplying the client with a copy of the completed and signed treatment plan for ongoing reference.

As mentioned earlier, many clients belong to insurance plans that will not pay for mental health services until the treatment plan is reviewed by the insurance company (this is usually called a utilization review). Helpers completing treatment plan forms need to know the company's diagnostic and treatment requirements, which may vary by month or by reviewer (Davis & Meier, 2001, p. 32). When a treatment plan is reviewed, two questions are typically asked (Leahy & Holland, 2000, p. 3):

1. Does the level of care match the severity of the client's symptoms and issues? (Recall, for example, the six client dimensions and the five levels of care that comprise the ASAM patient placement criteria for the treatment of substance-related disorders, discussed on page 283.)
2. Is the proposed treatment approach appropriate given the client's symptoms and issues?

Most clients will present complex problems with a diverse set of outcome goals. Addressing these will require a set of interventions and a combination of strategies designed to work with all the major target areas of a person's functioning. Both helper and client should be active participants in developing a treatment plan and selecting treatment strategies that are appropriate for the client's concerns and desired outcomes. The strategies reflected in the overall treatment plan should be relevant to the client's gender and culture, sufficient to deal with all the important target areas of change, and matched, as well as possible, to the response components of the defined issue as well as to the client's level of impairment, resistance, and coping style. After the strategies have been selected, the helper and client will continue to work together to implement the procedures, to evaluate the results, and to work toward a planned termination process once the client's goals are achieved. These are all consistent with shared decision making and collaborative cultural practice.

MODEL DIALOGUE: THE CASE OF ISABELLA

In this dialogue, the helper explores and helps Isabella plan some of the treatment strategies that could help Isabella decrease her nervousness about math class and her anticipation of rejection from her parents. Note that all three strategies suggested are based on Isabella's diagnostic pattern of specific (focal) anxiety, as opposed to generalized anxiety.

In the initial part of the interview, the helper summarizes the previous session and introduces Isabella to the idea of *exploring treatment strategies*. Notice the helper's emphasis on Isabella's *preferences*.

1. **Helper:** Last week, Isabella, we talked about some of the things you would like to see happen as a result of counseling. One of the things you indicated as pretty important to you was being able to do more initiating. You mentioned things like wanting to be able to ask questions or make responses, express your opinions, and express your feelings. We identified the fact that one thing that keeps you from doing these things more often is the apprehension you feel in certain situations with your parents or in math class. There are several ways we might deal with your apprehension. I thought today we might explore some of the procedures that may help. These procedures are things we can do together to help you get where you want to be. How does that sound?

Client: It's okay. So we'll find a way, maybe, that I could be less nervous and more comfortable at these times.

In the second response, the helper tries to explain to Isabella the collaborative process of treatment planning (notice the helper's use of "we"), which necessitates *Isabella's input*—that is, Isabella being able to verbalize in session (*in vivo* practice of targeted goal) what will be helpful for her.

2. **Helper:** Yes. One thing to keep in mind is that there are no easy answers and there is not necessarily one right way. What we can do today is explore some ways that are typically used to help people be less nervous in specific situations and try to come up with a way that *you* think is most workable for you. I'll be giving you some information about these procedures for your input in this decision.

Client: Okay.

In responses 3 and 4, the helper suggests possible strategies for Isabella to consider. The helper also explains how one intervention strategy, relaxation, *is related to Isabella's concerns and can help her achieve her goal.* Because Isabella's level of resistance is low (i.e., she appears open and receptive to the helper's advice), note throughout this process that the helper will be more directive and will offer guidance and suggestions.

3. **Helper:** From my experience, I believe that there are a couple of things that might help you manage your nervousness to the point where you don't feel as if you have to avoid the situation. First of all, when you're nervous, you're tense. Sometimes when you're tense, you feel bad or sick or just out of control. One thing we could do is to teach you some relaxation methods. The relaxation can help you learn to identify when you're starting to feel nervous, and it can help you manage this before it gets so strong you just skip class or refuse to speak up. Does this make sense?

Client: Yes, because when I really let myself get nervous, I don't want to say anything. Sometimes I force myself to, but I'm still nervous, and I don't feel like it.

4. **Helper:** That's a good point. You don't have the energy or desire to do something you're apprehensive about. Sometimes, for some people, just learning to relax and control your nervousness might be enough. If you want to try this first and it helps you be less nervous to the point where you can be more initiating, then that's fine. However, there are some other things we might do also, so I'd like you to know about these action plans too.

Client: Like what?

The helper proposes an additional intervention strategy in response 5 and indicates how this procedure can help Isabella decrease her nervousness by *describing how it is also related to Isabella's concern and goal.*

5. **Helper:** Well, one procedure has a very interesting name—it's called "stress inoculation." You know when you get a shot like a tetanus inoculation, the shot helps to prevent you from getting tetanus. Well, this procedure helps you to prevent yourself from getting so overwhelmed in a stressful situation, such as your math class or with your folks, that you want to avoid the situation or don't want to say anything.

Client: Is it painful like a shot?

The helper provides more information about what stress inoculation would involve from Isabella in terms of the *time, advantages, and risks of the procedure;* this information should help Isabella assess her preferences and be able to make an *empowered consent.* The helper also alludes to one of Isabella's *strengths* and how this can be used to facilitate the implementation of one of the recommended strategies.

6. **Helper:** No, not like that, although it would involve some work on your part. In addition to learning the

relaxation training I mentioned earlier, you would learn how to cope with stressful situations—through relaxing your body and thinking some thoughts that would help you handle these difficult or competitive situations. You are a bright young woman and so I am confident that, with practice here, you will be able to do this successfully with me. We'll then work on how you can start to do it in your math class and with your folks. Once you learn the relaxation, it will probably take several sessions to learn the other parts to it. The advantage of stress inoculation is that it helps you learn how to cope with rather than avoid a stressful situation. Of course, it does require you to practice the relaxation and the coping thoughts on your own, and this takes some time each day, but you strike me as someone who is up to meeting challenges. And, without this sort of daily practice, this procedure may not be that helpful.

Client: It does sound interesting. Have you used it a lot?

The helper indicates some *information and advantages* about the strategy based on the helper's *experience,* training, and use of it with others in this setting. The helper also makes reference to scientific reports (*evidence-based practice*) that it has been beneficial with a wide range of persons, adults *and* adolescents, male *and* female (therefore, *culturally appropriate*).

7. **Helper:** I believe I tend to use it, or portions of it, whenever I think people could benefit from learning to manage nervousness and not let stressful situations control them. I know other counselors have used it and found that people with different stresses can benefit from it. Some research even suggests that it is helpful for a lot of people. So it has a lot of potential if you're in a situation where your nervousness is getting the best of you and where you can learn to cope with the stress. Another advantage of this procedure is that it is pretty comprehensive. By that, I mean it deals with different parts of a nervous reaction—like the part of you that gets sweaty palms and butterflies in your stomach, the part of you that thinks girls are dumb in math or girls don't have much to say, and then the part of you that goes out of your way to avoid these sticky situations. It's kind of like going shopping and getting a whole outfit—jeans, shirt, and shoes—rather than just the shoes or just the shirt.

Client: Well, it sounds okay to me. I also like the idea of the relaxation that you mentioned earlier.

The helper moves on in response 8 to describe another possible treatment strategy, explaining what this involves

and how it might help Isabella manage her nervousness, and *relates the use of the procedure to her concern and goal.*

8. **Helper:** There's also another procedure called "desensitization" that is a pretty standard one to help a person decrease anxiety about situations. It is a way to help you desensitize yourself to the stress of your math class.

Client: How exactly does that work—to desensitize yourself to something?

The helper explains how this strategy can help Isabella decrease her nervousness and explains *elements, advantages, and risks* of this strategy (again, information provided so that Isabella can make an *empowered consent*).

9. **Helper:** It works on the principle that you can't be relaxed and nervous at the same time. So, after learning how to relax, then you imagine situations involving your math class—or with your folks. However, you imagine a situation only when you're relaxed. You practice this way to the point where you can speak up in class or with your folks without feeling all the nervousness you do now. In other words, you become desensitized. Most of this process is something we would do together in these sessions and is an advantage over something requiring a lot of outside work on your part.

Client: Does that take a long time?

The helper gives Isabella some information about the *time* or *duration* involved.

10. **Helper:** This may take a little longer than the other two procedures. This procedure has helped a great many people decrease their nervousness about specific situations—like taking a test or flying. Of course, keep in mind that any change plan takes some time.

Client: It sounds helpful.

The helper points out more of the *time factors* and the *mode (individual)* involved in these procedures. Also, notice the helper's continued reference to collaboration ("we" language).

11. **Helper:** We would be working together in these individual sessions for several months.

Client: That's okay. I have study hall during this period, and I usually just talk to my friends then anyway.

In response 12, the helper indicates *his or her preferences* (e.g., participation in *shared decision making*) and again makes reference to *evidence-based practice.*

12. **Helper:** I'd like us to make the decision together. I feel comfortable with all of these things I've mentioned. Also, all three of these procedures have been found to be pretty effective for many people who are concerned about working on their nervousness in situations so that it isn't a handicap. In fact, for some of these procedures there are even guidelines I can give you so you can practice on your own.

Client: I'm wondering exactly how to decide where to go from here.

In response 13, the helper elicits information about *client preferences*. Also, the helper alludes to a written document (*treatment plan*) that the helper and Isabella will be reviewing together (client–helper *collaboration*), one that is subject to change, and one that will help keep them "on track."

13. **Helper:** Perhaps if we reviewed the action plans I've mentioned and go over them, you can see which one you feel might work best for you, at least for now. We can always change something at a later point. How does that sound?

Client: Good. There's a lot of information, and I don't know if I remember everything you mentioned.

In response 14, the helper itemizes and summarizes the possible change strategies (which are entered on the written *treatment plan*), which help "map out" the "route" both Isabella and the helper have agreed to take on this "adventure." Note that the strategies are directed toward Isabella's predominant *coping style (internalizing)*, which also indicates the helper's attempt to *individualize care* by incorporating Isabella's *strengths and resources*.

14. **Helper:** Okay. We talked first about relaxation as something you could learn here and then do on your own to help you control the feelings and physical sensations of nervousness. Then we discussed stress inoculation, which involves giving you a lot of different skills to use to cope with the stressful situations in your math class. The third plan, desensitization, involves using relaxation first but also involves having you imagine the scenes related to your math class and to interactions with your parents. This procedure is something we would work on together, although the relaxation requires daily practice from you. What do you think would be most helpful to you at this point?

Client: I think maybe the relaxation might help, since I can practice with it on my own. It also sounds like the simplest to do, not so much in time but just in what is involved.

In the response 15, the helper pursues the option that Isabella has been leaning toward during the session, thus building on *client preferences*. Because Isabella's *level of impairment* is low, the helper will suggest *weekly sessions*.

15. **Helper:** That's a good point. Of the three procedures I mentioned, relaxation training is probably the easiest and simplest to learn to use. You have also mentioned once or twice before in our session that you were intrigued with this idea, so it looks as if you've been mulling it over for a little while and it still sounds appealing and workable to you. If so, we can start working with it today. Then I would like to see you once every week during this time if that is possible for you.

CHAPTER SUMMARY

Throughout this chapter, we offer several analogies to the process of treatment plan construction, as well as to the actual written document (i.e., the treatment plan form):

- Treatment planning is a joint venture or *journey* undertaken by both client and helper.
- Treatment planning is an integrative process that takes into consideration the "forest *and* the trees."
- The treatment plan is a *map* constructed jointly by the client and helper: each treatment goal is a destination (or vision of client improvement), and each intervention is the route or the vehicle taken to arrive at that destination.
- The treatment plan is a combination of a *course syllabus* (i.e., outlining the helper's and the client's respective "assignments") and a *report/grade card* (i.e., an evaluation of progress made, conducted at different points in time).

To this list we now add a fifth analogy, that of a household *grocery list*. This analogy emphasizes the importance of individualized client care because just as no two households are alike, no two grocery lists are alike! If a family member loses the grocery list on his or her way to the grocery store, it won't make sense to borrow another customer's list. In addition, when a household consists of more than one person, each member of the household may have some say in what gets entered on the list. In a similar manner, treatment plans represent the "collection site" or the "repository" of all persons involved in a particular client's care (e.g., referral source, parent/guardian, supervisor, members of a multidisciplinary treatment team). Furthermore, treatment plans, just like grocery lists, are time-sensitive. They are useful only for a specified period of time because they represent current client concerns, similar to current household needs. Now, unlike a grocery list, a new treatment plan is probably not needed every week! However, the treatment plan certainly needs to be reviewed and revised on a regular basis and, we suggest that it be updated with each client session and progress note completed.

There are clearly guidelines and decision rules to follow in the construction of a map, combined syllabus and grade/ report card, and grocery list. These include information presented in this chapter on common factors and differential treatments, evidence-based practice, and models of treatment planning (e.g., matching client to levels and types of care). Without these protocols, clients and helpers would be lost at sea! There are also spectacles or other visual aids to put on so as to consider both general and idiosyncratic information in clinical decision making and treatment planning. We have stated that this allows practitioners to be able to see both the "forest *and* the trees." These lenses include the vision proposed of a mainstream multicultural milieu, one that accounts for and prioritizes the cultural identities and contexts of all clients, and one that is realized in therapeutic proactivity and social justice efforts. Like any clinical activity conducted on behalf of another person's (or family's) well-being, clinical decision making and treatment planning should be entered into humbly and handled with great care.

REFERENCES

Adams, J. R., & Drake, R. E. (2006). Shared decision-making and evidence-based practice. *Community Mental Health Journal, 42,* 87–105.

Akutsu, P. D., Tsuru, G. K., & Chu, J. P. (2004). Predictors of nonattendance of intake appointments among five Asian American client groups. *Journal of Consulting and Clinical Psychology, 72,* 891–896.

American Counseling Association. (2005). *ACA code of ethics.* Alexandria, VA: Author.

American Psychiatric Association. (2000a). *Diagnostic and statistical manual of mental disorders* (4th ed., text revision). Washington, DC: Author.

American Psychiatric Association. (2000b). Practice guidelines of the treatment of patients with eating disorders (revision). *American Journal of Psychiatry, 157*(Suppl., January), 1–31.

American Psychological Association. (2003). Guidelines on multicultural education, training, research, practice, and organizational change for psychologists. *American Psychologist, 58,* 377–402.

APA Presidential Task Force on Evidence-Based Practice. (2006). Evidence-based practice in psychology. *American Psychologist, 61,* 271–285.

Atkinson, D. R., Thompson, C. E., & Grant, S. K. (1993). A three-dimensional model for counseling racial/ethnic minorities. *The Counseling Psychologist, 21,* 257–277.

Bergin, A. E., & Garfield, S. L. (1994). Overview, trends, and future issues. In A. E. Bergin & S. L. Garfield (Eds.), *Handbook of psychotherapy and behavior change* (4th ed., pp. 821–830). New York: Wiley.

Bernard, J. M., & Goodyear, R. K. (2004). *Fundamentals of clinical supervision* (3rd ed.). Boston: Allyn & Bacon.

Beutler, L. E., & Castonguay, L. G. (2006). The task force on empirically based principles of therapeutic change. In L. G. Castonguay & L. E. Beutler (Eds.), *Principles of therapeutic change that work* (pp. 3–12). New York: Oxford University Press.

Beutler, L., & Clarkin, J. (1990). *Systematic treatment selection.* New York: Brunner/Mazel.

Beutler, L., Clarkin, J., & Bongar, B. (2000). *Guidelines for the systematic treatment of the depressed patient.* New York: Oxford University Press.

Beutler, L. E., & Harwood, T. M. (2000). *Prescriptive psychotherapy: A practical guide to systematic treatment selection.* New York: Oxford University Press.

Bond, G. R., Drake, R. E., Mueser, K. T., & Latimer, E. (2001). Assertive community treatment for people with severe mental illness: Critical ingredients and impact on patients. *Disease Management and Health Outcomes, 9,* 141–159.

Boyer, S. L., & Bond, G. R. (1999). Does assertive community treatment reduce burnout? A comparison with traditional case management. *Mental Health Services Research, 1,* 31–45.

Brehm, J. W. (1966). *A theory of psychological reactance.* New York: Academic Press.

Brehm, S. S. (1976). *The application of social psychology to clinical practice.* Washington, DC: Hemisphere.

Brown, L. (2000). Feminist therapy. In C. Snyder & R. Ingram (Eds.), *Handbook of psychological change* (pp. 358–379). New York: Wiley.

Brown, L. S. (1994). *Subversive dialogues: Theory in feminist therapy.* New York: Basic.

Caldwell-Harris, C. L., & Ayçiçegi, A. (2006). When personality and culture clash: The psychological distress of allocentrics in an individualist culture and idiocentrics in a collectivist culture. *Transcultural Psychiatry, 43,* 331–361.

Castonguay, L. G., & Beutler, L. E. (2006a). Common and unique principles of therapeutic change: What do we know and what do we need to know? In L. E. Beutler & L. G. Castonguay (Eds.), *Principles of therapeutic change that work* (pp. 353–370). New York: Oxford University Press.

Castonguay, L. G., & Beutler, L. E. (2006b). (Eds.). *Principles of therapeutic change that work.* New York: Oxford University Press.

Chambless, D. L., & Holon, S. D. (1998). Defining empirically supported therapies. *Journal of Consulting and Clinical Psychology, 66,* 7–18.

Clarkin, J. F., & Levy, K. N. (2004). The influence of client variables on psychotherapy. In M. J. Lambert (Ed.), *Bergin and Garfield's handbook of psychotherapy and behavior change* (5th ed., pp. 194–226). New York: Wiley.

Comas-Díaz, L. (2006). Cultural variation in the therapeutic relationship. In C. D. Goodheart, A. E. Kazdin, & R. J. Sternberg (Eds.), *Evidence-based psychotherapy: Where practice and research meet* (pp. 81–105). Washington, DC: American Psychological Association.

Cummings, N. A. (1995). Impact of managed care on employment and training: A primer for survival. *Professional Psychology: Research and Practice, 26,* 10–15.

Davis, S., & Meier, S. (2001). *The elements of managed care.* Belmont, CA: Wadsworth.

De Bleser, L., Depreitere, R., De Waele, K., Vanhaecht, K., Vlayen. J., & Sermeus, W. (2006). Defining pathways. *Journal of Nursing Management, 14,* 553–563.

Eells, T. D., Lombart, K. G., Kendjelic, E. M., Turner, L. C., & Lucas, C. P. (2005). The quality of psychotherapy case formulations: A comparison of expert, experienced, and novice cognitive–behavioral and psychodynamic therapists. *Journal of Consulting and Clinical Psychology, 73,* 579–589.

Egan, G. (2007). *The skilled helper* (8th ed.). Belmont, CA: Thomson–Brooks/Cole.

Falvey, J. E. (2001). Clinical judgment in case conceptualization and treatment planning across mental health disciplines. *Journal of Counseling and Development, 79,* 292–303.

Gary, F. A. (2005). Stigma: Barriers to mental health care among ethnic minorities. *Issues in Mental Health Nursing, 26,* 979–999.

Goodheart, C. D., Kazdin, A. E., & Sternberg, R. J. (Eds.). (2006). *Evidence-based psychotherapy: Where practice and research meet.* Washington, DC: American Psychological Association.

Granello, P. F., & Witmer, J. M. (1998). Standards of care: Potential implications for the counseling profession. *Journal of Counseling & Development, 76,* 371–380.

Grave, R. D. (2005). A multi-step cognitive behaviour therapy for eating disorders. *European Eating Disorders Review, 13,* 373–382.

Greenberg, L. S., & Goldman, R. L. (1988). Training in experiential therapy. *Journal of Consulting and Clinical Psychology, 56,* 696–702.

Grella, C. E., & Stein, J. A. (2006). Impact of program services on treatment outcomes of patients with comorbid mental and substance use disorders. *Psychiatric Services, 57,* 1007–1015.

Grove Street Adolescent Residence of the Bridge of Central Massachusetts Inc. (2004). Using dialectical behavior therapy to help troubled adolescents return safely to their families and communities. *Psychiatric Services, 55,* 1168–1170.

Hansen, N. B., Lambert, M. J., & Forman, E. M. (2002). The psychotherapy dose-response effect and its implications for treatment delivery systems. *Clinical Psychology: Science and Practice, 9,* 329–343.

Harned, M. S., Banawan, S. F., & Lynch, T. R. (2006). Dialectical behavior therapy: An emotion-focused treatment for borderline personality disorder. *Journal of Contemporary Psychotherapy, 36,* 67–75.

Hays, P. (2001). *Addressing cultural complexities in practice: A framework for clinicians and counselors.* Washington, DC: American Psychological Association.

Hill, C. E. (2005). Therapist techniques, client involvement, and the therapeutic relationship: Inextricably intertwined in the therapy process. *Psychotherapy: Theory, Research, Practice, Training, 42,* 431–442.

Howard, K. I., Kopte, S. M., Krause, M. S., & Orlinsky, D. E. (1986). The dose-effect relationship in psychotherapy. *American Psychologist, 41,* 159–164.

Howard, K. I., Lueger, R. J., Maling, M. S., & Martinovich, Z. (1993). A phase model of psychotherapy outcome: Causal mediation of change. *Journal of Consulting and Clinical Psychology, 61,* 678–685.

Howard, K. I., Moras, K., Brill, P. L., Martinovich, Z., & Lutz, W. (1996). Evaluation of psychotherapy: Efficacy, effectiveness, and patient progress. *American Psychologist, 51,* 1059–1064.

Iguchi, M. Y., Belding, M. A., Morral, A. R., Lamb, R. J., & Husband, S. D. (1997). Reinforcing operants other than abstinence in drug abuse treatment: An effective alternative for reducing drug use. *Journal of Counseling and Clinical Psychology, 65,* 421–428.

Ingram, R., Hayes, A., & Scott, W. (2000). Empirically supported treatments: A critical analysis. In C. Snyder & R. Ingram (Eds.), *Handbook of psychological change* (pp. 40–60). New York: Wiley.

Ivey, A. E., & Brooks-Harris, J. E. (2005). Integrative psychotherapy with culturally diverse clients. In J. C. Norcross & M. R. Goldfried (Eds.), *Handbook of psychotherapy integration* (2nd ed.; pp. 321–339). New York: Oxford University Press.

Ivey, A. E., & Ivey, M. B. (2000). Developmental counseling and therapy and multicultural counseling and therapy: Metatheory, contextual consciousness, and action. In D. C. Locke, J. E. Myers, & E. L. Herr (Eds.), *The handbook of counseling* (pp. 219–236). Thousand Oaks, CA: Sage.

Kadera, S. W., Lambert, M. J., & Andrews, A. A. (1996). How much therapy is really enough? A session-by-session analysis of the psychotherapy dose-effect relationship. *Journal of Psychotherapy, Practice and Research, 5,* 132–151.

Kantrowitz, R., & Ballou, M. (1992). A feminist critique of cognitive–behavioral therapy. In L. S. Brown & M. Ballou (Eds.), *Personality and psychopathology: Feminist reappraisals* (pp. 70–87). New York: Guilford Press.

Kessler, R. C., Demler, O., Frank, R. G., Olfson, M., Pincus, H. A., Walters, E. E., et al. (2005). Prevalence and treatment of mental disorders, 1990 to 2003. *New England Journal of Medicine, 352*, 2515–2523.

Kim, D., Wampold, B. E., & Bolt, D. M. (2006). Therapist effects in psychotherapy: A random-effects modeling of the National Institute of Mental Health Treatment of Depression Collaborative Research Program data. *Psychotherapy Research, 16*, 161–172.

Kopta, S. M., Howard, K. I., Lowry, J. L., & Beutler, L. E. (1994). Patterns of symptomatic recovery in psychotherapy. *Journal of Consulting and Clinical Psychology, 62*, 1009–1016.

Lambert, M. J. (1992). Implications of outcome research for psychotherapy integration. In J. C. Norcross & M. R. Goldfried (Eds.), *Handbook of psychotherapy integration* (pp. 94–129). New York: Basic Books.

Lambert, M. J., & Ogles, B. M. (2004). The efficacy and effectiveness of psychotherapy. In M. J. Lambert (Ed.), *Bergin and Garfield's handbook of psychotherapy and behavior change* (5th ed., pp. 139–193). New York: Wiley.

Lambert, M. J., Whipple, J. L., Hawkins, E. J., Vermeersch, D. A., Nielsen, S. L., & Smart, D. W. (2003). Is it time for clinicians to routinely track patient outcome? A meta-analysis. *Clinical Psychology: Science and Practice, 10*, 288–301.

Lambert, M. J., Whipple, J. L., Smart, D. W., Vermeersch, D. A., Nielsen, S. L., & Hawkins, E. J. (2001). The effects of providing therapists with feedback on patient progress during psychotherapy: Are outcomes enhanced? *Psychotherapy Research, 11*, 49–68.

Leahy, R., & Holland, S. (2000). *Treatment plans and interventions for depression and anxiety disorders*. New York: Guilford Press.

Lee, C. C. (Ed.). (2007). *Counseling for social justice* (2nd ed.). Alexandria, VA: American Counseling Association.

Linehan, M. M. (1993). *Cognitive–behavioral treatment of borderline personality disorder*. New York: Guilford Press.

Lo, H., & Fung, K. P. (2003). Culturally competent psychotherapy. *Canadian Journal of Psychiatry, 48*, 161–170.

Lum, D. (2004). *Social work practice and people of color: A process approach* (5th ed.). Belmont, CA: Thomson–Brooks/Cole.

Lutz, W., Lowry, J., Kopta, S. M., Einstein, D. A., & Howard, K. I. (2001). Prediction of dose-response relations based on patient characteristics. *Journal of Clinical Psychology, 57*, 889–900.

Lutz, W., Saunders, S. M., Leon, S. C., Martinovich, Z., Kosfelder, J., Schulte, et al. (2006). Empirically and clinically useful decision making in psychotherapy: Differential predictions with treatment response models. *Psychological Assessment, 18*, 133–141.

Maruish, M. E. (2002). *Essentials of treatment planning*. New York: Wiley.

Maxie, A. C., Arnold, D. H., & Stephenson, M. (2006). Do therapists address ethnic and racial differences in cross-cultural psychotherapy? *Psychotherapy: Theory, Research, Practice, Training, 43*, 85–98.

Mee-Lee, D., Shulman, G. D., Fishman, M., Gastfriend, D. R., & Griffith, J. H. (Eds.). (2001). *ASAM patient placement criteria for the treatment of substance-related disorders* (2nd ed., revised). Chevy Chase, MD: American Society of Addiction Medicine.

Miller, B. (2007). What creates and sustains commitment to the practice of psychotherapy? *Psychiatric Services, 58*, 174–176.

Miller, T. W., Veltkamp, L. J., Lane, T., Bilyeu, J., & Elzie, N. (2002). Care pathway guidelines for assessment and counseling for domestic violence. *The Family Journal: Counseling and Therapy for Couples and Families, 10*, 41–48.

Miller, W. R., Sorensen, J. L., Selzer, J. A., & Brigham, G. S. (2006). Disseminating evidence-based practices in substance abuse treatment: A review with suggestions. *Journal of Substance Abuse Treatment, 31*, 25–39.

Mueser, K. T., Noordsy, D. L., Drake, R. E., & Fox, L. (2003). *Integrated treatment for dual disorders: A guide to effective practice*. New York: Guilford Press.

National Association of Social Workers. (1999). *Code of ethics*. Washington, DC: Author.

Neighbors, H. W., Trierweiler, S. J., Ford, B. C., & Muroff, J. R. (2003). Racial differences in DSM diagnosis using a semi-structured instrument: The importance of clinical judgment in the diagnosis of African Americans. *Journal of Health and Social Behavior, 43*, 237–256.

Nezu, A. M. (2005). Beyond cultural competence: Human diversity and the appositeness of asseverative goals. *Clinical Psychology: Science and Practice, 12*, 19–24.

Nezu, A. M., Nezu, C. M., & Lombardo, E. (2004). *Cognitive–behavioral case formulation and treatment design: A problem-solving approach*. New York: Springer.

Nezu, C. M., & Nezu, A. M. (1995). Clinical decision making in everyday practice: The science in the art. *Cognitive and Behavioral Practice, 2*, 5–25.

Paniagua, F. A. (2005). *Assessing and treating culturally diverse clients: A practical guide* (3rd ed.). Thousand Oaks, CA: Sage.

Reid, W. J., Kenaley, B. D., & Colvin, J. (2004). Do some interventions work better than others? A review of comparative social work experiments. *Social Work Research, 28*, 71–81.

Ridley, C. R. (2005). *Overcoming unintentional racism in counseling and therapy: A practitioner's guide to intentional intervention* (2nd ed.). Thousand Oaks, CA: Sage.

Rochkovski, O. (2006). Houses are a necessary illusion: Uncovering family process through asking families to draw a plan of their homes. *Australian and New Zealand Journal of Family Therapy, 27*, 10–15.

Safran, J. D., & Muran, J. C. (2000). *Negotiating the therapeutic alliance: A relational treatment guide.* New York: Guilford Press.

Sanchez, L. M., & Turner, S. M. (2003). Practicing psychology in the era of managed care: Implications for practice and training. *American Psychologist, 58*, 116–129.

Skovholt, T. M., & Jennings, L. (2004). *Master therapists: Exploring expertise in therapy and counseling.* Boston: Allyn & Bacon.

Smolar, A. I. (2003). When we give: Reflections on intangible gifts from therapist to patient. *American Journal of Psychotherapy, 57*, 300–323.

Substance Abuse and Mental Health Services Administration. (2006). *Results from the 2005 National Survey on Drug Use and Health: National findings.* (Office of Applied Studies, NSDUH Series H-30, DHHS Publication No. SMA 06-4194). Rockville, MD: Author.

Sue, D. W., & Sue, D. (1990). *Counseling the culturally different* (2nd ed.). New York: Wiley.

Task Force on Promotion and Dissemination of Psychological Disorders. (1993, October). Retrieved May 20, 2007, from http://www.apa.org/divisions/div12/est/chamble2.pdf

Thase, M. (2000). Psychopharmacology in conjunction with psychotherapy. In C. Snyder & R. Ingram (Eds.), *Handbook of psychological change* (pp. 475–497). New York: Wiley.

Torrey, W. C., Drake, R. E., Dixon, L., Burns, B. J., Flynn, L., Rush, A. J., et al. (2001). Implementing evidence-based practices for persons with severe mental illnesses. *Psychiatric Services, 52*, 45–50.

Virnig, B., Huang, Z., Lurie, N., Musgrave, D., McBean, A. M., & Dowd, B. (2004). Does Medicare managed care provide equal treatment for mental illness across races? *Archives of General Psychiatry, 61*, 201–205.

Wampold, B. E. (2001). *The great psychotherapy debate: Models, methods, and findings.* Mahwah, NJ: Lawrence Erlbaum.

Wampold, B. E., & Brown, G. S. (2005). Estimating variability in outcomes attributable to therapists: A naturalistic study of outcomes in managed care. *Journal of Consulting and Clinical Psychology, 73*, 914–923.

Whaley, A. L., & Davis, K. E. (2007). Cultural competence and evidence-based practice in mental health services: A complementary perspective. *American Psychologist, 62*, 563–574.

Wisniewski, L., & Kelly, E. (2003). The application of dialectical behavioral therapy to the treatment of eating disorders. *Cognitive and Behavioral Practice, 10*, 131–138.

Young, A., & Flower, L. (2001). Patients as partners: Patients as problem-solvers. *Health Communication, 14*, 69–97.

10   KNOWLEDGE AND SKILL BUILDER

Part One

In this section, we describe the case and treatment plan of David Chan (Sue & Sue, 1990, p. 259). After you read the case, identify (1) ways in which the selected treatment interventions used by the helper failed to address either contextual awareness or consciousness development; (2) how the helper interpreted the client's distress (and perhaps resistance); (3) which of Lum's (2004) five interventions (see Box 10.4 on page 292) the helper could have emphasized; and (4) the recommended type, duration, and mode of treatment you would follow as David's helper (Chapter Learning Outcome 1). Feedback follows on page 306.

David Chan is a 21-year-old student majoring in electrical engineering. He first sought counseling because he was having increasing study problems and was receiving failing grades. These academic difficulties became apparent during the first quarter of his senior year and were accompanied by headaches, indigestion, and insomnia. Because he had been an excellent student in the past, David felt that his lowered academic performance was caused by illness. However, a medical examination failed to reveal any organic disorder.

During the initial interview, David seemed depressed and anxious. He responded to inquiries with short, polite statements and seldom volunteered information about himself. He avoided any statements that involved feelings and presented his problem as strictly an education one. Although he never expressed it directly, David seemed to doubt the value of counseling and needed much reassurance and feedback about his performance in the interview.

After several sessions, the helper was able to discern one of David's major concerns. David did not like engineering and felt pressured by his parents to go into this field. Yet he was afraid to take responsibility for changing this decision without their approval; felt dependent on his parents, especially for bringing honor to them; and was afraid to express the anger he felt toward them. Using the Gestalt "empty chair" technique, the helper had David pretend that his parents were seated in empty chairs opposite him. The helper encouraged him to express his true feelings toward them. Initially, David found this very difficult to do, but he was able to ventilate some of his true feelings under constant encouragement by the helper. Unfortunately, the following sessions with David proved unproductive in that he seemed more withdrawn and guilt-ridden than ever.

Questions

1. How did the treatment intervention used by this helper (Gestalt "empty chair") not take into consideration David's cultural context and consciousness development?

2. How did the helper appear to interpret David's distress?

3. Which of Lum's (2004) five interventions (see Box 10.4) could the helper have emphasized in working with David?

4. If you were David's helper, what type, duration, and mode of treatment would you use? Provide information to support your choices.

Part Two

Learning Outcome 2 asks you to develop in writing a treatment plan for a given client case using a sample treatment planning form modeled after the one in Figure 10.1. Identify the presenting concern, strengths and resources, goals, measures, and treatment interventions. If you currently have a client caseload of your own, we suggest you do this for one of your actual clients and consult with your supervisor, a colleague, or your instructor after you and your client complete the treatment planning form. If you are a student and do not yet have clients, we suggest you use the case of Isabella based on the Model Dialogue that begins on page 298. After reviewing the dialogue between Isabella and her helper, identify at least two of Isabella's presenting concerns. Once you have done so, identify goals and measures that correspond to each of the concerns you listed. Assess Isabella's strengths and resources and incorporate these into your formulation of therapist interventions and client implementations. Feedback for the case of Isabella follows on page 302 (Figure 10.2).

10   KNOWLEDGE AND SKILL BUILDER **FEEDBACK**

Part One

1. It is not apparent that the helper engaged David in a discussion about David's contextual awareness or even oriented David to the helping process (e.g., helper's competencies and philosophy of professional care). No consideration seems to have been given to David's consciousness development, such as David's understanding of his Asian heritage, his acculturation status and language preference, and any connection he would identify between his academic performance and his relationship to his parents.

2. There is no indication that the helper took the time to ask David about the meaning of his distress, given his Asian heritage. It may be that David would have been more of an active participant in conversations with the helper if David's initial somatic complaints were taken seriously (i.e., validated). It appears that the helper "jumped right in" and assumed that David's decreased academic performance and his reported somatic complaints were the direct consequence of David not being able to speak honestly and forthrightly to his parents. David's presenting distress seems to have been dismissed as possibly being "all in his head" (particularly after negative medical reports).

3. We would have recommended that the helper use Lum's (2004) interventions of *maintenance of culture* (e.g., parental pride in his academic achievements) and *empowerment*. David may have been more amenable to the process of professional helping if various options had been explored with him, such as the consequences of extending his college career to accommodate a new academic major. This may have helped David feel empowered within his cultural context. Little is known, however, about David's cultural context (e.g., family composition, dynamics, parental expectations), which limits the helper's ability to encourage specific cultural practices. Taking the time to conduct a Cultural Analysis would have supplied this valuable information.

4. As David's helper, it is important first to clarify David's expectations for the helping process because they may be different from your own. It is also important to select a type of treatment that honors and respects David's traditional Asian cultural values—restraint of feelings, restraint of open discussion of problems with a stranger, and collective/family responsibility. Interventions that focus on behaviors and cognitions rather than on feelings are going to be more consistent with David's cultural beliefs. However, interventions that require individual self-assertion and expression of feelings are not useful because these clash with his worldview. It is also important to honor and validate the bicultural conflict that David is experiencing between obeying his parents' wishes for an engineering career and his own values and preferences. Because of this focus, the *duration* of treatment is likely to be short-term. Due to the nature of the conflict and also to the Asian value of belonging to a family, family consultation as a *mode* of treatment rather than individual counseling may be helpful. However, in working with David and his parents, it would be important not to force self-disclosure, to respect the family's hierarchy, and to try to arrive at a resolution that is mutually acceptable to all parties.

Part Two

If you used the case of Isabella, check your responses with the ones on Figure 10.2 (p. 307).

TREATMENT PLAN

Client Name: <u>Isabella</u>   Client File No.: _____

Therapist: _____   Supervisor: _____

Treatment Start Date: _____   Treatment End Date (Est.): _____

	Presenting Concerns	Strengths/Resources	Goals and Measures	Therapist Interventions and Client Implementations	Duration
1.	Decreased academic performance, irregular class attendance	Expressed desire to do well academically	Consecutive class attendance, next 2 weeks	A. Math teacher consultation B. Client meet with teacher after class, 2 × week	2 weeks
2.	Math anxiety	Awareness of symptoms related to anxiety	Reduce anxiety from 70 to 50 on 100-pt. SUDS scale	A. Exposure therapy B. Client implement new self-talk (replace "girls are dumb" with "girls are capable")	4 weeks
3.	Socially withdrawn, indecisive, acquiescent, inability to assert preferences and opinions	Self-perceptive, observant of others' behaviors, recognition of desired skills, openness to corrective feedback	Use of 4 initiating skills, at least 1 × week	A. Collaborative construction of therapist-observed and client-reported values, opinions, preferences B. In-session role play of conversation with peers C. Client videotape self standing up and verbalizing opinion and preference to peers, view 3 × week	4 weeks
4.	Parental pressure to succeed	Parental concern, client willingness to involve parents in sessions	Parental clarification of concerns, family session in 1 week	A. Schedule family session B. Client verbalize directly to parents one thing most helpful and one thing least helpful in their communications with her over past week	1 week

_____   _____   _____   _____
Client   Parent (if client under 18)   Therapist   Supervisor

Figure 10.2 Treatment-Planning From Applied to the Case of Isabella

Source: Adapted from Quin Curtis Center for Psychological Service, Training, and Research, Eberly College of Arts and Sciences, West Virginia University. Used with permission of William Fremouw, Ph.D., Director.

IMAGERY AND MODELING STRATEGIES

LEARNING OUTCOMES

After completing this chapter, you will be able to

1. Develop and try out a script for a modeling intervention in a role play or with an actual client; then use the Checklist for Developing Model Scripts at the end of the chapter to evaluate your script.
2. Describe how you would apply the four components of participant modeling in a simulated client case.
3. Demonstrate at least 14 out of 17 steps associated with participant modeling in a role play.
4. Identify which steps of the guided imagery procedure are alluded to in at least six out of seven helper leads.
5. Demonstrate 10 out of 13 steps of guided imagery in a role play; then use the Interview Checklist for Guided Imagery at the end of the chapter to assess your performance.
6. Describe how you would apply the five components of covert modeling, given a simulated client case.
7. Demonstrate at least 22 out of 28 steps associated with covert modeling in a role play; then use the Interview Checklist for Covert Modeling at the end of the chapter to assess your use of this strategy.

Picture the following: A young girl is asked what she wants to be when she grows up. Her reply: "A doctor, just like my mom." A child points a toy gun and says "Bang, bang, you're dead" after watching gunfire in an action program. Think of people flocking to stores to buy clothes that reflect the "outdoor," "sophisticated hipster," or "sleek spandex" look featured in some magazines. Consider a person reporting dysfunctional patterns of behaving similar to his or her own that were displayed by a family member when he or she was a child. All these events are examples of a process variously called imitation, copying, mimicry, vicarious learning, identification, observational learning, and modeling. In this chapter we review ways in which imagery and modeling strategies can help people acquire new behaviors or perform behaviors they already have in more appropriate ways or at more desirable times.

Rosenthal and Steffek (1991, p. 70) define *modeling* as "the processes by which information guides an observer (often

without messages conveyed through language), so that conduct is narrowed from 'random' trial-and-error toward an intended response. That is, much of the practice takes place covertly, through information-processing, decision making, and evaluative events *in advance* of visible or audible overt performance." Modeling is a process of observing an individual or group (observation learning) and imitating similar behaviors. The model acts as a stimulus for thoughts, beliefs, feelings, and actions of the observer.

Rosenthal and Steffek (1991) advise that "it is not enough to acquire the skills to earn desired outcomes. People must also gain enough self-efficacy (confidence) that they can perform the needed acts despite stresses, dangers, moments of doubts, and can persevere in the face of setbacks" (p. 75). They also emphasize the importance of restructuring vulnerable thoughts with positive coping statements and other cognitive aids to support the perseverance of the desired behavior. Higher self-efficacy is achieved by enhancing confidence for each component of the series or graduated hierarchy of behaviors to be acquired.

We present participant modeling, imagery, and covert modeling in this chapter. Box 11.1 is a sample of recent research on symbolic and participant modeling. With some client concerns, a helper may find that it is impossible or unrealistic to provide live or symbolic (e.g., media depiction) models or to have the client engage in overt practice of the goal behaviors. In symbolic modeling, the model is derived from media formats, such as stories, cartoons, films, advertisements, and information technology. In these cases, it may be more practical to employ strategies that use the client's imagination for the modeling or rehearsal. This chapter describes two therapeutic procedures. In both these strategies, scenes are developed that the client visualizes or rehearses by imagination. Initially, some people have trouble generating strong, vivid images or have reservations about doing so. We have found that most clients have the capacity to evoke vivid images and that with help from the helper they can elicit their visualization potential, but comfort and appropriateness must be assessed.

Often people use the terms *emotive imagery, visualization,* and *guided imagery* interchangeably. Visualization of mental images or pictures can be spontaneous or guided.

BOX 11.1   PARTICIPANT MODELING RESEARCH

Anxiety and Fear Reduction

Malgady, R., Rogler, T., & Costantino, G. (1990). Culturally sensitive psychotherapy for Puerto Rican children and adolescents: A program of treatment outcome research. *Journal of Consulting and Clinical Psychology, 58,* 704–712.

Mineka, S., Mystkowski, J. L., Hladek, D., & Rodriguez, B. I. (1999) The effects of changing contexts on return of fear following exposure therapy for spider fear. *Journal of Consulting and Clinical Psychology, 67*(4), 599–604.

Attitudes toward Mental Health Treatment

Buckley, G. I. & Malouff, J. M. (2005). Using modeling and vicarious reinforcement to produce more positive attitudes toward mental health treatment. *Journal of Psychology: Interdisciplinary and Applied, 139*(3),197–209.

Autism and Retardation

Bidwell, M. A., & Rehfeldt, R. A. (2004). Using video modeling to teach a domestic skill with an embedded social skill to adults with severe mental retardation. *Behavioral Interventions, 19*(4), 263–274.

Buggey, T. (2005). Video self-modeling applications with student with autism spectrum disorder in a small private school setting. *Focus on Autism and Other Developmental Disabilities, 20*(1), 52–63.

Gena, A., Couloura, S., & Kymissis, E. (2005). Modifying the affective behavior of preschoolers with autism using "in-vivo" or video modeling and reinforcement contingencies. *Journal of Autism and Developmental Disorders, 35*(5), 545–556.

Jones, C. D., & Schwartz, I. S. (2004). Siblings, peers, and adults: Differential effects of models for children with autism. *Topics in Early Childhood Special Education, 24*(4), 187–198.

HIV/AIDS Risk

Rhodes, F., & Humfleet, G. (1993). Using goal-oriented counseling and peer support to reduce HIV/AIDS risk among drug users not in treatment. *Drugs and Society, 7,* 185–204.

Interaction Skills

Trent, J. A., Kaiser, A. P., & Wolery, M. (2005). The use of responsive interaction strategies by siblings. *Topics in Early Childhood Special Educaiton, 25*(2), 107–118.

Parenting

Kliewer, W., & Lewis, H. (1995). Family influences on coping processes in children and adolescents with sickle cell disease. *Journal of Pediatric Psychology, 20,* 511–525.

Presentation Formats of Modeling

Doo, M. Y. (2005). The effects of presentation format for behavior modeling of interpersonal skills in online instruction. *Journal of Educational Multimedia and Hypermedia, 14*(3), 213–235.

Self-Efficacy

Newman, E. J., & Tuckman, B. W. (1997). The effects of participant modeling on self-efficacy, incentive, productivity, and performance. *Journal of Research and Development in Education, 31,* 38–45.

Stress

Romi, S., & Teichman, M. (1998). Participant modelling training programme: Tutoring the paraprofessional. *British Journal of Guidance and Counseling, 26*(2), 297–301.

Stuttering

Bray, M. A., & Kehle, T. J. (2001). Long-term follow-up of self-modeling as an intervention for stuttering. *School Psychology Review, 30*(1), 135–141.

Webber, M. J., Packman, A., & Onslow, M. (2004). Effects of self-modeling on stuttering. *International Journal of Language and Communication Disorders, 39*(4), 509–522.

Substance Use/Substance Prevention

Botvin, G., Baker, E., Botvin, E., & Dusenbury, L. (1993). Factors promoting cigarette smoking among black youth: A causal modeling approach. *Addictive Behaviors, 18,* 397–405.

Kalesan, B., Stine, J., & Alberg, A. J. (2006). The joint influence of parental modeling and positive parental concern on cigarette smoking in middle and high school students. *Journal of School Health, 76*(8), 402–407.

Mail, P. (1995). Early modeling of drinking behavior by Native American elementary school children playing drunk. *International Journal of the Addictions, 30,* 1187–1197.

Teaching Group Work

Riva, M. T., & Korinek, L. (2004). Teaching group work: Modeling group leader and member behaviors in the classroom to demonstrate group theory. *Journal for Specialists in Group Work, 29*(1), 55–63.

Violence

Kliewer, W., Parrish, K. A., Taylor, K. W., Jackson, K., Walker, J. M., & Shivy, V. A. (2006). Socialization of coping with community violence: Influences of caregiver coaching, modeling, and family context. *Child Development, 77*(3), 605–623.

Williams, O. (1994). Group work with African American men who batter: Toward more ethnically sensitive practice. *Journal of Comparative Family Studies, 25,* 91–103.

Visualizations or mental simulations that have emotive, emotional, or mental connections are increasingly being found fruitful in self-change and the ability to self-regulate (Taylor, Pham, Rivkin, & Armor, 1998). Building upon visualization (e.g., of a change in oneself or in one's circumstances), cognitive modeling provides a narrative of the task (e.g., talking a client through the steps necessary to make the change), which can then be followed by self-instructional training in which the client talks (aloud or mentally) herself or himself through the steps.

Collectively, these strategies have an extremely broad applicability and have achieved empirical support with a range of social problems and populations. Used appropriately, they can be important tools for collaborative, empowerment-oriented practice—for example, toward envisioning changed possibilities, gaining skills and insights for how to achieve desired change, and gaining independence from the practitioner in one's ability to undertake such imaging, rehearsal, and self-instruction alone or with supportive others in a client's social network. As we elaborate later in the chapter, cultural sensitivity and compatibility are important considerations in use of modeling techniques—for example, regarding the content of a modeled presentation as well as inclusion of models or aids that are credible and relevant within the context of a client's life experiences.

PARTICIPANT MODELING

Participant modeling consists of three components: modeled demonstration, guided practice, and successful experiences (Bandura, 1986). Participant modeling assumes that a person's successful performance is an effective means of producing change. Participant modeling has been used to reduce avoidance behavior and associated feelings about fearful activities or situations. For example, imagine an exterior house painter who develops acrophobia. Participant modeling could be used to help the painter gradually climb "scary" heights by dealing directly with the anxiety associated with being in high places. In participant modeling with phobic clients, successful performance in fearful activities or situations helps the person learn to cope with the feared situation.

Another application of participant modeling is with people who have behavioral deficits or who lack such skills as social communication, assertiveness, child management, or physical fitness. Some of these skills might be taught as preventive measures in schools or community agencies. For example, parents can be taught child-management skills by modeling and practicing effective ways of dealing with and communicating with their children.

The components are essentially the same whether the strategy is used to reduce fearful avoidance behavior or to increase some behavior or skill. Each component has several parts (see the Interview Checklist for Participant Modeling at the end of the chapter). We present a description of each

component, a hypothetical helper/client dialogue illustrating the implementation and use of participant modeling, and a Learning Activity about selecting a model. We first start with an illustration of a treatment rationale.

Treatment Rationale

Here is an example of a rationale that a helper might give for participant modeling:

> This procedure has been used to help other people overcome fears or acquire new behaviors [rationale]. There are three primary things we will do. First, you will see some people demonstrating. Next, you will practice this with my assistance in the interview. Then we'll arrange for you to do this outside the interview in situations likely to be successful for you. This type of practice will help you perform what is now difficult for you to do [overview]. Are you willing to try this now [client's willingness]?

Modeled Demonstration

The modeling component of participant modeling consists of five parts:

1. Division of the goal behavior, if complex, into separate tasks or subskills
2. Arrangement of subskills into a hierarchy
3. Selection of models
4. Instructing the client before the modeled demonstration
5. Modeled demonstration of each successive task with as many repetitions as necessary

Subdividing the Goal Behavior

Before the helper or someone else models the behavior to be acquired by the client, the helper must determine whether the behavior should be subdivided. Complex patterns of behavior should be broken down into subskills or separate tasks or small steps. Arranging tasks in order of difficulty may ensure that the client successfully performs the initial behaviors or tasks. The division of the goal behavior is a very important step in the participant modeling strategy. Start with a response or a behavior that the client will be able to perform.

For our house painter who fears heights, the target behavior might be engaging in house painting at a height of 30 feet off the ground. This response could be divided into subtasks of painting at varying heights. Each task might be elevated by several feet at a time.

Arranging Subskills or Tasks into a Hierarchy

The practitioner and client arrange the subskills or tasks into a hierarchy. The first task or subskill in the hierarchy is the least difficult or least threatening; tasks of greater complexity or greater threat follow. Usually, the first item in the hierarchy is worked on first. After the client has successfully practiced each task or subskill one at a time, he or she can practice them all. If the client is nonassertive, for example, the practitioner and client may agree that it would be best to work on eye contact first, then speech errors, then response latency, and finally all these behaviors at once. In phobic cases, the content and arrangement of each session can be a hierarchical list of feared activities or objects. The practitioner and client may agree to work first with the situation that poses the least threat to the client or provokes the least fear.

Selecting a Model

Before the modeling can begin, an appropriate model must be selected. Sometimes it may be most efficient, if appropriate, for the helper to be the model. However, therapeutic gains may be greater when multiple models who are somewhat similar to the client are used. For example, phobia clinics successfully employ participant modeling to extinguish phobias by using several formerly phobic clients as models. Learning Activity 11.1 provides an exercise with feedback in selecting or constructing a model.

Instructing the Client before the Demonstration

The helper tells the client that the model—the person doing the modeling—will be engaging in certain responses without experiencing any adverse consequences. For a nonassertive client, the instruction might be something like this: "Notice the way this person looks at you directly when refusing to type your paper." To the house painter, the helper might say, "Look to see how the model moves about the scaffolding easily at a height of five feet."

Modeled Demonstrations

In participant modeling, a live model demonstrates one subskill or task at a time. Often, repeated demonstrations of a response are necessary. Multiple demonstrations can be arranged for by having a single model repeat a demonstration or by having several models demonstrate the same subskill or task. For example, one model could show moving about on the scaffolding without falling several times, or several models could demonstrate this same activity. When it is feasible to use several models or models carefully selected with specific clients in mind, you should do so. Multiple models bring variety to the way the activity is performed and believability to the idea that adverse consequences will not occur. The helper needs to keep diversity in mind (e.g., sex, sexual orientation, disability status, race/ethnicity). Multiple models or models similar to the client may be particularly important, depending on the nature of the concern and the goal.

Guided Participation

After watching the demonstration of the behavior or activity, the client is given opportunities and the necessary guidance to perform the modeled behavior. Guided participation, or performance, is one of the most important components of learning to cope, to reduce avoidance of fearful situations, and to acquire new behaviors. The client must experience success in using what

has been modeled. The client's participation in the helping session should be structured in a nonthreatening manner.

Guided participation consists of the following five steps (Bandura, 1976, p. 262):

1. Client practice of the response or activity with helper assistance
2. Helper feedback
3. Use of various induction aids for initial practice attempts
4. Fading of induction aids
5. Client self-directed practice

Client Practice

After the model demonstrates the activity or behavior, the helper asks the client to do what was modeled. The helper has the client perform each activity or behavior in the hierarchy. The client performs each activity or behavior, starting with the first one, until he or she can do it skillfully and confidently.

It is possible that for an occasional client there will not need to be a subdivision of the goal behavior into graduated subskills or tasks. For such clients, guided practice of the entire goal behavior may be sufficient. Decisions about whether and to what extent to break the ultimate goal into small components or steps will be guided by the client's expression of comfort and ability to successfully undertake smaller or greater steps. This is often an iterative process of establishing how quickly to progress.

Our house painter would practice moving about on a ladder or scaffolding at a low height. Practices would continue at this height until the painter could move about easily and comfortably; then practices at the next height would ensue.

Helper Feedback

After each practice attempt by the client, the practitioner provides verbal feedback about the client's performance. There are two parts to the feedback: (1) praise or encouragement for successful practice and (2) suggestions for correcting or modifying errors. To the house painter, the practitioner might say, "You seem comfortable at this height. You were able to go up and down the ladder very easily. Even looking down didn't seem to bother you. That's really terrific."

Use of Induction Aids

Many people consider successful performance a good way to reduce anxiety, but most people are not going to participate in something they dread doing simply because they are told to do so. Suppose you really fear snakes. If we simply tell you to pick up a snake, you probably will be very reluctant to do so. But if someone is there with you and holds the snake first, and then holds the snake while you touch it, and then holds its head and tail while you hold the middle, and then holds its head while you hold the tail, and so on, you might surprise yourself with newfound courage. Similarly, the client may be more willing to do something he or she fears or dislikes if the helper uses some induction aids.

LEARNING ACTIVITY 11.1 — Selection of a Model

Your client is a young, biracial woman whose mother is Filipino and whose father is Mexican. Both of her parents are émigrés to the United States. Your client is the only child of these parents. She is applying for a job at a local child care center and is interested in learning some child care skills because she has no siblings and no babysitting experience.

1. Describe the type of model you would select, including age, gender, race, a coping or mastery model, and skills.

2. Develop an outline for a script you would use for the audiotaped model. The purpose of the script is to model child care skills, beginning with simple and progressing to more sophisticated levels. Include in the script instructions to the client, a description of the model, a brief example of one modeled scenario, an example of a practice opportunity, feedback about the practice, and a summarization of the script. Feedback follows on page 314.

To help our acrophobic painter reduce fear of heights, an initial induction aid might be joint practice. If actual practice with a ladder or scaffold is possible, nothing may be more supportive than having the model up on the scaffold with the painter standing directly behind or in front of the painter on a ladder. This behavior also functions as a type of protective aid. Of course, this scenario requires a model who is not afraid of heights.

If one member of a couple fears heights, the person who is nonacrophobic may induce the other to climb lighthouses, landmarks, and hills by going first and extending a hand. This type of induction aid enables both individuals to enjoy the experience together. As a result, the fears of one person do not interfere with the pleasures of the other, because continued practice efforts with some support reduce the fear level substantially.

Induction aids can be used in the counseling session, but they also should be applied in settings that closely approximate the natural setting. If at all possible, the helper or a model should accompany the client into the "field," where the client can witness further demonstrations and participate in the desired settings. For example, teaching assertive behavior to a client in an interview must be supplemented with modeling and guided participation in the natural setting in which the final goal behavior is to occur. It is doubtful that a helper would be equipped with scaffolds so that our acrophobic house painter could practice the modeled activities at different heights. The helper could use covert rehearsal instead of overt practice. Our point is that the helper who uses live participant modeling procedures must be prepared to provide supports that help the client practice as closely as possible the desired goal behavior. If this cannot be done, the next best alternative is to simulate those activities as closely as possible in the client's real situation.

Fading of Induction Aids

Induction aids can be withdrawn gradually. With a nonassertive client, the initial use of four induction aids might be gradually reduced to three, two, and one. With the painter, a very supportive aid, such as joint practice, could be replaced by a less supportive aid, such as verbal coaching. The gradual withdrawal of induction aids bridges the gap between helper-assisted and client-directed practice.

Client Self-Directed Practice

At some point, the client should be able to perform the desired activities or responses without any induction aids or assistance. A period of client self-directed practice may reinforce changes in the client's beliefs and self-evaluation and may lead to improved behavioral functioning. Therefore, the helper should arrange for the client to engage in successful performance of the desired responses independently and unassisted. Ideally, client self-directed practice would occur both within the interview and in the client's natural setting. For example, the house painter would practice moving on the ladder or scaffold alone. Client self-directed practice is likely to be superior to practitioner-directed practice toward gaining a sense of efficacy separate from the counselor's presence and support.

In addition to application of the participant modeling procedures in the counseling sessions, aiding the transfer of behavior from the training session to the natural environment should be an integral part of counseling. Generalization of desired changes can be achieved by success or by reinforcing experiences that occur as part of a transfer-of-training program.

Successful (Reinforcing) Experiences

The last component of the participant modeling procedure is successful (reinforcing) experiences. Clients must experience success in using what they are learning. Further, as Bandura points out, psychological changes "are unlikely to endure unless they prove effective when put into practice in everyday life" (1976, p. 248). Success experiences are arranged by tailoring a transfer-of-training program for each client. In an adequate transfer-of-training program, the client's new skills are used first in low-risk situations in the client's natural environment or in any situation in which the client will probably experience success or favorable outcomes. Gradually, the client extends the application of the skills to natural situations that are more unpredictable and involve a greater threat.

To summarize, success experiences are arranged through a program that transfers skill acquisition from the interview to the natural setting. This transfer-of-training program involves the following steps:

1. The practitioner and client identify situations in the client's environment in which the client desires to perform the target responses.
2. These situations are arranged in a hierarchy, starting with easy, safe situations in which the client is likely to be successful and ending with more unpredictable and risky situations.
3. The practitioner accompanies the client into the environment and works with each situation on the list by modeling and guided participation, often with use of induction aids. Gradually, the practitioner's level of participation is decreased.
4. The client is given a series of tasks to perform in a self-directed manner.

One advantage of participant modeling is that a broad range of resource persons, such as peers and former clients, can serve as therapeutic models. Participant modeling under lifelike conditions can help reduce the problems of transfer of learning from the interview to the client's real-life environment.

APPLICATIONS OF MODELING WITH DIVERSE GROUPS

Problem areas in which modeling has been studied with diverse populations are many and varied. Several of them are listed in Box 11.1. For example, Botvin, Baker, Botvin, and Dusenbury (1993) found among African American middle school students that social modeling—in the form of friends' smoking—was the most important early factor in the smoking *initiation* process. Helpers who are culturally similar to clients are likely to be most effective in modeling interventions, as indicated in HIV/AIDS prevention among sexual minorities (Rhodes and Humfleet, 1993) and African American men and family violence (Williams, 1994). Mail (1995) has suggested that substance use prevention programs include modeling as a major component within a context of culturally adapted programming.

Parental modeling is also an important factor in a variety of ways—for example, among Hispanic and African American families in supporting development of material teaching skills with young children, conveyance of parental values and positive role modeling, and helping children and adolescents cope with sickle cell disease (Kliewer & Lewis, 1995; Vargas & Busch-Rossnagel, 2003). Reyes, Routh, Jean-Gilles, and Sanfilippo (1991) have noted several differences among various ethnic groups in the use of parental modeling and have urged practitioners to be alert to both historical and cultural trends when using modeling approaches with a diverse group of parents.

As a treatment/intervention strategy, modeling has been an important component of child safety educational programs for African American, Asian American, Caucasian, and Hispanic parents (Alvarez & Jason, 1993) and in prosocial behavior training for Slovak school-age children (Reichelova & Baranova, 1994). An example of multicultural symbolic modeling involves Puerto Rican *cuentos* (folk tales) in which characters are used as therapeutic peer models depicting beliefs, values, and target behaviors that children can first attend to and then identify with and imitate (Malgady, Rogler, & Costantino, 1990). Applications have also been found useful with individuals and families involving disabilities such as autism (Buggey, 2005; Jones & Schwartz, 2004) and retardation (Bidwell & Rehfeldt, 2004).

GUIDELINES FOR USING MODELING WITH DIVERSE GROUPS OF CLIENTS

Here are some guidelines to consider when you are developing a social modeling intervention for culturally diverse clients. First, make sure that your live or symbolic (e.g., from television, movies, books, or computer games) model is culturally compatible with the client's background. For example, if you are developing a modeling program for African American youth with substance use issues, a model who is also African American, relatively young, and familiar with substance use issues will be more effective than an older, Caucasian model who knows little about or has had scant experience with substance use issues.

Second, make sure that the *content* of your modeled presentation is culturally relevant to the client and not simply a reflection of what may be your or your society's Eurocentric values. For example, the concept of social skills training is more relevant to many middle-class clients than it is to poorer clients and to some clients of color. Similarly, a model of assertion training may be more relevant to many Caucasian clients and less applicable to many Asian American clients. Modeling of boundary work is more relevant to some Caucasian clients and less relevant to some Native American clients.

Third, keep in mind cultural differences in the ways people attend to, learn from, and use modeling approaches. Determine whether your particular client or group of clients will find value in even having or seeing a model.

Malgady and colleagues (1990) found complex treatment effects when using culturally sensitive models with Puerto Rican children and adolescents. They noted that client process variables such as the client's cognitive responses and the client's familial context can affect treatment outcomes. (See Learning Activity 11.1.)

MODEL DIALOGUE FOR PARTICIPANT MODELING: THE CASE OF ISABELLA

Here is an example of the use of participant modeling with our client Isabella. Participant modeling is used to help Isabella perform the four behaviors in math class that she typically avoids. The rationales for the helper responses precede the responses.

Session 1

In the first response, the helper provides a *rationale* about the strategy and a brief *overview* of the procedure.

1. **Helper:** This procedure has been of help to other people who have trouble in classroom participation. We'll take each of the ways you would like to participate, and either I myself or maybe one of your classmates will show you a way to do this, then help you practice it. At first we'll just practice here. Then gradually you'll try this out in your other classes and, of course, finally in your math class. What do you think about this?

Client: It's okay with me. It's just something I know I can do but I don't because I'm a little nervous.

The helper picks up on Isabella's previous response and uses it to provide an *additional rationale* for the participant modeling strategy—noting both the sense of self-efficacy and the nervousness.

2. **Helper:** It sounds like you believe in your ability to accomplish this, but nervousness can keep you from doing something you want. This procedure helps you to learn to do something in small steps. As you accomplish each step, your confidence in yourself will increase and your nervousness will decrease.

Client: I think that will definitely help. Sometimes I just don't believe in myself.

In response 3, the helper ignores Isabella's previous self-effacing comment. The helper instead begins with the *modeling component* by reviewing the ways in which Isabella wanted to increase selected initiating skills in math class.

3. **Helper:** You know, last week I believe we found some ways that you would like to increase your participation in math class. And I think we arranged these in an order, starting with the one that you thought was easiest for you now, to the one that was hardest for you. Can you recall these things and this order?

Client: Yes, I believe it was like this: answering questions, going to the board, volunteering answers, and then volunteering opinions or ideas.

The helper asks the client *whether additional activities* need to be added or *whether the hierarchy order* needs to be rearranged.

4. **Helper:** After thinking about it for a week, have you thought of any other ways you'd like to participate, or do you think this order needs to be rearranged at all?

Client: Well, one more thing—I would like to be able to work the problems on my own after I ask Mr. Lamborne for help. That's where I want to begin. He usually takes over and works the problems for me.

In response 5, the helper explores a *potential model* for Isabella and obtains Isabella's input about this decision.

5. **Helper:** One thing we need to do now is to consider who might model and help you with these activities. I can do it, although if you can think of a classmate in math who participates the way you want to, this person

could assist you when you try this out in your class. What do you think?

Client: Is it necessary to have someone in the class with me? If so, I think it would be less obvious if it were someone already in the class.

The helper picks up on Isabella's discomfort about the helper's presence in her class and *suggests a classmate* as the model.

6. **Helper:** Well, there are ways to get around it, but it would be more helpful if someone could be there in your class, at least initially. I think you would feel more comfortable if this person were a classmate rather than me. If there is someone you could pick who already does a good job of participating, I'd like to talk to this person and have him or her help during our next sessions. So try to think of someone you like and respect and feel comfortable around.

Client: Well, there's Debbie. She's a friend of mine, and she hardly ever gets bothered by answering Mr. Lamborne's questions or going to the board. I could ask her. She'd probably like to do something like this. She works independently too on her math problems.

The helper provides *a rationale* for how Isabella's friend will be used as the model so that Isabella understands how her friend will be involved. Notice that Isabella's reaction to this is solicited. If Isabella were uncomfortable with this, another option would be explored.

7. **Helper:** If you ask her and she agrees, ask her to drop by my office. If that doesn't work out, stop back and we'll think of something else. If Debbie wants to do this, I'll train her to help demonstrate the ways you'd like to participate. At our session next week, she can start modeling these things for you. How does that sound?

Client: Okay. It might be kind of fun. I've helped her with her English themes before, so now maybe she can help with this.

The helper encourages the idea of these two friends' providing *mutual help* in the next response.

8. **Helper:** That's a good idea. Good friends help each other. Let me know what happens after you talk to Debbie.

After session 1, Isabella stops in to verify that Debbie will be glad to work with them. The helper then arranges a meeting with Debbie to explain her role in the participant modeling strategy. Specifically, Debbie practices modeling the other four participation goals Isabella identified. The helper gives Debbie instructions and feedback so that each behavior is modeled clearly and in a coping manner.

The helper also trains Debbie in ways to assist Isabella during the guided-participation phase. Debbie practices this, with the helper taking the role of Isabella. In these practice attempts, Debbie also practices various induction aids that she might use with Isabella, such as joint practice, verbal coaching, and graduated time intervals and difficulty of task. Debbie also practices having the helper (as Isabella) engage in self-directed practice. Classroom simulations of success experiences are also rehearsed so Debbie can learn her role in arranging for actual success experiences with Isabella. When Debbie feels comfortable with her part in the strategy, the next session with Isabella is scheduled.

Session 2

In response 1, the helper gives *instructions to Isabella about what to look for* during the modeled demonstration. Notice that the helper also points out the *lack of adverse consequences* in the modeling situation.

1. **Helper:** It's good to see you today, Isabella. I have been working with Debbie, and she is here today to do some modeling for you. What we'll do first is to work with one thing you mentioned last week: telling Mr. Lamborne you want to work the problems yourself after you ask him for an explanation. Debbie will demonstrate this first. So I'll play the part of Mr. Lamborne, and Debbie will come up to me and ask me for help. Note that she tells me what she needs explained, then firmly tells Mr. Lamborne she wants to try to finish it herself. Notice that this works out well for Debbie—Mr. Lamborne doesn't jump at her or anything like that. Do you have any questions?

Client: No, I'm ready to begin. [Modeling ensues.]

Debbie (as model): Mr. Lamborne, I would like some explanation about this problem. I need you to explain it again so I can work it out all right.

Helper (as Mr. Lamborne): Well, here is the answer. . . .

Debbie (as model, interrupts): I'd like to find the answer myself, but I'd like you to explain this formula again.

Helper (as Mr. Lamborne): Here's how you do this formula. . . .

Debbie (as model): That really helps. Thanks a lot. I can take it from here. [Debbie goes back to her seat.]

After the modeling, the helper *asks Isabella to react* to what she saw.

2. **Helper:** What reactions did you have to that, Isabella?

Client: Well, it looked fairly easy. I guess when I do ask him for help, I have a tendency just to let him take over. I am not really firm about telling him to let me finish the problem myself.

The helper picks up on Isabella's concern and *initiates a second modeled demonstration.*

3. **Helper:** That's an important part of it—first being able to ask for an additional explanation and then being able to let him know you want to apply the information and go back to your seat and try that out. It might be a good idea to have Debbie do this again—see how she initiates finishing the problem so Mr. Lamborne doesn't take over.

Client: Okay. [Second modeled demonstration ensues.]

In response 4, the helper asks Isabella for her opinion *about engaging in a practice.*

4. **Helper:** How ready do you feel now to try this out yourself in a practice here?

Client: I believe I could.

Before the first practice attempt, the helper introduces *one induction aid, verbal coaching,* from Debbie.

5. **Helper:** Now I believe one thing that might help you is to have Debbie sort of coach you. For instance, if you get stuck or start to back down, Debbie can step in and give you a cue or a reminder about something you can do. How does that sound?

Client: Fine. That makes it a little easier. [The first practice attempt begins.]

6. **Helper:** Let's begin. Now I'll be Mr. Lamborne, and you get up out of your seat with the problem.

Client: Mr. Lamborne, I don't quite understand this problem.

Helper (as Mr. Lamborne): Let me just give you the answer; you'll have one less problem to do then.

Client: Uh, I'm not sure the answer is what I need.

Helper (as Mr. Lamborne): What do you mean?

Debbie (intervenes to prompt): Isabella, you might want to indicate you would prefer to work out the answer yourself, but you do need another explanation of the formula.

Client: I'd like to find the answer myself. I do need another explanation of the formula.

Helper (as Mr. Lamborne): Well, it goes like this. . . .

Client: Okay, thanks.

Debbie: Now be sure you end the conversation there and go back to your seat.

The helper *assesses Isabella's reactions* to the practice.

7. **Helper:** What did you think about that, Isabella?

Client: It went pretty well. It was a help to have Debbie here. This is a good idea.

In the next response, the helper *provides positive feedback* to Debbie and to Isabella. *Another practice is initiated;* this also serves as an *induction aid.*

8. **Helper:** I think she helps too. You seemed to be able to start the conversation very well. You did need a little help in explaining to him what you wanted and didn't want. Once Debbie cued you, you were able to use her cue very effectively. Perhaps it would be a good idea to try this again. Debbie will prompt this time only if she really needs to. [Second practice ensues; Debbie's amount of prompting is decreased.]

The helper explores the idea of a *self-directed practice.*

9. **Helper:** That seemed to go very smoothly. I think you are ready to do this again without any assistance. How does that sound?

Client: I think so too.

After obtaining an affirmative response from Isabella, the helper asks Debbie to leave the room. Debbie's physical presence could be a protective condition for Isabella, which is another induction aid, so Debbie leaves to make sure that the *self-directed practice occurs.*

10. **Helper:** I'm going to ask Debbie to leave the room so you'll be completely on your own this time. [Self-directed practice ensues.]

Next the helper cues Isabella to provide herself with *feedback* about her self-directed practice.

11. **Helper:** How did you feel about that practice, Isabella?

Client: I realized I was relying a little on Debbie. So I think it was good to do it by myself.

The helper notes the link between self-directed performance and confidence and starts to work on *success experiences* outside counseling.

12. **Helper:** Right. At first it does help to have someone there. Then it builds your confidence to do it by yourself. At this point, I think we're ready to discuss ways you might actually use this in your class. How does that sound?

Client: Fine. A little scary, but fine.

The helper introduces the idea of *Debbie's assistance as an initial aid in Isabella's practice outside the session.*

13. **Helper:** It's natural to feel a little apprehensive at first, but one thing we will do to help you get started on the right foot is to use Debbie again at first.

Client: Oh, good. How will that work?

The helper *identifies a hierarchy of situations* in Isabella's math class. Isabella's first attempts will be assisted by Debbie to ensure success at each step.

14. **Helper:** Apparently, math is the only class where you have difficulty doing this, so we want to work on your using this in math class successfully. Since Debbie is in the class with you, instead of going up to Mr. Lamborne initially by yourself, first you can go with her. In fact, she could initiate the request for help the first time. The next time you could both go up, and you could initiate it. She could prompt you or fill in. Gradually, you would get to the point where you would go up by yourself. But we will take one step at a time.

Client: That really does help. I know the first time it would turn out better if she was there too.

15. **Helper:** Right. Usually in doing anything new, it helps to start slowly and feel good each step of the way. So maybe Debbie can come in now, and we can plan the first step.

Debbie will model and guide Isabella in using these responses in their math class. Next, the entire procedure will be repeated to work with the other initiating skills that Isabella wants to work on. This is a good time to try an exercise of your own in participant modeling (see Learning Activity 11.2).

CLIENT IMAGERY: ASSESSMENT AND TRAINING

To some extent, the success of both guided imagery and covert modeling may depend on the client's capacity to generate vivid mental images. That is why it is essential to assess the client's potential for using imagination and memory to form in his or her "mind's eye" not only visual images but also mental "images" related to hearing and the other senses. Some clients may be turned off by or reluctant to use imagery techniques (for example, on account of their personal beliefs). Others may have difficulty forming vivid

mental images or imagining themselves or their situations as significantly different from how they currently perceive them to be.

One way to assess the intensity and clarity of clients' mental imaging is to ask individuals to recall a recent event that they enjoyed or an event that made them feel relaxed and happy. Suggest that they close their eyes, take a couple of deep breaths to relax, and describe the event. After they describe it, ask them to rate its vividness, using either numbers (e.g., 4 indicates a very clear image, 0 indicates the inability to evoke an image) or words. The rating "highly vivid" would mean lots of detail and clarity, "moderately vivid" would mean a good bit of detail, "somewhat clear" would means that the client can imagine little more than the basic details, and "mixed or unclear" would mean that the client is struggling to provide enough detail to make the scene meaningful or evocative.

To train clients to enhance the vividness of their mental images, practitioner and the client together may develop practice scenes for the client to use. When clients have input into selecting and developing the details of a practice scene, they develop more self-efficacy and confidence. For example, the practitioner might instruct a client to "Picture in your mind's eye a place where you feel relaxed and at ease. Relax your body and mind, and try to be aware of all your senses while you visualize the image of this place." We have found that instructing clients about sensations associated with the scene is a powerful induction aid for enhancing the scene's vividness. The practitioner can provide sensory cues by asking questions like these: "What objects are visible in the scene?" "What colors do you see?" "How is the lighting in the scene—is it dark or bright?" "What is the degree of temperature that you feel in the scene?" "What odors do you experience?" "What sounds do you hear?" "What sensation of taste do you experience in your mouth?" "What sensations do you experience in your body?"

As practitioners assess clients' ability to visualize or when they train clients to have vivid images, they should be sure to suggest visualizing scenes or events that are enjoyable and pleasurable. We are much more aware of the sensations we experience in pleasurable events or situations. Table 11.1 lists dimensions of the senses and provides examples of sensory experiences. If clients have difficulty imagining specific details and providing training to enhance their imagery vividness would be too time-consuming, or if clients are reluctant to use or are uninterested in using imagery, a strategy that does not involve imagery may be more appropriate. But if a client has good feelings about imagery and is willing to practice it, then the practitioner and client may decide to use guided imagery or covert modeling, depending on the client's concern and goal behavior.

LEARNING ACTIVITY 11.2   Participant Modeling

This activity is designed to be completed so that you can acquire a new skill. You will need a partner.

1. Select a skill that you wish to acquire.
2. Define the skill by describing what you would be doing, thinking, and/or feeling differently. Decide whether the skill is so broad that it needs to be divided into a series of subskills. If so, identify them and arrange them in a hierarchy by order of difficulty.
3. Ask your partner to model or demonstrate the skill for you. (You can also arrange to observe other people you know and respect who might be likely to use similar skills in naturally occurring circumstances.)
4. With the help of your partner, prepare for your own initial practice of the skill or of the first subskill in the hierarchy. Your partner should aid your initial practice attempts with at least one or two induction aids, such as joint practice or verbal coaching. With successive practice attempts, these induction aids will gradually be removed. Your partner also needs to provide feedback after each practice.
5. With your partner, identify actual situations in which you want to apply your newly acquired skill. Rehearse such attempts, and identify any induction aids that may be necessary in your initial efforts at skill application in these situations.
6. Call or see your partner to report on how you handled your rehearsal efforts in step 5. Identify whether you need additional modeling, practice, or induction aids.

Some research has raised concern about "imagination inflation" resulting from visualization techniques. When adults vividly imagine the occurrence of fictional events from childhood (events assigned to them in experimental research) their confidence that these events actually happened to them increases (Paddock et al., 1999). Notably, imagination inflation is considerably more evident in young adult students than in middle-aged community samples (Clancy, McNally, & Schacter, 1999; Paddock et al., 1998).

Reviews are somewhat mixed with respect to concern about imagination inflation and strategies to limit it. Brown, Sheflin, and Hammond (1998) conclude that memory confusion or distortion associated with guided imagery is likely more a function of how the interviewing is conducted than of guided imagery per se. Reviewing a different set of findings, Arbuthnott, Arbuthnott, and Rossiter (2001a), express more caution about the use of guided imagery as a memory-recovery technique, as contrasted to uses such as assisting

TABLE 11.1	Sensations to Enhance Vividness of Imagery	
Senses	**Dimensions**	**Experiences**
Seeing	Colors, lightness, darkness, depth of field	Perception of proximity, distance, movement, stillness, physical objects, events, animals, people, nature
Hearing	Noise, sound, direction, pitch, loudness	Perception of sound: euphonious, unpleasant, from people, music, objects, nature
Smelling	Molecules of substances—odors, scent, or aroma	Airborne molecules drawn into the nose from substances, such as plants, animals, people, objects, nature, traffic, cooking, perfume, cologne, smoke, smog, moisture, pollution, fragrance of flowers, air
Tasting	Sour, bitter, sweet, salty	"Gruesome scene left bad taste in my mouth" or "The ocean breeze left a pleasant taste." Taste and smell provide experience of flavor.
Touching	Pressure, pain, temperature	Perception of touch: moisture and feelings of warmth or coolness, usually experienced as skin sensations
Moving and positioning of head and body	Motion, body's position in space	Which end is up? Different movements provide feedback on body's position.

exploration and problem solving of current issues, especially clarifying emotional and interpersonal themes and responses. They also suggest use of metaphorical imagery rather than realistic imagery in some cases to lessen the client's risk of confusing imagined and experienced events—for example, adding clearly fabricated but nonclinically significant detail, such as pink trees, to an imagery session to help the client maintain separation between the imagined and actual experienced events (Arbuthnott, Arbuthnott, & Rossiter, 2001b).

Courtois (2001) and Enns (2001) underscore cautions that memory recall or retrieval conditions should be carefully structured and monitored during treatment and that practitioners should be well versed in the issues and prepared for ethical use of techniques. Suggestions include assessing clients' susceptibility to dissociate, to have a strong sense of external control, or to be particularly oriented to pleasing the helper, and being particularly cautious with clients higher on these factors. The practitioner should make conditions as neutral or open-ended as possible and have no preconceived expectations; should use a term like *images* rather than *memories* when discussing the content of imagined events; should use a variety of therapeutic and assessment tools; and should initiate forthright discussion about memory distortion and the importance of appropriate expectations. In summary, recent contributions have reinforced the robust potential of imagery techniques and the strong empirical base, but offer caveats about ethical, constructive use.

APPLICATIONS OF IMAGERY WITH DIVERSE GROUPS

To date, imagery has been applied and tested with diverse samples. However, studies that provide distinctive findings about specific diverse groups are more limited. Herring and Meggert (1994) used imagery processes as a counseling strategy with Native American children. Andrada and Korte (1993) used imagery scenes with auditory, tactile, verbal, visual, and taste stimuli to enhance reminiscing among elderly Hispanic men and women living in a nursing home. Omizo, Omizo, and Kitaoka (1998) reported the effectiveness of a 10-session group intervention among children of Hawaiian ancestry in elevating self-esteem. Brigham (1994) describes specific imagery scenes for use with clients who are HIV-positive, and Eller (1999) found differential effects for guided imagery across the HIV disease cycle, with larger effects for those at midstage disease.

There are several guidelines to consider in using imagery with diverse groups of clients. Specific mode and content of imagery scenes appear to be correlated with a person's philosophical and cultural settings (Gaines & Price-Williams, 1990). Therefore, imagery must be viewed within the context of the client's notion of both self and culture. Also, the imagery used must be culturally relevant to the client. For example, a Native American client may choose to visualize the use of a "power shield" to ward off bad spirits and to enter into harmony with nature. Other clients may choose

to visualize themselves as "peace warriors." If healing symbols are used in imagery, they need to be culturally specific or at least universally recognized. One such symbol is the mandala, a circle of wholeness and sacred space (Brigham, 1994). Myths, folk tales, and legends indigenous to a client's culture can also be used in imagery. For example, Brigham (1994) uses the compact disc *Skeleton Woman,* in which the group Flesh and Bone has set music to the legend made so well known in *Women Who Run with the Wolves* (Estes, 1992). The Skeleton Woman tale can be read, and then the client can imagine some aspect of this legend.

GUIDED IMAGERY

In using the guided imagery procedure, a person focuses on positive thoughts or images while imagining a discomforting or anxiety-arousing activity or situation. By focusing on positive and pleasant images, the person is able to block the painful, fearful, or anxiety-provoking situation. One can think of blocking in emotive imagery as a process that takes advantage of the difficulty of focusing at the same time on pleasant thoughts and on anxiety, pain, or tension. This is difficult because these emotions are incompatible.

Self-initiated imagery has been used to help different types of concerns. Box 11.2 presents a sample of research illustrating uses for guided imagery. As you see, the uses are diverse, ranging from alleviation of health problems (asthma, cancer, COPD, osteoarthritis, migraine headaches), to helping people with abuse and chemical dependency, to improving memory and ability to process information, and to varied therapeutic uses. Also, like many other strategies presented in this text, guided imagery has been used to complement other treatment strategies, such as muscle relaxation, desensitization, eye movement desensitization and reprocessing, goal setting, and problem solving. The use of visualization in muscle relaxation training can create as great a physiological response as the actual experience of tightening and relaxing the muscles (Overholser, 1990, 1991).

Many people experience thoughts and emotions in the form of images or mental pictures. Judith Beck (1995) teaches clients to access their distressing images as a technique in assessment. She might say to the client, "When you had that thought or emotion, what image or picture did you have in your head?" (p. 230). If the practitioner and client can identify the distressing image, they can create a new image and later restructure the thought or emotions associated with the distressing image. Guided imagery has become very popular as a complementary strategy in medicine. Cognitive neuroscience on consciousness, thinking modalities, and imagination are also expanding means to apply imagery in psychotherapy (Singer, 2006). Finally, there are commercial audiotapes that offer ways for effective visualization, techniques for improving vividness of mental imagery, visualization and achieving goals, using one's inner adviser, and imagery exercises that contribute to alertness and mindfulness (Pulos, 1996).

BOX 11.2   GUIDED IMAGERY RESEARCH

Abuse Memory

Clancy, S., McNally, R. J., & Schacter, D. L. (1999). Effects of guided imagery on memory distortion in women reporting recovered memories of childhood sexual abuse. *Journal of Traumatic Stress, 12,* 559–569.

Anxiety

Marzillier, S. L., & Davey, G. C. L. (2005). Anxiety and disgust: Evidence for a unidirectional relationship. *Cognition and Emotion, 19*(5), 729–750.

Asthma

Dobson, R. L., Bray, M. A., Kehle, T. J., Theodore, L. A., & Peck, H. L. (2005). Relaxation and guided imagery as an intervention for children with asthma: A replication. *Psychology in the Schools, 42*(7), 707–720.

Cancer

Roffe, L., Schmidt, K., & Ernst, E. (2005). A systematic review of guided imagery as an adjuvant cancer therapy. *Psycho-Oncology, 14*(8), 607–617.

Chemical Dependency

Fox, H. C., Garcia, M., Kemp, K., Milivojevic, V., Kreek, M. J., & Sinha, R. (2006). Gender differences in cardiovascular and corticoadrenal response to stress and drug cues in cocaine dependent individuals. *Psychopharmacology, 185*(3), 348–357.

Fox, H. C., Talih, M., Malison, R., Anderson, G. M., Kreek, M. J., & Sinha, R. (2005). Frequency of recent cocaine and alcohol use affects drug craving and associated responses to stress and drug-related cues. *Psychoneuroendocrinology, 30*(9), 880–891.

Disease

Louie, S. W. (2004). The effects of guided imagery relaxation in people with COPD. *Occupational Therapy International, 11*(3), 145–159.

Eating Disorder

Esplen, M. J., Gallop, R., & Garfinkel, P. E. (1999). Using guided imagery to enhance self-soothing in women with bulimia nervosa. *Bulletin of the Menninger Clinic, 63,* 174–190.

Elderly in Nursing Homes

Crow, S., & Banks, D. (2004). Guided imagery: A tool to guide the way for the nursing home patient. *Advances in Mind–Body Medicine, 20*(4), 4–7.

Information Processing

Huder, J. A., Hudetz, A. G., & Klaymann, J. (2000). Relationship between relaxation by guided imagery and performance of working memory. *Psychological Reports, 28,* 15–20.

Memory

Hudetz, J. A., Hudetz, A. G., & Reddy, D. M. (2004). Effect of relaxation on working memory and the bispectral index of the EEG. *Psychological Reports, 95*(1), 53–70.

Osteoarthritis

Baird, C. L., & Sands, L. P. (2006). Effect of guided imagery with relaxation on health-related quality of life in older women with osteoarthritis. *Research in Nursing and Health, 29*(5), 442–451.

Partner Violence

Hahna, N. D., & Borling, J. E. (2003–2004). The Bonny Method of Guided Imagery and Music (BMGIM) with Intimate Partner Violence (IPV). *Journal of the Association for Music and Imagery, 9,* 41–57.

Sexual Assault Survivors

Kroese, B. S., & Thomas, G. (2006). Treating chronic nightmares of sexual assault survivors with an intellectual disability—two descriptive case studies. *Journal of Applied Research in Intellectual Disabilities, 19*(1), 75–80.

Stress/Tension Reduction

Mannix, L. K., Chandurkar, R. S., Rybicki, L. A., Tusek, D. L., & Solomon, G. D. (1999). Effect of guided imagery on quality of life for patients with chronic tension-type headache. *Headache, 39,* 326–334.

Supervision

Martenson-Blom, K. (2003–2004). Guided imagery and music in supervision: Applications of guided imagery and music (GIM) for supervision and professional development. *Journal of the Association for Music and Imagery, 9,* 97–118.

Therapy

Dowd, E. T. (2004). Expanding the cognitive therapy model: Imagery, meditation, and hypnosis. *Journal of Cognitive Psychotherapy, 18*(4), 351–359.

Singer, J. L. (2006). Expanding imagery in patient and therapist. In J. L. Singer, *Imagery in Psychotherapy* (pp. 161–186). Washington, DC: American Psychological Association.

Utay, J., & Miller, M. (2006). Guided imagery as an effective therapeutic technique: A brief review of its history and efficacy research. *Journal of Instructional Psychology, 33*(1), 40–43.

LEARNING ACTIVITY **11.3** | Guided Imagery

 This activity is designed to help you learn the process of guided imagery. It will be easier to do this with a partner, although you can do it alone if a partner is not available. You may wish to try it with a partner first and then by yourself.

Instructions for Dyadic Activity

1. One person takes the helper role; the other takes the part of the one helped. Switch roles after the first practice with the strategy.
2. The helper gives an explanation about the guided imagery procedure.
3. The helper determines the potential for imagination of the one being helped by asking the person to imagine several pleasant scenes and then probing for details.
4. The two together develop two imagery scenes that the person being helped can vividly imagine. Imagination of these scenes should produce pleasant, positive feelings and should be culturally relevant to the one being helped.

5. The person being helped practices imagining these scenes—as vividly and as intensely as possible.
6. The person being helped practices imagining a scene while the helper simulates a problem situation. For example, the helper can simulate an anxiety-provoking situation by describing it while the other engages in imagery, or the helper can simulate pain by squeezing the other person's arm during the imagination.

Instructions for Self-Activity

1. Think of two scenes you can imagine very vividly. These scenes should produce positive or pleasant feelings for you and be culturally relevant for you. Supply as many details for these scenes as you can.
2. Practice imagining these scenes as intensely as you can.
3. Practice imagining one of these scenes while simulating a problem (discomforting) situation such as grasping a piece of ice in your hands or holding your hands under cold water. Concentrate very hard on the imagery as you do so.
4. Practice this twice daily for the next three days. See how much you can increase your tolerance for the cold temperature with daily practice of the imagery scene.

Guided imagery involves five steps: a treatment rationale, assessment of the client's potential to use imagery, development of imagery scenes, practice of imagery scenes, and homework. See the Interview Checklist for Guided Imagery at the end of the chapter for some examples of practitioner leads associated with these steps. (See Learning Activity 11.3.)

Treatment Rationale

The following illustration of the purpose and overview of guided imagery can be used with people who have anxiety about a medical procedure and for relieving discomfort of such a procedure:

Here is how guided imagery works while you are having the procedure. Often people have a lot of anxiety about the procedure just before they go to the hospital. This is normal and natural. It is often very difficult to shake this belief. Usually the belief intensifies anxiety about the procedure. When some discomfort occurs, the result is even more anxiety.

Now, since the anxiety magnifies the effect of the medical procedure, the more anxious you become, the more actual pain you will probably experience. You can say the anxiety you experience escalates or intensifies the pain. This vicious circle happens often with patients undergoing this procedure. You can reverse the anxiety–pain cycle by using a technique called guided imagery. It works like this: You visualize a scene or an event that is pleasant for you and makes you feel relaxed while the procedure is occurring. You cannot feel calm, relaxed,

secure—or whatever other emotion the scene evokes—and anxious at the same time. You cannot experience feelings of anxiety and relaxation or calmness at the same time. These two different emotions are incompatible with each other.

So you select a scene that you can get into and that makes you feel relaxed, calm, and pleasant. You visualize the image or scene you have selected while the medical procedure is being performed. The imagery blocks the anxiety that can lead to increased discomfort while the procedure is being performed. People who have used guided imagery have reported that visualizing and holding a pleasant scene or image raises their threshold of pain. Using imagery while the medical procedure is performed on you eliminates anxiety-related discomfort and also has a dulling effect on what might be experienced as pain.

The rationale ends with a request for the client's willingness to try the strategy.

Assessment of Client's Imagery Potential

Because the success of the guided imagery procedure may depend on the amount of positive feeling and calmness that a client can derive from visualizing a particular scene, it is important for the practitioner to get a feeling for the client's potential for engaging in imagery. The practitioner can assess the client's imagery potential by the methods mentioned earlier in this chapter: a self-report questionnaire, a practice scene with client narration, or practitioner "probes" for details.

Development of Imagery Scenes

If the decision is made to continue with the guided imagery procedure, the client and practitioner develop imagery scenes. They should develop at least two scenes, although one might be satisfactory for some clients.

The scenario should promote calmness, tranquility, or enjoyment for the client. Such scenes might include skiing on a beautiful slope, hiking in a large forest, sailing on a sunny lake, walking on a secluded beach, or listening to and watching favorite music performed. The scene can involve the client as an active participant or as a participant observer or spectator. The more active some clients are in the scene, the greater is the degree of their involvement.

The scenario should be rich in sensory detail—colors, temperature, smell, touch, motion. The helper and client should decide on the particular senses that will be triggered by the imagery scene. Remember that the scene needs to be culturally relevant for the client.

The following imagery scene could be used with a client who experiences discomfort about a medical procedure. Notice the sensations described in the instructions. Bear in mind that this is an *illustration* only. The helper would need to assess in advance the degree to which the client is likely to experience various elements positively—such as comfort with being in water, being on a beach dressed in what one would assume to be swimwear, and being alone. The elements would need to be carefully reviewed.

> Close your eyes, sit back, take a couple of deep breaths [pause], and relax. With your eyes closed, sitting back in the chair and feeling relaxed, visualize yourself on a beautiful ocean beach. Visualize a few puffy clouds scattered throughout a dazzling blue sky. Notice the blue-green ocean water with the whitecaps of the surf rolling in toward the beach. See yourself wearing a bathing suit, and feel bright, warm rays of sun on your body. Take a deep breath, and experience the fresh and clean air. Hear the waves gently rolling in onto the beach and the water receding to catch the next wave. Smell the salt and moisture in the air. Experience the touch of a gentle breeze against your body. See yourself unfolding a beach towel, and feel the texture of the terry cloth material as you spread it on the sandy beach. Notice the sand on your feet; experience the warmth of the sand and feel the relaxing and soothing sensations the sand provides. Now visualize yourself walking toward the surf and standing in ankle-deep water, experiencing the wetness of the ocean. You experience the water as warm and comfortable. You are all alone, and you walk out in the surf up to your waist, then up to your chest. You hear the waves and see the sun glistening off the blue-green water. Smell the salt in the air as you surface dive into the oncoming surf. Experience the warmth of the water on your body as you swim out just beyond where the surf is breaking. See yourself treading water, and experience the gentle movement of going up and down on the surface of the water. Notice how warm the sun and water feel, and how relaxing it is just to linger there in the water. Experience the gentle motions of your arms and legs moving beneath the surface. Picture yourself slowly swimming back to the beach, catching a wave, and riding it in. Visualize yourself standing up and walking slowly toward your beach towel. Feel the warm sun and the air temperature of about 90 degrees on your wet body. You reach the beach towel, and you stretch out and lie down. You are alone; there is no else in the water or on the beach. You feel the warmth of the sun on the front of your body. Every muscle in your body feels totally relaxed. You look up at the sky, watching the large billowy clouds drifting by.

Practice of Imagery Scenes

After imagery scenes have been developed, the client is instructed to practice using them. There are two types of practice. In the first type, the client is instructed to focus on a scene for about 30 seconds, to picture all the detail that was developed for the scene, and to feel all the sensations associated with it. The helper cues the client after the time has elapsed. After the client uses the scene, the practitioner obtains an impression of the imagery experience—the client's feelings and sensory details of the scene. If other scenes are developed, the client can be instructed to practice imagining them. Variations on this type of practice might be to have the client use or hold a scene for varying lengths of time.

In the second type of practice, the client uses the scenes in simulated anxious, tense, fearful, or painful situations. The helper and client should simulate the target situations while using the imagery scenes. Practice under simulated conditions permits the practitioner and client to assess the effectiveness of the scenes for blocking out the discomfort or for reducing the anxiety or phobic reaction. Simulated situations can be created by describing vividly the details of an anxiety-provoking situation while the client uses a scene. For example, the practitioner can describe the pleasant scene while interweaving a description of the discomforting situation. The helper can simulate painful situations by squeezing the client's arm while the client focuses on a scene. Or, to simulate labor contractions, the labor coach squeezes the woman's thigh while she focuses on a pleasant image. Another simulation technique is to have clients hold their hands in ice water for a certain length of time. Simulated practice may aid in generalization of the scene application to the actual life situation. After the simulated practices, the practitioner assesses the client's reactions to using the scene in conjunction with the simulated discomfort or anxiety.

Homework and Follow-up

The helper instructs the client to apply guided imagery in vivo—that is, to use the scenes in the fearful, painful, tense, or anxious situation. The client can use a homework log to record the day, time, and situation in which he or she uses guided imagery. The client also can note reactions before and after using guided imagery with a 5-point scale, 1 representing *minimum discomfort* and 5 indicating *maximum discomfort*. The client should be told to bring the homework log to the next session or to a follow-up session.

MODEL EXAMPLE OF GUIDED IMAGERY

In this model example, we deviate from a clinical illustration to a normative life experience—specifically, the use of guided imagery before and during labor for childbirth. Part of our intent here is to illustrate ways in which clients can be assisted to apply intervention techniques in their lives outside of formal sessions, on their own or in cooperation with supportive others. This example involves a heterosexual couple, Jayne and Bob.

Treatment Rationale

Include a rationale for using guided imagery during labor in conjunction with the breathing and relaxation techniques that are commonly part of prepared-childbirth classes. Consider how and when the component of guided imagery may be needed. In this case, that might be at a point during labor when the breathing needs to be supplemented with something else. In conditions such as this, when verbal communication is likely to be constrained, consider working out in advance some signal that both parties will recognize, such as a finger-signaling system to use during contractions so that Jayne can inform Bob whether to continue or stop with the imagery scenes.

Assessment of Imagery Potential

Discuss what is likely to be realistic under circumstances of stress—in this case, the physical strain and intense emotionality associated with childbirth. Jayne and Bob discuss whether Jayne will be able to use fantasy effectively enough to concentrate during a labor contraction. They conduct a test by having Bob describe imagery stimuli and having Jayne imagine these, and they try to increase use of all sensations to make the imagery scenes as vivid as possible.

Development of Imagery Scenes

Together, the partners select two scenes to practice before labor and to use during labor. In one scene they are on a sailboat on a sunny, warm day and are sailing quite fast with a good breeze. This scene is selected because it evokes happy, relaxing memories for Jayne, has a lot of detailed sensory experience for her, and is one that she feels from practice helps her feel calmer. In the second scene it is nighttime, the boat lays anchored, and Jayne and Bob welcome a warm, soft breeze. Because both scenes represent actual experiences, Jayne and Bob feel they might work better than sheer fantasy.

Practice of Imagery Scenes

As with most techniques used during situations of stress, the success of guided imagery during labor depends on the degree to which the couple works with it before labor. Thus, they practice with the imagery scenes in two ways. First, Jayne imagines these scenes on her own, sometimes in conjunction with her self-directed practice in breathing and relaxation, and sometimes just as something to do—for instance, in a boring situ-

ation. Second, Jayne evokes the scenes deliberately while Bob simulates a contraction by tightly squeezing her upper arm.

Homework—in Vivo

There arrives, naturally, the time to put the preparation fully into service during labor itself. During the active phase of labor, Bob and Jayne start to use the guided imagery procedures they practiced—about midway through the time of labor, when the contractions are coming about every two minutes. Looking back, they believe guided imagery was a useful supplement to the breathing and relaxation typically taught in the Lamaze childbirth method. Jayne feels that a lot of the effectiveness had to do with the soothing effect of hearing Bob's vocal descriptions of the scenes—in addition to the images she produced during the scene descriptions.

Before moving on to covert modeling, review the self and dyadic exercises in Learning Activity 11.3 for implementing guided imagery.

COVERT MODELING

Covert modeling is a procedure in which the client imagines a model performing behaviors. Covert modeling has several advantages. The procedure does not require elaborate therapeutic or induction aids. Scenes can be developed to deal with a variety of problems. The scenes can be individualized to fit the unique concerns of the client. The client can practice the imagery scenes alone. The client can use the imagery scenes as a self-control procedure in troubling situations.

Covert modeling may be a good alternative when live or filmed models cannot be used or when it is difficult to use overt rehearsal in the interview. For an overview of the procedure, see the Interview Checklist for Covert Modeling at the end of the chapter.

Treatment Rationale

After the practitioner and client review the targets of change and the goal behaviors, the practitioner presents the rationale for covert modeling. Here is an example of an explanation for using covert modeling, in this case with someone seeking to complete school and successfully transition to steady work following incarceration:

We have discussed your goals and some of the concerns you have about achieving them. We have chosen covert modeling as a tool to mentally envision and "walk through" the steps you will need to be taking toward your goals. This is a kind of mental simulation in which we can help you rehearse scenes that you will be encountering. We will start this in session, and then you can practice it on your own. In this way, we can include difficulties you are likely to encounter and better prepare you to deal with them. You will likely experience the same kinds of thoughts and feelings (like anxiety and pride) in the imagined situations as you will experience when you actually encounter them. We can discuss these to help give you insight and preparation.

The following provides an illustration of detailing the steps involved in covert modeling:

> As we go through each situation, I'll ask you to close your eyes and try to imagine, as clearly as possible, that you are observing yourself in that situation. Try to use your senses in your visualization of each situation, including your emotions. I will give you prompts to focus and to experience the senses as you visualize going into each situation. After we complete visualizing a situation, I will ask you some questions concerning your thoughts and feelings about the sequence and any difficulties, insights, or questions you have. We will progressively work through a range of situations tied to your goals, adjusting the situations as needed.

Practice Scenes

The practitioner may then decide to try out the imagery process with several practice scenes. For some clients, imagining a scene may be a new experience and may seem foreign. Kazdin (1976, p. 478) suggests that practice scenes may help to familiarize clients with the procedure and sensitize them to focus on specific details of the imagery. Use of practice scenes also helps the practitioner assess the client's potential for carrying out instructions in the imagination.

The practice scenes usually consist of simple, straightforward situations that are unrelated to the goal behaviors. For example, if you are using covert modeling to help a client acquire job-interview skills, the practice scenes would be unrelated to job-seeking responses. You might use some of the following as practice scenes:

1. "Imagine watching a person at a golf match on the eighteenth hole of a beautiful golf course on a gorgeous day."
2. "Imagine someone hiking to the top of a mountain with a panoramic view."
3. "Imagine watching a comedian at a comedy club."
4. "Imagine someone taking a walk on a beautiful day."

In using practice scenes with a client, the helper usually follows six steps:

1. The helper instructs the client to close his or her eyes and to sit back and relax. The client is instructed to tell the helper when he or she feels relaxed. If the client does not feel relaxed, the helper may need to decide whether relaxation procedures should be introduced. The effect of relaxation on the quality of imagery in covert modeling has not been evaluated. However, live and symbolic modeling may be aided when the client is relaxed.
2. The helper describes a practice scene and instructs the client to imagine the scene and to raise an index finger when the scene has been imagined vividly. The practice scenes are

similar to the four examples listed above. The helper reads the scene or instructs the client about what to imagine.
3. The helper asks the client to open his or her eyes after the scene is vividly imagined (signal of index finger) and to describe the scene or to narrate the imagined events.
4. The helper probes for greater details about the scene—the clothes or physical features of a person in the imagery, the physical setting of the situation, the amount of light, colors of the furniture, decorative features, noises, or smells. This probing may encourage the client to focus on details of the imagery scene.
5. The helper may suggest additional details for the client to imagine during a subsequent practice. Working with practice scenes first can help with the development of the details in the actual treatment scenes.
6. Usually, each practice scene is presented several times. The number of practice scenes used before moving on to developing and applying treatment scenes will depend on several factors. If the client feels comfortable with the novelty of the imagined scenes after several presentations, the helper might consider this a cue to stop using the practice scenes. Additionally, if the client can provide a fairly detailed description of the imagery after several practice scenes, this may be a good time to start developing treatment scenes. If a client reports difficulty in relaxing, the helper may need to introduce relaxation training before continuing. For a client who cannot generate images during the practice scenes, another modeling strategy may be needed in lieu of covert modeling.

Developing Treatment Scenes

The treatment scenes used in covert modeling are developed in conjunction with the client and grow out of the desired client outcomes. The scenes consist of a variety of situations in which the client wants to perform the target response in the real-life environment. If a client wants to acquire effective job-interview skills, the treatment scenes are developed around job-interview situations. It is important for the client to help in the development of treatment scenes because client participation can provide many specifics about situations in which the goal behavior is to be performed.

Model Characteristics

Similarity between the model and the client—such as in sex, age, and race or ethnicity—contributes to client change. Clients who imagine several models may show more change than clients who imagine only one model. Coping models may be generally more effective in covert modeling than mastery models. A coping model who self-verbalizes his or her anxiety and uses covert self-talk for dealing with fear may enhance the behaviors to be acquired.

One of the most interesting questions about the covert model is the identity of the model: some clients imagine *themselves* as the model, and others imagine *another person* as the model. We believe that for most people, imagining themselves may be more powerful. However, data are not sufficient to indicate who the model should be in the covert modeling procedure. We suspect that the answer varies with clients, and we suggest that you give clients the option of deciding whether to imagine themselves or someone else as the model. You may need to ask multicultural or bicultural clients which parts of their culture they identify with the most or whether multiple identities are important to include. One key factor for any individual may be the particular identity that the client can imagine most easily or feels is most relevant. Factors such as gender, culture, or sexuality may or may not be key; other factors such as shyness or lack of confidence may be more salient for a given concern or goal. For clients who feel some stress at first in imagining themselves as models, imagining someone else might be introduced first and later replaced with self-modeling. Using oneself as the model is an option when culturally similar models are not readily available.

Individualized versus Standardized Scenes

The treatment scenes used in covert modeling can be either standardized or individualized. Standardized scenes cover different situations in everyday life and are presented to a group of clients or to all clients with the same target responses. For example, a practitioner can use a series of standardized scenes describing situations of job-interviewing behavior. Individualized scenes represent situations specifically tailored to suit an individual client. For example, one nonassertive client may need scenes developed around situations with strangers, and another may need scenes that involve close friends. Generally, treatment scenes should be individualized for those who have unique concerns and who are helped individually, for some standardized scenes may not be relevant for particular clients.

Specificity of Scenes

Some clients may benefit from very explicit instructions about the details of what to imagine. Other clients may derive more gains from covert modeling if the treatment scenes are more general and the clients are able to supply specific details. A risk of *not* providing clients with explicit instructions is that they might introduce scene material that is irrelevant to or detracts from the desired outcomes. We suggest this decision should consider the client's preferences.

Here is an example of a fairly general treatment scene for a prison inmate about to be released on parole who is seeking employment:

> Picture yourself (or someone else like you) in a job interview. The employer asks why you didn't complete high school. You tell the employer you got in some trouble, and the employer asks what kind of trouble. You feel a little uptight but tell her you have a prison record. The employer asks why you were in prison and for how long. The employer then asks what makes

you think you can stay out of trouble and what you have been doing while on parole. Imagine yourself saying that you have been looking for work while on parole and have been thinking about your life and what you want to do with it.

The generality of that treatment scene assumes that the client knows what type of response to make and what details to supply.

A more detailed treatment scene would specify more of the actual responses:

> Picture yourself (or someone else) in a job interview and imagine the following dialogue. The employer says, "I see that you have only finished three years of high school. You don't intend to graduate?"
>
> Picture yourself saying (showing some anxiety): "Well, no, I want to go to vocational school while I'm working." The employer asks: "What happened? How did you get so far behind in school?" Imagine yourself (or someone else) replying: "I've been out of school for a while because I've been in some trouble." Now imagine the employer is showing some alarm and asks: "What kind of trouble?" You decide to be up front as you imagine yourself saying: "I want you to know that I have a prison record." As the employer asks: "Why were you in prison?" imagine yourself feeling a little nervous but staying calm and saying something like "I guess I was pretty immature. Some friends and I got involved with drugs. I'm on parole now. I'm staying away from drugs, and I'm looking hard for a job. I really want to work."

Remember, the degree of specificity of each scene will depend largely on the client, the concern, and the goals for counseling.

Ingredients of the Scene

Three ingredients are required for a treatment scene in the covert modeling procedure: a description of the situation or context in which the behavior is to occur, a description of the model demonstrating the behavior to be acquired, and a depiction of some favorable outcome of the goal behavior.

> **Situation:** "Imagine yourself playing tennis on a bright, sunny day".
>
> **Description of model:** "You are playing in a tournament. Your opponent hits the ball to your forehand, and you return it. On your opponent's return, the ball is hit low to your backhand."
>
> **Demonstrating the desired behavior:** "You see yourself put both hands on the racket and pull your arms back ready to hit the low ball. You see yourself hit the ball across the net and inside the line. Notice the bodily sensation you experience while hitting the ball across the net."

Here is a covert modeling scene that includes a favorable outcome for an adult who wants to stop smoking:

> Imagine yourself in a restaurant having a drink with some friends before your reservation to be seated for dinner. All your

friends in the group are smoking, and the smell of the smoke makes you want a cigarette. You have been drinking with them for about 10 minutes, and one of them offers you a cigarette. In the past, you would have taken a cigarette if you did not have any of your own. Now cope with the situation in your imagination. Imagine yourself feeling the urge to smoke, but see yourself refuse and focus on what the group is discussing.

The inclusion of a favorable consequence as a scene ingredient is based on research indicating that a client who sees a model rewarded for the behavior or who feels good about the outcome of the behavior is more likely to perform the response. Moreover, specifying a possible favorable outcome to imagine may prevent a client from inadvertently imagining an unfavorable outcome.

We believe that the favorable outcome in the scene should take the form of some action initiated by the client or of covert self-reinforcement or praise. For example, the favorable outcome illustrated in the scene for the "stop smoking" client is the client's self-initiated action of refusing to take a cigarette. We prefer that the client or the model initiates the action (instead of someone else in the scene) because in a real situation it may be too risky for the client to rely on someone else to deliver a favorable outcome in the form of a certain response. As helpers, we cannot guarantee that clients will always receive favorable responses from someone else in the actual situation.

Another way to incorporate a favorable outcome into a treatment scene is to include an example of client (or model) self-reinforcement or praise. For instance, models might congratulate themselves by saying, "That is terrific. I am proud of myself for what I said to the hotel clerk." A favorable consequence in the form of model or client self-praise is self-administered. Again, in a real-life situation it may be better for clients to learn to reward themselves than to expect external encouragement, which might not be forthcoming.

The person who experiences the favorable outcomes will be the person the client imagines as the model. If the client imagines someone else as the model, then the client will also imagine that person initiating a favorable outcome or reinforcing himself or herself. Clients who imagine themselves as the models will imagine themselves receiving the positive consequences.

Number of Scenes

The practitioner and client can develop several scenes that portray the situation in which the client experiences difficulty or wants to use the newly acquired behavior. Multiple scenes can depict different situations in which the desired behavior is generally appropriate. The number of scenes that the practitioner and client develop depends on the client and his or her concerns. Although there is no set number of scenes that should be developed, certainly several scenes provide more variety than only one or two.

Applying Treatment Scenes

After all the scenes have been developed, the helper can apply the treatment scenes by having the client imagine each one. The basic steps in applying the treatment scenes are these:

1. Arranging scenes into a hierarchy
2. Instructing the client before scene presentation
3. Presenting one scene at a time from the hierarchy
4. Presenting a scene for a specified duration
5. Obtaining client reactions to the imagined scene, modifying as needed
6. Instructing the client to develop verbal summary codes and/or to personalize each treatment scene
7. Presenting each scene at least twice with the aid of the helper or a tape recorder
8. Having the client imagine each scene at least twice while directing himself or herself
9. Selecting and presenting scenes from the hierarchy in a random order

Creating a Scene Hierarchy

The scenes that the practitioner and client develop should be arranged in a hierarchy for presentation, beginning with a scene that is relatively easy for the client to imagine with little stress. The hierarchy reflects the client's sense of the relative difficulty or stressfulness of the scenes.

Instructing the Client before Scene Presentation

It may be necessary for the helper to repeat instructions about imagery to the client if a great amount of time has elapsed since using the practice scenes. To the adult who wants to stop smoking, for instance, the practitioner might say this:

Close your eyes, take a couple of deep breaths, and relax. I want you to imagine as vividly and clearly as possible that you are observing yourself having drinks with friends when you are offered a cigarette. Tune in and use all your senses. For example, try to envision the restaurant, who is there, the sounds around you. What odors or smells do you experience? What is the taste in your mouth? Notice the sensations you experience in your body. Notice your thoughts. In a moment, I will ask you some questions concerning your feelings about the entire sequence of the scene and how clearly you imagined it.

If a person other than the client is the model, the helper instructs the client to picture someone of his or her own age, gender, and culture. The client is told that the person who is pictured as the model will be used in all the treatment scenes. The practitioner also instructs the client to signal by raising an index finger as soon as the scene is pictured clearly and to hold the scene in imagery until the practitioner signals to stop.

Sequence of Scene Presentation

Starting at the lowest level, the scenes are presented one by one. When one scene has been covered sufficiently, the next scene in the hierarchy is presented. This process continues until all scenes in the hierarchy have been covered.

Duration of Scenes

There are no ground rules for how long to hold a scene in imagery once the client signals. For some clients, a longer duration may be more beneficial; for others, a shorter duration may be. We feel that the choice depends on the practitioner's assessment of any given client, the practitioner's experience with the covert modeling procedure, the nature of the client's concerns, the goal behavior for counseling, and—perhaps most important—the client's input about the scene duration. After one or two scenes have been presented, the practitioner can query the client about the suitability of the scene duration. Generally, a scene should be held long enough for the client to imagine the three scene ingredients vividly without rushing. We have found that visualizing a scene is perceived as lasting much longer than it lasts in "real" time.

Obtaining Client Reactions to the Scene with Modification as Needed

After the client imagines a particular scene, the practitioner queries the client about how clearly it was imagined. The client is asked to describe feelings during particular parts of the scene. The practitioner should also ask whether the scene was described too rapidly or whether the duration of the scene was adequate for the client to imagine the scene ingredients clearly. These questions enable the practitioner and client to modify aspects of a scene before it is presented the second time. Client input about possible scene revision can be very helpful. If particular episodes of the scene elicit intense feelings of anxiety, the content of the scene or the manner of presentation can be revised. Perhaps the order of the scenes in the hierarchy needs rearrangement.

Another way to deal with the client's unpleasant feelings or discomfort with a scene is to talk it over. If the client feels stressful when the model (or the self) is engaging in the behavior or activity in the scene, examine with the client what episode in the scene is producing the discomfort. In addition, if the client is the model and has difficulty performing the behavior or activity, discuss and examine the block. Focus on the adaptive behavior or the coping with the situational ingredient of the scene rather than on the anxiety or discomfort.

After presenting the first scene and making any necessary revisions, the helper may want to repeat the scene a couple of times. The number of scene repetitions may be dictated by the degree of comfort the client experiences while imagining the scene and by the complexity of the activities or behaviors the client imagines. Again, make the decision about the number of scene repetitions with client input. Scene repetition may also take place at a later point. If you use the verbal summary codes or personalization of the scene, remember to instruct the client to use the technique during later repetitions of each scene.

Verbal Summary Codes and Personalization

Verbal summary codes are brief descriptions, *in the client's own words*, about the behavior to be acquired and the context in which the behavior is to occur. Verbal coding of the modeling cues can help with acquisition and retention of the behaviors to be modeled and may maintain client performance during and after treatment by helping clients encode desired responses in their working memory. We recommend that clients rehearse using verbal summary codes with *practice* scenes and receive feedback from the helper about the descriptions of the practice scenes. The practice should occur before presentation of the *treatment* scenes. Then the treatment scenes are presented, and the client is instructed to develop his or her own verbal summary codes (descriptions of behavior and situation) for the scene. Have the client "try out" the treatment scene on the first presentation *without* the use of the summary code. On the second presentation of the scene, instruct the client to use the summary code and to say aloud exactly what it is.

Personalization of treatment scenes is another technique that can enhance covert modeling. After the scene has been presented once as developed, the client is instructed *to change the treatment scene in any way as long as the model responses to be acquired are represented in the scene.* As with verbal summary codes, the client is asked to rehearse personalizing (individualizing) or elaborating a scene using a practice scene, and he or she then receives feedback about the elaboration. The practitioner should encourage the client to use variations within the context of the situation presented by the scene. Variations include more details about the model responses and the situation in which the responses are to occur. The client is asked to elaborate the scene the second time the treatment scene is presented. Elaboration may lead to more client involvement because the scenes are individualized.

Remember to have the client experience imagining a scene first without instructions to use verbal summary codes or to personalize the scene. Then, on the second presentation of the treatment scene, the client is instructed to use one of these techniques. To verify that the client is complying with the instructions, the helper can instruct the client to say aloud the verbal summary code or elaboration being used.

Client-Directed Scene Repetition

In addition to helper-directed scene practice, the client should engage in self-directed scene practice. Again, the number of client practices is somewhat arbitrary, although perhaps two is a minimum. Generally, the client can repeat imagining the scenes alone until he or she feels comfortable in doing so. The client either can use the verbal summary codes without saying the codes aloud or can personalize the scenes. Overt rehearsal can help with acquisition and retention of the imagined behaviors. The client should be instructed to overtly enact (rehearse) the scene with the helper after the second or third time that each scene is presented.

Random Presentation of Scenes

After all the scenes in the hierarchy have been presented adequately, the practitioner can check out the client's readiness for self-directed homework practice by presenting some of the scenes in random order. This random presentation guards against any "ordering" effect that the hierarchy arrangement may have had in the scene presentation.

Homework and Follow-up

Self-directed practice in the form of homework is perhaps the most important therapeutic ingredient for generalization. If a person can apply or practice the procedure outside the counseling session, the probability of using the "new" behavior or of coping in the actual situation is greatly enhanced. Homework can consist of having clients identify several situations in their everyday lives in which they could use the desired responses.

In arranging the homework tasks, the helper and client should specify how often, how long, what times during the day, and where practice should occur. The helper should also instruct the client to record the daily use of the modeling scenes on log sheets. The helper should verify whether the client understands the homework and should arrange for a follow-up after some portion of the homework is completed.

MODEL DIALOGUE FOR COVERT MODELING: THE CASE OF ISABELLA

Here is an example of a covert modeling dialogue with our client Isabella to help her increase initiating skills in her math class. (See also Learning Activity 11.4.)

In response 1, the helper briefly describes the *rationale* and gives an *overview*.

1. **Helper:** Isabella, one way we can help you work on your initiating skills in math class is to help you learn the skills you want through practice. In this procedure, you will practice using your imagination. I will describe situations to you and ask you to imagine yourself or someone else participating in the way described in a situation. How does that sound?

Client: Okay. You mean I imagine things like daydreaming?

Further *instructions* about the strategy are provided in helper response 2.

2. **Helper:** It has some similarities. Instead of just letting your mind wander, you will imagine some of the skills you want to use to improve your participation in your math class.

Client: Well, I'm a pretty good daydreamer, so if this is similar, I will probably learn from it.

In response 3, the helper initiates the idea of using *practice scenes* to determine Isabella's level and style of imagery.

3. **Helper:** Let's see. I think it might help to see how easy or hard it is for you to actually imagine a specific situation as I describe it to you. So maybe we could do this on a try-out basis to see what it feels like for you.

Client: Okay, what happens?

In response 4, the helper instructs Isabella to *sit back and relax before imagining the practice scene.*

4. **Helper:** First of all, just sit back, close your eyes, and relax [gives Isabella a few minutes to do this]. You look pretty comfortable. How do you feel?

Client: Fine. It's never too hard for me to relax.

In response 5, the helper instructs Isabella *to imagine the scene vividly and to indicate this by raising her finger.*

5. **Helper:** Okay, now, Isabella, I'm going to describe a scene to you. As I do so, I want you to imagine the scene as vividly as possible. When you feel you have a very strong picture, then raise your index finger. Does that seem clear?

Client: Yes.

The helper offers a practice scene next. Notice that the *practice scene* is simple and relatively mundane. It asks Isabella only to imagine another person.

6. **Helper:** Imagine that someone is about to offer you a summer job. Just picture a person who might offer you a job like this [gives Isabella time until Isabella raises her index finger].

In response 7, the helper asks Isabella *to describe what she imagined.*

7. **Helper:** Isabella, now open your eyes. Can you tell me what you just imagined?

Consider the situation of a mother, Ms. Weare, who wishes to explain to her child's teacher a new strategy for dealing with a problem she is working on with her child and to request help and cooperation from the school. Specifically, Ms. Weare points out that one thing that may happen initially might be an increase in the child's tardiness at school. Assume that

Ms. Weare is hesitant to initiate the conference because she is unsure about what to say during the meeting. Describe how you would use covert modeling to help Ms. Weare achieve this goal. Describe specifically how you would use (1) a treatment rationale, (2) practice scenes, (3) development of treatment scenes, (4) application of treatment scenes, and (5) homework to help Ms. Weare in this objective. Feedback follows.

Client: I pictured myself with a man from the community center who asked me if I wanted to lifeguard this summer. Naturally I told him yes.

Isabella's imagery report was specific about the actions and dialogue, but Isabella didn't describe much about the man, so the helper *will probe for more details.*

8. **Helper:** Fine. What else did you imagine about the man? Did you mention his age? What was he wearing? Any physical characteristics you can recall?

Client: Well, he was about 35 and he was wearing shorts and a golf shirt—you see, we were by the pool. That's about it.

Isabella is able to describe the setting and the man's dress but no other physical characteristics, so the helper *suggests that Isabella add this to the next practice attempt.*

9. **Helper:** So you were able to see what he was wearing and also the setting where he was talking to you. I'd like to try another practice with this same scene. Imagine everything you did before, but this time try to imagine even more details about how this man actually looks. [Helper presents the same scene, which goes on until Isabella raises her finger.]

In response 10, the helper again *queries Isabella about the details of her imagery.*

10. **Helper:** Okay, let's stop. What else did you imagine this time about this person or the situation?

Client: He was wearing white shorts and a blue shirt. He was a tall man and very tan. He had dark hair, blue eyes, and had sunglasses on. He was also barefoot. We were standing on the pool edge. The water was blue, and the sun was out and it felt hot.

In response 11, the helper *tries to determine how comfortable Isabella is with imagery* and whether more practice scenes are necessary.

11. **Helper:** That's great. Looks like you were able to imagine colors and temperature—like the sun feeling hot. How comfortable do you feel now with this process?

Client: Oh, I like it. It was easier the second time you described the scene. I put more into it. I like to imagine this anyway.

In response 12, the helper decides Isabella can move ahead and *initiates development of treatment scenes.*

12. **Helper:** I believe we can go on now. Our next step is to come up with some scenes that describe the situations you find yourself in now with respect to participation in math class.

Client: And then I'll imagine them in the same way?

The helper sets the stage to *obtain all the necessary information to develop treatment scenes.* Notice the emphasis in response 13 on Isabella's *participation* in this process.

13. **Helper:** That's right. Once we work out the details of these scenes, you'll imagine each scene as you just did. Now we have sort of a series of things we need to discuss in setting up the scenes in a way that makes it easiest for you to imagine, so I'll be asking you some questions. Your input is very valuable here to both of us.

Client: Okay, shoot.

In response 14, the helper *asks Isabella whether she would rather imagine herself or someone else* as the model.

14. **Helper:** First of all, in that practice scene I asked you to imagine someone else. Now, you did that, but you were also able to picture yourself from the report you gave me. In using your class scenes, which do you feel would be easiest and least stressful for you to imagine—yourself going through the scene or someone else, maybe someone similar to you but another person? [Gives Isabella time to think.]

FEEDBACK

11.4   Covert Modeling

1. *Treatment rationale:* First, you would explain that covert modeling could help Ms. Weare find ways to express herself and could help her practice expressing herself before having the actual conference. Second, you would briefly describe the strategy, emphasizing that she will be practicing her role and responses in the school conference, using her imagination.

2. *Practice scenes:* You would explain that it is helpful to see how she feels about practicing through her imagination. You would select several unrelated scenes, such as imagining someone coming to her home, imagining an old friend calling her, or imagining a new television show about a policewoman. You would present one practice scene and instruct Ms. Weare first to close her eyes, imagine the scene intensely, and signal to you with her finger when she has a strong picture in her mind. After this point, you could tell her to open her eyes and to describe the details of what she imagined. You might suggest additional details and present the same scene again or present a different scene. If Ms. Weare is able to use imagery easily and comfortably, you could move on to developing the actual treatment scenes.

3. *Developing treatment scenes:* At this point, you would seek Ms. Weare's input about certain aspects of the scenes to be used as treatment scenes. Specifically, you would decide who would be used as the model, whether individualized or standardized scenes would be used, and whether Ms. Weare felt she could benefit from general or specific scenes. Our preference would be to use fairly specific, individualized scenes in which Ms. Weare imagines herself as the model, for she will ultimately be carrying out the action. Next, you should specify the three ingredients of the scenes: (a) the situation in which the behaviors should occur, (b) the behaviors to be demonstrated, and (c) a favorable outcome. For example, the scenes could include Ms. Weare calling the teacher to set up the conference, beginning the conference, explaining her strategy in the conference, and ending the conference. Specific examples of things she could say would be included in each scene. Favorable outcomes might take the form of covert self-praise or of relief from stressful, anxious feelings.

4. *Applying treatment scenes:* After all the treatment scenes have been developed, Ms. Weare would arrange them in a hierarchy from least to most difficult. Starting with the first scene in the hierarchy, you would again instruct Ms. Weare about how to imagine. After the first scene presentation, you would obtain Ms. Weare's reactions to the clearness of her imagery, the duration of the scene, and so on. Any needed revisions could be incorporated before a second presentation of the same scene. You would also encourage Ms. Weare to develop a verbal summary code for each scene after the initial presentation of that scene. You would present each scene to Ms. Weare several times, then have her self-direct her own scene imagining several times. After all the scenes in the hierarchy had been covered adequately, Ms. Weare would be ready for homework.

5. *Homework:* You would instruct Ms. Weare to continue to practice the scenes in her imagination outside the session. A follow-up should be arranged. You should be sure that Ms. Weare understands how many times to practice and how such practice can benefit her. Ms. Weare might record her practice sessions on log sheets. She could also call in and verbalize the scenes, using a phone mate.

Client: [pauses] Well, that's hard to say. I think it would be easier for me to imagine myself, but it might be a little less stressful to imagine someone else . . . [pauses again]. I think I'd like to try using myself.

In the next response, the helper *reinforces Isabella's choice and also points out the flexibility of implementing the procedure.*

15. **Helper:** That's fine. And besides, as you know, nothing is that fixed. If we get into this and that doesn't feel right and you want to imagine someone else, we'll change.

Client: Okey-dokey.

In response 16, the helper *introduces the idea of a coping model.*

16. **Helper:** Also, sometimes it's hard to imagine yourself doing something perfectly to start with, so when we get into this, I might describe a situation where you might have a little trouble but not much. That may seem more realistic to you. What do you think?

Client: That seems reasonable. I know what you mean. It's like learning to drive a car. In Driver's Ed, we take one step at a time.

In response 17, the helper *poses the option of individualizing the scenes* or using *standardized scenes.*

17. **Helper:** You've got the idea. Now we have another choice also in the scenes we use. We can work out

scenes just for you that are tailored to your situation, or we can use scenes on a cassette tape I have that have been standardized for many students who want to improve their class-participation skills. Which sounds like the best option to you?

Client: I really don't know. Does it really make a difference?

It is not that uncommon for a client not to know which route to pursue. In the next response, the helper *indicates a preference* and checks it out with Isabella.

18. **Helper:** Probably not, Isabella. If you don't have a choice at this point, you might later. My preference would be to tailor-make the scenes we use here in the session. Then, if you like, you could use the taped scenes to practice with at home later on. How does that sound to you?

Client: It sounds good, like maybe we could use both.

In responses 19 and 20, the helper asks Isabella to *identify situations in which Isabella desires to increase these skills.*

19. **Helper:** Yes, I think we can. Now let's concentrate on getting some of the details we need to make up the scenes we'll use in our sessions. First of all, let's go over the situations in math class in which you want to work on these skills.

Client: It's some of those things we talked about earlier, like being called on, going to the board, and so on.

Next, the helper *explores whether Isabella prefers a very general description or a very specific one.* Sometimes this makes a difference in how the person imagines.

20. **Helper:** Okay, Isabella, how much detail would you like me to give you when I describe a scene—a little detail, to let you fill in the rest, or do you want me to describe pretty completely what you should imagine?

Client: Maybe somewhere in between. I can fill in a lot, but I need to know what to fill in.

In response 21, the helper *asks about the specific situations* in which Isabella has trouble participating in her math class.

21. **Helper:** Let's fill out our description a little more. We're talking about situations you confront in your math class. I remember four situations in which you wanted to increase these skills. You want to answer more when Mr. Lamborne calls on you, volunteer more answers, go to the board, and tell Mr. Lamborne you want to work the problems yourself after you ask for an explanation. Any others, Isabella?

Client: I can't think of any offhand.

In responses 22–27, the helper asks Isabella to *identify the desired behaviors for these situations.*

22. **Helper:** So we've got about four different situations. Let's take each of these separately. For each situation, can we think of what you would like to do in the situation—like when Mr. Lamborne calls on you, for instance?

Client: I'd like to give him the answer instead of saying nothing or saying "I don't know."

23. **Helper:** Good. And if you did give him the answer—especially when you do know it—how would you feel?

Client: Good, probably relieved.

24. **Helper:** Okay. Now what about volunteering answers?

Client: Well, Mr. Lamborne usually asks who has the answer to this; then he calls on people who raise their hand. I usually never raise my hand even when I do know the answer, so I need to just raise my hand and, when he calls on me, give the answer. I need to speak clearly too. I think sometimes my voice is too soft to hear.

25. **Helper:** Now, how could you tell Mr. Lamborne to let you work out the problems yourself?

Client: Just go up to him when we have a work period and tell him the part I'm having trouble with and ask him to explain it.

26. **Helper:** So you need to ask him for just an explanation and let him know you want to do the work.

Client: Yup.

27. **Helper:** Now, what about going to the board?

Client: Well, I do go up. But I always feel like a fool. I get distracted by the rest of the class, so I hardly ever finish the problem. Then he lets me go back to my seat even though I didn't finish it. I need to concentrate more so I can get through the entire problem on the board.

Now that the content of the scenes has been developed, the helper asks Isabella to *arrange the four scenes in a hierarchy.*

28. **Helper:** So we've got four different situations in your math class where you want to improve your participation in some way. Let's take these four situations and arrange them in an order. Could you select the situation that right now is easiest for you and least stressful to you, and rank the rest in terms of difficulty and degree of stress?

Client: Sure, let me think. . . . Well, the easiest thing to do out of all of these would be to tell Mr. Lamborne I want to work out the problems myself. Then I guess it would be answering when he calls on me and then going to the board. I have a lot of trouble with volunteering answers, so that would be hardest for me.

The helper emphasizes the *flexibility of the hierarchy* and provides *general instructions to Isabella about how they will work with these scenes.*

29. **Helper:** Okay. Now, this order can change. At any point if you feel it isn't right, we can reorder these situations. What we will do is to take one situation at a time, starting with the easiest one, and I'll describe it to you in terms of the way you want to handle it and ask you to imagine it. So the first scene will involve your telling Mr. Lamborne what you need explained in order to work the problems yourself.

Client: So we do this just like we did at the beginning?

The helper *precedes the scene presentation with very specific instructions* to Isabella.

30. **Helper:** Right. Just sit back, close your eyes, and relax . . . [gives Isabella a few minutes to do so]. Now remember, as I describe the scene, you are going to imagine yourself in the situation. Try to use all your senses in your imagination—in other words, get into it. When you have a very vivid picture, raise your index finger. Keep imagining the scene until I give a signal to stop. Okay?

Client: Yeah.

The helper *presents the first scene in Isabella's hierarchy slowly* and with ample pauses to give Isabella time to generate the images.

31. **Helper:** Isabella, picture yourself in math class . . . [pause]. Mr. Lamborne has just finished explaining how to solve for *x* and *y*. . . . Now he has assigned problems

to you and has given you a work period. . . . You are starting to do the problems, and you realize there is some part of the equation you can't figure out. You take your worksheet and get up out of your seat and go to Mr. Lamborne's desk. You are telling Mr. Lamborne what part of the equation you're having trouble with. You explain to him you don't want him to solve the problem, just to explain the missing part. Now you're feeling good that you were able to go up and ask him for an explanation. [The helper waits for about 10 seconds after Isabella signals with her finger.]

The helper *signals Isabella to stop* and in responses 32–35 *solicits Isabella's reactions* about the imagery.

32. **Helper:** Okay, Isabella, open your eyes now. What did you imagine?

Client: It was pretty easy. I just imagined myself going up to Mr. Lamborne and telling him I needed more explanation but that I wanted to find the answers myself.

33. **Helper:** So you were able to get a pretty vivid picture?

Client: Yes, very much so.

34. **Helper:** What were your feelings during this—particularly as you imagined yourself?

Client: I felt pretty calm. It didn't really bother me.

35. **Helper:** So imagining yourself wasn't too stressful. Did I give you enough time before I signaled to stop?

Client: Well, probably. Although I think I could have gone on a little longer.

On the basis of Isabella's response about the length of the first scene, the helper will *modify the length during the next presentation.*

36. **Helper:** Okay, I'll give you a little more time the next time.

Before the helper presents the treatment scenes the second time, the helper explores whether the client would like to use *verbal summary codes* or to *personalize the treatment scenes.*

37. **Helper:** Isabella, there are two techniques that you can use to enhance your imagery scene of Mr. Lamborne's math class. One technique is to describe briefly the behavior you want to do and the situation in Mr. Lamborne's class when you will perform the behavior. All that you are doing is just describing the scene in

your own words. This process can help you remember what to do. With the other technique, you can change the scene or elaborate on the scene in any way as long as you still imagine engaging in the behaviors you want to do. Do you have any questions about these two techniques?

Client: You think these techniques might help me imagine the scene better?

38. **Helper:** That's right. Is there one technique you think might be more helpful to you?

Client: Yes, I think that for me to describe the scene in my own words might work better for me. It might help me to remember better what to do.

39. **Helper:** Okay, for the first scene, what verbal summary or description would you use?

Client: Well—after Mr. Lamborne explains how to solve for *x* and *y* and assigns problems, I might find something I can't figure out. I get out of my seat and go up to Mr. Lamborne and tell him I need more explanation but I want to find the answer myself.

40. **Helper:** That's great, Isabella!

The helper *presents the same scene again.* Usually each scene is presented *a minimum of two times* by the helper or on a tape recorder. If the client has chosen one or both treatment-scene enhancement techniques, instruct the client on the technique with each scene.

41. **Helper:** Let's try it again. I'll present the same scene, and I'll give you more time after you signal to me that you have a strong picture [presents the same scene again and checks out Isabella's reactions after the second presentation].

After the helper-presented scenes, the helper *asks Isabella to self-direct her own practice.* This also occurs a minimum of two times for each scene.

42. **Helper:** You seem pretty comfortable now in carrying out this situation the way you want to. This time, instead of my describing the scene orally to you, I'd like you just to go through the scene on your own—sort of a mental practice without my assistance.

Client: Okay [pauses to do this for several minutes].

43. **Helper:** How did that feel?

Client: It was pretty easy even without your instructions, and I think I can see where I can actually do this now with Mr. Lamborne.

The other scenes in the hierarchy are worked through in the same manner.

44. **Helper:** Good. Now we will work through the other three scenes in the same manner, sticking with each one until you can perform your desired behaviors in your imagination pretty easily. [The other three situations in the hierarchy are worked through.]

45. **Helper:** Well, how do you feel now that we've gone over every scene?

Client: Pretty good. I never thought that my imagination would help me in math class!

After the hierarchy has been completed, the helper *picks scenes to practice at random.* This is a way to see how easily the client can perform the scene when it is not presented in the order of the hierarchy.

46. **Helper:** Sometimes imagining yourself doing something helps you learn how to do it in the actual situation. Now I'd like to just pick a scene here at random and present it to you and have you imagine it again [selects a scene from the hierarchy at random and describes it].

Client: That was pretty easy too.

The helper *initiates homework practice* for Isabella.

47. **Helper:** I just wanted to give you a chance to imagine a scene when I took something out of the order we worked with today. I believe you are ready to carry out this imagination practice on your own during the week.

Client: Is this where I use the tapes?

The *purpose of homework* is explained to Isabella.

48. **Helper:** Sure. This tape has a series of scenes dealing with verbal class participation. So instead of me describing a scene, the tape can do this. I'd like you to practice with this daily, because daily practice will help you learn to participate more quickly and easily.

Client: So I just go over a scene the way we did today?

The helper instructs Isabella on *how to complete the homework practice.*

49. **Helper:** Go over the scenes one at a time—maybe about four times for each scene. Make your imagination as vivid as possible. Also, each time you go over a scene, make a check on your log sheets. Indicate the

time of day and place where you use this—also, the length of each practice. And after each practice session, rate the vividness of your imagery on this scale: 1 is not vivid, and 5 is very vivid. How about summarizing what you will do for your homework?

Client: Yes. I just do what we did today and check the number of times I practice each scene and assign a number to the practice according to how strongly I imagined the scene.

At the termination of the session, the helper *indicates that a follow-up on the homework* will occur at their next meeting.

50. **Helper:** Right. And bring your log sheets in at our next meeting, and we'll go over this homework then. Okay? We had a really good session today. You worked hard. I'll see you next Tuesday.

CHAPTER SUMMARY

The modeling strategies presented in this chapter can be used to help clients acquire new responses or extinguish fears or other barriers. The modeling procedures differ slightly. Participant modeling usually employs a live modeling demonstration designed to promote learning by providing a model of goal behaviors for the client. Guided imagery and covert modeling may be useful when live modeling is not feasible. These strategies can be used without elaborate therapeutic aids or expensive equipment. Both strategies involve imagery, which makes the procedures quite easy for a client to practice in a self-directed manner. The capacity of clients to generate vivid images may be important for the overall effectiveness of guided imagery and covert modeling. Assessing client potential to engage in imagery is a necessary prerequisite before using either of these procedures. Assuming that clients can produce clear images, helpers may use guided imagery to help them deal with fears or discomfort or to teach them covert modeling to promote desired responses.

Modeling appears to have applicability across diverse client groups and subgroups, although the research base is not yet highly developed. When modeling has been found to be an effective and appropriate intervention for a diverse group of clients—including but not limited to age and cognitive ability—the type of model should be culturally and/or contextually similar to the client, and the content of the modeled presentation should be culturally relevant. Although imagery has been used in limited ways with diverse clients, it is an intervention that can be helpful if the imagery is adapted to and relevant to the client's context and sense of self. Modeling and self-instructional techniques are quite amenable to educational and collaborative work styles between client and helper, yielding self-help tools that clients can use outside and beyond formal work with the practitioner.

REFERENCES

Alvarez, J., & Jason, L. (1993). The effectiveness of legislation, education, and loaners for child safety in automobiles. *Journal of Community Psychology, 21,* 280–284.

Andrada, P., & Korte, A. (1993). *En aquellas tiempos:* A reminiscing group with Hispanic elderly. *Journal of Gerontological Social Work, 20,* 25–42.

Arbuthnott, K. D., Arbuthnott, D. W., & Rossiter, L. (2001a). Guided imagery and memory: Implications for psychotherapists. *Journal of Counseling Psychology, 48,* 123–132.

Arbuthnott, K. D., Arbuthnott, D. W., & Rossiter, L. (2001b). Laboratory research, treatment innovation, and practice guidelines: A reply to Enns (2001) and Courtois (2001). *Journal of Counseling Psychology, 48,* 140–143.

Baird, C. L., & Sands, L. P. (2006). Effect of guided imagery with relaxation on health-related quality of life in older women with osteoarthritis. *Research in Nursing and Health, 29*(5), 442–451.

Bandura, A. (1976). Effecting change through participant modeling. In J. D. Krumboltz & C. E. Thoresen (Eds.), *Counseling methods* (pp. 248–265). New York: Holt, Rinehart and Winston.

Bandura, A. (1986). *Social foundations of thought and action: A social cognitive theory.* Englewood Cliffs, NJ: Prentice Hall.

Beck, J. S. (1995). *Cognitive therapy.* New York: Guilford Press.

Bidwell, M. A., & Rehfeldt, R. A. (2004). Using video modeling to teach a domestic skill with an embedded social skill to adults with severe mental retardation. *Behavioral Interventions, 19* (4), 263–274.

Botvin, G., Baker, E., Botvin, E., & Dusenbury, L. (1993). Factors promoting cigarette smoking among black youth: A causal modeling approach. *Addictive Behaviors, 18,* 397–405.

Bray, M. A., & Kehle, T. J. (2001). Long-term follow-up of self-modeling as an intervention for stuttering. *School Psychology Review, 30*(1), 135–41.

Brigham, D. (1994). *Imagery for getting well.* New York: Norton.

Brown, D., Scheflin, A., & Hammond, C. (1998). *Memory, trauma, treatment, and the law.* New York: Norton.

Buckley, G. I.; & Malouff, J. M. (2005). Using modeling and vicarious reinforcement to produce more positive attitudes toward mental health treatment. *Journal of Psychology: Interdisciplinary and Applied, 139*(3), 197–209.

Buggey, T. (2005). Video self-modeling applications with student with autism spectrum disorder in a small private school setting *Focus on Autism and Other Developmental Difficulties, 20*(1), 52–63.

Clancy, S. M., McNally, R. J., & Schacter, D. L. (1999). Effects of guided imagery on memory distortion in women reporting recovered memories of childhood sexual abuse. *Journal of Traumatic Stress, 12,* 559–569.

Courtois, C. A. (2001). Commentary on "Guided imagery and memory": Additional considerations. *Journal of Counseling Psychology, 48,* 133–135.

Crow, S., & Banks, D. (2004). Guided imagery: A tool to guide the way for the nursing home patient. *Advances in Mind–Body Medicine, 20*(4), 4–7.

Dobson, R. L., Bray, M. A., Kehle, T. J., Theodore, L. A., & Peck, H. L. (2005). Relaxation and guided imagery as an intervention for children with asthma: A replication. *Psychology in the Schools, 42*(7), 707–720.

Doo, M. Y. (2005). The effects of presentation format for behavior modeling of interpersonal skills in online instruction. *Journal of Educational Multimedia and Hypermedia, 14*(3), 213–235.

Dowd, E. T. (2004). Expanding the cognitive therapy model: Imagery, meditation, and hypnosis. *Journal of Cognitive Psychotherapy, 18*(4), 351–359.

Eller, L. S. (1999). Effects of cognitive–behavioral interventions on quality of life in persons with HIV. *International Journal of Nursing Studies, 36,* 223–233.

Enns, C. Z. (2001). Some reflections on imagery and psychotherapy implications. *Journal of Counseling Psychology, 48,* 136–139.

Esplen, M. J., Gallop, R., & Garfinkel, P. E. (1999). Using guided imagery to enhance self-soothing in women with bulimia nervosa. *Bulletin of the Menninger Clinic, 63,* 174–190.

Estes, C. (1992). *Women who run with the wolves.* New York: Ballantine.

Fox, H. C., Garcia, M., Kemp, K., Milivojevic, V., Kreek, M. J., & Sinha, R. (2006). Gender differences in cardiovascular and corticoadrenal response to stress and drug cues in cocaine dependent individuals. *Psychopharmacology, 185*(3), 348–357.

Fox, H. C., Talih, M., Malison, R., Anderson, G. M., Kreek, M. J., & Sinha, R. (2005). Frequency of recent cocaine and alcohol use affects drug craving and associated responses to stress and drug-related cues. *Psychoneuroendocrinology, 30*(9), 880–891.

Gaines, R., & Price-Williams, P. (1990). Dreams and imaginative processes in American and Balinese artists. *Psychiatric Journal of the University of Ottawa, 15,* 107–110.

Gena, A., Couloura, S., & Kymissis, E. (2005). Modifying the affective behavior of preschoolers with autism using "in-vivo" or video modeling and reinforcement contingencies. *Journal of Autism and Developmental Disorders, 35*(5), 545–556.

Hahna, N. D., & Borling, J. E. (2003–2004). The Bonny Method of Guided Imagery and Music (BMGIM) with Intimate Partner Violence (IPV). *Journal of the Association for Music and Imagery, 9,* 41–57.

Herring, R., & Meggert, S. (1994). The use of humor as a counselor strategy with Native American Indian children. *Elementary School Guidance and Counseling, 29,* 67–76.

Huder, J. A., Hudetz, A. G., & Klaymann, J. (2000). Relationship between relaxation by guided imagery and performance of working memory. *Psychological Reports, 28,* 15–20.

Hudetz, J. A., Hudetz, A. G., & Reddy, D. M. (2004). Effect of relaxation on working memory and the bispectral index of the EEG. *Psychological Reports, 95*(1), 53–70.

Jones, C. D., & Schwartz, I. S. (2004). Siblings, peers, and adults: Differential effects of models for children with autism. *Topics in Early Childhood Special Education, 24*(4), 187–198.

Kalesan, B., Stine, J., & Alberg, A. J. (2006). The joint influence of parental modeling and positive parental concern on cigarette smoking in middle and high school students. *Journal of School Health, 76*(8), 402–407.

Kazdin, A. E. (1976). Developing assertive behavior through covert modeling. In J. D. Krumboltz and C. E. Thoresen (Eds.). *Counseling methods* (pp. 475–486). New York: Holt, Rinehart and Winston.

Kliewer, W., & Lewis, H. (1995). Family influences on coping processes in children and adolescents with sickle cell disease. *Journal of Pediatric Psychology, 20,* 511–525.

Kliewer, W., Parrish, K. A., Taylor, K. W., Jackson, K., Walker, J. M., & Shivy, V. A. (2006). Socialization of coping with community violence: Influences of caregiver coaching, modeling, and family context. *Child Development, 77*(3), 605–623.

Kroese, B. S., & Thomas, G. (2006). Treating chronic nightmares of sexual assault survivors with an intellectual disability—two descriptive case studies. *Journal of Applied Research in Intellectual Disabilities, 19*(1), 75–80.

Louie, S. W. (2004). The effects of guided imagery relaxation in people with COPD. *Occupational Therapy International, 11*(3), 145–159.

Mail, P. (1995). Early modeling of drinking behavior by Native American elementary school children playing drunk. *International Journal of the Addictions, 30,* 1187–1197.

Malgady, R., Rogler, T., & Costantino, G. (1990). Culturally sensitive psychotherapy for Puerto Rican children and adolescents: A program of treatment outcome research. *Journal of Consulting and Clinical Psychology, 58,* 704–712.

Mannix, L. K., Chandurkar, R. S., Rybicki, L. A., Tusek, D. L., & Solomon, G. D. (1999). Effect of guided imagery on quality of life for patients with chronic tension-type headache. *Headache, 39,* 326–334.

Martenson-Blom, K. (2003–2004). Guided imagery and music in supervision: Applications of guided imagery and music (GIM) for supervision and professional development. *Journal of the Association for Music and Imagery, 9,* 97–118.

Marzillier, S. L., & Davey, G. C. L. (2005). Anxiety and disgust: Evidence for a unidirectional relationship. *Cognition and Emotion, 19*(5), 729–750.

Mineka, S., Mystkowski, J. L., Hladek, D., & Rodriguez, B. I. (1999). The effects of changing contexts on return of fear following exposure therapy for spider fear. *Journal of Consulting and Clinical Psychology, 67*(4), 599–604.

Newman, E. J., & Tuckman, B. W. (1997). The effects of participant modeling on self-efficacy, incentive, productivity, and performance. *Journal of Research and Development in Education, 31,* 38–45.

Omizo, M. M., Omizo, S. A., & Kitaoka, S. K. (1998). Guided affective and cognitive imagery to enhance self esteem among Hawaiian children. *Journal of Multicultural Counseling and Development, 26,* 52–62.

Overholser, J. C. (1990). Passive relaxation training with guided imagery: A transcript for clinical use. *Phobia Practice and Research Journal, 3,* 107–122.

Overholser, J. C. (1991). The use of guided imagery in psychotherapy: Modules for use with passive relaxation training. *Journal of Contemporary Psychotherapy, 21,* 159–172.

Paddock, J. R., Joseph, A. L., Chan, F. M., Terranova, S., Manning, C., & Loftus, E. F. (1998). When guided visualization procedures may backfire: Imagination inflation and predicting individual differences in suggestibility [Special issue]. *Applied Cognitive Psychology, 12,* S63–S75.

Paddock, J. R., Noel, M., Terranova, S., Eber, H. W., Manning, C., & Loftus, E. F. (1999). Imagination inflation and the perils of guided visualization. *Journal of Psychology, 133,* 581–595.

Picucci, M. (1992). Planning an experiential weekend workshop for lesbians and gay males in recovery. *Journal of Chemical Dependency Treatment, 5,* 119–139.

Pulos, L. (1996). *The power of visualization* [Audiotapes]. Niles, IL: Nightingale/Conant.

Reichelova, E., & Baranova, E. (1994). Training program for the development of prosocial behavior in children. *Psychologia a Patopsychologia Dietata, 29,* 41–50.

Reyes, M., Routh, D., Jean-Gilles, M., & Sanfilippo, M. (1991). Ethnic differences in parenting children in fearful situations. *Journal of Pediatric Psychology, 16,* 717–726.

Rhodes, F., & Humfleet, G. (1993). Using goal-oriented counseling and peer support to reduce HIV/AIDS risk among drug users not in treatment. *Drugs and Society, 7,* 185–204.

Riva, M. T., & Korinek, L. (2004). Teaching group work: Modeling group leader and member behaviors in the classroom to demonstrate group theory. *Journal for Specialists in Group Work, 29*(1), 55–63.

Roffe, L., Schmidt, K., & Ernst, E. (2005). A systematic review of guided imagery as an adjuvant cancer therapy. *Psycho-Oncology, 14*(8), 607–617.

Romi, S., & Teichman, M. (1998). Participant modelling training programme: Tutoring the paraprofessional. *British Journal of Guidance and Counseling, 26*(2), 297–301.

Rosenthal, T. L., & Steffek, B. D. (1991). Modeling methods. In F. H. Kanfer and A. P. Goldstein (Eds.), *Helping people change* (4th ed., pp. 70–121). New York: Pergamon.

Singer, J. L. (2006). Expanding imagery in patient and therapist. In J. L. Singer, *Imagery in Psychotherapy.* (pp. 161–186). Washington, DC: American Psychological Association.

Taylor, S. E., Pham, L. B., Rivkin, I., & Armor, D. A. (1998). Harnessing the imagination: Mental simulation and self-regulation of behavior. *American Psychologist, 53,* 429–439.

Trent, J. A., Kaiser, A. P., & Wolery, M. (2005). The use of responsive interaction strategies by siblings. *Topics in Early Childhood Special Education, 25*(2), 107–118.

Utay, J., & Miller, M. (2006). Guided imagery as an effective therapeutic technique: A brief review of its history and efficacy research. *Journal of Instructional Psychology, 33*(1), 40–43.

Vargas, M., & Busch-Rossnagel, N. A. (2003). Teaching behaviors and styles of low-income Puerto Rican mothers. *Applied Developmental Science, 7*(4), 229–238.

Webber, M. J., Packman, A., & Onslow, M. (2004). Effects of self-modeling on stuttering. *International Journal of Language and Communication Disorders, 39*(4), 509–522.

Williams, O. (1994). Group work with African American men who batter: Toward more ethnically sensitive practice. *Journal of Comparative Family Studies, 25,* 91–103.

11   KNOWLEDGE AND SKILL BUILDER

Part One

Learning Outcome 1 asks you to develop a script for a symbolic model. Your script should contain the following:

1. Examples of the modeled dialogue
2. Opportunities for practice
3. Feedback
4. Summarization

Use the Checklist for Developing Model Scripts as a guide.

Part Two

Learning Outcome 2 asks you to describe how you would apply the four components of participant modeling in a hypothetical client case. Describe how you would use the four components (treatment rationale, modeling, guided participation, and success experiences) to help a client acquire verbal and nonverbal skills necessary to initiate social contacts with someone he or she wants to ask out.

Part Three

Learning Outcome 3 asks you to demonstrate 14 out of 17 steps of participant modeling with a role-play client. The client might take the role of someone who is afraid to perform certain responses or activities in certain situations. You or an observer can assess your performance, using the Interview Checklist for Participant Modeling.

Checklist for Developing Model Scripts

Instructions: Determine whether you followed these guidelines when you constructed your model script. Check (✔) the guidelines you followed;

1. Determine which clients will use the symbolic modeling procedure, and identify their characteristics.

   a. Age
   b. Gender
   c. Ethnic origin, cultural practices, and race
   d. Coping or mastery model portrayed
   e. Possesses similar concern to that of client group or population

2. Goal behaviors to be modeled by client have been enumerated.
3. Medium is selected (for example, written script, imaginary character from film or other source, someone the client knows and can either envision or interact with, self).
4. Script includes the following ingredients:

   a. Instructions
   b. Modeled dialogue
   c. Practice
   d. Written feedback

   e. Written summarization of what has been modeled, with its importance for client

5. Written script has been field-tested.

Interview Checklist for Participant Modeling

Instructions: Determine which of the following leads the helper used in the interview. Check (✔) the leads that were used.

Treatment Rationale

1. Helper provides rationale for using participant modeling strategy.
   "This procedure has been used with other people who have concerns similar to yours. It is a way to help you overcome your fear or to help you acquire new skills."
2. Helper provides brief overview of participant modeling.
   "It involves three things. I'll model what you want to do, you'll practice this with my assistance, and then you'll try this out in situations that at first will be pretty easy for you so you can be successful."
3. Helper asks about client's willingness to use this strategy.
   "Are you willing to try this now?"

Modeling

4. Helper and client decide whether to divide the goal behavior into subskills or separate tasks.
   "Well, let's see . . . Right now you hardly ever go out of the house. You say it bothers you even to go out in the yard. Let's see whether we can identify different activities in which you would gradually increase the distance away from the house, like going to the front door, going out on the porch, out in the yard, out to the sidewalk, to the neighbor's house, and so on."
5. If a goal behavior is subdivided (step 4), helper and client arrange the subskills into a hierarchy according to increasing level of difficulty.
   "Perhaps we can take our list and arrange it in an order. Start with the activity that is easiest for you now, such as going to the door. Arrange each activity in order of increasing difficulty."
6. Helper and client identify and select an appropriate model.
   "I could help you learn to do this, or we could pick someone whom you know or someone similar to yourself to guide you through this. What are your preferences?"
7. Before the demonstration, helper provides instructions telling the client what to look for.
   "Notice that when the doorbell rings, I will go to the door calmly and quickly and open it without hesitation. Also notice that after I go to the door, I'm still calm; nothing has happened to me."

(continued)

(continued)

8. The model demonstrates the target response at least once; demonstrations are repeated if necessary. If a hierarchy is used, the first skill is modeled first, followed successively by all others skills. The model concludes with a demonstration combining all subskills.

"Okay, let me show this to you again." "Now that I've done the first scene, next I'll show you stepping out on the porch. Then we'll combine these two scenes."

Guided Participation

9. Client is asked to perform the target response. If a hierarchy is used, the first skill in the hierarchy is practiced first, successfully followed by the second, third, and so on.

"This time you try going to the door when the doorbell rings. I will assist you as you need help."

10. After each practice, the model or helper provides feedback consisting of positive feedback and error corrections.

"That was quite smooth. You were able to go to the door quickly. You still hesitated a little once you got there. Try to open the door as soon as you see who is there."

11. Initial practice attempts of each skill by the client are accompanied by induction aids, such as

a. Joint practice with model or helper:
"I'm going to assist you in your first few practices." "Let's do it together. I will walk with you to the door."

b. Verbal and/or physical coaching or guiding by model or helper:
"Let me give you a suggestion here. When you open the door, greet the person there. Find out what the person wants."

c. Repeated practice of one subtask until client is ready to move on to another:
"Let's work on this a few more times until you feel really comfortable."

d. Graduated time intervals for practice (short to long duration):
"This time we'll increase the distance you have to walk to the door. Let's start back in the kitchen."

e. Arrangement of protective conditions for practice to reduce likelihood of feared or undesired consequences:
"We'll make sure someone else is in the house with you."

f. Graduated levels of severity of threat:
"Okay, now we've worked with opening the door when a good friend is there. This time let's pretend it's someone you are used to seeing but don't know as a friend, like the person who delivers your mail."

12. In later practice attempts, the number of induction aids is gradually reduced.

"I believe now that you can do this without my giving you so many prompts."

13. Before moving on, client is able to engage in self-directed practice of all desired responses.

"This time I'm going to leave. I want you to do this by yourself."

Successful Experiences (Homework)

14. Helper and client identify situations in client's environment in which client desires to perform target responses.

"Let's list all the actual times and places where you want to do this."

15. Situations are arranged in a hierarchy from easy with least risk to difficult with greater risk.

"We can arrange these in an order. Put the easiest one first, and follow it by ones that are successively harder or more threatening for you."

16. Starting with the easiest and least risky situation, helper (or model) and client use live or symbolic modeling and guided practice in the client's real-life environment. Steps 4–11 are repeated outside session until gradually the helper (or model) reduces the level of assistance.

"Starting with the first situation, we're going to work with this when it actually occurs. At first I'll assist you until you can do it on your own."

17. Client is assigned a series of related tasks to carry out in a self-directed manner.

"Now you're ready to tackle this situation without my help. You have shown both of us you are ready to do this on your own."

Part Four

According to Learning Outcome 4, you should be able to identify accurately in six out of seven helper leads from the guided imagery steps that the helper is alluding to. Match each helper lead with the letter of the step of guided imagery that the helper is implementing. More than one helper lead may be associated with a step. Feedback follows:

Guided Imagery Steps

a. Treatment rationale
b. Determining the client's potential to use imagery
c. Developing imagery scenes
d. Practice of imagery scenes
e. Homework and follow-up

Helper Leads

1. "Can you think of several scenes you could imagine that give you calm and positive feelings? Supply as many details as you can. You can use these scenes later to focus on instead of the anxiety."

2. "It's important that you practice with this. Try to imagine these scenes at least several times each day."

3. "This procedure can help you control your anxiety. By imagining very pleasurable scenes, you can block out some of the fear."

11   KNOWLEDGE AND SKILL BUILDER

4. "Let's see whether you feel that it's easy to imagine something. Close your eyes, sit back, and visualize anything that makes you feel relaxed."

5. "Now, select one of these scenes you've practiced. Imagine this very intensely. I'm going to apply pressure to your arm, but just focus on your imaginary scene."

6. "What we will do, if you feel that imagination is easy for you, is to develop some scenes that are easy for you to visualize and that make you feel relaxed. Then we'll practice having you focus on these scenes while also trying to block out fear."

7. "Now I'd like you just to practice these scenes we've developed. Take one scene at a time, sit back, and relax. Practice imagining this scene for about 30 seconds. I will tell you when the time is up."

Part Five

Learning Outcome 5 asks you to demonstrate 10 out of 13 steps of guided imagery with a role-play client. You or an observer can assess your performance, assisted by the Interview Checklist for Guided Imagery.

Part Six

Learning Outcome 6 asks you to describe how you would use the five components of covert modeling with a simulated client case. Use the case of Mr. Huang (below), whose goal is to decrease his worrying about retirement and increase his positive thoughts about retiring, particularly in his work setting. Describe how you would use a treatment rationale, develop practice scenes, develop treatment scenes, apply treatment scenes, and assign homework to help Mr. Huang do this. Feedback follows the Knowledge and Skill Builder.

The Case of Mr. Huang

A 69-year-old Asian American man, Mr. Huang, came to counseling because he felt his performance on his job was "slipping." Mr. Huang had a job in a large automobile company. He was responsible for producing new car designs. Mr. Huang revealed that he noticed he had started having trouble about six months before, when the personnel director came in to ask him to fill out retirement papers. Mr. Huang, at the time he sought help, was due to retire in nine months. (The company's policy made it mandatory to retire at age 70.) Until this incident with the personnel director and the completion of the papers, Mr. Huang reported, everything seemed to be "Okay." He also reported that nothing seemed to be changed in his relationship with his family. However, on some days at work, he reported having a great deal of trouble completing

any work on his car designs. When asked what he did instead of working on designs, he said, "Worrying."

The "worrying" turned out to mean that he was engaging in constant repetitive thoughts about his approaching retirement, such as "I won't be here when this car comes out," and "What will I be without having this job?" Mr. Huang stated that there were times when he spent almost an entire morning or afternoon "dwelling" on these things and that this seemed to occur mostly when he was alone in his office actually working on a car design. As a result, he was not turning in his designs by the specified deadlines. Not meeting his deadlines made him feel more worried. He was especially concerned that he would "bring shame both to [his] company and to [his] family who had always been proud of [his] work record." He was afraid that his present behavior would jeopardize the opinion others had of him, although he didn't report any other possible "costs" to him.

In fact, Mr. Huang said it was his immediate boss who had suggested, after several talks and lunches, that he use the employee assistance program. Mr. Huang said his boss had not had any noticeable reactions to his missing deadlines, other than reminding him and being solicitous, as evidenced in the talks and lunches. Mr. Huang reported that he enjoyed this interaction with his boss and often wished he could ask his boss to go out to lunch with him. However, he stated that these meetings had all been at his boss's request. Mr. Huang felt somewhat hesitant about making the request himself.

In the last six months, Mr. Huang had never received any sort of reprimand for missing deadlines on his drawings. Still, he was concerned with maintaining his own sense of pride about his work, which he felt might be jeopardized since he'd been having this trouble.

Part Seven

Learning Outcome 7 asks you to demonstrate at least 22 out of 28 steps associated with covert modeling with a role-play client. The client might take the part of someone who wants to acquire certain skills or to perform certain activities. You or an observer can use the Interview Checklist for Covert Modeling to assess your interview.

Interview Checklist for Guided Imagery

Instructions: In a role-play helper/client interview, determine which of the following helper leads or questions were demonstrated. Indicate with a check (✔) the leads used by the helper.

Treatment Rationale

1. Helper describes the purpose of guided imagery.

(continued)

(*continued*)

"The procedure is called guided imagery because you can elicit pleasant thoughts or images in situations that evoke fear, pain, tension, anxiety, or routine boredom. The procedure helps you block your discomfort or reduce the anxiety that you experience in the difficult situation. The technique involves focusing on imaginary scenes that please you and make you feel relaxed while in the uncomfortable situation. This procedure works because it is extremely difficult for you to feel pleasant, calm, happy, secure, or whatever other emotion is involved in the scene and anxious (tense, fearful, stressed) at the same time. These emotions are incompatible."

2. Helper gives an overview of the procedure.

"What we will do first is to see how you feel about engaging in imagery and look at the details of the scene you used. Then we will decide whether guided imagery is a procedure we want to use. If we decide to use it, we will develop scenes that make you feel calm and good and generate positive feelings for you. We will practice using the scenes we have developed and try to rehearse using those scenes in a simulated fashion. Later, you will apply and practice using the scene in the real situation. Do you have any questions about my explanation?"

3. Helper assesses client's willingness to try the strategy.

"Would you like to go ahead and give this a try now?"

Assessment of Client's Imagery Potential

4. Helper instructs client to engage in imagery that elicits good feelings and calmness.

"Close your eyes, sit back, and relax. Visualize a scene or event that makes you feel relaxed and pleasant. Select something you really enjoy and feel good about. Try to be aware of all your sensations in the scene."

5. After 30 seconds to a minute, the helper probes to ascer-tain the sensory vividness of the client's imagined scene (colors, sounds, movement, temperature, smell). Helper asks client's feelings about imagery and about "getting into" the scene (feeling good with imaginal process).

"Describe the scene to me."

"What sensations did you experience while picturing the scene?"

"What temperature, colors, sounds, smells, and motions did you experience in the scene?"

"How do you feel about the imagery?"

"How involved could you get with the scene?"

6. Helper discusses with client the decision to continue or discontinue guided imagery. The decision is based on the client's attitude (feelings about imagery) and imaginal vividness.

"You seem to feel good with the imagery and are able to picture a scene vividly. We can go ahead now and develop some scenes just for you."

"Perhaps another strategy that would reduce tension without imagery would be better as it is hard for you to 'get into' a scene."

Development of Imagery Scenes

7. Helper and client develop at least two scenes that promote positive feelings for the client, involve many sensations (sound, color, temperature, motion, and smell), and are culturally relevant.

"Now I would like to develop an inventory of scenes or situations that promote calmness, tranquillity, and enjoyment for you. We want to have scenes that will have as much sensory detail as possible for you so that you can experience color, smell, temperature, touch, sound, and motion. Later, we will use the scenes to focus on instead of anxiety, so we want to find scenes for you that are also consistent with and meaningful to you culturally. What sort of scenes can you really get into?"

Practice of Imagery Scene

8. Helper instructs client to practice focusing on the scene for about 30 seconds.

"Take one of the scenes, close your eyes, sit back, and relax. Practice or hold this scene for about 30 seconds, picturing as much sensory detail as possible. I will cue you when the time is up."

9. Helper instructs client to practice focusing on the scene with simulated discomfort or anxiety.

"Let us attempt to simulate or create the difficult situation and to use the scenes. While I squeeze your arm to have you feel pain, focus on one of the imagery scenes we have developed."

"While I describe the feared situation or scene to you, focus on the scene."

10. Helper assesses client's reaction after simulated practice.

How did that feel?"

"What effects did my describing the discomforting situation [my application of pain] have on your relaxation?"

"Rate your ability to focus on the scene with the discomfort."

"How comfortable did you feel when you imagined this fearful situation then?"

11 KNOWLEDGE AND SKILL BUILDER

Homework and Follow-up

11. Helper instructs client to apply guided imagery in vivo.

    "For homework, apply the guided imagery scenes to the discomforting situation. Focus on the scene as vividly as possible while you are experiencing the activity or situation."

12. Helper instructs client to record use of guided imagery and to record level of discomfort or anxiety on log sheets.

    "After each time you use guided imagery, record the situation, the day, the time, and your general reaction on this log. For each occasion that you use imagery, record also your level of discomfort or anxiety, using a 5-point scale, with 5 equal to maximum discomfort and 1 equal to minimum discomfort."

13. Helper arranges a follow-up session.

    "Let's get together again in two weeks to see how your practice is going and to go over your homework log."

Observer Comments _____

_____

_____

Interview Checklist for Covert Modeling

Instructions: Determine which of the following leads the helper used in the interview. Check (✔) the leads that were used.

Treatment Rationale

1. Helper describes the purpose of the strategy.

   "This strategy can help you learn how to discuss your prison record in a job interview. I will coach you on some things you could say. As we go over this, gradually you will feel as if you can handle this situation when it comes up in an actual interview."

2. Helper provides an overview of the strategy.

   "We will be relying on your imagination a lot in this process. I'll be describing certain scenes and asking you to close your eyes and imagine that you are observing the situation I describe to you as vividly as you can."

3. Helper confirms client's willingness to use the strategy.

   "Would you like to give this a try now?"

Practice Scenes

4. Helper instructs client to sit back, close eyes, and relax in preparation for imagining practice scenes.

   "Just sit back, relax, and close your eyes."

5. Helper describes a practice scene unrelated to the goal and instructs client to imagine the scene as helper describes it and to raise index finger when scene is vividly imagined.

"As I describe this scene, try to imagine it very intensely. Imagine the situation as vividly as possible. When you feel you have a vivid picture, raise your index finger."

6. After client indicates vivid imagery, helper instructs client to open eyes and describe what was imagined during scene.

   "Okay, now let's stop—you can open your eyes. Tell me as much as you can about what you just imagined."

7. Helper probes for additional details about scene to obtain a very specific description from client.

   "Did you imagine the color of the room? What did the people look like? Were there any noticeable odors around you? How were you feeling?"

8. Helper suggests ways for client to attend to additional details during subsequent practice.

   "Let's do another scene. This time try to imagine not only what you see but what you hear, smell, feel, and touch."

9. Helper initiates additional practices of one scene or introduces practice of a new scene until client is comfortable with the novelty and is able to provide a detailed description of imagery.

   "Let's go over another scene. We'll do this for a while until you feel pretty comfortable with this."

10. After practice scenes, helper does one of the following:

    a. Decides to move on to developing treatment scenes:
       "Okay, this seems to be going pretty easily for you, so we will go on now."
    b. Decides that relaxation or additional imagery training is necessary:
       "I believe before we go on it might be useful to try to help you relax a little more. We can use muscle relaxation for this purpose."
    c. Decides to terminate covert modeling because of inadequate client imagery:
       "Judging from this practice, I believe another approach would be more helpful where you can actually see someone do this."

Developing Treatment Scenes

11. Helper and client decide on appropriate characteristics of the model, including

    a. Identity of model (client or someone else):
       "As you imagine this scene, you can imagine either yourself or someone else in this situation. Which would be easier for you to imagine?"
    b. Coping or mastery model:
       "Sometimes it's easier to imagine someone who doesn't do this perfectly. What do you think?"
    c. Single or multiple models:
       "We can have you imagine just one other person—someone like you—or several other people."
    d. Specific characteristics of model to maximize client/model similarity:

(continued)

(*continued*)

"Let's talk over the specific type of person you will imagine, someone similar to you."

12. Helper and client decide to use either

   a. Individualized scenes
   b. Standardized scenes

   "We have two options in developing the scenes you will imagine. We can discuss different situations and develop the scenes just to fit you, or we can use some standardized scenes that might apply to anyone with a prison record going through a job interview. What is your preference?"

13. Helper and client decide to use either

   a. General scene descriptions
   b. Specific, detailed scene descriptions

   "I can present the situations you've just described in one of two ways. One way is to give you a general description and leave it up to you to fill in the details. Or I can be very detailed and tell you specifically what to imagine. Which approach do you think would be best for you?"

14. Helper and client develop specific ingredients that will be in each scene, such as

   a. Situations or context in which behaviors should occur:
   "In the scene in which you are interviewing for a job, go over the type of job you might seek and the kind of employer who would be hard to talk to."
   b. Behaviors and coping methods to be demonstrated by the model:
   "Now, what you want to do in this situation is to discuss your record calmly, explaining what happened and emphasizing that your record won't interfere with your job performance."
   c. Favorable outcome of scene, such as
      1. Favorable client self-initiated action: "At the end of the scene you might want to imagine you have discussed your record calmly without getting defensive."
      2. Client self-reinforcement: "At the end of the scene, congratulate yourself or encourage yourself for being able to discuss your record."

15. Helper and client generate descriptions of multiple scenes. "Okay, now the job interview is one scene. Let's develop other scenes where you feel it's important to be able to discuss your record—for example, in establishing a closer relationship with a friend."

Applying Treatment Scenes

16. Helper and client arrange scenes in a hierarchy according to

   a. Client's degree of discomfort in the situation
   b. Client's view of the difficulty or complexity of the situation
   "Now I'd like you to take these six scenes we've developed and arrange them in an order. Start with the situation that you feel most comfortable with and that is easiest for you to discuss your record in now. End with the situation that is most difficult and gives you the most discomfort or tension."

17. Helper precedes scene presentation with instructions to client.

   "I'm going to tell you now what to do when the scene is presented."

   a. Instructions to sit back, relax, close eyes:
   "First, just sit back, close your eyes, and relax."
   b. Instructions on whom to imagine:
   "Now come up with an image of the person you're going to imagine, someone similar to you."
   c. Instructions to imagine intensely, using as many senses as possible:
   "As I describe the scene, imagine it as vividly as possible. Use all your senses—sight, smell, touch, and so on."
   d. Instructions to raise index finger when vivid imagery occurs: "When you start to imagine very vividly, raise your finger."
   e. Instructions to hold imagery until helper signals to stop:
   "And hold that vivid image until I tell you when to stop."

18. Helper presents one scene at a time, by describing the scene orally to client or by means of a tape recorder.

   "Here is the first scene. . . . Imagine the employer is now asking you why you got so far behind in school. Imagine that you are explaining what happened in a calm voice."

19. The duration of each scene is determined individually for the client and is held until client imagines the model performing the desired behavior as completely as possible (perhaps 20–30 seconds).

   "You should be able to imagine yourself saying all you want to about your record before I stop you."

20. After the first scene presentation, helper solicits client reactions about

   a. Rate of delivery and duration of scene:
   "How did the length of the scene seem to you?"
   b. Clearness and vividness of client imagery:
   "How intense were your images? What did you imagine?"
   c. Degree of discomfort or pleasantness of scene:
   "How did you feel while doing this?"

   If the client indicates difficulty or discomfort, the helper does one or more of the following:

   a. Revises scene or manner of presentation before second presentation:
   "Based on what you've said, let's change the type of employer. Also, I'll give you more time to imagine this the next time."
   b. Changes scene position in the hierarchy and presents another scene next:
   "Perhaps we need to switch the order of this scene and use this other one first."
   c. Precedes another presentation of the scene with relaxation or discussion of client discomfort:
   "Let's talk about your discomfort."

11 KNOWLEDGE AND SKILL BUILDER

21. Imagery enhancement techniques explained to client:

    a. Verbal summary codes:
    "You can briefly describe the scene in your own words, which can help you remember the behaviors to perform in the situation."

    b. Personalization or elaboration of treatment scene:
    "You can change or elaborate on the scene in any way as long as you still imagine the behavior you want to do."

22. Each scene is presented a minimum of two times by helper or on tape recorder.

    "Okay, now I'm going to present the same scene one or two more times."

23. Following helper presentations of scene, client repeats scene at least twice in a self-directed manner.

    "This time I'd like you to present the scene to yourself while imagining it, without relying on me to describe it."

24. After each scene in hierarchy is presented and imagined satisfactorily, helper presents some scenes to client in a random order, following steps 3, 4, and 5.

    "Now I'm just going to pick a scene at random and describe it while you imagine it."

Homework

25. Helper instructs client to practice scenes daily outside session and explains purpose of daily practice.

"During the week, I'd like you to take these cards where we've made a written description of these scenes and practice the scenes on your own. This will help you acquire this behavior more easily and quickly."

26. Instructions for homework include

    a. What to do:
    "Just go over one scene at a time—make your imagination as vivid as possible."

    b. How often to do it:
    "Go over this five times daily."

    c. When and where to do it:
    "Go over this two times at home and three times at school."

    d. A method for self-observation of homework completion:
    "Each time you go over the scene, make a tally on your log sheet. Also, after each practice session, rate the intensity of your imagery on this scale."

27. Helper arranges for a follow-up after completion of some amount of homework.

    "Bring these sheets next week so we can discuss your practices and see what we need to do as the next step."

Observer Comments _____

_____

_____

KNOWLEDGE AND SKILL BUILDER **FEEDBACK**

Part One

Check the contents of your script outline with the list in item 4 on the Checklist for Developing Model Scripts.

Part Two

Here is a brief description of how you might use participant modeling to help your client.

Treatment Rationale

First, you would explain to your client that the procedure can help him or her acquire the kinds of skills he or she will need to initiate social contacts with someone to ask out. You would also tell him or her that the procedure involves modeling, guided practice, and success experiences. You might emphasize that the procedure is based on the idea that change can occur when the desired activities are learned in small steps with successful performance emphasized at each step.

Modeling

You and your client would explore the verbal and nonverbal responses that might be involved in approaching people and asking them to lunch, for a drink, and so on. For example, these skills might be divided into making a verbal request, speaking without hesitation or errors, and speaking in a firm, strong voice. After specifying all the components of the desired response, you and your client would arrange them in a hierarchy according to order of difficulty.

You and your client would select a culturally appropriate model—yourself or an aide. The model selected would demonstrate to the client the first response in the hierarchy (followed by all the others). Repeated demonstrations of any response might be necessary.

Guided Participation

After the modeled demonstration of a response, you would ask your client to perform it. The first attempts would be assisted with induction aids administered by you or the model. For example, you might verbally coach the client to start with a short message and gradually increase it. After each practice, you would give your client feedback, being sure to encourage his or her positive performance and to make suggestions for improvement. Generally, your client would practice each response several times, and the number of induction aids would be reduced gradually. Before moving on to practice a different response, your client should be able to perform the response in a self-directed manner without your presence or support.

Success Experiences

You and your client would identify situations in his or her environment in which the client would like to use the learned skills. In this case, most of the applications would be in social situations. Some of these situations involve more risk than others. The situations should be arranged in order, from the least to the most risky. The client would work on the least risky situation until he or she was able to do that easily and successfully before going on. Ideally, it would help to have the helper or model go along with the client to model and guide. If the model was one of the client's colleagues, this would be possible. If this was not possible, the client could telephone the helper just before the "contact" to rehearse and to receive coaching and encouragement.

Part Three

Use the Interview Checklist for Participant Modeling to assess your performance or to have someone else rate you.

Part Four

1. c. Instructing the client to develop imagery scenes—used to focus on to block the unpleasant sensation.
2. e. Part of homework—in vivo application of imagery.
3. a. Treatment rationale—giving the client a reason for guided imagery.
4. b. The client's potential to use imagery—determining the level.
5. d. Imagery-scene practice—with a pain-provoking situation.
6. a. Treatment rationale—giving an overview of the procedure.
7. d. Imagery-scene practice—training the client to imagine the scenes very vividly before using them in simulation of anxiety-provoking situations.

Part Five

Use the Interview Checklist for Guided Imagery to assess your performance or to have someone else rate you.

Part Six

Rationale

First you would give Mr. Huang an explanation of covert modeling. You would briefly describe the process to him and explain how using his imagination to "see" someone doing something could help him perform his desired responses.

Practice Scenes

Next you would present a couple of unrelated practice scenes. You would instruct Mr. Huang to close his eyes, relax, and

11   KNOWLEDGE AND SKILL BUILDER **FEEDBACK**

imagine the scene as you describe it. When Mr. Huang signals that he is imagining the scene, you would stop and query him about what he imagined. You might suggest additional details for him to imagine during another practice scene. Assuming that Mr. Huang feels relaxed and can generate vivid images, you would go on to develop treatment scenes.

Developing Treatment Scenes

You and Mr. Huang would specify certain components to be included in the treatment scenes, including the identity of the model (Mr. Huang or someone else), type of model (coping or mastery), single or multiple models, and specific characteristics of the model to maximize client/model similarity. Next you would decide whether to use individualized or standardized scenes. Perhaps in Mr. Huang's case, his own scenes might work best. You would also need to decide how detailed the scene should be. In Mr. Huang's case, a scene might include some examples of positive thoughts and allow room for him to add his own. You and Mr. Huang would generate a list of scenes to be used, specifying the following:

1. The situation (which, for him, would be at work when the negative thoughts crop up)
2. The behavior and coping methods he would acquire (stopping interfering thoughts, generating positive thoughts about retirement, and getting back to his project at work)
3. Favorable outcomes (for Mr. Huang, this might be being able to get his work done on time, which would help him avoid shame and maintain pride in his work)

Applying Treatment Scenes

You and Mr. Huang would arrange the scenes in order—starting with a work situation in which his thoughts are not as interfering and proceeding to situations in which they are most interfering. Starting with the first scene, you would give Mr. Huang specific instructions on imagining. Then you would present the scene to him and have him hold the scene in imagination for a few seconds after he signals a strong image. After the scene presentation, you would get Mr. Huang's reactions to the scene and make any necessary revisions in duration, scene content, order in the hierarchy, and so on. At this time Mr. Huang could either develop a verbal summary code or personalize the scene by changing or elaborating on it in some way. The same scene would be presented to Mr. Huang at least one more time, followed by several practices in which he goes through the scene without your assistance. After you worked through all scenes in the hierarchy, you would present scenes to him in a random order.

Homework

After each scene presentation in the session, you would instruct Mr. Huang to practice the scenes daily outside the session. A follow-up on this homework should be arranged.

Part Seven

Assess your interview or have someone else assess it, using the Interview Checklist for Covert Modeling.

12

REFRAMING, COGNITIVE MODELING, AND PROBLEM-SOLVING STRATEGIES

LEARNING OUTCOMES

After completing this chapter, you will be able to

1. Demonstrate 8 out of 11 steps of reframing in a role-play interview.
2. Using a simulated client case, describe how you would apply the seven components of cognitive modeling and self-instructional training.
3. Demonstrate 16 out of 21 steps of cognitive self-instructional modeling in a role play; then use the Interview Checklist for Cognitive Modeling at the end of the chapter to rate your performance.
4. Identify which step of the problem-solving strategy is reflected in at least 8 of 10 helper interview responses.
5. Demonstrate 16 out of 19 steps of problem solving in a role-play interview; then use the Interview Checklist for Problem Solving at the end of the chapter to assess your performance.

THE PROCESS OF REFRAMING

People who grow up in chaotic, abusive, rejecting, or disorganized attachment-style environments will generally display distorted attribution processes. These people often perceive problems in living in ways that appear to have no workable solution for emotional relief. For example, Al, a man who experienced rejection from his parents while growing up, may say, "I don't have the skills to work with people." From Al's frame of reference, his "lack of interpersonal skills" is unchangeable, and he feels a sense of hopelessness about working with people. This habitual schema leads to self-limiting patterns of feeling, thinking, and behaving with people. If Al continues the cycle of self-indictment, he will experience a sense of despair and become regressive and withdrawn from social interactions. Al feels stuck in his schema, which was created at least in part by the state-dependent memory, learning, and behaving that he experienced in his family. The meaning and emotions that he experiences in social interactions lock him in a tenacious cycle that only limits his perceptions, beliefs, and options for alternative ways of behaving. Reframing might be one intervention that could help Al revise his way of perceiving and modify his interpersonal skills.

Reframing is exploring how an incident or situation is typically perceived and offering another view, or frame, for the situation. Reframing helps a client to change emotions, meaning, and perceived options. It can change clients' everyday conscious sets and perceptions of their personal limitations, of situations, and of others' entrenched behavior. Reframing goes beyond an intellectual shift to stimulate a sensed effect such as a weight being lifted, a physical freeing, and renewed energy to move forward. Opening this window of hope about being able to realize changes that previously felt stymied or impossible is part of what makes reframing an effective tool when paired with change strategies that build further insights, skills, and changed circumstances.

Box 12.1 presents a sample of recent research on reframing. A quick glance reveals that it has been used for many purposes. Reframing (sometimes also called *relabeling*) is an approach that modifies or restructures a client's perceptions of a difficult situation or a behavior. Efforts to reframe are implicitly constructivistic in that, rather than a single truth, they reflect that a circumstance can have multiple meanings across individuals and from the perspective of any one person. The aim is not self-deception but rather the search for *useful* ways to understand a circumstance, relative to a client's goals and/or perspectives that may be impeding the client's efforts to achieve those goals. Reframing is used frequently in family therapy as a way to redefine presenting problems so as to shift the focus away from an "identified patient" or "scapegoat" and onto the family as a whole, as a system in which each member is an interdependent part. When used in this way, reframing changes the way in which a family encodes an issue or a conflict.

With individual clients, reframing has a number of uses as well. By changing or restructuring what a client encodes and perceives, reframing can reduce defensiveness and mobilize the client's resources and forces for change. Second, it can shift the focus from overly simplistic trait attributions

BOX 12.1	RESEARCH ON REFRAMING

Cancer Survivors

Porter, L., S., Clayton, M. F., Belyea, M., Mishel, M., Gil, K. M., & Germino, B. B. (2006). Predicting negative mood state and personal growth in African American and White long-term breast cancer survivors. *Annals of Behavioral Medicine, 31*, 195–204.

Depression

Karasawa, K. (2003). Interpersonal reaction toward depression and anger. *Cognition and Emotion, 17*(1), 123–138.

Diabetes

Albarran, N. D., Ballesteros, M. N., Morales, G. G., & Ortega, M. I. (2006). Dietary behavior and type 2 diabetes care. *Patient Education and Counseling, 61*, 191–199.

Disability

Larson, E. (1998). Reframing the meaning of disability to families: The embrace of paradox. *Social Science and Medicine, 47*, 865–675.

Family Therapy

Fortune, D. G., Smith, J. V., & Garvey, K. (2005). Perceptions of psychosis, coping, appraisals, and psychological distress in the relatives of patients with schizophrenia: An exploration using self-regulation theory. *British Journal of Clinical Psychology, 44*, 319–331.

Group Counseling

Clark, A. J. (1998). Reframing: A therapeutic technique in group counseling. *Journal of Specialists in Group Work, 23*, 66–73.

Multicultural Consultation

Soo-Hoo, T. (1998). Applying frame of reference and reframing techniques to improve school consultation in multicultural settings. *Journal of Educational and Psychological Consultation, 9*, 325–245.

Older Adults

Motenko, A. K., & Greenberg, S. (1995). Reframing dependence in old age. *Social Work, 40*, 382–390.

Sexual Abuse

Maltz, W. (2001). Sex therapy with survivors of sexual abuse. In P. J. Kleinplatz, (Ed.), *New directions in sex therapy: Innovations and alternatives* (pp. 258–278). New York: Brunner-Routledge.

Stress

Devonport, T. J., & Lane, A. M. (2006). Cognitive appraisal of dissertation stress among undergraduate students. *The Psychological Record, 56*, 259–266.

Stroke Rehabilitation

Gillen, G. (2006). Coping during inpatient stroke rehabilitation: An exploratory study. *American Journal of Occupational Therapy, 60*(2), 136–145.

of behavior that clients are inclined to make ("I am lazy" or "I am not assertive") to analyses of important contextual and situational cues associated with the behavior. Finally, reframing can be a useful strategy for helping with clients' self-efficacy—their confidence that they can actually accomplish something important to them.

Reframing is often used as one part of a larger intervention to help clients come to grips with conflicts that are at the root of their issues. In one case example, Wachtel (1993) is working with a man who is confused by some of his interpersonal dynamics, juggling strong needs to please and be valued by others with an equally strong desire to have a clearer sense of what *he* values and who he sees his true self to be. The helper offers a reframe, suggesting that the client's confusion, rather indicating deficiency, was a legitimate and understandable feeling, an expression of the quest process he was engaged in, and a valuable resource to explore further. Reframing can also help one understand another person's experience, which may, in turn, make it easier for the client to behave differently toward the other and thus disrupt the negative cycles the two people are caught within. An

example involves a woman who felt hurt by a perception that her husband was not interested in her (Wachtel, 1993). After inquiring about recent fights between the couple, the practitioner offered a reframe of the husband's behavior, not as a sign of his not caring but as a sign that he felt hurt and was withdrawing to hide how hurt and vulnerable he felt. With the aid of the reframing, the woman was better positioned to see both sets of feelings and needs, to try out different interpretations she had not previously considered, and to consider new ways of communicating.

REFRAMING MEANING

Helpers reframe whenever they ask or encourage clients to see an issue from a different perspective. In this chapter, we propose a more systematic way for helpers to help clients reframe an issue. The most common method of reframing—and the one that we illustrate here—is to reframe the *meaning* of a problematic situation or behavior. When you reframe meaning, you are challenging the meaning that the client (or someone else) has assigned. Usually, the longer a particular meaning (or label) is attached to a behavior or situation, the more necessary the behavior or situation itself becomes in maintaining predictability and equilibrium in the client's functioning. Also, when meanings are attached to something over a long period of time, clients are more likely to develop "functional fixity"—that is, they see things from only one perspective or become fixated on the idea that this particular situation, behavior pattern, or attribute is *the* issue. Reframing helps clients by providing alternative ways to view the issue in question without directly challenging the behavior or situation itself and by loosening a client's perceptual frame, thus setting the stage for other kinds of intervention. Once the *meaning* of a behavior or situation changes, the person's response to it usually also changes, if the reframe is valid and acceptable to the client. The essence of a meaning reframe is to give a situation, a behavior, or some other issue of concern a new label or a new name that has a different meaning. This new meaning has a different connotation, and usually it is positive or at least less troubling to the client. For example, "stubbornness" might be reframed as "independence," or "greediness" might be reframed as "ambition." Reframing involves six steps:

1. Explanation of the treatment rationale: the purpose and an overview of the procedure
2. Identification of client perceptions and feelings in situations of concern
3. Deliberate enactment of selected perceptual features
4. Identification of alternative perceptions
5. Modification of perceptions in situations of concern
6. Homework and follow-up

A detailed description of the steps associated with these components is included in the Interview Checklist for Reframing at the end of this chapter and in Learning Activity 12.1.

Treatment Rationale

The rationale for reframing attempts to strengthen the client's belief that perceptions or attributions about the situation can cause emotional distress. Here is a rationale that can be used to introduce reframing:

> When we think about or when we are in a difficult situation, we automatically attend to *selected features* of the situation. As time goes on, we tend to get fixated on these same features of the situation and ignore other aspects of it. This can lead to some uncomfortable emotions, such as the ones you're feeling now. In this procedure, I will help you identify what you are usually aware of during these situations. Then we'll work on increasing your awareness of other aspects of the situation that you usually don't notice. As this happens, you will notice that your feelings about and responses to this issue will start to change. Do you have any questions?

Identification of Client Perceptions and Feelings

If the client accepts the rationale that the helper provides, the next step is to help the client become aware of what he or she automatically attends to in the problem situation. Clients are often unaware of what features or details they attend to in a situation and what information about the situation they encode. For example, clients who have a fear of water may attend to how deep the water is because they cannot see the bottom, and they may encode the perception that they might drown. Clients who experience test anxiety may attend to the large size of the room or to how quickly the other people seem to be working. The encoding of these perceptions leads to the clients' feeling overwhelmed, anxious, and lacking in confidence. In turn, these feelings can lead to impaired performance in or avoidance of the situation.

During the interview, the helper helps clients discover what they typically attend to in problem situations. The helper can use imagery or role play to help clients reenact situations in order to become aware of what they notice, interpret, and then do on the basis of that interpretation. While engaging in role play or in imagining the situation, the helper can help the client become more aware of typical encoding patterns by asking questions like these:

> "What are you attending to now?"
> "What are you aware of now?"
> "What are you noticing about the situation?"

In order to link feelings to individual perceptions, these questions can be followed with further inquiries, such as these:

> "What are you feeling at this moment?"
> "What do you feel in your body?"

The helper may need to assist clients to engage in role play or imagery several times so that they can reconstruct the situation and become more aware of salient encoded features. The helper may also suggest what the client might have felt and what the experience appears to mean to the client in order to bring these automatic perceptions into awareness. The practitioner also helps clients notice "marginal impressions"—fleeting images, sounds, feelings, and sensations that were passively rather than deliberately processed by the client yet affect the client's reaction to the situation.

Deliberate Enactment of Selected Perceptual Features

After clients become aware of their rather automatic attending, they are asked to reenact the situation and intentionally attend to the selected features that they have been processing automatically. For example, the water-phobic client reenacts (through role play or imagery) approach situations with the water and deliberately attends to the salient features such as the depth of the water and his or her inability to see the bottom of

| LEARNING ACTIVITY | **12.1** | **Reframing** |

 This activity is designed to help you use the reframing procedure with yourself.

1. Identify a situation that typically produces uncomfortable or distressing feelings for you— for example, you are about to initiate a new relationship with someone, or you are presenting a speech in front of a large audience.

2. Try to become aware of what you rather automatically attend to or focus on during this situation. Role-play it with another person, or pretend you're sitting in a movie theater and project the situation onto the screen in front of you. As you do so, ask yourself: "What am I aware of now?" "What am I focusing on now?" Be sure to notice fleeting sounds, feelings, images, and sensations.

3. Establish a link between these encoded features of the situation and your resulting feelings. As you reenact the situation, ask yourself: "What am I feeling at this moment?" "What am I experiencing now?"

4. After you have become aware of the most salient features of this situation, reenact it either in a role play or in your imagination. This time, deliberately attend to these selected features during the reenactment. Repeat this process until you feel that you have awareness and control of the perceptual process you engage in during this situation.

5. Select other features of the session (previously ignored) that you could focus on or attend to during this situation that would allow you to view and handle the situation differently. Consider images, sounds, and feelings as well as people and objects. Ask yourself questions such as "What other aspects of this same situation aren't readily apparent to me that would provide me with a different way to view the situation?" You may wish to query another person for ideas. After you have identified alternative features, again reenact the situation in a role play or your imagination—several times if necessary—in order to break old encoding patterns.

6. Construct a homework assignment for yourself that encourages you to apply this process as needed for use during actual situations.

the pool. By deliberately attending to these encoded features, a client is able to bring these habitual attentional processes fully into awareness and under direct control. This sort of "dramatization" seems to sharpen the client's awareness of existing perceptions. When these perceptions are uncovered and made more visible through this deliberate reenactment, it is harder for the client to maintain prior response habits. This step may need to be repeated several times during the session or assigned as a homework task.

Identification of Alternative Perceptions

The helper can help the client change his or her attentional focus by selecting other features of the target situation to attend to rather than ignore. For example, the water-phobic client who focuses on the depth of the water might be instructed to focus on how clear, clean, and wet the water appears. For the test-anxious client who attends to the size of the room, the helper can redirect the client's attention to how roomy (nonconstricting) the testing place is or how comfortable the seats are. Both clients and practitioners can suggest other features of the situation or person to use that have a positive or at least a neutral connotation. The practitioner can ask the client what features provide a felt sense of relief.

For reframing to be effective, the alternative perceptions must be acceptable to the client. Reframes should be linked to difficulties that the client is having in moving forward and are as valid a way of looking at the world as the way the person sees things now. All reframes or alternative perceptions have to be tailored to the client's values, style, and sociocultural context, and they have to fit the client's experience and model of his or her world. The alternative perceptions or reframes that you suggest also need to match the external reality of the situation closely enough to be plausible. If, for example, a husband is feeling very angry with his wife because of her extramarital affair, reframing his anger as "loving concern" is probably not representative enough of the external situation to be plausible to the client. A more plausible reframe might be something like "frustration from not being able to protect the (marital) relationship."

The delivery of a reframe is also important. When suggesting alternative perceptions to clients, it is essential that the practitioner's nonverbal behavior be congruent with the tone and content of the reframe. It is also important for the helper to use his or her voice effectively in delivering the reframe by emphasizing key words or phrases.

Modification of Perceptions in Situations of Concern

Modifying what clients attend to can be helped with role play or imagery. The helper instructs the client to attend to other features of the situation during the role play or imagery enactment. This step may need to be repeated several times. Repetition is designed to embody new perceptual responses so that the client gradually experiences a felt sense of relief, strength, or optimism.

Homework and Follow-up

The helper can suggest to the client that during in vivo situations, the client follow the same format used in their sessions. The client is instructed to become more aware of salient encoded features of a stressful or arousing situation, to link these to uncomfortable feelings, to engage in deliberate enactments or practice activities, and to try to make "perceptual shifts" during these situations to other features of the situation previously ignored.

As the client becomes more adept at this process, the helper will need to be alert to slight perceptual shifts and point these out to the client. Typically, clients are unskilled at detecting these shifts in encoding. Helping the client discriminate between old and new encodings of target situations can be very useful in promoting the overall goal of the reframing strategy: to alleviate and modify encoding or perceptual errors and biases.

REFRAMING CONTEXT

Although the steps we propose for reframing involve reframing meaning, another way in which you can reframe is to reframe the *context* of a concern. Reframing the context helps a client to explore and decide *when, where,* and *with whom* a given behavior, for example, is useful or appropriate. Context reframing is based on the assumption that many behaviors are useful in *some* but not all contexts or conditions. Thus, when a client states "I'm too lazy," a context reframe would be "In what situations (or with what people) is it useful or even helpful to be lazy?" The client may respond by noting that it is useful to be lazy whenever she wants to play with the children. At this point, the practitioner can help the client sort out and contextualize a given behavior so that the person can see where and when she or he does and does not want the behavior to occur. Context reframes are most useful for dealing with client generalizations—for example, "I'm *never* assertive" or "I'm *always* late."

APPLICATIONS OF REFRAMING WITH DIVERSE CLIENTS

For a reframe to be effective, it must be plausible and acceptable to the client. Client demographic factors such as age, gender, race or ethnicity, sexuality, and disability are important components to consider in developing reframes with diverse groups of clients. An excellent example of a culturally relevant meaning reframe is given by Oppenheimer (1992) in working with a severely depressed 67-year-old Latina. The woman was able to improve only after she could reframe her depression within the context of her Latino spiritualist beliefs. Her helper, also a Latina, not only refrained from labeling

as pathological the client's belief in the supernatural, but she used these beliefs to create a valid meaning reframe by taking the client's references to "intranquil spirits or ghosts" to reframe her pain surrounding a loss. Similar examples of culturally sensitive reframes have been used with Asian American adolescents to negotiate conflicting cultural values (Huang, 1994), with HIV-positive men to reframe stress around the threat of AIDS (Leserman, Perkins, & Evans, 1992), and with elderly people to reframe dependence (Motenko & Greenberg, 1995).

A good example of a multiculturally reframe is the feminist notion of the meaning of *resistance.* Rather than referring to resistance as a client's conscious and unconscious attempts "to avoid the truth and evade change," Brown (1994) suggests that it means instead "the refusal to merge with dominant cultural norms and to attend to one's own voice and integrity" (p. 15). The meaning of resistance shifts from something that is pathological to something that is healthy and desirable. In this sense, resistance means "learning the ways in which each of us is damaged by our witting or unwitting participation in dominant norms or by the ways in which such norms have been thrust upon us" (Brown, 1994, p. 25). An example might be what we do when our competent, conscientious, and loyal office manager is in danger of losing her or his job because of organizational restructuring and downsizing. Do we look the other way, do we ignore it, or do we speak on her or his behalf to persons holding the power in the dominant social structure of the organization? And as the office manager's helper, do we attempt to soothe the manager and have her or him adjust, or do we attempt to help the person to give voice to his or her anger and outrage?

In this sense, to resist means to tell the truth as we see it about what is actually happening and what is possible and available to each client as "avenues for change" (Brown, 1994, p. 26). Gay, lesbian, and bisexual clients are confronted with this sort of resistance daily in the "coming-out" process. Smith (1992) notes that as an African American girl she was brought up to be a "resister": to be honest and self-reliant and to stand up for herself, an experience echoed in research that many African American adolescent girls have a strong sense of healthy resistance (Taylor, Gilligan, & Sullivan, 1995). Robinson and Ward (1992) have made an important contribution to the notion of healthy resistance by distinguishing between resistance strategies for *survival* versus resistance strategies for *liberation.* They differentiate resistance strategies for survival as being crisis-oriented, short-term methods that include self-denigration, *excessive* autonomy at the expense of connectedness to one's collective culture, and "quick fixes" such as early and unplanned pregnancies, substance use, and school failure and/or dropping out. Resistance strategies for liberation include strategies in which problems of oppression are acknowledged, collectivity is valued, and demands for change are empowered. Robinson and Ward (1991) base their strategies for liberation on an African-centered Nguzo Saba

TABLE 12.1	Resistance Strategies
Survival/Oppression	**Liberation/Empowerment**
Isolation and disconnectedness from the larger African American community	Unity with African people that transcends age, socioeconomic status, geographic origin, and sexual orientation (Umoja)
Self defined by others (the media, educational system) in a manner that oppresses and devalues blackness	Self-determination through confrontation and repudiation of oppressive attempts to demean self. New models used to make active decisions that empower and affirm self and racial identity (Kujichagulia)
Excessive individualism and autonomy; racelessness	Collective work and responsibility; the self seen in connection with the larger body of African people, sharing a common destiny (Ujima)
"I've got mine, you get yours" attitude	Cooperative economics advocating a sharing of resources through the convergence of the "I" and the "we" (Ujaama)
Meaninglessness in life, immediate gratification to escape life's harsh realities; the use of "quick fixes"	Purpose in life that benefits the self and the collective, endorses delaying gratification as a tool in resistance (Nia)
Maintaining status quo, replicating existing models, although they may be irrelevant	Creativity through building new paradigms for the community through dialogue with other resisters (Kuumba)
Emphasis on the here and now, not looking back and not looking forward; myopic vision	Faith through an intergenerational perspective where knowledge of the history of Africa and other resisters and care for future generations gives meaning to struggle and continued resistance (Imani)

Source: "'A Belief in Self Far Greater than Anyone's Disbelief': Cultivating Resistance among African American Female Adolescents," by T. Robinson and J. V. Ward. In *Women, Girls, and Psychotherapy: Reframing Resistance,* by C. Gilligan, A. Rogers, and D. Tolman (Eds.), p. 99, Table 1. Copyright © 1992 by the Haworth Press, Inc., Binghamton, NY. Reprinted by permission.

value system (Karenga, 1980), as summarized in Table 12.1, although parallels to other groups and histories are evident.

Reframing within a framework of diversity and critical consciousness helps us see that "frame of reference" can involve multiple levels of analysis and contextualizing. For example, Soo-Hoo (1998) describes ways in which understanding differences in the frame of reference of people from varying cultural backgrounds and participatory roles is important to providing effective, efficient, and innovative solutions for school consultation in multicultural settings. Larson (1998) provides a compelling portrayal of how internal tensions in one's perspective and emotions surrounding issues need to be understood for reframing to be meaningful. This involved use of a life metaphor, the embrace of paradox, to help manage the internal conflicts of mothers parenting children with disabilities (e.g., loving one's children as they are versus wanting to erase the disability, dealing with incurability while seeking solutions, maintaining hope in the face of negative information and fear). In this case, reframing needed to incorporate both the internal sense of opposing forces and the contextual factors associated with culture and socioeconomics (the mothers were of Mexican origin living at or near poverty-level conditions).

MODEL CASE FOR REFRAMING

The model case of the Kim family (p. 352) illustrates the process of the reframing intervention. In it, the helper reframes the respective roles of a mother and her son in relationship

contexts. Notice how the reframes are grounded in the family's cultural values. The helper considers Asian American family ties in reframing Mrs. Kim's responsibilities as a mother and her son's duties as a son and a parent.

COGNITIVE MODELING WITH COGNITIVE SELF-INSTRUCTIONAL TRAINING

Cognitive modeling is a procedure in which practitioners show clients what to say to themselves while performing a task. Cognitive modeling and self-instructional training have been applied to a variety of client concerns and used with very diverse populations. Box 12.2 (p. 354) presents a list of recent research studies about cognitive modeling and self-instructional training. This listing is intended to provide illustrations: it is by no means complete and does not represent every type of problem for which this strategy can be used.

Applications for persons with various forms of disability have a long history. Applications among ethnic and culturally diverse groups can be difficult to discern because samples can include participants of varying heritages. Hains (1989) reports cognitive modeling with self-guiding verbalizations to teach anger control skills to African American, European American, and Hispanic male juvenile offenders. After training, 75 percent of the participants had an increased use of self-instruction and thinking-ahead statements during both provoking incidents and interpersonal conflicts. Rath (1998), Nagae et al., (1999), and Taylor and O'Reilly (1997) provide international perspectives from

MODEL EXAMPLE: THE KIM FAMILY*

Some months ago the local hospital asked the author to help with an elderly Korean lady who was about to be discharged. It appeared that the lady was very likeable and a good patient. She loved to be pampered by the staff, which concerned them because she appeared to be settling in for a long hospital stay. She was generally reluctant to use her weekend pass to go home, preferring to stay at the hospital and acting as if she were going to be there forever. She was becoming dependent on the staff and asking for more medication and care than she needed.

The hospitalization of 67-year-old Mrs. Kim had been precipitated by her attempted suicide (by cutting her throat with a butcher knife). She had been in the hospital for about a month, and her wound was healing nicely, a fact which the patient tended to minimize. The initially positive relationship between the patient and the staff appeared to be souring. Puzzled and frustrated by the lack of progress, the staff called the author, saying that there seemed to be a "family problem."

The staff had been encouraging Mrs. Kim to be independent and not to lean on her oldest son but to rely more on her husband. To their dismay, the husband seldom visited, but the oldest son came to see her every day even though he had a grueling schedule going to school, working full time, and raising two children as a single parent. They said they had talked to both mother and son to no avail and were getting somewhat frustrated with the dependent posture she was taking with her son.

The author decided that a joint session would be unproductive since mediated negotiation is often more productive than confrontation in working with Asian-American families. The therapeutic task for this family was two-fold: to find a way to help Mrs. Kim get back to live with her husband without losing face and to help her son find a way to get back to being a responsible father and a loyal son without "killing himself" in the process.

The separate interviews with the mother and son revealed the following. The son, the oldest of three sons, had come to this country about 12 years ago to seek honor for the family by earning a college degree and getting an important job. Instead, he fell in love with an American woman, married, had two children, and had to drop out of school in order to support the family. Only recently had he resumed his pursuit of his education part-time. The marriage had ended in divorce, and he had custody of the children. In order to show responsibility to his family, he had managed to bring his two younger brothers and his aging parents to the U.S. However unhappy and difficult their lives were here, none of the Kim family was in a position to return to Korea since the shame of failure in this country would be intolerable to face.

When the parents first came to this country a couple of years ago, they had moved in with the son and his children.

It appears that the grandchildren were not properly respectful to their grandparents; they were noisy, expressed their opinions freely, and did not appreciate the cultural heritage or customs, at times making rude remarks about the "old world" ways of the grandparents. They complained loudly to their father about their grandparents' "unreasonable" expectations, strange food, and strange way of doing things. In order to make things easier for everyone, the son made arrangements for his parents to move into a housing project for the elderly.

In order to pay deference to her status and age, the author met with Mrs. Kim alone first. Using the authority and status of a consultant brought in by the hospital, the author talked to her about how impressed she was with her dutiful son and what a fine job she had done raising such a bright, responsible son. The therapist and Mrs. Kim talked about her family and how much she must be suffering in a strange land so far away from home. The therapist commiserated with her about the young people nowadays, particularly those children who were born and raised in American ways, about how selfish they were and so on. This was designed to align the author with Mrs. Kim and to lay the groundwork for reframing her suicide attempt as a selfless sacrifice. In order to do so, the author joined with Mrs. Kim in her view of the situation she had tried to leave.

Mrs. Kim was reluctant to talk at first, but she gradually warmed up. By the second visit with her in the hospital, she was more willing to open up and talk about her sense of failure as a mother and humiliation at being pushed out of her son's home by the grandchildren. Seizing on this opportunity of her willingness to talk about the circumstances, the author reframed the son's behavior as an expression of his misguided but well-intentioned sense of responsibility toward his own children, which the author was sure that the mother had instilled in him. It was pointed out that no mother would want to see her son fail as a parent since that would surely mean that she had failed as a mother. Besides, had she succeeded in her suicide attempt, she would have left her son to fail permanently in his children's eyes, and she certainly cared about her son more than that. On the other hand, the author told her how impressed she was that she took her duty as a mother seriously enough to want to end her life.

The therapist reminded her that—as she well knew already—young people not only have a responsibility toward parents but we, as the older generation, have a duty to protect and encourage our children to succeed. The therapist added that this duty included being happy with our spouse so that we free our children from worrying about us. It is our responsibility to give our children all the chances they need to succeed. Mrs. Kim agreed and thanked me for coming.

Mrs. Kim's view was supported and reframed as her attempt to fulfill her cultural role as an elder of the family. Moreover,

---

THE KIM FAMILY*

her return to her husband was depicted as important and vital—a necessity for her son as he carried out the family honor in raising his children.

When talking with the son, the author complimented him on being a dutiful son and doing so much for his parents and his younger brothers. The author suggested that he must have been taught well by his mother since he was not only dutiful to his parents and to his brothers but also responsible to his children. Since a failure to take care of his children would indeed be a dishonor to his parents, he was urged to continue to work hard in order to help his own children to succeed. His world view was supported by the therapist and viewed as necessary.

Mrs. Kim was discharged to her husband's care soon after this session. A 1-year follow-up indicated that she was doing well and that there had been no recurrence of the depression.

The two interventions are interwoven and clearly address the norm of close-knit family ties often found in Asian-American families. Techniques of reframing in relationship contexts were used to respect the world view presented by each client. The tasks implied and suggested were designed to respect the client's view and failed attempts to solve the problem.

*Reprinted: From "Different and Same: Family Therapy with Asian-American Families," by I. K. Berg and A. Jaya. Reprinted from Volume 19, pp. 36–38, of the *Journal of Marital and Family Therapy.* Copyright © 1993 by the American Association for Marriage and Family Therapy. Reprinted with permission.

---

research in India, Japan, and Ireland on the utility of self-instructional training with reading-disabled children, for shyness, and acquiring shopping skills among persons with mild intellectual disabilities.

Cognitive modeling with a self-instructional training strategy is a five-steps process:

1. The helper serves as the model (or a symbolic model can be used) and first performs the task while talking aloud to himself or herself.
2. The client performs the same task (as modeled by the helper) while the helper instructs the client aloud.
3. The client is instructed to perform the same task again while instructing himself or herself aloud.
4. The client whispers the instructions while performing the task.
5. The client performs the task while instructing himself or herself covertly.

Cognitive modeling is reflected in step 1, whereas in steps 2–5, the client practices self-verbalizations while performing a task or behavior. The client's verbalizations are faded from an overt to a covert level.

We focus on seven components of cognitive modeling and self-instructional training:

Helper Groundwork

1. Treatment rationale
2. Cognitive modeling of the task and of the self-verbalizations

Client Practice:

3. Overt external guidance
4. Overt self-guidance
5. Faded overt self-guidance

6. Covert self-guidance
7. Homework and follow-up

We explain each of these in the rest of this section. Illustrations are also provided in the Interview Checklist for Cognitive Modeling on page 375.

Treatment Rationale

Here is an example of the practitioner's rationale for cognitive modeling:

It has been found that some people have difficulty in performing certain kinds of tasks. Often the difficulty is not because they don't have the ability to do it but because of what they say or think to themselves while doing it. In other words, a person's "self-talk" can get in the way or interfere with performance. For instance, if you get up to give a speech and you're thinking "What a flop I'll be," this sort of thought may affect how you deliver your talk. This procedure can help you perform something the way you want to by examining and coming up with some helpful planning or self-talk to use while performing [rationale]. I'll show what I am saying to myself while performing the task. Then I'll ask you to do the task while I guide or direct you through it. Next, you will do the task again and guide yourself aloud while doing it. The end result should be your performing the task while thinking and planning about the task to yourself [overview]. How does this sound to you [client willingness]?

After the rationale has been presented and any questions have been clarified, the helper begins by presenting the cognitive model.

Model of Task and Self-Guidance

First, the helper instructs the client to listen to what the helper says to herself or himself while performing the task. Next, the helper models performing a task while talking aloud:

BOX 12.2	COGNITIVE MODELING AND SELF-INSTRUCTIONAL TRAINING RESEARCH

Decision Making

Johnson, J. G. (2006). Cognitive modeling of decision making in sports. *Psychology of Sport and Exercise, 7*(6), 631–652.

Developmental Disabilities

Grote, I., & Baer, D. M. (2000). Teaching compliance with experimentally managed self-instructions can accomplish reversal shift. *Journal of Developmental and Physical Disabilities, 12*(3), 217–233.

Learning Disability

Johnson, L. A., Graham, S., & Harris, K. R. (1997). The effects of goal setting and self-instruction on learning a reading comprehension strategy: A study of students with learning disabilities. *Journal of Learning Disabilities, 30,* 80–91.

Levels of Cognitive Modeling

Sun, R., Coward, L. A., & Zenzen, M. J. (2005). On levels of cognitive modeling. *Philosophical Psychology, 18*(5), 613–637.

Multitasking

Kushleyeva, Y., Salvucci, D. D., Lee, F. J., & Schunn, C. (2005). Deciding when to switch tasks in time-critical multitasking. *Cognitive Systems Research, 6*(1), 41–49.

Obsessive–Compulsive Disorder

Fields, L. (1998). An integrative brief treatment approach for obsessive–compulsive disorder. *Journal of Psychotherapy Integration, 8*(3), 161–172.

Problem Solving

Gorrell, J. (1993). Cognitive modeling and implicit rules: Effects on problem-solving performance. *American Journal of Psychology, 106,* 51–65.

Self-Efficacy

Schwartz, L. S., & Gredler, M. E. (1998). The effects of self-instructional materials on goal-setting and self-efficacy. *Journal of Research and Development in Education, 31*(2), 83–89.

Shyness

Nagae, N., Nadate, L., & Sekiguchi, Y. (1999). Self-instructional training for shyness: Differences in improvements produced by different types of coping self-statements. *Japanese Journal of Counseling Science, 32,* 32–42.

Stress

Cary, M., & Dua, J. (1999). Cognitive–behavioral and systematic desensitization procedures in reducing stress and anger in caregivers for the disabled. *International Journal of Stress Management, 6*(2), 75–87.

Stroke Rehabilitation

Wenman, R., Bowen, A., Tallis, R. C., Gardener, E., Cross, S., & Niven, D. (2003). Use of a randomised single case experimental design to evaluate therapy for unilateral neglect. *Neuropsychological Rehabilitation, 13*(4), 441–459.

Teaching

Tao, X., Chongde, L., & Jiliang, S. (1999). Effect of cognitive self-instruction training on the improvement of teachers' teaching-regulated ability. *Psychological Science, 22,* 5–9.

Training and Supervision

Nutt-Williams, E., & Hill, C. E. (1996). The relationship between self-talk and therapy process variables for novice therapists. *Journal of Counseling Psychology, 43,* 170–177.

Helper's Modeled Self-Guidance

1. Poses a question about the task: "Okay, what is it I have to do?"
2. Answers the question about what to do: "You want me to copy the picture with different lines."
3. Self-guidance and focused attention: "I have to go slow and be careful. Okay, draw the line down, down, good; then to the right, that's it; now down some more and to the left."
4. Self-reinforcement: "Good. Even if I make an error I can go on slowly and carefully. Okay, I have to go down now. . . . Finished. I did it."
5. Coping self-evaluative statements with error correction options: "Now back up again. No, I was supposed to go down. That's okay. Just erase the line carefully."

As this example indicates, the helper's modeled self-guidance consists of five parts. The first part of the verbalization asks a question about the nature and demands of the task to be performed. The purposes of the question are to compensate for a possible deficiency in comprehending what to do, to provide a general orientation, and to create a cognitive set. The second part of the modeled verbalization answers the question about what to do. The answer is designed to model cognitive rehearsal and planning to focus the client's attention on relevant task requirements. Self-instruction in the form of self-guidance while performing the task is the third part of the modeled verbalization. The purpose of self-guidance is to concentrate attention on the task and to inhibit any possible overt or covert distractions or task irrelevancies. In the

---

LEARNING ACTIVITY **12.2** | Modeled Self-Guidance

The following helper verbalization is a cognitive model for a rehabilitation client with a physical challenge who is learning how to use a wheelchair. Identify the five parts of the message: (1) a question about what to do, (2) answers to the question in the form of planning, (3) self-guidance and focused attention, (4) coping self-evaluative statements, and (5) self-reinforcement. Feedback for this activity follows on page 357.

"What do I have to do to get from the parking lot, over the curb, onto the sidewalk, and then to the building?

I have to wheel my chair from the car to the curb, get over the curb and onto the sidewalk, and then wheel over to the building entrance. Okay, wheeling the chair over to the curb is no problem. I have to be careful now that I am at the curb. Okay, now I've just got to get my front wheels up first. They're up now. So now I'll pull up hard to get my back wheels up. Whoops, didn't quite make it. No big deal—I'll just pull up very hard again. Good. That's better, I've got my chair on the sidewalk now. I did it! I've got it made now."

---

example, modeled self-reinforcement is the fourth part and is designed to maintain task perseverance and to reinforce success. The last part in the modeled verbalization contains coping self-statements to handle errors and frustration, with an option for correcting errors. The example of the modeled verbalization used by Meichenbaum and Goodman (1971) depicts a coping model. In other words, the model does make an error in performance but corrects it and does not give up at that point. See whether you can identify these five parts of modeled self-guidance in Learning Activity 12.2.

Overt External Guidance

After the helper models the verbalizations, the client is instructed to perform the task (as modeled by the helper) while the helper instructs or coaches. The helper coaches the client through the task or activity, substituting the personal pronoun *you* for *I* (for example, "What is it that *you* . . .; *you* have to wheel your chair . . .; *you* have to be careful"). The helper should make sure that the coaching contains the same five parts of self-guidance that were previously modeled: question, planning, focused attention, coping self-evaluation, and self-reinforcement. Sometimes in the client's real-life situation, other people may be watching when the client performs the task—as could be the case whenever the client in a wheelchair appears in public. If the presence of other people appears to interfere with the client's performance, the helper might say, "Those people may be distracting you. Just pay attention to what you are doing." This type of coping statement can be included in the helper's verbalizations of overt external guidance in order to make this part of the procedure resemble what the client will actually encounter.

Overt Self-Guidance

The practitioner next instructs the client to perform the task while instructing or guiding himself or herself aloud. The purpose of this step is to have the client practice the kind of self-talk that will strengthen his or her attention to the demands of the

task and will minimize outside distractions. The practitioner should attend carefully to the content of the client's self-verbalizations. Again, as in the two preceding steps, these verbalizations should include the five component parts, and the client should be encouraged to use his or her own words. If the client's self-guidance is incomplete or if the client gets stuck, the practitioner can intervene and coach. If necessary, the practitioner can return to the previous steps—either modeling again or coaching the client while the client performs the task (overt external guidance). After the client completes this step, the practitioner should provide feedback about parts of the practice that the client completed adequately and about any errors or omissions. Another practice might be necessary before moving on to the next step: faded overt self-guidance.

Faded Overt Self-Guidance

The client next performs the task while whispering (lip movements). This part of cognitive modeling serves as an intermediate step between having the client verbalize aloud, as in overt self-guidance, and having the client verbalize silently, as in the next step, covert self-guidance. In other words, whispering the self-guidance is a way for the client to approximate successively the result of the procedure: thinking the self-guidance steps while performing them. In our own experience with this step, we have found that it is necessary to explain this rationale to an occasional client who seems hesitant or concerned about whispering. A client who finds the whispering to be too awkward, might prefer to repeat overt self-guidance several times and finally move directly to covert self-guidance. If the client has difficulty performing this step or leaves out any of the five parts, additional practice may be required before moving on.

Covert Self-Guidance

Finally, clients perform the task while guiding or instructing themselves covertly, or "in their heads." It is very important for clients to instruct themselves covertly after practicing the self-instructions overtly. After the client does this, the practitioner might ask for a description of the covert self-instructions. If distracting or inhibiting self-talk has occurred, the helper can offer suggestions for more appropriate verbalizations or self-talk and can initiate additional practice. Otherwise, the client is ready to use the procedure outside the session.

Homework and Follow-up

Assigning the client homework is essential for generalization from the interview to the client's environment to occur. The helper should instruct the client to use the covert verbalizations while performing the desired behaviors alone, outside the helping session. The homework assignment should specify what the client will do, how much or how often, and when and where. The helper should also provide a way for the client to monitor and reward himself or herself for completion of homework. The helper should also schedule follow-up on the homework task.

These seven components of cognitive modeling are modeled for you in the following dialogue with our client Isabella. Again, this strategy is used as one way to help Isabella achieve her goal of increasing her verbal participation in math class.

MODEL DIALOGUE FOR COGNITIVE MODELING WITH COGNITIVE SELF-INSTRUCTIONAL TRAINING: THE CASE OF ISABELLA

In response 1, the helper introduces the possible use of cognitive modeling to help Isabella achieve the goal of increasing initiating skills in her math class. The helper is giving a *rationale* about the strategy.

1. **Helper:** One of the goals we developed was to help you increase your participation level in your math class. One of the ways we might help you do that is to use a procedure in which I demonstrate the kinds of things you want to do—and also I will demonstrate a way to think or talk to yourself about these tasks. So this procedure will help you develop a plan for carrying out these tasks, as well as showing you a way to participate. How does that sound?

Client: Okay. Is it hard to do?

In response 2, the helper provides an *overview* of the procedure, which is also a part of the rationale.

2. **Helper:** No, not really, because I'll go through it before you do. And I'll sort of guide you along. The procedure involves my showing you a participation method, and while I'm doing that, I'm going to talk out loud to myself to sort of guide myself. Then you'll do that. Gradually, we'll go over the same participation method until you do it on your own and can think to yourself how to do it. We'll take one step at a time. Does that seem clear to you?

Client: Pretty much. I've never done anything like this, though.

In response 3, the helper determines *Isabella's willingness* to try out the procedure.

3. **Helper:** Would you like to give it a try?

Client: Sure.

In responses 4 and 5, the helper sets the stage for modeling of the task and accompanying self-guidance and *instructs the client in what will be done* and what to look for in this step.

4. **Helper:** We mentioned there were at least four things you could do to increase your initiating skills: asking Mr. Lamborne for an explanation only, answering more of Mr. Lamborne's questions, going to the board to do problems, and volunteering answers.

   Let's just pick one of these to start with. Which one would you like to work with first?

Client: Going to the board to work algebra problems. If I make a mistake there, it's visible to all the class.

5. **Helper:** Probably you're a little nervous when you do go to the board. This procedure will help you concentrate more on the task than on yourself. Now, in the first step, I'm going to pretend I'm going to the board. As I move out of my chair and up to the board, I'm going to tell you what I'm thinking that might help me do the problems. Just listen carefully to what I say, because I'm going to ask you to do the same type of thing afterward. Any questions?

Client: No, I'm just waiting to see how you handle this. I'll look like Mr. Lamborne. His glasses are always down on his nose, and he stares right at you. It's unnerving.

In responses 6 and 7, the helper *initiates and demonstrates* the task with accompanying *self-guidance*. Notice, in the modeled part of response 7, the *five components of the self-guidance process*. Also notice that a simple problem has been chosen for illustration.

6. **Helper:** You do that. That will help set the scene. Why don't you start by calling on me to go to the board?

Client (as teacher): Isabella, go to the board now and work this problem.

7. **Helper** (gets out of seat, moves to imaginary board on the wall, picks up the chalk, verbalizing aloud): What is it I need to do? He wants me to find *y*. Okay, I need to just go slowly, be careful, and take my time. The problem here reads $4x$ plus y equals 10, and x is 2.8. I can

12.2 ### F E E D B A C K
Modeled Self-Guidance

Question

"What do I have to do to get from the parking lot, over the curb, onto the sidewalk, and then to the building?"

Answers with Planning

"I have to wheel my chair from the car to the curb, get onto the curb and onto the sidewalk, and then wheel over to the building entrance."

Self-Guidance and Focused Attention

"Okay, wheeling the chair over to the curb is no problem. I have to be careful now that I am at the curb. Okay, now I've just got to get my front wheels up first. They're up now. So now I'll pull up hard to get my back wheels up."

Coping Self-Evaluation and Error-Correction Option

"Whoops, didn't quite make it. No big deal—I'll just pull up very hard again."

Self-Reinforcement

"Good. That's better; I've got my chair on the sidewalk now. I did it! I've got it made now."

---

use x to find y. [Helper asks *question* about task.] I'm doing fine so far. Just remember to go slowly. Okay, y has to be 10 minus $4x$. If x is 2.8, then y will be 10 minus 4 multiplied by 2.8. [Helper focuses *attention* and uses *self-guidance*.] Let's see, 4 times 2.8 is 10.2. Oops, is this right? I hear someone laughing. Just keep on going. Let me refigure it. No, it's 11.2. Just erase 10.2 and put in y equals 10 minus 11.2. Okay, good. If I keep on going slowly, I can catch any error and redo it. [Helper uses *coping self-evaluation* and makes *error correction*.] Now it's simple: 10 minus 11.2 is −1.2, and y is −1.2. Good, I did it, I'm done now, and I can go back to my seat. [Helper *reinforces self.*]

In responses 8 and 9, the helper initiates *overt external guidance*. The client performs the task while the helper continues to verbalize aloud the self-guidance, substituting *you* for I as used in the previous sequence.

8. **Helper:** That's it. Now let's reverse roles. This time I'd like you to get up out of your seat, go to the board, and work through the problem. I will coach you about what to plan during the process. Okay?

Client: Do I say anything?

9. **Helper:** Not this time. You just concentrate on carrying out the task and thinking about the planning I give you. In other words, I'm just going to talk you through this the first time.

Client: Okay, I see.

In response 10, the helper *verbalizes self-guidance while the client performs the problem.*

10. **Helper:** I'll be Mr. Lamborne. I'll ask you to go to the board, and then you go and I'll start coaching you. (As teacher.) Isabella, I want you to go to the board now and work out this problem: If $2x$ plus y equals 8 and x equals 2, what does y equal? [Isabella gets up from chair, walks to imaginary board, and picks up chalk.] Okay, first you write the problem on the board: $2x$ plus y equals 8, and x equals 2. Now ask yourself, "What do I have to do with this problem?" Now answer yourself [question].

You need to find the value of y [answer to question]. Just go slowly, be careful, and concentrate on what you're doing. You know x equals 2, so you can use x to find y. Your first step is to subtract: 8 minus $2x$. You've got that up there. You're doing fine—just keep going slowly [focuses attention and uses self-guidance].

Eight minus the quantity 2 multiplied by 2, you know, is 8 minus 4. Someone is laughing at you. But you're doing fine; just keep thinking about what you're doing. Eight minus 4 is 4, so y equals 4 [coping self-evaluation]. Now you've got y. That's great. You did it. Now you can go back to your seat [self-reinforcement].

In response 11, the helper *assesses the client's reaction* before moving on to the next step.

11. **Helper:** Let's stop. How did you feel about that?

Client: Well, it's such a new thing for me. I can see how it can help. See, usually when I go up to the board I don't think about the problem. I'm usually thinking about feeling nervous or about Mr. Lamborne or the other kids watching me.

In response 12, the helper reiterates the *rationale* for the cognitive modeling procedure.

12. **Helper:** Yes, those kinds of thoughts distract you from concentrating on your math problems. That's why this kind of practice may help. It gives you a chance to work on concentrating on what you want to do.

Client: I can see that.

In responses 13 and 14, the helper instructs the client to perform the task while verbalizing to herself (*overt self-guidance*).

13. **Helper:** This time I'd like you to go through what we just did—only on your own. In other words, you should get up, go to the board, work out the math problem, and as you're doing that, plan what you're going to do and how you're going to do it. Tell yourself to take your time, concentrate on seeing what you're doing, and give yourself a pat on the back when you're done. How does that sound?

Client: I'm just going to say something similar to what you said the last time—is that it?

14. **Helper:** That's it. You don't have to use the same words. Just try to plan what you're doing. If you get stuck, I'll step in and give you a cue. Remember, you start by asking yourself what you're going to do in this situation and then answering yourself. This time let's take the problem $5x$ plus y equals 10. With x equaling 2.5, solve for y.

Client (gets out of seat, goes to board, writes problem): What do I need to do? I need to solve for y. I know x equals 2.5. Just think about this problem. My first step is to subtract: 10 minus $5x$. Five multiplied by 2.5 is 12.5. So I'll subtract: 10 minus 12.5. [Helper laughs; Isabella turns around.] Is that wrong?

15. **Helper:** Check yourself but stay focused on the problem, not on my laughter.

Client: Well, 10 minus 12.5 is -2.5, so y equals -2.5. Let's see if that's right: 5 times 2.5 equals 12.5 minus 2.5 equals 10. I've got it. Yeah.

In response 15, the helper *gives feedback* to Isabella about her practice.

16. **Helper:** That was really great. You only stumbled one time—when I laughed. I did that to see whether you would still concentrate. But after that, you went right back to your work and finished the problem. It seemed pretty easy for you to do this. How did you feel?

Client: It really was easier than I thought. I was surprised when you laughed. But then, like you said, I just tried to keep going.

In responses 16–18, the helper instructs Isabella on how to *perform the problem while whispering instructions* to herself (*faded overt self-guidance).*

17. **Helper:** This time we'll do another practice. It will be just like you did the last time, with one change. Instead of talking out your plan aloud, I just want you to whisper it. Now you probably aren't used to whispering to yourself, so it might be a little awkward at first.

Client (laughs): Whispering to myself? That seems sort of funny.

18. **Helper:** I can see how it does. But it is just another step in helping you practice this to the point where it becomes a part of you—something you can do naturally and easily.

Client: Well, I guess I can see that.

19. **Helper:** Let's try it. This time let's take a problem with more decimals, since you get those too. If it seems harder, just take more time to think and go slowly. Let's take $10.5x$ plus y equals 25, with x equaling 5.5.

Client (gets out of seat, goes to board, writes on board, whispers): What do I need to do with this problem? I need to find y. This has more decimals, so I'm just going to go slowly. Let's see, 25 minus $10.5x$ is what I do first. I need to multiply 10.5 by 5.5. I think it's 52.75. [Helper laughs.] Let's see, just think about what I'm doing. I'll redo it. No, it's 57.75. Is that right? I'd better check it again. Yes, it's Okay. Keep going. 25 minus 57.75 is equal to -32.75, so y equals -32.75. I can check it. Yes, 10.5 times 5.5 is 57.75 minus 32.75 equals 25. I got it!

Helper *gives feedback* in response 19.

20. **Helper:** That was great, Isabella—very smooth. When I laughed, you just redid your arithmetic rather than turning around or letting your thoughts wander off the problem.

Client: It seems like it gets a little easier each time. Actually, this is a good way to practice math too.

In responses 20 and 21, the helper gives Isabella instructions on how to *perform the problem while instructing herself covertly (covert self-guidance).*

21. **Helper:** That's right—not only for what we do in here, but even when you do your math homework. Now, let's just go through one more practice today. You're really doing this very well. This time I'd like you to do the same thing as before—only this time I'd like you to just think about the problem. In other words, instead of talking out these instructions, just go over them mentally. Is that clear?

Client: You just want me to think to myself what I've been saying?

22. **Helper:** Yes—just instruct yourself in your head. Let's take the problem $12x$ minus y equals 36, with x equaling 4. Solve for y. [Isabella gets up, goes to the board, and takes several minutes to work through this.]

LEARNING ACTIVITY	**12.3**	**Cognitive Modeling with Cognitive Self-Instructional Training**

Ms. Weare wants to eliminate the assistance she gave her son Freddie in getting ready for school in the morning. One of Ms. Weare's concerns is to find a successful way to instruct Freddie about the new ground rules—mainly that she will not help him get dressed and will not remind him when the bus is five minutes away. Ms. Weare is afraid that after she tells Freddie, he will either pout or talk back to her. She is concerned that she will not be able to follow through with her plan or will not be firm in the way she delivers the rules to her son.

First, describe how you would use the seven components of cognitive modeling and self-instructional training to help Ms. Weare. Then write out an example of a cognitive modeling dialogue that Ms. Weare could use to accomplish this task. Make sure that this dialogue contains the five necessary parts of the self-guidance process: question, answer, focused attention, self-evaluation, and self-reinforcement. Feedback follows.

In response 22, the helper *asks the client to describe what happened during covert self-guidance practice.*

23. **Helper:** Can you tell me what you thought about while you did that?

Client: I thought about what I had to do, then what my first step in solving the problem would be. Then I just went through each step of the problem, and after I checked it, I thought I was right.

In response 23, the helper *checks to see whether another practice is needed* or whether they can move on to homework.

24. **Helper:** So it seemed pretty easy. That is what we want you to be able to do in class—to instruct yourself mentally like this while you're working at the board. Would you like to go through this type of practice one more time, or would you rather do this on your own during the week?

Client: I think on my own would help right now.

In response 24, the helper sets up Isabella's *homework assignment* for the following week.

25. **Helper:** I think it would be helpful if you could do this type of practice on your own this week—where you instruct yourself as you work through math problems.

Client: You mean my math homework?

In response 25, the helper *instructs Isabella on how to do homework,* including what to do, where, and how much.

26. **Helper:** That would be a good way to start. Perhaps you could take seven problems a day. As you work through each problem, go through these self-instructions mentally. (Do this at home.) Does that seem clear?

Client: Yes, I'll just work out seven problems a day the way we did here for the last practice.

In response 26, the helper instructs Isabella *to observe her homework completion* on log sheets and *arranges for a follow-up* of homework at their next session.

27. **Helper:** Right. One more thing. On these blank log sheets, keep a tally of the number of times you actually do this type of practice on math problems during the day. This will help you keep track of your practice. And then next week bring your log sheets with you, and we can go over your homework.

Now that you've seen an example, try the exercise in Learning Activity 12.3 applying cognitive modeling.

PROBLEM-SOLVING THERAPY

Problem-solving therapy or problem-solving training emerged in the late 1960s and early 1970s as a trend in the development of intervention and prevention strategies for enhancing competence in specific situations. D'Zurilla (1988) defines problem solving as a "cognitive–affective–behavioral process through which an individual (or group) attempts to identify, discover, or invent effective means of coping with problems encountered in every day living" (p. 86). Rose and LeCroy (1991) describe problem solving as a strategy whereby "the client learns to systematically work through a set of steps for analyzing a problem, discovering new approaches, evaluating those approaches, and developing strategies for implementing those approaches in the real world" (p. 439). Problem-solving therapy or training has been used with children, adolescents, adults, and elders as a treatment strategy, a treatment-maintenance strategy, or a prevention strategy. As a treatment strategy, problem solving has been used alone or in conjunction with other treatment strategies presented in this book.

The list in Box 12.3 shows a range of recently reported research involving problem-solving therapy used for many purposes.

FEEDBACK 12.3
Cognitive Modeling with Cognitive Self-Instructional Training

Description of the Seven Components

1. *Treatment rationale:* First, you would explain to Ms. Weare how cognitive modeling could help her in instructing Freddie and what the procedure would involve. You might emphasize that the procedure would be helpful to her in both prior planning and practice.

2. *Model of task and self-guidance:* You would model a way for Ms. Weare to talk to Freddie. You need to make sure that you use language that is relevant and acceptable to Ms. Weare. Your modeling would include both the task (what Ms. Weare could say to Freddie) and the five parts of the self-guidance process.

3. *Overt external guidance:* Ms. Weare would practice giving her instructions to Freddie while you coach her on the self-guidance process.

4. *Overt self-guidance:* Ms. Weare would perform the instructions while verbalizing aloud the five parts of the self-guidance process. If she gets stuck or if she leaves out any of the five parts, you can cue her. This step may need to be repeated.

5. *Faded overt self-guidance:* Assuming that Ms. Weare is willing to complete this step, she would perform the instructions to give Freddie while whispering the self-guidance to herself.

6. *Covert self-guidance:* Ms. Weare would practice giving the instructions to Freddie while covertly guiding herself. When she is able to do this comfortably, you would assign homework.

7. *Homework:* You would assign homework by asking Ms. Weare to practice the covert self-guidance daily and arranging for a follow-up after some portion had been completed.

Example of a Model Dialogue

"Okay, what is it I want to do in this situation [question]? I want to tell Freddie that he is to get up and dress himself without my help, that I will no longer come up and help him even when it's time for the bus to come [answer]. Okay, just remember to take a deep breath and talk firmly and slowly. Look at Freddie. Say, 'Freddie, I am not going to help you in the morning. I've got my own work to do. If you want to get to school on time, you'll need to decide to get yourself ready' [focused attention and self-guidance]. Now, if he gives me flak, just stay calm and firm. I won't back down [coping self-evaluation]. That should be fine. I can handle it" [self-reinforcement].

Problem-solving therapy or training has been used with a wide range of issues across multiple disciplines (Chang, D'Zurilla, & Sanna, 2004, provide a useful overview). It has been found useful across diverse groups and is explicitly collaborative in nature. Although the emphasis is on individuals (or groups or families), we see problem-solving training as a potentially valuable tool for supporting critical thinking and locating persons within their environments. The stresses of a problematic situation may stem to a greater or lesser degree from the environment (e.g., requirements, resource insufficiency, oppression) or from the person (e.g., personal goals, patterns, limitations). Problem-solving treatment tends to adopt a transactional view of problems in living as stemming from the nature of the person–environment relationship (e.g., imbalances and discrepancies). The same

---

BOX 12.3   PROBLEM-SOLVING RESEARCH

Aggression and Anger

D' Zurilla, T., Chang, E. C., & Sanna, L. J. (2003). Self-esteem and social problem solving as predictors of aggression in college students. *Journal of Social and Clinical Psychology, 22*(4), 424–440.

MacMahon, K. M. A., Jahoda, A., Espie, C. A., & Broomfield, N. M. (2006). The influence of anger-arousal level on attribution of hostile intent and problem solving capability in an individual with a mild intellectual disability and a history of difficulties with aggression. *Journal of Applied Research in Intellectual Disabilities, 19*(1), 99–107.

Sukhodolsky, D. G., Golub, A., Stone, E. C., & Orban, L. (2005). Dismantling anger control training for children: A randomized pilot study of social problem-solving versus social skills training components. *Behavior Therapy, 36*(1), 15–23.

Behavior Problems

Hemphill, S. A., & Littlefield, L. (2006). Child and family predictors of therapy outcome for children with behavioral and emotional problems. *Child Psychiatry and Human Development, 36*(3), 329–349.

Cancer

Nezu, A. M., Nezu, C. M., Houts, P. S., Friedman, S. H., & Faddis, S. (1999). Relevance of problem-solving therapy to psychosocial oncology. *Journal of Psychosocial Oncology, 16*(3–4), 5–6.

BOX 12.3   PROBLEM-SOLVING RESEARCH

Varni, J. W., Sahler, O. J., Katz, E. R., Mulhern, R. K., Copeland, D. R., Noll, R. B., et al. (1999). Maternal problem-solving therapy in pediatric cancer. *Journal of Psychosocial Oncology, 16*(3–4), 41–71.

Children

Steiner, H. H., & Carr, M. (2006). The development of problem solving strategies in gifted and average-ability children: Bringing research from cognitive development to educational practice. In A. V., Mittel (Ed.), *Focus on educational psychology* (pp. 235–250). Hauppauge, NY: Nova Science.

Couples and Parenting

Ronan, G. F., Dreer, L. E., Dollard, K. M., & Ronan, D. W. (2004). Violent couples: Coping and communication skills. *Journal of Family Violence, 19*(2), 131–137.

Stern, S. B. (1999). Anger management in parent-adolescent conflict. *American Journal of Family Therapy, 27,* 181–197.

Health

Cudney, S., Sullivan, T., Winters, C. A., Paul, L., & Oriet, P. (2005). Chronically ill rural women: Self-identified management problems and solutions. *Chronic Illness, 1*(1), 49–60.

Learning and Behavior Problems

Daunic, A. P., Smith, S. W., Brank, E. M., & Penfield, R. D. (2006). Classroom-based cognitive–behavioral intervention to prevent aggression: Efficacy and social validity. *Journal of School Psychology, 44*(2), 123–139.

Robinson, T. R., Smith, S. W., & Miller, M. D. (2002). Effect of a cognitive–behavioral intervention on responses to anger by middle school students with chronic behavior problems. *Behavioral Disorders, 27*(3), 256–271.

Mental Illness and Disability

Marshall, R. C., McGurk, S. R., Karow, C. M., Kairy, T. J., & Flashman, L. A. (2006). Performance of subjects with and without severe mental illness on a clinical test of problem solving. *Schizophrenia Research, 84*(2–3), 331–344.

Kern, R. S., Green, M. F., Mitchell, S., Kopelowicz, A., Mintz, J., & Liberman, R. P. (2005). Extensions of errorless learning for social problem-solving deficits in schizophrenia. *American Journal of Psychiatry, 162*(3), 513–519.

Meta-analytic Review

Thornton, W. J. L., & Dumke, H. A. (2005). Age differences in everyday problem-solving and decision-making effec-

tiveness: A meta-analytic review. *Psychology and Aging, 20*(1), 85–99.

Offenders

Bourke, M. L., & Van Hasselt, V. B. (2001). Social problem-solving skills training for incarcerated offenders: A treatment manual. *Behavior Modification, 25*(2), 163–188.

Older Adults

Blanchard-Fields, F., Stein, R., & Watson, T. L. (2004). Age differences in emotion-regulation strategies in handling everyday problems. *Journals of Gerontology: Series B: Psychological Sciences and Social Sciences, 59B*(6), 261–269.

Burton, C. L., Strauss, E., Hultsch, D. F., & Hunter, M. A. (2006). Cognitive functioning and everyday problem solving in older adults. *Clinical Neuropsychologist, 20*(3), 432–452.

Viskontas, I. V., Holyoak, K. J., & Knowlton, B. J. (2005). Relational integration in older adults. *Thinking and Reasoning, 11*(4), 390–410.

Palliative Care

Wood, B. C., & Mynors-Wallis, L. M. (1997). Problem-solving therapy in palliative care. *Palliative Medicine, 11,* 49–54.

Personality Disorders

McMurran, M., Duggan, C., Christopher, G., & Huband, N. (2007). The relationships between personality disorders and social problem solving in adults. *Personality and Individual Differences, 42*(1), 145–155.

Self-Harm

Hawton, K., Kingsburt, S., Steinhardt, K., James, A., & Fagg, J. (1999). Repetition of deliberate self-harm by adolescents: The role of psychological factors. *Journal of Adolescence, 22,* 369–378.

Stress Management

Bond, D. S., Lyle, R. M., Tappe, M. K., Seehafer, R. S., & D'Zurilla, T. J. (2002). Moderate aerobic exercise, T'ai Chi, and social problem-solving ability in relation to psychological stress. *International Journal of Stress Management, 9*(4), 329–343.

Panchanatham, N., Kumarasamy, N., & Vanitha, L. B. (2006). Stress management for problem solving executives with coercieve leadership style. *Journal of the Indian Academy of Applied Psychology, 32*(1), 33–36.

conditions are not inherently problematic for all people, or problems of the same type or level. "Solutions," then, must be situation- or context-specific if they are to be a realistic match for that person in that set of environmental conditions.

Perceptions and attitudes about problem solving can play either a helpful or a disruptive role. If perceptions and attitudes have a helpful role, the client is motivated to learn and engage in problem-solving behaviors. Clients who are unmotivated or avoid dealing with issues because of their perception about them may not want to learn the problem-solving strategy. In these cases, the helper will have to first help the client deal with these perceptions and attitudes. The helper can also help the client engage in some effective coping activities or behaviors that can contribute to the problem-solving process. It may be that intervention to change clients' self-appraisals about the value of problem solving and their ability to undertake problem solving will have benefits complementary to the problem-solving activities themselves. Dixon (2000), for example, found that appraisal of oneself to be an effective problem solver significantly corresponded with recovery from depression.

Many clients prefer to ignore or to avoid a significant issue because they believe it will probably go away by itself. Although some issues may simply dissipate, others will sustain if ignored or avoided. In fact, some may get worse and can become antecedents to greater issues if the client does not solve the initial difficulty. The role of the helper is to help clients take responsibility for solving problems within their means and commit to spending the time and energy needed to solve them by changing the client's attitudes and perceptions about these issues.

A variety of assessment tools have been developed in the area of social problem solving, several attending not only to outcomes but to process (e.g., attitudes, appraisals, skills) as well to help illuminate clients' strengths and gaps as they undertake problem-solving efforts. Chang et al. (2004) provide a useful overview of these assessment tools, including a Problem-Solving Self-Monitoring tool that assists clients in assessing the problem, emotional responses, solution options, and outcomes (D'Zurilla & Nezu, 1999).

APPLICATIONS OF PROBLEM SOLVING WITH DIVERSE CLIENTS

As Box 12.4 illustrates, problem solving has been researched as to its utility with diverse groups of clients in several areas, such as developing educational and academic achievement skills, supporting coping with adversity, conflict management, and managing mental health risks such as depression and suicide. Problem solving also has been incorporated as a component of various prevention programs, including HIV prevention, tobacco use prevention, and violence prevention.

Two studies specifically focused on culturally relevant educational processes and problem solving. Bell, Brown, and Bryant (1993) compared the performance of African American college students on a problem-solving task. Students were given both a traditional, analytic presentation of the task and a culturally relevant, holistic presentation. The students who received the culturally relevant presentation did better on the task than those given the traditional presentation. These authors note the impact of cultural factors on problem solving and also stress the importance for African American students of exposure to models of education that are Afrocentric rather than Eurocentric in nature. Mehan, Hubbard, and Villaneuva (1994) describe a program wherein African American and Latino students who took college preparatory classes were also offered a special elective class emphasizing collaborative instruction, writing, and problem solving. The students who went through the program enrolled in four-year colleges at a level well above the national average. The combination of collaborative support with skill development appeared important to fostering school achievement without compromising ethnic identity.

Other studies have explored nonacademic uses of problem solving. In one of these, Rao and Kramer (1993) interviewed African American mothers of infants with sickle cell anemia and infants with sickle cell trait to explore the coping skills that the mothers used to care for their children. Mothers of both groups reported using social support, positive reappraisal, and planned problem solving most frequently to cope with stressors related to parenting their children. Whitfield, Baker-Thomas, Heyward, Gatto, and Williams (1999) examined a measure of everyday problem solving with a community sample of African Americans and found that the measure achieved satisfactory psychometric support for use. We can also get some initial insights into cultural relevance through research with people of cultures outside the United States, such as Jiang, Sun, and Wu's (1999) findings of reduced problem-solving ability among elderly diabetics in China relative to matched healthy elders. A qualitative study with young African developmental activists in South Africa (Van Vlaenderen, 1999) showed not only the importance of cultural philosophy—in this case, Ubuntu notions of social harmony, holism, pursuit of practice purpose, and primacy of collective reality—in shaping perceptions of concepts of problems and problem solving, but also evidence of emerging assumptions that suggest shifts from traditional African philosophy toward a more Western philosophy.

Yang and Clum (1994) explored the relationship between a problem-solving model and a social-support model and stress, depression, hopelessness, and suicidal ideation among Asian international students (ages 18–40 years) living in the United States. The problem-solving model was related to stress, depression, hopelessness, and suicidal ideation. Specifically, students who were depressed and hopeless had deficits in problem-solving skills, suggesting that training in these skills for the international students could help them cope with stress and depression.

Watson, Bell, and Chavez (1994) explored differences in problem solving in the area of conflict-handling skills among Mexican American and White non-Hispanic high school students and dropouts. The White students generally used a competitive problem-solving approach to conflict management, whereas the Mexican American students and dropouts used a more cooperative problem-solving approach. These authors recommend that school systems provide opportunities for

BOX 12.4	PROBLEM-SOLVING RESEARCH WITH DIVERSE GROUPS

Developing Educational and Academic Achievement Skills

Bell, Y., Brown, R., & Bryant, A. (1993). Traditional and culturally relevant presentations of a logical reasoning task and performance among African-American students. *Western Journal of Black Studies, 17,* 173–178.

Malloy, C. E., & Jones, M. G. (1998). An investigation of African American students' mathematical problem solving. *Journal for Research in Mathematics Education, 29,* 143–163.

Mehan, H., Hubbard, L., & Villanueva, I. (1994). Forming academic identities: Accommodations without assimilation among involuntary minorities. *Anthropology and Education Quarterly, 25,* 91–117.

Developing Problem-Solving and Coping Skills

Chang, E. C. (1998). Cultural differences, perfectionism, and suicidal risk in a college population: Does social problem solving still matter? *Cognitive Therapy and Research, 22,* 237–254.

Rao, R., & Kramer, L. (1993). Stress and coping among mothers of infants with sickle cell condition. *Children's Health Care, 22,* 169–188.

Rixon, R., & Erwin, P. G. (1999). Measures of effectiveness in a short-term interpersonal cognitive problem solving programme. *Counselling Psychology Quarterly, 12,* 87–93.

Whitfield, K. E., Baker-Thomas, T., Heyward, K., Gatto, M., & Williams, Y. (1999). Evaluating a measure of everyday problem solving for use in African Americans. *Experimental Aging Research, 25,* 209–221.

Yang, B., & Clum, G. (1994). Life stress, social support, and problem-solving skills predictive of depression symptoms, hopelessness, and suicide ideation in an Asian student population: A test of a model. *Suicide and Life Threatening Behavior, 24,* 127–139.

Parenting

Cox, C. B. (2002). Empowering African American custodial grandparents. *Social Work, 47*(1), 45–54.

Problem Solving across Cultures

Anger-Diaz, B., Schlanger, K., Rincon, C., & Mendoza, A. B. (2004). Problem-solving across cultures: Our Latino experience. *Journal of Systemic Therapies, 23*(4), 11–27.

Promoting Conflict Management Skills

Watson, D., Bell, P., & Chavez, E. (1994). Conflict handling skills used by Mexican American and white non-Hispanic students in the educational system. *High School Journal, 78,* 35–39.

Prevention

Bracho-de-Carpio, A., Carpio-Cedraro, F., & Anderson, L. (1990). Hispanic families and teaching about AIDS: A participatory approach at the community level. *Hispanic Journal of Behavioral Sciences, 12,* 165–176.

Hammond, R., & Yung, B. (1991). Preventing violence in at-risk African American youth. *Journal of Health Care for the Poor and Underserved, 2,* 359–373.

Moncher, M., & Schinke, S. (1994). Group intervention to prevent tobacco use among Native American youth. *Research on Social Work Practice, 4,* 160–171.

St. Lawrence, J., Brasfield, T., Jefferson, K., Alleyne, E., O'Bannon, R., & Shirley, A. (1995). Cognitive–behavioral intervention to reduce African American adolescents' risk for HIV infection. *Journal of Consulting and Clinical Psychology, 63,* 221–237.

---

collaborative problem solving for all students, including students of various racial and ethnic groups.

Another major thrust in the use of problem-solving with diverse clients has been in the area of prevention. In an empirical study of HIV prevention programs, African American adolescents were given either education (EC) training only or behavioral skills training (BST) that included problem solving (St. Lawrence et al., 1995). For example, participants identified difficult situations they had encountered in the past as well as ones they anticipated in the future, then practiced problem-solving skills to deal with these situations. The outcomes in lowering the participants' risk for HIV infection evaluated at a one-year follow-up indicated significantly greater benefit for the youths in the skills-training program, with some gender differences. These authors conclude that because HIV risk behavior is influenced by a variety of "cognitive, interpersonal and situational determinants, multifaceted intervention approaches" are needed (p. 236). Also, for such training to be most effective with diverse groups of

clients, they must be "developmentally appropriate and culturally relevant" (p. 235).

Moncher and Schinke (1994) developed a group intervention for tobacco use prevention for Native American youth. The intervention included information on bicultural competence, coping skills, and problem-solving skills. Hammond and Yung (1991) developed a violence prevention program called PACT (Positive Adolescents Choices Training) targeted specifically at Black adolescents. In a pilot study of the PACT program, the participants' communication, problem-solving, and negotiation skills were improved.

GUIDELINES FOR USING PROBLEM SOLVING WITH DIVERSE GROUPS OF CLIENTS

Problem solving has been shown to be an effective intervention strategy with diverse groups of clients in different ways, but there are some guidelines to consider in enhancing its effectiveness. First, there is evidence that the specific nature of problem-solving skills varies according to gender, race, and ethnic group. It is unwise to assume that diverse groups of clients will solve issues in the same way. The traditional, individualistic Eurocentric and androcentric model of problem solving is used widely by some male and Caucasian clients, whereas many females and clients of color prefer a more collaborative and cooperative approach. As a result, both intervention and prevention programs that incorporate problem-solving training must be adapted for client characteristics such as age, gender, race, and ethnic affiliation to make problem solving both developmentally appropriate and culturally relevant.

Second, problem-solving training for clients from diverse cultures will be more effective for these clients when the training is conducted in a culturally sensitive manner—that is, in a way that respects the rituals and traditions of the client's culture, that promotes relevant cultural identity such as sexual and/or racial identity and also ethnic pride, that develops biracial and/or bicultural competence, and that helps these clients to acquire problem-solving skills without having to assimilate the norms of the mainstream culture.

As always, it is important with problem-solving intervention to be aware of intersections among factors such as culture, socioeconomic status, and other issues that may marginalize some people from supportive services. Gammon's (2000) study of rural caregivers of adults with severe developmental disabilities emphasized that to "empower caregiving families, particularly minorities, service providers must continually involve consumers in the assessment of needs and the design and delivery of programs" (p. 183). Noting significantly higher use of "passive" problem-solving strategies by non-Caucasian (predominantly African American) families, this study illustrates the value of considering the broader context within which families are striving to cope and their experience to date with seeking services; for example, relative inaccessibility or nonresponsiveness to needs fosters passive appraisals. In addition to engaging family members as collaborators in developing programs most needed by their children, Gammon (2000) argues that rural providers in particular need to be inventive in pulling together problem-solving supports, such as partnering with churches to help provide respite care, transportation, and socialization; coordinating caregiving exchanges among rural families; and encouraging use of the Internet to access self-advocacy groups and legal information.

STAGES OF PROBLEM SOLVING

D'Zurilla (1986) identifies the following stages:

1. *Treatment rationale (initial structuring):* to discuss the goals, rationale, and general format of the training; to begin training in recognizing and labeling concerns, including use of problem-solving self-monitoring; to discuss the limited capacity of the conscious mind during problem solving.

2. *Problem orientation:* to assess the client's problem-solving coping style; to educate clients about maladaptive and facilitative problem-solving coping skills; to determine cognitive and emotional obstacles to problem solving, and then to train the client to overcome these, attacking the concern from many different vantage points and assessing the time, energy, and commitment needed to resolve the difficulty.

3. *Problem definition and formulation:* to help the client gather relevant and factual information for understanding the issues, to identify problem-focused and/or emotion-focused components of the issues, and to identify problem-solving goals for each issue.

4. *Generation of alternative solutions:* to instruct the client to think about different ways to handle each goal and to use the deferment of judgment, quantity, and variety principles.

5. *Decision making:* to instruct the client to screen the list of alternative solutions, to evaluate (judge and compare) solution outcomes for each goal, and to select solution plans.

6. *Solution implementation and verification:* to encourage the client to carry out several alternative solutions simultaneously; to have the client self-monitor, evaluate, and reinforce the implementation of the solutions; and to help the client troubleshoot and recycle the problem-solving strategy if the solutions do not work.

Each of these stages is described in this section. For detailed descriptions of these stages, see the Interview Checklist for Problem Solving at the end of the chapter.

In addition, D'Zurilla and Nezu (1999) have been inclined to identify the use and control of emotions in problem solving as a discrete stage in which the goals are to discuss the roles of emotions, including ways in which emotion can be used to enhance problem-solving effectiveness, and to provide instruction in the use of coping methods to manage disruptive emotions. D'Zurilla and Nezu (1999) also recommend adding content to support maintenance and generalization of effective problem-solving performance.

Treatment Rationale

The rationale for using problem-solving therapy is that it attempts to strengthen the client's belief that problem solving can be an important coping skill for dealing with a variety of concerns. The overall goal is to help individuals increase their ability to apply problem-solving strategies designed to help them cope effectively with problematic situations that create stress for them. Here is an example of the rationale for problem-solving treatment:

Each of us is faced with both minor and important challenges. Some challenges are routine, such as trying to decide what to wear to a meeting or how to get the family out of the house more efficiently in the morning. Other challenges are more stressful, such as dealing with a difficult relationship. One way to enhance responsibility and self-control is to learn techniques for solving our difficulties. To take the time, energy, and commitment necessary to solve or deal with problems immediately may relieve future frustration and pain created by a concern.

Here is an example of an overview of the procedure. Keep in mind that this is a very general statement. The rationale and treatment overview must be relevant for the client's culture, beliefs, and life circumstances:

> You will learn how to become aware of how you see an issue. You will look at how much control, time and effort, and commitment you feel you have for solving the issue. We will need to gather information to understand and define the key problem. Also, we'll need to look at what might prevent you from solving the problem. It is important that we explore a variety of solutions for solving the problem. After obtaining several solutions, you will decide which solutions feel most reasonable to implement simultaneously. Finally, you will implement the solution plans. I'm wondering what your thoughts and feelings are regarding what I have described. Do you have any questions?

Problem Orientation

D'Zurilla (1988) provides guidance for implementing problem solving. After giving a rationale to the client, the helper asks the client to describe how she or he typically solves problems. The helper determines whether the client has a maladaptive or helpful problem-solving style and then helps the client distinguish between these two coping styles. People with maladaptive coping styles blame themselves or others for the issue or situation. These people often believe that something is wrong with them and may feel abnormal, hopeless, depressed, stupid, or unlucky. Maladaptive coping styles are often exhibited in persons who minimize the benefits of problem solving or who maximize or exaggerate the losses that may occur from failure to solve the issue successfully. Individuals with poor problem-solving skills often perceive the problem as hopeless and so avoid dealing with it. Also, poor problem solvers may feel inadequate or incompetent, and they prefer having someone else produce a solution. Some people have difficulty solving problems because they either never learned how or feel that the difficulty is overwhelming.

The role of the helper is to help the client with a maladaptive style of problem solving to change his or her perception about problem solving. However, the helper must do this in a culturally sensitive way, for problem-solving styles differ across gender, age, race, ethnicity, and religious affiliation. It is critical not to equate maladaptive problem solving with non-Eurocentric worldviews. Instead of viewing difficulties as a threat or a personal inadequacy, the helper assists the client to see them as an opportunity for personal growth and self-improvement. Clients may feel that it is easier not to solve the problem and just wait for things to get better. Helpers need to help these clients to realize that a problem that is not solved may come back to haunt them later. Clients need to believe that a solution exists and that they have the capacity and self-control

to find the solution independently and successfully. An expectation that one can cope with and solve a problem successfully will produce the ability to do so.

Problem solving takes time and energy. It is sometimes easier to avoid dealing with issues when they are influenced more by a person's feelings than by his or her reason. People often respond to issues impulsively and do not take time and effort to think about viable solutions. Problem solving requires time, energy, and commitment—a delay of gratification. The helper needs to assess the client's willingness to spend time and energy, to be committed, and to delay gratification, and the helper may have to motivate the client to make the necessary commitment to solve the problem.

Another component of problem orientation is discussing how the client's cognitions and emotions affect problem solving. Clients may be unmotivated to work on the problem because of how they think about it. Also, poor cognitions or self-talk such as "It is their fault," "It will go away," or "I can't work on it" inhibits the motivation to work on an issue. The purpose of this change intervention is to instruct and to train the client in positive coping methods, with the intent to overcome cognitive and/or emotional obstacles to problem solving. Strategies such as cognitive restructuring, reframing, stress inoculation, meditation, muscle relaxation, exposure or systematic desensitization, breathing exercises, and self-management, as well as environmental interventions, may help a client deal with cognitive and/or emotional barriers to problem solving. Once significant barriers have been minimized, the client is ready for the next stage of the problem-solving strategy.

Problem Definition and Formulation

In the defining and formulating stage of problem solving, the helper helps the client gather as much objective information about the problem as possible. In cases where a client has a distorted cognitive view or perception of the problem, the helper may have to use rational–emotive therapy or cognitive restructuring. The helper explains that problem solving is a skill and a practical approach whereby a person attempts to identify, explore, or create effective and adaptive ways of coping with everyday challenges (D'Zurilla, 1986). A problem can be viewed as a discrepancy between how a present situation is being experienced and how that situation should or could be experienced (D'Zurilla, 1988). In a shorthand version, this approach can be thought of as questions that provide the client's view of

> "What is"—what present conditions are unacceptable and to whom?
>
> "What should be"—what conditions are demanded or desired and by whom?
>
> What obstacles are influencing the availability of an effective response for reducing this discrepancy?

The client needs to obtain relevant information about the problem by identifying the obstacles that are creating the discrepancy or are preventing effective responses for reducing the discrepancy. It is also important to examine antecedent conditions or unresolved issues that may be contributing to or causing the present concern. These questions are then followed by goal-oriented "How can I—" or "What can I do to—" questions. These goals, like any change goals, need to be realistic and stated in specific, concrete terms. In some cases, however, goals that are overly specific may miss the mark by being too narrowly defined. For example, D'Zurilla and Nezu (1999) cite the example of a small church with limited finances that hired a painter to repaint the church in time for an important event. It soon became apparent that the painter worked very slowly and that the quality of the work was very poor. The members of the church committee initially framed their goal question as "How can we get the painter to improve the quality and efficiency of his work so that the church will be painted adequately in time for the celebration?" The question, however, could be framed differently to make available a greater range of alternative solutions: "How can we get the church painted adequately in time for the celebration at the lowest possible cost?" (p. 127).

Problems that have problem-focused definitions center on problem-solving goals, with the purpose of changing the problem situation for the better. Problems with emotion-focused definitions concentrate on changing the client's personal reactions to the problem. Alternatively, D'Zurilla (1988) suggests that if the problem situation is assessed as *changeable,* the problem-focused definition should be emphasized in therapy. If problem-focused problems are *unchangeable,* the helper helps the client deal with the client's reaction to the problem. In some cases, the client's problem is first assessed as problem focused, but later the helper and client discover the problem is unchangeable, and the goal of therapy then becomes changing the personal reaction.

It has been our experience that it is best to include both problem-focused and emotion-focused goals in defining the client's problem. Both problem-focused and emotion-focused definitions of a problem and corresponding goals seem to have some gender and cultural variation.

After the concern has been identified and defined, the practitioner and the client set realistic emotion-focused and/ or problem-focused goals. A goal is defined as what the client would like to have happen as a consequence of solving the problem. Goals should be realistic and attainable, and they should specify the type of behavior, level of behavior, and conditions under which the goal achievement will aid in solving the problem.

The practitioner should help the client identify obstacles that might interfere with problem-solving goals. Finally, the practitioner should help the client understand that the complexities of most problem situations usually require attacking the problem from many different vantage points (Nezu & Nezu, 1989). Establishing problem-solving goals will help the client during the next stage: creating alternative solutions.

Generation of Alternative Solutions

At this stage of problem, the client generates as many alternative solutions as possible. The helper instructs the client to think of *what* she or he could do, or *ways* to handle the situation. The helper also instructs the client not to worry about *how* to go about making a plan work or how to put the solution into effect; that will come later. The client is instructed to imagine a great variety of new and original solutions, no matter how ridiculous any given solution may seem. According to D'Zurilla (1986, 1988), the greater the quantity of alternative solutions that the client produces, the greater is the quality of the solutions available for the client to choose. Similarly, when the client defers judgment or critical evaluation of the solutions, greater-quality solutions are produced by the client.

After generating this list of alternative solutions, the client is asked to identify the number of different strategies represented. If too few strategies are represented, the client is instructed to generate more strategy solutions or more solutions for a specific strategy. This freewheeling or brainstorming process is intended to filter out functional fixity, practicality, and feasibility in generating solutions. If there are several goals, the helper encourages the client to generate several alternative solutions for each problem goal, the rationale being that most issues are complicated and a simple alternative is often inadequate.

Decision Making

During the decision-making stage, the helper helps the client decide on the best solution by judging and comparing all the alternatives. The client is first instructed to screen the list of available alternatives and to eliminate any solution that may pose a risk or is not feasible (D'Zurilla, 1988). The best solutions maximize benefits and minimize costs for the client's personal, immediate, and long-term welfare. The client is instructed to anticipate outcomes for each alternative and then is asked to evaluate each solution using the following four criteria: (1) Will the problem be solved? (2) What will be the status of the client's emotional well-being? (3) How much time and effort will be needed to solve the problem? (4) What effect will the solution have on the client's overall personal and social well-being? When working with diverse groups of clients, it is important not to impose your own values and culture on this process.

After the client selects and evaluates all the alternative solutions, D'Zurilla (1988) recommends that the helper instruct the client to answer these questions: (1) Can the problem be solved? (2) Is more information needed before a solution can be selected and implemented? (3) What solution or combination of solutions should be used to solve the problem? If the concern cannot be solved with one of the existing solutions, the helper may have to help the client redefine the issue and/or gather more information about the problem. When those three questions are answered satisfactorily, the client is ready to implement the solution, as long as the chosen solution is consistent with the goal for solving the concern as fully as possible.

Solution Implementation and Verification

During the first five stages of problem solving, the helper assumes a directive role with the client to ensure a thorough application of problem orientation, problem definition, generation of alternatives, and decision making. During the solution implementation stage, the helper assumes a less directive role. The therapeutic goal during the last stage of the strategy is for the client to become more responsible.

The purpose of solution implementation and verification is to test the chosen solutions and to verify whether they solve the problem. The client simultaneously implements as many solutions as possible. D'Zurilla (1988) describes four verification tasks. First, the client implements the chosen solution. If there are obstacles (behavioral deficits, emotional concerns, or dysfunctional cognitions) to implementing the solution, the client can acquire performance skills, defuse affective concerns, and restructure cognition to remove the obstacles.

Second, the client uses self-monitoring techniques to assess the effects of the chosen solution. The helper instructs the client to keep a daily log or journal of his or her self-talk or emotional reactions to the chosen solution. The self-talk or statements that the client records in the journal can be rated on a scale where 5 means *extremely negative,* 0 means *neutral,* and −5 means *extremely positive.* The accompanying affect state also can be noted, such as *loved, depressed, frustrated, guilty, happy,* or *neutral.* This task can increase the client's emotional awareness.

Third, the client assesses whether the chosen solution achieves the desired goal. The client considers these factors: (1) whether the solution resolved the problem, (2) the client's emotional well-being in the aftermath of the solution, (3) whether the time and effort exerted were worthwhile, and (4) the ratio of total benefit to cost (D'Zurilla, 1988).

Fourth, if the chosen solution meets all the criteria, the client engages in some form of self-reward for successfully solving the problem. However, if the chosen solution does not solve the concern, the helper and client try to pinpoint trouble areas and retrace the problem-solving steps. Common trouble areas for clients are emotional reactions to the problem, inadequate definitions of the problem, unresolved antecedent issues to the problem, problem-focused instead of emotion-focused definitions, and unsatisfactory solution choices.

Use and Control of Emotions in Problem Solving

Problematic situations are often stressful because they involve some difficulty, loss, conflict, or potential pain or harm. Emotions, positive or negative, inevitably are a part of problem solving and can either impede or aid problem-solving performance. Emotions can arise from several sources: (1) the problem situation itself; (2) clients' beliefs, appraisals, and expectations about the problem and about their ability to deal with it successfully; and (3) the problem-solving tasks used in attempting to solve the problem (D'Zurilla & Nezu, 1999).

Low or moderate levels of emotional arousal can be helpful to motivate problem-solving efforts. Sustained high levels of emotional stress, in contrast, are likely to impair problem solving and can result in negative outcomes of their own, such as fatigue, depression, and inertia. In addition, unchecked emotional experience can influence problem solving in ways not readily evident—for example, by narrowing or distorting how problems are labeled, how goals are set, and evaluations made along the way. With these issues in mind, D'Zurilla and Nezu (1999) identify ways in which clients can increase problem-solving effectiveness by viewing their emotional responses as

1. a cue for problem recognition, such as using negative emotional feelings as a trigger to look for what may be eliciting it
2. motivation to galvanize problem solving, such as purposefully using reframing to view the problem as a challenge rather than a threat
3. a problem-solving goal in its own right—if negative states such as anger or anxiety seem counterproductive, it is reasonable to set problem-solving goals to minimize these emotional responses and perhaps stimulate counterbalancing ones
4. a possible consequence of some parts of problem solving—for example, when evaluating solution alternatives, the emotions likely to be associated with various alternatives may be important to consider in decision making
5. a criterion for evaluating the solution outcome—expanding the point above, evaluating the effectiveness of a solution relative to a problem and goal may benefit from considering the emotional response to the outcome (e.g., sometimes a solution to one problem creates a new emotional outcome problem)
6. a reinforcer of effective problem-solving behavior—the counterpoint to point 5, achieving emotions such as hope, relief, and pride can be powerful outcomes of their own and reinforce subsequent problem-solving behavior.

An assessment can determine what kinds of resources clients have for reducing and controlling disruptive emotional effects of stressful issues—resources such as social support, adaptive avenues for distraction, exercise, and informational or tangible resources. Some individuals may need specialized emotion-focused coping techniques. Others may need more limited training in how to (1) recognize potentially disruptive feelings and thoughts, (2) identify various resources they have for coping with these negative effects, and (3) use these resources to reduce, manage, or prevent these effects.

Maintenance and Generalization

Supporting clients' ability to take training out of the context of formal helping and into their lives and futures is consistent with an empowering, collaborative approach to helping. D'Zurilla and Nezu (1999) suggest helping to consolidate maintenance and generalization of problem-solving training

LEARNING ACTIVITY 12.4 | Rapid Problem Solving

After initial problem-solving training, ongoing rapid practice can help you form quick-response habits and increase your ability to problem-solve in different kinds of situations. Give yourself very brief time limits for the following, literally 2 or 3 minutes. Think about a couple of relatively small dilemmas from your own life or something you can imagine (e.g., forgetting something important, an awkward situation, conflict about how to respond in a moment). Then walk through the steps of rapid problem solving either alone or with a student colleague, trying to stay within the time limits. Debrief afterwards. For example, did you draw a blank or get stuck at any step? It may help to write out some of your responses and review what might help you to be effective. Repeat the exercise with one or more training exercises until you have a good sense of the progression of steps and activities.

1. Make the following self-statements:

   "Take a deep breath and calm down."
   "There is no immediate catastrophe."
   "Think of this problem as a challenge."

"I can handle it."
"Stop and think."

2. Ask yourself the following questions:

   "What's the problem?" (State the discrepancy between "what is" and "what should be.")
   "What do I want to accomplish?" (State a goal.)
   "Why do I want to achieve this goal?" (Broaden the goal, if appropriate.)

3. Think of a solution. Then think of several other alternative solutions (at least two or three).

4. Think of the most important criteria for evaluating your solution ideas (at least two or three, such as "Will it achieve my goals?" "What effect will it have on others?" "How much time and effort will it take?"). Decide quickly on the solution alternative that seems best. Think of one or two quick ways to improve the solution.

5. Implement the solution. Are you satisfied with the outcome? If not, try out your second choice if you still have time (D'Zurilla & Nezu, 1999, p. 147).

---

by (1) continuing positive reinforcement and corrective feedback (identifying how and by whom this could be undertaken is one strategy), (2) reviewing positive problem orientation cognitions and strengthening them (for example, explicitly detailing significant gains made in learning how to generate these and in coping more effectively over the course of treatment), (3) directing attention to types of real-life issues that clients may encounter for which their problem-solving skills can be applied, and (4) anticipating and preparing for obstacles to implementing clients' problem-solving agenda in ways consistent with the problem-solving approach.

Practice followed by reflection and feedback is one strategy to develop skills and help generalize their use across different types of problems—such as use of a rapid problem-solving framework in the final sessions. Learning Activity 12.4 presents an example of how to consolidate problem-solving training into a rapid problem-solving format. We suggest spending time with these exercises to achieve a working feel for applying the method. It's not that all problems can be handled in a 1-to-5-minute span—not at all! Rather, repetitions of problem-solving steps with tricky but delimited problems can help make the steps easier to recall and use with more cumbersome problems. For a more thorough overview of problem-solving intervention and learning exercises, see Learning Activity 12.5 and the Interview Checklist for Problem Solving on page 377.

SOME CAUTIONS AND PROBLEM-SOLVING DO'S AND DON'TS

D'Zurilla (1988) offers three cautions about the problem-solving strategy. One concern is the possible failure of the practitioner to recognize when other strategies would be more appropriate. A client with a severe maladaptive behavior or environmental factors that cannot realistically be managed through problem solving will require other strategies. For example, a seriously depressed person may require intensive cognitive restructuring before problem-solving therapy could be considered an appropriate strategy, and a woman in imminent risk of harm from an abusive partner needs safety measures and advocacy assistance in addition to problem solving around longer-term decisions.

The second caution is the danger of viewing problem-solving therapy as a "rational," "intellectual," or "head-trip therapy or exercise" rather than as a coping strategy that involves behavior, cognition, and affect. The problem-solving strategy should be viewed as an overall or general system for personal change that must include the emotional, behavioral, and cognitive modes of a person and be culturally relevant as well.

The third caution is the potential failure of practitioners to recognize that rapport with the client or a positive therapeutic relationship is a necessary condition for successful therapy. The ingredients of ethical and sensitive therapy and the variables that enhance the therapeutic relationship

---

LEARNING ACTIVITY 12.5   Problem Solving

This activity provides an opportunity to try out problem solving. Think of a problem that you have, and apply the following steps to solve your problem. Do this in a quiet place when you will not be interrupted.

1. Determine how you solve problems. How is your approach affected by your gender and culture?
2. Assess your problem-solving style. How does it reflect your worldviews?
3. Use these questions to define the underlying discrepancy and your goals: What is? What should be? What obstacles might be barriers to solving problems? How can I . . . ?

4. How much time, energy, and commitment do you have for solving the problem?
5. Define your problem, and determine whether your problem is problem focused, emotion focused, or both.
6. Generate solutions for solving the problem. Be sure to think of a variety of solutions that fit your culture.
7. Select the best solutions, using the criteria in item 13 of the Interview Checklist for Problem Solving.
8. Implement your solutions to the problem, or at least think about how to implement the solutions. Choose a method for verifying the effectiveness of each solution.

---

are important for successful application of any strategy; the problem-solving strategy is no exception. Problem solving can sometimes be difficult for clients who are not accustomed to thinking of long-range effects, such as many adolescents and some clients with severe trauma histories who don't allow themselves to think much into the future. Bly (1996) contends that many Euro-Americans in the United States are shortsighted in problem solving and lack the *vertical gaze*—that is, the Native American custom of looking ahead to the possible effects of a given solution for the next seven generations. We add the reminder that many problems in living stem from environmental factors. Careful assessment must guide how much it is the environment rather that the person that needs to change, whether through problem solving or other change strategies.

Nezu, Nezu, and Perri (1989, pp. 133–136) offer some guidelines for implementing the problem-solving strategy, summarized also in D'Zurilla and Nezu (1999):

1. Training in problem solving should *not* be presented in a mechanistic manner. Training is best accomplished through interactive, engaging methods.
2. The helper should attempt to individualize the training and make it relevant to the specific needs of a client or group.
3. Homework and in vivo practice of the problem-solving components are crucial. Encourage as much between-session practice as possible. Handouts can be useful during and beyond formal intervention, for they remind clients of homework.
4. The helper should be caring and sensitive to the client's concerns and feelings. Correct implementation of the intervention is important to effectiveness, but the client's needs and responses must be the primary focus.

5. For the intervention to be most useful, the problems being targeted should not be only superficial but also include those most crucial for a given client.
6. The helper always needs to ensure that an accurate assessment of the problem has been obtained.
7. The helper should encourage the client to implement as many solutions as possible during training in order to obtain feedback about resolution or progress.
8. The helper must make a thorough evaluation of the patient's abilities and limitations in order to implement a solution alternative. The evaluation would also include how much control the client has over the problem situation.
9. Generally, both problem-focused coping and emotion-focused coping will be components of problem-solving coping. The helper must determine the forms or combination needed in the client's situation.

One role of the helper throughout the problem-solving process is to educate the client about the problem-solving strategy and to guide the client through the problem-solving steps. As we mentioned before, the helper is less directive with the client during the last stage of the problem-solving process in order to help the client become more independent and take responsibility for applying the chosen problem solutions and verifying their effectiveness. The helper can help the client to maintain these problem-solving skills and to generalize them to other concerns. The helper also can assist the client in anticipating obstacles to solving strategies and prepare the client for coping with them. The client should be able to cope fairly well if he or she takes the time to *examine critically and carefully* her or his orientation to the problem, to carefully define the concern, to generate a variety of alternative solutions, and to make a decision about solution alternatives that are compatible with goals or desired outcomes. Solution implementation may be easier if the first four stages of the problem-solving process have been thoroughly processed. (See also Learning Activity 12.5.)

MODEL EXAMPLE OF PROBLEM-SOLVING THERAPY

In this model example, we present a narrative account of how problem-solving therapy might be used with a 49-year-old male client. Yoshi, an air traffic controller, has reported that he would like to decrease the stress he experiences in his job. He believes that decreasing this stress will help his ulcer and help him cope better with his job. In addition to the physical signs of stress (insomnia), Yoshi also reports that he worries constantly about making mistakes in his job. He has also thought about taking early retirement, which would relieve him of the stress and worry.

Rationale

First, we explain to Yoshi that all of us face concerns and that sometimes we feel stuck because we don't know how to handle an issue. We tell Yoshi that solving problems as they occur can prevent future discomfort. We provide him with an overview of problem-solving therapy, telling him that we'll need to look at how he sees the problem and what obstacles there are to solving the problem. We tell him that we will need to define the concern, think of many different solutions, select several solutions, and try out the solutions and see how well the solutions solve the central concern. We emphasize that problem solving is a collaborative, cooperative process. Finally, we confirm Yoshi's willingness to use problem-solving strategy, and we answer any questions he may have about the procedure.

Problem Orientation

We determine how Yoshi typically solves problems. We ask him to give an example of a concern he has had in the past and how and what he did to solve it. Then we describe for Yoshi the difference between maladaptive and helpful problem solving. We explain to him that most people inherently have problem-solving ability but something blocks the use of it. We tell him that problem-solving therapy removes the blocks or obstacles that are maladaptive for good problem solving. We explain that healthy problem solving is the capacity to view issues as an opportunity. If Yoshi is encountering cognitive or emotional obstacles in his problem-solving attempts, we would introduce appropriate strategies to help remove them. Finally, we assess how much time, energy, and commitment Yoshi has for solving the issue.

Problem Definition and Formulation

We briefly describe the problem-solving strategy for Yoshi. We explain to him that we need to gather information about the concern, such as his thoughts and feelings on the matter,

what unresolved issues are contributing, how intense the issue is, what has been done to solve the issue, and when and where the issue occurs. We ask Yoshi what other information is needed to define the problem. If he has distorted views or perceptions of the issue, we would have to help him reframe his perception. We have to determine whether Yoshi's problem is problem focused, emotion focused, or both. For example, we can probably change his emotional and cognitive reaction to the work situation and help him reduce the stress, but he cannot change the job requirements unless he leaves or retires. We can help Yoshi identify problem-solving goals or what he would like to have happen so that the problem would be solved. For Yoshi, one of the most attainable and realistic goals might be to reduce job stress.

Generation of Alternative Solutions

Yoshi is instructed to generate as many alternative solutions as possible for solving the problem. We inform him not to worry about how to go about making the alternatives work or how to put the solution into effect. Also, he is instructed to defer judgment about how good or feasible his ideas or solutions are until later, to generate as many alternatives as he can think of (because quantity produces quality), and to be creative and to think of nontraditional and unconventional solutions as well.

Decision Making

We instruct Yoshi to screen the list of alternatives and to use the following criteria for evaluating each solution: Will the concern be solved with this solution? What will be the status of his emotional well-being? How much time and effort will be needed to use the alternative solutions? What will be his overall personal and social well-being from using each of these alternative solutions? Yoshi is reminded that it is important to evaluate each solution by answering these four criteria questions. Finally, he is instructed to select the best solutions that are compatible with the problem-solving goals and that fit best with his own culture.

Solution Implementation and Verification

We instruct Yoshi to try his chosen solutions for solving the concern. We also instruct him to self-monitor the alternative solutions he chose to solve the problem in order to determine their effectiveness. Suppose that he chooses to reduce his stress in the workplace by using meditation as one solution. We instruct Yoshi to self-monitor by keeping a written log or journal of the effectiveness of meditation using the following criteria questions: How effective is meditation in reducing job stress? How well does he feel emotionally about the meditative experience? Are the time and effort spent with daily meditation worth it? Are there more benefits for using meditation than costs, and what are his thoughts, feelings, and behavior in relationship to the solution implementation? Yoshi is instructed to complete the self-monitoring or journal each day just before bedtime. He is instructed to rate each of the criteria questions on a five-point scale, with descriptive words for each point on the scale. We tell him that he needs to reward himself after successfully solving the problem (reducing the stress) by selecting rewarding things or activities. Also, we tell him to determine the best time to receive something or to engage in rewarding activity. If, for example, the meditation did not contribute to solving the issue, we instruct Yoshi to look at trouble areas that might be obstacles to solving the problem, such as his emotional reactions, the fact that the issue may not be well defined, or unresolved issues that may be contributing.

CHAPTER SUMMARY

Reframing is a useful strategy to help the client develop alternative ways to view a concern. To be effective, the reframe must be plausible, acceptable, and culturally meaningful to the client. An example of a meaning reframe is the notion of "healthy resistance," meaning clients' empowerment to resist oppression and to stand up for themselves and their beliefs. Reframing can serve as an important complement to other intervention strategies. For example, new ways to view an issue or goal can foster motivation to undertake subsequent change efforts such as cognitive modeling or problem solving. Cognitive modeling and self-instruction go a step further than modeling strategies: aiming to help people learn how to use self-talk to enhance performance. In this strategy, implicit or covert responses as well as overt responses are modeled. Self-instructional training can be paired with a great many interventions and can be very useful toward supporting collaborative and person-in-environment helping approaches. For example, envisioning oneself undertaking the desired actions within one's social context can help illuminate potential difficulties that can be addressed before the client works toward enacting these steps in their actual circumstances.

Problem-solving therapy or training provides clients with a formalized system for viewing issues more constructively. As a treatment strategy, problem solving can be used alone or in conjunction with other treatment strategies presented in this book. Problem solving has been used in a number of ways with diverse groups of clients. Some differences in problem-solving styles are apparent in client characteristics such as age, gender, race, and ethnicity. Culturally sensitive problem-solving training also includes elements of ethnic identity, critical consciousness, and multicultural competence. Problem solving is often about changing aspects of one's environment—tangible, relational, power, sociocultural, or other dimensions—that are the root or at least a considerable part of the client's problem. The breadth of applicability, environmental sensitivity, empirical support, collaborative nature, and nurturance of creative critical thinking situate problem solving, at its best, firmly within the practice nexus.

REFERENCES

Albarran, N. D., Ballesteros, M. N., Morales, G. G., & Ortega, M. I. (2006). Dietary behavior and type 2 diabetes care. *Patient Education and Counseling, 61,* 191–199.

Anger-Diaz, B., Schlanger, K., Rincon, C., & Mendoza, A. B. (2004). Problem-solving across cultures: Our Latino experience. *Journal of Systemic Therapies, 23*(4), 11–27.

Bell, Y., Brown, R., & Bryant, A. (1993). Traditional and culturally relevant presentations of a logical reasoning task and performance among African-American students. *Western Journal of Black Studies, 17,* 173–178.

Bly, R. (1992). *The sibling society.* Reading, MA: Addison-Wesley.

Bracho-de-Carpio, A., Carpio-Cedraro, F., & Anderson, L. (1990). Hispanic families and teaching about AIDS: A participatory approach at the community level. *Hispanic Journal of Behavioral Sciences, 12,* 165–176.

Brown, L. S. (1994). *Subversive dialogues: Theory in feminist therapy.* New York: Basic.

Cary, M., & Dua, J. (1999). Cognitive–behavioral and systematic desensitization procedures in reducing stress and anger in caregivers for the disabled. *International Journal of Stress Management, 6*(2), 75–87.

Chang, E. C. (1998). Cultural differences, perfectionism, and suicidal risk in a college population: Does social problem solving still matter? *Cognitive Therapy and Research, 22,* 237–254.

Chang, E. C., D'Zurilla, T. J., & Sanna, L. J. (Eds.). (2004). *Social problem solving: Theory, research, and training.* Washington, DC: American Psychological Association.

Clark, A. J. (1998). Reframing: A therapeutic technique in group counseling. *Journal of Specialists in Group Work, 23,* 66–73.

Cox, C. B. (2002). Empowering African American custodial grandparents. *Social Work, 47*(1), 45–54.

Devonport, T. J., & Lane, A. M. (2006). Cognitive appraisal of dissertation stress among undergraduate students. *The Psychological Record, 56,* 259–266.

Dixon, W. A. (2000). Problem-solving appraisal and depression: Evidence for a recovery model. *Journal of Counseling and Development, 78,* 87–91.

D'Zurilla, T. J. (1986). *Problem-solving therapy: A social competence approach to clinical intervention.* New York: Springer.

D'Zurilla, T. J. (1988). Problem-solving therapies. In K. S. Dobson (Ed.), *Handbook of cognitive–behavioral therapies* (pp. 85–135). New York: Guilford Press.

D'Zurilla, T. J., & Nezu, C. M. (1999). *Problem-solving therapy: A social competence approach to clinical intervention* (2nd ed.). New York: Springer.

Fields, L. (1998). An integrative brief treatment approach for obsessive–compulsive disorder. *Journal of Psychotherapy Integration, 8*(3), 161–172.

Fortune, D. G., Smith, J. V., & Garvey, K. (2005). Perceptions of psychosis, coping, appraisals, and psychological distress in the relatives of patients with schizophrenia: An exploration using self-regulation theory. *British Journal of Clinical Psychology, 44,* 319–331.

Gammon, E. A. (2000). Examining the needs of culturally diverse rural caregivers who have adults with severe developmental disabilities living with them. *Families in Society, 81,* 174–185.

Gillen, G. (2006). Coping during inpatient stroke rehabilitation: An exploratory study. *American Journal of Occupational Therapy, 60*(2), 136–145.

Gorrell, J. (1993). Cognitive modeling and implicit rules: Effects on problem-solving performance. *American Journal of Psychology, 106,* 51–65.

Grote, I., & Baer, D. M. (2000). Teaching compliance with experimentally managed self-instructions can accomplish reversal shift. *Journal of Developmental and Physical Disabilities, 12*(3), 217–233.

Hains, A. (1989). An anger-control intervention with aggressive delinquent youths. *Behavioral Residential Treatment, 4,* 213–230.

Hammond, R., & Yung, B. (1991). Preventing violence in at-risk African American youth. *Journal of Health Care for the Poor and Underserved, 2,* 359–373.

Huang, L. N. (1994). An integrative approach to clinical assessment and intervention with Asian-American adolescents. *Journal of Clinical Child Psychology, 23,* 21–31.

Jiang, T., Sun, C., & Wu, Z. (1999). Difference in problem solving between elderly diabetics and elderly healthy people. *Chinese Journal of Clinical Psychology, 7,* 204–207.

Johnson, J. G. (2006). Cognitive modeling of decision making in sports. *Psychology of Sport and Exercise, 7*(6), 631–652.

Johnson, L. A., Graham, S., & Harris, K. R. (1997). The effects of goal setting and self-instruction on learning a reading comprehension strategy: A study of students with learning disabilities. *Journal of Learning Disabilities, 30,* 80–91.

Karasawa, K. (2003). Interpersonal reaction toward depression and anger. *Cognition and Emotion, 17*(1), 123–138.

Karenga, M. (1980). *Kawaida theory.* Los Angeles: Kawaida.

Kushleyeva, Y., Salvucci, D. D., Lee, F. J., & Schunn, C. (2005). Deciding when to switch tasks in time-critical multitasking. *Cognitive Systems Research, 6*(1), 41–49.

Larson, E. (1998). Reframing the meaning of disability to families: The embrace of paradox. *Social Science and Medicine, 47,* 865–675.

Leserman, J., Perkins, D., & Evans, D. (1992). Coping with the threat of AIDS: The role of social support. *American Journal of Psychiatry, 149,* 1514–1520.

Malloy, C. E., & Jones, M. G. (1998). An investigation of African American students' mathematical problem solving. *Journal for Research in Mathematics Education, 29,* 143–163.

Maltz, W. (2001). Sex therapy with survivors of sexual abuse. In P. J. Kleinplatz, (Ed.), *New directions in sex therapy: Innovations and alternatives* (pp. 258–278). New York: Brunner-Routledge.

Mehan, H., Hubbard, L., & Villanueva, I. (1994). Forming academic identities: Accommodations without assimilation among involuntary minorities. *Anthropology and Education Quarterly, 25,* 91–117.

Meichenbaum, D. H., & Goodman, J. (1971). Training impulsive children to talk to themselves: A means of developing self-control. *Journal of Abnormal Psychology, 77,* 115–126.

Moncher, M., & Schinke, S. (1994). Group intervention to prevent tobacco use among Native American youth. *Research on Social Work Practice, 4,* 160–171.

Motenko, A. K., & Greenberg, S. (1995). Reframing dependence in old age. *Social Work, 40,* 382–390.

Nagae, N., Nadate, L., & Sekiguchi, Y. (1999). Self-instructional training for shyness: Differences in improvements produced by different types of coping self-statements. *Japanese Journal of Counseling Science, 32,* 32–42.

Nezu, A. M., & Nezu, C. M. (Eds.). (1989). *Clinical decision making in behavior therapy: A problem-solving perspective.* Champaign, IL: Research Press.

Nezu, A. M., Nezu, C. M., Houts, P. S., Friedman, S. H., & Faddis, S. (1999). Relevance of problem-solving therapy to psychosocial oncology. *Journal of Psychosocial Oncology, 16*(3–4), 5–6.

Nezu, A. M., Nezu, C. M., & Perri, M. G. (1990). Psychotherapy for adults within a problem-solving framework: Focus on depression. *Journal of Cognitive Psychotherapy, 4,* 247–256.

Nutt-Williams, E., & Hill, C. E. (1996). The relationship between self-talk and therapy process variables for novice therapists. *Journal of Counseling Psychology, 43,* 170–177.

Oppenheimer, M. (1992). Alma's bedside ghost: Or the importance of cultural similarity. *Hispanic Journal of Behavioral Sciences, 14,* 496–501.

Porter, L., S., Clayton, M. F., Belyea, M., Mishel, M., Gil, K. M., & Germino, B. B. (2006). Predicting negative mood state and personal growth in African American and White long-term breast cancer survivors. *Annals of Behavioral Medicine, 31,* 195–204.

Rao, R., & Kramer, L. (1993). Stress and coping among mothers of infants with sickle cell condition. *Children's Health Care, 22,* 169–188.

Rath, S. (1998). Verbal self-instructional training: An examination of its efficacy, maintenance, and generalization. *European Journal of Psychology of Education, 13,* 399–409.

Rixon, R., & Erwin, P. G. (1999). Measures of effectiveness in a short-term interpersonal cognitive problem solving programme. *Counselling Psychology Quarterly, 12,* 87–93.

Robinson, T., & Ward, J. V. (1991). "A belief in self far greater than anyone's disbelief": Cultivating resistance among African American female adolescents. Women, girls and psychotherapy: Reframing resistance. [Special issue]. *Women and Therapy, 11*(3–4), 87–103.

Rose, S. D., & LeCroy, C. W. (1991). Group methods. In F. H. Kanfer & A. P. Goldstein (Eds.), *Helping people change* (pp. 422–453). New York: Pergamon.

St. Lawrence, J., Brasfield, T., Jefferson, K., Alleyne, E., O'Bannon, R., & Shirley, A. (1995). Cognitive–behavioral intervention to reduce African American adolescents' risk for HIV infection. *Journal of Consulting and Clinical Psychology, 63,* 221–237.

Schwartz, L. S., & Gredler, M. E. (1998). The effects of self-instructional materials on goal-setting and self-efficacy. *Journal of Research and Development in Education, 31*(2), 83–89.

Smith, B. (1992). Raising a resister. In C. Gilligan, A. Rogers, & D. Tolman (Eds.), *Women, girls and psychotherapy: Reframing resistance* (pp. 137–148). Binghamton, NY: Haworth Press.

Soo-Hoo, T. (1998). Applying frame of reference and reframing techniques to improve school consultation in multicultural settings. *Journal of Educational and Psychological Consultation, 9,* 325–245.

Stern, S. B. (1999). Anger management in parent–adolescent conflict. *American Journal of Family Therapy, 27,* 181–193.

Sun, R., Coward, L. A., & Zenzen, M. J. (2005). On levels of cognitive modeling. *Philosophical Psychology, 18*(5), 613–637.

Tao, X., Chongde, L., & Jiliang, S. (1999). Effect of cognitive self-instruction training on the improvement of teachers' teaching-regulated ability. *Psychological Science, 22,* 5–9.

Taylor, I., & O'Reilly, M. F. (1997). Toward a functional analysis of private verbal self-regulation. *Journal of Applied Behavior Analysis, 30,* 43–58.

Taylor, J., Gilligan, C., & Sullivan, A. (1995). *Between voice and silence: Women and girls, race and relationships.* Cambridge, MA: Harvard University Press.

Van Vlaenderen, H. (1999). Problem solving: A process of reaching common understanding and consensus. *South African Journal of Psychology, 29,* 166–177.

Varni, J. W., Sahler, O. J., Katz, E. R., Mulhern, R. K., Copeland, D. R., Noll, R. B., et al. (1999). Maternal problem-solving therapy in pediatric cancer. *Journal of Psychosocial Oncology, 16*(3–4), 41–71.

Wachtel, P. L. (1993). *Therapeutic communication: Principles and effective practice.* New York: Guilford Press.

Watson, D., Bell, P., & Chavez, E. (1994). Conflict handling skills used by Mexican American and white non-Hispanic students in the educational system. *High School Journal, 78,* 35–39.

Wenman, R., Bowen, A., Tallis, R. C., Gardener, E., Cross, S., & Niven, D. (2003). Use of a randomised single case experimental design to evaluate therapy for unilateral neglect. *Neuropsychological Rehabilitation, 13*(4), 441–459.

Whitfield, K. E., Baker-Thomas, T., Heyward, K., Gatto, M., & Williams, Y. (1999). Evaluating a measure of everyday problem solving for use in African Americans. *Experimental Aging Research, 25,* 209–221.

Wood, B. C., & Mynors-Wallis, L. M. (1997). Problem-solving therapy in palliative care. *Palliative Medicine, 11,* 49–54.

Yang, B., & Clum, G. (1994). Life stress, social support, and problem-solving skills predictive of depression symptoms, hopelessness, and suicide ideation in an Asian student population: A test of a model. *Suicide and Life Threatening Behavior, 24,* 127–139.

12   KNOWLEDGE AND SKILL BUILDER

Part One

Learning Outcome 1 asks you to demonstrate 8 out of 11 steps of the reframing procedure with a role-play client. Use the Interview Checklist for Reframing to assess your interview.

Interview Checklist for Reframing

Instructions: Determine whether the helper demonstrated the lead listed in the checklist. Check (✔) the leads that were used.

Treatment Rationale

____ 1. Helper explains purpose of reframing.

"Often when we think about a problem situation, our initial or intuitive reaction can lead to emotional distress. For example, we focus only on the negative features of the situation and overlook other details. By focusing only on the selected negative features of a situation, we can become nervous or anxious about the situation."

____ 2. Helper provides overview of reframing.

"We'll identify what features you attend to when you think of the situation. Once you become aware of these features, we will look for other neutral or positive aspects of the situation that you may ignore or overlook. Then we will work on incorporating these other things into your perceptions of the problem situation."

____ 3. Helper confirms client's willingness to use the strategy.

"How does this all sound? Are you ready to try this?"

Identification of Client Perceptions and Feelings in Problem Situations

____ 4. Helper has client identify features typically attended to during situation (may have to use imagery with some clients).

"When you think of the situation or one like it, what features do you notice or attend to? What is the first thing that pops into your head?"

____ 5. Helper has client identify typical feelings during situation.

"How do you usually feel?" "What do you experience [or are you experiencing] during this situation?"

Deliberate Enactment of Selected Perceptual Features

____ 6. Helper asks client to reenact situation (by role play or imagery) and to deliberately attend to selected features. (This step may need to be repeated several times.)

"Let's set up a role play [or imagery] in which we act out this situation. This time I want you to deliberately focus on these aspects of the situation we just identified. Notice how you attend to _____."

Identification of Alternative Perceptions

____ 7. Helper instructs client to identify positive or neutral features of situation. The new reframes are plausible and acceptable to the client and fit the client's values and age, gender, race, and ethnicity.

"Now, I want us to identify other features of the situation that are neutral or positive. These are things you have forgotten about or ignored. Think of other features." "What other aspects of this situation that aren't readily apparent to you could provide a different way to view the situation?"

Modification of Perceptions in Problem Situations

____ 8. Helper instructs client to modify perceptions of situation by focusing on or attending to the neutral or positive features. (Use of role play or imagery can help with this process for some clients. This step may need to be repeated several times.)

"When we act out the situation, I want you to change what you attend to in the situation by thinking of the positive features we just identified. Just focus on these features."

Homework and Follow-up

____ 9. Helper encourages client to practice modifying perceptions during in vivo situations.

"Practice is very important for modifying your perceptions. Every time you think about or encounter the situation, focus on the neutral or positive features of the situation."

____ 10. Helper instructs client to monitor aspects of the strategy on homework log sheet.

"I'd like you to use this log to keep track of the number of times you practice or use this. Also record your initial and resulting feelings before and after these kinds of situations."

____ 11. Helper arranges for a follow-up. (During follow-up, helper comments on client's log and points out small perceptual shifts.)

"Let's get together in two weeks. Bring your log sheet with you. Then we can see how this is working for you."

Observer Comments

_____

_____

_____

Part Two

Describe how you would use the seven components of cognitive modeling and self-instructional training to help

12 KNOWLEDGE AND SKILL BUILDER

Mr. Huang initiate social contacts with his boss (Learning Outcome 2). These are the seven components:

1. Rationale
2. Model of task and self-guidance
3. Overt external guidance
4. Overt self-guidance
5. Faded overt self-guidance
6. Covert self-guidance
7. Homework and follow-up

See Feedback section for answers.

Part Three

Learning Outcome 3 asks you to demonstrate 16 out of 21 steps of the cognitive self-instructional modeling procedure with a role-play client. You can audiotape your interview or have an observer assess your performance using the Interview Checklist for Cognitive Modeling.

Part Four

Learning Outcome 4 asks you to identify the steps of the problem-solving strategy represented by at least 8 out of 10 helper interview responses. Match each helper response with the letter of the step of the problem-solving procedure that is being used. More than one helper response may be associated with a step. See Feedback section for answers.

Steps of Problem Solving

 a. Rationale for problem solving
 b. Problem orientation
 c. Problem definition and formulation
 d. Generation of alternative solutions
 e. Decision making
 f. Solution implementation and verification

Helper Responses

____ 1. "Self-monitoring involves keeping a diary or log about your thoughts, feelings, and behaviors."
____ 2. "To help you assess each solution, you can answer several questions about how effective the solution will be in solving the problem."
____ 3. "Be creative and freewheeling. Let your imagination go. Write down whatever comes into your mind."
____ 4. "What goals do you want to set for your emotional or personal reaction to the issue?"
____ 5. "When you have concerns, give me an example of the concern and describe how you typically solve it."
____ 6. "Solving problems as they occur can prevent future discomfort."

____ 7. "Most people have an ability to solve problems, but often they block the use of it and become poor problem solvers."
____ 8. "What unresolved issues may be contributing to the problem? When does the problem occur? Where does it occur?"
____ 9. "Look over your list of solutions to see how much variety is on your list; think of new and original ones."
____ 10. "You need to think about what you can reward yourself with after you complete this step."

Part Five

Learning Outcome 5 asks you to demonstrate 16 out of 19 steps associated with the problem-solving strategy in a role-play interview. You can audiotape your interview or have an observer rate it using the Interview Checklist for Problem Solving.

Interview Checklist for Cognitive Modeling

Instructions: Determine which of the following leads the helper used in the interview. Check (✔) the leads that were used.

Treatment Rationale

____ 1. Helper provides a rationale for the strategy.
"This strategy is a way to help you do this task and also plan how to do it. The planning will help you perform better and more easily."
____ 2. Helper provides overview of strategy.
"We will take it step by step. First, I'll show you how to do it, and I'll talk to myself aloud while I'm doing it so you can hear my planning. Then you'll do that. Gradually, you'll be able to perform the task while thinking through the planning to yourself at the same time."
____ 3. Helper checks client's willingness to use strategy.
"Would you like to go ahead with this now?"

Model of Task and Self-Guidance

____ 4. Helper instructs client in what to listen and look for during modeling.
"While I do this, I'm going to tell you orally my plans for doing it. Just listen closely to what I say as I go through this."
____ 5. Helper engages in modeling of task, verbalizing self-guidance aloud, using language relevant to the client.
"Okay, I'm walking in for the interview. [Helper walks in.] I'm getting ready to greet the interviewer and then wait for his cue to sit down" [sits down].
____ 6. Self-guidance demonstrated by helper includes five components:

(continued)

12   KNOWLEDGE AND SKILL BUILDER

(continued)

_____ a. *Question* about demands of task:

"Now what is it I should be doing in this situation?"

_____ b. *Answer to* question mentions planning what to do:

"I just need to greet the person, sit down on cue, and answer the questions. I need to be sure to point out why they should take me."

_____ c. *Focused attention* to task and *self-guidance* during task:

"Okay, remember to take a deep breath, relax, and concentrate on the interview. Remember to discuss my particular qualifications and experiences and try to answer questions completely and directly."

_____ d. *Coping self-evaluation* and, if necessary, *error correction:*

"Okay, now, if I get a little nervous, just take a deep breath. Stay focused on the interview. If I don't respond too well to one question, I can always come back to it."

_____ e. *Self-reinforcement* for completion of task:

"Okay, doing fine. Things are going pretty smoothly."

Overt External Guidance

_____ 7. Helper instructs client to perform task while helper coaches.

"This time you go through the interview yourself. I'll be coaching you on what to do and on your planning."

_____ 8. Client performs task while helper coaches by verbalizing self-guidance, changing *I* to *you.*

"Now just remember you're going to walk in for the interview. When the interview begins, I'll coach you through it." Helper's verbalization includes the five components of self-guidance:

_____ a. Question about task:

"Okay, you're walking into the interview room. Now ask yourself what it is you're going to do."

_____ b. Answer to question:

"Okay, you're going to greet the interviewer. [Client does so.] Now he's cuing you to sit down." [Client sits.]

_____ c. Focused attention to task and self-guidance during task:

"Just concentrate on how you want to handle this situation. He's asking you about your background. You're going to respond directly and completely."

_____ d. Coping self-evaluation and error correction:

"If you feel a little nervous while you're being questioned, take a deep breath. If you don't respond to a question completely, you can initiate a second response. Try that now."

_____ e. Self-reinforcement:

"That's good. Now remember you want to convey why you should be chosen. Take your time to do that. [Client does so.] Great. Very thorough job."

Overt Self-Guidance

_____ 9. Helper instructs client to perform task and instruct self aloud.

"This time I'd like you to do both things. Talk to yourself as you go through the interview in the same way we have done before. Remember, there are five parts to your planning. If you get stuck, I'll help you."

_____ 10. Client performs task while simultaneously verbalizing aloud self-guidance process. Client's verbalization includes five components of self-guidance:

_____ a. Question about task:

"Now what is it I need to do?"

_____ b. Answer to question:

"I'm going to greet the interviewer, wait for the cue to sit down, then answer the questions directly and as completely as possible."

_____ c. Focused attention and self-guidance:

"Just concentrate on how I'm going to handle this situation. I'm going to describe why I should be chosen."

_____ d. Coping self-evaluation and error correction:

"If I get a little nervous, just take a deep breath. If I have trouble with one question, I can always come back to it."

_____ e. Self-reinforcement:

"Okay, things are going smoothly. I'm doing fine."

_____ 11. If client's self-guidance is incomplete or if client gets stuck, helper

_____ a. Either intervenes and cues client:

"Let's stop here for a minute. You seem to be having trouble. Let's start again and try to . . ."

_____ b. Or recycles client back through step 10:

"That seemed pretty hard, so let's try it again. This time you go through the interview, and I'll coach you through it."

_____ 12. Helper gives feedback to client about overt practice.

"That seemed pretty easy for you. You were able to go through the interview and coach yourself. The one place you seemed a little stuck was in the middle, when you had trouble describing yourself. But overall, it was something you handled well. What do you think?"

Faded Overt Self-Guidance

13. Counselor instructs client on how to perform task while whispering.

"This time I'd like you to go through the interview and whisper the instructions to yourself as you go along. The

12 | KNOWLEDGE AND SKILL BUILDER

whispering may be a new thing for you, but I believe it will help you learn to do this."

14. Client performs task and whispers simultaneously.

"I'm going into the room now, waiting for the interviewer to greet me and to sit down. I'm going to answer the questions as completely as possible. Now I'm going to talk about my background."

15. Counselor checks to determine how well client performed.

   a. If client stumbled or left out some of the five parts, client engages in faded overt practice again:

"You had some difficulty with _____. Let's try this type of practice again."

   b. If client performed practice smoothly, counselor moves on to next step:

"You seemed to do this easily and comfortably. The next thing is . . . ."

Covert Self-Guidance

16. Counselor instructs client to perform task while covertly (thinking only) instructing self.

"This time while you practice, simply *think* about these instructions. In other words, instruct yourself mentally or in your head as you go along."

17. Client performs task while covertly instructing. Only the client's actions are visible at this point.

18. After practice (step 17), counselor asks client to describe covert instructions.

"Can you tell me what you thought about as you were doing this?"

19. On the basis of client report (step 18)

   a. Counselor asks client to repeat covert self-guidance:

"It's hard sometimes to begin rehearsing instructions mentally. Let's try it again so you feel more comfortable with it."

   b. Counselor moves on to homework:

"Okay, you seemed to do this very easily. I believe it would help if you could apply this to some things that you do on your own this week. For instance . . ."

Homework

20. Counselor instructs client on how to carry out homework.

"What I'd like you to do this week is to go through this type of mental practice on your own."

   a. What to do:

"Specifically, go through a simulated interview where you mentally plan your responses as we've done today."

   b. How much or how often to do the task:

"I believe it would help if you could do this two times each day."

   c. When and where to do it:

"I believe it would be helpful to practice at home first, then practice at school [or work]."

   d. A method for self-monitoring during completion of homework:

"Each time you do this, make a check on this log sheet. Also, write down the five parts of the self-instructions you used."

21. Counselor arranges for a face-to-face or telephone follow-up after completion of homework assignment.

"Bring in your log sheets next week, or give me a call at the end of the week, and we'll go over your homework then."

Interview Checklist for Problem Solving

Instructions: Determine whether the helper demonstrated each of the leads listed in the checklist. Check (✔) the leads that were used.

Treatment Rationale

_____ 1. Helper explains purpose of problem-solving therapy in a way that is consistent with the client's culture.

"All of us are faced with little and big concerns. Sometimes we feel stuck because we don't know how to handle a concern. This procedure can help you identify and define a difficulty and examine ways of solving it. You can be in charge of the issue instead of the issue being in charge of you. Solving difficulties as they occur can prevent future discomfort."

_____ 2. Helper provides brief overview of procedure in a way that is consistent with the client's culture.

"There are five steps we'll do in using this procedure. Most problems in living are complex, and achieving changes often requires many different perspectives. First, we'll need to look at how you see the problem. We'll examine what are unhelpful and helpful problem-solving skills. Another part of this step is to explore how to overcome thoughts and feelings that could be obstacles to achieving your goals. We'll also need to see how much time and energy you are willing to use to solve the problem. Second, we will define the problem by gathering information about it. Third, we'll want to see how many different solutions we can come up with for solving the problem. Next, we'll examine the solutions and decide which one to use. Finally, you will try out the chosen solutions and see how well they solve the problem. What are your thoughts about what I have described? Do you have any questions?"

Problem Orientation

_____ 3. Helper determines how the client solves problems.

(continued)

12   KNOWLEDGE AND SKILL BUILDER

(*continued*)

"When you have concerns or problems, give me an example of the problem and describe how you typically solve it."

_____ 4. Helper describes the difference between maladaptive and helpful problem solving, recognizing variations across gender, age, and culture and worldviews.

"Most people have the ability to solve problems, but often they block the use of it. Problem-solving therapy helps to remove blocks or obstacles and helps bring important issues into focus. Problem-solving therapy provides a formalized system for viewing problems differently. People who don't solve problems very well may feel inadequate or incompetent to solve their problem. Often these people want to avoid the problem or want someone else to solve it. People sometimes feel that it is easier not to solve the problem and that things will get better. At times, poor problem solvers feel hopeless, depressed, or unlucky. If you feel like a poor problem solver, we'll have to consider ways that make you feel like you are in charge. You can solve problems; they are a part of daily living. There are usually a variety of solutions to every problem, and you have the capacity to find the solution. It can be helpful to think of problems as an opportunity."

_____ 5. Helper determines what cognitive and emotional obstacles the client might have as barriers to solving the problem.

"When you think about your problem, what thoughts do you have concerning the problem? What are you usually thinking about during this problem? Do you have any 'shoulds' or beliefs concerning the problem? What feelings do you experience when thinking about the problem? Are there any holdover or unfinished feelings from past events in your life that still affect the problem? How do your thoughts and feelings affect the problem and your ability to solve it? You may not be aware of it, but think about some past issues or unfinished business you may have as we do problem solving." (If there are any obstacles, the helper introduces a strategy or strategies [for example, rational emotive therapy, cognitive restructuring, reframing, meditation, muscle relaxation] to help the client remove cognitive or emotional obstacles to problem solving.)

_____ 6. Helper assesses the client's time, energy, and commitment to solving the problem.

"Any problem usually takes time, effort, and commitment to solve. But it is often important to solve the problem now rather than wait and solve it later—or not at all. It is important to know how committed you are to solving the problem. [Wait

for the answer.] Also, solving a problem takes time. Do you feel you have enough time to work on the problem? [Pause; wait for answer.] Thinking about and working on a problem can take a lot of energy. How energized do you feel about working on this problem?" [Pause for answer.]

Problem Definition and Formulation

_____ 7. Helper describes the problem-solving strategy for the client in a culturally relevant way.

"People have problems or concerns. Some concerns are minor, and some are major. Problem solving is a skill and a practical approach. People use problem solving to identify, explore, or create effective ways of dealing with everyday concerns or difficult situations."

_____ 8. Helper helps the client gather information about the problem.

"We want to gather as much information about the concern as we can. What type of issue or situation is it? What thoughts do you have when the difficulty occurs? What feelings do you experience? How often does the difficulty occur, or is it ongoing? What unresolved issues may be contributing? Who or what other people are involved? When does the problem occur? Where does it occur? How long has this been going on? How intense is the problem? What have you done to solve the problem? What obstacles can you identify that prevent you from making desired changes? Tell me, how do you see the issue or troubling situation?" What other information do we need to define the problem? What is your definition of the problem?"

_____ 9. Helper determines whether the client's problem is problem focused, emotion focused, or both.

"From the way you have defined the problem, how can the problem be changed? What aspects of the problem can be changed? What emotional reactions do you have about the problem? How would you like to change your personal/emotional reaction to the problem? There may be some things about the problem that you cannot change. Some problem situations are unchangeable. If there are aspects of the problem that are changeable, we will work on those things that can be changed. One thing we can change is your emotional or personal reaction to the problem."

_____ 10. Helper helps the client identify culturally relevant problem-solving goals.

"Now that we have identified and defined the problem, we need to set some goals. A goal is what you would like to have happen so that the problem would be solved. The goals should be things you can do or things that are attainable and realistic."

"How many obstacles are there that prevent you from setting problem-solving goals? How can you remove these obstacles?

12   K N O W L E D G E   A N D   S K I L L   B U I L D E R

What goals do you want to set for your emotional or personal reaction to the problem? What behaviors do you want to change? How much or what level of behavior is going to change? Under what condition or circumstance will the behavior change occur? What goals do you want to set for things that are changeable in the problem situation? What behaviors or goals do you want to set for yourself, the frequency of these behaviors, and in what problem conditions? These goals will help us in the next stage of problem solving."

Generation of Alternative Solutions

_____ 11. Helper presents guidelines for generating alternative solutions.

"We want to generate as many alternative solutions for solving the problem as possible. We do this because problems are often complicated and a single alternative is often inadequate. We need to generate several alternative solutions for each problem-solving goal."

_____ a. What options:

"Think of what you could do or ways to handle the problem. Don't worry about how to go about making your plan work or how to put the solution into effect—you'll do that later."

_____ b. Defer judgment:

"Defer judgment about your ideas or solutions until later. Be loose and open to any idea or solution. You can evaluate and criticize your solutions later."

_____ c. Quantity:

"Quantity breeds quality. The more alternative solutions or ideas you can think of, the better. The more alternatives you produce, the more quality solutions you'll discover."

_____ d. Variety:

"Be creative and freewheeling. Let your imagination go. Write down whatever comes into your mind. Allow yourself to think of a variety of unusual or unconventional solutions as well as more traditional or typical ones. Look over your list of solutions, and see how much variety there is. If there is little variety on your list, generate more and think of new and original solutions."

Decision Making

_____12. Helper instructs the client to screen the list of alternative solutions.

"Now you need to screen and look over your list of alternative solutions for solving the problem. You want to look for the *best* solutions. The best solutions are the ones that maximize benefits and minimize costs for your personal, social, immediate, and long-term welfare."

_____ 13. Helper provides criteria for evaluating each solution.

"To help you assess *each* solution, answer the following four questions:

_____ a. Will the problem be solved with this particular solution?

_____ b. By using this solution, what will be the status of my emotional well-being?

_____ c. If I use this solution, how much time and effort will be needed to solve the problem?

_____ d. What will be my overall personal and social well-being if I use this solution?

Remember that it is important to evaluate *each* solution by answering the four questions."

_____ 14. Helper instructs the client to make a decision and select the best solutions compatible with problem-solving goals and the client's culture.

"Select every solution that you think will work or solve the problem. Answer these questions:

_____ a. Can the problem be solved reasonably well with these solutions?

_____ b. Is more information about the problem needed before these solutions can be selected and implemented?

Decide whether the solutions fit with the problem-solving goals." (If the answers to question a and question b are *yes* and *no*, respectively, move on to step 15. Answers of *no* to question a and *yes* to question b may require recycling by redefining the problem, gathering more information, and determining problem obstacles.)

Solution Implementation and Verification

_____ 15. Helper instructs the client to carry out chosen solutions.

"For the last stage of problem solving, try out the solutions you have chosen. If there are obstacles to trying out the solutions, we'll have to remove them. You can use several alternative solutions at the same time. Use as many solutions as you can."

_____ 16. Helper informs the client about self-monitoring strategy.

"We'll need to develop a technique for you to see whether the solution solves the problem. Self-monitoring involves keeping a diary or log about your thoughts, feelings, and behavior. You can record these behaviors as you implement your chosen solutions. We'll need to discuss what responses you'll record, when you'll record them, and the method of recording."

_____ 17. Helper instructs the client to use certain criteria to assess whether the solution achieves the desired goal for solving the problem.

(continued)

12   KNOWLEDGE AND SKILL BUILDER

(*continued*)

"You'll need to determine whether your solution solves the problem. One way to do this is to ask yourself the following:

____ a. Problem resolved:

"Did the solution solve the problem?"

____ b. Emotional well-being:

"How is your emotional well-being after you used the solution?"

____ c. Time and effort exerted:

"Was the time and effort you exerted worth it?"

____ d. Ratio of total benefits to total costs:

"Were there more benefits for using the solution than costs?"

____ 18. Helper instructs the client about self-reward.

"You need to think about how you can reward yourself after successfully solving the problem. What types of things or activities are rewarding to you? When would be the best time to receive something or to engage in a rewarding activity?"

____ 19. Helper instructs the client on what to do if solutions do not solve the problem.

"When the solutions do not solve the problem, we need to look at some trouble areas that might be obstacles to solving the problem. What is your emotional reaction to the problem? The problem may not be defined well. There may be old unresolved problems that are contributing to the present problem."

12   KNOWLEDGE AND SKILL BUILDER **FEEDBACK**

Part One

Use the Interview Checklist for Reframing to assess your interview.

Part Two

1. *Rationale:* First, you would explain the steps of cognitive modeling and self-instructional training to Mr. Huang. Then you would explain how this procedure could help him practice and plan the way he might approach his boss.

2. *Model of task and self-guidance:* You would model for Mr. Huang a way he could approach his boss to request a social contact. You would model the five parts of the self-guidance process: (a) the question about what he wants to do, (b) the answer to the question in the form of planning, (c) focused attention on the task and guiding himself through it, (d) evaluating himself and correcting errors or making adjustments in his behavior in a coping manner, and (e) reinforcing himself for adequate performance. In your modeling, it is important to use language that is relevant to Mr. Huang.

3. *Overt external guidance:* Mr. Huang would practice making an approach or contact while you coach him through the five parts of self-guidance as just described.

4. *Overt self-guidance:* Mr. Huang would practice making a social contact while verbalizing aloud the five parts of the self-guidance process. If he got stuck, you could prompt him, or you could have him repeat this step or recycle step 3.

5. *Faded overt self-guidance:* Mr. Huang would engage in another practice attempt, but this time he would whisper the five parts of the self-guidance process.

6. *Covert self-guidance:* Mr. Huang would make another practice attempt while using the five parts of the self-guidance process covertly. You would ask him afterward to describe what happened. Additional practice with covert self-guidance or recycling to step 4 or step 5 might be necessary.

7. *Homework:* You would instruct Mr. Huang to practice the self-guidance process daily before actually making a social contact with his boss.

Part Three

Rate an audiotape of your interview or have an observer rate you, using the Interview Checklist for Cognitive Modeling in the Knowledge and Skill Builder.

Part Four

1. f. Solution implementation and verification
2. e. Decision making
3. d. Generation of alternative solutions
4. c. Problem definition and formulation
5. b. Problem orientation
6. a. Rationale for problem solving
7. b. Problem orientation
8. c. Problem definition and formulation
9. d. Generation of alternative solutions
10. f. Solution implementation and verification

Part Five

Rate an audiotape of your interview or have someone else rate it, using the Interview Checklist for Problem Solving in the Knowledge and Skill Builder.

13

COGNITIVE CHANGE AND COGNITIVE RESTRUCTURING STRATEGIES

LEARNING OUTCOMES

After completing this chapter, you will be able to

1. Identify and describe the six components of cognitive restructuring from a written case description.
2. Teach the six components of cognitive restructuring to another person, or demonstrate them in a role-play interview.
3. Describe ways in which schemas are involved in cognitive functioning.

Since the first edition of this book, 30 years ago, considerable changes have emerged in the concept and practice of cognitive therapy—change strategies that assume problematic emotions and behaviors to be the result of how clients perceive and interpret events. Three levels of cognition are believed to play a significant role in producing emotional and behavioral difficulties: (1) automatic thoughts, (2) schemas or underlying assumptions, and (3) cognitive distortions. Clinical improvement depends on *cognitive restructuring*—changes in these three levels of cognition—which is the focus of this chapter.

Prochaska and Norcross (2007) characterize cognitive–behavioral therapies as "the fastest growing and most heavily researched system of psychotherapy on the contemporary scene" (p. 348). Features such as client collaboration, specification of how-to strategies to guide implementation, sensitivity to brevity and cost effectiveness, commitment to empirical evaluation, openness to integration with other therapeutic techniques to augment effectiveness, and a steadily growing track record of comparative effectiveness are some of the reasons for its growth. Computer-administered cognitive treatments are on the rise as are cognitive therapies in self-help and web-accessed formats. The breadth of applicability of cognitive therapies, their demonstrated effectiveness for wide-ranging problems, and their adaptability for diverse populations are part of why cognitive interventions are a mainstay of this book. Cognitive therapies tend to be approached in psychoeducationally oriented ways that

can be consistent with collaborative practice. In addition to establishing a collaborative relationship, the client and therapeutic helper work together as an investigative team—for example, treating problematic automatic thoughts and schemas as hypotheses to be assessed relative to evidence that seems to be consistent or inconsistent. Some developers of therapy models strive for "deepening" cognitively oriented therapies through approaches to tap less easily accessed core aspects of personal knowledge, the complexity of personal meaning systems, and the social embeddedness of people, problems, and meaning (see Neimeyer and Raskin, 2001, and Mahoney, 2003, for examples).

Although there is an exceptionally strong foundation of support for cognitive therapies (Beck, 2005), we encourage you to keep in mind that there is no one-size-fits-all or "silver bullet" set of change strategies. Cognitively oriented interventions have their share of limitations. For example, although helpers can well use cognitive therapies in a contextualized manner, consistent with assessing and helping people within circumstances that may themselves be part of the problem, the emphasis tends to be inwardly directed—focusing on distorted, maladaptive, or otherwise nonproductive thinking (Prochaska & Norcross, 2007). However, even in social conditions that are unhealthy, there are often dimensions to how people are carrying the effects of these conditions in their patterns of thought and feeling that will benefit from attention. We urge you to maintain your own critical consciousness in applying these or other interventions and to balance attention to environmental contributors, including sociopolitical and cultural factors that can easily be devalued or overlooked (Berlin, 2001).

A word about terminology: The definitional boundaries can be unclear—between cognitive and cognitive–behavioral interventions, for example. By and large, we see the interventions that we present as being consistent with three propositions considered fundamental to cognitive–behavioral therapy: (1) Cognitive activity affects behavior. (2) Cognitive activity may be monitored and altered. (3) Desired behavior change may be affected through cognitive change

(Dobson & Dozois, 2001). In this chapter, we use the term *cognitive therapy* not so much to distinguish these interventions from cognitive–behavioral ones as to focus more attention on the underpinnings of human cognition and how it works (in normative and problematic ways) and on strategies targeting cognitive change.

RECOGNIZING CULTURE, CONTEXT, AND "HOT" FACTORS IN COGNITIVE THERAPY

Mahoney (1995) suggests that

> the major conceptual developments in the cognitive psychotherapies over the past three decades have been (a) the differentiation of rationalist and constructivist approaches to cognition; (b) the recognition of social, biological, and embodiment issues; (c) the reappraisal of unconscious processes; (d) an increasing focus on self and social systems; (e) the reappraisal of emotional and experiential processes; and (f) the contribution of the cognitive psychotherapies to the psychotherapy integration movement. (p. 6).

More recently, Goodheart (2006) illustrates the blending of concepts from cognitive–behavioral therapy and other approaches such as motivational interviewing, behavioral change couples treatment, strengths-based approaches, and elements of psychodynamic theory, as well as attention to diversity factors and context.

Cognitive restructuring, sometimes referred to as *cognitive replacement,* involves fundamental cognitive change yet is integrally inclusive of "hot" factors such as emotion, motivation, goals, and values, reflecting the integration of findings from arenas such as physiology, neuroanatomy, linguistics, computer science, and cultural anthropology. Recent work has advanced understanding of the profound interdependence of mind and culture. Markus, Kitayama, and Heiman (1996) provide a detailed review of the multiple ways in which culture influences structures, systems, and transactional dynamics of cognition and meaning making. They emphasize that

> Cultural, societal, or collective contexts provide the very frames within which psychological systems can develop, and the psychological systems of the person develop in ways that are culturally resonant and that help establish the person as a member in good standing in any given group or social context. Understanding culturally mediated psychological processes necessarily involves an analysis of the meanings (the metaphors, the values, the beliefs, the goals, the schemas) and the practices (the tacit patterns of living) within which any given event or act can be made meaningful. (p. 903)

We emphasize a contextualized and culturally sensitive approach to understanding variation not only in cognitive content (e.g., schemas, beliefs, and goals as well as whether we would evaluate these as "distorted" or "maladaptive") but also in the circumstances, norms, and power dynamics that constitute the surrounding environment and conventions of daily life. Keep in mind also that the notion of culture may usefully be applied to many collectives beyond those defined by national or racial heritage—for example, cultural dimensions related to disability, older age, sexual orientation, religion, and small town or rural life. Recent discussions of the practice of cognitive therapy are provided by Beck, Freeman, Davis, et al. (2004), Dobson (2001), Leahy (2003), Mennuti, Freeman, and Christner (2006), Nurius and Macy (2007), Sperry (2006), and Young, Klosko, and Weishaar (2003).

USES OF COGNITIVE RESTRUCTURING

Cognitive restructuring has its roots in the elimination of distorted or invalid inferences, disputing irrational thoughts or beliefs, and developing new, healthier cognitions and patterns of responding. Cognitive restructuring is considered an essential component of almost every cognitive–behavioral procedure. For a sample of recent cognitive restructuring research, see Box 13.1. Inspection of this list of research reveals the variety of concerns to which cognitive restructuring has been applied. Broader reviews point to applications with depression (unipolar and bipolar), anxiety, panic disorders, trauma, social phobia, suicidality, obsessive–compulsive disorder, schizophrenia, eating disorders, anger, pain, substance abuse, gambling, self-esteem problems, stress and coping, and relapse prevention, among others. We also refer you to sources such as Guralnick & Neville (1997), Kendall (2000), Mash & Barkley (2006), and Ollendick and King (2000) for instruction specific to children and adolescents, including disabilities. This is a complex and highly evolving arena of therapeutic care. There is still much to be learned about the types of strategies that are most effective with specific problems, diverse populations, and differing conditions.

APPLICATIONS OF COGNITIVE THERAPY AND COGNITIVE RESTRUCTURING WITH DIVERSE CLIENTS

In recent years, the use of cognitive therapy with diverse groups of clients has received increased attention, although the need continues to outstrip availability (Hays, 1995; Zane, Hall, Sue, Young, & Nunez, 2004). Critiquing cognitive therapy from a multicultural viewpoint, Hays (1995) observed that the values embraced in this approach may be reflective of those supported by the status quo of the mainstream culture and should be thoughtfully applied. As an example, the emphasis on self-control that fits with the Euro-American value of personal autonomy may be empowering for some clients but may also "imply placing blame on

BOX 13.1 COGNITIVE RESTRUCTURING RESEARCH

Anxiety

Watt, M. C., Stewart, S. H., Lefaivre, M. J., & Uman, L. S. (2006). A brief cognitive–behavioral approach to reducing anxiety sensitivity decreases pain related anxiety. *Cognitive Behaviour Therapy, 35*(4), 48–256.

Gosch, E. A., Flannery-Schroeder, E., Mauro, C. F., & Compton, S. N. (2006). Principles of cognitive–behavioral therapy for anxiety disorders in children. *Journal of Cognitive Psychotherapy, 20*(3), 247–262.

Body Dysmorphic Disorder

Geremia, G. M., & Neziroglu, F. (2001). Cognitive therapy in the treatment of body dysmorphic disorder. *Clinical Psychology and Psychotherapy, 8*(4), 243–251.

Chronic Pain

Merlijn, V. P. B. M., Hunfeld, J. A. M., van der Wouden, J. C., Hazebroek-Kampschreur, A. A. J. M., van Suijlekom-Smit, L. W. A., Koes, B. W., & Passchier, J. (2005). A cognitive–behavioural program for adolescents with chronic pain—a pilot study. *Patient Education and Counseling, 59*(2), 126–134.

Controlling Mental Contamination

David, D., Macavei, B., Szentagotai, A., & McMahon, J. (2005). Cognitive restructuring and mental contamination: An empirical re-conceptualization. *Journal of Rational–Emotive and Cognitive Behavior Therapy, 23*(1), 21–56.

Couples and Family Treatment

Dattilio, F. M. (2005). The critical component of cognitive restructuring in couples therapy: A case study. *Australian and New Zealand Journal of Family Therapy, 26*(2), 73–78.

Dattilio, F. M. (2006). A cognitive–behavioral approach to reconstructing intergenerational family schemas. *Contemporary Family Therapy: An International Journal, 28*(2), 191–200.

Illness

Baarnhielm, S. (2005). Making sense of different illness realities: Restructuring of illness meaning among Swedish-born women. *Nordic Journal of Psychiatry, 59*(5), 350–356.

Insomnia

Backhaus, J., Hohagen, F., Voderholzer, U., & Riemann, D. (2001). Long-term effectiveness of a short-term cognitive–behavioral group treatment for primary insomnia. *European Archives of Psychiatry and Clinical Neuroscience, 251*(1), 35–42.

Bélanger, L., Savard, J., & Morin, C. M. (2006). Clinical management of insomnia using cognitive therapy. *Behavioral Sleep Medicine, 4*(3), 179–202.

Nightmares

Spoormaker, V. I., & van den Bout, J. (2006). Lucid dreaming treatment for nightmares: A pilot study. *Psychotherapy and Psychosomatics, 75*(6), 389–394.

Obesity

Hayward, L. M., Nixon, C., Jasper, M. P., Murphy, K. M., Harlan, V., Swirda, L., & Hayward, K. (2000). The process of restructuring and the treatment of obesity in women. *Health Care for Women International, 21*(7), 615–630.

Offenders

Wilson, D. B., Bouffard, L. A., & Mackenzie, D. L. (2005). A quantitative review of structured, group-oriented, cognitive–behavioral programs for offenders. *Criminal Justice and Behavior, 32*(2), 172–204.

Paraprosopia

Kemp, S., Young, A. W., Szulecka, K., & de Pauw, K. W. (2003). A case of paraprosopia and its treatment. *Cognitive Neuropsychiatry, 8*(1), 43–57.

Personality Disorders

Kellogg, S. H., & Young, J. E. (2006). Schema therapy for borderline personality disorder. *Journal of Clinical Psychology, 62*(4), 445–458.

Posttraumatic Stress Disorder

Foa, E. B., Hembree, E. A., Cahill, S. P., Rauch, S. A. M., Riggs, D. S., Feeny, N. C., & Yadin, E. (2005). Randomized trial of prolonged exposure for posttraumatic stress disorder with and without cognitive restructuring: Outcome at academic and community clinics. *Journal of Consulting and Clinical Psychology, 73*(5), 953–964.

Massad, P. M., & Hulsey, T. L. (2006). Causal attributions in posttraumatic stress disorder: Implications for clinical research and practice. *Psychotherapy: Theory, Research, Practice, Training, 43*(2), 201–215.

Power, K., McGoldrick, T., Brown, K., Buchanan, R., Sharp, D., Swanson, V., & Karatzias, A. (2002). A controlled comparison of eye movement desensitization and reprocessing versus exposure plus cognitive restructuring versus waiting list in the treatment of post-traumatic stress disorder. *Clinical Psychology and Psychotherapy, 9*(5), 299–318.

Smith, P., Perrin, S., & Yule, W. (1999). Cognitive behaviour therapy for post traumatic stress disorder. *Child and Adolescent Mental Health, 4*(4), 177–182.

BOX 13.1	COGNITIVE RESTRUCTURING RESEARCH

Somatization

Nakao, M., Nakao, M., Myers, P., Fricchione, G., Zuttermeister, P. C., Barsky, A. J., & Benson, H. (2001). Somatization and symptom reduction through a behavioral medicine intervention in a mind/body medicine clinic. *Behavioral Medicine, 26*(4), 169–176.

Trauma

Peres, J., Mercante, J., & Nasello, A. G. (2005). Psychological dynamics affecting traumatic memories: Implications in psychotherapy. *Psychology and Psychotherapy: Theory, Research and Practice, 78*(4), 431–447.

the individual for problems that are previously a result of unjust social conditions" (Hays, 1995, p. 311; Ivey, Ivey, & Simek-Morgan, 1997).

Cognitive therapy and cognitive restructuring have also been critiqued by feminist therapists. In the early days of feminism, cognitive–behavioral therapy was seen as admirable "for teaching women new ways of behaving" (Brown, 1994, p. 55). This was in the era when individual change was viewed as a primary solution for societal problems. More recent views in feminist therapy, multicultural therapy, and ecological therapy note dangers in an overly individualistic approach and in assisting people to accommodate to what may fundamentally be unjust or otherwise problematic environments and circumstances. If applied in a highly rationalistic manner, cognitive therapy could serve to reinforce worldviews and cognitive processes that are stereotypically Euro-American and masculine, risking devaluation of worldviews and cognitive processing styles of some women and some persons of differing heritages. Alternatively, these change strategies can be applied to support empowerment and a sense of efficacy. Similarly, cognitive therapy/restructuring employ strategies such as challenging one's beliefs and thoughts. As Kantrowitz and Ballou (1992) suggest, this challenging may not fit with some culture and gender socialization patterns, whereas others find challenging negative cognitions to be consistent with some collectivistic cultural views and codes of conduct (Comas-Diaz, 1992).

With sensitivity to cautions in mind, there is growing attention to diversity factors in cognitive practice and promising evidence (Comas-Diaz, 2006). Practice scholars are recommending use of cognitive therapies infused with gender and multicultural awareness and cultural adaptations (Bernal & Scharron del Rio, 2001; Hays, 1995; Lewis, 1994). Cognitive behavioral therapies have been pursued to assess and intervene with issues related to racism, oppression, loss, stress, and coercion (Comas-Dias, 2006, in press) and have been adapted to respond to a wide range of problems in living. Box 13.2 offers a sampling of recent literature in this regard. Ahijevych and Wewers (1993) suggested the use of cognitive restructuring as an intervention for nicotine-dependent African American women who want to stop smoking. Addressing a different problem, Hatch and Paradis

(1993) developed a 12-week group treatment incorporating cognitive restructuring, breathing, and relaxation for African American women with panic disorder. They found that the women in the group particularly valued audiovisual aids and self-help material but noted the small number of African Americans represented in television programs as well as among the group facilitators who were the role models. An African American woman who had completed successful treatment for panic attacks was invited to speak to the group. Addressing racial issues and providing access to other African Americans for both education and support seem to be critical parts of this cognitive intervention.

Iwamasa (1993) contends that cognitive restructuring can be culturally compatible for some Asian American clients, especially those who are well educated and achievement oriented. He notes that part of the appeal of this intervention is that it is structured (versus unstructured), emphasizes thoughts and behaviors, and does not require the Asian American client to oppose the traditional Asian value of not revealing personal and/or familial difficulties to strangers.

Some developments urge caution in assuming that Western treatment approaches are not suitable for ethnically diverse clients, noting the risk of cultural stereotyping. Ma (2000), for example, urges Western therapists to increase their knowledge about the diversity of lives of ethnic families to help guide use of treatments with efficacious and promising empirical support. Sonderegger & Barrett (2004) describe such an undertaking, targeting the prevention of mental health disorders, emotional distress, and impaired social functioning of immigrant and refugee children and adolescents. In this life skills program, key components of cognitive behavioral treatment are integrated with family and interpersonal components as well as developmental understanding of acculturation, including issues relevant for those from non-English-speaking backgrounds.

Johnson and Ridley (1992) have described an adaptation of cognitive restructuring for clients who sought "Christian counseling." The clients were encouraged to challenge problematic beliefs by using biblical scriptures as the basis for the disputation. These authors contended that cognitive restructuring can be adapted to culture-specific values of

BOX 13.2	COGNITIVE THERAPY RESEARCH WITH DIVERSE GROUPS

African American Clients

Ginsburg, G. S., & Drake, K. L. (2002). School-based treatment for anxious African-American adolescents: A controlled pilot study. *Journal of the American Academy of Child and Adolescent Psychiatry, 41*(7), 768–775.

Haley, W., Roth, D., Coleton, M., & Ford, G. (1996). Appraisal, coping and social support as mediators of well-being in black and white family caregivers of patients with Alzheimer's disease. *Journal of Consulting and Clinical Psychology, 64,* 121–129.

Asian American Clients

Iwamasa, G. Y. (1993). Asian Americans and cognitive behavioral therapy. *The Behavior Therapist, 16,* 233–235.

Yoo, H. C., & Lee, R. M. (2005). Ethnic identity and approach-type coping as moderators of the racial discrimination/well-being relation in Asian Americans. *Journal of Counseling Psychology, 52*(4), 497–506.

Clients with Physical Challenges

Ellis, A. (1997). Using rational emotive behavior therapy techniques to cope with disability. *Professional Psychology, 28,* 17–22.

Disabled Persons with Chronic Pain

Ehde, D. M., & Jensen, M. P. (2004). Feasibility of a cognitive restructuring intervention for treatment of chronic pain in persons with disabilities. *Rehabilitation Psychology, 49*(3), 254–258.

Elderly Clients

Lopez, M., & Mermelstein, R. (1995). A cognitive–behavioral program to improve geriatric rehabilitation outcome. *Gerontologist, 35,* 696–700.

Rapp, S., Brenes, G., & Marsh, A. P. (2002). Memory enhancement training for older adults with mild cognitive impairment: A preliminary study. *Aging and Mental Health, 6*(1), 5–11.

Rybarczyk, B., DeMarco, G., DeLaCruz, M., Lapidos, S., & Fortner, B. (2001). A classroom mind/body wellness intervention for older adults with chronic illness: Comparing immediate and 1-year benefits. *Behavioral Medicine, 27*(1), 15–28.

Thompson, L. W. (1996). Cognitive–behavioral therapy and treatment for late-life depression. *Journal of Clinical Psychiatry, 57,* 29–37.

Villa, K. K., & Abeles, N. (2000). Broad spectrum intervention and the remediation of prospective memory declines in the able elderly. *Aging and Mental Health, 4*(1), 21–29.

Latino Clients

De Rios, M. D. (2002). What we can learn from shamanic healing: Brief psychotherapy with Latino immigrant clients. *American Journal of Public Health, 92*(10), 1576–1578.

Native American Clients

Renfrey, G. S. (1992). Cognitive–behavior therapy and the Native American client. *Behavior Therapy, 23,* 321–340.

Religion

Tix, A. P., & Frazier, P. A. (1998). The use of religious coping during stressful life-events: Main effects, moderation, and mediation. *Journal of Consulting and Clinical Psychology, 66,* 411–422.

some Christian clients. In examining the role of religious coping during stressful life events, Tix and Frazier (1998) discuss the varied forms this can take and the importance of targeting both social support and cognitive restructuring and perceived control to help people make needed adjustments over time.

Increasingly, cognitive restructuring is being used with the elderly, especially those with major depressive disorders (Thompson, 1996). This use of the technique is especially important because many older people experience serious side effects with some antidepressant medications. The best attempts at using cognitive restructuring with older persons have presented the intervention as an educational rather than a therapeutic experience (Freiberg, 1995), with sensitivity to the older clients' fears and biases about disclosing concerns and dealing with their beliefs about being old

(Arean, 1993). Group modes of cognitive therapies are especially useful because they provide greater social involvement and support (Arean, 1993; Freiberg, 1995). Also, the delivery of the intervention may need to be modified depending on the client's hearing and seeing abilities and other special needs (Thompson, 1996). Cognitive therapy has also been used to improve rehabilitation outcomes in elderly persons (Lopez & Mermelstein, 1995) and to aid with life-review work by the elderly (Weiss, 1995).

Cognitive restructuring has also been used with gay, lesbian, and bisexual clients, attending to special developmental challenges and ethical considerations (Martell, Safren, & Prince, 2004). Ussher (1990) and Kuehlwein (1992) have used cognitive restructuring to help gay male clients examine and correct internalized heterosexist beliefs and thoughts. Wolfe (1992) has described the use of cognitive restructuring with a lesbian client who was dealing with both parental and social discrimination as a result of her sexual orientation.

Organista, Dwyer, and Azocar (1993) describe some very specific modifications of cognitive restructuring for Latino clients. First, it is important to have a linguistic match between predominantly Spanish-speaking clients and their helpers. Second, Organista and colleagues have found consistent issues and theories for Latino clients related to marriage and family and acculturation stress. Culture- and gender-related issues are common with Latinas and often produce depression, partly because of the culture's emphasis on *marianismo*—a cultural trait that values a Latina's role in the family as a person who is self-sacrificing and willing to endure suffering—and also because of the concept of *guadar,* holding in rather than expressing anger. These authors do use cognitive restructuring, but with Latino clients they recommend a one-step rather than a multistep disputational process to challenge errors in thinking such as "yes, but." Miranda and Dwyer (1993) discuss the use of cognitive therapy with low-income medical patients. They also note the importance of having bilingual and multicultural treatment staff available. They use treatment manuals to teach cognitive restructuring, and they recommend that the content and reading level be adapted to the client. For example, rather than using the term *generalization,* they use the phrase "thinking all bad things means everything will be bad" (Miranda & Dwyer, 1993, p. 227). They also note the importance of dealing with psychosocial stressors as well as with cognitions. They find that group rather than individual cognitive treatment is more effective for most of their clients.

Renfrey (1992) discusses the use of cognitive therapy with Native American clients. Renfrey (1992) notes that current mental health needs of many Native Americans are great, largely because of acculturation and deculturation stressors brought on by the European American culture. Native Americans' mental health needs are also underserved. Renfrey (1992) recommends that a helper collaborate with traditional healers in the Native American community. He believes that culturally sensitive cognitive therapy can be useful because it is specific and direct, involves homework, and focuses on altering present actions rather than emotional states. He recommends making an initial assessment of the client's acculturation status prior to any intervention because this variable will affect treatment process and outcomes. At the very least, cognitive restructuring must be offered in a way that promotes bicultural competence so that treatment begins with enhancement of the Native American's traditional identity and focuses on skills to help the client meet the demands of the indigenous culture, the mainstream culture, and the transculture (Renfrey, 1992, p. 330).

GUIDELINES FOR USING COGNITIVE RESTRUCTURING WITH DIVERSE GROUPS OF CLIENTS

As Hays (1995) has noted, cognitive therapy and cognitive restructuring are potentially quite applicable to diverse groups of clients, depending on the way the procedure is implemented and on the "therapist's sensitivity to diverse perspectives" (p. 312). We offer the following guidelines for using cognitive restructuring in a culturally sensitive way.

First, be very careful about the language you use when describing client cognitions. Although we don't recommend the use of the terms *rational* and *irrational* with any client, we consider these terms—and even others, such as *maladaptive* and *dysfunctional*—to be particularly inappropriate for women, gays, lesbians, clients of color, and all others who feel marginalized by the mainstream culture. These terms can further diminish a sense of self-efficacy and increase a sense of marginalization.

Second, present a rationale for cognitive restructuring that is educational rather than therapeutic to help remove the stigma that some clients of some cultural groups may have learned about mental health treatment. A didactic approach that includes specific and direct homework assignments is useful.

Third, adapt the language presented in cognitive restructuring to the client's primary language, age, educational level, and hearing, seeing, and reading abilities. Avoid jargon. Consider streamlining the procedure, focusing on one or two steps rather than multistep processes such as challenging self-defeating thoughts. Provide examples of skills and coping thoughts that are bicultural and transcultural as appropriate.

Fourth, use and/or collaborate with bilingual, ethnically similar helpers and/or traditional healers who can help you address issues of psychosocial stressors, race, and discrimination. Remember that for clients who feel marginalized, addressing these issues is as important as addressing issues of internal cognition. Also consider the usefulness for some of these clients of cognitive restructuring offered in a group rather than an individual setting.

Finally, Comas-Diaz (2006) notes that effective multicultural therapeutic relationships need extension beyond cognitive and affective empathy to include cultural empathy. Cultural empathy involves perspective taking using a cultural framework as a guide for understanding the client "from the outside in," an ability to gain and convey an understanding of the self-experience of clients from other cultures, informed by helpers interpretations of cultural data (Ridley & Lingle, 1996).

SIX COMPONENTS OF COGNITIVE RESTRUCTURING

Our presentation of cognitive restructuring reflects research findings as well as our own adaptations of cognitive restructuring based on clinical usage. We describe six components of cognitive restructuring:

1. Treatment rationale: purpose and overview of the procedure
2. Identification of client thoughts in problem situations
3. Introduction and practice of coping thoughts
4. Shifting from self-defeating to coping thoughts
5. Introduction and practice of reinforcing self-statements
6. Homework and follow-up

Each of these parts is described in this section. For a detailed description of these six components see the Interview Checklist for Cognitive Restructuring at the end of the chapter and Learning Activity 13.3.

Treatment Rationale

The rationale used in cognitive restructuring attempts to strengthen the client's belief that "self-talk" can influence performance and particularly that self-defeating thoughts or negative self-statements can cause emotional distress and interfere with performance. The examples used should be relevant to the client's gender and culture.

Rationale

The following general performance anxiety rationale can be used with clients with different concerns. You can fashion the rationale based on the specific client concern.

> One of our goals is for you to become aware of your thoughts or what you say to yourself that seems to maintain your anxiety when you are doing this activity (or while you are performing). Once we have identified these automatic thoughts, we can replace or change them. The thoughts about your performance are probably contributing to your anxiety. The performance situation may create these automatic thoughts, or perhaps the feelings you have about the situation create these thoughts. In either case, the thoughts or the feelings create physiological responses in your body, and these responses, as well as your feelings and thoughts, influence your performance. When we become aware of these automatic thoughts, we can deal with them by changing what you think about.

Overview

Here is an example of an overview of the procedure:

> We will learn how to deal with your automatic thoughts by becoming aware of when the thoughts occur or discovering what you say to yourself and what these internal self-statements are. Awareness of self-defeating automatic thoughts is one of the first steps in changing and decreasing the anxiety while performing. Once we know what the self-defeating statements are, they can act as a red flag for you to shift your self-talk to more self-enhancing performance statements. In other words, we will generate self-enhancing thoughts to shift to when you become aware of the automatic self-defeating thoughts. By shifting to the self-enhancing statements, your physiological

and emotional responses will also become self-enhancing, and this will help you perform with less self-defeating anxiety. We will learn how to shift to self-enhancing statements while you are performing, and before and after your performances.

The Difference between Self-Defeating and Self-Enhancing Thoughts

In addition to providing a standard rationale such as the one just illustrated, the helper should preface the cognitive restructuring procedure by drawing some contrast between self-enhancing thoughts and self-defeating thoughts. In some literature, the contrast is between rational and irrational thinking. Our reading of cognitive behavioral principles tells us that the helper's goal is to help focus clients on the available evidence for the automatic thoughts (e.g., noting contradictions between thoughts such as "I'm hopelessly incompetent" with evidence of achievement and effectiveness in various life roles) and distinguish between self-enhancing and self-defeating thoughts in terms of how helpful or hurtful any given thoughts are to the client and his or her goals. This explanation may help clients discriminate between their own self-enhancing and self-defeating thoughts during treatment. Many clients who could benefit from cognitive restructuring are all too aware of their self-defeating thoughts but are unaware of or unable to generate self-enhancing thoughts. Providing a contrast may help them see that they can develop more realistic thinking styles.

One way to contrast these two types of thinking is to model some examples of positive, enhancing self-talk and of negative, defeating self-talk. The examples can come out of your personal experiences or can relate to the client's problem situations. Again, providing culturally relevant examples is important. The examples might occur *before, during,* or *after* a problem situation. For instance, you might say to the client that in a situation that makes you a little uptight, such as meeting a person for the first time, you could get caught up in very negative thoughts:

Before Meeting

"What if I don't come across very well?"

"What if this person doesn't like me?"

"I'll just blow this chance to establish a good relationship."

During Meeting

"I'm not making a good impression on this person."

"This person is probably wishing our meeting were over."

"I'd just like to leave and get this over with."

"I'm sure this person won't want to see me after this."

After Meeting

"Well, that's a lost cause."

"I can never talk intelligently to a stranger."

"I might as well never bother to set up this kind of meeting again."

"How stupid I must have sounded!"

In contrast, you might demonstrate examples of positive, self-enhancing thoughts about the same situation:

Before Meeting

"I'm just going to try to get to know this person."

"I'm just going to be myself when I meet this person."

"I'll find something to talk about that I enjoy."

"This is only an initial meeting. We'll have to get together more to see how the relationship develops."

During Meeting

"I'm going to try to get something out of this conversation."

"This is a subject I know something about."

"This meeting is giving me a chance to talk about. . . ."

"It will take some time for me to get to know this person, and vice versa."

After Meeting

"That went Okay; it certainly wasn't a flop."

"I can remember how easy it was for me to discuss topics of interest to me."

"Each meeting with a new person gives me a chance to see someone else and explore new interests."

"I was able just to be myself then."

The Influence of Self-Defeating Thoughts on Performance

The last part of the rationale for cognitive restructuring should be an *explicit* attempt to point out how self-defeating thoughts or negative self-statements are unproductive and can influence emotions and behavior. You are trying to convey to the client that we are likely to believe and to act on whatever we tell ourselves. However, it is also useful to point out that in some situations, people don't *literally* tell themselves something. In many situations, our thoughts are so well learned that they reflect our core beliefs or schemas. For this reason, you might indicate that you will often ask the client to monitor or log what happens during actual situations between sessions.

The importance of providing an adequate rationale for cognitive restructuring cannot be overemphasized. If you begin implementing the procedure too quickly, or without the client's agreement, the process can backfire. One way to prevent difficulty in implementing the procedure is to enhance the client's self-efficacy. The helper can do this by practicing with the client in the session so that the client is comfortable with the shifting facets of the procedure. With repeated practice, the client can gain enough experience that

the self-enhancing thoughts become almost as automatic as the self-defeating ones. Practice helps loosen the grip on self-defeating thoughts and enables the client to formulate experiences more realistically (Beck, 1995). Also, repeated practice can enhance the client's self-efficacy with the procedure. The helper should not move ahead until the client's commitment to work with the strategy is obtained.

Identifying Client Thoughts in Problem Situations

Assuming that the client accepts the rationale provided about cognitive restructuring, the next step involves an analysis of the client's thoughts in anxiety-provoking or otherwise difficult situations. Both the range of situations and the content of the client's thoughts in these situations should be explored.

Description of Thoughts in Problem Situations

Within the interview, the practitioner should query the client about the particular distressing situations encountered and the things the client thinks about before, during, and after these situations. The practitioner might say something like this: "Sit back and think about the situations that are really upsetting to you. What are they?" Then: "Can you identify exactly what you are thinking about or telling yourself before you go to_____? What are you thinking during the situation? And afterward?"

In identifying negative or self-defeating thoughts, the client might be aided by a description of possible cues that compose a self-defeating thought. The practitioner can point out that a negative thought may have a "worry quality" such as "I'm afraid" or a "self-oriented quality" such as "I won't do well." Negative thoughts may also include elements of catastrophizing ("If I fail, it will be awful") or exaggerating ("I *never* do well" or "I *always* blow it"). Box 13.3 identifies several types of thoughts that may become habitual or automatic for clients, particularly in problem situations, and contribute to their difficulties. Each category is followed by a general description of the type of thought and an example. It may be useful to see if clients recognize their own thought patterns among these. Examine with the client what evidence may or may not be available to support such a thought and how helpful this type of thought pattern is or isn't, based on how it affects coping and distress. Clients can identify the extent to which such thoughts contribute to situational anxiety by asking themselves, "Do I (1) make unreasonable demands of myself, (2) feel that others are evaluating my performance or actions, and (3) forget that this is only one small part of my life?"

Modeling of Links between Events and Emotions

If clients have trouble identifying negative thoughts, Guidano (1995) suggests that they engage in what he calls the "movieola"

BOX 13.3   CATEGORIES OF DISTORTED AUTOMATIC THOUGHTS: A GUIDE FOR PATIENTS

1. *Mind reading:* You assume that you know what people think without having sufficient evidence of their thoughts. "He thinks I'm a loser."

2. *Fortune-telling:* You predict the future negatively: Things will get worse, or there is danger ahead. "I'll fail that exam," or "I won't get the job."

3. *Catastrophizing:* You believe that what has happened or will happen will be so awful and unbearable that you won't be able to stand it. "It would be terrible if I failed."

4. *Labeling:* You assign global negative traits to yourself and others. "I'm undesirable," or "He's a rotten person."

5. *Discounting positives:* You claim that the positive things you or others do are trivial. "That's what wives are supposed to do—so it doesn't count when she's nice to me," or "Those successes were easy, so they don't matter."

6. *Negative filtering:* You focus almost exclusively on the negatives and seldom notice the positives. "Look at all of the people who don't like me."

7. *Overgeneralizing:* You perceive a global pattern of negatives on the basis of a single incident. "This generally happens to me. I seem to fail at a lot of things."

8. *Dichotomous thinking:* You view events or people in all-or-nothing terms. "I get rejected by everyone," or "It was a complete waste of time."

9. *Shoulds:* You interpret events in terms of how things should be, rather than simply focusing on what is. "I should do well. If I don't, then I'm a failure."

10. *Personalizing:* You attribute a disproportionate amount of the blame to yourself for negative events, and you fail to see that certain events are also caused by others. "The marriage ended because I failed."

11. *Blaming:* You focus on the other person as the *source of* your negative feelings, and you refuse to take responsibility for changing yourself. "She's to blame for the way I feel now," or "My parents caused all my problems."

12. *Unfair comparisons:* You interpret events in terms of standards that are unrealistic—for example, you focus primarily on others who do better than you and find yourself inferior in the comparison. "She's more successful than I am," or "Others did better than I did on the test."

13. *Regret orientation:* You focus on the idea that you could have done better in the past, rather on what you can do better now. "I could have had a better job if I had tried," or "I shouldn't have said that."

14. *What if?:* You keep asking a series of questions about "what if" something happens, and you fail to be satisfied with any of the answers. "Yeah, but what if I get anxious?" or "What if I can't catch my breath?"

15. *Emotional reasoning:* You let your feelings guide your interpretation of reality. "I feel depressed; therefore, my marriage is not working out."

16. *Inability to disconfirm:* You reject any evidence or arguments that might contradict your negative thoughts. For example, when you have the thought "I'm unlovable," you reject as *irrelevant* any evidence that people like you. Consequently, your thought cannot be refuted. "That's not the real issue. There are deeper problems. There are other factors."

17. *Judgment focus:* You view yourself, others, and events in terms of evaluations as good–bad or superior–inferior, rather than simply describing, accepting, or understanding. You are continually measuring yourself and others according to arbitrary standards, and finding that you and others fall short. You are focused on the judgments of others as well as your own judgments of yourself. "I didn't perform well in college," or "If I take up tennis, I won't do well," or "Look how successful she is. I'm not successful."

Source: Treatment Plans and Interventions for Depression and Anxiety Disorders, by R. H. Leahy and S. J. Holland, p. 299. Copyright © 2000 The Guilford Press. Reprinted with permission.

technique. Clients are instructed to run scenes of the situation in their heads: "Then, as if [he or she] were in an editing room, the client is instructed to 'pan' the scenes, going back and forth in slow motion, thereby allowing the client to 'zoom in' on a single scene, to focus on particular aspects" of the scene (p. 157). The therapist may need to point out that the thoughts are the link between the situation and the resulting emotion, and ask the client to notice explicitly what this link seems to be. If the client is still unable to identify thoughts, the practitioner can model this link, using either the client's situations or situations from the practitioner's life. For example, the practitioner might say this:

Here is one example that happened to me. I was a music major in college, and several times a year I had to present piano recitals that were graded by several faculty members and attended by faculty, friends, and strangers. Each approaching recital got worse—I got more nervous and more preoccupied with failure. Although I didn't realize it at the time, the link between the event of the recital and my resulting feelings of nervousness was things I was thinking that I can remember now—like "What if I get out there and blank out?" or "What if my arms get so stiff I can't perform the piece?" or "What if my shaking knees are visible?" Now can you try to recall the specific thoughts you had when you felt so upset about_____?

In working with the client to identify and even elicit automatic thoughts in problem situations, the practitioner can note and bring to the client's attention any emotional responses or changes during the session, such as increases in anxiety, anger, or sadness. Getting a working sense of the paired nature of certain types of activating events, thoughts, emotions, and behaviors can be a significant step toward self-observation and change efforts outside the helping session.

Identifying Client Schemas Underlying Distorted Thoughts

Developments in cognitive therapy note layers of cognitive content and process important for treatment. Underlying automatic thoughts, for example, are assumptions and, fundamentally, our schemas. Assumptions are the if-then understandings of how things work, the conclusions, the "shoulds" that we all carry with us but that can become maladaptive in their effects. For example, a heterosexual woman who finds social situations stressful may experience an automatic thought ("He'll reject me") based on a maladaptive assumption ("I need the approval of men to like myself") fueled by schemas of self and others ("I'm unlovable. Men are rejecting.") (Leahy & Holland, 2000).

Our *schemas* are mental representations of our experiences with situations or people. Schemas contain and organize conceptually related elements to form complex constructs that are stored in memory and are activated to help us interpret new experiences. Rather than being passive repositories of information, schemas shape what we attend to, how we interpret ourselves and our world, and how we incorporate new information. For example, a client who has a schema of being inferior and abandoned will use selective attention to focus on information related to failure, isolation, and rejection, and will tend to overlook or dismiss information related to success, relational connection, and acceptance (Leahy, 1996). Thus, it is not enough to assess the cognitive content of problematic schemas; it also is necessary to identify the perceptual and interpretive habits the client may unwittingly be engaging in that are consistent with the schema and that tend to reinforce the schema's depiction of self, others, and what can be expected in the world.

Figure 13.1 illustrates ways in which schemas can function (Persons & Davidson, 2001, p. 98). External situational events, such as the behavior of others, or internal ones, such as our own thoughts or bodily sensations, activate schemas,

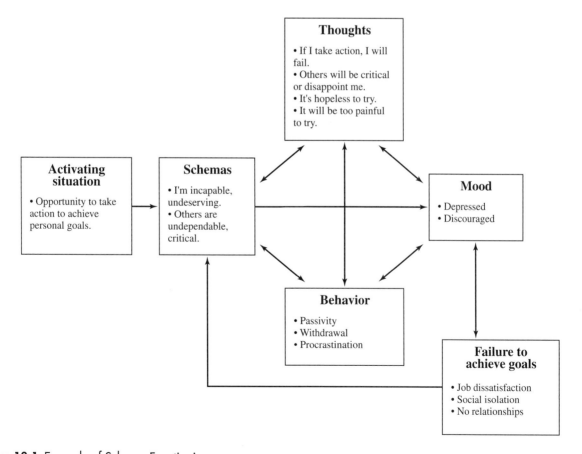

Figure 13.1 Example of Schema Functioning
Source: "Cognitive–Behavioral Case Formulation," by J. B. Persons and J. Davidson. In K. S. Dobson (Ed.), *Handbook of Cognitive-Behavioral Therapies* (2nd ed.), pp. 86–110. Copyright © 2001 by the Guilford Press. Reprinted with permisson.

drawing them out of memory storage and into an active state (although we may not be wholly aware that this is happening). These schemas become part of what is salient at the moment (making up "working memory") and influence our information processing and behavior at that particular point in time. This process works the same for adaptive and maladaptive schemas, but the outcomes from the two types are obviously different. Thus, it is important for helper and client to assess what types of situations tend to be problematic for the client, because the problematic situations will trigger maladaptive schemas (e.g., "I'm incapable, undeserving").

Schemas carry with them emotional valences (e.g., depressed, discouraged feeling) from prior experiences that influence how the client is feeling in the moment. Schemas contain understandings or assumptions about oneself, others, and the world ("If I take action I will fail; others will be critical or disappoint me") that influence a person's observations, expectations, and interpretations in the moment. Collectively, activated schemas and their content-consistent thoughts and mood bias the behaviors that the person will take in this moment and situation (e.g., passivity, withdrawal). The experience itself and its outcomes (e.g., failure to achieve goals) serve to confirm the felt "reality" represented by the schema and thus reinforce its strength and increase the likelihood of its future activation under similar circumstances.

Schemas can be tenaciously resistant to challenge and change. By and large, this stability is a strength. It is part of what helps us all to retain a sense of the coherence, understandability, and predictability of ourselves, others, and the world. However, it means that a client and helper who are collaborating to target and reconstruct or replace long-standing schemas and habits of thinking and feeling that may be central to a client's identity or worldview are working against the grain of cognitive functioning. It is believed that some schemas about self and others grow out of object representations and experiences in childhood, including early attachment styles, that are carried forward as internal working models of relationships (Bowlby, 1988). These schemas serve as foundations on which subsequent learning and representation take cognitive form, rendering the early schemas more and more elaborated and networked with other schemas, sensory states (e.g., moods, sights, smells, bodily sensations), and complex understandings. We are continuously developing and accessing schemas, and problematic schemas are not necessarily rooted in childhood or in traumatic experiences. However, schemas that have become broad based in their negative impact are generally those that the client has been living with and through for some time and that have become deeply integrated with multiple understandings, aspects of self, and a range of life situations.

The cultural context and the sociopolitical context of a person's life are other examples of powerful environmental forces that can influence developing schemas. These may take many normative forms due to exposure to different languages, traditions, norms for interaction, codes of behavior, priorities, and so forth. These differences may also offer a better understanding of difficulties. For example, children who experience or witness instances of discrimination and oppression or traumatic events probably develop different schemas than children who are not affected in those ways. In a longitudinal study, Nolen-Hoeksema, Girgus, and Seligman (1992) found that stressful life events caused children to develop a negative cognitive style that was predictive of later depression if additional stressors occurred. Differing developmental histories may also hold different sources of strength, resilience, or conceptualizations to build on. For example, identity research (Oyserman, Gant, & Ager, 1995) illuminates times when social context is limiting and group memberships such as race, gender, and socioeconomic status carry challenges (such as stigma or difficulty in managing combinations of identities) to the kinds of selves that one experiments with and develops. Within these circumstances, conceptualizing oneself as a group member, having awareness of stereotypes and limitations, and developing a schema-based vision of oneself succeeding *as a group member* contribute to healthy outcomes such as academic achievement among youth.

Leahy (1996) notes the difficulty in challenging schemas that were established when the client was operating at a pre-operational level of processing, such as childhood, "marked by egocentrism, centration, magical thinking and moral realism" (p. 192). Nonetheless, understanding how schema development and processing works is an important part of cognitive therapy. This understanding can help normalize in clients' eyes how they arrived at their current struggle as well as help guide their cognitive reconstruction efforts. An "investigative" approach is fundamental to cognitive therapy, whereby the practitioner helps the client to systematically gather data, evaluate evidence, draw conclusions, and generate alternatives. These steps are indeed constituent parts of the ongoing self-observation and cognitive–affective–behavioral change process that the client will need to continue after the end of formal helping. Consistent with this investigative aim, Leahy (1996) provides some sample questions to illustrate this identification process:

> How did your parents (siblings, peers, teachers) teach you that you are _____? (Fill in the word that best describes the client's schema.)
>
> When you learned the schema, you were 5 years old. Do you think it is wise to guide your life by what a 5-year-old thinks?
>
> What evidence is there that you are not _____?
>
> Or that you are _____? (Fill in the word that best describes the client's schema.)

What is the consequence of demanding this of yourself? Is it ever OK to be helpless? To fail? To depend on others? To be disapproved of?

How would you challenge your mother and father, now that you are an adult, if they were to describe you as_____? (Fill in the word that best describes the client's schema.) (Leahy, 1996, p. 194)

Schema-focused treatment has been referred to as relapse prevention. Even after clients began to feel better from depression, for example, they remain vulnerable to future similar difficulties due to maladaptive schemas that, unless identified and modified, could pull them back into negative patterns of information processing and social interaction. Young, Beck, and Weinberger (1998) describe schema assessment consisting of

1. A focused review of the client's history, with the aim of linking past experiences to current problems through the formation and reinforcement of maladaptive schemas
2. Use of a questionnaire designed to assess schemas
3. An experiential component to trigger schemas—that is, to activate them from long-term memory into active working memory.

Young and colleagues (1998) describe a case example with a woman (Michelle) whose problems included the inability to express herself and ask for things, especially with her husband, and recurrent thoughts that her husband had "one step out the door" of their marriage. The focused life review probed Michelle's childhood relative to the onset of her emotional difficulties and previous experiences with psychotherapy and depression. Part of the goal was to determine if a series of experiences contributed to the development of schemas that were subsequently activated and reinforced, creating a vicious cycle. The life review revealed themes of an "absentee" father, emotional isolation, anxiety about self-expression, and devaluation. The therapist hypothesized that these experiences generated schemas of "disconnection and rejection" domain (see Box 13.4).

The Schema Questionnaire (Young, 1999; Young et al., 1998) consists of 205 items and is used to formally assess the 18 underlying schemas listed in Box 13.4. This tool allows clients to indicate the extent to which they see statements operationalizing the schema as representing them. The practitioner can review responses carefully with the client for clarification, to gain additional information, and to ensure that the responses line up well with the issues of greatest concern to the client. Through the focused life review and use of the Schema Questionnaire, the helper and client, Michelle, identified four schemas that seemed most salient to the problems of concern to Michelle.

An experiential exercise can be useful by activating schemas to help the client more directly experience their content and intensity, including a high degree of affect. As Beck and associates (1990) noted, "The arousal of a strong feeling suggests not only that a core schema has been exposed, but also that the dysfunctional thinking is more accessible to modification" (quoted in Young et al., 1998, p. 299). After the helper provides a rationale for the exercise, strategies such as relaxation and guided imagery can be useful for these purposes. An excerpt from the case of Michelle provides an illustration (Young et al., 1998, p. 299). The practitioner and client were aiming to identify origins of Michelle's abandonment schema:

T: Michelle, why don't you close your eyes now and see if you can get a visual image of anything that comes into your mind.

M: Do I have to see it?

T: Yes, it's not thoughts but pictures that we want. It could be a picture of a person, of a place, anything at all; almost as if you were looking at a movie in your head.

M: What is the point of all this again?

T: Well, the point is to try to discover feelings and themes, buttons if you like, that are getting pushed, but that you're not aware of right now, like, right now you told me you're feeling butterflies but you don't know why. We often find that when people close their eyes, they get pictures that tell them why they're feeling those butterflies, why they're nervous, so it's a way of sort of getting to the deeper issues without directly talking about them, but rather through picturing them. . . .

M: I'm seeing something. I see my father leaving the house. He doesn't want to come in and be with me.

T: You're actually picturing him leaving the house?

M: Yeah, he's outside the house now leaving, and he knows I'm inside, he knows I want to be with him, but he just doesn't care to be with me. (Cries)

The therapist continued to use guided imagery to assess whether there was a link between these childhood experiences and the client's current problems with her husband.

T: Now Michelle, please keep your eyes closed and see if you can get an image of Jim and tell me what you see.

M: Well, as you said that, what I saw Jim doing was just walking out the door and just slamming the door. He had his suitcase packed and with him, and he just walked out the door and there I was in the house all alone by myself.

T: Just like you were with your father, the same feeling that you had before?

M: Yeah, it feels exactly the same.

| BOX 13.4 | EARLY MALADAPTIVE SCHEMAS |

Disconnection and Rejection

(Expectation that one's needs for security, safety, stability, nurturance, empathy, sharing of feelings, acceptance, and respect will not be met in a predictable manner. Typical family origin is detached, cold, rejecting, withholding, lonely, explosive, unpredictable, or abusive.)

1. *Abandonment/Instability (AB):* The perceived *instability* or *unreliability* of those available for support and connection. Involves the sense that significant others will not be able to continue providing emotional support, connection, strength, or practical protection because they are emotionally unstable and unpredictable (e.g., angry outbursts), unreliable, or erratically present; because they will die imminently; or because they will abandon the patient in favor of someone better.

2. *Mistrust/Abuse (MA):* The expectation that others will hurt, abuse, humiliate, cheat, lie, manipulate, or take advantage. Usually involves the perception that the harm is intentional or the result of unjustified and extreme negligence. May include the sense that one always ends up being cheated relative to others or "getting the short end of the stick."

3. *Emotional Deprivation (ED):* Expectation that one's desire for a normal degree of emotional support will not be adequately met by others. The three major forms of deprivation are

   A. *Deprivation of Nurturance:* Absence of attention, affection, warmth, or companionship.

   B. *Deprivation of Empathy:* Absence of understanding, listening, self-disclosure, or mutual sharing of feelings from others.

   C. *Deprivation of Protection:* Absence of strength, direction, or guidance from others.

4. *Defectiveness/Shame (DS):* The feeling that one is defective, bad, unwanted, inferior, or invalid in important respects; or that one would be unlovable to significant others if exposed. May involve hypersensitivity to criticism, rejection, and blame; self-consciousness, comparisons, and insecurity around others; or a sense of shame regarding one's perceived flaws. These flaws may be *private* (e.g., selfishness, angry impulses, unacceptable sexual desires) or *public* (e.g., undesirable physical appearance, social awkwardness).

5. *Social Isolation/Alienation (SI):* The feeling that one is isolated from the rest of the world, different from other people, and/or not part of any group or community.

Impaired Autonomy and Performance

(Expectations about oneself and the environment that interfere with one's perceived ability to separate, survive, function independently, or perform successfully. Typical family origin is enmeshed, undermining of child's confidence, overprotective, or failing to reinforce child for performing competently outside the family.)

6. *Dependence/Incompetence (DI):* Belief that one is unable to handle one's *everyday responsibilities* in a competent manner, without considerable help from others (e.g., take care of oneself, solve daily problems, exercise good judgment, tackle new tasks, make good decisions). Often presents as helplessness.

7. *Vulnerability to Harm or Illness (VH):* Exaggerated fear that *imminent* catastrophe will strike at any time and that one will be unable to prevent it. Fears focus on one or more of the following: (A) *medical catastrophes*: e.g., heart attacks, AIDS; (B) *emotional catastrophes*: e.g., going crazy; (C) *external catastrophes*: e.g., elevators collapsing, victimized by criminals, airplane crashes, earthquakes.

8. *Enmeshment/Undeveloped Self (EM):* Excessive emotional involvement and closeness with one or more significant others (often parents), at the expense of full individuation or normal social development. Often involves the belief that at least one of the enmeshed individuals cannot survive or be happy without the constant support of the other. May also include feelings of being smothered by, or fused with, others *or* insufficient individual identity. Often experienced as a feeling of emptiness and floundering, having no direction, or in extreme cases questioning one's existence.

9. *Failure (FA):* The belief that one has failed, will inevitably fail, or is fundamentally inadequate relative to one's peers, in areas of *achievement* (school, career, sports, etc.). Often involves beliefs that one is stupid, inept, untalented, ignorant, lower in status, less successful than others, etc.

Impaired Limits

(Deficiency in internal limits, responsibility to others, or long-term goal-orientation. Leads to difficulty respecting the rights of others, cooperating with others, making commitments, or setting and meeting realistic personal goals. Typical family origin is characterized by permissiveness, overindulgence, lack of direction, or a sense of superiority—rather than appropriate confrontation, discipline, and limits in relation to taking responsibility, cooperating in a reciprocal manner, and setting goals. In some cases, child may not have been pushed to tolerate normal levels of discomfort, or may not have been given adequate supervision, direction, or guidance.)

BOX 13.4   EARLY MALADAPTIVE SCHEMAS

10. *Entitlement/Grandiosity (ET):* The belief that one is superior to other people; entitled to special rights and privileges; or not bound by the rules of reciprocity that guide normal social interaction. Often involves insistence that one should be able to do or have whatever one wants, regardless of what is realistic, what others consider reasonable, or the cost to others; *or* an exaggerated focus on superiority (e.g., being among the most successful, famous, wealthy)—in order to achieve *power* or *control* (not primarily for attention or approval). Sometimes includes excessive competitiveness toward, or domination of, others: asserting one's power, forcing one's point of view, or controlling the behavior of others in line with one's own desires—without empathy or concern for others' needs or feelings.

11. *Insufficient Self-Control/Self-Discipline (IS):* Pervasive difficulty or refusal to exercise sufficient self-control and frustration tolerance to achieve one's personal goals, or to restrain the excessive expression of one's emotions and impulses. In its milder form, patient presents with an exaggerated emphasis on *discomfort-avoidance:* avoiding pain, conflict, confrontation, responsibility, or overexertion—at the expense of personal fulfillment, commitment, or integrity.

Other-Directedness

(An excessive focus on the desires, feelings, and responses of others, at the expense of one's own needs—in order to gain love and approval, maintain one's sense of connection, or avoid retaliation. Usually involves suppression and lack of awareness regarding one's own anger and natural inclinations. Typical family origin is based on conditional acceptance; children must suppress important aspects of themselves in order to gain love, attention, and approval. In many such families, the parents' emotional needs and desires—or social acceptance and status—are valued more than the unique needs and feelings of each child.)

12. *Subjugation (SB):* Excessive surrendering of control to others because one feels *coerced*—usually to avoid anger, retaliation, or abandonment. The two major forms of subjugation are

    A. *Subjugation of Needs:* Suppression of one's preferences, decisions, and desires.

    B. *Subjugation of Emotions:* Suppression of emotional expression, especially anger.

    Usually involves the perception that one's own desires, opinions, and feelings are not valid or important to others. Frequently presents as excessive compliance, combined with hypersensitivity to feeling trapped. Generally leads to a buildup of anger, manifested in maladaptive symptoms

(e.g., passive–aggressive behavior, uncontrolled outbursts of temper, psychosomatic symptoms, withdrawal of affection, "acting out," substance abuse).

13. *Self-Sacrifice (SS):* Excessive focus on *voluntarily* meeting the needs of others in daily situations, at the expense of one's own gratification. The most common reasons are to prevent causing pain to others; to avoid guilt from feeling selfish; or to maintain the connection with others perceived as needy. Often results from an acute sensitivity to the pain of others. Sometimes leads to a sense that one's own needs are not being adequately met and to resentment of those who are taken care of. (Overlaps with concept of co-dependency.)

14. *Approval-Seeking/Recognition-Seeking (AS):* Excessive emphasis on gaining approval, recognition, or attention from other people, or fitting in, at the expense of developing a secure and true sense of self. One's sense of esteem is dependent primarily on the reactions of others rather than on one's own natural inclinations. Sometimes includes an overemphasis on status, appearance, social acceptance, money, or achievement—as means of gaining *approval, admiration,* or *attention* (not primarily for power or control). Frequently results in major life decisions that are inauthentic or unsatisfying; or in hypersensitivity to rejection.

Overvigilance and Inhibition

(Excessive emphasis on suppressing one's spontaneous feelings, impulses, and choices or on meeting rigid, internalized rules and expectations about performance and ethical behavior—often at the expense of happiness, self-expression, relaxation, close relationships, or health. Typical family origin is grim, demanding, and sometimes punitive: performance, duty, perfectionism, following rules, hiding emotions, and avoiding mistakes predominate over pleasure, joy, and relaxation. There is usually an undercurrent of pessimism and worry—that things could fall apart if one fails to be vigilant and careful at all times.)

15. *Negativity/Pessimism (NP):* A pervasive, lifelong focus on the negative aspects of life (pain, death, loss, disappointment, conflict, guilt, resentment, unsolved problems, potential mistakes, betrayal, things that could go wrong, etc.) while minimizing or neglecting the positive or optimistic aspects. Usually includes an exaggerated expectation—in a wide range of work, financial, or interpersonal situations—that things will eventually go seriously wrong, or that aspects of one's life that seem to be going well will ultimately fall apart. Usually involves

(continued)

BOX 13.4	EARLY MALADAPTIVE SCHEMAS

(continued)

an inordinate fear of making mistakes that might lead to financial collapse, loss, humiliation, or being trapped in a bad situation. Because potential negative outcomes are exaggerated, these patients are frequently characterized by chronic worry, vigilance, complaining, or indecision.

16. *Emotional Inhibition (EI):* The excessive inhibition of spontaneous action, feeling, or communication—usually to avoid disapproval by others, feelings of shame, or losing control of one's impulses. The most common areas of inhibition involve (a) inhibition of *anger* and aggression; (b) inhibition of *positive impulses* (e.g., joy, affection, sexual excitement, play); (c) difficulty expressing *vulnerability* or *communicating* freely about one's feelings, needs, etc.; or (d) excessive emphasis on *rationality* while disregarding emotions.

17. *Unrelenting Standards/Hypercriticalness (US):* The underlying belief that one must strive to meet very high *internalized standards* of behavior and performance, usually to avoid criticism. Typically results in feelings of pressure or difficulty slowing down; and in hypercriticalness toward oneself and others. Must involve significant impairment in pleasure, relaxation, health, self-esteem, sense of accomplishment, or satisfying relationships.

Unrelenting standards typically present as (a) *perfectionism,* inordinate attention to detail, or an underestimate of how good one's own performance is relative to the norm; (b) *rigid rules* and "shoulds" in many areas of life, including unrealistically high moral, ethical, cultural, or religious precepts; or (c) preoccupation with *time and efficiency,* so that more can be accomplished.

18. *Punitiveness (PU):* The belief that people should be harshly punished for making mistakes. Involves the tendency to be angry, intolerant, punitive, and impatient with those people (including oneself) who do not meet one's expectations or standards. Usually includes difficulty forgiving mistakes in oneself or others because of a reluctance to consider extenuating circumstances, allow for human imperfection, or empathize with feelings.

Source: Copyright 1998, Jeffrey Young, PhD. Unauthorized reproduction without written consent from the author is prohibited. For more information, write: Cognitive Therapy Center of New York, 120 East 56th Street, Suite 530, New York, NY 10022.

Putting together all the information, the practitioner develops a formulation of the schemas that appear to be centrally involved in the most troubling issues and situations. This formulation needs to be reviewed with the client to determine if it seems to be accurate and to be functioning in the manner that the practitioner believes. This assessment then informs subsequent schema content and activation change efforts. (See Learning Activity 13.1.)

Client Monitoring of Thoughts

The practitioner can also have the client identify situations and thoughts by monitoring and recording events and thoughts outside the interview in the form of homework. An initial homework assignment might be to have the client observe and record for one week at least three self-defeating statements and emotions per day in the stressful situation. The client could record on a daily log the self-defeating self-statements and the emotions for each situation in which the statements were noted (see Figure 13.2).

Using the client's data, the practitioner and client can determine which of the thoughts were self-enhancing and productive and which were self-defeating and unproductive. The practitioner should try to have the *client* discriminate between the two types of statements and identify why the negative ones are unproductive. The identification serves several purposes. First, it is a way to determine whether the client's present repertory consists of both positive and negative self-statements or whether the client is generating or recalling only negative thoughts. These data may also provide information about the client's degree of distress in a particular situation. If some self-enhancing thoughts are identified, the client becomes aware that alternatives are already present in his or her thinking style. If no self-enhancing thoughts are reported, this is a cue that some specific attention may be needed in this area. The practitioner can demonstrate how the client's unproductive thoughts can be changed by showing how self-defeating thoughts can be restated more constructively.

Introduction and Practice of Coping Thoughts

At this point in the procedure, the focus shifts from the client's self-defeating thoughts to other kinds of thoughts that are incompatible with the self-defeating ones. These incompatible thoughts may be called *coping thoughts, coping statements,* or *coping self-instructions.* They are developed for and with each client. There is no attempt to have all clients accept a common core of rational beliefs, as is often done in rational–emotive therapy.

The introduction and practice of coping statements are, as far as we know, crucial to the overall success of the cognitive restructuring procedure. Rehearsal of coping statements, by itself, is almost as effective as the combination of identifying negative statements and replacing them with incompatible coping thoughts.

LEARNING ACTIVITY	**13.1**	**Schema Identification**

 Learning Activity 13.3 addresses the overall array of steps involved in cognitive restructuring, asking you to personalize and get familiar with these steps by applying them to yourself. Here we ask you to begin by focusing on the schema component. Our purpose is to give you a working understanding of schemas as a critical building foundation of both adaptive and maladaptive perceptions and cognitive functioning.

1. Follow the instructions for Part One of Learning Activity 13.3 on page 403. Decide which of the eight statements are self-defeating. Then decide how you would categorize those self-defeating statements according to the five domains of maladaptive schemas listed in Box 13.4.

2. Examine the self-defeating thoughts you record in your weekly log as part of Learning Activity 13.3 (see Part Two). How would you categorize them relative to the five domains of maladaptive schemas? If you have difficulty with this, try a guided imagery exercise such as the one depicted in the case example of Michelle. What feeling states are evoked? Do these emotional reactions aid you in identifying the schema that may cognitively represent self-defeating thoughts that trouble you?

Explanation and Examples of Coping Thoughts

The helper should explain the purpose of coping thoughts clearly. The client needs to understand that it is difficult to think of failing at an experience (a self-defeating thought) while concentrating on doing one's best regardless of the outcome (a coping thought). Here's an example explaining the purpose and use of coping thoughts:

> So far we've worked at identifying some of the self-defeating things you think during _____. As long as you're thinking about those kinds of things, they can make you feel anxious. But as soon as you replace these with coping thoughts, then the coping thoughts take over, because it is almost impossible to concentrate on both failing at something and coping with the situation at the same time. The coping thoughts help you to manage the situation and to cope if you start to feel overwhelmed.

The helper should also model some examples of coping thoughts so that the client can clearly differentiate between a self-defeating and a coping thought. Here are some examples of coping thoughts to use *before* a situation:

Before Situation
"I've done this before, and it is never as bad as I think."
"Stay calm in anticipating this."

"Do the best I can. I'm not going to worry how people will react."
"This is a situation that can be a challenge."
"It won't be bad—only a few people will be there."

Here are examples of coping thoughts to use *during* a situation:

During Situation
"Focus on the task."
"Just think about what I want to do or say."
"What is it I want to accomplish now?"
"Relax so I can focus on the situation."
"Step back a minute, take a deep breath."
"Take one step at a time."
"Slow down, take my time, don't rush."
"Okay, don't get out of control. It's a signal to cope."

If you go back and read over these lists of coping examples, you may notice some subtle differences. There are four types of coping statements: (1) *Situational coping statements* help the client reduce the potential level of threat or the severity of the anticipated situation. Examples are "It won't be too bad" or "Only a few people will be watching me." (2) *Task-oriented coping statements* refer more to the plans, steps, or behaviors that the person will need to demonstrate during the

Date: _____ Week: _____

Situations	*Emotions*	*Self-Defeating Statements*
1. _____	1. _____	1. _____
2. _____	2. _____	2. _____
3. _____	3. _____	3. _____

Figure 13.2 Example of a Daily Log

situation, such as "Concentrate on what I want to say or do," "Think about the task," or "What do I want to accomplish?" (3) *Statements to cope with being overwhelmed* are another type, such as "Keep cool," "Stay calm," or "Relax and take a deep breath." *Positive self-statements* allow clients to reinforce or encourage themselves for having coped. Examples include "Great, I did it" or "I managed to get through that all right." Positive self-statements can be used during a stressful situation and especially after the situation. Later in this chapter we describe the use of positive self-statements in cognitive restructuring in more detail.

In explaining about and modeling potential coping thoughts, you may want to note the difference between *coping* thoughts and *mastery* thoughts. Coping thoughts help a client deal with or manage a situation, event, or person adequately. Mastery thoughts are directed toward helping a person "conquer" or master a situation in an almost flawless manner. For some clients, mastery self-instructions may function as perfectionistic standards that are, in reality, too difficult to attain. Use of mastery thoughts can make these clients feel more pressured rather than more relieved. For these reasons, we recommend that helpers avoid modeling mastery self-statements and also remain alert to clients who may spontaneously use mastery self-instructions in subsequent practice sessions during the cognitive restructuring procedure.

Client Examples of Coping Thoughts

After providing some examples, the practitioner should ask the client to think of additional coping statements. The client may come up with self-enhancing or positive statements that she or he has used in other situations. The helper should encourage the client to select coping statements that feel most natural. Clients can identify coping thoughts by discovering convincing counterarguments for their unrealistic thoughts.

Client Practice

Using client-selected coping statements, the practitioner should ask the client to practice verbalizing coping statements aloud. Doing this is important because most clients are not accustomed to using coping statements. Such practice may reduce some of the client's initial discomfort and can strengthen confidence in being able to produce different "self-talk." In addition, clients who are "formally" trained to practice coping statements systematically may use a greater variety of coping thoughts, may use more specific coping thoughts, and may report more consistent use of coping thoughts in vivo.

At first, the client can practice verbalizing the individual coping statements that she or he selected to use before and during the situation. Gradually, as the client gets accustomed to coping statements, the coping thoughts should be practiced in the natural sequence in which they would be used. First, the client would anticipate the situation and practice coping statements before the situation to prepare for it. Then the client would practice coping thoughts during the situation—focusing on the task and coping with feeling overwhelmed.

It is important for the client to be actively involved in these practice sessions. Try to ensure that the client does not simply rehearse the coping statements by rote. Instead, the client should use these practices to try to internalize the meaning of the coping statements. One way to encourage more client involvement and self-assertion in these practice attempts is to suggest that the client pretend he or she is talking to an audience or a group of persons and needs to speak in a persuasive, convincing manner to get his or her point across.

Shifting from Self-Defeating to Coping Thoughts

After the client has identified negative thoughts and has practiced alternative coping thoughts, the practitioner introduces the rehearsal of shifting from self-defeating to coping thoughts during stressful situations. Practice of this shift helps the client use a self-defeating thought as a cue for an immediate switch to coping thoughts. The importance of repeated and supported practice both within and outside of sessions, the latter being where most of the naturally occurring stressful situations will occur, cannot be overstated. New response patterns have to compete with older ones to gain their accessibility and salience at times most needed. Practice with support is essential to forming these new patterns.

Helper Demonstration of the Shift

The helper should model this process before asking the client to try it. This gives the client an accurate idea of how to practice this shift. Here is an example of modeling for a high school student who constantly "freezes up" in competitive situations:

> Okay, I'm sitting here waiting for my turn to try out for cheerleader. Ooh, I can feel myself getting very nervous [anxious feeling]. Now, wait, what am I so nervous about? I'm afraid I'm going to make a fool of myself [self-defeating thought]. Hey, that doesn't help [cue to cope]. It will take only a few minutes, and it will be over before I know it. Besides, only the faculty sponsors are watching. It's not like the whole school [situation-oriented coping thoughts].

> Well, the person before me is just about finished. Oh, they're calling my name. Boy, do I feel tense [anxious feelings]. What if I don't execute my jumps [self-defeating thought]? Okay, don't think about what I'm not going to do. Okay, start out it's my turn. Just think about my routine—the way I want it to go [task-oriented coping thoughts].

Client Practice of the Shift

After the demonstration, the client should practice identifying and stopping self-defeating thoughts and replacing them with coping thoughts. The practitioner can monitor the client's progress and coach if necessary. Rehearsal of this shift involves four steps:

1. The client imagines the stressful situation or carries out his or her part in the situation by means of a role play.
2. The client is instructed to recognize the onset of any self-defeating thoughts and to signal this by raising a hand or finger.
3. The client is told to stop these thoughts or to reframe these thoughts.
4. After the self-defeating thought is stopped, the client immediately replaces it with the coping thoughts. The client should be given some time to concentrate on the coping thoughts. Initially, it may be helpful for the client to verbalize coping thoughts; later, this can occur covertly.

As the client seems able to identify, stop, and replace the self-defeating thoughts, the practitioner can gradually decrease the amount of assistance. Before homework is assigned, the client should be able to practice and carry out this shift in the interview setting in a completely self-directed manner. Social support, such as friends or family members, can also support the client in this self-directed goal—for example, by anticipating stressful situations and walking through them, reviewing situations, and reinforcing use of the coping thoughts identified with the helper. This kind of contextual support is best formulated with the helper and can be a powerful resource toward situating clients' change efforts within their support systems and working realistically with their social environments.

Introduction and Practice of Reinforcing Self-Statements

The next-to-last part of cognitive restructuring involves teaching clients how to reinforce themselves for having coped. This is accomplished by modeling by the practitioner—and possibly by others, if relevant—and by client practice of positive, or reinforcing, self-statements. Many clients who could benefit from cognitive restructuring report not only frequent self-defeating thoughts but also few or no positive or rewarding self-evaluations. Some clients may learn to replace self-defeating thoughts with task-oriented coping ones and feel better but not be satisfied with their progress. The purpose of including positive self-statements in cognitive restructuring is to help clients learn to praise or congratulate themselves for signs of progress. Although the helper can provide social reinforcement in the interview, as can others in the support network, the client cannot always be dependent on encouragement from someone else when confronted with a stressful situation.

Purpose and Examples of Positive Self-Statements

The helper should explain the purpose of reinforcing self-statements to the client and provide some examples. An explanation might sound like this:

> You know, Isabella, you've really done very well in handling these situations and learning to stop those self-defeating ideas and to use some coping thoughts. Now it's time to give yourself credit for your progress. I will help you learn to encourage yourself by using rewarding thoughts so that each time you're in this situation and you cope, you also give yourself a pat on the back for handling the situation and not getting overwhelmed by it. This kind of self-encouragement helps you to note your progress and prevents you from getting discouraged.

Then the helper can give some examples of reinforcing self-statements:

Positive Self-Statements
"Gee, I did it."
"Hey, I handled that Okay."
"I didn't let my emotions get the best of me."
"I made some progress, and that feels good."
"See, it went pretty well after all."

Client Selection of Positive Self-Statements

After the helper provides some examples, the client should be asked for additional positive statements. The client should select the statements that feel suitable. This is particularly important in using reinforcing statements because the reinforcing value of a statement may be very idiosyncratic.

Helper Demonstration of Positive Self-Statements

The helper should demonstrate how the client can use a positive self-statement after coping with a situation. Here is an example of modeling the use of positive self-statements during and after a stressful situation. In this case, the client was an institutionalized adolescent who was confronting her parents in a face-to-face meeting:

> Okay, I can feel them putting pressure on me. They want me to talk. I don't want to talk. I just want to get the hell out of here [self-defeating thought]. Slow down; wait a minute. Don't pressure yourself. Stay cool [coping with being overwhelmed]. Good. That's better [positive self-statement].
>
> Well, it's over. It wasn't too bad. I stuck it out. That's progress [positive self-statement].

Client Practice of Positive Self-Statements

The client should be instructed to practice using positive self-statements during and after the stressful situation. The practice occurs first within the interview and gradually outside the interview with in vivo assignments. Learning Activity 13.3

Like Learning Activity 13.1, this activity focuses on one aspect of cognitive restructuring —specifically, to prepare you to help clients build on their self-observations of problematic patterns toward brainstorming and trying out alternative ones.

Figure 13.3 provides an example of a homework log sheet to use with a client. Review that example. Notice that one part of the homework is to use questions at the bottom to compose an alternative response to a problematic automatic thought.

Use the six questions at the bottom of Figure 13.3 in your own cognitive restructuring exercise. Answer each question. Do these questions help you gain a new way of looking at yourself or at the situation that was unpleasant or distressing? Develop one or more alternative responses to the distressing situation that would be more adaptive. How readily can you do this? If generating adaptive alternatives is something of a struggle, consider what might be helpful (e.g., having a professional helper generate examples, playing either the client or the helper role, hearing examples from others who have made some gains with similar kinds of issues).

provides illustrations of negative self-defeating and positive self-enhancing statements that you can use as models for those you identify or develop with clients.

Homework and Follow-up

Although homework is an integral part of every step of the cognitive restructuring procedure, the client should ultimately be able to use cognitive restructuring whenever it is needed in actual distressing situations. The client should be instructed to use cognitive restructuring in vivo but cautioned not to expect instant success. Clients can be reminded of the time they have spent playing the old tape over and over in their heads and of the need to make frequent and lengthy substitutions with the new tape. The client can monitor and record the instances in which cognitive restructuring was used over several weeks.

The practitioner can help with the written recording by providing a homework log sheet that might look something like Figure 13.3. The client's log data can be reviewed at a follow-up session to determine the number of times the client is using cognitive restructuring and the amount of progress that has occurred. The helper can also use the follow-up session to encourage the client to apply the procedure to stressful situations that could arise in the future. This may encourage the client to generalize the use of cognitive restructuring to situations other than those that are presently considered problematic. Learning Activity 13.2 provides you an opportunity to use Figure 13.2 in your own cognitive restructuring exercise.

Occasionally, a client's level of distress may not diminish even after repeated practice in restructuring self-defeating thoughts. In some cases, negative self-statements do not precede or contribute to the person's strong feelings. Some emotions may be classically conditioned and therefore may be better treated by a counterconditioning procedure, such as exposure or systematic desensitization. However, cognitive processes may even play some role in maintaining or reducing strong emotions such as classically conditioned fears.

When cognitive restructuring does not reduce a client's level of distress, depression, or anxiety, the practitioner and client may need to redefine the concern and goals. Perhaps treatment may need to focus more on external psychosocial stressors rather than on internal events. The helper should consider the possibility that his or her assessment has been inaccurate and that there are, in fact, no persistent thought patterns that are functionally tied to this particular client's issue. Remember that the assessment of initial issues in living may not always turn out to be valid or accurate, that changes over the course of helping affect an intervention plan, and that flexibility is needed to meet each client's unique needs.

If the helper believes that the original problem assessment is accurate, perhaps a change in parts of the cognitive restructuring procedure is necessary. Here are some possible revisions:

1. The amount of time the client uses to shift from self-defeating to coping thoughts and to imagine coping thoughts can be increased.
2. The coping statements selected by client may not be very helpful. The practitioner may need to help the client change the type of coping statements.
3. Cognitive restructuring should be supplemented either with additional coping skills, such as deep breathing or relaxation, or with skill training.

Another reason for failure of cognitive restructuring may be that the client's behaviors result from errors in encoding rather than errors in reasoning. In that case, a different strategy—reframing, designed to alter encoding or perceptual errors—may be useful, as may be such strategies as reverse role plays, guided imagery, or individualized flash cards, all with prompts to attend to in order to "read" situational cues in different ways.

Directions: When you notice your mood getting worse, ask yourself, "What's going through my mind right now?" Then as soon as possible jot down the thought or mental image in the "Automatic thought(s)" column.

Date/time	Situation	Automatic thought(s)	Emotion(s)	Adaptive response	Outcome
	1. What actual event or stream of thoughts, or daydreams or recollection led to the unpleasant emotion?	1. What thought(s) and/or image(s) went through your mind?	1. What emotion(s) (sad/ anxious/ angry/ etc.) did you feel at the time?	1. (optional) What cognitive distortion did you make?	1. How much do you now believe each automatic thought?
	2. What (if any) distressing physical sensations did you have?	2. How much did you believe each one at the time (0 to 100%)?	2. How intense (0-100%) was the emotion?	2. Use questions at bottom to compose a response to the automatic thought(s). 3. How much do you believe each response?	2. What emotion(s) do you feel now? How intense (0 to 100%) is the emotion? 3. What will you do (or did you do)?
Friday 2/23 10 A.M. Tuesday 2/27 12 P.M. Thursday 2/29 5 P.M.	*Talking on the phone with Donna. Studying for my exam. Thinking about my economics class tomorrow. Noticing my heart beating fast and my trouble concentrating.*	*She must not like me anymore. 90% I'll never learn this. 100% I might get called on and I won't give a good answer. 80% What's wrong with me?*	*Sad 80% Sad 95% Anxious 80% Anxious 80%*		

Questions to help you compose an alternative response: (1) What is the evidence that the automatic thought is true? Not true? (2) Is there an alternative explanation? (3) What's the worst that could happen? Could I live through it? What's the best that could happen? What's the most realistic outcome? (4) What's the effect of my believing the automatic thought? What could be the effect of my changing my thinking? (5) What should I do about it? (6) If _____ [friend's name] was in the situation and had this thought, what would I tell him/her? (See also Learning Activity 13.2.)

Figure 13.3 Example of a homework log sheet
Source: Cognitive Therapy: Basics and Beyond, by J. S. Beck, p. 126. Copyright © 1995 by The Guilford Press. Reprinted by permission

MODEL DIALOGUE FOR COGNITIVE RESTRUCTURING: THE CASE OF ISABELLA

We demonstrate cognitive restructuring with Isabella, who is having problems in math class. The interview is directed toward helping Isabella replace self-defeating thoughts with coping thoughts. This is the nuts and bolts of cognitive restructuring.

1. **Helper:** Good to see you again, Isabella. How did your week go?

Client: Pretty good. I did a lot of practice. I also tried to do this in math class. It helped some, but I still felt nervous. Here are my logs.

In response 2, the helper gives a *rationale* for cognitive restructuring, *explains the purpose of "coping" thoughts* to Isabella, and gives an *overview* of the strategy.

2. **Helper:** Today we're going to work on having you learn to use some more constructive thoughts. I call these coping thoughts. You can replace the negative thoughts with coping thoughts that will help you when you're anticipating your class, in your class itself, and when things happen in your class that are especially hard for you—like taking a test or going to the board. What questions do you have about this?

Client: I don't think any—although I don't know if I know exactly what you mean by a coping thought.

The helper, in response 3, *explains and gives some examples of coping thoughts* and particular times when Isabella might need to use them.

3. **Helper:** Let me explain about these and give you some examples. Then perhaps you can think of your own examples. The first thing is that there are probably different times when you could use coping thoughts—like before math class, when you're anticipating it. Only, instead of worrying about it, you can use this time to prepare to handle it. For example, some coping thoughts you might use before math class are "No need to get nervous. Just think about doing okay" or "You can manage this situation" or "Don't worry so much—you've got the ability to do okay." Then, during math class, you can use coping thoughts to get through the class and to concentrate on what you're doing, such as "Just psych yourself up to get through this" or "Look at this class as a challenge, not a threat" or "Keep your cool; you can control your nervousness." Then, if there are certain times during math class that are especially hard for you, like taking a test or going to the board, there are coping thoughts you can use to help you deal with really hard things, like "Think about

staying very calm now" or "Relax, take a deep breath" or "Stay as relaxed as possible. This will be over shortly." After math class, or after you cope with a hard situation, you can learn to encourage yourself for having coped by thinking things like "You did it" or "You were able to control your negative thoughts" or "You're making progress." Do you get the idea?

Client: Yes, I think so.

In responses 4–7, the helper instructs Isabella *to select and practice coping thoughts at each critical phase,* starting with *preparing for class.*

4. **Helper:** Isabella, let's take one thing at a time. Let's work just with what you might think before your math class. Can you come up with some coping thoughts you could use when you're anticipating your class?

Client: Well [pauses]. I could think about just working on my problems and not worrying about myself. I could think that when I work at it, I usually get it even if I'm slow.

5. **Helper:** Okay, good. Now just to get the feel for these, practice using them. Perhaps you could imagine you are anticipating your class—just say these thoughts aloud as you do so.

Client: I'm thinking that I could look at my class as a challenge. I can think about just doing my work. When I concentrate on my work, I usually do get the answers.

6. **Helper:** Good! How did that feel?

Client: Okay, I can see how this might help. Of course, I don't usually think these kinds of things.

7. **Helper:** I realize that, and later on today we'll practice actually having you use these thoughts. You'll get to the point where you can use your nervousness as a signal to cope. You can stop the self-defeating thoughts and use these coping thoughts instead. Let's practice this some more. [Additional practice ensues.]

In responses 8–10, the helper asks Isabella *to select and practice verbalizing coping thoughts* she can use during class.

8. **Helper:** Isabella, now you seem to have several kinds of coping thoughts that might help you when you're anticipating math class. What about some coping thoughts you could use during the class? Perhaps some of these could help you concentrate on your work instead of your tenseness.

LEARNING ACTIVITY	**13.3**	**Cognitive Restructuring**

Part One

Listed below are eight statements. Read each statement carefully, and decide whether it is a self-defeating or a self-enhancing statement. A *self-defeating thought* is a negative, unproductive way to view a situation. A *self-enhancing thought* is a realistic, productive interpretation of a situation or of oneself. Write down your answers. Then compare your responses to those in Feedback box 13.3.

1. "Now that I've had this accident, I'll *never* be able to do anything I want to do again."
2. "How can I ever give a good speech when I don't know what I want to say?"
3. "Using a wheelchair is not as hard as it looks. I can get around wherever I want to go."
4. "I had to come to this country without my son and now that he is coming here too, I know he won't want to have anything to do with me."
5. "What I need to think about is what I want to say, not what I think I *should* say."
6. "If I just weren't a diabetic, a lot more opportunities would be available to me."
7. "Why bother? She probably wouldn't want to go out with me anyway."
8. "Of course I would prefer that my daughter marries a man, but if she chooses to be single or be with another woman, I'm okay with that too. It's her life, and I love her no matter what."

Part Two

This part of the Learning Activity is designed to help you personalize cognitive restructuring in some way by using it yourself.

1. Identify a problem situation for yourself—a situation in which you don't do what you want to, not because you don't have the skills but because of your negative, self-defeating thoughts. Some examples:

a. You need to approach your boss about a raise, promotion, or change in duties. You know what to say, but you are keeping yourself from doing it because you aren't sure it would have any effect and you aren't sure how the person might respond.
b. You have the skills to be an effective helper, yet you constantly think that you aren't.
c. You continue to get positive feedback about the way you handle a certain situation, yet you are constantly thinking you don't do this very well.

2. For about a week, every time this situation comes up, monitor all the thoughts you have *before, during,* and *after* the situation. Write these thoughts in a log. At the end of the week, do the following:

a. Identify which of the thoughts are self-defeating.
b. Identify which of the thoughts are self-enhancing.
c. Determine whether the greatest number of self-defeating thoughts occur before, during, or after the situation.

3. In contrast to the self-defeating thoughts you have, identify some possible coping or self-enhancing thoughts you could use. On paper, list some you could use *before, during,* and *after* the situation, with particular attention to the time period when you tend to use almost all self-defeating thoughts. Make sure that you include in your list some positive or self-rewarding thoughts too—for coping.

4. Imagine the situation—*before, during,* and *after* it. As you do this, stop any self-defeating thoughts and replace them with coping and self-rewarding thoughts. You can even practice this in a role play. Practice this step until you can feel your coping and self-rewarding thoughts taking hold.

5. Construct a homework assignment for yourself that encourages you to apply this as needed when the self-defeating thoughts occur.

Client: Well, I could tell myself to think about what I need to do—like to get the problems. Or I could think—just take one situation at a time. Just psych myself up 'cause I know I really can do well in math if I believe that.

9. **Helper:** It sounds like you've already thought of several coping things to use during class. This time, why don't you pretend you're sitting in your class? Try out some of these coping thoughts. Just say them aloud.

Client: Okay. I'm sitting at my desk; my work is in front of me. What steps do I need to take now? I could just think

about one problem at a time, not worry about all of them. If I take it slowly, I can do okay.

10. **Helper:** That seemed pretty easy for you. Let's do some more practice like this just so these thoughts don't seem unfamiliar to you. As you practice, try hard to think about the meaning of what you're saying to yourself. [More practice occurs.]

Next, Isabella *selects and practices coping thoughts* to help her deal with especially *stressful or critical situations* that come up in math class (responses 11–13).

11. **Helper:** This time, let's think of some particular coping statements that might help you if you come up against some touchy situations in your math class—things that are really hard for you to deal with, like taking a test, going to the board, or being called on. What might you think at these times that would keep the lid on your nervousness?

Client: I could think about just doing what is required of me—maybe, as you said earlier, taking a deep breath and just thinking about staying calm, not letting my anxiety get the best of me.

12. **Helper:** Okay, great. Let's see—can you practice some of these aloud as if you were taking a test or had just been asked a question or were at the board in front of the class?

Client: Well, I'm at the board. I'm just going to think about doing this problem. If I start to get really nervous, I'm going to take a deep breath and just concentrate on being calm as I do this.

13. **Helper:** Let's practice this several times. Maybe this time you might use another tense moment, like being called on by your teacher. [Further practice goes on.]

Next, the helper *points out how Isabella may discourage or punish herself after class* (responses 14 and 15). Isabella selects and *practices encouraging or self-rewarding thoughts* (responses 16–18).

14. **Helper:** Isabella, there's one more thing I'd like you to practice. After math class, what do you usually think?

Client: I feel relieved. I think about how glad I am it's over. Sometimes I think about the fact that I didn't do well.

15. **Helper:** Well, those thoughts are sort of discouraging too. What I believe might help is if you could learn to encourage yourself as you start to use these coping thoughts. In other words, instead of thinking about not doing well, focus on your progress in coping. You can do this during class or after class is over. Can you find some more positive things you could think about to encourage yourself—like giving yourself a pat on the back?

Client: You mean like I didn't do as bad as I thought?

16. **Helper:** Yes, anything like that.

Client: Well, it's over, and it didn't go too badly. Actually I handled things Okay. I can do this if I believe it. I can see progress.

17. **Helper:** Now let's assume you've just been at the board. You're back at your seat. Practice saying what you might think in that situation that would be encouraging to you.

Client: I've just sat down. I might think that it went fast and I did concentrate on the problem, so that was good.

18. **Helper:** Now let's assume class is over. What would be positive, self-encouraging thoughts after class?

Client: I've just gotten out. Class wasn't that bad. I got something out of it. If I put my mind to it, I can do it. [More practice of positive self-statements occurs.]

In response 19, the helper instructs Isabella *to practice the entire sequence* of stopping a self-defeating thought and using a coping thought before, during, and after class. Usually the client practices this by *imagining the situation.*

19. **Helper:** So far we've been practicing these coping thoughts at the different times you might use them so you can get used to them. Now let's practice this in the sequence that it might actually occur—like before your class, during the class, coping with a tough situation, and encouraging yourself after class. If you imagine the situation and start to notice any self-defeating thoughts, you can practice stopping these. Then switch immediately to the types of coping thoughts that you believe will help you most at that time. Concentrate on the coping thoughts. How does this sound?

Client: Okay, I think I know what you mean [looks a little confused].

Sometimes long instructions are confusing. Modeling may be better. In responses 20 and 21, the helper *demonstrates how Isabella can apply coping thoughts in practice.*

20. **Helper:** Well, I just said a lot, and it might make more sense if I showed this to you. First, I'm going to imagine I'm in English class. It's almost time for the bell; then it's math class. Wish I could get out of it. It's embarrassing. Stop! That's a signal to use my coping thoughts. I need to think about math class as a challenge. Something I can do okay if I work at it. [Pauses.] Isabella, do you get the idea?

Client: Yes, now I do.

21. **Helper:** Okay, I'll go on and imagine now I'm actually in the class. He's given us a worksheet to do in 30 minutes. Whew! How will dumb me ever do that! Wait a minute. I know I can do it, but I need to go slowly and concentrate on the work, not on me. Just take one problem at a time. Well, now he wants us to read our answers. What if he calls on me? I can feel my heart pounding. Oh

13.3 FEEDBACK
Cognitive Restructuring

Part One

1. *Self-defeating:* The word *never* indicates the person is not giving himself or herself any chance for the future.

2. *Self-defeating:* The person is doubting both his or her ability to give a good speech and his or her knowledge of the subject.

3. *Self-enhancing:* The person is *realistically* focusing on what she or he can do.

4. *Self-defeating:* The person is saying with certainty, as evidenced by the word *know,* that there is no chance to regain a relationship with his or her son. This is said without supporting evidence.

5. *Self-enhancing:* The client is realistically focusing on his or her own opinion, not on the assessment of others.

6. *Self-defeating:* The person is viewing the situation only from a negative perspective.

7. *Self-defeating:* The person predicts a negative reaction without supporting evidence.

8. *Self-enhancing:* The person recognizes a preference yet focuses on her love for her daughter.

well, if I get called on, just take a deep breath and answer. If it turns out to be wrong, it's not the end of the world.

Well, the bell rang. I am walking out. I'm glad it's over. Now, wait a minute—it didn't go that badly. Actually I handled it pretty well. Now, why don't you try this? [Isabella practices the sequence of coping thoughts several times, first with the helper's assistance, gradually in a completely self-directed manner.]

Before terminating the session, the helper *assigns daily homework practice.*

22. **Helper:** This week I'd like you to practice this several times each day—just like you did now. Keep track of your practices on your log. And you can use this whenever you feel it would be helpful—such as before, during, or after math class. Jot these times down too, and we'll go over this next week.

THIRD-GENERATION DEVELOPMENTS

In closing, we feel it is important to note the development of intervention approaches that some scholars have characterized as third-generation developments (following,

first, behavior therapy and, second, cognitive therapies). Third-wave interventions have developed in part in reaction to gaps or shortcomings noted in cognitive/cognitive–behavioral intervention research (Hayes, Strosahl, Bunting, Twohig, & Wilson, 2004). Rather than focusing on content, form, or frequency of cognitions, emotions, sensations, and memories, new treatments focus more on their *function,* on fostering psychological flexibility, and they emphasize concepts such as dialectics, spirituality, relationship, mindfulness, and acceptance. Acceptance and commitment therapy (ACT), for example, focuses on people's inclinations to avoid distressing problems, feelings, and situations (which can often lead to worsening of conditions). Common goals include assisting clients to increase (1) their capacity to tolerate exposure to thoughts and feelings that are highly uncomfortable, (2) the capacity for mindfulness or awareness that allows observation of distressing events while maintaining a sense of neutrality, and (3) the capacity to change their own attitudes about their own internal responding (negative emotions and thoughts), fostering greater acceptance, relaxation, and openness (Hayes, Follette, & Linehan, 2004).

ACT draws from theory and research—a core being Relational Theory Frame (RFT; Hayes, Barnes-Holmes, & Roche, 2001)—on linkages between language, cognition, and subsequent psychological problems. Rather than specific intervention strategies per se, ACT draws on six core clinical processes, which are implemented across a range of disorders in a contextually sensitive manner. ACT treatment seeks to help clients with (Strosahl, Hayes, Wilson, & Gifford, 2004):

- *Acceptance:* fostering acceptance and willingness while reducing the prominence of attempts at emotional control and avoidance—e.g., of difficult thoughts/feelings—in clients' response habits

- *Defusion:* breaking down processes based on excessively literal language that causes private experiences (thoughts, feelings, sensations) to function as psychological barriers—e.g., through unhelpful evaluations, fusion/confusion between what one directly experiences and how one's use of language shapes interpretation of experience in negative ways

- *Getting in contact with the present moment:* living more in the moment, gaining skills in noticing what is being experienced in the present moment through the ongoing flow of experiences

- *The notion of self as context:* distinguishing between conceptualizations of self (one's life story, self-evaluations, the content of troubled thinking/feeling) and the context within which these conceptualizations occur; gaining experience with mindfulness that helps discriminate the thoughts from "I am the person having these thoughts"

- *Values:* focusing on valued outcomes, ways in which current patterns are blocking valued actions, clarifying values that legitimize confronting previously avoided psychological barriers

- *Committed action:* beginning and increasingly building larger patterns of committed action that are consistent with valued life goals and ends

At this writing, systematic clinical application of acceptance and commitment therapy is growing. Hayes & Strosahl (2004), for example, provide practical guides for application with anxiety, substance abuse, posttraumatic stress disorder, serious mental illness, stress, and pain, with varied populations such as children and adolescents, and in medical settings. The coming years will undoubtedly bring greater specification of intervention strategies, how strategies are theorized to effect desired change, and comparative analysis to discern for what problems and populations acceptance-based therapies are efficacious as well as their time and outcome effectiveness relative to other interventions such as cognitive–behavioral therapies (Nurius & Macy, 2007).

Similar emphasis on mindfulness and experiential acceptance can also be seen in dialectical behavior therapy (DBT; Linehan, 1993; Hayes, Masuda, Bissett, Luoma, & Guerrero, in press), integrative behavioral couple therapy (Christensen et al., 2004), and mindfulness-based cognitive therapy (MBCT; Segal, Williams, & Teasdale, 2002). Mindfulness as a core feature has considerable overlap with cognitive–behavioral strategies that strive to assist clients to move away from an "autopilot" mode of responding and toward greater awareness of one's own thinking and a decentered perspective that allows individuals to look at their own thoughts, feelings, and bodily sensations in a more removed manner—for example, as simply thoughts rather than being "you" or "reality." In its simplest form, mindfulness involves "paying attention in a particular way: on purpose, in the present moment, and nonjudgmentally" (Kabat-Zinn, 1994, p. 4); and it is a central dimension to meditation and stress reduction (see also Kabat-Zinn, 1990). Augmenting from the original stress focus, mindfulness-based cognitive therapy has been applied with depression within a relapse prevention framework, acknowledging that sad moods can activate thinking patterns associated with previous sad moods that, unexamined, can serve to intensify and maintain vicious cycles of depressive spirals (Segal et al., 2002). At this point, the evidence base for third-generation developments is preliminary but growing. We bring this emerging intervention approach to your attention so that you can monitor developments and, over time, gauge their value for your clientele.

CHAPTER SUMMARY

Various cognitive change procedures of cognitive modeling, problem solving, reframing, stress inoculation, and cognitive restructuring are used with considerable frequency in helping practice. A cognitive perspective sees an individual's construction of a particular situation to be like a photograph. The individual's emotional states and patterns of responding in the person's thinking, feeling, and interacting can affect this mental picture—blurring, coloring, or distorting the images and what they represent in ways that do not serve the client well. Cognitive restructuring is akin to assisting clients to examine how their photographs take shape and to develop other pictures or different constructions of themselves, others, or situations. Cognitive structural change can be more than modifying habitual cognitions, rules, expectancies, assumptions, and imperatives. It is also about providing emotional relief, fostering hopefulness, and supporting a view of options and agency in changing those parts of a problem that are linked to one's own self and worldviews.

As with any intervention, adaptations need to be made depending on client characteristics and context. What challenges people are exposed to as well as the meaning these hold and options for change or difference are deeply affected by race, culture, sociodemographic status, gender, sexual orientation, abledness, and many others factors. Cognitive change techniques should be collaboratively applied with thoughtful attention to how diversity factors may bear on assessment and use of strategies. Moreover, conditions of inequality, marginalization, and other forms of stress and/or injustice argue for a critical consciousness to environmental contributors while assisting people to undertake cognitive changes in the service of their own goals and well-being. Finally, as basic research rapidly advances in illuminating the complex transactions among memories, thoughts, feelings, sensations, physical embodiment, and the social/material world, so too will clinical models need to evolve. We anticipate important developments in the coming decade relevant to effective practice.

REFERENCES

Ahijevych, K., & Wewers, M. (1993). Factors associated with nicotine dependence among African American women cigarette smokers. *Research in Nursing and Health, 16,* 283–292.

Arean, P. A. (1993). Cognitive behavioral therapy with older adults. *The Behavior Therapist, 16,* 236–239.

Baarnhielm, S. (2005). Making sense of different illness realities: Restructuring of illness meaning among Swedish-born women. *Nordic Journal of Psychiatry, 59*(5), 350–356.

Backhaus, J., Hohagen, F., Voderholzer, U., & Riemann, D. (2001). Long-term effectiveness of a short-term cognitive–behavioral group treatment for primary insomnia. *European Archives of Psychiatry and Clinical Neuroscience, 251*(1), 35–42.

Beck, A. T. (2005). The current state of cognitive therapy: A 40-year perspective. *Journal of the American Medical Association, 62,* 953–959.

Beck, A. T., Freeman, A., Davis, D. D., & associates (2004). *Cognitive therapy of personality disorders.* New York: Guilford Press.

Beck, J. S. (1995). *Cognitive therapy.* New York: Guilford Press.

Bélanger, L., Savard, J., & Morin, C. M. (2006). Clinical management of insomnia using cognitive therapy. *Behavioral Sleep Medicine, 4*(3), 179–202.

Berlin, S. (2001). *Clinical social work: A cognitive–integrative perspective.* New York: Oxford University Press.

Bernal, G., & Scharron del Rio, M. R. (2001). Are empirically supported treatments valid for ethnic minorities? Toward an alternative approach for treatment research. *Cultural Diversity and Ethnic Minority Psychology, 7*, 328–342.

Bowlby, J. (1988). *A secure base: Parent–child attachments and healthy human development.* New York: Basic.

Brown, L. S. (1994). *Subversive dialogues: Theory in feminist therapy.* New York: Basic.

Christensen, A., Atkins, D. C., Berns, S., Wheeler, J., Baucom, D. H., & Simpson, L. E. (2004). Traditional versus integrative behavioral couple therapy for significantly and chronically distressed married couples. *Journal of Consulting and Clinical Psychology. 72*(2), 176–191.

Comas-Diaz, L. (1992). The future of psychotherapy with ethnic minorities. *Psychotherapy, 29*, 88–94.

Comas-Diaz, L. (2006). Cultural variation in the therapeutic relationship. In C. D. Goodheart, A. E. Kazdin, & R. J. Sternberg (Eds.), *Evidence-based psychotherapy: Where practice and research meet* (pp. 81–105). Washington, DC: American Psychological Association.

Comas-Diaz, L. (in press). Ethnopolitical psychology. In E. Aldarondo (Ed.), *Promoting social justice in mental health practice.* Mahwah, NJ: Lawrence Erlbaum.

Dattilio, F. M. (2005). The critical component of cognitive restructuring in couples therapy: A case study. *Australian and New Zealand Journal of Family Therapy, 26*(2), 73–78.

Dattilio, F. M. (2006). A cognitive–behavioral approach to reconstructing intergenerational family schemas. *Contemporary Family Therapy: An International Journal, 28*(2), 191–200.

David, D., Macavei, B., Szentagotai, A., & McMahon, J. (2005). Cognitive restructuring and mental contamination: An empirical re-conceptualization. *Journal of Rational–Emotive and Cognitive Behavior Therapy, 23*(1), 21–56.

De Rios, M. D. (2002). What we can learn from shamanic healing: Brief psychotherapy with Latino immigrant clients. *American Journal of Public Health, 92*(10), 1576–1578.

Dobson, K. S. (Ed.). (2001). *Handbook of cognitive–behavioral therapies* (2nd ed.). New York: Guilford Press.

Dobson, K. S., & Dozois, D. J. A. (2001). Historical and philosophical bases of the cognitive–behavioral therapies. In K. S. Dobson (Ed.), *Handbook of cognitive–behavioral therapies* (2nd ed., pp. 3–39). New York: Guilford Press.

Ehde, D. M., & Jensen, M. P. (2004). Feasibility of a cognitive restructuring intervention for treatment of chronic pain in persons with disabilities. *Rehabilitation Psychology, 49*(3), 254–258.

Ellis, A. (1997). Using rational emotive behavior therapy techniques to cope with disability. *Professional Psychology, 28*, 17–22.

Foa, E. B., Hembree, E. A., Cahill, S. P., Rauch, S. A. M., Riggs, D. S., Feeny, N. C., & Yadin, E. (2005). Randomized trial of prolonged exposure for posttraumatic stress disorder with and without cognitive restructuring: Outcome at academic and community clinics. *Journal of Consulting and Clinical Psychology, 73*(5), 953–964.

Freiberg, P. (1995, May). Older people thrive with the right therapy. *American Psychological Association Monitor,* p. 38.

Geremia, G. M., & Neziroglu, F. (2001). Cognitive therapy in the treatment of body dysmorphic disorder. *Clinical Psychology and Psychotherapy, 8*(4), 243–251.

Ginsburg, G. S., & Drake, K. L. (2002). School-based treatment for anxious African-American adolescents: A controlled pilot study. *Journal of the American Academy of Child and Adolescent Psychiatry, 41*(7), 768–775.

Goodheart, C. D. (2006). Evidence, endeavor, and expertise in psychology practice. In C. D. Goodheart, A. E. Kazdin, & R. J. Sternberg (Eds.), *Evidence-based psychotherapy: Where practice and research meet* (pp. 37–61). Washington, DC: American Psychological Association.

Gosch, E. A., Flannery-Schroeder, E., Mauro, C. F., & Compton, S. N. (2006). Principles of cognitive–behavioral therapy for anxiety disorders in children. *Journal of Cognitive Psychotherapy, 20*(3), 247–262.

Guidano, V. F. (1995). Self-observation in constructivist psychotherapy. In R. A. Neimeyer & M. J. Mahoney (Eds.), *Constructivism in psychotherapy* (pp. 155–168). Washington, DC: American Psychological Association.

Guralnick, M., & Neville, B. (1997). Designing early intervention programs to promote children's social competence. In M. J. Guralnick (Ed.), *The effectiveness of early intervention* (pp. 579–610). Baltimore: Brookes.

Haley, W., Roth, D., Coleton, M., & Ford, G. (1996). Appraisal, coping and social support as mediators of well-being in black and white family caregivers of patients with Alzheimer's disease. *Journal of Consulting and Clinical Psychology, 64*, 121–129.

Hatch, M., & Paradis, C. (1993). Panic disorder with agoraphobia. A focus on group treatment with African Americans. *The Behavior Therapist, 16,* 240–242.

Hayes, S. C., Barnes-Holmes, D., & Roche, B. (Eds.). (2001*). Relational frame theory: A post-Skinnerian account of human language and cognition.* New York: Plenum.

Hayes, S. C., Folette, V. M., & Linehan, M. M. (Eds.). (2004). *Mindfulness and acceptance: Expanding the cognitive–behavioral tradition.* New York: Guilford Press.

Hayes, S. C., Masuda, A., Bissett, R., Luoma, J., & Guerrero, L. F. (in press). DBT, FAP, and ACT: How empirically oriented are the new behavior therapy technologies? *Behavior Therapy.*

Hayes, S. C., & Strosahl, K. D. (Eds.). (2004). *A practical guide to acceptance and commitment therapy.* New York: Springer.

Hayes, S. C., Strosahl, K. D., Bunting, K., Twohig, M., & Wilson, K. G. (2004). What is acceptance and commitment therapy? In S. C. Hayes & K. D. Strosahl (Eds.), *A practical guide to acceptance and commitment therapy* (pp. 1–29). New York: Springer.

Hays, P. (1995). Multicultural applications of cognitive behavior therapy. *Professional Psychology, 26,* 309–315.

Hayward, L. M., Nixon, C., Jasper, M. P., Murphy, K. M., Harlan, V., Swirda, L., & Hayward, K. (2000). The process of restructuring and the treatment of obesity in women. *Health Care for Women International, 21*(7), 615–630.

Ivey, A. E., Ivey, M. B., & Simek-Morgan, L. (1997). *Counseling and psychotherapy: A multicultural perspective* (4th ed.). Boston: Allyn & Bacon.

Iwamasa, G. Y. (1993). Asian Americans and cognitive behavioral therapy. *The Behavior Therapist, 16,* 233–235.

Johnson, W. B., & Ridley, C. R. (1992). Brief Christian and non-Christian rational–emotive therapy with depressed Christian clients: An exploratory study. *Counseling and Values, 36,* 220–229.

Kabat-Zinn, J. (1990). *Full catastrophe living.* New York: Dell.

Kabat-Zinn, J. (1994). *Wherever you go, there you are: Mindfulness meditation in everyday life.* New York: Hyperion.

Kantrowitz, R., & Ballou, M. (1992). A feminist critique of cognitive–behavioral therapy. In L. S. Brown & M. Ballou (Eds.), *Personality and psychopathology: Feminist reappraisals* (pp. 70–87). New York: Guilford Press.

Kellogg, S. H., & Young, J. E. (2006). Schema therapy for borderline personality disorder. *Journal of Clinical Psychology, 62*(4), 445–458.

Kemp, S., Young, A. W., Szulecka, K., & de Pauw, K. W. (2003). A case of paraprosopia and its treatment. *Cognitive Neuropsychiatry, 8*(1), 43–57.

Kendall, P. C. (Ed.). (2000). *Child and adolescent therapy: Cognitive behavioral procedures* (2nd ed.). New York: Guilford Press.

Kuehlwein, K. T. (1992). Working with gay men. In A. Freeman & F. M. Dattillio (Eds.), *Comprehensive casebook of cognitive therapy* (pp. 249–255). New York: Plenum.

Leahy, R. (1996). *Cognitive therapy: Basic principles and implications.* Northvale, NJ: Aronson.

Leahy, R. (Ed.). (2003). *Roadblocks in cognitive–behavioral therapy: Transforming challenges into opportunities for change.* New York: Guilford Press.

Leahy, R., & Holland, S. (2000). *Treatment plans and interventions for depression and anxiety disorders.* New York: Guilford Press.

Lewis, S. Y. (1994). Cognitive–behavioral therapy. In L. Comas-Diaz & B. Greene (Eds.), *Women of color: Integrating ethnic and gender identities in psychotherapy* (pp. 223–238). New York: Guilford Press.

Linehan, M. M. (1993). *Cognitive–behavioral treatment of borderline personality disorder.* New York: Guilford Press.

Lopez, M., & Mermelstein, R. (1995). A cognitive–behavioral program to improve geriatric rehabilitation outcome. *Gerontologist, 35,* 696–700.

Ma, J. I. (2000). Treatment expectations and treatment experience of Chinese families towards family therapy: Appraisal of a common belief. *Journal of Family Therapy, 22,* 296–307.

Mahoney, M. J. (1995). Theoretical developments in the cognitive psychotherapies. In M. J. Mahoney (Ed.), *Cognitive and constructive psychotherapies* (pp. 3–19). New York: Springer.

Mahoney, M. J. (2003). *Constructive psychotherapy: A practical guide.* New York: Guilford Press.

Markus, H. R., Kitayama, S., & Heiman, R. J. (1996). Culture and basic psychological principles. In E. T. Higgens & A. W. Kruglanski (Eds.), *Social psychology: Handbook of basic principles* (pp. 857–914). New York: Guilford Press.

Martell, C. R., Safren, S. A., & Prince, S. E. (2004). *Cognitive–behavioral therapies with lesbian, gay, and bisexual clients.* New York: Guilford Press.

Mash, E. J., & Barkley, R. A. (Eds.). (2006). *Treatment of childhood disorders.* New York: Guilford Press.

Massad, P. M., & Hulsey, T. L. (2006). Causal attributions in posttraumatic stress disorder: Implications for clinical research and practice. *Psychotherapy: Theory, Research, Practice, Training, 43*(2), 201–215.

Mennuti, R. B., Freeman, A., & Christner, R. W. (Eds.). (2006). *Cognitive behavioral interventions in educational settings: A handbook for practice.* New York: Routledge.

Merlijn, V. P. B. M., Hunfeld, J. A. M., van der Wouden, J. C., Hazebroek-Kampschreur, A. A. J. M., van Suijlekom-Smit, L.W. A., Koes, B. W., & Passchier, J. (2005). A cognitive–behavioural program for adolescents with chronic pain—a pilot study. *Patient Education and Counseling, 59*(2), 126–134.

Miranda, J., & Dwyer, E. V. (1993). Cognitive behavioral therapy for disadvantaged medical patients. *The Behavior Therapist, 16,* 226–228.

Nakao, M., Nakao, M., Myers, P., Fricchione, G., Zuttermeister, P. C., Barsky, A. J., & Benson, H. (2001). Somatization and symptom reduction through a behavioral medicine intervention in a mind/body medicine clinic. *Behavioral Medicine, 26*(4), 169–176.

Neimeyer, R. A., & Raskin, J. D. (2001). Varieties of constructivism in psychotherapy. In K. S. Dobson (Ed.), *Handbook of cognitive–behavioral therapies* (2nd ed., pp. 393–430). New York: Guilford Press.

Nolen-Hoeksema, S., Girgus, J. S., & Seligman, M. (1992). Predictors and consequences of childhood depressive symptoms: A 5-year longitudinal study. *Journal of Abnormal Psychology, 101,* 405–422.

Nurius, P. S., & Macy, R. J. (2007). Cognitive behavioral therapies. In K. M. Sowers & C. N. Dulmus (Eds.), *Comprehensive handbook of social work and social welfare, Vol. 2: Human behavior in the social environment.* New York: Wiley.

Ollendick, T. H., & King, N. J. (2000). Empirically supported treatments for children and adolescents. In P. C. Kendall (Ed.), *Child and adolescent therapy: Cognitive behavioral procedures* (2nd ed., pp. 386–425). New York: Guilford Press.

Organista, K., Dwyer, E. V., & Azocar, F. (1993). Cognitive behavioral therapy with Latino outpatients. *The Behavior Therapist, 16,* 229–232.

Oyserman, D., Gant, L., & Ager, J. (1995). A socially contextualized model of African American identity: Possible selves and school persistence. *Journal of Personality and Social Psychology, 69,* 1216–1232.

Peres, J., Mercante, J., & Nasello, A. G. (2005). Psychological dynamics affecting traumatic memories: Implications in psychotherapy. *Psychology and Psychotherapy: Theory, Research and Practice, 78*(4), 431–447.

Persons, J. B., & Davidson, J. (2001). Cognitive–behavioral case formulation. In K. S. Dobson (Ed.), *Handbook of cognitive–behavioral therapies* (2nd ed., pp. 86–110). New York: Guilford Press.

Power, K., McGoldrick, T., Brown, K., Buchanan, R., Sharp, D., Swanson, V., & Karatzias, A. (2002). A controlled comparison of eye movement desensitization and reprocessing versus exposure plus cognitive restructuring versus waiting list in the treatment of posttraumatic stress disorder. *Clinical Psychology and Psychotherapy, 9*(5), 299–318.

Prochaska, J. O., & Norcross, J. C. (2007). *Systems of psychotherapy: A transtheoretical analysis* (6th ed.). Pacific Grove, CA: Brooks/Cole.

Rapp, S., Brenes, G., & Marsh, A. P. (2002). Memory enhancement training for older adults with mild cognitive impairment: A preliminary study. *Aging and Mental Health, 6*(1), 5–11.

Renfrey, G. S. (1992). Cognitive–behavior therapy and the Native American client. *Behavior Therapy, 23,* 321–340.

Ridley, C., & Lingle, D. W. (1996). Cultural empathy in multicultural counseling: A multidimensional process model. In P. B. Pedersen, J. G. Draguns, W. J. Lonner, & J. E. Trimble (Eds.), *Counseling across cultures* (4th ed., pp. 21–46). Thousand Oaks, CA: Sage.

Rybarczyk, B., DeMarco, G., DeLaCruz, M., Lapidos, S., & Fortner, B. (2001). A classroom mind/body wellness intervention for older adults with chronic illness: Comparing immediate and 1-year benefits. *Behavioral Medicine, 27*(1), 15–28.

Segal, Z. V., Williams, J. M., & Teasdale, J. D. (2002). *Mindfulness-based cognitive therapy for depression: A new approach to preventing relapse.* New York: Guilford Press.

Smith, P., Perrin, S., & Yule, W. (1999). Cognitive behaviour therapy for post traumatic stress disorder. *Child and Adolescent Mental Health, 4*(4), 177–182.

Sonderegger, R., & Barrett, P. M. (2004). Assessment and treatment of ethnically diverse children and adolescents. In P. M. Barrett & T. H. Ollendick (Eds.), *Handbook of interventions that work with children and adolescents: Prevention and treatment* (pp. 89–111). New York: Wiley.

Sperry, L. (2006). *Cognitive behavior therapy of DSM-IV-TR personality disorders: Highly effective interventions for the most common personality disorders* (2nd ed.). New York: Routledge.

Spoormaker, V. I., & van den Bout, J. (2006). Lucid dreaming treatment for nightmares: A pilot study. *Psychotherapy and Psychosomatics, 75*(6), 389–394.

Strosahl, K. D., Hayes, S. C., Wilson, K. G., & Gifford, E. V. (2004). An ACT primer: Core therapy processes, intervention strategies, and therapist competencies. In S. C. Hayes & K. D. Strosahl (Eds.), *A practical guide to acceptance and commitment therapy* (pp. 31–58). New York: Springer.

Thompson, L. W. (1996). Cognitive–behavioral therapy and treatment for late-life depression. *Journal of Clinical Psychiatry, 57,* 29–37.

Tix, A. P., & Frazier, P. A. (1998). The use of religious coping during stressful life-events: Main effects, moderation, and mediation. *Journal of Consulting and Clinical Psychology, 66,* 411–422.

Ussher, J. (1990). Cognitive behavioral couples therapy with gay men referred for counseling in an AIDS setting: A pilot study. *AIDS-Care, 2,* 43–51.

Villa, K. K., & Abeles, N. (2000). Broad spectrum intervention and the remediation of prospective memory declines in the able elderly. *Aging and Mental Health, 4*(1), 21–29.

Watt, M. C., Stewart, S. H., Lefaivre, M. J., & Uman, L. S. (2006). A brief cognitive–behavioral approach to reducing anxiety sensitivity decreases pain related anxiety. *Cognitive Behaviour Therapy, 35*(4), 48–256.

Weiss, J. (1995). Cognitive therapy and life-review therapy. *Journal of Mental Health Counselors, 17,* 157–172.

Wilson, D. B., Bouffard, L. A., & Mackenzie, D. L. (2005). A quantitative review of structured, group-oriented, cognitive–behavioral programs for offenders. *Criminal Justice and Behavior, 32*(2), 172–204.

Wolfe, J. L. (1992). Working with gay women. In A. Freeman & F. M. Dattilio (Eds.), *Comprehensive casebook of cognitive therapy* (pp. 249–255). New York: Plenum.

Yoo, H. C., & Lee, R. M. (2005). Ethnic identity and approach-type coping as moderators of the racial discrimination/well-being relation in Asian Americans. *Journal of Counseling Psychology, 52*(4), 497–506.

Young, J. E. (1999). *Cognitive therapy for personality disorders: A schema-focused approach* (3rd ed.). Sarasota, FL: Professional Resource Press.

Young, J. E., Beck, A. T., & Weinberger, A. (1998). Depression. In D. H. Barlow (Ed.), *Clinical handbook of psychological disorders: A step-by-step treatment manual* (3rd ed.). New York: Guilford Press.

Young, J. E., Klosko, J. S., & Weishaar, M. E. (2003). *Schema therapy: A practitioner's guide.* New York: Guilford Press.

Zane, N., Hall, G. C., Sue, S., Young, K., & Nunez, J. (2004). Research on psychotherapy with culturally diverse populations. In M. J. Lambert (Ed.), *Handbook of psychotherapy and behavior change* (5th ed., pp. 767–804). New York: Wiley.

13   KNOWLEDGE AND SKILL BUILDER

Part One

Learning Outcome 1 asks you to identify and describe the six components of cognitive restructuring in a client case. Using the case described here, explain briefly how you would use the steps and components of cognitive restructuring with *this* client, Doreen. You can use the six questions following the client case to describe your use of the procedure. Feedback follows on page 415.

Doreen is a junior in college; she is majoring in education and getting very good grades. She reports that she has an active social life and has some good close friendships with both males and females. Despite obvious "pluses," the client reports constant feelings of being worthless and inadequate. Her standards for herself seem to be unrealistically high. Although she has almost a straight-A average, she still chides herself that she does not have all A's. Although she is attractive and has an active social life, she thinks that she should be more attractive and more talented. At the end of the initial session, she adds that as an African American woman she always has felt as though she has to prove herself more than the average person.

1. How would you explain the rationale for cognitive restructuring to this client?
2. Give an example you might use with this client to point out the difference between a self-defeating and a self-enhancing thought. Try to base your example on the client's self-description.
3. How would you have the client identify her thoughts about herself—her grades, appearance, social life, and so on? How would you help her identify schemas underlying maladaptive ways of thinking?
4. What are some coping thoughts this client might use?
5. Explain how, in the session, you would help the client practice shifting from self-defeating to coping thoughts.
6. What kind of homework assignment would you use to help the client increase her use of coping thoughts about herself?

Part Two

Learning Outcome 2 asks you to teach the six components of cognitive restructuring to someone else or to demonstrate these components with a role-play client. Use the Interview Checklist for Cognitive Restructuring as a teaching and evaluation guide.

Part Three

Learning Outcome 3 asks you to describe ways in which schemas are involved in cognitive functioning. In client-accessible terms, briefly describe your understanding of how schemas are formed, how they are drawn into play in cognitive operations, and why they can be difficult to change. Feedback follows the Knowledge and Skill Builder.

Interview Checklist for Cognitive Restructuring

Instructions: Determine whether the helper demonstrated the lead listed in the checklist. Check (✔) the leads that the helper used.

Treatment Rationale and Overview

_____ 1. Helper explains purpose and rationale of cognitive restructuring.

"You've reported that you find yourself getting anxious and depressed during and after these conversations with the people who have to evaluate your work. This procedure can help you identify some things you might be thinking in this situation that are just beliefs, not facts, and are unproductive. You can learn more realistic ways to think about this situation that will help you cope with it in a way that you want to."

_____ 2. Helper provides brief overview of procedure.

"There are several things we'll do in using this procedure. *First,* this will help you identify the kinds of things you're thinking before, during, and after these situations that are self-defeating. *Second,* we'll work to determine ways that these self-defeating beliefs (schemas) developed over time and what conditions tend to activate them. *Third,* this will help us develop cues and strategies for you to catch a self-defeating thought and replace it with a coping thought. *Fourth,* this will help you see ways to break long-standing patterns of responding and learn how to give yourself credit for changing these self-defeating thoughts."

_____ 3. Helper explains difference between self-enhancing thoughts and self-defeating thoughts and provides culturally relevant examples of both.

"A self-defeating thought is one way to interpret the situation, but it is usually negative and unproductive, like thinking that the other person doesn't value you or what you say. In contrast, a self-enhancing thought is a more constructive and realistic way to interpret the situation—like thinking that what you are talking about has value to you."

_____ 4. Helper explains influence of irrational and self-defeating thoughts on emotions and performance.

"When you're constantly preoccupied with yourself and worried about how the situation will turn out, this can affect your feelings and your behavior. Worrying about the situation can make you feel anxious and upset. Concentrating on the situation and not worrying about its outcome can help you feel more relaxed, which helps you handle the situation more easily."

(continued)

13 KNOWLEDGE AND SKILL BUILDER

(continued)

_____ 5. Helper confirms client's willingness to use strategy. "Are you ready to try this now?"

Identifying Client Thoughts in Problem Situations

_____ 6. Helper asks client to describe problem situations and identify examples of self-enhancing thoughts and of self-defeating thoughts that client typically experiences in these situations.

"Think of the last time you were in this situation. Describe for me what you think before you have a conversation with your evaluator . . . . What are you usually thinking during the conversation? . . . What thoughts go through your mind after the conversation is over? Now let's see which of those thoughts are actual facts about the situation or are constructive ways to interpret the situation. Which ones are your beliefs about the situation that are unproductive or self-defeating?"

_____ 7. If client is unable to complete step 6, helper models examples of thoughts or "links" between event and client's emotional response.

"Okay, think of the thoughts that you have while you're in this conversation as a link between this event and your feelings afterward of being upset and depressed. What is the middle part? For instance, it might be something like 'I'll never have a good evaluation, and I'll lose this position' or 'I always blow this conversation and never make a good impression.' Can you recall thinking anything like this?"

_____ 8. Helper instructs client to monitor and record content of thoughts *before, during,* and *after* stressful or upsetting situations before the next session.

"One way to help you identify this link or your thoughts is to keep track of what you're thinking in these situations as they happen. This week I'd like you to use this log each day. Try to identify and write down at least three specific thoughts you have in these situations each day, and bring this in with you next week."

_____ 9. Using client's monitoring, helper and client identify client's self-defeating thoughts.

"Let's look at your log and go over the kinds of negative thoughts that seem to be predominant in these situations. We can explore how these thoughts affect your feelings and performance in this situation—and whether you feel there is any evidence or rational basis for these."

_____ 10. Helper assesses client's schemas.

In some cases, more focal assessment of underlying schemas is needed. In-depth assessment of schemas (adaptive or maladaptive) can involve multiple tools such as a focused review of the client's history relative to the current problem, use of schema inventories, experiential exercises to trigger certain schemas, and client education about schemas

(Young et al., 1998). As part of a case conceptualization, Leahy (1996, p. 194) suggests the following questions to get a better sense of how the client sees this. On each blank line, fill in the word that describes the schema in question.

"How did your (parents, other family members, peers, teachers, partner as relevant) teach you that you were _____? What evidence is there that you are not _____? How would you rate yourself on a continuum from _____ to (the opposite)? Does this depend on the situation or other factors? If so, how and why? What is the consequence of believing or demanding this of yourself? Is it ever okay to be _____? How would you challenge your (parent, teacher, as appropriate) now that you are an adult, if they were to describe you as _____?"

Introduction and Practice of Coping Thoughts

_____ 11. Helper explains purpose and potential use of coping thoughts and gives some examples of coping thoughts to be used:
_____ a. Before the situation—preparing for it
_____ b. During the situation
_____ 1. Focusing on task
_____ 2. Dealing with feeling overwhelmed

"Up to this point, we've talked about the negative or unproductive thoughts you have in these situations and how they contribute to your feeling uncomfortable, upset, and depressed. Now we're going to look at some alternative, more constructive ways to think about the situation—using coping thoughts. These thoughts can help you prepare for the situation, handle the situation, and deal with feeling upset or overwhelmed in the situation. As long as you're using some coping thoughts, you avoid giving up control and letting the old self-defeating thoughts take over. Here are some examples of coping thoughts."

_____ 12. Helper instructs client to think of additional coping thoughts that client could use or has used before.

"Try to think of your own coping thoughts—perhaps ones you can remember using successfully in other situations, ones that seem to work for you."

_____ 13. Helper instructs client to practice verbalizing selected coping statements.

"At first you will feel a little awkward using coping statements. It's like learning to drive a stick shift after you've been used to driving an automatic. So one way to help you get used to this is for you to practice these statements aloud."

_____ a. Helper instructs client first to practice coping statements individually. Coping statements to use before a situation are practiced, then coping statements to use during a situation:

"First, just practice each coping statement separately. After you feel comfortable with saying these aloud, practice the ones you could use before this conversation. Okay, now practice the ones you could use during this conversation with your evaluator."

_____ b. Helper instructs client to practice sequence of coping statements as they would be used in actual situation:

"Now let's put it all together. Imagine it's an hour before your meeting. Practice the coping statements you could use then. We'll role-play the meeting. As you feel aroused or overwhelmed, stop and practice coping thoughts during the situation."

_____ c. Helper instructs client to become actively involved and to internalize meaning of coping statements during practice:

"Try to really put yourself into this practice. As you say these new things to yourself, try to think of what these thoughts really mean."

Shifting from Self-Defeating to Coping Thoughts

_____ 14. Helper models shift from recognizing a self-defeating thought and stopping it to replacing it with a coping thought.

"Let me show you what we will practice today. First, I'm in this conversation. Everything is going okay. All of a sudden I can feel myself starting to tense up. I realize I'm starting to get overwhelmed about this whole evaluation process. I'm thinking that I'm going to blow it. No, I stop that thought at once. Now, I'm just going to concentrate on calming down, taking a deep breath, and thinking only about what I have to say."

_____ 15. Helper helps client practice shift from self-defeating to coping thoughts. Practice consists of four steps:

"Now let's practice this. You will imagine the situation. As soon as you start to recognize the onset of a self-defeating thought, stop it. Verbalize the thought aloud, and tell yourself to stop. Then verbalize a coping thought in place of it and imagine carrying on with the situation."

_____ a. Having client imagine situation or carry it out in a role play (behavior rehearsal)

_____ b. Recognizing self-defeating thought (which could be signaled by a hand or finger)

_____ c. Stopping self-defeating thought (which could be supplemented with a hand clap)

_____ d. Replacing thought with coping thought (possibly supplemented with deep breathing)

_____ 16. Helper helps client practice using shift for each problem situation until anxiety or stress felt by client while practicing the situation is decreased to a reasonable or negligible level and client can

carry out practice and use coping thoughts in a self-directed manner.

"Let's keep working with this situation until you feel pretty comfortable with it and can shift from self-defeating to coping thoughts without my help."

Introduction and Practice of Reinforcing Self-Statements

_____ 17. Helper explains purpose and use of positive self-statements and gives some examples of these to client.

"You have really made a lot of progress in learning to use coping statements before and during these situations. Now it's time to learn to reward or encourage yourself. After you've coped with a situation, you can pat yourself on the back for having done so by thinking a positive or rewarding thought like 'I did it' or 'I really managed that pretty well.'"

_____ 18. Helper instructs client to think of additional positive self-statements and to select some to try out.

"Can you think of some things like this that you think of when you feel good about something or when you feel like you've accomplished something? Try to come up with some of these thoughts that seem to fit for you."

_____ 19. Helper models application of positive self-statements as self-reinforcement for shift from self-defeating to coping thoughts.

"Okay, here is the way you reward yourself for having coped. You recognize the self-defeating thought. Now you're in the situation using coping thoughts, and you're thinking things like 'Take a deep breath' or 'Just concentrate on this task.' Now the conversation is finished. You know you were able to use coping thoughts, and you reward yourself by thinking 'Yes, I did it' or 'I really was able to manage that.'"

_____ 20. Helper instructs client to practice use of positive self-statements in interview following practice of shift from self-defeating to coping thoughts. This should be practiced in sequence (coping *before* and *during* situation and reinforcing oneself *after* situation).

"Okay, let's try this out. As you imagine the conversation, you're using the coping thoughts you will verbalize . . . . Now, imagine the situation is over, and verbalize several reinforcing thoughts for having coped."

Homework and Follow-up

_____ 21. Helper instructs client to use cognitive restructuring procedure (identifying self-defeating thought, stopping it, shifting to coping thought, reinforcing with positive self-statement) in situations outside the interview.

(continued)

13   KNOWLEDGE AND SKILL BUILDER

(continued)

"Okay, now you're ready to use the entire procedure whenever you have these conversations in which you're being evaluated—or any other situation in which you recognize your negative interpretation of the event is affecting you. In these cases, you recognize and stop any self-defeating thoughts, use the coping thoughts before the situation to prepare for it, and use the coping thoughts during the situation to help focus on the task and deal with being overwhelmed. After the situation is over, use the positive self-thoughts to reward your efforts."

_____ 22. Helper instructs client to monitor and record on log sheet the number of times client uses cognitive restructuring outside the interview.

"I'd like you to use this log to keep track of the number of times you use this procedure and to jot down the situation in which you're using it. Also rate your tension level on a 1- to-5 scale before and after each time you use this."

_____ 23. Helper arranges for follow-up.

"Do this recording for the next two weeks. Then let's get together for a follow-up session."

Observer Comments

_____

_____

_____

_____

13   KNOWLEDGE AND SKILL BUILDER **FEEDBACK**

Part One

1. One overall goal may be for Doreen to feel more empowered about herself and to feel less pressure to have to constantly prove herself as a black woman. You can explain that cognitive restructuring (CR) would help her identify some of her thoughts about herself that are beliefs, not inherent "facts," and are contestable—perhaps unrealistic thoughts, leading to feelings of depression and worthlessness. In addition, CR would help her learn to think about herself in more realistic, self-enhancing ways in line with her values. See the Interview Checklist for Cognitive Restructuring for another example of the CR rationale.

2. A core issue for Doreen to challenge is her belief system about her race and gender—that as an African American and as a woman she must constantly prove herself in order to be a worthy person. Thinking that she is not good enough is self-defeating. Self-enhancing or positive thoughts about herself are more realistic interpretations of her experiences—good grades, close friends, active social life, and so on. Recognition that she is intelligent and attractive is a self-enhancing thought.

3. You could ask the client to describe different situations and the thoughts she has about herself in them. She could also observe this during the week. You could model some possible thoughts she might be having. See leads 6–9 in the Interview Checklist for Cognitive Restructuring. For schema identification, several tools and sample questions are listed in lead 10.

4. There are many possible coping thoughts she could use. Here are some examples: "Hey, I'm doing pretty well as it is." "Don't be so hard on myself. I don't have to be perfect." "That worthless feeling is a sign to cope—recognize my assets." "What's more attractive anyway? I am attractive." "Don't let that one B get me down. It's not the end of the world." "I'm an African American woman, and I'm proud of it. I feel okay about myself the way I am. I don't have to prove my worth to anyone."

5. See leads 14–16 on the Interview Checklist for Cognitive Restructuring.

6. Many possible homework assignments might help. Here are a few examples:

a. Every time Doreen uses a coping thought, she could record it on her log.

b. She could cue herself to use a coping thought by writing these down on note cards and reading a note before doing something else, like getting a drink or making a phone call, or by using a phone-answering device to report and verbalize coping thoughts.

c. She could enlist the aid of a close friend or roommate. If the roommate notices that the client starts to "put herself down," she could interrupt her. Doreen could then use a coping statement.

Part Two

Use the Interview Checklist for Cognitive Restructuring to assess your teaching or counseling demonstration of this procedure.

Part Three

You could explain that the word *schema* refers to how information gets organized and stored in memory. Schemas are built up over time and experience, from input we get from others as well as from our own reflections and evaluations. Not all but many of the deeply problematic schemas have their beginnings in childhood and youth, when identity and attachment styles are being formed. Schemas are not passive "file drawers" of recorded information; they are more like complex filters that screen, direct, and shape what we notice, how we interpret ourselves and our world, and how we respond. We have too many schemas for them all to be actively working at any one time. Rather, because we tend to develop patterns and habits, some schemas get punched much like buttons under trigger situations. When these get punched, other schemas that are related get activated as well, and we are filled with the sense of them. This subset of active schemas influences our thoughts, feelings, and behaviors in the moment, and it is hard to access schemas that run counter to them. For example, when our schema of inadequacy is pushed, it brings with it related schemas such as shame and worthlessness, which make it difficult to access schemas about our talent, promise, and hope.

STRESS MANAGEMENT STRATEGIES

LEARNING OUTCOMES

After completing this chapter, you will be able to

1. Assess your own breathing by using four of the five awareness-of-breathing instructions.
2. Demonstrate five of the six steps for diaphragmatic breathing.
3. Using a simulated client case, describe how the five components of stress inoculation would be used with a client.
4. Demonstrate 17 of the 21 steps of stress inoculation in a role-play interview.

Feel anxious? Stressful? Wired?

Do you have tension headaches?

Do you abuse "soft" drugs—alcohol or tobacco?

Do you feel chronic fatigue?

Are you irritable, with low frustration tolerance?

Do you have high blood pressure in certain situations or at certain times?

Does your immune system seem not to be working well?

A great number of people would respond "yes" to one or more of these questions. Anxiety is one of the most common concerns reported by clients, and stress is related to physiological discomfort such as headaches and indigestion. Stress is also correlated with heart disease, cancer, and other serious diseases. Perhaps as a consequence of the "stress syndrome," the last several years have produced an explosion in procedures for management of stress or anxiety, originally introduced in 1929 as "progressive relaxation" (Jacobson, 1929). There has been a considerable amount of research exploring the relative strengths and weaknesses of stress management approaches, and a number of guides applicable to children and adults are available (Casey & Benson, 2004; Crum, 2000; Fink, 2000; Kahn, 2006; Kendall-Tackett,

2005; McGuigan, 1999; Rice, 2000; Smith, 2002; Wong & Wong, 2006).

This chapter addresses stress and its management. We look at forms that stress takes, including cultural variations, and we examine both physiological and cognitive dimensions of stress management. Our coverage includes the physiology of breathing and techniques applicable in broad-based practice as well as stress inoculation therapy. Like other cognitive therapies, stress inoculation assumes that maladaptive emotions and thinking are influenced or mediated by a person's core beliefs, schemas, perceptions, and cognitions. Stress inoculation has components of cognitive restructuring as well as coping skills. These procedures help to identify how clients interpret their situations and experiences, and to urge clients to substitute a new interpretive frame (Gendlin, 1996, p. 242). We also attend to the growing recognition of spirituality as an important dimension of coping and stress management for many people.

STRESS AND COPING

Widely studied in recent decades, stress has become a commonplace concept in our daily lives and language ("I am so stressed out!"). Stress essentially refers to conditions stemming from demands exceeding capacity. This definition covers a lot of ground, such as roles, tasks, and expectations from one's environment, from oneself, or from others that exceed a person's abilities or conditions. Stress can stem from something that we regard as positive (e.g., a desired job promotion, marriage or partnering, parenthood, a holiday, a move) as well as from something that we regard as negative (e.g., significant losses; injuries or illnesses; serious financial, relationship, or mental health threats). Stress has multiple levels of effects. We are all aware of what being stressed feels like—elevated heart rate, muscle tension, effects on breathing, anxiety, rumination. Stress also gives rise to psychophysiological effects and processes involving the brain, the endocrine, autonomic nervous, cardiovascular, gastrointestinal, and immunological systems as well as muscles, skin, and perceptual receptors (e.g., vision, hearing, touch) (Greenberg, 1996).

Although we do not review all these dimensions of the causes and effects of stress, it is useful to recognize that there is enormous variability in factors that may be fostering stress, in how stress is experienced, in what stress and stressors mean to the people involved, in underlying mind–body connections in stress and its management, and in choices for how to handle stressful issues. As with self-management, many of the interventions that we describe in this book may be useful components of stress management, depending on the assessment and match of intervention plan to needs and conditions. Stress management may involve managing the symptoms or phenomenology of stress itself (relaxation, exercise, biofeedback), affecting factors that are creating the stress (problem solving, advocacy, conflict resolution, changing environmental stressors), fostering factors that will help buffer or otherwise weather or transform the stress (social supports networking, spirituality, meditation), and a whole range of methods for decreasing one's own stressful behavior, lifestyle characteristics, or ways of perceiving and responding to targeted stressors.

One's cognitive interpretations or appraisals of a life situation and its implications are crucial components of the meaning that the situation holds for an individual, of emotional reactions, of physiological responses, of attributions and perceptions of options and likely outcomes, and of actions taken or not taken. Figure 14.1 illustrates the process of coping with stress. This depiction is rooted in a transactional, ecological view (Lazarus, 1990; Lazarus & Folkman, 1984) wherein the helper considers both person and environment characteristics as well as comparatively "objective" factors (e.g., the mix of resources and demands in place, situational factors, the client's own and others' behaviors) and ways in which those factors are uniquely interpreted (perceived, appraised) and experienced by the people involved. All the boxes and arrows in Figure 14.1 make for a complex picture—but an important one for showing that there are typically multiple points of helping that may make a significant difference in achieving improved outcomes or bolstering resiliency, *if* the helper understands the relationships among the person and environment factors relative to coping. For example, focusing only on resources (including social currency, as illustrated,

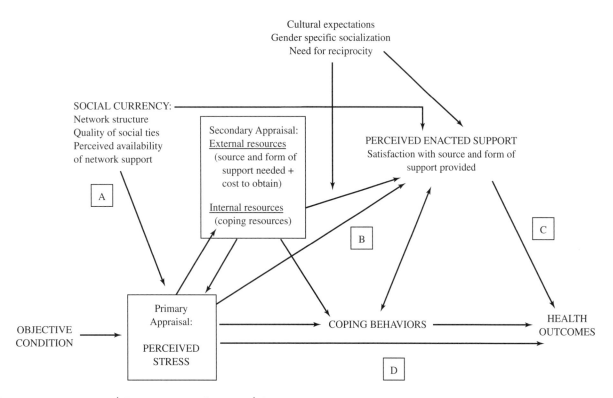

Figure 14.1 Person and Environment in Stress and Coping
Source: From "Social Support: The Promise and the Reality," by P. W. Underwood. In V. H. Rice (Ed.), *Handbook of Stress, Coping, and Health: Implications for Nursing Research, Theory, and Practice,* pp. 367–391. Copyright © 2000 and is held by Patricia W. Underwood. Reprinted with permission of P. W. Underwood.

but possibly including many other types of resources) is unlikely to be sufficient if the helper does not take other coping, contextual, and sociocultural factors into account. Similarly, if the helper works only to change certain coping behaviors, this strategy alone is likely insufficient, given factors influencing those behaviors as well as outcomes separate from coping behaviors. Although health outcomes are used in Figure 14.1, the problematic or desired outcomes could take many forms, such as mental health, social/family well-being, or employment functioning.

Let us briefly review some of the features of stress and coping relevant to assessment and intervention planning. What is the antecedent profile of person and environment strengths and vulnerabilities involved? What is the client's perceived social support relative to the stress and needs in question? What is his or her sense of self-efficacy? "Primary appraisal" in Figure 14.1 refers to whether the stressor itself is perceived as a threat of harm or loss or is perceived more as a positive challenge. "Secondary appraisals" involve questions like these: Who or what is responsible for this situation? Does the person have what is needed to handle this? What are the likely outcomes—positive and negative? The nature of a person's emotions can make a huge difference (e.g., feeling angry versus feeling guilty positions one very differently for how one is likely to respond), and emotions stem in part from how the circumstances have been appraised and the meaning they hold for the individual (family, group, community) in question.

A distinction has often been made between problem-focused coping and emotion-focused coping. Although an oversimplification, these two types can be thought of as actions to manage the stressor and actions to manage emotions associated with the stressor and the context. Coping is not a one-shot step but rather an ongoing, constantly changing process that includes how people reappraise (naturally occurring or through helping interventions) the stress context, themselves, and their anticipated future. These appraisal, emotion, and behavioral components of grappling with stress mediate the effects of stressors on the person's outcomes and well-being. And this whole set of experiences positions the individual—positively or negatively—in a different place relative to encountering the next life stressor (Fink, 2000; Kahn, 2006; Nurius, 2000; Rice, 2000; and Wong & Wong, 2006, offer overviews of stress and coping).

Current views generally recognize that both stress and coping are dynamic, with individual uniqueness and environmental forces important at each step and changing as they interact (Moos & Schaefer, 1993). Social support is a good example of this. Figure 14.1 shows a number of ways in which social support is being examined relative to the different ways in which it may relate, positively or negatively, to perceived stress, secondary appraisals, cop-

ing behaviors, and outcomes (Underwood, 2000). For example, having social resources (the notion of "social currency") may buffer the effect of stress ("A" in the model); for example, as with informational and material resources, people high in helpful and available social support may experience lower stress from the same threatening circumstances than those low in social currency. How satisfied one is with the source and type of support will likely influence how much and in what ways that support affects outcomes ("C" in the model—for example, not all "support" is helpful and some forms can actually exacerbate a problem or undermine adaptive coping whereas other forms may provide important benefits). Perceived social support may directly mediate perceived stress, on its own or in relation to coping behaviors ("D" in the model). And, of course, there are many individual differences that people bring (personality, coping preferences, gender and cultural socialization, and beliefs or expectations) that can influence how social support is conceptualized and experienced ("B" in the model).

By the time clients seek professional help, their level of stress and the salience of avoiding or minimizing negative outcomes may understandably be running very high. In addition to focusing on reducing negative outcomes, stress management research is suggesting the value of looking also at potential positive outcomes that may follow or come from coping with adversity or traumatic events. Davis, Nolen-Hoeksema, and Larson (1998) distinguish between two forms of meaning making. Both of them appear to be important to adjustment but are not correlated: (1) "making sense" of the event in terms of an explanation or deeper comprehension and (2) achieving an increased sense of meaning through finding some kind of positive outcome or benefit. Tedeschi and Calhoun's (1995; Calhoun & Tedeschi, 1998, 1999) work on perceived growth following trauma argues that intervention can build on the shattering and trauma-related disruption to help clients build new conceptions of self, meaning, and future. As Antoni and colleagues (2001) and others (Folkman, 1997) have pointed out, this trend reinforces the importance of carefully considering with clients the unique meaning that an adverse or traumatic experience holds for them as part of assessment, including perceived positive as well as negative possibilities or outcomes.

The point of these illustrations is not to cause you worry about understanding all that is involved in stress and coping! Rather, it is to underscore that individuals are continuously embedded in contexts, histories, and multilayered environments. We may think of stress as something that happens to us, but we need to appreciate that how we approach stress and what we bring with us to the coping process can markedly affect what we experience and our outcomes. As Figure 14.1 illustrates, there are a number of points in and contributors to the stress process to consider for intervention, including external and internal factors that may have mediating effects of stressful life events on subsequent health and well-being outcomes. Recent years have seen growing attention to these potential mediators. Particularly within cognitive–behavioral interventions there has been growing attention to clients' cognitive appraisals of their stress-provoking life situations as well as to their appraisal-related habits or patterns that may have become part of the stress cycle and outcomes, such as triggered anxiety, anger, or sense of helplessness or hopelessness that is impeding desired actions. Stress inoculation training, presented later in this chapter, builds on the notion of a mediated process, combining coping skills training with an educational phase regarding stress and ways in which a person's appraisals, emotions, and supports (or lack thereof) influence how the person experiences and responds to stress.

CULTURAL AND LIFE COURSE VARIATIONS IN STRESS

The model of stress and the particular interventions that we present in this chapter derive, as does much of practice-related research, predominantly from Euro-American roots. Therefore, particular care is needed in how stress is assessed and in deciding what may and may not be appropriate or useful for various clients. The need to attend to cultural, historical, life course, and other forms of diversity in order to understand the stress experience and how coping works is becoming increasingly apparent. Leininger (1988) views culture as the "learned, shared, and transmitted values, beliefs, norms, and life practices of a particular group that guides thinking, decisions, and actions in patterned ways" (p. 156) and has developed a model of cultural care diversity and universality. Cultural care involves understanding beliefs, values, and patterned expressions that "assist, support, or enable another individual or group to maintain well-being, improve a human condition or lifeway, or face death and disabilities" (p. 156, cited in Cohen & Welch, 2000). The historical, cultural, and social contexts of people influence expressions of care as well as patterns and practice of well-being and holistic health through ethnohistory, language, and environmental contexts. Folk or other culturally specific resources or systems may be important components of helping, alone or combined with professional systems such as those that you work in or anticipate working in. In short, this model helps us think about the ways in which culture is infused throughout current and historical dimensions of people's lives. This infusion, in turn, shapes and colors the encounter and experience of stress, as well as helping interventions.

Cultural differences exist, both globally and within the United States, in the concept and management of stress and the values and ideologies involved in stress reactions, perceptions of control or influence, and coping mechanisms. Examples of presentations of anxiety and stress in other countries, as summarized by Castillo (1997), include the following:

1. The *dhat* syndrome in India, characterized by somatic symptoms and anxiety over a loss of semen (which is thought to result in loss of spiritual power)
2. *Nervios* in Latin American countries, characterized by generalized anxiety along with a range of principal symptoms
3. *Hwa-byung* syndrome in Korea, characterized by anxiety and somatic symptoms often associated with the suppression of anger. (See Castillo's book for a complete discussion of these cultural variations.)

Among some cultural groups in India, for example, stress is not viewed as a major problem and certainly not a concern to bring to an "expert" (Laungani, 1993). Instead, stress is viewed as an integral part of life. Within this culture, one may see a widespread acceptance of a magical or more spiritually based explanation of stress and of coping, and persons particularly qualified to remove spells and exorcise evil spirits are often used. As in many cultures, people seeking relief from various concerns also make offerings to deities, make pilgrimages to shrines, or access what would be referred to in the United States as alternative resources such as faith healers, gurus, and homeopathic practitioners. Further, there is a greater reliance on self-healing forms of managing stress such as meditation and yoga. This illustration is intended to indicate the importance of a cultural lens (including but not limited to racial and national heritage) in understanding how stress is being experienced, what targets of change are likely to result in reduced stress, and what interventions and resources are likely to be most appropriate for clients' goals and contexts.

Lam and Palsane (1997) have reviewed contemporary research on stress and coping undertaken in Asian societies. They note both similarities and differences in the conceptualization and findings from research that applies Western findings in an Asian context (e.g., whether social support buffers effects of stress) and that which aims to identify indigenous patterns of stress and coping relative to culture-specific manifestations (e.g., exploring the nature and function of social support in specific cultures). They make the important point that cultural examinations of stress, coping, and implications for well-being need to be undertaken with structural and quality-of-life conditions in mind. For example, factors such as incidence of poverty, malnutrition, inaccessible or poor medical services, poor housing quality, and limited protection from injustices create contexts of adversity that may confound cultural dimensions. Differences among Asian and

Western societies (e.g., differences in stress proneness and stress resistance, in how stress is experienced, in ways of coping) warrant further examination, but so too do differences among different Asian cultures and within each society. We see many of these points applying to practitioners within the United States. Our pluralistic society will become even more varied in years to come, including marked differentials in economic and political issues as well as in cultural factors.

There are also variations in the prevalence of stress and stressors among various cultural groups. For example, in the United States, a much higher number of women than men are diagnosed with anxiety and stress-related disorders (Barlow & Durand, 1995). Stress syndromes are also highly prevalent among refugee and veteran groups because of related traumas, including torture, which has lagged in empirical study yet holds potential for informing concepts of coping and adaptation (Basoglu, 1997). Posttraumatic stress disorders (PTSDs) are also seen in non-Western civilian populations—for example, associated with natural disasters and with systems of social order involving widespread violence against women or other targeted hardships or injustices. Boehnlein and Kinzie (1997) point out complexities in cross-cultural analysis and treatment of PTSD. For example, although reconstructing meaning and purpose in lives affected by trauma is highly culturally determined (e.g., cultural symbols, communication patterns, identity and values, and healing approaches), the cognitive disruption and existential pain constitute a universal human response to severe traumatic events. Issues of diagnostic and measurement appropriateness across cultures also remain in question, signaling the importance of cultural consultation in rendering culturally sensitive assessment and intervention with highly stressed and trauma-related cases.

Diversity is, of course, layered, as illustrated by Sharma and Sud's (1990) findings of consistently higher test anxiety among girls, irrespective of culture (the United States and four Asian and four European nations), as well as differences in the levels and patterns of test anxiety both within and among the various Asian and European and American samples. Although understanding values, beliefs, or norms that appear to be generally patterned within a group can be helpful, stereotyped or overly generalized expectations can lead to error. For example, Alferi, Carver, Antoni, Weiss, and Duran (2001) report that Hispanic cultural norms of family serving as a key source of support were not reflected in their findings of support beyond spouses among low-income Hispanic women in early stages of breast cancer. The reasons for this outcome were not clear in the study, illustrating the importance of case-by-case assessment and the appreciation that coping and social support are dynamic phenomena that can change over the course of sustained stress and distress.

People who feel marginalized from the sociocultural and political mainstream, such as persons of color, gays and lesbians, the elderly, and the physically and mentally challenged, "are more likely to experience increased numbers of stressful events in the form of discrimination, poverty, humiliation, and harassment" (Castillo, 1997, p. 173). Broad-based exposure to prejudice and to inequalities not only poses the threat of negative health outcomes such as elevated blood pressure, heart conditions, low birth weight, higher infant mortality, HIV/AIDS, other somatic health problems, and mental health (e.g., depression, distress); it can also include differential exposure, susceptibility, and responses—both social and biological—to factors such as those (Krieger, 1999, p. 332). Moreover, minority groups, particularly ethnic minorities, are at substantially elevated risk of chronic exposure to cumulative forms of adversity that can have significant effects not only on the manifestations of stress but also on the body's neurophysiological ability to respond. Such forms of adversity include

- *Economic and social deprivation:* at work, at home, in the neighborhood, and other relevant socioeconomic regions
- *Toxic substances and hazardous conditions* (pertaining to physical, chemical, and biological agents): at work, at home, and in the neighborhood
- *Socially inflicted trauma* (mental, physical, or sexual, ranging from verbal to violent): at work, at home, in the neighborhood, and in society at large
- *Targeted marketing of legal and illegal psychoactive substances* (alcohol, tobacco, other drugs) and other commodities (e.g., junk food)
- *Inadequate health care,* by health care facilities and by specific providers (including access to care, diagnosis, and treatment)

Issues related to life course development and to the various roles and circumstances we inhabit over a lifetime are also important considerations in understanding stress, its costs or effects, and how we attempt to manage stress. For example, Greenberg (1996) reviews a range of life domains and roles relative to some of the factors that can contribute to stress:

- *Stress and educational attainment:* pressure for grades, performance, or competition; combined pressure for many of work, school, and family life; lifestyle changes that often involve health risks; debt; self-doubt; loss of support relationships and the need to create new ones; developmental challenges that often correspond with the years one is in school; confrontation with challenges to one's beliefs, values, and expectations; additional stressors for minority students (e.g., people of color, those for whom

English is not a first language, older students, students with disabilities).

- *Family stress:* the changing definition and form of family (e.g., nuclear, extended, blended, family of choice, multigenerational, dual career, single parent); financial concerns; separation/divorce; family planning; parenting; relationship conflict; role overload or conflict.
- *Aging and stress:* loss and adjustment in later years—for example, loss of valued roles, independence, health and physical strength, and mobility; loss of others and grief; the need to accept caregiving, role reversals, death and dying; losses of dignity; stereotyping or condescending attitudes or behavior from others.
- *Occupational stress:* stressors directly related to work, such as work overload or conflict, time pressures, poor working conditions, exposure to dangers of various kinds, lack of job security, thwarted goals or advancement, constraints on decision making or options, poor relations with boss/subordinate/coworkers, office politics, and so on.

However, occupational stress is often used to convey not just stress due to the job but also stress that workers bring to the job. Increasingly, employers are becoming attentive to the cumulative and dangerous effects of unchecked stress on workers. Table 14.1 provides an illustration of multiple levels and life domains that can carry stress and need to be considered for an inclusive assessment. This stress evaluation grid is by no means totally comprehensive, but it does provide a useful reminder that stress is best thought of in pluralistic ways and that interventions can, similarly, span a wide range of options that are well suited to the persons and circumstances. (See also Learning Activity 14.1.)

THE PHYSIOLOGY OF BREATHING AND STRESS

An overview of the physiology of breathing is helpful in explaining what happens to the mind/body when breathing is disordered. The function of breathing is to supply the body, including, of course, the brain, with oxygen. Respiration (inspiration) oxygenates body cells, and ventilation (expiration) removes excess carbon dioxide. Inhalation or respiration brings air into the lungs. The heart and lungs work together. The heart takes the oxygen-rich blood from the lungs and pumps the blood through the aorta to all parts of the body. The oxygen-poor blood—carrying carbon dioxide—is pumped to the lungs for the exchange of gases. From the lungs, some of the oxygen moves from the air into the bloodstream. At the same time, carbon dioxide moves from the blood into air and is breathed out (ventilation).

Metabolic activity provides oxygenation to the body, a process achieved by blood circulation or by the oxygen transport system that adjusts the amount of oxygen de-

livery needed. When there is an increase in metabolic demand, a homeostatic—a stable state of equilibrium or balance—adjustment can contribute to physiological responding leading to problems related to hypoxia. Fried (1993) notes a range of hypoxia from varying amount of decreased oxygen availability to anoxia (no oxygen). Hyperventilation can be viewed as evidence of hypoxia and as one manifestation of a continuum of stress reactions. Contrary to common usage of the term, *hyperventilation* does not refer to behaviors—such as short, shallow breathing—but rather refers to the outcome, specifically to hypocapnia, or decreased alveolar carbon dioxide. Hypocapnia carries serious risk of impairment to all bodily systems, particularly those of blood/arteries, potentially leading to significant reduction of blood flow to body extremities and to the brain (Fried, 1993). Thus, we see the danger of a vicious cycle in some patterns of stress responding that include disordered breathing leading to conditions of hypoxia and hypocapnia, which significantly impair the individual's capacity to reason and function effectively, which may lead to exacerbated stress and eroded health. Box 14.1 lists the various symptoms reported by stress sufferers that were identical to symptoms of the hyperventilation syndrome. As Box 14.1 reveals, disordered breathing influences emotions and can contribute to psychophysiological disorders.

The practice of diaphragmatic or abdominal breathing, in contrast to chest or shallow breathing, balances the sympathetic and parasympathetic nervous systems. These two systems govern the internal organs and blood vessels, affecting heart rate, blood pressure, unconscious breathing, and digestion. The sympathetic nervous system (SNS) activates the stress response and disordered breathing. The SNS is critically important for self-protection, and the altered breathing is a normal part of the stress response. The SNS responds to threatening situations. The parasympathetic nervous system (PNS) produces the relaxation response that can evoke deep, abdominal breathing. The PNS performs a homeostatic and balancing function.

In short, our patterns of breathing are related in a variety of ways to our well-being—physiologically as we have illustrated here but also emotionally and psychologically. Many of us have had experiences where we could not get our breath or breathe well and feel a rising sense of panic; or find what may have started as low anxiety quickly accelerated when we could not effectively manage our physical responding such as breathing and heart rate. Chest or shallow breathing created by stress or by learned breathing patterns is a common element of problematic stress responding. Tools such as diaphragmatic or abdominal breathing training can help an individual learn or reestablish effective breathing, thereby avoiding the hypoxia-related maladies and helping to foster mental relaxation.

TABLE 14.1	Occupational Stress Evaluation Grid

Levels	Stressors	Interventions	
		Formal	**Informal**
Sociocultural	Racism; sexism Ecological shifts Economic downturns Political changes Military crises	Elections Lobbying/political action Public education Trade associations	Grassroots organizing Petitions Demonstrations Migration Spouse employment
Organizational	Hiring policies Plant closings Layoffs, relocation Automation, market shifts, retraining Organizational priorities	Corporate decision Reorganization New management model Management consultant (inservice/ retraining)	Social activities Contests, incentives Manager involvement and ties with workers Continuing education Moonlighting
Work setting	Task (time, speed, autonomy, creativity) Supervision Coworkers Ergonomics Participation in decision making	Supervisor meetings Health/safety meetings Union grievance Employee involvement Quality circles Job redesign Inservice training	Slowdown/speedup Redefine tasks Support of other workers Sabotage, theft Quit, change jobs
Interpersonal	Divorce, separation, marital discord Conflict, family/friend Death, illness in family Intergenerational conflict Legal/financial difficulties Early parenthood	Legal/financial services Leave of absence Counseling, psychotherapy Insurance plans Family therapy Loans/credit unions Day care	Seek social support/advice Seek legal/financial assistance Self-help groups Vacation/sick days Child care
Psychological	Neurosis, mental illness Disturbance of affect, cognition, or behavior Ineffective coping skills Poor self-image Poor communication Addictive behavior	Employee assistance (referral/in house) Counseling, psychotherapy Medication Supervisory training Stress management workshop	Seek support from friends, family, church Self-help groups/books Self-medication Recreation, leisure Sexual activity "Mental health" days
Biological	Disease, disability Sleep, appetite disturbance Chemical dependency Biochemical imbalance Pregnancy	Preplacement screening Counseling Medical treatment Health education Employee assistance Maternity leave	Change sleep/wake habits Bag lunch Self-medication Cosmetics Diets, exercise Consult physician
Physical/environmental	Poor air, climate Noise exposure Toxic substance exposure Poor lighting Radiation exposure Poor equipment design Bad architecture	Protective clothing/equipment Climate control Health/safety committee Interior decoration Muzak Union grievance	Own equipment, decoration Walkman, radio Consult personal physician Letters of complaint

Source: "A Review of NIOSH Psychological Stress Research—1997," by M. J. Smith et al., March 1978, NIOSH Proceedings of Occupational Stress Conference (Cincinnati, OH: National Institute of Occupational Stress and Health), pp. 27–28. Cited in *Comprehensive Stress Management* by J. S. Greenberg, p. 249, Brown & Berchmark, 1996.

LEARNING ACTIVITY **14.1** **Cultural and Life Course Variations in Stress**

In this activity, we ask you to reflect alone and with colleagues on ways in which differences in culture and life course development can affect what is experienced as stressful and subsequent implications for stress management relevant to these differences.

First, on your own, think of two personally stressful times of life that are separated by at least a few years. Consider environmental context, language, and ethnohistory factors (e.g., education, economics, political and legal, cultural values and lifestyle, kinship and social relations, religion and philosophy, technology) that you believe may have been shaping why and how that event or set of conditions was stressful. For example, were there values about responsibility, threats to something cherished, or external constraints that were prominent?

Repeat this exercise with the second stressful time of life. What are some differences you notice that may be partly due to the different points of life—for example, differences due to experience, personal power or resources, or changed roles from one's youth to adulthood? What are some implications for these contextual differences in stress and coping for directions you would see appropriate for stress management intervention?

In a group exercise, compare selected parts of your self-analysis with those of student colleagues. What differences do you notice in environmental, cultural, or life course development factors that may be related to how stress arose, to how it was experienced, to coping efforts, and to what would be most useful?

STEPS FOR BREATHING

Take a little time to answer these questions:

Do you inflate your chest when you take a deep breath?

Do you experience queasy sensations in your chest or stomach?

Is your breath mostly up in your chest?

Is your breathing shallow?

Do you often feel that you are not getting a full breath?

Do you get mild or more severe headaches, often in the afternoon?

Do you sometimes have painful sensations in your rib cage or shooting pains that make you want to hold your breath?

Are your muscles often tense or sore to the touch?

Do you sigh often?

Do you feel breathless fairly often?

Do you tire easily or wake up tired?

When you are calm and restful, do you breathe more than 15 times a minute? (Hendricks 1995, p. ix)

A client with a "yes" answer to any of those questions may benefit from breathing exercises. We review diaphragmatic breathing here. Hendricks (1995) offers a more extensive review of additional breathing exercises. You can discuss with the client whether breathing exercises might help with his or her presenting concerns. Benefits of conscious breathing exercises can be one or a combination of the following: releases stress and tension, builds energy and endurance, contributes to emotional mastery, prevents and heals physical problems, manages pain, contributes to graceful aging, enhances mental concentration and physical performance,

---

BOX 14.1   SYMPTOMS REPORTED BY STRESS SUFFERERS THAT ARE IDENTICAL TO THE HYPERVENTILATION SYNDROME

- Tension (a "feeling of tension," muscle ache)
- Irritability, low frustration tolerance
- Anxiety (apprehension, heightened vigilance)
- Dyspnea (inability to catch one's breath, choking sensation, feeling of suffocation, frequent sighing, chest heaving, lump in throat)

- Fatigue, tiredness, burnout
- Insomnia
- Heart palpitations (pounding in chest, seemingly accelerated pulse rate, sensation of heaviness or weight on the chest, diffuse chest pain)
- Depression, restlessness, nervousness
- Dizzy spells, shakiness, trembling
- Coldness of the hands and feet, occasional tingling sensations
- Inability to concentrate
- Bloating

Source: Adapted from "The Role of Respiration in Stress and Stress Control: Toward a Theory of Stress as a Hypoxic Phenomenon," by R. Fried. In *Principles and Practice of Stress Management* (2nd ed.), by P. M. Lehrer and R. L. Woolfolk, pp. 310–311. Copyright © 1993 by The Guilford Press. Used by permission.

TABLE 14.2 How to Work with the Breath			
Dimensions of the Breath	**Problems in Breathing**	**Relaxed Breathing**	**Levels of Interaction**
Location of breath	Chest	Belly	Observe only
Depth of breath	Shallow	Deep	Bring to awareness
Rate of breath	Fast	Slow	Teach or use one of the breath exercises to modify problems in breathing
Exhalation of breath	Holding or rapid	Released (often with sound) slowly	Teach or use one of the breath exercises to modify problems in breathing
Inhalation of breath	Choppy and shallow	Deep and smooth	Teach or use one of the breath exercises to modify problems in breathing

Note: All the above apply to both the helper and the client.

and promotes psychospiritual transformation (Hendricks, 1995, pp. 7–31).

When you are teaching awareness orientation to breathing or are teaching breathing exercises, consider the client's age, gender, class, and ethnicity. Also, determine whether the client has any medical or physical condition that could make these breathing exercises inappropriate. If you or the client has any doubts, instruct the client to confer with his or her primary care physician and receive approval to engage in the exercise *before* you begin the instruction. Also, refer to the "Contraindications and Adverse Effects of Diaphragmatic Breathing" later in the chapter.

Awareness of Breathing

The awareness-of-breathing orientation is a technique used to help a person become aware and conscious of her or his breathing. The orientation process has five steps:

1. Ask the client to get into a comfortable position (in a recliner chair or whatever is comfortable) with legs apart, the feet relaxed and off to the side; one arm is bent at the elbow and placed on the navel; the other arm and hand are relaxed and alongside the body.
2. Instruct the client to breathe slowly through the nose and to become aware and conscious; he or she is to feel the movement of the abdomen when inhaling and exhaling.
3. Instruct the client to keep breathing slowly and deeply, and to be relaxed.
4. After several minutes of the client's breathing while lying down, instruct the client to sit up straight with spine erect; he or she is to place one hand below the navel and the other hand on the upper chest.
5. Ask the client to notice the movement of the hands during inhalation and exhalation, and to assess which hand moves more. If the hand on the upper chest moves more than the other hand, it probably means the client is breathing from the chest rather than the

abdomen, in which case the breathing is shallow and not as deep as diaphragmatic or abdominal breathing.

For some clients, this exercise brings awareness or consciousness of breathing before the rationale for diaphragmatic breathing and training is presented. We have found that this awareness exercise will enhance diaphragmatic breathing training for some clients. For other clients, the practitioner can begin with the rationale and overview for breathing and start the diaphragmatic breathing training without the awareness exercise.

How to Work with Breath

Table 14.2 presents ways to work with breath, differentiating among dimensions of breath and types of problems in breathing. For example, the practitioner can (1) observe the location of the client's breath—chest for problem breathing, belly for relaxed breathing; (2) bring awareness to the client of the depth of breath—shallow for problem breathing, deep for relaxed breathing; (3) determine the rate of breathing—fast for problem breathing, slow for relaxed breathing; (4) observe whether the client holds or has a rapid exhalation of the breath; and (5) observe whether the client's inhalation is choppy and shallow. For any of these issues, the helping practitioner can teach one of the appropriate exercises in Table 14.2 and in Learning Activity 14.2.

Empowered Consent for Breathing Exercises

The helper needs to act in good faith to protect clients' rights and welfare by informing clients adequately about the breathing exercises. The helper should obtain clients' consent and willingness to use the exercises prior to offering any instruction. As part of the consent process, the helper should give clients the following information:

1. Description of breathing exercises
2. Rationale, purpose, and potential benefits of the breathing exercises

LEARNING ACTIVITY 14.2 Breathing Exercises

In this activity, you will use a breathing exercise so that your practice with conscious breathing will help with your teaching of others.

1. Try the breathing awareness exercise and the diaphragmatic breathing exercise presented in the chapter. Do each exercise for several days so that you become familiar with it and experience its effects.

2. Try to use the diaphragmatic breathing in real, stressful situations: whenever you need to feel calmer, feel more in control, or become energized.
3. During a two-week period, keep a journal or log of each practice session, describing what you experienced in your practice. Record your overall energy and level of relaxation in what you perceive as a consequence of your practice with the breathing exercises.

---

3. Description of the helper's role
4. Description of the client's role
5. Description of possible risks or discomforts
6. Description of expected benefits
7. Estimated time needed for the exercise
8. Answers to client's questions about the breathing exercises
9. Explanation of client's right to discontinue the exercises at any time
10. Summary and clarification/exploration of client's reactions

You can use these items to construct a written consent form that clients will sign indicating that they received this information. Also, refer to the contraindications section for the use of diaphragmatic breathing. If you or any client has doubts about performing these exercises, the client should consult with his or her primary care physician.

Rationale and Overview for Breathing Training

The rationale and overview for breathing training could be presented like this:

A lot of people do not breathe deeply enough. Learning to breathe with greater use of your diaphragm or abdomen can increase your oxygen intake. This way of breathing uses the full capacity of the lungs and enables you to inhale about seven times more oxygen than with normal shallow breathing. Also, you can practice this any time during the day—while you are waiting in a line or in your car stuck in traffic. Increased oxygen capacity can have many mental and physical benefits. Breathing training stimulates the PNS or relaxation response, and calms the central nervous system. In the beginning you might experience a little discomfort or lightheadedness, but such discomfort is rare. Effective breathing can help release stress and tension, build energy and endurance, contribute to emotional mastery, prevent and heal physical problems, help with pain management, and enhance mental concentration and physical performance. There are no known risks in learning and practicing breathing exercises, although for some

clients there may be contraindications. If you feel any pain or discomfort, which is very unlikely, we will stop immediately. The process will include training you in abdominal breathing, or breathing with your diaphragm. We can explore other breathing exercises that you might find helpful. You will practice the breathing exercises during the week. If you practice once a day, you will spend five or six minutes. The time is doubled if you practice twice a day. Also, you will learn to use deep breathing when you are in stressful situations, or when you need a break, or for a refreshing relief to reenergize yourself. You can be trained to use the breathing exercises in one session. You can practice during the week, and if you feel the need, we can check in by phone to see how you are doing. Practice helps you incorporate deep breathing in your everyday life and in stressful situations. How does that sound?

Diaphragmatic Breathing

It may be useful to start training either by describing how a diaphragm works or with a picture that illustrates the diaphragm as a wide, fan-shaped muscle below the lungs that contracts and relaxes, pulling air in or pushing it out, respectively. You can use the following steps as a guide in teaching this exercise. (Also see Learning Activity 14.2.)

1. The helper provides the client with a *rationale*. You can say to the client, "Notice that at the start of each breath your stomach rises and the lower edge of your rib cage expands. If your breathing is too shallow, diaphragmatic breathing should help you acquire a deeper pattern of breathing." The helper explains to the client that when one inhales, the muscle fibers of the diaphragm contract and are drawn downward toward the abdomen. A picture may help the client to visualize the movement of the diaphragm at the beginning of diaphragmatic training.
2. The helper instructs the client to get in a *comfortable position and to breathe through the nose*. Legs are comfortably apart, with feet relaxed and off to the side. The helper focuses the client on the bodily sensations of

breathing in and out, noting movement in the abdomen. This is also called belly or abdominal breathing because the movement of the abdomen is out during inhalation and in during exhalation.

3. The helper demonstrates *placement of hands and visualization*. The client is told to bend the arms at the elbow and place the thumbs gently below the rib cage; the rest of the hand and fingers are pointing toward each other and perpendicular to the body. Then the client is asked to visualize the diaphragm upon inhaling to see its muscular fibers contract and draw downward. The helper tells the client upon exhalation to visualize the diaphragm being drawn upward as the air is pushed out of the lungs and forms a cone shape: "As you inhale, extend your abdomen outward, and as you exhale, allow your abdomen to come inward. You may wish to exaggerate this movement. Always breathe through your nostrils in an even and smooth manner. When you start, it is helpful to focus on the rise and fall of your hand as you inhale and exhale. Focus on each inhalation: your hand goes up, and your belly comes out. On your exhalation, press in and back on your abdominal muscles (allowing the abdomen to draw inward toward the spine), and your hand goes down. Remember, the diaphragm is a muscle, and like any muscle it can be trained and strengthened."

4. The client is instructed to *simulate the movement of the diaphragm* with the hands. The thumbs are just below the rib cage on the abdomen, and the fingers are slightly interlaced. As the client inhales, the interlaced fingers are flattened to simulate the diaphragm being drawn downward. On the exhalation, the client is instructed to curve the fingers so they are cone shaped, simulating the movement of the diaphragm being drawn upward as the air is being pushed out of the lungs. On the inhalation, the muscle fibers of the diaphragm contract and are drawn downward. The diaphragm becomes less cone shaped and almost flat. As the diaphragm descends, it presses on the stomach, liver, and other organs, and gently massages and stimulates them: "When you exhale, the muscles contract and the diaphragm becomes cone shaped and pushes upward toward the lungs. Visualize your diaphragm working and exercising the internal organs of digestion and elimination, massaging and kneading them for each inhalation and exhalation, forcing the blood into the organs and then squeezing the blood out. This way of breathing uses the full capacity of your lungs" (Birch, 1995, p. 45).

5. The client is instructed to sit up with spine erect and eyes closed, to *visualize the diaphragm's position while sitting*—inhaling and exhaling, and to feel the abdomen rising and falling like the tide.

6. The helper instructs the client to *practice daily* diaphragmatic breathing for homework, at least twice each day. The helper reminds the client to find a time and place to practice that will be free of distractions and interruptions. The client is also instructed to use abdominal or diaphragmatic breathing when in a stressful situation or to reenergize the mind or body. This way of breathing uses the full capacity of the lungs. It enables one to inhale about seven times more oxygen than with normal shallow breathing. Instruct the client to use diaphragmatic breathing at any time during the day. Learning Activity 14.2 outlines activities for implementing breathing exercises.

CONTRAINDICATIONS AND ADVERSE EFFECTS OF DIAPHRAGMATIC BREATHING

Deep abdominal/diaphragmatic breathing may not be helpful for everyone. For example, some people doing these exercises may develop cramps. Fried (1993) offers clients the following instructions:

> If an exercise causes pain or discomfort, stop it immediately. Also, do not do any exercise if you have any physical or medical condition or any injury that would contraindicate its safety. Among such conditions are the following:
>
> 1. Muscle or other tissue or organ malformation or injury— for example, sprained or torn muscles, torticolis, fractures, or recent surgery.
> 2. Any condition causing metabolic acidosis, where hyperventilation may be compensatory such as diabetes, kidney disease, heart disease, severe hypoglycemia, etc. If you are in doubt, please bring your condition to my attention.
> 3. Low blood pressure or any related condition, such as syncope (fainting). Deep abdominal breathing may cause a significant decrease in blood pressure.
> 4. Insulin-dependent diabetes. If you are an insulin-dependent diabetic, you should not do this or any other deep relaxation exercise without the expressed approval by your physician and his or her close monitoring of your insulin needs. (Fried, 1993, p. 323)

Pregnancy also may affect a client's capacity to do some of the breathing. Smokers too have more trouble with breathing exercises, and Hendricks (1995) does not use breathing exercises until after a person stops smoking.

MODEL EXAMPLE FOR DIAPHRAGMATIC BREATHING

In this model example, we present a narrative account of how two breathing exercises might be used with Yoshi, a 49-year-old male Japanese American air traffic controller.

Rationale

First, we explain to Yoshi that learning to breathe with his diaphragm or abdomen can increase his oxygen intake. We tell him that this way of breathing uses the full capacity of the lungs and enables him to inhale about seven times more oxygen than with normal shallow breathing. We tell him that the benefits of diaphragmatic breathing include releasing stress and tension and enhancing mental concentration. We provide an overview by telling him that the process will include training in diaphragmatic breathing. We tell Yoshi that he can practice during the week and use deep breathing in stressful situations. We confirm Yoshi's willingness to try diaphragmatic breathing and answer any questions he may have about the procedure. We provide all the elements of information illustrated in the example of a rationale previously described.

Instructions about Position and Breathing Through the Nose

We show Yoshi a diagram of the position of the diaphragm for exhalation and inhalation. Yoshi is instructed to get into a comfortable position and to breathe through his nose. We request that he breathe through his nose, notice his breath (while breathing through his nose), and observe what happens as he exhales and inhales. We ask Yoshi what the movement is like near his navel and below his rib cage. We explain to him that if he is breathing diaphragmatically, a hand placed on the navel will move more during the exhalation and inhalation than a hand below the rib cage. We ask Yoshi to relax and just notice his breathing.

Placement of the Hands and Visualization

We ask Yoshi to bend his arms and place his thumbs gently below his rib cage (we model the position of the hands for him). Yoshi is instructed to place the rest of his fingers on each hand perpendicular to his body. We ask him to visualize the diaphragm, and as he inhales, we remind him that the muscular fibers of the diaphragm contract and are drawn downward. We describe—as he exhales—the diaphragm being drawn upward and forming a cone shape as the air is pushed out of the lungs.

Simulation of the Diaphragm with the Fingers

Yoshi is instructed to simulate the movement of the diaphragm with his hands. We tell him, as he inhales, to straighten his fingers out flat. As he exhales, he is to curve his fingers so that they become cone shaped. We ask him to do this for several breaths, simulating the movement of the diaphragm while his breathing is gentle and relaxed.

Diaphragmatic Breathing While Sitting

Yoshi is instructed to sit up with spine erect, eyes closed, and his hands on his lap, on his knees, or wherever is comfortable for him. We ask him to visualize his abdomen expanding or rising and falling like the tide, and to breathe in this relaxed fashion for a couple of minutes.

Daily Practice and in Vivo Use

Yoshi is instructed to practice diaphragmatic breathing twice a day for five minutes, once after getting up in the morning and once in the late afternoon or early evening. We remind Yoshi to find a quiet place to practice that is free of distractions and interruptions. Yoshi is instructed to visualize the movement of his diaphragm while he is practicing and when he uses abdominal breathing in stressful situations.

STRESS INOCULATION: PROCESSES AND USES

Stress management can, and typically does, involve change interventions that are incorporated into an integrated set, by the helper and the client, that is appropriate to case-specific factors such as the nature of the stressors and goals. For example, Antoni and colleagues (2001) describe a stress management intervention for women diagnosed with breast cancer that includes 10 two-hour sessions with in-session didactic material, experiential components, and between-session assignments (e.g., practicing relaxation techniques and monitoring stress responses). This applies both problem-focused (e.g., active coping and planning, replacement of doubt appraisals with a sense of confidence via cognitive restructuring) and emotion-focused (e.g., relaxation training, emotional expression, and use of social support) coping strategies. This is an intervention designed for a certain kind of life stress. The specific array for a different type of condition or clients may be revised accordingly. For example, many forms of stress are due to more chronic and pervasive factors, such as poverty, oppression, trauma, and long-standing conditions of need. Understanding how stress is experienced and what is typically involved in the coping process (both the person and environmental factors)—content that we reviewed earlier in this chapter—will guide your selection of change strategies. Level of severity is a very important consideration. Evidence indicates, for example, that individuals experiencing posttraumatic stress disorder benefit from exposure therapy and stress-focused cognitive restructuring, or integration of these two strategies (Moore, Zoellner, & Bittinger, 2004).

Stress inoculation is an approach to teaching both physical and cognitive coping skills. As the name implies, the aim is to enhance resistance to stress by better preparing the client to respond more effectively when stressors are encountered. Meichenbaum (1993) states that stress inoculation training "helps clients acquire sufficient knowledge, self-understanding, and coping skills to facilitate better ways of handling expected stressful encounters. Stress inoculation training combines elements of Socratic and didactic teaching, client self-monitoring, cognitive restructuring, problem solving, self-instructional and relaxation training, behavioral and imagined rehearsal, and environmental change" (p. 381). Eliot and Eisdorfer (1982) and Meichenbaum (1993) classify stressful events as follows:

1. One event that is time limited and not chronic, such as a medical biopsy, surgery, a dental procedure, an oral examination.
2. One event that triggers a series of stressful reactions, such as job loss, divorce, death of loved one, natural or manmade disaster, or sexual assault.
3. Chronic and intermittent events, such as musical performances, athletic competitions, military combat, recurrent headaches.
4. Chronic and continual events, such as chronic medical or mental illness, marital conflict, chronic physical–emotional or psychological abuse, some professions—nursing, teaching, or police work. (Meichenbaum, 1993, p. 373)

Stress inoculation training varies with the type of stress involved and the particular coping and stress management skills incorporated, but it is consistent in having (1) an educational phase (helping the client better understand the nature of stress and stress effects), (2) a skill acquisition and rehearsal phase (developing and practicing a repertoire of coping skills), and (3) an application and generalization phase (using coping skills in conditions approximating problem situations as well as conditions with potential stress effects). In a meta-analytic review, Saunders, Driskell, Johnston, and Salas (1996) found stress inoculation training to be an effective means of reducing performance anxiety, reducing more generalized anxiety, and enhancing performance under stress, with no evidence among the studies reviewed of limitations on the application of stress inoculation to applied training environments. Box 14.2 presents a sample of stress inoculation research used with a variety of concerns. These include academic performance, anger management and reduction, anxiety associated with wide-ranging life experiences, child and family issues, athletic performance, exercise, pain management, stress burnout, dental treatment, use with older adults, hypertension, and trauma.

Although Saunders and colleagues (1996) specifically tested for differences in populations in terms of high and low anxiety, their review does not speak to other dimensions of client populations that could make a difference relative to good fit or effectiveness. In one of a limited number of culture-specific studies, Chiu (1997) concluded that the basic principles of stress inoculation, such as fostering realistic advance preparation for future stressors, will have cross-cultural applicability, although content and selection of training components should be reflective of individual differences and cultural characteristics. In her study of changes over time of newly arrived Asian students during their first year at a U.S. university, Chiu found outcome differences for students with low, moderate, and high levels of anticipatory fear. Implications of this research include tailoring interventions to clients with different needs (such as anticipatory fear) and different coping histories, as well as exploration of specific coping strategies likely to be more readily applied by people of different cultures.

SEVEN COMPONENTS OF STRESS INOCULATION

Stress inoculation* has seven components:

1. Treatment rationale
2. Information giving by the helper
3. Client learning and practice of direct-action coping strategies
4. Client learning and practice of cognitive coping strategies
5. Application of all coping skills to problem-related situations
6. Application of all coping skills to potential problem situations
7. Homework and follow-up

Each of these components is described in this section. For detailed descriptions of the steps associated with each part see Interview Checklist for Stress Inoculation at the end of this chapter and Learning Activity 14.3.

Treatment Rationale

Here is an example of a rationale that a helping practitioner might use for stress inoculation.

Purpose

The helper might explain as follows the purpose of stress inoculation for a client having trouble with hostility:

> You find yourself confronted with situations in which your temper gets out of hand. You have trouble managing your anger, especially when you feel provoked. This procedure can help you learn to cope with provoking situations and can help you manage the intensity of your anger when you're in these situations so it doesn't control you.

Overview

Then the helper can give the client a brief overview of the procedure:

> First, we will try to help you understand the nature of your feelings and how certain situations may provoke your feelings and lead from anger to hostility. Next, you will learn some ways to manage this and to cope with situations in which you feel this way. After you learn these coping skills, we will set up situations where you can practice using these skills to help you control your anger. How does this sound to you?

*We wish to acknowledge the work of Meichenbaum (1993, 1994) in our presentation of stress inoculation training.

BOX 14.2   STRESS INOCULATION RESEARCH

Anger

Timmons, P. L., Oehlert, M. E., Sumerall, S. W., Timmons, C. W., et al. (1997). Stress inoculation training for maladaptive anger: Comparison of group counseling versus computer guidance. *Computers in Human Behavior, 13,* 51–64.

Anxiety and Panic

Fontana, A. M., Hyra, D., Godfrey, L., & Cermak, L. (1999). Impact of a peer-led stress inoculation training intervention on state anxiety and heart rate in college students. *Journal of Applied Biobehavioral Research, 4,* 45–63.

Lopez Alonso, J. C., & Gomez-Jarabo, G. (2000). A model of therapeutic action in panic disorders. *European Journal of Psychiatry, 14*(1), 42–51.

Children and Adolescents

Gottman, J. M., & Katz, L. F. (2002). Children's emotional reactions to stressful parent–child interactions: The link between emotion regulation and vagal tone. *Marriage and Family Review, 34*(3–4), 265–283.

Maag, J. W., & Kotlash, J. (1994). Review of stress inoculation training with children and adolescents: Issues and recommendations. *Behavior Modification, 18,* 443–469.

Health Conditions

Garcia, J., Simon, M. A., Duran, M., Canceller, J., & Aneiros, F. J. (2006). Differential efficacy of a cognitive–behavioral intervention versus pharmacological treatment in the management of fibromyalgic syndrome. *Psychology, Health and Medicine, 11*(4), 498–506.

Garcia-Vera, M. P., Labrador, F. J., & Sanz, J. (1997). Stress management training for essential hypertension: A controlled study. *Applied Psychophysiology and Biofeedback, 22*(4), 261–283.

Military Training

Cigrang, J. A., Todd, S. L., & Carbone, E. G. (2000). Stress management training for military trainees returned to duty after a mental health evaluation: Effect on graduation rates. *Journal of Occupational Health Psychology, 5*(1), 48–55.

Offenders

Bourke, M. L., & Van Hasselt, V. B. (2001). Social problem-solving skills training for incarcerated offenders: A treatment manual. *Behavior Modification, 25*(2), 163–188.

Pain Reduction

Milling, L. S., Kirsch, I., Meunier, S. A., & Levine, M. R. (2002). Hypnotic analgesia and stress inoculation training: Individual and combined effects in analog treatment of experimental pain. *Cognitive Therapy and Research, 26*(3), 355–371.

Posttraumatic Stress Disorder

Foa, E. B., Dancu, C. V., Hembree, E. A., Jaycox, L. H., Meadows, E. A., & Street, G. P. (1999). A comparison of exposure therapy, stress inoculation training, and their combination for reducing posttraumatic stress disorder in female assault victims. *Journal of Consulting and Clinical Psychology, 67*(2), 194–200.

Lee, C., Gavriel, H., Drummond, P., Richards, J., & Greenwald, R. (2002). Treatment of PTSD: Stress inoculation training with prolonged exposure compared to EMDR. *Journal of Clinical Psychology, 58*(9), 1071–1089.

Litz, B. T., Williams, L., Wang, J., Bryant, R., & Engel, C. C. (2004). A therapist-assisted Internet self-help program for traumatic stress. *Professional Psychology: Research and Practice, 35*(6), 628–634.

Trzepacz, A. M., & Luiselli, J. K. (2004). Efficacy of stress inoculation training in a case of posttraumatic stress disorder (PTSD) secondary to emergency gynecological surgery. *Clinical Case Studies, 3*(1), 83–92.

Posttraumatic Stress Disorder and Anger

Cahill, S. P., Rauch, S. A., Hembree, E. A., & Foa, E. B. (2003). Effect of cognitive–behavioral treatments for PTSD on anger. *Journal of Cognitive Psychotherapy, 17*(2), 113–131.

Posttraumatic Stress Disorder and Substance Abuse

Triffleman, E. (2000). Gender differences in a controlled pilot study of psychosocial treatments in substance dependent patients with post-traumatic stress disorder: Design considerations and outcomes. *Alcoholism Treatment Quarterly, 18*(3), 113–126.

Triffleman, E., Carroll, K., & Kellogg, S. (1999). Substance dependence posttraumatic stress disorder therapy: An integrated cognitive–behavioral approach. *Journal of Substance Abuse Treatment, 17*(1–2), 3–14.

Preventing Mental Illness

Schiraldi, G. R., & Brown, S. L. (2001). Primary prevention for mental health: Results of an exploratory cognitive–behavioral college course. *Journal of Primary Prevention, 22*(1), 55–67.

Traumatic Brain Injury

Aeschleman, S. R., & Imes, C. (1999). Stress inoculation training for impulsive behaviors in adults with traumatic brain injury. *Journal of Rational–Emotive and Cognitive Behavior Therapy, 17*(1), 51–65.

Williams, W. H., Evans, J. J., & Wilson, B. A. (2003). Neurorehabilitation for two cases of post traumatic stress disorder following traumatic brain injury. *Cognitive Neuropsychiatry, 8*(1), 1–18.

Information Giving by the Helper

Before learning and applying various coping strategies, the client needs to be given some information about the nature of a stress reaction and the possible coping strategies that might be used. It is helpful for the client to understand the nature of a stress reaction and how various coping strategies can help manage the stress. The education phase of stress inoculation helps the client conceptualize reactions to stressful events and lays a foundation for understanding the other components.

The helper should provide a conceptual framework for the client's emotional reaction, information about the phases of reacting to stress, and examples of coping skills and strategies.

Conceptual Framework for the Client's Reaction

In setting a framework, the helper should first explain the nature of the client's reaction to a stressful situation. Although understanding one's reaction may not be sufficient for changing it, the conceptual framework lays some groundwork for beginning the change process. An explanation of some kind of stress (anxiety, hostility, pain) usually involves describing the stress as having two components: physiological arousal and covert self-statements or thoughts that provoke anxiety, hostility, or pain. This explanation may help the client realize that coping strategies must be directed toward the arousal behaviors *and* the cognitive processes. For example, to describe such a framework to a client who has trouble controlling hostility, the helper could say something like this:

> Perhaps you could think about what happens when you get very angry. You might notice that certain things happen to you physically—perhaps your body feels tight, your face may feel warm, you may experience more rapid breathing, or your heart may pound. This is the physical part of your anger. However, there is another thing that probably goes on while you're very angry—that is, what you're thinking. You might be thinking such things as "He had no right to attack me; I'll get back at him; boy, I'll show him who's boss; I'll teach her to keep her mouth shut." These kinds of thoughts only intensify your anger. So the way you interpret and think about an anger-provoking situation also contributes to arousing hostile feelings.

(Note that in this and related examples, we are differentiating between appropriate, legitimate feelings of anger and hostility that leads to abuse or damage.)

Phases of Stress Reactions

After explaining a framework for emotional arousal, the helper should describe the kinds of times or phases when the client's arousal level may be heightened. For example, phobic clients may view their anxiety as one "massive panic reaction." Similarly, clients who are angry, depressed, or in pain may interpret their feelings as one large, continuous reaction that has a certain beginning and end. Clients who interpret their reactions in this way may perceive the reaction as too difficult to change because it is so massive and overwhelming.

One way to help the client see the potential for coping with feelings is to describe the feelings by individual stages or phases of reacting to a situation. Meichenbaum (1993, 1994) used four stages to help the client conceptualize the various critical points of a reaction: (1) preparing for a stressful, painful, or provoking situation; (2) confronting and handling the situation or the provocation; (3) coping with critical moments or with feelings of being overwhelmed or agitated during the situation; and (4) rewarding oneself after the stress for using coping skills in the first three phases. Explanation of these stages in the preliminary part of stress inoculation helps the client understand the sequence of coping strategies to be learned. To explain the client's reaction as a series of phases, the helper might say something like this:

> When you think of being angry, you probably just think of being angry for a continuous period of time. However, you might find that your anger is probably not just one big reaction but comes and goes at different points during a provoking situation. The first critical point is when you anticipate the situation and start to get angry. At this point, you can learn to prepare yourself for handling the situation in a manageable way. The next point may come when you're in the middle of the situation and you're very angry. Here you can learn how to confront a provoking situation in a constructive way. There might also be times when your anger really gets intense and you can feel it starting to control you—and perhaps feel yourself losing control. At this time, you can learn how to cope with intense feelings of agitation. Then, after the situation is over, instead of getting angry with yourself for the way you handled it, you can learn to encourage yourself for trying to cope with it. In this procedure, we'll practice using the coping skills at these especially stressful or arousing times.

Coping Skills and Strategies

The helper should provide some information about the kinds of coping skills and strategies that can be used at these critical points. The helper should emphasize that there is a *variety* of useful coping skills and that clients' input in selecting and tailoring these skills for themselves is *most* important. Allow clients to choose coping strategies that reflect their own preferences. In using stress inoculation, teach both "direct-action" and "cognitive" coping skills (Meichenbaum, 1993). *Direct-action* coping strategies are designed to help the client use coping behaviors to handle the stress; *cognitive* coping skills are used to give the client coping thoughts (self-statements) to handle the stress. The client should understand that *both* kinds of coping skills are important and that the two serve different functions, although some clients may prefer to rely more on one type than on the other, depending on their gender and culture. To provide the client with information about the usefulness of these coping skills, the helper might explain them in this way:

> In the next phase of this procedure, you'll be learning a lot of different ways to prepare for and handle a provoking situation. Some of these coping skills will help you learn to cope with provoking situations by your actions and behaviors; others will help you handle these situations by the way you interpret and think about the situation. Not all the strategies you learn may be useful or necessary for you, so your input in selecting the ones you prefer to use is important.

Client Learning and Practice of Direct-Action Coping Strategies

In this phase of stress inoculation, the client learns and practices some direct-action coping strategies. The helper first discusses and models possible action strategies; the client selects some to use and practices them with the helper's encouragement and assistance. Direct-action coping skills are designed to help the client acquire and apply coping behaviors in stressful situations. The most commonly used direct-action coping strategies are

1. Collecting objective or factual information about the stressful situation
2. Identifying escape routes or ways to decrease the stress
3. Palliative coping strategies
4. Mental relaxation methods
5. Physical relaxation methods

Information Collection

Collecting objective or factual information about a stressful situation may help the client evaluate the situation more realistically. The assessment process is very helpful in collecting information. Moreover, information about a situation may reduce the ambiguity for the client and indirectly reduce the level of threat. For example, for a client who may be confronted with physical pain, information about the source and expected timing of pain can reduce stress. This coping method is widely used in childbirth classes. The women and their "labor coaches" are taught and shown that the experienced pain is actually a uterine contraction. They are given information about the timing and stages of labor and the timing and intensity of contractions so that when labor occurs, their anxiety will not be increased by misunderstanding or a lack of information about what is happening in their bodies.

Collecting information about an anxiety- or anger-engendering situation serves the same purpose. For example, in using stress inoculation to help clients control anger, collecting information about the people who typically provoke them may help. Clients collect information that can help them view provocation as a *task* or a problem to be solved, rather than as a *threat* or a personal attack.

Identification of Escape Routes

Identifying escape routes is a way to help the client cope with stress before it gets out of hand. The idea of an escape route is to short-circuit the explosive or stressful situation or to deescalate the stress before the client behaves in a way that may "blow it." This coping strategy may help abusive clients learn to identify cues that elicit their physical or verbal abuse and to take some preventive action before striking out. This is similar to the stimulus-control self-management strategy. These escape or prevention routes can be very simple things that the client can *do* to prevent losing control or losing face in the situation. An abusive client could perhaps avoid striking out by counting to 60, leaving the room, or talking about something humorous.

Palliative Coping Strategies

Meichenbaum (1993, 1994) describes palliative coping strategies that may be particularly useful for aversive or stressful situations that cannot be substantially altered or avoided, such as chronic or life-threatening illnesses:

> Train emotionally focused palliative coping skills, especially when the client has to deal with unchangeable and uncontrollable stressors; e.g., perspective taking, selective attention diversion procedures, as in the case of chronic pain patients; adaptive modes of affective expression such as humor, relaxation, and reframing the situation. (Meichenbaum, 1993, p. 384)

Mental Relaxation methods

Mental relaxation can also help clients cope with stress. This technique may involve attention-diversion tactics: Angry clients can control their anger by concentrating on a problem to solve, counting floor tiles in the room, thinking about a funny or erotic joke, or thinking about something positive about themselves. Attention-diversion tactics are commonly used to help people control pain. Instead of focusing on the pain, the person may concentrate very hard on an object in the room or on the repetition of a word (a mantra) or a number. Again, in the Lamaze method of childbirth, women are taught to concentrate on a "focal point" such as an object in the room or on a picture. In this way, the woman's attention is directed to an object instead of to the tightening sensations in her lower abdomen.

Some people find that mental relaxation is more successful when they use imagery or fantasy. People who enjoy daydreaming or who report a vivid imagination may find imagery a particularly useful way to promote mental relaxation. Generally, imagery as a coping method helps the client go on a fantasy trip instead of focusing on the stress, the provocation, or the pain. For example, instead of thinking about how anxious or angry he feels, the client might learn to fantasize about lying on a warm beach, being on a sailboat, making love, or eating a favorite food. For pain control, the person can imagine different things about the pain. A woman in labor can picture the uterus contracting like a wave instead of thinking about pain. Or a person who experiences pain from a routine source, such as the extraction of a wisdom tooth, can use imagery to change the circumstances producing the pain. Instead of thinking about how terrible and painful it is to have a tooth pulled, the person can imagine that the pain is only the aftermath of intense training for a marathon race or comes from the person being the underdog who was hit in the jaw during a boxing match with the world champion.

Physical Relaxation Methods

Physical relaxation methods are particularly useful for clients who report physiological components of anxiety and anger, such as sweaty palms, rapid breathing or heartbeat, or nausea. Physical relaxation is also a very helpful coping strategy for pain control, because body tension will heighten the sensation of pain. Physical relaxation can be supported by various strategies such as breathing techniques, muscle relaxation, meditation, and exercise.

Each direct-action strategy should first be explained to the client, with discussion of its purpose and procedure. Several sessions may be required to discuss and model all the possible direct-action coping methods. After the strategies have been described and modeled, the client should select the particular methods to be used. The number of direct-action strategies used by a client will depend on the intensity of the reaction, the nature of the stress, and the client's preferences. With the helper's assistance, the client should practice using each skill in order to be able to apply it in simulated and in vivo situations.

Client Learning and Practice of Cognitive Coping Strategies

This part of stress inoculation—the learning and practice of cognitive coping strategies—is very similar to cognitive restructuring. The helper models examples of coping thoughts that the client can use during stressful phases of problem situations; then the client selects and practices substituting coping thoughts for negative or self-defeating thoughts.

Description of Four Phases of Cognitive Coping

As you remember from our discussion of information giving, the helper helps the client understand the nature of an emotional reaction by conceptualizing the reaction by phases. In helping the client acquire cognitive coping skills, the helper may first wish to review the importance of learning to cope at crucial times. The helper can point out that the client can learn a set of cognitive coping skills for each important phase: preparing for the situation, confronting and handling the situation, coping with critical moments in the situation, and rewarding himself or herself after the situation. Note that the first phase concerns coping skills *before*

the situation, the second and third phases deal with coping *during* the situation, and the fourth phase concerns coping *after* the situation. The helper can describe these four phases to the client with an explanation similar to this:

Earlier we talked about how your anger is not just one giant reaction but something that peaks at certain stressful points when you feel provoked or attacked. Now you will learn a method of cognitive control that will help you control any negative thoughts that may lead to hostility and also help you use coping thoughts at stressful points. There are four times that are important in your learning to use coping thoughts, and we'll work on each of these four phases. First is how you interpret the situation initially, and how you think about responding or preparing to respond. Second is actually dealing with the situation. Third is coping with anything that happens during the situation that *really* provokes you. After the situation, you learn to encourage yourself for dealing with your feelings in a way that is not hurtful.

Helper Modeling of Coping Thoughts

After explaining the four phases of cognitive coping to the client, the helper models examples of coping statements that are especially useful during each phase. Meichenbaum (1994) and Meichenbaum and Turk (1976) have provided an excellent summary of the coping statements used by Meichenbaum and Cameron (1973) for anxiety control, by Novaco (1975) for anger control, and by Turk (1975) for pain control. These statements, presented in Table 14.3, are summarized for each of the four coping phases: preparing for the situation, confronting the situation, coping with critical moments, and reinforcing oneself for coping. (Also see Learning Activity 14.3.)

Client Selection of Coping Thoughts

After the helper models some possible coping thoughts for each phase, the client should add some or select those that fit. The helper should encourage the client to try on and adapt the thoughts in whatever way feels most natural. The client might look for coping statements that he or she has used in other stress-related situations. At this point in the procedure, the helper should be working to tailor a coping program *specifically* for this client. If the client's self-statements are too general, they may lead only to rote repetition and not function as effective self-instructions. Also, specific coping statements are more likely to be culturally relevant. The helper might explain the importance of the client's participation like this:

You know, your input in finding coping thoughts that work for you is very important. I've given you some examples. Some of these you might feel comfortable with, and there may be others you can think of too. What we want to do now is to come up with some specific coping thoughts you can and will use during these four times that fit for *you,* not me or someone else.

TABLE 14.3	Examples of Coping Thoughts Used in Stress Inoculation

Anxiety	Anger	Pain
I. Preparing for a stressor (Meichenbaum & Cameron, 1973) What is it you have to do? You can develop a plan to deal with it. Just think about what you can do about it. That's better than getting anxious. No negative self-statements; just think rationally. Don't worry; worry won't help anything. Maybe what you think is anxiety is eagerness to confront it.	**Preparing for a provocation** (Meichenbaum, 1994) This is going to upset me, but I know how to deal with it. What is it that I have to do? I can work out a plan to handle this. If I find myself getting upset, I'll know what to do. There won't be any need for an argument. Try not to take this too seriously. This could be a testy situation, but I believe in myself. Time for a few deep breaths of relaxation. Feel comfortable, relaxed, and at ease. Easy does it. Remember to keep your sense of humor.	**Preparing for the painful stressor** (Turk, 1975) What is it you have to do? You can develop a plan to deal with it. Just think about what you have to do. Just think about what you can do about it. Don't worry; worrying won't help anything. You have lots of different strategies you can call upon.
II. Confronting and handling a stressor (Meichenbaum & Cameron, 1973) Just "psych" yourself up—you can meet this challenge. One step at a time; you can handle the situation. Don't think about fear; just think about what you have to do. Stay relevant. This anxiety is what the doctor said you would feel. It's a reminder to use your coping exercises. Relax. You're in control; take a slow deep breath. Ah, good.	**Impact and confrontation** (Meichenbaum, 1994) Stay calm. Just continue to relax. As long as I keep my cool, I'm in control. Just roll with the punches; don't get bent out of shape. Think of what you want to get out of this. You don't need to prove yourself. There is no point in getting mad. Don't make more out of this than you have to. I'm not going to let him get to me. Look for the positives. Don't assume the worst or jump to conclusions. It's really a shame that he has to act like this. For someone to be that irritable, he must be awfully unhappy. If I start to get mad, I'll just be banging my head against the wall. So I might as well relax. There is no need to doubt myself. What he says doesn't matter. I'm on top of this situation, and it's under control.	**Confronting and handling the pain** (Turk, 1975) You can meet the challenge. One step at a time; you can handle the situation. Just relax, breathe deeply, and use one of the strategies. Don't think about the pain, just what you have to do. This tenseness can be an ally, a cue to cope. Relax. You're in control. Take a slow deep breath. Ah, good. This anxiety is what the trainer said you might feel. That's right; it's the reminder to use your coping skills.
III. Coping with the feeling of being overwhelmed (Meichenbaum & Cameron, 1973) When fear comes, just pause. Keep the focus on the present; what is it you have to do? Label your fear from 0 to 10, and watch it change. You should expect your fear to rise. Don't try to eliminate fear totally; just keep it manageable. You can convince yourself to do it. You can reason your fear away. It will be over shortly. It's not the worst thing that can happen. Just think about something else. Do something that will prevent you from thinking about fear. Describe what is around you. That way you won't think about worrying.	**Coping with arousal** (Meichenbaum, 1994) My muscles are starting to feel tight. Time to relax and slow things down. Getting upset won't help. It's just not worth it to get so angry. I'll let him make a fool of himself. I have a right to be annoyed, but let's keep the lid on. Time to take a deep breath. Let's take the issue point by point. My anger is a signal of what I need to do. Time to instruct myself. I'm not going to get pushed around, but I'm not going haywire either. Try to reason it out. Treat each other with respect. Let's try a cooperative approach. Maybe we are both right. Negatives lead to more negatives. Work constructively. He'd probably like me to get really angry. Well, I'm going to disappoint him. I can't expect people to act the way I want them to. Take it easy, don't get pushy.	**Coping with feelings at critical moments** (Turk, 1975) When pain comes, just pause; keep focusing on what you have to do. What is it you have to do? Don't try to eliminate the pain totally; just keep it manageable. You were supposed to expect the pain to rise; just keep it under control. Just remember, there are different strategies; they'll help you stay in control. When the pain mounts, you can switch to a different strategy; you're in control.

(continued)

TABLE 14.3	Examples of Coping Thoughts Used in Stress Inoculation

(continued)

IV. Reinforcing self-statements
(Meichenbaum & Cameron, 1973)
It worked; you did it.
Wait until you tell your therapist about this.
It wasn't as bad as you expected.
You made more out of the fear than it was worth.
Your damn ideas—that's the problem. When you control them, you control your fear.
It's getting better each time you use the procedures.
You can be pleased with the progress you're making.
You did it!

Reflecting on the provocation
(Meichenbaum, 1994)
a. When conflict is unresolved
Forget about the aggravation. Thinking about it only makes you upset.
These are difficult situations, and they take time to straighten out.
Try to shake it off. Don't let it interfere with your job.
I'll get better at this as I get more practice.
Remember relaxation. It's a lot better than anger.
Don't take it personally.
Take a deep breath.
b. When conflict is resolved or coping is successful
I handled that one pretty well. It worked!
That wasn't as hard as I thought.
It could have been a lot worse.
I could have gotten more upset than it was worth.
I actually got through that without getting angry.
My pride can sure get me into trouble, but when I don't take things too seriously, I'm better off.
I guess I've been getting upset for too long when it wasn't even necessary.
I'm doing better at this all the time.

Reinforcing self-statements
(Turk, 1975)
Good, you did it.
You handled it pretty well.
You knew you could do it!
Wait until you tell the trainer about which procedures worked best.

Source: From *A Clinical Handbook: Practical Therapist Manual for Assessing and Treating Adults with Posttraumatic Stress Disorder,* by D. Meichenbaum, pp. 407–408. Copyright 1994 by Institute Press. Originally published in "The Cognitive–Behavioral Management of Anxiety, Anger, and Pain," by D. Meichenbaum and D. Turk, in *The Behavioral Management of Anxiety, Depression, and Pain,* by P. O. Davidson (Ed.). Copyright 1976 by Brunner/Mazel. Reprinted by permission of the author.

Client Practice of Coping Thoughts

After the client selects coping thoughts to use for each phase, the helper instructs the client to practice these self-statements by saying them aloud. This verbal practice is designed to help the client become familiar with the coping thoughts and accustomed to the words. After this practice, the client should also practice the selected coping thoughts in the sequence of the four phases. This practice helps the client learn the timing of the coping thoughts in the application phase of stress inoculation.

The helper can say something like this:

First, I'd like you to practice using these coping thoughts just by saying them aloud to me. This will help you get used to the words and ideas of coping. Next, let's practice these coping thoughts in the sequence in which you would use them when applying them to a real situation. I'll show you. Okay, first I'm anticipating the situation, so I'm going to use coping statements that help me prepare for the situation, like "I know this type of situation usually upsets me, but I have a plan now to handle it" or "I'm going to be able to control my anger even if this situation is rough." Next, I'll pretend I'm actually into the situation. I'm going to cope so I can handle it. I might say something to myself like "Just stay calm. Remember who I'm dealing with. This is her style. Don't take it personally" or "Don't overreact. Just relax."

Now the person's harassment is continuing. I am going to cope with feeling more angry. I might think "I can feel myself getting more upset. Just keep relaxed. Concentrate on this" or "This is a challenging situation. How can I handle myself in a way I don't have to apologize for?" Okay, now afterward I realize I didn't get abusive or revengeful. So I'll think something to encourage myself, like "I did it" or "Gee, I really kept my cool."

Now you try it. Just verbalize your coping thoughts in the sequence of preparing for the situation, handling it, coping with getting really agitated, and then encouraging yourself.

Application of All Coping Skills to Problem-Related Situations

During this part of stress inoculation, the client applies both the direct-action and the cognitive coping skills in the face of stressful, provoking, or painful situations. Before the client is instructed to apply the coping skills in vivo, she or he practices applying coping skills under simulated conditions with the helper's assistance. The application phase of stress inoculation appears to be important for the overall efficacy of the procedure. Simply having a client rehearse coping skills *without* opportunities to apply them in stressful situations seems to result in an improved but limited ability to cope.

The application phase involves modeling and rehearsing to provide the client with exposure to simulations of problem-related situations. For example, the client who wanted to manage hostility would have opportunities to practice

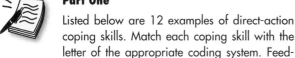

LEARNING ACTIVITY   14.3   Stress Inoculation

Part One

Listed below are 12 examples of direct-action coping skills. Match each coping skill with the letter of the appropriate coding system. Feedback follows on page 437.

Codes

a. Information (I)

b. Escape route (ER)

c. Social support network (SSN)

d. Ventilation (V)

e. Perspective taking (PT)

f. Attention diversion (AD)

g. Imagery manipulations (IM)

h. Muscle relaxation (MR)

i. Breathing techniques (B)

Direct-Action Coping Skills

_____ 1. "Learn to take slow, deep breaths when you feel especially tense."

_____ 2. "Instead of thinking just about the pain, try to concentrate very hard on one spot on the wall."

_____ 3. "Imagine that it's a very warm day and the warmth makes you feel relaxed."

_____ 4. "If it really gets to be too much, just do the first part only—leave the rest for a while."

_____ 5. "You can expect some pain, but it is really only the result of the stitches. It doesn't mean that something is wrong."

_____ 6. "Just tighten your left fist. Hold it and notice the tension. Now relax it—feel the difference."

_____ 7. "Try to imagine a strong, normal cell attacking the weak, confused cancer cells when you feel the discomfort of your treatment."

_____ 8. "When it gets very strong, distract yourself— listen hard to the music or study the picture on the wall."

_____ 9. "If you talk about it and express your feelings about the pain, you might feel better."

_____10. "Your initial or intuitive reaction might cause you to see only selected features of the situation. There are also some positive aspects we need to focus on."

_____11 ."It would be helpful to have your family and neighbors involved to provide you feedback and another perspective."

_____12. "Social skills are important for you to learn in order to develop the support you need from other people. Others can lessen the effects of the aversive situation."

Part Two

Listed below are eight examples of cognitive coping skills used at four phases of cognitive coping. Match each coping skill with the letter of the appropriate phase. Feedback follows.

Phases

a. Preparing for a situation

b. Confronting or handling the situation

c. Dealing with critical moments in the situation

d. Self-encouragement for coping

Cognitive Coping Skills

_____1. "By golly, I did it."

_____2. "What will I need to do?"

_____3. "Don't lose your cool even though it's tough now. Take a deep breath."

_____4. "Think about what you want to say—not how people are reacting to you now."

_____5. "Relax; it will be over shortly. Just concentrate on getting through this rough moment now."

_____6. "Can you feel this—the coping worked!"

_____7. "When you get in there, just think about the situation, not your anxiety."

_____8. "That's a signal to cope now. Just keep your mind on what you're doing."

coping in a variety of hostility-provoking situations. During this application practice, the client needs to be faced with a stressful situation in which to practice the skills. In other words, the application should be arranged and conducted as realistically as possible. The hostile client can be encouraged to practice feeling very agitated and to rehearse even starting to lose control—but then applying the coping skills to gain control (Novaco, 1975). This type of application practice is viewed as the client's providing a self-model of how to behave in a stressful situation. By imagining faltering or losing control, experiencing anxiety, and then coping with this, the person practices the thoughts and feelings as they are likely to occur in a real-life situation (Meichenbaum, 1994). In the application phase of stress inoculation, the client's anxiety, hostility, or distressful emotions are used as a cue or reminder to cope.

Helper Modeling of Application of Coping Skills

The helper should first model how the client can apply the newly acquired skills when faced with a stressful situation. Here is an example of a helper demonstration of this process with a client who is working toward hostility control (in this case, with his family):

> I'm going to imagine that the police have just called and told me that my 16-year-old son was just picked up again for breaking and entering. I can feel myself start to get really hot. Whoops, wait a minute. That's a signal [arousal cue for coping]. I'd better start thinking about using my relaxation methods to stay calm and using my coping thoughts to prepare myself for handling this situation constructively.
>
> Okay, first of all, sit down and relax. Let those muscles loosen up. Count to 10. Breathe deeply [direct-action coping methods]. Now I'll be seeing my son shortly. What is it I have to do? I know it won't help to lash out or to hit him. That won't solve anything. So I'll work out another plan. Let him do most of the talking. Give him the chance to make amends or find a solution [cognitive coping: preparing for the situation].
>
> Now I can see him walking in the door. I feel sort of choked up. I can feel my fists getting tight. He's starting to explain. I want to interrupt and let him have it. But wait [arousal cue for coping]. Concentrate on counting and on breathing slowly [direct-action coping]. Now just tell myself—keep cool. Let him talk. It won't help now to blow up [cognitive coping: confronting situation].
>
> Now I can imagine myself thinking back to the last time he got arrested. Why in hell doesn't he learn? No son of mine is going to be a troublemaker [arousal]. Whew! I'm pretty angry. I've got to stay in control, especially now [cue for coping]. Just relax, muscles! Stay loose [direct-action coping]. I can't expect him to live up to my expectations. I can tell him I'm disappointed, but I'm not going to blow up and shout and hit him [cognitive coping: feelings of greater agitation]. Okay, I'm doing a good job of keeping my lid on [cognitive coping: self-reinforcement].

Client Application of Coping Skills in Imaginary and Role-Play Practice

After the helper modeling, the client should practice a similar sequence of both direct-action and cognitive coping skills. The practice can occur in two ways: imagination and role play. We find that it is often useful to have the client first practice the coping skills while imagining problem-related situations. This practice can be repeated until the client feels very comfortable in applying the coping strategies to imagined situations. Then the client can practice the coping skills with the helper's aid in a role play of a problem situation. The role-play practice should be similar to the in vivo situations that the client encounters. For instance, our angry client could identify particular situations and people with whom he or she is most likely to blow up or lose control. The client can imagine each situation (starting with the most manageable one) and imagine using the coping skills. Then, with the helper taking the part of someone else such as a provoker, the client can practice the coping skills in a role play.

Application of All Coping Skills to Potential Problem Situations

Any therapeutic procedure should be designed not only to help clients deal with current concerns but also to help them anticipate constructive handling of potential concerns. In other words, an adequate therapeutic strategy should help prevent future problems in living as well as resolve current ones. The prevention aspect of stress inoculation is achieved by having clients apply the newly learned coping strategies to situations that are not problematic now but could be in the future. If this phase of stress inoculation is ignored, the effects of the inoculation may be very short-lived. In other words, if clients do not have an opportunity to apply the coping skills to situations other than the current problem-related ones, their coping skills may not generalize beyond the present problem situations.

The application of coping skills to other potentially stressful situations is accomplished in the same way as application to the present problem areas. First, after explaining the usefulness of coping skills in other areas of the client's life, the helper demonstrates the application of coping strategies to a potential, hypothetical stressor. The helper might select a situation the client has not yet encountered, one that would require active coping by anyone who might encounter it, such as not receiving a desired job promotion or raise, facing a family crisis, moving to a new place, anticipating retirement, or being very ill. After the helper has modeled application of coping skills to these sorts of situations, the client would practice applying the skills in these situations or in similar ones that she or he identifies. The practice can occur in imagination or in role-play enactments. A novel way to practice is to switch roles: the client plays the helper, and the helper plays the client. The client helps or trains the helper to use the coping skills. Placing the client in the role of a helper or a trainer can provide another kind of application opportunity that may also have benefits for the client's acquisition of coping strategies and bolster the client's self-efficacy. Some version of Learning Activity 14.3 may be useful as part of training for clients as well as helpers.

Stress inoculation training is one of a number of cognitive–behavioral interventions for which computer-assisted programs have been developed and tested. Timmons and associates (1997), for example, evaluated the effectiveness of using a computer guidance program to treat male veterans with maladaptive anger. Both this and a group counseling approach were developed using Novaco's (1975) stress inoculation training. Results indicated that both venues

---

14.3	**F E E D B A C K**
	Stress Inoculation

Part One

1. i. B
2. f. AD
3. g. IM
4. b. ER
5. a. I
6. h. MR
7. g. IM
8. f. AD
9. d. V
10. e. PT
11. c. SSN
12. c. SSN

If this exercise was difficult for you, you might review the information presented in the text on direct-action coping skills.

Part Two

1. d. Encouraging phase
2. a. Preparing for the situation
3. c. Dealing with a critical moment
4. b. Confronting the situation
5. c. Dealing with a critical moment
6. d. Encouragement for coping
7. a. Preparing for the situation
8. b. Confronting the situation

If you had trouble identifying the four phases of cognitive coping, you may want to review Table 14.3.

---

were equally effective in reducing self-reported anger as well as anger suppression, with no differences in treatment satisfaction.

Homework and Follow-Up

When the client has learned and used stress inoculation within the interviews, she or he is ready to use coping skills in vivo. The helper and client should discuss the potential application of coping strategies to actual situations. The helper might caution the client not to expect to cope beautifully with every problematic situation. The client should be encouraged to use a daily log to record the particular situations and the number of times that the coping strategies are used. The log data can be used in a later follow-up as one way to determine the client's progress.

In our opinion, stress inoculation training is one of the most comprehensive therapeutic treatments presently in use. Teaching clients both direct-action and cognitive coping skills that they can use in current and potential problematic situations provides skills that are under the clients' control and are applicable to future as well as current situations.

A MODEL DIALOGUE FOR STRESS INOCULATION: THE CASE OF ISABELLA

Session 1

In this session, the helper teaches Isabella some direct-action coping skills for mental and physical relaxation to help her cope with her physical sensations of nervousness about her math class. Imagery manipulations and slow, deep breathing are used.

1. **Helper:** Hi, Isabella. How was your week?

Client: Pretty good. You know, this, well, whatever you call it, it's starting to help. I took a test this week and got an 85. I usually get a 70 or 75.

The helper introduces the *idea of other coping skills to deal with Isabella's nervousness.*

2. **Helper:** That really is encouraging. And that's where the effects of this count—on how you do in class. Because what we did last week went well for you, I believe today we might work with some other coping skills that might help you decrease your nervous feelings.

Client: What would this be?

In responses 3 and 4, the helper explains and *models possible direct-action coping skills.*

3. **Helper:** One thing we might do is help you learn how to imagine something that gives you very calm feelings, and while you're doing this to take some slow, deep breaths—like this. [Helper models closing eyes, breathing slowly and deeply.] When I was doing that, I thought about curling up in a chair with my favorite book—but there are many different things you could think of. For instance, to use this in your math class, you might imagine that you are doing work for which you will receive some prize or award. Or you might imagine that you are learning problems so you'll be in a position to be a helper for someone else. Do you get the idea?

Client: I think so. I guess it's like trying to imagine or think about math in a pretend kind of way.

4. **Helper:** Yes—and in a way that reduces rather than increases the stress of it for you.

Client: I think I get the idea. It's sort of like when I imagine that I'm doing housework for some famous person instead of just at my house—it makes it more tolerable.

In response 5, the helper asks Isabella to *find some helpful imagery manipulations to promote calm feelings.*

5. **Helper:** That's a good example. You imagine that situation to prevent yourself from getting too bored. Here, you find a scene or scenes to think about to prevent yourself from getting too nervous. Can you take a few minutes to think about one or two things you could imagine—perhaps about math—that would help you feel calm instead of nervous?

Client [Pauses]: Well, maybe I could pretend that math class is part of something I need in order to do something exciting, like being an Olympic downhill skier.

In responses 6 and 7, the helper instructs Isabella to *practice these direct-action coping skills.*

6. **Helper:** Okay, good. We can work with that, and if it doesn't help, we can come up with something else. Why don't you try first to practice imagining this while you also breathe slowly and deeply, as I did a few minutes ago? [Isabella practices.]

7. **Helper:** How did that feel?

Client: Okay—it was sort of fun.

In response 8, the helper gives *homework*—asks Isabella to engage in *self-directed practice* of these coping skills before the next session.

8. **Helper:** Good. Now, this week I'd like you to practice this in a quiet place two or three times each day. Keep track of your practice sessions in your log, and also rate your tension level before and after you practice. Next week we will go over this log and then work on a way you can apply what we did today—and the coping thoughts we learned in our two previous sessions. So I'll see you next week.

Session 2

In this session, the helper helps Isabella integrate the strategies of some previous sessions (coping thoughts, imagery, and breathing coping skills). Specifically, Isabella learns to apply all these coping skills in imagery and role-play practices of some stressful situations related to math class. Application of coping skills to problem-related situations is a part of stress inoculation and helps the client to generalize the newly acquired coping skills to in vivo situations as they occur.

In responses 1 and 2, the helper *reviews Isabella's use of the direct-action skills homework.*

1. **Helper:** How are things going, Isabella?

Client: Okay. I've had a hard week—one test and two pop quizzes in math. But I got 80s. I also did my imagination and breathing practice. You know, that takes a while to learn.

2. **Helper:** That's natural. It does take a lot of practice before you really get the feel of it. So it would be a good idea if you continued the daily practice again this week. How did it feel when you practiced?

Client: Okay—I think I felt less nervous than before.

The helper introduces the idea of *applying all the coping skills in practice situations and presents a rationale for this application phase.*

3. **Helper:** That's good. As time goes on, you will notice more effects from it. Up to this point, we've worked on some things to help you in your math class—stopping self-defeating thoughts and using imagination and slow breathing to help you cope and control your nervousness. What I think might help now is to give you a chance to use all these skills in practices of some of the stressful situations related to your math class. This will help you use the skills when you need to during the class or related situations. Then we will soon be at a point where we can go through some of these same procedures for the other situations in which you want to express yourself differently and more frequently, such as with your folks. Does this sound Okay?

Client: Yes.

Next, the helper *demonstrates (models) how Isabella can practice her skills in an imaginary practice.*

4. **Helper:** What I'd like you to do is to imagine some of the situations related to your math class and try to use your coping thoughts and the imagination scene and deep breathing to control your nervousness. Let me show you how you might do this. I'm imagining that it's almost time for math class. I'm going to

concentrate on thinking about how this class will help me train for the Olympic downhill program. If I catch myself thinking I wish I didn't have to go, I'm going to use some coping thoughts. Let's see—class will go pretty fast. I've been doing better. It can be a challenge. Now, as I'm in class, I'm going to stop thinking about not being able to do the work. I'm going to just take one problem at a time. One step at a time. Oops! Mr. Lamborne just called on me. Boy, I can feel myself getting nervous. Just take a deep breath. . . . Do the best I can. It's only one moment anyway. Well, it went pretty well. I can feel myself starting to cope when I need to. Okay, Isabella, why don't you try this several times now? [Isabella practices applying coping thoughts and direct action with different practice situations in imagination.]

In response 5, the helper *checks Isabella's reaction* to applying the skills in practice through imagination.

5. **Helper:** Are you able to really get into the situation as you practice this way?

Client: Yes, although I believe I'll have to work harder to use this when it really happens.

Sometimes *role play makes the practice more real.* The helper introduces this next. Notice that the helper adds a stress element by calling on Isabella at unannounced times.

6. **Helper:** That's right. This kind of practice doesn't always have the same amount of stress as the "real thing." Maybe it would help if we did some role-play practice. I'll be your teacher this time. Just pretend to be in class. I'll be talking, but at an unannounced time, I'm going to call on you to answer a question. Just use your coping thoughts and your slow breathing as you need to when this happens. [Role-play practice of this and related scenarios occurs.]

The helper *assesses Isabella's reaction* to role-play practice and *asks Isabella to rate her level of nervousness* during the practice.

7. **Helper:** How comfortable do you feel with these practices? Could you rate the nervousness you feel as you do this on a 1-to-5 scale, with 1 being *not nervous* and 5 being *very nervous*?

Client: Well, about a 2.

The helper encourages Isabella to *apply coping statements in the math-related problem situations* as they occur, assigns *homework,* and schedules a *follow-up.*

8. **Helper:** I think you are ready to use this as you need to during the week. Remember, any self-defeating thought or body tenseness is a cue to cope, using your coping thoughts and imagination and breathing skills. I'd like you to keep track of the number of times you use these on your log sheets. Also, rate your level of nervousness before, during, and after math class on the log sheet. How about coming back in two weeks to see how things are going?

Client: Fine.

SPIRITUALITY IN PRACTICE

Many of the strategies discussed here for managing and coping with stress are familiar both to helping professionals and to the lay public. Another dimension of coping and stress management that is familiar to many, but is less clearly established in counseling-related helping services, involves spirituality. Research indicates that religion and spirituality may be important correlates of health and well-being in general, as well as of how people cope with life stressors. Young, Cashwell, and Shcherbakova (2000), for example, report findings that spirituality provides a moderating effect for both depression and anxiety. George, Larson, Koenig, and McCullough (2000) identify relationships between religious practices and reduced onset of physical and mental illnesses, reduced mortality, and likelihood of recovery from or adjustment to physical and mental illness. Pursuit of spiritual comfort or guidance is commonly included in assessing people's coping repertoires. Spiritual beliefs, activities (e.g., prayer; reading spiritual texts; meditation; participating in services, rituals, or traditions), and involvement in a faith community (e.g., for spiritual purposes, mutual assistance, and/or social purposes) are examples of religion or spirituality as a coping strategy. We use the term *spirituality* here to encompass values, activities, and personal experiences that may have a religious base, but don't necessarily.

National surveys indicate that most Americans hold some kind of spiritual values and engage in activities such as prayer. Many, particularly older adults, use prayer to help cope with various types of problems. Even in the United States, however, there are important cultural differences in the importance and in forms of spirituality. African Americans, for instance, tend to be more religiously active than European Americans (Taylor, Chatters, Jayakody, & Levin, 1996). And although the religions of the world have a great-deal in common, there are considerable differences among religions and spiritual traditions (e.g., Judaism, Christianity, Islam, Buddhism, Hinduism, and Confucianism; Smart, 1993, 1994).

Religious or spiritual issues constitute a recent diagnostic category in the 1994 *DSM-IV,* and helpers are likely to see an increase in the number of clients seeking help for spiritual problems or requesting inclusion of spiritual concerns as part of their work with helping professionals (see Lukoff, Lu, & Turner, 1999). The positive potential of clients' spiritual or religious values and behaviors as resources for coping, well-being, and helping services has stimulated increased research in recent years. Research topics include the spiritual aspects of coping with serious illness, disabling conditions, caretaking and loss of loved ones, personal crisis, managing ongoing chronic health and mental health conditions, alcohol and other substance use problems, identity development, end-of-life factors, and professional issues such as ethics and assessment tools (see Box 14.3). Recent work is illustrating the range of life venues in which spirituality may be important to stress management—such as decisions and preparation for military missions (Hathaway, 2006), application of solution-focused methods for spiritual issues (Guterman & Leite, 2006), and use of online forums to support spiritual dimensions of life (McKenna & West, 2007). Forgiveness is an example of an emerging practice focus that connects with spirituality but can be applied outside that frame as well. Luskin, Ginzburg, and Thoresen (2005), for example, combining rational–emotive group therapy with an emotional refocusing forgiveness intervention, found significant improvements in subsequent forgiveness, level of hurt, anger, perceived efficacy, hope, and spiritual growth. Miller and Thoresen (2003) describe the study of spirituality and its relationship to health as a true frontier with high public interest, and they provide an overview of literature linking spirituality to health and addressing a range of critiques and promising directions.

Diversity has been notably apparent in research on spirituality. As Box 14.4 illustrates, there has been increased examination of cultural group differences as well as spiritual factors relevant to gender, sexual minorities, religions, and specific cultural groups. Particularly prominent has been research with African Americans and with elders. Research has also focused on spiritual growth as a constructive consequence of highly stressful life experiences (e.g., James & Samuels, 1999). Some research aims to distinguish varied spiritual resources to better understand what dimensions of spirituality are most likely to be useful at different stages of adversity (such as breast cancer; Simon, Crowther, & Higgerson, 2007). Spiritual experiences appear, for example, to be associated with fewer depressive symptoms, a pattern that is affected by stress and age but maintains across gender and race (Mofidi et al., 2006).

Maintaining a positive outlook and a generally positive emotional state in the context of chronic and serious stressors has been significantly associated with using coping strategies that are more likely to produce good outcomes and with healing, even transformative, outcomes. It may be that spiritual values and activities foster situational appraisals or personal meanings that are emotionally comforting, help infuse ordinary events with positive meaning, and stimulate positive reframing and goal-directed problem-focused coping—important ingredients for adaptive stress manage-

ment outcomes (Folkman & Moskowitz, 2000). Attention has also been directed to populations such as gay and lesbian individuals who may be "caught in the middle" between sexual orientations and rejecting religious beliefs. Roseborough (2006), for example, illustrates a developmental approach to integrating these intrinsic elements of oneself toward healthier outcomes, often framed as experiences of spiritual growth.

Although it is not yet clear whether spirituality is exerting a direct influence or how it may be exerting indirect influence, researchers are beginning to look more closely at this subject. George and colleagues (2000) suggest three mechanisms that may be at work—specifically, that religiousness generally (1) promotes healthy behaviors, (2) is associated with stronger social supports, and (3) fosters a sense of coherence or meaning. For example, adherence to spiritual beliefs may prompt a person to lifestyle and interpersonal behaviors that lead to healthy outcomes and, conversely, may discourage risky behaviors likely to result in negative outcomes. A spiritual orientation may prompt people to seek out and participate with others who share or value this orientation, which helps build a network of supportive relationships. And, as described above, spiritual beliefs and ways of relating may help people interpret negative events in ways that make sense to them or even provide solace, thus helping them to better cope with adversity, loss, and other troubling experiences. For example, in a study of African Americans diagnosed with hypertension, Brown (2000) found that a majority of participants used their religious beliefs as protective, control, and coping mechanisms in the management of their illness. They felt protected from immediate and long-term negative consequences but also felt better able to find meaning in and cope with having hypertension and to exert control over its management. Consistent with coping theory, this combination of solace, hope, and positivity in how a threat and one's ability to handle the threat are appraised may then help individuals persevere and continue the hard behavioral work of learning what they need to learn and doing what they need to do.

There is need for caution, however. Research to date has generally used a lot of different ways of assessing spirituality. This reduces our ability to generalize conclusions from findings across studies. One basic issue is that although spiritual experiences are often conceived as part of religion, spirituality is not seen as dependent on religious beliefs. A study of differences in how medically ill people define what they mean by *spiritual* and *religious* revealed some similarities but also significant differences in overall belief systems as well as interpretations of how individuals' beliefs affected their health and recovery. For example, those identifying themselves as spiritual saw recovery and healing happening *through* them whereas those identifying themselves as religious were more prone to see it as happening *to* them (Hill & Nutt Williams, 2000; Woods & Ironson, 1999). Published work under the heading "assessment" in Box 14.3 illustrates recent efforts

BOX 14.3	RESEARCH ON SPIRITUALITY

Assessment

Freiheit, S. R., Sonstegard, K., Schmitt, A., & Vye, C. (2006). Religiosity and spirituality: A psychometric evaluation of the Santa Clara Strength of Religious Faith Questionnaire. *Pastoral Psychology, 55*(1), 27–33.

Prest, L. A., & Robinson, W. D. (2006). Systemic assessment and treatment of depression and anxiety in families: The BPSS model in practice. *Journal of Systemic Therapies, 25*(3), 4–24.

Cancer

Mako, C., Galek, K., & Poppito, S. R. (2006). Spiritual pain among patients with advanced cancer in palliative care. *Journal of Palliative Medicine, 9*(5), 1106–1113.

Puig, A., Lee, S. M., Goodwin, L., & Sherrard, P. A. D. (2006). The efficacy of creative arts therapies to enhance emotional expression, spirituality, and psychological well-being of newly diagnosed Stage I and Stage II breast cancer patients: A preliminary study. *Arts in Psychotherapy, 33*(3), 218–228.

Depression

Briggs, M. K., & Shoffner, M. F. (2006). Spiritual wellness and depression: Testing a theoretical model with older adolescents and midlife adults. *Counseling and Values, 51*(1), 5–20.

Eating Disorders

Marsden, P., Karagianni, E., & Morgan, J. F. (2007). Spirituality and clinical care in eating disorders: A qualitative study. *International Journal of Eating Disorders, 40*(1), 7–12.

Richards, P. S., Berrett, M. E., Hardman, R. K., & Eggett, D. L. (2006). Comparative efficacy of spirituality, cognitive, and emotional support groups for treating eating disorder inpatients. *Eating Disorders: The Journal of Treatment and Prevention, 14*(5), 401–415.

Health Management

Arcury, T. A., Quandt, S. A., McDonald, J., & Bell. R. A. (2000). Faith and health self-management of rural older adults. *Journal of Cross-Cultural Gerontology, 15*(1), 55–74.

Brown, C. M. (2000). Exploring the role of religiosity in hypertension management among African Americans. *Journal of Health Care for the Poor and Underserved, 11*(1), 19–32.

Woods, T. E., & Ironson, G. H. (1999). Religion and spirituality in the face of illness: How cancer, cardiac, and HIV patients describe their spirituality/religiosity. *Journal of Health Psychology, 4,* 393–412.

Young, S. J., Cashwell, C. S., & Shcherbakova, J. (2000). The moderating relationship of spirituality on negative life events and psychological adjustment. *Counseling and Values, 45*(1), 49–57.

Forgiveness

Luskin, F. M., Ginzburg, K., & Thoresen, C. E. (2005). The efficacy of forgiveness intervention in college age adults: Randomized controlled study. *Humbolt Journal of Social Relations, 29,* 163–184.

Identity

Kiesling, C., Sorell, G. T., Montgomery, M. J., & Colwell, R. K. (2006). Identity and spirituality: A psychosocial exploration of the sense of spiritual self. *Developmental Psychology, 42*(6), 1269–1277.

Internet

McKenna, K. Y. A., & West, K. J. (2007). Give me that online-time religion: The role of the Internet in spiritual life. *Computers in Human Behavior, 23*(2), 942–954.

Military

Hathaway, W. L. (2006). Religious diversity in the military clinic: Four cases. *Military Psychology, 18*(3), 247–257.

Spiritual Competency

Hodge, D. R., Baughman, L. M., & Cummings, J. A. (2006). Moving toward spiritual competency: Deconstructing religious stereotypes and spiritual prejudices in social work literature. *Journal of Social Service Research, 32*(4), 211–232.

Solution-Focused Counseling

Guterman, J. T., & Leite, N. (2006). Solution-focused counseling for clients with religious and spiritual concerns. *Counseling and Values, 51*(1), 39–52.

Substance Abuse

Sussman, S., Skara, S., Rodriguez, Y., & Pokhrel, P. (2006). Non drug use- and drug use-specific spirituality as one-year predictors of drug use among high-risk youth. *Substance Use and Misuse, 41*(13), 1801–1816.

Webb, J. R., Robinson, E. A. R., Brower, K. J., & Zucker, R. A. (2006). Forgiveness and alcohol problems among people entering substance abuse treatment. *Journal of Addictive Diseases, 25*(3), 55–67.

Terminal Illness

Leung, K., Chiu, T., & Chen, C. (2006). The influence of awareness of terminal condition on spiritual well-being in terminal cancer patients. *Journal of Pain and Symptom Management, 31*(5), 449–456.

Oliver, D. P. (2003). Social work and spiritual counseling: Results of one state audit. *Journal of Palliative Medicine, 6*(6), 919–925.

Use in Helping Services

Gilligan, P., & Furness, S. (2006). The role of religion and spirituality in social work practice: Views and experiences of social workers and students. *British Journal of Social Work, 36*(4), 617–637.

Miller, W. R., & Thoresen, C. E. (2003). Spirituality, religion, and health: An emerging research field. *American Psychologist, 58,* 24–35.

BOX 14.4	SPIRITUALITY AND DIVERSITY

African Americans

Henry, A. (2006). "There's salt-water in our blood": The "Middle Passage" epistemology of two Black mothers regarding the spiritual education of their daughters. *International Journal of Qualitative Studies in Education, 19*(3), 329–345.

Milner, H. R. (2006). Culture, race and spirit: A reflective model for the study of African-Americans. *International Journal of Qualitative Studies in Education, 19*(3), 367–385.

Simon, C. E., Crowther, M., & Higgerson, H. (2007). The stage-specific role of spirituality among African American Christian women throughout the breast cancer experience. *Cultural Diversity and Ethnic Minority Psychology, 13*(1), 26–34.

Washington, G., Johnson, T., Jones, J., & Langs, S. (2007). African-American boys in relative care and a culturally centered group mentoring approach. *Social Work with Groups, 30*(1), 45–68.

Depression

Mofidi, M., DeVellis, R. F., Blazer, D. G., DeVellis, B. M., Panter, A. T., & Jordan, J. M. (2006). Spirituality and depressive symptoms in a racially diverse US sample of community-dwelling adults. *Journal of Nervous and Mental Disease, 194*(12), 975–977.

Elders

Chang, B., Noonan, A. E., & Tennstedt, S. L. (1998). The role of religion/spirituality in coping with caregiving for disabled elders. *Gerontologist, 38*, 463–470.

Langer, N. (2000). The importance of spirituality in later life. *Gerontology and Geriatrics Education, 20*(3), 41–50.

Musick, M. A., Traphagan, J. W., Koenig, H. G., & Larson, D. B. (2000). Spirituality in physical health and aging. *Journal of Adult Development, 7*(2), 73–86.

Estonians

Teichmann, M., Murdvee, M., & Saks, K. (2006). Spiritual needs and quality of life in Estonia. *Social Indicators Research, 76*(1), 147–163.

Filipino

Shimabukuro, K. P., Daniels, J., & D'Andrea, M. (1999). Addressing spiritual issues from a cultural perspective:

The case of the grieving Filipino boy. *Journal of Multicultural Counseling and Development, 27*, 221–239.

Illness

Harvey, I. S. (2006). Self-management of a chronic illness: An exploratory study on the role of spirituality among older African American women. *Journal of Women and Aging, 18*(3), 75–88.

Moadel, A., Morgan, C., Fatone, A., Grennan, J., Carter, J., Laruffia, G., et al., (1999). Feeling meaning and hope: Self-reported spiritual and existential needs among an ethnically diverse cancer patient population. *Psycho-Oncology, 8*, 378–385.

Ramer, L., Johnson, D., Chan, L., & Barrett, M. T. (2006). The effect of HIV/AIDS disease progression on spirituality and self-transcendence in a multicultural population. *Journal of Transcultural Nursing, 17*(3), 280–289.

Maternity Issues in Greek Culture

Paxson, H. (2006). Reproduction as spiritual kin work: Orthodoxy, IVF, and the moral economy of motherhood in Greece. *Culture, Medicine and Psychiatry, 30*(4), 481–505.

Latino

Comas-Diaz, L. (2006). Latino healing: The integration of ethnic psychology into psychotherapy. *Psychotherapy: Theory, Research, Practice, Training, 43*(4), 436–453.

Rehm, R. S. (1999). Religious faith in Mexican-American families dealing with chronic childhood illness. *IMAGE: Journal of Nursing Scholarship, 311*, 33–38.

Native Americans

Salois, E. M., Holkup, P. A., Tripp-Reimer, T., & Weinert, C. (2006). Research as spiritual covenant. *Western Journal of Nursing Research, 28*(5), 505–524.

St. Clair, D. M., & Castro, L. (2005). Native men, spirituality, and cancer recovery. *Journal of Cancer Education, 20*(1), 33–36.

Sexual Minorities

Roseborough, D. J. (2006). Coming out stories framed as faith narratives, or stories of spiritual growth. *Pastoral Psychology, 55*(1), 47–59.

to develop tools that remedy the fuzziness of current distinctions between spirituality and religiousness and among dimensions of spirituality, and to better understand cultural and contextual uniqueness as well as more universally shared elements. Stanard, Sandhu, and Painter (2000) see spirituality as an emerging fifth force in counseling and psychotherapy and provide a review of instruments currently in use and their psychometric properties and potential uses. Kier and Davenport

(2004) note that much of recent research has focused on the Judeo-Christian majority, leaving open questions as to the components and roles of spirituality from other traditions.

Similarly, we cannot yet sufficiently determine possible confounding or other moderating factors that may be involved with spirituality and health or mental health outcomes, nor has the field yet accounted for failures to find significant outcomes (Thoresen, 1999). Although spirituality is by no means new, growth of the practice-focused research base is comparatively recent (e.g., Oman, Hedberg, and Thoresen's, 2006, randomized controlled trial). As with other ways of coping, there are likely to be complex relationships, individual and group differences, and situational factors that will make a difference in the roles that spirituality plays in problem development as well as in problem solving and improved well-being. It would be important to know, for example, the extent to which a positive association between spirituality and well-being was due to higher levels of healthy behavior (and thus less exposure to certain risks), to family or friendship activities that yielded certain kinds of social support that buffered effects of stress, to cognitive schemas that shaped how a person viewed the world and interpreted stressors, or to some combination of those factors or to something entirely different. As with any factor, there are negative as well as positive potentials. Spirituality, for example, may incline a client toward rigidity, distortion, or zealotry, which would impede rather than support progress in managing stressful life circumstances or undertaking needed changes.

Spirituality may enter into practice in a number of ways. In addition to (1) including spirituality as part of assessment, Meador and Koenig (2000) note (2) incorporating spirituality into the treatment plan, (3) assessing the clinician's beliefs, (4) examining the clinical implications of the client's spirituality, (5) using religion or spirituality to cope with stress, (6) employing cognitive therapeutic models, and (7) avoiding clinician bias or proselytizing. Although there are competing views about the use of spirituality in professional helping, it has a longer and more widespread acceptance in some arenas than in others—for example, related to death and dying, and with 12-step programs such as Alcoholics Anonymous (Tonigan, Toscova, & Connors, 1999).

Embedded throughout are ethical issues and the need for safeguards. Spirituality entails values on the part of the client, helper, and any others involved—values that may conflict, that may not be well examined or understood, that may carry costs or dangers as well as benefits. You will need to be careful with professional, ethical, and legal issues when working with spiritual values and interventions in psychotherapy. Examples include questions about (1) the nature of the helper's role and appropriate accountability oversight, (2) making helpers' and clients' values and differences explicit, (3) determining the setting and conditions of therapy, (4) how the presenting concern and goals of the client are construed and determined, (5) confronting unhealthy client values or addressing deficiencies or confusion, (6) obtaining informed consent and evaluating a helper's competency relative to spiritual dimensions, (7) maintaining professional and scientific responsibility, (8) respecting the client's religious values, (9) documenting use of spiritual interventions, (10) evaluating therapy outcome and termination, (11) making appropriate financial arrangements, and (12) treatment issues such as those that may arise in family therapy or mental health problems like dissociative disorders (e.g., ethical factors in dealing with spiritual issues such as distorted views of God or feelings of being demonized) (Chappelle, 2000; Haug, 1998; Mungadze, 2000; Richards, Rector, & Tjeltveit, 1999). Finally, it is important to be aware that differences in religious or spiritual perspectives may have substantial implications for inclusion as part of helping services.

CHAPTER SUMMARY

In this chapter, we examine various forms that stress takes, including cultural variations of stress as well as current models of factors that affect stress and coping. We have seen ways in which stress and its management relate to many other assessment and intervention strategies described in this book. Understanding current models of stress and coping should help guide you in developing an intervention plan appropriate to specific client needs, depending on the factors that appear most important either in how stress is being experienced or in what types of stress management are likely to best achieve client goals.

Specific to stress management, we present breathing interventions to help address physiological dimensions. Clients can achieve greater awareness of their breathing and can undertake breathing exercises that will help calm the central nervous system, reduce symptoms such as dizziness, and better prepare them to undertake additional steps in managing their stressful circumstances. We also describe stress inoculation as an approach to teaching both physical and cognitive coping strategies. Stress inoculation training pulls together a number of strategies to increase knowledge about stress and coping, self-monitoring, cognitive change, problem solving, relaxation training, rehearsal preparation, and environmental change.

As with any intervention, you will need to assess the appropriateness of each component as well as additional ones. For example, spirituality may be an important resource to consider for use in stress management intervention. Moreover, although cultural diversity is becoming much more explicit in practice involving stress and coping, much of the research and intervention development is rooted in a Western framework—for example, that stress is viewed as a "problem" requiring the assistance of an external source such as a professional helper and some "training" in order to be alleviated or managed. Some clients may view stress more as a part of life, and to them self-healing practices such as meditation, movement, or one or more forms of self-management (perhaps anchored within one's personal network or community) may be attractive and relevant.

REFERENCES

Aeschleman, S. R., & Imes, C. (1999). Stress inoculation training for impulsive behaviors in adults with traumatic brain injury. *Journal of Rational–Emotive and Cognitive Behavior Therapy, 17*(1), 51–65.

Alferi, S. M., Carver, C. S., Antoni, M. H., Weiss, S., & Duran, R. E. (2001). An exploratory study of social support, distress, and life disruption among low-income Hispanic women under treatment for early stage breast cancer. *Health Psychology, 20,* 41–46.

Antoni, M. H., Lehman, J. M., Kilbourn, K. M., Boyers, A. E., Culver, J. L., Alferi, S. M., et al. (2001). Cognitive–behavioral stress management intervention decreases the prevalence of depression and enhances benefit finding among women under treatment for early-stage breast cancer. *Health Psychology, 20,* 20–32.

Arcury, T. A., Quandt, S. A., McDonald, J., & Bell. R. A. (2000). Faith and health self-management of rural older adults. *Journal of Cross-Cultural Gerontology, 15*(1), 55–74.

Barlow, D. H., & Durand, V. M. (1995). *Abnormal psychology: An integrative approach.* Pacific Grove, CA: Brooks/Cole.

Basoglu, M. (1997). Torture as a stressful life event: A review of the current status of knowledge. In T. W. Miller (Ed.), *Clinical disorders and stressful life events* (pp. 45–69). Madison, CT: International Universities Press.

Birch, B. B. (1995). *Power yoga.* New York: Fireside.

Boehnlein, J. K., & Kinzie, J. D. (1997). Clinical perspectives on posttraumatic stress disorder. In T. W. Miller (Ed.), *Clinical disorders and stressful life events* (pp. 19–43). Madison, CT: International Universities Press.

Bourke, M. L., & Van Hasselt, V. B. (2001). Social problem-solving skills training for incarcerated offenders: A treatment manual. *Behavior Modification, 25*(2), 163–188.

Briggs, M. K., & Shoffner, M. F. (2006). Spiritual wellness and depression: Testing a theoretical model with older adolescents and midlife adults. *Counseling and Values, 51*(1), 5–20.

Brown, C. M. (2000). Exploring the role of religiosity in hypertension management among African Americans. *Journal of Health Care for the Poor and Underserved, 11*(1), 19–32.

Cahill, S. P., Rauch, S. A., Hembree, E. A., & Foa, E. B. (2003). Effect of cognitive–behavioral treatments for PTSD on anger. *Journal of Cognitive Psychotherapy, 17*(2), 113–131.

Calhoun, L. G., & Tedeschi, R. G. (1998). Beyond recovery from trauma: Implications for clinical practice and research. *Journal of Social Issues, 54,* 357–371.

Calhoun, L. G., & Tedeschi, R. G. (1999). *Facilitating posttraumatic growth: A clinician's guide.* Mahwah, NJ: Lawrence Erlbaum.

Casey, A., & Benson, H. (2004). *Mind your heart: A mind/body approach to stress management, exercise, and nutrition for heart health.* New York: Free Press.

Castillo, R. J. (1997). *Culture and mental illness.* Pacific Grove, CA: Brooks/Cole.

Chang, B., Noonan, A. E., & Tennstedt, S. L. (1998). The role of religion/spirituality in coping with caregiving for disabled elders. *Gerontologist, 38,* 463–470.

Chappelle, W. (2000). A series of progressive legal and ethical decision-making steps for using Christian spiritual interventions in psychotherapy. *Journal of Psychology and Theology, 28,* 43–53.

Chiu, M. L. (1997). The influence of anticipatory fear on foreign student adjustment: An exploratory study. *International Journal of Intercultural Relationships, 19,* 1–44.

Cigrang, J. A., Todd, S. L., & Carbone, E. G. (2000). Stress management training for military trainees returned to duty after a mental health evaluation: Effect on graduation rates. *Journal of Occupational Health Psychology, 5*(1), 48–55.

Cohen, J. A., & Welch, L. M. (2000). Attitudes, beliefs, values, and culture as mediators of stress. In V. H. Rice (Ed.), *Handbook of stress, coping, and health: Implications for nursing research, theory, and practice* (pp. 335–366). Thousand Oaks, CA: Sage.

Comas-Diaz, L. (2006). Latino healing: The integration of ethnic psychology into psychotherapy. *Psychotherapy: Theory, Research, Practice, Training, 43*(4), 436–453.

Crum, A. (2000). *The 10-step method of stress relief: Decoding the meaning and significance of stress.* Boca Raton, FL: CRC.

Davis, C. G., Nolen-Hoeksema, S., & Larson, J. (1998). Making sense of loss and benefiting from the experience: Two construals of meaning. *Journal of Personality and Social Psychology, 75,* 561–574.

Eliot, G. R., & Eisdorfer, C. (1982). *Stress and human health.* New York: Springer-Verlag.

Fink, G. (2000). *Encyclopedia of stress.* San Diego, CA: Academic Press.

Foa, E. B., Dancu, C. V., Hembree, E. A., Jaycox, L. H., Meadows, E. A., & Street, G. P. (1999). A comparison of exposure therapy, stress inoculation training, and their combination for reducing posttraumatic stress disorder in female assault victims. *Journal of Consulting and Clinical Psychology, 67*(2), 194–200.

Folkman, S. (1997). Positive psychological states and coping with severe stress. *Social Science and Medicine, 38,* 309–316.

Folkman, S., & Moskowitz, J. T. (2000). Positive affect and the other side of coping. *American Psychologist, 55,* 647–654.

Fontana, A. M., Hyra, D., Godfrey, L., & Cermak, L. (1999). Impact of a peer-led stress inoculation training intervention on state anxiety and heart rate in college students. *Journal of Applied Biobehavioral Research, 4,* 45–63.

Freiheit, S. R., Sonstegard, K., Schmitt, A., & Vye, C. (2006). Religiosity and spirituality: A psychometric evaluation of the Santa Clara Strength of Religious Faith Questionnaire. *Pastoral Psychology, 55*(1), 27–33.

Fried, R. (1993). The role of respiration in stress and stress control: Toward a theory of stress as a hypoxic phenomenon. In P. M. Lehrer & R. L. Woolfolk (Eds.), *Principles and practice of stress management* (2nd ed., pp. 301–331). New York: Guilford Press.

Garcia, J., Simon, M. A., Duran, M., Canceller, J., & Aneiros, F. J. (2006). Differential efficacy of a cognitive–behavioral intervention versus pharmacological treatment in the management of fibromyalgic syndrome. *Psychology, Health and Medicine, 11*(4), 498–506.

Garcia-Vera, M. P., Labrador, F. J., & Sanz, J. (1997). Stress management training for essential hypertension: A controlled study. *Applied Psychophysiology and Biofeedback, 22*(4), 261–283.

Gendlin, E. T. (1996). *Focusing-oriented psychotherapy: A manual of the experiential method.* New York: Guilford Press.

George, L. K., Larson, D. B., Koenig, H. G., & McCullough, M. E. (2000). Spirituality and health: What we know, what we need to know. *Journal of Social and Clinical Psychology, 19,* 102–116.

Gilligan, P., & Furness, S. (2006). The role of religion and spirituality in social work practice: Views and experiences of social workers and students. *British Journal of Social Work, 36*(4), 617–637.

Gottman, J. M., & Katz, L. F. (2002). Children's emotional reactions to stressful parent–child interactions: The link between emotion regulation and vagal tone. *Marriage and Family Review, 34*(3–4), 265–283.

Greenberg, J. S. (1996). *Comprehensive stress management.* Madison, WI: Brown and Benchmark.

Guterman, J. T., & Leite, N. (2006). Solution-focused counseling for clients with religious and spiritual concerns. *Counseling and Values, 51*(1), 39–52.

Harvey, I. S. (2006). Self-management of a chronic illness: An exploratory study on the role of spirituality among older African American women. *Journal of Women and Aging, 18*(3), 75–88.

Hathaway, W. L. (2006). Religious diversity in the military clinic: Four cases. *Military Psychology, 18*(3), 247–257.

Haug, I. (1998). Including a spiritual dimension in family therapy: Ethical considerations. *Contemporary Family Therapy: An International Journal, 20,* 181–194.

Hendricks, G. (1995). *Conscious breathing.* New York: Bantam.

Henry, A. (2006). "There's salt-water in our blood": The "Middle Passage" epistemology of two Black mothers regarding the spiritual education of their daughters. *International Journal of Qualitative Studies in Education, 19*(3), 329–345.

Hill, C., & Nutt Williams, E. (2000). The process of individual therapy. In S. D. Brown & R. W. Lent (Eds.), *Handbook of counseling psychology* (3rd ed., pp. 670–710). New York: Wiley.

Hodge, D. R., Baughman, L. M., & Cummings, J. A. (2006). Moving toward spiritual competency: Deconstructing religious stereotypes and spiritual prejudices in social work literature. *Journal of Social Service Research, 32*(4), 211–232.

Jacobson, E. (1929). *Progressive relaxation.* Chicago: University of Chicago Press.

James, B. J., & Samuels, C. A. (1999). High stress life events and spiritual development. *Journal of Psychology and Theology, 27,* 250–260.

Kahn, A. P. (2006). *The encyclopedia of stress and stress-related diseases.* New York: Facts on File.

Kendall-Tackett, K. A., (Ed.). (2005). *Handbook of women, stress, and trauma.* New York: Brunner-Routledge.

Kier, F. J., & Davenport, D. S. (2004). Unaddressed problems in the study of spirituality and health. *American Psychologist, 59,* 53–54.

Kiesling, C., Sorell, G. T., Montgomery, M. J., & Colwell, R. K. (2006). Identity and spirituality: A psychosocial exploration of the sense of spiritual self. *Developmental Psychology, 42*(6), 1269–1277.

Krieger, N. (1999). Embodying inequality: A review of concepts, measures, and methods for studying health consequences of discrimination. *International Journal of Social Welfare, 29,* 295–352.

Lam, D. J., & Palsane, M. N. (1997). Research on stress and coping: Contemporary Asian approaches. In H. S. R. Kao & D. Sinha (Eds.), *Asian perspectives on psychology* (pp. 265–281). Thousand Oaks, CA: Sage.

Langer, N. (2000). The importance of spirituality in later life. *Gerontology and Geriatrics Education, 20*(3), 41–50.

Laungani, P. (1993). Cultural differences in stress and its management. *Stress-Medicine, 9,* 37–43.

Lazarus, R. S. (1990). Theory-based stress measurement. *Psychological Inquiry, 1,* 3–13.

Lazarus, R. S., & Folkman, S. (1984). *Stress, appraisal, and coping.* New York: Springer.

Lee, C., Gavriel, H., Drummond, P., Richards, J., & Greenwald, R. (2002). Treatment of PTSD: Stress inoculation training with prolonged exposure compared to EMDR. *Journal of Clinical Psychology, 58*(9), 1071–1089.

Leininger, M. M. (1988). Leininger's theory of nursing: Culture care diversity and universality. *Nursing Science Quarterly, 1,* 152–160.

Leung, K., Chiu, T., & Chen, C. (2006). The influence of awareness of terminal condition on spiritual well-being in terminal cancer patients. *Journal of Pain and Symptom Management, 31*(5), 449–456.

Litz, B. T., Williams, L., Wang, J., Bryant, R., & Engel, C. C. (2004). A therapist-assisted internet self-help program for traumatic stress. *Professional Psychology: Research and Practice, 35*(6), 628–634.

Lopez Alonso, J. C., & Gomez-Jarabo, G. (2000). A model of therapeutic action in panic disorders. *European Journal of Psychiatry, 14*(1), 42–51.

Lukoff, D., Lu, F., & Turner, R. (1999). From spiritual emergency to spiritual problem: The transpersonal roots of the new *DSM-IV* category. *Journal of Humanistic Psychology, 38,* 21–50.

Luskin, F. M., Ginzburg, K., & Thoresen, C. E. (2005). The efficacy of forgiveness intervention in college age adults: Randomized controlled study. *Humbolt Journal of Social Relations, 29,* 163–164.

Maag, J. W., & Kotlash, J. (1994). Review of stress inoculation training with children and adolescents: Issues and recommendations. *Behavior Modification, 18,* 443–469.

Mako, C., Galek, K., & Poppito, S. R. (2006). Spiritual pain among patients with advanced cancer in palliative care. *Journal of Palliative Medicine, 9*(5), 1106–1113.

Marsden, P., Karagianni, E., & Morgan, J. F. (2007). Spirituality and clinical care in eating disorders: A qualitative study. *International Journal of Eating Disorders, 40*(1), 7–12.

McGuigan, F. J. (1999). *Encyclopedia of stress.* Boston: Allyn & Bacon.

McKenna, K. Y. A., & West, K. J. (2007). Give me that online-time religion: The role of the Internet in spiritual life. *Computers in Human Behavior, 23*(2), 942–954.

Meador, K. G., & Koenig, H. G. (2000). Spirituality and religion in psychiatric practice: Parameters and implications. *Psychiatric Annals, 30,* 549–555.

Meichenbaum, D. H. (1993). Stress inoculation training: A 20-year update. In P. M. Lehrer & R. L. Woolfolk (Eds.), *Principles and practice of stress management* (2nd ed., pp. 373–406). New York: Guilford Press.

Meichenbaum, D. H. (1994). *A clinical handbook/practical therapist manual for assessing and treating adults with posttraumatic stress disorder (PTSD).* Waterloo, Ontario, Canada: Institute Press.

Meichenbaum, D. H., & Cameron, R. (1983). Stress inoculation training: Toward a general paradigm on training coping skills. In D. H. Meichenbaum & M. E. Jaremko (Eds.), *Stress reduction and prevention* (pp. 115–157). New York: Plenum.

Meichenbaum, D. H., & Turk, D. (1976). The cognitive–behavioral management of anxiety, anger, and pain. In P. O. Davidson (Ed.), *The behavioral management of anxiety, depression and pain.* New York: Brunner/Mazel.

Miller, W. R., & Thoresen, C. E. (2003). Spirituality, religion, and health: An emerging research field. *American Psychologist, 58,* 24–35.

Milling, L. S., Kirsch, I., Meunier, S. A., & Levine, M. R. (2002). Hypnotic analgesia and stress inoculation training: Individual and combined effects in analog treatment of experimental pain. *Cognitive Therapy and Research, 26*(3), 355–371.

Milner, H. R. (2006). Culture, race and spirit: A reflective model for the study of African-Americans. *International Journal of Qualitative Studies in Education, 19*(3), 367–385.

Moadel, A., Morgan, C., Fatone, A., Grennan, J., Carter, J., Laruffia, G., et al. (1999). Feeling meaning and hope: Self-reported spiritual and existential needs among an ethnically diverse cancer patient population. *Psycho-Oncology, 8,* 378–385.

Mofidi, M., DeVellis, R. F., Blazer, D. G., DeVellis, B. M., Panter, A. T., & Jordan, J. M. (2006). Spirituality and depressive symptoms in a racially diverse US sample of community-dwelling adults. *Journal of Nervous and Mental Disease, 194*(12), 975–977.

Moore, S. A., Zoellner, L. A., & Bittinger, J. N. (2004). Combining cognitive restructuring and exposure therapy: Toward an optimal integration. In S. Taylor (Ed.), *Advances in the treatment of posttraumatic stress disorder: Cognitive behavioral perspectives* (pp. 129–149). New York: Springer.

Moos, R. H., & Schaefer, J. A. (1993). Coping resources and processes: Current concepts and measures. In L. Goldberger & S. Breznitz (Eds.), *Handbook of stress: Theoretical and clinical aspects* (2nd ed., pp. 234–257). New York: Free Press.

Mungadze, J. (2000). Is it dissociation or demonization? Sorting out spiritual and clinical issues in the treatment of dissociative disorders. *Journal of Psychology and Christianity, 19,* 139–143.

Musick, M. A., Traphagan, J. W., Koenig, H. G., & Larson, D. B. (2000). Spirituality in physical health and aging. *Journal of Adult Development, 7*(2), 73–86.

Novaco, R. W. (1975). *Anger control: The development and evaluation of an experimental treatment.* Lexington, MA: Heath.

Nurius, P. S. (2000). Coping. In P. Allen-Meares & C. Garvin (Eds.), *The handbook of social work direct practice* (pp. 349–372). Thousand Oaks, CA: Sage.

Oliver, D. P. (2003). Social work and spiritual counseling: Results of one state audit. *Journal of Palliative Medicine, 6*(6), 919–925.

Oman, D., Hedberg, J., & Thoresen, C. E. (2006). Passage meditation reduces perceived stress in health professionals: A randomized, controlled trial. *Journal of Consulting and Clinical Psychology, 74,* 714–719.

Paxson, H. (2006). Reproduction as spiritual kin work: Orthodoxy, IVF, and the moral economy of motherhood in Greece. *Culture, Medicine and Psychiatry, 30*(4), 481–505.

Prest, L. A., & Robinson, W. D. (2006). Systemic assessment and treatment of depression and anxiety in families: The BPSS model in practice. *Journal of Systemic Therapies, 25*(3), 4–24.

Puig, A., Lee, S. M., Goodwin, L., & Sherrard, P. A. D. (2006). The efficacy of creative arts therapies to enhance emotional expression, spirituality, and psychological well-being of newly diagnosed Stage I and Stage II breast cancer patients: A preliminary study. *Arts in Psychotherapy, 33*(3), 218–228.

Ramer, L., Johnson, D., Chan, L., & Barrett, M. T. (2006). The effect of HIV/AIDS disease progression on spirituality and self-transcendence in a multicultural population. *Journal of Transcultural Nursing, 17*(3), 280–289.

Rehm, R. S. (1999). Religious faith in Mexican-American families dealing with chronic childhood illness. IMAGE: *Journal of Nursing Scholarship, 311*, 33–38.

Rice, V. H. (Ed). (2000). *Handbook of stress, coping, and health: Implications for nursing research, theory, and practice.* Thousand Oaks, CA: Sage.

Richards, P. S., Berrett, M. E., Hardman, R. K., & Eggett, D. L. (2006). Comparative efficacy of spirituality, cognitive, and emotional support groups for treating eating disorder inpatients. *Eating Disorders: The Journal of Treatment and Prevention, 14*(5), 401–415.

Richards, P. S., Rector, J. M., & Tjeltveit, A. C. (1999). Values, spirituality, and psychotherapy. In W. R. Miller (Ed.), *Integrating spirituality into treatment: Resources for practitioners* (pp. 133–160). Washington, DC: American Psychological Association.

Roseborough, D. J. (2006). Coming out stories framed as faith narratives, or stories of spiritual growth. *Pastoral Psychology, 55*(1), 47–59.

St. Clair, D. M., & Castro, L. (2005). Native men, spirituality, and cancer recovery. *Journal of Cancer Education, 20*(1), 33–36.

Salois, E. M., Holkup, P. A., Tripp-Reimer, T., & Weinert, C. (2006). Research as spiritual covenant. *Western Journal of Nursing Research, 28*(5), 505–524.

Saunders, T., Driskell, J. E., Johnston, J. H., & Salas, E. (1996). The effect of stress inoculation training on anxiety and performance. *Journal of Occupational Health Psychology, 1*, 170–186.

Schiraldi, G. R., & Brown, S. L. (2001). Primary prevention for mental health: Results of an exploratory cognitive–behavioral college course. *Journal of Primary Prevention, 22*(1), 55–67.

Sharma, S., & Sud, A. (1990). Examination stress and test anxiety: A cross-cultural perspective. *Psychology and Developing Societies, 2*, 183–201.

Shimabukuro, K. P., Daniels, J., & D'Andrea, M. (1999). Addressing spiritual issues from a cultural perspective: The case of the grieving Filipino boy. *Journal of Multicultural Counseling and Development, 27*, 221–239.

Simon, C. E., Crowther, M., & Higgerson, H. (2007). The stage-specific role of spirituality among African American Christian women throughout the breast cancer experience. *Cultural Diversity and Ethnic Minority Psychology, 13*(1), 26–34.

Smart, N. (1993). *Religions of Asia.* Englewood Cliffs, NJ: Prentice Hall.

Smart, N. (1994). *Religions of the West.* Englewood Cliffs, NJ: Prentice Hall.

Smith, J. C. (2002). *Stress management: A comprehensive handbook of techniques and strategies.* New York: Springer.

Stanard, R. P., Sandhu, D. S., & Painter, L. C. (2000). Assessment of spirituality in counseling. *Journal of Counseling and Development, 78*, 204–210.

Sussman, S., Skara, S., Rodriguez, Y., & Pokhrel, P. (2006). Non drug use– and drug use–specific spirituality as one-year predictors of drug use among high-risk youth. *Substance Use and Misuse, 41*(13), 1801–1816.

Taylor, R. J., Chatters, L. M., Jayakody, R., & Levin, J. S. (1996). Black and white differences in religious participation: A multisample comparison. *Journal for the Scientific Study of Religion, 35*, 403–410.

Tedeschi, R. G., & Calhoun, L. G. (1995). *Trauma and transformation: Growing in the aftermath of suffering.* Thousand Oaks, CA: Sage.

Teichmann, M., Murdvee, M., & Saks, K. (2006). Spiritual needs and quality of life in Estonia. *Social Indicators Research, 76*(1), 147–163.

Thoresen, C. E. (1999). Spirituality and health: Is there a relationship? *Journal of Health Psychology, 43*, 291–300.

Timmons, P. L., Oehlert, M. E., Sumerall, S. W., Timmons, C. W., et al. (1997). Stress inoculation training for maladaptive anger: Comparison of group counseling versus computer guidance. *Computers in Human Behavior, 13*, 51–64.

Tonigan, J. S., Toscova, R. T., & Connors, G. J. (1999). Spirituality and the 12-step programs: A guide for clinicians. In W. R. Miller (Ed.), *Integrating spirituality into treatment: Resources for practitioners* (pp. 111–131). Washington, DC: American Psychological Association.

Triffleman, E. (2000). Gender differences in a controlled pilot study of psychosocial treatments in substance dependent patients with post-traumatic stress disorder: Design considerations and outcomes. *Alcoholism Treatment Quarterly, 18*(3), 113–126.

Triffleman, E., Carroll, K., & Kellogg, S. (1999). Substance dependence posttraumatic stress disorder therapy: An integrated cognitive–behavioral approach. *Journal of Substance Abuse Treatment, 17*(1–2), 3–14.

Trzepacz, A. M., & Luiselli, J. K. (2004). Efficacy of stress inoculation training in a case of posttraumatic stress disorder (PTSD) secondary to emergency gynecological surgery. *Clinical Case Studies, 3*(1), 83–92.

Turk, D. (1975). *Cognitive control of pain: A skills training approach for the treatment of pain.* Unpublished master's thesis, University of Waterloo. Waterloo, Ontario, Canada.

Underwood, P. W. (2000). Social support: The promise and the reality. In V. H. Rice (Ed.), *Handbook of stress, coping, and health: Implications for nursing research, theory, and practice* (pp. 367–391). Thousand Oaks, CA: Sage.

Washington, G., Johnson, T., Jones, J., & Langs, S. (2007). African-American boys in relative care and a culturally centered group mentoring approach. *Social Work with Groups, 30*(1), 45–68.

Webb, J. R., Robinson, E. A. R., Brower, K. J., & Zucker, R. A. (2006). Forgiveness and alcohol problems among people entering substance abuse treatment. *Journal of Addictive Diseases, 25*(3), 55–67.

Williams, W. H., Evans, J. J., & Wilson, B. A. (2003). Neurorehabilitation for two cases of post-traumatic stress disorder following traumatic brain injury. *Cognitive Neuropsychiatry, 8*(1), 1–18.

Wong, P. T. P., & Wong, L. C. (Eds). (2006). *Handbook of multicultural perspectives on stress and coping.* New York: Springer.

Woods, T. E., & Ironson, G. H. (1999). Religion and spirituality in the face of illness: How cancer, cardiac, and HIV patients describe their spirituality/religiosity. *Journal of Health Psychology, 4,* 393–412.

Young, S. J., Cashwell, C. S., & Shcherbakova, J. (2000). The moderating relationship of spirituality on negative life events and psychological adjustment. *Counseling and Values, 45*(1), 49–57.

14   KNOWLEDGE AND SKILL BUILDER

Part One

Learning Outcome 1 asks you to assess your own breathing by using four of the five awareness-of breathing instructions.

Part Two

Learning Outcome 2 asks you to demonstrate five of the six steps for diaphragmatic breathing. Use the Checklist for Diaphragmatic Breathing to assess your performance.

Checklist for Diaphragmatic Breathing

1. Rationale

   a. If you have doubts, check with your primary care physician before starting.
   b. Think about the purposes and benefits of abdominal breathing.

2. Comfortable Position and Breathing through the nose

   a. Get in a comfortable position to experience and feel the movement of your abdomen.
   b. Breathe through your nose. Just notice your breath.
   c. As you inhale, notice how cool the air feels, and how much warmer the air feels when you exhale.

3. Placement of Hands

   a. Bend your arms and place your thumbs below your rib cage. Place the rest of the fingers of each hand perpendicular to your body.
   b. Visualize the movement of the diaphragm. It contracts and is drawn downward as you inhale. When you exhale, the air is pushed out of the lungs, and the diaphragm is drawn upward.

4. Simulate Movement of the Diaphragm

   a. To simulate movement of the diaphragm, place your fingers interlaced on your abdomen, thumbs just under your rib cage. Straighten the fingers as you inhale, and curve outward as you exhale.

5. Diaphragmatic Breathing while Sitting

   a. Continue to breathe diaphragmatically without your hand gestures or movement. Place your hands in your lap or beside your body.
   b. As you breathe diaphragmatically, visualize the movement of the diaphragm as the abdomen rises and falls like the tide.

6. Daily Practice and Use in Stressful Situations

   a. Select a time and place to practice daily for a week.
   b. When you are in a stress situation, start breathing diaphragmatically.

Part Three

Learning Outcome 3 asks you to describe how you would use the five components of stress inoculation with a client case.

Read the client description below; then respond to the five questions following the case description as if you were using stress inoculation with this client. Feedback follows on page 453.

The client has been referred to you by Family Services. He is unemployed, is receiving welfare support, and has three children. He is married to his second wife; the oldest child is hers by another marriage. He has been referred because of school complaints that the oldest child, a seventh grader, has arrived at school several times with obvious facial bruises and cuts. The child has implicated the stepfather in this matter. After a long period of talking, the client reports that he has little patience with this boy and sometimes does strike him in the face as his way of disciplining the child. He realizes that maybe, on occasion, he has gone too far. Still, he gets fed up with the boy's "irresponsibility" and "lack of initiative" for his age. At these times, the client reports, his impatience and anger get the best of him.

1. Explain the purpose of stress inoculation as you would to this client.
2. Briefly give an overview of the stress inoculation procedure.
3. Describe and provide one example of each of the following direct-action coping strategies that might be useful to this client:

   a. Information collection
   b. Escape route
   c. Attention diversion
   d. Imagery manipulation
   e. Physical relaxation
   f. Palliative coping (perspective taking, social support, ventilation)

4. Explain to this client the four times or phases when his level of emotional arousal may be heightened. For each phase, provide two examples of cognitive coping skills (thoughts) for this client. The four phases are (a) preparing for a disagreement or argument with the boy, (b) confronting the situation, (c) dealing with critical moments or overwhelming feelings, and (d) rewarding himself for using coping skills.
5. Describe how you would set up opportunities during the interview with this client to help him practice direct-action and cognitive coping strategies in a role play of the provoking situations.

Part Four

Learning Outcome 4 asks you to demonstrate 17 out of 21 steps of the stress inoculation procedure with a role-play client. Use the Interview Checklist for Stress Inoculation to assess your role-play interview.

(continued)

(*continued*)

Interview Checklist for Stress Inoculation

Instructions: Determine which steps the helper demonstrated in using stress inoculation with a client or in teaching stress inoculation to another person. Check (✔) any step the helper demonstrated in the application of the procedure.

Treatment Rationale

1. Helper explains purpose of stress inoculation.
   "Stress inoculation is a way to help you cope with feeling anxious so that you can manage your reactions when you're confronted with these situations."
2. Helper provides brief overview of stress inoculation procedure.
   "First, we'll try to understand how your anxious feelings affect you now. Then you'll learn some coping skills that will help you relax physically—and help you use coping thoughts instead of self-defeating thoughts. Then you'll have a chance to test out your coping skills in stressful situations we'll set up."
3. Helper checks to see whether client is willing to use the strategy.
   "How do you feel now about working with this procedure?"

Information Giving by Helper

4. Helper explains nature of client's emotional reaction to a stressful situation.
   "Probably you realize that when you feel anxious, you are physically tense. Also, you may be thinking in a worried way—worrying about the situation and how to handle it. Both the physical tenseness and the negative or worry thoughts create stress for you."
5. Helper explains possible *phases* of reacting to a stressful situation.
   "When you feel anxious, you probably tend to think of it as one giant reaction. Actually, you're probably anxious at certain times or phases. For example, you might feel very uptight just anticipating the situation. Then you might feel uptight during the situation, especially if it starts to overwhelm you. After the situation is over, you may feel relieved—but down on yourself too."
6. Helper explains specific kinds of coping skills to be learned in stress inoculation and the importance of client's input in tailoring coping strategies.
   "We'll be learning some action kinds of coping strategies—like physical or muscle relaxation, mental relaxation, and just commonsense ways to minimize the

stress of the situation. Then also you'll learn some different ways to view and think about the situation. Not all these coping strategies may seem best for you, so your input in selecting the ones you feel are best for you is important."

Client Learning and Practice of Direct-Action Coping Strategies

7. Helper discusses and models direct-action coping strategies (or uses a symbolic model).
   "First, I'll explain and we can talk about each coping method. Then I'll demonstrate how you can apply it when you're provoked."
   a. Collecting objective or factual information about stressful situation:
   "Sometimes it helps to get any information you can about things that provoke and anger you. Let's find out the types of situations and people that can do this to you. Then we can see whether there are other ways to view the provocation. For example, what if you looked at it as a situation to challenge your problem-solving ability rather than as a personal attack?"
   b. Identifying escape routes—alternative ways to deescalate stress of situation:
   "Suppose you're caught in a situation. You feel it's going to get out of hand. What are some ways to get out of it or to deescalate it *before* you strike out? For example, little things like counting to 60, leaving the room, using humor, or something like that."

Mental Relaxation

   c. Attention diversion:
   "Okay, one way to control your anger is to distract yourself—take your attention away from the person you feel angry with. If you have to stay in the same room, concentrate very hard on an object in the room. Think of all the questions about this object you can."
   d. Imagery manipulations:
   "Another way you can prevent yourself from striking out at someone is to use your imagination. Think of something very calming and very pleasurable, like listening to your favorite record or being on the beach with the hot sun."

Physical Relaxation

   e. Muscle relaxation:
   "Muscle relaxation can help you cope whenever you start to feel aroused and feel your face getting flushed or your body tightening up. It can help you learn to relax your body, which, in turn, can help you control your anger."
   f. Breathing techniques:
   "Breathing is also important in learning to relax physically. Sometimes, in a tight spot, taking slow, deep breaths can give you time to get yourself together before saying or doing something you don't want to."

Palliative Coping Strategies

   g. Perspective taking:
   "Let's try to look at this situation from a different perspective. What else about the situation might you be overlooking?"
   h. Social support network:

"Let's put together some people and resources you could use as a support system."

i. Ventilation of feelings:

"Perhaps it would be helpful just to spend some time getting your feelings out in the open."

8. Client selects most useful coping strategies and practices each strategy under helper's direction.

"We've gone over a lot of possible methods to help you control your anger so it doesn't result in abusive behavior. I'm sure that you have some preferences. Why don't you pick the methods that you think will work best for you? We'll practice with these so you can get a feel for them."

Client Learning and Practice of Cognitive Coping Strategies

9. Helper describes four phases of using cognitive coping strategies to deal with a stressful situation.

"As you may remember from our earlier discussion, we talked about learning to use coping procedures at important points during a stressful or provoking situation. Now we will work on helping you learn to use coping thoughts during these four important times: preparing for the situation, handling the situation, dealing with critical moments during the situation, and encouraging yourself after the situation."

10. For each phase, helper models examples of coping statements.

"I'd like to give you some ideas of some possible coping thoughts you could use during each of these four important times. For instance, when I'm trying to psych myself up for a stressful situation, here are some things I think about."

11. For each phase, client selects the most natural coping statements.

"The examples I gave may not feel natural for you. I'd like you to pick or add ones that you could use comfortably, that wouldn't seem foreign to you."

12. Helper instructs client to practice using these coping statements for each phase.

"Sometimes, because you aren't used to concentrating on coping thoughts at these important times, it feels a little awkward at first. So I'd like you to get a feel for these by practicing aloud the ones you selected. Let's work first on the ones for preparing for a provoking situation."

13. Helper models and instructs client to practice sequence of all four phases and verbalize accompanying coping statements.

"Next I'd like you to practice verbalizing the coping thoughts aloud in the sequence that you'll be using when you're in provoking situations. For example, [helper models].

Now you try it."

Application of All Coping Skills to Problem-Related Situations

14. Using coping strategies and skills selected by client, helper models how to apply these in a coping manner while imagining a stressful (problem-related) situation.

"Now you can practice using all these coping strategies when confronted with a problem situation. For example, suppose I'm you and my boss comes up to me and gives me criticism based on misinformation. Here is how I might use my coping skills in that situation."

15. Client practices coping strategies while imagining problem-related stressful situations. (This step is repeated as necessary.)

"This time, why don't you try it? Just imagine this situation—and imagine that each time you start to lose control, that is a signal to use some of your coping skills."

16. Client practices coping strategies in role play of problem-related situation. (This step is repeated as necessary.)

"We could practice this in role play. I could take the part of your boss and initiate a meeting with you. Just be yourself and use your coping skills to prepare for the meeting. Then, during our meeting, practice your skills whenever you get tense or start to blow up."

Application of All Coping Skills to Potential Problem Situations

17. Helper models application of client-selected coping strategies to non-problem-related or other potentially stressful situations.

"Let's work on some situations now that aren't problems for you but could become problems in the future. This will give you a chance to see how you can apply these coping skills to other situations you encounter in the future. For instance, suppose I just found out I didn't get a promotion that I believe I really deserved. Here is how I might cope with this."

18. Client practices, as often as needed, applying coping strategies to potentially stressful situations by

a. Imagining a potentially stressful situation:

"Why don't you imagine you've just found out you're being transferred to a new place? You are surprised by this. Imagine how you would cope."

b. Taking part in a role-play practice:

"This time let's role-play a situation. I'll be your husband and tell you I've just found out I am very ill. You practice your coping skills as we talk."

c. Assuming the role of a teacher of coping strategies:

"This time I'm going to pretend that I have chronic arthritis and am in constant pain. It's really getting to me. I'd like you to be my trainer or helper and teach me how I could learn to use some coping skills to deal with this chronic discomfort."

(continued)

14   KNOWLEDGE AND SKILL BUILDER

(continued)

Homework and Follow-up

19. Helper and client discuss application of coping strategies to in vivo situations.
    "I believe now you could apply these coping skills to problem situations you encounter during a typical day or week. You may not find that they work as quickly as you'd like, but you should find yourself coping more and not losing control as much."
20. Helper shows client how to use log to record uses of stress inoculation for in vivo situations.

"Each time you use the coping skills, mark it down on the log and briefly describe the situation in which you used them."

21. Helper arranges for a follow-up.
    "We could get together next week and go over your logs and see how you're doing."

Observer Comments _____

_____

_____

14   KNOWLEDGE AND SKILL BUILDER **FEEDBACK**

Part One

See if you can repeat the awareness-of-breathing exercise without reviewing notes. See if you understand what to look for and feel sufficiently so you can easily show it to another person. If you have difficulty, review the section "Awareness of Breathing."

Part Two

Use the Checklist for Diaphragmatic Breathing to assess how completely you covered each step in your demonstration.

Part Three

1. Your rationale to this client might sound something like this: "You realize that there are times when your anger and impatience do get the best of you. This procedure can help you learn to control your feelings at especially hard times—when you're very upset with this child—so that you don't do something you will regret later."

2. Here is a brief overview of stress inoculation: "First, we'll look at the things the child can do that really upset you. When you realize you're in this type of situation, you can learn to control how upset you are—through keeping yourself calm. This procedure will help you learn different ways to keep calm and not let these situations get out of hand."

3. For each strategy, see the indicated leads on the Interview Checklist for Stress Inoculation:

   a. Information collection—lead 7, part a
   b. Escape route—lead 7, part b
   c. Attention diversion—lead 7, part c
   d. Imagery manipulation—lead 7, part d
   e. Physical relaxation—lead 7, parts e and f
   f. Palliative coping—lead 7, parts g, h, and i

4. Here is a list and explanation of the four phases of emotional arousal, followed by cognitive coping skills you might present to this client.

   a. *Preparing for a provoking situation:* Before a disagreement or discussion begins, plan how you want to handle it.
   "What do I want to say to him that gets my point across?"
   "I can tell him how I feel without shouting".

   b. *Confronting a provoking situation:* When you're talking to your son, think about how to stay in control.
   "Just keep talking in a normal voice, no yelling."
   "Let him talk, too. Don't yell a lot; it doesn't help."

   C. *Dealing with a very provoking moment:* If you feel very angry, think of some things to keep you from blowing your cool.
   "Wait a minute. Slow down. Don't let the lid off."
   "Keep those hands down. Stay calm now."

   d. *Rewarding self for coping:* When you are successful, acknowledge your success. Give yourself a pat on the back when you manage to keep your cool.
   "I kept my cool that time!"
   "I could feel myself getting angry, but I kept in control then."

5. Practice opportunities can be carried out by the client in imagination or by you and the client in a role-play. In a role-play practice, you could take the part of the child. See leads 14, 15, and 16 on the Interview Checklist for Stress Inoculation for some examples of this type of practice.

Part Four

Use the Interview Checklist for Stress Inoculation to assess your role-play interview.

15

MEDITATION AND RELAXATION STRATEGIES

LEARNING OUTCOMES

After completing this chapter, you will be able to

1. Identify which step of the relaxation response is reflected by nine helper responses, accurately identifying at least seven of the nine examples.
2. Identify which step of the mindfulness meditation procedure is reflected by eight helper responses.
3. Select either mindfulness meditation or relaxation response, and teach the procedure to another person. Audiotape your teaching and assess your steps with the Interview Checklist for Mindfulness Meditation or the Interview Checklist for Relaxation Response, or have an observer evaluate your teaching, using the checklist.
4. Describe how you would apply the seven components of the muscle-relaxation procedure, given a simulated client case.
5. Demonstrate 13 out of 15 steps of muscle relaxation with a role-play client, using the Interview Checklist for Muscle Relaxation to assess your performance.
6. Using the body-scan script, demonstrate the body scan with a role-play client.

This chapter extends the focus on stress and its management. We all know from experience that it is difficult to focus, learn, be open to and feel energized for change, or take on the hard work involved in helping interventions when we are wound up, fragmented, overwhelmed, and exhausted from stress. Thus, strategies such as those described in this chapter are increasingly used in conjunction with the cognitively intensive strategies that are part of the cognitive–behavioral repertoire. This is especially true for stress management training and as adjuncts to other interventions when skills in self-calming, physical awareness, emotional regulation, and help with focus and presence are needed. It is important to keep in mind the value of these strategies for helpers. We previously noted the importance of self-care, and it may be particularly important when we are relatively new to the helper role, anxious, and scrambling to juggle

the multiple roles of student, professional helper, family, and so forth.

First, we present meditation procedures, specifically for mindfulness meditation and relaxation response. In addition, we discuss approaches to muscle relaxation training. As you will see, muscle relaxation, including the body scan, can be used with other interventions or as one component of meditation. Similarly, mindful meditating can be a useful element to achieving muscle relaxation. Mindfulness meditation is not about inducing relaxation per se; it promotes nonjudgmental observation of current conditions such as intrusive thoughts, physiological arousal, or muscle tension. Achieving a more nonjudgmental state is compatible with relaxation, facilitating reduction of muscular tension and development of skills in managing the physical experience of stress.

MEDITATION: PROCESSES AND USES

The usefulness of meditation for attaining mental calmness and physical relaxation has long been recognized, and meditation is receiving increasing clinical and empirical support for its use with a range of issues—particularly stress-related issues—commonly encountered in direct service practice. What is growing in use and empirical support is the application of meditation to develop mindfulness, a potentially important intervention strategy complementary to others presented in this book. Although no one intervention strategy is a silver bullet or is appropriate for all people or circumstances, meditation is becoming a common tool in medicine, psychology, education, and self-development (Goleman, 1988).

Practitioners and researchers define meditation strategy in different ways. Fontana (1991) describes what meditation is not and what it is: "Meditation *isn't*: falling asleep, going into a trance, shutting yourself off from reality and becoming unworldly, being selfish, doing something 'unnatural,' becoming lost in thought, forgetting where you are. Meditation *is*: keeping the mind alert and attentive, keeping the mind focused and concentrated, becoming aware of the world, becoming more human, knowing where you are" (p. 17). Focusing on implementation, Patel (1993) describes meditation as a practice of "taking a comfortable position—either sitting, lying down, or standing, although sitting is the most usual posture. It then involves being in a quiet environment, regulating the breath, adopting a physically relaxed and mentally passive attitude, and dwelling single-mindedly upon an object. The object of meditation does not have to be physical. It can be an idea, image, or happening; it can be mental repetition of a word or phrase, as in mantra meditation; it can be observing one's own thoughts, perception, or reaction; or it can be concentrating on some bodily generated rhythm (e.g., breathing)" (p. 127).

Borysenko (1987) broadens this definition: "meditation is any activity that keeps the attention pleasantly anchored in the present moment. . . . To develop a state of inner awareness, to witness and to let go of the old dialogues, you need an observation point. If you went out in a boat to view offshore tides but neglected to put down an anchor, you would soon be carried off to sea. So it is with the mind. Without an anchor to keep the mind in place, it will be carried away by the torrent of thoughts. Your ability to watch what is happening will be lost. The practice of meditation, which calms the body through the relaxation response and fixes the mind through dropping the anchor of attention, is the most important tool of self-healing and self-regulation" (p. 36).

Although consistent with other cognitive–behavioral methods described in this book, meditation therapy provides distinct and complementary tools. For example, whereas some cognitive interventions focus on changing the content of a client's problematic thoughts (e.g., "I am a failure"), meditation therapy focuses more on altering the client's attitude or relationship to the thought. This approach may include regarding thoughts as similar to the five senses in that negative thoughts are noticed as "thought stimuli" (akin to smell or hearing stimuli) and accepted as natural behavior of the mind but not as inherently defining the self or dictating subsequent feelings or actions (Epstein, 1995; Marlatt and Kristeller, 1999). We provide overviews here of mindfulness meditation: and the relaxation response. Some meditation, such as relaxation response, is purposefully concentrative. The person focuses on a certain image or sound and on his or her breathing patterns to foster relaxation and calmness. Offering a contrast, mindfulness meditation is less like a laser beam and more like a searchlight that illuminates a wide range of thoughts or sensations, one at a time, as they arise in awareness—fostering a relaxed, choiceless awareness of the movement of awareness among the changing elements of experience (Germer, 2005). Two main aspects of this form of meditation are an experiential perspective of the fluid, changing nature of perceived reality and a capacity to self-monitor as a present-centered, nonevaluative observer.

Carrington (1993) reviews some of the symptoms or difficulties for which a person might benefit from meditation:

tension and/or anxiety states, psychophysiological disorders, chronic fatigue states, insomnias and hypersomnias, alcohol, drug, or tobacco abuse, excessive self-blame, chronic low-grade depressions or subacute reaction depressions, irritability, low frustration tolerance, strong submissive trends, poor developed psychological differentiation, difficulties with self-assertion, pathological bereavement reactions, separation anxiety, blocks to productivity or creativity, inadequate contact with affective life, a need to shift emphasis from client's reliance on therapist to reliance on self—of particular use when terminating psychotherapy. (pp. 150–151)

Several reviews of the physical and psychological applications of meditation and mindfulness illustrate the range of its uses (Baer, 2003; Bishop, 2002; Germer, Siegel, & Fulton, 2005). Also, as you can see from the list in Box 15.1, recent research on meditation reflects a wide range of applications: treatment of health conditions such as cancer, heart functioning, HIV/AIDS, and late-stage diseases, use with varying populations such as the elderly and youth in school settings, negative mood, anxiety, and stress reduction in a wide range of situations, and treatment for substance abuse, aggression, eating disorders, and relapse prevention.

APPLICATIONS OF MEDITATION AND RELAXATION WITH DIVERSE CLIENTS

Many meditation techniques have Eastern origins, and a global perspective is evident in research from India, Thailand, and other Asian countries (e.g., Emavardhana & Tori, 1997; Vigne, 1999). Meditation is increasingly used in health care settings. Ott (Ott, 2004; Ott, Longobucco-Hynes, & Hynes, 2002) illustrates the value of mindfulness meditation in health care, including pediatric medicine, with issues such as pain, anxiety, and sleep disturbance; and von Weiss (2002) advocates use in cases of fibromyalgia. Integration is also apparent in academic settings. With a focus on issues of disability in education, Holland (2004) reports promising outcomes integrating mindfulness meditation and somatic education. Hall (1999) found that meditation interventions (consisting of natural breathing techniques, relaxation, and attention-focusing techniques) were associated with a significant increase in overall academic performance with African American college students, whereas Ruben (1989) found that relaxation training incorporated into a classroom guidance program for Hispanic and African American fifth-grade students was associated with enhanced self-esteem and reduced the dropout rate of these students. Meditation has also been used with the elderly in various ways, including the extension of longevity (Alexander, Robinson, Orme-Johnson, & Schneider, 1994), the management of respiratory problems

BOX 15.1   RESEARCH ON MEDITATION

Cancer
Carlson, L. E., & Garland, S. N. (2005). Impact of mindfulness-based stress reduction (MBSR) on sleep, mood, stress and fatigue symptoms in cancer outpatients. *International Journal of Behavioral Medicine, 12*(4), 278–285.

Counselor Education
Christopher, J. C., Christopher, S. E., Dunnagan, T., & Schure, M. (2006). Teaching self-care through mindfulness practices: The application of yoga, meditation, and Qigong to counselor training. *Journal of Humanistic Psychology, 46*(4), 494–509.
Kurash, C., & Schaul, J. (2006). Integrating mindfulness meditation within a university counseling center setting. *Journal of College Student Psychotherapy, 20*(3), 53–67.

Dysphoric Mood
Broderick, P. C. (2005). Mindfulness and coping with dysphoric mood: Contrasts with rumination and distraction. *Cognitive Therapy and Research, 29*(5), 501–510.

Emotional Awareness
Nielsen, L., & Kaszniak, A. W. (2006). Awareness of subtle emotional feelings: A comparison of long-term meditators and nonmeditators. *Emotion, 6*(3), 392–405.

Habitual Responding
Wenk-Sormaz, H. (2005). Meditation can reduce habitual responding. *Advances in Mind–Body Medicine, 21*(3–4), 33–49.

Health
Ditto, B., Eclache, M., & Goldman, N. (2006). Short-term autonomic and cardiovascular effects of Mindfulness Body Scan Meditation. *Annals of Behavioral Medicine, 32*(3), 227–234.

Heart Rate Variability
Sarang, P., & Telles, S. (2006). Effects of two yoga based relaxation techniques on heart rate variability (HRV). *International Journal of Stress Management, 13*(4), 460–475.
Telles, S., Mohapatra, R. S., & Naveen, K. V. (2005). Heart rate variability spectrum during vipassana mindfulness meditation. *Journal of Indian Psychology, 23*(2), 1–5.

HIV/AIDS
Brazier, A., Mulkins, A., & Verhoef, M. (2006). Evaluating a yogic breathing and meditation intervention for individuals living with HIV/AIDS. *American Journal of Health Promotion, 20*(3), 192–195.

Quality of Life
Curiati, J. A., Bocchi, E., Freire, J. O., Arantes, A. C., Braga, M., Garcia, Y., et al. (2005). Meditation reduces sympathetic activation and improves the quality of life in elderly patients with optimally treated heart failure: A prospective randomized study. *Journal of Alternative and Complementary Medicine, 11*(3), 465–472.

Williams, A. L., Selwyn, P. A., Liberti, L., Molde, S., Njike, V. Y., Mccorkle, R., et al. (2005). A randomized controlled trial of meditation and massage effects on quality of life in people with late-stage disease: A pilot study. *Journal of Palliative Medicine, 8*(5), 939–952.

Meditation Combined with Cognitive Therapies
Hamilton, N. A., Kitzman, H., & Guyotte, S. (2006). Enhancing health and emotion: Mindfulness as a missing link between cognitive therapy and positive psychology. *Journal of Cognitive Psychotherapy, 20*(2), 123–134.
Lau, M. A., & McMain, S. F. (2005). Integrating mindfulness meditation with cognitive and behavioural therapies: The challenge of combining acceptance- and change-based strategies. *Canadian Journal of Psychiatry, 50*(13), 863–869.

Medication
Walsh, R., Victor, B., & Bitner, R. (2006). Emotional effects of Sertraline: Novel findings revealed by meditation. *American Journal of Orthopsychiatry, 76*(1), 134–137.

Mindfulness Assessment
Baer, R. A., Smith, Gregory T., Hopkins, J., Krietemeyer, J., & Toney, L. (2006). Using self-report assessment methods to explore facets of mindfulness. *Assessment, 13*(1), 27–45.

Neurophysiologic Effects
Cahn, B. R., & Polich, J. (2006). Meditation states and traits: EEG, ERP, and neuroimaging studies. *Psychological Bulletin, 132*(2), 180–211.
Takahashi, T., Murata, T., Hamada, T., Omori, M., Kosaka, H., Kikuchi, M., et al. (2005). Changes in EEG and autonomic nervous activity during meditation and their association with personality traits. *International Journal of Psychophysiology, 55*(2), 199–207.

Partner Violence
Kane, K. E. (2006). The phenomenology of meditation for female survivors of intimate partner violence. *Violence against Women, 12*(5), 501–518.

Social Phobia
Bogels, S. M., Sijbers, G. F. V. M., & Voncken, M. (2006). Mindfulness and task concentration training for social phobia: A pilot study. *Journal of Cognitive Psychotherapy, 20*(1), 33–44.

Stress Reduction
Galantino, M. L., Baime, M., Maguire, M., Szapary, P. O., & Farrar, J. T. (2005). Association of psychological and physiological measures of stress in health-care professionals during an 8-week mindfulness meditation program: Mindfulness in practice. *Stress and Health: Journal of the International Society for the Investigation of Stress, 21*(4), 255–261.

BOX 15.1	RESEARCH ON MEDITATION

Oman, D., Hedberg, J., & Thoresen, C. E. (2006). Passage meditation reduces perceived stress in health professionals: A randomized, controlled trial. *Journal of Consulting and Clinical Psychology, 74*(4), 714–719.

Rausch, S. M., Gramling, S. E., & Auerbach, S. M. (2006). Effects of a single session of large-group meditation and progressive muscle relaxation training on stress reduction, reactivity, and recovery. *International Journal of Stress Management, 13*(3), 273–290.

Shigaki, C. L., Glass, B., & Schopp, L. H. (2006). Mindfulness-based stress reduction in medical settings. *Journal of Clinical Psychology in Medical Settings, 13*(3), 209–216.

Wall, R. B. (2005). Tai Chi and mindfulness-based stress reduction in a Boston public middle school. *Journal of Pediatric Health Care, 19*(4), 230–237.

Substance Use

Bowen, S., Witkiewitz, K., Dillworth, T. M., Chawla, N., Simpson, T. L., Ostafin, B. D., et al. (2006). Mindfulness meditation and substance use in an incarcerated population. *Psychology of Addictive Behaviors, 20*(3), 343–347.

Witkiewitz, K., Marlatt, G. A., & Walker, D. (2005). Mindfulness-based relapse prevention for alcohol and substance use disorders. *Journal of Cognitive Psychotherapy, 19*(3), 211–228.

(Connolly, 1993), and the reduction of hypertension (Alexander et al., 1994). Extending application of mindfulness meditation with substance abuse, Bowen et al. (2006) provide intervention recommendations with incarcerated populations. Research has also been exploring the biophysiological mechanisms through which meditation may be producing effects (Tooley, Armstrong, Norman, & Sali 2000; Lazar et al., 2000; Seeman, Dubin, & Seeman, 2003). Although diversity is present in research samples in applying mindfulness meditation, we do not yet find a clear body of evidence that explicitly addresses effectiveness across cultural groups in the United States. This is one topic we advise attention to in following future developments and in your own practice applications.

MEDITATION BASICS

Patel (1993) describes seven recommended preconditions for meditation:

1. Meditate in a place free of distracting noise, movement, light, telephones, and activity of other people.
2. Make sure you are comfortable and the room is warm; wear loose clothes, empty your bladder and bowel, and do not practice for at least two hours after a meal.
3. Make sure your back is straight, your body is relaxed, and your eyes are half or fully closed.
4. Breathe through the nostrils and down into the abdomen. Make sure that your breathing is regular, slow, and rhythmical.
5. Dwell on a single object, word, phrase, or your breath.
6. Develop a passive and relaxed attitude toward distractions.
7. Practice regularly. (p. 130)

Table 15.1 provides an overview of the two meditation strategies that we describe in this chapter: first, mindfulness, and then relaxation responses. Patel's recommendations provide useful starting points for both strategies.

MINDFULNESS MEDITATION

Focusing on mindfulness meditation in particular, Marlatt and Kristeller (1999) note the element of being aware of the full range of experiences that exist in the here-and-now. They add that "mindful awareness is based on an attitude of acceptance. Rather than judging one's experiences as good or bad, healthy or sick, worthy or unworthy, mindfulness accepts all personal experiences (e.g., thoughts, emotions, events) as just 'what is' in the present moment" (p. 68). One important clinical application of mindfulness is developing the capacity of an "observing self" that can see thoughts as "just thinking" rather than as facts or directives.

We focus on mindfulness meditation because of its explicit linkage with thought and feeling processes, its rapidly growing application in psychological practice, and promising evidence of effectiveness (Baer, 2003). Although deriving from Buddhist meditative traditions, mindfulness training and meditation have largely been pursued in a secularized form, often being incorporated with other intervention strategies such as mindfulness-based stress reduction, mindfulness-based cognitive therapy, and Dialectical Behavior Therapy (Dimidjian & Linehan, 2003).

There are levels of mindfulness. We can periodically disengage from the tumble of our ongoing experiences to purposefully stop and deliberately focus our attention on what we are sensing, feeling, thinking at the moment—to what is going on and how are we responding. Because you are likely to be using these techniques with clients for whom this is a new experience, we focus on beginning levels. Examples of more intensive approaches can be found in Germer et al. (2005) and Segel, Williams, and Teasdale (2002). Kabat-Zinn (2003) provides an overview of the background of mindfulness practice, issues related to culture, and recommendations for training. Hamilton, Kitzman, and Guyotte (2006) provide a summary of mechanisms through which mindfulness meditation is

| TABLE 15.1 | Instructions for the Mindfulness Meditation of Kabat-Zinn (1990) and for the Relaxation Response of Benson (1987) and Benson and Stuart (1992) |

Mindfulness Meditation	Relaxation Response
1. Rationale—about nondoing, watching whatever comes up in the mind; provides energy and self-knowledge. Give overview of procedure. Confirm client's willingness to use.	1. Rationale—give purpose and overview; meditation is a way to elicit the relaxation response; sit quietly, get a focus word or phrase, and focus on breathing. Confirm client's willingness to try.
2. Instruct client about attitudinal foundations for mindfulness practice: nonjudging, patience, beginner's mind, trust, nonstriving, acceptance, and letting go.	2. Instruct client about when, where, and how long to practice.
3. Instruct about commitment, self-discipline, and energy.	3. Instruct about focus word, phrase, or prayer. Give examples.
4. Instruct about preparations for meditation.	4. Instruct about position for meditation, and about eyes.
5. Do a quick body scan to relax client's muscles.	5. Request the client to relax her or his muscles, or do a quick body scan.
6. Provide instructions for breathing.	6. Provide instructions for breathing.
7. Instruct about a wandering mind, focus on breathing to control the mind.	7. Instruct about a passive attitude when meditating.
8. Instruct client to sit quietly, close eyes, be present in the moment, 10 to 20 minutes, come out slowly.	8. Instruct client to meditate for about 10 to 20 minutes.
9. Inquire about the just-completed meditation experience. How did it feel? How did client handle distracting thoughts?	9. Inquire about the just-completed meditation experience. How did it feel? Did client handle distracting thoughts?
10. Homework—instruct client to meditate every day or 6 days a week, for 8 weeks, and about 15 to 30 minutes a day. Instruct about informal meditation.	10. Homework—instruct client to practice meditation once or twice daily for the next week. Not within one hour after eating; use quiet place, several hours before bedtime. Instruct how to apply in vivo.

understood to help support stress reduction, cognitive change, and adaptive coping response patterns.

Attitudinal Foundations for Practice

Mindfulness meditation is about letting go and watching or witnessing whatever comes up from one moment to the next. The client is told to select a quiet place to meditate—with eyes closed, focusing on his or her breathing, allowing thoughts to flow freely—for about 10 to 20 minutes. To enhance the practice of meditation, a participant needs definitions about core concepts of mindfulness (Kabat-Zinn,1990). Experience suggests that understanding and valuing these concepts is essential to successful meditation. Moreover, it is not uncommon for people reared in U.S. culture to struggle with incorporating the underlying attitudes and "habits of mind."

1. *Nonjudging* means that mindfulness is aided by being an impartial witness or observer to one's own experience. We have a habit of categorizing or judging our experiences, which locks us into unaware "knee jerk" or mechanical reactions that often do not have an objective basis. For example, you can be practicing and think about all the things you have to do and how boring the practice is. These are judgments that take you away from observing whatever comes up. If you pursue these thoughts, it takes you away from moment-by-moment awareness. To remedy this, just watch your breathing.

2. *Patience* means that we often have to allow things to unfold in their own time. Practicing patience means that we don't have to fill our lives with moments of doing and activity.

3. *Expectations of the beginner's mind* are often based on our past experiences or cognitive schema, but prevent us from seeing things as they really are. It is important for beginning meditators to be open to moment-by-moment experiences without framing the moment with expectations of how we think the moment will be.

4. *Trust* is about developing trust in your feelings and intuition. Clients are instructed to trust their feelings and wisdom, not discount them. For example, if you are sitting in a particularly uncomfortable posture while meditating, change to another posture that feels better. If your intuition says do this, follow what your intuition is telling you and experiment to find a way that matches your needs. The message is to obey and trust what your body or feelings are telling you.

5. *Nonstriving* means that mindfulness meditation is about the process of practice and not about striving to achieve something or get somewhere. Instruct clients to experience the moments; they do not have to get anywhere—just attend to or be with whatever comes up.

6. *Acceptance* means don't worry about results. Instruct the client to just focus on seeing and accepting things as they are, moment by moment, and in the present.

7. *Letting go* means nonattachment or not holding on to thoughts. If, for example, a client becomes judgmental, instruct the client to let go and just observe the judging mind. (pp. 33–40)

Instruction about Commitment, Self-Discipline, and Energy

Mindfulness meditation is insight oriented, intended to enhance well-being and awareness and to discipline one's mind and emotions. Kabat-Zinn (1990) asks his clients to make a commitment to the practice of mindfulness meditation similar to the commitment that would be required in athletic training. Clients are advised of the importance of making a serious commitment to working on themselves, recognizing the importance of self-discipline, perseverance, and sustained energy. Kabat-Zinn tells his clients, "You don't have to like it; you just have to do it" (pp. 41–42). Then, after eight weeks of practice, the client can say whether the practice was useful.

Preparations for Meditation

Clients are instructed to set aside a particular *block of time* every day—at least six days a week for at least eight consecutive weeks—to practice. We find that a three-week period is necessary for the practice to take hold. Clients are given instruction about making a *special place* in their homes to meditate. The place should be comfortable and free of interruptions. The recommended pose for mindfulness meditation is a *sitting posture* on a chair or on the floor. Clients are instructed to sit erect with head, neck, and back aligned vertically; this posture allows the breath to flow easily. If sitting in a chair, the person should sit away from the back of the chair so their spine is self-supporting (Kabat-Zinn, 1990, pp. 61–62). If sitting on the floor, the person should sit on a cushion to raise the buttocks off the floor. Some clients prefer to meditate while lying on their backs. We find that some clients who meditate lying down often fall asleep. They associate relaxation with sleep, and they lose consciousness. After meditating for a couple of weeks, however, these clients start to maintain awareness and decrease their urge to sleep.

Body Scan to Relax the Muscles

The helper typically begins mindfulness mediation by introducing the body scan, which involves focusing on one's breath and systematically directing attention to each part of one's body—attending to sensations, whether of pleasure or discomfort, without judgment of these sensations. The body scan helps the client to discover his or her body and to bring mind–body awareness to the moment. (See the next section of this chapter for a body-scan script.)

Breathing Instructions

The client is instructed to focus on the breath as it flows in and out. Ask the client to notice the difference in temperature of the exhaled breath and the inhaled breath, and to feel the sensations of the air as it moves in and out of the nostrils.

Instructions about the Mind Wandering

Attention is often carried away by thoughts cascading through the mind. Instruct clients that when this happens, they are to return their attention to the flow of breathing and let go of the thoughts. Note that this level of meditation is designed to focus on breathing. Initially, what matters is whether you are aware of your thoughts and feelings during meditation and how you handle them. Mindfulness meditation is not intended to stimulate thinking per se, nor analysis of one's thinking. Rather, the intent is to make room for awareness—without reactance or analysis—of one's thoughts, emotions, and sensations on a moment-to-moment basis. If the client gets stuck in a thought, feeling, sensation, sound, pain, or discomfort, instruct the client to bring his or her attention back to breathing and to let go by exhaling these distractions. As the client gains experience with meditation, a shift can be made to following the stream of thoughts, to noticing—without judgment or attempt to control—what predominates in awareness.

Instructions for Meditating

Instruct clients to close their eyes and to meditate for 10 to 20 minutes. After they conclude the meditation, they may wish to sit quietly, then move or stretch, and just relax for a few moments before opening their eyes.

Discussion of the Meditation Experience

Discuss or probe the client's reaction to meditation. Clients may be unsure of themselves because they are judging the process. Discuss with them how they felt with their first meditative experience. The helper should be nonjudgmental about what clients experience. For example, if clients say that most of their experience was chasing after thoughts, encourage them to continue meditating. Every practice will be different, and it is the process of the experience that is important.

The helper should instruct the client to select a quiet place and time and to determine how often to meditate, using the instructions from the previous mindfulness meditation experience. The helper should instruct the client not to meditate within one hour after eating. If meditation is done in the evening, it should occur several hours before bedtime. Finally, encourage the client to bring mindful awareness throughout the day while, for example, eating, getting stuck in traffic, doing everyday tasks, and interacting with people. The mantra is "to be here now," "be in the moment," "be present with what you are experiencing—in feeling and thought."

Kabat-Zinn (1990) describes four other types of mindfulness meditation in addition to the breath meditation described above:

1. Sitting with the breath and the body as a whole.
2. Sitting with sound from the environment, nature, or music—it is not about listening for sounds, but hearing what is in the moment.
3. Sitting with thoughts and feelings, which means perceiving them as events in your mind and noting their content and their change.
4. Sitting with choiceless awareness—just being open and receptive to whatever comes into your field of awareness, allowing it to come and to go. (pp. 72–74)

Integration of Mindfulness with Other Interventions

Mindfulness meditation is increasingly being incorporated into intervention modalities applicable for both physical and psychological disorders. Baer (2003) and Bishop (2002) offer overviews. Major areas of development include mindfulness-based stress reduction (Kabat-Zinn, 1990), Dialectical Behavior Therapy for difficult-to-treat disorders such as borderline personality disorder (Linehan, 1993), acceptance and commitment therapy (Hayes & Strosahl, 2004), mindfulness-based cognitive therapy developed for depression (Segal, Williams, & Teasdale, 2002), incorporation into extant treatments for generalized anxiety disorder (Borkovec, Alcaine, & Behar, 2004) and posttraumatic stress disorder (Orsillo & Batten, 2005), and addiction treatment (Witkiewitz, Marlatt, & Walker, 2005).

Dialectical Behavior Therapy (DBT), for example, is designed for individuals with heightened sensitivity to and intense experience of emotion, often high risk for self-injury and suicide. The word *dialectical* refers to a balance or middle place that must be achieved between, for example, acceptance and change; of balancing and regulating conflicting thoughts, feelings, and behaviors. A wise mind provides a metaphor as middle ground between the extremes of a completely rational mind and the tumultuous currents of a wholly emotional mind. DBT includes four foundational modules of coping behavior (Linehan, 1993): (1) developing skills of nonjudgmental mindfulness, (2) ability to tolerate distress, (3) ability to regulate one's emotions, and (4) skills of interpersonal effectiveness. The combination of interventive strategies such as behavioral contracting, exposure-based methods, and cognitive modification with acceptance and mindfulness-oriented procedures has proven highly effective and serves as an illustration of integrated practice models that are increasingly becoming important parts of a clinician's skill set.

RELUCTANCE, CONTRAINDICATIONS, AND ADVERSE EFFECTS OF MEDITATION

Meditation does not come naturally for many people steeped in American culture. American predilections to "do" something, to actively "dig in" to solve problems, present a potentially discordant starting point. Progress through meditation strategies often does not come quickly. It generally takes time to feel less self-conscious about use of the techniques and to slow down and reorient one's habits of responding to thoughts, emotions, physical sensations, and external phenomena to experience the benefits. Thus, it is important to alert clients to the incremental nature of change and to encourage discipline and persistence through the initial stages.

It is also important to be aware of cautions about using meditation. For example, although meditation and mindfulness have demonstrated effectiveness for stress and a range of emotional disorders, beginners should be aware that these are strategies not to avoid their difficulties but rather to better come to grips with them. Although a relaxed state can be one outcome, meditation also increases our awareness and the salience of our internal entanglements, and the process of achieving a relaxed

openness with this state can prove challenging. Carrington (1993) has also found that some people may be "hypersensitive to meditation" and may need a shorter period of time to meditate than other people (p. 153). Some may release emotional material that is difficult for them to handle, particularly if they meditate for a very long period of time.

Goleman (1988) points out that some clients with a schizoid disorder may become overly absorbed in inner realities and less connected with reality if they meditate (p. 171). People "in acute emotional states may be too agitated to begin meditation, and obsessive–compulsive clients might become overzealous with the new experience of meditation" (pp. 171–172). Marlatt and Kristeller (1999) see mindfulness meditation as being useful for a broad range of clients but note that some cautions are important. Some clients, for example, may become disconcerted with sensations of dissociation (e.g., feelings of floating or of being in a trance, sometimes with disturbing thoughts flooding the mind). Marlatt and Kristeller also caution use of meditation with individuals with histories of obsessive-compulsive disorder or past trauma (see also Carrington, 1998), but they point out that individuals with some types of severe psychiatric disturbance may use meditation effectively.

Finally, for some clients, the action of certain drugs may be enhanced by meditation. Carrington (1993) recommends monitoring patients practicing meditation if they are also using antianxiety, antidepressant, antihypertensive, or thyroid-regulating drugs (p. 154). The continued practice of meditation may allow some of these patients to lower their dosage of some drugs. The practitioner should be aware of any medication the client is taking and know what potential interaction might occur with a particular drug or medication and what intervention strategy might be needed. It is important for the helper to individualize the meditative process to address specific client needs and concerns.

MODEL EXAMPLE OF MINDFULNESS MEDITATION

In this model example, we present a narrative account of how mindfulness meditation might be used with a 49-year-old Japanese American male client. Yoshi, an air traffic controller, has reported that he would like to decrease the stress he experiences in his job. He believes that decreasing his stress will help to heal his ulcer and allow him to cope better with the demands of his job. In addition to describing the physical signs of stress (hypertension), Yoshi reports that he worries constantly about making mistakes at work.

Treatment Rationale

First, we explain to Yoshi that mindfulness meditation is used to help people cope with job-related stress. We tell him that the procedure is also used to help people with high blood pressure and anxiety as well as those who want to feel more alert. We give him an overview of mindfulness meditation, telling him that the procedure is a process of focusing on breathing in a quiet place, with eyes closed, allowing thoughts to flow freely. We explain that he should focus on breathing if his thoughts become too distracting, and we tell him that most people using this technique meditate for 10 to 20 minutes a day. We tell Yoshi that to help the practice of meditation, participants need a foundation of attitudes on which to build a meditative practice. Finally, we confirm his willingness to use meditation, and we answer any questions he has about the process.

Attitudinal Foundations for Practice

We describe to Yoshi seven attitudes that are conducive to mindfulness meditation. We tell him that mindfulness is helped if we are nonjudgmental and if, when we meditate, we strive to be impartial witnesses or observers of our experiences and avoid the human tendency to categorize experiences. We explain to Yoshi that we don't have to fill our lives with moments of doing and activity, and we ask him to be patient and to allow things to unfold in their own time while he is meditating. We tell him that beginners usually have expectations about what will happen while they are meditating, and we urge him simply to be open to the moment-by-moment experiences without injecting expectations based on past experience. We tell him to trust his feeling and intuition: there is no "right" or "correct" way to meditate. We ask him to experiment with the process to learn what fits his needs, and to obey and trust what his feelings and intuition tell him. We explain that mindfulness meditation is about the process of practice and is not about striving to achieve something or to get somewhere. All Yoshi has to do is to be "in the moment," to attend to or be with whatever comes up. We talk to him about acceptance and tell him not to worry about the outcome—to instead see and accept the way things are, moment by moment, in the present. Finally, we talk to Yoshi about letting go and experiencing nonattachment—not holding on to thoughts and feelings; we ask him to observe whatever comes up and to observe the judging mind.

Instruction about Commitment, Self-Discipline, and Energy

We tell Yoshi to commit to practicing mindfulness in much the same way an athlete would commit to training. Yoshi understands that he must make a firm commitment, discipline himself to persevere, and generate enough energy so that he can develop a strong meditative practice.

Preparations for Meditation

We ask Yoshi to set aside a block of time every day and meditate for at least six days a week, to find a quiet and special place to meditate without interruption, and to meditate in a sitting position with his back straight. We tell him to meditate for eight weeks so that he can become adjusted to the process. We instruct him not to meditate within one hour after eating and to wear comfortable clothing during the practice time.

Body Scan to Relax the Muscles

We conduct a body scan with Yoshi and tell him that we will scan different muscle groups of his body as a purification process. We tell him that this relaxes his body and brings mind–body awareness into the moment.

Breathing Instructions

We ask Yoshi to breathe deeply and notice how his belly expands on the inhaled breath and falls on the exhaled breath. We ask him to feel the difference in temperature of the outgoing breath and the incoming breath, and to feel the sensation of the air as it goes in and out of his nostrils.

Instructions about the Mind Wandering

Yoshi says that his attention is often carried away by cascading thoughts. We tell him that there is nothing wrong with that; when it happens, he is just to return his attention to the flow of breathing and let the thoughts go. We tell him to be aware of his thoughts and feelings during meditation. If he gets stuck in a thought, feeling, bodily sensation, sound, pain, or discomfort, he is to bring his attention back to breathing, and exhale these distractions.

Instructions for Meditating

We instruct Yoshi to sit quietly and get relaxed for about a minute. Then he is to close his eyes and focus his breathing. The air comes in and goes out, and he is to "ride" the tide of his breath. We tell Yoshi that mindfulness meditation is not an exercise and requires no effort; he can't force it. We mention to him that if distracting thoughts, feelings, sensations, or sounds occur, he should allow them to come and not try to influence them. He should observe them, then return to his breathing: "The air comes in and goes out." We tell Yoshi that he will meditate for 10 to 20 minutes. When the time is up, we ask him to come out of the meditation slowly by sitting with his eyes closed for about a minute; he may want to move and stretch. We instruct Yoshi to absorb what he is experiencing and then to open his eyes slowly.

Inquiring about the Just-Completed Meditation Experience

We ask Yoshi a series of questions about his experience: "How did you feel about the experience? How did you handle distractions? What are your feelings right now?"

Homework

We instruct Yoshi to meditate once a day, preferably in the morning soon after he wakes up. We remind him of the things to do to prepare: find a quiet environment, select a special time,

Meditation (Relaxation Response and Mindfulness Meditation)

Part One

The teaching of mindfulness meditation or the relaxation response is a psychoeducational process. The helper provides the instructions, and the client engages in meditation in a self-directed manner. To practice giving instructions to someone about meditation, select a partner or a role-play client, and give instructions as described in the Interview Checklist for Mindfulness Meditation or the Interview Checklist for Relaxation Response—both at the end of the chapter. Then assess how well your partner was able to implement your instructions. If you wish, reverse roles so that you can experience being instructed by another person.

Part Two

This activity provides an opportunity to try formal meditation. Do this in a quiet, restful place where you will not be interrupted for 20 minutes. Do *not* do this within

one hour after a meal or within two hours of going to sleep.

1. Get into a comfortable sitting position, and close your eyes.
2. Relax your entire body. Think about all the tension draining out of your body.
3. Meditate for 15 to 20 minutes.
   a. Breathe easily and naturally through your nose.
   b. Focus on your breathing with the thought of a number (one) or a word. Say (think) your word silently each time you inhale and exhale.
   c. If other thoughts or images appear, don't dwell on them but don't force them away. Just relax and focus on your word or breathing.
4. Try to assess your reactions to your meditative experience:
   a. How do you feel about it?
   b. How did you feel afterward?
   c. What sorts of thoughts or images come into your mind?
   d. How much difficulty did you have with distractions?
5. Practice the relaxation response systematically—twice daily for a week, if possible.

---

do a quick body scan, and remember the seven attitudes and commitment, discipline, and energy. We tell him not to meditate within an hour after eating and instruct him to try to be mindful and aware throughout the day, moment to moment.

Before we turn to muscle relaxation, review Learning Activity 15.1 for meditation. Try to make time for these exercises either on your own or with another person.

THE RELAXATION RESPONSE

The relaxation response is a physical state of rest and calm that alters our emotional and physical responses to stress.

The following steps illustrate the relaxation response (Benson, 1987; Benson & Stuart, 1992); they are summarized in Table 15.1.

Treatment Rationale

Here is an example of a rationale for meditation adapted from Benson and Stuart (1992, p. 46):

> Meditation is one technique for eliciting the relaxation response. It builds upon a process of focusing the mind on an object or activity, something you naturally do most of the time. In this use of meditation, you turn your attention inward, concentrating on a repetitive focus such as a word, a phrase, a sound or breathing. Your body and your mind begin to quiet down. A state of physiological and mental rest ensues. But, as we all know too well, the mind is usually very active and difficult to focus.

Instructions about When, Where, and How Long to Practice

According to Benson and Stuart (1992), before breakfast is the best time to meditate. Meditating before the daily schedule begins sets a positive tone for the day; this period is usually uncluttered with events and activities. Choosing a regular time is best, so that a routine is developed. Where you practice is very important. Benson and Stuart (1992) recommend selecting a place that is attractive and quiet and feels safe. The place also should be a location where you will be free from distractions and interruptions. Ideally, a person would practice from 10 to 20 minutes once or twice a day. In the beginning, clients may have difficulty setting aside a specific time to meditate and committing to meditate for a particular length of time. They should experiment with different approaches to learn what works best for them.

Instructions about Focusing on a Word, Phrase, or Prayer

One way to focus your mind is to link the focusing to breathing, either by concentrating on the breath or by attending closely to something else. You can focus on a word, phrase, or prayer. You might draw the focal word or sound from your belief system, stemming, for example, from spiritual or religious views, cultural background, or a relationship to nature and the environment. Focus on a positive or calming word such as *love, warm,* or *calm* or simply on calm breathing.

Instructions about Body Position and Eyes

Any posture that is comfortable is appropriate for meditation—lying down on one's back or sitting up. We prefer to meditate while sitting up comfortably, with back straight and well supported. Clients are asked to close their eyes so they can more easily be in the present moment.

Body Scan Relax the Muscles

With the client focused on breathing, the helper can do a quick body scan, from head to feet, or from feet to head. Any of the muscle relaxation procedures described later in the chapter can be used as a prelude to meditation. Basically, the client focuses on different muscle groups and breathes tension out as she or he exhales.

Breathing Instructions

When you instruct clients in breathing, ask them to notice the rising and falling of the abdomen. Have them focus on the air coming in and going out through the nostrils and notice the slightly cooler air entering the nose and the warmer air leaving. As their breathing becomes quieter and more regular, clients may notice a subtle pause when the inhalation ends and before the exhalation begins, and vice versa (Benson & Stuart, 1992, p. 43).

Instructions about a Passive Attitude

Benson and Stuart (1992, p. 47) say that meditation can be like going to a movie: you can choose to become emotionally involved in the movie, or you can pull back, noting that it's just a movie. The practice of meditation allows people to observe or witness their thoughts, feelings, or bodily sensations. In *Thoughts without a Thinker,* Epstein (1995), describes attention during meditation as "diminishing reactivity. . . . Separating out the reactive self from the core experience, the practice of bare attention eventually returns the meditator to a state of unconditional openness" (p. 117). It is like watching a train—just standing or sitting and looking at one car at a time go by without changing your position. You are simply witnessing or observing without using the judging part of your mind. As quickly as one car of the train enters your sight, you let it go and attend to the next car that comes into view. Also, you can instruct clients not to worry about whether the meditation is going "correctly" or how they are doing. Tell them to maintain a passive attitude, let go, and return to their word or breath if judgmental thoughts come to mind.

Instructions about Length of Meditation

Clients are instructed to meditate for 10 to 20 minutes. The helper and client may want to select the length of time for the first meditation before the client begins. We find that 10 minutes may be long enough for the first in-session meditation, although some clients prefer a longer period.

Discussion of Meditation Experience

The helper gets the client's reaction to the just-completed meditative experience. How did the client feel? How did the client handle the distractions? Were any aspects of the experience challenging? If so, which ones? What might be ways to reduce the challenges next time? Were any aspects of the experience positive? If so, which ones? How might this kind of exercise be combined with other change strategies?

Homework and Follow-up

The helper recommends that the client meditate twice or at least once daily for the next week. The helper can help the client identify a quiet place and time to practice during the next week, reminding the client that regular meditation is an important part of the therapeutic and healing process. If there are remaining questions or concerns (e.g., questions about making time, logistics to finding a quiet place, any discomfort), address them and encourage a genuine effort.

MUSCLE RELAXATION: PROCESSES AND USES

Muscle relaxation teaches a person to relax by becoming aware of the sensations of tensing and relaxing major muscle groups. Take a few moments to feel and to become aware of some of these sensations. Make a fist with your preferred (dominant) hand. Clench the fist of that hand. Clench it tightly, and study the tension in your hand and forearm. Feel the sensations of tension. Now release the tension in your fist, hand, and forearm. Relax your hand and rest it. Notice the difference between tension and relaxation. Do the exercise once more, but this time close your eyes. Clench your fist tightly, become aware of the tension in your hand and forearm, and then relax your hand and let the tension flow away. Notice the different sensations of relaxing and tensing your fist.

When you did this exercise, did you notice that your hand and forearm *cannot* be tense and relaxed at the same time? Relaxation is incompatible with tension. Did you notice that you instructed your hand to tense up and then to relax. You sent messages from your head to your hand to impose tension and then to create relaxation. You can cue a muscle group (the hand and forearm, in this case) to perform or respond in a particular manner (tense up and relax). Probably, this exercise was too brief for you to notice changes in other bodily functions. Tension and relaxation can affect blood pressure, heart rate, and respiration rate and also can influence covert processes and the way a person performs or responds overtly: "The long-range goal of muscle relaxation is for the body to monitor instantaneously all of its numerous control signals, and automatically to relieve tensions that are not desired" (McGuigan, 1993, p. 21).

Relaxation training is not new, but it is an increasingly popular technique for dealing with a variety of client concerns. Muscle relaxation has been used to address many emotional and physical states (see Box 15.2). Among them

BOX 15.2 MUSCLE RELAXATION RESEARCH

Aggression

Lopata, C. (2003). Progressive muscle relaxation and aggression among elementary students with emotional or behavioral disorders. *Behavioral Disorders, 28*(2), 162–172.

To, M. Y. F., & Chan, S. (2000). Evaluating the effectiveness of progressive muscle relaxation in reducing the aggressive behaviors of mentally handicapped patients. *Archives of Psychiatric Nursing, 14,* 39–46.

Anger

Nickel, C., Lahmann, C., Tritt, K., Loew, T. H., Rother, W. K., & Nickel, M. K. (2005). Short communication: Stressed aggressive adolescents benefit from progressive muscle relaxation: A random, prospective, controlled trial. *Stress and Health: Journal of the International Society for the Investigation of Stress, 21*(3), 169–175.

Anxiety

Cheung, Y. L., Molassiotis, A., & Chang, A. M. (2003). The effect of progressive muscle relaxation training on anxiety and quality of life after stoma surgery in colorectal cancer patients. *Psycho-Oncology, 12*(3), 254–266.

Asthma

Aboussafy, D., Campbell, T. S., Lavoie, K., Aboud, F. E., & Ditto, B. (2005). Airflow and autonomic responses to stress and relaxation in asthma: The impact of stressor type. *International Journal of Psychophysiology, 57*(3), 195–201.

Nickel, C., Kettler, C., Muehlbacher, M., Lahmann, C., Tritt, K., Fartacek, R., et al. (2005). Effect of progressive muscle relaxation in adolescent female bronchial asthma patients: A randomized, double-blind, controlled study. *Journal of Psychosomatic Research, 59*(6), 393–398.

Nickel, C., Lahmann, C., Muehlbacher, M., Gil, F. P., Kaplan, P., Buschmann, W., et al. (2006). Pregnant women with bronchial asthma benefit from progressive muscle relaxation: A randomized, prospective, controlled trial. *Psychotherapy and Psychosomatics, 75*(4), 237–243.

Children

Klein-Hessling, J., & Lohaus, A. (2002). Benefits and interindividual differences in children's responses to extended and intensified relaxation training. *Anxiety, Stress and Coping: An International Journal, 15*(3), 275–288.

Lohaus, A., & Klein-Hessling, J. (2003). Relaxation in children: Effects of extended and intensified training. *Psychology and Health, 18*(2), 237–249.

Lohaus, A., Klein-Hessling, J., Vogele, C., and Kuhn-Hennighausen, C. (2001). Psychophysiological effects of relaxation training in children. *British Journal of Health Psychology, 6*(2), 197–206.

Creativity

Friedman, R. S., & Forster, J. (2000). The effects of approach and avoidance motor actions on the elements of creative insight. *Journal of Personality and Social Psychology, 79*(4), 477–492.

Fear

Hazlett-Stevens, H., & Borkovec, T. D. (2001). Effects of worry and progressive relaxation on the reduction of fear in speech phobia: An investigation of situational exposure. *Behavior Therapy, 32*(3), 503–517.

Frustration Tolerance

Nakaya, N., Kumano, H., Minoda, K., Koguchi, T., Tanouchi, K., Kanazawa, M., & Fukudo, S. (2004). Preliminary study: Psychological effects of muscle relaxation on juvenile delinquent. *International Journal of Behavioral Medicine, 11*(3), 176–180.

Headache

Grazzi, L., Andrasik, F., D'Amico, D., Leone, M., Usai, S., Kass, S. J., & Bussone, G. (2002). Behavioral and pharmacologic treatment of transformed migraine with analgesic overuse: Outcome at 3 years. *Headache: The Journal of Head and Face Pain, 42*(6), 483–490.

Insomnia

Waters, W. F., Hurry, M. J., Binks, P. G., Carney, C. E., Lajos, L. E., Fuller, K. H. (2003). Behavioral and hypnotic treatments for insomnia subtypes. *Behavioral Sleep Medicine, 1*(2), 81–101.

Music-Assisted Interventions

Robb, S. L. (2000). Music assisted progressive muscle relaxation, progressive muscle relaxation, music listening, and silence: A comparison of relaxation techniques. *Journal of Music Therapy, 37*(1), 2–21.

Nausea

Molassiotis, A. (2000). A pilot study of the use of progressive muscle relaxation training in the management of post-chemotherapy nausea and vomiting. *European Journal of Cancer Care, 9*(4), 230–234.

Stress Reduction

Ghoncheh, S., & Smith, J. C. (2004). Progressive muscle relaxation, yoga stretching, and ABC relaxation theory. *Journal of Clinical Psychology, 60*(1), 131–136.

Marr, A. J. (2006). Relaxation and muscular tension: A biobehavioristic explanation. *International Journal of Stress Management, 13*(2), 131–153.

Matsumoto, M., & Smith, J. C. (2001). Progressive muscle relaxation, breathing exercises, and ABC relaxation theory. *Journal of Clinical Psychology, 57*(12), 1551–1557.

Rausch, S. M., Gramling, S. E., & Auerbach, S. M. (2006). Effects of a single session of large-group meditation and progressive muscle relaxation training on stress reduction, reactivity, and recovery. *International Journal of Stress Management, 13*(3), 273–290.

are aggression, emotionality such as anxiety, anger, frustration tolerance, and fear, as part of exercise interventions, and a range of stress and health problems—asthma, cancer, headaches, HIV/AIDS, hypertension, and insomnia. Also, body-scan relaxation, a technique for muscle relaxation, is an integral part of meditation and yoga training (Kabat-Zinn, 1990; LePage, 1994; Patel, 1993).

The effects of muscle relaxation, like those of any other strategy, are related to satisfactory problem assessment, client characteristics, and the helper's ability to apply the procedure competently and confidently. Practitioners should also heed other cautions: they should not apply relaxation training indiscriminately without first exploring the causes of the client's reported tension. The practitioner probably made a reasonable determination of these root causes during the assessment process. For example, is muscle relaxation a logical strategy for alleviating the client's discomfort? Is it a meaningful component of a broader intervention plan? If the client is experiencing tension in a job situation, the practitioner and client may need to deal first with the client's external situation (the job). If the client is experiencing tension as a result of oppression and discrimination, this condition will need to be targeted for change. Bernstein and Borkovec (1973) point out the difference between dealing with the tension of daily hassles or difficulties and handling the tension of someone who is on the verge of financial disaster. In the latter case, combinations of therapeutic strategies may be necessary.

MUSCLE-RELAXATION PROCEDURE

The muscle-relaxation procedure consists of the following seven components:

1. Treatment rationale
2. Instructions about client dress
3. Creation of a comfortable environment
4. Helper modeling of relaxation exercises
5. Instructions for muscle relaxation
6. Posttraining assessment
7. Homework and follow-up

Each component is described in this section. For detailed descriptions of the steps associated with each part see the Interview Checklist for Muscle Relaxation at the end of the chapter.

Treatment Rationale

Here is an example of one way a helper might explain the *purpose* of relaxation: "This process, if you practice it regularly, can help you become relaxed. The relaxation benefits you derive can help you sleep better at night." An *overview* of the procedure might be this: "The procedure involves

learning to tense and relax different muscle groups in your body. By doing this, you can compare the difference between tenseness and relaxation. This will help you to recognize tension so you can instruct yourself to relax."

In addition, the helper should explain that muscle relaxation is a *skill*. The process of learning will be gradual and will require regular practice. The helper might explain that some discomfort may occur during the relaxation process. If so, the client can move his or her body into a more comfortable position. Finally, the client may experience some floating, warming, or heavy sensations. The helper should inform the client about these possible sensations. The explanation of the rationale for muscle relaxation should be concluded with a probing of the client's willingness to try the procedure.

Instructions about Client Dress

Before the actual training session, clients should be instructed about appropriate clothing. They should wear comfortable clothes such as slacks, a loose-fitting blouse or shirt, or any apparel that will not be distracting during the exercises. Clients who wear contact lenses should be told to wear their regular glasses for the training. They can take off the glasses while going through the exercises. It is uncomfortable to wear contact lenses when your eyes are closed.

Creation of a Comfortable Environment

A comfortable environment is necessary for effective muscle-relaxation training. The training environment should be quiet and free of distracting noises such as ringing telephones, street repair work outside, and airplane sounds. A padded recliner chair should be used, if possible. If the facility cannot afford one, an aluminum lawn chair or recliner covered with a foam pad may be satisfactory. If relaxation training is applied to groups, pads or blankets can be placed on the floor, with pillows to support each client's head. The clients can lie on the floor on their backs, with their legs stretched out and their arms along their sides with palms down.

Helper Modeling of Relaxation Exercises

Just before the relaxation training begins, the helper should model briefly at least a few of the muscle exercises that will be used in training. The helper can start with either the right or the left hand (make a fist, and then relax the hand, opening the fingers; tense and relax the other hand; bend the wrists of both arms and relax them; shrug the shoulders and relax them) and continue demonstrating some of the rest of the exercises. The helper should tell the client that the demonstration is going much faster than the speed at which the client will perform the exercises. The helper should also punctuate the demonstration with comments like "When I clench my biceps like this, I feel the tension in my biceps muscles, and now, when I relax and drop my arms to my side, I notice the difference between the tension that was in my biceps and the relative relaxation I feel now." These comments are used to show clients how to discriminate between tension and relaxation.

Instructions for Muscle Relaxation

Muscle-relaxation training can start after the helper gives the client the rationale for the procedure, answers any questions about relaxation training, instructs the client about what to wear, creates a comfortable environment for the training, and models some of the various muscle-group exercises. In delivering (or reading) the instructions for the relaxation training exercises, the helper's voice should be conversational, not dramatic. We recommend that the helper practice along with the client during the beginning exercises. Practicing initial relaxation exercises with the client can give the helper a sense of timing for delivering the verbalizations of relaxation and tension and may decrease any awkwardness that the client feels about doing "body" exercises.

In instructing the client to tense and relax muscles, remember that you do *not* want to instruct the client to tense up as hard as possible. You do not want the client to strain a muscle. Be careful of your vocabulary when giving instructions. Do not use phrases like "as hard as you can," "sagging or drooping muscles," or "tense the muscles until they feel like they could snap." Sometimes you can supplement instructions to tense and relax with comments about the client's breathing or the experiencing of warm or heavy sensations. These comments may help the client to relax.

The various muscles used for client training can be categorized into 17 groups, 7 groups, or 4 groups (see Table 15.2; Bernstein & Borkovec, 1973). Generally, in initial training sessions, the helper instructs the client to exercise all 17 muscle groups. This may help the client to discriminate sensations of tension and relaxation in different parts of the body. When the client can alternately tense and relax any of the 17 muscles on command, you can gradually reduce the number of muscle groups involved. You can shorten the procedure and train the client in using 7 muscle groups. After learning this process, the client can practice relaxation using only 4 groups. When the client gets to the point of using the relaxation in vivo, exercising 4 muscle groups is much less unwieldy than exercising 17!

We next describe how you, as helper, can instruct the client in relaxation of all 17 muscle groups. First, ask the client to settle back as comfortably as possible—either in a recliner chair or on the floor with the client's head on a pillow. The arms can be alongside the body, resting on the arms of the chair or on the floor, with the palms of the hands down. Then instruct the client to close her or his eyes. Some clients may not wish to do this, or helper and client may decide that it might be more therapeutic for the client's eyes to remain open during training. In such cases, the client can focus on some object in the room or on the ceiling. Tell the client to

listen and to *focus* on your instructions. When presenting instructions for each muscle group, direct the client's attention to the tension, which is held for 5 to 7 seconds, and then to the feelings of relaxation that follow when the client is instructed to relax. Allow about 10 seconds for the client to enjoy the relaxation of each muscle group before you deliver another instruction. Intermittently throughout the instructions, make muscle-group comparisons—for example, "Is your forehead as relaxed as your biceps?" While delivering the instructions, gradually lower your voice and slow the pace of delivery. Usually each muscle group is presented twice in initial training sessions.

Here is a way the helper might proceed with initial training in muscle relaxation, using the 17 muscle groups listed in Table 15.2:

1. *Fist of dominant hand:* "First think about your right arm, your right hand in particular. Clench your right fist. Clench it tightly and study the tension in the hand and in the forearm. Study those sensations of tension. [Pause.] Now let go. Just relax the right hand and let it rest on the arm of the chair [or floor]. [Pause.] And notice the difference between the tension and the relaxation." [10-second pause]

2. *Fist of nondominant hand:* "Now we'll do the same with your left hand. Clench your left fist. Notice the tension [5-second pause], and now relax. Enjoy the difference between the tension and the relaxation." [10-second pause]

3. *One or both wrists:* The helper instructs the client to bend both wrists at the same time or to bend each wrist separately. You might start with the dominant arm if you instruct the client to bend the wrists one at a time. "Now bend both hands back at the wrists so that you tense the muscles in the back of the hand and in the forearm. Point your fingers toward the ceiling. Study the tension, and now relax. [Pause.] Study the difference between tension and relaxation." [10-second pause]

4. *Biceps of one or both arms:* The helper instructs the client to work with both biceps or one at a time. If you train the client to exercise one at a time, start with the dominant biceps. "Now clench both your hands into fists and bring them toward your shoulders. As you do this, tighten your biceps muscles, the ones in the upper part of your arm. Feel the tension in these muscles. [Pause.] Now relax. Let your arms drop down to your sides. See the difference between the tension and the relaxation." [10-second pause]

5. *Shoulders:* Usually the client is instructed to shrug both shoulders. However, the client could be instructed to shrug one shoulder at a time. "Now we'll move to the shoulder area. Shrug your shoulders. Bring them up to your ears. Feel and hold the tension

TABLE 15.2	Relaxation Exercises for 17, 7, and 4 Muscle Groups	
17 Muscle Groups	**7 Muscle Groups**	**4 Muscle Groups**
1. Clenching *fist* of dominant *hand*	1. Hold *dominant arm* in front with elbow bent at about a 45-degree angle while making a *fist* (hand, lower arm, and biceps muscles).	1. Right and left *arms, hands,* and *biceps* (same as 1 and 2 in 7-muscle group)
2. Clenching *fist* of nondominant *hand*	2. Same exercise with *nondominant arm.*	2. *Face* and *neck* muscles. Tense all *face* muscles (same as 3 and 4 in 7-muscle group)
3. Bending *wrist* of one or both arms	3. Facial muscle groups. Wrinkle *forehead* (or frown), squint *eyes,* wrinkle up *nose,* clench *jaws* or press *tongue* on roof of mouth, press *lips* or pull corners of mouth back.	3. *Chest, shoulders, back,* and *stomach* muscles (same as 5 in 7-muscle group)
4. Clenching *biceps* (one at a time or together)	4. Press or bury *chin* in chest (neck and throat).	4. Both left and right upper *leg, calf,* and *foot* (combines 6 and 7 in 7-muscle group)
5. Shrugging *shoulders* (one at a time or together)	5. *Chest, shoulders, upper back,* and *abdomen.* Take deep breath, hold it, pull shoulder blades back and together, while making stomach hard (pulling in).	
6. Wrinkling *forehead*	6. *Dominant thigh, calf,* and *foot.* Lift foot off chair or floor slightly while pointing toes and turning foot inward.	
7. Closing *eyes* tightly	7. Same as 6, with *nondominant thigh, calf,* and *foot.*	
8. Pressing *tongue* or clenching *jaws*		
9. Pressing *lips* together		
10. Pressing *head* back (on chair or pillow)		
11. Pushing *chin* into chest		
12. Arching *back*		
13. Inhaling and holding *chest muscles*		
14. Tightening *stomach* muscles		
15. Contracting *buttocks**		
16. Stretching *legs*		
17. Pointing *toes* toward head		

*This muscle group can be eliminated; its use is optional.

Source: Progressive Relaxation Training: A Manual for Helping Professions, by D. A. Bernstein and T. D. Borkovec. Copyright 1973 by Research Press. Used by permission.

in your shoulders. [Pause.] Now, let both shoulders relax. Notice the contrast between the tension and the relaxation that's now in your shoulders." [10-second pause]

6. *Forehead:* This and the next three exercises are for the facial muscles. Here are the instructions for the forehead: "Now we'll work on relaxing the various muscles of the face. First, wrinkle up your forehead and brow. Do this until you feel your brow furrow. [Pause.] Now relax. Smooth out the forehead. Let it loosen up." [10-second pause]

7. *Eyes:* The purpose of this exercise is to allow the client to recognize the difference between tension and relaxation of the muscles that control eye movements. "Now close your eyes tightly. Can you feel tension all around your eyes? [5-second pause] Now relax those muscles, noticing the difference between the tension and the relaxation." [10-second pause]

8. *Tongue or jaws:* You can instruct some clients to clench their jaws: "Now clench your jaw by biting your teeth together. Pull the corners of your mouth back. Study the tension in your jaw. [5-second pause] Relax your jaw now. Can you tell the difference between tension and relaxation in your jaw area?" [10-second pause] This exercise may be difficult for some clients who wear dentures. An alternative exercise is to instruct them to "Press your tongue into the roof of your mouth. Notice the tension within your mouth. [5-second pause] Relax your mouth and tongue now. Just concentrate on the relaxation." [10-second pause]

9. *Lips:* The last facial exercise involves the mouth and chin muscles. "Now press your lips together tightly. As you do this, notice the tension all around the mouth. [Pause.] Now relax those muscles around the mouth. Enjoy this relaxation in your mouth area and

your entire face. [Pause.] Is your face as relaxed as your biceps [intermuscle-group comparison]?"

10. *Head:* "Now we'll move to the neck muscles. Press your head back against your chair. Can you feel the tension in the back of your neck and in your upper back? Hold the tension. [Pause.] Now let your head rest comfortably. Notice the difference. Keep on relaxing." [10-second pause]

11. *Chin in chest:* This exercise focuses on the muscles in the neck, particularly the front of the neck. "Now continue to concentrate on the neck area. Bring your head forward. See whether you can bury your chin into your chest. Notice the tension in the front of your neck. Now relax and let go." [10-second pause]

12. *Back:* Be careful: you don't want the client to get a sore back. "Now direct your attention to your upper back area. Arch your back as if you were sticking out your chest and stomach. Can you feel tension in your back? Study that tension. [Pause.] Now relax. Notice the difference between the tension and the relaxation." [10-second pause]

13. *Chest muscles:* Inhaling (filling the lungs) and holding the breath focuses the client's attention on the muscles in the chest and down into the stomach area. "Now take a deep breath, filling your lungs, and hold it. Feel the tension all through your chest and into your stomach area. Hold that tension. [Pause.] Now relax and let go. Let your breath out naturally. Enjoy the pleasant sensations." [10-second pause]

14. *Stomach muscles:* "Now think about your stomach. Tighten up the muscles in your abdomen. Hold this tension. Make your stomach like a knot. Now relax. Loosen those muscles now. [10-second pause] Is your stomach as relaxed as your back and chest [muscle-group comparison]?" An alternative instruction is to tell the client to "pull in your stomach" or "suck in your stomach."

15. *Buttocks:* Moving down to other areas of the body, the helper instructs or coaches the client to tighten the buttocks. Exercising this muscle group, however, is optional. With some clients, the helper may ignore it and move on to the legs. The model instructions are as follows: "Focus now on your buttocks. Tense your buttocks by pulling them together or contracting them. Notice the tension. And now relax. Let go and relax." [10-second pause]

16. *Legs:* "I'd like you now to focus on your legs. Stretch both legs. Feel tension in your thighs. [5-second pause] Now relax. Study the difference again between tension in the thighs and the relaxation you feel now." [10-second pause]

17. *Toes:* "Now concentrate on your lower legs and feet. Tighten both calf muscles by pointing your toes toward your head. Pretend a string is pulling your toes up. Can you feel the pulling and the tension? Notice that tension. [Pause.] Now relax. Let your legs relax deeply.

Enjoy the difference between tension and relaxation." [10-second pause]

After each muscle group has been tensed and relaxed twice, the helper usually concludes relaxation training with a summary and review. The helper goes through the review by listing each muscle group and asking the client to dispel any tension that is noted as the helper names the muscle area. Here is an example:

Now I'm going to go over once more the muscle groups that we've covered. As I name each group, try to notice whether there is any tension in those muscles. If there is any, try to concentrate on those muscles and tell them to relax. Think of draining any remaining tension out of your body as we do this. Now relax the muscles in your feet, ankles, and calves. [Pause.] Get rid of tension in your knees and thighs. [Pause.] Loosen your hips. [Pause.] Let the muscles of your lower body go. [Pause.] Relax your abdomen, waist, lower back. [Pause.] Drain the tension from your upper back, chest, and shoulders. [Pause.] Relax your upper arms, forearms, and hands. [Pause.] Loosen the muscles of your throat and neck. [Pause.] Relax your face. [Pause.] Let all the tension drain out of your body. [Pause.] Now sit quietly with your eyes closed.

The practitioner can conclude the training session by evaluating the client's level of relaxation on a scale from 0 to 5 or by counting aloud to the client to instruct him or her to become successively more alert. For example:

Now I'd like you to think of a scale from 0 to 5, where 0 is *complete relaxation* and 5 is *extreme tension*. Tell me where you would place yourself on that scale now. I'm going to count from 5 to 1. When I reach the count of 1, open your eyes. Five . . . four . . . three . . . two . . . one. Open your eyes now.

Posttraining Assessment

After the session of relaxation training, the helper asks the client about the experience: "What is your reaction to the procedure?" "How do you feel?" "What reaction did you have when you focused on the tension?" "What about relaxation?" "How did the contrast between the tension and relaxation feel?" The helper should be encouraging about the client's performance, praise the client, and build positive expectations about the training and practice.

People experiencing relaxation training may have several difficulties or symptoms of stress (Bernstein & Borkovec, 1973). Some potential difficulties are cramps, excessive laughter or talking, spasms or tics, intrusive thoughts, falling asleep, inability to relax individual muscle groups, unfamiliar sensations, and holding the breath. If the client experiences muscle cramps, possibly too much tension is being created in the muscle group being exercised. In this case, the helper can instruct the client to decrease the amount of tension. If spasms and tics occur in certain muscle groups, the helper can mention that these occur commonly, as in one's sleep, and that possibly the reason the client is aware of them now is that he or she is awake. Excessive laughter or talking are most likely to occur in group-administered relaxation training. Possibly the best solution is to ignore it or to discuss how such behavior can be distracting.

A common training issue is for the client to fall asleep during relaxation training. The client should be informed that continually falling asleep can impede learning the skills associated with muscle relaxation. By watching the client throughout training, the helper can confirm whether the client is awake. The helper also can tell the client to "stay awake" during the muscle-relaxation process.

If the client has difficulty or is unable to relax a particular muscle group, the helper and client might work out an alternative exercise for that muscle group. If intrusive client thoughts become too distracting, the helper might suggest changing the focus of thought to something less distracting or to more positive or pleasant thoughts. It might be better for some clients to gaze at a picture of their choosing placed on the wall or ceiling throughout the training. Another strategy for dealing with interfering or distracting thoughts is to help the client use task-oriented coping statements or thoughts that would aid in focusing on the relaxation training.

Another potential difficulty is the occurrence of unfamiliar sensations, such as floating, warmth, and headiness. The helper should point out that these sensations are common and that the client should not fear them. Finally, some clients have a tendency to hold their breath while tensing a muscle. The helper needs to observe the client's breathing during muscle relaxation. If the client is holding the breath, the helper can instruct the client to breathe freely and easily.

Homework and Follow-up

The last step in muscle relaxation is assigning homework. Four or five training sessions with two daily home practice sessions between training sessions are probably sufficient. Some practitioners have found that minimal helper contact with the client and home-based relaxation training using manuals and audiotapes with telephone consultation were just as effective in reducing tension headaches as six hours of helper-assisted training. Regardless of the amount of time or the number of training sessions with the client, the helper should inform the client that relaxation training, like learning any skill, requires a great deal of practice.

The more the client practices the procedure, the more proficient he or she will become in gaining control over tension, anxiety, or stress. The client should be instructed to select a quiet place for practice, free from distracting noise. The client should be encouraged to practice the muscle-relaxation exercises about 15 to 20 minutes twice a day. The exercises should be done when there is no time pressure.

Some clients may not be willing to practice twice a day. The practitioner can encourage these clients to practice several times or as often as they can during the week. The exercises can be done in a recliner chair or on the floor, with a pillow supporting the head.

The client should be encouraged to complete a homework log after each practice. Figure 15.1 is an example of a homework log. Clients can rate their reactions on a scale from 1 (little or no tension) to 5 (extremely tense) before and after each practice. They can practice the relaxation exercises using a tape recording of the relaxation instructions or from memory. After client homework practices, a follow-up session should be scheduled.

A practitioner can use several techniques to promote client compliance with relaxation homework assignments. One technique is to ask the client to demonstrate during the training session how the exercises for the muscles in the neck or the calf, for example, were done during last week's home practice. The helper can select randomly from four or five muscle groups for the client to demonstrate. If the exercises are demonstrated accurately, the client probably practiced.

CONTRAINDICATIONS AND ADVERSE EFFECTS OF MUSCLE RELAXATION

Generally, muscle relaxation is benign and pleasant, but for some people it can have adverse side effects—for example, clients with generalized anxiety disorder, panic disorder, or a history of hyperventilation (Bernstein & Carlson, 1993, p. 66). Some clients with certain muscles or connective tissues that have been damaged or are chronically weak will have difficulty in tensing and relaxing a particular muscle group. Also, some clients are incapable of exercising voluntary control over all muscles in the body because of a neuromuscular disability. Finally, a medical consultation may be necessary before beginning muscle-relaxation training with clients who are taking certain types of medication. Some clients who are taking medications for diabetes or for hypertension may require a change in the amount of medication they need (Bernstein & Carlson, 1993, p. 67). Be sure to seek a medical consultation if there is a question about medications.

In cases of anxiety or panic disorders, the helping practitioner can start with stress reduction breathing exercises such as diaphragmatic breathing (Patel, 1993). If a client has difficulty with a particular muscle group, the helper can avoid that group or do a body scan. Herman (1994) notes that relaxation is often contraindicated for clients who present with severe trauma histories, because of their need to maintain some degree of vigilance in order to feel safe. Similarly, Taylor's (2004) findings indicate relaxation training is relatively ineffective in treatment of posttraumatic stress disorder and exposure treatment is highly effective both in short- and longer-term outcomes.

					Level of Tension (1–5)	
			Homework Log Sheet			
Date	Tape Number	Exercised Muscle Groups	Practice Session Number	Session Location	Before Session	After Session

Figure 15.1 Example of Homework Log Sheet for Relaxation Training

Note: 1 = slightly or not tense; 2 = somewhat tense; 3 = moderately tense; 4 = very tense; 5 = extremely tense.

VARIATIONS OF MUSCLE RELAXATION

There are several variations of the muscle-relaxation procedure as we've described it. These variations—recall, counting, differential relaxation, and body scan—are introduced, first explaining these relaxation skills, having the client practice them in session, and then the client applying these skills in real-life situations. The 4-muscle-group exercises listed in Table 15.2 can be used in combination with the recall and counting procedures described by Bernstein and Borkovec (1973).

Recall

Recall proceeds according to the relaxation exercises for the 4 muscle groups (see Table 15.2). The helper first provides the client with the rationale for using this variation of relaxation training: "To increase your relaxation skills without needing to tense up your muscles." The client is asked to focus on one of the 4 muscle groups (arms; face and neck; chest, shoulders, back, and stomach; or legs and feet) and to relax and recall what it was like in the previous session when the client released the tension in that particular group of muscles. The helper might suggest that when there is tension in a particular muscle group, the client should relax or send a message for the muscle to relax and should allow the tension to "flow away." The helper gives similar instructions for all 4 muscle groups, encouraging, the client to recall how the relaxation of each group felt. Clients can use recall after learning the tension/relaxation-contrast procedure for the 4 muscle groups. Gradually, the client is able to use recall to induce relaxation in self-directed practice. Recall also can be used in combination with counting.

Counting

The rationale for counting is that it helps the client become very deeply relaxed. The helper explains this rationale. Then the helper says that she or he will count from 1 to 10 and that the client is likely to become increasingly relaxed after each number. The helper might say the following, slowly:

> One—you are becoming more relaxed; two—notice that your arms and hands are becoming more and more relaxed; three—feel your face and neck becoming more relaxed; four, five—more and more relaxed are your chest and shoulders; six—further and further relaxed; seven—back and stomach feel deeply relaxed; eight—further and further relaxed; nine—your legs and feet are more and more relaxed; ten—just continue to relax as you are—relax more and more.

The helper can use counting with recall and can instruct the client to use counting in real situations that provoke tension. Counting is a direct-action coping skill used in stress inoculation; it can increase relaxation and decrease tension, and the client should be encouraged to practice it outside the session. For a more detailed presentation of counting, see Bernstein and Borkovec (1973).

Differential Relaxation

Differential relaxation may contribute to generalization of relaxation training from the treatment session to the client's world. The purpose of differential relaxation is to help the client distinguish the muscles that are needed in various situations, body positions, and activities from the muscle groups that are not used. Table 15.3 describes two levels of differential relaxation.

TABLE 15.3	Levels of Differential Relaxation	
Situation	**Body Position**	**Activity Level**
Quiet	Sitting	Low—inactive
Noisy	Standing	High—routine movements

Here is an example of the differential-relaxation procedure. The helper has the client, Jake, sit in a regular chair (not a recliner) and asks Jake to identify which muscles are used and which are not used when he is sitting. If Jake feels tension in muscles (face, legs, and stomach) that are *not* required for what he is doing (sitting), the helper instructs him to induce and to maintain relaxation in those muscles. The helper instructs Jake to engage in the differential-relaxation procedure in different settings and levels of activity—for example, sitting in a quiet place while he is inactive, and standing in a noisy place. When practicing differential relaxation, Jake tries to recognize whether any tension exists in *nonessential* muscle groups. If there is tension in the *nonengaged* muscles, he concentrates on dispelling it. After several practice sessions, the client can be assigned homework to practice differential relaxation in various places, such as while sitting in a quiet cafeteria, sitting in a noisy cafeteria while eating, standing in line to buy a ticket for some event, and walking in a busy shopping center.

Body Scan

Body scaning can be a powerful technique for reestablishing contact with the body because it provides a way to develop concentration and flexibility of attention simultaneously (Kabat-Zinn, 1990, p. 77). The purpose of the body scan is to permit the client to feel each region of the body or each muscle group. Listening to the helper's instructions, the client focuses every breath on a region of the body, inhaling into the region and exhaling out of the region. If the client feels tension in one region, the helper instructs the client to breathe the tension out on the exhalation. In Box 15.3 we offer a script for body scanning (LePage, 1994, pp. 6.15–6.16) using cues to focus on the breath throughout the instructions. Body scans are useful variations of the traditional method of muscle relaxation for clients who tend to hold their breath while tensing their muscles. Instructions for deep muscle relaxation with little focus on breathing can be found in Patel (1993, pp. 123–124).

MODEL DIALOGUE FOR MUSCLE RELAXATION: THE CASE OF ISABELLA

In this dialogue, the helper demonstrates relaxation training to help Isabella deal with her physical sensations of nervousness. First, the helper gives Isabella a *rationale* for relaxation.

The helper explains the *purpose* of muscle relaxation and provides a brief *overview* of the procedure.

1. **Helper:** Basically, we all learn to carry around some body tension. Some is okay. But in a tense spot, usually your body becomes even more tense, although you may not realize this. If you can learn to recognize muscle tension and relax your muscles, this state of relaxation can help to decrease your nervousness or anxiety. What we'll do is to help you recognize when your body is relaxed and when it is tense by deliberately tensing and relaxing different muscle groups in your body. We should get to the point where, later on, you can recognize the sensations that mean tension and use them as a signal to yourself to relax. Does this make sense?

Client: I think so. You'll sort of tell me how to do this?

Next, the helper *"sets up"* the relaxation by attending to details about the room and the client's comfort.

2. **Helper:** Yes. At first I'll show you so you can get the idea of it. One thing we need to do before we start is for you to get as comfortable as possible. So that you won't be distracted by light, I'm going to turn off the light. If you are wearing your contact lenses, take them out if they're uncomfortable, because you may feel more comfortable if you go through this with your eyes closed. Also, I use a special chair for this. You know the straight-backed chair you're sitting on can seem like a rock after a time. That might distract too. So I have a padded chaise you can use for this. [Gets lounge chair out.]

Client (sits in chaise): Umm. This really is comfortable.

Next, the helper begins *to model the muscle relaxation* for Isabella. This demonstration shows her how to do it and may alleviate any embarrassment on her part.

3. **Helper:** Good. That really helps. Now I'm going to show you how you can tense and then relax your muscles. I'll start first with my right arm. [Clenches right fist, pauses and notes tension, relaxes fist, pauses and notes relaxation; models several other muscle groups.] Does this give you an idea?

| BOX 15.3 | BODY-SCAN SCRIPT |

Allow the body to begin to completely relax. . . . Inhale and feel the breath flow from the soles of the feet to the crown of the head, like a gentle slow motion wave. With each exhalation allow tension to flow out of the body. Bring your awareness to the fingers of the left hand. Inhale breath and awareness through the fingers and up the left arm. Exhale, release the arm into the support of the earth. . . . Allow relaxation to deepen with each exhalation. Now bring your awareness to the right fingertips and inhale the breath up the arm, exhale and completely relax. As you relax the arms, become more aware of all the feelings and sensations. . . . Focus all of your awareness into these sensations and then relax into them.

Now bring your awareness down to the toes of the left foot, drawing the wave of breath up to the top of the leg, and on exhalation relax the leg fully. Now bring your awareness into the right leg, and allow the wave of breath to flow up the right leg, and with the exhalation completely surrender the weight of the leg. Feel and see both legs now and with each breath become more aware of all the sensations in the legs, with each exhalation relax even more deeply. Listen to the sound of the waves as the breath flows through the body.

Now bring the breath and your awareness up into the hips, pelvis and buttocks. On the inhalation feel the pelvis area naturally expand and exhaling allow it rest down into the earth. . . . With each inhalation feel the pelvic floor being drawn gently up into the abdomen and with each exhalation allow it to completely release. Feel the wave of breath rising up from the pelvis filling the abdomen. Feel the abdomen rise and fall, and explore the abdomen with your awareness. With each exhalation the abdomen becomes softer and softer. Feel this softness touch the lower back and feel the breath there. Explore the sensations in the low back and then allow this area to soften into the earth.

Now allow breath and awareness to flow up the spine. With each inhalation, the spine fills with sensation. With each exhalation, the spine relaxes into the earth. Feeling the breath now through the entire back. Inhaling, sensing; exhaling, completely relaxing.

Now bring your awareness again to the rising and falling of the abdomen. As you inhale draw the breath up into the solar plexus filling that area fully with breath and awareness. And as you exhale, relax into the center of that awareness. Now focus the breath up into the heart and lungs, and with each exhalation relax deeper and deeper into the center of the heart.

Draw the breath into the neck and throat. Exhale, allowing any tension to be released. . . . Allow the breath to flow up through the head, with each inhalation become more aware of the sensations, with each exhalation, relax. Relax the jaw, the eyes, the forehead and the back of the head, soften the inner ears, and relax into the earth.

Feel the entire body now washed by a gentle wave of breath from the soles of the feet and the tips of the fingers, all the way to the crown of the head. Feel the peace and complete relaxation as the breath becomes softer and softer. Feel the sensations in the body becoming softer and more subtle and relax into them.

Now allow the wave of breath to be felt a little more strongly, rising up through the soles of the feet, and rising and falling in the abdomen. As the breath becomes stronger allow the sensations in the body to increase. Let the body gently begin to move with the breath. Move the toes and fingers. . . . Allow the whole body to begin to gently stretch. Remaining with the eyes closed, begin to gently roll over onto the right side. Let every movement be an experience of awareness. Over the next minute come up into a seated position. And as you come to the seated position, feel the deep three-part breath and experience how the body, breath and mind are in balance.

Source: Integrative Yoga Therapy Manual, by Joseph LePage, pp. 6.22–6.23. Copyright © 1994 by Integrative Yoga Therapy, Aptos, CA. Used by permission.

Client: Yes. You don't do your whole body?

The helper provides *further information about muscle relaxation, describes sensations* Isabella might feel, and checks to see whether she is completely clear about the procedure before going ahead.

4. **Helper:** Yes, you do. But we'll take each muscle group separately. By the time you tense and relax each muscle group, your whole body will feel relaxed. You will feel like you are "letting go," which is very important when you tense up—to let go rather than to tense even more. Now, you might not notice a lot of difference right away—but you might. You might even feel like you're floating. This really depends on the person. The most important thing is to remain as comfortable as possible while I'm instructing you. Do you have any questions before we begin, anything you don't quite understand?

Client: I don't think so. I think that this is maybe a little like yoga.

The helper proceeds with *instructions to alternately tense and relax* each of 17 muscle groups.

5. **Helper:** Right. It's based on the same idea—learning to soothe away body tension. Okay, get very comfortable in your chair, and we'll begin. [Gives Isabella several minutes to get comfortable, then uses the relaxation instructions. Most of the session is spent in instructing Isabella in muscle relaxation as described earlier in this chapter.]

LEARNING ACTIVITY 15.2 | Muscle Relaxation

Because muscle relaxation involves the alternate tensing and relaxing of muscle groups, learning the procedure well enough to use it with a client is sometimes difficult. The easiest way for you to learn muscle relaxation is to do it yourself. This not only helps you learn what is involved but also may bring indirect benefits for you—increased relaxation!

In this activity, you will apply the muscle-relaxation procedure you've just read about to yourself. You can do this by yourself or with a partner. You may wish to try it out alone and then with someone else.

By Yourself

1. Get in a comfortable position, wear loose clothing, and remove your glasses or contact lenses.
2. Use the written instructions in this chapter to practice muscle relaxation. You can do this by putting the instructions on tape or by reading the instructions to yourself. Go through the procedure quickly to get a feel for the process; then do it again slowly without trying to rely too much on having to read the instructions. As you go through the procedure, study the differences between tension and relaxation.
3. Try to assess your reactions after the relaxation. On a scale from 0 to 5 (0 being *very relaxed* and 5 being *very tense*), how relaxed do you feel? Were there any particular muscle groups that were hard for you to contract or relax?
4. One or two times through muscle relaxation is not enough to learn it or to notice any effects. Try to practice this procedure on yourself once or twice daily over the next several weeks.

With a Partner

One person takes the role of helper; the other person is the client learning relaxation. Switch roles so you can practice helping someone else through the procedure and trying it out on yourself.

1. The helper gives you an explanation and a rationale for muscle relaxation and any instructions about it before beginning the procedure.
2. The helper reads the instructions on muscle relaxation to you. The helper should give you ample time to tense and relax each muscle group and should encourage you to notice the different sensations associated with tension and relaxation.
3. After going through the process, the helper should query you about your relaxation level and your reactions to the process.

After the relaxation, the helper *queries Isabella* about her feelings during and after the relaxation. It is important to find out how the relaxation affected the client.

6. **Helper:** Isabella; how do you feel now?

Client: Pretty relaxed.

7. **Helper:** How did the contrast between the tensed and relaxed muscles feel?

Client: It was pretty easy to tell. I guess sometimes my body is pretty tense, and I don't think about it.

The helper assigns *relaxation practice* to Isabella as *daily homework.*

8. **Helper:** As I mentioned before, this takes regular practice in order for you to use it when you need it—and to really notice the effects. I have put these instructions on this audiotape, and I'd like you to practice with this tape each day during the next week. Do the practice in a quiet place at a time when you don't feel pressured, and use a comfortable place when you do practice. Do you have any questions about the practice?

Client: No, I think I understand.

Helper *explains the use of the log.*

9. **Helper:** Also, I'd like you to use a log sheet with your practice. Mark down where you practice, how long you practice, what muscle groups you use, and your tension level before and after each practice on this 5-point scale. Remember, zero means *complete relaxation,* and 5 means *complete or extreme tension.* Let's go over an example of how you use the log. . . . Now, any questions?

Client: No. I can see this will take some practice.

Finally, the helper arranges a *follow-up.*

10. **Helper:** Right, it really is like learning any other skill. It doesn't just come automatically. Why don't you try this on your own for two weeks and then come back, Okay?

Learning Activity 15.2 outlines exercises that can help familiarize you with muscle relaxation.

CHAPTER SUMMARY

In this chapter we describe two meditation strategies—mindfulness meditation and the relaxation response—a procedure for muscle relaxation, and two body-scan scripts. These and other meditation strategies can be used in vivo. Helpers must be aware that techniques such as meditation and muscle relaxation can have contraindications and adverse effects for some clients. The muscle-relaxation strategy can be used with 17, 7, or 4 muscle groups. All these strategies are often used as a single treatment to prevent stress and to deal with stress-related situations. In addition, they can be used as complements to other stress management interventions, exposure therapies, and other interventions (such as problem solving and self-management) in which additional aids for relaxation or mindfulness appear indicated.

REFERENCES

Aboussafy, D., Campbell, T. S., Lavoie, K., Aboud, F. E., & Ditto, B. (2005). Airflow and autonomic responses to stress and relaxation in asthma: The impact of stressor type. *International Journal of Psychophysiology, 57*(3), 195–201.

Alexander, C. N., Robinson, P., Orme-Johnson, D. W., & Schneider, R. (1994). The effects of transcendental meditation compared to other methods of relaxation and meditation in reducing risk factors, morbidity, and mortality. *Homeostasis in Health and Disease, 35,* 243–263.

Baer, R. A. (2003). Mindfulness training as a clinical intervention: A conceptual and empirical review. *Clinical Psychology: Science and Practice, 10*, 125–143.

Baer, R. A., Smith, Gregory T., Hopkins, J., Krietemeyer, J., & Toney, L. (2006). Using self-report assessment methods to explore facets of mindfulness. *Assessment, 13*(1), 27–45.

Benson, H. (1987). *Your maximum mind.* New York: Avon.

Benson, H., & Stuart, E. M. (1992). *The wellness book: The comprehensive guide to maintaining health and treating stress-related illness.* New York: Birch Lane.

Bernstein, D. A., & Borkovec, T. D. (1973). *Progressive relaxation training: A manual for helping professions.* Champaign, IL: Research Press.

Bernstein, D. A., & Carlson, C. R. (1993). Progressive relaxation: Abbreviated methods. In P. M. Lehrer & R. L. Woolfolk (Eds.), *Principles and practice of stress management* (2nd ed., pp. 53–87). New York: Guilford Press.

Bishop, S. R. (2002). What do we really know about mindfulness-based stress reduction? *Psychosomatic Medicine, 64,* 71–84.

Bogels, S. M., Sijbers, G. F. V. M., & Voncken, M. (2006). Mindfulness and task concentration training for social phobia: A pilot study. *Journal of Cognitive Psychotherapy, 20*(1), 33–44.

Borkovec, T. D., Alcaine, O., & Behar, E. (2004). Avoidance theory of worry and generalized anxiety disorder. In R. G. Heimberg, C. L. Turk, & D. S. Mennin (Eds.), *Generalized anxiety disorder: Advances in research and practice* (pp. 77–108). New York: Guilford Press.

Borysenko, J. (1987). *Minding the body, mending the mind.* New York: Bantam.

Bowen, S., Witkiewitz, K., Dillworth, T. M., Chawla, N., Simpson, T. L., Ostafin, B. D., et al. (2006). Mindfulness meditation and substance use in an incarcerated population. *Psychology of Addictive Behaviors, 20*(3), 343–347.

Brazier, A., Mulkins, A., & Verhoef, M. (2006). Evaluating a yogic breathing and meditation intervention for individuals living with HIV/AIDS. *American Journal of Health Promotion, 20*(3), 192–195.

Broderick, P. C. (2005). Mindfulness and coping with dysphoric mood: Contrasts with rumination and distraction. *Cognitive Therapy and Research, 29*(5), 501–510.

Cahn, B. R., & Polich, J. (2006). Meditation states and traits: EEG, ERP, and neuroimaging studies. *Psychological Bulletin,132*(2), 180–211.

Carlson, L. E., & Garland, S. N. (2005). Impact of mindfulness-based stress reduction (MBSR) on sleep, mood, stress and fatigue symptoms in cancer outpatients. *International Journal of Behavioral Medicine, 12*(4), 278–285.

Carrington, P. (1993). Modern forms of meditation. In P. M. Lehrer & R. L. Woolfolk (Eds.), *Principles and practice of stress management* (2nd ed., pp. 139–168). New York: Guilford Press.

Carrington, P. (1998). *The book of meditation.* Boston: Element.

Cheung, Y. L., Molassiotis, A., & Chang, A. M. (2003). The effect of progressive muscle relaxation training on anxiety and quality of life after stoma surgery in colorectal cancer patients. *Psycho-Oncology, 12*(3), 254–266.

Christopher, J. C., Christopher, S. E., Dunnagan, T., & Schure, M. (2006). Teaching self-care through mindfulness practices: The application of yoga, meditation, and Qigong to counselor training. *Journal of Humanistic Psychology, 46*(4), 494–509.

Connolly, M. J. (1993). Respiratory rehabilitation in the elderly patient. *Reviews in Clinical Gerontology, 3,* 281–294.

Curiati, J. A., Bocchi, E., Freire, J. O., Arantes, A. C., Braga, M., Garcia, Y., et al. (2005). Meditation reduces sympathetic activation and improves the quality of life in elderly patients with optimally treated heart failure: A prospective randomized study. *Journal of Alternative and Complementary Medicine, 11*(3), 465–472.

Dimidjian, S., & Linehan, M. M. (2003). Defining an agenda for future research on the clinical application of mindfulness practice. *Clinical Psychology: Science and Practice, 10*, 166–171.

Ditto, B., Eclache, M., & Goldman, N. (2006). Short-term autonomic and cardiovascular effects of mindfulness body scan meditation. *Annals of Behavioral Medicine, 32*(3), 227–234.

Emavardhana, T., & Tori, C. D. (1997). Changes in self-concept, ego defense mechanisms, and religiosity following seven-day Vipassana meditation retreats. *Journal for the Scientific Study of Religion, 36,* 194–206.

Epstein, M. (1995). *Thoughts without the thinker.* New York: Basic.

Fontana, D. (1991). *The elements of meditation.* New York: Element.

Friedman, R. S., & Forster, J. (2000). The effects of approach and avoidance motor actions on the elements of creative insight. *Journal of Personality and Social Psychology, 79*(4), 477–492.

Galantino, M. L., Baime, M., Maguire, M., Szapary, P. O., & Farrar, J. T. (2005). Association of psychological and physiological measures of stress in health-care professionals during an 8-week mindfulness meditation program: Mindfulness in practice. *Stress and Health: Journal of the International Society for the Investigation of Stress, 21*(4), 255–261.

Germer, C. K. (2005). Mindfulness: What is it? What does it matter? In C. K. Germer, R. D. Siegel, & P. R. Fulton (Eds.), *Mindfulness and psychotherapy* (pp. 3–27). New York: Guilford Press.

Germer, C. K., Siegel, R. D., & Fulton, P. R. (Eds.). (2005). *Mindfulness and psychotherapy.* New York: Guilford Press.

Ghoncheh, S., & Smith, J. C. (2004). Progressive muscle relaxation, yoga stretching, and ABC relaxation theory. *Journal of Clinical Psychology, 60*(1), 131–136.

Goleman, D. (1988). *The meditative mind.* New York: Jeremy P. Tarcher/Perigee.

Grazzi, L., Andrasik, F., D'Amico, D., Leone, M., Usai, S., Kass, S. J., & Bussone, G. (2002). Behavioral and pharmacologic treatment of transformed migraine with analgesic overuse: Outcome at 3 years. *Headache: The Journal of Head and Face Pain, 42*(6), 483–490.

Hall, P. (1999). The effect of meditation on the academic performance of African American college students. *Journal of Black Studies, 29,* 408–415.

Hamilton, N. A., Kitzman, H., & Guyotte, S. (2006). Enhancing health and emotion: Mindfulness as a missing link between cognitive therapy and positive psychology. *Journal of Cognitive Psychotherapy, 20*(2), 123–134.

Hayes, S. C., & Strosahl, K. D. (Eds.). (2004). *A practical guide to acceptance and commitment therapy.* New York: Springer.

Hazlett-Stevens, H., & Borkovec, T. D. (2001). Effects of worry and progressive relaxation on the reduction of fear in speech phobia: An investigation of situational exposure. *Behavior Therapy, 32*(3), 503–517.

Herman, J. L. (1994, April). *Women's pathways to healing.* Paper presented at the Learning from Women Conference, Boston.

Holland, D. (2004). Integrating mindfulness meditation and somatic awareness into a public educational setting. *Journal of Humanistic Psychology 44*(4), 468–484.

Kabat-Zinn, J. (1990). *Full catastrophe living.* New York: Dell.

Kabat-Zinn, J. (2003). Mindfulness-based interventions in context: Past, present, and future. *Clinical Psychology: Science and Practice, 10,* 144–156.

Kane, K. E. (2006). The phenomenology of meditation for female survivors of intimate partner violence. *Violence against Women, 12*(5), 501–518.

Klein-Hessling, J., & Lohaus, A. (2002). Benefits and interindividual differences in children's responses to extended and intensified relaxation training. *Anxiety, Stress and Coping: An International Journal, 15*(3), 275–288.

Kurash, C., & Schaul, J. (2006). Integrating mindfulness meditation within a university counseling center setting. *Journal of College Student Psychotherapy, 20*(3), 53–67.

Lau, M. A., & McMain, S. F. (2005). Integrating mindfulness meditation with cognitive and behavioural therapies: The challenge of combining acceptance- and change-based strategies. *Canadian Journal of Psychiatry, 50*(13), 863–869.

Lazar, S. W., Bush, G., Gollub, R. L., Fricchione, G. L., Khalsa, G., & Benson, H. (2000). Functional brain mapping of the relaxation response and meditation. *Neuroreport: For Rapid Communication of Neuroscience Research, 11,* 1581–1585.

LePage, J. (1994). *Integrative yoga therapy manual.* Aptos, CA: Integrative Yoga Therapy.

Linehan, M. M. (1993). *Cognitive–behavioral treatment of borderline personality disorder.* New York: Guilford Press.

Lohaus, A., & Klein-Hessling, J. (2003). Relaxation in children: Effects of extended and intensified training. *Psychology and Health, 18*(2), 237–249.

Lohaus, A., Klein-Hessling, J., Vogele, C., & Kuhn-Hennighausen, C. (2001). Psychophysiological effects of relaxation training in children. *British Journal of Health Psychology, 6*(2), 197–206.

Lopata, C. (2003). Progressive muscle relaxation and aggression among elementary students with emotional or behavioral disorders. *Behavioral Disorders, 28*(2), 162–172.

Marlatt, G. A., & Kristeller, J. L. (1999). Mindfulness and meditation. In W. R. Miller (Ed.), *Integrating spirituality into treatment: Resources for practitioners* (pp. 67–84). Washington, DC: American Psychological Association.

Marr, A. J. (2006). Relaxation and muscular tension: A biobehavioristic explanation. *International Journal of Stress Management, 13*(2), 131–153.

Matsumoto, M., & Smith, J. C. (2001). Progressive muscle relaxation, breathing exercises, and ABC relaxation theory. *Journal of Clinical Psychology, 57*(12), 1551–1557.

McGuigan, F. J. (1993). Progressive relaxation: Origins, principles, and clinical applications. In P. M. Lehrer & R. L. Woolfolk (Eds.), *Principles and practice of stress management* (pp. 17–52). New York: Guilford Press.

Molassiotis, A. (2000). A pilot study of the use of progressive muscle relaxation training in the management of post-chemotherapy nausea and vomiting. *European Journal of Cancer Care, 9*(4), 230–234.

Nakaya, N., Kumano, H., Minoda, K., Koguchi, T., Tanouchi, K., Kanazawa, M., & Fukudo, S. (2004). Preliminary study: Psychological effects of muscle relaxation on juvenile delinquent. *International Journal of Behavioral Medicine, 11*(3), 176–180.

Nickel, C., Kettler, C., Muehlbacher, M., Lahmann, C., Tritt, K., Fartacek, R., et al. (2005). Effect of progressive muscle relaxation in adolescent female bronchial asthma patients: A randomized, double-blind, controlled study. *Journal of Psychosomatic Research, 59*(6), 393–398.

Nickel, C., Lahmann, C., Muehlbacher, M., Gil, F. P., Kaplan, P., Buschmann, W., et al. (2006). Pregnant women with bronchial asthma benefit from progressive muscle relaxation: A randomized, prospective, controlled trial. *Psychotherapy and Psychosomatics, 75*(4), 237–243.

Nickel, C., Lahmann, C., Tritt, K., Loew, T. H., Rother, W. K., & Nickel, M. K. (2005). Short communication: Stressed aggressive adolescents benefit from progressive muscle relaxation: A random, prospective, controlled trial. *Stress and Health: Journal of the International Society for the Investigation of Stress, 21*(3), 169–175.

Nielsen, L., & Kaszniak, A. W. (2006). Awareness of subtle emotional feelings: A comparison of long-term meditators and nonmeditators. *Emotion, 6*(3), 392–405.

Oman, D., Hedberg, J., & Thoresen, C. E. (2006). Passage meditation reduces perceived stress in health professionals: A randomized, controlled trial. *Journal of Consulting and Clinical Psychology, 74*(4), 714–719.

Orsillo, S. M., & Batten, S. V. (2005). ACT in the treatment of PTSD. *Behavioral Modification, 29*, 95–129.

Ott, J. J. (2004). Mindfulness meditation: A path of transformation and healing. *Journal of Psychosocial Nursing and Mental Health Services, 42*(7), 22–29.

Ott, M. J., Longobucco-Hynes, S., & Hynes, V. A. (2002). Mindfulness meditation in pediatric clinical practice. *Pediatric Nursing, 28*(5), 487–490.

Patel, C. (1993). Yoga-based therapy. In P. M. Lehrer & R. L. Woolfolk (Eds.), *Principles and practice of stress management* (2nd ed., pp. 89–137). New York: Guilford Press.

Rausch, S. M., Gramling, S. E., & Auerbach, S. M. (2006). Effects of a single session of large-group meditation and progressive muscle relaxation training on stress reduction, reactivity, and recovery. *International Journal of Stress Management, 13*(3), 273–290.

Robb, S. L. (2000). Music assisted progressive muscle relaxation, progressive muscle relaxation, music listening, and silence: A comparison of relaxation techniques. *Journal of Music Therapy, 37*(1), 2–21.

Ruben, A. (1989). Preventing school dropouts through classroom guidance. *Elementary School Guidance and Counseling, 24*, 21–29.

Sarang, P., & Telles, S. (2006) Effects of two yoga based relaxation techniques on heart rate variability (HRV). *International Journal of Stress Management, 13*(4), 460–475.

Seeman, T. E., Dubin, L. F., & Seeman, M. (2003). Religiosity/spirituality and health: A critical review of the evidence for biological pathways. *American Psychologist, 58*(1), 53–63.

Segal, Z. V., Williams, J. M. G., & Teasdale, J. D. (2002). *Mindfulness-based cognitive therapy for depression: A new approach to preventing relapse.* New York: Guilford Press.

Shigaki, C. L., Glass, B., & Schopp, L. H. (2006). Mindfulness-based stress reduction in medical settings. *Journal of Clinical Psychology in Medical Settings, 13*(3), 209–216.

Takahashi, T., Murata, T., Hamada, T., Omori, M., Kosaka, H., Kikuchi, M., et al. (2005). Changes in EEG and autonomic nervous activity during meditation and their association with personality traits. *International Journal of Psychophysiology, 55*(2), 199–207.

Taylor, S. (2004). Efficacy and outcome predictors for three PTSD treatments: Exposure therapy, EMDR, and relaxation training. In S. Taylor (Ed.), *Advances in the treatment of posttraumatic stress disorder: Cognitive behavioral perspectives* (p. 13–37). New York: Springer.

Telles, S., Mohapatra, R. S., & Naveen, K. V. (2005). Heart rate variability spectrum during Vipassana mindfulness meditation. *Journal of Indian Psychology, 23*(2), 1–5.

To, M. Y. F., & Chan, S. (2000). Evaluating the effectiveness of progressive muscle relaxation in reducing the aggressive behaviors of mentally handicapped patients. *Archives of Psychiatric Nursing, 14*, 39–46.

Tooley, G. A., Armstrong, S. M., Norman, T. R., & Sali, A. (2000). Acute increases in night-time plasma melatonin levels following a period of meditation. *Biological Psychology, 53,* 69–78.

Vigne, J. (1999). Meditation and mental health. *Indian Journal of Clinical Psychology, 24,* 46–51.

von Weiss, D. (2002). Use of mindfulness meditation for fibromyalgia. *American Family Physician, 65*(3), 380–384.

Wall, R. B. (2005). Tai Chi and mindfulness-based stress reduction in a Boston public middle school. *Journal of Pediatric Health Care, 19*(4), 230–237.

Walsh, R., Victor, B., & Bitner, R. (2006). Emotional effects of Sertraline: Novel findings revealed by meditation. *American Journal of Orthopsychiatry, 76*(1), 134–137.

Waters, W. F., Hurry, M. J., Binks, P. G., Carney, C. E., Lajos, L. E., Fuller, K. H., et al. (2003). Behavioral and hypnotic treatments for insomnia subtypes. *Behavioral Sleep Medicine, 1*(2), 81–101.

Wenk-Sormaz, H. (2005). Meditation can reduce habitual responding. *Advances in Mind–Body Medicine, 21*(3–4), 33–49.

Williams, A. L., Selwyn, P. A., Liberti, L., Molde, S., Njike, V. Y., Mccorkle, R., et al. (2005). A randomized controlled trial of meditation and massage effects on quality of life in people with late-stage disease: A pilot study. *Journal of Palliative Medicine, 8*(5), 939–952.

Witkiewitz, K., Marlatt, G. A., & Walker, D. (2005). Mindfulness-based relapse prevention for alcohol and substance use disorders. *Journal of Cognitive Psychotherapy, 19*(3), 211–228.

15 KNOWLEDGE AND SKILL BUILDER

Part One

Learning Outcome 1 asks you to identify the steps of the relaxation response procedure represented by at least seven out of nine helper responses. Match each helper response with the letter of the step that is being implemented. Feedback follows on page 485:

Relaxation Response Steps

a. Treatment rationale
b. Instructions about when, where, and how long to practice
c. Instructions about focusing on a word, phrase, or prayer
d. Breathing instructions
e. Instructions about a passive attitude
f. Meditating for 10 to 20 minutes
g. Probing about the meditative experience
h. Homework and practice

Helper Responses

1. "It is very important that you practice this at home regularly. Usually there are no effects without regular practice—about twice daily."
2. "Find a comfortable place in your home to practice, one free of interruptions and noise."
3. "This procedure has been used to help people with high blood pressure and people who have trouble sleeping and just as a general stress reduction process."
4. "Breathe through your nose and focus on your breathing. If you can concentrate on one word as you do this, it may be easier."
5. "Be sure to practice at a quiet time when you don't think you'll be interrupted. And do not practice within two hours after a meal or within two hours before going to bed."
6. "Continue now to meditate like this for 10 or 15 minutes. Then sit quietly for several minutes after you're finished."
7. "How easy or hard was this for you to do?"
8. "There may be times when other images or thoughts come into your mind. Try to maintain a passive attitude. If you're bothered by other thoughts, don't dwell on them, but don't force them away. Just focus on your breathing and your word."
9. "Pick a word like *one* or *zum* that you can focus on—something neutral to you."

Part Two

Learning Outcome 2 asks you to identify the steps of the mindfulness meditation procedure represented by eight helper responses. Match each helper response with the letter of the step of the meditation procedure that is being implemented. Feedback follows:

Mindfulness Meditation Steps

a. Rationale
b. Instructions about attitude
c. Preparations for meditation
d. Instructions about commitment, self-discipline, and energy
e. Breathing instructions
f. Body-scan instructions
g. Discussion of client's reaction to first meditation
h. Homework and practice

Helper Responses

1. "Meditation has benefited people by reducing tension, anxiety, stress, and headaches."
2. "Meditate for eight weeks and at the same times once or twice a day."
3. "Allow distracting thoughts to flow. Allow memories, images, and thoughts to occur. Don't try to influence them."
4. "Find a comfortable position in which to meditate."
5. "Notice as the air you breathe enters and exits your nostrils."
6. "Come out of meditation slowly. Sit with your eyes closed for two minutes. Slowly open your eyes. How do you feel?"
7. "Allow the wave of your breath to enter your body from the tip of your toes to the crown of your head."
8. "At first it will be like you are in training."

Part Three

Learning Outcome 3 asks you to teach a meditation procedure to another person. Select either the relaxation response or mindfulness meditation to teach. You can have an observer evaluate you, or you can audiotape your teaching session and rate yourself. You can use the Interview Checklist for Mindfulness Meditation or the Interview Checklist for Relaxation Response as a teaching guide and evaluation tool.

Part Four

Learning Outcome 4 asks you to describe how you would apply the seven parts of the muscle-relaxation procedure. Using the client description below and the seven questions following it, describe how you would use the procedure with this person. Feedback follows.

The client is a middle-age man who is concerned about his inability to sleep at night. He has tried sleeping pills but does not want to rely on medication.

1. Provide a rationale for the use of muscle relaxation. Include the purpose and an overview of the strategy.
2. What instructions would you give this client about appropriate dress for relaxation training?

15 KNOWLEDGE AND SKILL BUILDER

3. List any special environmental factors that may affect the client's use of muscle relaxation.
4. Model some of the relaxation exercises for the client.
5. Describe some of the important muscle groups that you would instruct the client to tense and relax alternately.
6. Give two examples of probes you might use after relaxation to assess the client's use of and reactions to the strategy.
7. What instructions for homework would you give to this client?

Part Five

Learning Outcome 5 asks you to demonstrate 13 out of 15 steps of muscle relaxation with a role-play client. An observer or the client can assess your performance, or you can assess yourself, using the Interview Checklist for Muscle Relaxation.

Part Six

Learning Outcome 6 asks you to demonstrate with a role-play client the body-scan procedure. An observer can assess you, or you can tape-record this activity using the script presented.

Interview Checklist for Mindfulness Meditation

Instructions: Determine which of the following helper leads or questions were demonstrated in the interview. Check (✔) each of the leads that the helper used.

Treatment Rationale

1. Helper describes purpose of procedure.

"I would like to teach you mindfulness meditation. This type of meditation has been used to relieve fatigue caused by anxiety, to decrease stress that leads to high blood pressure, and to bring balance and focus in your life. Meditation helps you become more relaxed and deal more effectively with your tension and stress. It may bring you new awareness about yourself and a new way of seeing and doing in your life."

2. Helper gives client an overview.

"First we will select a quiet place in which to meditate. You will then get into a relaxed and comfortable position. With your eyes closed, you will focus on your breathing, and allow your thoughts to flow freely. If your mind wanders off, you can bring it back by focusing on the breath. You will meditate for 10 to 20 minutes. Then, we will talk about the experience."

3. Helper confirms client's willingness to use strategy.

"How do you feel now about practicing meditation?"

Attitudinal Foundations for Practice

4. Helper instructs client about attitudes to help the practice of meditation.

"There are seven attitudes that will help with your practice of meditation."

5. Helper instructs the client about being nonjudging.

"First, it is best to be nonjudging. We have a tendency to categorize or judge people, things, or our experiences. These judgments take you away from observing whatever comes up while you are meditating. Judging steals energy from the moment-by-moment awareness. To remedy this, focus on your breathing."

6. Helper instructs the client about patience.

"Second, have patience, which means just allow things to unfold in their own time. We don't have to fill our lives with moments of doing and activity."

7. Helper instructs the client about beginner's mind and basing moment-by-moment awareness on past experiences.

"Third, as a beginner, what we experience in the moment is often based on our past experiences and ways of doing things. Just be open to moment-by-moment experience. Don't let past experiences judge and steal energy from moment-by-moment awareness."

8. Helper instructs client about trusting feelings and intuition.

"Fourth, trust your feelings and intuition while meditating. For example, if your body tells you that your posture for meditating is not comfortable, change to another posture that feels better."

9. Helper instructs the client to be nonstriving.

"Fifth, try to be nonstriving, which means that mindfulness meditation is about the process of practice; every practice will be different. You don't want a mindset that requires you to achieve something or get somewhere. Just be in the moment, and attend to whatever comes up."

10. Helper instructs the client about acceptance.

"Sixth, just focus on seeing and accepting things as they are, moment by moment, and in the present."

11. Helper instructs the client about letting go.

"Seventh, just let go, which means nonattachment or not holding on to thoughts."

Instructions about Commitment, Self-Discipline, and Energy

12. Helper instructs client about commitment, self-discipline, and energy.

"You want to make the kind of commitment required in athletic training. This strong commitment is about working on your self. You have to summon enough self-discipline to generate enough energy that you can develop a strong meditative practice and a high degree of mindfulness. You don't have to like it; you just have to do it. Then, at the end of eight weeks of practice, we can see whether the practice was useful."

(continued)

15   K N O W L E D G E   A N D   S K I L L   B U I L D E R

(*continued*)

Preparations for Meditation

13. Helper instructs the client about time, place, and posture.
    "Select a particular time every day to meditate. Meditate for at least six days a week, and for eight weeks. Find a place to meditate that will be free of interruptions and that will be comfortable. When you meditate, sit erect in a chair or on the floor. Try to have your back so that it is self-supporting."

Body-Scan Instructions

14. Helper instructs client to do a body scan.
    "Allow the body to begin to relax completely. Inhale and feel the breath flow from the soles of the feet to the crown of the head, like a gentle slow motion wave. With each exhalation, allow tension to flow out of the body." (Continue from the script presented earlier in the chapter.)

Breathing Instructions

15. Helper instructs the client about breathing.
    "Observe your breathing as it flows in and flows out. Notice the difference in temperature of the out breath and in breath. Feel the sensation of the air as it goes in and out of the nostrils."

Instructions about the Mind Wandering

16. Helper instructs client about what to do with cascading thoughts, feelings, sensations, sounds, pain, or discomfort.
    "If you find yourself getting stuck in thoughts, feelings, sensations, sounds, pain, or discomfort, this is normal; just bring your attention to breathing, and let go by exhaling these distractions."

Instructions for Meditating

17. Helper instructs client about sitting quietly and relaxed for a minute. You can do a quick body scan to help with relaxation.
    "Sit quietly for a while; just relax; focus on your breathing."
18. Helper instructs client to close eyes, focus on breathing, and get in a comfortable position.
    "Close your eyes, get in a comfortable position, and focus on your breathing; the air comes in and flows out."
19. Helper instructs client to be in the moment, to have awareness and observe what comes up, and not give distractions any energy.
    "Just be in the moment; be aware and observe whatever comes to mind. If distractions of thoughts, feelings, sounds, pain, or discomfort steal energy, just breathe

them out and continue to observe and not move with the flow of these distractions."
20. Helper tells the client that she or he will meditate for 10 to 20 minutes.
    "Meditate for 10 to 20 minutes. I will keep time and tell you when to stop."
21. Helper instructs client to come out of meditation slowly.
    "I want you to come out of the meditation Just sit slowly. there with your eyes closed for a while; take time to absorb what you experienced. You may wish to stretch and open your eyes slowly."

Discussion of Client's Reaction to Mindfulness Meditation

22. Helper asks client about experience with mindfulness meditation.

    "What was the experience like for you?"

    "How did you handle distractions?"

    "How did you feel about mindfulness

Homework

23. Helper instructs client to meditate at home once a day and reminds client about preparation for meditation.
    "Practice mindfulness meditation once a day at least 5 days a week. Remember to select a quiet environment without distractions. Do not take any alcoholic beverages or nonprescription drugs at least 24 hours before meditating. Wait for an hour before meditating after eating solid foods or drinking beverages containing caffeine. Be in the moment when you meditate; just observe what comes up without being carried away."
24. Helper instructs client about informal meditation.
    "You can meditate informally when you are stressed out in stressful situations that may occur daily. Just relax and focus on your breathing; be aware and observe what is going on without giving energy to stress, and be peaceful in the situation."

Observer Comments _____

_____

_____

Interview Checklist for Relaxation Response

Instructions: Determine which of the following helper leads or questions were demonstrated in the interview. Check (✔) each of the leads that the helper used.

15   KNOWLEDGE AND SKILL BUILDER

Treatment Rationale

1. Helper describes purpose of meditation.

   "The relaxation response has been used to relieve anxiety, to decrease stress that can lead to high blood pressure, and to become more relaxed. It may give you a new focus and awareness about your self and your world."

2. Helper gives client an overview.

   "You will select a focus word; then you will get in a comfortable position, relax your body, and focus on your breathing. You will maintain a passive attitude while meditating, which will elicit the relaxation response. You will meditate for 10 to 20 minutes. Then, we will talk about the experience."

3. Helper confirms client's willingness to use relaxation response.

   "How do you feel about working with meditation that will elicit the relaxation response?"

Instructions about When, Where, and How Long to Practice

4. Helper instructs client about when, where, and how long to practice.

   "One of the best times to practice is before breakfast because it sets a positive tone for the day. This time is uncluttered with events and activities of the day. Relaxation works best if a regular time is chosen for it so that a routine is developed. Select a place to practice that is quiet and free from distractions and interruptions. Try to practice 10 to 20 minutes at least once and, better, twice a day."

Instructions about a Focus Word, Phrase, or Prayer

5. Helper provides rationale for mental word, phrase, or prayer.

   "One major way to focus your mind is to link it to breathing either by concentrating on the breath or by focusing on something. You can focus on a word, phrase, or prayer."

6. Helper gives examples of focus word, phrase, or prayer.

   "You might prefer a neutral calming word or phrase such as 'love' or 'peace' or 'warm'; or you can use a phrase—'the air flows in, and the air flows out.' Or you could focus on a phrase consistent with your belief system, or a sound you find calming or pleasing."

Instructions about Body Position and Eyes

7. Helper instructs client about body posture and eyes.

   "There are several ways to meditate. I'll show you one. I want you to get into a comfortable position while you are sitting there."

Body Scan

8. Helper does quick body scan with the client.

   "Relax all the muscles in your body; relax [said slowly] your head, face, neck, shoulders, chest, your torso, thighs, calves, and your feet. Relax your body." (You can use the body scan script presented under that section in the chapter).

Breathing Instructions

9. Helper gives instructions about how to breathe.

   "Breathe through your nose and focus on (or become aware of) your breathing. It is sometimes difficult to be natural when you are doing this. Just let the air come to you. Breathe easily and naturally. As you do this, say your focus word for each inhalation and exhalation. Say your focus word silently to yourself each time you breathe in and out."

Instructions about a Passive Attitude

10. Helper instructs client about passive attitude.

    "Be calm and passive. If distracting thoughts or images occur, attempt to be passive about them by not dwelling on them. Return to repeating your focus word, phrase, or prayer. Try to achieve effortless breathing. After more practice, you will be able to examine these thoughts or images with greater detachment. Do not attempt to keep the thoughts out of your mind; just let them pass through. Keep your mind open; don't try to solve problems or think things over. Allow thoughts to flow smoothly into your mind and then drift out. Say your focus word and relax. Don't get upset with distracting thoughts. Just return to your focus word, phrase, or prayer."

Instructions about Length of Meditation

11. Helper instructs client to meditate 10 to 20 minutes.

    "Now, meditate for 10 to 20 minutes. You can open your eyes to check on the time. After you have finished, sit quietly for several minutes. You may wish to keep your eyes closed for a couple of minutes and later open them. You may not want to stand up for a few minutes."

Discussion of Client's Reaction to Relaxation Response

12. Helper asks client about experience with relaxation response.

    "How do you feel about the experience?" "What sorts of thoughts or images flowed through your mind?" "What did you do when the distracting thoughts drifted in?" "How did you feel about your focus word, phrase, or prayer?"

(continued)

(*continued*)

Homework

13. Helper instructs client to meditate daily for the next week.
    "Practice the relaxation response two times a day. Get comfortable in your relaxation response position. Practice in a quiet place away from noise and interruptions. Do not meditate within two hours after eating or within a couple of hours before bedtime."

14. Helper instructs client to apply relaxation
    "Also, it would be helpful for you to apply an informal response *in vivo* meditation in problem or stressful situations that may occur daily. You can do this by becoming detached and passive in the stressful situation. Observe yourself and focus on being calm and on your breathing. Be relaxed in situations that evoke stress."

Observer Comments _____

_____

_____

Interview Checklist for Muscle Relaxation

Instructions: Indicate with a check (✔) each helper lead demonstrated in the interview.

Treatment Rationale

1. Helper explains purpose of muscle relaxation.
    "The name of the strategy that I believe will be helpful is *muscle relaxation*. Muscle relaxation has been used very effectively to benefit people who have a variety of concerns like insomnia, high blood pressure, anxiety, or stress, or people who are bothered by everyday tension. Muscle relaxation will be helpful in decreasing your tension. It will benefit you because you will be able to control and to dispel tension that interferes with your daily activities."

2. Helper gives overview of how muscle relaxation works.
    "I will ask you to tense up and relax various muscle groups. All of us have some tensions in our bodies—otherwise, we could not stand, sit, or move around. Sometimes we have too much tension. By tensing and relaxing, you will become aware of and compare the feelings of tension and relaxation. Later we will train you to send a message to a particular muscle group to relax when nonessential tension creeps in. You will learn to control your tension and relax when you feel tension."

3. Helper describes muscle relaxation as a skill.
    "Muscle relaxation is a skill. And, as with any skill, learning it well will take a lot of practice. A lot of repetition and training are needed to acquire the muscle-relaxation skill."

4. Helper instructs client about moving around if uncomfortable and informs client of sensations that may feel unusual.
    "At times during the training and muscle exercises, you may want to move while you are on your back on the floor [or on the recliner]. Feel free to do this so that you can get more comfortable. You may also feel heady sensations as we go through the exercise. These sensations are not unusual. Do you have any questions concerning what I just talked about? If not, do you want to try this now?"

Instructions about Client Dress

5. Helper instructs client about what to wear for a training session.
    "For the next session, wear comfortable clothing. Wear regular glasses instead of your contact lenses."

Creation of a Comfortable Environment

6. Helper provides a quiet environment, a padded recliner chair, or a pillow if the client lies on the floor.
    "During training, I'd like you to sit in this recliner chair. It will be more comfortable and less distracting than this wooden chair."

Helper Modeling of Relaxation Exercises

7. Helper models some exercises for specific muscle groups.
    "I would like to show you [some of] the exercises we will use in muscle relaxation. First, I make a fist to create tension in my right hand and forearm and then relax it."

Instructions for Muscle Relaxation

8. Helper reads or recites instructions from memory in a conversational tone and practices along with client.

9. Helper instructs client to get comfortable, close eyes, and listen to instructions.
    "Now, get as comfortable as you can, close your eyes, and listen to what I'm going to be telling you. I'm going to make you aware of certain sensations in your body and then show you how you can reduce these sensations to increase feelings of relaxation."

10. Helper instructs client to tense and relax alternately each of 17 muscle groups (*two* times for each muscle group in initial training). Also, helper occasionally makes muscle-group comparisons.

    a. Fist of dominant hand:
    "First think about your right arm, your right hand in particular. Clench your right fist. Clench it tightly and study the tension in the hand and in the forearm. Study those sensations of tension. [Pause.] Now let go. Just relax the right hand and let it rest on the arm of the chair. [Pause.] And notice the difference between the tension and the relaxation." [10-second pause]

b. Fist of nondominant hand:

"Now we'll do the same with your left hand. Clench your left fist. Notice the tension [5-second pause], and now relax. Enjoy the difference between the tension and the relaxation." [10-second pause]

c. One or both wrists:

"Now bend both hands back at the wrists so that you tense the muscles in the back of the hand and in the forearm. Point your fingers toward the ceiling. Study the tension, and now relax. [Pause.] Study the difference between tension and relaxation." [10-second pause]

d. Biceps of one or both arms:

"Now clench both your hands into fists and bring them toward your shoulders. As you do this, tighten your biceps muscles, the ones in the upper part of your arm. Feel the tension in these muscles. [Pause.] Now relax. Let your arms drop down again to your sides. See the difference between the tension and the relaxation." [10-second pause]

e. Shoulders:

"Now we'll move to the shoulder area. Shrug your shoulders. Bring them up to your ears. Feel and hold the tension in your shoulders. [Pause.] Now let both shoulders relax. Notice the contrast between the tension and the relaxation that's now in your shoulders. [10-second pause] Are your shoulders as relaxed as your arms?"

f. Forehead:

"Now we'll work on relaxing the various muscles of the face. First, wrinkle up your forehead and brow. Do this until you feel your brow furrow. [Pause.] Now relax. Smooth out the forehead. Let it loosen up." [10-second pause]

g. Eyes:

"Now close your eyes tightly. Can you feel tension all around your eyes? [5-second pause] Now relax those muscles, noticing the difference between the tension and the relaxation." [10-second pause]

h. Tongue or jaw:

"Now clench your jaw by biting your teeth together. Pull the corners of your mouth back. Study the tension in your jaw. [5-second pause] Relax your jaw now. Can you tell the difference between tension and relaxation in your jaw area?" [10-second pause]

i. Lips:

"Now press your lips together tightly. As you do this, notice the tension all around the mouth. [Pause.] Now relax those muscles around the mouth. Just enjoy the relaxation in your mouth area and your entire face." [Pause.]

j. Head:

"Now we'll move to the neck muscles. Press your head back against your chair. Can you feel the tension in the back of your neck and in your upper back? Hold the tension. [Pause.] Now let your head rest comfortably. Notice the difference. Keep on relaxing." [10-second pause]

k. Chin into chest:

"Now continue to concentrate on the neck area. Bring your head forward. See whether you can bury your chin into your chest. Notice the tension in the front of your neck. Now relax and let go." [10-second pause]

l. Back:

"Now direct your attention to your upper back area. Arch your back as if you were sticking out your chest and stomach. Can you feel tension in your back? Study that tension. [Pause.]

Now relax. Notice the difference between the tension and the relaxation." [10-second pause]

m. Chest muscles:

"Now take a deep breath, filling your lungs, and hold it. See the tension all through your chest and into your stomach area. Hold that tension. [Pause.] Now relax and let go. Let your breath out naturally. Enjoy the pleasant sensations. Is your chest as relaxed as your back and shoulders?" [10-second pause]

n. Stomach muscles:

"Now think about your stomach. Tighten up the muscles in your abdomen. Hold this tension. Make your stomach like a knot. Now relax. Loosen those muscles now." [10-second pause]

o. Buttocks:

"Focus now on your buttocks. Tense your buttocks by pulling them together or contracting them. Notice the tension. And now relax. Let go and relax." [10-second pause]

p. Legs:

"I'd like you now to focus on your legs. Stretch both legs. Feel tension in your thighs. [5-second pause] Now relax. Study the difference again between the tension in the thighs and the relaxation you feel now." [10-second pause]

q. Toes:

"Now concentrate on your lower legs and feet. Tighten both calf muscles by pointing your toes toward your head. Pretend a string is pulling your toes up. Can you feel the pulling and the tension? Notice that tension. [Pause.] Now relax. Let your legs relax deeply. Enjoy the difference between tension and relaxation." [10-second pause]

11. Helper instructs client to review and relax all muscle groups.

"Now, I'm going to go over again the different muscle groups that we've covered. As I name each group, try to notice whether there is any tension in those muscles. If there is any, try to concentrate on those muscles and tell them to relax. Think of draining any remaining tension out of your body as we do this. Now relax the muscles in your feet, ankles, and calves. [Pause.] Get rid of tension in your knees and thighs. [Pause.] Loosen your hips. [Pause.] Let the muscles of your lower body go. [Pause.] Relax your abdomen, waist, and lower back. [Pause.] Drain the tension from your upper back, chest, and shoulders. [Pause.] Relax your upper arms, forearms, and hands. [Pause.] Loosen the muscles of your throat and neck. [Pause.] Relax your face. [Pause.] Let all the tension drain out of your body. [Pause.] Now sit quietly with your eyes closed."

12. Helper asks client to rate his or her relaxation level following training session.

"Now I'd like you to think of a scale from 0 to 5, where 0 is *complete relaxation* and 5 *extreme tension*. Tell me where you would place yourself on that scale now."

(continued)

(continued)

Posttraining Assessment

13. Helper asks client about first session of relaxation training and discusses problems with training if client has any.

   "How do you feel?"

   "What is your overall reaction to the procedure?"

   "Think back about what we did. Did you have problems with any muscle group?"

   "What reaction did you have when you focused on the tension?

   What about relaxation?"

   "How did the contrast between the tension and relaxation feel?"

Homework and Follow-up

14. Helper assigns homework and requests that client complete homework log for practice sessions.

"Relaxation training, like any skill, takes a lot of practice. I would like you to practice what we've done today. Do the exercises twice a day for 15 to 20 minutes each time. Do them in a quiet place in a reclining chair, on the floor with a pillow, or on your bed with a head pillow. Also, try to do the relaxation at a time when there is no time pressure—like arising, after school or work, or before dinner. Try to avoid any interruptions, like phone calls and people wanting to see you. Complete the homework log I have given you. Make sure you fill it in for each practice session. Do you have any questions?"

15. Helper arranges for follow-up session.

   "Why don't you practice with this over the next two weeks and come back then?"

Notations for Problems Encountered or Variations Used _____

_____

_____

15   KNOWLEDGE AND SKILL BUILDER **FEEDBACK**

Part One

1. h. Homework (practice)
2. b. Instruction about where to practice
3. a. Rationale—telling the client how the procedure is used
4. d. Breathing instructions
5. h. Homework—giving the client instructions about how to carry out the practice
6. c. Instructing the client to meditate for 10 to 20 minutes
7. g. Probing about the meditative experience—assessing the client's reactions
8. e. Instruction about a passive attitude
9. c. Instruction about focusing on word or phrase

Part Two

1. a. Rationale—reason
2. h. Homework—when to practice
3. b. Instructions about attitude
4. c. Preparation about position for meditating
5. e. Breathing instructions
6. g. Discussion about reactions to meditation
7. f. Body scan
8. d. Instructions about self-discipline and commitment

Part Three

Use the Interview Checklist for Relaxation Response or the Interview Checklist for Mindfulness Meditation as a guide to assess your teaching.

Part Four

1. Rationale for client

   a. Purpose: "This procedure, if you practice it regularly, can help you become relaxed. The relaxation benefits you derive can help you sleep better."
   b. Overview: "This procedure involves learning to tense and relax different muscle groups in your body. By doing this, you can contrast the difference between tenseness and re-laxation. This will help you to recognize tension so you can instruct yourself to relax."

2. Instructions about dress: "You don't want anything to dis-tract you, so wear comfortable, loose clothes for training. You may want to remove your glasses or contact lenses."
3. Environmental factors: (a) a quiet room with a reclining chair, (b) no obvious distractions or interruptions.
4. Modeling of exercises: "Let me show you exactly what you'll be doing. Watch my right arm closely. I'm going to clench my fist and tighten my forearm, studying the tension as I do this. Now I'm going to relax it like this [hand goes limp], letting all the tension drain out of the arm and hand and fingertips."
5. Muscle groups used in the procedure include arms, hands, and biceps; face and neck muscles; chest, shoul-ders, back, and stomach muscles; and upper legs, calf, and foot muscles.
6. Possible probes

   a. "On a scale from 0 to 100, 0 being *very relaxed* and 100 *very tense,* how do you feel now?"
   b. "What is your overall reaction to what you just did?"
   c. "How did the contrast between the tensed and relaxed mus-cles feel?"
   d. "How easy or hard was it for you to do this?"

7. Homework instructions: (a) Practice twice daily. (b) Prac-tice in a quiet place, and avoid interruptions. (c) Use a reclining chair or lie on the floor or on a bed with pillow support for your head.

Part Five

Use the Interview Checklist for Muscle Relaxation to assess your performance.

Part Six

Use the body scan script to assess the way you used the body scan with a role-play client.

EXPOSURE STRATEGIES
BY DANIEL W. McNEIL AND BRANDON N. KYLE
WEST VIRGINIA UNIVERSITY

LEARNING OUTCOMES

After completing this chapter, you will be able to

1. Describe to a client the rationale for the use of exposure and provide at least one theoretical explanation for how exposure may work.
2. Name and describe at least one gradual method and at least one intensive method for exposure.
3. Name at least three issues a helper should consider in choosing an exposure method with a client.
4. List and describe at least 8 of the 11 steps in implementing exposure therapy, as outlined in Figure 16.1.
5. Articulate issues of informed consent and be able to detail at least one caution in the use of exposure.

Exposure is an inclusive term that refers to a variety of treatment methods, as well as to a basic process in human behavior change. Various modalities can be involved in treatment, such as imaginal exposure in the form of systematic desensitization, or actual exposure to objects, events, or situations that cause distress to clients. Whatever the modality, exposure involves some form of contact between the client and what he or she finds anxiety provoking, frightening, or otherwise distressing. Classically, exposure often took the form of *imaginal* desensitization, followed by *in vivo* exposure outside of the therapy room. If our client Isabella was fearful of going for a dental visit, for example, a thorough, individualized assessment first would be conducted. Then the helper might assist her in learning a relaxation response that is incompatible with anxiety, perhaps through progressive muscle-relaxation training. A few or several therapy sessions would be devoted to Isabella learning to relax herself, and Isabella would have homework assignments and self-monitor her relaxation practice. Then, Isabella and the helper working together would construct a hierarchy of emotionally evocative situations ranging from least to most fear provoking. Over the course of a number of sessions, the helper would "expose" Isabella to these situations in her imagination, by reading the descriptions to her in a systematic way. Once the hierarchy was completed, or

perhaps while it was in progress, Isabella would have homework assignments to do self-exposure to dental situations. For example, the first assignment might be to simply call for information about dental services. Then she might visit a dental office without scheduling dental treatment. Later, she could meet the dentist or hygienist in the office, and later still she could actually receive dental services.

This chapter addresses exposure in its many forms, from systematic desensitization, to one-session flooding, and beyond. We discuss definitions of exposure, theoretical mechanisms that may underlie exposure, and methods by which both gradual and intensive exposure can evoke change. Various contemporary applications of exposure therapy are described, as are current exciting new areas of research. It is important to note that exposure has been utilized most commonly for the treatment of both anxiety and fear. Although these states are similar, they represent unique constructs: fear is more present oriented and psychophysiologically focused (as in a fight–flight reaction), and anxiety is more future oriented and involved with worry and other cognitive processes (Barlow, 2002; Craske, 2003). Nevertheless, for the sake of simplicity and readability, these terms are used interchangeably in this chapter, for exposure is an effective treatment for both anxiety and fear.

WHAT IS EXPOSURE?

Exposure is a key process in the treatment of a broad spectrum of problems with anxiety and fear, extreme manifestations of these states in anxiety disorders, as well as other emotional disorders. Both psychosocial and pharmacological treatments depend on the mechanism of exposure to help clients relearn adaptive responses to objects, situations, and people that cause arousing emotional distress. *Exposure therapy* is defined as

a form of behavior therapy that is effective in treating anxiety disorders. Exposure therapy involves systematic confrontation with a feared stimulus, either *in vivo* (live), or in the imagination. It works by (a) habituation, in which repeated exposure reduces anxiety over time by a process of extinction; (b) disconfirming fearful predictions; (c) deeper processing of the feared stimulus; and (d) increasing feelings of self-efficacy and mastery. Exposure therapy may encompass any of a number behavioral interventions, including systematic desensitization, flooding, implosive therapy, and extinction-based techniques. (APA, 2007, p. 357).

The extinction that may be inherent to exposure occurs after repeated or prolonged contact with whatever it is that evokes fear (be it a small animal like a snake, a place such as a glass elevator overlooking a large city, or a situation such as receiving dental treatment) without any aspects that would lead to aversive reactions, such as a snake bite, the elevator dropping a number of floors uncontrollably, or pain during dental care. A variety of anxiety problems are addressed by exposure, but other emotional issues such as grief and depression also can be targeted with this strategy. There are elements of exposure in treatment for alcohol and other drug problems as well, such as when cue desensitization is used, exposing individuals to the sights, sounds, smells, and other aspects of alcohol and drug consumption situations, using response prevention so that actual substance use does not occur in association with those stimuli.

Phobias, however, are disorders that perhaps are most commonly addressed by exposure; they are regarded as "a persistent and irrational fear of a specific situation, object, or activity (e.g., heights, dogs, water, blood, driving, flying) which is consequently either strenuously avoided or endured with marked distress. In *DSM-IV TR* the many types of individual phobias are classified under the heading of 'Specific Phobia.' See also 'Social Phobia.'" (APA, 2007, p. 697). Traumatic reactions, including posttraumatic stress disorder, also are treated using exposure; it is "in *DSM-IV TR,* a disorder that results when an individual lives through or witnesses an event in which he or she believes that there is a threat to life or physical integrity and safety and experiences fear, terror, or helplessness" (APA, 2007, p. 717). Treatment of obsessive–compulsive disorder also includes exposure for the compulsions or obsessions associated with it. In the case of a client with hand-washing rituals, for example, there can be exposure to dirt or germs, followed by response prevention for excessive hand washing or other cleansing rituals.

Exposure leads to changes in an individual's responses to the objects, situations, and/or people that previously elicited fear or anxiety. Behavioral changes typically are emphasized over others, for actually performing the desired action is seen as the ultimate outcome. Moreover, there is some evidence that overt-motor behavioral changes often precede physiological and cognitive changes in the treatment process (Mavissakalian & Michelson, 1982; Rachman & Hodgson, 1974); if a person can first outwardly behave in a certain way, then his or her frightening thoughts and physiological responses will calm as well. Nevertheless, cognitive and psychophysiological changes

are extremely important too, and often are direct targets for change in the helping process.

The broad term *exposure* not only describes a key process in psychological changes but also is an omnibus term referring to a variety of treatment methods, including systematic desensitization. Systematic desensitization is a method in which there is gradual exposure over time; it can be conducted using imagery, virtual reality, role plays, or *in vivo* (i.e., in the client's actual environment). Other treatment methods that are subsumed under *exposure* are flooding and implosive therapy, which are considered to be intensive exposure methods, typically involving repeated, long-lasting, or extremely emotionally evocative exposure.

An example may help to illustrate how exposure might be used in a helping situation to counteract a phobia. If during childhood Isabella had been a victim of a dog attack, she may have developed a dog phobia. (It is possible to develop such phobias, however, even without direct traumatic experience [Lichtenstein & Annas, 2000; Öst & Hugdahl, 1983; Rachman, 1977].) In conducting exposure with Isabella to help her with the dog phobia, after completing an appropriate assessment and providing the client with a thorough rationale, the helper might assist Isabella in learning relaxation skills which she could implement to prevent or combat later anxious responses. Then the helper might use a psychoeducational approach, providing information about dogs and knowledge about different breeds and rules for interacting with dogs. Even this discussion about dogs would be a form of exposure, albeit a mild one. Imaginal exposure might then take place, first involving construction of a hierarchy of fearful events involving dogs, ranging from very mild situations (e.g., walking through the dog accessories section of a retail store) to situations that are highly fear evoking (e.g., having a large, snarling dog break its chain and come running toward you, mouth agape and teeth flashing). The helper then would expose the client to these scenes in a systematic way for brief periods of time, describing the scenes while the client imagines them with eyes closed, to limit visual distraction. The relaxation skills would be used before, during, and after imaginal exposure, to help the client respond without undue physiological distress. Exposure to actual dog stimuli then would take place, *in vivo.* Isabella may have homework assignments from the clinician to visit retail stores, and to spend time in the dog section, looking at and holding collars, leashes, and other dog-related items. Then Isabella may be asked to visit pet stores and to view dogs that are in cages. She also may be asked to go to a local dog park and to view the dogs and owners from outside the fence. The clinician may open the possibility of Isabella inviting a friend with a nice dog to a helping session, so that the clinician could work directly with Isabella to interact with a dog in real life. In such a session, the clinician and/or friend may model how to interact with a dog, in such ways as petting it or scratching it. The friend might rub the dog, and Isabella would place her hand on top of the friend's hand, with the knowledge that over time, the friend would remove her hand, allowing Isabella to touch the dog directly. Future hierarchy steps might include walking a friend's dog or going to a park where there frequently are dogs running loose but with their owners. The client may be encouraged to maintain an "exposure-based lifestyle" involving dogs, so that fear would be unlikely to return. For example, Isabella might be encouraged to get a puppy, so that she could enjoy a dog, learning to live with it day in and day out.

From a developmental perspective, exposure can happen naturalistically in a person's life, providing the individual with opportunities to learn adaptive responses without ever having to go through the angst of a learned, encapsulated anxiety response. For example, if, when Isabella was a young child, she had been exposed to dental care by a professional before any dental problems developed, then she may never have had an opportunity to directly learn a phobic response to dental situations. (Nevertheless, there are ample societal messages in the form of cartoons and advertisements, as well as social learning from family members, peers, and others, that can lead to the indirect, vicarious acquisition of dental phobia.) In pediatric dentistry, for example, it is best if a child's first appointment includes such simple activities as being given a "ride" up and down on the dental chair, tooth-counting by the dentist or hygienist, receiving a bright new toothbrush, and other fun activities that help the child to learn positive expectations of the dental experience. In this way, as a child, Isabella may have learned to seek out dental care on a regular basis, rather than avoid it because of negative societal messages or unpleasant situations related to symptomatic care.

In other instances, life situations bring new opportunities, which may actually be challenges to which a person must respond (leading to exposure), or from which a person may choose to retreat (representing avoidance). For example, in the case of Isabella, if she was interested in running for student council at her high school, but campaigning required her to speak publicly in front of a school assembly, she may find herself experiencing fear or even phobia related to the possibility of the public speaking. The new demand poses both a challenge and an opportunity. Isabella may choose to attempt to "get through" the public speaking assignments with considerable dread and endure the unpleasant physiological and cognitive sequelae, and perhaps over time, exposure will operate so that she feels more comfortable doing public speaking. (This outcome, however, is uncertain, because many times such phobias maintain over time, even with periodic exposure.) Alternately, she may choose to seek out professional treatment for her phobia. Or she may choose to decline the possibility of running for student council to avoid the phobic situation.

THEORETICAL BACKGROUND FOR EXPOSURE

Exposure therapy is considered an empirically supported treatment strategy (Chambless et al., 1997). Debate has raged over decades of research regarding how exposure reduces distress and improves functioning (Tryon, 2005). Although this chapter emphasizes how to effectively implement exposure as a method of treatment, it is important to briefly examine possible mechanisms through which exposure exerts an influence on anxiety, fear, and other negative emotional states. The importance of understanding how and why exposure works lies in being able to apply the general principles of exposure-based treatments to a wide variety of clients and in a multitude of situations. A helper well versed in the theoretical background of exposure can properly adapt treatment to many therapeutic situations. Additionally, helpers will want to provide clients with a rationale for exposure-based treatment, and an understanding of the theoretical background of exposure is essential to a proper explanation.

Reciprocal Inhibition

The first explanation put forth for how exposure could exert an influence on fear and anxiety was reciprocal inhibition (Wolpe, 1958). Exposure to fear-provoking stimuli (i.e., images) was paired with relaxation because the physiological response of relaxation in the parasympathetic nervous system was believed to directly oppose the physiological activity of fear or anxiety in the sympathetic nervous system. (Briefly and simply explained, the sympathetic nervous system is generally associated with arousal and excitation, and the parasympathetic nervous system controls opposing physiological responses.) Thus, the connection between fear or anxiety and the targeted stimulus would be severed while the connection between relaxation and the stimulus would be bolstered, and the feared stimulus would no longer evoke a fearful or anxious response.

The theory of reciprocal inhibition was found to be problematic for explaining the effects of exposure (Tryon, 2005). First, reciprocal conditioning was thought to have short-term effects in the nervous system, yet some people maintained improvements made in treatment over an extended period of time. Second, people who were treated by repeated and/or prolonged exposure to feared stimuli without being taught relaxation skills showed treatment gains comparable to the gains of people trained to relax in conjunction with exposure (e.g., Yates, 1975). Reciprocal inhibition theory, however, would hold that treatment without relaxation should be ineffective because an incompatible physiological state was not paired with fear-provoking stimuli. These two problems also suggested that physiology was not the only component of fear and anxiety.

Counterconditioning

Another early suggestion for the mechanism underlying exposure therapy's effectiveness was counterconditioning (Davison,

1968; Tryon, 2005). Like reciprocal inhibition, counterconditioning involved training clients to relax during exposure to feared stimuli. Rather than completely inhibiting anxiety, however, counterconditioning was supposed to affect change by teaching clients a response intended to manage fear they experienced. Counterconditioning, then, was thought to effect a long-term change broadly at behavioral and emotional levels instead of solely a physiological change.

Difficulties also arose in trying to explain the effects of exposure with counterconditioning as a theoretical mechanism. The primary objection to counterconditioning was similar to the main objection against reciprocal inhibition: it could not explain the improvements made by clients who were exposed to fear-provoking stimuli without training in relaxation skills. The evidence, which did not support reciprocal inhibition and counterconditioning, led researchers to look beyond relaxation as the component through which change occurred during exposure.

Habituation

As evidence grew that relaxation might not be an essential component of exposure therapy, focus shifted to other possible mechanisms through which exposure worked. One of the mechanisms suggested was habituation, or decrease in physiological reactivity in response to a fear-provoking stimulus during prolonged exposure (Emmelkamp & Felten, 1985; Lader & Matthews, 1968; Watts, 1979). Simply put, the physiological arousal experienced by a client in the presence of a feared stimulus could not be maintained for an extended period of time. When a client experienced decreased arousal in the presence of a stimulus, that stimulus lost its association with physiological arousal and thus its ability to evoke arousal and fear or anxiety.

Habituation might explain decrease in fear or in anxiety within a session; it does not explain decrease in fear or in anxiety over an extended period of time, between sessions (Tryon, 2005). The inability of habituation to explain the effectiveness of exposure therapy in the long term leaves it as an insufficient explanation on its own, especially in light of evidence that between-session decrease in fear and anxiety could be a vital component of exposure therapy (Kamphuis & Telch, 2000). Some evidence also suggests that physiological arousal might not be a *necessary* component of exposure therapy for all individuals (Lang & Craske, 2000).

Extinction

One of the simpler yet more comprehensive explanations for why exposure therapy works has been extinction, in both the respondent and the operant conditioning sense (Hazlett-Stevens & Craske, 2003; McGlynn, Mealiea, & Landau, 1981). A client might develop a fear of a neutral stimulus (a conditioned stimulus, or CS) when that neutral stimulus is paired with another stimulus (an unconditioned stimulus, or US) that naturally elicits an unpleasant response (an unconditioned response, or UR) that a client finds aversive, such as intense physiological arousal or pain. With repeated pairings of the US and CS (or with only one pairing, if the client found the event extremely aversive), the CS begins to elicit a conditioned response (CR) of fear that the client finds aversive, like the UR. As the client finds the CR unpleasant, he or she typically escapes or avoids the CS to avoid experiencing the CR. The client's escape and avoidance of the CS is negatively reinforced through the removal or avoidance of the CR. Consider the example of a child and thunderstorms. The cues signaling an approaching storm (dark clouds, lightning, etc.) are not inherently aversive. Many children find the loud noise from thunder accompanying storms to be naturally aversive, though. Through repeated pairings of other storm cues and thunder, these storm cues can come to elicit fear and arousal in the child. The child might seek to avoid the unpleasant fear and arousal associated with storm cues by hiding in a closet or by seeking reassurance from adults whenever a storm is approaching.

Exposure therapy creates repeated and extended presentations of the CS without the US, which decreases and can even eliminate the CR. Continued exposure to the CS without negative reinforcement for escape or avoidance decreases the association for escape and avoidance with reinforcement as well. For example, the child might be exposed to storms without thunder, thus experiencing the CS without the US. Additionally, the child properly exposed to storm cues other than thunder should have lasting fear reduction over time due to extinction, not temporary fear reduction related to escape or avoidance. Eventually, through extinction, the child should experience less fear related to storms, and should experience little or no distress about dark clouds and wind.

Possible difficulties also exist for the extinction theory of exposure. First, not all clients suffering from fear and anxiety can recall their feared stimulus (CS) being associated with a US. Second, it can be difficult to identify what CR a client is attempting to eliminate by escaping or avoiding a CS, especially in the cases when clients demonstrate minimal physiological reactivity in response to their feared stimulus (Hodgson & Rachman, 1974; Rachman & Hodgson, 1974). Finally, under the extinction framework of exposure, eliciting a CR of physiological arousal would not be a necessary component of exposure, for the two important factors are presence of the CS and absence of the US.

Acceptance

In recent years, acceptance and commitment therapy (ACT) has been proposed as a new form of psychotherapy, growing out of the behavioral tradition (the founders of ACT refer to it as the third wave of behavior therapy), which is offered as an alternative to contemporary forms of cognitive–behavioral therapy

(Eifert & Forsyth, 2005; Hayes, Strosahl, & Wilson, 1999). ACT practitioners hold that psychopathology arises when people attempt to avoid the unavoidable: negative private events (i.e., distressing cognitions, private verbal behavior, or physiological states). The founders of ACT believe that traditional cognitive–behavioral therapy often furthers client suffering by suggesting clients can and should control their private events. Contrastingly, clinicians following an ACT framework suggest exposure therapy can work by teaching people to accept the aversive private events they experience in the presence of their feared stimuli, allowing the clients to learn to engage in valued tasks while experiencing aversive private events. Rather than emphasizing decrease of aversive private states elicited by feared stimuli, ACT places importance on accepting private events as normal, natural, and (most important) not necessarily capable of dictating a person's overt-motor behavior. Whereas traditional cognitive–behavioral therapy rationales for exposure have altering the *form* of private events as the goal of therapy (e.g., decrease physiological arousal in the presence of feared stimuli), ACT rationales for exposure have altering the *function* of private events as therapy's goal (e.g., not allowing physiological arousal to prevent a client with acrophobia from enjoying a beautiful but high scenic view). Clients supposedly learn new relations between their private events and their overt behavior, without emphasis on decreasing or altering their private events. Decrease in fear and arousal typically does take place during exposure exercises using ACT, but this decrease in the frequency and intensity of private events is considered a secondary side-effect of the exposure.

To date, acceptance and commitment therapy has received support from most studies as an effective form of psychotherapy (e.g., Eifert & Forsyth, 2005; Hayes, Luoma, Bond, Masuda, & Lillis, 2006). Proponents and the skeptical alike agree, however, that more well-designed research must be conducted to demonstrate that ACT is equivalent or superior to current effective treatments (Hayes et al., 2006), and critics further maintain that it remains to be seen if ACT is truly different from traditional cognitive and behavioral therapies. One criticism that could be leveled at the ACT explanation for exposure therapy is that, although lessening physiological arousal might not be the stated goal of exposure in ACT, decrease in physiological arousal likely occurs. Thus, it seems difficult to determine if, despite having differently stated goals than cognitive–behavioral therapy, ACT works through its proposed mechanism (altering the function, not the form, of private events) or through mechanisms similar to those of cognitive–behavioral therapy (altering the form of private events through learning mechanisms such as extinction). Also, practitioners of cognitive–behavioral therapy might argue that proponents of ACT misrepresent the therapeutic goals of cognitive–behavioral therapy. Clinicians practicing the latter emphasize a decrease in fear and anxiety that allows a person to function adaptively in daily living; they often do not require or expect a complete and permanent elimination of fear and anxiety.

Relearning

Emotional processing theory suggests exposure therapy accesses and modifies a client's "fear structure," a set of propositions and behaviors a person associates with a feared stimulus (Foa & Kozak, 1986; Foa & McNally, 1996; Lang, 1977; Rachman, 1980). Under this theory, it is important to elicit fear and anxiety as comprehensively as possible in order to more thoroughly access, and hence alter more completely, a client's fear structure. Relatedly, other researchers emphasize that exposure should be viewed as new learning, which can be enhanced through general principles of learning (repeated trials, multiple contexts, spaced rehearsal, etc.), and not seen as "unlearning" of the original fear and anxiety response to stimuli (Mystkowski, Craske, & Echiverri, 2002).

For the present, the skilled practitioner can benefit greatly by being familiar with the conceptual foundations for exposure, which allow for proper and effective application of exposure in a multitude of novel therapy situations. For further reading regarding the theoretical issues underlying exposure, we recommend a 2006 book edited by Craske, Hermans, and Vansteenwegen.

METHODS BY WHICH EXPOSURE CAN EVOKE CHANGE

Exposure therapy can take two general forms: gradual and intensive. Gradual exposure therapies present increasingly fear- or anxiety-provoking stimuli in a steadily increasing fashion over several shorter sessions. Intensive exposure therapies place the client in contact with more intense fear- or anxiety-provoking stimuli almost immediately and for an extended period of time, sometimes even during only one or a very few sessions. Both clients and helpers tend to be more comfortable with gradual exposure. More caution is necessary in using intensive exposure, including greater focus on preparing the client, and even greater emphasis on informed consent. Gradual exposure is accepted more readily and may be more palatable to clients, thus increasing satisfaction, at least early in treatment, perhaps with fewer dropouts. Nevertheless, the efficacy and efficiency of intensive methods are appealing to many clients, who may have dropped out if treatment seemed to plod along.

Gradual Exposure or Desensitization

Gradual exposure therapy has been used efficaciously and effectively to reduce fear and anxiety for decades. Proper implementation of gradual exposure, which also could be referred to as *desensitization,* is vital to achieve the most success with clients exhibiting anxiety problems. Each disorder has its own nuances related to exposure therapy, and we direct helpers to established and user-friendly manuals (typically accompanied by informative client workbooks) to answer any questions about tailoring the strategies discussed here to clients with particular disorders. It is our experience, however, that while the specifics of gradual exposure change with each client, the general principles remain the same across individuals and contexts. Therefore, we present the underlying strategies and techniques of exposure therapy, but the helper must determine how best to use these principles to assist a client in overcoming fear and anxiety.

Gradual exposure can take one of three forms, each of them described in further detail below. First, clients can be exposed to *imaginal* stimuli (i.e., fear- or anxiety-provoking stimuli of which the client creates a mental image). Second, clients can

engage in what we call *in vitro* exposure, in which clients are exposed to more tangible but simulated stimuli. For example, client and helper can role-play an interaction with the client's boss that caused the client anxiety in the past or that the client worries about occurring in the future. Finally, clients can be exposed to the actual situations and stimuli that elicit fear and anxiety, a process referred to as *in vivo* exposure. A client who has a fear of spiders might allow a spider to crawl over his or her hand, or even over his or her face. Additionally, these three forms of gradual exposure therapy can be used sequentially, in tandem, or independently.

Regardless of the particular combination of different forms of gradual exposure a helper chooses to utilize, the general sequence of therapy remains similar (see Figure 16.1). First,

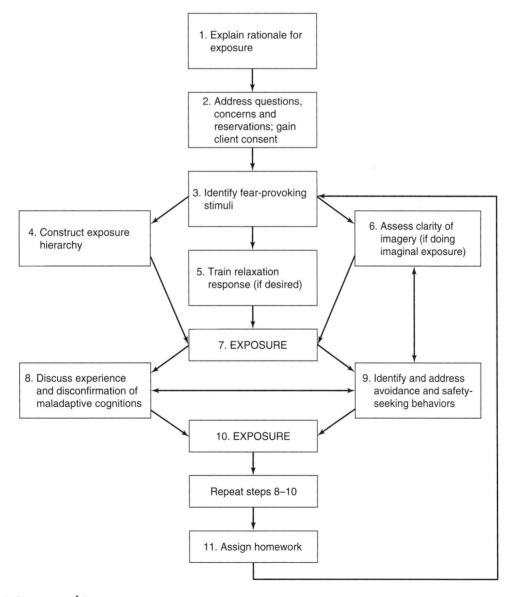

Figure 16.1 Sequence of Exposure

the helper explains the rationale for exposure, which will be impacted by the theoretical viewpoint the helper holds regarding exposure. Generally, it can be explained to the client that anxiety and fear are natural, normal, and sometimes helpful human emotions. For example, being scared of a bear in the woods helps people run away and escape harm. Sometimes, though, excessive fear and anxiety can become associated with a variety of stimuli or situations and impair daily functioning. Simply put, a person "learns" to be afraid. Exposure therapy can be used to help clients break the pairing of fear and anxiety with certain stimuli or situations and learn a different response to fear and anxiety (or anticipation thereof) besides avoidance.

After explaining the rationale for exposure therapy, helpers should address client questions and concerns, and gain informed consent from clients before proceeding. Rushing into exposure therapy without adequately addressing reasonable concerns and questions can damage rapport and the therapeutic alliance. Some common concerns clients might have are that exposure-based treatment will (1) progress too quickly, (2) make them worse, and (3) fail to address the underlying or original cause of their problem. No one answer will satisfy all clients, but helpers can have some general responses prepared ahead of time. Concerns about the pacing of progress can typically be addressed by assuring the client that, although the helper will challenge the client to push him- or herself outside of his or her comfort zone, treatment ultimately will move at the client's pace. In regards to concerns about getting worse, clients can be informed that the effort they put forth in therapy now will lead to less anxiety in the future. Essentially, exposure will not be easy for most clients, nor will it always be a pleasant experience. Although the helper should not guarantee success, he or she can point to the empirical evidence supporting exposure treatments and honestly suggest that many clients receive great benefits from exposure therapy. As for the underlying or original cause of the client's fear, the helper can candidly explain that although information about the history of the client's problem will be gathered and should prove useful in understanding the client's problems, treatment will focus more on the situations in the client's current environment that maintain fear and/or avoidance. It can be communicated that while the past cannot be changed, one can gain at least some degree of control over one's current behaviors. An opportunity to practice explaining exposure therapy is presented in Learning Activity 16.1.

After gaining informed consent for treatment, the helper begins the process by identifying precisely what are fear-provoking stimuli for a client. Clients suffering from problems with anxiety can generally be grouped into diagnostic categories, but no two clients are exactly alike. Helpers should take care to discover precisely what "it" is that leads to a client's fear and avoidance. Although this sounds deceptively simple on the surface (e.g., "What are you afraid of?"), helpers must be aware of several barriers to information gathering. Many clients have engaged in avoidance behaviors for years and might no longer be certain precisely what frightens them most. Further, mere discussion of feared topics during therapy can be distressing for some clients. Verbal and cognitive representations of feared stimuli often are aversive, much like the actual situation (e.g., conversations about the traumatic event for a client with posttraumatic stress disorder), or they are *the* aversive stimuli (e.g., the obsessive thoughts that a client with obsessive–compulsive disorder finds disturbing). Specifying precisely what aspects of a situation are distressing also can be difficult for clients with more complex anxiety reactions. For example, a client might report a fear of elevators. A skilled helper must not let this statement stand on its own, though. Instead, it should be determined what specifically about the elevator distresses the client. Is it the enclosed space, or the motion of the elevator and subsequent physiological sensations, or an overwhelming sense of dread that the elevator will fall or get stuck for an extended period of time?

Although a helper must take care not to push the client for information too quickly, the preceding types of questions should be answered to effectively conduct the next step of exposure: constructing an exposure hierarchy. The client and helper must work together to rank or order the situations the client fears. A good tool for helping the client rank stimuli is a subjective units of discomfort scale (SUDS) (Wolpe, 1990). SUDS ratings generally range from 0 to 100 and have verbal anchors at each end to assist the client in making ratings. Typical anchors used for the purposes of exposure therapy would be "No fear/anxiety" and "Most fear/anxiety possible" or "No distress" and "Most distress possible." Most clients can quickly understand SUDS ratings, and these ratings can become a fast and simple tool for self-report of fear and anxiety. Ideally, the client should be able to list at least 10 fear-provoking situations, each no more than 10 units away from the next situation listed. For each situation, clients should attempt to be as specific as possible. Other information important to gather for each situation on the hierarchy includes the client's typical thoughts related to the situation, the client's typical response to the situation (an especially important piece of information for particularly avoidant clients or clients with obsessive–compulsive disorder who engage in compulsive rituals), and the client's typical physiological reaction to the situation. Such data provide the helper with a clear vision of the client's perspective and assist the client in rationally deciding which situations provoke the most fear or anxiety (e.g., "My palms sweat when I see a spider in the basement; but my palms sweat, my heart races, and I can't stop thinking 'It will get me while I sleep' when I see a spider in my bedroom"). Situations can be written on a paper form for

---

LEARNING ACTIVITY   16.1   Explaining Exposure Therapy

 This activity is designed to give you some practice in explaining exposure therapy to a client. You can do this activity with a colleague, a fellow student, or a friend. Someone who is not a professional may be a good choice, as that interaction may most closely resemble explaining exposure to a client.

Part One: *Developing a Script*
Write or, better yet, type into a computer a sample script, emphasizing bullet points so that you are not tempted to read the script. Order the points from most to least important. Include several opportunities throughout the explanation for comments or questions from the client.

Part Two: *Practicing the Explanation*
You may wish to go through the explanation out loud several times in a private setting, hearing yourself and finding the best word combinations for yourself.

Part Three: *Delivering the Explanation*
Sit facing the person whom you have found to participate in this role play. Deliver the explanation as if you are in a real situation with an actual client. (Do you realize that this role play is a form of exposure for yourself?!)

Part Four: *Getting Feedback*
This is the time to listen! Ask the person you involved in your practice what he or she understands exposure to be. Give them time and encourage them to think. Ask what questions about exposure remain unanswered. Is there anything else the person wants to know?

Part Five: *Feedback*
Here are some important aspects of exposure therapy to mention in your explanation:

- Fear is learned.
- Because fear is learned, there must be new learning to replace what was inaccurately learned.
- Exposure is a learning-based therapeutic approach that has been found to be very successful in treating fear, anxiety, and other problems.
- Exposure may be a good choice to help you with your problems.
- What are your thoughts so far?
- Various types of exposure: imaginal, role play, in real life.
- Exposure can be gradual or intensive.
- Comments and questions? Thoughts about the best way for you to use exposure.
- Homework assignments likely.
- Let's plan together a course of exposure to help you with your problems.

---

future reference or, better yet, may be recorded using a word processing program to allow future revision and addition. Figure 16.2 provides an example of such a form. Learning Activity 16.2 provides a chance to practice developing scenes for exposure therapy.

At this point in treatment, the helper has the option of training the client how to engage in a relaxation response to be used in conjunction with exposure. Many resources exist, including relaxation training exercises such as progressive muscle relaxation and breathing retraining (e.g., O'Donohue, Fisher, & Hayes, 2003). Although literature exists to suggest that training a relaxation response is not necessary for exposure therapy to result in a reduction of fear and avoidance (Tryon, 2005), we recommend considering relaxation training for several reasons. To the degree that exposure works through the mechanism of learned self-efficacy, training in a relaxation response can foster a client's sense of mastery and control during exposure. Next, relaxation exercises can help clients learn to be aware of their physiological sensations. Awareness of bodily sensations can help put clients in contact with such sensations and learn that arousal typically does not lead to a permanently debilitating state ("If my heart keeps racing and my head keeps spinning, I'm gonna go crazy") and that both arousal and relaxation occur and cycle naturally. Finally, many clients with anxiety problems also report stress from various sources in their lives. Practicing relaxation exercises daily can reduce a client's overall level of stress, which in turn can have positive effects on anxiety.

With an exposure hierarchy constructed and a relaxation response trained, the client and helper are ready to begin exposure. It is our experience that, given the option, clients will typically attempt to delay exposure as much as possible. This avoidance behavior can take the form of asking repeated questions about the exposure or bringing in a "crisis" to discuss at the beginning of the therapy session. Although extraordinary crises (e.g., a death in the family, job loss) warrant attention, the skilled helper begins exposure as soon as possible while politely and professionally curtailing avoidance ("I understand that you still have some questions about the process, but I really think that we've covered it

LEARNING ACTIVITY   **16.2**   **Developing Scenes for Use in Exposure Therapy**

This activity is designed to give you practice in detailing a situation that may be used in exposure. You can do this activity by yourself, for almost everyone harbors at least some degree of fear or anxiety about something. Focusing on yourself also provides a different perspective on fear and allows you to respect the privacy of others.

Part One: *Describing the General Situation*
Write or, better yet, type into a computer a description of a situation that you find anxiety provoking, including any relevant parameters, such as time of day, weather, the presence or absence of others. It may be best not to choose a situation that is truly phobic for you, because the degree of emotionality may be counterproductive to this exercise.

Part Two: *Describing Your Behavioral Reactions*
Describe how you typically behave in this situation, such as asking others for reassurance, moving away from the glass wall of the elevator, or closing your eyes.

Part Three: *Describing Your Thoughts*
What thoughts do you have before, during, and after this situation? List anything you can remember regarding the situation, whether rational or not.

Part Four: *Describing Your Physiological Reactions*
How does your body respond in this situation? Review your bodily systems, and list all of your reactions.

enough and that at this point the best way to answer any further questions you have is to begin" or "That sounds like a topic really worth devoting some attention to, and we can discuss it more later, but for now I think we should move on to beginning exposure").

Exposure treatment usually begins with the selection of a situation from the client's exposure hierarchy that elicits a SUDS rating close to zero. The exact method by which the client can be exposed to the stimuli depends on the type of exposure being conducted. Constant across all methods of exposure, however, is the general formula of the client being fully exposed to each situation from his or her hierarchy

until his or her SUDS level declines to an acceptable level, regardless of the original level of SUDS. What constitutes "an acceptable level" depends on the goals and model of the exposure therapy. A model focused on *mastery* would emphasize a high level of proficiency in minimizing the anxiety response and would have as a goal a SUDS rating close to zero. In contrast, a *coping* model of exposure would focus on reducing anxiety to a manageable level, not on complete anxiety reduction, and a SUDS rating 10 points less than the original value might be an acceptable goal for each item. Regardless of the model and goal the helper uses, helper and client should discuss and agree on what the goals of exposure

---

Scene Description Information

Brief description _____ SUDS _____

Describe the scene in detail using all senses (sight, sound, smell, taste, touch) _____
_____
_____

What are your typical behavioral responses? _____
_____

What are your thoughts? _____

What are your physiological responses? _____

(After the client spontaneously reports such responses, inquire about bodily systems not mentioned, and about potential physiological activation, such as increased heart rate, elevated muscle tension, rapid breathing, sweating, and blurry vision.)

Figure 16.2 Exposure Scene Description Form

Exposure Record

Name _____ Day/Date _____ Time Start/Finish _____

Location _____   Persons Present _____

Stimulus/Situation _____

SUDS	Thoughts	Physical Sensations
Start _____		
5 min _____		
10 min _____		
15 min _____		
20 min _____		
25 min _____		
30 min _____		
35 min _____		
40 min _____		
45 min _____		
50 min _____		
55 min _____		
60 min _____		
65 min _____		
70 min _____		
75 min _____		

Figure 16.3 Exposure Record Sheet

therapy will be. Each exposure session should be recorded on a sheet similar to the example in Figure 16.3.

When a client's SUDS rating has reduced to a predetermined level, the stimulus can be presented again. The helper should take care to encourage the client to remain in the exposure situation until he or she experiences a reduction in anxiety and distress, even if this takes some time. If the client or the clinician terminates exposure prematurely, several negative outcomes are likely: the client will be reinforced for escape/avoidance behavior, the clinician will be reinforcing distorted cognitions that the stimulus is dangerous and worthy of fear and avoidance, new learning severing the connection between fear and the stimulus will not occur, and client self-efficacy will be decreased even further.

In managing time, the helper should have a period set aside at the end of the session to discuss the client's experience and to identify behaviors detrimental to the exposure therapy. The helper and the client can benefit by reviewing the client's perspective of the session because disconfirmation of the client's problematic cognitions can be highlighted. For example, a client with panic disorder might

have the belief that he will "go crazy" or suffer a heart attack if he experiences a panic attack. During interoceptive exposure (a form of exposure therapy where clients who are prone to being fearful of bodily sensations, especially sensations signaling arousal, are exposed to these very sensations through physical exercises that mimic some of the symptoms of a panic attack, such as rapid heart rate and shortness of breath), the client could be exposed to an increased heart rate through doing step-up exercises (Such procedures should be undertaken only after current assessment of the client's medical status.) These exercises increase heart rate and can lead to client fear and anxiety that subsequently subside. After interoceptive exposure, the client and helper can discuss the experience and relate it to expectations beforehand ("What did you expect would happen during the exposure?" "What did you think would happen if you experienced the symptoms of a panic attack?" "How did it feel to experience an increased heart rate and more rapid breathing?" "What happened after the exposure?" "What do you think will happen the next time you experience increased heart rate and breathing?"). It is important to facilitate the client drawing his or her own conclusions, rather than telling the client what to say and think. Exposure is *experiential* learning; it contradicts the spirit of the therapy to engage in a didactic component at the end instead of allowing the client to reach his or her own conclusions independently at his or her own pace.

The helper also must be watchful for signs the client is engaging in avoidance or safety-seeking behaviors during exposure. Such actions delay progress in therapy and reinforce behaviors detrimental to coping effectively with anxiety. Avoidance and safety-seeking behaviors come in all shapes and sizes, and helpers are strongly encouraged to examine the function a given behavior serves rather than focus solely on the form of the behavior. Some avoidance and safety-seeking behaviors are more common than others, though, and there are several "red flags" a helper can be vigilant about that probably indicate a client is not fully benefiting from exposure therapy. If a client's SUDS ratings do not rise near the anticipated level, the client could possibly be engaging in overt (e.g., looking away from the stimulus) or covert (e.g., thinking of something else) avoidance. Although some clients have learned to avoid a stimulus so proficiently that they overestimate their SUDS rating ahead of time, helpers will need to gently but firmly address the possibility of avoidance. A helper also should take note when clients talk excessively during exposure sessions or repeatedly ask questions such as "Are you sure this is safe?" or "You're sure that snake can't get out of the terrarium?" Excessive talking typically acts as a form of distraction and indicates the client is not fully experiencing the stimulus. Repeated questions, in contrast, often are an attempt to seek reassurance from the helper. Although it can be tempting to answer the client's questions to allay client fears, such behavior can have a detrimental effect by implicitly reinforcing the belief that the stimulus is unsafe and deserving of worry. Clients also could learn to become dependent on the helper to complete exposure exercises ("If it hadn't been for you letting me know it was safe, I don't think I could have done it"). Clients should be learning that they are capable of independently coping effectively with the feared stimuli, not that exposure is possible only with the assistance of an "expert."

After assessing the client's first exposure session and addressing any difficulties that arise, the helper typically utilizes exposure again and again, session after session. When the client gains competence with one stimulus from the hierarchy by showing a minimal SUDS rating and minimal avoidance, the client and helper should move on to the next item on the exposure hierarchy. After each session, the client and helper should take time to discuss the exposure and any insights the client had, as well as address any safety-seeking or avoidance behaviors. Gradual exposure therapy is an iterative process and evolves over time as new issues arise and are addressed. Moreover, as therapy progresses, the client should engage in independent, self-directed exposure exercises outside of the therapeutic context, which should be recorded on an exposure record (see Figure 16.3). Such homework assignments can include stimuli with which the client already has demonstrated some proficiency in session while still "pushing" the client out of his or her comfort zone. These homework assignments allow the client to experience a decrease in anxiety in the presence of a fear-provoking stimulus in multiple contexts. Such learning is vital to ensure the client generalizes new associations made between stimuli and the absence of anxiety.

This sequence of steps in exposure therapy allows helpers to gain an initial understanding of the how-to of exposure. No substitute exists, though, for supervised experiences. As exposure therapy rests on the assumption that several sessions of experiential learning can begin the process of reversing learned habits of fear and avoidance, learning and mastering exposure therapy skills also requires learning by doing. Further, the particulars of specific forms of gradual exposure therapy deserve further discussion to better highlight specific advantages and disadvantages, as well as subtle nuances and areas of current research and debate. Described below are three specific forms of gradual exposure therapy: imaginal, *in vitro*, and *in vivo* exposure.

Imaginal Exposure

In this form of exposure the client is exposed to imagined scenes that provoke anxiety. Commonly, the client describes anxiety-provoking scenes in detail, and the helper or client can record the information. Note cards historically were used, but there are many advantages to typing and storing the information electronically using a laptop computer, allowing for ongoing revisions. To make the image as realistic as possible, the client should attempt to explain the scene with reference to as much sensory and response information as possible. A client who has suffered a motor vehicle accident and now fears driving might describe the scene of simply sitting behind the wheel of an automobile. In addition to being able to list all the visual cues present when behind the wheel (the color of the dashboard and upholstery, the different gauges behind the steering column, the view from the rearview mirror, etc.), the client also should attempt to recall smells (e.g., the smell of leather upholstery), sounds (e.g., the sound of the engine idling), tactile sensations (e.g., the softness of the seats), and even tastes when possible (e.g., the taste of mint chewing gum if the client sometimes chews gum while driving). The ability to imagine a scene with great detail allows exposure to as many cues as possible to elicit anxiety, which then allows for subsequent anxiety reduction and new learning.

Imaginal exposure can be especially potent for clients whose primary fear-provoking stimuli are cognitions. For example, someone who witnessed the traumatic event of a fatal car accident could be fearful about his or her memories of the accident. In these cases, special care should be taken to walk the client through imaginal exposure in a supportive environment while establishing evidence for the new belief and understanding that thoughts themselves cannot cause harm nor must they necessarily lead to overt-motor behaviors.

The usual sequence of imaginal exposure is to establish a neutral or positive image selected by the client that elicits a SUDS rating of zero. Sitting back in a chair with eyes closed at the start of the exposure session, the client can imagine this scene to assist with relaxation. When the client is relaxed with a SUDS rating at or near zero, he or she should give some signal to the helper (e.g., raise index finger), preferably a nonverbal signal to minimize the strain on the client's attention. The helper then asks the client to imagine a scene from the exposure hierarchy. When the client signals the scene is a clear image, the helper continues the exposure for a brief period of time (typically 15 to 30 seconds) before asking the client to erase the image. Following this, the helper quickly but unobtrusively asks for a SUDS rating before asking the client to imagine the neutral scene again for a minute or two. When the client signals relaxation again, the helper asks the client to return to the scene from the hierarchy. Once the SUDS rating that the scene elicits diminishes significantly, the helper and client move on to the next scene. It is best to end sessions with successful completion of an anxiety scene, followed by a neutral or relaxing scene. The next session should begin with the last scene from the previous session that elicited a minimal amount of anxiety.

With imaginal exposure, much depends on the helper being a good storyteller, eliciting images in the client and reading the scripts in an evocative manner, to spark the client's imagination. Client avoidance can take the form of refusal to clearly imagine an anxiety-provoking scene. The helper and client should discuss the client's concerns regarding clearly picturing the scene, and care should be taken to make sure the hierarchy is not ascended too quickly. Homework for imaginal exposure typically takes the form of practicing at home with items successfully completed in therapy.

Imaginal exposure can be either used alone or in conjunction with (and typically before) *in vitro* or *in vivo* exposure. If all the client's fear-provoking stimuli are cognitive, imaginal exposure alone would make sense. Usually, though, even for clients whose anxiety-provoking stimuli are primarily cognitive, real-world events tend to increase the likelihood of such cognitions. Victims of posttraumatic stress disorder who experience anxiety and distress from memories of the trauma might experience the memories more often in the context of stimuli that remind them of the event, for example. Usually, imaginal exposure should be used as a stepping-stone to more realistic exposure so new learning can better generalize to the client's everyday life.

Advantages of Imaginal Exposure Imaginal exposure offers several advantages to helpers. It might be the only form of exposure that clients with severe cases of anxiety are willing to endure at first. Disconfirming negative expectations and building self-efficacy can occur through imaginal exposure, which can then allow for the client to progress to more reality-based exposure. Another benefit derives from the element of control present. Imagined scenes can be created to conform precisely with how the helper and client would like to see exposure progress. Unforeseen occurrences that could potentially hinder progress for some clients (e.g., a client with obsessive–compulsive disorder falling ill subsequent to a session involving touching a bathroom door handle, or a client with a specific phobia of dogs inadvertently getting bitten) have much less likelihood of occurring with imaginal exposure. Imaginal exposure also presents the most direct form of exposure for fear-provoking stimuli that are primarily cognitive.

Finally, imaginal exposure is more practically implemented, as some situations are impossible to reliably produce (e.g., flying on an airplane with severe turbulence) or ethically inappropriate to recreate (e.g., trauma in combat or physical assault) *in vivo*.

Limitations of Imaginal Exposure Though offering some distinct benefits, imaginal exposure certainly has limitations. Some clients less skilled in creating mental images might have a difficult time fully immersing themselves in anxiety-provoking scenes, and may view the process as "hokey" or overly contrived. If the scene does not evoke a sufficient amount of anxiety or does not closely resemble the actual anxiety-provoking stimuli, new learning capable of overriding old learning might not occur. Imagined scenes might be quite realistic for clients with vivid imaginations, but they still are symbols and representations of actual stimuli. The best (i.e., longest-lasting and most likely to generalize) learning likely occurs in the presence of real stimuli, as research suggests that in vivo exposure may be the most effective (Davey, 1997; Zoellner, Abramowitz, & Moore, 2003). Finally, although the helper can monitor a client's SUDS ratings and infer from self-report that the client is picturing certain scenes, the only person with complete access to precisely what the client is imagining is the client. With real stimuli, conversely, the clinician at the least can directly observe and quantify their presentation (e.g., timing how long a patient with dental phobia can allow a dentist to hold a dental instrument in his or her mouth).

Imagery Ability and Assessment The efficacy of imaginal therapies depends at least in part on the client's ability to vividly imagine. What is in the imagination has the power to evoke emotions, including psychophysiological responses in the form of heart rate change, muscle tension, and sweat gland activity, among others. The use of imagery in therapy often takes the form of "visualization," focusing on visual images, or "pictures in the head." Nevertheless, imagery transcends all sensory modalities, including smell, taste, hearing, and touch. In the case of dental phobia, for example, the client not only may have memories of visual images of the dentist, dental chair, and instruments, but also may remember the smell of the dental office, the taste in the mouth associated with different dental procedures, hearing the dental drill, the touch of the instruments on her teeth and gums, and the feeling of the dentist's gloved fingers inside her mouth. These images may be distressing to the individual with dental phobia, but it is precisely this material that provides the basis for positive therapeutic change. These images actually are "grist for the mill" of imaginal desensitization. In fact, the more psychophysiologically evocative such images are, the greater is the likelihood of successful imaginal exposure. It should be noted that these images are stored in a client's memory and may be based on actual experiences of the client, but also they may originate from vicariously learned material, such as stories from friends and relatives, or they may have been created from the client's own fearful anticipation of "what might be," based on media reports or other incidental-learning.

Peter Lang and colleagues have done a tremendous amount of work on imagery in therapy (Lang, 1977), and they have found that images of the client, across sensory modalities, are powerful tools that can be used effectively in therapy. Images often are prompted by the clinician, who helps the client manage them so that they are evocative when necessary but thinking about them does not spiral out of control. Typically, personally relevant imagery scenes are more evocative than generic ones. In fact, helpers should be cognizant of the fact that there is a great deal of personal relevance in imagery. Relaxing scenes, for example, are highly individual, and the clinician should elicit them from the client, rather than assuming that what he or she considers relaxing would also be so for the client. An image of spending a lazy day lounging by a waterfall may seem relaxing to the helper, but it would not be so for a client who has a phobia of water or for a client who remembers a nasty breakup with a romantic partner after a day spent together at a waterfall.

In using imagery in therapy, it is important to know the imagery ability of one's client. Imagery ability differs across individuals, likely along a continuum, ranging from some people who are quite proficient with imagery and are able to elicit and control images quite well, to those who report little or no ability to "see pictures in the head" and do not respond to even the most seemingly evocative prompts. The helper can assess imagery ability informally by taking a client through a brief trial of mildly evocative imagery and following up with questions about the client's degree of engagement and ability to think and feel "as if" the situation

actually were happening. There also are self-report instruments that assess imagery ability (e.g., Questionnaire upon Mental Imagery; Sheehan, 1976).

It is possible to do "imagery training" in clients, although it rarely may be necessary because when imagery ability is low, other forms of exposure typically are better alternatives than devoting time to helping the client to learn imagery skills. Nevertheless, in certain instances when the actual stimuli are difficult to access for practical or ethical reasons, training in imagery may be a good choice. In such training, clients are given some brief instructions by the clinician, such as trying to act "as if" the situation actually was happening, rather than being a passive, distant observer of an event. Clients also are encouraged to use the full range of sensory modalities, trying to create not only the sights but the smells, tastes, sounds, and physical feelings associated with the situation. Imagery trials are conducted, using emotionally positive scenes. The client is asked to imagine and then is asked to report on his or her experiences in imagery, particularly physiological responses. These responses are the focus of attention for the practitioner, who praises them and encourages the client to accentuate such responses in future trials.

Imagery can be a powerful tool in imaginal desensitization and other forms of therapy. It also has been incorporated into new therapeutic applications.

Eye Movement Desensitization and Reprocessing   What some might consider a form of imaginal exposure, EMDR (eye movement desensitization and reprocessing) has received plenty of controversial attention in the literature over the past couple decades (Shapiro, 2001). Briefly explained, EMDR is a form of therapy primarily designed for clients suffering from traumatic memories. The client recalls the traumatic memories while the helper moves his or her finger rapidly back and forth across the client's field of vision. While continuing to remember the traumatic event, the client follows the helper's finger. Proponents of EMDR claim that clients "reprocess" memories of the traumatic event until the memories no longer evoke anxiety and fear. (According to EMDR experts, special training is required to properly conduct EMDR sessions, and no helper should attempt to perform EMDR therapy without first receiving proper training. It is of course true for any helper employing any therapeutic technique that appropriate prior training and supervision are necessary. Whether special certification is necessary is a matter of contention and professional practice.)

The empirical support for EMDR has been mixed. Some articles and reviews support the efficacy and effectiveness of EMDR (e.g., Davidson & Parker, 2001), and the APA lists it as a probably efficacious treatment for posttraumatic stress disorder (Chambless et al., 1997). Many other articles and reviews claim EMDR is less successful than traditional exposure

LEARNING ACTIVITY	16.3	Developing an Example Imaginal Exposure Session

This activity is designed to give you some practice in using imaginal exposure. Assume that Isabella, the model client, has a phobia about receiving a dental injection.

Part One: *Developing a Hierarchy of Situations*
Write or, better yet, type into a computer a list of likely situations that Isabella would find uncomfortable related to needles and oral injections.

Part Two: *Develop the Scenes*
Use the sample form (see Figure 16.2) to help fully develop the description of each situation, including

behavioral, verbal, and physiological aspects of Isabella's response.

Part Three: *Conducting Exposure*
Read the situations out loud with appropriate feeling and a persuasive, storytelling voice designed to engage the client. Use appropriate pauses to allow the hypothetical (but absent) client to think about and fully experience the scene.

---

therapy (e.g., Devilly, 2002; Taylor et al., 2003). Some critics have expressed the belief that EMDR is simply imaginal exposure with unnecessary eye movements, and some literature exists to support this position (Devilly, 2002). Other researchers take exception to the ambiguity about what constitutes EMDR. EMDR proponents have rejected research critiques because they claim the critics conducted the procedure improperly.

Although it is not yet possible to draw firm conclusions about the success or failure of EMDR, several important issues must be addressed by both sides. If EMDR is to be considered supported or refuted by science, then it must be subject to scientific investigative principles. What constitutes EMDR must be explicitly stated (preferably manualized) so that treatment can reliably be replicated. Clinician adherence to EMDR protocol should be documented and meet adequate levels. If possible, research participants should be randomly assigned to an EMDR treatment group or to a group undergoing an already established treatment (preferred), receiving a psychological or pill placebo (less preferred), or serving as a wait-list control (least preferred). It is preferable that the research be conducted by various independent research teams. Dismantling studies also should be conducted to determine the necessary and sufficient components of treatment. Finally, researchers should agree beforehand what evidence would and would not support acceptance of EMDR as an empirically supported treatment. Having conducted our discussion of imaginal exposure, we provide an opportunity to practice an imaginal exposure session in Learning Activity 16.3.

In Vitro Exposure (Simulated Situations)

Although *in vitro* technically refers to "in the test tube," we use that term to refer to exposure that happens in an office situation, using role plays or other simulated situations. *In vitro* exposure, which consists of exposure to stimuli and

situations meant to simulate actual fear-provoking stimuli, lies between imaginal exposure and *in vivo* exposure in degree of realism. Role plays are used extensively in Cognitive Behavioral Group Therapy for Social Phobia (Hope, Heimberg, Juster, & Turk, 2000), as they allow exposure to simulated social situations in the safety of a group therapy session. To the best of his or her ability, the helper attempts to re-create in the therapy the events that the client reports as eliciting an anxiety response. The complexity and degree of realism of these simulated situations can vary greatly. A helper who has a thorough understanding of the habits and mannerisms of an individual whom a client associates with anxiety can create a fairly realistic and anxiety-provoking stimulus. Similarly, a helper with the proper resources can create realistic faux vomit for a client with a fear of vomiting by others (e.g., one's child).

One way to conduct *in vitro* exposure is to begin by examining the scenes and stimuli described by the client as part of his or her exposure hierarchy. The helper should decide which scenes are better suited for *in vitro* exposure and which scenes are better suited for *in vivo* exposure. Additionally, some scenes lend themselves well to both *in vitro* and *in vivo* exposure. For example, a client with social anxiety disorder might experience anxiety in relation to speaking with coworkers (SUDS = 40) and speaking with the boss (SUDS = 60). Most likely, *in vivo* exposure would be recommended as a homework assignment, perhaps later in therapy. *In vitro* exposure, however, offers the chance to ease into *in vivo* exposure, to practice social skills, and to gain exposure to a variety of reactions from coworkers and the boss (warmth and support, indifference, hostility, etc.).

As *in vitro* exposure is typically meant to imitate real-life scenes and stimuli that elicit anxiety, it is important to make the situations as real as possible for the client. Properly trained and ethically sanctioned confederates can be enlisted to simulate situations involving strangers or people of the opposite sex. In addition, as in vitro exposure mirrors reality, it is important to usually have the express goal with *in vitro* exposure of eventually moving on to *in vivo* exposure. Sometimes, moving on to *in vivo* exposure will prove challenging. A helper using *in vitro* exposure with a client who has a fear of flying will most likely not move on to *in vivo* exposure until toward the end of therapy, whereas a helper using role plays to expose a client to social interactions might use a format in which situations for *in vivo* exposure homework are practiced first in session via *in vitro* exposure, and then practiced as homework prior to the next session.

In vitro exposure also can focus on interoceptive cues—that is, internal physiological sensations that the client fears. Interoceptive exposure involves the client engaging in activities that produce physiological sensations such as dizziness or heart rate increase (e.g., by spinning in a chair or or doing "step-up" exercises with a stool [Barlow, 2002]. It can be argued that this exposure actually is *in vivo*, but we classify it as *in vitro* because it typically takes place in the helper's office, under the helper's supervision, not in a naturalistic environment.

Helpers should be vigilant against attempts to escape and avoid *in vitro* exposure. A refusal by the client to attempt to immerse her- or himself in simulated situations could be related to a fear of the consequences of immersion. When using virtual-reality technology, clients might protest with claims of motion sickness. Clients also might protest against repeated role plays of the same scenario, claiming not to understand why it is necessary to conduct the exercise again and again if it went well the first time. Although client concerns with *in vitro* exposure might be legitimate, helpers need to be prepared to deal with resistance.

Advantages of *In Vitro* Exposure *In vitro* exposure offers the skilled helper several distinct advantages. Clients can be exposed to situations and stimuli through *in vitro* exposure that would be very difficult to conduct using *in vivo* exposure. Unlike imaginal exposure, *in vitro* exposure presents the helper with the ability to directly observe the stimuli to which the client is exposed. Moreover, the helper can execute more control during *in vitro* exposure than during most *in vivo* or imaginal exposure sessions. For example, the helper is limited only by his or her imagination as to how a role play can be directed. Initially, a positive and reinforcing experience can be crafted for the client; later, a situation designed to challenge the client's ability to cope with adverse circumstances can be orchestrated. This element of control permits the helper to direct exposure with a degree of precision and certainty not possible with most *in vivo* exposure.

Limitations of *In Vitro* Exposure Perhaps one of the biggest disadvantages of *in vitro* exposure can be the time

and resources sometimes required to properly conduct the exposure. Not all helpers have ready access to virtual-reality equipment, nor can all helpers easily enlist the help of confederates to assist with the exposure. The amount of time and effort required to conduct *in vitro* exposure in addition to or instead of *in vivo* exposure can seem not to be worthwhile, especially as not all forms of *in vitro* exposure have received the same amount of empirical support as *in vivo* exposure. Finally, not all clients will be able to take *in vitro* exposure seriously or fully immerse themselves in the experience, potentially not benefiting as much as they could from *in vivo* exposure.

Role play Role plays are simulated interactions between two or more people meant to approximate interactions that have happened or will potentially happen in the future. The client typically "plays" him- or herself while the helper and confederates "play" other people in the client's everyday environment. Sometimes, especially for clients with skills deficits accompanying anxiety problems, the helper can assume the role of the client at first in order to model proficient social and coping skills. Role plays have proven useful in treatment for anxiety disorders (e.g., Foa, 1997).

Role plays can be conducted in several ways, based on the client's current skill level and the experience the helper wishes the client to have. If the client's skill level appears to be low, approximately less than 60 percent proficient, it probably will be a better learning experience to watch the helper perform the task first. Similarly, if the client's anxiety level will most likely prevent a somewhat competent performance, the helper probably will want to perform the role play first to demonstrate the correct way to do it. But if the client appears to possess a minimum level of skill and will likely not be hindered too greatly by anxiety, it might be best to have the client perform the task first, without the helper modeling it.

An additional decision that helpers must face with role plays is the level of proficiency to expect during the role play. If the emphasis is on the client being able to perform certain tasks while still experiencing some anxiety, then perfection certainly would not be a realistic goal for the role play. When modeling the role play, the helper also might portray him- or herself as coping with the situation despite anxiety. Alternatively, if the emphasis of treatment is on almost complete anxiety reduction, role plays might be repeated until no anxiety seems apparent. Modeled role plays might be performed with greater mastery by the helper in order to create a higher standard.

Virtual Reality A form of in vitro exposure gaining attention in recent years has been virtual-reality exposure (Wiederhold & Wiederhold, 2005). Virtual-reality exposure (VRE) involves using electronic media equipment to

BOX 16.1	RESEARCH ON EXPOSURE THERAPY

Distraction and Safety-Seeking Behavior

Kamphuis, J. H., & Telch, M. J. (2000). Effects of distraction and guided threat reappraisal on fear reduction during exposure-based treatments for specific fears. *Behaviour Research and Therapy, 38,* 1163–1181.

Sloan, T., & Telch, M. J. (2005). The effects of safety-seeking behavior and guided threat reappraisal on fear reduction during exposure: An experimental investigation. *Behaviour Research and Therapy, 40,* 235–251.

Telch, M. J., Valentine, D. P., Ilai, D., Young, P. R., Powers, M. B., & Smits, J. A. J. (2004). Fear activation and distraction during the emotional processing of claustrophobic fear. *Journal of Behavior Therapy and Experimental Psychiatry, 35,* 219–232.

Virtual-Reality Exposure

Price, M., & Anderson, P. (2007). The role of presence in virtual reality exposure therapy. *Journal of Anxiety Disorders, 21,* 742–751.

Rothbaum, B. O. (2006). Virtual reality exposure therapy. In B. O. Rothbaum (Ed.), *Pathological anxiety: Emotional processing in etiology and treatment* (pp. 227–244). New York: Guilford Press.

Rothbaum, B. O., Anderson, P., Zimand, E., Hodges, L., Lang, D., & Wilson, J. (2006). Virtual reality exposure therapy and standard (in vivo) exposure therapy in the treatment of fear of flying. *Behavior Therapy, 37,* 80–90.

Wiederhold, B. K., & Wiederhold, M. D. (2005). *Virtual reality therapy* for *anxiety disorders: Advances in evaluation and treatment.* Washington, DC: American Psychological Association.

D-cycloserine

Davis, M., Myers, K. M., Ressler, K. J., & Rothbaum, B. O. (2005). Facilitation of extinction of conditioned fear by d-cycloserine. *Current Directions in Psychological Science, 14,* 214–219.

Hofmann, S. G., Pollack, M. H., & Otto, M. W. (2006). Augmentation treatment of psychotherapy for anxiety disorders with d-cycloserine. *CNS Drug Reviews, 12,* 208–217.

Otto, M. W., Basden, S. L., Leyro, T. M., McHugh, R. K., & Hofmann, S. G. (2007). Clinical perspectives on the combination of d-cycloserine and cognitive–behavioral therapy for the treatment of anxiety disorders. *CNS Spectrums, 12,* 51–56, 59–61.

Ressler, K. J., Rothbaum, B. O., Tannenbaum, L., Anderson, P., Graap, K., Zimand, E., et al. (2004). Cognitive enhancers as adjuncts to psychotherapy: Use of d-cycloserine in phobic individuals to facilitate extinction of fear. *Archives of General Psychiatry, 61,* 1136–1144.

Woods, A. M., & Bouton, M. E. (2006). D-cycloserine facilitates extinction but does not eliminate renewal of the conditioned emotional response. *Behavioral Neuroscience, 120,* 1159–1162.

create a realistic, three-dimensional environment in which a person can be immersed. Either the helper or the client can control the client's progress through the virtual-reality environment. Depending on the level of technology being used, VRE can be an experience closely resembling real life for some clients. Even if the VRE environment does not precisely resemble a real-world setting, many clients can still experience a large amount of anxiety and fear in response to VRE stimuli, creating the opportunity for new learning to occur.

VRE can be especially useful for exposing clients to situations and stimuli not easily done through *in vivo* exposure. Further, it presents the opportunity to expose clients to a variety of situations without needing to leave the treatment setting. A helper assisting a client with a paralyzing fear of heights does not need to locate an appropriate tall building or other height-related stimulus in the surrounding area and arrange a "field trip." Instead, the client can come to the helper's normal work setting, and suitable stimuli can be created with VRE equipment (a tall building with an observation deck, a bridge, a cliff, a glass elevator, a hot air

balloon ride, etc.). The stimuli the client can gain exposure to are limited only by imagination and technology.

Virtual-reality exposure has become a "hot" area of research in recent years, and early research on its efficacy and effectiveness appears promising. Research on VRE also could have implications for the way helpers understand the underlying mechanisms of exposure techniques. Further work must be done to better understand and to invest more confidence in VRE as a form of exposure therapy, though. Readers are directed to Box 16.1 for more research on VRE. Ending our discussion of *in vitro* exposure, Learning Activity 16.4 focuses on practicing an *in vitro* exposure session.

In Vivo Exposure

In vivo exposure therapy involves exposure to the actual stimuli and situations that provoke anxiety and fear for a client. *In vivo* exposure can be conducted in or out of the therapy setting depending on the nature of the client's problem. It might be feasible to conduct *in vivo* exposure in session with a client who has a fear of spiders by bringing in different spider stimuli. With a client who has a fear of riding in a motor vehicle, *in vivo* exposure ultimately must take place outside of the therapy setting in an actual automobile. (As noted elsewhere, in such instances, it typically is prudent for the exposure sessions to be guided by professionals from a driving school.)

In vivo exposure is conducted in much the same way as imaginal and *in vitro* exposure, and it generally follows the steps described above (see Figure 16.1). Perhaps an important aspect of *in vivo* exposure is that the helper should take steps to ensure the client remains in the presence of the feared stimulus until his or her SUDS rating decreases. Often the helper is assisting the client in overcoming years of avoidance, and ensuring that the client remains in the presence of the fear-provoking stimuli for an extended period of time can require skilled exercise of the helper's clinical acumen. If the client is to break the association of escape or avoidance and anxiety reduction, he or she should engage in new learning where anxiety reduction occurs in the presence of the feared stimulus.

As with other forms of exposure, helpers must be on the lookout for escape, avoidance, and safety-seeking behaviors from the client. Clients might attempt to delay exposure by talking about it rather than doing it. During exposure, clients might not look directly at the stimulus or engage in other sensory avoidance (e.g., not listening, thinking about something else). Clients also could engage in distraction by conversing with the helper. Helpers should note that clients can learn to escape *in vivo* exposure by reporting lower SUDS ratings despite minimal reduction in actual fear and distress. If a helper notices a disparity between a client's self-reported distress and overt-motor behavior (e.g., looking away from the stimulus) or physiological response

(e.g., sweating profusely), the helper should attempt to bring this disparity to the client's attention in a nonaccusatory manner.

In vivo exposure has the additional advantage of lending itself well to homework assignments. A client being seen for a one-hour therapy session once a week is living the other 167 hours of his or her life outside of the therapy session. With evidence suggesting learning from exposure therapy has a strong contextual component (Mystkowski et al., 2002), it is essential for clients to engage in exposure exercises outside of the therapy context and in the settings in which they live their daily lives. Homework can be assigned to a client based on progress in therapy, although the client can complete exposure exercises with a particular stimulus for the first time outside of the therapy context. In order to create a palatable title for the exercise and to reduce unrealistic all-or-none expectations of success, homework assignments even can be referred to as behavioral experiments. Consider the example of a client with social anxiety speaking with a colleague at work. The helper can present the exposure exercise of conversing with the colleague as a behavioral experiment to test the client's beliefs and assumptions. This way, the helper can create a situation in which the client seldom fails. If the exposure experience goes well, the client builds self-efficacy and engages in new learning suggesting he or she can cope with social anxiety. If the conversation goes poorly, the client and helper can discuss perhaps why the experience went poorly and what can be done differently in the future to create a more positive experience.

One consideration that is discussed in more detail later in the chapter is the presence or absence of the helper during in vivo exposure. The therapist's presence early in a course of

LEARNING ACTIVITY **16.5**   **Developing an Example *In Vivo* Exposure Session**

This activity is designed to give you some practice in using *in vivo* exposure. Again assume that Isabella, the model client, has a phobia about receiving a dental injection.

Part One: *Developing a Hierarchy of Situations*
Write or, better yet, type into a computer a list of likely situations that Isabella would find uncomfortable related to needles and oral injections. (This list may be the same one you constructed for a previous Learning Activity.)

Part Two: *Develop the In Vivo Steps*
Write or, better yet, type into a computer a list of likely steps that Isabella would take in this exposure. If Isabella is in need of dental treatment that will require the use of a dental injection, then in vivo exposure involves actually visiting a

dentist for the necessary treatment. Ideally, there would not be time pressure to complete the appointment immediately, although that sometimes is the case. Collaboration with Isabella's dentist is necessary, with the written permission of Isabella and her parents. Possible steps associated with in vivo exposure may be entering the dental office, talking to the dentist about the injection, receiving education about dental injections and how they are best completed, having a topical substance applied in the area of the mouth for the injection as a physically desensitizing agent, having the dentist touch the part of Isabella's mouth in which the injection will take place, having the dentist use good chairside technique and not showing Isabella the syringe and needle but bringing them into her mouth for the length of time an injection would take place, and then actually performing the injection.

---

in vivo therapy can help to make the exposure more gradual and palatable. In some instances, a team of two or more practitioners (one of whom may be in training) may be helpful, adding generalization to the situation so that the client's success completing an activity is not ascribed to the presence of a specific individual such as the primary helper.

In vivo exposure can come after imaginal and/or in vitro exposure, or *in vivo* exposure can be the sole means of exposure used during treatment. As discussed above, some clients might find it easier to engage in less realistic forms of exposure first before facing their real anxiety-provoking stimuli. Other times, the situation might lend itself quite well to *in vivo* exposure from the beginning. The ultimate use of *in vivo* exposure methods remains up to the clinical judgment of the helper and the informed preference of the client.

Advantages of *In Vivo* Exposure Despite disagreement over the precise mechanism through which exposure works, most researchers could probably agree that the most effective learning during exposure likely occurs in the presence of the actual anxiety-provoking stimuli. As the goal of treatment typically involves improving the client's adaptive functioning and reducing his or her distress in daily living, it makes sense to engage in exposure to the stimuli from the client's day-to-day life that have resulted in impaired functioning and increased distress. Finally, *in vivo* exposure involves exposure to tangible stimuli that can objectively be quantified to document the client's treatment gains. A helper utilizing *in vivo* exposure can note that a client who began therapy unable to remain in a room with a caged, common garden snake one foot in length was able to drape

a python of six feet in length over his or her shoulders for a period of five minutes.

Limitations of *In Vivo* Exposure Many clients have reservations about engaging in *in vivo* exposure, especially without any sort of "preparation" through imaginal or *in vitro* exposure. First, because the helper cannot exercise complete control over *in vivo* exposure exercises, the potential always exists that unforeseen events will cause a temporary setback in the client's progress. Second, behavioral experiment homework assignments can be an aversive experience for a client who meets with a high degree of "failure," and the helper might have to spend therapy time repairing the client's damaged self-confidence and faith in exposure treatment. Third, the primary anxiety-provoking stimuli for some clients can be imaginal in nature, and *in vivo* exposure might not be the best form of exposure therapy for eliciting the greatest amount of client anxiety to promote the most new learning. Fourth, there are practical and ethical limitations that sometimes prohibit use of *in vivo* exposure. As with imaginal and *in vitro* exposure, we present an opportunity to practice *in vivo* exposure in Learning Activity 16.5.

Intensive Exposure

In addition to the methods of gradual exposure described above, exposure can be conducted in a much more time-limited, intense fashion. Whereas gradual exposure procedures emphasize moving at a pace that slowly "pushes" the client beyond his or her zone of comfort, intensive exposure procedures can be used during which clients encounter more fear or anxiety-provoking stimuli in a more compressed amount of time. Rather than bringing the client in for approximately an hour a week for several weeks to ascend the exposure hierarchy, the clinician (with informed and voluntary consent from the client) can begin therapy with exposure to items the client reports as being the most fear provoking.

To date, much evidence indicates that intensive exposure seems to be effective in reducing fear and avoidance (Zoellner et al., 2003), with gains maintained over time. With evidence supporting various ways of conducting exposure, the method selected for an individual client will be decided by several factors. First, and perhaps most important, it is our experience that gradual exposure techniques tend to be more palatable for many clients. Clients who have engaged in avoidance and worry for years typically balk at the idea of immediately being exposed to the worst situations they can conceive. Yet some clients enter therapy so motivated to change that they are willing to do whatever is required to help that change occur as quickly as possible. Second, the timing of the different sessions required for the two general methods of exposure must be considered. Gradual exposure will most likely require one or two shorter (1 to 1.5 hours) sessions a week for several weeks, depending on the rate of client progress and attendance. Intensive exposure demands blocks of several hours (often a minimum of 3), but usually fewer sessions are required. Third, some presenting problems lend themselves more readily to gradual or to intensive exposure. For example, a helper more skilled with *in vivo* exposure with access to a zoo or pet shop might readily consider intensive exposure for a client with a fear of snakes. But a helper who has a client with an intense fear of flying might not be able to conduct intensive exposure through flying on an airplane because of the implications of the client experiencing panic on a plane crowded with other passengers.

It remains, then, for the helper and client to decide together which form of exposure is appropriate for the client's specific difficulties in living. The gradual exposure methods may be more acceptable to a broader range of clientele, but intensive exposure has its place, both historically and presently. With clients who desire rapid change, intensive exposure methods such as flooding and implosive therapy may be more direct and efficient and may provide relief much more quickly.

Flooding

Flooding essentially is an intensive exposure therapy form of *in vivo* exposure therapy. Clients are presented with fear-provoking stimuli for an extended period of time until they experience a reduction in anxiety and distress (Zoellner et al., 2003). Several important differences from *in vivo* exposure therapy involve the nature and order of the stimuli presented, the training of a relaxation response, the length of the session, and the more likely explanation of why

the technique works. Whereas *in vivo* exposure typically involves a gradual ascent up the exposure hierarchy beginning with the *least* fear-provoking stimuli, flooding begins exposure with the stimuli that elicit the *most* fear from a client. Whereas a typical *in vivo* exposure session might last an hour and a half at most, a session of flooding often lasts for several hours, as the session continues until the client's fear reaction subsides almost completely. Finally, emphasis on treatment gains for *in vivo* exposure often focuses on a client's between-session reductions in physiological responses and SUDS ratings in response to fear-provoking stimuli, which likely suggests that extinction could be the method of learning. Helpers using flooding, in contrast, emphasize within-session reduction in SUDS ratings and physiological reaction.

One example of how *in vivo* exposure and flooding differ could be in the treatment of a fear of spiders. *In vivo* exposure might progress over several sessions from cartoon images of spiders, to photographs of spiders, to being in a room with a spider, to holding a spider. Flooding would more likely involve being in a room with a spider and ultimately touching it over the course of several hours during one session.

Implosive Therapy

If flooding is analogous to *in vivo* exposure, then implosive therapy would probably be best described as related to imaginal exposure. Rather than gradually ascending a client's hierarchy with short presentations of fear-provoking imagined scenes, implosive therapy utilizes prolonged and clinician-facilitated imagination of more intense fear-eliciting scenes (Levis & Krantweiss, 2003). The images are highly evocative and may tap into psychodynamically based conflict areas that are supposed to be related to the avoidance behavior. Many of the same distinctions between *in vivo* exposure and flooding hold up similarly for imaginal exposure and implosive therapy. One advantage that implosive therapy can offer is the ability to imagine distressing scenarios a clinician would be incapable of re-creating in real life. In treating a fear of spiders, for example, a helper using implosive therapy might ask a client to imagine being in the presence of a giant spider the size of a house. Nevertheless, the images can be quite horrific, and the treatment extremely stressful for both client and helper.

CONDUCTING EXPOSURE

Conducting exposure must be undertaken with adequate preparation by both helper and client, including plans for assessing progress over time. The most effective treatment is developed from a strong theoretical base, with plans for ongoing evaluation, and a clear goal in place. The preparation phase should not be taken lightly, as adequate planning is necessary to ensure that this often stressful procedure is executed properly and sensitively.

1. First, the clinician must develop a preliminary plan for exposure that will address the client's problems. Consideration must be given to the client's type of problem, as well as the client's characteristics, including both strengths (e.g., strong verbal and imaginative abilities) and limitations (e.g., depression), that may affect treatment progress. The type of problem likely will dictate at least the initial approach to exposure. For example, in the case of flying phobia, our experience is that imaginal approaches are typically best as an initial approach, for they can be readily utilized within in-office sessions. Nevertheless, the availability of local resources, such as a nearby airport, or airline programs to help (potential) customers to be more comfortable about flight, should be considered in this treatment planning. Also important is the timeline for the treatment. In our experience, clients with phobias sometimes present for treatment only when there is a looming real-life exposure, such as an essential business trip a considerable distance from the client's home, necessitating travel by air, or an upcoming speech that is unavoidable.

2. A second but perhaps the most important step is to obtain the expressed consent of the client: exposure must be conducted only with the client's informed agreement. Above and beyond any treatment contracts in writing, the client must understand the rationales for exposure and appreciate its likely effectiveness. It is necessary too for the client to be dedicated to the process of change. According to Heimberg and colleagues (Hope et al., 2000), clients participating in exposure must willingly "invest anxiety in a calmer future" (p. 9). We find that adage quite useful, sharing it with clients and reminding them of it over the course of treatment. Over time, as exposure leads to improved functioning in a client's everyday life, we encourage the idea of an exposure-based lifestyle. For the client to remain healthy in regard to a phobia or other problem, there must be ongoing exposure at periodic intervals, to lessen the possibility of return of fear. Typically, reaching agreement about exposure requires the clinician to share the conceptual background and mention at least some of the research support for this treatment. Also, the clinician explains the general approach (e.g., imaginal exposure first, followed by later *in vivo* exposure).

3. After there is agreement between client and helper, working on the specifics of the plan for exposure is the next step. Like other parts of this therapy, this process is best implemented as a collaborative one in which client and clinician work together, rather than the clinician being highly directive and imposing specific steps. In many cases, and depending on the client's verbal and writing abilities, the client is asked to do homework by bringing in a list of objects or situations that relate to the phobia or other clinical target problem. Often, we ask clients to construct a list that includes 10–15 stimuli or situations, in sequential order from least to most anxiety provoking. If a client appears to be highly avoidant or to have less well-developed paper-and-pencil or verbal skills, we construct this list in session. Some clients construct their lists and bring them in on paper or in an electronic format, allowing easier revision and addition. Typically, we first explain a SUDS rating system (e.g., 0–100; Wolpe, 1990), and we ask clients to have a representation of 10–15 objects or situations that fall across the range of possible scores, again with no greater than 10 points between items.

Discussed below are several areas of particular importance to consider ahead of time when planning exposure treatment.

Individual Approach

Like other forms of psychotherapy, exposure almost always is best individualized to the particular client and his or her problems. Typically, phobias that require clinical intervention are highly idiosyncratic, such as in the case of a client who feared green snakes but not brown ones, based on a belief about their relative dangerousness.

Preparation and Flexibility of the Clinician

As with any treatment, the clinician should be appropriately trained in exposure prior to implementing it with a client. Supervision of a clinician's first cases and of unusual or challenging cases is recommended. Some degree of anxiety on the part of the clinician in conducting exposure is normal and natural. Such anxiety may help motivate the clinician to the highest levels of practice. It is not necessary for a helper to be a master of the situation confronting the client, or to be fearless or a "paragon of mental health" vis-à-vis the client's problem. In fact, a therapist's sharing her own mild discomfort about some aspects of the phobic situation may be helpful to the client, normalizing the client's reactions and leading the client to believe that he too may be able to develop coping.

The helper must be flexible in developing and implementing exposure treatments, to respond to changing information about the client's phobia or other problem. As treatment progresses, both client and clinician learn more about the client's problem, and that insight often demands change in the way in which exposure is implemented. Often, the imagery scenes or actual *in vivo* stimuli must be changed somehow to more closely reflect what the client truly fears. For example, imagery scenes often are embellished over time, as clients remember new details, ones that perhaps were cognitively unavailable to them because of anxiety or related avoidance processes.

Repeated Exposure

The research on the underlying mechanisms of exposure treatment (e.g., Emmelkamp & Felten, 1985; Hazlett-Stevens & Craske, 2003; Mystkowski et al., 2002) has frequently indicated that, to be effective, exposure must be of sufficient intensity, duration, and repetition. Gradually evolving the intensity of exposure is fine in many cases and may be more palatable to clients who wish to "ease in" to this form of treatment. Nevertheless, ultimately the stimuli or situations that clients confront must be highly evocative to allow them to fully experience the greatest possible anxiety response (Forsyth & Fusé, 2003). Only in doing so will they *learn* that they can "survive" and even "conquer" that which they most fear (or find distressing).

Length of exposure is a critical factor, both within sessions and across the entire course of treatment. Related to avoidance, some clients delay exposure by talking about it rather than doing it. This delay can take place before any exposures in a session or between exposures. This is not to say that clients' discourse about their thoughts and feelings should be ignored or even discouraged from discussion. It is the case, however, that clinicians should be cognizant of the possibility of subtle avoidance behavior, about which the client may be unaware. Avoidance also can result from clinicians' own discomfort or fear of doing exposure! Our experience with beginning clinicians is that they often are uncomfortable with exposing clients to thoughts and tangible stimuli and situations that can be highly distressing. Sometimes, then, both client and helper "conspire" to approach exposure very gradually, then to have very brief exposures, and then to spend considerable time thereafter in discussing the exposure and its emotional consequences in the client. This situation is a trap, however, for the outcome is less exposure than would be ideal to help the client. Typically, repeated and/or continuing exposures are recommended within single treatment sessions. Similarly, the client must experience the confrontation with the stimuli or situation for a long enough time to allow an anxiety (or related) response to fully develop, be manifested, and then dissipate through extinction or habituation.

Response Prevention

Particularly with obsessive–compulsive disorder, but with other clinical problems as well, it is important for the client not to engage in anxiety-reducing activities during or after exposure (Roth, Foa, & Franklin, 2003). A client with an obsession about germs, and compulsive hand-washing behaviors, for example, should not wash his hands for some period of time after exposure to dirt or other "germy" stimuli during exposure. This response prevention allows the anxiety about exposure to be fully operative and not diminished by a potentially detrimental, although immediately and temporarily reinforcing, reaction to the anxiety by the client. During exposure, clients typically also should not engage in activities that distract them from the anxiety, such as counting or thinking about something else other than that which is causing them distress. To do so may ameliorate or remove the anxiety, which can be counterproductive. The literature on distraction during exposure, however is mixed and awaits further clarification (Rodriguez & Craske, 1993).

Return of Fear

Although exposure therapy has proven to be an effective treatment for many clients suffering from problems with anxiety, some clients experience a return of fear after treatment concludes (Hermans et al., 2005). There are several possible reasons why some clients experience a return of fear, and helpers should be aware of them so that they might try to prevent such return. The animal literature on which much exposure therapy work has been based suggests that repeated presentations of the unconditioned stimulus after extinction learning will lead to return of fear, and similar work with humans has found the same results (Hermans et al., 2005). For example, consider a person with a phobia of flying on airplanes for whom exposure treatment was effective. If the client did not fly again for several years after treatment, the phobia could return in response to newspaper and other media reports about airline disasters. Additionally, it is important for helpers to remember that exposure therapy may involve the learning of new information incompatible with old information, not the unlearning of the previous fear response (Mystkowski et al., 2002). Therefore, the general rules of learning should apply, and helpers should make every attempt to take advantage of what is currently known about learning. Fear has returned for clients who were exposed to a fear-provoking stimulus in a context different from the context of exposure treatment (Mystkowski et al., 2002). A client who learns how to manage her fear in the presence of spiders in the helper's office might experience intense fear when encountering a spider during a picnic outdoors. Additionally, Tsao and Craske (2000) found that uniformly spaced sessions and "expanding-spaced" sessions—in which the time length between sessions increases over time—produce longer retention-of-treatment gains than do massed sessions that occur in close temporal proximity to one another, possibly because these schedules require more effort by the client to retrieve information learned between sessions and contextual cues can be more varied. In general, to prevent return of fear, helpers should encourage clients to engage in exposure exercises in a variety of contexts at various times, with as much repetition as possible, in order to increase the odds of greater learning and generalization to the greatest number of possible future contexts.

Sequencing of Stimuli Presentations

The traditional order of presentation of stimuli during gradual methods of exposure therapy has been to move from presenting less fear-provoking to more fear-provoking stimuli. As discussed above, part of the rationale for this sequencing has been to build client self-efficacy and increase client acceptance of exposure therapy. Certainly, these considerations are important in developing an exposure-based treatment plan. Just as importantly, though, helpers should consider the empirical support for certain sequencing of stimuli. Although exposure therapy often utilizes graded hierarchies, the success of flooding treatments that begin with the most fear-provoking stimuli (e.g., Miller, 2002) serves as an indication that presenting less fear-provoking stimuli first is not always necessary for clients to overcome their fears. Other research has suggested that hierarchies adapted to the individual or to particular methods of presenting hierarchies do not necessarily influence the successful outcome of exposure treatments (Yates, 1975). Some research has even suggested that fears summate—that is, when a stimulus eliciting less fear is followed by a stimulus eliciting more fear, the subsequent simultaneous presentation of both stimuli together results in a greater fear response (Rachman & Lopatka, 1986). A client reports a SUDS rating of 50 for a spider crawling on her hand and reports a SUDS rating of 90 for a spider crawling up her arm. When the client is exposed to a spider on her hand and then to a spider crawling up her arm, she might report an even higher SUDS rating (maybe 95) if during the next exposure the spider crawls from her hand up her arm. Rachman and Lopatka also found that the opposite order of stimulus presentation (i.e., a stimulus eliciting more fear preceded a stimulus eliciting less fear) resulted in a lower fear level when the two stimuli were presented together. Although most helpers probably will continue to rely on graded exposure to stimuli from client hierarchies, helpers should consider the evidence supporting alternate orders of stimuli presentation when they are deciding on the order of stimulus presentation, especially for clients who might not respond well to initial attempts at exposure therapy.

CAUTIONS, PERILS, AND LIMITATIONS
Informed Consent

Any form of helping, including psychological treatment, requires the client to be fully informed and to consent to the treatment that is being provided (i.e., to give informed consent). This step may be particularly important in exposure treatment, which often is highly emotionally evocative and involves clients' behaving in ways that are directly antagonistic to what their cognitive or physiological state "tells" them to do (e.g., to immediately leave the situation, as part of a "fight or flight" reaction, so as not to encounter that which they most fear). At some level, then, exposure is counterintuitive to the client, so it is extremely important for the helper to provide a thorough rationale and to periodically remind the client of the rationale over the course

of treatment. It is imperative to help the client understand that avoidance is reinforcing in the short term but allows the phobia to be maintained. It should be emphasized that exposure, as noted earlier, is an investment of anxiety at the present time for greater calmness in the future (Hope et al., 2000).

The Client's Right to Choose

When you are treating clients, it may be best to inform them that they are "in control" at all times and that you as the helper will not "force them" to do anything: "Not that I could, as you ultimately are in charge of your life and your actions. I am here as a guide, certainly to encourage you, but always to respect you and your right to your own decisions." At the same time, it may be wise to share with your clients that you will encourage them, sometimes repeatedly, to "touch" (sometimes psychologically) that which they most fear, because that is the route to change and greater ultimate comfort. Rather than trying to cajole or "guilt" a client into some action, it may be wise to break the action down into its component parts and to have the client gradually experience it.

When to "Push" and When Not

It is a matter of individual client characteristics, helper style, and clinical judgment as to when a helper should "push" (psychologically, not physically) and when the helper should be patient and allow the client to consolidate his or her gains. Some clients depend on the clinician to provide this encouragement and consider it a valued part of treatment. Other clients want any movement to be of their own accord and resist any clinician encouragement except prior to entering an evocative situation.

Presence or Absence of the Clinician

The presence or absence of the clinician is a critical element in many exposure treatments. In agoraphobia, obsessive–compulsive disorder, and some other anxiety disorders, the presence of the clinician or another "safe person" can prevent the occurrence of any anxiety whatsoever—and subverts the therapeutic aspects of exposure. Sometimes, however, the presence of the clinician can allow the client to take those "baby steps" necessary to begin the steps of exposure. One common dimension of hierarchies is the presence or absence of others, with the involvement of "safe" others being included early, in the less anxiety-provoking part of the list.

There certainly are ethical, legal, and safety issues involved in the presence of the clinician during in vivo exposure. In some instances, for safety reasons, two clinicians should be present. Also, merely being in the presence of the clinician in the community can cue others that the client is under the care of a helper, compromising confidentiality. This is not to say that it then precludes such an approach, only that the client must be made aware of this possibility, and that the ramifications of this choice be considered by both client and clinician. This form of exposure, *in vivo*, can be extremely powerful, and often the clinician's presence is necessary, particularly in the early stages of treatment.

The client's safety, and that of the public and the clinician, must be a paramount concern during *in vivo* exposure. A client with an elevator phobia who rides a few floors on an elevator in a five-story building has less potential for problems than an individual with agoraphobia, who has not traveled alone for years, driving by herself in a urban area. (In the latter case, the *in vivo* exposure likely would be best handled by a driving school, for such an organization provides expertise in the physical aspects of driving.) Clients sometimes ask (and even plead), for example, for clinicians to accompany them on airplane flights. The clinician may or may not be able to "make it all right" during such encounters, is "on someone else's turf," and is subject to the rules and regulations of that situation. Prior permission for such therapeutic work may be necessary from the company or entity that provides the activity.

Avoidance

Avoidance comes in many forms. It can be quite overt and obvious, or it can be subtle, leaving the helper wondering if there is discomfort and related avoidance. The work of Isaac Marks (1987) provides a conceptual and practical basis for understanding the many faces of avoidance and escape. The "fight or flight" reaction is perhaps the most salient demonstration of avoidance-like behaviors. Leaving a situation in which anxiety occurs is a behavioral form of withdrawal that often is obvious.

Avoidance can be differentiated from escape. Avoidance behaviors involve not entering a situation in which contact with the phobic stimulus would take place, and thereby avoiding anticipatory anxiety. When escape behaviors occur, in contrast, the individual already is in the situation and leaves because of anxiety associated with actual contact with the object, event, or situation. Both avoidance and escape are detrimental to the client and lead to a cyclical reinforcement of the anxiety.

Freezing is another type of phobic reaction that is a form of avoidance. One sometimes sees freezing in public speaking situations or in dental situations. Functionally, freezing allows the individual to avoid interaction and to insulate himself or herself from the ongoing situation.

Camouflage is a form of avoidance in which clients, consciously or nonconsciously, attempt to minimize their impact in social situations. If an individual is less noticed, then there is less opportunity for social demand. Our client, Isabella, for example, may choose to wear inconspicuous clothing at a school dance, so that she is less noticed by potential dancing partners. Not being noticed allows her to avoid social encounters and to not have the social demand

of accepting or declining such invitations. Actually, Isabella may avoid the dance altogether if she experiences social phobia. Alternately, she may escape the dance by leaving early, perhaps saying that "it was boring," a form of reason-giving.

As human beings, we may avoid not only uncomfortable objects, situations, and events, but our own distressing physiological and cognitive reactions to them, or to the prospect of them. From an ACT perspective, there can be experiential avoidance, in which the client withdraws from experiencing negative cognitive and psychophysiological reactions (Hayes et al., 1999). Not allowing oneself to experience such states, however, is a problem in that it reinforces the fear, allowing it to continue and perhaps to grow.

Cognitive avoidance can be an outgrowth of worry (Borkovec, 1994) and can occur as well during imaginal desensitization, either during scene construction or during imagery itself. The client may find it impossible to conjure up distressing images, to maintain imagery for a sufficiently long period, or to consistently imagine without intrusive thoughts.

Certainly not all forms of avoidance are direct; many are passive and can be quite subtle. Avoidance interacts with other factors that influence behavior, and it can be a determinant of behavior that combines with others. For example, avoidance of dental care is commonplace, but acknowledging that avoidance is due to fear is less common because of the social desirability of portraying oneself as "in control" and competent. A person can indicate that she does "not have the time to go to the dentist right now," or she might suggest that cost prevents her from securing timely dental care. Although the latter issue may be accurate for some individuals, for others it is a form of reason-giving that belies the true function of the behavior, which is to avoid encountering the fear of exposure to dental care.

PRACTICE AND RESEARCH WITH DIVERSE GROUPS

With its emphasis on basic learning processes, and its practical, commonsense basis, exposure is appropriate for a broad range of groups. Special sensitivity may be required, however, when the clinician is a member of some dominant group and is employing exposure with a client who is a member of a less-dominant group and the subject of the exposure is potentially related to social issues involving these groups. For example, conducting exposure related to assertive behavior in a client who is a member of an ethnic/racial minority group by a European American therapist has some social considerations that should be considered in treatment.

Anxiety disorders have been the subject of interest in African Americans, due to their relative prevalence in this group, with some unique features (e.g., sleep paralysis). Exposure has been explored in this group, and it appears to be an effective therapeutic modality (Friedman, 1994). There are, however, unique challenges that face many African American clients for whom exposure may be the treatment of choice, in terms of daily hassles related to racism and to treatment delivery barriers (Friedman, 1994).

Posttraumatic stress disorder and its treatment have been the subject of considerable attention across ethnocultural groups, specifically including American Indians, Hispanics, Asian Americans, and African Americans (Marsella, Friedman, Gerrity, & Scurfield, 1996). The greater presence of post-traumatic stress disorder in refugee groups makes exposure a likely treatment option. Great care should be taken, however, in understanding the ecological issues involved in the clinician, as an authority figure, exposing survivors of traumatic events to emotionally evocative images and situations.

Exposure, particularly gradual methods, has been effectively utilized with children's phobias (Beidel & Turner, 2005). Intensive exposure methods with children typically are shied away from because of ethical concerns. *In vivo* exposure can be effective with children who do not have the language or conceptual abilities to benefit from imaginal approaches, such as some individuals with developmental disabilities. Issues of informed consent, and other ethical concerns, must of course be carefully considered in such cases. Gradual exposure may be especially preferred in these instances, allowing the clinician to slowly and carefully consider the impact of exposure on an ongoing basis.

CURRENT STATUS OF RESEARCH ON EXPOSURE

Much work continues to be conducted on exposure: its efficacy and effectiveness, its limitations and barriers, its underlying mechanisms and basic behavior processes, and its expansion into new areas and new technologies. A complete review of all recently published work on exposure would extend well beyond the scope of this chapter. Three areas that currently seem to be "hot topics" in the exposure literature are methods for increased effectiveness, virtual-reality exposure (VRE), and the use of d-cycloserine (a chemical compound and antibiotic that is approved for the treatment of tuberculosis). (See Box 16.1.)

Much of the recent research of exposure therapy has focused on factors that lead to more or less efficacy in reducing fear and anxiety. One variable that has received some attention is the use of safety cues (Powers, Smits, & Telch, 2004). The work done in this area conceptualizes safety cues, such as the ability to immediately escape an exposure session or divert attention to distracting stimuli, as forms of overt and/or covert avoidance. It appears that even the mere presence of these safety cues, not necessarily their utilization by clients, decreases the effectiveness of exposure and the maintenance of gains over time. Another variable that

has been manipulated in exposure has been the spacing of sessions. According to Tsao and Craske (2000), uniformly spaced and "expanding-spaced" treatment sessions appear to lead to longer-lasting fear reduction. The context of exposure can be an important variable as well, and helpers should ensure that clients practice exposure in multiple contexts to promote generalization of learning (Mystkowski et al., 2002). Finally, researchers have suggested that exposure therapy alone, without the addition of a cognitive therapy component, is more successful in reducing a client's fear than is the combination of exposure therapy and cognitive treatments (Foa, Rothbaum, & Furr, 2003; Moore, Zoellner, & Bittinger, 2004).

The use of virtual-reality equipment has become more common in exposure in recent years, and the literature on the efficacy of this approach is growing. From a theoretical perspective, many researchers hypothesize that if the mechanism through with exposure works is by accessing the fear structure, in a manner consistent with the work of Lang (1977), Rachman (1980), and Foa and Kozak (1986), then any medium that adequately accesses a person's fear structure should be capable of eliciting change. Virtual-reality exposure offers several advantages to helpers, including the ability to create situations impractical to replicate in reality, to create situations of greater intensity than commonly found in real life, and to create situations that can be directly controlled by the helper for manipulation of key variables (e.g., number of spiders present for a client with a phobia of spiders). Alternatively, VRE presents disadvantages, including high costs for the initial purchase of equipment, possible technical errors associated with most electronic equipment, time and effort to learn how to use the equipment, and potential difficulties in creating situations "real" enough for clients. Initial research in the area of VRE has proven promising, especially in regards to VRE for fear of flying and fear of heights (Krijn, Emmelkamp, Olafsson, & Biemond, 2004). Krijn et al. also note, however, that most work in VRE has been exploratory with small sample sizes and little use of random assignment. The initial success of VRE indicates that it warrants further, more thorough research to better empirically determine its ability to effect change in clients.

Finally, there has been recent interest in the use of a drug, d-cycloserine (DCS), to enhance exposure exercises. The DCS literature is based on basic laboratory experiments with animals and extinction. Initial translational research (e.g., Hofmann et al., 2006) examining the use of DCS in humans has proven promising. Participants who were administered DCS before exposure exercises recorded faster initial decreases in fear and anxiety. The early gains made under the influence of DCS were maintained over time, although in several additional sessions participants who did not use DCS "caught up with" participants using DCS.

Thus, the early and ongoing work in this area indicates that DCS might be useful for speeding up the process of extinction learning during exposure.

Several cautions about DCS should be mentioned, including the fact it must be physician prescribed and monitored. It must be made explicitly clear to clients that DCS is not meant to replace exposure and that DCS is still in the experimental phase; the long-term consequences of use in this application are not known. Some researchers have concerns that DCS will detract from self-efficacy gains made during exposure, and that research on DCS will detract from time potentially spent researching basic behavioral mechanisms of expose. For psychologists, the potential utility of DCS may further fuel the debate over prescription authority. Still, many researchers see DCS as a ripe topic for discussion, one that could possibly impact the way exposure therapy is conducted in the future. It should be noted, however, that there are alternative behavioral means of augmenting exposure therapy.

MODEL DIALOGUE FOR EXPOSURE THERAPY: THE CASE OF ISABELLA

To get a sense of how a clinician might conduct exposure therapy, examine the following dialogue between a helper and Isabella, who experiences anxiety related to mathematics, including doing calculations and being in a math class. First, the helper reminds Isabella of the process of *identifying fear-provoking stimuli, creating a hierarchy, and practicing a relaxation response.* Additionally, the helper gives a brief overview of what to expect from the exposure exercise and asks about any questions Isabella might have.

1. **Helper:** Isabella, we've discussed your anxiety surrounding doing calculations and being in your math class, and identified many different aspects of that class that lead to you feeling anxious. You rated these stimuli based on how much you fear them using the SUDS system I explained to you. You also have been doing a wonderful job practicing relaxation through deep breathing. You've shared that you feel fairly comfortable using it to help you relax and remain calm. So here's how we can proceed. First, I'll ask you to get comfortable in your chair and take a moment to really focus your attention on what we're doing. Then I'll ask you to envision your neutral scene we developed earlier in therapy that has a SUDS of zero for you. When you feel relaxed and ready, just signal with your finger. After I get the ready signal from you, I'll ask you to begin imagining a lower scene from your hierarchy, sitting in math class before the bell rings to start class. When you feel you are really imagining the scene clearly, I'll ask you to signal me again with your finger. Please keep imagining the scene for about half a minute until

I indicate you can clear the scene from your mind. At that point, I'll ask you to give your SUDS rating before switching back to your neutral scene. When you feel relaxed again, with a SUDS close to zero, I'll ask you to imagine the scene again. We'll continue until the scene causes you a minimal amount of fear, and then move on to the next higher item on your hierarchy and repeat the process. How does all of this sound?

Isabella: How many items will we do today? We won't do the items at the top of my list today, will we? I'm really worried about my math class later this week. We might have a pop quiz!

Isabella's response here could be interpreted as an attempt to delay and avoid exposure. The helper takes care to briefly and adequately address Isabella's concern while gently but firmly redirecting the session to exposure. The helper also creates an expectancy for success.

2. **Helper:** You pose a good question. I also understand that exposure brings up some anxiety as it causes us to think about the very thing that makes us the most anxious and upset. We'll move through your hierarchy at a pace that is comfortable enough, but one that will allow you to make progress. You'll be in control the entire time. The pace will be set by how quickly your fear decreases; I can't really say for sure how many items we'll get through, but I can say we won't move on to the next item until you're ready for it. I do expect you'll move through the items faster than you might initially expect.

Isabella: Okay, I think I can handle that.

The helper inquires about relaxation and imagery before beginning to assess and determine if Isabella has the relaxation and imagery skills necessary for successful exposure treatment.

3. **Helper:** Great! Now, how has practicing relaxation been going for you?

Isabella: I have been practicing a couple of times a day at home. It has even helped me to calm down when I feel under pressure from my parents.

4. **Helper:** Excellent, practicing your breathing in a real-world setting "under pressure" will really help you apply deep breathing today during our session. We also discussed imagery techniques to help build your skills in making imagined scenes as real as possible for you. What are some of the different ways you can make images clearer for yourself?

Isabella: I imagine the scene, not just in a picture, but I try to make it as if I'm really there, thinking about all my senses: asking myself what I would smell, hear, taste, and feel, not just see. I also think about how my body would respond in that situation. The more detail and the more specific I can make the scene, the better.

The helper verbally praises Isabella's relaxation and imagery abilities, and presents one last opportunity to address client concerns.

5. **Helper:** Precisely! You've really grasped the importance of focusing on details when imagining the situation itself, and your own bodily responses. You also can focus on the thoughts you would have in the scene that would clue you in as to how you're feeling. Now we're ready to begin exposure to imagined scenes from the hierarchy you constructed. I know that you have concerns about your ability to handle this exposure, and we've discussed these fears and why engaging feared images now can be beneficial to you in the long term. It sounds like you really feel skilled with relaxation and are well prepared to experience a reduction in your fear. Are you ready to begin?

Isabella: I'm still a bit worried about how this will go, but I also believe it could really help me overcome my fears. Let's do it.

The helper reinforces Isabella's positive attitude and moves through the steps of imaginal exposure with her. First, a positive or neutral scene is established. Next, the helper moves to a lower scene from Isabella's hierarchy, waiting for the scene to become clear for Isabella and recording a SUDS rating after Isabella erases the scene from her mind. The helper instructs Isabella to return to the neutral scene before repeating the exposure, and this cycle continues until the end of the exposure therapy portion of the session.

6. **Helper:** Great. That's an attitude that should help you really succeed with imaginal exposure. Let's begin then. Go ahead and take moment to get settled in your chair and focused on the here-and-now. Whenever you're ready, allow your eyes to close. [Isabella closes her eyes and assumes a relaxed position in the chair]. Okay, go ahead and breathe deeply like you've been practicing while you imagine yourself on the beach. [The helper previously established that this scene is positive for her and does not involve any fear, such as fear of water.] The waves roll in and out without a cloud in the sky, you smell the salty sea breeze as it brushes your face, and the sand is soft and warm beneath your bare feet. Just signal me with your finger when the scene is clear. [Helper waits for Isabella's signal, acknowledges it, and allows 30 to 60 seconds to pass.]

Okay, Isabella, now it's time to move on to something else. [Pause for approximately 10 seconds.] Now, please imagine you're in your math classroom before the bell rings. You can see the chalkboard, you wonder what will happen when class begins, and you can feel butterflies in your stomach as your shoulders tense. Signal me with your finger when the scene is vivid for you. [Helper waits patiently until Isabella raises her finger.] Good, you should really be able to smell the chalk, see the trees outside the classroom window, and feel your heartbeat increasing. Now, stick with imagining the scene, Isabella. [Helper waits 15 to 30 seconds.] Great, now go ahead and erase the scene from your mind, Isabella. Please tell me your SUDS rating. [Helper records Isabella's SUDS rating of 15.] Thank you. Please go ahead and imagine your beach scene again, Isabella, and let me know when you're relaxed by raising your finger. [Helper waits for Isabella's signal, and the cycle repeats until Isabella's SUDS rating decreases to 10 or lower. The helper proceeds through the hierarchy, with multiple presentations, until the end of the session.]

In the final fear scene presentation of the session, the helper attempts to bring the appointment to a close with an exposure in which the client does not signal fear, or a desire to terminate the image, to end with a success. As the conclusion to the imagery part of the session, the helper again presents the positive scene, to allow the client to end the session on a positive note.

After the exposure part of the session ends, the clinician can discuss the experience with Isabella before assigning homework and talking about the next session.

The helper begins discussion in an open-ended manner so as to allow Isabella to reach her own conclusions, which begin with disconfirmation of her maladaptive cognitions.

7. **Helper:** Well, Isabella, tell me a little bit about what your thoughts and feelings are about the session. What did you notice about your anxiety related to math class?

Isabella: That wasn't as bad as I had imagined it was going to be. I thought it was going to be terrible to even imagine anything related to math class, but I stopped feeling anxious pretty quickly. The whole thing made me think that maybe I can deal with math class things in real life, even doing calculations!

The helper reinforces Isabella in response 8.

8. **Helper:** Wonderful! A lot of people feel the same way as you do after their first exposure session. Many times we've avoided something so much we anticipate more anxiety than we actually experience when we confront the situation. How does that fit with your experiences?

Isabella: Yeah, I think that really matches with how I feel about today's session.

The helper capitalizes on Isabella's success in session by proposing a homework exercise for in vivo exposure.

9. **Helper:** Good, I'm glad you feel that way. I would like to propose an exercise I would like you to try this coming week. You say you normally avoid sitting in math class before the bell rings, like we just imagined, because it makes you feel nervous and worried. I would like you to see what happens if you do sit in class before the bell. Do you think you could try that?

Isabella: I am a little scared to try that out. I know how important you said it was to practice things outside of therapy, though. Plus, maybe it'll be like today: how worried I am ahead of time will be worse than how it will actually be.

Once again, the helper praises Isabella's choice of an exposure-based lifestyle and moves on to discussing *in vitro* exposure, in the form of a role play, for the next session.

10. **Helper:** That's a wonderful attitude to have, Isabella. I can't say exactly how you'll feel while you sit in class before the bell, but I can say that expecting the best will assist you greatly in this exercise. And, before you go, I'd like to quickly discuss what we'll be doing together during our next session. You've mentioned that asking questions and going to the board during math class make you feel anxious and worried, correct?

Isabella: Yeah, I really am afraid I'll look foolish or do something to embarrass myself.

11. **Helper:** Well, next time, I'd like to role-play you asking questions and going to the board. In order for the role play to work as well as possible, I'd like you to think some about different ways these situations could turn out, what the probability of each outcome is, how the different outcomes would make you feel, and what you would do if each outcome occurred. How does that sound?

Isabella: I think I can do that.

12. **Helper:** Wonderful! I'll see you next week.

CHAPTER SUMMARY

Exposure is a powerful therapeutic approach that can be of great benefit to clients suffering from phobias, posttraumatic stress disorder, obsessive–compulsive disorder, and other clinical problems such as excessive and prolonged grief. Exposure can be employed in gradual or intensive ways, depending on the problem at hand as well as on the characteristics and preferences of the client. One form of exposure is imaginal, such as in systematic desensitization. Another form of exposure is what we have termed *in vitro*, suggesting exposure in an office or laboratory setting that occurs under tightly controlled circumstances, such as in role play or involving phobic stimuli that are introduced into a setting in which they typically do not exist (e.g., viewing and touching dental instruments in a mental health clinician's office). Finally, exposure in its strongest form is *in vivo*. This real-life exposure offers the greatest potential benefit when it is practical and when the client is ready for it. Regardless of the type of exposure, the amount of contact with whatever causes fear seems to be the operative factor. The implication then is clear: greater exposure, whether it is repeated or prolonged, is associated with better treatment outcome. Successful treatment must be followed by an "exposure-based lifestyle" to prevent return of fear and to ensure that treatment gains are maintained. There are ethical and practical issues that must be addressed in conducting exposure treatment, including issues of informed consent and therapist presence or absence. With proper implementation and follow-through, exposure has great potential to expand clients' range of activities and comfort and to enhance quality of life generally.

REFERENCES

Barlow, D. H. (2002). *Anxiety and its disorders: The nature and treatment of anxiety and panic* (2nd ed.). New York: Guilford Press.

Beidel, D. C., & Turner, S. M. (2005). *Childhood anxiety disorders: A guide to research and treatment.* New York: Routledge.

Borkovec, T. D. (1994). The nature, functions, and origins of worry. In G. C. L. Davey & F. Tallis (Eds.), *Worrying: Perspectives on theory, assessment, and treatment* (pp. 5–33). New York: Wiley.

Chambless, D. L., Baker, M. J., Baucom, D. H., Beutler, L. E., Calhoun, K. S., Crits-Cristoph, P., et al. (1997). *Update on empirically validated therapies, II.* Retrieved July 5, 2007, from http://www.apa.org/divisions/div12/est/97report.pdf.

Craske, M. G. (2003). *Origins of phobias and anxiety disorders: Why more women than men?* New York: Elsevier.

Craske, M. G., Hermans, D., & Vansteenwegen (Eds.). (2006). *Fear and learning: From basic processes to clinical implications.* Washington, DC: American Psychological Association.

Davey, G. C. L. (Ed.). (1997). *Phobias: A handbook of theory, research and treatment.* New York: Wiley.

Davidson, P. R., & Parker, K. C. H. (2001). Eye movement desensitization and reprocessing (EMDR): A meta-analysis. *Journal of Consulting and Clinical Psychology, 69,* 305–316.

Davis, M., Myers, K. M., Ressler, K. J., & Rothbaum, B. O. (2005). Facilitation of extinction of conditioned fear by d-cycloserine. *Current Directions in Psychological Science, 14,* 214–219.

Davison, G. C. (1968). Systematic desensitization as a counterconditioning process. *Journal of Abnormal Psychology, 73,* 91.

Devilly, G. J. (2002). Eye movement desensitization and reprocessing: A chronology of its development and scientific standing. *The Scientific Review of Mental Health Practice, 1,* 113–138.

Eifert., G. H., & Forsyth, J. P. (2005). *Acceptance and commitment therapy for anxiety disorders: A practitioner's treatment guide to using mindfulness, acceptance, and values-based behavior change strategies.* Oakland, CA: New Harbinger.

Emmelkamp, P. M. G., & Felten, M. (1985). The process of exposure in vivo: Cognitive and physiological changes during treatment of acrophobia. *Behaviour Research and Therapy, 23,* 219–223.

Foa, E. B. (1997). Trauma and women: Course, predictors, and treatment. *Journal of Clinical Psychiatry, 58,* 25–28.

Foa, E. B., & Kozak, M. S. (1986). Emotional processing of fear: Exposure to corrective information. *Psychological Bulletin, 99,* 20–35.

Foa, E. B., & McNally, R. J. (1996). Mechanisms of change in exposure therapy. In M. Rapee (Ed.), *Current controversies in the anxiety disorders* (pp. 329–343). New York: Guilford Press.

Foa, E. B., Rothbaum, B. O., & Furr, J. M. (2003). Augmenting exposure therapy with other CBT procedures. *Psychiatric Annals, 33,* 47–53.

Forsyth, J. P., & Fusé, T. (2003). Interoceptive exposure for panic disorder. In W. O'Donohue, J. E. Fisher, & S. C. Hayes (Eds.), *Cognitive behavior therapy: Applying empirically supported techniques in your practice* (pp. 212–222). Hoboken, NJ: Wiley.

Friedman, S. (Ed.). (1994). *Anxiety disorders in African Americans.* New York: Springer.

Hayes, S. C., Luoma, J. B., Bond, F. W., Masuda, A., & Lillis, J. (2006). Acceptance and commitment therapy: Model, processes, and outcomes. *Behaviour Research and Therapy, 44,* 1–25.

Hayes, S. C., Strosahl, K. D., & Wilson, K. G. (1999). *Acceptance and commitment therapy: An experiential approach to behavior change.* New York: Guilford Press.

Hazlett-Stevens, H., & Craske, M. G. (2003). Live (in vivo) exposure. In W. O'Donohue, J. E. Fisher, & S. C. Hayes (Eds.), *Cognitive behavior therapy: Applying empirically supported techniques in your practice* (pp. 223–228). Hoboken, NJ: Wiley.

Hermans, D., Dirikx, T., Vansteenwegenin, D., Baeyens, F., Van den Bergh, O., & Eelen, P. (2005). Reinstatement of fear responses in human aversive conditioning. *Behaviour Research and Therapy, 43,* 533–551.

Hodgson, R., & Rachman, S. (1974). II. Desynchrony in measures of fear. *Behaviour Research and Therapy, 12,* 319–326.

Hofmann, S. G., Meuret, A. E., Smits, A. J., Simon, N. M., Pollack, M. H., Eisenmenger, K., et al. (2006). Augmentation of exposure therapy with d-cycloserine for social anxiety disorder. *Archives of General Psychiatry, 63,* 298–304.

Hofmann, S. G., Pollack, M. H., & Otto, M. W. (2006). Augmentation treatment of psychotherapy for anxiety disorders with d-cycloserine. *CNS Drug Reviews, 12,* 208–217.

Hope, D. A., Heimberg, R. G., Juster, H. R., & Turk, C. L. (2000). *Managing social anxiety: A cognitive–behavioral therapy approach. Client workbook.* San Antonio, TX: Psychological Corporation.

Kamphuis, J. H., & Telch, M. J. (2000). Effects of distraction and guided threat reappraisal on fear reduction during exposure-based treatments for specific fears. *Behaviour Research and Therapy, 38,* 1163–1181.

Krijn, M., Emmelkamp, P. M. G., Olafsson, R. P., & Biemond, R. (2004). Virtual reality exposure therapy of anxiety disorders: A review. *Clinical Psychology Review, 24,* 259–281.

Lader, M. H., & Matthews, A. M. (1968). A physiological model of phobic anxiety and desensitization. *Behaviour Research and Therapy, 32,* 817–823.

Lang, A. J., & Craske, M. G. (2000). Manipulations of exposure-based therapy to reduce return of fear: A replication. *Behaviour Research and Therapy, 38,* 1–12.

Lang, P. J. (1977). Imagery in therapy: An information processing analysis of fear. *Behavior Therapy, 8,* 862–886.

Levis, D. J., & Krantweiss, A. R. (2003). Working with implosive (flooding) therapy: A dynamic cognitive–behavioral exposure psychotherapy treatment approach. In W. O'Donohue, J. E. Fisher, & S. C. Hayes (Eds.), *Cognitive behavior therapy: Applying empirically supported techniques in your practice* (pp. 463–470). Hoboken, NJ: Wiley.

Lichtenstein, P., & Annas, P. (2000). Heritability and prevalence of specific fears and phobias in childhood. *Journal of Child Psychology and Psychiatry, 41,* 927–937.

Marks, I. M. (1987). *Fears, phobias, and rituals: Panic, anxiety, and their disorders.* New York: Oxford University Press.

Marsella, A. J., Friedman, M. J., Gerrity, E. T., & Scurfield, R. M. (Eds.). (1996). *Ethnocultural aspects of posttraumatic stress disorder.* Washington, DC: American Psychological Association.

Mavissakalian, M., & Michelson, L. (1982). Patterns of psychophysiological change in the treatment of agoraphobia. *Behaviour Research and Therapy, 20,* 347–356.

McGlynn, F. D., Mealiea, W. L., Jr., & Landau, D. L. (1981). The current status of systematic desensitization. *Clinical Psychology Review, 1,* 149–179.

Miller, C. (2002). Flooding. In M. Hersen & W. Sledge (Eds.), *Encyclopedia of psychotherapy, vol. 1* (pp. 809–813). New York: Elsevier Science.

Moore, S. A., Zoellner, L. A., & Bittinger, J. N. (2004). Combining cognitive restructuring and exposure therapy:

Toward an optimal integration. In S. Taylor (Ed.), *Advances in treatment of posttraumatic stress disorder: Cognitive behavioral perspectives* (pp. 129–149). New York: Springer.

Mystkowski, J. L., Craske, M. G., & Echiverri, A. M. (2002). Treatment context and return of fear in spider phobia. *Behavior Therapy, 33,* 399–416.

O'Donohue, W., Fisher, J. E., & Hayes, S. C. (Eds.). (2003). *Cognitive behavior therapy: Applying empirically supported techniques in your practice.* Hoboken, NJ: Wiley.

Öst, L. G., & Hugdahl, K. (1983). Acquisition of agoraphobia, mode of onset and anxiety response patterns. *Behaviour Research and Therapy, 21,* 623–631.

Otto, M. W., Basden, S. L., Leyro, T. M., McHugh, R. K., & Hofmann, S. G. (2007). Clinical perspectives on the combination of d-cycloserine and cognitive-behavioral therapy for the treatment of anxiety disorders. *CNS Spectrums, 12,* 51–56, 59–61.

Powers, M. B., Smits, J. A., & Telch, M. J. (2004). Disentangling the effects of safety-behavior utilization and safety-behavior availability during exposure-based treatment: A placebo-controlled protocol. *Journal of Consulting and Clinical Psychology, 72,* 448–454.

Price, M., & Anderson, P. (2007). The role of presence in virtual reality exposure therapy. *Journal of Anxiety Disorders, 21,* 742–751.

Rachman, S. (1977). The conditioning theory of fear-acquisition: A critical examination. *Behaviour Research and Therapy, 15,* 375–387.

Rachman, S. (1980). Emotional processing. *Behaviour Research and Therapy, 18,* 51–60.

Rachman, S., & Hodgson, R. (1974). I. Synchrony and desynchrony in fear and avoidance. *Behaviour Research and Therapy, 12,* 311–318.

Rachman, S., & Lopatka, C. (1986). Do fears summate?, III. *Behaviour Research and Therapy, 24,* 653–660.

Ressler, K. J., Rothbaum, B. O., Tannenbaum, L., Anderson, P., Graap, K., Zimand, E., et al. (2004). Cognitive enhancers as adjuncts to psychotherapy: Use of d-cycloserine in phobic individuals to facilitate extinction of fear. *Archives of General Psychiatry, 61,* 1136–1144.

Rodriguez, B. I., & Craske, M. G (1993). The effects of distraction during exposure to phobic stimuli. *Behaviour Research and Therapy, 31,* 549–558.

Roth, D. A., Foa, E. B., & Franklin, M. E. (2003). Response prevention. In W. O'Donohue, J. E. Fisher, & S. C. Hayes (Eds.), *Cognitive behavior therapy: Applying empirically supported techniques in your practice* (pp. 341–348). Hoboken, NJ: Wiley.

Rothbaum, B. O. (2006). Virtual reality exposure therapy. In B. O. Rothbaum (Ed.). *Pathological anxiety: Emotional processing in etiology and treatment* (pp. 227–244). New York: Guilford Press.

Rothbaum, B. O., Anderson, P., Zimand, E., Hodges, L., Lang, D., & Wilson, J. (2006). Virtual reality exposure therapy and standard (in vivo) exposure therapy in the treatment of fear of flying. *Behavior Therapy, 37,* 80–90.

Shapiro, F. (2001). *Eye movement desensitation and reprocessing: Basic principles, protocols, and procedures* (2nd ed.). New York: Guilford.

Sheehan, P. W. (1967). A shortened form of Betts' Questionnaire upon Mental Imagery. *Journal of Clinical Psychology, 223,* 380–389.

Sloan, T., & Telch, M. J. (2005). The effects of safety-seeking behavior and guided threat reappraisal on fear reduction during exposure: An experimental investigation. *Behaviour Research and Therapy, 40,* 235–251.

Taylor, S., Thordarson, D. S., Maxfield, L., Fedoroff, I. C., Lovell, K., & Ogrodniczuk, J. (2003). Comparative efficacy, speed, and adverse effects of three PTSD treatments: Exposure therapy, EMDR, and relaxation training. *Journal of Consulting and Clinical Psychology, 2,* 330–338.

Telch, M. J., Valentine, D. P., Ilai, D., Young, P. R., Powers, M. B., & Smits, J. A. J. (2004). Fear activation and distraction during the emotional processing of claustrophobic fear. *Journal of Behavior Therapy and Experimental Psychiatry, 35,* 219–232.

Tryon, W. W. (2005). Possible mechanisms for why desensitization and exposure therapy work. *Clinical Psychology Review, 25,* 67–95.

Tsao, J. C., & Craske, M. G. (2000). Timing of treatment and return of fear: Effects of massed, uniform-, and expanding-spaced exposure schedules. *Behavior Therapy, 31,* 479–497.

VandenBos, G. R. (Ed.). (2007). *APA dictionary of psychology.* Washington, DC: American Psychological Association.

Watts, F. N. (1979). Habituation model of systematic desensitization. *Psychological Bulletin, 86,* 627–637.

Wiederhold, B. K., & Wiederhold, M. D. (2005). *Virtual reality therapy for anxiety disorders: Advances in evaluation and treatment.* Washington, DC: American Psychological Association.

Wolpe, J. (1958). *Psychotherapy by reciprocal inhibition.* Stanford, CA: Stanford University Press.

Wolpe, J. (1990). *The practice of behavior therapy* (4 ed.). New York: Pergamon Press.

Woods, A. M., & Bouton, M. E. (2006). D-cycloserine facilitates extinction but does not eliminate renewal of the conditioned emotional response. *Behavioral Neuroscience, 120,* 1159–1162.

Yates, A. J. (1975). *Theory and practice in behavior therapy* (pp. 152–182). New York: Wiley.

Zoellner, L. A., Abramowitz, J. S., & Moore, S. A. (2003). Flooding. In W. O'Donohue, J. E. Fisher, & S. C. Hayes (Eds.), *Cognitive behavior therapy: Applying empirically supported techniques in your practice* (pp. 160–166). Hoboken, NJ: Wiley.

16   KNOWLEDGE AND SKILL BUILDER

The questions in this Knowledge and Skill Builder are based directly on the Learning Outcomes described at the beginning of the chapter. Suggested answers for the following questions can be found in the feedback section on page 516.

1. You have are seeing a client with a fear of spiders. She says she developed this fear after "nearly dying" from a poisonous spider bite as a child. She avoids all situations involving spiders. She is interested in exposure therapy after seeing a special about it on a television news program, but she wants more information before beginning treatment. How might you describe the rationale for treatment using exposure? Be sure to include at least one theoretical explanation for how exposure might work.

2. You are being asked about different forms of exposure therapy by a new client who has accessed a few Internet sources about treatment for a phobia about speaking in public in front of groups. Name and describe at least one gradual and one intensive method for exposure.

3. You are trying to decide on an exposure method for a client with a fear of flying. Name at least three issues you would consider in choosing an exposure method with this client.

4. What are the steps of exposure therapy you use in implementing an exposure treatment with a client who has an extreme fear of heights?

5. What are the issues of informed consent you should cover with your client in doing exposure therapy? What is at least one caution you should consider in using this form of treatment?

16   KNOWLEDGE AND SKILL BUILDER **FEEDBACK**

1. You can explain the client's fear of spiders as developing from experiencing the spider in combination with an aversive event (i.e., "almost dying"). This pairing led to learning that associated spiders with fear and, subsequently, to avoidance. The avoidance in which the client has been engaging for years has prevented new learning that breaks the previous associations made. The goal of exposure therapy will be to create new learning, in which the client associates spiders with nonaversive outcomes and learns she can deal effectively with the presence of spiders. Exposure might possibly work for the client through respondent and operant extinction. Spiders will be presented without any aversive consequence, and the client will no longer be negatively reinforced with decreased arousal through escape/avoidance.

2. A gradual exposure method a helper might use is *in vivo* exposure, in which a client is progressively exposed to real stimuli (as opposed to imagined or simulated stimuli) that provoke fear and anxiety. Alternatively, a client can be treated with the intensive exposure method of flooding, in which a client is exposed for an extended period of time to his most fear-provoking stimuli until fear and arousal decrease.

3. In choosing an exposure method to use with your client, you need to consider at least some of the following issues: practical considerations such as the availability of a local airport, access to virtual-reality equipment, other resources such as flying-related DVDs, the motivation level of the client, the willingness of the client to engage in different forms of exposure therapy, and the client's health status.

4. Briefly, explain the rationale behind exposure therapy to the client, and then address the client's concerns before gaining the client's informed consent to treatment. The next step will be to identify precisely what situations and stimuli involving heights evoke fear and anxiety for the client, using the information to construct a hierarchy of feared items with the client. If appropriate, you can train the client in relaxation skills to use in conjuction with exposure exercises. If you are using imaginal exposure, the client's imagery ability should be assessed. Exposure to the items identified by the client as fear provoking should then begin. After exposures, encourage the client to discuss thoughts and feelings, emphasizing how maladaptive thoughts were disconfirmed, providing discussion time at the end of session to address client insights, avoidance, and safety-seeking behavior. Using information gained during initial exposure, you can continue and modify later exposure exercises, and homework exercises can be created.

5. The three components of informed consent to remember when you are discussing exposure therapy with a client are ensuring the client is competent to give consent, has adequate information on which to base consent, and gives consent voluntarily and is not forced or coerced by the helper. One caution the helper should be aware of in using exposure treatment is that clients with certain health conditions, such as cardiac problems, may be at increased risk from the physiological activation sometimes seen in exposure therapy. Medical clearance is necessary for exposure treatment with such clients.

17

SELF-MANAGEMENT STRATEGIES
SELF-MONITORING, STIMULUS CONTROL, SELF-REWARD, AND SELF-EFFICACY

LEARNING OUTCOMES

After completing this chapter, you will be able to

1. Given a written client case description, describe the use of self-monitoring and stimulus control for the client.
2. Teach another person how to engage in self-monitoring as a self-change strategy.
3. Given a written client case description, be able to describe the use of a culturally relevant self-management program for the client.
4. Teach another person how to use self-monitoring, stimulus control, and self-reward.

In self-management, the helping professional aids the client to better understand naturally occurring processes (predominantly behavioral and psychological) that are believed to exert considerable influence over behaviors or responses that have become problematic for the client. Self-management is a very teaching-oriented approach. *During* formal sessions, the helper teaches clients about processes that are fueling problems and about processes that will lead to desired changes after clients undertake stages of activities *outside* formal sessions to achieve sustainable changes. Thus, the client does most of the work *between* sessions. One of the major goals of self-management intervention is to assist clients in gaining a greater capacity for self-determined initiative, or "agency," relative to their goals and to achieve increasing independence in their desired functioning.

In several respects, self-management draws on various tools and interventions; a meaningful set is pulled together by the client and helper, depending on assessment, goals, and conditions. Self-management is a strongly collaborative, environmentally attentive strategy that has been used across a wide range of specific problems in living and with varying clientele (e.g., age groups, disability status, problem severity, cultural heritage). We do urge caution, for self-management strategies can be presented or approached in a decontextualized manner—inattentive, for example, to current or historical environmental inequities or stressors that are as much if not more the true source of the issues that the client

is struggling with. We see the emphasis on "self" here to be valuable toward empowering, goal-achieving awareness, and skill building, not as a question of approaching clients as selves that need to be managed to accommodate flawed circumstances.

Definitions of self-management vary in part because different theorists emphasize different processes and strategies, and in part because of overlap among related terms that are sometimes used interchangeably and can be confusing. For example, self-change methods have been referred to as *self-control, self-regulation,* and *self-management.* We use *self-management* because it conveys the notion of handling one's life within a set of life conditions and because literature searches on this term will turn up applications of change techniques more than basic research on underlying processes. Also, the term *self-management* avoids the concepts of inhibition and restriction often associated with the words *control* and *regulation*—although these associations can be misleading as in some self-regulatory applications that are more about insight, opening up new options, and integrative linkages among physiology, psychology, and social phenomena.

In spite of differing emphases, self-management tends to be anchored in social learning and social cognitive theories underlying cognitive–behavioral models. According to Bandura (1986, 1997), for example, the social cognitive theory holds that human behavior is extensively motivated and regulated by the ongoing exercise of self-influence. The major self-management processes operate through four principal subfunctions: (1) self-monitoring of one's behavior, its components, and its effects; (2) judgment of one's behavior; (3) affective self-reactions; and (4) self-efficacy. Self-efficacy plays a central role in the exercise of personal agency by its strong impact on thought, affect, motivation, and action. Self-efficacy is very important in helping clients achieve treatment goals and enhancing their confidence and ability to execute the self-management strategies. Behavioral change is very often challenging and frequently not pleasant. If clients are involved in negotiating treatment planning and setting goals, they are much more likely to implement the strategies and to achieve the change goals successfully. Of course, there are also situation difficulties or symptoms that cannot be readily changed. Part of the goal then may be assisting clients to achieve coping strategies to handle these intractable situations as effectively as realistically possible.

Self-management strategies have several client outcomes that may include the following: (1) to use more effective task, interpersonal, cognitive, and emotional behaviors; (2) to alter perceptions of and judgmental attitudes toward problematic situations or persons; and (3) either to change or to learn to cope with a stress-inducing situation (Kanfer & Gaelick-Buys, 1991, p. 307). We focus here on

Self-monitoring: observing and recording your own particular behaviors (thoughts, feelings, and actions) about yourself and your interactions with environmental events

Stimulus control: prearranging antecedents or cues to increase or decrease your performance of a target behavior

Self-reward: giving yourself a positive stimulus following a desired response

Self-efficacy: increasing one's beliefs and expectations of being able to perform certain things under certain situations

These strategies may be viewed as self-management because in each procedure the client, in a self-directed fashion, monitors, alters, rewards, models, and possesses self-efficacy to perform a specific task to produce the desired behavioral changes. Of course, none of these strategies is entirely independent of the client's personal history, gender, age, culture, ethnicity, and environmental variables. In fact, because self-management treatment planning is so greatly dependent on careful assessment of concerns and needs and also on the client's ability to take on a self-manager role, diversity and contextualizing factors are particularly important considerations.

In addition to these four self-management procedures, a wide range of other change strategies are often found in the clinical literature (e.g., problem solving, coping, stress management). Broadly speaking, a client can use nearly any helping strategy in a self-directed manner. For example, a client could apply relaxation training to manage anxiety by using a relaxation training CD or DVD without the assistance of a helper. In fact, some degree of client self-management may be a necessary component of many significant change efforts. However, not all change strategies are predicated on the same degree of understanding the learning principles underlying processes that self-management is. These self-managed aspects of any formal change procedure typically include the following:

1. Client self-directed practice in the interview
2. Client self-directed practice in the in vivo setting (often through homework tasks)
3. Client self-observation and recording of target behaviors or of homework
4. Client self-reward (verbal or material) for successful completion of action steps and homework assignments

CLINICAL USES OF SELF-MANAGEMENT STRATEGIES

Self-management strategies have been used for a wide range of clinical concerns (see Box 17.1). They have been applied to many health problems, including arthritis, asthma, breast cancer, comorbid medical conditions, diabetes, and irritable bowel syndrome. Among the psychological problems for which self-management strategies have recently been investigated are attention-deficit/hyperactivity disorder (ADHD), anger, anxiety, depression, and chronic mental illness. Self-management has also been used to decrease substance and alcohol abuse, to help compensate for developmental disabilities, and to improve effectiveness in classroom behavior of students with emotional or behavioral disorders. Measures of self-management, self-regulation, and self-efficacy have been developed and are available for use in practice.

APPLICATIONS OF SELF-MANAGEMENT WITH DIVERSE GROUPS

Self-management has been used with diverse groups of clients in areas such as health management, school success, relationship conflict, and HIV intervention. Jacob, Penn, Kulik, and Spieth (1992) researched the effects of self-management and positive reinforcement on the self-reported compliance rate of African American women who performed breast self-examinations over a nine-month period. Both self-management and positive reinforcement were associated with high compliance rates, especially for women who were designated initially as "monitors" (e.g., more likely to "track" things about themselves).

Yip and colleagues (2007) used an arthritis self-management program combined with exercise in a Chinese population suffering from osteoarthritis. The authors tailored the program to be culturally relevant in several ways, including omitting a typically Western component of cognitive emotional therapy, because a pilot study revealed that many of the participants did not feel that learning emotional management was relevant to their needs. Instead, the patients desired to learn how to use exercise, including the tradition of Tai Chi, to control their arthritis symptoms. The intervention group showed significant improvement on most measures compared to a control group, and the authors

BOX 17.1	RESEARCH ON SELF-MANAGEMENT

ADHD

Gureasko-Moore, S., DuPaul, G. J., & White, G. P. (2006). The effects of self-management in general education classrooms on the organizational skills of adolescents with ADHD. *Behavior Modification, 30*(2), 159–183.

Arthritis

Goodacre, L. (2006). Women's perceptions on managing chronic arthritis. *British Journal of Occupational Therapy, 69*(1), 7–14.

Yip, Y. B., Sit, J. W., Fung, K. K. Y., Wong, D. Y. S., Chong, S. Y. C., Chung, L. H., & Ng, T. P. (2007). Impact of an arthritis self-management programme with an added exercise component for osteoarthritic knee sufferers on improving pain, functional outcomes, and use of health care services: An experimental study. *Patient Education and Counseling, 65*(1), 113–121.

Asthma

Clark, N. M., Gong, M., Kaciroti, N., Yu, J., Wu, G., Zeng, Z., & Wu, Z. (2005). A trial of asthma self-management in Beijing schools. *Chronic Illness, 1*(1), 31–38.

Horner, S. D. (2006). Home visiting for intervention delivery to improve rural family asthma management. *Journal of Community Health Nursing, 23*(4), 213–223.

Breast Cancer Survivors

Cimprich, B., Janz, N. K., Northouse, L., Wren, P. A., Given, B., & Given, C. W. (2005). Taking charge: A self-management program for women following breast cancer treatment. *Psycho-Oncology, 14*(9), 704–717.

Damush, T. M., Perkins, A., & Miller, K. (2006). The implementation of an oncologist referred, exercise self-management program for older breast cancer survivors. *Psycho-Oncology, 15*(10), 884–890.

Career Development

Kuijpers, M. A. C. T., & Scheerens, J. (2006). Career competencies for the modern career. *Journal of Career Development, 32*(4), 303–319.

Chronic Illness

Harvey, I. S. (2006). Self-management of a chronic illness: An exploratory study on the role of spirituality among older African American women. *Journal of Women and Aging, 18*(3), 75–88.

Swerissen, H., Belfrage, J., Weeks, A., Jordan, L., Walker, C., Furler, J., et al. (2006). A randomised control trial of a self-management program for people with a chronic illness from Vietnamese, Chinese, Italian and Greek backgrounds. *Patient Education and Counseling, 64*(1–3), 360–368.

Comorbid Medical Conditions

Bayliss, E. A., Ellis, J. L., Steiner, J. F., & Main, D. S. (2005). Initial validation of an instrument to identify barriers to self-management for persons with co-morbidities. *Chronic Illness, 1*(4), 315–320.

Depression

Bachman, J., Swenson, S., Reardon, M. E., & Miller, D. (2006). Patient self-management in the primary care treatment of depression. *Adminstration and Policy in Mental Health and Mental Health Services Research, 33*(1), 76–85.

Scholz, U., Knoll, N., Sniehotta, F. F., & Schwarzer, R. (2006). Physical activity and depressive symptoms in cardiac rehabilitation: Long-term effects of a self-management intervention. *Social Science and Medicine, 62*(12), 3109–3120.

Diabetes

Bell, R. A., Stafford, J. M., Arcury, T. A., Snively, B. M., Smith, S. L., Grzywacz, J. G., & Quandt, S. A. (2006). Complementary and alternative medicine use and diabetes self-management among rural older adults. *Complementary Health Practice Review, 11*(2), 95–106.

Nagelkerk, J., Reick, K., & Meengs, L. (2006). Perceived barriers and effective strategies to diabetes self-management. *Journal of Advanced Nursing, 54*(2), 151–158.

Oster, N. V., Welch, V., Schild, L., Gazmararian, J. A., Rask, K., & Spettell, C. (2006). Differences in self-management behaviors and use of preventive services among diabetes management enrollees by race and ethnicity. *Disease Management, 9*(3),167–175.

HIV/AIDS

Kemppainen, J. K., Eller, L. S., Bunch, E., Hamilton, M. J., Dole, P., Holzemer, W., et al. (2006). Strategies for self-management of HIV-related anxiety. *AIDS Care, 18*(6), 597–607.

Irritable Bowel Syndrome

Bogalo, L., & Moss-Morris, R. (2006). The effectiveness of homework tasks in an irritable bowel syndrome cognitive behavioural self-management programme. *New Zealand Journal of Psychology, 35*(3), 120–125.

Medication Management

Muir-Cochrane, E., Fereday, J., Jureidini, J., Drummond, A., & Darbyshire, P. (2006). Self-management of medication for mental health problems by homeless young people. *International Journal of Mental Health Nursing, 15*(3), 163–170.

Mental Retardation

Chapman, R. A., Shedlack, K. J., & France, J. (2006). Stop–think–relax: An adapted self-control training strategy for

(continued)

BOX 17.1	RESEARCH ON SELF-MANAGEMENT

(*continued*)

individuals with mental retardation and coexisting psychiatric illness. *Cognitive and Behavioral Practice, 13*(3), 205–214.

Pain

Austrian, J. S., Kerns, R. D., & Reid, M. C. (2005). Perceived barriers to trying self-management approaches for chronic pain in older persons. *Journal of the American Geriatrics Society, 53*(5), 856–861.

Buck, R., & Morley, S. (2006). A daily process design study of attentional pain control strategies in the self-management of cancer pain. *European Journal of Pain, 10*(5), 385–398.

Students with Behavior and Emotional Disorders

Mooney, P., Ryan, J. B., Uhing, B. M., Reid, R., & Epstein, M. H. (2005). A review of self-management interventions targeting academic outcomes for students with emotional and behavioral disorders. *Journal of Behavioral Education, 14*(3), 203–221.

Substance Abuse

Koerkel, J. (2006). Behavioural self-management with problem drinkers: One-year follow-up of a controlled drinking group treatment approach. *Addiction Research and Theory, 14*(1), 35–49.

Sobell, M. B., & Sobell, L. C. (2005). Guided self-change model of treatment for substance use disorders. *Journal of Cognitive Psychotherapy, 19*(3), 199–210.

posited that the cultural relevance and specificity of the intervention was crucial.

Swerissen et al. (2006) tested the effectiveness of a chronic disease self-management program with four immigrant populations living in Victoria, Australia. This community-based intervention was delivered in the native languages of the immigrant groups—Chinese, Greek, Italian, and Vietnamese—and consisted of symptom management, problem solving, dealing with disease-related emotions, exercise and relaxation, meditation, healthy eating, and communication skills. Participants had better outcomes on a variety of measures, including energy, exercise, pain, and fatigue. Results varied by group, however, with the Chinese and Vietnamese participants demonstrating greater benefits. The authors argue that self-management techniques may not be equally effective across all populations. Given the variability in how self-management interventions are operationalized, further research is required to understand more about which components and strategies are more or less well suited for differing populations.

Harvey (2006) conducted a qualitative, exploratory study of the use of spirituality in the self-management of chronic illness by African American women. In her interviews, four themes emerged: (1) using spiritual practices in combination with traditional medicine in self-management; (2) empowerment to health-promotive practices; (3) using prayer as a mediator of illness; and (4) spirituality as a coping mechanism. Harvey argues that spirituality should be an important aspect of interventions with older African American women, and that it can be used to improve self-efficacy, coping, and health-promotive activities.

Roberson (1992) also explored the role of compliance and self-management in adult rural African Americans who had been diagnosed with chronic health conditions. She found that the patients and their health professionals had different notions of compliance and also different treatment goals. The patients defined compliance in terms of apparent "good health" and wanted treatments that were manageable, viable, and effective. They developed systems of self-management to cope with their illnesses that were suitable to their lifestyles, belief patterns, and personal priorities. They believed they were managing their illnesses and treatment regimens effectively. Roberson (1992) suggested that as professionals we need to focus less on noncompliance rates per se and more on understanding differing perspectives and enhancing clients' efforts to manage their own illnesses and to live effectively with them.

Asthma has been a health focus. Haire-Joshu, Fisher, Munro, and Wedner (1993) explored attitudes toward asthma care within a sample of low-income African American adults receiving services at a public acute care facility versus patients receiving services at a private setting that stressed preventive self-management. Those persons in the acute care setting were more likely to engage in self-treatment (such as relying on over-the-counter medication) or to avoid or delay care, compared to the patients who had learned preventive asthma self-management techniques—findings that urge attention to factors such as access to resources and differential histories with service providers in planning interventions. An innovative computer-assisted instructional program (the main character in the game could match the subject on gender and ethnicity; the protagonist's asthma could be tailored similarly to the subjects) to improve asthma self-management in inner-city children has achieved promising initial results in both self-management behaviors and health outcomes (Bartholomew et al., 2000). Rao and Kramer (1993) found self-control to be an important aspect of stress reduction and coping among African American mothers who had infants with sickle cell conditions. Notably, other strategies complementary to self-control (positive reappraisal, seeking social support, problem solving) were also found useful.

Self-management has also been found to be an effective component of HIV-infection risk reduction training with gay men (Kelly & St. Lawrence, 1990; Martin, 1993). In a study of several hundred African American youth, self-management was part of an eight-week HIV-risk-reduction program that compared receiving either information or skills training versus both information and skills training (St. Lawrence et al., 1995). Youth who received both information and skills training lowered their risk to a greater degree, maintained risk reduction changes better, and deferred the onset of sexual activity to a greater extent than those who received only one component of training. However, issues of dropout and perceived self-relevance have also been raised in HIV-prevention interventions for inner-city heterosexual African American men (Kalichman, Rompa, & Coley, 1997).

Research has indicated the utility of broadening the view of resources to be included in self-management interventions—to draw upon environmental resources such as social support people and networks, spirituality, and opportunities to work with families or communities to develop culturally relevant approaches. A computer-assisted program applied to asthma self-management is one such example. In addition to research findings, Bartholomew and colleagues (2000) also offer an overview of applying theory (e.g., about self-efficacy and self-regulatory processes) to a self-management need in a culturally sensitive manner. Wang and Abbott (1998) describe a project to work with a Chinese community group toward developing a culturally sensitive community-based self-management program for chronic diseases such as diabetes and hypertension. Faith, prayer, and religious activities were demonstrated to be importantly associated with health management among a racially diverse group of rural older adults (Arcury, Quandt, McDonald, & Bell, 2000), arguing for the need to consider such factors in developing self-management plans. In related work, factors that need to be considered in working with rural populations, particularly among vulnerable elders such as those widowed, have been addressed relative to nutritional self-management (Quandt, McDonald, Arcury, Bell, & Vitolins, 2000).

It would seem that self-management could be incorporated as a culturally effective intervention with many clients from diverse groups, especially as self-management is time limited, deals with the present, and focuses on pragmatic problem resolution (Sue & Sue, 2003). Similarly, focus on behavioral patterns as well as beliefs or orientations to promote action and not just "talk" and self-exploration would be consistent with the use of a self-management intervention. However, we would note that self-management need not be construed to be a "lone ranger" or nonreflective method, but rather one that can sensibly build on environmental resources and cultural perspectives about self and problem solving. Self-management may also appeal to some clients who do not like or feel comfortable with traditional mental health services. Keep in mind that in self-management efforts, the work is client managed, and most of it occurs outside helping sessions. Values and belief systems (e.g., that self-reliance, faith, and inclusion in community are important general strategies for living) as well as characteristics of the client's environment—social, material, informational, sociopolitical—can be important dimensions of assessment to guide appropriate self-management intervention planning.

However, caution must be used in selecting self-management as an appropriate intervention for all clients from diverse cultural groups. McCafferty (1992) has suggested that the process of self-regulation varies among cultures and societies. Some of the notions involved in self-management strategies are decidedly Eurocentric. Casas (1988) asserts that the basic notion underlying self-management may "not be congruent with the life experiences of many racial/ethnic minority persons. More specifically, as a result of life experiences associated with racism, discrimination, and poverty, people may have developed a cognitive set (e.g., an external locus of control, an external locus of responsibility, and learned helplessness) that . . . is antithetical to any self-control approaches" (pp. 109–110). For example, within a framework of worldviews, there are four quadrants in Sue and Sue's (2003) cultural identity model based on the dimensions of locus of control and the locus of responsibility. These quadrants range from *internal control* to *external control* and from *internal responsibility* to *external responsibility*. Thus, locus of control and locus of responsibility seem to be mediating variables that affect the appropriateness of using self-management for some women clients and for some clients of color. In an innovative study conducted by St. Lawrence (1993), African American female and male youth completed measures of knowledge related to AIDS, attitudes toward the use of condoms, vulnerability to HIV infection, peer sexual norms, personal sexual behavior, contraceptive preferences, and locus of control. Condom use as prevention was associated with greater internal locus of control, which was higher for the African American girls than for the boys. In addition to the mediating variables of locus of control and locus of responsibility, the client's identification with his or her cultural (collective) identity, acculturation status, and assimilation may also be mediating variables that affect the use of self-management for non-Euro-American clients.

GUIDELINES FOR USING SELF-MANAGEMENT WITH DIVERSE GROUPS OF CLIENTS

We recommend the following guidelines in using self-management approaches with diverse groups of clients.

First, consider the client's lifestyle, beliefs, behavioral patterns, and personal priorities in assessing the usefulness of self-management. For example, if the client is interested in following the progress of events, a strategy such as self-monitoring may be relevant to his or her personal and cognitive style. For clients who have no interest in such tracking, self-monitoring may appear to be a waste of time, an activity that is personally and culturally irrelevant.

Second, adapt the intervention to the client's culture and background. Some clients have been socialized to be very private and would feel most uncomfortable in publicly displaying their self-monitoring data. Other clients would be unlikely to discipline themselves to go to one place to obtain stimulus control, such as using a smoking chair to help control smoking. And, depending on the client's history, the idea of using self-rewards may be awkward or benefit from reframing. At the very least, the rewards must be tailored to the client's gender, age, and culture.

Third, discover the client's worldview and consider the relevance of self-management based on this perception of the world. For clients whose cultural identity or the targeted issue is shaped by an external locus of control and an external locus of responsibility, self-management may not be a good match or may need to be discussed as an option with such factors in mind.

Fourth, consider the relevance of self-management against the client's goals for helping intervention and also the context of the client's life. If the client is also struggling with multiple problems in living, aversive external structures and discrimination, serious vulnerabilities, or overwhelming pressures, self-management would have a limited role, if deemed appropriate at all. Consider, for example, how it might feel if you were a low-income mother with no social support and few resources and were regularly beaten by your live-in male partner—and your helping practitioner told you to engage in some form of self-management. One or more self-management strategies, however, may provide some concrete relief—perhaps in better managing a health problem or in helping her child better manage troubling classroom behavior—that can be a meaningful part of a larger set of goals.

Fifth, consider the client's access to resources, and be aware that resources may differ for oppressed individuals within society. Barriers can be due to personal characteristics, such as literacy, disability, or transportation, as well as to structural problems such as racism, homophobia, or similar prejudices and inequities that may make it more difficult for some clients to self-manage.

CHARACTERISTICS OF AN EFFECTIVE SELF-MANAGEMENT PROGRAM

Well-constructed and well-executed self-management programs have some advantages over helper-administered procedures. For instance, the use of a self-management procedure may increase a person's perceived control over the environment and decrease dependence on the helper or others. Perceived control over the environment often motivates and supports a person to take some action. Second, self-management approaches are practical—inexpensive and portable (Thoresen & Mahoney, 1974, p. 7). Third, such strategies are usable. By this we mean that a person will occasionally refuse to go "into therapy" or formalized helping to stop drinking or to lose weight but will agree to use the self-administered instructions that a self-management program provides. This may be particularly advantageous with some clients who are mistrustful of therapy or related forms of professional helping. Finally, self-management strategies may enhance generalization of learning—both from the interview to the environment and from problematic to nonproblematic situations (Thoresen & Mahoney, 1974, p. 7). These are some of the possible advantages of self-management that have spurred both researchers and practitioners to apply and explore some of the components and effects of successful self-management programs.

Although many questions remain unanswered, we can tentatively say that the following factors may be important in an effective self-management program:

1. A combination of strategies, some focusing on antecedents of behavior and others on consequences
2. Consistent use of strategies over a period of time
3. Evidence of client self-evaluation, goal setting, and self-efficacy
4. Use of covert, verbal, or material self-reinforcement
5. Some degree of external or environmental support

Combination of Strategies

We have mentioned that self-management is often combined with other change strategies and that a combination of self-management strategies is usually more useful than a single strategy. In a weight-control study, Mahoney, Moura, and Wade (1973) found that the addition of self-reward significantly enhanced the procedures of self-monitoring and stimulus control, and that those who combined self-reward and self-punishment lost more weight than those who used just one of the procedures. Stress inoculation training includes application of self-management principles within a multicomponent package, with considerable support across a variety of concerns (Meichenbaum, 1994) and with children and adolescents (Ollendick & King, 2000). Examples include combining self-management strategies with meditation, relaxation methods, coping skill supports, reframing techniques, cognitive restructuring, education, and exercise.

Consistent, regular use of the strategies is a very important component of effective self-management. Seeming ineffectiveness may be partly attributable to sporadic or inconsistent use. Some individuals may be more likely than others to apply self-management strategies with the regularity that is needed. Lack of positive outcomes in a self-management program may be due to lack of clarity about how best to use the procedures, or it may reflect lack of efficacy even with consistent application. Also, if self-management efforts are not used over a certain period of time, their effectiveness may be too limited to produce any change. Ongoing assessment as to the fit of these techniques for clients is needed. Those who have external supports and encouragement for consistency of use are also likely to have a more successful experience.

Self-Evaluation, Standard Setting, and Self-Efficacy

Self-evaluation in the form of standard setting (or goal setting) and intention statements seems to be an important component of a self-management program. Some evidence also suggests that self-selected stringent standards affect performance more positively than do lenient standards (Bandura, 1971). It is important to distinguish *outcome* expectations (one's beliefs about whether a certain behavior or event will produce a particular outcome) from *self-efficacy* expectations (the belief or level of confidence a person has in his or her ability to develop intentions, set behavioral goals, and successfully execute the behaviors in question). A client may have confidence that she or he can manage a certain action but may not undertake it because of a belief that it will not accomplish the desired outcome (or that obstacles will intervene to prevent the desired outcome). In some cases, these readings of a situation may be realistic, underscoring the importance of careful assessment of a client's circumstances and other agents or factors that may have significant roles in the desired outcome.

In general, however, perceived self-efficacy is seen by many as a centrally important component. Without this, it is difficult at best to build an intervention program that requires substantial client involvement or to achieve incrementally successful, reinforcing outcomes along the way. Strengthening efficacy expectations can augment an internal resource crucial to subsequent successes in a self-management intervention. For example, successful self-controllers usually set higher goals and criteria for change than unsuccessful self-controllers do. However, the standards set should be realistic and within reach; otherwise, it is unlikely that self-reinforcement will ever occur. Bandura (1997) offers a discussion of sources through which self-efficacy expectations are typically influenced: (1) one's own performance accomplishments, (2) vicarious experience (e.g., observing others, reading stories, imagining), (3) verbal persuasion, and (4) physiological and affective states (e.g., strategies to pair a positive mood and a relaxed state with conditions under which self-efficacy is needed).

Use of Self-Reinforcement

Self-reinforcement, whether covert, verbal, or material, appears to be an important ingredient of an effective self-management program. Being able to praise oneself covertly or to note positive improvement seems to be correlated with self-change. In contrast, self-criticism (covert and verbal) seems to mitigate against change (Mahoney & Mahoney, 1976). It is important to consider what any given client will experience as genuinely reinforcing. For example, some people may find that material self-reward (such as money or valued items) may be more effective than either self-monitoring or self-punishment; others may find various forms of social support or pride to be more effective. Self-reinforcement must also be relevant to the client's gender and culture.

Environmental Support

Some degree of external support is necessary to effect and maintain the changes resulting from a self-management program. For example, public display of self-monitoring data and the help of another person provide opportunities for social reinforcement that often augment behavior change. Successful self-controllers may report receiving more positive feedback from others about their change efforts than do unsuccessful self-controllers. To maintain any self-managed change, there must be some support from the social and physical environment, although how this is best achieved may vary for clients from different cultural backgrounds, age cohorts, or life circumstances. We previously used examples to illuminate variability in how "self" may be conceptualized differently among people and how self-management may be embedded for some within networks, communities, historical legacies, or current conditions that should be considered. The examples illustrated ways that faith and spirituality may be important along with support networks and cultural identities (Gartett, 1999, provides an example for Native American youth).

STEPS IN DEVELOPING A CLIENT SELF-MANAGEMENT PROGRAM

We have incorporated those five characteristics of effective self-management into a description of the steps associated with a self-management program. The steps are applicable to any program in which the client uses stimulus control, self-monitoring, or self-reward. Figure 17.1 summarizes the steps associated with developing a self-management program; the characteristics of effective self-management reflected in the steps are noted in the left column of the figure.

For developing a self-management program, steps 1 and 2 both involve aspects of standard setting and self-evaluation.

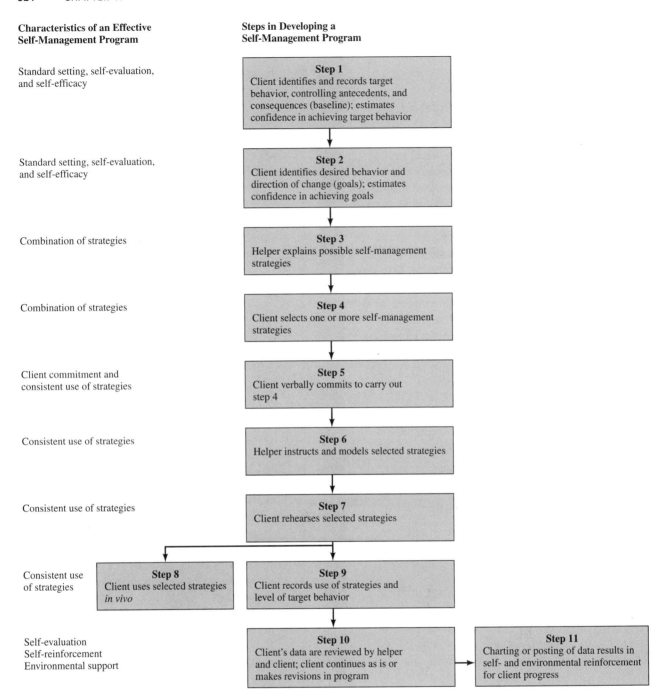

Figure 17.1 Developing an Effective Self-management Program

In step 1, the client identifies and records the target behavior and its antecedents and consequences. This step involves self-monitoring, in which the client collects baseline data about the behavior to be changed. If baseline data have not been collected as part of assessment, it is imperative that such data be collected now, before using any self-management strategies. In step 2, the client explicitly iden-

tifies the desired behavior, conditions, and level of change. The behavior, conditions, and level of change are the three parts of a counseling outcome goal. Defining the goal is an important part of self-management because of the possible motivating effects of standard setting. Establishing goals may interact with some of the self-management procedures and contribute to the desired effects.

Steps 3 and 4 are directed toward helping the client select a combination of self-management strategies to use. The helper will need to explain all the possible self-management strategies to the client (step 3). The helper should emphasize that the client should select some strategies that involve prearrangement of the antecedents and some that involve manipulation and self-administration of consequences. Ultimately, the client is responsible for selecting which self-management strategies should be used (step 4). Client selection of the strategies is an important part of the overall *self-directed* nature of self-management, although this step may benefit from assistance from the professional helper or others involved in supporting the client's efforts in sorting through the choices.

Steps 5–9 all involve procedural considerations that may strengthen client commitment and may encourage consistent use of the strategies over time. First, the client commits himself or herself verbally by specifying what and how much change is desired and the action steps (strategies) the client will take to produce the change (step 5). Next, the helper instructs the client in how to carry out the selected strategies (step 6). (The helper can follow the guidelines listed later in the chapter for self-monitoring, those for stimulus control, and those for self-reward.) Explicit instructions and modeling by the helper may encourage the client to use a procedure more accurately and effectively. The instructional set given by a helper may contribute to some degree to the overall treatment outcome. The client also may use the strategies more effectively if there is an opportunity to rehearse the procedures in the interview under the helper's direction (step 7). Finally, the client applies the strategies in vivo (step 8) and records (monitors) the frequency of use of each strategy and the level of the target behavior (step 9). Some of the treatment effects of self-management may also be a function of the client's self-recording.

Steps 10 and 11 involve aspects of self-evaluation, self-reinforcement, and environmental support. The client has an opportunity to evaluate progress toward the goal by reviewing the self-recorded data collected during strategy implementation (step 10). Review of the data may indicate that the program is progressing smoothly or that some adjustments are needed. When the data suggest that some progress toward the goal is being made, the client's self-evaluation may set the occasion for self-reinforcement. Charting or posting the data (step 11) can enhance self-reinforcement and can elicit important environmental support for long-term maintenance of client change.

In the next section we describe how self-monitoring can be used to record the target behavior. Such recording can occur initially for problem assessment and goal setting, or it can be introduced later as a self-change strategy. We discuss how self-monitoring can be specifically used to promote behavior change.

SELF-MONITORING: PURPOSES, USES, AND PROCESSES

Purposes of Self-Monitoring

Self-monitoring is a process in which clients observe and record things about themselves and their interactions with environmental situations. Self-monitoring is a useful adjunct to assessment because the observational data can verify or change the client's verbal report about the target behavior. We recommend that clients record their daily self-observations over a designated time period on a behavior log. Usually, the client observes and records the target behavior, the controlling antecedents, and the resulting consequences.

Self-monitoring is a core first step in any self-change program. The client must be able to discover what is happening *before* implementing a self-change strategy, just as the helper must know what is going on before using any other therapeutic procedure. In other words, any self-management strategy, like any other strategy, should be preceded by a baseline period of self-observation and recording. During this period, the client collects and records data about the behavior to be changed (B), the antecedents (A) of the behavior, and the consequences (C) of the behavior. In addition, the client may wish to note how much or how often the behavior occurs. For example, a client might record the daily amount of study time or the number of times he or she left the study time and place to do something else. Behavior logs used to collect assessment data can also be used by a client to collect baseline data before implementing a self-management program. If the helper introduces self-management strategies *after* assessment, these self-observation data should be already available.

Self-monitoring is also very useful for evaluation of goals or outcomes. When a client self-monitors the target behavior either before or during a treatment program, "the primary utility of self-monitoring lies in its assessment or data collection function" (Ciminero, Nelson, & Lipinski, 1977, p. 196). However, practitioners and researchers have realized that the mere act of self-observation can produce change. As one collects data about oneself, the data collection may influence the behavior being observed. We now know that self-monitoring is useful not only to collect data but also to promote client change. If properly structured and executed, self-monitoring can be used as one type of self-management strategy. (See Learning Activity 17.1.)

Clinical Uses of Self-Monitoring

A number of research reports and clinical studies have explored self-monitoring as a major change strategy. Box 17.2 indicates a variety of subjects for which self-monitoring has been recently investigated as a change strategy. These include ADHD, binge eating, obesity, classroom behavior, depression, psychosis, spinal cord injury, and stress. Other recently

LEARNING ACTIVITY   17.1   Self-Monitoring

This activity is designed to help you use self-monitoring yourself. The instructions describe a self-monitoring plan for you to try out.

1. *Discrimination of a target response:*
   a. Specify one target behavior you would like to change. Pick either the positive or the negative side of the behavior to monitor—depending on which you value more and whether you want to increase or decrease this response.
   b. Write down a definition of this behavior. How clear is your definition?
   c. Can you write some examples of this behavior? If you had trouble with these, try to tighten up your definition—or contrast positive and negative instances of the behavior.

2. *Recording of the response:*
   a. Specify the *timing* of your self-recording. Remember the rules of thumb:
      (1) Use prebehavior monitoring to decrease an undesired response.
      (2) Use postbehavior monitoring to increase a desired response.
      (3) Record immediately—don't wait.
      (4) Record when there are no competing responses.

   b. Select a *method* of recording (frequency, duration, and so on). Remember:
      (1) Frequency counts for clearly separate occurrences of the response
      (2) Duration or latency measures for responses that occur for a period of time
      (3) Intensity measures to determine the severity of a response
   c. Select a *device* to assist you in recording. Remember that the device should be
      (1) Portable
      (2) Accessible
      (3) Economical
      (4) Obtrusive enough to serve as a reminder to self-record
   d. After you have made these determinations, engage in self-monitoring for at least a week (preferably two). Then complete steps 3, 4, and 5.

3. *Charting of the response:* Take your daily self-recording data and chart them on a simple line graph for each day that you self-monitored.

4. *Displaying of data:* Arrange a place (that you feel comfortable with) to display your chart.

5. *Analysis of data:* Compare your chart with your stated desired behavior change. What has happened to the behavior?

---

investigated applications include alcohol consumption, self-injurious behavior, obsessive–compulsive behaviors, smoking cessation, suicidal ideation, managing conditions such as inflammatory bowel disease, and panic. Self-monitoring has been used with many different populations. Examples from recent research include people with a range of disabilities, people with chronic mental illness, immigrants, children, elders, and caregivers, and across cultures. Attention to self-monitoring may help achieve a more nuanced understanding of processes—such as Kosic, Mannetti, and Sam's (2006) finding that self-monitoring plays a role in moderating between differing acculturation strategies and the sociocultural and psychological adaptation outcomes of immigrants.

Factors Influencing the Reactivity of Self-Monitoring

Two issues involved in self-monitoring are the reliability of the self-recording and its reactivity. Reliability, the accuracy of the self-recorded data, is important when self-monitoring is used to evaluate the goal behaviors. However, when self-monitoring is used as a change strategy, the accuracy of the data may be less crucial. From a helping perspective, the reactivity of self-monitoring can support its use as a change strategy. As an example of reactivity, Kanfer and Gaelick-Buys (1991) noted that a married or partnered couple using self-monitoring to observe their frequent arguments reported that whenever the monitoring device (a camcorder) was turned on, the argument was avoided. Similarly, the process of carefully monitoring one's habits raises self-awareness, which in itself can support self-control strategies that change these habits (cf. Karoly, 2005).

Although the reactivity of self-monitoring can be a dilemma in data collection, it can be an asset when self-monitoring is used intentionally as a helping strategy. In using self-monitoring as a change strategy, try to maximize the reactive effects of self-monitoring—at least to the point of producing desired behavioral changes. Self-monitoring for *long* periods of time maintains reactivity. A number of factors seem to influence the reactivity of self-monitoring.

BOX 17.2   RESEARCH ON SELF-MONITORING

ADHD

Harris, K. R., Friedlander, B. D., Saddler, B., Frizzelle, R., & Graham, S. (2005). Self-monitoring of attention versus self-monitoring of academic performance: Effects among students with ADHD in the general education classroom. *Journal of Special Education, 39*(3), 145–156.

Binge Eating

Hildebrandt, T., & Latner, J. (2006). Effect of self-monitoring on binge eating: Treatment response or "binge drift"? *European Eating Disorders Review, 14*(1), 17–22.

Child Obesity

Germann, J. N., Kirschenbaum, D. S., & Rich, B. H. (2007). Child and parental self-monitoring as determinants of success in the treatment of morbid obesity in low-income minority children. *Journal of Pediatric Psychology, 32*(1), 111–121.

Classroom Behavior

Amato Zech, N. A., Hoff, K. E., & Doepke, K. J. (2006). Increasing on-task behavior in the classroom: Extension of self-monitoring strategies. *Psychology in the Schools, 43*(2), 211–221.

Classroom Social Skills

Peterson, L. D., Young, K. R., Salzberg, C. L., West, R. P., & Hill, M. (2006). Using self-management procedures to improve classroom social skills in multiple general education settings. *Education and Treatment of Children, 29*(1), 1–21.

Classroom Staff

Petscher, E. S., & Bailey, J. S. (2006). Effects of training, prompting, and self-monitoring on staff behavior in a classroom for students with disabilities. *Journal of Applied Behavior Analysis, 39*(2), 215–226.

Depression

Chen, H., Guarnaccia, P. J., & Chung, H. (2003). Self-attention as a mediator of cultural influences on depression. *International Journal of Social Psychiatry, 49*(3), 192–203.

Dunn, B. D., Dalgleish, T., Lawrence, A. D., & Ogilvie, A. D. (2007). The accuracy of self-monitoring and its relationship to self-focused attention in dysphoria and clinical depression. *Journal of Abnormal Psychology, 116*(1), 1–15.

Kocovski, N. L., & Endler, N. S. (2000). Self-regulation: Social anxiety and depression. *Journal of Applied Biobehavioral Research, 5*(1), 80–91.

Immigrant Adaptation

Kosic, A., Mannetti, L., & Sam, D. L. (2006). Self-monitoring: A moderating role between acculturation strategies and adaptation of immigrants. *International Journal of Intercultural Relations, 30*(2), 141–157.

Psychophysiology

Hofmann, S. G. (2006). The emotional consequences of social pragmatism: The psychophysiological correlates of self-monitoring. *Biological Psychology, 73*(2), 169–174.

Psychosis

Johns, L. C., Gregg, L., Allen, P., & McGuire, P. K. (2006). Impaired verbal self-monitoring in psychosis: Effects of state, trait and diagnosis. *Psychological Medicine, 36*(4), 465–474.

Self-Prophecy

Spangenberg, E. R., & Sprott, D. E. (2006). Self-monitoring and susceptibility to the influence of self-prophecy. *Journal of Consumer Research, 32*(4), 550–556.

Social Interactions

Flynn, F. J., Reagans, R. E., Amanatullah, E. T., & Ames, D. R. (2006). Helping one's way to the top: Self-monitors achieve status by helping others and knowing who helps whom. *Journal of Personality and Social Psychology, 91*(6), 1123–1137.

Ickes, W., Holloway, R., Stinson, L. L., & Hoodenpyle, T. G. (2006). Self-monitoring in social interaction: The centrality of self-affect. *Journal of Personality, 74*(3), 659–684.

Spinal Cord Injury

Lee, Y., & McCormick, B. P. (2006). Examining the role of self-monitoring and social leisure in the life quality of individuals with spinal cord injury. *Journal of Leisure Research, 38*(1), 1–19.

Stress

Huflejt-Lukasik, M., & Czarnota-Bojarska, J. (2006). Short communication: Self-focused attention and self-monitoring influence on health and coping with stress. *Stress and Health: Journal of the International Society for the Investigation of Stress, 22*(3), 153–159.

A summary of these factors suggests that self-monitoring is most likely to produce positive behavioral changes when change-motivated subjects continuously monitor a limited number of discrete, positively valued target behaviors; when performance feedback and goals or standards are made available and are unambiguous; and when the monitoring act is both salient and closely related in time to the target behaviors.

Nelson (1977) has identified eight variables that seem to be related to the occurrence, intensity, and direction of the reactive effects of self-monitoring:

1. *Motivation:* Clients who are interested in changing the self-monitored behavior are more likely to show reactive effects when they self-monitor.
2. *Valence of target behaviors:* Behaviors that a person values positively are likely to increase with self-monitoring; negative behaviors are likely to decrease; neutral behaviors may not change.
3. *Type of target behaviors:* The nature of the behavior that is being monitored may affect the degree to which self-monitoring procedures effect change.
4. *Standard setting (goals), reinforcement, and feedback:* Reactivity is enhanced for people who self-monitor in conjunction with goals and the availability of performance reinforcement or feedback.
5. *Timing of self-monitoring:* The time when the person self-records can influence the reactivity of self-monitoring. Results may differ depending on whether self-monitoring occurs before or after the target response.
6. *Devices used for self-monitoring:* More obtrusive or visible recording devices seem to be more reactive than unobtrusive devices.
7. *Number of target responses monitored:* Self-monitoring of only one response increases reactivity. As more responses are concurrently monitored, reactivity decreases.
8. *Schedule for self-monitoring:* The frequency with which a person self-monitors can affect reactivity. Continuous self-monitoring may result in more behavior change than intermittent self-recording.

Three factors may contribute to the reactive effects of self-monitoring:

1. *Client characteristics:* Client intellectual and physical abilities may be associated with greater reactivity when self-monitoring.
2. *Expectations:* Clients seeking help may have some expectations for desirable behavior changes. However, it is probably impossible to separate client expectations from implicit or explicit therapeutic "demands" to change the target behavior.
3. *Behavior change skills:* Reactivity may be influenced by the client's knowledge and skills associated with behavior change. For example, the reactivity of addictive behaviors may be affected by the client's knowledge of simple, short-term strategies such as fasting or abstinence. These are general guidelines, and their effects may vary with the gender, class, race, and ethnicity of each specific client.

STEPS OF SELF-MONITORING

Self-monitoring involves at least six important steps: (1) rationale for the strategy, (2) discrimination of a response, (3) recording of a response, (4) charting of a response, (5) displaying of data, and (6) analysis of data. Each of these six steps and guidelines for their use are discussed here and summarized in Table 17.1. Remember that the steps are interactive and that the presence of all of them may be required for a person to use self-monitoring effectively. Also, remember that any or all of these steps may need to be adapted, depending on the client's gender and culture.

Treatment Rationale

First, the practitioner explains the rationale for self-monitoring. Before using the strategy, the client should be aware of what the self-monitoring procedure will involve and how the

---

TABLE 17.1   Steps of Self-Monitoring

1. Rationale for self-monitoring
  A. Purpose
  B. Overview of procedure
2. Discrimination of a response
  A. Selection of target response to monitor
    (1) Type of response
    (2) Valence of response
    (3) Number of responses
3. Recording of a response
  A. Timing of recording
    (1) Prebehavior recording to decrease a response; postbehavior recording to increase a response
    (2) Immediate recording
    (3) Recording when no competing responses distract recorder
  B. Method of recording
    (1) Frequency counts
    (2) Duration measures
      (a) Continuous recording
      (b) Time sampling
  C. Devices for recording
    (1) Portable
    (2) Accessible
    (3) Economical
    (4) Somewhat obtrusive
4. Charting of a response
  A. Charting and graphing of daily totals of recorded behavior
5. Displaying of data
  A. Chart for environmental support
6. Analysis of data
  A. Accuracy of data interpretation
  B. Knowledge of results for self-evaluation and self-reinforcement

procedure will help with the client's concern. An example, adapted from Benson and Stuart (1992), follows:

> The purpose of self-monitoring is to increase your awareness of your sleep patterns. Research has demonstrated that people who have insomnia benefit from keeping a self-monitoring diary. Each morning for a week you will record the time you went to bed the previous night; approximately how many minutes it took you to fall asleep; if you awakened during the night, how many minutes you were awake; the total number of hours you slept; and the time you got out of bed in the morning. Also, on a scale you will rate how rested you feel in the morning, how difficult it was to fall asleep the previous night, the quality of sleep, your level of physical tension when you went to bed the previous night, your level of mental activity when you went to bed, and how well you think you were functioning the previous day. The diary will help us evaluate your sleep and remedy issues. This kind of awareness helps in correcting factors that might contribute to your insomnia. How does that sound?

Discrimination of a Response

When a client engages in self-monitoring, an observation, or discrimination, of a response is required first. For example, a client who is monitoring fingernail biting must be able to discriminate instances of nail biting from instances of other behavior. Discrimination of a response indicates awareness, reflecting the client's ability to identify the presence or absence of the behavior and whether it is overt, like nail biting, or covert, like a positive self-thought.

Discrimination of a response involves helping the client identify *what* to monitor. This decision will often require helper assistance. The type of the monitored response may affect the results of self-monitoring. For example, self-monitoring may produce greater weight loss for people who recorded their daily weight and daily caloric intake than for those who recorded only daily weight. What works for individuals may vary; thus, the selection of target responses remains a pragmatic choice as to what seems to work well. Mahoney (1977, pp. 244–245) points out that there may be times when self-monitoring of certain responses could detract from intervention effectiveness, as in asking a suicidal client to monitor depressive thoughts.

The effects of self-monitoring also vary with the valence of the target response. There are always "two sides" of a behavior that could be monitored—the positive and the negative. There also seem to be times when one side is more important for self-monitoring than the other. Unfortunately, there are very few data to guide a decision about the exact type and valence of responses to monitor. Because the reactivity of self-monitoring is affected by the value assigned to a behavior (Watson & Tharp, 2007), one guideline might be to have the client monitor the behavior that she or he cares *most* about changing. Generally, it is a good idea to encourage the client

to limit monitoring to one response, at least initially. If the client engages in self-monitoring of one behavior with no difficulties, then more items can be added.

Recording of a Response

After the client has learned to make discriminations about a response, the helper can provide instructions and examples about the method for recording the observed response. Most clients have probably never recorded their behavior *systematically*. Systematic recording is crucial to the success of self-monitoring, so it is imperative that the client understand the importance and methods of recording. The client needs instructions about when and how to record and about devices for recording. The timing, method, and recording devices can all influence the effectiveness of self-monitoring.

Timing of Self-Monitoring: When to Record

One of the least understood processes of self-monitoring involves timing, or the point when the client actually records the target behavior. Instances have been reported of both prebehavior and postbehavior monitoring. In prebehavior monitoring, the client records the intention or urge to engage in the behavior *before* doing so. In postbehavior monitoring, the client records each completed instance of the target behavior—*after* the behavior occurs. Kazdin (1974, p. 239) points out that the precise effects of self-monitoring may depend on the point at which monitoring occurs in the chain of responses relative to the response being recorded. Effects of the timing of self-monitoring may depend partly on whether other responses are competing for the person's attention at the time the response is recorded. Another factor influencing the timing of self-monitoring is the amount of time between the response and the actual recording. There is general agreement that delayed recording of the behavior weakens the efficacy of the monitoring process.

We suggest four guidelines that may help the helper and client decide when to record. First, if the client is using monitoring as a way to *decrease* an undesired behavior, prebehavior monitoring may be more effective, for this seems to interrupt the response chain early in the process. An example for self-monitoring an undesired response would be to record whenever you have the urge to smoke or to eat. Prebehavior monitoring may result in more change than postbehavior monitoring. Second, if the client is using self-monitoring to *increase* a desired response, then postbehavior monitoring may be more helpful. Postbehavior monitoring can make a person more aware of a low-frequency, desirable behavior. Third, recording instances of a desired behavior as it occurs or immediately after it occurs may be most helpful. The guideline is to "Record *immediately* after you have the urge to smoke—or *immediately* after you have covertly praised yourself; do not wait even for 15 or 20 minutes, as the impact of recording may be lost." Fourth, the client should be encouraged to record the response when not distracted by the situation or by other competing responses. The client should be instructed to record the behavior in vivo as it occurs, if possible, rather than at the end of the day, when he or she is dependent on recall. In vivo recording may not always be feasible, however, and in some cases the client's self-recording may have to be performed later.

Method of Self-Monitoring: How to Record

The helper needs to instruct the client in a *method* for recording the target responses. McFall (1977) points out that the method of recording can vary in a number of ways:

> It can range from a very informal and unstructured operation, as when subjects are asked to make mental notes of any event that seems related to mood changes, to something fairly formal and structured, as when subjects are asked to fill out a mood-rating sheet according to a time-sampling schedule. It can be fairly simple, as when subjects are asked to keep track of how many cigarettes they smoke in a given time period; or it can be complex and time-consuming, as when they are asked to record not only how many cigarettes they smoke, but also the time, place, circumstances, and affective response associated with lighting each cigarette. It can be a relatively objective matter, as when counting the calories consumed each day; or it can be a very subjective matter, as when recording the number of instances each day when they successfully resist the temptation to eat sweets. (p. 197)

Ciminero and associates (1977, p. 198) suggest that the recording method should be "easy to implement, must produce a representative sample of the target behavior, and must be sensitive to changes in the occurrence of the target behavior." Keep the method informal and unstructured for clients who are not "monitors" or who do not value "tracking" in such a systematic way.

Frequency, duration, and intensity can be recorded with either a continuous recording or a time-sampling method. Selection of one of these methods will depend mainly on the type of target response and the frequency of its occurrence. To record the *number* of target responses, the client can use a frequency count. Frequency counts are most useful for monitoring responses that are discrete, do not occur all the time, and are of short duration (Ciminero et al., 1977, p. 190). For instance, clients might record the number of times they have an urge to smoke or the number of times they praise or compliment themselves covertly.

Other kinds of target responses are recorded more easily and accurately by duration. Anytime a client wants to record the amount or length of a response, a duration count can be used. Ciminero and associates (1977, p. 198) recommend the use of a duration measure whenever the target response is not discrete and it varies in length. For example, a client might use a duration count to note the amount of time

spent reading textbooks or practicing a competitive sport. Or a client might want to keep track of the length of time spent in a "happy mood."

Sometimes a client may want to record two different responses and use both the frequency and the duration methods. For example, a client might use a frequency count to record each urge to smoke and a duration count to monitor the time spent smoking a cigarette. Watson and Tharp (2007) suggest that the helper can recommend frequency counts whenever it is easy to record clearly separate occurrences of the behavior and duration counts whenever the behavior continues for long periods.

Clients also can self-record the intensity of responses whenever data are desired about the relative severity of a response. For example, a client might record the intensity of happy, anxious, or depressed feelings or moods.

Format of Self-Monitoring Instruments

There are many formats of self-monitoring instruments that a client can use to record the frequency, duration, and/or intensity of the target response as well as information about contributing variables. The particular format of the instrument can affect reactivity and can increase client compliance with self-monitoring. The format of the instrument should be tailored to the client situation and goal and to the client. Figure 17.2 shows three formats for monitoring instruments. Each format can use a variety of self-recording devices. Watson and Tharp (2007) provide a range of additional examples.

Example 1 shows a format useful for relatively frequent recordings—for example, with couples for self-monitoring of the content and quality of their interactions. In this format, each person records the content of the interaction with the partner (for example, having dinner together, talking about finances, discussing work, going to movies, dealing with a parenting issue) and rates the quality of that interaction. This kind of format aims to capture all substantial interactions and characterize them. Other approaches may focus on certain types of interactions, such as discussing a sensitive topic or dealing with conflict, or may track aspects of interactions, such as the use of active listening skills.

Example 2 shows a format useful when more detail is needed and the client is likely to benefit from having her or his attention directed to components (e.g., What was I saying to myself just then?), to connections (e.g., the types of events that seem to systematically trigger certain reactions), and to the level of one's reaction and views about how it was handled. This example is designed for anxiety responses, but it could readily be modified for a range of other affective states, thinking patterns, or behaviors.

Example 3 illustrates a brief diary format. This integrates attention to the triggering event but also includes recording coping efforts and self-administered praise or reinforcement as well as affective states before and after the coping efforts.

Example 1: Content and Quality of Partnered Interactions
(Record the type of interaction under "Content." For each interaction, circle one category that best represents the quality of that interaction.)

Time	Content of Interaction	Quality of Interaction					
		Very Pleasant	**Pleasant**	**Neutral**	**Unpleasant**	**Very Unpleasant**	
___	___	++	+	0	-	- -	
___	___	++	+	0	-	- -	
___	___	++	+	0	-	- -	
___	___	++	+	0	-	- -	

Example 2: Self-Monitoring Log for Recording Anxiety Responses (This could be adapted for other feeling/thought/behavior targets.)

Date and Time	Situation Features	Internal Dialogue (Self-Statements)	Degree of Feeling	Behavioral Factors	Satisfaction in Handling Situation	Alternatives to Consider
	Describe each problematic situation; note what seemed to trigger anxiety	Note your thoughts or things you said to yourself when this occurred	Rate the intensity of the anxiety: (1) a little intense, (2) somewhat intense, (3) very intense, (4) extremely intense	Note how you responded—what you did	Rate how effectively you believe you handled the situation: (1) a little, (2) somewhat, (3) very, (4) extremely	What different thoughts or behaviors seem useful to try? What would help you prepare to try this next time?

Example 3: Brief Diary Format

Instructions: For each situation in which you experience a headache, record the following. After several episodes, reflect on what you see to be trends and what seems to be associated with reduced tension.

Headache Diary:

Stressful situation: _____

Negative thoughts: _____

Tension level rated   1   2   3   4   5   6   7   8   9   10

Coping strategies: _____

Praising self for coping: _____

Resulting tension level   1   2   3   4   5   6   7   8   9   10

Figure 17.2 Examples of Formats for Self-Monitoring Instruments
Source: Adapted from *Self-Directed Behavior* (9th ed.), by *D. L. Watson & R. G. Tharp*, p. 87. Copyright © 2007 Thomson.

The illustration uses headaches as a physical manifestation of stress, but, again, the general format could be applied to any number of targets.

Devices for Self-Monitoring

Clients often report that one of the most intriguing aspects of self-monitoring is the device or mechanism used for recording. For recording to occur systematically and accurately, the client must have access to some recording device. A variety of devices have been used to help clients keep accurate records. Note cards, daily log sheets, and diaries can be used to make written notations. A popular self-recording device is a wrist counter, such as a golf counter. The golf counter can be used for self-recording in different settings. If several behaviors are being counted simultaneously, the client can wear several wrist counters or use knitting tallies. A wrist counter with rows of beads permits the recording of several behaviors. Toothpicks, small plastic tokens, or cell phone text messaging can also be used as recording devices. Watson and Tharp (2007) report the use of coins: a client can carry coins in one pocket and transfer one coin to another pocket each time a behavior occurs. Children can record frequencies by pasting stars on a chart or by using a countoon, which has pictures and numbers for three recording columns: "What do I do," "My count," and "What happens." Clocks, watches, and kitchen timers can be used for duration counts. The nature of the device depends, of course, on what kind of observations are most useful (e.g., notes about thoughts, feelings, circumstances, and reactions require different devices than those needed for frequency or duration).

Not surprisingly, information technology is opening up new mediums. Many if not most paper-and-pencil formats can be used via a computer and a common word processing program, and some of the multimedia capabilities of computers allow for more engaging devices. For some people, this is a quicker and more accessible approach. As an example, the form can be sent electronically as can responses (aiding with communication between client and helper between sessions, a particularly important issue for people living in more remote or rural locations or with transportation constraints) and is always available in a file or at a website. A computer-based format may be easier to keep up with than a piece of paper that's gotten lost in the pile on the dining room table. As with computer-assisted assessment tools, there is some evidence that computers can have a positive impact. For example, Calam, Cox, Glasgow, Jimmieson, and Larsen (2000) discuss benefits for children and for people with disabilities. McGuire and colleagues (2000) describe advantages of using touchscreen technology that does not require keyboard use. Newman and colleagues (Newman, Consoli, & Taylor, 1997; Newman, Kenardy, Herman, & Taylor, 1997) review the advantages and dis-

advantages of a number of computer tools in this regard, including the use of palmtop computers that are sufficiently small to be carried at all times (and, thus, more likely to be available in target situations relevant to intervention). Amato Zech, Hoff, and Doepke, (2006) describe the use of an electronic, vibrating beeper as a tactile reminder to self-monitor attention in a special-education classroom.

The helper and client select a recording device. Here is an opportunity to be inventive! There are several practical criteria to consider in helping a client. The device should be portable and accessible so that it is present whenever the behavior occurs (Watson & Tharp, 2007). It should be easy, convenient, and economical. The obtrusiveness of the device should also be considered. The recording device can function as a cue (discriminative stimulus) for the client to self-monitor, so it should be noticeable enough to remind the client. However, a device that is too obtrusive may draw attention from others who could reward or punish the client for self-monitoring. Finally, the device should be capable of giving cumulative frequency data so that the client can chart daily totals of the behavior. Many of the devices used for practice assessment may be useful for ongoing self-monitoring.

After the client has been instructed in the timing and method of recording, and after a recording device has been selected, the client should practice using the recording system. Breakdowns in self-monitoring often occur because a client does not understand the recording process clearly. Rehearsal of the recording procedures may ensure that the client will record accurately. Generally, a client should engage in self-recording for three to four weeks. Usually, the effects of self-monitoring are not apparent in only one or two weeks' time.

Charting of a Response

The data recorded by the client should be translated onto a more permanent storage record such as a chart or graph that will enable the client to inspect the self-monitored data visually.

This type of visual guide may provide the occasion for client self-reinforcement (Kanfer & Gaelick-Buys, 1991), which, in turn, can influence the reactivity of self-monitoring. The data can be charted by days, using a simple line graph. For example, a client counting the number of urges to smoke a cigarette could chart these by days, as in Figure 17.3. A client recording the amount of time spent studying each day could use the same sort of line graph to chart duration of study time. The vertical axis would be divided into time intervals such as 15 minutes, 30 minutes, 45 minutes, or 1 hour.

The client should receive either oral or written instructions on a way to chart and graph the daily totals of the recorded response. The helper can assist the client in interpreting the chart in the sessions on data review and analysis. If a client

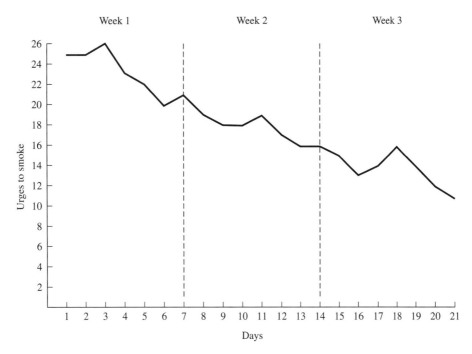

Figure 17.3 Self-monitoring Chart

is using self-monitoring to increase a behavior, the line on the graph should go up gradually if the self-monitoring is having the desired effect. If self-monitoring is influencing an undesired response to decrease, the line on the graph should go down gradually.

Displaying of Data

After the graph has been made, the client has the option of displaying the completed chart. If the chart is displayed in a "public" area, this display may prompt environmental reinforcement, a necessary part of an effective self-management program. The effects of self-monitoring are usually augmented when the data chart is displayed as a public record. However, some clients will not want to make their data public for reasons of confidentiality or shame avoidance.

Analysis of Data

If the client's recording data are not reviewed and analyzed, the client may soon feel as if he or she was told to make a graph just for practice in drawing straight lines! A very important facet of self-monitoring is the information that it can provide to the client. There is some evidence that people who receive feedback about their self-recording change more than those who do not. The recording and charting of data should be used *explicitly* to provide the client with knowledge of results about behavior or performance. Specifically, the client should bring the data to weekly sessions for review and

analysis. In these sessions, the helper can encourage the client to compare the data with the desired goals and standards. The client can use the recorded data for self-evaluation and determine whether the data indicate that the behavior is within or outside the desired limits. The helper can also aid in data analysis by helping the client interpret the data correctly. Guidance on ways to meaningfully display and analyze client self-monitoring data has been growing in sophistication over the years. In general, many of the methods and guidelines used for identifying, defining, and evaluating outcome goals can be adapted for client self-monitoring.

MODEL EXAMPLE OF SELF-MONITORING: THE CASE OF ISABELLA

Our case example, Isabella, indicated the goal of increasing her positive thoughts (and simultaneously decreasing her negative thoughts) about her ability to do well with math. This goal lends itself to the application of self-management strategies for several reasons. First, the goal represents a covert behavior (positive thoughts), which is observable only by Isabella. Second, the flip side of the goal (the negative thoughts) represents a very well-learned habit. Probably most of these negative thoughts occur *outside* the sessions. To change this thought pattern, Isabella needs to use strategies she can apply frequently (as needed) in vivo, and she needs to use strategies that she can administer to herself.

Here is a description of the way in which Isabella could use self-monitoring to achieve this goal:

1. *Treatment rationale:* The helper provides an explanation of what Isabella will self-monitor and why, emphasizing that this is a strategy she can apply herself, can use with a "private" behavior, and can use as frequently as possible in the actual setting.
2. *Discrimination of a response:* The helper needs to help Isabella define the target response explicitly. One definition could be "Anytime I think about myself doing math or working with numbers successfully." The helper provides some possible examples of this response, such as "Gee, I did well on my math homework today" or "I was able to balance my checkbook today." The helper also encourages Isabella to identify some examples of the target response. Because Isabella wants to increase this behavior, the target response will be stated in the "positive."
3. *Recording of a response:* The helper instructs Isabella in timing, a method, and a device for recording. In this case, because Isabella is using self-monitoring to increase a desired behavior, she will use postbehavior monitoring. Isabella is instructed to record *immediately* after a target thought occurs. She is interested in recording the *number* of such thoughts, so she will use a frequency count. A tally on a note card or a wrist counter can be selected as the device for recording. After these instructions, Isabella will practice recording before actually doing it. The helper instructs her to engage in self-monitoring for about four consecutive weeks.
4. *Charting of a response:* After each week of self-monitoring, Isabella can add her daily frequency totals and chart them by days on a simple line graph, as shown in Figure 17.4.

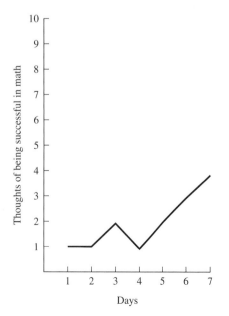

Figure 17.4 Simple Line Graph for Self-monitoring

Isabella is using self-monitoring to increase a behavior; as a result, if the monitoring has the desired effect, the line on her graph will gradually rise. It is just starting to do so here; additional data for the next few weeks will show a greater increase if the self-monitoring is influencing the target behavior in the desired direction.

5. *Displaying of data:* After Isabella makes a data chart, she may wish to post it in a place such as her room, although this is a very personal decision.
6. *Analysis of data:* During the period of self-monitoring, Isabella brings in her data for weekly review sessions with the helper. The helper provides reinforcement and helps Isabella interpret the data accurately. Isabella can use the data for self-evaluation by comparing the "story" of the data with her stated desired behavior and level of change.

STIMULUS CONTROL

Kanfer and Gaelick-Buys (1991, p. 335) define *stimulus control* as the predetermined arrangement of environmental conditions that makes it impossible or unfavorable for an undesired behavior to occur. Stimulus-control methods emphasize rearranging or modifying environmental conditions that serve as cues or antecedents of a particular response. Within the ABC model of behavior, a behavior is often guided by certain things that precede it (antecedents) and is maintained by positive or negative events that follow it (consequences). Remember also that both antecedents and consequences can be external (overt) or internal (covert). For example, an antecedent could be a situation, an emotion, a cognition, or an overt or covert verbal instruction.

Clinical Uses of Stimulus Control

Stimulus-control procedures have been used for a wide range of concerns; see Box 17.3 for a sample of recent research on stimulus control. This procedure has been used to treat issues related to autism, eating disorders, insomnia, obesity, fitness activities, anxiety, additive supports for attending and learning, and resistance and compliance responses. One study (Almeida et al., 2005) provided an interesting example of ways in which self-management strategies can also be helpful in supporting desired changes in the behavior of service providers. Within the context of a busy clinical setting, members of a physician group used a stimulus-control intervention to help prompt their attention to assessing and considering referrals for physical activity. The effort resulted in significantly higher referrals to as well as initiation of physical activity—suggesting such interventions may be practical methods for supporting service-provider attention to areas of particular need.

How Antecedents Acquire Stimulus Control

When antecedents are consistently associated with a behavior that is reinforced in the *presence* (not the absence) of

| BOX 17.3 | RESEARCH ON STIMULUS CONTROL |

Autism

Green, G. (2001). Behavior analytic instruction for learners with autism: Advances in stimulus control technology. *Focus on Autism and Other Developmental Disabilities, 16*(2), 72–85.

Matthews, B., Shute, R., & Rees, R. (2001). An analysis of stimulus overselectivity in adults with autism. *Journal of Intellectual and Developmental Disability, 26*(2), 161–176.

Brain Injury

Schlund, M. W. (2000). When instructions fail: The effects of stimulus control training on brain injury survivors' attending and reporting during hearing screenings. *Behavior Modification, 24*(5), 658–672.

Child Obesity

Epstein, L. H., Paluch, R. A., Kilanowski, C. K., & Raynor, H. A. (2004). The effect of reinforcement or stimulus control to reduce sedentary behavior in the treatment of pediatric obesity. *Health Psychology, 23*(4), 371–380.

Insomnia

Hajak, G., Bandelow, B., Zulley, J., & Pittrow, D. (2002). "As needed" pharmacotherapy combined with stimulus control treatment in chronic insomnia—Assessment of a novel intervention strategy in a primary care setting. *Annals of Clinical Psychiatry, 14*(1), 1–7.

Pallesen, S., Nordhus, I. H., Kvale, G., Nielsen, G. H., Havik, O. E., Johnsen, B. H., & Skjotskift, S. (2003). Behavioral treatment of insomnia in older adults: An open clinical trial comparing two interventions. *Behaviour Research and Therapy, 41*(1), 31–48.

Intellectual Disabilities

Dickson, C. A., Wang, S. S., Lombard, K. M., & Dube, W. V. (2006). Overselective stimulus control in residential school students with intellectual disabilities. *Research in Developmental Disabilities, 27*(6), 618–631.

Pathological Gambling

Echeburua, E., & Fernandez-Montalvo, J. (2002). Psychological treatment of slot machine pathological gambling: A case study. *Clinical Case Studies, 1*(3), 40–253.

Phobia

Johnstone, K. A., & Page, A. C. (2004). Attention to phobic stimuli during exposure: The effect of distraction on anxiety reduction, self-efficacy and perceived control. *Behaviour Research and Therapy, 42*(3), 249–275.

Physician Referral

Almeida, F. A., Smith-Ray, R. L., Van Den Berg, R., Schriener, P., Gonzales, M., Onda, P., & Estabrooks, P. A. (2005). Utilizing a simple stimulus control strategy to increase physician referrals for physical activity promotion. *Journal of Sport and Exercise Psychology, 27*(4), 505–514.

Reading Ability

Chafouleas, S. M., Martens, B. K., Dobson, R. L., Weinstein, K. S., & Gardner, K. B. (2004). Fluent reading as the improvement of stimulus control: Additive effects of performance-based interventions to repeated reading on students' reading and error rates. *Journal of Behavioral Education, 13*(2), 67–81.

these antecedent stimuli, they gain control over the behavior. You might think of this as an antecedent working as a stimulus for a certain response. When an antecedent gains stimulus control over the response, there is a high probability that the response will be emitted in the presence of these particular antecedent events. For example, most of us automatically slow down, put our foot on the brake, and stop the car when we see a red traffic light. The red light is a stimulus that has gained control over our stopping-the-car behavior. Generally, the fact that antecedents exert stimulus control is helpful, as it is in driving: we go when we see a green light and stop at the sight of a red light.

Inappropriate Stimulus Control in Troubling Behavior

Behaviors that trouble clients may occur because of *inappropriate* stimulus control. Inappropriate stimulus control may be related to obesity, for example. Eating responses of overweight people tend to be associated with many environmental cues. If a person eats something not only at the dining table but also when working in the kitchen, watching television, walking by the refrigerator, and stopping at a Dairy Queen, the sheer number of eating responses could soon result in obesity. Too many environmental cues are often related to other client difficulties, particularly "excesses" such as substance use. In these cases, the primary aim of a self-management stimulus-control method is to reduce the number of cues associated with the undesired response, such as eating or smoking.

Other troubling behaviors have been observed that seem to involve excessively narrow stimulus control. At the opposite pole from obesity are people who eat so little that their physical and psychological health suffers (anorexia nervosa). For these people, there are too few eating cues, among other elements involved with this issue. Lack of exercise can be a function of too narrow stimulus control. For some people, the paucity of environmental cues associated with exercise results in very little physical activity. In these cases, the primary

TABLE 17.2	Principles and Examples of Stimulus-Control Strategies
Principle of change	**Example**

To decrease a behavior: Reduce or narrow the frequency of cues associated with the behavior.	1. Prearrange or alter cues associated with the place of the behavior:
	   a. Prearrange cues that make it hard to execute the behavior. Place fattening foods in high, hard-to-reach places.
	   b. Prearrange cues so that they are controlled by others. Ask friends or family to serve you only one helping of food and to avoid serving fattening foods to you.
	2. Alter the time or sequence (chain) between the antecedent cues and the resulting behaviors:
	   a. Break up the sequence. Buy and prepare food only on a full stomach.
	   b. Change the sequence. Substitute and engage in nonfood activities when you start to move toward snacking (toward refrigerator, cupboard, or candy machine).
	   c. Build pauses into the sequence. Delay second helpings of food or snacks for a pre-determined amount of time.

To increase a behavior: Increase or prearrange the cues associated with the response.	1. Seek out these cues deliberately to perform the desired behavior. Initially arrange only one room with a desk to study. When you need to study, go to this place. 2. Concentrate on the behavior when in the situation. Concentrate only on studying in the room. If you get distracted, get up and leave. Don't mix study with other activities, such as listening to records or talking. 3. Gradually extend the behavior to other situations. When you have control over studying in one room, extend the behavior to another conducive room or place. 4. Promote the occurrence of helpful cues by other people or by self-generated reminders. Ask your roommate to remind you to leave the desk when you are talking or distracted. Remind yourself of good study procedures by posting a list over your study desk or by using verbal or covert self-instructions.

aim of a stimulus-control strategy is to establish or increase the number of cues that will elicit the desired behavior.

To summarize, stimulus-control self-management involves reducing the number of antecedent stimuli associated with an undesirable behavior and simultaneously increasing the antecedent cues associated with a desirable response (Watson & Tharp, 2007). Table 17.2 shows the principal methods of stimulus control and some examples.

Using Stimulus Control to Decrease Behavior

To decrease the rate of a behavior, the antecedent cues associated with the behavior should be reduced in frequency or altered in time and place of occurrence. When cues are separated from the habitual behavior by alteration or elimination, the old, undesired habit can be terminated (Watson & Tharp, 2007). Many behavioral "excesses," such as eating, smoking, drinking, or self-criticism, are tied to a great number of antecedent situations. Reducing these cues can restrict the occurrence of the undesired behavior. Existing cues can be prearranged to make the target behavior so hard to execute that the person is unlikely to do it. An example would be altering the place of smoking by moving one's smoking chair to an inconvenient place like the basement. The smoker would have to go downstairs each time she or he wanted a cigarette. A person can

prearrange cues by placing their control in the hands of someone else. Giving your pack of cigarettes to a friend is an example of this method. The friend should agree to help you reduce smoking and should agree not to reinforce or punish any instances of your smoking behavior (the undesired response).

A behavior can also be reduced through stimulus control by interrupting the learned pattern or sequence that begins with one or more antecedent cues and results in the undesired response. This sequence may be called a *chain*. A troubling behavior is often the result of a long chain of events. For example, a variety of behaviors make up the sequence of smoking. Before puffing on a cigarette, a person has to go to a store, buy cigarettes, remove one cigarette from the pack, and light up.

A chain might be interrupted in a number of ways—for example by breaking up or unlinking the chain of events, changing the chain, or building pauses into the chain (Watson & Tharp, 2007). All these methods involve prearranging or altering the nature of the sequence and the way in which the behavior in question is tied to stimuli events and to patterned ways of responding. A chain of events can be broken up by discovering and interrupting an event early in the sequence or by scrambling the typical order of events. For example, the smoker could break up the chain by not going to stores that sell cigarettes. Or if the smoker typically smokes at certain times, the usual order of events leading to smoking could be mixed up. The smoker could also change the typical chain of events. People who start to light up a cigarette whenever they are bored, tense, or lacking something to do with their hands could perform a different activity at this point, such as calling a friend when bored, relaxing when tense, or knitting or playing cards to provide hand activity. Finally, smokers could interrupt the chain by deliberately building pauses into it.

As you may recall, when antecedents exert control over a behavior, the behavior occurs almost automatically. One way to deal with this automatic quality is to pause before responding to a cue. For instance, whenever the smoker has an urge to light up in response to a stress cue, a deliberate pause of 10 minutes can be built in before the person actually does light up. Gradually, this time interval can be increased. Deliberately building in pauses to make a record (in a journal, computer notebook, or other monitoring tool) can be useful toward building in reflection—for example, about how one is feeling, thoughts in the moment, environmental conditions of the moment—which can help in breaking behavior chains. Sometimes you can even strengthen the pause procedure by covertly instructing yourself on what you want to do or by thinking about the benefits of not smoking. The pause itself can then become a new antecedent.

Using Stimulus Control to Increase Behavior

Stimulus-control methods can also be used to increase a desired response. As noted in Table 17.2, to increase the rate of a response, a person increases or prearranges the antecedent cues associated with the desired behavior. The person deliberately seeks out these cues to perform the behavior and concentrates only on this behavior when in the situation. Competing or distracting responses must be avoided. Gradually, as stimulus control over the behavior in one situation is achieved, the person can extend the behavior by performing it in another, similar situation. This process of stimulus generalization means that a behavior learned in one situation can be performed in different but similar situations (Watson & Tharp, 2007). The person can promote the occurrence of new antecedent cues by using reminders from others, self-reminders, or overt or covert self-instructions. The rate of a desired response is increased by increasing the times and places in which the person performs the response.

Suppose that you are working with a client who wants to increase his or her amount of daily exercise. First, more cues would be established to which the person would respond with isometric or physical activity. For example, the person might perform isometric activities whenever sitting in a chair or waiting for a traffic light. Or the person might perform physical exercises each morning and evening on a special exercise mat. The client would seek out these prearranged cues and concentrate on performing the activity while

in the situation. Other behaviors should not be performed while in these situations, for a competing response could interfere with the exercise activity (Watson & Tharp, 2007). Gradually, the client could extend the exercise activities to new but similar situations—for example, doing isometrics while sitting on the floor or waiting for a meeting to start. The person could also promote exercise behavior in these situations by reminders—posting an exercise chart on the wall or carrying it around in a pocket or wallet.

Stimulus-control instructions have also been used to increase sleep. Clients were instructed as follows: (1) Go to bed or lie down to sleep only when sleepy. (2) Do not read, watch TV, or eat in bed. Use the bed only for sleeping and/or sexual activities. (3) If unable to fall asleep after 10 to 20 minutes, get out of bed and engage in some activity. Return to bed only when sleepy, and continue this procedure throughout the night as necessary. (4) Set the alarm clock and get up at the same time every morning regardless of the amount of sleep obtained during the night. (5) Do not take naps during the day.

According to Kanfer and Gaelick-Buys (1991), one advantage of stimulus control is that only minimal self-initiated steps are required to trigger environmental changes that effect desired or undesired responses. However, stimulus-control methods are often insufficient to modify behavior without the support of other strategies. Stimulus-control methods are usually not sufficient for long-term self-change unless accompanied by other self-management methods that exert control over the *consequences* of the target behavior. One self-management method that involves self-presented consequences is discussed in the following section and illustrated in Learning Activity 17.2.

MODEL EXAMPLE OF STIMULUS CONTROL: THE CASE OF ISABELLA

This model example illustrates how stimulus control can be used to help Isabella achieve her goal of increasing positive thoughts about her math ability. Recall that the principle of change in using stimulus control to increase a behavior is to increase the cues associated with the behavior. Here's how the helper will implement this principle with Isabella:

1. The helper will establish at least one cue that Isabella can use as an antecedent for positive thoughts. The helper might suggest something like putting a piece of tape over her watch.
2. Isabella and the helper will develop a list of several positive thoughts about math. Each thought can be written on a blank card that Isabella can carry with her.
3. The helper will instruct Isabella to read or think about a thought on one card *each* time she looks at her watch. The helper will instruct her to seek out the opportunity deliberately by looking at her watch frequently and then concentrating on one of the positive thoughts.

LEARNING ACTIVITY   **17.2**   **Stimulus Control**

The purpose of this activity is to help you reduce an unwanted behavior by using stimulus-control methods.

1. Specify a behavior that you find undesirable and wish to decrease. It can be an overt one, such as smoking, eating, biting your nails, or making sarcastic comments, or it can be a covert behavior, such as thinking about yourself in negative ways or thinking how great food or smoking tastes.
2. Select one or more stimulus-control methods to use for behavior reduction from the list and examples given in Table 17.2. Remember, you will be reducing the number of cues or antecedent events associated with this behavior by altering the times and places the undesired response occurs.

3. Implement these stimulus-control methods daily for two weeks.
4. During the two weeks, engage in self-monitoring of your target response. Record the type and use of your method and the amount of your target behavior, using frequency or duration methods of recording.
5. At the end of two weeks, review your recorded data. Did you use your selected method consistently? If you did not, what contributed to your infrequent use? If you used it consistently, did you notice any gradual reduction in the target behavior by the end of two weeks? What problems did you encounter in applying a stimulus-control method with yourself? What did you learn about stimulus control that might help you when using it with clients?

---

4. When Isabella gets to the point where she automatically thinks of a positive thought after looking at her watch, other cues can be established that she can use in the same way. For instance, she can put a smiley face on her math book. Each time she gets out her math book and sees the smiley face, she can use this cue to concentrate on another positive thought.
5. Isabella can promote more stimulus control over these thoughts by using reminders. For instance, she can put a list of positive thoughts on the mirror or on the closet door in her room. Each time she sees the list, it serves as a reminder. Or she can ask a friend or classmate to remind her to "think positively" whenever the subject of math or math class is being discussed.

SELF-REWARD: PROCESSES AND USES

Self-monitoring and stimulus-control procedures may be enough to maintain the desired goal behavior for many people. However, for some people with low self-esteem, depression, strong emotional reactions, environmental consequences, or low self-efficacy, self-monitoring may not always be effective in regulating behavior (Kanfer & Gaelick-Buys, 1991). In such cases, self-reward procedures are used to help clients regulate and strengthen their behavior with the aid of self-produced consequences. Many actions of an individual are controlled by self-produced consequences as much as by external consequences.

According to Bandura (1971), there are three necessary conditions of self-reinforcement, or self-reward:

1. The individual (rather than someone else) determines the criteria for adequacy of her or his performance and for resulting reinforcement.
2. The individual (rather than someone else) controls access to the reward.
3. The individual (rather than someone else) is his or her own reinforcing agent and administers the rewards.

Notice that self-reward involves both the self-determination and the self-administration of a reward. This distinction has, at times, been overlooked in self-reinforcement research and application. Nelson, Hayes, Spong, Jarrett, and McKnight (1983, p. 565) propose that "self-reinforcement is effective primarily because of its stimulus properties in cuing natural environmental consequences."

As a self-management procedure, self-reward is used to strengthen or increase a desired response. The operations involved in self-reward are assumed to parallel those that occur in external reinforcement. In other words, a self-presented reward, like an externally administered reward, is defined by the function it exerts on the target behavior. A reinforcer (self- or external) is something that when administered following a target response, tends to maintain or increase the probability of that response in the future. A major advantage of self-reward over external reward is that a person can use and apply this strategy independently.

Self-rewards can be classified into two categories: positive and negative. In positive self-reward, one presents oneself with a positive stimulus (to which one has free access) *after* engaging in a specified behavior. Examples of positive reward include praising yourself after you have completed a long and difficult task, buying yourself a new compact disk after you have engaged in a specified amount of piano practice, or imagining that you are resting in your favorite spot after you have completed your daily exercises. Negative self-reward involves the removal of a negative stimulus after execution of a target response. Taking down an uncomplimentary picture or chart from your wall after performing the target response is an example of negative self-reward.

Our discussion of self-reward as a therapeutic strategy is limited to the use of positive self-reward for several reasons. First, there has been very little research to validate the negative self-reward procedure. Second, by definition, negative self-reward involves an aversive activity. It is usually unpleasant for a person to keep suet in the refrigerator or to put an ugly picture on the wall. Many people will not use a strategy that is aversive. Third, we do not recommend that helpers suggest strategies that seem aversive, because the client may feel that terminating the helping relationship is preferable to engaging in an unpleasant change process.

Like other management strategies, self-reward has been used in many clinical applications. Degotardi et al. (2006), for example, explored the use of self-reward in the context of a cognitive–behavioral therapy intervention with juvenile fibromyalgia. Children reported significant decreases in pain, somatic symptoms, anxiety, fatigue, and sleep disturbances. Kocovski and Endler (2000) found a significant negative relationship between self-reinforcing behavior and anxiety and depression in a sample of college-age students. In some instances, self-reward is part of a cluster of interventions—for example, as one component used with developmental disabilities (Harchik, Sherman, & Sheldon, 1992), promoting physical activity and behavioral control with elementary-age children (Cromie & Baker, 1997; Marcoux et al., 1999), and enhancing the academic productivity of secondary students with learning problems (Seabaugh & Schumaker, 1994). Other research has explored moderating variables and alternative reward sources. For example, Enzle, Roggeveen, and Look (1991) found that ambiguous standards of performance coupled with self-administration of rewards reduced intrinsic motivation, whereas clear standards with self-administration of rewards maintained high levels of intrinsic motivation. Research also has examined factors that may interfere with one's capacity to productively use self-reward, such as depression and self-defeating attitudes (Karoly & Lecci, 1997; Schill & Kramer, 1991). Finally, variables have been examined relative to their likely support of self-reward, such as the importance of explicit goals (preferably self-chosen) as part of change strategies involving self-reward (Fuhrmann & Kuhl, 1998; Kuhl & Baumann, 2000).

Some of the clinical effects typically attributed to the self-reinforcement procedure may also be due to certain external factors, including a client's previous reinforcement history, client goal setting, the role of client self-monitoring, surveillance by another person, external contingencies in the client's environment, and the instructional set given to the client about the self-reward procedure. The exact role that these external variables may play in self-reward is still relatively unknown. However, a helper should acknowledge and perhaps try to capitalize on some of these factors to heighten the clinical effects of a self-reward strategy.

COMPONENTS OF SELF-REWARD

Self-reward involves planning by the client of appropriate rewards and of the conditions in which they will be used. Four components of self-reward are (1) selection of appropriate self-rewards, (2) delivery of self-rewards, (3) timing of self-rewards, and (4) planning for self-change maintenance. These components are described in this section and summarized in the following list. Although we discuss them separately, keep in mind that all of them are integral parts of an effective self-reward procedure.

1. Selection of appropriate self-rewards
   a. Individualize the reward.
   b. Use accessible rewards.
   c. Use several rewards.
   d. Use different types of rewards (verbal/symbolic, material, imaginal, current, potential).
   e. Use potent rewards.
   f. Use rewards that are not punishing to others.
   g. Match rewards to the target response.
   h. Use rewards that are relevant to the client's culture, gender, age, class, and so on.
2. Delivery of self-rewards
   a. Self-monitor for data of the target response.
   b. Specify what and how much is to be done for a reward.
   c. Specify frequent reinforcement in small amounts for different levels of target response.
3. Timing of self-rewards
   a. Reward should come after, not before, behavior.
   b. Rewards should be immediate.
   c. Rewards should follow performance, not promises.
4. Planning for self-change maintenance
   a. Enlist help of others in sharing or dispensing rewards (if desired).
   b. Review data with helper.

Selection of Appropriate Self-Rewards

In helping a client to use self-reward effectively, the therapist must devote some time and planning to selecting rewards that are appropriate for the client and for the desired target behavior. Selecting rewards can be time-consuming. However, effective use of self-reward is somewhat dependent on the availability of events that are truly reinforcing to the client. The helper can assist the client in selecting appropriate self-rewards; however, the client should have the major role in determining the specific contingencies.

Rewards can take many different forms. A self-reward may be verbal/symbolic, material, or imaginal. One verbal/symbolic reward is self-praise, such as thinking or telling oneself, "I did a good job." This sort of reward may be especially useful with a very self-critical client (Kanfer & Gaelick-Buys, 1991). A material reward is something tangible—an event (such as a movie), a purchase (such as a banana split), or a token or point that can be exchanged for a reinforcing event or purchase. An imaginal reinforcer is the covert visualization of a scene or situation that is pleasurable and produces good feelings. Imaginal reinforcers might include picturing yourself as a thin person after losing weight or imagining that you are water-skiing on a lake you have all to yourself.

Self-rewards can also be classified as current or potential. A current reward is something pleasurable that happens routinely or occurs daily, such as eating, talking to a friend, or reading a newspaper. A potential reward is something that would be new and different if it happened, something that a person does infrequently or anticipates doing in the future. Examples of potential rewards include going on a vacation or buying a "luxury" item (something you love but rarely buy for yourself, not necessarily something expensive). Engaging in a "luxury" activity—something you rarely do—can be a potential reinforcer. For a person who is very busy and constantly working, "doing nothing" might be a luxury activity that is a potential reinforcer.

In selecting appropriate self-rewards, a client should consider the availability of these various kinds of rewards. We believe that a well-balanced self-reward program involves a *variety* of types of self-rewards. A helper might encourage a client to select both verbal/symbolic and material rewards. Relying only on material rewards may ignore the important role of positive self-evaluations in a self-change program. Further, material rewards have been criticized for overuse and misuse. Imaginal reinforcers may not be so powerful as verbal/symbolic and material ones. However, they are completely portable and can be used to supplement verbal/symbolic and material rewards when it is impossible for an individual to use these other types (Watson & Tharp, 2007).

In selecting self-rewards, a client should also consider the use of both current and potential rewards. One of the easiest ways for a client to use current rewards is to observe what daily thoughts or activities are reinforcing and then to rearrange these so that they are used in contingent rather than noncontingent ways (Watson & Tharp, 2007). However, whenever a client uses a current reward, some deprivation or self-denial is involved. For example, agreeing to read the newspaper only after cleaning the kitchen involves initially denying oneself some pleasant, everyday event in order to use it to reward a desired behavior. As Thoresen and Mahoney (1974) point out, this initial self-denial introduces an aversive element into the self-reward strategy. Some people do not respond well to any aversiveness associated with self-change or self-directed behavior. One of the authors, in fact, consistently "abuses" the self-reward principle by doing the reward before the response (reading the paper before cleaning the kitchen)—precisely as a reaction against the aversiveness of this "programmed" self-denial. One way to prevent self-reward from becoming too much like programmed abstinence is to have the client select novel or potential reinforcers to use in addition to current ones.

A helper can help a client identify and select various kinds of self-rewards in several ways. One way is simply with verbal report. Helper and client can discuss current self-reward practices and desired luxury items and activities (Kanfer & Gaelick-Buys, 1991). The client can also identify rewards by using in vivo observation. The client should be instructed to observe and list current consequences that seem to maintain some behaviors. Finally, the client can identify and select rewards by completing preference and reinforcement surveys.

A preference survey is designed to help the client identify preferred and valued activities. Here is one that Watson and Tharp (2007, pp. 210–211) recommend:

1. What will be the rewards of achieving your goal?
2. What kind of praise do you like to receive, from yourself or from others?
3. What kinds of things do you like to have?
4. What are your major interests?
5. What are your hobbies?
6. What people do you like to be with?
7. What do you like to do with those people?
8. What do you do for fun?
9. What do you do to relax?
10. What do you do to get away from it all?
11. What makes you feel good?
12. What would be a nice present to receive?
13. What kinds of things are important to you?
14. What would you buy if you had an extra $20? $50? $100?
15. On what do you spend your money each week?
16. What behaviors do you perform every day? (Don't overlook the obvious or the commonplace.)
17. Are there any behaviors that you usually perform instead of the target behavior?
18. What would you hate to lose?
19. Of the things you do every day, which would you hate to give up?
20. What are your favorite daydreams and fantasies?
21. What are the most relaxing scenes you can imagine?

The client can complete this sort of preference survey in writing or in a discussion. Clients who find it difficult to identify rewarding events might also benefit from completing a more formalized reinforcement survey, such as the Reinforcement Survey Schedule or the Children's Reinforcement Survey Schedule, written by Cautela (1977). The client can be given homework assignments to identify possible verbal/symbolic and imaginal reinforcers. For instance, the client might be asked to make a daily list for a week of positive self-thoughts or of the positive consequences of desired change. Or the client could make a list of all the things about which she or he likes to daydream or of some imagined scenes that would be pleasurable (Watson & Tharp, 2007).

Sometimes a client may seem thwarted in initial attempts to use self-reward because of difficulties in identifying rewards. Watson and Tharp (2007) note that people whose behavior consumes the reinforcer (such as smoking or eating), whose behavior is reinforced intermittently, or whose avoidance behavior is maintained by negative reinforcement may not be able to identify reinforcing consequences readily. Individuals who are locked into demanding schedules may not be able to find daily examples of reinforcers. Depressed people sometimes have trouble identifying reinforcing events. In these cases, the helper and client have several options that can be used to overcome difficulties in selecting effective self-rewards.

A client who does not have the time or money for material rewards might use imaginal rewards. Imagining pleasant scenes following a target response has been described by Cautela (1970) as *covert positive reinforcement.* Using this procedure, the client usually imagines performing a desired behavior, then imagines a reinforcing scene. A helper might consider use of imaginal reinforcers only when other kinds of reinforcers are not available.

A second option is to use a client's everyday activity as a self-reward. Some clinical cases have used a mundane activity such as answering the phone or opening the daily mail as the self-reward. If a frequently occurring behavior is used as a self-reward, it should be a desirable or at least a neutral activity. As Watson and Tharp (2007) note, clients should not use as a self-reward any high-frequency behavior that they would stop immediately if they could. Using a negative high-frequency activity as a reward may seem more like punishment than reinforcement.

No thought, event, or imagined scene is reinforcing for everyone. Often, what one person finds rewarding is very different from the rewards selected by someone else. When self-rewards are used, it is important to help clients choose rewards that will work well for *them*—not for the helper, a friend, or a spouse. Kanfer and Gaelick-Buys (1991) note the importance of considering the client's history and also of taking into account the client's gender, culture, age, class, and personal preferences.

The practitioner should use the following guidelines to help the client determine some self-rewards that might be used effectively.

1. *Individualize* the reward to the client.
2. The reward should be *accessible* and *convenient* to use after the behavior is performed.
3. *Several* rewards should be used interchangeably to prevent satiation (a reward can lose its reinforcing value because of repeated presentations).
4. Different *types* of rewards should be selected (verbal/symbolic, material, imaginal, current, potential).
5. The rewards should be *potent* but not so valuable that an individual will not use them contingently.
6. The rewards should not be *punishing* to others. Watson and Tharp (2007) suggest that if a reward involves someone else, the other person's agreement should be obtained.
7. The rewards should be *compatible* with the desired response (Kanfer & Gaelick-Buys, 1991). For instance, a person losing weight might use new clothing as a reward or thoughts of a new body image after weight loss. Using eating as a reward is not a good match for a weight-loss target response.
8. The rewards should be *relevant* to the client's values and circumstances as well as appropriate to her or his culture, gender, age, socioeconomic status, and any other salient features (e.g., personality and personal philosophy).

Delivery of Self-Rewards

Specifying the conditions and method of delivering the self-rewards is the second part of working out a self-reward strategy with a client. A client cannot deliver or administer a self-reward without some data. Self-reward delivery is dependent on systematic data gathering, so self-monitoring is an essential first step.

Second, the client needs to identify the precise conditions under which a reward will be delivered. The client, in other words, needs to state the rules of the game: *what* and *how much* has to be done before administering a self-reward. Self-reward is usually more effective when clients reward themselves for small steps of progress. Performance of a subgoal should be rewarded. Waiting to reward oneself for demonstration of the overall goal usually introduces too much of a delay between responses and rewards.

Finally, the client needs to indicate how much and what kind of reward will be given for performing various responses or different levels of the goals. The client needs to specify that doing so much of the response results in one type of reward and how much of it. Reinforcement is usually most effective when broken down into small units such as tokens or points that are self-administered frequently. After a certain amount of points or tokens is accumulated, these units can be exchanged for a "larger" reinforcer. Learning Activity 17.3 walks you through a self-reward exercise with questions to consider.

LEARNING ACTIVITY 17.3   Self-Reward

 This activity is designed to have you engage in self-reward.

1. Select a target behavior you want to increase. Write down your goal (the behavior to increase, the desired level of increase, and conditions in which behavior will be demonstrated).
2. Select several types of self-rewards to use, and write them down. The types to use are verbal/symbolic, material (both current and potential), and imaginal. See whether your selected self-rewards meet the following criteria:
   a. Individually tailored to you?
   b. Accessible and convenient to use?
   c. Several self-rewards?
   d. Different types of self-rewards?
   e. Potent rewards?
   f. Rewards not punishing to others?
   g. Rewards compatible with your desired goal?
   h. Rewards relevant to your gender and culture?
3. Set up a plan for delivery of your self-reward: What type of reinforcement and how much will be administered? How much and what demonstration of the target behavior are required?
4. When do you plan to administer a self-reward?
5. How could you enlist the aid of another person?
6. Apply self-reward for a specified time period. Did your target response increase? To what extent?
7. What did you learn about self-reward that might help you in suggesting its use to diverse groups of clients?

Timing of Self-Rewards

The helper needs to instruct the client about the timing of self-reward: when a self-reward should be administered. There are three ground rules for the timing of a self-reward:

1. The client should administered a self-award *after* performing the specified response, not before.
2. The client should administer a self-award *immediately* after the response. Long delays may render the procedure ineffective.
3. A self-reward should follow *actual performance,* not promises to perform.

Planning for Self-Change Maintenance

Self-reward, like any self-change strategy, needs environmental support for long-term maintenance of change. The last part of using self-reward involves helping the client find ways to plan for self-change maintenance. First, the helper can give the client the option of enlisting the help of others in a self-reward program. Other people can share in or dispense some of the reinforcement if the client is comfortable with this idea (Watson & Tharp, 2007). Some evidence indicates that certain people may benefit more from self-reward if initially in the program they received their rewards from others (Mahoney & Thoresen, 1974). Second, the client should plan to review with the helper the data collected during self-reward. The review sessions give the helper a chance to reinforce the client and to help the client make any necessary revisions in the use of the strategy. Helper expectations and approval for client progress may add to the overall effects of the self-reward strategy if the helper serves as a reinforcer to the client.

SOME CAUTIONS IN USING REWARDS

The use of rewards as a motivational and informational device is a controversial issue (Eisenberger & Cameron, 1996). Using rewards, especially material ones, as incentives has been criticized on the grounds that tangible rewards are overused, are misused, and often discourage rather than encourage the client.

As a change strategy, self-reward should not be used indiscriminately. Before suggesting self-reward, the helper should carefully consider the individual client, the client's previous reinforcement history, and the client's desired change. Self-reward may not be appropriate for clients from cultural backgrounds in which the use of rewards is considered "undesirable or immodest" (Kanfer & Gaelick-Buys, 1991, p. 338). When a helper and client do decide to use self-reward, two cautionary guidelines should be followed. First, material rewards should not be used solely or indiscriminately. The helper should seek ways to increase a person's intrinsic satisfaction in performance before automatically resorting to extrinsic rewards as a motivational technique. Second, the helper's role in self-reward should be limited to providing instructions about the procedure and encouragement for progress. The client should be the one who selects the rewards and determines the criteria for delivery and timing of reinforcement. When the target behaviors and the contingencies are specified by someone other than the person using self-reward, the procedure can hardly be described accurately as a self-change operation.

MODEL EXAMPLE OF SELF-REWARD: THE CASE OF ISABELLA

This example illustrates how self-reward can be used to help Isabella increase her positive thoughts about her ability to do well in math:

1. *Selection of self-rewards:* First, the helper helps Isabella select some appropriate rewards to use for reaching her predetermined goal. The helper encourages Isabella to identify some self-praise she can use to reward herself symbolically or verbally ("I did it"; "I can gradually see my attitude about math changing"). Isabella can give herself points for daily positive thoughts. She can accumulate and exchange the points for material rewards, including current rewards (such as engaging in a favorite daily event) and potential rewards (such as a purchase of a desired item). These are suggestions; Isabella is responsible for the actual selection. The helper suggests that Isabella identify possible rewards through observation or completion of a preference survey. The helper makes sure that the rewards that Isabella selects are accessible and easy to use. Several rewards are selected to prevent satiation. The helper also makes sure that the rewards selected are potent, compatible with Isabella's goal, not punishing to anyone else, and relevant to Isabella.

2. *Delivery of self-rewards:* The helper helps Isabella determine guidelines for delivery of the rewards selected. Isabella might decide to give herself a point for each positive thought. This allows for reinforcement of small steps toward the overall goal. A predetermined number of daily points, such as 5, might result in delivery of a current reward, such as watching TV or going over to her friend's house. A predetermined number of weekly points could mean delivery of a potential self-reward, such as going to a movie or purchasing a new item. Isabella's demonstration of her goal beyond the specified level could result in the delivery of a bonus self-reward.

3. *Timing of self-rewards:* The helper instructs Isabella to administer the reward *after* the positive thoughts or after the specified number of points is accumulated. The helper emphasizes that the rewards follow performance, not promises. The helper should encourage Isabella to engage in the rewards as soon as possible after the daily and weekly target goals are met.

4. *Planning for self-change maintenance:* The helper helps Isabella find ways to plan for self-change maintenance.

One way is to schedule periodic "check-ins" with the helper. In addition, Isabella might select a friend who can help her share in the reward by watching TV or going shopping with her or by praising Isabella for her goal achievement.

SELF-EFFICACY

Self-efficacy is viewed as a cognitive process that mediates behavioral change. *Self-efficacy* refers to our judgments and subsequent beliefs of how capable we are of performing certain things under specific situations. These capabilities include but are not limited to overt behaviors—for example, how capable we believe we are in managing our thoughts or feelings in specific situations as well as how capably we can undertake particular actions. If our self-efficacy beliefs are broad, we think we can accomplish something in most situations (like walking, being able to communicate in our native language). If our self-efficacy beliefs are situation specific, we may believe we can be assertive or resist temptation in some situations but not in others.

There are some important distinctions to keep in mind. Self-efficacy beliefs foster expectations about our personal abilities to accomplish something. They are related to but are different from *outcome* expectations—that is, our beliefs that our actions will result in desired outcomes (Bandura, 1986). We may feel that we have the ability to accomplish a task—say, at school or work—and, thus we have high self-efficacy in this regard. But if we believe that this ability alone is not sufficient for achieving the desired outcome—like succeeding in a change or recognition of a job well done—then we have low outcome expectations (due perhaps to beliefs that the outcome is dependent on other people, events, or forces that are not predictable or are not likely to be efficacious). Including outcome expectations and factors likely to affect the outcome of an attempted task is clearly important to assessment. As important as self-efficacy is to fueling people's pursuits of what is important to them, so too is realistic consideration of whether this is enough: Consideration of barriers that can thwart success regardless of the skills and beliefs that an individual can bring to the effort.

Self-efficacy is not the same as self-esteem. For example, we can have high self-efficacy beliefs about certain tasks or abilities but low overall self-esteem. Low self-esteem can be due to a lot of reasons, such as not valuing things we do well as much as things we believe we are not able to successfully accomplish, or input from others that devalues what we believe we can do well. In general, however, self-esteem is enhanced when our self-efficacy is high in domains of life that we care most about and in which we desire to exert personal control—when we feel capable of doing what is required to achieve success, or when we realize that we have reached our goal. Underlying self-efficacy is either optimism

BOX 17.4   RESEARCH ON SELF-EFFICACY

Alcohol Use

Holloway, A. S., Watson, H. E., & Starr, G. (2006). How do we increase problem drinkers' self-efficacy? A nurse-led brief intervention putting theory into practice. *Journal of Substance Use, 11*(6), 375–386.

Assessment

Pajares, F. (2007). Empirical properties of a scale to assess writing self-efficacy in school contexts. *Measurement and Evaluation in Counseling and Development, 39*(4), 239–249.

Scherbaum, C. A., Cohen-Charash, Y., & Kern, M. J. (2006). Measuring general self-efficacy: A comparison of three measures using item response theory. *Educational and Psychological Measurement, 66*(6), 1047–1063.

Cardiac Illness

Joekes, K., Van Elderen, T., & Schreurs, K. (2007). Self-efficacy and overprotection are related to quality of life, psychological well-being and self-management in cardiac patients. *Journal of Health Psychology, 12*(1), 4–16.

Lau-Walker, M. (2006). Predicting self-efficacy using illness perception components: A patient survey. *British Journal of Health Psychology, 11*(4), 643–661.

Career Decisions

Bandura, A., Barbaranelli, C., Vittorio Caprara, G., & Pastorelli, C. (2001). Self-efficacy beliefs as shapers of children's aspirations and career trajectories. *Child Development, 72*(1), 187–206.

Nauta, M. M., & Kahn, Jeffrey H. (2007). Identity status, consistency and differentiation of interests, and career decision self-efficacy. *Journal of Career Assessment, 15*(1), 55–65.

Chronic Illness

Davis, A. H. T., Carrieri-Kohlman, V., Janson, S. L., Gold, W. M., & Stulbarg, M. S. (2006). Effects of treatment on two types of self-efficacy in people with chronic obstructive pulmonary disease. *Journal of Pain and Symptom Management, 32*(1), 60–70.

Creativity

Beghetto, R. A. (2006). Creative self-efficacy: Correlates in middle and secondary students. *Creativity Research Journal, 18*(4), 447–457.

Depression

Pomaki, G., ter Doest, L., & Maes, S. (2006). Goals and depressive symptoms: Cross-lagged effects of cognitive versus emotional goal appraisals. *Cognitive Therapy and Research, 30*(4), 499–513.

Diabetes

Griva, K., Myers, L. B., & Newman, S. (2000). Illness perceptions and self-efficacy beliefs in adolescents and young adults with insulin dependent diabetes mellitus. *Psychology and Health, 15*, 733–750.

Dietary Behavior

Annesi, J. J., & Unruh, J. L. (2006). Correlates of mood changes in obese women initiating a moderate exercise and nutrition information program. *Psychological Reports, 99*(1), 225–229.

Hagler, A. S., Norman, G. J., Zabinski, M. F., Sallis, J. F., Calfas, K. J., & Patrick, K. (2007). Psychosocial correlates of dietary intake among overweight and obese men. *American Journal of Health Behavior, 31*(1), 3–12.

Epilepsy

Elliott, J. O., Jacobson, M. P., & Seals, B. F. (2006). Self-efficacy, knowledge, health beliefs, quality of life, and stigma in relation to osteoprotective behaviors in epilepsy. *Epilepsy and Behavior, 9*(3), 478–491.

Exercise

Beauchamp, M. R., Welch, A. S., & Hulley, A. J. (2007). Transformational and transactional leadership and exercise-related self-efficacy: An exploratory study. *Journal of Health Psychology, 12*(1), 83–88.

HIV/AIDS

Wolf, M. S., Davis, T. C., Osborn, C. Y., Skripkauskas, S., Bennett, C. L., & Makoul, G. (2007). Literacy, self-efficacy, and HIV medication adherence. *Patient Education and Counseling, 65*(2), 253–260.

Maternal Self-Efficacy

Noel-Weiss, J., Bassett, V., & Cragg, B. (2006). Developing a prenatal breastfeeding workshop to support maternal breastfeeding self-efficacy. *Journal of Obstetric, Gynecologic, and Neonatal Nursing: Clinical Scholarship for the Care of Women, Childbearing Families, and Newborns, 35*(3), 349–357.

Mental Health Nurses

Dunn, K., Elsom, S., & Cross, W. (2007). Self-efficacy and locus of control affect management of aggression by mental health nurses. *Issues in Mental Health Nursing, 28*(2), 201–217.

Pain

Hadjistavropoulos, H., Dash, H., Hadjistavropoulos, T., & Sullivan, T. (2007). Recurrent pain among university students: Contributions of self-efficacy and perfectionism to

BOX 17.4	RESEARCH ON SELF-EFFICACY

the pain experience. *Personality and Individual Differences, 42*(6), 1081–1091.

Taylor, W. J., Dean, S. G., & Siegert, R. J. (2006). Differential association of general and health self-efficacy with disability, health-related quality of life and psychological distress from musculoskeletal pain in a cross-sectional general adult population survey. *Pain, 125*(3), 225–232.

Parenting

Streisand, R., Swift, E., Wickmark, T., Chen, R., & Holmes, C. S. (2005). Pediatric parenting stress among parents of children with type 1 diabetes: The role of self-efficacy, responsibility, and fear. *Journal of Pediatric Psychology, 30*(6), 513–521.

Whittaker, K. A., & Cowley, S. (2006). Evaluating health visitor parenting support: Validating outcome measures for parental self-efficacy. *Journal of Child Health Care, 10*(4), 296–308.

Smoking

Victoir, A., Eertmans, A., Van den Broucke, S., & Van den Bergh, O. (2006). Smoking status moderates the contribution of social–cognitive and environmental determinants to adolescents' smoking intentions. *Health Education Research, 21*(5), 674–687.

Teaching

Caprara, G. V., Barbaranelli, C., Steca, P., & Malone, P. S. (2006). Teachers' self-efficacy beliefs as determinants of job satisfaction and students' academic achievement: A study at the school level. *Journal of School Psychology, 44*(6), 473–490.

Work Performance

Judge, T. A., Jackson, C. L., Shaw, J. C., Scott, B. A., & Rich, B. L. (2007). Self-efficacy and work-related performance: The integral role of individual differences. *Journal of Applied Psychology, 92*(1), 107–127.

and hope that yield high efficacy, or helplessness and despair that contribute to low efficacy.

We can have high self-efficacy in some life domains but low self-efficacy in others, believing, for example, that we are capable of being successful at work but are lousy at parenting. In general, efficacy beliefs also build on experience, whether vicarious or actual, and draw from our cognitive schemas about who we are (e.g., my experiences with and input from others about my academic ability incline me to have high or low self-efficacy about mastering an academic challenge, depending on the nature of that experience and input). Thus, self-efficacy is not fixed but is largely learned and shaped by life experience, and it can be relearned and reshaped through focused intervention. Part of the reason why self-efficacy is so important is that it has been found to be a significant component in many issues germane to well-being, like tackling versus avoiding challenges and opportunities, degree of effort expended, persistence with the task, problem solving, coping, performance, confidence, determination, optimism, hopefulness, and enthusiasm.

Over the last several years, research about self-efficacy has flourished. Box 17.4 lists a selected sample of these studies. Here we see wide-ranging life domains and clinical concerns such as substance use, health conditions (asthma, cancer, cardiovascular, chronic illness, diabetes, epilepsy, HIV/AIDS), achievement and performance, vocational and work issues, dietary behavior, depression, maternity and parenting, teaching, and outcome effec-

tiveness across a range of life domains. The list of self-efficacy research is far greater than we can present here. Thus, we encourage you to undertake your own literature searches on problems, goals, or populations of particular relevance to you.

Several sources contribute to self-efficacy and to similar concepts in the constellation of one's personality or personal constructs. According to Bandura (1997), four factors influence efficacy expectations: (1) actual performance accomplishments, (2) mind–body states such as emotional arousal, (3) environmental experiences such as vicarious learning, and (4) verbal installation—as a prelude to treatment. Verbal installation is the persuasion process that the helper uses to enhance a client's confidence or self-efficacy expectations about performing specific tasks. A helping professional might foster positive self-efficacy by talking with the client about his or her past success in performing similar or related tasks. Or the helper can attempt to build confidence by discussing any of the client's successful experiences if the client has not engaged in tasks for which self-confidence or efficacy was needed.

Performance Accomplishments

There is huge variability in how people perform. People who have a high degree of self-efficacy recoup very quickly from failure. At one extreme are people who are motivated, energized, and risk taking despite the possibility of failure—partly because they do not anticipate failure or are able to interpret failure in ways that do not significantly diminish their future self-efficacy expectations. At the other extreme are people who fall into a state of learned helplessness (Seligman, 1990). These people are plagued with depressed feelings that contribute to pessimism, a low level of energy, negative internal dialogue, vulnerability, and hopelessness, resulting in low levels of attempted performance. When these people experience failure, they are more likely to interpret it as further evidence that they are not capable ("It's my fault," "I always screw things up," "This is just another example that I can never do anything right"), thus deepening future low efficacy expectations. You can see the cognitive underpinnings of self-efficacy and ways in which self-schemas, cognitive processing habits, and interactions with the world can contribute either positively or negatively to self-efficacy beliefs.

Most of us fall somewhere between these two extremes. Perceived self-efficacy is a major determinant of whether people engage in a task, the amount of effort they exert if they do engage, and how long they will persevere with the task if they encounter adverse circumstances. For example, people who frequently surf the Internet on their personal computers in search of a particular webpage feel competent in performing this task. They may feel quite confident in their abilities and persevere for some time in their search, even when they are unsuccessful in locating a specific webpage. However, the same people may feel less competent in programming software and may avoid programming tasks. Sometimes people feel competent at performing a task but do not perform it because there is no incentive for doing so. Also, some people may have unrealistic expectations about performing a task simply because they are unfamiliar with the task. For example, some people may feel *overconfident* about doing something, and others may experience *less* confidence. Generally, when we develop competence of any kind, we enhance and strengthen our self-efficacy, confidence, self-esteem, willingness to take risks, and ability to perform the task.

Mind–Body Link to Self-Efficacy

What we are feeling emotionally and the bodily sensations and phenomena accompanying differing emotions have important implications for what cognitions we are likely to access from memory and to generate in that context. If we are feeling highly anxious, for example, we will have a different set of cognitions salient to our information processing in the moment than if we are feeling calm or excited. Thus, if we are feeling anxious in a situation, it will be difficult to access memories of when we were successful in the past or to focus on aspects of the situation that address how we might be successful, which, in turn, will result in a set of schemas and perceptions active in that situation that are unlikely to support high self-efficacy expectations. Thus, one's ability to be aware of and manage one's emotional state (e.g., to shift

from a high level of emotional arousal to a lower level, from anxiety more toward determination) is a valuable tool for managing self-efficacy beliefs and expectations.

Similarly, we are becoming increasingly aware of the ways in which our thoughts, feelings, and behaviors interact, and how these affect and are affected by many bodily systems, such as biochemistry and neurological processes. For example, there are chain reactions and interactions within the mind–body information-processing system. Some of this work involves the information molecules, peptides, and receptors that serve as biochemicals of emotion (Pert, 1993) and ways in which messenger molecules or neuropeptides influence self-efficacy. As we've noted, a person who has a high degree of self-confidence and higher perceptions of personal control, compared with someone of lower self-confidence, is inclined to attempt more difficult tasks, use more energy, persevere longer at solutions when faced with adversity, and refuse to blame himself or herself when encountering failure. One hypothesis here is that the production of endogenous morphine (endorphins) in the brain is high and that the production of catecholamines (stress hormones) is low—relevant because production of endorphins is positively correlated with confidence. It has an analgesic effect, which spreads throughout the body, reducing sensitivity to pain and lessening automatic activities like cardiac reactivity and blood pressure (Bandura, Cioffi, Taylor, & Brouillard, 1988; Pert, 1993).

In contrast, people without feelings of control have low levels of perceived self-efficacy, avoid difficult tasks, have lower expectancies, and have a weak commitment to achieving a goal. They are more vulnerable to dwelling on their personal inadequacies, allowing negative self-talk, putting forth less effort, having little energy for a task, and taking longer to recover from failure on some task. They are very susceptible to stress and depression. When we feel we are not in control, our feelings of low self-efficacy can increase the production of catecholamines (Bandura, Taylor, Williams, Mefford, & Barchas, 1985). Our emotional state affects our perceived level of self-efficacy; this state, in turn, causes information molecules or neuropeptides to produce either stress hormones or brain opioids, depending on our emotional state. The degree of perceived self-efficacy and biochemical reactivity have many contributors, including origins in the family (on both a genetic and a social basis) and the environmental and cultural context in which the family resides. Needless to say, this is but one small part of the complex relationships of our psychoneuroendocrinology, thoughts, feelings, and actions (Zillmann & Zillmann, 1996).

Although self-efficacy fundamentally refers to beliefs, it, like other cognitions, is far from being "all in the head." Thinking and feeling (such as hope, forgiveness, optimism, and determinism) are intricately interwoven with our physiology and genetic makeup, which collectively interact with our social conditions to shape our behaviors and outcomes (Snyder & Lopez, 2007).

Environmental Influences

A person's self-efficacy is influenced by reciprocal interactions of cognitive, affective, behavioral, relational, and environmental and/or cultural variables. Family of origin, culture, and environmental setting mold a person's perceived self-efficacy, which contributes to cognitive development and functioning. Bandura (1993) proposed that perceived self-efficacy exerts a powerful influence on four major developmental processes: cognitive, motivational, affective, and perceptual selection. For example, Bandura (1993) illustrates ways in which perceived self-efficacy can operate at multiple levels, both individual and collective. Relative to academic development, for example, we can see the following: (1) Individual students' beliefs in their efficacy to regulate their own learning and to master academic activities determine their level of motivation and academic accomplishments. (2) Individual teachers' beliefs in their efficacy to motivate and promote learning affect the types of learning environments that teachers create and the degree of their students' academic progress. (3) Whole faculties' beliefs in their collective instructional efficacy contribute significantly to their schools' level of achievement. (4) Collective student body characteristics can influence school-level achievement in part by altering faculties' beliefs in their collective efficacy.

Note that these four levels of perceived self-efficacy are also affected by a person's worldview, often reflective of one's cultural perspective (Bandura, 1995). Oettingen (1995), for example, examines cultural effects on self-efficacy relative to differences based on individualism versus collectivism, power differential, masculinity, and avoidance of uncertainty. In collectivist cultures, members of core groups are likely to be a primary source of efficacy information for each individual. In contrast, in individualistic cultures, there is higher reliance on one's own evaluations and emotional reactions. Cultures or social conditions in which there are large power differentials are likely to find those with greater power as stronger sources of environmental influences as opposed to conditions with less power disparity. In the latter, individuals may be more inclined to see their actions and outcomes as more closely tied to their skill, and efficacy belief and less vulnerable to external impediments. Although a centrally important therapeutic factor, it is essential to realize that real-world factors have historically and continue to impinge differently on people's actual ability to be efficacious. For some, even if one can be successful in accomplishing a task, this may not be sufficient to achieving desired goals given more powerful external factors that can negatively affect actual outcomes.

Self-Efficacy as a Prelude for Treatment

A client's expectations, based on his or her perceived self-efficacy, shape the underlying cognitive process that accounts, at least in part, for changes in therapeutic outcomes and the achievement of treatment goals. Clients must acquire self-efficacy (confidence) to perform the specific skills associated with a particular therapeutic strategy so that they can achieve their therapeutic goals. Self-efficacy has been found associated with planning for change, harder effort, better problem solving, and greater persistence even in the face of failure (Cervone, 2000). Self-efficacy is a mental precondition that has a striking influence on the successful application of treatment. We believe that if the helper can maximize the client's perceived self-efficacy and expectancies about treatment, the client will be confident about using the specific steps associated with the treatment protocol, and that confidence will enhance the potential benefits and effectiveness of treatment. Although the success of achieving therapeutic goals may be largely a function of a client's self-efficacy, factors such as a client's age, gender, social class, and cultural and ethnic background may influence the degree of efficacy or confidence he or she brings to the therapeutic tasks.

APPLICATIONS OF SELF-EFFICACY WITH DIVERSE GROUPS

Increasingly, self-efficacy is being investigated with diverse groups of clients and research participants. As is evident in Box 17.5, the topics on which self-efficacy has been empirically studied with diverse groups are varied. In the area of prevention and risk reduction, for example, self-efficacy has been examined as a factor relative to drug and alcohol use, smoking, HIV and other sexually transmitted diseases, cardiovascular disease, and other health conditions. Depression, social support, mental distress, and other dimensions of emotional and psychological well-being include self-efficacy as a factor. Studies of academic performance and various aspects of job seeking, work, and career have long implicated self-efficacy, and continue with diverse client samples. Increasingly, older adults, people with disabilities, and those struggling with poverty are included in self-efficacy research, in addition to examination of cultural differences, both in the United States and elsewhere.

The concept of resilience is gaining attention, and self-efficacy appraisals are a part of that analysis. Zimmerman, Ramirez-Valles, and Maton (1999), for example, tested the protective effects of African American male adolescents' beliefs about their efficacy in social and political systems (termed *sociopolitical control*) on the link between helplessness and mental health (psychological symptoms and self-esteem). They found that high sociopolitical self-efficacy beliefs limited the negative consequences of helplessness

BOX 17.5   APPLICATION OF SELF-EFFICACY WITH DIVERSE GROUPS

Academic Achievement

Reed, M. C. (2003). The relation of neighborhood variables, parental monitoring, and school self-efficacy on academic achievement among urban African American girls. *Dissertation Abstracts International: Section B: The Sciences and Engineering, 64*(6-B), 2987.

Zimmerman, B. J., & Kitsantas, A. (2005). Homework practices and academic achievement: The mediating role of self-efficacy and perceived responsibility beliefs. *Contemporary Educational Psychology, 30*(4), 397–417.

Alcoholism

Oei, T. P. S., & Jardim, C. L. (2007). Alcohol expectancies, drinking refusal self-efficacy and drinking behaviour in Asian and Australian students. *Drug and Alcohol Dependence, 87*(2–3), 281–287.

Spiller, V., Zavan, V., & Guelfi, G. P. (2006). Assessing motivation for change in subjects with alcohol problems: The MAC2-A Questionnaire. *Alcohol and Alcoholism, 41*(6), 616–623.

Career Decisions

Gushue, G. V., & Whitson, M. L. (2006). The relationship among support, ethnic identity, career decision self-efficacy, and outcome expectations in African American high school students: Applying social cognitive career theory. *Journal of Career Development, 33*(2), 112–124.

Condom Use

Barkley, T. W., Jr., & Burns, J. L. (2000). Factor analysis of the Condom Use Self-Efficacy Scale among multicultural college students. *Health Education Research, 15*, 485–489.

Bogart, L. M., Cecil, H., & Pinkerton, S. D. (2000). Intentions to use the female condom among African American adults. *Journal of Applied Social Psychology, 30*, 1923–1953.

Cultural Differences

Durndell, A., Haag, Z., & Laithwaite, H. (2000). Computer self-efficacy and gender: A cross-cultural study of Scotland and Romania. *Personality and Individual Differences, 28*, 1037–1044.

Piontkowski, U., Florack, A., Hoelker, P., & Obdrzalek, P. (2000). Predicting acculturation attitudes of dominant and non-dominant groups. *International Journal of Intercultural Relations, 24*(1), 1–26.

Schaubroeck, J., Lam, S. S., & Xie, J. L. (2000). Collective efficacy versus self-efficacy in coping responses to stressors and control: A cross-cultural study. *Journal of Applied Psychology, 85*, 512–525.

Depression

Casten, R. J., Rovner, B. W., Pasternak, R. E., & Pelchat, R. (2000). A comparison of self-reported function assessed before and after depression treatment among depressed geriatric patients. *International Journal of Geriatric Psychiatry, 15*, 813–818.

Makaremi, A. (2000). Self-efficacy and depression among Iranian college students. *Psychological Reports, 86*, 386–388.

Diabetes

Kara, M., van der Bijl, J. J., Shortridge-Baggett, L. M., Asti, T., & Erguney, S. (2006). Cross-cultural adaptation of the diabetes management self-efficacy scale for patients with type 2 diabetes mellitus: Scale development. *International Journal of Nursing Studies, 43*(5), 611–621.

Educational Technology

Wu, Y., & Tsai, C. (2006). University students' Internet attitudes and Internet self-efficacy: A study at three universities in Taiwan. *CyberPsychology and Behavior, 9*(4), 441–450.

Gender

Blanchard, C. M., Reid, R. D., Morrin, L. I., Beaton, L. J., Pipe, A., Courneya, K. S., & Plotnikoff, R. C. (2007). Barrier self-efficacy and physical activity over a 12-month period in men and women who do and do not attend cardiac rehabilitation. *Rehabilitation Psychology, 52*(1), 65–73.

HIV

Barclay, T. R., Hinkin, C. H., Castellon, S. A., Mason, K. I., Reinhard, M. J., Marion, S. D., et al. (2007). Age-associated predictors of medication adherence in HIV-positive adults: Health beliefs, self-efficacy, and neurocognitive status. *Health Psychology, 26*(1), 40–49.

HIV/AIDS Education

Kyrychenko, P., Kohler, C., & Sathiakumar, N. (2006). Evaluation of a school-based HIV/AIDS educational intervention in Ukraine. *Journal of Adolescent Health, 39*(6), 900–907.

Meyer-Weitz, A. (2005). Understanding fatalism in HIV/AIDS protection: The individual in dialogue with contextual factors. *African Journal of AIDS Research, 4*(2), 75–82.

Older Adults

Lucidi, F., Grano, C., Barbaranelli, C., & Violani, C. (2006). Social–cognitive determinants of physical activity attendance in older adults. *Journal of Aging and Physical Activity, 14*(3), 344–359.

Stretton, C. M., Latham, N. K., Carter, K. N., Lee, A. C., & Anderson, C. S. (2006). Determinants of physical health in

BOX 17.5	APPLICATION OF SELF-EFFICACY WITH DIVERSE GROUPS

frail older people: The importance of self-efficacy. *Clinical Rehabilitation, 20*(4), 357–366.

Physical Impairment

Sanford, J. A., Griffiths, P. C., Richardson, P., Hargraves, K., Butterfield, T., & Hoenig, H. (2006). The effects of in-home rehabilitation on task self-efficacy in mobility-impaired adults: A randomized clinical trial. *Journal of the American Geriatrics Society, 54*(11), 1641–1648.

Racism

Lightsey, O. R., & Barnes, P. W, (2007). Discrimination, attributional tendencies, generalized self-efficacy, and assertiveness as predictors of psychological distress among African Americans. *Journal of Black Psychology, 33*(1), 27–50.

Rollins, V. B., & Valdez, J. N. (2006). Perceived racism and career self-efficacy in African American adolescents. *Journal of Black Psychology, 32*(2), 176–198.

Sexual Behaviors

Ozakinci, G., & Weinman, J. A. (2006). Determinants of condom use intentions and behavior among Turkish youth: A theoretically based investigation. *Journal of HIV/AIDS Prevention in Children and Youth, 7*(1), 73–95.

Traeen, B., & Kvalem, I. L. (2007). Investigating the relationship between past contraceptive behaviour, self-efficacy, and anticipated shame and guilt in sexual contexts among Norwegian adolescents. *Journal of Community and Applied Social Psychology, 17*(1), 19–34.

Smoking

Chang, F., Lee, C., Lai, H., Chiang, J., Lee, P., & Chen, W. (2006). Social influences and self-efficacy as predictors of youth smoking initiation and cessation: A 3-year longitudinal study of vocational high school students in Taiwan. *Addiction, 101*(11), 1645–1655.

Social Development

Yuen, M., Hui, E. K. P., Lau, P. S. Y., Gysbers, N. C., Leung, T. M. K., Chan, R. M. C., & Shea, P. M. K. (2006). Assessing the personal–social development of Hong Kong Chinese adolescents. *International Journal for the Advancement of Counselling, 28*(4), 317–330.

on mental health, suggesting the value of this form of self-efficacy in buffering or protecting youth from negative consequences of feeling helplessness.

One of the premises behind self-efficacy theory is that its effect is often one of mediating the relationship of background variables to outcomes. Smith, Walker, Fields, Brookins, and Seay (1999) found support for this among a sample of male and female early adolescents from different racial/ethic backgrounds. Specifically, they found that, ethnic identity and self-esteem, though related, were distinct from each other and that both contributed to prosocial attitudes about goal attainment operating through (and mediated by) self-efficacy of their ability to achieve. This type of finding supports the argument that efforts to foster healthy identity and positive self-esteem, though critically important, may not be sufficient in supporting achievement of outcome goals if self-efficacy beliefs do not correspond.

Attention has also been directed to environmental and contextual factors, for these influence or interact with self-efficacy. Boardman and Robert (2000) focused on people's socioeconomic status, questioning whether neighborhood socioeconomic characteristics were related to individuals' self-efficacy. Their findings showed that lower socioeconomic status (SES) corresponded with lower self-efficacy.

Of particular note was the finding that neighborhood indicators of lower SES (high proportions of unemployment and public assistance) were associated with lower self-efficacy above and beyond the relationship of individual-level SES to self-efficacy. Findings also indicate, however, that structural factors are not inherently predictive. Bandura, Barbaranelli, Caprara, and Pastorelli (2001), for example, found that effects of socioeconomic status were mediated by parent's expectations of and aspirations for their adolescent children and were powerful predictors of their children's perceived self-efficacy and career aspirations. Reed (2003) found that parental monitoring and self-efficacy significantly related to youths' academic achievement whereas neighborhood characteristics such as crime and impoverishment did not. Wolf et al. (2007) found that patient illiteracy could be positively mediated by positive self-efficacy relative to successful HIV-medication adherence. Findings such as these remind us that helping efforts with individuals and their families are best pursued with the critical awareness that people are always embedded in many types of environments—social, material, cultural, political—that are important considerations in assessment and intervention.

Considerable research on HIV/AIDS continues, including diverse samples relative to race, sexual orientation, and socioeconomic status. The bulk of research continues to suggest the importance of self-efficacy to predict HIV-related risk behaviors as well as predicting treatment adherence (Barclay et al., 2007). However, findings are also indicating complexities, including the need for theoretical models of behavior change to include dimensions of diversity and identity. To illustrate, Faryna and Morales (2000) found within an ethnically diverse sample of high school students that ethnicity consistently appeared a stronger predictor of HIV-related risk behaviors than did gender, self-efficacy, or knowledge, attitudes, and beliefs regarding sexual activity and substance use. Cochran and Mays (1993) discuss some potential issues in the application of models to predict risk behaviors, noting that many of these models emphasize the importance of individualistic, direct control of behavioral choices and de-emphasize external factors such as racism and poverty that are particularly relevant to many communities at highest risk of HIV infection. Other researchers have also discussed the need for AIDS education and prevention that mobilize the will of members of communities of color, acknowledging the role of environment in conditioning behavior (Gasch, Poulson, Fullilove, & Fullilove, 1991).

In a related vein, Van-Hasselt, Hersen, Null, and Ammerman (1993) describe a drug use prevention program for African American children that focuses on the development of family-based alternative activities to promote self-efficacy, achievement, and self-esteem. Investigating the relationship of self-efficacy to career decisions, ethnic identity, and parental and teacher support in African American high school students, Gushue and Whiston (2006) found that parental/ and teacher support were related to self-efficacy but ethnic identity was not. Health has been a significant focus of study, indicating the importance of self-efficacy about one's ability to successfully undertake specific health promotive activities to be significantly predictive of those activities and intentions to sustain them—such as exercise (Chou, Macfarlane, Chi, & Cheng, 2006; Lucidi, Grano, Barbaranelli, & Violani, 2006), falls (Stretton, Latham, Carter, Lee, & Anderson, 2006), and mobility (Sanford et al., 2006).

Self-efficacy is also an important variable in academic success. Bryan and Bryan (1991) found self-efficacy and positive mood induction to be related to performance of both junior high and high school students with a learning disability. At the postsecondary level, college self-efficacy—or the degree of confidence that one can successfully complete college—was an important determinant of student adjustment for Mexican American and Latino American college students (Solberg, O'Brien, Villareal, & Kennel, 1993). With an ethnically mixed group of high school equivalency students (predominantly Hispanic and Native American girls and boys) from seasonal farmwork backgrounds, students' interests, perceived incentives, and self-efficacy expectations (beliefs about their ability to learn to engage in an occupation successfully) predicted their willingness to consider future occupations (Church, Teresa, Rosebrook, & Szendre, 1992). Among an ethnically mixed high school population of over 800 rural girls and boys (Hispanic, Native American, and White youth), Lauver and Jones (1991) found differences in self-efficacy estimates for career choice among varied ethnic groups, with efficacy lowest for 7 of the 18 occupations studied among the Native American youth.

From a multicultural standpoint, the goal of strengthening self-efficacy, when used alone, raises questions meriting careful attention. Out of context, the self-efficacy model can be seen to assume direct control of behavioral choices, reflecting a worldview that is high in internal locus of control and internal locus of responsibility. People from cultures that stress collectivity and unity may not feel comfortable with this model, and neither may individuals who have experienced unjust societal conditions such as racism and poverty. Increasingly, self-efficacy is being researched and approached from a life-span perspective and in a more contextualized manner. This includes more attention to historical, cultural, developmental, linguistic, social network, privilege, and other environmental factors that are likely to exert influence on individuals' evolving sense of self-efficacy as well as how their self-efficacy schemas and appraisals are activated or interpreted in specific situations.

MODEL EXAMPLE OF SELF-EFFICACY: THE CASE OF ISABELLA

One of Isabella's goals—asking questions and making reasonable requests—has four subgoals: (1) to decrease anxiety ratings associated with anticipation of failure in math class and rejection by parents, (2) to increase positive self-talk and thoughts that "girls are capable" in math class and other competitive situations from zero or two times a week to four or five times a week over the next two weeks, (3) to increase attendance in math class from two or three times a week to four or five times a week during treatment, and (4) to increase verbal participation and initiation in math class and with her parents from none or once a week to three or four times a week over the next two weeks during treatment. Verbal participation is defined as asking and answering questions posed by teachers or parents, volunteering answers or offering opinions, or going to the chalkboard.

The helper can determine the extent of Isabella's self-efficacy (confidence) for each of the goal behaviors. Self-efficacy can be measured by asking Isabella to give a verbal rating of her confidence for each goal on a scale from 0 (no confidence) to 100 (a great deal of confidence). Alternatively, the helper can design a rating scale and ask Isabella to circle her rating of confidence for each goal (see Learning Activity 17.4). Three examples for goals are shown with the metric

| LEARNING ACTIVITY | **17.4** | **Self-Efficacy** |

In this activity, you are to determine and assess your self-efficacy.

1. Select some goals you would like to achieve. Your general goal may have to be divided into subgoals.
2. Write down your goals and/or subgoals. Make sure that your written goals are behaviorally defined, specify the context or circumstances in which the behavior is to occur, and identify the level or amount or change sought for any given step.
3. For the goal you would like to achieve, make a scale (0 to 100) to measure your self-efficacy (confidence) in performing your goal behaviors, thoughts, or feelings for each subgoal, and for each person with whom and each setting in which the goal is to be performed.
4. Assess your self-efficacy by circling the number on each scale that reflects your degree of uncertainty or certainty (confidence) in performing each goal.
5. You might wish to use the self-efficacy scales to self-monitor your confidence over a period of time as you gain more experience in performing the goal behaviors.

below; they are followed by other examples shown without the 0–100 metric to conserve space.

Sample Goals for Math Class or Parents

Confidence in *decreasing anxiety* (from 70 to 50) about possible failure in *math class*

0 10 20 30 40 50 60 70 80 90 100

Uncertain   Total certainty

Confidence to *increase positive self-talk and thoughts*— "girls are capable"—to four or five times a week in *math class*

0 10 20 30 40 50 60 70 80 90 100

Uncertain   Total certainty

Confidence in *answering questions asked by parents*

0 10 20 30 40 50 60 70 80 90 100

Uncertain   Total certainty

Other Examples

- Confidence in *decreasing anxiety* (from 70 to 50) about possible *rejection by parents*
- Confidence to *increase attendance* in *math class* to four or five times a week
- Confidence in *asking* questions in *math class*
- Confidence in *answering* questions in *math class*
- Confidence in *volunteering answers* in *math class*
- Confidence in *going to the chalkboard* in *math class*
- Confidence in *asking parents questions*
- Confidence in *offering opinions to parents*

As Isabella becomes more successful in achieving her goal behaviors, measures of her self-efficacy or confidence will increase.

CHAPTER SUMMARY

Self-management is a process in which clients direct their own behavior change by using any one change intervention strategy or a combination of strategies. Four strategies are reviewed here: self-monitoring, stimulus-control procedures, self-reward techniques, and self-efficacy enhancement. Promoting client commitment to using self-management strategies can be achieved by introducing these strategies later in the helping process, assessing the client's motivation for change, creating a social support system to aid the client in the use of the strategy, and maintaining contact with the client while self-management strategies are being used. All of these self-management strategies are affected by self-efficacy, a cognitive process that mediates behavioral change. These change strategies and tools can—and, we argue, *should*—be applied collaboratively with clients and in the service of building on strengths, supporting empowerment and self-determination, and being critically attentive to environmental factors that may be relevant targets of change as well as potential resources. Processes involved in self-regulation appear to vary across cultures and societies, and factors such as the client's cultural or collective identity and acculturation and assimilation status may affect the appropriateness of self-management or ways in which these tools and interventions are applied.

REFERENCES

Almeida, F. A., Smith-Ray, R. L., Van Den Berg, R., Schriener, P., Gonzales, M., Onda, P., & Estabrooks, P. A. (2005). Utilizing a simple stimulus control strategy to increase physician referrals for physical activity promotion. *Journal of Sport and Exercise Psychology, 27*(4), 505–514.

Amato Zech, N. A., Hoff, K. E., & Doepke, K. J. (2006). Increasing on-task behavior in the classroom: Extension of self-monitoring strategies. *Psychology in the Schools, 43*(2), 211–221.

Annesi, J. J., & Unruh, J. L. (2006). Correlates of mood changes in obese women initiating a moderate exercise and nutrition information program. *Psychological Reports, 99*(1), 225–229.

Arcury, T. A., Quandt, S. A., McDonald, J., & Bell, R. A. (2000). Faith and health self-management of rural older adults. *Journal of Cross-Cultural Gerontology, 15,* 55–74.

Austrian, J. S., Kerns, R. D., & Reid, M. C. (2005). Perceived barriers to trying self-management approaches for chronic pain in older persons. *Journal of the American Geriatrics Society, 53*(5), 856–861.

Bachman, J., Swenson, S., Reardon, M. E., & Miller, D. (2006). Patient self-management in the primary care treatment of depression. *Adminstration and Policy in Mental Health and Mental Health Services Research, 33*(1), 76–85.

Bandura, A. (1971). Vicarious and self-reinforcement processes. In R. Glaser (Ed.), *The nature of reinforcement.* New York: Academic.

Bandura, A. (1986). *Social foundations of thought and action: A social cognitive theory.* Englewood Cliffs, NJ: Prentice Hall.

Bandura, A. (1993). Perceived self-efficacy in cognitive development and functioning. *Educational Psychologist, 28,* 117–148.

Bandura, A. (Ed.). (1995). *Self-efficacy in changing societies.* New York: Cambridge University Press.

Bandura, A. (1997). *Self-efficacy: The exercise of self-control.* New York: Freeman.

Bandura, A., Barbaranelli, C., Vittorio Caprara, G., & Pastorelli, C. (2001). Self-efficacy beliefs as shapers of children's aspirations and career trajectories. *Child Development, 72*(1), 187–206.

Bandura, A., Cioffi, D., Taylor, C., & Brouillard, M. E. (1988). Perceived self-efficacy in coping with cognitive stressors and opioid activation. *Journal of Personality and Social Psychology, 55,* 477–488.

Bandura, A., Taylor, C., Williams, S. L., Mefford, I. N., & Barchas, J. D. (1985). Catecholamine secretion as function of perceived coping self-efficacy. *Journal of Consulting and Clinical Psychology, 53,* 406–415.

Barclay, T. R., Hinkin, C. H., Castellon, S. A., Mason, K. I., Reinhard, M. J., Marion, S. D., et al. (2007). Age-associated predictors of medication adherence in HIV-positive adults: Health beliefs, self-efficacy, and neurocognitive status. *Health Psychology, 26*(1), 40–49.

Barkley, T. W., Jr., & Burns, J. L. (2000). Factor analysis of the Condom Use Self-Efficacy Scale among multicultural college students. *Health Education Research, 15,* 485–489.

Bartholomew, L. K., Gold, R. S., Parcel, G. S., Czyewski, D. I., Sockrider, M. M., Fernandez, M., et al. (2000). Watch, discover, think, and act: Evaluation of computer-assisted instruction to improve asthma self-management in inner-city children. *Patient Education and Counseling, 39,* 269–280.

Bayliss, E. A., Ellis, J. L., Steiner, J. F., & Main, D. S. (2005). Initial validation of an instrument to identify barriers to self-management for persons with co-morbidities. *Chronic Illness, 1*(4), 315–320.

Beauchamp, M. R., Welch, A. S., & Hulley, A. J. (2007). Transformational and transactional leadership and exercise-related self-efficacy: An exploratory study. *Journal of Health Psychology, 12*(1), 83–88.

Beghetto, R. A. (2006). Creative self-efficacy: Correlates in middle and secondary students. *Creativity Research Journal, 18*(4), 447–457.

Bell, R. A., Stafford, J. M., Arcury, T. A., Snively, B. M., Smith, S. L., Grzywacz, J. G., & Quandt, S. A. (2006). Complementary and alternative medicine use and diabetes self-management among rural older adults. *Complementary Health Practice Review, 11*(2), 95–106.

Benson, H., & Stuart, E. M. (Eds.). (1992). *The wellness book: The comprehensive guide to maintaining health and treating stress-related illness.* New York: Birch Lane.

Blanchard, C. M., Reid, R. D., Morrin, L. I., Beaton, L. J., Pipe, A., Courneya, K. S., & Plotnikoff, R. C. (2007). Barrier self-efficacy and physical activity over a 12-month period in men and women who do and do not attend cardiac rehabilitation. *Rehabilitation Psychology, 52*(1), 65–73.

Boardman, J. D., & Robert, S. A. (2000). Neighborhood socioeconomic status and perceptions of self-efficacy. *Sociological Perspectives, 43,* 117–136.

Bogalo, L., & Moss-Morris, R. (2006). The effectiveness of homework tasks in an irritable bowel syndrome cognitive behavioural self-management programme. *New Zealand Journal of Psychology, 35*(3), 120–125.

Bogart, L. M., Cecil, H., & Pinkerton, S. D. (2000). Intentions to use the female condom among African American adults. *Journal of Applied Social Psychology, 30,* 1923–1953.

Bryan, T., & Bryan, J. (1991). Positive mood and math performance. *Journal of Learning Disability, 24,* 490–494.

Buck, R., & Morley, S. (2006). A daily process design study of attentional pain control strategies in the self-management of cancer pain. *European Journal of Pain, 10*(5), 385–398.

Calam, R., Cox, A., Glasgow, D., Jimmieson, P., & Larsen, S. G. (2000). Assessment and therapy work with children: Can computers help? *Clinical Child Psychology and Psychiatry, 5,* 329–343.

Caprara, G. V., Barbaranelli, C., Steca, P., & Malone, P. S. (2006). Teachers' self-efficacy beliefs as determinants of job satisfaction and students' academic achievement: A study at the school level. *Journal of School Psychology, 44*(6), 473–490.

Casas, J. M. (1988). Cognitive behavioral approaches: A minority perspective. *The Counseling Psychologist, 16,* 106–110.

Casten, R. J., Rovner, B. W., Pasternak, R. E., & Pelchat, R. (2000). A comparison of self-reported function assessed before and after depression treatment among depressed geriatric patients. *International Journal of Geriatric Psychiatry, 15,* 813–818.

Cautela, J. R. (1970). Covert reinforcement. *Behavior Therapy, 1,* 33–50.

Cautela, J. R. (1977). *Behavior analysis forms for clinical intervention* (Vol. 2). Champaign, IL: Research Press.

Cervone, D. (2000). Thinking about self-efficacy. *Behavior Modification, 24*(1), 30–56.

Chafouleas, S. M., Martens, B. K., Dobson, R. L., Weinstein, K. S., & Gardner, K. B. (2004). Fluent reading as the improvement of stimulus control: Additive effects of performance-based interventions to repeated reading on students' reading and error rates. *Journal of Behavioral Education, 13*(2), 67–81.

Chang, F., Lee, C., Lai, H., Chiang, J., Lee, P., & Chen, W. (2006). Social influences and self-efficacy as predictors of youth smoking initiation and cessation: A 3-year longitudinal study of vocational high school students in Taiwan. *Addiction, 101*(11), 1645–1655.

Chapman, R. A., Shedlack, K. J., & France, J. (2006). Stop–think–relax: An adapted self-control training strategy for individuals with mental retardation and coexisting psychiatric illness. *Cognitive and Behavioral Practice, 13*(3), 205–214.

Chen, H., Guarnaccia, P. J., & Chung, H. (2003). Self-attention as a mediator of cultural influences on depression. *International Journal of Social Psychiatry, 49*(3), 192–203.

Church, A., Teresa, J., Rosebrook, R., & Szendre, D. (1992). Self-efficacy for careers and occupational consideration in minority high school equivalency students. *Journal of Counseling Psychology, 39,* 498–508.

Ciminero, A. R., Nelson, R. O., & Lipinski, D. P. (1977). Self-monitoring procedures. In A. R. Ciminero, K. S. Calhoun, & H. E. Adams (Eds.), *Handbook of behavioral assessment* (pp. 195–232). New York: Wiley.

Cimprich, B., Janz, N. K., Northouse, L., Wren, P. A., Given, B., & Given, C. W. (2005). Taking charge: A self-management program for women following breast cancer treatment. *Psycho-Oncology, 14*(9), 704–717.

Clark, N. M., Gong, M., Kaciroti, N., Yu, J., Wu, G., Zeng, Z., & Wu, Z. (2005). A trial of asthma self-management in Beijing schools. *Chronic Illness, 1*(1), 31–38.

Cochran, S., & Mays, V. (1993). Applying social psychological models to predicting HIV-related sexual risk behaviors among African Americans. *Journal of Black Psychology, 19,* 142–154.

Cromie, S. D., & Baker, L. J. V. (1997). The behavioural self-control of study in third-level students: A review. In K. Dillenburger, M. F. O'Reilly, et al. (Eds.), *Advances in behaviour analysis* (pp. 113–133). Dublin, Ireland: University College Dublin Press.

Damush, T. M., Perkins, A., & Miller, K. (2006). The implementation of an oncologist referred, exercise self-management program for older breast cancer survivors. *Psycho-Oncology, 15*(10), 884–890.

Davis, A. H. T., Carrieri-Kohlman, V., Janson, S. L., Gold, W. M., & Stulbarg, M. S. (2006). Effects of treatment on two types of self-efficacy in people with chronic obstructive pulmonary disease. *Journal of Pain and Symptom Management, 32*(1), 60–70.

Degotardi, P. J., Klass, E. S., Rosenberg, B. S., Fox, D. G., Gallelli, K. A., & Gottlieb, B. S. (2006). Development and evaluation of a cognitive–behavioral intervention for juvenile fibromyalgia. *Journal of Pediatric Psychology, 31*(7), 714–723.

Dickson, C. A., Wang, S. S., Lombard, K. M., & Dube, W. V. (2006). Overselective stimulus control in residential school students with intellectual disabilities. *Research in Developmental Disabilities, 27*(6), 618–631.

Dunn, B. D., Dalgleish, T., Lawrence, A. D., & Ogilvie, A. D. (2007). The accuracy of self-monitoring and its relationship to self-focused attention in dysphoria and clinical depression. *Journal of Abnormal Psychology, 116*(1), 1–15.

Dunn, K., Elsom, S., & Cross, W. (2007). Self-efficacy and locus of control affect management of aggression by mental health nurses. *Issues in Mental Health Nursing, 28*(2), 201–217.

Durndell, A., Haag, Z., & Laithwaite, H. (2000). Computer self-efficacy and gender: A cross-cultural study of Scotland and Romania. *Personality and Individual Differences, 28,* 1037–1044.

Echeburua, E., & Fernandez-Montalvo, J. (2002). Psychological treatment of slot machine pathological gambling: A case study. *Clinical Case Studies, 1*(3), 40–253.

Eisenberger, R., & Cameron, J. (1996). Detrimental effects of reward: Reality or myth? *American Psychologist, 51,* 1153–1166.

Elliott, J. O., Jacobson, M. P., & Seals, B. F. (2006). Self-efficacy, knowledge, health beliefs, quality of life, and stigma in relation to osteoprotective behaviors in epilepsy. *Epilepsy and Behavior, 9*(3), 478–491.

Enzle, M. E., Roggeveen, J. P., & Look, S. C. (1991). Self-versus other-reward administration and intrinsic motivation. *Journal of Experimental Social Psychology, 27,* 468–479.

Epstein, L. H., Paluch, R. A., Kilanowski, C. K., & Raynor, H. A. (2004). The effect of reinforcement or stimulus control to reduce sedentary behavior in the treatment of pediatric obesity. *Health Psychology, 23*(4), 371–380.

Faryna, E. L., & Morales, E. (2000). Self-efficacy and HIV-related behaviors among multiethnic adolescents. *Cultural Diversity and Ethnic Minority Psychology, 6,* 42–56.

Flynn, F. J., Reagans, R. E., Amanatullah, E. T., & Ames, D. R. (2006). Helping one's way to the top: Self-monitors achieve status by helping others and knowing who helps whom. *Journal of Personality and Social Psychology, 91*(6), 1123–1137.

Fuhrmann, A., & Kuhl, J. (1998). Maintaining a healthy diet: Effects of personality and self-reward versus self-punishment on commitment to and enactment of self-chosen and assigned goals. *Psychology and Health, 13,* 651–686.

Gartett, M. T. (1999). Soaring on the wings of the eagle: Wellness of Native American high school students. *Professional School Counseling, 3,* 57–64.

Gasch, H., Poulson, D., Fullilove, R., & Fullilove, M. (1991). Shaping AIDS education and prevention programs for African Americans amidst community decline. *Journal of Negro Education, 60,* 85–96.

Germann, J. N., Kirschenbaum, D. S., & Rich, B. H. (2007). Child and parental self-monitoring as determinants of success in the treatment of morbid obesity in low-income minority children. *Journal of Pediatric Psychology, 32*(1), 111–121.

Goodacre, L. (2006). Women's perceptions on managing chronic arthritis. *British Journal of Occupational Therapy, 69*(1), 7–14.

Green, G. (2001). Behavior analytic instruction for learners with autism: Advances in stimulus control technology. *Focus on Autism and Other Developmental Disabilities, 16*(2), 72–85.

Griva, K., Myers, L. B., & Newman, S. (2000). Illness perceptions and self-efficacy beliefs in adolescents and young adults with insulin dependent diabetes mellitus. *Psychology and Health, 15,* 733–750.

Gureasko-Moore, S., DuPaul, G. J., & White, G. P. (2006). The effects of self-management in general education classrooms on the organizational skills of adolescents with ADHD. *Behavior Modification, 30*(2), 159–183.

Gushue, G. V., & Whitson, M. L. (2006). The relationship among support, ethnic identity, career decision self-efficacy, and outcome expectations in African American high school students: Applying social cognitive career theory. *Journal of Career Development, 33*(2), 112–124.

Hadjistavropoulos, H., Dash, H., Hadjistavropoulos, T., & Sullivan, T. (2007). Recurrent pain among university students: Contributions of self-efficacy and perfectionism to the pain experience. *Personality and Individual Differences, 42*(6), 1081–1091.

Hagler, A. S., Norman, G. J., Zabinski, M. F., Sallis, J. F., Calfas, K. J., & Patrick, K. (2007). Psychosocial correlates of dietary intake among overweight and obese men. *American Journal of Health Behavior, 31*(1), 3–12.

Haire-Joshu, D., Fisher, E., Munro, J., & Wedner, J. (1993). A comparison of patient attitudes toward asthma self-management among acute and preventive care settings. *Journal of Asthma, 30,* 359–371.

Hajak, G., Bandelow, B., Zulley, J., & Pittrow, D. (2002). "As needed" pharmacotherapy combined with stimulus control treatment in chronic insomnia—Assessment of a novel intervention strategy in a primary care setting. *Annals of Clinical Psychiatry, 14*(1), 1–7.

Harchik, A. E., Sherman, J. A., & Sheldon, J. B. (1992). The use of self-management procedures by people with developmental disabilities: A brief review. *Research in Developmental Disabilities, 13,* 211–227.

Harris, K. R., Friedlander, B. D., Saddler, B., Frizzelle, R., & Graham, S. (2005). Self-monitoring of attention versus self-monitoring of academic performance: Effects among students with ADHD in the general education classroom. *Journal of Special Education, 39*(3), 145–156.

Harvey, I. S. (2006). Self-management of a chronic illness: An exploratory study on the role of spirituality among older African American women. *Journal of Women and Aging, 18*(3), 75–88.

Hildebrandt, T., & Latner, J. (2006). Effect of self-monitoring on binge eating: Treatment response or "binge drift"? *European Eating Disorders Review, 14*(1), 17–22.

Hofmann, S. G. (2006). The emotional consequences of social pragmatism: The psychophysiological correlates of self-monitoring. *Biological Psychology, 73*(2), 169–174.

Holloway, A. S., Watson, H. E., & Starr, G. (2006). How do we increase problem drinkers' self-efficacy? A nurse-led brief intervention putting theory into practice. *Journal of Substance Use, 11*(6), 375–386.

Horner, S. D. (2006). Home visiting for intervention delivery to improve rural family asthma management. *Journal of Community Health Nursing, 23*(4), 213–223.

Huflejt-Lukasik, M., & Czarnota-Bojarska, J. (2006). Short communication: Self-focused attention and self-monitoring influence on health and coping with stress. *Stress and Health: Journal of the International Society for the Investigation of Stress, 22*(3), 153–159.

Ickes, W., Holloway, R., Stinson, L. L., & Hoodenpyle, T. G. (2006). Self-monitoring in social interaction: The centrality of self-affect. *Journal of Personality, 74*(3), 659–684.

Jacob, T., Penn, N., Kulik, J., & Spieth, L. (1992). Effects of cognitive style and maintenance strategies of breast self-examination (BSE) practice by African American women. *Journal of Behavioral Medicine, 15,* 589–609.

Joekes, K., Van Elderen, T., & Schreurs, K. (2007). Self-efficacy and overprotection are related to quality of life, psychological well-being and self-management in cardiac patients. *Journal of Health Psychology, 12*(1), 4–16.

Johns, L. C., Gregg, L., Allen, P., & McGuire, P. K. (2006). Impaired verbal self-monitoring in psychosis: Effects of state, trait and diagnosis. *Psychological Medicine, 36*(4), 465–474.

Johnstone, K. A., & Page, A. C. (2004). Attention to phobic stimuli during exposure: The effect of distraction on anxiety reduction, self-efficacy and perceived control. *Behaviour Research and Therapy, 42*(3), 249–275.

Judge, T. A., Jackson, C. L., Shaw, J. C., Scott, B. A., & Rich, B. L. (2007). Self-efficacy and work-related performance: The integral role of individual differences. *Journal of Applied Psychology, 92*(1), 107–127.

Kalichman, S. C., Rompa, D., & Coley, B. (1997). Lack of positive outcomes from a cognitive–behavioral HIV and AIDS prevention intervention for inner-city men: Lessons from a controlled pilot study. *AIDS Education and Prevention, 9,* 299–313.

Kanfer, F. H., & Gaelick-Buys, L. (1991). Self-management methods. In F. H. Kanfer & A. P. Goldstein (Eds.), *Helping people change* (4th ed., pp. 305–360). New York: Pergamon.

Kara, M., van der Bijl, J. J., Shortridge-Baggett, L. M., Asti, T., & Erguney, S. (2006). Cross-cultural adaptation of the diabetes management self-efficacy scale for patients with type 2 diabetes mellitus: Scale development. *International Journal of Nursing Studies, 43*(5), 611–621.

Karoly, P. (2005). Self-monitoring. In M. Hersen & J. Rosquist (Eds.), *Encyclopedia of behavior modification and cognitive behavior therapy* (vol. 1, pp. 521–525). Thousand Oaks, CA: Sage.

Karoly, P., & Lecci, L. (1997). Motivational correlates of self-reported persistent pain in young adults. *Clinical Journal of Pain, 13,* 104–109.

Kazdin, A. E. (1974). Self-monitoring and behavior change. In M. J. Mahoney & C. E. Thoresen (Eds.), *Self-control: Power to the person* (pp. 218–246). Pacific Grove, CA: Brooks/Cole.

Kelly, J., & St. Lawrence, J. (1990). The impact of community-based groups to help persons reduce HIV infection risk behaviors. *AIDS Care, 2,* 25–36.

Kemppainen, J. K., Eller, L. S., Bunch, E., Hamilton, M. J., Dole, P., Holzemer, W., et al. (2006). Strategies for self-management of HIV-related anxiety. *AIDS Care, 18*(6), 597–607.

Kocovski, N. L., & Endler, N. S. (2000). Self-regulation: Social anxiety and depression. *Journal of Applied Biobehavioral Research, 5*(1), 80–91.

Koerkel, J. (2006). Behavioural self-management with problem drinkers: One-year follow-up of a controlled drinking group treatment approach. *Addiction Research and Theory, 14*(1), 35–49.

Kosic, A., Mannetti, L., & Sam, D. L. (2006). Self-monitoring: A moderating role between acculturation strategies and adaptation of immigrants. *International Journal of Intercultural Relations, 30*(2), 141–157.

Kuhl, J., & Baumann, N. (2000). Self-regulation and rumination: Negative affect and impaired self-accessibility. In W. J. Perrig & A. Grob (Eds.), *Control of human behavior, mental processes, and consciousness: Essays in honor of the 60th birthday of August Frammer* (pp. 283–305). Mahwah, NJ: Lawrence Erlbaum.

Kuijpers, M. A. C. T., & Scheerens, J. (2006). Career competencies for the modern career. *Journal of Career Development, 32*(4), 303–319.

Kyrychenko, P., Kohler, C., & Sathiakumar, N. (2006). Evaluation of a school-based HIV/AIDS educational intervention in Ukraine. *Journal of Adolescent Health, 39*(6), 900–907.

Lau-Walker, M. (2006). Predicting self-efficacy using illness perception components: A patient survey. British *Journal of Health Psychology, 11*(4), 643–661.

Lauver, P., & Jones, R. (1991). Factors associated with perceived career options in American Indian, white and Hispanic rural high school students. *Journal of Counseling Psychology, 38,* 159–166.

Lee, Y., & McCormick, B. P. (2006). Examining the role of self-monitoring and social leisure in the life quality of individuals with spinal cord injury. *Journal of Leisure Research, 38*(1), 1–19.

Lightsey, O. R., & Barnes, P. W. (2007). Discrimination, attributional tendencies, generalized self-efficacy, and assertiveness as predictors of psychological distress among African Americans. *Journal of Black Psychology, 33*(1), 27–50.

Lucidi, F., Grano, C., Barbaranelli, C., & Violani, C. (2006). Social–cognitive determinants of physical activity attendance in older adults. *Journal of Aging and Physical Activity, 14*(3), 344–359.

Mahoney, K., & Mahoney, M. J. (1976). Cognitive factors in weight reduction. In J. D. Krumboltz & C. E. Thoresen (Eds.), *Counseling methods* (pp. 99–105). New York: Holt, Rinehart and Winston.

Mahoney, M. J. (1977). Some applied issues in self-monitoring. In J. Cone & R. Hawkins (Eds.), *Behavioral assessment: New directions in clinical psychology* (pp. 241–254). New York: Brunner/Mazel.

Mahoney, M. J., Moura, N. G., & Wade, T. C. (1973). Relative efficacy of self-reward, self-punishment, and self-monitoring techniques for weight loss. *Journal of Consulting and Clinical Psychology, 40,* 404–407.

Mahoney, M. J., & Thoresen, C. E. (Eds.). (1974). *Self-control: Power to the Person.* Pacific Grove, CA: Brooks/Cole.

Makaremi, A. (2000). Self-efficacy and depression among Iranian college students. *Psychological Reports, 86,* 386–388.

Marcoux, M. F., Sallis, J. F., McKenzie, T. L., Marshall, S., Armstrong, C. A., & Goggin, K. J. (1999). Process evaluation of a physical self-management program for children: SPARK. *Psychology and Health, 14,* 659–677.

Martin, D. (1993). Coping with AIDS-risk reduction efforts among gay men. *AIDS Education and Prevention, 5,* 104–120.

Matthews, B., Shute, R., & Rees, R. (2001). An analysis of stimulus overselectivity in adults with autism. *Journal of Intellectual and Developmental Disability, 26*(2), 161–176.

McCafferty, S. (1992). The use of private speech by adult second language learners: A cross-cultural study. *Modern Language Journal, 76,* 179–189.

McFall, R. M. (1977). Parameters of self-monitoring. In R. B. Stuart (Ed.), *Behavioral self-management: Strategies, techniques and outcomes* (pp. 196–214). New York: Brunner/Mazel.

McGuire, M., Bakst, K., Fairbanks, L., McGuire, M., Sachinvala, N., Von Scotti, H., & Brown, N. (2000). Cognitive, mood, and functional evaluations using touchscreen technology. *Journal of Nervous and Mental Disease, 188,* 813–817.

Meichenbaum, D. H. (1994). *A clinical handbook/practical therapist manual for assessing and treating adults with posttraumatic stress disorder (PTSD).* Waterloo, Ontario, Canada: Institute Press.

Meyer-Weitz, A. (2005). Understanding fatalism in HIV/AIDS protection: The individual in dialogue with contextual factors. *African Journal of AIDS Research, 4*(2), 75–82.

Mooney, P., Ryan, J. B., Uhing, B. M., Reid, R., & Epstein, M. H. (2005). A review of self-management interventions targeting academic outcomes for students with emotional and behavioral disorders. *Journal of Behavioral Education, 14*(3), 203–221.

Muir-Cochrane, E., Fereday, J., Jureidini, J., Drummond, A., & Darbyshire, P. (2006). Self-management of medication for mental health problems by homeless young people. *International Journal of Mental Health Nursing, 15*(3), 163–170.

Nagelkerk, J., Reick, K., & Meengs, L. (2006). Perceived barriers and effective strategies to diabetes self-management. *Journal of Advanced Nursing, 54*(2), 151–158.

Nauta, M. M., & Kahn, J. H. (2007). Identity status, consistency and differentiation of interests, and career decision self-efficacy. *Journal of Career Assessment, 15*(1), 55–65.

Nelson, R. O. (1977). Methodological issues in assessment via self-monitoring. In J. D. Cone & R. P. Hawkins (Eds.), *Behavioral assessment: New directions in clinical psychology* (pp. 217–254). New York: Brunner/Mazel.

Nelson, R. O., Hayes, S. C., Spong, R. T., Jarrett, R. B., & McKnight, D. L. (1983). Self-reinforcement: Appealing misnomer or effective mechanism. *Behaviour Research and Therapy, 21,* 557–566.

Newman M. G., Consoli, A., & Taylor, C. B. (1997). Computers in assessment and cognitive behavioral treatment of clinical disorders: Anxiety as a case in point. *Behavior Therapy, 28,* 211–235.

Newman, M. G., Kenardy, J., Herman, S., & Taylor, C. B. (1997). Comparison of palmtop-computer-assisted brief cognitive–behavioral treatment to cognitive behavioral treatment for panic disorder. *Journal of Consulting and Clinical Psychology, 65,* 178–183.

Noel-Weiss, J., Bassett, V., & Cragg, B. (2006). Developing a prenatal breastfeeding workshop to support maternal breastfeeding self-efficacy. *Journal of Obstetric, Gynecologic, and Neonatal Nursing: Clinical Scholarship for the Care of Women, Childbearing Families, and Newborns, 35*(3), 349–357.

Oei, T. P. S., & Jardim, C. L. (2007). Alcohol expectancies, drinking refusal self-efficacy and drinking behaviour in Asian and Australian students. *Drug and Alcohol Dependence, 87*(2–3), 281–287.

Oettingen, G. (1995). Cross-cultural perspectives on self-efficacy. In A. Bandura (Ed.), *Self-efficacy in changing societies* (pp. 149–176). New York: Cambridge University Press.

Ollendick, T. H., & King, N. J. (2000). Empirically supported treatments for children and adolescents. In P. C. Kendall (Ed.), *Child and adolescent therapy: Cognitive behavioral procedures* (2nd ed., pp. 386–425). New York: Guilford Press.

Oster, N. V., Welch, V., Schild, L., Gazmararian, J. A., Rask, K., & Spettell, C. (2006). Differences in self-management behaviors and use of preventive services among diabetes management enrollees by race and ethnicity. *Disease Management, 9*(3), 167–175.

Ozakinci, G., & Weinman, J. A. (2006). Determinants of condom use intentions and behavior among Turkish youth: A theoretically based investigation. *Journal of HIV/AIDS Prevention in Children and Youth, 7*(1), 73–95.

Pajares, F. (2007). Empirical properties of a scale to assess writing self-efficacy in school contexts. *Measurement and Evaluation in Counseling and Development, 39*(4), 239–249.

Pallesen, S., Nordhus, I. H., Kvale, G., Nielsen, G. H., Havik, O. E., Johnsen, B. H., & Skjotskift, S. (2003). Behavioral treatment of insomnia in older adults: An open clinical trial comparing two interventions. *Behaviour Research and Therapy, 41*(1), 31–48.

Pert, C. (1993). The chemical communicators. Interview by B. Moyers with C. Pert, in *Healing and the mind* (pp. 177–193). New York: Doubleday.

Peterson, L. D., Young, K. R., Salzberg, C. L., West, R. P., & Hill, M. (2006). Using self-management procedures to improve classroom social skills in multiple general education settings. *Education and Treatment of Children, 29*(1), 1–21.

Petscher, E. S., & Bailey, J. S. (2006). Effects of training, prompting, and self-monitoring on staff behavior in a classroom for students with disabilities. *Journal of Applied Behavior Analysis, 39*(2), 215–226.

Piontkowski, U., Florack, A., Hoelker, P., & Obdrzalek, P. (2000). Predicting acculturation attitudes of dominant and non-dominant groups. *International Journal of Intercultural Relations, 24*(1), 1–26.

Pomaki, G., ter Doest, L., & Maes, S. (2006). Goals and depressive symptoms: Cross-lagged effects of cognitive versus emotional goal appraisals. *Cognitive Therapy and Research, 30*(4), 499–513.

Quandt, S. A., McDonald, J., Arcury, T. A., Bell, R. A., & Vitolins, M. Z. (2000). Nutritional self-management of elderly widows in rural communities. *Gerontologist, 40,* 86–96.

Rao, R., & Kramer, L. (1993). Stress and coping among mothers of infants with a sickle cell condition. *Children's Health Care, 22,* 169–188.

Reed, M. C. (2003). The relation of neighborhood variables, parental monitoring, and school self-efficacy on academic achievement among urban African American girls. *Dissertation Abstracts International: Section B: The Sciences and Engineering, 64*(6-B), 2987.

Roberson, M. (1992). The meaning of compliance: Patient perspectives. *Qualitative Health Research, 2,* 7–26.

Rollins, V. B., & Valdez, J. N. (2006). Perceived racism and career self-efficacy in African American adolescents. *Journal of Black Psychology, 32*(2), 176–198.

Sanford, J. A., Griffiths, P. C., Richardson, P., Hargraves, K., Butterfield, T., & Hoenig, H. (2006). The effects of in-home rehabilitation on task self-efficacy in mobility-impaired adults: A randomized clinical trial. *Journal of the American Geriatrics Society, 54*(11), 1641–1648.

Schaubroeck, J., Lam, S. S., & Xie, J. L. (2000). Collective efficacy versus self-efficacy in coping responses to stressors and control: A cross-cultural study. *Journal of Applied Psychology, 85,* 512–525.

Scherbaum, C. A., Cohen-Charash, Y., & Kern, M. J. (2006). Measuring general self-efficacy: A comparison of three measures using item response theory. *Educational and Psychological Measurement, 66*(6), 1047–1063.

Schill, T., & Kramer, J. (1991). Self-defeating personality, self-reinforcement, and depression. *Psychological Reports, 69,* 137–138.

Schlund, M. W. (2000). When instructions fail: The effects of stimulus control training on brain injury survivors' attending and reporting during hearing screenings. *Behavior Modification, 24*(5), 658–672.

Scholz, U., Knoll, N., Sniehotta, F. F., & Schwarzer, R. (2006). Physical activity and depressive symptoms in cardiac rehabilitation: Long-term effects of a self-management intervention. *Social Science and Medicine, 62*(12), 3109–3120.

Seabaugh, G. O., & Schumaker, J. B. (1994). The effects of self-regulation training on the academic productivity of secondary students with learning problems. *Journal of Behavioral Education, 4,* 109–133.

Seligman, M. (1990). *Learned optimism.* New York: Pocket.

Smith, E. P., Walker, K., Fields, L., Brookins, C. C., & Seay, R. C. (1999). Ethnic identity and its relationship to self-esteem, perceived efficacy, and prosocial attitudes in early adolescence. *Journal of Adolescence, 22,* 867–880.

Snyder, C. R., & Lopez, S. J. (2007). *Positive psychology: The scientific and practical explorations of human strengths.* Thousand Oaks, CA: Sage.

Sobell, M. B., & Sobell, L. C. (2005). Guided self-change model of treatment for substance use disorders. *Journal of Cognitive Psychotherapy, 19*(3), 199–210.

Solberg, V., O'Brien, K., Villareal, P., & Kennel, R. (1993). Self-efficacy and Hispanic college students: Validation of the College Self-Efficacy Instrument. *Hispanic Journal of Behavioral Sciences, 15,* 80–95.

Spangenberg, E. R., & Sprott, D. E. (2006). Self-monitoring and susceptibility to the influence of self-prophecy. *Journal of Consumer Research, 32*(4), 550–556.

Spiller, V., Zavan, V., & Guelfi, G. P. (2006). Assessing motivation for change in subjects with alcohol problems: The MAC2-A Questionnaire. *Alcohol and Alcoholism, 41*(6), 616–623.

St. Lawrence, J. (1993). African American adolescents' knowledge, health-related attitudes, sexual behavior, and contraceptive decisions: Implications for the prevention of adolescent HIV infection. *Journal of Consulting and Clinical Psychology, 61,* 104–112.

St. Lawrence, J., Brasfield, T., Jefferson, K., Alleyne, E., O'Bannon, R., & Shirley, A. (1995). Cognitive–behavioral intervention to reduce African American adolescents' risk for HIV infection. *Journal of Consulting and Clinical Psychology, 63,* 221–237.

Streisand, R., Swift, E., Wickmark, T., Chen, R., & Holmes, C. S. (2005). Pediatric parenting stress among parents of children with type 1 diabetes: The role of self-efficacy, responsibility, and fear. *Journal of Pediatric Psychology, 30*(6), 513–521.

Stretton, C. M., Latham, N. K., Carter, K. N., Lee, A. C., & Anderson, C. S. (2006). Determinants of physical health in frail older people: The importance of self-efficacy. *Clinical Rehabilitation, 20*(4), 357–366.

Sue, D. W. , & Sue, D. (2003). *Counseling the culturally diverse:* (4th ed.). New York: Wiley.

Swerissen, H., Belfrage, J., Weeks, A., Jordan, L., Walker, C., Furler, J., et al. (2006). A randomised control trial of a self-management program for people with a chronic illness from Vietnamese, Chinese, Italian and Greek backgrounds. *Patient Education and Counseling. 64*(1–3), 360–368.

Taylor, W. J., Dean, S. G., & Siegert, R. J. (2006). Differential association of general and health self-efficacy with disability, health-related quality of life and psychological distress from musculoskeletal pain in a cross-sectional general adult population survey. *Pain, 125*(3), 225–232.

Thoresen, C. E., & Mahoney, M. J. (1974). *Behavioral self-control.* New York: Holt, Rinehart and Winston.

Traeen, B., & Kvalem, I. L. (2007). Investigating the relationship between past contraceptive behaviour, self-efficacy, and anticipated shame and guilt in sexual contexts among Norwegian adolescents. *Journal of Community and Applied Social Psychology,17*(1), 19–34.

Van Hasselt, V., Hersen, M., Null, J., & Ammerman, R. (1993). Drug abuse prevention for high risk African American children and their families: A review and model program. *Addictive Behaviors, 18,* 213–234.

Victoir, A., Eertmans, A., Van den Broucke, S., & Van den Bergh, O. (2006). Smoking status moderates the contribution of social–cognitive and environmental determinants to adolescents' smoking intentions. *Health Education Research, 21*(5), 674–687.

Wang, C., & Abbott, L. J. (1998). Development of a community-based diabetes and hypertension preventive program. *Public Health Nursing, 15,* 406–414.

Watson, D. L., & Tharp, R. G. (2007). *Self-directed behavior* (9th ed.). Pacific Grove, CA: Thomson/Wadsworth.

Whitaker, K. A., & Cowley, S. (2006). Evaluating health visitor parenting support: Validating outcome measures for parental self-efficacy. *Journal of Child Health Care, 10*(4), 296–308.

Wolf, M. S., Davis, T. C., Osborn, C. Y., Skripkauskas, S., Bennett, C. L., & Makoul, G. (2007). Literacy,

self-efficacy, and HIV medication adherence. *Patient Education and Counseling, 65*(2), 253–260.

Wu, Y., & Tsai, C. (2006). University students' Internet attitudes and Internet self-efficacy: A study at three universities in Taiwan. *CyberPsychology and Behavior, 9*(4), 441–450.

Yip, Y. B., Sit, J. W., Fung, K. K. Y., Wong, D. Y. S., Chong, S. Y. C., Chung, L. H., & Ng, T. P. (2007). Impact of an arthritis self-management programme with an added exercise component for osteoathritic knee sufferers on improving pain, functional outcomes, and use of health care services: An experimental study. *Patient Education and Counseling, 65*(1), 113–121.

Yuen, M., Hui, E. K. P., Lau, P. S. Y., Gysbers, N. C., Leung, T. M. K., Chan, R. M. C., & Shea, P. M. K. (2006). Assessing the personal–social development of Hong Kong Chinese adolescents. *International Journal for the Advancement of Counselling, 28*(4), 317–330.

Zillmann, D., & Zillmann, M. (1996). Psychoneuro-endocrinology of social behavior. In E. T. Higgins & A. W. Kruglanski (Eds.), *Social psychology: Handbook of basic principles* (pp. 39–71). New York: Guilford Press.

Zimmerman, B. J., & Kitsantas, A. (2005). Homework practices and academic achievement: The mediating role of self-efficacy and perceived responsibility beliefs. *Contemporary Educational Psychology, 30*(4), 397–417.

Zimmerman, M. A., Ramirez-Valles, J., & Maton, K. I. (1999). Resilience among urban African American male adolescents: A study of protective effects of sociopolitical control on their mental health. *American Journal of Community Psychology, 27,* 733–751.

17   KNOWLEDGE AND SKILL BUILDER

Part One

For Learning Outcome 1, describe the use of self-monitoring and stimulus control in the following client case. Feedback follows on page 560.

The client, Maria, is a 30-something Puerto Rican woman who was physically separated from her husband of 15 years when they came to the United States in separate trips. Although they were reunited about a year ago, Maria reports that during the past year she has had "*ataques de nervios*"—which she describes as trembling and faintness. She worries that her husband will die young and she will be left alone. Her history reveals no evidence of *early* loss or abandonment; however, she experienced losses with her immigration. Also, she seems to be self-sacrificing and dependent on Juan, her husband. She reports being very religious and praying a lot about this.

Maria asks for assistance in gaining some control over her "*ataques de nervios.*" How would you use self-monitoring and stimulus control to help her decrease them?

What else would you focus on in addition to the use of these two strategies, given Maria's cultural background and the case description?

Part Two

Learning Outcome 2 asks you to teach another person how to engage in self-monitoring. Your teaching should follow the six guidelines listed in Table 17.1: rationale, response discrimination, self-recording, data charting, data display, and data analysis. Feedback follows.

Part Three

Learning Outcome 3 asks you to describe the application of a culturally relevant self-management program (self-efficacy, self-monitoring, self-reward, and stimulus control) in a given client case. Feedback follows.

The client, Thad, is a young African American man who recently identified himself as gay. Thad has been working with you in coming to terms with his sexual orientation. He has visited some gay bars and has participated in some gay activities, but he has not asked anyone out. He would like to go out at least once a week with a male partner. You have discussed with Thad the use of self-monitoring and self-reward as possible interventions for this goal. He is interested in these strategies.

How would you use and adapt the interventions of self-monitoring, self-reward, stimulus control, and self-efficacy with this particular client?

Part Four

Learning Outcome 4 asks you to teach another person how to use self-reward, self-monitoring, and stimulus control. You can use the steps of self-monitoring, the stimulus-control principles, and the components for self-reward. Feedback follows.

Part One

Self-Monitoring

1. *Treatment rationale:* In the rationale, you would emphasize how this strategy can help provide information about the client's direction. You would explain that Maria will be recording defined *"ataques de nervios"* in vivo on a daily basis for several weeks. You need to be careful to frame the rationale in a way that respects Maria's cultural values.

2. *Discrimination of a response:* Response-discrimination training would involve selecting, defining, and giving examples of the response to be monitored. You should model some examples of the defined behavior and elicit some others from the client. Specifically, you would help Maria define the nature and content of the behaviors she will be recording, such as feeling faint.

3. *Timing of self-monitoring:* Because this client is using self-monitoring to decrease an undesired behavior, she will engage in prebehavior monitoring. Each time she feels faint or worried, she will record.

4. *Method of self-monitoring:* The client should be instructed to use a frequency count and record the number of times she feels faint or worried. If she is unable to discern when these start and end, she can record with time sampling. For example, she can divide a day into equal time intervals and use the "all or none" method. If such thoughts occurred during an interval, she would record "yes"; if they did not, she would record "no". Or, during each interval, she could rate the approximate frequency of these behaviors on a numerical scale, such as 0 for *never occurring*, 1 for *occasionally*, 2 for *often*, and 3 for *very frequently*.

5. *Device for self-monitoring:* There is no one right device to assist this client with recording. She could use tallies on a note card, a golf wrist counter, or a handheld computer to count the frequency. Or she could use a daily log sheet to keep track of interval occurrences.

6. *Charting of a response:* A simple chart might have days along the horizontal axis and frequency of behaviors along the vertical axis.

7. *Displaying of data:* This client may not wish to display the data in a public place at home. She could carry the data in her purse or backpack.

8. *Analysis of data:* The client could engage in data analysis by reviewing the data with the helper or by comparing the data with the baseline or with her goal (desired level of behavior change). The latter involves self-evaluation and may set the stage for self-reinforcement.

Stimulus Control

You can explain the use of stimulus control as another way to help Maria gain some feeling of personal control surrounding her *"ataques de nervios"* by confining them to particular places and times so that they don't occur so randomly and unpredictably. You could suggest the use of a worry spot or worry chair that she goes to at a designated time to do her worrying, and you would tell her that she is to stop worrying when she leaves this place or chair.

In addition to those two self-management interventions, it would be useful to explore Maria's feelings of loss and safety surrounding her immigration experience, the adaptations she is having to make to a different culture, and the conflicts she may be experiencing between the two cultures.

Part Two

Use Table 17.1 as a guide to assist your teaching. You might determine whether the person you taught implemented self-monitoring accurately.

Part Three

You need to determine how well the use of self-management "fits" with Thad's beliefs, values, worldview, and lifestyle. If Thad is receptive to the use of self-management and is oriented toward an internal rather than an external locus of control and responsibility, you can proceed. (However, it is important to explore whether any external social factors may be contributing to his sense of discomfort.) You may first wish to assess and work with self-efficacy, or Thad's confidence in himself and the contacts he will make with other men. Notice that Thad's sense of self-efficacy is related to his identity development as a gay male and as an African American. We anticipate that as Thad uses various self-management tools, his sense of self-efficacy will increase.

Self-reward can be used in conjunction with times Thad actually makes social contacts with men and goes out with a man. *Verbal symbolic rewards* used by Thad could consist of self-praise or covert verbalizations about the positive consequences of his behavior. Here are some examples: "I did it! I asked him out." "I did just what I wanted to do." "Wow! What a good time I'll have with _____."

Material rewards would be things or events that Thad indicates he prefers or enjoys, such as watching TV, listening to music, or playing sports. Both current and potential rewards should be used. Of course, these activities are only possibilities; Thad has to decide whether they are reinforcing.

17 KNOWLEDGE AND SKILL BUILDER **FEEDBACK**

Imaginal rewards may include pleasant scenes or scenes related to going out: imagining oneself on a raft on a lake, imagining oneself on a football field, imagining oneself with one's partner at a movie, imagining oneself with one's partner lying on a warm beach.

Self-monitoring can be used to help Thad track the number of social contacts he has with other men.

Stimulus control can be used to help Thad increase the number of cues associated with increasing his social contacts with other men. For example, he might start in one place or with one activity where he feels most comfortable; then gradually he can increase his visits to other places and activities where he will find other gay men.

Part Four

Use the following:

Self-monitoring steps—see Table 17.1 and the related section of the chapter.

Principles of stimulus control—see Table 17.2 and the related section of the chapters.

Components of self-reward—see the section with this title.

CHAPTER
18

STRATEGIES FOR WORKING WITH RESISTANCE
SOLUTION-FOCUSED THERAPY AND MOTIVATIONAL INTERVIEWING

LEARNING OUTCOMES

After completing this chapter, you will be able to identify, in writing, using a client case description and client–helper dialogue, three examples of

1. Solution-focused therapy approaches.
2. Motivational interviewing approaches.
3. Combined solution-focused therapy and motivational interviewing approaches.

Think back to a time when you were annoyed by someone's suggestion that you do something different or change something about yourself. Perhaps a good friend advised you to make what you considered to be a drastic and an unnecessary change in your appearance (e.g., hairstyle, wardrobe). Maybe a family member strongly suggested that you change a certain habit or change the status of a relationship you are in with someone else (e.g., sever ties with a significant other). Although the suggestion may have been well intentioned, you may have been frustrated with what you interpreted as another's interference in your life.

This experience may not be too unlike that of many clients when they first seek out professional help (e.g., counseling). A good number of them may arrive at the helper's office to appease someone else or to comply with a mandate. They may enter into a helping relationship feeling angry or fearful about what is to come; they may think they do not need to be talking to a helper, let alone making any significant changes in their lives. Although some type of change may be necessary (i.e., to ensure mental and physical health), it may not always be welcomed with enthusiasm or embraced wholeheartedly. It may be stalled for a period of time, entered into begrudgingly, or defied altogether. This is true for clients and helpers alike.

In this chapter we discuss these responses to change as *resistance, reluctance,* and *ambivalence,* and we describe them as normal features of the change process. The helping relationship is presented as a partnership between client and helper, and therefore both partners are involved in a process of change. We depict this change process as a type of dance between client and helper, wherein the helper works and moves with the client (rather than against the client) toward change. Rather than regarding resistance, reluctance, and ambivalence as missteps or stumbles, we see them as dance steps that both clients and helpers use in their work together, and how the helper proposes using them will determine how the client and helper dance together. Two helping styles that are conducive to working with and through resistance, reluctance, and ambivalence are offered and discussed here: solution-focused therapy and motivational interviewing. Specific strategies are described so as to assist helpers learn how to dance with their clients toward positive change.

RESISTANCE, RELUCTANCE, REACTANCE, AND AMBIVALENCE

Resistance in therapy is often and automatically associated with and descriptive of client behavior, due in part to helpers typically being the ones to make an interpretation of resistance. Indeed, the noun *resistance* is rarely presented without the modifier *client,* and the adjective *resistant* commonly precedes *client.* Clients who pose particular challenges in session, who are thought of as "difficult," are often regarded as "resistant." This might be true for clients who habitually cancel or arrive late for sessions, appear unwilling to recognize problems and accept responsibility, and contest the helper's expertise or integrity. Clients described as resistant may be ones who do not follow through on tasks discussed in previous sessions and are not particularly forthcoming with information in session or do not actively participate in individual or group therapy conversations.

Rather than being a unitary construct, resistance is a complex phenomenon that defies a quick and simple definition (Arkowitz, 2002; Engle & Arkowitz, 2006). Newman (2002) suggested that resistance is difficult to define because it is linked to helpers' theoretical orientations. From a cognitive–behavioral perspective, resistance is generally defined as the client's attempts to prevent or restore losses (e.g., sense of freedom, safety, integrity, power) anticipated during a personal change process (e.g., therapy; Beutler & Harwood, 2000). Indeed, Engle and Arkowitz (2006) defined resistance as "behaviors that interfere with making progress toward desired changes" (p. 2).

Ritchie (1986) proposed that resistance may actually signify a reservation about change or a reluctance to change, and Egan (2007) defined reluctance as the client's "hesitancy to engage in the work demanded by the stages and steps of the helping process" (p. 184). Egan distinguished reluctance from resistance, defining the latter as "the push-back from clients when they feel they are being coerced" (p. 184). Cullari (1996) also differentiated the two concepts, with resistance representing a client's intrapsychic and unconscious process (consistent with a psychoanalytic perspective) and reluctance being the "conscious ambivalence" (p. 4) that occurs between client and helper.

A related concept is that of reactance, described as "a motivational state . . . [with] energizing properties that drive individuals to engage in freedom-restoration behaviors" (Miron & Brehm, 2006, p. 10). Reactance comprises the behaviors exhibited (e.g., opposition, defiance) and the feelings experienced (e.g., frustration, rage) when an individual's personal freedom (e.g., ability to choose among several options) has been threatened or eliminated (e.g., all but one option has been restricted). Instances when persons might be expected to demonstrate some type and degree of reactance include losing one's driving privileges, custodial rights of a child, or employment. Clients informed that they will be involuntarily hospitalized in a psychiatric facility or that they will be imprisoned if they do not participate in counseling are also likely to exhibit some form of reactance.

Rather than being pathological, reactance is considered an expected response and a normal process intended to protect one's personal freedom. Such threats can be interpreted as painful feelings, personally revealing material, insight or self-understanding, and even change itself, resulting in client opposition to these forces, including the helper's effort to be of assistance (Mahalik, 1994).

In cognitive–behavioral therapy, client resistance is often understood as not cooperating or being noncompliant with treatment recommendations. Frequently cited examples of client noncompliance are not completing homework assignments, not adhering to a medication regimen, attempting to prolong therapy unnecessarily, or dropping out of therapy prematurely. Client demonstrations of noncompliance in session include interrupting and confronting helpers, placing unreasonable demands on helpers, presenting a negative attitude, repeatedly misinterpreting helpers' comments, and maintaining their own agendas (Newman, 2002; Patterson & Forgatch, 1985). Kemp, David, and Hayward (1996) described "Compliance Therapy" as a clinical program that integrates cognitive therapy and motivational interviewing

principles to increase insight and maintain medication compliance among patients with psychosis. Although the term *compliance* has been criticized for its connotation of client passivity and servitude (see Donohue, 2006), its use and that of *noncompliance* will likely continue in medical and mental health practice until satisfactory alternatives are identified.

Ambivalence has been characterized as fluctuating compliance (Westra & Dozois, 2006) and is another form of resistance generally defined as feeling or thinking two ways about something. More specifically, ambivalence reflects a tension between two equally attractive yet opposing feelings or attitudes, resulting in indecision, confusion, and a sense of being stuck, indicative of behavioral procrastination. It is therefore a prime characteristic of persons who are aware of a need to make a lifestyle change (e.g., exercise, vocation/career, diet, intimate relationship, addictive behavior), are seriously considering or contemplating change (specifically in the next six months; Prochaska & DiClemente, 1982), but have not yet taken the steps necessary to change their current regimen or circumstance. The experience of ambivalence can be likened to the hyperbole of being "in-between a rock and a hard place," reflecting what Arkowitz (2002) described as "conflicts between desires and fears, and between 'shoulds' and oppositional attitudes toward change" (p. 221).

DiClemente (2003) suggested that ambivalence be thought of as the opposite of impulsivity and therefore regarded as a necessary and welcome step in the process of change, particularly for persons prone to making hasty decisions and engaging in risk-taking and health-compromising behaviors (e.g., persons addicted to alcohol, other drugs, gambling, or sex). From this perspective, ambivalence could signal a time-out or a rest stop from problematic behavior and therefore could represent a relief from the debilitating and exhausting consequences of a "problem saturated" pattern of living. This alternative depiction of ambivalence appears to support Arkowitz's (2002) proposal that the term *ambivalence* replace *resistance* because of the former's more neutral and less pejorative connotation. As a form of resistance denoting a normal and expected stage in the process of change, ambivalence represents a resource in the helping process, a dance step that beckons for utilization by both helper and client.

Although reluctance, reactance, and ambivalence may represent varying gradations or at least types of client participation and cooperation in the helping process, we do not believe that as an overarching concept resistance is exclusively a client characteristic. This clarification is important because Arkowitz (2002) reminded helpers that "The way we conceptualize resistance clearly influences how we work with it" (p. 224). Resistance attributed solely to clients implies that resistance is something that resides in clients and is therefore entirely under their control. Such thinking absolves the helper of any responsibility for creating or contributing to resistance and can then be used by helpers as a convenient explanation for lack of therapeutic progress.

Take for example a client who refuses to give permission for his helper to contact his wife. The client may be labeled resistant until, upon reviewing his case in supervision, the supervisor learns that the helper failed to explain to the client her reasons for wanting to contact the wife or neglected to assure the client that she would not keep any of his wife's information a secret from him. Because the helper did not clarify her need to talk with the client's wife and did not carefully review with the client the contents of the release-of-information form—including what would be done with all information obtained from his wife—it is understandable that this client would question his helper's request to speak with his wife and thus withhold his consent. Rather than portraying this *client* as resistant, we would characterize the helping *interaction* as resistant or, more precisely, as generating resistance. The helper's failure to be direct and explicit more than likely contributed to the client's reluctance to give consent and to the subsequent resistance experienced in session.

Resistance, therefore, is not a one-person operation. Just as it "takes two to tango," it takes two to resist. This perspective is supported in the literature (e.g., Cullari, 1996) and underscores a primary assumption of motivational interviewing—namely that helper style is a powerful determinant of resistance and change (W. R. Miller, 1999; W. R. Miller & Rollnick, 1991, 2002). Motivational interviewing interprets resistance as an interactional occurrence, as something that takes place between the client and helper and is a product of that interaction, such as when the client and helper do not agree on the goals for therapy. This implies that helpers contribute to resistance (e.g., failure to establish and maintain a healthy helping relationship) and that clients should not be held entirely responsible for its occurrence. Rappaport (1997) similarly proposed that although "the client is *ultimately* responsible for changing or not changing, the influence of the therapist is paramount in altering the client's level of motivation at any given time" (p. 11). He contended that facilitating movement toward positive change is "the greatest challenge" for helpers.

The helper's awareness of his or her role in resistance is critical in addressing what Safran and Muran (2000) referred to as therapeutic alliance ruptures, which we might interpret as resistance gone awry. When resistance does occur, this indicates that something is important for the client, the helping relationship, or both, and that whatever these things are need to be respected and understood (Arkowitz, 2002). It is critical therefore for helpers to pick up on cues that the helping alliance is in trouble and then address those concerns with clients in a way that does not amplify anxiety, confusion, or frustration. Periodically saying "I'm not sure

if this makes sense" can signify the helper's attentiveness as well as his or her interest in understanding the client's perspective. Likewise asking "How is this sitting with you so far?" can elicit valuable information from clients that they may not have offered on their own. Rather than learning of a client's dissatisfaction when he or she announces termination or simply fails to return, helpers are advised to intentionally check in with clients and invite feedback throughout each session.

It is important to note that resistance can take many forms and may not always be amenable to change. Beutler and Harwood (2000) discussed resistance traits (i.e., stable, enduring disposition) and resistance states (i.e., varying reactions to situation-specific occurrences), the former being more descriptive of one's personality (and thus less subject to change) and the latter being fluid and transitory (and thus more receptive to change). Helpers must be able to distinguish between enduring and temporary forms of resistance and adapt their style of interaction accordingly. Although Beutler and Harwood equate trait resistance with high client resistance and state resistance with low client resistance, there are occasions when situation-specific resistance can be quite acute and likewise when more stable resistance that is consistent with one's personality can go unnoticed. For example, client cooperation may exemplify an acquiescent or people-pleasing personality style that over time may resist the helper's attempts to cultivate in the client greater autonomy and self-reliance. Resistance may therefore not be easily discernible. What the helper may have initially welcomed as client compliance may have actually been the client distancing him- or herself from the helper by engaging in "intellectualization, shifting the topic, justification, compliance, or immediate agreement with the therapist's statement without exploration or elaboration" (Safran, Muran, & Samstag, 1994, p. 231). Indeed, based on interviews with 14 clients about their first or second therapy session, Rennie (1994) associated client compliance with one form of client deference or negative politeness wherein the client felt pressure from the therapist's demands or apparent expectations and either submitted to them (i.e., complied) or rebelled against them (e.g., not returning for a subsequent session).

To more fully understand the concept of resistance so as to effectively work with and through it, the notion of two-way resistance is worth reinforcing. Resistance is an interactional phenomenon between the client and helper or, as Cullari (1996) offered: "Resistance is viewed as being due primarily to conflicts arising from simultaneous attempts at self-preservation and self-transformation both within the client and between the client, the therapist, and society" (p. 9). Trait and state resistance, therefore, must be interpreted and addressed relationally. A helper–client relationship characterized by trait or enduring resistance may require more structure and planning, more concrete and explicit parameters for interaction (e.g., written attendance agreement), consultation with other persons involved in the case (e.g., supervisor, referral source), and more objective measures of progress (e.g., specific behaviors to be implemented) than a relationship characterized by state or situation-specific resistance. The latter could be addressed through ongoing and deliberate client and helper conversations, wherein the helper initiates and facilitates in-the-moment discussion about observed disagreements and other indications of lack of therapeutic cohesion.

Regardless of which type of resistance is present in the client–helper relationship, the helper must remain observant to both content (i.e., actual words spoken) and meta-communication (i.e., interpretation of content, as well as nonverbal expressions), reflect on his or her own interactions with clients, be able to address the resistance appropriately rather than simply ignoring its existence, and remain nonjudgmental and nonpunitive. Questions such as "What do I need to hear from you that would help me better understand what you're going through?" and "What needs to change so that you are getting something out of our time together?" demonstrate the helper's interest in the client–helper interaction and can keep resistance to a minimum, use resistance productively (e.g., view it as signaling interest in and creating momentum for some type of change), and prevent alliance ruptures. Beutler and Harwood (2000) identified three general helper practices for addressing resistance (see Box 18.1). Additional and specific strategies for working through trait and state types of resistance are discussed throughout the remainder of this chapter. These strategies are informed by solution-focused therapy, motivational interviewing, and an integration of the two.

To better illustrate the helper's contribution to resistance and likewise to therapeutic rapport, we encourage you to participate in Learning Activity 18.1. You will need two other people to participate with you, each one selecting the role of client, counselor, or observer. If conducted in a classroom setting, this activity can help explain the occurrence of resistance between client and helper, and highlight specific helper behavior to help manage and lessen resistance. The observer's feedback is critical in this particular activity.

RESEARCH ON SOLUTION-FOCUSED THERAPY AND MOTIVATIONAL INTERVIEWING

In their review of 35 studies investigating resistance, Beutler, Moleiro, and Talebi (2002) concluded that nondirective or supportive therapeutic interventions generally work best for clients demonstrating high levels of resistance. Two helping styles that reflect a humanistic, nondirective, and client–helper collaborative philosophy—and are therefore well suited for clients who are less than eager to be in counseling—are solution-focused therapy (SFT) and motivational interviewing (MI). Both styles have been characterized as strengths-based approaches and comprise models proposed that intentionally integrate the two (Lewis & Osborn, 2004) and are used in concert with cognitive–behavioral therapy (Corcoran, 2005). The integration or combined use of SFT and MI has been recommended with African American women in drug treatment (Roberts & Nishimoto, 2006) and has been used to study such things as diabetes management among adolescents (Viner, Christie, Taylor, & Hey, 2003).

The future of both SFT and MI appears promising. Using a Delphi survey technique, Norcross, Hedges, and Prochaska (2002) asked 62 experts in psychotherapy to predict the use (i.e., popularity) of 29 theoretical orientations by the year 2010. Predictions were based on a 7-point scale (1 = *great decrease*, 4 = *remain the same*, 7 = *great increase*), and all theories were eventually ranked according to predicted increases in use. Of the 29 theories listed, the mean prediction score for SFT was 4.70 and that for MI was 4.47, resulting in an overall ranking for these two theories of 10 and 11, respectively. This means that the psychotherapy experts predicted that the popularity of both SFT and MI would remain about the same or would increase very slightly, suggesting at the very least their stability as applied theories in the next few years. In this same study, cognitive–behavioral therapy was ranked first (mean prediction score of 5.67), indicating that its use was predicted to increase more than any of the other 28 theories listed.

SFT Research

Despite its popularity, solution-focused therapy (SFT) has been criticized for its lack of an empirical research base (Fish, 1997; Shoham, Rohrbaugh, & Patterson, 1995; Stalker, Levene, & Coady, 1999). Many reports of SFT's effectiveness over the years have been promulgated by the founders of SFT and by clinicians who participated in intensive training at the Brief Family Therapy Center in Milwaukee, Wisconsin, the "home" of SFT. These reports must be interpreted cautiously because as S. D. Miller (1994) noted, they are "substantiated solely by reference to 'subjective clinical experience'" and are often presented in anecdotal form (p. 21). Claims of SFT's

BOX 18.1	THREE RESPONSES TO CLIENT EXPRESSIONS OF RESISTANCE

1. Acknowledge and reflect client's concerns and anger.
2. Discuss the therapeutic relationship.

3. Renegotiate the therapeutic contract regarding goals and therapeutic roles.

Source: Beutler & Harwood, 2000.

The purpose of this activity is to recognize the helper's role in both generating and managing resistance in the helping relationship. It can be conducted in groups of three, with one person portraying a client who decided to attend counseling rather than go to jail for a crime committed (e.g., neglect of children, assault, driving while intoxicated). The client, however, is not pleased to be in counseling and doesn't think it will do any good. A second person in this activity is to portray a counselor who is meeting with this client for the first time. The counselor should do his or her best to convince the client that the client needs to be in counseling, needs to change his or her behavior now, and should take heed of all of the counselor's recommendations. Client excuses are not acceptable!

The third person in this activity serves as an observer, attending to the interaction taking place between the client and the counselor by considering the following questions: How is the client's displeasure or irritation at needing to be in counseling received by the counselor? What does the counselor say and do to convince the client of the need for immediate change, akin to an overhaul of the client's life? How did the client respond to the counselor's definitive language (e.g.,

"You really need to change things around now or else something worse will happen")? What nonverbal communication is evident between the two of them?

Allow just 5 minutes for this exercise. The observer keeps time and then provides his or her observations to both the client and the counselor about their interaction.

Staying in the same three-person group and using the same client scenario, the observer and counselor switch roles. The new counselor's role is to acknowledge the client's aggravation about needing to be in counseling, emphasize that the client and counselor will be working together to help the client reach his or her goals, and acknowledge that change may take some time. The observer is to notice how the client responds to the new counselor's engagement. Again, after 5 minutes, the observer stops the interaction and asks the client these questions: What did this counselor say that stood out for you (or was helpful for you)? What did you notice about this counselor's interpersonal style (tone of voice, facial expression, posture, and other nonverbal expressions)? How did this counselor's style compare to the first counselor's style? Who would you be more willing to work with? Why? What specific aspects of these two counselors stood out to you?

utility and efficacy, therefore, are primarily theoretical and have not been subjected to sound empirical testing.

In their review of 15 studies conducted through 1999, Gingerich and Eisengart (2000) located only 5 studies that met criteria as well controlled (e.g., focused on a specific disorder, used randomized group design or acceptable single-case design, used treatment manual and procedures for monitoring treatment adherence). Four of the 5 studies found SFT to be significantly better than no treatment or than standard treatment services, and the remaining study reported that SFT demonstrated equivalent outcomes when compared to another treatment intervention (interpersonal psychotherapy for depression). Although the 15 studies as a whole "fall short of what is needed to establish efficacy" (i.e., favorable outcomes when compared to another therapeutic approach), Gingerich and Eisengart argued that the studies reviewed "provide some evidence of treatment effectiveness—evidence that [solution-focused therapy] works in typical practice settings" (p. 495).

In light of what Trepper, Dolan, McCollum, and Nelson (2006) characterized as SFT's "promising early findings" (p. 136), SFT research would do well to consider the specific processes involved in actual practice, processes that may contribute to client improvement. One such process is that of questioning style. Bishop and Fish (1999) conducted a video analogue study in which the same therapist

actor was videotaped using three different questioning styles (Socratic, solution-focused, and diagnostic) in her work with the same client actor presenting the same complaint (i.e., fear of asking a woman for a date). Psychology trainees ($n = 67$) and undergraduate nontherapists ($n = 115$) watched all three videotapes and rated solution-focused questioning more favorably (using a therapeutic questions measure developed for the study) than either Socratic questioning (associated with Rational Emotive Behavioral Therapy) or diagnostic interviewing. Specifically, participants perceived the therapist actor's solution-focused questions to the client actor as more helpful than the other two questioning styles. The most frequent reason given for preferring the solution-focused questioning style was that "it enhanced the client's autonomy and participation in therapy" (p. 134), alluding "to the advantage of maintaining a positive focus" (p. 135). Participant comments supporting this rationale included: "The client was given a lot of time to speak and think for himself," "The therapist let the client try to figure out the problem on his own," and "The client gained confidence and insight on his own."

Additional SFT processes already investigated include client report of change prior to initiating therapy (also known as pretreatment change). In two different studies (Lawson, 1994; Weiner-Davis, de Shazer, & Gingerich, 1987), clients presenting for their initial counseling appointment were asked about positive changes experienced since contacting the agency by telephone to schedule the appointment. The majority of clients in both studies reported pretreatment improvement, leading to the researchers' recommendations that practitioners routinely inquire about such change with new clients so as to build on existing change and to credit clients with initiating their own change.

Other research has focused on eliciting client strengths and resources, as well as honoring client preferences, and results suggest beneficial client outcomes. de Shazer and Isebaert (2003) studied chemically dependent patients receiving help from nurse therapists in Belgium who subscribed to a solution-focused approach. Treatment focused on identifying exceptions to the presenting problem and honoring clients' preferences for therapy—that is, what patients wanted from treatment. At 4-year follow-up (former patients contacted by telephone), 50 percent ($n = 36$) of the former patients reported being abstinent, and 32 percent reported success at controlled drinking. Although not explicitly SFT research, two additional studies underscore the importance of inquiring about and utilizing client strengths in the helping process. Opioid-dependent clients who received vouchers (redeemable for bus passes, groceries, movie tickets) for engaging in positive behaviors (e.g., attending self-help support group meetings) were more likely to be abstinent over the four 6-week evaluation periods than two comparison groups (Iguchi, Bilding, Morral, Lamb, & Husband, 1997). In another study, Bray and Kehle (1996) found that when children who stutter viewed three different 5-minute video tapes of themselves *not* stuttering and were encouraged to engage in more of these "exemplary behaviors," "all students' stuttering decreased in school and in various nonacademic settings" (p. 364). It appears that an intentional focus on and an incorporation of clients' exceptions (i.e., strengths and capacities) can be useful in initiating and maintaining positive change.

Despite the lack of quality or well-controlled SFT research, existing studies do suggest that clients benefit when specific aspects of a solution-focused approach (e.g., inquiring about occasions when the presenting concern was nonproblematic) are incorporated into the helping process. Solution-focused practitioners, therefore, are encouraged to reframe resistance as a useful resource in the helping process—that is, as an indication that the client is interested in or curious about and committed to some type of change. Helpers who adopt this perspective are then more inclined to solicit client preferences, offer genuine concern in the spirit of collaboration that supports client autonomy, and reinforce client steps toward change.

MI Research

Motivational interviewing (MI) has a more extensive and impressive record of well-conducted and compelling research than SFT. At least five reviews of MI studies have been conducted thus far: the earliest one (Noonan & Moyers, 1997) reviewed 11 studies, and the most recent one (Hettema, Steele, & Miller, 2005) reviewed 72 studies. In the latter review, the majority of studies conducted (72 percent, $n = 51$) investigated MI (or components or adaptations of MI) when applied to alcohol and other drug concerns. Other studies using MI included in Hettema et al.'s meta-analysis addressed HIV/AIDS, treatment compliance, gambling, intimate relationships, water purification/safety, eating disorders, and diet and exercise. Based on their review, Hettema et al. concluded that 53 percent ($n = 38$) of the studies demonstrated a significant effect favoring MI. The strongest support for MI was found in studies focused on substance use, specifically alcohol abuse. Although MI appears to have been helpful in reducing or abstaining from illicit drug use, studies on smoking cessation using MI have not yielded consistently positive or beneficial results. Burke, Arkowitz, and Menchola (2003) reported similar findings in their meta-analysis of 30 MI studies. Overall, reviews of MI suggest that this helping style has broad application across behavioral domains and, more often than not, the practice of MI (including elements of MI combined with other treatment methods) leads to positive client outcomes.

Despite what Burke, Dunn, Atkins, and Phelps (2004) regarded as "promising beginnings" (p. 313) to MI practice and research, they remarked that little is still known about *how* MI actually works. This is particularly noteworthy given Hettema et al.'s (2005) observation of wide variability in effects of MI across treatment sites and populations. Additional observations are that the effects of MI tend to be noticeable early in treatment and then diminish over time (i.e., over 12 months), are significantly larger among ethnically diverse populations than among White populations, and appear to persist or increase over time when added to another form of treatment. Speculations about beneficial components of MI include MI's usefulness as a precursor or adjunct to treatment (e.g., psychotherapy of depression; see Zuckoff, Swartz, & Grote, 2008). Specifically, MI appears to assist persons in the early stages of change, such as those who are not quite sure whether or not to invest in the helping process. Arkowitz and Westra (2004) argued that MI can assist ambivalent clients prepare to actively participate in cognitive–behavioral therapy. Indeed, Westra and Dozois (2006) found that when MI was used as a prelude to cognitive–behavioral therapy for anxiety, clients were significantly more likely to expect positive benefits from the latter, complete cognitive–behavioral therapy homework assignments, and effectively manage their anxiety symptoms than were clients who did not participate in MI prior to cognitive–behavioral therapy. It appears, therefore, that MI can assist clients make a commitment to the helping process, thereby improving client engagement, adherence, and retention in cognitive–behavioral and other action-oriented therapies.

Recent MI research has focused on the importance of client speech. As Amrhein, Miller, Yahne, Palmer, and Fulcher (2003) noted, "Measuring strength of commitment language is a particularly appropriate way to assess the dynamic events in MI, given that strengthening client commitment to change is the stated primary goal of this approach" (p. 865). In their review of videotapes of counseling sessions with drug-abusing clients, Amrhein (2004) and his colleagues (Amrhein et al., 2003) found that it was not the *frequency* of client talk about commitment to change that predicted eventual abstinence; rather, it was the *strength* of such commitment talk that resulted in abstinence. For example, the statement "I'm not going to use" is much stronger than the utterance "I might stop using." Furthermore, commitment language expressed near the end of counseling sessions indicated eventual abstinence more so than did commitment language spoken earlier in sessions. The authors suggested that their findings support MI's emphasis on clients rather than therapists vocalizing the reasons for change and that helpers can assist clients in their efforts by attending to hints of change or commitment talk and promoting or encouraging such language from their clients.

Both SFT and MI have evolved from intuitive and somewhat isolated practices (i.e., originating from their founders' reflections on their own therapeutic experiences and observations) to well-known approaches used today by a variety of helping professionals in a variety of settings with diverse populations. The ongoing development of both approaches has been strengthened by their fidelity to their theories-of-origin (i.e., humanistic, client centered, systemic) and their adaptability or "willingness to play" with other treatment methods (e.g., cognitive–behavioral therapy). The scholarly scrutiny both SFT and MI have undergone in research investigations has also bolstered their appeal and relevance; this is particularly true for MI (see Box 18.2 for a list of MI research studies). Although SFT and MI would benefit from continued and systematic inquiry concerning their respective and possibly shared "active ingredients," both appear to be well-established and well-respected methods for helping people through the process of change. Additional research on SFT and MI is discussed in the remainder of this chapter as it relates to specific helper strategies.

WORKING WITH RESISTANCE, RELUCTANCE, AND AMBIVALENCE

Solution-focused therapy and motivational interviewing have offered over the course of their respective stylistic developments slightly differing perspectives on resistance. SFT has historically had an aversion to resistance, regarding its discussion as an unnecessary and unhelpful focus on the problem, and believing that even considering resistance percolates its existence. O'Hanlon and Weiner-Davis (2003)

commented that "If you are focused on finding resistance, you will almost certainly be able to find something that looks like it" (p. 29). Resistance, therefore, was dismissed by some early solution-focused practitioners, even to the point of declaring it dead (de Shazer, 1984) and ceremoniously mourning its death (O'Hanlon & Weiner-Davis, 2003). The concept of resistance is considered moot by some solution-focused practitioners (e.g., Corcoran, 2005) when the helper invests his or her attention and energies instead on honoring client preferences and collaborating with clients to achieve their goals. Others, however (e.g., Shilts & Thomas, 2005), have entertained the notion of resistance as a form of curiosity. This suggests that both clients and helpers are intrigued by or at least interested in something and the task thus becomes identifying a shared interest (e.g., client regaining custody of her children, extending the client's time in-between psychiatric hospitalizations). Once a common curiosity has been established in session, therapeutic collaboration is underway.

Unlike some solution-focused practitioners, MI regards resistance as a natural and expected part of the change process, recognized in "client speech that defends and expresses commitment to status quo" (Hettema et al., 2005, p. 93). In addition, MI asserts that both the client and the helper are part of the development and resolution of resistance. Indeed, W. R. Miller and Rollnick (2002) contend that if resistance increases during session, it is very likely in response to something the *helper* is doing. Although MI recommends that helpers "roll with resistance" or otherwise "sidestep resistance," this simply means that resistance should not be met with direct confrontation but with reflection and appropriate reframing instead. In contrast to solution-focused practitioners, MI practitioners would declare that resistance is "alive and well" and therefore must be acknowledged, carefully handled and processed, and ultimately resolved. The importance of attending to resistance is reinforced by Arkowitz (2002) in his suggestion that resistance has meaning, signals that something is important to the client or helper or both, and therefore serves a function or purpose in the helping process.

Both SFT and MI offer a framework from which helpers can work with clients through resistance. Both approaches regard client–helper cooperation and collaboration not simply as preferable by-products of therapy but as essential ingredients to the helping process. Cooperation and collaboration between clients and helpers are intentionally established and monitored and are included as appropriate goals in treatment plans. It is safe to assume that when clients and helpers have established a productive working alliance and are collaborating, resistance is nonexistent or at least minimal.

SFT and MI have extended refreshing and welcome characterizations of the client–helper relationship, and they do

BOX 18.2	MOTIVATIONAL INTERVIEWING RESEARCH

Adolescents

Peterson, P. P. L., Baer, J. S., Wells, E. A., Ginzler, J. A., & Garrett, S. B. (2006). Short-term effects of a brief motivational intervention to reduce alcohol and drug risk among homeless adolescents. *Psychology of Addictive Behaviors, 20,* 254–264.

Stein, L. A. R., Colby, S. M., Barnett, M. P., Monti, P. M., Golembeske, C., Lebeau-Craven, R., & Miranda, R. (2006). Enhancing substance abuse treatment engagement in incarcerated adolescents. *Psychological Services, 3,* 25–34.

College Students

Baer, J. S., Kivlahan, D. R., Blume, A. W., McKnight, P., & Marlatt, G. A. (2001). Brief intervention for heavy-drinking college students: 4-year follow-up and natural history. *American Journal of Public Health, 91,* 1310–1316.

Carey, K. B., Carey, M. P., Maisto, S. A., & Henson, J. M. (2006). Brief motivational interventions for heavy college drinkers: A randomized controlled trial. *Journal of Consulting and Clinical Psychology, 74,* 943–954.

LaBrie, J. W., Lamb, T. F., Pedersen, E. R., & Quinlan, T. (2006). A group motivational interviewing intervention reduces drinking and alcohol-related consequences in adjudicated college students. *Journal of College Student Development, 47,* 267–280.

Michael, K. D., Curtin, L., Kirkley, D. E., Jones, D. L., & Harris, R., Jr. (2006). Group-based motivational interviewing for alcohol use among college students: An exploratory study. *Professional Psychology: Research and Practice, 37,* 629–634.

Alcohol Use

John, U., Veltrup, C., Driessen, M., Wetterling, T., & Dilling, H. (2003). Motivational intervention: An individual counseling vs. a group treatment approach for alcohol-dependent inpatients. *Alcohol and Alcoholism, 38,* 263–269.

Schilling, R. F., El-Bassel, N., Finch, J. B., Roman, R. J., & Hanson, M. (2002). Motivational interviewing to encourage self-help participation following alcohol detoxification. *Research on Social Work Practice, 12,* 711–730.

Vasilaki, E. I., Hosier, S. G., & Cox, W. M. (2006). The efficacy of motivational interviewing as a brief intervention for excessive drinking: A meta-analytic review. *Alcohol and Alcoholism, 41,* 328–335.

Cocaine Use

Stotts, A. L., Potts, G. F., Ingersoll, G., George, M. R., & Martin, L. E. (2007). Preliminary feasibility and efficacy of a brief motivational intervention with psychophysiological feedback for cocaine abuse. *Substance Abuse, 27*(4), 9–20.

Stotts, A., L., Schmitz, J. M., Rhoades, H. M., & Grabowski, J. (2001). Motivational interviewing with cocaine-dependent patients: A pilot study. *Journal of Consulting and Clinical Psychology, 69,* 858–862.

Smoking Cessation

Kelly, A. B., & Lapworth, K. (2006). The HYP program—Targeted motivational interviewing for adolescent violations of school tobacco policy. *Preventive Medicine: An International Journal Devoted to Practice and Theory, 43,* 466–471.

Steinberg, M. L., Ziedonis, D. M., Krejci, J. A., & Brandon, T. H. (2004). Motivational interviewing with personalized feedback: A brief intervention for motivating smokers with schizophrenia to seek treatment for tobacco dependence. *Journal of Consulting and Clinical Psychology, 72,* 723–728.

Stotts, A. L., DiClemete, C. C., & Dolan-Mullen, P. (2002). One-to-one: A motivational intervention for resistant pregnant smokers. *Addictive Behaviors, 27,* 275–292.

Co-Occurring Disorders

Baker, A., Bucci, S., Lewin, T. J., Kay-Lambkin, F., Constable, P. M., & Carr, V. J. (2006). Cognitive–behavioural therapy for substance use disorders in people with psychotic disorders: Randomised controlled trial. *British Journal of Psychiatry, 188,* 439–448.

Bellack, A. S., Bennett, M. E., Gearon, J. S., Brown, C. H., & Yang, Y. (2006). A randomized clinical trial of a new behavioral treatment for drug abuse in people with severe and persistent mental illness. *Archives of General Psychiatry, 63,* 426–432.

Graeber, D. A., Moyers, T. B., Griffith, G., Guajardo, E., & Tonigan, S. (2003). A pilot study comparing motivational interviewing and an educational intervention in patients with schizophrenia and alcohol use disorders. *Community Mental Health Journal, 39,* 189–202.

HIV/AIDS Prevention

Kiene, S. M., & Barta, W. D. (2006). A brief individualized computer-delivered sexual risk reduction intervention increases HIV/AIDS preventive behavior. *Journal of Adolescent Health, 39,* 404–410.

Picciano, J. F., Roffman, R. A., Kalichman, S. C., Rutledge, S. E., & Berghuis, J. P. (2001). A telephone based brief intervention using motivational enhancement to facilitate HIV risk reduction among MSM: A pilot study. *AIDS and Behavior, 5,* 251–262.

Medication Adherence

Parsons, J. T., Rosof, E., Punzalan, J. C., & Di Maria, L. (2005). Integration of motivational interviewing and cognitive

(continued)

| BOX 18.2 | MOTIVATIONAL INTERVIEWING RESEARCH |

(continued)

behavioral therapy to improve HIV medication adherence and reduce substance use among HIV-positive men and women: Results of a pilot project. *AIDS Patient Care and STDs, 19,* 31–39.

Thrasher, A. D., Golin, C. E., Earp, J. A. L., Tien, H., Porter, C., & Howie, L. (2006). Motivational interviewing to support antiretroviral therapy adherence: The role of quality counseling. *Patient Education and Counseling, 62,* 64–71.

Sustained Breastfeeding

Wilhelm, S. L., Stepans, M. B. F., Hertzog, M., Rodehorst, T. K. C., & Gardner, P. (2006). Motivational interviewing to promote sustained breastfeeding. *Journal of Obstetric, Gynecologic, and Neonatal Nursing: Clinical Scholarship for the Care of Women, Childbearing Families, and Newborns, 35,* 340–348.

Diabetes Management

Knight, K. M., Bundy, C., Morris, R., Higgs, J. F., Jameson, R. A., Unsworth, P., & Jayson, D. (2003). The effects of group motivational interviewing and externalizing conversations for adolescents with type-1 diabetes. *Psychology, Health and Medicine, 8,* 149–157.

Cardiac Care

Riegel, B., Dickson, V. V., Hoke, L., McMahon, J. P., Reis, B. F., & Sayers, S. (2006). A motivational counseling approach to improving heart failure self-care: Mechanisms of effectiveness. *Journal of Cardiovascular Nursing, 21,* 232–241.

Weight Loss

Carels, R. A., Darby, L., Cacciapaglia, H. M., Konrad, K., Coit, C., Harper, J., et al. (2007). Using motivational interviewing as a supplement to obesity treatment: A stepped-care approach. *Health Psychology, 26,* 369–374.

Nutrition/Diet

Resnicow, K., Jackson, A., Wang, T., De, A. K., McCarty, F., Dudley, W. N., & Baranowski, T. (2001). A motivational interviewing intervention to increase fruit and vegetable intake through Black churches: Results of the Eat for Life trial. *American Journal of Public Health, 91,* 1686–1693.

Physical Activity

Bennett, J. A., Lyons, K. S., Winters-Stone, K., Nail, L. M., & Scherer, J. (2007). Motivational interviewing to increase physical activity in long-term cancer survivors: A randomized controlled trial. *Nursing Research, 56,* 18–27.

so with the assistance of analogies to two different types of physical activity, each activity involving two people. SFT regards the helping relationship as a "multidisciplinary collaboration between experts" (Prochaska & Norcross, 2007, p. 459) in that the client and helper, according to de Shazer (1984), are not opponents but are like tennis partners playing on the same side of the net. Similarly, MI is "like dancing: rather than struggling against each other, the partners move together smoothly. The fact that one of them is leading is subtle and is not necessarily apparent to an observer. Good leading is gentle, responsive, and imaginative" (W. R. Miller & Rollnick, 2002, p. 22). It seems that for SFT and MI the focus is more on *how* helpers interact with clients rather than on *what* helpers do with or to clients. Helper style—and the interactional style that develops between client and helper over time—appears to be more important than specific and prescribed interventions (e.g., techniques) in working with and through resistance, reluctance, and ambivalence. Drawing on the analogies of two physical activities (i.e., tennis and dancing), it may be that the helping process is about the client and helper learning to (1) be successful tennis partners and together beating the client's presenting concern, or at least successfully managing the debilitating influence of such an opponent on the other side

of the net; and (2) dance together and in so doing, composing their own steps, rhythm, lyrics, and music that are helpful to the client. Box 18.3 presents a snapshot of alternative definitions of resistance and suggestions for how to work with it, informed by and reflecting the philosophies of SFT and MI presented in this chapter.

Certainly playing doubles tennis and learning to dance with a partner require that both participants learn and apply specific skills. When applied to the helping relationship for the purpose of establishing and maintaining an alliance and thereby working through reluctance, ambivalence, and resistance, it is the professional helper who is expected to take the lead and apply certain interpersonal skills integral to the practice of SFT and MI. These might include (1) informing the client about certain aspects of the helping process (e.g., client and helper roles and responsibilities), (2) affirming the client's right to make decisions regarding his or her participation in therapy, (3) reflecting accurate empathy, (4) inquiring about discrepancies (e.g., client's current behavior pattern and his or her desired lifestyle) and client ambivalence, and (5) identifying exceptions to the presenting concern (including past, current, and future client accomplishments) and conveying these observations to the client. In turn, clients would be encouraged to (1) engage in

---

BOX 18.3   **REFRAMING AND WORKING WITH RESISTANCE**

Definitions of Resistance

Ambivalence

- Uncertainty, confusion about change.
- Tension between maintaining status quo and engaging in new and beneficial activities.
- Normal, expected occurrence in the process of change.
- Welcome time-out from impulsivity; opportunity for reflection.

Curiosity

- Something is important to and has meaning for both helper and client.

- Both helper and client are interested in some type of change.

Functional and Interactive Definition

- Resistance has meaning and serves a purpose in the helping process.
- Both helper and client contribute to the occurrence and resolution of resistance.

Working with Resistance in the Helping Process

- Helper and client playing doubles tennis.
- Helper and client learning to dance together.

---

self-disclosure, (2) explore the discrepancies between making a healthy change in their lives and maintaining the status quo (i.e., remaining the same), (3) permit the helper to have contact with other persons in the client's life (e.g., spouse, referral source), and (4) visualize (and eventually rehearse) an actual day when the client is implementing new and more positive behaviors.

SFT and MI are discussed in more detail in the following sections with respect to applications with diverse populations and cultivating and maintaining a positive helping relationship. Specific helper strategies or practices intended to work with and through resistance are discussed.

SOLUTION-FOCUSED THERAPY

As its name implies, SFT is less interested in the origin and maintenance of a presenting concern than it is in constructing pathways through or around the concern that clients report. Rather than talking about resolving issues, SFT speaks of constructing solutions. This type of language shifts the spotlight from deficiencies, liabilities, and seemingly insurmountable hurdles to strengths, resources, and possibilities. Indeed, G. Miller and de Shazer (1998) stated that concerns, issues, or problems may be "unconnected" and even "irrelevant to the change process" (p. 370). Presenting concerns might be likened to merely an entry pass to an event—that is, they get persons in the therapy door, but a focus on the concern or issue doesn't help clients move through the helping process and out the therapy door. In SFT, helpers concentrate on *exceptions* to the presenting concern, occasions when it is not problematic (past or present) or times when the client has taken or can envision taking a break or a vacation from the concern. S. D. Miller (1992) referred to such occasions as "problem irregularit[ies]" (p. 2), times when the problem cycle was or had been disrupted. Inquiring about and amplifying these exception times is part of

the process of solution construction, and this can have the effect of rendering as inconsequential problem clarification and understanding.

SFT is often referred to as a nonpathological approach. However, rather than defining something by what it is not (and in so doing allowing the problem or concern to remain the protagonist), we prefer to speak of SFT as a salutary and strengths- or competency-based approach to helping. The client's assets and resources are regarded as ingredients for building solutions, and the helper remains confident in the client's ability to make positive changes in his or her life by continually accessing and utilizing identified assets and resources. The client is regarded as the expert on what will be helpful, and the helper is viewed as the client's student, learning from the client what his or preferences are and what may and may not be useful. This notion "challenges the prevailing idea that the therapist dispenses wisdom and brings about cures" (McGarty, 1985, p. 149) and explains in part SFT's characterization as "client-determined" (Berg & Miller, 1992b, p. 7).

The reversal of client and helper roles in SFT (compared to a traditional model of helper as expert and client as passive student) encourages cooperation and collaboration in the helping process, thus minimizing or at least effectively managing resistance. Indeed, Milton Erickson, whose work in hypnotherapy informed the early development of SFT, regarded resistance as client responsiveness and cooperation (Haley, 1967). For example, a client who voices her skepticism about the benefits of therapy is actually making her preferences known and, if she remains for the entire session, is at least demonstrating her willingness to hear the helper's perspective. Erickson also believed that resistance serves a purpose, such as the active engagement of both the client and helper. In addition, resistance can signal to the helper that a readjustment of the treatment or helping plan is necessary. Cooperation is possible when both client and helper are willing to acknowledge, work through, and understand the purpose of resistance. This is certainly necessary for tennis partners to be successful against their opponents! When the client is allowed to voice his or her opinion and the helper conveys an interest in the client's perspective, resistance is addressed directly and cooperation is in motion.

Utilization of Resistance in SFT

An enduring assumption of SFT is that of *utilization,* coined by Milton Erickson (1954) as the involvement and "acceptance of what the [client] represents and presents" (p. 127). This means that who the client is and what he or she brings to sessions should be acknowledged, validated, and factored into the helping process. Utilization can also be understood as acknowledging and intentionally incorporating into the helping process all resources represented and presented by both client and helper. This would include resistance and would imply that resistance can serve a beneficial purpose, such as clarifying goals and objectives, establishing a strong and durable helping relationship, and demonstrating the client's ability to take action. In reframing resistance as curiosity, Shilts and Thomas (2005) highlight the investment of both client and helper in the process of change, proposing that each person is interested in a positive outcome and therefore the momentum represented can be fostered and funneled in productive ways.

Types of Helping Relationships

It is worth mentioning again that SFT refers to types of helping relationships rather than to types of clients or types of helpers. This speaks rather convincingly to SFT's prioritization of the client–helper relationship. Berg and Miller (1992b) described three types of client–helper relationships: (1) the customer-type relationship, (2) the complainant-type relationship, and (3) the visitor-type relationship. Each one is determined by both client and helper, is subject to change, and requires the helper to assume more responsibility for managing and making use of the relationship for the client's benefit.

A *customer-type relationship* characterizes the interaction of client and helper who have jointly identified and agreed on a workable goal. The helper has acknowledged and validated the client's needs and preferences and has agreed to serve in the role of ally and consultant in an effort to assist the client in constructing a realistic and relevant solution. In turn, the client recognizes the strengths and resources that he or she brings to the process and views him- or herself as an active participant in solution construction.

A *complainant-type relationship* describes the client and helper's agreement on preliminary goals, minus the identification of specific steps to be taken to realize a solution. The helper may be expecting the client to initiate or get moving with the process of change, and the client may be looking to

the helper or to someone else (e.g., school principal) to make change happen. In other words, the client and helper "may not readily see themselves as part of the solution and, in fact, may believe that the only solution is for someone other than themselves to change" (Berg & Miller, 1992b, p. 23).

A *visitor-type relationship* occurs when the client and helper have neither jointly identified a need or concern nor agreed on a goal to work toward. This type of relationship may characterize the early phase of interaction when a client is perhaps vague about the purpose of professional care or may not even believe that such care is necessary. The helper in turn is unclear about what might be helpful for the client but remains willing to assist through the process.

To assist the solution-focused helper facilitate each of these relationships, Osborn (1999) described 12 helper practices or postures in SFT. These were generated specifically for use in visitor- and complainant-type relationships (e.g., when clients have been mandated to participate in professional help or are otherwise regarded as "involuntary" clients), but they are also useful for moving toward and amplifying the customer-type relationship. These practices include (1) soliciting the client's story (i.e., his or her perspectives, opinions), (2) acknowledging the client's aggravation and commiserating with his or her circumstance (e.g., being told by someone else that therapy is required), (3) commending the client's decision to pursue professional help even with reservations and perhaps hostility, (4) encouraging the client's full participation and engagement, (5) contacting the referral source and recruiting that person's recommendations for client care and goals, and (6) generating clear and realistic goals with the client.

Before proceeding to the next section, we encourage you to participate in Learning Activity 18.2. This activity invites you to consider how four helper roles can facilitate the three client-helper relationships described in SFT.

Specific Strategies of SFT That Foster Collaboration

Throughout an SFT session, the helper retains a posture of curiosity or wonderment, a keen interest in the client as a person, in his or her concerns and preferences, in his or her strengths and resources, and in the possibilities that can be cultivated and considered for the client's well-being. Establishing, maintaining, and making full use of client and helper collaboration is a priority in SFT, and strategies are therefore viewed as joint activities and not solely in the helper's purview. The practice of SFT is known for its creative use of questions (questions for both client and helper to consider, intended to stimulate possibility thinking) and for the attention given to the language used by both client and helper. The conversations between client and helper are therefore fluid, not scripted, and reflect a mutual inquisitiveness about alternative perspectives and realities.

The purpose of this activity is to consider further how helpers can work within the three client–helper relationships described in SFT. Feedback is provided on page 574.

Prochaska and Norcross (2001) described four roles that helpers can assume in working with a variety of clients at various stages of change. The *nurturing parent* acknowledges and joins with the client's opposition or reluctance to change, as well as the client's ambivalence about change. The *Socratic teacher* encourages clients to consider and achieve their own insights into their circumstance and options, and the *experienced coach* provides clients with a proposed plan of action and reviews clients' own proposals for solution construction.

Finally, the *consultant* provides helpful advice and support when the plan of action is not progressing as smoothly as anticipated.

Which of the four helper roles described by Prochaska and Norcross (2001) would be helpful in managing and making use of the three client–helper relationships described by Berg and Miller (1992b): (1) customer-type relationship, (2) complainant-type relationship, and (3) visitor-type relationship? How would the helper know which role or stance to emulate or to operate from, given the type of client–helper relationship? How would the helper know that a particular role had been beneficial for the client? How might the helper combine two of these roles in each of the client–helper relationships?

Asking Constructive Questions

In SFT, encouraging client engagement and coconstructing realistic goals or solutions go hand in hand. This is most often done by the helper carefully crafting and then posing to the client unique questions for the specific purpose of engaging the client in the process of solution generation. Indeed, "Questions are perceived as better ways to create open space for clients to think about and evaluate situations and solutions for themselves" (Lee, 2003, p. 390). Known as constructive questions, these questions introduce possibilities and new, more satisfactory and beneficial realities, and they are intended to build solutions by developing "different enough differences" (Lipchik & de Shazer, 1986, p. 97). The purpose of constructive questions, therefore, is to "engage clients in conversation, while inviting consideration of extraordinary perspectives" (e.g., client preferences; Strong, 2000, p. 29) so as "to prompt, promote, or elicit change or information about change" (Lipchik & de Shazer, 1986, p. 97).

Several types of questions are often used to invite client participation in the construction of solutions. Chief among these are *exception questions*. Exception questions presume that clients' lives are not always the same and that problems are neither pervasive nor permanent. Lipchik and de Shazer (1986) defined exceptions as any "behaviors, perceptions, thoughts and expectations that are outside the complaint's constraints . . . [which] can be used as building blocks for constructing a solution" (p. 89). Exceptions can be situated in the past or future, can be new, and can be recurring (Nunnally, 1993). For example, to assist a client who has assumed the full-time responsibility of caring for her ailing mother, the helper may ask: "Tell me about the last time you were able to take a break from your constant caretaking. How did you arrange that and how was that time helpful for you?" In posing this past-exception question, the helper

is curious about the client's description of a nonproblem occasion, a time when the client benefited—even for a brief moment—from not having to be on call. Once the client is able to identify an exception, the helper might encourage her to expand on the benefits and then envision a time in the future when similar benefits would be possible.

Another example of a past-exception question is the question asked in the first session of SFT when the helper is curious about pretreatment change. Weiner-Davis et al. (1987, p. 360) posed the following question to new clients: "Many times people notice in between the time they make the appointment for therapy and the first session that things already seem different. What have you noticed about your situation?" When clients responded in the affirmative, they were then asked: "Do these changes relate to the reason you came for therapy? Are these the kinds of changes you would like to continue to have happen?" In asking such questions, Lawson (1994) observed that "a counselor can significantly influence a client's expectation about a preexisting solution to a problem by communicating a definite expectancy" (p. 247). And Weiner-Davis et al. emphasized that client depictions of pretreatment change are regarded not as "flights into health" but as "real change (although admittedly new and somewhat 'out of character')," and they described their subsequent work with clients as attempts "to 'keep 'em flying' by transforming these 'flights' into real lasting change" (p. 362).

To help construct a vision of client improvement in a complainant-type relationship, the helper may ask: "Let's say that you and I have agreed on a goal for the use of our time together and our conversations are helpful to you. How will you know when this has occurred? What will tell you that we haven't been wasting our time?" This future-exception (or "fast-forward") question presumes there will be a time when

FEEDBACK
Helper Roles in the Helping Relationship

Helpers are encouraged to be intentional about the roles they assume and prioritize in a given type of client–helper relationship. Within the three client–helper relationships that Berg and Miller (1992b) described, one or more of Prochaska and Norcross's (2001) helper roles are recommended. The diagram here depicts which helper role may be best suited for managing each of the three types of client–helper relationships. Notice that the Socratic teacher role may be beneficial for both the visitor-type relationship and the complainant-type relationship, and that the experienced coach role may likewise be beneficial for both the complainant-type relationship and the customer-type relationship.

The nurturing parent role, however, would be emphasized in the visitor-type relationship, given that this relationship often characterizes an early phase of the helping process wherein the helper would concentrate on establishing him- or herself as a caring companion for the client as the two determine how to proceed. The consultant role would likely be prioritized in the customer-type relationship in light of the helper and client having established and agreed on a direction for change and having worked together over a certain period of time and having already experienced preliminary change.

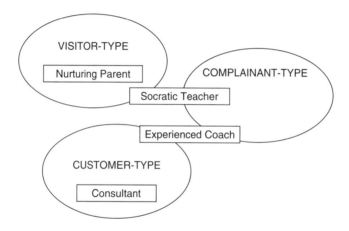

the client will derive benefit from the helping relationship. Fashioned in this way, exception questions resemble presuppositional questions (O'Hanlon & Weiner-Davis, 2003) or questions that presuppose the emergence of a positive or hopeful reality, as in "*When* you sense our conversations have been helpful for you . . ." as opposed to "*If* you think our conversations have been helpful for you. . . ." Exception and presuppositional questions, therefore, are used to "amplify . . . exceptions, to convey the inevitability of change to clients, to elicit the client's outcome goal, and to cocreate a future client reality without problems" (Selekman, 1993, p. 61).

The best-known exception question and perhaps the most distinctive feature of SFT is the *miracle question* (de Shazer, 1985). The client is invited to imagine that his or her life has been changed "miraculously" (e.g., "Tonight, while you are asleep") in a desired direction (e.g., "the problem that brought you in to counseling has been solved") and is then asked to describe how he or she will know that his or her life

has changed (e.g., "When you wake up tomorrow morning, how will you know that a miracle has occurred while you were sleeping? What will be different that will clue you in?"). The value of the miracle question is in its ability to elicit idiosyncratic and detailed behavioral descriptions of a nonproblem future, perhaps capturing elements of a solution that, unbeknownst to the client, are already occurring.

Clients who initially respond to the miracle question with "I don't know" can be encouraged to "pretend" or "give it your best shot" so as to entertain the improbability of such a miracle actually occurring. "I know it may seem like a weird question, way out there in left field," the helper might say, "but use your imagination or put your magician's hat on." Whatever snippet of difference (i.e., exception) the client is able to provide (e.g., "Well, I would have gotten some sleep, actually") is intentionally deconstructed or clarified by the helper and then amplified so as to create the increasing likelihood of such a day actually occurring. For example, the helper may encourage the client to describe the feeling of waking up knowing that he or she had slept well the night before (e.g., "How will you know? How is that different?") and then inquire about client contributions to having slept well (e.g., "What would you have done the day or the night before to help make this happen? What would you be credited with doing?"). In asking such questions, the helper is assuming that such a miracle day is a possibility and is helping the client prepare for its arrival, engaging in a type of "dress rehearsal." The focus is on client behavior so as to encourage and empower the client to summon forth positive change.

Coping questions (also "getting by" questions, G. Miller, 1997) represent a third type of solution-focused question. These inquire about how clients are already managing the concerns they have raised in counseling and how they might build on current successes for the future, such as "Given your recent struggle, how were you able to accomplish that?" Implicit in these questions are commendations of client strength, skill, and progress already at work. The client is asked about past or current successes and in so doing is complimented on being able to manage a difficult task.

Tyson and Baffour (2004) asked 108 adolescents in an acute-care psychiatric hospital to make a list of exceptions or strengths they had used in past situations. From this list, they were then asked to identify up to three of the most frequent things they did that "stopped the negative emotion or behavior from pushing them around when the negative event happened" (p. 219). An occasion when a crisis occurred that did not require hospitalization was described by therapists as an exception and strength. Such a reframe introduced the idea to the youth that they were probably more equipped to handle challenges than they had previously thought, that they had more resources at their disposal to fend off a crisis than perhaps they realized. Most of the youth identified artistic strengths, such as listening to music, writing (e.g., poetry, music lyrics), artwork, and singing/playing an instrument, that had been helpful in stalling or preventing a crisis.

Scaling questions encourage clients to quantify feelings and aspirations on a numerical scale (e.g., 1 to 10) anchored by diametrically opposed endpoints, such as 1 representing "no confidence at all" and 10 representing "as confident as you can be." Scaling questions have been described as the "work horses of solution-focused therapy because they are frequently asked . . . to achieve a variety of therapeutic ends" (G. Miller, 1997, p. 12). Their purpose is to help clients express previously unexplainable feelings, clarify the next desired steps for clients, and assess client progress (Davis & Osborn, 2000). In visitor-type helping relationships, scaling questions can be used to ascertain the degree of client investment in the process of change and to crystallize the direction needed to arrive at some realization of progress. For example, the helper may ask, "On a scale from 1 to 10, with 1 being 'clueless' and 10 being 'clear as a bell,' how clear are you about what needs to happen so that you don't feel like you're in a mess again?" If the client answers "1," the helper may respond with "Okay, so it's still cloudy or murky to you about what needs to happen. Let's fast-forward then to 2 weeks from now and let's say that your answer to the same question is a '2.' What would have happened in the next 2 weeks for you to have answered that question honestly?" Scaling questions can therefore be used to investigate exceptions for the purpose of constructing solutions.

Carefully constructed and purposeful questions in SFT not only address but also make use of client–helper resistance. This means that questions are not only regarded as an intervention in SFT, they are also the product of client–helper interaction. Said in another way, resistance—or what Shilts and Thomas (2005) regard as curiosity—is the intended recipient or target of constructive questions as well as the germination or yeast for such questions. The questions described are intended to engage clients in the helping process by tapping into client resources and strengths.

You are encouraged to try your hand at developing constructive questions. Learning Activity 18.3 describes the case of Susan and asks you to formulate possible exception, coping, and scaling questions to pose to Susan. Review the material on these three types of questions before you participate in Learning Activity 18.3.

Offering Legitimate Commendations

Mention has been made of complimenting clients on managing or accomplishing difficult tasks. The use of such compliments is important in SFT to the extent that some researchers have suggested that "all of solution-focused therapy is compliments" (Campbell, Elder, Gallagher, Simon, & Taylor, 1999, p. 36). Compliments—or our preferred term, *commendations*—acknowledge client strengths and competencies and are used to normalize a client's experience, help the client think differently about the problem or concern at hand, and exemplify the client's own ability to construct a solution. "Sounds like you did what you knew to do at the time" points out the client's use of his or her own decision-making skills and may serve to ease the client's concern about "not knowing what to do" or "not doing enough." In addition, a commendation such as "You've been through a lot and have somehow managed to keep your head above water" conveys to the client that past and perhaps lingering challenges have not gotten the best of the client, that the client has been able to draw on and mobilize available resources to rise above difficulties. Hearing such an observation from a helper may offer the client a new perspective, one that may reinforce the client's ability to participate in his or her own solution-construction. This is certainly empowering.

Our concern about "compliments" (as well as SFT's reference to "cheerleading") is that they may be constructed

This activity gives you a chance to practice writing several SFT constructive questions using the case of Susan and following these four steps. Feedback follows on page 578.

1. Read through Susan's case and, consistent with SFT, identify or take an inventory of what you think are Susan's strengths and resources. These will constitute the "ingredients" for your constructive questions.
2. Formulate and write down three different *exception* questions: one intended to highlight past strengths and resources, another focused on current strengths and resources, and the third intended to elicit from Susan existing or anticipated strengths and resources for use in the future. This third exception question might be phrased as a miracle question.
3. Formulate and write down three different *coping* questions. How are these different from the exception questions?
4. Formulate and write down three different *scaling* questions. What are the endpoints or the anchors for each scaling question? In other words, what will represent 1 and what will represent 10 on each scale?

Susan is a 35-year-old Native American who has experienced faint tremors in her arms, hands, and face all of her life, a condition she says her father has as well. She quit her job as a waitress a year ago because the tremors were getting noticeably worse. She has entered counseling on the advice of her medical doctor, and also because she wants to get back to work. She is very apprehensive, though, about talking with a counselor and is not sure what can be done that will be helpful to her. She is quiet, reserved, speaks softly and only when spoken to, and sits in a closed position with her hands clasped tightly in her lap.

Susan has been divorced for four years, after experiencing years of physical abuse. She says she finally left her ex-husband when he started hitting their son, Matt, now 14 years old. Matt currently lives with Susan's father some distance away, choosing to stay with his grandfather when Susan moved to her current residence a year-and-a-half ago (Matt didn't want to leave his school and friends). Susan doesn't see Matt often because she and her current boyfriend do not own a car, she hasn't been driving anyway, and Matt is busy with football and basketball at school. Susan tears up easily when she talks about Matt and says she hasn't been a good mother. She says that when she gets back to work, she'll be able to provide more for Matt and be more of the mother she says he deserves.

and articulated rather hastily and thus be interpreted as superficial. Clients who are not yet engaged in and are skeptical about the process of change, and may still be "testing out" the credibility and trustworthiness of the helper, may construe statements of praise (e.g., "You did great!") as disingenuous. Indeed, the client may regard the helper as ingratiating or being too eager to "win over" the client, which may actually result in the client withdrawing from the helping process.

We believe commendations connote the recognition of genuine or authentic material. Whereas compliments can be interpreted as flattery or showcasing rather shallow characteristics of the speaker (what some might think of as "feel-good warm fuzzies"), commendations are intended to draw out and put the spotlight on substantive client qualities. In addition, compliments may be ephemeral, whereas commendations are designed to be enduring. We believe that commendations are more respectful of clients and, in the long run, promote client engagement and investment in the change process.

Speaking the Client's Language

As a humanistic and client-directed approach, SFT is dedicated to recognizing, appreciating, and validating each client's unique experiences and perspectives. Furthermore, SFT has been informed by constructivistic or poststructuralist thought (Berg & de Shazer, 1993; de Shazer & Berg, 1992)—namely social constructionism, which postulates that reality is constructed in the moment through human interaction and dialogue. This means that reality is constantly changing and "constructed," not static or discovered, and that client and helper together determine what is real or true and helpful for the client. Clients, therefore, do not meet with helpers to "get answers" or to "find solutions" (although some clients may expect this), as if some "truth" or "recipe" already exists and is simply waiting for the client's knock or access code. Rather, through their conversations, client and helper together create or construct a new, preferred reality for the client, one the client authors and the helper edits. This means that what clients say and how they express what they mean deserve the helper's careful attention.

Therapy has been characterized as "a language system and a linguistic event" (Anderson, 1997, p. 2), and helpers have been described as "linguistic detectives" (Efran & Cook, 2000, p. 140). Solution-focused helpers, therefore, are perpetually tuning in to clients' expressions of their unique experiences and perspectives. This requires a genuine and "focused curiosity" (Strong, 2002) on the helper's part, referred to in SFT as a position of "not knowing" (Anderson & Goolishian, 1992). This means that helpers do not presume to know what would be helpful for their clients and do not try to impose their ideas or recommendations on clients. Rather, they assume the role of student of the client's subjectivity (e.g., "Tell me what it's been like for you" or "How would you describe what you're going through?"), attentive to the verbal and nonverbal expressions of that inner reality so as to fashion with the client—through conversation —a one-of-a-kind solution. As Walter and Peller (2000) have noted, "Creating a positive image, description, or experience arises from within the conversation and is never forced" (p. 76).

The process of solution construction is aided by the helper's ability to speak the client's language, which essentially means respecting, understanding, and appreciating what the client wants and needs. O'Hanlon and Weiner-Davis (2003) refer to this as "matching the client's language" (p. 61) or using the client's words to join with the client and build rapport. Rather than expecting the client to adopt the helper's understanding of panic disorder, for example, the helper remains inquisitive about how the client experiences what might be described in medical terminology as panic disorder and uses the client's own words (e.g., "a fog," "stuck," "freeze frame") to discuss this reality. Client and helper discussions might then focus on what to use as "fog lights," how to get "unstuck," and what to do to "defrost" or "thaw out." In this example, it's the client's experience and the words he or she has used to describe that experience that are incorporated into ongoing client–helper conversations.

Exploring the Client's "Instead"

SFT assumes that clients do want to change, that they do not want things to remain as they are. The word *instead,* therefore, is a wonderful tool for helping clients envision and plan for change. It also is consistent with one characteristic of well-formulated goals—namely that goals describe what is desired or preferred rather than what is to be avoided or eliminated. Asking about a client's "instead" is therefore a means of eliciting client wants and preferences. For example, rather than being advised to "abstain from all mood/mind altering substances" (i.e., what to *avoid* or what *not* to do), clients would be encouraged to "initiate and actively participate in a sober lifestyle" (i.e., behaviors to engage in or what *to* do). The difference is that clients and helpers can envision the presence of positive behaviors (e.g., attending Alcoholics Anonymous meetings, taking medications as prescribed, engaging in physical exercise, journaling) more so than they can describe absent or even diminished problems. The absence of something can be fathomed only by what will take its place. Therefore, it is much more productive and promising to discuss what the client will be doing *instead of*

drinking and in so doing to describe positive rather than problematic behaviors.

Honoring the Client's Preferences

Given that SFT is a client-directed form of helping, emphasis is placed on what the client wants to address, what the client wants to accomplish from talking with the helper. Inventory of the client's wants, desires, and preferences is therefore taken at the beginning of the helping process, and these are given full consideration throughout the process of helping. Walter and Peller (2000) refer to this practice as "preferencing." Client preferences may be to talk through concerns and troubles, and Walter and Peller allow for this, stating that it may be more important to the client that he or she feels understood than to have the helper move the conversation (prematurely) toward solutions, a practice referred to as "solution-*forced* therapy" (Nylund & Corsiglia, 1994).

Eliciting client preferences and honoring what the client brings forth "invites a discussion of purpose, of what [the client] wants from coming to the consultation" (Walter & Peller, 2000, p. 65). This may be to "get my probation officer off my back" or "keep our family from falling apart," client preferences that may initially attribute the responsibility of constructing and implementing the solution to someone else or something else. Such utterances, however, should not be squelched. Rather, the solution-focused practitioner pursues discussion about how such an eventuality would be helpful and what the client could do to begin the journey to such an envisioned destination. Questions such as "What will make it possible for your probation officer to be off your back?" and "What are some things you have already tried to keep your family from falling apart?" honor the client's preferences while considering client contributions to the solution under construction.

MODEL DIALOGUE FOR DECONSTRUCTING SOLUTIONS: THE CASE OF ISABELLA

Isabella and her helper have established a customer-type relationship thus far, given Isabella's cooperation and investment in the change process. The helper has therefore assumed the role of consultant and in this dialogue is interested in identifying the pieces and parts of their coconstructed solutions. This process of deconstruction allows both Isabella and the helper to locate the "active ingredients" of the solutions Isabella employed so that specific behaviors within her control can be replicated once therapy has concluded. The helper is hopeful that Isabella will be able to recognize her (Isabella's) active role in the change process—that is, that the solutions realized weren't chance events but were the result of Isabella's own instrumentality. This realization can be very empowering for clients.

1. Susan's strengths and resources (reflecting the helper's observations and impressions)

- Access to medical care
- Has followed medical doctor's recommendation to enter counseling, despite her apprehension about its benefits; is willing to give counseling a try
- Has desire and motivation to work again
- Wants to be a good mother to Matt
- Was able to leave an abusive marriage
- Other strengths and resources? _____

2. Examples of exception questions to ask Susan

- *Past-exception question:* "Tell me about a time in your life that was pretty special to you, a time that you still value and treasure. What made that time special? What about it set it apart from other times?"

- *Present-exception question:* "Since the time you made the appointment to come in and talk with me, what have you noticed that's been going well in your life?"

- *Future-exception question:* "Let's fast-forward to three months from now and imagine that things are going pretty well for you. Describe for me what that will be like. How will you know that things are going pretty well for you? What will be taking place that will tell you this?"

- *Miracle question:* "Let's say that tonight, when you go to bed and you are fast asleep, a miracle happens, and the miracle is that the main concern that you brought in with you today, to our session, simply disappears. It vanishes or just evaporates. That's the miracle. But you don't know that a miracle has occurred right then and there because you're sound asleep. When you wake up tomorrow morning, what will be the first thing you will notice? What will indicate to you that something has changed, that something is different?"

3. Examples of coping questions to ask Susan

- "What made it possible for you to come on in and talk with me today despite not being convinced that counseling would help?"

- "You say you've had these tremors all of your life. When was a time, even in the past week, that you were able to manage the tremors pretty well?"

- "What made it possible for you to leave your abusive husband? How were you able to finally do that?"

- "When you picture yourself being the good mother that you say Matt deserves, what do you see yourself doing? What are some of those things that you can say you're doing even now, maybe even in a small measure?"

Notice that the coping questions make use of what the helper has already identified as some of Susan's strengths and resources (e.g., managing tremors, leaving an abusive husband), whereas the exception questions leave it up to Susan to determine what she regards as being different from, or the exception to, what some of her concerns are. The exception questions ask about differences in general (e.g., a special time in her life), whereas the coping questions inquire about specific instances that imply or presuppose that Susan is or will be doing something (or has already done something) to control, cope with, or manage some of her concerns. Both types of questions are intended to illustrate for the client that he or she is responsible and gets the credit for changes made.

4. Examples of scaling questions to ask Susan

- "Let's say that 1 equals 'not helpful at all' and 10 equals 'extremely helpful.' How helpful would you say our conversation today, our session, has been for you?"

- "On a scale from 10 to 1, with 10 being 'tremors out of control' and 1 being 'tremors not in the way at all,' tell me about how the tremors have been for you, on average, in the past week. What do you notice is responsible for a drop in a point, say, from a 6 to a 5, when the tremors are easing off a bit?"

- "Given what you know about waitressing, how confident are you that in, say, three months you can return to that line of work and do well at it? On a scale from 1 to 10, with 1 being 'not confident at all,' and 10 being 'very confident,' how confident are you right now about this?"

- "If Matt were here today, what would he tell me about the kind of mother you have been to him? Let's say that 10 is 'the best mom ever!' and 1 is 'not a good mother at all.' How do you think Matt would rate you as a mom?"

1. **Helper:** We've had several sessions together, Isabella, and I thought it might be helpful today to review the work we've done so far and for me to hear from you what's been helpful.

Client: Okay.

2. **Helper:** You really have worked hard and have made good progress at school with your math class. [Helper is *commending* Isabella for her progress.] What would you say is the main thing that's made it possible for you to do well in school?

Client: Well, it hasn't been an all-at-once thing, you know? You broke things down for me so that speaking up in math class, for example, didn't seem overwhelming.

3. **Helper:** So doing things little by little, step-by-step, makes it possible for you to accomplish things that are important to you.

Client: Yeah. And you've been very patient with me. Respectful too. I mean, you haven't been in my face demanding that I do certain things.

4. **Helper:** So small steps taken that aren't rushed or forced is also helpful for you.

Client: Yeah. I didn't get all nervous and hyped up in here. You always took your time explaining things to me in a way that wasn't talking down to me.

5. **Helper:** What do you think made it possible for you to cooperate in here, participate in all the practice sessions we had?

In response 5, the helper is attempting to redirect the conversation back to *Isabella's active role in solution construction and implementation.* The helper does not want to assume credit for Isabella's progress. Notice that in responses 3 and 4 the helper kept the verb tense in the present to counter Isabella's past-tense reference to the solution. Also notice in these responses that the helper kept the focus on Isabella's behaviors, not those of the helper. These are subtle attempts to reinforce Isabella's instrumentality—that is, her ability to continue to instigate positive change.

Client: I guess I had to.

6. **Helper:** You had to. I'm not sure what you mean. Help me with that.

Client: I mean if I didn't, I probably would have failed math and maybe even gotten kicked out of school for pathetic grades. My parents would really have been upset with me then. So, I had to.

7. **Helper:** You wanted to stay in school and do well. The only alternative you saw was unacceptable to you.

Client: I guess you could say it like that. I just didn't want to fail.

8. **Helper:** And you certainly haven't. In fact, you've done quite well grade-wise from what you've told me. So let's fast-forward to the beginning of your junior year. What will be two or three things you'll catch yourself doing in advanced algebra that will tell you this time meeting with me, all the practice sessions we had, that this was all worth it?

Client: Wow. That's a great question!

In response 8, the helper asks a *future-oriented question* intended to help Isabella visualize her continued enactment of positive behaviors learned in therapy. The question *presupposes that positive change will endure* and will be done naturally, without too much effort (i.e., Isabella will "catch" herself maintaining positive behaviors).

9. **Helper:** It may take you a little while to think about it.

Client: Let's see. I guess I'll raise my hand in class when I have a question, and I'll ask to meet with the teacher after class if I'm still not clear on something.

10. **Helper:** That's great to hear. You didn't have to think too long on that, which tells me that one thing you'll be taking away from our work together is a lot of self-confidence and evidence of success from your work this year in math. This is very encouraging!

MOTIVATIONAL INTERVIEWING

It is important to emphasize that motivational interviewing (MI) is a style of helping and a method of communication, not a set of techniques. Beginning helpers are often eager to identify and try out specific interventions and then store them in their helper "toolbox." MI, however, is actually a belief system or a set of assumptions about human nature and the process of human change more so than simply a collection of helper strategies. This means that helpers themselves are influential participants in the change process and cannot attribute client progress or decline to an isolated technique brought out of storage and applied in session. Who the helper is (e.g., cultural identity), what he or she believes (e.g., theoretical orientation, extent of human agency), and how he or she communicates and interacts in a consistent fashion with clients may have more of an impact on the change process than any specific (and perhaps impersonal) intervention. Practicing MI, therefore, suggests embracing or identifying with a certain philosophy of helping rather than simply implementing a set of prescribed interventions.

MI "Spirit"

To highlight the intended contributions of MI, priority is given to what is often referred to as the "spirit" of MI (W. R. Miller & Rollnick, 2002). This core or essence comprises the guiding assumptions that "flavor" the practice of MI. Moyers and Rollnick (2002) likened this spirit to a song's melody rather than the lyrics: MI cannot be broken down into separate words or musical notes; rather, it can be appreciated and dutifully practiced only as a gestalt, a composite belief system, or an entire musical score.

An appropriate classification of MI is that of "a cognitive–emotive psychotherapy" (W. R. Miller & Rollnick, 2004, p. 306). Within this theoretical framework is the working definition of MI: "a directive, client-centered counselling style for eliciting behaviour change by helping clients to explore and resolve ambivalence" (Rollnick & Miller, 1995, p. 326). This description of MI, a richly laden song title, captures the spirit or essence of MI, and each component (or each musical note) is discussed (or sounded) so as to gain full appreciation for (and hear) the entire MI melody.

Themes of MI

Four guiding assumptions or themes of MI inform its practice. These are presented in Box 18.4 and discussed in this section.

First and foremost, MI is a *humanistic, client-centered helping style*, a testimonial to its roots in person-centered therapy. William R. Miller, the psychologist instrumental in developing MI, has described (in Moyers, 2004) his early years of clinical practice as primarily listening to clients with alcohol use disorders because "I didn't know anything" (p. 292). His investment in purposeful listening without admonishing

clients to change resulted in what Miller described as "an 'interesting and intense' learning experience . . . [and] an 'immediate chemistry' in talking with these clients" (Moyers, 2004, p. 292). He found he really enjoyed listening to and learning from his clients, and they seemed to appreciate and benefit from his attentive, listening stance.

This same listening and learning posture is emphasized today in MI and is referred to as the "learning-to-learn" model (W. R. Miller, Yahne, Moyers, Martinez, & Pirritano, 2004; W. R. Miller & Moyers, 2006). In essence, helpers are trained to learn from their clients how to engage in MI. Specifically, helpers are encouraged to attend to shifts in their clients' speech and behavior that may signify change talk and cooperation (thereby reinforcing the helper's attempts to practice MI purposefully and faithfully) or suggest resistance and client contentment with the status quo. The latter would indicate that the helper is the one who needs to shift his or her stance so as to cultivate or restore consonance. The "learning-to-learn" model, therefore, casts the helper in the role of student, the one who needs to be attentive to and learn from the client's words and behavior in session. This expands the meaning of "client-centered" in that the client is charged with teaching the helper about the helping process. Or, as W. R. Miller et al. (2004) stated, "Once counselors are attuned to these cues [e.g., shifts in client speech and behavior], their clients in essence teach them MI" (p. 1054).

Ambivalence is a central focus of MI and is considered a normal experience and a natural phase in the process of change. This is the second of four MI themes offered by W. R. Miller and Rollnick (2004). Ambivalence refers to having simultaneous and conflicting or contradictory attitudes or feelings about something. An example might be relishing the learning of graduate school while also finding graduate studies to be taxing and draining and at times doubting one's decision to pursue a graduate degree. Ambivalence is also a defining characteristic of the contemplation stage of change (Prochaska & DiClemente, 1982). Although some persons are able to sort through and move beyond the confusion of ambivalence on their own, others can get stuck and remain entrenched in the tension and the push–pull of ambivalence for

---

BOX 18.4	THEMES OF MOTIVATIONAL INTERVIEWING

1. Motivational interviewing is client-centered. Emphasis is placed on the client's ability to make his or her own decisions about change.
2. Motivational interviewing is designed to evoke and explore ambivalence (or confusion, uncertainty, confliction, discrepancy).
3. Motivational interviewing is directive or, more precisely, it has direction and is intentional. Its purpose

is to elicit and strengthen client motivation for positive change.
4. Motivational interviewing focuses on client speech, listening for both sides of ambivalence (i.e., arguments for and against change) and assisting the client in voicing the argument for change.

Source: W. R. Miller & Rollnick, 2004.

quite some time. The latter group may then require professional assistance. This is true of persons in abusive relationships, those engaged in addictive behaviors (e.g., nicotine smoking), and those experiencing other medically related concerns (e.g., eating disorders, diabetes, bipolar disorder). For these and other challenges that often include delayed action or behavioral procrastination (i.e., stalling positive change, another characteristic of the contemplation stage of change), MI represents an appropriate intervention.

As a helping style intended to assist clients through the process of change, MI is "designed to evoke and explore ambivalence, and to help the person resolve it in the direction of positive change" (W. R. Miller & Rollnick, 2004, p. 300). It is the helper's ability to elicit and hear both sides of the ambivalence, explore with the client the tensions involved, remain patient as the client considers his or her options, and guide the client through a decision-making process that may determine whether the client gets unstuck. Such movement beyond indecision may take some time and therefore require the helper's extreme patience, which W. R. Miller (2000) characterized as waiting with the client. On other occasions, however, the decision to change in a positive direction may take place after a brief encounter (e.g., 5–10 minutes) between a person in distress and a practitioner in an emergency waiting room, for example. Such a conversation usually entails the practitioner acknowledging the client's confusion and fear, expressing his or her concern about the client's well-being, providing the client with feedback (e.g., lab results, practitioner's own assessment of the client's situation) only after obtaining the client's permission to do so, and then reviewing with the client options available to him or her. This form of brief negotiation, an adaptation of motivational interviewing because of the element of feedback, represents a "teachable moment" and has demonstrated promising results in clinical studies (see Burke et al., 2003; Dunn, Deroo, & Rivara, 2001; Hettema et al., 2005; Resnicow et al., 2002). Ambivalence, therefore, should be considered not an intractable conundrum

but a fairly common occurrence requiring a helper's care and sensitivity (and sometimes time) to explore with the client and hopefully resolve.

A third theme of MI is that it is *directive*. This means that MI has direction and is intentional in its application. Its purpose is to elicit and strengthen client motivation for positive change. Although "directive" may be interpreted as confrontational or prescriptive, MI is far from that. As a humanistic and client-centered helper, the MI practitioner encourages the client to determine if change will occur and, if so, what that change will be. MI is directive in that the helper steers the conversation in the direction of considering change without installing or forcing such change on the client. Indeed, W. R. Miller (2000) harkens back to a core belief of Carl Rogers "that the therapist is not the author of change in clients so much as a witness to its emergence" (p. 12). The target of change is the client's perceptions—that is, changes once viewed as unacceptable or impossible to the client are now entertained and undertaken. This highlights the exploration phase of MI.

The fourth and final MI theme proposed by W. R. Miller and Rollnick (2004) is that MI *focuses on client speech*. Specifically, the helper listens to both sides of the ambivalence, that which argues for the status quo (i.e., not changing or resistance) and that which favors change (i.e., self-motivational statements or change talk). In one sense, then, the MI practitioner engages in selective listening—that is, listens for both sides of ambivalence. This implies that the helper "responds in particular ways to change talk in order to reinforce it, and to resistance in order to diminish it, both in the service of resolving ambivalence and promoting behavior change" (W. R. Miller & Rollnick, 2002, p. 51). Both sides of the ambivalence are explored by considering their advantages and disadvantages (referred to as a cost/benefit analysis or a decisional balance; W. R. Miller & Rollnick, 2002), and the helper assesses the strength or intensity of both.

Figure 18.1 offers an example of a cost/benefit analysis completed by one client, Heather, and her counselor. Notice

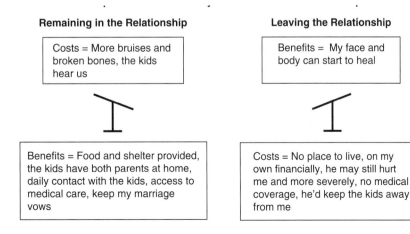

Remaining in the Relationship

Costs = More bruises and broken bones, the kids hear us

Benefits = Food and shelter provided, the kids have both parents at home, daily contact with the kids, access to medical care, keep my marriage vows

Leaving the Relationship

Benefits = My face and body can start to heal

Costs = No place to live, on my own financially, he may still hurt me and more severely, no medical coverage, he'd keep the kids away from me

Figure 18.1 Sample Cost/Benefit Analysis of an Abusive Relationship

that the benefits to Heather of remaining in an abusive relationship outweigh the costs and that the costs of leaving the relationship outweigh the benefits. Given this, it is likely that Heather is not ready to leave the relationship at this time and that any movement toward change (i.e., leaving the relationship) will be the result of the depicted seesaws or scales tipping in their opposite directions. In other words, the costs of staying where she is will need to outweigh the benefits, and likewise the benefits of leaving will need to outweigh the costs for Heather to leave the abusive relationship.

Using open-ended questions, affirmations, reflective statements or empathic reflections, and summarizations (often referred to by the acronym OARS; W. R. Miller & Rollnick, 2002), the MI practitioner encourages clients like Heather to consider as much as possible the full spectrum of change—that is, the pros and cons of not changing and the pros and cons of changing. The helper listens more than talks and evokes rather than instills a consideration of change by making use of the client's own resources (e.g., values, words) and undergirding or amplifying client strengths (e.g., motivation). It is important for the client to utter words of commitment to positive behavior change because, as Amrhein (2004) noted, "by making a verbal commitment to change, the client is announcing that the current state of his or her emotions and beliefs justifies the risk of personal and public humiliation and disappointment that would result if change did not occur" (p. 325). Through such a process, W. R. Miller and Rollnick (2004) contend, the client can literally talk himself or herself into change.

The types and strength of client speech have been a focus of MI research over the past 15 years, and results suggest that not only what the client says but also what the client *doesn't* say is important. For example, in one study with problem drinkers, W. R. Miller, Benefield, and Tonigan (1993) found that the *absence* of client resistant or uncooperative speech (i.e., interrupting, arguing, off-task responses such as silence or sidetracking, and negative responses such as disagreeing and blaming others) "was more strongly related to outcome than was the *presence* of client verbal responses ("positive") commonly thought to mark motivation for change (i.e., agreeing with the therapist and expressing concern, determination, or optimism)" (p. 460). This means that helpers should not be quick to latch on to what initially sounds like change talk but should be able to discern genuine change talk from yea-saying or acquiescence (i.e., a client saying only what he or she thinks the helper wants to hear). Genuine change talk will include expressions of a desire, ability, reason, and need for change (all four of which predict a commitment to change and are often referred to by the acronym DARN-C; Amrhein et al., 2003) *without* resistance (i.e., conveying cooperation), whereas insincere change talk will evince remnants of resistance (e.g., compliance or withdrawal).

To further differentiate genuine from inauthentic change talk, the helper should also listen for the strength or intensity of change talk. In a study with drug-addicted clients mentioned earlier in this chapter, Amrhein et al. (2003) found that the strength of a client's commitment to change (particularly toward the end of an MI session) predicted client outcome, namely drug abstinence. Higher-intensity change talk included statements such as "I won't be using" or "I promise" whereas lower-intensity change talk included comments such as "I'll try" or "I'll think about it." MI practitioners encourage clients to vocalize increasingly stronger change talk, not by putting words in their mouths but by reflecting and supporting a client's own stated reasons for change.

The importance of client speech in the process of change is evident in the three hypotheses that Hettema et al. (2005) proposed are related to an emerging MI theory:

1. Practitioners who practice MI will elicit increased levels of change talk and decreased levels of resistance from clients, relative to more overtly directive or confrontational counseling styles.
2. The extent to which clients verbalize arguments against change (resistance) during MI will be inversely related to the degree of subsequent behavior change.
3. The extent to which clients verbalize change talk (arguments for change) during MI will be directly related to the degree of subsequent behavior change.

Notice the emphasis on invitation or evocation (i.e., summoning forth genuine change talk from clients) and the association between client speech and eventual behavior change. MI is clearly a highly interactive process, one that reflects more of a partnership between client and helper than an authoritarian or paternalistic enterprise. The MI practitioner is one who can carefully discern types and gradations of client speech and buttress even the mere whispers of client change talk. This is all done in a manner or style that respects the client's autonomy, empathizes with the client's circumstance (e.g., ambivalence), and remains resolute in the client's ability to effect positive change.

Before reading further about specific MI practices, take a moment to inspect Box 18.5. The five methods listed on the left are recommended practices for helpers to use from the start with clients and throughout the helping process. In many ways, these five methods reflect MI's theoretical allegiance and philosophy that a directive or intentional helper stance, coupled with client–counselor collaboration, is curative or helpful. The five types of client speech listed on the right side of Box 18.5 are the result of MI research. Amrhein et al. (2003) found that these four underlying dimensions of client speech (i.e., client desire, perceived ability, reasons for change, and need for change; DARN) collectively influence the strength of commitment language, which in turn accounts

BOX 18.5	HELPER CONTRIBUTIONS TO CLIENT CHANGE TALK

Methods That Influence Client Talk about Change	Dimensions of Client Change Talk
OARS + 1	DARN-C
Ask **O**pen-ended Questions	**D**esire
Affirm	**A**bility
Offer **R**eflective Statements	**R**easons
Summarize	**N**eed
Listen for Change Talk	**C**ommitment

Source: Amrhein et al., 2003; W. R. Miller & Rollnick, 2002.

for client behavioral change. The assumption, therefore, is that by intentionally using the five methods, helpers cultivate the five types of client speech concerning change that, when genuinely uttered, can lead to positive change. Said in another way, helpers who intentionally practice OARS + 1 (the five methods listed on the left side of Box 18.5) will more than likely eventually hear their clients talk about change in one or more of its five dimensions (desire, ability, reasons, need, and commitment; DARN-C), listed on the right side of Box 18.5.

Learning Activity 18.4 on page 584 is designed to help you recognize client change talk and, when identified, assess its strength. Before you participate in this activity, you may wish to review the case of Susan described in Learning Activity 18.3.

Specific Strategies of MI That Cultivate Positive Change

Although MI is more of a helping style or a way of being with clients than it is a collection of techniques, there are specific strategies that MI practitioners engage in or postures they assume in their work with clients. In their review of 72 studies, Hettema et al. (2005) identified 12 interventions associated with MI and used these to determine whether a therapeutic approach (incorporating an average of 3.6 of the 12 interventions) was "MI-like." These interventions are

1. Being collaborative
2. Being client-centered
3. Being nonjudgmental
4. Building trust
5. Reducing resistance
6. Increasing readiness for change
7. Increasing self-efficacy
8. Increasing perceived discrepancy
9. Engaging in reflective listening
10. Eliciting change talk
11. Exploring ambivalence
12. Listening empathically

Moyers, Miller, and Hendrickson (2005) offered greater specificity in their distillation from 12 helper behaviors to 7,

all representing an MI-consistent style determined to contribute to increased client involvement in counseling sessions. These 7 helper postures are listed in Box 18.6, along with 5 MI-inconsistent therapist behaviors. Because they are conducive to working with and through resistance, the 7 MI-consistent behaviors are discussed in more detail and are viewed in contrast to the 5 MI-inconsistent behaviors.

Advising Only with Permission

The concept of offering clients advice may initially seem counterintuitive to the values of MI. Although described as a directive approach, the provision of advice in MI does not equate with telling the client what to do. Recall that being directive in MI means that the helper is purposeful or intentional in his or her (1) promotion of client discrepancy, (2) exploration of both sides of the ambivalence, and (3) elicitation of client change talk. Advice giving in MI, therefore, is directive insofar as it assists the client in decision making and the process of change. MI practitioners offer their clients advice—when appropriate—as an expression of concern for their clients' well-being.

W. R. Miller and Rollnick (1991) developed three specific guidelines for offering advice (pp. 118–119): (1) Helpers should not be too eager to give advice (and in so doing, play a bit "hard to get") and should wait for a direct invitation or request for information. (2) Helpers should qualify any suggestions made and present advice in a deliberately nonpersonal way. For example, the helper can say, "I don't know if this would work for you or not, but I can give you an idea of what has worked for some other people in your situation" (or "You'll have to try it to see if it'll work for you"). (3) Helpers should offer not one piece of advice but a cluster or a menu of options. Offering more than one option (and preferably three at the most rather than two) not only conveys respect for a client's autonomy but also signifies the practitioner's effort to tailor care to the individual client. In addition, clients are more likely to feel empowered when given the opportunity to make choices about their care and may be more likely to adhere to a specific course of action when they are able to select it from among alternatives. The helper is following this third

LEARNING ACTIVITY 18.4 — Detecting Dimensions of Client Change Talk

This activity provides an opportunity to practice detecting and then ranking the strength of types of client change talk identified in MI research. The client statements listed below were uttered by Susan, the client described earlier in this chapter. As you read through the statements, determine which of the five dimensions of client change talk each statement illustrates. Is Susan's talk about change an example of her *desire*, *ability*, *reason*, *need*, or *commitment* to change? After you determine which dimension each statement represents, rank the strength of each statement on a scale from −3 to +3, with −3 indicating *lowest strength possible* (e.g., "There's absolutely no need for me to change at all"), +3 indicating *highest strength possible* (e.g., "I really need to do something differently now"), and 0 reflecting *neutral strength* (e.g., "I don't know what needs to happen. I guess I'll just wait and see"). Feedback follows on page 586.

1. "I only came in today because of Matt. He's a good kid and deserves a good mother."

   Change Talk Dimension _____
   Strength _____

2. "I can't keep going on like this. Something really has to change."

   Change Talk Dimension _____
   Strength _____

3. "I did okay for a while carrying trays and pouring coffee. I don't think I could start right back, though, and not shake at all in front of customers."

   Change Talk Dimension _____
   Strength _____

4. "My doctor said it would be good to see someone, but I kept putting it off. I didn't want to have to talk about really personal things with a perfect stranger."

   Change Talk Dimension _____
   Strength _____

5. "I'm going to stop in a restaurant tomorrow that has a 'hiring' sign out front."

   Change Talk Dimension _____
   Strength _____

6. "I wish I could drive again so I could go see Matt."

   Change Talk Dimension _____
   Strength _____

7. "I guess I have thought that if I could leave Matt's father, I should be brave and stand up for myself in other ways."

   Change Talk Dimension _____
   Strength _____

8. "I need to find something because we can't continue to live off my boyfriend's pay much longer."

   Change Talk Dimension _____
   Strength _____

9. "Maybe I'll talk with my former boss. I guess it couldn't hurt."

   Change Talk Dimension _____
   Strength _____

10. "I'm tired of sitting around all day."

    Change Talk Dimension _____
    Strength _____

BOX 18.6 — HELPER BEHAVIORS CONSISTENT AND NOT CONSISTENT WITH MI

MI-Consistent Behaviors
1. Advise only with permission
2. Affirm
3. Emphasize personal choice and control/encourage client autonomy
4. Ask open-ended questions
5. Reflect
6. Reframe
7. Support

MI-Inconsistent Behaviors
1. Confront
2. Direct
3. Warn
4. Advise without permission
5. Raise concern without permission

Source: Moyers, Miller, & Hendrickson, 2005.

guideline when he or she states: "Let me describe a number of possibilities, and you tell me which of these makes the most sense to you."

Paramount to advice giving—indeed, to all helper strategies in MI—is that the helper offers advice only after the client grants permission for the helper to do so. Again, this reflects the humanistic, client-centered values of MI. The helper can request permission by saying, for example: "I've thought about this, and I have some suggestions about what might be helpful for you. Would you like to hear what I've been thinking about?" Permission is implied in the first of three occasions when the provision of advice is considered appropriate (Denise Ernst, cited in W. R. Miller & Rollnick, 2002, p. 277):

1. The recipient asks for information.
2. The practitioner has information that might be helpful to a client.
3. The practitioner feels ethically compelled to provide advice.

The practitioner may feel compelled to offer advice after reviewing the results of medical tests (e.g., blood work indicating high cholesterol, liver disease, anemia), hearing the client speak of being in a physically abusive relationship or suicidal ideation, and learning of the client's legal history and current status (e.g., on court probation). Regardless of the circumstance, it is recommended that advice be provided in a manner that conveys concern for the client's well-being.

Affirming

A second MI practice is to affirm client efforts toward positive change—that is, to impart appreciation, reinforcement, or confidence (W. R. Miller, Moyers, Ernst, & Amrhein, 2003). This practice dovetails nicely with solution-focused therapy's recommendation that helpers notice the difference (i.e., exceptions to client accounts of problem-saturated stories), or otherwise discern client strengths and resources, and then convey their observations or assessments to clients. As discussed earlier in the chapter, we prefer "commendations" or "affirmations" to SFT's reference to "compliments" or "cheerleading." The former two terms imply genuine observations based on certain evidence (e.g., client's demonstration of a certain skill), whereas compliments could be construed as general or hollow accolades representing the helper's wishful thinking. Notice the difference between "You've done a fantastic job" and "You persevered and accomplished a difficult task." The first statement is non-specific and may be interpreted as overly optimistic. By contrast, the second statement identifies a specific client characteristic utilized (i.e., perseverance) that contributed to the client's positive outcome. In this manner, affirmations are used to direct the client's attention to assets already in his or her possession, intrinsic or at least accessible resources that can be fostered and mobilized in future circumstances.

Helpers who are able to recognize client strengths, who remain hopeful about their client's ability to realize positive change, and who deliver affirmations or words of appreciation that convey their confidence with reference to specific observations are practicing what W. R. Miller (2000) depicted as "other-efficacy." Whereas *self-efficacy* refers to confidence in oneself, *other-efficacy* is confidence in another person's abilities. Affirmations, therefore, are examples of the helper's other-efficacy.

Emphasizing Personal Choice and Control

Consistent with MI's humanistic philosophy is the practice of emphasizing to clients that they alone are the ones to decide how to invest in and make use of the helping process, including whether or not—or to what extent—they will make changes in their lives. This practice exemplifies the ethical principle of autonomy in the helping professions (Kitchener, 2000)—that is, respecting the client's right to make decisions about his or her care when the client is competent to do so. Emphasizing the client's autonomy can be conveyed in a comment such as "Well, it really is your choice what to do next. We've talked about several possibilities, but you alone are the one to say what's going to happen. I couldn't decide for you, let alone make you do anything." W. R. Miller and Rollnick (2002) contend that a reassuring statement such as this may be "the best antidote" (p. 106) for persons who feel threatened and are thus opposing the mandates or suggestions of others to behave differently. Furthermore, the helper is conveying the truth and that which respects the client's autonomy. This is best reflected in W. R. Miller's (1999) admonition to practitioners:

> In a motivational approach to counseling, it is not your task to *give* a client a choice—choice is not yours to give but the client's to make. You do not *allow* a client to choose because the choice is already and always belongs with the client. The *client* chooses. Your task is to help clients make choices that are in their best interests. (p. 90)

Asking Open-Ended Questions

This particular intervention is mentioned here because of its emphasis in MI, particularly in working with resistance. Open-ended questions are intended to open the door to further conversation by seeking information, inviting the client's perspective, or encouraging self-exploration (W. R. Miller et al., 2003). As opposed to closed-ended questions (which usually can be answered with only "yes" or "no"), open-ended questions are designed to elicit many possible answers and in this manner are similar to the constructive questions in solution-focused therapy.

FEEDBACK	
18.4	**Detecting Dimensions of Client Change Talk**

Change Talk Dimension	Strength
1. Reason	+2 or +1
2. Need	+3
3. Ability	−2 or −1
4. Desire	−2
5. Commitment	+3 or +2
6. Desire (maybe also Reason)	0
7. Ability	+1 or 0
8. Need or Reason	+1
9. Commitment	−2
10. Reason	0

Note: Lower strength ratings reflect indecisiveness (e.g., "maybe"), lack of commitment or confidence, and minimal interest. Higher strength ratings reflect determination, specific plans for change, or clear reasons to change. Neutral ratings reflect either general "wishful thinking," without temporal or otherwise concrete specificity, or vague explanations.

Open-ended questions usually begin with "What" (e.g., "What are your thoughts about being here and having to talk to me?") and "How" (e.g., "How would you like things to be different?"). Rather than to interrogate (often implied when questions begin with "Why"), open-ended questions are designed to invite the client's opinion and encourage elaboration. Because of this intent, they need not always be in the form of a question. "Tell me about—" and "Say more about—" are both examples of invitational statements categorized as open-ended questions in MI because they are designed to elicit further information, including the client's thoughts and feelings, and to keep the client talking. By asking open-ended questions and posing invitational statements, the MI practitioner is able to do more listening than talking, an important goal when working with resistance. Indeed, Hettema et al. (2005) describe MI as "a complex clinical style for eliciting the client's own values and motivations for change. It is far more about listening than telling, about evoking rather than instilling" (p. 108).

Although asking open-ended questions may appear to be a simple or "no brainer" activity, they do require the helper's vigilance. For one thing, the helper's tone of voice must convey genuine inquisitiveness and not incredulity. This can be monitored by paying attention to which words in the question are emphasized. In addition, an open-ended question may inadvertently turn into a closed-ended question as in "Tell me about your smoking. How old were you when you started?" Notice that what begins as a statement inviting a wealth of unlimited information quickly turns into a search for a specific type and a limited amount of information. Such a detour is regarded as a "spoiled open question" (W. R. Miller et al., 2003). Now, in their defense, closed-ended questions are useful when the helper knows what he or she is looking for (e.g., "Do you mean to say that. . . ?"), to either confirm or disconfirm the helper's hypothesis, and so can expedite the pace of gathering information. When the helper is facing resistance, however, open-ended questions are preferred, particularly in the beginning phases of the helping process, because they convey respect for the client's perspective, encourage participation and collaboration, and do not send the message that the practitioner "knows best."

Reflecting

W. R. Miller and Rollnick (2002) characterize reflective listening as "one of the most important and most challenging skills required for motivational interviewing" (p. 67). Indeed, reflections are the product of meaning making and therefore require discernment and thoughtfulness from the helper. One way to appreciate the need for and the function of reflections is to liken them to hitting the space bar on the keyboard so as to separate words in a sentence and make sense of their connections. Without spaces between words, all the words in a sentence run together and any message intended is difficult, if not impossible, to interpret. Reflections, similarly, are pauses or spaces in a conversation that allow both client and helper to interrupt a train of thought and make sense of what has been discussed or shared thus far. They separate concepts, thoughts, and feelings and may foster understanding and empathy. Like the space bar on a keyboard, reflections create space for discernment and meaning making. Given this function served by reflections, it is no wonder that reflective listening during the course of a session is challenging!

Reflections—also known as reflective or empathic statements—capture and return to the client something that the client has said (W. R. Miller et al., 2003) and in so doing verify that the client has been heard. The essence of reflective statements is that they make a guess as to what the speaker means (e.g., thoughts, feelings, intentions), but the guess is phrased in the form of a statement, not a question, so that the speaker's voice tone goes down at the end (i.e., ends with a period rather than a question mark).

Practice for a moment by saying out loud the statement "You are confused about what to do next." Now say the same words again by intentionally placing a question mark at the end. Notice the difference? The question mark (i.e., voice tone going up at the end) makes the statement into a question, and a closed-ended question at that, resembling

W. R. Miller et al.'s (2003) "spoiled open question" mentioned earlier. Repeating the phrase and placing a period at the end (i.e., voice tone going down at the end) does not question the client's feeling or intention; rather, it leaves the door open for the client to agree or disagree and possibly elaborate. In this manner, reflective statements serve to "continue the paragraph" of conversation in the helping process (W. R. Miller & Rollnick, 2002, p. 70).

Although several types of reflections are offered in MI, three basic reflective statements are discussed here and examples are provide in Box 18.7. *Simple reflections* mirror and acknowledge the client's emotion, opinion, or perception and thus repeat or rephrase what the client has said. *Complex reflections* go beyond simple reflections by adding substantial meaning or emphasis to what the client has said. One way in which helpers do this is to use metaphors or analogies (ones not used by the client). Another way is to exaggerate or amplify certain words so as to convey that the extent of the client's thinking or the intensity of his or her emotion has been heard. Responding in this way may encourage the client to "cool down" or back off a bit from the saturated feeling or the certainty of thought (i.e., serve as a space bar or a pause from the emotion or certainty). Inflecting one's voice and using overgeneralizations (e.g., "never," "only," "always," or "nothing") in a straightforward and empathic manner can help communicate to the client that his or her perspectives matter. Complex reflections, therefore, are designed to validate the client's experience and also offer an alternative perspective.

Double-sided reflections are categorized in MI as a specific type of complex reflections and are used when the client has voiced some ambivalence. The helper listens carefully for both sides of the ambivalence and then reflects both sides, not discounting or dismissing either one, and in so doing the helper allows the client to wrestle with the tension. One signal that a double-sided reflection is in order is the client's use of the word "but," suggesting that there are two conflicting or at least nonparallel views at work. In response, the helper may retain the "but," although using "and" to connect the two sides may initially help the client come face-to-face with the full weight or tension of both sides, resulting in a realization that "something's gotta give."

When used to shed light on both sides of a discrepancy or ambivalence, reflections can resemble a form of confrontation, which W. R. Miller (1999) reframed as an invitation for clarification. This means that clients are encouraged to come face-to-face "with a difficult and often threatening reality, to 'let in' rather than 'block it out,' and to allow this reality to change them. That makes confrontation a *goal* of counseling rather than a particular *style* or *technique*" (p. 10). Three helpful words that can be used as a preface to a reflective statement, one that confronts or invites clarification, are "Help me understand." The word "Help" signals an invitation (or a request for permission), "me" personalizes the request, and "understand" indicates that the helper is intent on empathizing with the client's struggle. To practice using this preface, insert these three words at the beginning of the example of a double-sided reflection in Box 18.7. Notice how these words may catch the client's attention and then soften the effect of the double-sided reflection. We encourage you to periodically use "Help me understand" as a genuine request for shared clarity.

Although reflective statements may be likened to a mild or gentle form of confrontation, it is important to remember that their intention is to convey understanding and empathy. Perhaps one reason reflective listening can be a challenge is that it requires practitioners to be patient and to stay with the client's emotion or experience. Helpers may be more ready for clients to change than they are to change themselves, a differential Skovholt (2001) described as the "readiness gap," only 1 of 20 "hazards" of working as a helping professional. Indeed, helpers may be so eager to speed up the process of change (because of pressure to document client improvement, difficulty managing many clients on a caseload, or simply impatience) that they fail to hear or fully appreciate the magnitude of the client's emotion and circumstance (e.g., anger, confusion, anxiety, depression). Just as reflective statements may not always be easy for the client to hear, reflective listening may not be easy for the helper to do. Both imply looking in a mirror that may reflect a not-too-pleasant or an otherwise unsettling reality, one the client must come face-to-face with and one the helper must vicariously participate in if authentic and enduring change is to occur. Kenneth Minkoff (featured in the Mental

---

BOX 18.7   EXAMPLES OF THREE TYPES OF REFLECTIVE STATEMENTS

Client: "Coming here is a bunch of crap. It's all political. I wouldn't mind getting some help to stay sober, but you know, the only reason I'm here is because that damn prosecutor is up for reelection! It's just not right."

Simple reflection: "You're frustrated about having to come here, especially when it's to help a politician get reelected."

Complex reflection: "Coming here is a total waste of your time because you feel it doesn't have anything to do with you. You're frustrated about being the guinea pig for someone else's career advancement, not your own well-being."

Double-sided reflection: "You'd like to get sober, but [or *and*] you're also angry about being told to do it for the sole purpose of helping the prosecutor get reelected."

Illness Education Project, 2000) said it best when he implored practitioners working with clients with co-occurring disorders (substance use and mental illness) to "have the courage to join them [clients] in the reality of their despair." Well-formulated reflections, therefore, not only challenge clients to face up to and work through their ambivalence; reflective listening challenges helpers to press the space bar and join or come alongside clients in the experience of their ambivalence. Such empathic alignment may be the most difficult dance step for helpers to learn, but it may be the most important one for them to engage in as they guide clients through resistance.

To help implement the practices of asking open-ended questions and reflective listening (two important strategies in MI), W. R. Miller and Rollnick (2002, p. 183) offered four general guidelines:

1. Talk less than your client does.
2. Offer two to three reflections for every question that you ask.
3. Ask twice as many open questions as closed questions.
4. When you listen empathically, more than half of the reflections you offer should be deeper, more complex reflections (paraphrase) rather than simpler repetition or rephrasing of what the client offered.

Reframing

Reframing is mentioned here because it is particularly useful in addressing and working with resistance. Reframing is similar to reflecting in the sense that both convey understanding. The difference is that reframes "also change the valence or emotional charge of a client statement" (W. R. Miller et al., 2003, p. 40) from a negative to a positive meaning or vice versa. Reframes offer a new meaning or interpretation and recast the client's information in a new light that is more likely to support change (W. R. Miller & Rollnick, 2002). Take for example a client who says, "I've reached my limit and I don't know if I can go on like this." A complex reflection might be something like "You've hit a wall, or at least a stumbling block, and now you're wondering if you can keep going in the same direction or at the same pace." A reframe, however, might be phrased as "You're at a crossroads and you're thinking you need to take another route." Whereas the reflection makes a guess as to the client's current circumstance or emotional state, the reframe offers new meaning and introduces an alternative perspective (i.e., "at a crossroads" and "you need to take another route") that is more hopeful

(i.e., the client has an opportunity to make a change, and another course of action is possible) than simply validating the client's feeling of "hitting a wall."

Reframes can also alert clients to risks or dangers that they were not aware of or heretofore considered advantageous or at least "no big deal." For example, "holding one's liquor" may not necessarily be a source of pride when reframed as "tolerance" or the body's warning device that it is accommodating a toxin (W. R. Miller & Rollnick, 2002). In addition, being the "good daughter" may have its toll on being the "good wife and mother" if caring for an aging parent is depriving other family members of care and attention. Likewise, "keeping up with the Joneses" or pursuing the status of "super Mom" or "super Dad" may actually create a divide between parent and child valuing extraneous and transient things and modeling superficial character. Additional examples of possible reframes are provided in Box 18.8.

Supporting

Supportive statements are regarded in MI as expressions of agreement, sympathy, and compassion. "I'm here to help you with this" conveys an intention to lend comfort and reassurance and "That must have been difficult" reflects a sympathetic or agreeing quality. In MI, supportive statements differ from affirmations in that supportive comments reflect more of the helper's concern for or investment in the client's well-being, whereas affirmations are intended to point out to the client strengths and resources already in his or her possession. Supportive statements may say more about the helper's qualities (e.g., compassionate, concerned) than about those of the client, whereas affirmations are intended to emphasize the client's qualities.

Support for MI-Consistent Practices

Motivational interviewing was originally conceptualized as a preparation for chemical dependency treatment and mental health services, to increase client engagement and retention in the therapeutic process. Thus, MI is a logical or at least an appropriate approach to use with persons in the early stages of change and with clients who may not see a need to change, may dismiss any offers of assistance, or are otherwise reluctant or ambivalent about change. In addition, MI has demonstrated its adaptability to various settings, populations, and presenting concerns, and it has established itself as a helpful "playmate" when coupled or integrated

BOX 18.8	EXAMPLES OF POSSIBLE REFRAMES	
• Not making a decision right now = Being careful		• Compulsivity = Persistence
• Stubborn = Determined		• Nagging = Concerned
• Selfishness = Self-care		• Failure = Lesson learned
• "Do not resuscitate" = "Allow natural death"		• Dinner leftovers = Extreme makeovers

with cognitive–behavioral and other therapies (Arkowitz & Westra, 2004; Arkowitz, Westra, W. R. Miller, & Rollnick, 2008; Baker et al., 2006; Westra & Dozois, 2006). Indeed, "When MI is used as a prelude to treatment . . . its effects appear to endure across time, suggesting a synergistic effect of MI with other treatment approaches" (Hettema et al., 2005, p. 104). This is particularly true when MI is introduced at the outset of therapy, suggesting that its additive effect is in treatment retention and adherence.

As has been emphasized throughout this chapter, MI is a style of helping, a way of being with and speaking to clients, rather than simply a collection of techniques applied to or on clients (see Rollnick, 2001). Although we have reviewed seven specific strategies of MI (likened to individual musical notes within a song), none contain its essence or its "spirit." MI can be understood and appreciated only by stepping back to see the gestalt or to hear the entire musical score.

Prominent in MI is the theme, strand, or melody of client-centered humanism that emphasizes respect and empathy for others, particularly in the midst of resistance, reluctance, and ambivalence. Although mentioned earlier, the centrality of this value to MI was made evident in a recent study of MI practitioners. Moyers et al. (2005) determined that therapist demonstration of both MI-preferred interpersonal characteristics and MI-consistent behaviors predicted client involvement in sessions, providing support for "particular clinician skills that can be expected to increase client collaboration, disclosure, and expression of affect" (p. 596). Surprisingly, however, MI-inconsistent behaviors did not decrease client involvement in session when clinicians demonstrated such characteristics as warmth, empathy, and acceptance. MI-inconsistent therapist behaviors (e.g., confrontation, directing clients, or giving advice without permission) that occur within an empathic, accepting, and egalitarian interpersonal context "may be consistent with a genuine and authentic stance that is well received by clients and therefore elicits cooperation and increased expression of affect and disclosure" (p. 59). Put in another way, therapists who confront or direct clients within an atmosphere of empathy and acceptance may actually "convey a sense of honesty and transparency on the part of the clinician that may facilitate, rather than suppress, the alliance with the client" (p. 596).

In another study, Moyers and Martin (2006) found that three MI-consistent helper behaviors resulted in an immediate increase in client change talk: (1) generously affirming client strengths, (2) emphasizing personal choice and control or encouraging the client's autonomy in the change process, and (3) seeking permission first before offering advice. These helper behaviors were found to increase the client's verbalization of a desire, ability, reason, and need to change. Notice that they are the first three of seven listed on the left side of Box 18.6. According to Moyers and Martin's research findings, then, these three would be the most important MI-consistent helper behaviors to use in conversations with clients.

MODEL DIALOGUE FOR AFFIRMING, EMPHASIZING AUTONOMY, AND ADVISING ONLY WITH PERMISSION: THE CASE OF ISABELLA

Isabella has indicated that she wants to express herself better in the classroom and with her parents. Specifically, she wants to express differences of opinion and positive feelings. From the work that Isabella has done so far with her helper, it appears that she has made progress toward implementing these skills at school, specifically in her math class. Because of this, the helper now inquires about Isabella's readiness to implement some of these same skills at home with her parents. A motivational interviewing style seems appropriate here because Isabella is ambivalent about talking to her parents about changing her college preparation curriculum.

1. **Helper:** I've been very pleased with how well you've practiced and followed through on many of the skills we've worked on together. From what you've told me, it sounds like you've been able to participate more in math class and have been getting better grades on your assignments.

Client: Yeah, I'm kinda pleased with myself too. It feels good to not feel all out of sorts and worried so much about things when I'm in school.

2. **Helper:** That's great to hear! You have been very open to trying out all these exercises I've suggested. Your cooperation tells me that doing better at school is something that's very important to you. And it sounds like your diligence is now paying off in ways that are evident to you. I'm sure it must feel good to be able to pat yourself on the back for a job well done.

Client: I am kind of proud of myself. And it does feel good to know this is something I've done, that I can give myself credit for, not something someone else has done for me.

The helper has been intentional to offer Isabella several *affirmations* about the progress she has made thus far.

3. **Helper:** I remember that in addition to being able to speak up in math class, you wanted to be able to talk with your parents more confidently about things. We haven't talked about that in a while. How is that going?

Client: Well, of course they're really happy about how I'm doing now in school. They've said, "See, we knew you could do it. You just had to put your mind to it." So now the pressure's on to continue to do well, to not disappoint them. It's like they've had in mind what I should be doing, what I should be studying, and they're pleased as punch that I've "come around" to finally see things their way. But I don't know if I want to do what they want me to do.

4. **Helper:** You'd like to be able to make some of your own decisions about what to study.

In response 4, the helper offers a *simple reflection* that can serve to affirm Isabella, for its purpose is to convey that she has been heard and understood. In addition, the helper validates Isabella's desire to have some control over deciding what she wants to study.

Client: Exactly. Doing better in math has made me think that there are other things I can do well that I hadn't considered before. But I know my parents, especially my dad, would go ballistic if he knew what I've been thinking I'd really like to study someday.

5. **Helper:** Your increased self-confidence has fueled your interest in other areas, areas that may not be in sync with those your parents have in mind for you.

Notice that in response 5, the helper does not ask Isabella what it is she'd like to study someday. Instead, the helper offers another *simple reflection*. Recall that reflections should be at least twice the number of questions asked in motivational interviewing. The helper may be thinking that the specific area of study Isabella has in mind is secondary to Isabella's concern about her parents' reaction. Asking about the area of study may only satisfy the helper's curiosity. Isabella is free to disclose this information without being asked directly about it.

Client: Yeah. It's like they'll only support me if I'm studying what they want me to study.

6. **Helper:** And you want to have a little more control over what that is but not lose their support entirely.

In response 6, the helper uses a *double-sided reflection* that acknowledges both sides of Isabella's ambivalence—having more control on the one hand and not losing her parents' support on the other.

Client: Maybe that's selfish, though. Maybe I should just give in and do what they want me to do, especially if I want them to pay for it—college, that is.

7. **Helper:** Well, I have some thoughts about this. Would you like to hear what they are? [Helper *asks for permission* before offering any observation, insight, or advice.]

Client: Sure.

8. **Helper:** I could be wrong, but I don't think you "just gave in" to your anxieties about math class. Seems to me you tackled them head-on by using some of the relaxation, imagery, and coping thought skills we practiced together. So, I'm sitting here wondering how you can not "just give in" to what you think are your parents' expectations and use some of the same skills in your conversation with your parents that you've used to help you in math class. What do you think? [Helper ends by inviting feedback from the client.]

Client: You mean do some of the same things that have helped me in math with my parents?

9. **Helper:** Yes. I'm wondering if what's been helpful to you in math class might be helpful to you in your conversations with your parents. You've been able to speak up in class, for example. And it doesn't sound like you've done this inappropriately. So, I wonder how you can speak up or voice your own interests to your parents about what you really want to study and do this appropriately—in a calm, confident, and matter-of-fact manner. Does this make sense?

Client: I think so. Although I'm not sure I could do it.

10. **Helper:** You're not sure *right now* that you can. [Helper offers an *amplified reflection,* emphasizing the temporal aspect of Isabella's uncertainty. This opens up the possibility that she may not remain uncertain, that it may be just right now that she's not quite sure.]

Client: [Sighs] I do want to be able to talk to my parents. And I would like to be able to study what I want to study.

11. **Helper:** Talking with your parents in a way you'd like to be able to is something we could practice in here, just like we practiced the skills you've used for school. You don't have to do this, though. It is your choice.

In response 11, the helper reinforces Isabella's *autonomy,* saying that it is her decision whether to practice initiating skills to be used in her conversations with her parents.

Client: Well, maybe it's worth a try. I mean I didn't think a while ago that I'd be able to speak up in math class, and now I'm able to do it. So, maybe this is possible too.

12. **Helper:** Step-by-step, right?

Client: Yep. That's one of the things I've learned—that change takes time and that it's definitely not a piece of cake!

| LEARNING ACTIVITY | **18.5** | **Practicing MI Consistently** |

This activity lets you try your hand at detecting MI-consistent helper behaviors and offer alternative responses to those that are MI-inconsistent. Read through each of the following client statements, and then determine whether the helper responses *are* consistent with MI or not. If they are, identify what *types,* of helper responses they are from the 7 presented in Box 18.6. If the helper responses are *not* consistent with MI, identify what kinds they are (from the list of 5 presented in Box 18.6), then *rewrite* different responses that are MI-consistent, and explain what types of response they are. Feedback follows on pages 592–593.

1. **Client:** Why are you giving me this booklet? Are you telling me I have to use condoms?
   a. "It's just information. What you do with it is up to you. Naturally, no one can make you use condoms."
   b. "I've thought that if you don't start wearing condoms, you're eventually going to have more than one child support payment to make."
   c. "I'm concerned about you and want you to have some information that you might find helpful."

2. **Client:** I was told I only had to come here for an "evaluation." No one said anything to me about attending "therapy." So, you telling me I have to come back for some group therapy sessions is a load of crap!
   a. "You're not happy about my recommendation and believe you've been misinformed about—maybe even tricked into—coming here."
   b. "I do have another thought here. I could be off, but see what you think. Because you said you feel like no one's taking you seriously, I'm wondering if you at least attended one group session, just to try it

out, I'm wondering if that might show that you are serious about doing something. Again, I could be wrong, but I'm thinking your attendance in at least one session would actually be in your favor."
   c. "Well, I do think it would be good for you to attend at least one group session."

3. **Client:** I really don't know what all the fuss is about. All of my friends drink and we have a good time. Isn't that what college is for? Yeah, my grades could be better, I'd have more money to spend on other things, and my parents would back off.
   a. "Sounds like you've given this a lot of thought, and you see some connection between your drinking and the hassles you've been dealing with."
   b. "You are young, though, and I wouldn't want to see you get into any more trouble."
   c. "Sounds like you've been having too much fun and not concentrating enough on your studies. I guess I think that *studying* is what college is for, not partying."

4. **Client:** My boss says *I'm* the one with the "anger management" problem. Hell, *he's* the guy who's always out of control!
   a. "Well, you're the one who's here, not your boss, so we'll need to focus on you in our conversations, not him."
   b. "What do you think are your boss's reasons for saying you needed to come to counseling?"
   c. "It's not fair to you that you've gotten the short end of the stick, but I'm thinking you might have some advantage here. Who knows? You might just be able to model appropriate behavior to him as you learn more about anger management here."

To help you determine whether certain helper responses are MI-consistent or MI-inconsistent, we encourage you to participate in Learning Activity 18.5. This activity also challenges you to offer alternative and more appropriate helper responses in your effort to practice MI consistently. Feedback follows on pages 592–593.

APPLICATIONS OF SFT AND MI WITH DIVERSE GROUPS

Both SFT and MI have been heralded as suitable and helpful therapeutic approaches for diverse populations. This is particularly encouraging given the barriers to accessing proper mental health services faced by many racial and ethnic mi-

norities (U.S. Department of Health and Human Services, 2001). Among these barriers are cost of care, societal stigma, clinician's lack of awareness of cultural issues, and the client's fear and mistrust of professional help. Working with resistance may therefore allow SFT and MI to be particularly useful for clients from cultural backgrounds who are initially skeptical or suspicious of such care. The humanistic, nondirective, and client–helper collaborative philosophy of both SFT and MI can serve as a nonthreatening invitation to prospective and recent clients to engage in services.

SFT has been described as appropriate for use with ethnic minority (namely African American, Mexican American, Asian American) families (Corcoran, 2000; Lee & Mjelde-Mossey, 2004) and individuals (Berg & Miller, 1992a),

	FEEDBACK		
18.5	**Practicing MI Consistently**		

MI-Consistent? or MI-Inconsistent?	**Type of MI-Consistent Helper Behavior**	**Type of MI-Inconsistent Helper Behavior**	**Rewrite of MI-Inconsistent Helper Response**
1. a. MI-Consistent	Emphasize persona choice and control/ Encourage client autonomy		
1. b. MI-Inconsistent		Warn	No, I'm not here to tell you what to do. You strike me as one who wants to make his own decisions, so I thought this booklet might help you in the process. (Affirm)
1. c. MI-Consistent	Support		
2. a. MI-Consistent	Reflect		
2. b. MI-Consistent	Advise with permission		
2. c. MI-Inconsistent		Advise without permission	It really is your choice whether or not you want to take me up on my recommendation. (Emphasize personal choice and control)
3. a. MI-Consistent	Affirm		
3. b. MI-Inconsistent		Raise concern without permission	On the one hand, you're having a good time drinking. On the other hand, you're able to see some specific benefits to you of not drinking. (Double-sided reflection)
3. c. MI-Inconsistent		Direct	You're confused about why your drinking is such a concern. (Simple reflection)

18.5	**F E E D B A C K** **Practicing MI Consistently**			
4. a. MI-Inconsistent			Confront	Sounds like you're pretty perceptive about others and you have some insight about what could be helpful in our work together. (Affirm)
4. b. MI-Consistent	Ask open-ended questions			
4. c. MI-Consistent	Reframe			

Appalachian individuals (Gunn, 2001), and Hispanic children of incarcerated parents (Springer, Lynch, & Rubin, 2000). Given SFT's emphasis on the utilization of client (and community) strengths and resources, it certainly represents an empowerment approach typically recommended for working with diverse populations. In addition, the pragmatic features of SFT may make it somewhat appealing (or professional care less stigmatizing) to those from various cultural backgrounds. Indeed, Lee (2003) explained that "Solution-focused therapy is goal-oriented and emphasizes clear indicators of progress, consistent with the pragmatic, problem-solving orientation shared by ethnic and racial groups that stress collectivism" (p. 390).

As the review of MI research earlier in this chapter indicated (see Hettema et al., 2005), MI and adaptations of MI appear to result in beneficial outcomes for minorities more so than for White clients. Although this differential has not been fully explained, it may be that MI's primary focus on ambivalence makes it particularly suitable for persons who are quite familiar with a life of tension and struggling against opposing forces. It may also be that MI's respectful manner that evokes rather than installs change is received as a breath of fresh air by those who have experienced various forms of discrimination and oppression.

Roberts and Nishimoto (2006) recommended a combination of SFT and MI in working with African American women (specifically postpartum) in drug treatment. They described SFT as useful in providing hope by helping female clients focus more on "high-success" situations or "multiple episodes of sobriety" than on "high-risk" situations or "chronic relapses" (see Berg & Miller, 1992b; Mason, Chandler, & Grasso, 1995) and that MI is helpful in exploring with clients their internal motivation. Roberts and Nishimoto stated that "examining internal barriers may be associated with blaming

the victim, but this is not necessarily so. Examining internal barriers provides opportunities for. . . . practitioners to become competent in exploring and addressing issues of inner motivation, especially in light of the reality that a number of subjects are mandated to treatment" (p. 67).

CHAPTER SUMMARY

Perhaps resistance has been presented in a new or different light in this chapter, not as something to be attacked head-on or avoided but as something to be accepted and worked through in collaboration with clients. It may also be that understanding resistance as a "two-person operation" (i.e., something that client and helper generate and participate in together) rather than as solely a client characteristic and problem may open up more options for helpers. There may be more ways of working with resistance than practitioners may have first thought.

Solution-focused therapy (SFT) and motivational interviewing (MI) do represent what we believe are helpful ways to work with resistance with our clients. Their shared and complementary philosophies allow them to work in tandem for the benefit of clients and helpers. Indeed, Lewis and Osborn (2004) presented seven similarities between SFT and MI and five differences, all of them listed in Box 18.9. They further described the integration of SFT and MI as a confluence and proposed three features of such a "synergistic emergence" (p. 45). First, they noted that *honoring client stories* bolsters the full participation of both client and helper in the helping process. Second, *motivation* and *ambivalence* are regarded as *resources for change*, and third, *change occurs in relation*. They stated that when SFT and MI are intertwined, "change is understood in terms of conversational or relational movements or fluctuations

BOX 18.9	COMPARISON OF SFT AND MI

SFT and MI Similarities

1. Nonpathological, salutary focus
2. Multiple perspectives
3. Anchored in change
4. Reframing "resistance"
5. Cooperation is key
6. Use of client strengths and resources
7. Temporal sensitivity

SFT and MI Differences

1. Social construction through language
2. Concept of change
3. Counselor focus and goals
4. Temporal focus
5. Reflectivity

Source: Lewis & Osborn, 2004.

over time, illustrating the systemic, holistic, dynamic or interactional, and recursive nature of counseling and the counseling process" (p. 46).

Lewis and Osborn (2004) conjectured that the confluence of SFT and MI can bolster the process of change by offering multiple passages through the challenges and impasses experienced during the change process. Client strengths and the resources present in the helping relationship itself can be utilized to work with and through resistance, representing an example of solution construction.

As we have reflected on SFT and MI, a vivid and compelling image has emerged to describe their integrated approach to working with resistance: "dancing with curiosity." This image combines W. R. Miller and Rollnick's (2002) characterization of the helping relationship as a dance and Shilts and Thomas's (2005) reframe of resistance as curiosity. We believe that both clients and helpers benefit when they assume a posture of intrigue or curiosity during their collaborative effort (i.e., dance) to construct a more manageable and hopeful reality for the client.

REFERENCES

Amrhein, P. C. (2004). How does motivational interviewing work? What client talk reveals. *Journal of Cognitive Psychotherapy, 18,* 323–336.

Amrhein, P. C., Miller, W. R., Yahne, C. E., Palmer, M., & Fulcher, L. (2003). Client commitment language during motivational interviewing predicts drug use concerns. *Journal of Consulting and Clinical Psychology, 71,* 862–878.

Anderson, H. (1997). *Conversation, language, and possibilities: A postmodern approach to therapy.* New York: Basic.

Anderson, H., & Goolishian, H. (1992). The client is the expert: A not-knowing approach to therapy. In S. McNamee & K. J. Gergen (Eds.), *Therapy as social construction* (pp. 25–39). Newbury Park, CA: Sage.

Arkowitz, H. (2002). Toward an integrative perspective on resistance to change. *Journal of Clinical Psychology, 58,* 219–227.

Arkowitz, H., & Westra, H. A. (2004). Integrating motivational interviewing and cognitive behavioral therapy in the treatment of depression and anxiety. *Journal of Cognitive Psychotherapy, 18,* 337–350.

Arkowitz, H., Westra, H. A., Miller, W. R., & Rollnick, S. (Eds.). (2008). *Motivational interviewing in the treatment of psychological problems.* New York: Guilford Press.

Baer, J. S., Kivlahan, D. R., Blume, A. W., McKnight, P., & Marlatt, G. A. (2001). Brief intervention for heavy-drinking college students: 4-year follow-up and natural history. *American Journal of Public Health, 91,* 1310–1316.

Baker, A., Bucci, S., Lewin, T. J., Kay-Lambkin, F., Constable, P. M., & Carr, V. J. (2006). Cognitive–behavioural therapy for substance use disorders in people with psychotic disorders: Randomised controlled trial. *British Journal of Psychiatry, 188,* 439–448.

Bellack, A. S., Bennett, M. E., Gearon, J. S., Brown, C. H., & Yang, Y. (2006). A randomized clinical trial of a new behavioral treatment for drug abuse in people with severe and persistent mental illness. *Archives of General Psychiatry, 63,* 426–432.

Bennett, J. A., Lyons, K. S., Winters-Stone, K., Nail, L. M., & Scherer, J. (2007). Motivational interviewing to increase physical activity in long-term cancer survivors: A randomized controlled trial. *Nursing Research, 56,* 18–27.

Berg, I. K., & de Shazer, S. (1993). Making numbers talk: Language in therapy. In S. Friedman (Ed.), *The new language of change: Constructive collaboration in psychotherapy* (pp. 5–24). New York: Guilford Press.

Berg, I. K., & Miller, S. D. (1992a). Working with Asian American clients: One person at a time. *Families in Society: The Journal of Contemporary Human Services, 73*(6), 356–363.

Berg, I. K., & Miller, S. D. (1992b). *Working with the problem drinker: A solution-focused approach.* New York: Norton.

Beutler, L. E., & Harwood, T. M. (2000). *Prescriptive psychotherapy: A practical guide to systematic treatment selection.* New York: Oxford University Press.

Beutler, L. E., Moleiro, C. M., & Talebi, H. (2002). Resistance. In J. C. Norcross (Ed.), *Psychotherapy relationships that work: Therapist contributions and responsiveness to patients* (pp. 129–143). New York: Oxford University Press.

Bishop, W., & Fish, J. M. (1999). Questions as interventions: Perceptions of Socratic, solution focused, and diagnostic questioning styles. *Journal of Rational–Emotive & Cognitive–Behavior Therapy, 17*, 115–140.

Bray, M. A., & Kehle, T. J. (1996). Self-modeling as an intervention for stuttering. *School Psychology Review, 25*, 358–369.

Burke, B. L., Arkowitz, H., & Menchola, M. (2003). The efficacy of motivational interviewing: A meta-analysis of controlled clinical trials. *Journal of Consulting and Clinical Psychology, 71*, 843–861.

Burke, B. L., Dunn, C. W., Atkins, D. C., & Phelps, J. S. (2004). The emerging evidence base for motivational interviewing: A meta-analytic and qualitative inquiry. *Journal of Cognitive Psychotherapy, 18*, 309–322.

Campbell, J., Elder, J., Gallagher, D., Simon, J., & Taylor, A. (1999). Crafting the "tap on the shoulder": A compliment template for solution-focused therapy. *American Journal of Family Therapy, 27*, 35–47.

Carels, R. A., Darby, L., Cacciapaglia, H. M., Konrad, K., Coit, C., Harper, J., et al. (2007). Using motivational interviewing as a supplement to obesity treatment: A stepped-care approach. *Health Psychology, 26*, 369–374.

Carey, K. B., Carey, M. P., Maisto, S. A., & Henson, J. M. (2006). Brief motivational interventions for heavy college drinkers: A randomized controlled trial. *Journal of Consulting and Clinical Psychology, 74*, 943–954.

Corcoran, J. (2000). Solution-focused family therapy with ethnic minority clients. *Crisis Intervention, 6*, 5–12.

Corcoran, J. (2005). *Building strengths and skills: A collaborative approach to working with clients.* New York: Oxford University Press.

Cullari, S. (1996). *Treatment resistance: A guide for practitioners.* Boston: Allyn & Bacon.

Davis, T. E., & Osborn, C. J. (2000). *The solution-focused school counselor: Shaping professional practice.* Philadelphia: Accelerated Development/Taylor & Francis.

de Shazer, S. (1984). The death of resistance. *Family Process, 23*, 11–17.

de Shazer, S. (1985). *Keys to solution in brief therapy.* New York: W. W. Norton.

de Shazer, S., & Berg, I. K. (1992). Doing therapy: A post-structural re-vision. *Journal of Marital and Family Therapy, 18*, 71–81.

de Shazer, S., & Isebaert, L. (2003). The Bruges Model: A solution-focused approach to problem drinking. *Journal of Family Psychotherapy, 14*(4), 43–52.

DiClemente, C. C. (2003). *Addiction and change: How addictions develop and addicted people recover.* New York: Guilford Press.

Donohoe, G. (2006). Adherence to antipsychotic treatment in schizophrenia: What role does cognitive behavioral therapy play in improving outcomes? *Disease Management and Health Outcomes, 14*, 207–214.

Dunn, C., Deroo, L., & Rivara, F. P. (2001). The use of brief interventions adapted from motivational interviewing across behavioral domains: A systematic review. *Addiction, 96*, 1725–1742.

Efran, J. S., & Cook, P. F. (2000). Linguistic ambiguity as a diagnostic tool. In R. A. Neimeyer & J. D. Raskin (Eds.), *Constructions of disorder: Meaning-making frameworks for psychotherapy* (pp. 121–144). Washington, DC: American Psychological Association.

Egan, G. (2007). *The skilled helper* (8th ed.). Belmont, CA: Thomson–Brooks/Cole.

Engle, D. E., & Arkowitz, H. (2006). *Ambivalence in psychotherapy: Facilitating a readiness to change.* New York: Guilford Press.

Erickson, M. H. (1954). Special techniques of brief hypnotherapy. *Journal of Clinical and Experimental Hypnosis, 2*, 109–129.

Fish, J. M. (1997). Paradox for complainants? Strategic thoughts about solution-focused therapy. *Journal of Systemic Therapies, 16*, 266–273.

Gingerich, W. J., & Eisengart, S. (2000). Solution-focused brief therapy: A review of the outcome research. *Family Process, 39*, 477–498.

Graeber, D. A., Moyers, T. B., Griffith, G., Guajardo, E., & Tonigan, S. (2003). A pilot study comparing motivational interviewing and an educational intervention in patients with schizophrenia and alcohol use disorders. *Community Mental Health Journal, 39*, 189–202.

Gunn, C. (2001). Chapter 2: Flight of the Appalachian bumblebee: Solution-oriented brief therapy with a young adult. *Journal of College Student Psychotherapy, 16*, 13–25.

Haley, J. (Ed.). (1967). *Advanced techniques of hypnosis and therapy: Selected papers of Milton H. Erickson, M. D.* Boston: Allyn & Bacon.

Hettema, J., Steele, J., & Miller, W. R. (2005). Motivational interviewing. *Annual Review of Clinical Psychology, 1*, 91–111.

Iguchi, M. Y., Belding, M. A., Morral, A. R., Lamb, R. J., & Husband, S. D. (1997). Reinforcing operants other than abstinence in drug abuse treatment: An effective alternative for reducing drug use. *Journal of Counseling and Clinical Psychology, 65*, 421–428.

John, U., Veltrup, C., Driessen, M., Wetterling, T., & Dilling, H. (2003). Motivational intervention: An individual counseling vs. a group treatment approach for alcohol-dependent in-patients. *Alcohol and Alcoholism, 38*, 263–269.

Kelly, A. B., & Lapworth, K. (2006). The HYP program–Targeted motivational interviewing for adolescent violations of school tobacco policy. *Preventive Medicine: An International Journal Devoted to Practice and Theory, 43,* 466–471.

Kemp, R., David, A., & Hayward, P. (1996). Compliance therapy: An intervention targeting insight and treatment adherence in psychotic patients. *Behavioural and Cognitive Psychotherapy, 24,* 331–350.

Kiene, S. M., & Barta, W. D. (2006). A brief individualized computer-delivered sexual risk reduction intervention increases HIV/AIDS preventive behavior. *Journal of Adolescent Health, 39,* 404–410.

Kitchener, K. S. (2000). *Foundations of ethical practice, research, and teaching in psychology.* Mahwah, NJ: Lawrence Erlbaum.

Knight, K. M., Bundy, C., Morris, R., Higgs, J. F., Jameson, R. A., Unsworth, P., & Jayson, D. (2003). The effects of group motivational interviewing and externalizing conversations for adolescents with type 1 diabetes. *Psychology, Health and Medicine, 8,* 149–157.

LaBrie, J. W., Lamb, T. F., Pedersen, E. R., & Quinlan, T. (2006). A group motivational interviewing intervention reduces drinking and alcohol-related consequences in adjudicated college students. *Journal of College Student Development, 47,* 267–280.

Lawson, D. (1994). Identifying pretreatment change. *Journal of Counseling and Development, 72,* 244–248.

Lee, M. Y. (2003). A solution-focused approach to cross-cultural clinical social work practice: Utilizing cultural strengths. *Families in Society, 84,* 385–395.

Lee, M. Y., & Mjelde-Mossey, L. (2004). Cultural dissonance among generations: A solution-focused approach with East Asian elders and their families. *Journal of Marital and Family Therapy, 30,* 497–513.

Lewis, T. F., & Osborn, C. J. (2004). Solution-focused counseling and motivational interviewing: A consideration of confluence. *Journal of Counseling and Development, 82,* 38–48.

Lipchik, E., & de Shazer, S. (1986). The purposeful interview. *Journal of Strategic and Systemic Therapies, 5*(1 and 2), 88–99.

Mahalik, J. R. (1994). Development of the client resistance scale. *Journal of Counseling Psychology, 41,* 58–68.

Mason, W. H., Chandler, M. C., & Grasso, B. C. (1995). Solution based techniques applied to addictions: A clinic's experience in shifting paradigms. *Alcoholism Treatment Quarterly, 13*(4), 39–49.

McGarty, R. (1985). Relevance of Ericksonian psychotherapy to the treatment of chemical dependency. *Journal of Substance Abuse Treatment, 2,* 147–151.

Mental Illness Education Project. (Producer). (2000). *Dual diagnosis: An integrated model for the treatment of people with co-occurring psychiatric and substance disorders. A lecture by Kenneth Minkoff, M.D.* (Video available from Mental Illness Education Project Videos, 22-D Hollywood Ave., Hohokus, NJ 07423).

Michael, K. D., Curtin, L., Kirkley. D. E., Jones, D. L., & Harris, R., Jr. (2006). Group-based motivational interviewing for alcohol use among college students: An exploratory study. *Professional Psychology: Research and Practice, 37,* 629–634.

Miller, G. (1997). Systems and solutions: The discourses of brief therapy. *Contemporary Family Therapy, 19*(1), 5–22.

Miller, G., & de Shazer, S. (1998). Have you heard the latest rumor about . . . ? Solution-focused brief therapy as a rumor. *Family Process, 37,* 363–377.

Miller, S. D. (1992). The symptoms of solution. *Journal of Strategic and Systemic Therapies, 11,* 1–11.

Miller, S. D. (1994). The solution conspiracy: A mystery in three installments. *Journal of Systemic Therapies, 13,* 18–37.

Miller, W. R. (Ed.). (1999). *Enhancing motivation for change in substance abuse treatment,* Treatment Improvement Protocol Series 35 (DHHS Publication No. SMA 99-3354). Rockville, MD: U.S. Department of Health and Human Services.

Miller, W. R. (2000). Rediscovering fire: Small interventions, large effects. *Psychology of Addictive Behaviors, 14,* 6–18.

Miller, W. R., Benefield, R. G., & Tonigan, J. S. (1993). Enhancing motivation for change in problem drinking: A controlled comparison of two therapist styles. *Journal of Consulting and Clinical Psychology, 61,* 455–461.

Miller, W. R., & Moyers, T. B. (2006). Eight stages in learning motivational interviewing. *Journal of Teaching in the Addictions, 5,* 3–17.

Miller, W. R., Moyers, T. B., Ernst, D., & Amrhein, P. (2003). *Manual for the motivational interviewing skill code (MISC).* Center on Alcoholism, Substance Abuse and Addiction (CASAA), University of New Mexico. Retrieved from http://casaa.unm.edu/download/misc.pdf

Miller, W. R., & Rollnick, S. (1991). *Motivational interviewing: Preparing people to change addictive behavior.* New York: Guilford Press.

Miller, W. R., & Rollnick, S. (2002). *Motivational interviewing: Preparing people for change* (2nd ed.). New York: Guilford Press.

Miller, W. R., & Rollnick, S. (2004). Talking oneself into change: Motivational interviewing, stages of change, and therapeutic process. *Journal of Cognitive Psychotherapy, 18,* 299–308.

Miller, W. R., Yahne, C. E., Moyers, T. B., Martinez, J., & Pirritano, M. (2004). A randomized trial of methods to help clinicians learn motivational interviewing. *Journal of Consulting and Clinical Psychology, 72,* 1050–1062.

Miron, A. M., & Brehm, J. W. (2006). Reactance theory—40 years later. *Zeitschrift für Sozialpsychologie, 37,* 9–18.

Moyers, T. B. (2004). History and happenstance: How motivational interviewing got its start. *Journal of Cognitive Psychotherapy, 18,* 291–298.

Moyers, T. B., & Martin, T. (2006). Therapist influence on client language during motivational interviewing sessions. *Journal of Substance Abuse Treatment, 30,* 245–251.

Moyers, T. B., Miller, W. R., & Hendrickson, S. M. L. (2005). How does motivational interviewing work? Therapist interpersonal skill predicts client involvement within motivational interviewing sessions. *Journal of Consulting and Clinical Psychology, 73,* 590–598.

Moyers, T. B., & Rollnick, S. (2002). A motivational interviewing perspective on resistance in psychotherapy. *Journal of Clinical Psychology, 58,* 185–193.

Newman, C. F. (2002). A cognitive perspective on resistance in psychotherapy. *Journal of Clinical Psychology, 58,* 165–174.

Noonan, W. C., & Moyers, T. B. (1997). Motivational interviewing. *Journal of Substance Misuse, 2,* 8–16.

Norcross, J. C., Hedges, M., & Prochaska, J. O. (2002). The face of 2010: A Delphi poll on the future of psychotherapy. *Professional Psychology: Research and Practice, 33,* 316–322.

Nunnally, E. (1993). Solution focused therapy. In R. A. Wells and V. J. Giannetti (Eds.), *Casebook of the brief psychotherapies* (pp. 271–286). New York: Plenum.

Nylund, D., & Corsiglia, V. (1994). Becoming solution-focused forced in brief therapy: Remembering something important we already knew. *Journal of Systemic Therapies, 13,* 5–12.

O'Hanlon, B., & Weiner-Davis, M. (2003). *In search of solutions: A new direction in psychotherapy* (Rev. ed.). New York: Norton.

Osborn, C. J. (1999). Solution-focused strategies with "involuntary" clients: Practical applications for the school and clinical setting. *Journal of Humanistic Education and Development, 37,* 169–181.

Parsons, J. T., Rosof, E., Punzalan, J. C., & Di Maria, L. (2005). Integration of motivational interviewing and cognitive behavioral therapy to improve HIV medication adherence and reduce substance use among HIV-positive men and women: Results of a pilot project. *AIDS Patient Care and STDs, 19,* 31–39.

Patterson, G. R., & Forgatch, M. S. (1985). Therapist behavior as a determinant for client noncompliance: A paradox for the behavior modifier. *Journal of Consulting and Clinical Psychology, 53,* 846–851.

Peterson, P. P. L., Baer, J. S., Wells, E. A., Ginzler, J. A., & Garrett, S. B. (2006). Short-term effects of a brief motivational intervention to reduce alcohol and drug risk among homeless adolescents. *Psychology of Addictive Behaviors, 20,* 254–264.

Picciano, J. F., Roffman, R. A., Kalichman, S. C., Rutledge, S. E., & Berghuis, J. P. (2001). A telephone based brief intervention using motivational enhancement to facilitate HIV risk reduction among MSM: A pilot study. *AIDS and Behavior, 5,* 251–262.

Prochaska, J. O., & DiClemente, C. (1982). Transtheoretical therapy: Towards a more integrative model of change. *Psychotherapy, 19,* 276–278.

Prochaska, J. O., & Norcross, J. C. (2001). Stages of change. *Psychotherapy, 38,* 443–448.

Prochaska, J. O., & Norcross, J. C. (2007). *Systems of psychotherapy: A transtheoretical analysis* (6th ed.). Belmont, CA: Brooks/Cole.

Rappaport, R. L. (1997). *Motivating clients in therapy: Values, love, and the real relationship.* New York: Routledge.

Rennie, D. L. (1994). Clients' deference in psychotherapy. *Journal of Counseling Psychology, 41,* 427–437.

Resnicow, K., DiIorio, C., Soet, J. E., Borrelli, B., Ernst, D., Hecht, J., & Thevos, A. K. (2002). Motivational interviewing in medical and public health settings. In W. R. Miller & S. Rollnick (Eds.), *Motivational interviewing: Preparing people for change* (pp. 251–269). New York: Guilford Press.

Resnicow, K., Jackson, A., Wang, T., De, A. K., McCarty, F., Dudley, W. N., & Baranowski, T. (2001). A motivational interviewing intervention to increase fruit and vegetable intake through Black churches: Results of the Eat for Life trial. *American Journal of Public Health, 91,* 1686–1693.

Riegel, B., Dickson, V. V., Hoke, L., McMahon, J. P., Reis, B. F., & Sayers, S. (2006). A motivational counseling approach to improving heart failure self-care: Mechanisms of effectiveness. *Journal of Cardiovascular Nursing, 21,* 232–241.

Ritchie, M. H. (1986). Counseling the involuntary client. *Journal of Counseling and Development, 64,* 516–518.

Roberts, A. C., & Nishimoto, R. (2006). Barriers to engaging and retaining African-American post-partum women in drug treatment. *Journal of Drug Issues, 36,* 53–76.

Rollnick, S. (2001). Enthusiasm, quick fixes and premature controlled trials: A commentary. *Addiction, 96,* 1769–1775.

Rollnick, S., & Miller, W. R. (1995). What is motivational interviewing? *Behavioural and Cognitive Psychotherapy, 23,* 325–334.

Safran, J. D., & Muran, J. C. (2000). *Negotiating the therapeutic alliance: A relational treatment guide.* New York: Guilford Press.

Safran, J. D., Muran, C., & Samstag, L. W. (1994). Resolving therapeutic alliance ruptures: A task analytic investigation. In A. O. Horvath & L. S. Greenberg (Eds.), *The working alliance: Theory, research, and practice* (pp. 225–255). New York: Wiley.

Schilling, R. F., El-Bassel, N., Finch, J. B., Roman, R. J., & Hanson, M. (2002). Motivational interviewing to encourage self-help participation following alcohol detoxification. *Research on Social Work Practice, 12,* 711–730.

Selekman, M. D. (1993). *Pathways to change: Brief therapy solutions with difficult adolescents.* New York: Guilford Press.

Shilts, L., & Thomas, K. A. (2005). Becoming solution-focused: Some beginning thoughts. *Journal of Family Psychotherapy, 16*(1–2), 189–197.

Shoham, V., Rohrbaugh, M., & Patterson, J. (1995). Problem- and solution-focused couple therapies: The MRI and Milwaukee models. In N. S. Jacobson & A. E. Gurman (Eds.), *Clinical handbook of couple therapy* (pp. 142–163). New York: Guilford Press.

Skovholt, T. M. (2001). *The resilient practitioner: Burnout prevention and self-care strategies for counselors, therapists, teachers, and health professionals.* Boston: Allyn & Bacon.

Springer, D. W., Lynch, C., & Rubin, A. (2000). Effects of a solution-focused mutual aid group for Hispanic children of incarcerated parents. *Child and Adolescent Social Work Journal, 17,* 431–442.

Stalker, C. A., Levene, J. E., & Coady, N. F. (1999). Solution-focused brief therapy—One model fits all? *Families in Society, 80,* 468–477.

Stein, L. A. R., Colby, S. M., Barnett, M. P., Monti, P. M., Golembeske, C., Lebeau-Craven, R., & Miranda, R. (2006). Enhancing substance abuse treatment engagement in incarcerated adolescents. *Psychological Services, 3,* 25–34.

Steinberg, M. L., Ziedonis, D. M., Krejci, J. A., & Brandon, T. H. (2004). Motivational interviewing with personalized feedback: A brief intervention for motivating smokers with schizophrenia to seek treatment for tobacco dependence. *Journal of Consulting and Clinical Psychology, 72,* 723–728.

Stotts, A. L., DiClemete, C. C., & Dolan-Mullen, P. (2002). One-to-one: A motivational intervention for resistant pregnant smokers. *Addictive Behaviors, 27,* 275–292.

Stotts, A. L., Potts, G. F., Ingersoll, G., George, M. R., & Martin, L. E. (2007). Preliminary feasibility and efficacy of a brief motivational intervention with psychophysiological feedback for cocaine abuse. *Substance Abuse, 27*(4), 9–20.

Stotts, A. L., Schmitz, J. M., Rhoades, H. M., & Grabowski, J. (2001). Motivational interviewing with cocaine-dependent patients: A pilot study. *Journal of Consulting and Clinical Psychology, 69,* 858–862.

Strong, T. (2002). Constructive curiosities. *Journal of Systemic Therapies, 21*(1), 77–90.

Thrasher, A. D., Golin, C. E., Earp, J. A. L., Tien, H., Porter, C., & Howie, L. (2006). Motivational interviewing to support antiretroviral therapy adherence: The role of quality counseling. *Patient Education and Counseling, 62,* 64–71.

Trepper, T. S., Dolan, Y., McCollum, E. E., & Nelson, T. (2006). Steve de Shazer and the future of solution-focused therapy. *Journal of Marital and Family Therapy, 32,* 133–139.

Tyson, E. H., & Baffour, T. D. (2004). Arts-based strengths: A solution-focused intervention with adolescents in an acute-care psychiatric facility. *The Arts in Psychotherapy, 31,* 213–227.

U.S. Department of Health and Human Services. (2001). *Mental health: Culture, race, and ethnicity—A supplement to mental health: A report of the Surgeon General.* Rockville, MD: U.S. Department of Health and Human Services, Public Health Service, Office of the Surgeon General.

Vasilaki, E. I., Hosier, S. G., Cox, W. M. (2006). The efficacy of motivational interviewing as a brief intervention for excessive drinking: A meta-analytic review. *Alcohol and Alcoholism, 41,* 328–335.

Viner, R. M., Christie, D., Taylor, V., & Hey, S. (2003). Motivational/solution-focused intervention improves HbA_{1c} in adolescents with Type 1 diabetes: A pilot study. *Diabetic Medicine, 20,* 739–742.

Walter, J. L., & Peller, J. E. (1992). *Becoming solution-focused in brief therapy.* New York: Brunner/Mazel.

Weiner-Davis, M., de Shazer, S., & Gingerich, W. J. (1987). Building on pretreatment change to construct the therapeutic solution: An exploratory study. *Journal of Marital and Family Therapy, 13,* 359–363.

Westra, H. A., & Dozois, D. J. A. (2006). Preparing clients for cognitive–behavioral therapy: A randomized pilot study of motivational interviewing for anxiety. *Cognitive Therapy and Research, 30,* 481–498.

Wilhelm, S. L., Stepans, M. B. F., Hertzog, M., Rodehorst, T. K. C., & Gardner, P. (2006). Motivational interviewing to promote sustained breastfeeding. *Journal of Obstetric, Gynecologic, and Neonatal Nursing: Clinical Scholarship for the Care of Women, Childbearing Families, and Newborns, 35,* 340–348.

Zuckoff, A., Swartz, H. A., & Grote, N. K. (2008). Motivational interviewing as a prelude to psychotherapy of depression. In H. Arkowitz, H. A. Westra, W. R. Miller, & S. Rollnick (Eds.), *Motivational interviewing in the treatment of psychological problems* (pp. 109–144). New York: Guilford Press.

18

 This activity is intended to address Learning Outcomes 1, 2, and 3. It is designed to assess your ability to identify solution-focused-therapy (SFT) and motivational interviewing (MI) intervention approaches in a client–helper interaction.

Read through the case of Vince and the recent conversation he and his helper (a middle-age Caucasian female) had in session. What three strategies of SFT did the helper use? What three strategies of MI did the helper use? What three strategies used by Vince's helper reflect a *combination* or *integration* of SFT and MI? For each response, provide a rationale for its use. For those intervention approaches that combine SFT and MI, describe how they illustrate a primary theme of this chapter—that "dancing with curiosity" is a recommended helping style for working with resistance. Feedback follows on page 602.

Vince is a 25-year-old biracial (African American and Caucasian) male who is a high school graduate and currently a student in his first quarter at a local technical college. He is on parole for assault with a deadly weapon after serving a four-year sentence in a prison in another state. As a condition of his parole, Vince is to obtain counseling at the local drug and alcohol treatment facility where you work. He states that "weed" (i.e., marijuana) is his drug of choice and that it's not going to be easy staying clean ("It helps calm me down") in order to pass the monthly urine screens his probation officer will administer. He last used two weeks ago right before his release from the local jail, where he was serving time for an alleged drug possession charge. The charges have been dropped. Vince acknowledges a five-year "career" in cocaine trafficking, but he denies a history of cocaine use, stating that profits were used, in part, to support his use of marijuana. He says he started smoking cigarettes at age 8 and started smoking marijuana regularly at about age 10. He acknowledges occasional use of alcohol but states he really doesn't care for it.

Vince was adopted at age 2 by a Caucasian couple who already had two biological children of their own (6 and 8 years old at the time). Vince's dad is a college professor, and his mother is a social worker. Vince says his parents continue to be concerned about him and want him to stay out of prison and finally get away from drugs. His relationship with them is estranged, and Vince acknowledges that he has never been able to trust anybody. He lives alone in his own apartment, just recently started working for a local trash collection company, and states he wants to get back to boxing, a talent he says won him a Golden Gloves competition when he was 19.

Helper: You know, I'm really glad you decided to come in today. I wasn't sure if you would because last week was the first time that we talked about you being adopted. I sensed that you weren't too happy with me for bringing it up. You didn't say much at the end of our session and headed right out the main door without saying good-bye, which is unusual for you. I could have been reading that all wrong.

Vince: Naw, I was a little pissed.

Helper: You were upset with me for bringing up the adoption thing.

Vince: Yeah.

Helper: I appreciate you letting me know. I'm curious, though, what made you decide to come back in today, given that you were upset with me last week?

Vince: [Shrugging shoulders] I have to.

Helper: You don't want to break parole and have to go back to prison.

Vince: Yeah.

Helper: So you decided to do what you have to do to stay out of prison.

Vince: You got it.

Helper: I wonder, then, what you were thinking about, what you had in mind we'd be talking about, when you came in today.

Vince: Anything else but stuff back then. The past is the past, you know? I just want to keep movin' forward and not keep lookin' back all the time.

Helper: You've got your sights set on what's ahead, and looking back would trip you up or maybe even just be a waste of time.

Vince: Yeah. You know, I figure I've done my time. No use digging stuff up and going through what's already happened. What's done is done.

Helper: You're a man on a mission. You've probably been on a mission for most of your life.

Vince: Maybe.

Helper: Well, if so, what would you say that mission has been?

Vince: [Shrugging shoulders] I guess to be on my own. To not have to depend on anyone, you know? I guess just to be left alone.

Helper: Which has its advantages and disadvantages.

Vince: [Looking up at the helper] What doesn't?

Helper: Most things in life have their up and down sides.

Vince: Yeah. You gotta take the bad with the good, the good with the bad, or whatever.

Helper: That's one thing I like about you, Vince, and one thing I think you have going for you. You're pretty realistic. I mean, you're not out there with your head in the clouds,

(continued)

(continued)

your head filled with all these fancy, far-fetched ideas. You're down to earth. Pretty practical, getting done what you think needs to get done. I get the impression, though, that this is fueled by a lot of anger, that you're constantly fighting something, always on the attack.

Vince: [Hands tightly grasping his chair's arm rests] You'd be too, if you came from where I came from. Look [Starting to get up from his chair], I don't need you to try to get inside my head to try to figure me out. You're talking like my mom now and [Standing up now and walking to the office door] I don't need another White woman telling me who I am and what I need to do. I should have known this would happen again today. [Hand holding the knob of the office door, pausing, not turning the doorknob]

Helper: [Still seated but turning to face Vince] You're free to go; you know that, Vince. No one's going to stop you. I just need to know what happened or what I just said just now that made you want to leave.

Vince: [Still holding the doorknob] Look, I thought this "treatment" stuff was about my smokin' weed, about helping me stay clean, not about this "psycho-talk" of my past and my anger.

Helper: They're all connected, Vince, in some way. You weren't in prison for smoking pot.

[Silence]

Vince: Look, you've been dealing with a lot of stuff for a long, long time; heck, for most of your life. It's still there too—probably will be for a long time. I just want to help you deal with some of that. I'm not your mother; I don't want to be your mother. And I can't help it if I'm White. I just want to offer what help I can so that you can stay clean, stay out of prison, and do some of the good things with your life that you've wanted to do for a long time.

[Silence. Vince still in the room, holding the doorknob]

Helper: What do you say? Will you stay in the ring for now so that we can box this out without using fists or gloves or any force? Can we talk this out without fighting?

Vince: [Releasing hand from doorknob, folding his arms across his chest, and leaning against the back of the door with his shoulder] I just want to be left alone. I don't need anybody telling me what to do or how to live my life. I'm tired of all that.

Helper: You're able to do things on your own, figure things out on your own.

Vince: And no one seems to get it.

Helper: There's more for us to talk about, Vince. I wonder if we can keep talking with both of us sitting down.

Vince: [Standing up straight now, shrugging shoulders, and walking slowly back to his chair] Sure, whatever. [Sitting down]

Helper: Thank you. [Pause] Okay, so you tell me what about yourself you have figured out. I'm the student here. I have more to learn about you and you have more to teach me about you.

Vince: What do you want to know?

Helper: Well, for starters, I am still curious about what keeps you going, what your fuel is. I threw out the notion of anger earlier, and that may have been the curveball. It was probably presumptuous on my part. I need to hear from you instead.

Vince: Naw, you're not off. There's a lot inside that's been burning. Anger, I guess.

Helper: Say more about that.

Vince: I don't know. It's been like that for as long as I can remember. [Pause] It builds up, like a pressure cooker, and I have to get it out somehow.

Helper: Boxing helped, and so did smoking pot.

Vince: Yeah, and now I can't do either one.

Helper: You said you were "a little pissed" at me after last week's session. What did you do with that anger instead of smoking?

Vince: Oh, I don't know. I went to the gym, lifted weights, jumped rope.

Helper: Good. That's good. And how exactly did that help?

Vince: Release. Just working the muscles again, sweating, and doing it myself.

Helper: Something you could give yourself credit for. Not a joint.

Vince: Huh. Yeah, I guess so. Never thought of it that way before.

Helper: So there are some things you're already doing, even just last week, to help with that anger or tension or burning inside that you talk about. What else do you think could be helpful?

Vince: [Sighs] Talking, I guess.

Helper: Talking in here, with me.

Vince: Yeah.

Helper: And you decided to do that today. You could have left, but you stayed.

Vince: I was that close to leaving.

Helper: It looked like you were. What made you decide to stay?

Vince: You gave me the choice. You didn't tell me what to do.

Helper: You were free to decide. What else?

Vince: You just said it straight. That I wasn't doing time for smoking pot.

Helper: And you didn't argue with me.

Vince: Naw. They're connected, I know. I just need to deal with it on my own.

Helper: Which has its advantages and disadvantages.

Vince: Huh?

Helper: Well, let's talk about the advantages of dealing with this stuff on your own—your anger, your attempt to stay clean, your staying in school. [Vince identifies feeling in control, taking all the credit, pride, proving others wrong.] Okay, so what are the disadvantages? What are the drawbacks of dealing with all of this stuff on your own? [Vince talks about loneliness, sense of failure, getting tired, feeling depressed.] Let's look at the other side: What would be the advantages of having others help you deal with all this stuff? What would be helpful about that?

Vince: Maybe it wouldn't seem so hard all the time.

Helper: Others would help carry the load. What else?

Vince: I wouldn't feel all alone all the time.

Helper: You'd have some company. Good. Now, there probably would also be some drawbacks, some disadvantages, to having others help you with what you're dealing with. It won't always be smooth sailing.

Vince: You got that right. As you can see, I can get ticked off pretty easy.

Helper: So even having others help you deal with your anger, for instance, can get you angry.

Vince: I guess so. It sounds stupid when you say it like that, but I guess that's true.

Helper: You've got some insight about that, and that's good. The challenge, then, may be how to let others help you—at various times, in different ways, to certain degrees—without getting ticked off by them.

Vince: May not be possible.

Helper: It may be. You've stayed here today. You've worked with me on this advantages–disadvantages thing, and, I could be wrong, but it doesn't look like you're ticked off at me.

Vince: Naw, it's cool. I'm okay.

18   KNOWLEDGE AND SKILL BUILDER **FEEDBACK**

Strategies of SFT

1. Asked *coping questions:* "What made you decide to come back in today, given that you were upset with me last week?"
   Rationale: Intended to draw out client's methods of managing concerns, behaviors that client is already implementing to address concerns or challenges.
2. Offered *legitimate commendations:* "You're down to earth. Pretty practical, getting done what you think needs to get done."
   Rationale: Highlights client's strengths and resources, capacities or abilities that are already in client's possession.
3. Engaged in "role-switching"*: helper as student, client as teacher:* "I'm the student here. I have more to learn about you, and you have more to teach me about you."
   Rationale: Emphasizes that the helping relationship is a partnership, that the helper is not a know-it-all, and that the client has valuable information to contribute.
4. Inquired about the *client's "instead":* "What did you do with that anger instead of smoking?"
   Rationale: Highlights client involvement in solution construction—that is, that Vince is already engaged in "exceptional behaviors" or positive behaviors that, when repeated, may "drown out" the presenting concern.
5. *Spoke the client's language:* In her responses, the helper used the client's own words to describe his experience or thinking, such as "burning inside" and "ticked off."
   Rationale: Helper's attempt to convey that client has been understood, that his experiences are valid and accepted at face value.

Strategies of MI

1. Offered *reflective or empathic statements:* "You don't want to break parole and have to go back to prison" (simple reflection) and "You've got your sights set on what's ahead, and looking back would trip you up or maybe even just be a waste of time" (complex reflection).
   Rationale: Intended to verify that what the client was meaning to say has been heard and understood. The simple reflection was intended to mirror the client's experience, and the complex reflection offered an alternative perspective (e.g., "sights set on what's ahead" as opposed to "not keep looking back") or added meaning (e.g., "looking back" might be "a waste of time") to what the client had said.
2. Emphasized *personal choice and control:* "You're free to go. . . . No one's going to stop you."
   Rationale: Reminded or reinforced for client what is already true: he has the right to decide whether or not

to remain in session, to continue with counseling. This was particularly important for Vince to hear given that he values his freedom to choose, his right to make his own decisions. He says he stayed in session because "You gave me the choice. You didn't tell me what to do."
3. Provided *affirmations:* The client stated that "release" was a benefit of going to the gym and exercising. The helper's interpretation that this experienced benefit was something he could give himself credit for (i.e., a positive outcome that he was responsible for) appeared appealing to Vince ("Never thought of it that way before").
   Rationale: Like commendations in SFT, affirmations highlight the client's abilities and strengths.
4. Asked *open-ended questions:* "Say more about that." "What else?" "What made you decide to stay?"
   Rationale: Intended to solicit more information from client without being prescriptive.
5. Offered *support:* "I just want to offer what help I can so that you can stay clean, stay out of prison, and do some of the good things with your life that you've wanted to do for a long time."
   Rationale: Intended to convey to the client the helper's concern for his well-being and her commitment to stick with him through the helping and change process.

Combined or Integrated Strategies of SFT and MI

1. *Client's preferences (or goals, ambitions) honored:* The helper does not push "back then" topics (e.g., client's adoption) because the client made it clear at the beginning of this session that he was "a little pissed" about "lookin' back" in the previous session. The helper instead inquires about the alternative perspective—that is, what's ahead. She does this by introducing the reframe "You're a man on a mission" and then inquiring about what his "mission" has been. The helper follows the client's lead (exemplifying the humanistic, person-centered philosophy of both SFT and MI) while introducing new territory to consider.
2. *Ambivalence regarded as resource:* Although Vince acknowledges that talking with the helper has been helpful to him, he's still not sold on the idea of counseling (he explains that he returned to this session because "I have to"). He is therefore ambivalent about the helping process. He is also ambivalent about how to deal with his anger, wanting others to help him but also wanting to deal with it on his own. The helper uses this ambivalence as a resource in session by exploring with Vince both sides of the ambivalence in the form of a cost/benefit analysis (i.e., advantages/disadvantages of others helping, and the advantages/disadvantages of Vince dealing with his

anger on his own). Ambivalence was therefore regarded as normal, and its exploration may have encouraged the client's participation in session. Notice the helper's use of the word "curious" as an invitation for the client to offer his perspective. His ambivalence was regarded with intrigue and curiosity rather than dismissed or attacked head-on. The client may have experienced this approach as welcoming and encouraging his participation in session.

3. *Change in relation:* Throughout the session, the helper's style emphasized collaboration and that change was not experienced solo. This is particularly evident in the helper's frequent use of "I" statements, signifying her participation as a partner in the helping process. She also acknowledged that raising the issue of Vince's anger "fueling" his "practicality" and "mission" may have been a "curveball" and "presumptuous." Although raising this issue may have triggered Vince to get up and almost leave the session, it appears that the helper's observation was valid (Vince said her observation was not "off"). This may have been a time when she took the lead in their dance. Another occasion when she stepped out and took the lead was when she said, "You weren't in prison for smoking pot." This gentle confrontation, offered in an atmosphere of acceptance, may have contributed to Vince changing his mind about leaving the session. He intimated this when he said he decided to stay because the helper was "straight" with him. Although Vince doesn't like to be told what to do, it appears that he appreciates people being honest and up-front with him, and he is open to help when it is offered to him rather than imposed or forced on him. Perhaps both client and helper are learning to work together as dance and doubles tennis partners so as to effectively manage the anger that Vince apparently has been struggling with for a long time.

APPENDIX: CODES OF ETHICS

Codes of ethics and related standards of professional practice can be found on the websites for the following helping professions. This list refers you to the websites of the major helping professions organizations.

American Association of Marriage and Family Therapy
(www.aamft.org)

American Association of Pastoral Counselors
(www.aapc.org)

American Counseling Association
(www.counseling.org)

American Mental Health Counselors Association
(www.amhca.org)

American Psychological Association
(www.apa.org)

American School Counselor Association
(www.schoolcounselor.org)

Association for Multicultural Counseling and Development
(www.bgsu.edu/colleges/edhd/programs/AMCD)

Canadian Psychological Association
(www.cpa.ca)

Code of Professional Ethics for Rehabilitation Counselors
(http://crcertification.com)

International Association of Marriage and Family Counselors
(www.iamfc.com)

International Society for Mental Health Online
(www.ismho.org)

National Association of Social Workers
(www.naswdc.org)

National Organization for Human Services Education
(www.nohse.com)

NAME INDEX

SUBJECT INDEX